RETURN TO TRADITION

A facsimile reproduction in a limited edition for
homeschooling and other educational use.
Originally published in 1948

RETURN TO
TRADITION

A DIRECTIVE
ANTHOLOGY

EDITED BY
FRANCIS BEAUCHESNE THORNTON, M.A.; B.LITT. (OXON.)

Roman Catholic Books

Distribution Center: Post Office Box 2286, Fort Collins, CO 80522

ISBN 0-912141-70-0

TO

REVEREND MOTHER MARY FIDELIS

AND THE SCHOOL SISTERS OF NOTRE DAME

ON THE HUNDREDTH ANNIVERSARY

OF THEIR FOUNDING IN THE UNITED STATES

AND

TO ED AND JEAN FOLEY

WHO HELPED MAKE THIS BOOK POSSIBLE

INTRODUCTION

BY *Frank O'Malley*

THE crisis of the modern world has brought many of our most serious artists to a genuine or apparently genuine search for values in man and his society. These values have not been found because modern society has lacked them. In this group might be included such writers as Aldous Huxley, W. H. Auden, Thomas Wolfe, and Thomas Mann. Thomas Wolfe, after a huge, surging, and great romantic quest is dead. Aldous Huxley has played with the Christian tradition and more recently has been fascinated by the mystique of orientalism. W. H. Auden has revealed himself to have found the Word, much, it is said, to the confusion of his friend, Stephen Spender who, disturbed by Auden's essays in Theology, now experiments with rather feeble "Spiritual Exercises" directed toward "Transparent Light." Thomas Mann, negative as he is, has analyzed the whole range of modern hedonistic experience, the modern civilized man's indifference to spiritual life and his love of death, his masochistic zest for the withering of his own life and culture. In *The Magic Mountain* and in the Joseph series, Thomas Mann has shown that his finest aims are the ordered revitalizing of human and communal concepts, the drawing together of the remotest past and dissipated present, and the vivifying of these efforts in the measures of literature. It is not at all foolish to say of him that he has tried to be the thinker, the synthesist, for his time. Indeed, it is notable that in a civilization in which the religious man has been repudiated, the man of letters often deems himself a spiritual and intellectual substitute and offers to men the integrating power of art for want of the integrating power of religion.

Yet there is an impressive number of modern writers in whose work shines the integrating power of a real faith and truth. It is possible in this world, as Etienne Gilson once remarked, to be a philosopher and an artist without a knowledge of religion, but it is impossible without this knowledge to become a Christian philosopher or artist. Writers like Charles Peguy, Leon Bloy, Georges Bernanos, Eric Gill, G. M. Hopkins, Francois Mauriac, Sigrid Undset, to mention only a few, work within the Christian Catholic tradition and have complete and genuine concepts of God, Man, and the Universe, concepts that underlie and underline all their art. They have not neglected their readers by denying absolute values or by omitting all sign of them in their works; neither have they searched fruitlessly for them, emitting only a vaguely defined intelligibility and responsibility or a dubious authority in what they have said. And they are not opportunists, sentimental spiritualists of the Lloyd Douglas type.

Sometimes, of course, their Christian orthodoxy is appraised with a cold eye, an appraisal natural in a civilization that has limited its vision to the physical and the technological, that has rejected the spiritual values that the Church authoritatively protects. There is, for instance, today in our country a fine young poet, Robert Lowell, who is "consciously a Catholic poet," that is, his beliefs as a Catholic enter importantly into his poetry. In an introductory comment to Lowell's first work, Allen Tate said that this poet's intellectualized Christian symbolism "points to the disappearance of the Christian experience from the modern world and stands, perhaps for the poet's own effort to recover it" and that "in a young man like Lowell, whether we like his Catholicism or not, there is at last a memory of the spiritual dignity of man, now sacrificed to mere secularization and a craving for mechanical order." Conrad Aiken, however, declared that he found "this predilection intellectually embarrassing and retrogressive," and that where two writers of equal talent are concerned, "that one will be greater, the more wholly sustaining, whose range of reference is wider than any orthodoxy would endow, freer than it would permit." Frankly, I would take the opposite point-of-view. I grow very tired of the constant assertion that orthodoxy in religion or philosophy is intellectually devitalizing. I don't think that Hopkins and Bernanos and Sigrid Undset are "crippled" because of their orthodoxy. Their beliefs enter vitally into the spiritual and intellectual form of their works and are clearly part of their power. What is this "wider range of reference" to which Aiken refers? It is indeed unlimited. It is so unlimited, so unboundaried that ultimately it is *chaos,* signifying the anarchy of culture and art. I do not think that chaos gives very much sustenance or order or animation. The great writers of the world give contrary evidence: Chaucer, Langland, Dante, Shakespeare, John Donne, Novalis, Dostoievski, and Paul Claudel — all of whom are, in one way or another, orthodox writers, that is, writers in whom a principle of authority and intelligibility, a stable frame of reference for values and for actions can be discerned.

A true conception of matter and form could give to modern poetry the needed intellectual and spiritual strength that it has already given to Hopkins and Eliot and that it is now giving to W. H. Auden and to Robert Lowell. For, as a critic in the *Nation* once pointed out, commenting on the Ern Malley frauds in the Australian literary quarterly, *Angry Penguins,* "Modern poetry because of its apparent lack of a discipline, certainly gives scope to the charlatan, to the pretentious, the precious, and the stupid." It seems to me, too, that the Greek, Jewish, and Christian conception of man — certainly orthodox — as Maritain has described it, is not for writers a "crippling" conception: "Man as an animal endowed with reason, whose supreme dignity is in the intellect; and man as a free individual in personal relation with God, whose supreme righteousness consists in voluntarily obeying the law of God; and man as a sinful creature called to divine life and to the freedom of grace, whose supreme perfection consists of love." Surely the novelist and the dramatist (and the critic) cannot be *limited or frustrated* by this powerful religious conception of the person:

To the Christian thinker and artist, man, as grasped by Jacques Maritain, is "never simply his natural self. He is a being out of joint and wounded — wounded by the desire with the wound of concupiscence and by God's wound of love. In the one hand he carries the burden of original sin, he is born dispossessed of the gifts of grace, not indeed corrupted in the substance of his being, but wounded in his nature. On the other hand he is made for a supernatural end: to see God as God beholds Himself, to reach even to the very life of God, he is traversed by the calls of actual grace, and if he does not turn against God by his power of refusal, he bears within him even here below the truly divine life of sanctifying grace and of its gifts. Hence, in point of existence, we may say that man is at once a natural and supernatural being."

Should one prefer perhaps the point-of-view of Ernest Hemingway? Which conception will permit or provide its greatest possibility of really serious, human, tragic art? Maritain's or Hemingway's? This is Hemingway writing in *A Farewell to Arms:* "If people bring so much courage to this world, the world has to kill them to break them; so, of course, it kills them. The world breaks everyone and afterwards many are strong at the broken places. But those that will not break it kills. It kills the very good and the very gentle and the very brave impartially. If you are none of these you can be very sure it will kill you too but there will be no special hurry." Now this is what Hemingway believes about men and their society. He has only a dark, agonized, almost brutish standard for existence; there is nothing nobly human or spiritual or metaphysical about his understanding of reality. And this want he shares with other contemporary writers and artists: with their pitiable and hopeless devotion to a pitiable and hopeless mankind, they cannot go beyond their grim scrutiny of the fearsome phenomena of time; they are themselves blinded and scarred by events and driven by them into a hideous, self-conscious discussion of their plight and the plight of society, attacking, defending, brooding forever. They do not appear to realize that before they can become great again as artists, empowered to create man and his destiny, they will have to unearth and repossess *reality*. Obviously for this rediscovery political zeal and social frenzy will not avail them much. Only that nurturing philosophy which penetrates and stabilizes the surface of society may renew their souls and minds and renew their art. That is why the light of Aristotle and St. Thomas and their modern interpreters like Jacques Maritain can do more today for artists than they can do for themselves. Artists today, returning to the Church and to the tradition of the Church, will find that their spirit is protected and accelerated rather than impeded. And this anthology, compiled and "directed" with sensitive, graceful intelligence by Father Thornton, is a remarkably varied and full record of the power of the faith for the serious thinkers and artists who have lived in the religious underworld of our amazing — and terrifying — civilization.

AUTHOR'S INTRODUCTION

IN A certain sense the term "Catholic Literature" seems narrowly inexpressive. To large groups of people, within the Church and outside her boundaries, it has come to denote a kind of narrow dogmatism seen against a background of pietism and apologetic.

Since it is in combinations that individual words take on their fullness of meaning, perhaps the connection of the term *Catholic* with the word *literature* has much to do with narrowing the original content of the word Catholic. Originally Catholic meant universal; that is its true sense. But when the pond of Protestantism grew into such an enormous body of water that it engulfed practically all English writers, the term *Catholic* combined with the term *literature* came to be used to describe not the ocean but only a puddle. It acquired a sectarian use quite foreign to its first meaning. And because the great English writers from the seventeenth to the nineteenth century were the first fruits of the Reformation and were widely advertised and touted in histories of literature, the phrase Catholic literature has been unjustly applied to certain backwashes of the literary scene, almost unknown bays and inlets of literary interest, adequately treated, so pundits thought, in a paragraph or a footnote of faint praise. The flight from supernaturalism first, and later from the natural law, added further notes of distaste and understatement to the originally expressive phrase Catholic literature.

Perhaps the best way to widen and re-emphasize the term Catholic literature is to review its use historically. Before the Reformation men of the Western world would not have used these words. If they spoke of literature they meant Catholic literature; a literature based on the natural law irradiated by the Incarnation, not only as it was seen in a period of time in Palestine but in the living Church as well. The medieval beatification of Aristotle, Plato, and Virgil was no quaintly childish outlook growing from an obscure knowledge of Greek and Roman writers. The Christian world exalted many of the great pagan writers because the scholars of the Middle Ages appreciated men who, without revelation, had, however obscurely, seen into divine things. Through their understanding of the natural law, they had in a sense paved the way for the power of the Word of God.

In writing his treatises Augustine quite naturally used the works of Plato, Aristotle, and Plotinus; when Thomas Aquinas made his survey of knowledge, he took as his foundation the works of Aristotle.

The literary and philosophical modes of the Greeks and Romans were perpetuated and developed in medieval culture. They flowered as expressively in the *Divine Comedy* as in the Cathedrals of Santa Sofia and Chartres. By an entirely natural growth Western literature and Catholic literature became parts of the same thing, the culture of the West. The maliciously conceived statement of the famous German scholar Troeltsch, who maintained that the Catholic Church does not belong to the Middle Ages but is rather the last creative effort of classical antiquity, which may be said to have died in giving birth to it, is only a partial expression of a fact which, partial as it is, contains a basic description of the continuity of Western culture that lies outside the purviews of those who deal with Western literature.

From the historical point of view, however, it is easy to see that Western literature is Catholic literature. The opinions and personal beliefs of individuals are important only in so far as they reflect the fundamental truths of Western culture: Alexander Pope is less Catholic than Shakespeare because Pope reflects an embalmed view of Greek and medieval life, while Shakespeare, regardless of the faith he professed, if any, refracts the living glory of both Greek and medieval times.

When Luther shut the North from the

living tradition of Western culture, a new dynamism developed which, from the sixteenth to the eighteenth century, attempted an evident distortion of history. Medieval times were labeled the "Dark Ages," a term sufficiently belied by the cathedrals of Chartres and Rheims, the Book of Kells, and the mosaics at Ravenna! Writers like Aquinas, Scotus, and Albert were lumped together under the tag "Schoolmen." There was less than faint praise in the word. All along the line Reformation quarrels engendered misappraisal, at least understatement. During this time the Church, being on the defensive, concentrated all her efforts on reform. Her best talents, seen in men like Ignatius and Borromeo, were spent in the activities of mending her bastions within and without. Literary and creative spirit flowed into the channel of apologetic. During those years the term Catholic literature came to be applied to this narrowed field of writing. The burnish left the term when it was associated with the specific rather than the universal.

As time went on and Reformation hatreds were blunted with years, people from the North once more turned toward the southern lands. Men like Horace Walpole and Addison made the "grand tour" and were enchanted with what they saw. Mountains, scenery, cathedrals, and castles filled them with a warmth of wonder. The heat was not without a spark of malice, as the journals and diaries of the eighteenth century attest. The South was lovely, the cathedrals impressive in their floridness; the frigidity of the northern imagination thawed and burgeoned, but reluctantly. This reluctance is evident in the first popular literature which appeared as a result of the opening of southern lanes of travel, the so-called "Novel of Terror." Italian castles crammed with secret passages and trap doors, specters, highly spiced bishops, slippery abbots, and gingerbread ladies became the literary ancestors of Sir Walter Scott's impossible pictures of the Middle Ages. Much has been made of Scott's contribution to the revival of Catholic Traditionalism in England; as a matter of fact, the revival was well started before

Scott appeared, and Romanticism itself principly owes its rise to increasing southern travel. Scott popularized and lent glamour to the revival.

As many scholars have pointed out, the nineteenth-century Romanticists do have a connection with the spirit of the troubadours and trouvers; the connection is, however, superficial in the extreme. At the period when the troubadours flourished, dialectic toughmindedness was the solid background of the Latin culture. Courts and noble houses rested and refreshed themselves with the *nouvelle,* the love lyric, and personalized poetry. In such soft moments of relaxation the senses reached out for endless treasure, but this treasure was seen as a means of diversion, not an entire mode of life.

In their southern travels men like Shelley and Byron grasped the surface glitter but, unfortunately, their learning and their reading were insufficient to show them the hard, intellectual core of the time they sought to emulate; nor did their much-touted intuitions aid them with faint flashes of insight into the double outlook of the ages they admired. Peter Abelard to them was Peter Abelard by a river brim; nothing more than the stuff for a poem or story.

As a consequence of this misapprehension regarding the mental toughness of medieval and Renaissance times, the nineteenth-century romanticists tried to build a universe founded almost completely on the senses and emotions. It was so dangerously short-lived a world that within sixty years the full-bodied and lusty cynicism of Byron had become the nerve-shattered outlook of Swinburne and Wilde, the sensism and altruism of Keats and Shelley had degenerated into the escapism of Morris and Rossetti.

While the noble patrons of literature traveled south with skirts lifted in true northern contempt of southern cleanliness and customs, while Shelley and Byron were building up their false universe of torrid sentiment and vague aspiration, dons from German universities and Oxford and Cambridge as well, were busy with the study of Dante. He opened to them and to their world the riches of medieval culture.

Even as early as the days when Alexander Pope and his Bolingbroke cackled at the inanities of metaphysic, northern scholars were already finding delight in the thought of Thomas and Abelard. Grand tours in the South produced Romanticism, the scholars laid the ground for the genuine Catholic revival.

Because he was a scholar in the truest sense of the term, Kenelm Digby stands out as one of the most important figures in the English return to Traditionalism. Cambridge University turned his mind to the past, and the deeper he went into it the more sweetly mellow became his love of a living thing. This is the point about Digby which eludes most students of the man. Though he was loved by his intimates, he has been consistently patronized by Catholic critics ever since his death. Dear old Digby, they exclaim; he was a sweet soul, so polite, affable, and, unfortunately, pedestrian. He pottered about in boats along the green shores of the Thames, rooted in old monasteries on the continent and left a library of discursive volumes full of pious tales about the Middle Ages. To a great many able people he seemed to be a sort of historical Turveydrop, but entirely without scientific method. The phrase "scientific method" has been used to cover more than a mortal number of deficiencies among historians.

In the hands of genuinely intelligent men the scientific method serves a good purpose, but to those of deficient time-sense and perspective it has become an end and a curse. Laundry bills, lists of household articles, deeds of land, processes for weaving, itemization of tawdry intrigues, these are too often the litanies of the so-called workers in the field. The blood of things and ages passes through their fingers, and like Coulton, they become sifters of dry bones. To good historical scholars an age is only as vivid as its spirit. Digby's books do ramble; he is forever led aside into digressions that interest him, but he proves conclusively that in the Middle Ages a great many people lived the Beatitudes and joyed in the spirit of the Word and its application in the social sphere. And, as Jacques Maritain has pointed out, the important thing about the Middle Ages is not the absence of absolute perfection, but the amazing fact that so large a percentage of people lived almost entirely in the spirit of Christ.

Digby's works are the best possible proof of this, and as our age is driven back to the things of the spirit the credit of Digby should rise. He was no nostalgic escapist looking at the past "through the pathos of distance." As a spiritual man he saw the *whole* before he assembled the multitudinous parts. Lingard, Newman, and others in the revival have overshadowed him with the sheer glitter of personality, but he is the true father of the movement.

With the advent of Newman the first purely historical phase of the revival closes. The personality of the leader of the Oxford movement starts into life a new current whose main aspects were devotional and apologetic. The lambent Faber wrote hymns and treatises on the spiritual life; Ward and Manning made the controversial welkin ring; De Vere sang of Our Lady far better than his master Wordsworth tinkled of Lucy Gray. Only Hopkins, struggling with himself, agonized over English prosody and genuine poetry.

With the advent of Mrs. Meynell the revival of Catholic Traditionalism became socially respectable. If she brought the revival into the drawing room, she also took it into the empyrean of pure literature. Into her drawing room at Palace Court came the shy Thompson with mingled flight and adoration in his eyes; Meredith sent her strawberries; Patmore discussed mystical love; Catherine Tynan and Yeats warmed to the silver of her smile and the gold of her candle glow. She was a great spirit. Behind the disciplined wall of her words burned intense emotional fires. She banked them under the wise eyes of her husband, but her thoughts were "doves that went with the hour" to enchant a whole circle. In many ways she is the most important person in the English return to Traditionalism. During the last years of her life, when World War I jangled her nerves and frayed her mind, she must have looked with pleasure on the fourth and present phase of the Catholic revival which was already taking shape.

It may justly be called the age of Belloc, for though Chesterton became the poet and arch popularizer of the period, Belloc is the great inspirer standing craggily in the background. In him the work of Digby and Newman bears full fruit. His historical studies glitter in the sword blade of his perfect prose. His conversation and advice have drawn to the movement people as diversely talented as Chesterton, Waugh, D. B. Wyndham Lewis, Woodruff, and Bruce Marshall. No more does Traditionalism seem archaic and foreign, as Newman pictured it in the moving music of *The Second Spring.* Under the leadership of Belloc, Traditionalism has assumed the offensive through the development of compelling satire in the works of Waugh and other writers. Respected Catholic publishing houses have arisen to carry on the work of disseminating Traditionalist productions. Through their efforts the English revival is losing certain of its provincial qualities. English Traditionalism, often too strongly wedded to local aspects of the "tight little Isle," has seen the measure of its greatness in the works of Maritain, Claudel, Bloy, and Rimbaud.

The last tinctures of parochialism and puritanism begin to disappear as the English stream flows into the full river of Continental philosophy and mysticism.

Traditionalism has definitely arrived. Its abounding life has drawn to its center such choice spirits as Bergson and Maritain; into its orbit have moved men of the stamp of T. S. Eliot and C. S. Lewis.

The Irish revival has not been so fortunate. In that country the movement got off to a bad beginning through the gyrations of the "twilight group." Ignoring the written traditions of the Irish, A. E. and Yeats went back to the monolithic tenuities of Irish legend. Pearse and MacDonough bade fair to cure these unrealists, but the abortive revolution of 1916 cut off their promise. Since this time only Robert Farren and Kate O'Brien have measured their greatness.

The movement in America, so long a pale reflex of English Traditionalist thought, appears on the verge of casting its own shadow. Apologies and imitations have both been thrown away. Men like William Walsh, the historian, and Leonard Feeney, the poet, are making genuine contributions to traditionalist thought. A true spirit of creation is abroad in the land. Poetry of utter maturity walks softly among its small audience, competent prose works show the first signs of complexity and artistic promise, the novel bids fair to shake off its hobbles of sweetness and light.

With the exception of France the Continent agonizes under the terrible blows inflicted by two wars and the continued struggles of rival tyrannies. Though the literary revival in Continental Europe had no consciousness of itself such as took form in England, Ireland, France, and America, it made such strides in the social field as to be the only massive force capable of opposing publicly brown or red inhumanism.

Of course, it did more than this, particularly in the field of liturgy. Here the self-consciousness did demonstrate itself and under Adams and Guardini, Herwegen and Parsch the Liturgical Movement spotlighted the bourgeois conception of religion and life. As a movement its critical and destructive aspects were secondary. So strong was its dynamic force and integrating qualities that it overflowed its own boundaries and affected philosophy, art, and architecture and strongly impregnated the social consciousness and the labor movement. It was a shaping and a shaking force as was the Liturgy in the early Church.

In a short essay of this kind it is impossible to estimate the influence of the Liturgical Movement. One can only generalize and pass on. This is but scant justice to a movement which even in the field of religious art made the Beuronese influence everywhere significant and in other specific spheres did immeasurably more, especially in the field of plain song under Dom Mocquereau.

But its consciousness of self was totally liturgical. In its main currents it was largely didactic and begot no literary school as the revival did in France and England. As a consequence of this, Catholic literary achievement on the continent seemed a scattered effort too small to catalogue, unless the work of Sigrid Undset, Maria Von Le Fort, Papini, and Rilke were to be placed in some common framework of reference, which it could not be.

It was not alone on the continent of Europe that lack of self-consciousness as a movement failed to unify purpose and beget opportunity. The British Commonwealth of nations offers significant examples of the same thing in the poetry of Eileen Duggan and the prose of Louis Hemon.

French Canada with its characteristic inwardness has produced excellent folk tales and superb historical writing, but even in these fields the parochial qualities of the French Canadian mind have been largely responsible for failure to translate their own excellences into the larger circle of Catholic thought which would make the French Canadian Movement in letters more dynamic and less defensive. Though they fight "a good fight," the strategy is narrowing and the achievement, so far, creatively barren.

One could wish it otherwise, for the French Canadians have been a long time on the North American continent and they are steeped in the purples they brought from old France.

Perhaps here, as in the United States, the last barriers to full literary consciousness await only time and complete education for their full release.

Surveying the massive achievement of the Catholic revival in the last hundred years, one finds little cause for discouragement. As the national spirit in many lands reveals itself for the monstrous thing it is, as the last vestiges of culturally uprooted liberalism slowly disappear, the balanced and spiritual dynamism of Traditionalism seems the only force capable of restoring men to sanity. Though wars threaten and the Red tides move over continental Europe, Western culture cannot be totally destroyed while living Traditionalism sends its light abroad over the world.

St. Paul, Minn.
February, 1948

CONTENTS

PART I. THE ENGLISH REVIVAL

CONTENTS

CONTENTS

CONTENTS

PART II. THE FRENCH INFLUENCE

CONTENTS

PART III. THE IRISH REVIVAL

CONTENTS

PART IV. THE AMERICAN REVIVAL

CONTENTS

CONTENTS

CONTENTS

Part V. The Liturgical Revival

RETURN
TO
TRADITION

PART

I

THE ENGLISH REVIVAL

AS GEORGE SHUSTER has observed in *The Catholic Spirit in Modern Literature,* the position of English Catholicism at the close of the eighteenth century was lamentable. "Recently freed from the penal code, their small handful — 60,000 — was torn with dissension which separated the laity from the clergy and prelates one from the other. There was no such thing as Catholic opinion. Scorned by the mass of Englishmen, accused of every sort of villainy and more than occasionally threatened with dire penalties, the faithful went their way, reduced to an impotent silence."

Within a century all this was miraculously changed: the Catholic laity was thoroughly united, the hierarchy had been re-established, and a flood of converts, in their writings, were amazing and charming the whole English speaking world. London was treated to the unusual spectacle of two cardinals entering the most exclusive clubs and scientific societies, long the holy of holies of liberalism and privilege. Pugin became the acknowledged head of the architectural revival, Lingard set the pace in factual and scholarly history, Alice Meynell had almost as large a popular following as Kipling.

All this called for endless labor. History as recorded by Hume and others had almost completely obscured the true facts of the English reformation and the correct picture of the Church and her doctrines. The rubbish of decades had to be cleared away. This was done necessarily in the first period of the revival of Catholic letters.

Lingard was first in the field. He uncovered the plain truth concerning the English reformation. One might expect the truth to be unpalatable to Englishmen steeped in half-truths and distortions, but Lingard stated his thesis with such moderation that it came to be accepted by all.

What Lingard had done for the English scene Kenelm Digby did for the concept of the Church in general. He made the Middle Ages live again; he revealed them sweetly with all their religious implications and social overtones.

Once these historical labors were well under way, Newman and his circle took another important step forward. They brought theology and philosophy out of the libraries and universities where they had been banished, revealing to the world the perennial newness of Church doctrine as well as its psychological subtlety.

On Catholic artists the effect of all this was startling. They sang once more the songs of merrie England. Nor was their singing without its lesson, for they taught poets that poetry itself is more a matter of content than a preoccupation with word glitter. Hopkins, Thompson, Alice Meynell, and Lionel Johnson are still read by the new generation, while the somewhat wordy lines of the "lords of language," such as Tennyson and Browning, seem to have fallen into popular neglect.

Belloc and his school are thus enabled to move about the field of literature with something of the quiet arrogance of free men. They continue to sing, to write history, biography, and philosophy. In addition to these things they have found time for satire which has placed on the defensive liberalism and a too-smug Protestantism. In a hundred years Catholics in England have almost completely reversed their situation. The labor has been great, but the achievement is no less extraordinary.

JOHN LINGARD

(1771–1851)

JOHN LINGARD, son of a Lincolnshire yeoman, was born at Winchester, February 5, 1771. After some years spent in London the family returned again to Winchester.

Lingard entered Douai College, September 30, 1782. His scholastic career was unusually brilliant. With the closing of the college, due to the advent of the French Revolution, Lingard escaped to England, becoming first a tutor to Lord Stourton and later, assistant to the Rev. John Eyre. It was under Eyre that Lingard first discovered his historical bent. Lectures and informal fireside conversations about the fire grew into his *History of the Anglo-Saxon Church*.

In 1811 Lingard retired to Hornby, a country parish some eight miles from Lancaster. Here he developed his scientific approach to history, and between missions abroad he devoted all his time to the examination and comparison of original documents.

His first three volumes of English history, extending to the death of Henry VII, were published in 1819. They achieved a phenomenal success. Lingard was honored by both Pope and crown and by the time of the publication of the eighth and concluding volume of his work, his fame was international. Learned societies at home and abroad honored him; he became a member of the French Academy and, quite probably,

was created a cardinal *in petto* by Leo XIII.

In the years remaining, Lingard incessantly revised his *History,* which two years before his death had already reached a fifth edition. He died in 1851 and was buried at Ushaw College, which he had aided with imperial munificence.

It is hardly necessary to praise the work of Lingard. His clarity of style does admirable service to the factual correctness of his *History of England*. By sheer honesty and a quiet tone he pioneered the way for scientific history and did much to remove that science out of the realms of opinion and bias. He cleared away the clutter of misapprehension and misstatement which had choked the life of the Church in England since the Reformation.

There were five editions of his *History* published in his lifetime. The final edition which he oversaw and corrected, was published 1849–1851 and may be considered the definitive edition of his great work. Though some of its pages were hastily written, and though his history of the Anglo-Saxon and Norman periods has been largely superseded, his *History* is still a standard work for a complete knowledge of the fourteenth and fifteenth centuries. His life may be followed in the study written by Hughes, Lancaster, 1907.

MARY*

IT WAS on the evening of the sixth of July that Edward expired at Greenwich. With the view of concealing his death for some

*Lingard, John, D.D., *A History of England From the First Invasion by the Romans to the Accession of William and Mary* (New York: P. O'Shea, 1887), Vol. 5.

days from the knowledge of the public, the guards had been previously doubled in the palace, and all communication intercepted between his chamber and the other apartments. Yet that very night, while the lords sat in deliberation, the secret was communicated to Mary by a note, probably from the earl of Arundel, unfolding the design of the conspirators. She was then at Hoddesdon, in the neighbourhood of London, and, had she hesitated, would by the next morning have been a prisoner in the Tower. Without losing a moment she mounted her horse, and rode with the servants of her household to Kennighall, in Norfolk.

The council broke up after midnight; and Clinton, the lord admiral, took possession of the Tower, with the royal treasures, the munitions of war, and the prisoners of state. The three next days were employed in making such previous arrangements as were thought necessary for the success of the enterprise. While the death of Edward was yet unknown, the officers of the guards and of the household, the lord mayor, six aldermen, and twelve of the principal citizens, were summoned before the council. All were informed of the recent settlement of the crown, and required to take an oath of allegiance to the new sovereign; the latter were dismissed with an injunction not to betray the secret, and to watch over the tranquillity of the city. On the fourth morning it was determined to publish the important intelligence; and the chief of the lords, attended by a numerous escort, rode to Sion House to announce to the Lady Jane her succession to the throne of her royal cousin.

Jane has been described to us as a young woman of gentle manners, and superior talents, addicted to the study of the Scriptures and the classics, but fonder of dress than suited the austere notions of the reformed preachers. Of the designs of the duke of Northumberland in her favour, and of the arts by which he had deceived the simplicity of Edward, she knew nothing; nor had she suffered the dark and mysterious predictions of the duchess to make any impression on her mind. Her love of privacy had induced her to solicit, what in the uncertain state of the king's health was readily granted, permission to leave London, and to spend a few days at Chelsea; she was indulging herself in this retirement, when she received by the lady Sydney, her husband's sister, an order from the council to return immediately to Sion House, and to await there the com-

mands of the king. She obeyed; and the next morning was visited by the duke of Northumberland, the marquess of Northhampton, and the earls of Arundel, Huntingdon, and Pembroke. At first, the conversation turned on indifferent subjects, but there was in their manner an air of respect, which awakened some uneasiness in her mind, and seemed to explain the hints already given to her by her mother-in-law. Soon afterwards that lady entered, accompanied by the duchess of Suffolk and the marchioness of Northampton; and the duke, addressing the Lady Jane, informed her that the king her cousin was dead; that before he expired, he had prayed to God to preserve the realm from the infection of papistry, and the misrule of his sisters Mary and Elizabeth; that, on account of their being bastards, and by act of parliament incapable of the succession, he had resolved to pass them by, and to leave the crown in the right line; and that he had therefore commanded the council to proclaim her, the Lady Jane, his lawful heir, and in default of her and her issue, her two sisters, Catherine and Mary. At the words the lords fell on their knees, declared that they took her for their sovereign, and swore that they were ready to shed their blood in support of her right. The reader may easily conceive the agitation of spirits which a communication so important and unlooked for was likely to create in a young woman of timid habits and delicate health.

She trembled, uttered a shriek, and sank to the ground. On her recovery she observed to those around her, that she seemed to herself a very unfit person to be a queen; but that, if the right were hers, she trusted God would give her strength to wield the sceptre to his honour and the benefit of the nation. Such is the account of this transaction given, about a month afterwards, by Jane herself, in a letter from the Tower to Queen Mary. The feelings which she describes are such as we might expect; surprise at the annunciation, grief for the death of her royal cousin, and regret to quit a station in which she had been happy. But modern writers have attributed to her much of which she seems to have been ignorant herself. The beautiful language which they put into her mouth, her forcible reasoning in favour of the claim of Mary, her philosophic contempt of the splendour of royalty, her refusal to accept a crown which was not her right, and her reluctant submission to the commands of her parents, must be considered as the fictions of historians, who, in their zeal to exalt the character of the heroine, seem to have forgotten that she was only sixteen years of age.

About three in the afternoon, the young queen was conducted by water to the Tower, the usual residence of our kings preparatory to their coronation. She made her entry in state. Her train was borne by her mother, the duchess of Suffolk; the lord treasurer presented her with the crown; and her relations saluted her on their knees. At six the same evening, the heralds proclaimed the death of Edward and the succession of Jane; and a printed instrument with her signature was circulated, to acquaint the people with the grounds of her claim. It alleged, (1) That though the succession, by the thirty-fifth of Henry VIII, stood limited to the ladies Mary and Elizabeth, yet neither of them could take any thing under that act, because, by a previous statute of the twenty-eighth of the same reign, which still remained in force, both daughters had been pronounced bastards, and incapable of inheriting the crown; (2) That even, had they been born in lawful wedlock, they could have no claim to the succession after Edward, because being his sisters only by the half-blood, they could not inherit from him according to the ancient laws and customs of the realm; (3) That the fact of their being single women ought to be a bar to their claim, as by their subsequent marriages they might place the sovereign power in the hands of a foreign despot, who would be able to subvert the liberties of the people, and to restore the jurisdiction of the bishop of Rome; (4) That these considerations had moved the late king to limit, by his letters patent, the inheritance of the crown in the first place to the lawful issue of the duchess of Suffolk, her male issue, if any were born to her during his life, otherwise to her daughters and their issue

in succession, and after them to the daughter of the late countess of Cumberland, sister to the said duchess, and to her issue, inasmuch as the said ladies were nigh to him of blood, and "naturally born within the realm;" (5) And that therefore the lady Jane, the eldest daughter of the duchess of Suffolk, had now taken upon herself, as belonging to her of right, the government of the kingdoms of England and Ireland, and of all their dependencies. To the arguments contained in this laboured proclamation the people listened in ominous silence. They had so long considered Mary the presumptive heir, that they did not comprehend how her claim could be defeated by any pretensions of a daughter of the house of Suffolk. Not a single voice was heard in approbation; a vintner's boy had the temerity to express his dissent, and the next day paid the forfeit of his folly with the loss of his ears.

The following morning arrived at the Tower a messenger from Mary, the bearer of a letter to the lords, in which, assuming the style and tone of their sovereign, she upbraided them with their neglect to inform her of the death of her brother, hinted her knowledge of their disloyal intention to oppose her right, and commanded them, as they hoped for favour, to proclaim her accession immediately in the metropolis, and as soon as possible, in all other parts of the kingdom.

This communication caused no change in their counsels, awakened no apprehension in their minds. Mary was a single and defenseless female, unprepared to vindicate her right, without money, and without followers. *They* had taken every precaution to insure success. The exercise of the royal authority was in their hands; the royal treasures were at their disposal; the guards had sworn obedience; a fleet of twenty armed vessels lay in the river; and a body of troops had been assembled in the Isle of Wight, ready at any moment to execute their orders. Depending on their own resources, contrasted with the apparent helplessness of their adversary, they affected to dread her flight more than her resistance, and returned an answer under the signatures of the archbishop, the chancellor, and twenty-one councillors, requiring her to abandon her false claim, and to submit as a dutiful subject to her lawful and undoubted sovereign.

In a few hours the illusion vanished. The mass of the people knew little of the lady Jane, but all had heard of the ambition of Northumberland. His real object, it was said, was now unmasked. To deprive the late king of his nearest relatives and protectors, he had persuaded Somerset to take the life of the lord admiral, and Edward to take that of Somerset. The royal youth was the next victim. He had been removed by poison to make room for the lady Jane, who, in her turn, would be compelled to yield the crown to Northumberland himself. These reports were circulated and believed, and the public voice, wherever it might be expressed with impunity, was unanimous in favour of Mary. The very day on which the answer to her letter had been despatched brought the alarming intelligence that she was already joined by the earls of Bath and Sussex, and by the eldest sons of the lords Wharton and Mordaunt; that the gentlemen of the neighbouring counties were hastening to her aid with their tenants and dependants; and that in a short time a numerous and formidable army would be embattled under her banners. Northumberland saw the necessity of despatch: but how could he venture to leave the capitol, where his presence awed the disaffected and secured the co-operation of his colleagues? He proposed to give the command of the forces to the duke of Suffolk, whose affection for his daughter was a pledge of his fidelity, and whose want of military experience might be supplied by the knowledge of his associates. But he could not deceive the secret partisans of Mary, who saw his perplexity, and to liberate themselves from his control, urged him to take the command upon himself. They praised his skill, his valour, and his good fortune; they exaggerated the insufficiency of Suffolk, and the consequences to be apprehended from a defeat; and they prevailed upon Jane, through anxiety for her father, to unite with them in their entreaties to Northumberland. He gave a tardy and re-

luctant consent. When he took leave of his colleagues he exhorted them to fidelity with an earnestness which betrayed his apprehensions; and, as he rode through the city at the head of the troops, he remarked, in a tone of despondency, to Sir John Gates, "The people crowd to look upon us, but not one exclaims, 'God speed ye.'"

From the beginning the duke had mistrusted the fidelity of the citizens: before his departure he requested the aid of the preachers, and exhorted them to appeal from the pulpit to the religious feelings of their hearers. By no one was the task performed with greater zeal than by Ridley, bishop of London, who, on the following Sunday, preached at St. Paul's Cross before the lord mayor, the aldermen, and a numerous assemblage of the people. He maintained that the daughters of Henry VIII. were, by the illegitimacy of their birth, excluded from the succession. He contrasted the opposite characters of the present competitors, the gentleness, the piety, the orthodoxy of the one, with the haughtiness, the foreign connections, and the popish creed of the other. As a proof of Mary's bigotry, he narrated a chivalrous but unsuccessful attempt, which he had made within the last year, to withdraw her from the errors of popery; and in conclusion, he conjured the audience, as they prized the pure light of the gospel, to support the cause of the lady Jane, and to oppose the claim of her idolatrous rival. But the torrent of his eloquence was poured in vain. Among his hearers there were many indifferent to either form of worship. Of the rest, the Protestants had not yet learned that religious belief could affect hereditary right; and the Catholics were confirmed by the bishop's arguments in their adhesion to the interest of Mary.

That princess, to open a communication with the emperor in Flanders, had unexpectedly left Kenninghall; and, riding forty miles without rest, had reached, on the same evening, the castle of Framlingham. There her hopes were hourly cheered with the most gratifying intelligence. The earl of Essex, the lord Thomas Howard, the Jerninghams, Bedingfelds, Sulyards, Pastons, and most of the neighbouring gentlemen, successively arrived, with their tenants, to fight under her standard. Sir Edward Hastings, Sir Edmund Peckham, and Sir Robert Drury had levied ten thousand men in the counties of Oxford, Buckingham, Berks, and Middlesex, and purposed to march from Drayton for Westminster and the palace; her more distant friends continued to send her presents of money, and offers of service; Henry Jerningham prevailed on a hostile squadron, of six sail, which had reached the harbour of Yarmouth, to acknowledge her authority; and a timely supply of arms and ammunition from the ships relieved the more urgent wants of her adherents. In a few days Mary was surrounded by more than thirty thousand men, all volunteers in her cause, who refused to receive pay, and served through the sole motive of loyalty.

In this emergency, doubt and distrust seem to have unnerved the mind of Northumberland, who had marched from Cambridge, in the direction of Framlingham, accompanied by his son the earl of Warwick, by the marquess of Northampton, the earl of Huntingdon, and the lord Grey. With an army of eight thousand infantry, and two thousand cavalry, inferior, indeed, in number to his opponents, but infinitely superior in military appointments and discipline, he might, by a bold and immediate attack, have dispersed the tumultuary force of the royalists, and have driven Mary across the sea, to the court of her imperial cousin. But he saw, as he advanced, the enthusiasm of the people in her cause; he heard that he had been proclaimed a rebel, and that a price had been fixed on his head; and he feared that Sir Edward Hastings would, in a few days, cut off his communication with the capital. At Bury his heart failed him. He ordered a retreat to Cambridge, and wrote to the council for a numerous and immediate reinforcement. The men perceived the irresolution of their leader; their ignorance of his motives gave birth to the most disheartening reports; and their ranks were hourly thinned by desertion.

In the council there appeared no diminution of zeal, no want of unanimity. It was resolved to send for a body of mercenaries, which had been raised in Picardy, to issue commissions for the levying of troops in the vicinity of the metropolis, and to offer eight crowns per month, besides provisions, to volunteers. But, as such tardy expedients did not meet the urgency of the case, the lords proposed to separate, and hasten to the army, at the head of their respective friends and dependants. Though Suffolk had been instructed to detain them within the walls of the Tower, he either saw not their object, or dared not oppose their pleasure. The next morning the lord treasurer and lord privy seal, the earls of Arundel, Shrewsbury, and Pembroke, Sir Thomas Cheney, and Sir John Mason left the fortress under the pretence of receiving the French ambassador at Baynard's Castle, a fitter place, it was said, for that purpose than the Tower.

There they were joined by the lord mayor, the recorder, and a deputation of aldermen, who had been summoned by a trusty messenger; and the discussion was opened by the earl of Arundel, who, in a set speech, declaimed against the ambition of Northumberland, and asserted the right of the two daughters of Henry VIII. The moment he had finished, the earl of Pembroke drew his sword, exclaiming, "If the arguments of my lord of Arundel do not persuade you, this sword shall make Mary queen, or I will die in her quarrel." He was answered with shouts of approbation, and Suffolk, who had been sent for, signed with the others the proclamation of Mary. The whole body then rode in procession through the city. At St. Paul's Cross the earl of Pembroke proclaimed the new queen amidst the deafening acclamations of the populace. Te Deum was sung in the cathedral; beer, wine, and money were distributed among the people; and the night was ushered in with bonfires, illuminations, and the accustomed demonstrations of public joy.

While the earl of Arundel and the lord Paget carried the intelligence of this revolution to Framlingham, the earl of Pembroke, with his company of the guard, took possession of the Tower. The next morning the lady Jane departed to Sion House. Her reign had lasted but nine days; and they had been days of anxiety and distress. She had suffered much from her own apprehensions of an unfortunate result, more from the displeasure of her husband, and the imperious humour of his mother. The moment she was gone, the lords, without any distinction of party, united in sending an order to Northumberland to disband his forces, and to acknowledge Mary for his sovereign. But he had already taken the only part which prudence suggested. Sending for the vice-chancellor, Dr. Sands, who, on the preceding Sunday, had preached against the daughters of Henry, he proceeded to the market-place, where, with tears of grief running down his cheeks, he proclaimed the Lady Mary, and threw his cap into the air, in token of joy. During the night he was prevented from making his escape by the vigilance of his own men; and on the following morning he was arrested on a charge of high treason, by the earl of Arundel, and conducted, with several of his associates, to the Tower. It required a strong guard to protect the prisoners from the vengeance of the populace.

The Lady Elizabeth had taken no part in this contest. To a messenger, indeed, from Northumberland, who offered her a large sum of money, and a valuable grant of land, as the price of her voluntary renunciation of all right to the succession, she replied, that she had no right to renounce, as long as her elder sister was living. But, if she did not join the Lady Jane, she did nothing in aid of the Lady Mary. Under the excuse of a real or feigned indisposition, she confined herself to her chamber, that, whichever party proved victorious, she might claim the negative merit of non-resistance. Now, however, the contest was at an end: the new queen approached her capital; and Elizabeth deemed it prudent to court the favour of the conqueror. At the head of a hundred and fifty horse, she met her at Aldgate. They rode together in triumphal procession through the streets, which were lined with the different crafts in their gayest attire. Every eye was directed towards the royal sisters. Those who had seen Henry VIII. and Catherine could discover little in the queen to remind them of the majestic port of her father, or of the beautiful features and graceful carriage of her mother. Her figure was short and small; the lines of care were deeply impressed on her countenance; and her dark piercing eyes struck with awe all those on whom they were fixed. In personal appearance Elizabeth had the advantage. She was in the bloom of youth, about half the age of the queen. Without much pretension to beauty, she could boast of agreeable features, large blue eyes, a tall and portly figure, and of hands, the elegant symmetry of which she was proud to display on every occasion. As they passed, their ears were stunned with the acclamations of the people; when they entered the Tower, they found kneeling on the green, the state prisoners, the duchess of Somerset, the duke of Norfolk, the son of the late marquess of Exeter, and Tunstall and Gardiner, the deprived bishops of Durham and Winchester. The latter pronounced a short congratulatory address. Mary burst into tears, called them *her* prisoners, bade them rise and, having kissed them, gave them their liberty. The same day she ordered a dole to be distributed, of eight pence, to every poor householder. . . .

In the appointment of her official advisers, the new queen was directed by necessity as much as choice. If the lords who, escaping from the Tower, had proclaimed her in the city, expected to retain their former situations, the noblemen and gentlemen who had adhered to her fortunes, when every probability was against her, had still more powerful claims on her gratitude. She sought to satisfy both classes, by admitting them into her council; and to these she successively added a few others, among whom the chief were the bishops Gardiner and Tunstall, who, under her father, had been employed in offices of trust, and had discharged them with fidelity and success. The acknowledged abilities of the former soon raised him to the post of prime minister. He first received the custody of the seals, and was soon afterwards appointed chancellor. The next to him, in ability and influence in the council, was the lord Paget.

Though the queen found herself unexpectedly in debt from the policy of Northumberland, who had kept officers and servants of the crown three years in arrear of their salaries, she issued two proclamations, which drew upon her the blessings of the whole nation. By the first she restored a depreciated currency to its original value, ordered a new coinage of sovereigns and half-sovereigns, angels and half-angels, of fine gold, and of silver groats, half-groats, and pennies of the standard purity; and charged the whole loss and expense to the treasury. By the other she remitted to her people, in gratitude for their attachment to her right, the subsidy of four shillings in the pound on land, and two shillings and eight pence on goods, which had been granted to the crown by the late parliament. As the time of her coronation approached, the queen introduced within the palace an innovation highly gratifying to the younger branches of the female nobility, though it foreboded little good to the reformed preachers. Under Edward, their fanaticism had given to the court a sombre and funeral appearance. That they might exclude from it the pomps of the devil, they had strictly forbidden all richness of apparel, and every fashionable amusement. But Mary, who recollected with pleasure the splendid gaieties of her father's reign, appeared publicly in jewels and coloured silks; the ladies, emancipated from restraint, copied her example; and the courtiers, encouraged by the approbation of their sovereign, presumed to dress with a splendour that became their rank in the state. A new impulse was thus communicated to all classes of persons, and considerable sums were expended by the citizens in public and private decorations, preparatory to the coronation. That ceremony was performed after the ancient rite, by Gardiner, bishop of Winchester, and was concluded in the usual manner, with a magnificent banquet in Westminster Hall. The same day a general pardon was proclaimed, with the exception, by name, of sixty individuals who had been committed to prison, or confined to their own houses, by order of council, for treasonable or seditious offenses committed since the queen's accession.

But though Mary was now firmly seated on the throne, she found herself without a friend to whom she could open her mind with freedom and safety. Among the leading members of her council there was not one who had not, in the reigns of her father or her brother, professed himself her enemy; nor did she now dare to trust them with her confidence, till she had assured herself of their fidelity. In this distress she had recourse to the prince who had always proved himself her friend, and who, she persuaded herself, could have no interest in deceiving her. She solicited the advice of the emperor on three very important questions; the punishment of those who had conspired to deprive her of the crown, the choice of her future husband, and the restoration of the ancient worship. It was agreed between them that the correspondence on these subjects should pass through the hands of the imperial ambassador, Simon de Renard, and that he, to elude suspicion, should live in comparative privacy, and very seldom make his appearance at court.

KENELM HENRY DIGBY

(1800–1880)

KENELM DIGBY was the youngest son of the Very Rev. William Digby, dean of Clonfert, who belonged to the Irish branch of Lord Digby's family, and was descended from the ancient Leicestershire family of the same name. He received his education at Trinity College, Cambridge, where he took the degree of B.A. in 1819. While a student at the university he entered into an examination of the antiquities of the Middle Ages, and subsequently made a searching inquiry into the scholastic system of theology, the result being that at an early age he became a convert to Roman Catholicism. Most of his subsequent life was spent in literary leisure in the metropolis, and he died at his residence, Shaftesburg House, Kensington, March 22, 1880.

The works of Digby deserve more than the casual praise usually bestowed upon them. While other historians were laboring on the identification of persons in Dante's *Inferno*, Digby was led by love and admiration to the very heart of the Middle Ages.

For humanity the significance of these times is based upon religious causes: the sweetness and rightness of Christ's doctrine as explained and lived in His Church. From these flows the social enlightenment of the times, as well as the artistic refulgence still visible in Chartres and the little parish church at Iffley. What may seem a mosaic of quotation in Digby, is merely the accumulation of factual evidence proving his main thesis.

Of his works, *The Broadstone of Honour* has been most highly praised. Published in 1822 when Digby was still a student at Cambridge, it was later revised and amplified. It has been called "the bible of the Christian gentleman." Less known and much more important than any of his other works is the *Mores Catholici*. Digby supports his thesis with an amazing wealth of evidence. In this work his scholarship and ability to write are seen at their best. Digby wrote much verse, but it would scarcely entitle him to a place among the immortals. The romantic character of the man is best savored in the *Memoir of Kenelm Henry Digby,* by Bernard Holland.

MORUS*

IN A work by the amiable Mr. Alban Butler, there is the following anecdote: "During the civil War, the famous Marquis of Worcester marching once in Cardiganshire, near the ruins of a monastery, at Strata Florida, a woman who was a hundred years old was presented to him, who had remembered the monks in Catholic times, and had lived above three-score years in great regret for the loss of the public service of the altar, and in constant private devotion, without seeing a priest, nor thinking that any could be found in England. The Marquis asked her, 'When the religion altered, you altered with the religion?' She answered, 'No, master, I stayed to see whether or not the people of the new religion would be better than the people of the old; and could see them in nothing, but grow worse and worse, and charity to wax colder and colder, and so I kept me to my old religion, I thank God, and mean, by God's grace, to live and die in it.' When the Marquis told her he would take her to Ragland Castle (his seat in Monmouthshire), where she would find a priest, and might hear mass every day, she was so transported with joy, that she died before the next morning. The Marquis wept when he heard of her death, and said, 'If this poor soul died where she might have served God, how joyfully will she serve him in a place where she will never die.'"

"It is wonderful," says Vogt, "with what knowledge of human nature the whole discipline and form of the Church was moulded. The year had its four grand festivals: Christmas for winter, Easter for the spring, Whitsuntide for summer, All-hallows and All-souls for autumn. The three weeks before Christmas, or Advent, were devoted to prayer and repentance. Then followed the pomp and joy of the great feast, and the third day after that, Holy Innocents; both

*Digby, Kenelm Henry, *The Broadstone of Honour or Rules for the Gentlemen of England,* first appeared in 1822. It was later enlarged into four closely printed volumes titled respectively *Godefridus, Tancredus, Morus,* and *Orlandus. Godefridus* treats of chivalry and government; *Tancredus* explains the religion and discipline of the Middle Ages; *Morus* answers modern objections to the practice of knighthood and *Orlandus* exposes the virtues of chivalrous character as it grows under the influence of religion. The above selection is from the third book.

of which were peculiarly the feasts of the young, when children were taught to associate happiness with obedience and duty and love," Christmas, on many accounts, was peculiarly the feast of youth: for then we celebrate, as the boy would say, for whom Erasmus wrote a beautiful declamation, *"Our emperor Jesus."* We commemorate, "pueri puerum." Then men were reminded that they must become like children; that as their blessed Saviour was at that time born in the flesh, so they should pray that he might be born spiritually in their hearts. . . . The very circumstance of its vacation from ordinary employment, which dispersed the boys of all nations throughout their respective districts, served to infuse the freshness and air of youth over the scene of nature.

"Christmas was succeeded by the Feast of Kings, when kings and great men made their offerings at the altar, and kept hospitable court. In every family a king was chosen, who ruled for the day. The rest of the winter was the Carnival, or the time of feasting and joy. The three last days usually gave occasion for dancing and song, and other innocent diversions. But now came on the time of fasting, with Ash-Wednesday. The people flocked to church, and priests strewed them, as they knelt, with ashes, and signed them with the Cross, and said 'Memento homo quia pulvis est, et in pulverem reverteris." Now the songs of joy gave place to the seven penitential psalms, which were solemnly repeated in all churches and chapels. The plentiful board was exchanged for strict temperance, and the overplus given to the poor. Instead of the music of the bower and hall, the chant of 'miserere' was heard, with the eloquent warnings of the preacher. Forty days' fast overcame the lust of the people. Kings, princes, and lords were humbled with their domestics, and dressed in black instead of their gorgeous habits. In Holy Week the mourning was still more strongly expressed. The chant became more solemn, the fast stricter; no altar was decorated, no bell sounded, and no pompous equipage rolled in the streets. Princes and vassals, rich and poor, went on foot in habits of deep mourning. On Palm Sunday, after reading out of the history of Christ, every one bore his palm, and nothing else was heard but the sufferings of the Messiah."

In Provence, before the Revolution, it was usual to see all the children and all the youths carrying branches of palm in triumph, curiously entwined and mixed with ribands.

"After receiving the sacrament of Maundy Thursday, the bishops and priests, king and princes, proceeded to wash the feet of the poor, and to serve them at table. On Good Friday, the holy sepulchre was represented, the halls hung with black, and but a few lights burning, while verses were chanted out of Jeremiah. The same was continued on Saturday, till twelve o'clock struck at midnight, and then the church resounded with the joyful cry, 'He is risen!' The bells sounded from the towers, the organs made the vaults echo with triumphant harmony, and three times the whole chorus sang 'Allelujah! Allelujah! Allelujah!' On Easter Sunday every one appeared again in his festive apparel, and all the expressions of mourning were laid aside. It was a festivity of Church and State from Easter till Whitsuntide. Divine service was performed with all the pomp and beauty of the Church; and the political assemblies called Fields of March and May were held on the banks of the Rhine. All splendid ceremonies now took place; peace was proclaimed, kings were crowned, nobles gave chivalrous games, the people enjoyed themselves at their sports." Then the knights and noble dames walking in their garden, as the bright rays of a Sunday morning gilded all the opening blossoms of rose and jasmine, of tulip and narcissus, of Naiad-like lily and purple hyacinth, would feel and understand why Religion also decked her altars, and sent forth to the blue heaven her sweet frankincense, while

. . . the spring arose on the garden fair,
Like the spirit of love felt everywhere;
And each flower and herb on earth's dark breast,
Rose from the dreams of its winter's rest.

Then the music and the soul, as it were, of the Church, harmonized with the universal beauty; for like the poet's blood, her spirit ever moved,

> . . . in mystic sympathy
> With nature's ebb and flow.

"On the first day of May, processions went into the fields to beg a blessing for the crops. The summer commenced with Ascension-day, and the thoughts of men were directed to the gifts of the Holy Ghost on the day of Pentecost. The feast of the Trinity was only an ordinary Sunday; for it was held to be presumptuous to represent so incomprehensible a doctrine by a festival: yet, in a later age, Corpus Christi day was employed in festive pomp, when the Host was carried about in grand procession, while the streets were hung with richest tapestry, every householder displaying his most beautiful pageantry, and kings and queens, princes and princesses, followed in humility to mark their reverence and loyalty for the Lord of all. Now came on harvest-time, and the blessing of God was then petitioned for at the Kirmess, or feast of Consecration, when the Church and people rejoiced together. After the Assumption, the harvest being brought home, the hunting season commenced; though, at first, only that of small game, hares, quails, etc.; but after St. Ægidius, or the holy hunter, St. Hubert, the nobles hastened to the woods in quest of the wolf, the wild boar, and the stag. At the end of the vintage, rents were paid and wordly accounts transacted. All-Hallowne day closed the festivity of the harvest. As the labourer and vintner had now received the fruit of their pains, so it was proper that the labourers in the Lord's vineyard should be honoured with praises. The face of the country was now changed by the advance of the year, and the success of the husbandmen. The fields were naked, and the leaves were falling fast from the trees, the dark clouds poured down with rain, the brooks were swoln to rivers."

And the leaves, brown, yellow, and grey,
   and red,
And white with the whiteness of what is dead,
Like troops of ghosts on the swift wind past;
Their whistling noise made the birds aghast.

And yet still the Christian pilgrim had bright views; for while he felt the influence of the ghastly change, and listened to the howl of winds which made his path so awful through the sullen night, he would love to recall and to view by the light of faith those sublime and beautiful images with which his youthful fancy had been fed and nourished. . . .

"All-Hallowne day was the last joyful feast of the year, the next day was All-Souls' day, devoted to prayer for the dead, and to the remembrance of the dead which awaited the living. A mournful colouring spread over nature, highly favourable to romantic feelings, high thoughts, and generous deeds. The altars were hung with black, men kneeled upon the graves of their relations, and strewed them with flowers, and held lonely vigils, and strengthened their hearts." The dark grass, and the flowers among the grass, were bright with tears as they wandered by.

From their sighs the wind caught a mournful
   tone,
And sate in the pines, and gave groan for groan.

This solemn season continued till Advent, and the birth of Christ, when the year again commenced.

The wisdom of the Church, in setting apart these particular seasons for the commemoration of subjects which must have so deeply interested all who had an affection for its faith, will for ever accord with the spirit and religious feelings of chivalry. Some of these seasons, ordained to remind the soul of heaven, were abandoned even by those reformed theologians who had imbibed the least contempt for antiquity; but by the more general consent of the moderns, nearly all have been laid aside.

MORES CATHOLICI*

MODERN writers in their contempt for these [Middle Ages] ages, besides having confounded causes together which had no connection, have shown that they never rightly understood society as it had been formed by the Catholic religion. The greatest enemies of this religion of truth must admit a fact which De Saint Victor says is as clear as the light of the sun — that it has developed the intelligence in all ranks of the social hierarchy, and to a degree of which no society of pagan antiquity can offer an example. Hence it followed that the people, properly speaking, could among Christian nations become free and enter into civil society, because every Catholic Christian, however ignorant and rude, has in himself, by his faith and by the perpetuity of instruction, a rule of manners and a principle of order sufficient to maintain him in this society without disturbing it; whereas the pagan multitude who had no such moral law, or who at least had very incomplete notions of it, was obliged to remain in a state of slavery, in order that it might not overthrow society. The moral history of the ages of faith proves the truth of this observation. In referring to it, reader, you are journeying to a Catholic land, that is, we may add, in the language of Pliny, and with far greater justice than when he used it, "to men who have obeyed nature's law in virtue, goodness, friendship, loyalty, and religion." You are going to behold a state that is earthly, and therefore imperfect, composed of men, and therefore liable to a thousand disorders and afflictions; but it is a state constituted with an especial view to all the spiritual necessities and to all the noble capacities of the redeemed race that is destined to rise to a life immortal: it is a state in conformity with the principles of nature, in which the imagination, the purity and the happiness of the youngest member are deemed of greater importance than the thoughts and interest of the highest in the walks of commerce and ambition, and one in which gloom and proud severity, and merciless industry, are never suffered to enter under the mask of virtue. The apostles of nations, and the saintly kings who placed their crowns at the foot of the altar, founded these old Catholic monarchies, and as Pindar says of Hieron establishing the new city of Aetna upon the genuine Doric principles, they founded them "with heaven-built freedom."

"Your solicitude for the public good," says St. Hilary of Poitiers to a government that was disposed to abuse its power, "your imperial vigils, in a word, the whole labor of your sovereignty should have for object to secure for all those over whom it extends the sweetest of all treasures, liberty. There is no mode of appeasing troubles, and of reuniting what is divided, unless everyone, emancipated from all the fetters of servitude, be able to live according to his choice." "Dishonorable and cruel is he who does not favor liberty," was the old Catholic maxim of English law. "Nothing is more glorious than liberty, except virtue," says John of Salisbury, adding, "if liberty be properly derived from virtue, for to all wise persons it is clear," he continues, "that true liberty can proceed from nothing else: so that a man is virtuous as far as he is free, and free as far as he is virtuous. Vices alone bring men into slavery, to persons, and to things. What, therefore, is more amiable than liberty? What more favorable to one who has any reverence for virtue? We read that all good princes have promoted it, and that none have ever trampled upon liberty, but the manifest enemies of virtue." To think that the new religious systems, which dissolved the ancient union of society, have been favorable to political liberty, would in nations under their influence be every man's thought; no doubt, as Prince Henry says

*Digby, Kenelm Henry, *Mores Catholici*, or *Ages of Faith* (New York: P. O'Shea, 1888), Vol. I, Bk. II, pp. 263–271.

Mores Catholici was first published by Digby 1831–1840. In this work Digby shows that the Middle Ages exemplified the Eight Beatitudes.

to Poins, he is "a blessed fellow who thinks as every man thinks"; and we may add, never a man's thought in the world kept the roadway better than that of Blackstone, who in eulogizing Edward VI, and in reviling Mary, records the most oppressive and tyrannical laws enacted by the former, and the most just and mild laws enacted by the latter. Their principle has on the contrary been favorable to anarchy and despotism, though it may have met with contrary causes to neutralize its effects; for as the learned father Ventura observes, "There are some people of Europe who although they have ceased for three centuries to believe, and to think catholically, yet in many respects have continued hitherto to live catholically; and there are others who after monarchy has been destroyed, yet continue to be governed monarchally; so that if they retain any thing true in matter of religion, or right in politics, it is not to be ascribed to their inventions or rebellions, whose institutions are of no weight, but to the ancient traditions of the Catholic religion, and of monarchy, which have not as yet been totally effaced; but when these traditions and manners shall have vanished, then it will be manifest how pernicious was their departure from the true religion and from their just institutions." With regard to the religious element that entered into the constitution of a Catholic state, we may observe that Leibnitz recognized its necessity, and admired the exterior society of God and man, which he calls "the state the most perfect under the most perfect of monarchs"; under which it is impossible for men to live as Isocrates described the Persians, "all their lives either insulting over others, or else servilely enslaved to others, which must of all things corrupt the nature of men." This really secured that spiritual excellence of government which Tacitus ascribed in a material sense to Nerva, saying, "Then the state had what are now incompatible: authority and liberty." It was this element which inspired the desire and enhanced the real value of political freedom; witness what Don Savedra testifies of the Belgians in his time, that "they love religion and liberty,

neither deceiving others nor allowing themselves to be deceived." The liberty, however, which was loved in these ages was not an abstraction, but a real personal exemption and immunity from the inconvenience and indignity of servitude. This is expressed even on the tomb of the Norman hero, Jourdan, son of Roger, on which was inscribed, "Quantus fuit auctor domesticae libertatis ipse devicta à Barbaris Sicilia demonstrat." That under the influence of Christianity even the remains of pagan servitude were unattended with individual misery may be inferred from the fact, that when Louis X published his ordinance, very few of the serfs desired to redeem themselves, so that the king by letters declared afterwards "that many have not known the greatness of the benefit which was offered to them." It must be remembered that until the fifth century there were in Gaul two distinct societies, the civil and religious, which differed not only in their object but also because they were governed by different principles. The civil society seemed to be Christian like the religious, but it was in fact pagan; it derived its institutions, its laws, and its manners from paganism.

The Christian civil society, as Guizot remarks, was not developed till later, after the invasion of the barbarians; and we must carefully distinguish its action and institutions from the influence of the ancient legislation; for the founders of Christian states had not the advantage which Plato ascribes to his ideal legislators: when a necessity fell upon the Christian clergy to apply the things which they contemplated in the regions of universal truth and order to the manners of men in public as well as in private, and not merely to form themselves, they were not, indeed, found bad artists to form temperance and justice, and all that belongs to the virtue of a people; for in employing their pencil, and in tracing that picture from a divine model, they constituted states which were highly favorable to the sanctification and eternal beatitude of men; but they were not permitted in the first instance, as Socrates required, to take as a piece of plain canvas the city and the manners of men, and make it clean, which he acknowledges would be no easy matter: they enjoyed no such distinction over all legislators, that they never were required to touch either an individual or a state, or to make laws before they either received or made it pure and clean. They found the world polluted with all the vices of the old pagan civilization, and the new elements entrusted to them were wild and barbarous; yet their deep and sweet colors succeeded at last in overpowering the almost inveterate and loathsome forms over which they had to work: their labor cannot be better described than in the very words of Plato: "While painting the form of the state, they continually turned their eyes from one to the other, that is, from what is essentially just and beautiful and wise, and all such things, to what actually takes place among men, blending and fashioning, from these models the ideal of humanity. Parts they effaced and parts they refreshed and repainted, until they rendered the manners of men as far as is possible worthy of being the object of divine love." This was their noble painting of a government, not "the unhistoric rational state on the revolutionary destructive principle, which Frederick Schlegel well denounces as clearly irreconcilable with Christianity and in opposition to it," but the Christian Catholic and holy state, according to whose law man was contained in the family, the family in the nation, the nation in the religion, the religion in the universe, the universe in the immensity of God: — the holy, just, and happy state, which really enjoyed what the ancient sages and poets ascribe without reason to some of their people. . . . Here was really found that unity, of the importance of which Plato had so profound a sense, that to secure it he had recourse in his speculations to those wild and extravagant conceits which are the disgrace of his noble work on the republic; to have unity he sacrifices everything, even the moral law of nature. His plan is ridiculous to the last degree, detestable, monstrous; but so much the more does it prove the depth of his conviction, that unity in a state was essential to its happiness. Let it not be thought that I exaggerate in ascrib-

ing to the Catholic states of ages of faith, the advantage which seemed so admirable and so unattainable to Plato. Guizot is struck with observing the moral unity which prevailed in France during a period of such multitudinous divisions of territory as took place under the feudal system. He endeavors to account for it in this way. "It is because in the life of a people, the exterior and visible unity, the unity of name and of government, however important, is not the first; the most real is that which truly constitutes a nation. There is a unity more profound, more powerful; that which results, not from an identity of government and destiny, but from the similitude of social elements, from similitude of institutions, manners, ideas, sentiments and languages, the unity which resides in the men themselves who are reunited, in society, and not in the form of their approximation; in short, moral unity, far superior to political unity, and which can alone form its solid foundation." Perhaps the fact admitted might be accounted for in fewer words, but its decided recognition by such a writer is sufficiently remarkable.

In a Catholic state one might have looked upon every person in every rank as one of a great but closely united family, possessing the same affections, entrusted with the same secrets, and acting from the same motives for the same end: this poor laborer, this young apprentice, this student, this soldier, this artisan, this king, had all the same sources of instruction and consolation as yourself. In the tribunal of penance, they had all been taught the same lessons and traditions, and had been all directed to the same end. In every other state, whether heathen or modern, each man has his own motives, his own rule of right and wrong, his own end in view; perhaps he thinks virtues what you regard as sins, and sins against his type of perfection what you regard as the highest virtue; in the Catholic states there was only one standard even amidst desertions, only one morality understood even by those who departed from it, as there was but one faith. What an increase of public and social happiness resulted from such unity! It is true, meek obedience was a prominent feature in this painting, but that this was not opposed to real freedom, or a source of servitude, has, perhaps, already been sufficiently shown. Muller says, "With the Dorians, that comparatively free and noble people of antiquity, so great was the desire of unity in the state, that greater importance was attached to obedience than to the assertion of individual freedom." In fact, the Spartans considered an immunity from labor as constituting entire liberty. True, in Christian states there was degree and subordination of ranks, necessarily attended with an unequal distribution of the goods of this world:

But government, though high, and low, and
    lower,
Put into parts, did keep in one concert,
Congruing in a full and natural close
Like music. . . .

"Old men participate by the very law of nature in paternity," says Bonald, "and young men owe them deference: persons weak in mind or body, participate in the claims of childhood, and require protection. Society is all paternity and dependence, rather than fraternity and equity." The Gallic rioters of the talk of the fraternal action of nations just as the great depopulators of the earth always effect to attach great importance to population. The Church reminded men of a real fraternity, "This is true brotherhood which is never broken by strife, which follows the Lord in giving up life."

We have seen that in the theory and practice of ecclesiastical rule, from which the civil was in a great measure modeled, the advice and interests of the community governed were always to be consulted. Accordingly we find in an article of a capitulary of Charlemagne that the emperor, not content with ordering his officers to read *"in mallo publico,"* to the citizens of each territory, the laws newly made, desires besides that their opinion should be asked, and that each person should testify either by his signature or by his seal his acquiescense in the new ordinance. However the modern politicians may deem such a reference unnecessary, we can only understand the reason and spirit of this ancient government by looking back to the origin and elements of the Christian society. In the first place, then, the people had priority of claims to its advantages inasmuch as religion commenced with them. The modern systems, unlike Christianity, began with the great and noble. In the first assembly of Huguenots in the year 1557, which was discovered in the street of St. James, at Paris, and dispersed by the populace, there were found among them many persons of the highest rank, and several ladies of the court, some of whom were in waiting upon the queen. From the first they had many gentlemen in their ranks who were ever ready to draw their swords and rush out upon the people as in the affair of the church of St. Marceau, where their fury was excited by hearing the bells tolling for vespers. In England and Germany, Protestantism introduced itself by the head of the state, by princes, and nobles, and magistrates, and men of letters, and descended slowly into the lower ranks. Christianity followed an opposite course; it commenced in the plebeian classes, with the poor and ignorant, the faith ascended by degrees into the higher ranks, and reached at length the imperial throne. It is a remark of Chateaubriand, too, just to be rejected, "that the two impressions of these two origins have remained distinct in the two communions." The same difference continues in the propagation of the two religions. By the preaching and miracles of St. Francis Xavier, the whole kingdom of Travancore embraced the Catholic religion with the exception of the king and the chief men of his court. In the missions of the Protestants, it is invariably the higher classes which furnish them with a favorable soil. So little alive are they to the natural inference from this startling fact, that in magnifying their national religions, they always speak of their happy effects in giving some certain tone to high society or to literature or in contributing to some worldly advantage, which virtually belongs alone to the ranks above the poor. There is in truth always a secret tendency in the higher classes to disdain the company of the shepherds at Bethlehem. The poor shepherds believed the angel, but the rich will not believe apostles, prophets, angels or the triune eternal God who sends them.

. . . To the observation of Chateaubriand, we may add that in the political doctrine of states and legislations the two impressions of the two religions are still discernible. While the moderns have alternately rejected or exaggerated the doctrine of the popular power, the great writers of the Middle Age maintain it within its *just* proportion. St. Thomas, for instance, said, that "since law was given for the general good, it was not the reason of any individual that could make law, but that of the multitude or of the prince who stood in place of it." Cardinal Bellarmine placed no mediate power between the people and God, but he supposed the people to be between the king and God. Suarez confirms this doctrine by the authority of St. Ambrose, St. Gregory the Great and St. Augustine. St. Alphonsus Liguori speaks to the same effect: "It is certain," he says, "that power is given to men of making laws, but this power as it respects civil laws belongs by nature to no one, but only to the community, and from this it is transferred to one or to more by whom the community is governed." Fénelon also says: "The temporal power comes from the community which is called the nation," and Bossuet asserts: "No one denies that the power of kings is not in such a manner from God, but that it is also by the consent of the people." The Abbé la Mennais shows that this doctrine of St. Thomas and other theologians is not to be confounded with that of Jurieu and Rousseau, which they defended under the name of sovereignty of the people, which supposes that the people have no other law but their own will, which creates justice, whereas Catholic theologians lay down as a principle that the people as well as an individual are subject to the divine law of justice, essentially independent of its will.

Aware of all the abuses to which the exercise of that right is open, which cannot, however, destroy that right, they have with St. Thomas endeavored to guard against them, saying, "A tyrannical government is unjust, being ordained not for the common good, but for the private good of the ruler. Therefore, the disturbance of this rule is not sedition, unless when the overthrow of tyranny is so inordinately pursued that the multitude suffers more from the disturbance than from the existence of the government." In fact, during the ages of faith, though the popular power was generally exercised in a legal resistance, which sufficiently preserved society from the dangers of a reckless revolution, yet the greatest monarchs had occasion to feel the necessity of guarding against its expression in a less orderly form; but true to the origin of its emancipation, it was seldom formidable excepting in defense of its religion. Hence it was that Don Savedra warns kings and their ministers never to meddle with religion because "this will kindle the fury of the people against them." Charles V so feared the people, that he decreed public prayers and processions throughout all Spain to obtain the deliverance of the Pontiff, whom his own troops kept prisoner in Italy.

With the heathen sentiments of a false and unattainable liberty, the moderns also adopted their expressions of contempt and hatred for the lower orders of the state; expressions which, in a Christian society, are both unjust and opposed to the original laws and institutions of government. In the ages of faith, the people were not the vulgar crowd spoken of by Cicero, in whom "is no counsel, no reason, no discrimination, no diligence; whose actions were seldom to be praised." . . . They were not that Athenian people described by Demosthenes as "the most treacherous of all things"; not that democracy whose gifts, as the moderns would infer, are always a Cyclopian grace, to destroy others first and their friends last.

The divine Saviour taught men not to be so proudly ready to rail at the multitude, and had left them His example in those gracious words benign," *misereor super turbam.*" Moreover, the constitution of a Christian state recognized them as entitled to every protection, and secured the perpetuity of institutions founded by charity for their advantage. The Church claimed them as the objects of her especial love, and formed them by her discipline to become what they still continue in every Catholic country, when not perverted by the policy and driven to exasperation by the injustice of rulers, a most innocent, joyous, and engaging race, whose name might no longer be taken for that of a nation, but seems to be rather that of Christian intelligence. The Church prayed oftener for the people than for the kings. She wished that their approval might accompany her elections, and she indicated the necessity of her approval for kings in the ceremony of their coronation. The first grand objects which meet the eye in the capital of her government derive their title from the people, as if to remind men of that ancient discipline which lasted in practice till the 13th century.

CARDINAL WISEMAN
(1802–1865)

NICHOLAS PATRICK WISEMAN was born in Seville August 2, 1802. His father was a merchant, and upon his death Mrs. Wiseman removed the family to Waterford, Ireland.

Wiseman was educated at St. Cuthbert's College, Ushaw, and made further studies for the priesthood at the English College in Rome. He was ordained in 1825 and soon achieved fame as a linguist. In 1827 he was appointed vice-rector of the English College, and he became rector in 1828. In 1836, during a leave of absence, he founded the *Dublin Review.* In 1840 he was made president of Oscott College and also bishop-coadjutor. By his writings, charm, and learning he had a profound effect on the course of the Oxford Movement.

In 1850 he became archbishop of Westminster and was soon after named a cardinal. This honor caused great excitement in England. There was a great outcry of bigotry which was finally dispelled by time and the diplomatic dignity of Wiseman who at the time of his death in 1865 was quite generally beloved.

The principal works of Wiseman: *Science and Revealed Religion,* 1836; *Essays on Various Subjects,* 1853; *Recollections of the Last Four Popes,* 1858, are but little read today.

One work, however, still holds a measure of popularity, his novel *Fabiola,* 1854, which first made his fame as a popular writer. It is a story of the early church, and though it suffers from excessive romanticism and woodenness of character delineation, *Fabiola* still is worthy of study as one of the first of the historical novels which achieved instant success and continental fame.

THE DEATH OF AGNES*

IT WAS still early in the morning when she stood again before the tribunal of the prefect, in the Roman Forum; unchanged and unscathed, without a blush upon her smiling countenance, or a pang of sorrow in her innocent heart. Only her unshorn hair, the symbol of virginity, which had been let loose, flowed down, in golden waves, upon her snow-white dress.

It was a lovely morning. Many will remember it to have been a beautiful day on its anniversary, as they have walked out of the Nomentan Gate, now the Porta Pia,

*Wiseman, Nicholas Cardinal, *Fabiola* (New York: P. O'Shea, 1854), pp. 405–410.

towards the church which bears our virgin martyr's name, to see blessed upon her altar the two lambs, from whose wool are made the palliums sent by the Pope to the archbishops of his communion. Already the almond-trees are hoary, not with frost, but with blossoms; the earth is being loosened round the vines, and spring seems latent in the swelling buds, which are watching for the signal from the southern breeze, to burst and expand. The atmosphere, rising into a cloudless sky, has just the temperature that one loves, of a sun, already vigorous, not heating, but softening, the slightly frosty air. Such we have frequently experienced St. Agnes's day, together with joyful thousands, hastening to her shrine.

The judge was sitting in the open Forum, and a sufficient crowd formed a circle round the charmed space, which few, save Christians, loved to enter. Among the spectators were two whose appearance attracted general attention; they stood opposite each other, at the ends of the semicircle formed by the multitude. One was a youth, enveloped in his toga, with a slouching hat over his eyes, so that his features could not be distinguished. The other was a lady of aristocratic mien, tall and erect, such as one does not expect to meet on such an occasion. Wrapped close about her, and so ample as to veil her from head to foot, like the beautiful ancient statue, known among artists by the name of Modesty, she had a scarf or mantle of Indian workmanship, woven in richest pattern of crimson purple, and gold, a garment truly imperial, and less suitable, than even female presence, to this place of doom and blood. A slave or servant, of superior class attended her, carefully veiled also like her mistress. The lady's mind seemed intent on one only object, as she stood immovable, leaning with her elbow on a marble post.

Agnes was introduced by her guards into the open space, and stood intrepid, facing the tribunal. Her thoughts seemed to be far away; and she took no notice even of those two who, till she appeared, had been objects of universal observation.

"Why is she unfettered?" asked the prefect, angrily.

"She does not need it: she walks so readily." answered Catulus; "and she is so young."

"But she is as obstinate as the oldest. Put manacles on her hands at once."

The executioner turned over a quantity of such prison ornaments — to Christian eyes really such — and at length selected a pair as light and small as he could find, and placed them round her wrists. Agnes playfully, and with a smile, shook her hands, and they fell, like St. Paul's viper, clattering at her feet.

"They are the smallest we have, sir," said the softened executioner: "one so young ought to wear other bracelets."

"Silence, man!" rejoined the exasperated judge, who, turning to the prisoner, said in a blander tone:

"Agnes, I pity thy youth, thy station, and the bad education thou hast received. I desire, if possible, to save thee. Think better while thou hast time. Renounce the false and pernicious maxims of Christianity, obey the imperial edicts, and sacrifice to the gods."

"It is useless," she replied, "to tempt me longer; my resolution is unalterable. I despise thy false divinities, and can only love and serve the one living God. Eternal Ruler, open wide the heavenly gates, until lately closed to man. Blessed Christ, call to Thee the soul that cleaveth unto Thee: victim first to Thee by virginal consecration; now to Thy Father by martyrdom's immolation."

"I waste time, I see," said the impatient prefect, who saw symptoms of compassion rising in the multitude. "Secretary, write the sentence. We condemn Agnes, for contempt of the imperial edicts, to be punished by the sword."

"On what road, and at what mile-stone shall the judgment be executed?" asked the headsman.

"Let it be carried into effect at once," was the reply.

Agnes raised for one moment her hands and eyes to heaven, then calmly knelt down. With her own hands she drew forward her silken hair over her head, and exposed her neck to the blow. A pause ensued, for the executioner was trembling with emotion, and could not wield his sword. As the child knelt alone, in her white robe, with her head inclined, her arms modestly crossed upon her bosom, and her amber locks hanging almost to the ground, and veiling her features, she might not unaptly have been compared to some rare plant, of which the slender stalk, white as the lily, bent with the luxuriancy of its golden blossom.

The judge angrily reproved the executioner for his hesitation, and bid him at once do his duty. The man passed the back of his rough left hand across his eyes, as he raised his sword. It was seen to flash for an instant in the air; and the next moment, flower and stem were lying scarcely displaced on the ground. It might have been taken for the prostration of prayer, had not the white robe been in that minute dyed into rich crimson — washed in the blood of the Lamb.

The man on the judge's right hand had looked with unflinching eye upon the stroke, and his lip curled in a wicked triumph over the fallen. The lady opposite had turned away her head, till the murmur, that follows a suppressed breath in a crowd, told her all was over. She then boldly advanced forward, unwound from round her person her splendid brocaded mantle, and stretched it, as a pall, over the mangled body. A burst of applause followed this graceful act of womanly feeling, as the lady stood, now in the garb of deepest mourning, before the tribunal.

"Sir," she said, in a tone clear and distinct, but full of emotion, "grant me one petition. Let not the rude hands of your servants again touch and profane the hallowed remains of her, whom I have loved more than anything on earth; but let me bear them hence to the sepulchre of her fathers; for she was noble as she was good."

Tertullus was manifestly irritated, as he replied: "Madam, whoever you may be, your request cannot be granted. Catulus, see that the body be cast, as usual, into the river, or burnt."

"I entreat you, sir," the lady earnestly insisted, "by every claim which female virtue has upon you, by any tear which a mother has shed over you, by every soothing word which a sister has ever spoken to you, in ill-ness or sorrow; by every ministration of their gentle hands, I implore you to grant my humble prayer. And if, when you return home this evening, you will be met at the threshold by daughters, who will kiss your hand, though stained with the blood of one, whom you may feel proud if they resemble, be able to say to them, at least, that this slightest tribute to the maidenly delicacy which they prize, has not been refused."

Such common sympathy was manifested, that Tertullus, anxious to check it, asked:

"Pray, are you, too, a Christian?"

She hesitated for one instant, then replied, "No, sir, I am not; but I own that if anything could make me one, it would be what I have seen this day."

"What do you mean?"

"Why, that to preserve the religion of the empire such beings as she whom you have slain" (her tears interrupted her for a moment) "should have to die; while monsters who disgrace the shape and name of man should have to live and flourish. Oh, sir, you know not what you have blotted out from earth this day! She was the purest, sweetest, holiest, thing I ever knew upon it, the very flower of womanhood, though yet a child. And she might have lived yet, had she not scorned the proffered hand of a vile adventurer; who pursued her with his loathsome offers, into the seclusion of her villa, into the sanctuary of her home, and even into the last retreat of her dungeon. For this she died, that she would not endow with her wealth, and ennoble by her alliance, that Asiatic spy."

She pointed with calm scorn at Fulvius, who bounded forward, and exclaimed with fury: "She lies, foully and calumniously, sir. Agnes openly confessed herself a Christian."

"Bear with me, sir," replied the lady, with noble dignity, "while I convict him; and look on his face for proof of what I say. Didst thou not, Fulvius, early this morning, seek that gentle child in her cell, and deliberately tell her (for unseen, I heard you) that if she would but accept your hand, not only would you save her life, but, despising the imperial commands, she should still remain a Christian?"

Fulvius stood, pale as death: *stood,* as one does for a moment who is shot through the heart, or struck by lightning. He stood like a man on whom sentence is going to be pronounced — not of death, but of perpetual pillory, as the judge addressed him, saying:

"Fulvius, thy very look confirms this grievous charge. I could arraign thee on it, for thy head, at once. But take my counsel, begone hence forever. Flee, and hide thyself, after such villainy, from the indignation of all just men, and from the vengeance of the gods. Show not thy face again here, nor in the Forum, nor in any public place of Rome. If this lady pleases, even now, I will take her deposition against thee. Pray, madam," he asked, most respectfully, "may I have the honor of knowing your name?"

"Fabiola," she replied.

The judge was now all complacency, for he saw before him, he hoped, his future daughter-in-law. "I have often heard of you, madam," he said, "and of your high accomplishments, and exalted virtues. You are, moreover, nearly allied to this victim of treachery, and have a right to claim her body. It is at your disposal." This speech was interrupted at its beginning by a loud hiss and yell that accompanied Fulvius's departure; he was pale with shame, fear, and rage.

Fabiola gracefully thanked the prefect, and beckoned to Syra, who attended her. The servant again made a signal to some one else; and presently four slaves appeared bearing a lady's litter. Fabiola would allow no one but herself and Syra to raise the relics from the ground, place them on the litter, and cover them with their precious pall. "Bear this treasure to its own home," she said, and followed as mourner with her maid. A little girl, all in tears, timidly asked if she might join them. "Who art thou?" asked Fabiola. "I am poor Emerentiana, her foster sister," replied the child; and Fabiola led her kindly by the hand.

The moment the body was removed, a crowd of Christians, children, men, and women, threw themselves forward, with sponges and linen cloths, to gather up the blood. In vain did the guards fall on them, with whips, cudgels, and even sharper weapons, so that many mingled their own blood with that of the martyr. When a sovereign, at his coronation, or on first entering his capital, throws, according to ancient custom, handfuls of gold and silver coins among the crowd, he does not create a more eager competition for his scattered treasures, than there was among those primitive Christians, for what they valued more than gold or precious stones, the ruby drops which a martyr had poured from his heart for his Lord. But all respected the prior claim of one; and here it was the deacon Reparatus, who, at risk of life, was present, phial in hand, to gather the blood of Agnes's testimony; that it might be appended, as a faithful seal, to the record of martyrdom on her tomb.

ROBERT STEPHEN HAWKER
(*1803–1875*)

ROBERT STEPHEN HAWKER, British poet and antiquary, was born at Plymouth in 1803, the son of Dr. Hawker. After an early education at Liskeard Grammar School, he was placed with a solicitor in Plymouth. Finding the study of law distasteful, the youthful Hawker entered Pembroke College, Oxford, to begin his training for the English clergy. Less than a year later he married Charlotte D'ans.

He continued his undergraduate studies at Oxford and took his degree in 1828. He was appointed vicar of Morwenstow, a rocky parish in northwest Cornwall, where he labored until his death. Hawker's life was an active one — he restored the church and parsonage, cared for the survivors of the numerous shipwrecks on the rugged coast, and gave much time to the study of the history and legends of the Cornish people.

Following the publication of his first important work, *Records of the Western Shore,* in 1832, he produced a long series of romantic and religious poems, the finest of which is *The Quest of Sangraal.* On his deathbed, in 1875, he entered the Church.

Hawker's poetry is full of dash and feeling. It sparkles from the line with an almost mystical fire. In his *Quest of the Sangraal* he traces the effect of the loss of the Blessed Sacrament upon˙ England. The grail is the symbol of the Sacrament, and all the evils in the land are traced back to the loss of the Eucharistic domination of England's fortunes. Though the poem is incomplete, it is a better expression of Arthurian times than are the *Idylls of the King.* Tennyson is too concerned with a pure universe of feeling, his symbolism is vague; in short, his is a stiflingly bourgeois conception of the men and ages of faith.

The *Life and Letters of R. S. Hawker,* by C. E. Byles, London, 1905, gives a pleasing picture of Hawker, which may be amplified by Paul Elmer More's study in the *Shelburne Essays* (Fourth Series).

THE QUEST OF THE SANGRAAL*

(*King Arthur Concludes His Speech*)
"Be this our cry! the battle is for God!
If bevies of foul fiends withstand your path,
Nay! if strong angels hold the watch and ward,
Plunge in their midst, and shout, 'A Sangraal.'"

He ceased; the warriors bent a knightly knee,
And touched, with kiss and sign, Excalibur;
Then turned, and mounted for their perilous way!

That night Dundagel shuddered into storm—
The deep foundations shook beneath the sea:
Yet there they stood, beneath the murky moon,
Above the bastion, Merlin and the King.
Thrice waved the sage his staff, and thrice they saw
A peopled vision throng the rocky moor.

First fell a gloom, thick as a thousand nights,
A pall that hid whole armies; and beneath
Stormed the wild tide of war; until on high
Gleamed red the dragon, and the Keltic glaive
Smote the loose battle of the roving Dane!
Then yelled a fiercer fight: for brother blood
Rushed mingling, and twin dragons fought the field!

The grisly shadows of his faithful knights
Perplext their lord: and in their midst, behold!
His own stern semblance waved a phantom brand,
Drooped, and went down the war. Then cried the King,

"Ho! Arthur to the rescue!" and half drew
Excalibur; but sank, and fell entranced.

A touch aroused the monarch: and there stood
He, of the billowy beard and awful eye,
The ashes of whole ages on his brow—
Merlin the bard, son of a demon-sire!
High, like Ben Amram at the thirsty rock,
He raised his prophet staff: that runic rod,
The stem of Igdrasil—the crutch of Raun—
And wrote strange words along the conscious air.

Forth gleamed the east, and yet it was not day!
A white and glowing horse outrode the dawn;
A youthful rider ruled the bounding rein,
And he, in semblance of Sir Galahad shone:
A vase he held on high; one molten gem,
Like massive ruby or the chrysolite:
Thence gushed the light in flakes; and flowing, fell
As though the pavement of the sky brake up,
And stars were shed to sojourn on the hills,

*Cormist Ballads and Other Poems (London: John Lane, 1905).

From grey Morwenna's stone to Michael's
  tor,
Until the rocky land was like a heaven.

Then saw they that the mighty Quest was
  won!
The Sangraal swoon'd along the golden air:
The sea breathed balsam, like Gennesaret:
The streams were touched with supernatural
  light:
And fonts of Saxon rock, stood, full of God!
Altars arose, each like a kingly throne,
Where the royal chalice, with its lineal blood,
The Glory of the Presence, ruled and reigned.
This lasted long: until the white horse fled,
The fierce fangs of the libbard in his loins:
Whole ages glided in that blink of time,
While Merlin and the King, looked, wonder-
  ing, on.

But see! once more the wizard-wand arise,
To cleave the air with signals, and a scene.

Troops of the demon-north, in yellow garb,
The sickley hue of vile Iscariot's hair,
Mingle with men, in unseen multitudes!
Unscared, they throng the valley and the
  hill;
The shrines were darkened and the chalice
  void:
That which held God was gone: Maran-atha!
The awful shadows of the Sangraal, fled!
Yet giant-men arose, that seemed as gods,
Such might they gathered from the swarthy
  kind:
The myths were rendered up: and one by
  one,

The Fire — the Light — the Air — were
  tamed and bound
Like votive vassals at their chariot-wheel.
Then learnt they war: yet not that noble
  wrath,
That brings the generous champion face to
  face
With equal shield, and with a measured
  brand,
To peril life for life, and do or die;
But the false valour of the lurking fiend
To hurl a distant death from some deep den:
To wing with flame the metal of the mine:
And, so they rend God's image, reck not
  who!

"Ah! haughty England! lady of the wave!"
Thus said pale Merlin to the listening King,
"What is thy glory in the world of stars?
To scorch and slay: to win demoniac fame,
In arts and arms; and then to flash and die!
Thou art the diamond of the demon-crown,
Smitten by Michael upon Abarim,
That fell; and glared, an island of the sea.
Ah! native England! wake thine ancient cry;
Ho! for the Sangraal! vanish'd Vase of
  Heaven,
That held, like Christ's own heart, an hin
  of blood!"

He ceased; and all around was dreamy night:
There stood Dundagel, throned; and the
  great sea
Lay, a strong vassal at his master's gate,
And, like a drunken giant, sobb'd in sleep!

JOHN HENRY CARDINAL NEWMAN
(1801–1890)

JOHN HENRY NEWMAN was of
French and English extraction. The severity of his early Calvinistic training was considerably modified by his own imaginative
bent. Though his banker father had destined
him for the bar, Newman's inclination toward the church was clearly in evidence by
the time he entered Oxford University, 1816.
He was ordained in the Established Church,
1821, and after a brilliant career as cleric
and fellow at Oriel College, was appointed
Vicar of St. Mary's in Oxford. His new

appointment and his graduation into the highest circles of the English Church fixed him in the spotlight of public esteem. His *Parochial Sermons* electrified Oxford. Students reverently pointed him out in the streets, and his sincerity and reserved charm gradually gave him the leadership of the Oxford Movement, which had already created a stir under Keble and Hurrell Froude. The stir became a storm with the publication of *Tracts of the Times,* a series of pamphlets designed for the reform of the Established church. Newman's attempt to steer a middle course (*via media*) in religion seemed, in Tract 90, to be a tendency toward Rome. His bishop mildly censured the tract. Newman stopped publication of the series, resigned his living, and retired to Littlemore. In 1845 he was received into the Catholic Church and was ordained in Rome the following year. His first years as a Catholic were anything but happy. His former friends Manning and Ward misunderstood him at every turn; nearly all his enterprises broke in his hand. Because of the prejudice of some of the Irish bishops he was unsuccessful as rector of the newly created National University in Ireland, although his lectures on the *Idea of a University* were universally acclaimed.

His controversy with Charles Kingsley, the English writer, led to no small triumph with Newman's publication of the *Apologia Pro Vita Sua,* his greatest work. With the election of Leo XIII the cloud lifted from Newman. He was created a cardinal, 1879, and spent his last years revising his writings. He died quietly, 1890, in the complete esteem of the whole English-speaking world.

Newman is of first importance to the Catholic Revival because of his personality as well as his works. He was the ideal Englishman: sensitive, mentally alive to every shade of thought, gracious, reserved, retiringly magnificent. In an age of great Englishmen he brought home to the English mind the living possibilities of the race. His entrance into the Catholic literary field communicated notes of value and weight which at once made Catholic literature respectable in the eyes of the general public. The sweet reasonableness and psychological acuteness of his writings and their outer form so logically arranged and beautifully lucid all pointed to Newman as the ideal leader in the struggle for a return to living traditionalism.

Newman's life is best seen in his works: *Collected Works* (36 vols., popular edition, London, 1895). Among these of first importance is the *Apologia,* marvelously concise history of his religious progress from Calvinism to Catholicism. It is in the grand tradition of Augustine's *Confessions.* His *Idea of a University* is one of the best educational treatises in the language, and his *Historical Sketches,* with their clarity of thought and arrangement of ideas, have influenced writers of history since his time, notably Hilaire Belloc. Of his sermons the *Second Spring* is perhaps best; its inner drama is wonderfully clothed in verbal melodies which follow the inner rhythm of ideas.

As a poet Newman was not of first rank. The *Dream of Gerontius,* a felicitous blending of liturgical and psychological insight, hardly approaches the architectural massiveness of Dante, though it has often been referred to as Dantesque. Newman's hymn, *Lead Kindly Light,* still retains perennial popularity in both Protestant and Catholic churches. Wilfrid Ward's *The Life of Newman* is the best biography of the man.

THE SECOND SPRING*

(Preached in St. Mary's, Oscott)

Surge, propera, amica mea, columba mea, formosa mea, et veni. Jam enim hiems transiit, imber abiit et recessit. Flores apparuerunt in terra nostra. (Cant. 2:10–12.)

Arise, make haste, my love, my dove, my beautiful one, and come. For the winter is now past, the rain is over and gone. The flowers have appeared in our land.

WE HAVE familiar experience of the order, the constancy, the perpetual renovation of the material world which surrounds us. Frail and transitory as is every part of it, restless and migratory as are its elements, never-ceasing as are its changes, still it abides. It is bound together by a law of permanence, it is set up in unity; and, though it is ever dying, it is ever coming to life again. Dissolution does but give birth to fresh modes of organization, and one death is the parent of a thousand lives. Each hour, as it comes, is but a testimony, how fleeting, yet how secure, how certain, is the great whole. It is like an image on the waters, which is ever the same, though the waters ever flow. Change upon change — yet one change cries out to another, like the alternate Seraphim, in praise and in glory of their Maker. The sun sinks to rise again; the day is swallowed up in the gloom of the night, to be born out of it, as fresh as if it had never been quenched. Spring passes into summer, and through summer and autumn into winter, only the more surely, by its own ultimate return, to triumph over that grave, towards which it resolutely hastened from its first hour. We mourn over the blossoms of May, because they are to wither: but we know, withal, that May is one day to have its revenge upon November, by the revolution of that solemn circle which never stops — which teaches us in our height of hope, ever to be sober, and in our depth of desolation, never to despair.

And forcibly as this comes home to every one of us, not less forcible is the contrast which exists between this material world, so vigorous, so reproductive, amid all its changes, and the moral world, so feeble, so downward, so resourceless, amid all its aspirations. That which ought to come to nought, endures; that which promises a future, disappoints and is no more. The same sun shines in heaven from first to last, and the blue firmament, the everlasting mountains, reflect his rays; but where is there upon earth the champion, the hero, the lawgiver, the body politic, the sovereign race, which was great three hundred years ago, and is great now? Moralists and poets, often do descant upon this innate vitality of matter, this innate perishableness of mind. Man rises to fall: he tends to dissolution from the moment he begins to be; he lives on, indeed, in his children, he lives on in his name, he lives not on in his own person. He is, as regards the manifestations of his nature here below, as a bubble that breaks, and as water poured out upon the earth. He was young, he is old, he is never young again. This is the lament over him, poured forth in verse and in prose, by Christians and by heathen. The greatest work of God's hands under the sun, he, in all the manifestations of his complex being, is born only to die.

His bodily frame first begins to feel the power of this constraining law, though it is the last to succumb to it. We look at the bloom of youth with interest, yet with pity; and the more graceful and sweet it is, with pity so much the more; for, whatever be its excellence and its glory, soon it begins to be deformed and dishonoured by the very force of its living on. It grows into exhaustion and collapse, till at length it crumbles into that dust out of which it was originally taken.

So is it, too with our moral being, a far higher and diviner portion of our natural constitution; it begins with life, it ends with what is worse than the mere loss of life,

*Newman, John Henry Cardinal, *Complete Works.*

with a living death. How beautiful is the human heart, when it puts forth its first leaves, and opens and rejoices in its spring-tide. Fair as may be the bodily form, fairer far, in its green foliage and bright blossoms, is natural virtue. It blooms in the young, like some rich flower, so delicate, so fragrant, and so dazzling. Generosity and lightness of heart and amiableness, the confiding spirit, the gentle temper, the elastic cheer-fulness, the open hand, the pure affection, the noble aspiration, the heroic resolve, the romantic pursuit, the love in which self has no part, — are not these beautiful? and are they not dressed up and set forth for ad-miration in their best shapes, in tales and in poems? and ah! what a prospect of good is there! who could believe that it is to fade! and yet, as night follows upon day, as de-crepitude follows upon health, so surely are failure, and overthrow, and annihilation, and issue of this natural virtue, if time only be allowed to it to run its course. There are those who are cut off in the first opening of this excellence, and then, if we may trust their epitaphs, they have lived like angels; but wait a while, let them live on, let the course of life proceed, let the bright soul go through the fire and water of the world's temptations and seductions and corruptions and transformations; and, alas for the in-sufficiency of nature! alas for its powerless-ness to persevere, its waywardness in disap-pointing its own promise! Wait till youth has become age; and not more different is the miniature which we have of him when a boy, when every feature spoke of hope, put side by side with the large portrait painted to his honour, when he is old, when his limbs are shrunk, his eye dim, his brow furrowed, and his hair grey, than differs the moral grace of that boyhood from the for-bidding and repulsive aspect of his soul, now that he has lived to the age of man. For moroseness, and misanthropy, and selfish-ness, is the ordinary winter of that spring.

Such is man in his own nature, and such, too, is he in his works. The noblest efforts of his genius, the conquests he has made, the doctrines he has originated, the nations he has civilized, the states he has created, they outlive himself, they outlive him by many centuries, but they tend to an end, and that end is dissolution. Powers of the world, sovereignties, dynasties, sooner or later come to nought; they have their fatal hour. The Roman conqueror shed tears over Carthage, for in the destruction of the rival city he discerned too truly an augury of the fall of Rome; and at length, with the weight and the responsibilities, the crimes and the glories, of centuries upon centuries, the Imperial City fell.

Thus man and all his works are mortal; they die, and they have no power of renovation.

But what is it, my Fathers, my Brothers, what is it that has happened in England just at this time? Something strange is passing over this land, by the very surprise, by the very commotion, which it excites. Were we not near enough the scene of action to be able to say what is going on — were we the inhabitants of some sister planet possessed of a more perfect mechanism than this earth has discovered for surveying the transactions of another globe — and did we turn our eyes thence towards England just at this season, we should be arrested by a political phenomenon as wonderful as any which the astronomer notes down from his physical field of view. It would be the oc-currence of a national commotion, almost without parallel, more violent than has hap-pened here for centuries — at least in the judgments and intentions of men, if not in act and deed. We should note it down, that soon after St. Michael's day, 1850, a storm arose in the moral world, so furious as to demand some great explanation, and to rouse in us an intense desire to gain it. We should observe it increasing from day to day, and spreading from place to place, without remission, almost without lull, up to this very hour, when perhaps it threatens worse still, or at least gives no sure prospect of alleviation. Every party in the body politic undergoes its influence — from the Queen upon her throne, down to the little ones in the infant or day school. The ten thousands of the constituency, the sum-total of Protes-tant sects, the aggregate of religious societies and associations, the great body of established clergy in town and country, the bar, even the medical profession, nay, even literary and scientific circles, every class, every interest, every fireside, gives tokens of this ubiquitous storm. This would be our report of it, seeing it from the distance, and we should speculate on the cause. What is it all about? against what is it directed? what wonder has happened upon earth? what prodigious, what preternatural event is adequate to the burden of so vast an effect?

We should judge rightly in our curiosity about a phenomenon like this; it must be a portentous event, and it is. It is an innovation, a miracle, I may say, in the course of human events. The physical world revolves year by year, and begins again; but the political order of things does not renew itself, does not return; it continues, but it proceeds; there is no retrogression. This is so well understood by men of the day, that with them progress is idolized as another name for good. The past never returns — it is never good — if we are to escape existing ills, it must be by going forward. The past is out of date; the past is dead. As well may the dead live to us, as well may the dead profit us, as the past return. This, then, is the cause of this national transport, this national cry, which encompasses us. The past has returned, the dead live. Thrones are overturned, and are never restored; States live and die, and then are matter only for history. Babylon was great, and Tyre, and Egypt, and Nineveh, and shall never be great again. The English Church was, and the English Church was not, and the English Church is once again. This is the portent, worthy of a cry. It is the coming in of a Second Spring; it is a restoration in the moral world, such as that which yearly takes place in the physical.

Three centuries ago, and the Catholic Church, that great creation of God's power, stood in this land in pride of place. It had the honours of near a thousand years upon it; it was enthroned on some twenty sees up and down the broad country; it was based in the will of a faithful people; it energized through ten thousand instruments of power and influence; and it was ennobled by a host of Saints and Martyrs. The Churches, one by one, recounted and rejoiced in the line of glorified intercessors, who were the respective objects of their grateful homage. Canterbury alone numbered perhaps some sixteen, from St. Augustine to St. Dunstan and St. Elphege, from St. Anselm and St. Thomas down to St. Edmund. York had its St. Paulinus, St. John, St. Wilfred, and St. William; London, its St. Erconwald; Durham, its St. Cuthbert; Winton, its St. Swithun. Then there were St. Aidan of Lindisfarne, and St. Hugh of Lincoln, and St. Chad of Lichfield, and St. Thomas of Hereford, and St. Osmund of Salisbury, and St. Birinus of Dorchester, and St. Richard of Chichester. And then, too, its religious orders, its monastic establishments, its universities, its wide relations all over Europe, its high prerogatives in the temporal state, its wealth, its dependencies, its popular honours — where was there in the whole of Christendom a more glorious hierarchy? Mixed up with the civil institutions, with kings and nobles, with the people, found in every village and in every town — it seemed destined to stand, so long as England stood, and to outlast, it might be, England's greatness.

But it was the high decree of heaven, that the majesty of that presence should be blotted out. It is a long story, my Fathers and Brothers — you know it well. I need not go through it. The vivifying principle of truth, the shadow of St. Peter, the grace of the Redeemer, left it. That old Church in its day became a corpse (a marvellous, an awful change!); and then it did but corrupt the air which once it refreshed, and cumber the ground which once it beautified. So all seemed to be lost; and there was a struggle for a time, and then its priests were cast out or martyred. There were sacrileges innumerable. Its temples were profaned or destroyed; its revenues seized by covetous nobles, or squandered upon the ministers of a new faith. The presence of Catholicism was at length simply removed — its grace disowned, — its power despised, — its name, except as a matter of history, at length almost unknown. It took a long time to do this thoroughly; much time, much thought, much labour, much expense; but at last it was done. Oh, that miserable day, centuries before we were born! What a martyrdom to live in it and see the fair form of Truth, moral and material, hacked piece-meal, and every limb and organ carried off, and burned in the fire, or cast into the deep! But at last the work was done. Truth was disposed of, and shovelled away, and there was a calm, a silence, a sort of peace;—and such was about the state of things when we were born into this weary world.

My Fathers and Brothers, you have seen it on one side, and some of us on another; but one and all of us can bear witness to the fact of the utter contempt into which Catholicism had fallen by the time that we were born. You, alas, know it far better than I can know it; but it may not be out of place, if by one or two tokens, as by the strokes of a pencil, I bear witness to you from without, of what you can witness so much more truly from within. No longer the Catholic Church in the country; nay, no longer, I may say, a Catholic community;—but a few adherents of the Old Religion, moving silently and sorrowfully about, as memorials of what had been. "The Roman Catholics;"—not a body, however small, representative of the Great Communion abroad,—but a mere handful of individuals, who might be counted, like the pebbles and detritus of the great deluge, and who, forsooth, merely happened to retain a creed which, in its day indeed, was the profession of a Church. Here a set of poor Irishmen, coming and going at harvest time, or a colony of them lodged in a miserable quarter of the vast metropolis. There, perhaps an elderly person, seen walking in the streets, grave and solitary, and strange, though noble in bearing, and said to be of good family, and a "Roman Catholic." An old-fashioned house of gloomy appearance, closed in with high walls, with an iron gate, and yews, and the report attaching to it that "Roman Catholics" lived there; but who they were, or what they did, or what was meant by calling them "Roman Catholics," no one could tell;—though it

had an unpleasant sound, and told of form and superstition. And then, perhaps, as we went to and fro, looking with a boy's curious eyes through the great city, we might come to-day upon some Moravian chapel, or Quaker's meeting-house, and to-morrow on a chapel of the "Roman Catholics:" but nothing was to be gathered from it, except that there were lights burning there, and some boys in white, swinging censers; and what it all meant could only be learned from books, from Protestant Histories and Sermons; and they did not report well of "the Roman Catholics," but, on the contrary, deposed that they had once had power and had abused it. And then, again, we might on one occasion hear it pointedly put out by some literary man, as the result of his careful investigation, and as a recondite point of information, which few knew, that there was this difference between the Roman Catholics of England and the Roman Catholics of Ireland, that the latter had bishops, and the former were governed by four officials, called Vicars-Apostolic.

Such was about the sort of knowledge possessed of Christianity by the heathen of old time, who persecuted its adherents from the face of the earth and then called them a *gens lucifuga,* a people who shunned the light of day. Such were Catholics in England, found in corners, and alleys, and cellars, and the housetops, or in the recesses of the country; cut off from the populous world around them, and dimly seen, as if through a mist or in twilight, as ghosts flitting to and fro, by the high Protestants, the lords of the earth. At length so feeble did they become, so utterly contemptible, that contempt gave birth to pity; and the more generous of their tyrants actually began to wish to bestow on them some favour, under the notion that the opinions were simply too absurd ever to spread again, and that they themselves, were they but raised in civil importance, would soon unlearn and be ashamed of them. And thus, out of mere kindness to us, they began to vilify our doctrines to the Protestant world, that so our very idiocy or our secret unbelief might be our plea for mercy.

A great change, an awful contrast, between the time-honoured Church of St. Augustine and St. Thomas, and the poor remnant of their children in the beginning of the nineteenth century! It was a miracle, I might say, to have pulled down that lordly power; but there was a greater and a truer one in store. No one could have prophesied its fall, but still less would any one have ventured to prophecy its rise again. The fall was wonderful; still after all it was in the order of nature; — all things come to nought: its rise again would be a different sort of wonder, for it is in the order of grace, — and who can hope for miracles, and such a miracle as this? Has the whole course of history a like to show? I must speak cautiously and according to my knowledge, but I recollect no parallel to it. Augustine, indeed, came to the same island to which the early missionaries had come already; but they came to Britons, and he to Saxons. The Arian Goths and Lombards, too, cast off their heresy in St. Augustine's age, and joined the Church; but they had never fallen away from her. The inspired word seems to imply the almost impossiblity of such a grace as the renovation of those who have crucified to themselves again, and trodden under foot, the Son of God. Who then could have dared to hope that, out of so sacrilegious a nation as this is, a people would have been formed again unto their Saviour? What signs did it show that it was to be singled out from among the nations? Had it been prophesied some fifty years ago, would not the very notion have seemed preposterous and wild?

My Fathers, there was one of your own order, then in the maturity of his powers and his reputation. His name is the property of this diocese; yet is too great, too venerable, too dear to all Catholics, to be confined to any part of England, when it is rather a household word in the mouths of all of us. What would have been the feelings of that venerable man, the champion of God's ark in an evil time, could he have lived to see this day? It is almost presumptuous for one who knew him not, to draw pictures about him, and his thoughts, and his friends, some of whom are even here present; yet am I wrong in fancying that a day such as this, in which we stand, would have seemed to him a dream, or, if he prophesied of it, to his hearers nothing but a mockery? Say that one time, rapt in spirit, he had reached forward to the future, and that his mortal eye had wandered from that lowly chapel in the valley which had been for centuries in the possession of Catholics, to the neighbouring height, then waste and solitary. And let him say to those about him: "I see a bleak mount, looking upon an open country, over against that huge town, to whose inhabitants Catholicism is of so little account. I see the ground marked out, and ample enclosure made; and plantations are rising there, clothing and circling in the space.

"And there on that high spot, far from the haunts of men, yet in the very centre of the island, a large edifice, or rather pile of edifices, appears with many fronts, and courts, and long cloisters and corridors, and story upon story. And there it rises, under the invocation of the same sweet and powerful name which has been our strength and consolation in the Valley. I look more attentively at that building, and I see it is fashioned upon that ancient style of art which brings back the past, which had seemed to be perishing from off the face of the earth, or to be preserved only as a curiosity, or to be imitated only as a fancy. I listen, and I hear the sound of voices, grave and musical, renewing the old chant, with which Augustine greeted Ethelbert in the free air upon the Kentish strand. It comes from a long procession, and it winds along the cloisters. Priests and Religious, theologians from the schools, and canons from the Cathedral, walk in due precedence. And then there comes a vision of well-nigh twelve mitred heads; and last I see a Prince of the Church, in the royal dye of empire and of martyrdom, a pledge to us from Rome of Rome's unwearied love, a token that that goodly company is firm in Apostolic faith and hope. And the shadow of the Saints is there; — St Benedict is there, speaking to us by the voice of bishop and of priest, and counting over the long ages through which he has prayed, and studied, and laboured; there, too, is St. Dominic's white wool, which no blemish can impair, no stain can dim: — and if St. Bernard be not there, it is only that his absence may make him be remembered more. And the princely patriarch, St. Ignatius, too, the St. George of the modern world, with his chivalrous lance run through his writhing foe, he, too, sheds his blessing upon that train. And others, also, his equals or his juniors in history, whose pictures are above our altars, or soon shall be, the surest proof that the Lord's arm has not waxen short, nor His mercy failed, — they, too, are looking down from their thrones on high upon the throng. And so that high company moves on into the holy place; and there, with august rite and awful sacrifice, inaugurates the great act which brings it thither." What is that act? it is the first synod of a new Hierarchy; it is the resurrection of the Church.

O my Fathers, my Brothers, had that revered Bishop so spoken then, who that had heard him but would have said that he spoke what could not be? What! those few scattered worshippers, the Roman Catholics, to form a Church! Shall the past be rolled back? Shall the grave open? Shall the Saxons live again to God? Shall the shepherds, watching their poor flocks by night, be visited by a multitude of the heavenly army, and hear how their Lord has been new-born in their own city? Yes; for grace can, where nature cannot. The world grows old, but the Church is ever young. She can, in any time, at her Lord's will, "inherit the Gentiles, and inhabit the desolate cities." "Arise, Jerusalem, for thy light is come, and the glory of the Lord is risen upon thee. Behold, darkness shall cover the earth, and a mist the people; but the Lord shall rise upon thee, and His glory shall be seen upon thee. Lift up thine eyes round about, and see; all these are gathered together, they come to thee; thy sons shall come from afar, and thy daughters shall rise up at thy side." "Arise, make haste, my love, my dove, my beautiful one, and come. For the winter is now past and the rain is over and gone. The

flowers have appeared in our land. . . . the fig-tree hath put forth her green figs; the vines in flower yield their sweet smell. Arise, my love, my beautiful one, and come." It is the time for thy Visitation. Arise, Mary, and go forth in thy strength into that north country, which once was thine own, and take possession of a land which knows thee not. Arise, Mother of God, and with thy thrilling voice, speak to those who labor with child, and are in pain, till the babe of grace leaps within them. Shine on us, dear Lady, with thy bright countenance, like the sun in his strength, *O stella matutina*, O harbinger of peace, till our year is one perpetual May. From thy sweet eyes, from thy pure smile, from thy majestic brow, let ten thousand influences rain down, not to confound or overwhelm, but to persuade, to win over thine enemies. O Mary, my hope, O Mother undefiled, fulfil to us the promise of this Spring. A second temple rises on the ruins of the old. Canterbury has gone its way, and York is gone, and Durham is gone, and Winchester is gone. It was sore to part with them. We clung to the vision of past greatness, and would not believe it could come to nought; but the Church in England has died, and the Church lives again. Westminster and Nottingham, Beverley and Hexham, Northampton and Shrewsbury, if the world lasts, shall be names as musical to the ear, as stirring to the heart, as the glories we have lost; and Saints shall rise out of them, if God so will, and Doctors once again shall give the law to Israel, and Preachers call to penance and to justice, as at the beginning.

Yes, my Fathers and Brothers, and if it be God's blessed will, not Saints alone, not Doctors only, not Preachers only, shall be ours — but Martyrs, too, shall re-consecrate the soil to God. We know not what is before us, ere we win our own; we are engaged in a great, a joyful work, but in proportion to God's grace is the fury of His enemies. They have welcomed us as the lion greets his prey. Perhaps they may be familiarized in time with our appearance, but perhaps they may be irritated the more. To set up the Church again in England is too great an act to be done in a corner. We have had reason to expect that such a boon would not be given to us without a cross. It is not God's way that great blessings should descend without the sacrifice first of great sufferings. If the truth is to be spread to any wide extent among this people, how can we dream, how can we hope, that trial and trouble shall not accompany its going forth? And we have already, if it may be said without presumption, to commence our work withal, a large store of merits. We have no slight outfit for our opening warfare. Can we religiously suppose that the blood of our martyrs, three centuries ago and since, shall never receive its recompense? Those priests, secular and regular, did they suffer for no end? or rather, for an end which is not yet accomplished? The long imprisonment, the fetid dungeon, the weary suspense, the tyrannous trial, the barbarous sentence, the savage execution, the rack, the gibbet, the knife, the cauldron, the numberless tortures of those holy victims, O my God, are they to have no reward? Are Thy martyrs to cry from under Thine altar for their loving vengeance on this guilty people, and to cry in vain? Shall they lose life, and not gain a better life for the children of those who persecuted them? Is this Thy way, O my God, righteous and true? Is it according to Thy promise, O King of saints, if I may dare talk to Thee of justice? Didst not Thou Thyself pray for Thine enemies upon the cross, and convert them? Did not Thy first Martyr win Thy great Apostle, then a persecutor, by his loving prayer? And in that day of trial and desolation for England, when hearts were pierced through and through with Mary's woe, at the crucifixion of Thy body mystical, was not every tear that flowed, and every drop of blood that was shed, the seeds of a future harvest, when they who sowed in sorrow were to reap in joy?

And as that suffering of the Martyrs is not yet recompensed, so perchance, it is not yet exhausted. Something, for what we know, remains to be undergone, to complete the necessary sacrifice. May God forbid it, for this poor nation's sake! But still could

we be surprised, my Fathers and my Brothers, if the winter even now should not yet be quite over? Have we any right to take it strange, if, in this English land, the springtime of the Church should turn out to be an English spring, an uncertain, anxious time of hope and fear, of joy and suffering — of bright promise and budding hopes, yet withal, of keen blasts, and cold showers, and sudden storms?

One thing alone I know — that according to our need, so will be our strength. One thing I am sure of, that the more the enemy rages against us, so much the more will the Saints in Heaven plead for us; the more fearful are our trials from the world, the more present to us will be our Mother Mary, and our good Patrons, and Angel Guardians; the more malicious are the devices of men against us, the louder cry of supplication will ascend from the bosom of the whole Church to God for us. We shall not be left orphans; we shall have within us the strength of the Paraclete, promised to the Church and to every member of it. My Fathers, my Brothers in the priesthood, I speak from my heart when I declare my conviction, that there is no one among you here present but, if God so willed, would readily become a martyr for His sake. I do not say you would wish it; I do not say that the natural will would not pray that that chalice might pass away; I do not speak of what you can do by any strength of yours; — but in the strength of God, in the grace of the Spirit, in the armor of justice, by the consolations and peace of the Church, by the blessing of the Apostles Peter and Paul, and in the name of Christ, you would do what nature cannot do. By the intercession of the Saints on high, by the penances and good works and the prayers of the people of God on earth, you would be forcibly borne up as upon the waves of the mighty deep, and carried on out of yourselves by the fulness of grace, whether nature wished it or no. I do not mean violently, or with unseemly struggle, but calmly, gracefully, sweetly, joyously, you would mount up and ride forth to battle, as on the rush of Angel's wings, as your fathers did before you, and gained the prize. You, who day by day offer up the Immaculate Lamb of God, you who hold in your hands the Incarnate Word under the visible tokens which He has ordained, you who again and again drain the chalice of the Great Victim; who is to make you fear? what is to startle you? what to seduce you? who is to stop you, whether you are to suffer or to do, whether to lay the foundations of the Church in tears, or to put the crown upon the work in jubilation?

My Fathers, my Brothers, one word more. It may seem as if I were going out of my way in thus addressing you; but I have some sort of plea to urge in extenuation. When the English College at Rome was set up by the solicitude of a great Pontiff in the beginning of England's sorrows, and missionaries were trained there for confessorship and martyrdom here, who was it that saluted the fair Saxon youths as they passed by him in the streets of the great City, with the salutation, "Salvete flores martyrum"? And when the time came for each in turn to leave that peaceful home, and to go forth to the conflict, to whom did they betake themselves before leaving home, to receive a blessing which might nerve them for their work? They went for a Saint's blessing; they went to a calm old man, who had never seen blood, except in penance; who had longed indeed to die for Christ, what time the great St. Francis opened

the way to the far East, but who had been fixed as if a sentinel in the holy city, and walked up and down for fifty years on one beat, while his brethren were in the battle. Oh! the fire of that heart, too great for its frail tenement, which tormented him to be kept at home when the whole Church was at war! and therefore came those bright-haired strangers to him, ere they set out for the scene of their passion, that the full zeal and love pent up in that burning breast might find a vent, and flow over, from him who was kept at home, upon those who were to face the foe. Therefore one by one, each in his turn, those youthful soldiers came to the old man; and one by one they persevered and gained the crown and the palm, — all but one, who had not gone, and would not go, for the salutary blessing.

My Fathers, my Brothers, that old man was my own St. Philip. Bear with me for his sake. If I have spoken too seriously, his sweet smile shall temper it. As he was with you three centuries ago in Rome, when our Temple fell, so now surely when it is rising, it is a pleasant token that he should have even set out on his travels to you; and that, as if remembering how he interceded for you at home, and recognizing the relations he then formed with you, he should now be wishing to have a name among you, and to be loved by you, and perchance to do you a service, here in your own land.

ST. CHRYSOSTOM*

JOHN OF ANTIOCH, from his sanctity and his eloquence called Chrysostom, was approaching sixty years of age, when he had to deliver himself up to the imperial officers, and to leave Constantinople for a distant exile. He had been the great preacher of the day now for nearly twenty years; first at Antioch, then in the metropolis of the East; and his gift of speech, as in the instance of the two great classical orators

before him, was to be his ruin. He had made an Empress his enemy, more powerful than Antipater — as passionate, if not so vindictive, as Fulvia. Nor was this all; a zealous Christian preacher offends not individuals merely, but classes of men, and much more so when he is pastor and ruler too, and has to punish as well as to denounce. Eudoxia, the Empress, might be taken off suddenly — as indeed she was taken off a few weeks after the Saint arrived at the place of exile, which she personally, in spite of his entreaties, had marked out for

*Newman, John Henry Cardinal, *Complete Works,* Historical Sketches.

him—but her death did but serve to increase the violence of the persecution directed against him. She had done her part in it, perhaps she might have even changed her mind in his favour; probably the agitation of a bad conscience was, in her critical condition, the cause of her death. She was taken out of the way; but her partisans, who had made use of her, went on vigorously with the evil work which she had begun. When Cacusus would not kill him, they sent him on his travels anew, across a far wilder country than he had already traversed, to a remote town on the eastern coast of the Euxine; and he sank under this fresh trial.

The Euxine! that strange mysterious sea, which typifies the abyss of outer darkness, as the blue Mediterranean basks under the smile of heaven in the centre of civilization and religion. The awful, yet splendid drama of man's history has mainly been carried on upon the Mediterranean shores; while the Black Sea has ever been on the very outskirts of the habitable world, and the scene of wild unnatural portents; with legends of Prometheus on the savage Caucasus, of Medea gathering witch-herbs in the moist meadows of the Phasis, and of Iphigenia sacrificing the shipwrecked stranger in Taurica; and then again, with the more historical, yet not more grateful visions of barbarous tribes, Goths, Huns, Scythians, Tartars, flitting over the steppes and wastes which encircle its inhospitable waters. To be driven from the bright cities and sunny clime of Italy or Greece to such a region, was worse than death; and the luxurious Roman actually preferred death to exile. The suicide of Gallus, under this dread doom, is well known; Ovid, too cowardly to be desperate, drained out the dregs of a vicious life on the cold marshes between the Danube and the sea. I need scarcely allude to the heroic Popes who patiently lived on in the Crimea, till a martyrdom, in which they had no part but the suffering, released them.

But banishment was an immense evil in itself. Cicero, even though he had liberty of person, the choice of a home, and the prospect of a return, roamed disconsolate through the cities of Greece, because he was debarred access to the senate-house and forum. Chrysostom had his own *rostra,* his own *curia;* it was the Holy Temple, where his eloquence gained for him victories not less real, and more momentous, than the detection and overthrow of Catiline. Great as was his gift of oratory, it was not by the fertility of his imagination, or the splendour of his diction that he gained the surname of "Mouth of Gold." We shall be very wrong if we suppose that fine expressions, or rounded periods, or figures of speech, were the credentials by which he claimed to be the first doctor of the East. His oratorical power was but the instrument, by which he readily, gracefully, adequately expressed—expressed without effort and with felicity—the keen feelings, the living ideas, the earnest practical lessons which he had to communicate to his hearers. He spoke, because his heart, his head, were brimful of things to speak about. His elocution corresponded to that strength and flexibility of limb, that quickness of eye, hand, and foot, by which a man excels in manly games or in mechanical skill. It would be a great mistake, in speaking of it, to ask whether it was Attic or Asiatic, terse or flowing, when its distinctive praise was that it was natural. His unrivalled charm, as that of every really eloquent man, lies in his singleness of purpose, his fixed grasp of his aim, his noble earnestness.

A bright, cheerful, gentle soul; a sensitive heart, a temperament open to emotion and impulse; and all this elevated, refined, transformed by the touch of heaven,—such was St. John Chrysostom; winning followers, riveting affections, by his sweetness, frankness, and neglect of self. In his labours, in his preachings, he thought of others only. "I am always in admiration of that thrice-blessed man," says an able critic, "because he ever in all his writings puts before him as his object, to be useful to his hearers; and as to all other matters, he either simply put them aside, or took the least possible notice of them. Nay, as to his seeming ignorant of some of the thoughts of Scripture, or careless of entering into its depths, and similar defects all this he utterly disregarded in comparison of the profit of his hearers."

There was as little affectation of sanctity in his dress or living as there was effort in his eloquence. In his youth he had been one of the most austere of men; at the age of twenty-one, renouncing bright prospects of the world, he had devoted himself to prayer and study of the Scriptures. He had retired to the mountains near Antioch, his native place, and had lived among the monks. This had been his home for six years, and he had chosen it in order to subdue the daintiness of his natural appetite. "Lately," he wrote to a friend at the time — "lately, when I had made up my mind to leave the city and betake myself to the tabernacle of the monks, I was for ever inquiring and busying myself how I was to get a supply of provisions; whether it would be possible to procure fresh bread for my eating, whether I should be ordered to use the same oil for my lamp and for my food, to undergo the hardship of peas and beans, or of severe toil, such as digging, carrying wood or water, and the like; in a word, I made much account of bodily comfort." Such was the nervous anxiety and fidget of mind with which he had begun; but this rough discipline soon effected its object, and at length, even by preference, he took upon him mortifications which at first were a trouble to him. For the last two years of his monastic exercise, he lived by himself in a cave; he slept, when he did sleep, without lying down; he exposed himself to the extremities of cold. At length he found he was passing the bounds of discretion, nature would bear no more; he fell ill, and returned to the city.

A course of ascetic practice such as this would leave its spiritual effects upon him for life. It sank deep into him, though the surface might not show it. His duty at Constantinople was to mix with the world; and he lived as others, except as regards such restraints as his sacred office and archiepiscopal station demanded of him. He wore shoes, and an undergarment; but his stomach was ever delicate, and at meals he was obliged to have his own dish, such as it was, to himself. However, he mixed freely with all ranks of men; and he made friends, affectionate friends, of young and old, men and women, rich and poor, by condescending to all of every degree.

How he was loved at Antioch is shown by the expedient used to transfer him thence to Constantinople. Asterius, count of the East, had orders to send for him, and ask his company to a church without the city. Having got him into his carriage, he drove off with him to the first station on the high-road to Constantinople, where imperial officers were in readiness to convey him thither. Thus he was brought upon the scene of those trials which have given him a name in history, and a place in the catalogue of the Saints. At the imperial city he was as much followed, if not as popular, as at Antioch. "The people flocked to him," says Sozomen, "as often as he preached; some of them to hear what would profit them, others to make trial of him. He carried them away, one and all, and persuaded them to think as he did about the Divine Nature. They hung upon his words, and could not have enough of them; so that, when they thrust and jammed themselves together in an alarming way, every one making an effort to get nearer to him, and to hear him more perfectly, he took his seat in the midst of them, and taught from the pulpit of the Reader." He was, indeed, a man to make both friends and enemies; to inspire affection, and to kindle resentment; but his friends loved him with a love "stronger" than "death," and more burning than "hell"; and it was well to be so hated, if he was so beloved.

IDEA OF A UNIVERSITY*

In 1851 Newman was appointed rector of the newly established National University in Ireland, which was under the control of the Irish hierarchy. In 1852 he gave in Ireland the addresses making up the *Idea of a University*. The lectures end abruptly, but they are, as William Barry has said, "the best defense of Catholic educational theories in any language."

DISCOURSE V

KNOWLEDGE ITS OWN END

I

I HAVE said that all branches of knowledge are connected together, because the subject-matter of knowledge is intimately united in itself, as being the acts and the work of the Creator. Hence it is that the Sciences, into which our knowledge may be said to be cast, have multiplied bearings one on another, and an internal sympathy, and admit, or rather demand, comparison and adjustment. They complete, correct, balance each other. This consideration, if well-founded, must be taken into account, not only as regards the attainment of truth, which is their common end, but as regards the influence which they exercise upon those whose education consists in the study of them. I have said already, that to give undue prominence to one is to be unjust to another; to neglect or supersede these is to divert those from their proper object. It is to unsettle the boundary lines between science and science, to disturb their action, to destroy the harmony which binds them together. Such a proceeding will have a corresponding effect when introduced into a place of education. There is no science but tells a different tale, when viewed as a portion of a whole, from what it is likely to suggest when taken by itself, without the safeguard, as I may call it of others.

Let me make use of an illustration. In the combination of colours, very different effects are produced by a difference in their selection and juxta-position; red, green, and white, change their shades, according to the contrast to which they are submitted. And, in like manner, the drift and meaning of a branch of knowledge varies with the company in which it is introduced to the student. If his reading is confined to one subject, however, such division of labour may favour the advancement of a particular pursuit, a point into which I do not here enter, certainly it has a tendency to contract his mind. If it is incorporated with others, it depends on those others as to the kind of influence which it exerts upon him. Thus the Classics, which in England are the means of refining the taste, have in France subserved the spread of revolutionary and deistical doctrines. In Metaphysics, again, Butler's Analogy of Religion, which has had so much to do with the conversion to the Catholic faith of members of the University of Oxford, appeared to Pitt and others, who had received a different training, to operate only in the direction of infidelity. And so again, Watson, Bishop of Llandaff, as I think he tells us in the narrative of his life, felt the science of Mathematics to indispose the mind to religious belief, while others see in its investigations the best parallel, and thereby defence, of the Christian Mysteries. In like manner, I suppose, Arcesilas would not have handled logic as Aristotle, nor Aristotle have criticized poets as Plato; yet reasoning and poetry are subject to scientific rules.

It is a great point then to enlarge the range of studies which a University professes, even for the sake of the students; and, though they cannot pursue every subject which is open to them, they will be the gainers by living among those and under those who represent the whole circle. This I conceive to be the advantage of a seat of universal learning, considered as a place of education. An assemblage of learned men, zealous for their own sciences, and rivals of each other, are brought, by familiar intercourse and for the sake of intellectual peace, to adjust together the claims and relations of their respective subjects of investigation. They learn to respect, to consult, to aid each other. Thus

*Newman, John Henry Cardinal, *Collected Works*, Lectures.

is created a pure and clear atmosphere of thought, which the student also breathes, though in his own case he only pursues a few sciences out of the multitude. He profits by an intellectual tradition, which is independent of particular teachers, which guides him in his choice of subjects, and duly interprets for him those which he chooses. He apprehends the great outlines of knowledge, the principles on which it rests, the scale of its parts, its lights and its shades, its great points and its little, as he otherwise cannot apprehend them. Hence it is that his education is called "Liberal." A habit of mind is formed which lasts through life, of which the attributes are, freedom, equitableness, calmness, moderation, and wisdom; or what in a former Discourse I have ventured to call a philosophical habit. This then I would assign as the special fruit of the education furnished at a University, as contrasted with other places of teaching or modes of teaching. This is the main purpose of a University in its treatment of its students.

And now the question is asked me, What is the *use* of it? and my answer will constitute the main subject of the Discourses which are to follow.

2

Cautious and practical thinkers, I say, will ask of me, what, after all, is the gain of this Philosophy, of which I make such account, and from which I promise so much. Even supposing it to enable us to exercise the degree of trust exactly due to every science respectively, and to estimate precisely the value of every truth which is anywhere to be found, how are we better for this master view of things, which I have been extolling? Does it not reverse the principle of the division of labour? will practical objects be obtained better or worse by its cultivation? to what then does it lead? where does it end? what does it do? how does it profit? what does it promise? Particular sciences are respectively the basis of definite arts, which carry on to results tangible and beneficial the truths which are the subjects of the knowledge attained; what is the Art of this science of

sciences? what is the fruit of such a Philosophy? what are we proposing to effect, what inducements do we hold out to the Catholic community, when we set about the enterprise of founding a University?

I am asked what is the end of University Education, and of the Liberal or Philosophical Knowledge which I conceive it to impart: I answer, that what I have already said has been sufficient to show that it has a very tangible, real and sufficient end, though the end cannot be divided from the knowledge itself. Knowledge is capable of being its own end. Such is the constitution of the human mind, that any kind of knowledge, if it be really such, is its own reward. And if this is true of all knowledge, it is true also of that special Philosophy, which I have made to consist in a comprehensive view of truth in all its branches, of the relations of science to science, of their mutual bearings, and their respective values. What the worth of such an acquirement is, compared with other objects which we seek, — wealth or power or honour or the conveniences and comforts of life, I do not profess here to discuss; but I would maintain, and mean to show, that it is an object, in its own nature so really and undeniably good, as to be the compensation of a great deal of thought in the compassing, and a great deal of trouble in the attaining.

Now, when I say that knowledge is not merely a means to something beyond it or the preliminary of certain arts into which it naturally resolves, but an end sufficient to rest in and to pursue for its own sake, surely I am uttering no paradox, for I am stating what is both intelligible in itself, and has ever been the common judgment of philosophers and the ordinary feeling of mankind. I am saying what at least the public opinion of this day ought to be slow to deny, considering how much we have heard of late years, in opposition to Religion, of entertaining, curious, and various knowledge. I am but saying what whole volumes have been written to illustrate, viz., by a "selection from the records of Philosophy, Literature, and Art, in all ages and countries, of a body of examples, to show how the most unpropitious circumstances have been unable to conquer an ardent desire for the acquisition of know-ledge." That further advantages accrue to us and redound to others by its possession, over and above what it is in itself, I am very far indeed from denying; but, independent of these, we are satisfying a direct need of our nature in its very acquisition; and, whereas our nature, unlike that of the inferior crea-tion, does not at once reach its perfection, but depends, in order to it, on a number of external aids and appliances, Knowledge, as one of the principal of these, is valuable for what its very presence in us does for us after the manner of a habit, even though it be turned to no further account, nor subserve any direct end.

3

Hence it is that Cicero, in enumerating the various heads of mental excellence, lays down the pursuit of Knowledge for its own sake, as the first of them. "This pertains most of all to human nature," he says, "for we are all of us drawn to the pursuit of Knowledge; in which to excel we consider excellent, whereas to mistake, to err, to be ignorant, to be deceived, is both an evil and a disgrace." And he considers Knowledge the very first object to which we are attracted, after the supply of our physical wants. After the calls and duties of our animal existence, as they may be termed, as regards ourselves, our family, and our neighbours, follows, he tells us, "the search after truth. Accordingly, as soon as we escape from the pressure of neces-sary cares, forthwith we desire to see, to hear, and to learn; and consider the knowledge of what is hidden or is wonderful a condition of our happiness."

This passage, though it is but one of many similar passages in a multitude of authors, I take for the very reason that it is so familiarly known to us; and I wish you to observe, Gentlemen, how distinctly it separates the pursuit of Knowledge from those ulterior objects to which certainly it can be made to conduce, and which are, I suppose, solely contemplated by the persons who would ask of me the use of a University or Liberal Education. So far from dreaming of the cul-tivation of Knowledge directly and mainly in

order to our physical comfort and enjoyment, for the sake of life and person, of health, of the conjugal and family union, of the social tie and civil security, the great Orator implies, that it is only after our physical and political needs are supplied, and when we are "free from necessary duties and cares," that we are in a condition for "desiring to see, to hear, and to learn." Nor does he contemplate in the least degree the reflex or subsequent action of Knowledge, when acquired, upon those material goods which we set out by securing before we seek it; on the contrary, he ex-pressly denies its bearing upon social life altogether, strange as such a procedure is to those who live after the rise of the Baconian philosophy, and he cautions us against such a cultivation of it as will interfere with our duties to our fellow-creatures. "All these methods," he says, "are engaged in the investi-gation of truth; by the pursuit of which to be carried off from public occupations is a transgression of duty. For the praise of virtue lies altogether in action; yet intermissions often occur, and then we recur to such pur-suits; not to say that the incessant activity of the mind is vigorous enough to carry us on in the pursuit of knowledge, even without any exertion of our own." The idea of benefiting society by means of "the pursuit of science and knowledge" did not enter at all into the motives which he would assign for their cultivation.

This was the ground of the opposition which the elder Cato made to the intro-duction of Greek Philosophy among his countrymen, when Carneades and his com-panions, on occasion of their embassy, were charming the Roman youth with their elo-quent expositions of it. The fit representative of a practical people, Cato estimated every thing by what it produced; whereas the Pur-suit of Knowledge promised nothing beyond Knowledge itself. He despised that refine-ment or enlargement of mind of which he had no experience.

4

Things, which can bear to be cut off from every thing else and yet persist in living, must have life in themselves; pursuits, which issue in nothing, and still maintain their ground for ages, which are regarded as admirable, though they have not as yet proved themselves to be useful, must have their sufficient end in themselves, whatever it turn out to be. And we are brought to the same conclusion by considering the force of the epithet, by which the knowledge under consideration is popularly designated. It is common to speak of "*liberal* knowledge," of the "*liberal* arts and studies," and of a "*liberal* education," as the especial characteristic or property of a University and of a gentleman; what is really meant by the word? Now, first, in its grammatical sense it is opposed to *servile;* and by "servile work" is understood, as our catechisms inform us, bodily labour, mechanical employment, and the like, in which the mind has little or no part. Parallel to such servile works are those arts, if they deserve the name, of which the poet speaks, which owe their origin and their method to hazard, not to skill; as, for instance, the practice and operations of an empiric. As far as this contrast may be considered as a guide into the meaning of the word, liberal education and liberal pursuits are exercises of mind, of reason, of reflection.

But we want something more for its explanation, for there are bodily exercises which are liberal, and mental exercises which are not so. For instance, in ancient times the practitioners in medicine were commonly slaves; yet it was an art as intellectual in its nature, in spite of the pretence, fraud, and quackery with which it might then, as now, be debased, as it was heavenly in its aim. And so in like manner, we contrast a liberal education with a commercial education or a professional; yet no one can deny that commerce and the professions afford scope for the highest and most diversified powers of mind. There is then a great variety of intellectual exercises, which are not technically called "liberal;" on the other hand, I say, there are exercises of the body which do receive that appellation. Such, for instance, was the palaestra, in ancient times; such the Olympic games, in which strength and dexterity of body as well as of mind gained the prize. In

Xenophon we read of the young Persian nobility being taught to ride on horseback and to speak the truth; both being among the accomplishments of a gentleman. War, too, however rough a profession, has ever been accounted liberal, unless in cases when it becomes heroic, which would introduce us to another subject.

Now comparing these instances together, we shall have no difficulty in determining the principle of this apparent variation in the application of the term which I am examining. Manly games, or games of skill, or military prowess, though bodily, are, it seems, accounted liberal; on the other hand, what is merely professional, though highly intellectual, nay, though liberal in comparison of trade and manual labour, is not simply called liberal, and mercantile occupations are not liberal at all. Why this distinction? because that alone is liberal knowledge, which stands on its own pretensions, which is independent of sequel, expects no complement, refuses to be *informed* (as it is called) by any end, or absorbed into any art, in order duly to present itself to our contemplation. The most ordinary pursuits have this specific character, if they are self-sufficient and complete; the highest lose it, when they minister to something beyond them. It is absurd to balance, in point of worth and importance, a treatise on reducing fractures with a game of cricket or a fox-chase; yet of the two the bodily exercise has that quality which we call "liberal," and the intellectual has it not. And so of the learned professions altogether, considered merely as professions; although one of them be the most popularly beneficial, and another the most politically important, and the third the most intimately divine of all human pursuits, yet the very greatness of their end, the health of the body, or of the commonwealth, or of the soul, diminishes, not increases, their claim to the appellation "liberal," and that still more, if they are cut down to the strict exigencies of that end. If, for instance, Theology, instead of being cultivated as a contemplation, be limited to the purposes of the pulpit or be represented by the catechism, it loses — not its usefulness, not its divine character, not its meritoriousness (rather it gains a claim upon these titles by such charitable condescension) — but it does lose the particular attribute which I am illustrating; just as a face worn by tears and fasting loses its beauty, or a labourer's hand loses its delicateness; for Theology thus exercised is not simple knowledge, but rather is an art or a business making use of Theology. And thus it appears that even what is supernatural need not be liberal, nor need a hero be a gentleman, for the plain reason that one idea is not another idea. And in like manner the Baconian Philosophy, by using its physical sciences in the service of man, does thereby transfer them from the order of Liberal Pursuits to, I do not say the inferior, but the distinct class of the Useful. And, to take a different instance, hence again, as is evident, whenever personal gain is the motive, still more distinctive an effect has it upon the character of a given pursuit; thus racing, which was a liberal exercise in Greece, forfeits its rank in times like these, so far as it is made the occasion of gambling.

All that I have been now saying is summed up in a few characteristic words of the great Philosopher. "Of possessions," he says, "those rather are useful, which bear fruit; those *liberal, which tend to enjoyment.* By fruitful, I mean, which yield revenue; by enjoyable, where *nothing accrues of consequence beyond the using.*"

5

Do not suppose, that in thus appealing to the ancients, I am throwing back the world two thousand years, and fettering Philosophy with the reasonings of paganism. While the world lasts, will Aristotle's doctrine on these matters last, for he is the oracle of nature and of truth. While we are men, we cannot help, to a great extent, being Aristotelians, for the great Master does but analyze the thoughts, feelings, views and opinions of human kind. He has told us the meaning of our own words and ideas, before we were born. In many subject-matters, to think correctly, is to think like Aristotle; and we are his disciples whether we will or no, though

we may not know it. Now, as to the particular instance before us, the word "liberal" as applied to Knowledge and Education, expresses a specific idea, which ever has been, and ever will be, while the nature of man is the same, just as the idea of the Beautiful is specific, or of the Sublime, or of the Ridiculous, or of the Sordid. It is in the world now, it was in the world then; and, as in the case of the dogmas of faith, it is illustrated by a continuous historical tradition, and never was out of the world, from the time it came into it. There have indeed been differences of opinion from time to time, as to what pursuits and what arts came under that idea, but such differences are but an additional evidence of its reality. That idea must have a substance in it, which has maintained its ground amid these conflicts and changes, which has ever served as a standard to measure things withal, which has passed from mind to mind unchanged, when there was so much to colour, so much to influence any notion or thought whatever, which was not founded in our very nature. Were it a mere generalization, it would have varied with the subjects from which it was generalized; but though its subjects vary with the age, it varies not itself. The palaestra may seem a liberal exercise to Lycurgus, and illiberal to Seneca; coach-driving and prize-fighting may be recognized in Elis, and be condemned in England; music may be despicable in the eyes of certain moderns, and be in the highest place with Aristotle and Plato — (and the case is the same in the particular application of the idea of Beauty, or of Goodness, or of Moral Virtue, there is a difference of tastes, a difference of Judgments) — still these variations imply, instead of discrediting, the archetypal idea, which is but a previous hypothesis or condition, by means of which issue is joined between contending opinions, and without which there would be nothing to dispute about.

I consider, then, that I am chargeable with no paradox, when I speak of a Knowledge which is its own end, when I call it liberal knowledge, or a gentleman's knowledge, when I educate for it, and make it the scope of a University. And still less am I incurring such a charge, when I make this acquisition consist, not in Knowledge in a vague and ordinary sense, but in that Knowledge which I have especially called Philosophy or, in an extended sense of the word, Science; for whatever claims Knowledge has to be considered as a good, these it has in a higher degree when it is viewed not vaguely, not popularly, but precisely and transcendently as Philosophy. Knowledge, I say, is then especially liberal, or sufficient for itself, apart from every external and ulterior object, when and so far as it is philosophical, and this I proceed to show.

6

Now bear with me, Gentlemen, if what I am about to say, has at first sight a fanciful appearance. Philosophy, then, or Science, is related to Knowledge in this way: Knowledge is called by the name of Science or Philosophy, when it is acted upon, informed, or if I may use a strong figure, impregnated by Reason. Reason is the principle of that intrinsic fecundity of Knowledge, which, to those who possess it, is its especial value, and which dispenses with the necessity of their looking abroad for any end to rest upon external to itself. Knowledge indeed, when thus exalted into a scientific form, is also power; not only is it excellent in itself, but whatever such excellence may be, it is something more, it has a result beyond itself. Doubtless, but that is a further consideration, with which I am not concerned. I only say that, prior to its being a power, it is a good; that it is, not only an instrument, but an end. I know well it may resolve itself into an art, and terminate in a mechanical process, and in tangible fruit; but it also may fall back upon that Reason which informs it, and resolve itself into Philosophy. In one case it is called Useful Knowledge, in the other Liberal. The same person may cultivate it in both ways at once; but this again is a matter foreign to my subject; here I do but say that there are two ways of using Knowledge, and in matter of fact those who use it in one way are not likely to use it in the

other, or at least in a very limited measure. You see, then, here are two methods of Education; the end of the one is to be philosophical, of the other to be mechanical; the one rises towards general ideas, the other is exhausted upon what is particular and external. Let me not be thought to deny the necessity, or to decry the benefit, of such attention to what is particular and practical, as belongs to the useful or mechanical arts; life could not go on without them; we owe our daily welfare to them; their exercise is the duty of the many, and we owe to the many a debt of gratitude for fulfilling that duty. I only say that Knowledge, in proportion as it tends more and more to be particular, ceases to be Knowledge. It is a question whether Knowledge can in any proper sense be predicated of the brute creation; without pretending to metaphysical exactness of phraseology, which would be unsuitable to an occasion like this, I say, it seems to me improper to call that passive sensation, or perception of things, which brutes seem to possess, by the name of Knowledge. When I speak of Knowledge, I mean something intellectual, something which grasps what it perceives through the senses; something which takes a view of things; which sees more than the senses convey; which reasons upon what it sees, and while it sees; which invests it with an idea. It expresses itself, not in a mere enunciation, but by an enthymeme: it is of the nature of science from the first, and in this consists its dignity. The principle of real dignity in Knowledge, its worth, its desirableness, considered irrespectively of its results, is this germ within it of a scientific or a philosophical process. This is how it comes to be an end in itself; this is why it admits of being called Liberal. Not to know the relative disposition of things is the state of slaves or children; to have mapped out the Universe is the boast, or at least the ambition, of Philosophy.

Moreover, such knowledge is not a mere extrinsic or accidental advantage, which is ours to-day and another's to-morrow, which may be got up from a book, and easily forgotten again, which we can command or communicate at our pleasure, which we can borrow for the occasion, carry about in our hand, and take into the market; it is an acquired illumination, it is a habit, a personal possession, and an inward endowment. And this is the reason, why it is more correct, as well as more usual, to speak of a University as a place of education, than of instruction, though, when knowledge is concerned, instruction would at first sight have seemed the more appropriate word. We are instructed, for instance, in manual exercises, in the fine and useful arts, in trades, and in ways of business; for these are methods, which have little or no effect upon the mind itself, are contained in rules committed to memory, to tradition, or to use, and bear upon an end external to themselves. But education is a higher word; it implies an action upon our mental nature, and the formation of a character; it is something individual and permanent, and is commonly spoken of in connexion with religion and virtue.

When, then, we speak of the communication of Knowledge as being Education, we thereby really imply that that Knowledge is a state or condition of mind; and since cultivation of mind is surely worth seeking for its own sake, we are thus brought once more to the conclusion, which the word "Liberal" and the word "Philosophy" have already suggested, that there is a Knowledge, which is desirable, though nothing come of it, as being of itself a treasure, and a sufficient remuneration of years of labour.

HISTORY OF MY RELIGIOUS OPINIONS*

The *Apologia* came into being because of a book review. Charles Kingsley, reviewing Froude's *History of England*, in *Macmillan's Magazine*, Jan., 1864, asserted that, "Father Newman informs us that truth for its own sake need not be, and on the whole ought not to be a virtue of the Roman clergy." Newman was quick to take up this challenge to his honesty and the sincerity of the Roman clergy. Working under the stress of his indignation, he composed swiftly. The world was astonished at the psychological subtlety of his self-knowledge as revealed in the *Apologia*, of which the American critic, George Shuster, has said, "In these pages words seem to burn not with the morbid light of Byron's verse, but with the full radiance of indignation aroused to the defense of a holy cause." Kingsley was completely silenced upon the publication of this work. It was first issued in seven parts which appeared bi-monthly between April 21 and June 2, 1864.

IT MAY easily be conceived how great a trial it is to me to write the following history of myself; but I must not shrink from the task. The words "Secretum meum mihi," keep ringing in my ears; but as men draw towards their end, they care less for disclosures. Nor is it the least part of my trial, to anticipate that my friends may, upon first reading what I have written, consider much in it irrelevant to my purpose; yet I cannot help thinking that, viewed as a whole, it will effect what I wish it to do.

I was brought up from a child to take great delight in reading the Bible; but I had no formed religious convictions till I was fifteen. Of course I had perfect knowledge of my Catechism.

After I was grown up, I put on paper such recollections as I had of my thoughts and feelings on religious subjects, at the time that I was a child and a boy. Out of these I select two, which are at once the most definite among them, and also have a bearing on my later convictions.

In the paper to which I have referred, written either in the long vacation of 1820, or in October 1823, the following notices of my school days were sufficiently prominent in my memory for me to consider them worth recording: — "I used to wish the Arabian Tales were true: my imagination ran on unknown influences, on magical powers, and talismans. . . . I thought life might be a dream, or I an Angel, and all this world a deception, my fellow-angels by a playful device concealing themselves from me, and

*Newman, John Henry Cardinal, *Collected Works, Apologia Pro Vita Sua*.

deceiving me with the semblance of a material world."

Again, "Reading in the Spring of 1816 a sentence from (Dr. Watts's) *Remnants of Time,* entitled 'the Saints unknown to the world,' to the effect, that 'there is nothing in their figure or countenance to distinguish them,' etc., etc., I suppose he spoke of Angels who lived in the world, as it were disguised."

The other remark is this: "I was very superstitious, and for some time previous to my conversion" (when I was fifteen) "used constantly to cross myself on going into the dark."

Of course I must have got this practice from some external source or other; but I can make no sort of conjecture whence; and certainly no one had ever spoken to me on the subject of the Catholic religion, which I only knew by name. The French master was an *émigré* priest, but he was simply made a butt, as French masters too commonly were in that day, and spoke English very imperfectly. There was a Catholic family in the village, old maiden ladies we used to think; but I knew nothing but their name. I have of late years heard that there were one or two Catholic boys in the school; but either we were carefully kept from knowing this, or the knowledge of it made simply no impression on our minds. My brother will bear witness how free the school was from Catholic ideas.

I had once been into Warwick Street Chapel, with my father, who, I believe, wanted to hear some piece of music; all that I bore away from it was the recollection of a pulpit and a preacher and a boy swinging a censer.

When I was at Littlemore, I was looking over old copybooks of my school days, and I found among them my first Latin verse-book; and in the first page of it there was a device which almost took my breath away with surprise. I have the book before me now, and have just been showing it to others. I have written in the first page, in my schoolboy hand, "John H. Newman, February 11th, 1811, Verse Book;" then follow my first verses. Between "Verse" and "Book" I have

drawn the figure of a solid cross upright, and next to it is, what may indeed be meant for a necklace, but what I cannot make out to be anything else than a set of beads suspended, with a little cross attached. At this time I was not quite ten years old. I suppose I got the idea from some romance, Mrs. Radcliffe's or Miss Porter's; or from some religious picture; but the strange thing is, how, among the thousand objects which meet a boy's eyes, these in particular should so have fixed themselves in my mind, that I made them thus practically my own. I am certain there was nothing in the churches I attended, or the prayer books I read, to suggest them. It must be recollected that churches and prayer books were not decorated in those days as I believe they are now.

When I was fourteen, I read Paine's *Tracts against the Old Testament,* and found pleasure in thinking of the objections which were contained in them. Also, I read some of Hume's *Essays;* and perhaps that on *Miracles.* So at least I gave my father to understand; but perhaps it was a brag. Also, I recollect copying out some French verses, perhaps Voltaire's, against the immortality of the soul, and saying to myself something like "How dreadful, but how plausible!"

When I was fifteen (in the autumn of 1816) a great change of thought took place in me. I fell under the influences of a definite creed, and received into my intellect impressions of dogma, which, through God's mercy, have never been effaced or obscured. Above and beyond the conversations and sermons of the excellent man, long dead, who was the human means of this beginning of divine faith in me, was the effect of the books which he put into my hands, all of the school of Calvin. One of the first books I read was a work of Romaine's; I neither recollect the title nor the contents, except one doctrine, which of course I do not include among those which I believe to have come from a divine source, viz. the doctrine of final perseverance. I received it at once, and believed that the inward conversion of which I was conscious (and of which I am still more certain than that I have hands and feet) would last into the next life, and that I was elected to eternal glory. I have no consciousness that this belief had any tendency whatever to lead me to be careless about pleasing God. I retained it till the age of twenty-one, when it gradually faded away; but I believe that it had some influence on my opinions, in the direction of those childish imaginations which I have already mentioned, viz. in isolating me from the objects which surrounded me, in confirming me in my mistrust of the reality of material phenomena, and making me rest in the thought of two and two only supreme and luminously self-evident beings, myself and my Creator; — for while I considered myself predestined to salvation, I thought others simply passed over, not predestined to eternal death. I only thought of the mercy to myself.

The detestable doctrine last mentioned is simply denied and adjured, unless my memory strangely deceives me, by the writer who made a deeper impression on my mind than any other, and to whom (humanly speaking) I almost owe my soul — Thomas Scott of Aston Sandford. I so admired and delighted in his writings, that, when I was an undergraduate, I thought of making a visit to his parsonage, in order to see a man whom I so deeply revered. I hardly think I could have given up the idea of this expedition, even after I had taken my degree; for the news of his death in 1821 came upon me as a disappointment as well as a sorrow. I hung upon the lips of Daniel Wilson, afterwards Bishop of Calcutta, as in two sermons at St. John's Chapel he gave the history of Scott's life and death. I had been possessed of his *Essays* from a boy; his *Commentary* I bought when I was an undergraduate.

What, I suppose, will strike any reader of Scott's history and writings, is his bold unworldliness and vigorous independence of mind. He followed truth wherever it led him, beginning with Unitarianism, and ending in a zealous faith in the Holy Trinity. It was he who first planted deep in my mind that fundamental truth of religion. With the assistance of Scott's *Essays,* and the admirable work of Jones of Nayland, I made a

collection of Scripture texts in proof of the doctrine, with remarks (I think) of my own upon them, before I was sixteen; and a few months later I drew up a series of texts in support of each verse of the Athanasian Creed. These papers I have still.

Besides his unworldliness, what I also admired in Scott was his resolute opposition to Antinomianism, and the minutely practical character of his writings. They show him to be a true Englishman, and I deeply felt his influence; and for years I used almost as proverbs what I considered to be the scope and issue of his doctrine, Holiness rather than peace, and *Growth the only true evidence of life.*

Calvinists make a sharp separation between the elect and the world; there is much in this that is parallel or cognate to the Catholic doctrine; but they go on to say, as I understand them, very differently from Catholicism, — that the converted and the unconverted can be discriminated by man, that the justified are conscious of their state of justification, and that the regenerate cannot fall away. Catholics on the other hand shade and soften the awful antagonism between good and evil, which is one of their dogmas, by holding that there are different degrees of justification that there is a great difference in point of gravity between sin and sin, that there is the possibility and the danger of falling away, and that there is no certain knowledge given to any one that he is simply in a state of grace, and much less that he is to persevere to the end: — of the Calvinistic tenets the only one which took root in my mind was the fact of heaven and hell, divine favour and divine wrath, of the justified and the unjustified. The notion that the regenerate and the justified were one and the same, and that the regenerate, as such, had the gift of perseverance, remained with me not many years, as I have said already.

This main Catholic doctrine of the warfare between the city of God and the powers of darkness was also deeply impressed upon my mind by a work of a very opposite character, Law's *Serious Call.*

From this time I have given a full inward

assent and belief to the doctrine of eternal punishment, as delivered by our Lord Himself, in as true a sense as I hold that of eternal happiness; though I have tried in various ways to make that truth less terrible to the reason.

Now I come to two other works, which produced a deep impression on me in the same autumn of 1816, when I was fifteen years old, each contrary to each, and planting in me the seeds of an intellectual inconsistency which disabled me for a long course of years. I read Joseph Milner's *Church History,* and was nothing short of enamoured of the long extracts from St. Augustine and the other Fathers which I found there. I read them as being the religion of the primitive Christians: but simultaneously with Milner I read Newton *On the Prophecies,* and in consequence became most firmly convinced that the Pope was the Antichrist predicted by Daniel, St. Paul, and St. John. My imagination was stained by the effects of this doctrine up to the year 1843; it had been obliterated from my reason and judgment at an earlier date; but the thought remained upon me as a sort of false conscience. Hence came that conflict of mind, which so many have felt besides myself; — leading some men to make a compromise between two ideas, so inconsistent with each other — driving others to beat out the one idea or the other from their minds — and ending in my own case, after many years of intellectual unrest, in the gradual decay and extinction of one of them — I do not say in its violent death, for why should I not have murdered it sooner, if I murdered it at all?

I am obliged to mention, though I do it with great reluctance, another deep imagination, which at this time, the autumn of 1816, took possession of me — there can be no mistake about the fact; — viz. that it was the will of God that I should lead a single life. This anticipation, which has held its ground almost continuously ever since — with the break of a month now and a month then, up to 1829, and, after that date, without any break at all — was more or less connected, in my mind, with the notion that my calling in life would require such a sacrifice as celibacy involved; as for instance, missionary work among the heathen, to which I had a great drawing for some years. It also strengthened my feeling of separation from the visible world, of which I have spoken above.

THE DREAM OF GERONTIUS*

GERONTIUS

The Dream of Gerontius is Newman's most ambitious attempt at verse writing. It owes its excellence to Newman's understanding of psychology, and the union of its verse forms with the medieval concept seen in the play Everyman. Gerontius was set to music by Elgar. In its oratorio form it is still popular in church circles and choral societies.

Jesu, Maria — I am near to death,
    And Thou art calling me; I know it now —
Not by the token of this faltering breath,
    This chill at heart, this dampness on my
        brow,
(Jesu, have mercy! Mary, pray for me!) —
    'Tis this new feeling, never felt before,
(Be with me, Lord in my extremity!)
    That I am going, that I am no more.

'Tis this strange innermost abandonment,
    (Lover of souls! great God! I look to Thee,)
This emptying out of each constituent
    And natural force, by which I come to be.
Pray for me, O my friends; a visitant
    Is knocking his dire summons at my door,
The like of whom, to scare me and to daunt,
    Has never, never come to me before;
'Tis death, — O loving friends, your prayers!
        — 'tis he! . . .
As though my very being had given way,
    As though I was no more a substance now,
And could fall back on nought to be my stay,
    (Help, loving Lord! Thou my sole Refuge,
        Thou,)
And turn no whither, but must needs decay
    And drop from out the universal frame
Into that shapeless, scopeless, blank abyss,

That utter nothingness, of which I came:
This is it that has come to pass in me;
  O horror! this it is, my dearest, this;
So pray for me, my friends, who have not
    strength to pray.

ASSISTANTS

Kyrie eleison, Christe eleison, Kyrie eleison.
Holy Mary, pray for him.
All holy Angels, pray for him.
Choirs of the righteous, pray for him.
Holy Abraham, pray for him.
St. John Baptist, St. Joseph, pray for him.
St. Peter, St. Paul, St. Andrew, St. John,
All Apostles, all Evangelists, pray for him.
All holy Disciples of the Lord, pray for him.
All holy Innocents, pray for him.
All holy Martyrs, all holy Confessors,
All holy Hermits, all holy Virgins,
All ye Saints of God, pray for him.

GERONTIUS

Rouse thee, my fainting soul, and play
    the man;
  And through such waning span
Of life and thought as still has to be trod,
  Prepare to meet thy God.
And while the storm of that bewilderment
  Is for a season spent,
And, ere afresh the ruin on thee fall,
  Use well the interval.

ASSISTANTS

Be merciful, be gracious, spare him, Lord.
Be merciful, be gracious; Lord, deliver him.
  From the sins that are past;
      From Thy frown and Thine ire;
      From the perils of dying;
      From any complying
      With sin, or denying
      His God, or relying
  On self, at the last;
      From the nethermost fire;
  From all that is evil;
From power of the devil;
Thy servant deliver,
For once and for ever.

  By Thy birth, and by Thy Cross,
  Rescue him from endless loss;
  By Thy death and burial,

Save him from a final fall;
By Thy rising from the tomb,
  By Thy mounting up above,
  By the Spirit's gracious love,
Save him in the day of doom.

GERONTIUS

Sanctus fortis, Sanctus Deus,
  De profundis oro te,
Miserere, Judex meus,
  Parce mihi, Domine
Firmly I believe and truly
  God is Three, and God is One;
And I next acknowledge duly
  Manhood taken by the Son.
And I trust and hope most fully
  In that Manhood crucified;
And each thought and deed unruly
  Do to death, as He has died.

Simply to His grace and wholly
  Light and life and strength belong,
And I love, supremely, solely,
  Him the holy, Him the strong.
Sanctus fortis, Sanctus Deus,
  De profundis oro te,
Miserere, Judex meus,
  Parce mihi, Domine.
And I hold in veneration,
  For the love of Him alone,
Holy Church, as His creation,
  And her teachings, as His own.
And I take with joy whatever
  Now besets me, pain or fear,
And with strong will I sever
  All the ties which bind me here.
Adoration aye be given
  With and through the angelic host,
To the God of earth and heaven,
  Father, Son, and Holy Ghost,
Sanctus fortis, Sanctus Deus,
  De profundis oro te,
Miserere, Judex meus,
  Mortis in discrimine.

I can no more; for now it comes again,
That sense of ruin, which is worse than pain,
That masterful negation and collapse
Of all that makes me man; as though I bent
Over the dizzy brink
Of some sheer infinite descent;
Or worse, as though

Down, down for ever I was falling through
The solid framework of created things,
And needs must sink and sink
Into the vast abyss. And, crueller still,
A fierce and restless fright begins to fill
The mansion of my soul. And, worse
　　and worse,
Some bodily form of ill
Floats on the wind, with many a loath-
　　some curse

Tainting the hallowed air, and laughs,
　　and flaps
Its hideous wings,
And makes me wild with horror and dismay.
O Jesu, help! pray for me, Mary, pray!
Some angel, Jesu! such as came to Thee
In Thine own agony. . . .
Mary, pray for me. Joseph, pray for me.
　　Mary, pray for me.

THE PILLAR OF THE CLOUD

Lead, Kindly Light, amid the encircling
　　gloom
　　　　Lead Thou me on!
The night is dark, and I am far from
　　home —
　　　　Lead Thou me on!
Keep Thou my feet; I do not ask to see
The distant scene — one step enough for me.

I was not ever thus, nor pray'd that Thou
　　　　Shouldst lead me on.
I loved to choose and see my path, but now
　　Lead Thou me on!

I loved the garish day, and, spite of fears,
Pride ruled my will: remember not past years.
So long Thy power hath blest me, sure it still
　　　　Will lead me on,
O'er moor and fen, o'er crag and torrent, till
　　　　The night is gone;
And with the morn those angel faces smile
Which I have loved long since, and lost
　　awhile.

At Sea
June 16, 1833

AUBREY THOMAS DE VERE

(1814–1902)

AUBREY DE VERE, third son of a noble Irish family, was born in Ireland and educated at Trinity College, Dublin. As a young man he came under the Romantic influence of Coleridge and Wordsworth. On a journey to Oxford Newman captivated him and he later entered the Church, 1857. His first book, an arraignment of English misdeeds in Ireland during the potato famine, was praised by Mill and Carlyle. His poems give him his chief title to fame, although in his own day his essays on Wordsworth and the Romantic school were more popular with the general public. His charming personality

made for him a large circle of friends, including Wordsworth and Sara Coleridge.

His best poems are found in the volume *May Carols,* 1857, which he wrote at the instance of Pius IX. They illustrate his mastery of the lyric form, his complete Catholicity, and wild ecstasy in the presence of nature. De Vere's *Medieval Records and Sonnets,* 1898, though dedicated to Digby, lack the sweet unconsciousness of his master's attitude toward the Middle Ages. The blank verse of his longer pieces is on the tedious side, the sonnets slightly wooden.

His essays on the Romantic poets are not

of great importance as essays. They do, however, illustrate the influence of the Romantic poets on the men of their own time. Wilfrid Ward's *Aubrey de Vere: a Memoir* offers a pleasant commentary on his life and importance.

SANCTA MARIA*

IV

Mary! To thee the humble cry.
  What seek they? Gifts to Pride unknown.
They seek thy help — to pass thee by: —
  They murmur, "Show us but thy Son."

*The above and following poem is from *May Carols*, by Aubrey de Vere (London: Longmans, Brown, Green, Longmans & Roberts, 1857).

The childlike heart shall enter in;
  The virgin soul its God shall see: —
Mother, and maiden pure from sin,
  Be thou the guide: the Way is He.

The mystery high of God made Man
  Through thee to man is easier made:
Pronounce the consonant who can
  Without the softer vowel's aid!

MATER SALVATORIS

XII

O Heart with His in just accord!
  O Soul His echo, tone for tone!
O Spirit that heard, and kept His word!
  O Countenance moulded like His own!

Behold, she seemed on Earth to dwell;
  But, hid in light, alone she sat
Beneath the Throne ineffable,
  Chanting her clear Magnificat.

Fed from the boundless heart of God,
  The joy within her rose more high
And all her being overflowed,
  Until the awful hour was nigh.

Then, then, there crept her spirit o'er
  The shadow of that pain world-wide
Whereof her Son the substance bore: —
  Him offering, half in Him she died;

Standing like that strange Moon, whereon
  The mask of Earth lies dim and dead,

An orb of glory, shadow-strewn,
  Yet girdled with a luminous thread.

XX

When April's sudden sunset cold
  Through boughs half clothed with watery sheen
Bursts on the high, new-cowslipped wold,
  And bathes a world half gold, half green,

Then shakes the illuminated air
  With din of birds; the vales far down
Grow phosphorescent here and there;
  Forth flash the turrets of the town;

Along the sky thin vapors scud;
  Bright zephyrs curl the choral main;
The wild ebullience of the blood
  Rings joy-bells in the heart and brain:

Yet in that music discords mix;
  The unbalanced light like meteors play;
And, tired of splendors that perplex,
  The dazzled spirit sighs for May.

TOTA PULCHRA*

XII

A broken gleam on wave and flower —
  A music that in utterance dies —
O Poets, and O Men! what more
  Is all that Beauty which ye prize?

And ah! how oft Corruption works
  Through that brief Beauty's force or wile!
How oft a gloom eternal lurks
  Beneath an evanescent smile!

But thou, serene and smiling light
  Of every grace redeemed from Sense,
In thee all harmonies unite
  That charm a pure Intelligence.

Whatever teaches mind or heart
  To God by loveliest types to mount,
Mary, is thine. Of each true Art
  The parent art thou, and the fount.

Those pictures, fair as moon or star,
  The ages dear to Faith brough forth,
Formed but the illumined calendar
  Of her, that Church which knows thy
    worth.

Not less doth Nature teach through thee
  That mystery hid in hues and lines:
Who loves thee not hath lost the key
  To all her sanctuaries and shrines.

*Hymns and Poems.

MATER CHRISTI*

"Behold thy Mother!" From the Cross
  He gave her — not to one alone:
We are His Brethren; unto us
  He gave a mother as to John.

Behold the greatest gift of Christ,
  Save that wherein Himself He gives,
The wonder-working Eucharist,
  Sole life of each that truly lives.

Mysterious Bread, not joined and knit
  With him that eats, like mortal food,
But, fire-like, joining him with it,
  And blending with the Church of God.

Mary! from thee the Saviour took
  That Flesh He gives! The mercies twain,
Like streams of a divided brook,
  But separate to meet again.

*Mediaeval Records and Sonnets.

SAINT THOMAS AQUINAS*

He left the fortress-palace of his sires:
The blood of princes coursing through
  his veins
Flushed him no more with pride's insurgent
  fires
Than streams, hill-born, make proud the
  sundered plains:
He loved that lowly life the world disdains;
Contemned the insensate pomp that world
  admires; —

He walked, in soul conversing with those
  choirs
That sing where peace eternal lives and
  reigns.
Tender Loretto to her breast elate
Caught him a youngling. Silent, meek,
  serene,
His small feet sought the poor beside
  her gate

That wondered at the brightness of his mien
Even then a holy creature dedicate
To Wisdom's sovran seat and sacred Queen.

Beauteous Campania! In the old Roman
  morn
The great ones of the nations rush to thee:
In thy rich gardens by the full-voiced sea
Wearied they slept, and woke like men
  re-born.
Not so the greatest of thy sons! In scorn
He passed the snare; his spirit strong and free
Less honouring Pestum's roses than that
  thorn
The crown of Calvary's Victim. Who
  was he?
The Ascetic who refused a prelate's throne
Lest worldly aims with cares divine should
  mix;
The Builder lifting fanes of thought not
  stone,
Far less poor Babel Towers of sun-burnt
  bricks;
The man who summed all Truth, yet drew
  alone

His sacred science from his crucifix.

Great Saint! In pictures old a sun there
  flamed
Soft sphere of radiance on thy vest of snow;
It taught us that from hearts by sin un-
  shamed,
The mind's inspirer best, alone could flow
Sapience like thine. "Master of those who
  know!"
At heaven's high mark alone thy shaft was
  aimed:
Therefore, by thee unwoo'd by thee
  disclaimed
Science terrestrial sought thy threshold low.
Beneath thy cell she knelt: all pagan lore
From mines of Plato and the Stagyrite
To thee she tendered. Thou, with spiritual
  light
Piercing each ingot of that golden ore,
To gems didst change them meet to pave
  the floor
Of God's great Temple on the empyreal
  height.

Mediaeval Records and Sonnets.

FREDERICK WILLIAM FABER

(1814–1863)

FATHER FABER'S hymns are so numerous and so long that it might be said
he was almost a choir of angels by himself.
Faber was a priest's priest, and religious interests dominated his life from earliest years.
During his time at Oxford he was drawn
into the center of the Oxford Movement.

Like his much admired friend, Newman,
Faber left Anglicanism for the Catholic
Church. In 1848 he joined the Oratorians.
His spiritual conferences and skill as a direc-
tor of souls gave him a large following.

Hymn writers are not born every day.
The craft of hymn writing calls for a disarming simplicity, a feeling for rhythm, and
an exaltation which are given to few men.
Faber had the gift *in excelsis* and he embalmed the liturgical year in canticles of
praise. Many of the most loved hymns sung
in our churches were the work of Father
Faber. Protestants, too, admired his songs
and they often took them over and revamped
them to suit their own tastes.

Several of Father Faber's books of instruction have become spiritual classics.
Among these latter is *Growth In Holiness*
which has lost none of its luster with the
changing times.

FAITH OF OUR FATHERS*

Faith of our Fathers! living still
  In spite of dungeon, fire and sword:
O how our hearts beat high with joy
  Whene'er we hear that glorious word:
Faith of our Fathers! Holy Faith!
We will be true to thee till death.

Our Fathers, chained in prisons dark,
  Were still in heart and conscience free:
How sweet would be their children's fate,
  If they, like them, could die for thee!
Faith of our Fathers! Holy Faith!
We will be true to thee till death.

Faith of our Fathers! Mary's prayers
  Shall win our country back to thee;
And through the truth that comes from God
  England shall then indeed be free.
Faith of our Fathers! Holy Faith!
We will be true to thee till death.

Faith of our Fathers! We will love
  Both friend and foe in all our strife:
And preach thee too, as love knows how
  By kindly words and virtuous life:
Faith of our Fathers! Holy Faith!
We will be true to thee till death.

---

*The above, and following hymns have been selected from Faber, Frederick William, D.D., *Hymns* (Baltimore: Murphy & Co., 1880).

A DAILY HYMN TO MARY

For the Children of St. Philip's Home

Mary! dearest Mother!
  From thy heavenly height
Look on us thy children,
  Lost in earth's dark night.

Mary! purest creature!
  Keep us all from sin:
Help us erring mortals
  Peace in heaven to win.

Mary! Queen and Mother!
  Get us still more grace,
With still greater fervor
  Now to run our race.

Daughter of the Father!
  Lady kind and sweet!
Lead up to our Father,
  Leave us at His Feet.

Mother of our Saviour,
  Joy of God above!
Jesus bade thee keep us
  In His fear and love.

Mary! Spouse and servant
  Of the Holy Ghost!
Keep for Him His creatures
  Who would else be lost.

Holy Queen of angels!
  Bid thine angels come
To escort us safely
  To our heavenly home.

Bid the saints in heaven
  Pray for us their prayers;
They are thine, dear Mother!
  That thou mayst be theirs.

Oh we love thee, Mary!
  Trusting all to thee,
What is past, or present,
  What is yet to be.

Get us what thou pleasest,
  What we cannot know,
What we most are needing
  Every day below.

Thou didst make for Jesus
  To this earth a road;
Make us love our Saviour,
  Make us love our God.

Cause of all our gladness!
  Make us glad in Him;
Fill our hearts with fervor,
  Fill them to the brim.

Sweeter still and sweeter
  Dost thou grow to us, —

Will it, dearest Mother,
  Evermore be thus?

O not yet, sweet Mother!
  Is our love of thee
What it will be one day
  In eternity.

Jesus! hear Thy children
  From Thy throne above;
Give us love of Mary,
  As thou wouldst have us love.

THANKSGIVING AFTER COMMUNION

Jesus, gentlest Saviour!
  God of might and power!
Thou Thyself art dwelling
  In us at this hour.

Nature cannot hold Thee,
  Heaven is all too strait
For Thine endless glory,
  And Thy royal state.

Out beyond the shining
  Of the furthest star,
Thou art ever stretching
  Infinitely far.

Yet hearts of children
  Hold what worlds cannot,
And the God of wonders
  Loves the lowly spot.

As men to their gardens
  Go to seek sweet flowers,
In our hearts dear Jesus
  Seeks them at all hours.

Jesus, gentlest Saviour!
  Thou art in us now;
Fill us full of goodness,
  Till our hearts o'erflow.

Pray the prayer within us
  That to heaven shall rise;
Sing the song that angels
  Sing above the skies.

Multiply our graces,
  Chiefly love and fear,
And, dear Lord! the chiefest —
  Grace to persevere.

Oh, how can we thank Thee
  For a gift like this,
Gift that truly maketh
  Heaven's eternal bliss?

Ah! when wilt Thou always
  Make our hearts Thy home?
We must wait for heaven, —
  Then the day will come.

Now at least we'll keep Thee
  All the time we may;
But thy grace and blessing
  We will keep alway.

When our hearts Thou Leavest,
  Worthless though they be,
Give them to Thy Mother
  To be kept for Thee.

THE IMMACULATE CONCEPTION

O purest of creatures! sweet Mother! sweet
Maid
The one spotless womb wherein Jesus was
laid!
Dark night hath come down on us, Mother!
and we
Look out for thy shining, sweet Star of the
Sea!

Deep night hath come down on this rough-
spoken world,
And the banners of Darkness are boldly
unfurled:
And the tempest-tost Church — all her eyes
are on thee,
They look to thy shining, sweet Star of the
Sea!

The Church doth what God had first taught
her to do;
He looked o'er the world to find hearts that
were true;
Through the ages He looked, and He found
none but thee,
And He loved thy clear shining, sweet Star
of the Sea!

He gazed on thy soul; it was spotless and
fair;
For the empire of sin — it had never been
there;
None had e'er owned thee, dear Mother, but
He,
And He blessed thy clear shining, sweet Star
of the Sea!

Earth gave Him one lodging; 'twas deep in
thy breast,
And God found a home where the sinner
finds rest;
His home and His hiding-place, both were
in thee;
He was won by thy shining, sweet Star of
the Sea!

Oh blissful and calm was the wonderful rest
That thou gavest thy God in thy virginal
breast;
For the heaven He left He found heaven in
thee,
And He shone in thy shining, sweet Star of
the Sea!

To sinners what comfort, to angels what
mirth,
That God found one creature unfallen on
earth,
One spot where His Spirit untroubled could
be,
The depths of thy shining, sweet Star of the
Sea!

So age after age in the Church has gone
round,
And the saints new inventions of homage
have found,
New titles of honor, new honors for thee,
New love for thy shining, sweet Star of the
Sea!

And now from the Church of all lands thy
dear name
Comes borne on the breath of one mighty
acclaim;
Men call on their Father, that He should
decree
A new gem to thy shining, sweet Star of the
Sea!

O shine on us brighter than ever, then, shine!
For the primest of honors, dear Mother! is
thine;
"Conceived without sin," thy new title shall
be,
Clear light from thy birth-spring, sweet Star
of the Sea!

So worship we God in these rude latter days;
So worship we Jesus our Love, when we
Praise
His wonderful grace in the gifts He gave
thee,
The gift of clear shining, sweet Star of the
Sea!

Deep night hath come down on us, Mother,
deep night,
And we need more than ever the guide of
thy light;
For the darker the night is, the brighter
should be
Thy beautiful shining, sweet Star of the Sea!

THE INFANT JESUS

Dear Little One! how sweet Thou art,
  Thine eyes how bright they shine,
So bright they almost seem to speak
  When Mary's look meets Thine!

How faint and feeble is thy cry,
  Like plaint of harmless dove,
When Thou dost murmur in Thy sleep
  Of sorrow and of love.

When Mary bids Thee sleep Thou sleepest,
  Thou wakest when she calls;
Thou art content upon her lap,
  Or in the rugged stalls.

Simplest of Babes! with what a grace
  Thou dost Thy Mother's will!
Thine infant fashions well betray
  The Godhead's hidden skill.

When Joseph takes Thee in his arms,
  And smooths Thy little cheek,
Thou lookest up into his face
  So helpless and so meek.

Yes! Thou art what Thou seemst to be,
  A thing of smiles and tears:
Yet Thou art God, and heaven and earth
  Adore Thee with their fears.

Yes! dearest Babe! those tiny hands
  That play with Mary's hair,

The weight of all the mighty world
  This very moment bear.

While Thou art clasping Mary's neck
  In timid tight embrace,
The boldest Seraphs veil themselves
  Before Thine infant Face.

When Mary hath appeased Thy thirst,
  And hushed Thy feeble cry,
The hearts of men lie open still
  Before Thy slumbering eye.

Art Thou, weak Babe! my very God?
  Oh I must love Thee then,
Love Thee, and yearn to spread Thy love
  Among forgetful men.

O sweet, O wakeful-hearted Child!
  Sleep on, dear Jesus! sleep;
For Thou must one day wake for me .
  To suffer and to weep.

A Scourge, a Cross, a cruel Crown
  Have I in store for Thee;
Yet why? one little tear, O lord!
  Ransom enough would be.

But no! death is Thine own sweet will,
  The price decreed above;
Thou wilt do more than save our souls,
  For Thou wilt die for Love.

Chapter X

HUMAN RESPECT*

TO GIVE ourselves up to the spiritual life is to put ourselves out of harmony with the world around us. We make a discord even with much that is amiable and affectionate, and with which, as natural virtue, we cannot be altogether without sympathy. We live in a different world, have

*Faber, Frederick William, D.D., *Growth In Holiness* (New York: John Murphy Co.).

different interests and speaks a different language, and the two worlds will not mingle. Grace holds us in one world, nature draws us down again into the other. This is the secret of the immense power which human respect has over us; and of the three dispositions which compose the normal state of the spiritual life, fatigue is the one which lays us most open to its attacks. We are weary of interior things and weakened by long combat, and a vigorous charge from an enemy who gets close to us under friendly colours is more than for the most part we can withstand. The good spirit, then, which should be the faithful satellite of our fatigue, is the presence of God, or singleness of purpose, or simplicity, but which I prefer to designate merely the absence of human respect, because no word seems so exactly to describe this spirit as the negative appellation in question.

There is much to be said of human respect. It is a fault most keenly felt by spiritual persons, and comparatively little felt by others. It is more like an atmosphere than anything else, and can hardly be caught and punished in distinct acts. Yet it is a thing of which there can be no doubt. We have an infallible consciousness of it. It gives undeniable evidences of its own existence. It destroys all' liberty, and becomes the positive tyrant of a man's life. Yet if we look well into it, nothing can be more stupid than our submission to it. For we set little or no value on the separate opinions of individuals; and when the judgment is in our favour, it can do us no good, neither, unless true, can it afford us any rational pleasure. Indeed, its power is altogether in the prospect, and not in the present possession. Yet it is a most universal, and must be dealt with as one of the most inconvenient facts of the spiritual life. Look at a person who is completely under its domination. Watch him in society and public life, or in the bosom of his family, or in the intimacies of friendship, or at confession and in conference with his director, or even with God in prayer, or in utter solitude. It is as if the omnipresence of God was spunged out all round him, and that some other powerful eye was fixed upon him, ruling him with a power like that of the solar light, and causing in him at all times an almost preternatural uneasiness.

It is not difficult to see the evils of this miserable world-presence, this spirit which gathers all mankind up into an eye, and throws its portentous fascination upon our souls. It causes men to be false and insincere in their mutual relations, and to act inconsiderately with others. It destroys all generous enthusiasm either for charity or penance. It puts a man under the despotism of ridicule, which becomes a kind of false god to him. It is the contradictory of perfection, and while it is in force, renders it impossible; for it is always drawing us off from God to creatures. A brood of sins of omission follow it wherever it goes, sprung from shame and the fear of ridicule, and another brood of sins of commission, from the desire to please. In process of time, and the process is not slow, it establishes itself as an habitual distraction in prayer and meditation; and as to examination of conscience, it almost seems to supply food to the voracity of human respect.

It is as miserable as it is evil. The bondage of Carthusian austerity would be easier to bear. No slavery is more degraded and unhappy. What a misery to be ashamed of our duties and our principles! What a misery that every action should have a flaw in it, and a blight upon it! What a misery to lose at last, as we must inevitably do, the very thing for which all our sacrifices have been made, the respect of others! Misery of miseries, thus to lose even respect of self! Religion, which ought to be our peace, becomes our torment. The very sacraments have a feeling of incompleteness about them, as if we did not, as we do not, use them rightly; and our communication with our director, which should be medicinal, is poisoned by this spirit. Surely we must try to get to the bottom of the matter, and to study the various phases of this disease of pious souls. A general wish to please, a laying ourselves out in particular subject matters in order to please, building castles in the air and imagining heroic acts, reflecting on the praise bestowed upon us, and giving way to low spirits when dispraised, — these are all manifestations of this horrible human respect.

Human respect, however, is not so much a particular fault, as a whole world of faults. It is the death of all religion. We shall never have an adequate horror of it until we admit that these hard words are no exaggeration. Let us therefore look at the place which it occupies in the grand struggle between good and evil. First of all, let us trace its rise; for this is a difficult problem, considering how in detail we all disbelieve in each other. The especial task of Christians is the realization of the invisible world. They have different standards of right and wrong from the votaries of earth. They live inextricably mixed up with the children of the world, as men using the same language with different meanings, and the confusion and apparent deceit grow worse every day, and the world, the owner of the territory or its lessee, more and more angry, and inclined, in spite of its theory of haughty toleration, to persecute those who thus wilfully put themselves at variance with the public peace. Men feel that religious people are right, and on that very account they will not look the fact in the face, and realize it. They feel it, because they feel that they are not irresponsible. Yet they chafe at the judgments of God, and His incessant interference; at the quiet way in which He gives His judgments, and takes His own time to execute His verdicts. So, not being able to do without the judicial power, they consolidate God from Three Divine Persons into a function, a cause, a pantheistic fluid, or a mechanical force, and transfer the judicial power to mankind in a body. This seems to be the account of human respect in the mind. Men in all generations fret under God's judicial power. It seems as if, because of this fretfulness, it were one of the most unutterable of His compassions that He should have confided his ultimate judicial rights to our Lord as Man, and that in virtue of the Sacred Humanity He should be our judge. Looked at in a human point of view, men's transfer of the judicial power to themselves may be said to have worked admirably. Social comfort, a standard of endurable morals, and generally what may be called for the moment *live-ableness,* have come of it. It causes a certain amount of individual unhappiness, because its police is harsh and rough, and the procedures of its court unkindly, and of the Draconian School. But men have a compensation for this in its giving over to them, utterly unquestioned, the whole region of thought. Under the administration of God, thoughts were acts, and were tried and found guilty as such. They

furnished the most abundant materials for its tribunals, and were just what caused His jurisdiction to press so heavily upon the soul. Now all this is free. Calumny, detraction, rash judgments, spiteful criticism, — they make us wince as they visit our outward acts; but we may be as base as we please in thought, and yet walk through human courts with proud eye, and head erect.

No wonder that when once human respect had taken its place among the powers of the world, it should cause especial desolation in the religious mind, and becomes a worse evil and a greater misery there than elsewhere. For it is itself a sort of spurious counterfeit religion. For what is religiousness but the sensible presence of God, and religion the worship of Him? In religion, the presence of God is our atmosphere. Sacraments, and prayer, and mortification, and all the exercises of the spiritual life are so many appointments, not only for realizing it, but for substantially introducing it both into body and soul. The respiration of our soul depends upon it. It produces a certain kind of character, a type of its own sort and easily recognized, a supernatural character which inspires other men with awe, love, hatred, or contempt, according to the different points of view from which they look at it. To the pure-minded, it is the greatest possible amount of happiness on earth; for it infuses into us a certain marvellous unreasoning instinct for another world, as being faith's sight of Him who is invisible. Yet it is hardly conscious what it is it sees. Now is not human respect, in its own way, a simple copy and caricature of all this? A something which undertakes to perform for the world every function which the presence of God performs for the enlightened soul? It is in fact a mental paganism.

It is this similarity to a false religion which makes human respect so peculiarly dangerous. It does not alarm us by any grossness. On the contrary it forces sin into concealment. Not that this is any real boon to the best interests of men, for certain of the deadliest sins thrive best under cover. It confuses the boundaries between public opinion and itself, and pretends an alliance with prudence and discretion. This is a stratagem to be guarded against. For public opinion is within limits a legitimate power; and the man who because he was devout, should lay it down as a principle that he would never respect public opinion or be swayed by it, would be paving the way for the triumphs of delusion. Nothing can be more alien to the moderation of the Church. There is a vast difference between what my fellow-citizens expect of me and show beforehand that they expect and give reasons for expecting, and the criticism they may pass upon my actions and my doing them rather with reference to that criticism than to the wish of God. Moreover, human respect unsupernaturalizes actions which are good in substance. It kills the nerve of the intention; but it gives us no such smart warning as the nerve of a tooth does in dying. It is like a worm in a nut; it eats away the kernel of our motive, and lets the fruit hang as fairly from the tree as ever. Religion is so much a matter of motives that this amounts to destroying it altogether, and as human respect introduces a directly wrong motive in lieu of the right one, it destroys spirituality in the most fatal way. Thus it is one of the completest instruments, which corrupt nature puts into the devil's hands and at his disposal for the destruction of souls. What can be more hateful than this, and what more odious in the sight of God? A caricature is always odious, and it is odious in proportion to the beauty and dignity of what it caricatures; and as we have seen, human respect is a caricature of the presence and judicial power of God.

Few are aware until they honestly turn to God, how completely they are the slaves of this vice. Then they wake up to a sense of it, and see how it is in their blood, as if it were their life and their identity, an inexplicable unconquerable vital thing. Its rise is a mystery, for which we can only invent a theory. No one can tell for sure how it rose, or when, or why; it has been like an exhalation from corrupt humanity, the spreading of a silent pestilence that has no external symptoms. There is not a class of society which it has not mastered, no corner of

private life that it has not invaded, no convent cell but its air is freighted with the poisonous influence. It rivals, what theologians call the pluri-presence of Satan. Its strength is so great that it can get the better of God's commandments and of the precepts of His Church, nay, of a man's own will, which last conquest even grace and penance find it difficult to achieve. It appears to increase with civilization, and with the extension of all means of locomotion and publicity. In modern society men systematize it, acknowledge it as a power, uphold its claims, and punish those who refuse submission. God is an ex-king amongst us, legitimate perhaps but deposed. It is much as if we build Him in His own kingdom a house made with hands that He may dwell therein, and keep Himself within-doors. Surely if the evil one has not preternaturally helped human respect, he has at least concentrated his energies on its spread and success. He is never more a prince than when he stoops to be the missionary of human respect.

Look into your own soul, and see how far this power has brought you into subjection. Is there a nook in your whole being, wherein you can sit down unmolested and breathe fresh air? Is there any exercise however spiritual, any occupation however sacred, any duty however solemn, over which the attractive influence of human respect is not being exercised? Have you any sanctuary, the inside of which it has never seen? When you have thought it conquered, how often has it risen up again, as if defeat refreshed it like sleep? Does it not follow you as your shadow, as a perpetual black spot in the sweet sunshine? Yet how long is it since you turned to God, and became spiritual? How many Lents and Months of Mary have you passed, how many sacraments received, how many indulgences gained? And yet this human respect so active, so robust, so unwearied, so ubiquitous. Can there be any question nearer your heart than what concerns the remedies for this evil?

The Church provides remedies for us in two ways: in her general system, and in her dealing with individual souls. She begins by boldly pronouncing a sentence of excommunication against the world, ignores its judgments in her own subject-matter of religion, and proclaims its friendship nothing less than a declaration of war against God. She gives her children different standards of right and wrong from the world, and an opposite rule of conduct. All her positive precepts and her obligations of outward profession of faith arc so many protests against human respect, and she canonizes just those men who have been heroes in their contempt for it. The world feels and understands the significance of these things, and shows it by anger, exhibiting all the quick jealousy of a conscious usurper.

But of far greater efficacy are the remedies which she administers to single souls in the confessional and in spiritual direction. The world dreads the secret power of that benign, cogent, and unreported tribunal. First of all, the practice of the presence of God is pitted against this universal human respect. We are taught how to act slowly, and to unite all our actions to God by a pure intention. We are bidden to take this fault as the subject of our particular examination of conscience, to pray earnestly against it, and to be full about our falls when we accuse ourselves in confession. Even in indifferent things we are recommended to adopt that line of conduct which tells most against human respect, were it only for the sake of mortification. This is often the rationale of the seemingly absurd and childish mortifications imposed in religious houses. For human respect is but a veiled worship of self, which we seem to transfer to the world, because self is even to us so small an object. And whatever kills this worship of self, as such mortifications do, is a blow to human respect. In casting out devils, the saints have often delighted to use puerile means; so also may we cast this devil out of ourselves. Once let our souls be possessed by a timid, child-like devotion to the Eye of God, eternal and unsleeping, and human respect will die away and disappear, as the autumnal leaves waste in the rain, and enrich the soil for the coming spring.

When we give ourselves up to God, we deliberately commit ourselves to live a supernatural life. Now what does a supernatural life mean? It means giving up this life altogether, as seeing we cannot have both worlds. Altogether! I hear you say. Yes! altogether. For how would you have me qualify it? Not that we shall not be a thousand times happier and sunnier even in this life; but it is from out the other life that the sunshine and happiness will come. This life must go, and altogether. There is no smoothing the word down. A supernatural life means that we do not make sin the limit of our freedom, but that we draw the line much nearer home, by the evangelical counsels. It means mortification, and mortification is the inflicting of voluntary punishment on ourselves, as if passing sentence on ourselves and executing it before the day of wrath. We put other interests, other loves, other enjoyments, in the place of those of the world. A conviction of our own weakness is the ground work of all our actions, and we lean our whole weight on supernatural aids and sacramental assistances, as depending solely upon them. To a certain extent we even become unsocial by silence, or solitude, or penance, or seeming eccentricity, or vocation. In a word, we deliberately become members of a minority, knowing we shall suffer for it.

Now, realizing this significance of the spiritual life, what is the view the world will naturally take of us and how will it feel towards us? The world, half unconsciously, believes in its own infallibility. Hence it is first of all surprised and then irritated with our venturing to act on different principles from itself. Such a line of action denies the world's supremacy, and contradicts its narrow code of prudence and discretion. Our conduct is therefore a reflection on the world, as if God had outlawed it, which He has. Its fashions, its sects, its pursuits, its struggles, its tyranny and its conceits are to us no better than a self-important, grandiloquent puerility. Meanwhile, though we ignore the world, the world cannot ignore us, for we are a fact, intruding on its domain and interfering with its hypothesis. We ignore the world, and ignoring is the policy of the extremes of weakness and strength. In our case it is of both, natural weakness, supernatural strength.

What sort of treatment then must we expect at the world's hands? It will have its phases and varieties according to circumstances. But on the whole we must expect as follows. If we succeed in what we undertake for God, or have influence, or convert persons, or take any high line, or reproach others by our examples, we must make our account to be hated. We shall be feared, and with an angry fear, when men see we have a view and go on a principle, which they do not; and they fear it because they prognosticate our success. Men will fear us also, when they think we are working for God in secret, and they cannot find out how, and this they call jesuitism, a holy and a good word to ears wise and true! They will moreover suspect us of all manner of strange misdemeanours. They can hardly help it; for the disproportion of means to ends in supernatural conduct is ever a teasing, baffling problem to the carnal mind. They will blame us; for blame is easy; and we swerve from man's usual standard of praise. Moreover, condemnation of us is safe; for even so-called moderate men on our own side throw us overboard. With them indiscretion means provoking the world, and not being friends with that whose friendship the Holy Ghost tells us is enmity with God. We shall be misunderstood, because even those who would naturally take a good-natured view of us cannot see what we see. They have no grasp of our principle — so they often think they have got logical proof of our inconsistency. Besides which, we cannot even give a good account of ourselves. We must expect also, hard as we must strive to hinder it, to be more or less at variance with flesh and blood. Vocations, devotions and penances have a sad though inculpable liability to disturb family peace. Parents are slow to give in to God, even long after children are come to years of ripe discretion. For instance, if a son marries, he will have liberty, because the world bids it; if he enters orders or religion, he will not, because only the Church bids it then. Yet they are good people, and religious in their way; why should not we be like them? So they think, and others say. We cannot see things in their light, and they cannot see things in ours.

Now to something of this kind, more or less, we committed ourselves when we took up the spiritual life in earnest. We knew what we were about. From that hour we parted company with the world, nevermore to do aught but fly from it as a plague, or face it as a foe. Human respect, therefore, must henceforth be for us either an impossibility, or an inconsistency, or a sin. What have we to do with giving or taking the world's respect, which we have bound ourselves eternally to disrespect? Enough for us that we have taken ourselves out of the world's hands, and out of our own, and put ourselves into the hands of God, and we have felt those hands, O happy we! gently but firmly close over us, and hold us fast.

CARDINAL MANNING

(1808–1892)

HENRY EDWARD MANNING was born into the most exclusive circles of Anglicanism at a time when great things were stirring in the English Church. Very early in his life he demonstrated his vocation for the clerical state and an ability for administrative work which marked him as a coming leader.

Caught up into the Oxford Movement, Manning found himself mentally convinced of Catholic truth and came into the Church in 1845. Though his career in the Established

Church had promised great things, they were no more astonishing than the things which Catholicism brought to Manning. He was ordained priest, 1851, became archbishop of Westminster, 1865, and cardinal, in 1875. At Rome, Manning was not only *persona grata,* but also the confidant of Pius IX and of Leo XIII.

His genius for affairs and aristocratic bearing made Manning an admired champion of the Church in England. He was far more than a mere manager as so many have implied. His fearless championship of labor marked him as a pioneer in a movement which had as its leader Leo XIII.

Much has been made of the rivalry which existed between Newman and Manning, though this rivalry often existed more in the idle chatter of the two factions in the Church which had been emotionally drawn to one or other of these two great men. As a matter of fact, the only real rivalry between them was a difference of talent and outlook; Newman's idea of the priest's role was intellectual and aristocratic, Manning's practical and social.

Manning's conception of the priesthood, exposed in his book *The Eternal Priesthood,* is quite as exalted as anything in Newman's works. Manning much more easily fell in with the Roman and continental idea of the training for clerical life and the safeguards which should surround it, while Newman remained to the end of his course an individualist and an eclectic.

In expressing his ideas, whether in sermons, lectures, or books, Manning had very little of the genius and insight which marked Newman. He did, however, display balance, prudence, and good judgment which gave his words and works a practical value in an age already weary of incertitude and overcome with life in a world of liberal thinking and harsh living.

LECTURE 1

REVEALED TRUTH DEFINITE AND CERTAIN*

This is life everlasting, that they may know Thee, the only true God, and Jesus Christ whom Thou hast sent. (St. John 17:3).

MY PURPOSE is to speak of the grounds of Faith; I do not mean of the special doctrines of the Catholic theology, but of the grounds or foundation upon which all Faith rests.

This is a subject difficult to treat: partly, because it is of a dry and preliminary nature; and partly, because it is not easy to touch upon a matter so long controverted, without treating it likewise in a controversial tone. But I should think it a dishonor to the sacredness of truth itself, if I could treat a matter so sacred and so necessary in a tone of mere argument. I desire to speak, then, for the honor of our Lord, and, if God so will, for the help of those who seek the truth. To lay broad and sure the foundations

*Manning, Most Rev. Henry Edward, *Manning's Lectures* (Baltimore: Kelly Piet and Co., 1872).

on which we believe is necessary at all times, because as the end of man is life eternal, and as the means to that end is the knowledge of God, and of Jesus Christ whom He hath sent, our whole being, moral, intellectual, and spiritual demands that we should rightly know, and by knowledge be united with, the mind and will of God. And what is necessary at all times is especially so at this. For this land, once full of light, once united to the great commonwealth of Christendom, and grafted into the mystical vine, through whose every branch and spray life and truth circulate, three hundred years ago, by evil men for evil ends, was isolated from the Christian world, and torn from the unity of Christ. Since that time, what has been the religious history of England? The schism which rent England from the Divine Tradition of Faith, rent it also from the source of certainty; the division which severed England from the unity of the Church throughout the world planted the principle of schism in England, itself. England, carried away from Catholic unity, fell as a landslip from the shore, rending itself by its weight and mass. England, Scotland, Ireland, parted from each other, each with a religion of its own, each with its rule of faith. With schism came contradiction; with contradiction uncertainty, debate, and doubt.

Nor did it stop here. That same principle of schism which rent asunder these three kingdoms propagated itself still further. In each country division followed division. Each Protestant church, as it was established, contained within itself the principle both of its creation and dissolution, namely, private judgment. And private judgment, working out its result in individual minds, caused schism after schism; until we are told by a writer, Protestant himself, that in the seventeenth century, during the high time of Protestant ascendency, the sects of England amounted to between one and two hundred.

But there are causes and events nearer to our day which render it more than ever necessary to turn back again to the only foundations of certainty, and lay once more the basis of faith. The establishment so long by many believed to be a Church, a body with a tradition of three hundred years, upheld by the power of this mighty nation, maintained by the sanction of law and legislature, invested with dignity and titles of state, possessing vast endowments, not of land or gold alone, but of that which is more precious, of treasures which the Catholic Church had gathered, and of which it was rudely spoiled; universities, colleges, and school: that vast body, cultivated in intellect, embracing the national life in all its strength and ripeness, in an hour of trial was questioned of its faith, and prevaricated in its answer. It was bid to speak as a teacher sent from God; it could not, because God had not sent it. And thus the last remaining hope of certainty among Protestant bodies in this land revealed its own impotence to teach. The body which men fondly believed to partake of the divine office of the Church, proclaimed that alike in its mission and its message it was human.

What then do we see in this land? Sects without number, perpetually subdividing; each equally confident, all contradictory; and the dominant communion which claims to be authoritative in teaching, itself confounded by internal contradictions of its own. How has this come to pass? It is because the rule of faith is lost, and the principle of certainty destroyed. Put a familiar illustration: suppose that in this teeming commercial city, where men, in fret and fever from sunrise to sunset, buy and sell, barter and bargain, the rules of calculation and the laws of number were to become extinct; what error would ensue, what litigation, what bankruptcy, and what ruin! Or suppose that in this great mercantile empire, whose fleets cover the seas, the science of astronomy and the art of navigation were to perish; the shores of all the world would be strewn with our wrecks. So it is in the spiritual world. The Rule of Faith once lost, souls wander and perish. The effect of this is that men have come to state, as scientifically certain, that there is no definite doctrine in revelation. As if, indeed, truth had no definite outline. And we find in serious and even good men an enmity against the definite statement of religious truth. They call it dogmatism. The Athanasian Creed they cannot away with. It is too precise and too presumptuous. They feel as men who turn suddenly upon the image of our crucified Lord. They start at it from its very definiteness; and as the sight of a crucifix unexpectedly produces a shock, so will the definite statement of truth. It forces home the reality of faith. People now-a-days assume that religious truth can have no definite outline, and that each man must discover and define it for himself. And however definite he may choose to be, one law is binding equally upon us all. No one must be certain. Each must concede to his neighbor as much certainty as he claims for himself. The objective certainty of truth is gone. The highest rule of certainty to each is the conviction of his own understanding. And this, in the revelation of God; in the knowledge which is life eternal.

I. In answer, then, I say, that all knowledge must be definite; that without definiteness there is no true knowledge. To tell us that we may have religious knowledge which is not definite, is to tell us that we may have color which is not distinguishable. Every several truth is as distinct as the several colors in the rainbow. Blend them, and you have only confusion. So it is in religious knowledge. Doctrines definite as the stars in heaven, when clouded by the obscurities of the human mind, lose their definiteness, and pass from sight.

Is not this true in every kind of knowledge? Take science, for example. What would a mathematician think of a diagram which is not definite? What would any problem of physical science be, as in optics, or in mechanics, or engineering, or in any of the arts whereby man subjugates nature to his use, if it were not definite? How could it be expressed, by what calculus could it be treated? What, again, is history which is not definite? History which is not the record of definite fact is mythology, fable, and rhapsody. Where history ceases to be definite, it begins to be fabulous. Or take moral science; what are moral laws which are not definite? A law which is not definite carries with it no obligation. If the law cannot be stated, it cannot be known; if not known, it has no claim on our obedience. Unless it definitively tells me what I am to do and what I am not to do, it has no jurisdiction over my conscience. And as in human knowledge, so, above all, in divine. If there be any knowledge which is severely and precisely definite, it is the knowledge which God has revealed of Himself. Finite indeed it is, but definite always: finite as our sight of the earth, the form of which is round; and yet because our narrow sight can compass no more, to us it seems one broad expanse.

Again, take an example from the highest knowledge. When we speak of wisdom, goodness, or power, we carry our mind upward to the attributes of God. When we see these moral qualities reproduced in a finite being, we call them still by the same titles. So with knowledge. What is knowledge in God but an infinite and definite apprehension of uncreated and eternal truth? The knowledge which God has of himself and of His works is a science divine, the example and type of all. To descend from the divine perfection; what is knowledge in the angels but equally definite, though in a finite intelligence? And what was the knowledge of man before the fall, but, though finite, definite still? What, then, is the knowledge which God has restored to man through revelation but a definite knowledge, a participation of His own? The truth which has been revealed, what is it in the mind of God who reveals it, but one, harmonious and distinct? What was that knowledge as revealed by the Holy Spirit on the day of Pentecost, but one, harmonious and distinct? What was the conception of that knowledge in inspired men, but one, harmonious and distinct also? And what was that knowledge when communicated by those who were inspired to those who believed, but one, harmonious and distinct as before? And what is this unity and harmony and distinctness of knowledge, which God revealed of Himself through Jesus Christ, but the faith we confess in our creed? Our baptismal faith, its substance and its letter, the explicit and the implicit meaning, article by article, is as definite, severe, and precise, as any problem in science. It is of the nature of truth to be so; and where definiteness ends, knowledge ceases.

Observe the distinction between finite knowledge and definite knowledge. Is not science definite? Yet it is also finite. The gravitation, definite as it is, is finite too. The theory of electricity is definite as far as we know it, but finite also. Go through the whole range of physical sciences, what is it but an example of the same condition of knowledge, definiteness in conception with finiteness of reach? What has astronomy revealed to us? The starry heavens, in which we trace the laws and revolutions of heavenly bodies. We find centre after centre, and orbit beyond orbit, until at last we reach what has been long fixed upon as the centre of the universe; and yet even here, science now tells us that probably this, our central point, which we believed to be fixed, is again itself a planet revolving around some mightier centre which science cannot attain. Here, then, are the conditions of definiteness and finiteness combined. So in revealed truth. If we have not a definite knowledge of what we believe, we may be sure we have no true knowledge of it.

GERARD MANLEY HOPKINS, S.J.
(1844-1889)

GERARD MANLEY HOPKINS was born July 28, 1844, at Stratford, near London. He began his education at Newgate and completed it at Balliol College, Oxford. Under the influence of the Oxford Movement he entered the Catholic Church in 1866. In order to prepare himself to enter the Society of Jesus, Hopkins left Balliol and entered the Birmingham Oratory, where he was further influenced by the association and friendship of Father Newman.

His religious vocation led him to the priesthood and the Society of Jesus in 1868. Following his ordination he was sent to work among the poor in Liverpool. After a period as preacher in London he was stationed at St. Aloysius Church, Oxford. Later came his appointment as a Fellow of the Royal University of Ireland, from which post he went to Dublin, where he acted as classical examiner until his death in 1889.

The poems of Hopkins, though few in number, have caused a sensation in the world of letters. His system of verse writing, adequately explained in his preface to his poems, a system which Hopkins himself did not follow with any degree of faithfulness, has done much to give comfort to poets of the twentieth century bent on creating a new school of poetry. Basically Hopkins' system is a free system of verse, though it appears not to be. For its effect it depends upon a double mechanic: first, the normally half-heard measure of words with their regular accents and emphases; second, the mind or tone accent of ideas which may be based on the importance of the ideas or, as in nursery rhymes, upon mere caprice and solely for the clash of word sounds. His poems have, therefore, both an inscape and an outscape: the outscape what is called normal scansion; the inscape, idea emphasis. Hopkins adds to the freedom of this system by breaking his lines where he wills, even in the first foot of a new line, and by adding extra feet at the end of his lines as sense or double rhythm dictates. His use of compound words is uniquely original and adds much to the crowded opulence of his lines.

It is not without point that Hopkins constantly refers to his system as a restoration, or, if you will, a return to pre-Shakespearean standards both for our spoken and verse language. As a matter of fact, he is not entirely accurate, though he did see vaguely that those who attempted to make of English verse a mere follower of Latin and Greek measures neither fully understood their own language nor its musical possibilities. In the composition of Latin and Greek poems the first requirements are those of measure and the correctness of endings, in English verse the emphasis is: first, on the inscape or musical quality of the idea pattern; second, in the half-heard outscape of scansion which may be altered as words are combined in phrases. Greek and Latin words have absolute measure, English words have duration and measure of a sort, depending upon the ideas they serve.

As it stands, Hopkins' verse system more nearly fits the nature and demands of our language than any other system set down by any English poet or critic.

The Wreck of the Deutschland remains his greatest poem not merely because of its length, but because of the complication of the idea it embodies. As Job discovered, the power and wrath of God are only understood by understanding His mercy. This was the lesson the nuns taught in *The Wreck*.

The so-called "Terrible Sonnets" have been somewhat overestimated. Half the seeming anguish of them is due to Hopkins' use of exclamations and the unusual ways in which he breaks his lines. Whether they sum up his "dark night of the soul," spiritual dryness, or anguish at his lack of inspiration, they are good sonnets though somewhat pale beside the perfect beauty of *The Windhover*.

Hopkins' poems are indeed a horn book of prosody for anyone who is interested in English poetry. Packed with ideas, as they are, and ornamented with the most lambent flowers of rhetoric, doubly lovely in their originality, the poems must be taken slowly and read often before yielding their full felicity.

The best edition of the poems is that edited by Robert Bridges.

As a letter writer, Hopkins also stood in the first rank. His letters are spontaneous, witty, and they range up and down the whole field of the arts. They were published by the Oxford Press in two volumes, 1935, and were edited by C. Collier Abbot.

The story of Hopkins' life is a story of reticences. The official life is that of Father Lahey, S.J.

For those who find Hopkins a "difficult poet," the competent study of the man and his work by Dr. John Pick, the Oxford Press, is indispensable.

THE WRECK OF THE DEUTSCHLAND*

PART THE FIRST

1

Thou mastering me
God! giver of breath and bread;
World's strand, sway of the sea;
Lord of living and dead;
Thou hast bound bones and veins in me, fastened me flesh,
And after it almost unmade, what with dread,
Thy doing: and dost thou touch me afresh?
Over again I feel thy finger and find thee.

2

I did say yes
O at lightning and lashed rod;
Thou heardst me truer than tongue confess
Thy terror, O Christ, O God;
Thou knowest the walls, altar and hour and night:
The swoon of a heart that the sweep and the hurl of thee trod
Hard down with a horror of height:
And the midriff astrain with leaning of, laced with fire of stress.

---

*The above and following poems have been selected from *Poems of Gerard Manley Hopkins*, edited by Robert Bridges (London: Oxford University Press, 1938).

3

Tho frown of his face
Before me, the hurtle of hell
Behind, where, where was a, where was a place?
I whirled out wings that spell
And fled with a fling of the heart to the heart of the Host.
My heart, but you were dovewinged, I can tell,
Carrier-witted, I am bold to boast,
To flash from the flame to the flame then, tower from the grace to the grace.

4

I am soft sift
In an hourglass — at the wall
Fast, but mined with a motion, a drift
And it crowds and it combs to the fall;
I steady as a water in a well, to a poise, to a pane,
But roped with, always, all the way down from the tall
Fells or flanks of the voel, a vein
Of the gospel proffer, a pressure, a principle, Christ's gift.

5

I kiss my hand
To the stars, lovely-asunder
Starlight, wafting him out of it; and
Glow, glory in thunder;
Kiss my hand to the dappled-with-damson west:
Since, tho' he is under the world's splendour and wonder,
His mystery must be instressed, stressed;
For I greet him the days I meet him, and bless when I understand.

6

Not out of his bliss
Springs the stress felt
Nor first from heaven (and few know this)
Swings the stroke dealt —
Stroke and a stress that stars and storms deliver,
That guilt is hushed by, hearts are flushed by and melt —
But it rides time like riding a river
(And here the faithful waver, the faithless fable and miss).

7

It dates from day
Of his going in Galilee;
Warm-laid grave of a womb-life grey;
Manger, maiden's knee;
The dense and the driven Passion, and frightful sweat;
Thence the discharge of it, there its swelling to be,
Though felt before, though in high flood yet —
What none would have known of it, only the heart, being hard at bay,

8

Is out with it! Oh,
  We lash with the best or worst
    Word last! How a lush-kept plush-capped sloe
      Will, mouthed to flesh-burst,
Gush! — flush the man, the being with it, sour or sweet,
Brim, in a flash, full! — Hither then, last or first,
    To hero of Calvary, Christ's feet —
Never ask if meaning it, wanting it, warned of it — men go.

9

Be adored among men,
  God, three-numbered form;
    Wring thy rebel, dogged in den,
      Man's malice, with wrecking and storm.
Beyond saying sweet, past telling of tongue,
Thou art lightning and love, I found it, a winter and warm;
    Father and fondler of heart thou hast wrung:
Hast thy dark descending and most art merciful then.

10

With an anvil-ding
  And with fire in him forge thy will
    Or rather, rather then, stealing as Spring
      Through him, melt him but master him still:
Whether at once, as once at a crash Paul,
Or as Austin, a lingering-out sweet skill,
    Make mercy in all of us, out of us all
Mastery, but be adored, but be adored King.

PART THE SECOND

11

'Some find me a sword; some
  The flange and the rail; flame,
    Fang, or flood' goes Death on drum,
      And storms bugle his fame.
But we dream, we are rooted in earth — Dust!
Flesh falls within sight of us, we, though our flower the same,
    Wave with the meadow, forget that there must
The sour scythe cringe, and the blear share come.

12

On Saturday sailed from Bremen,
  American-outward-bound,
    Take settler and seamen, tell men with women,
      Two hundred souls in the round —
O Father, not under thy feathers nor ever as guessing
The goal was a shoal, of a fourth the doom to be drowned;
    Yet did the dark side of the bay of thy blessing
Not vault them, the millions of rounds of thy mercy not reeve even them in?

13

Into the snows she sweeps,
　Hurling the haven behind,
The Deutschland, on Sunday; and so the sky keeps,
　For the infinite air is unkind,
And the sea flint-flake, black-backed in the regular blow,
Sitting Eastnortheast, in cursed quarter, the wind;
　Wiry and white-fiery and whirlwind-swivelled snow
Spins to the widow-making unchilding unfathering deeps.

14

She drove in the dark to leeward,
　She struck — not a reef or a rock
But the combs of a smother of sand: night drew her
　Dead to the Kentish Knock;
And she beat the bank down with her bows and the ride of her keel:
The breakers rolled on her beam with ruinous shock;
　And canvas and compass, the whorl and the wheel
Idle for ever to waft her or wind her with, these she endured.

15

Hope had grown grey hairs,
　Hope had mourning on,
Trenched with tears, carved with cares,
　Hope was twelve hours gone;
And frightful a nightfall folded rueful a day
Nor rescue, only rocket and lightship, shone,
　And lives at last were washing away:
To the shrouds they took, — they shook in the hurling and horrible airs.

16

One stirred from the rigging to save
　The wild woman-kind below,
With a rope's end round the man, handy and brave —
　He was pitched to his death at a blow,
For all his dreadnought breast and braids of thew:
They could tell him for hours, dandled the to and fro
　Through the cobbled foam-fleece, what could he do
With the burl of the fountains of air, buck and the flood of the wave?

17

They fought with God's cold —
　And they could not and fell to the deck
(Crushed them) or water (and drowned them) or rolled
　With the sea-romp over the wreck.
Night roared, with the heart-break hearing a heart-broke rabble
The woman's wailing, the crying of child without check —
　Till a lioness arose breasting the babble,
A prophetess towered in the tumult, a virginal tongue told.

18

Ah, touched in your bower of bone
    Are you! turned for an exquisite smart,
Have you! make words break from me here all alone,
    Do you! — mother of being in me, heart.
O unteachable after evil, but uttering truth,
    Why, tears! is it? tears; such a melting, a madrigal start!
    Never-eldering revel and river of youth,
What can it be, this glee? the good you have there of your own?

19

Sister, a sister calling
    A master, her master and mine! —
And the inboard seas run swirling and hawling;
    The rash smart sloggering brine
Blinds her; but she that weather sees one thing, one;
Has one fetch in her: she rears herself to divine
    Ears, and the call of the tall nun
To the men in the tops and the tackle rode over the storm's brawling.

20

She was first of a five and came
    Of a coifèd sisterhood.
(O Deutschland, double a desperate name!
    O world wide of its good!
But Gertrude, lily, and Luther, are two of a town,
Christ's lily and beast of the waste wood:
    From life's dawn it is drawn down,
Abel is Cain's brother and breasts they have suckled the same.)

21

Loathed for a love men knew in them,
    Banned by the land of their birth,
Rhine refused them. Thames would ruin them;
    Surf, snow, river and earth
Gnashed: but thou art above, thou Orion of light;
Thy unchancelling poising palms were weighing the worth,
    Thou martyr-master: in thy sight
Storm flakes were scroll-leaved flowers, lily showers — sweet heaven was astrew
    in them.

22

Five! the finding and sake
    And cipher of suffering Christ.
Mark, the mark is of man's make
    And the word of it Sacrificed.
But he scores it in scarlet himself on his own bespoken,
Before-time-taken, dearest prizèd and priced —
    Stigma, signal, cinquefoil token
For lettering of the lamb's fleece, ruddying of the rose-flake.

23

Joy fall to thee, father Francis,
    Drawn to the Life that died;
  With the gnarls of the nails in thee, niche of the lance, his
      Lovescape crucified
And seal of his seraph-arrival! and these thy daughters
And five-livèd and leavèd favour and pride,
    Are sisterly sealed in wild waters,
To bathe in his fall-gold mercies, to breathe in his all-fire glances.

24

Away in the loveable west,
    On a pastoral forehead of Wales,
  I was under a roof here, I was at rest,
    And they the prey of the gales;
She to the black-about air, to the breaker, the thickly
Falling flakes, to the throng that catches and quails
    Was calling 'O Christ, Christ, come quickly':
The cross to her she calls Christ to her, christens her wild-worst Best.

25

The majesty! what did she mean?
    Breathe, arch and original Breath.
  Is it love in her of the being as her lover had been?
    Breathe, body of lovely Death.
They were else-minded then, altogether, the men
Woke thee with a *we are perishing* in the weather of Gennesareth.
    Or is it that she cried for the crown then,
The keener to come at the comfort for feeling the combating keen?

26

For how to the heart's cheering
    The down-dugged ground-hugged grey.
  Hovers off, the jay-blue heaven appearing
    Of pied and peeled May!
Blue-beating and hoary-glow height; or night, still higher,
With belled fire and the moth-soft Milky Way,
    What by your measure is the heaven of desire,
The treasure never eyesight got, nor was ever guessed what for the hearing?

27

No, but it was not these.
    The jading and jar of the cart,
  Time's tasking, it is fathers that asking for ease
    Of the sodden-with-its-sorrowing heart,
Not danger, electrical horror; then further it finds
The appealing of the Passion is tenderer in prayer apart:
    Other, I gather, in measure her mind's
Burden, in wind's burly and beat of endragonèd seas.

28

But how shall I . . . make me room there:
   Reach me a . . . Fancy, come faster —
Strike you the sight of it? look at it loom there,
   Thing that she . . . there then! the Master,
Ipse, the only one, Christ, King, Head:
He was to cure the extremity where he had cast her;
   Do, deal, lord it with living and dead;
Let him ride, her pride, in his triumph, despatch and have done with his
   doom there.

29

Ah! there was a heart right!
   There was single eye!
Read the unshapeable shock night
   And knew the who and the why;
Wording it how but by him that present and past,
Heaven and earth are word of, worded by? —
   The Simon Peter of a soul! to the blast
Tarpeian-fast, but a blown beacon of light.

30

Jesu, heart's light,
   Jesu, maid's son,
What was the feast followed the night
   Thou hadst glory of this nun? —
Feast of the one woman without stain,
For so conceived, so to conceive thee is done;
   But here was heart-throe, birth of a brain,
Word, that heard and kept thee and uttered thee outright.

31

Well, she has thee for the pain, for the
   Patience; but pity of the rest of them!
Heart, go and bleed at a bitterer vein for the
   Comfortless unconfessed of them —
No not uncomforted: lovely-felicitous Providence
Finger of a tender of, O of a feathery delicacy, the breast of the
   Maiden could obey so, be a bell to, ring of it, and
Startle the poor sheep back! is the shipwreck then a harvest, does tempest carry
   the grain for thee?

32

I admire thee, master of the tides,
   Of the Yore-flood, of the year's fall;
The recurb and the recovery of the gulf's sides,
   The girth of it and the wharf of it and the wall;
Stanching, quenching ocean of a motionable mind;
Ground of being, and granite of it: past all
   Grasp God, throned behind
Death with a sovereignty that heeds but hides, bodes but abides;

33

With a mercy that outrides
The all of water, an ark
For the listener; for the lingerer with a love glides
Lower than death and the dark;
A vein for the visiting of the past-prayer, pent in prison,
The-last-breath penitent spirits — the uttermost mark
Our passion-plunged giant risen,
The Christ of the Father compassionate, fetched in the storm of his strides.

34

Now burn, new born to the world,
Doubled-naturèd name,
The heaven-flung, heart-fleshed, maiden-furled
Miracle-in-Mary-of-flame,
Mid-numbered He in three of the thunder-throne!
Not a dooms-day dazzle in his coming nor dark as he came;
Kind, but royally reclaiming his own;
A released shower, let flash to the shire, not a lightning of fire hard-hurled.

35

Dame, at our door
Drowned, and among our shoals,
Remember us in the roads, the heaven-haven of the Reward:
Our King back, oh, upon English souls!
Let him easter in us, be a dayspring to the dimness of us,
be a crimson-cresseted east,
More brightening her, rare-dear Britain, as his reign rolls,
Pride, rose, prince, hero of us, high-priest.
Our hearts' charity's heart's fire, our thoughts' chivalry's throng's Lord.

THE STARLIGHT NIGHT

Look at the stars! look, look up at the skies!
O look at all the fire-folk sitting in the air!
The bright boroughs, the circle-citadels there!
Down in dim woods the diamond delves! the elves'-eyes!
The grey lawns cold where gold, where quickgold lies!
Wind-beat whitebeam! airy abeles set on a flare!
Flake-doves sent floating forth at a farmyard scare! —
Ah well! it is all a purchase, all is a prize.
Buy then! bid then! — What? — Prayer, patience, alms, vows.
Look, look: a May-mess, like on orchard boughs!
Look! March-bloom, like on mealed-with-yellow sallows!
These are indeed the barn; withindoors house
The shocks. This piece-bright paling shuts the spouse
Christ home, Christ and his mother and all his hallows.

THE WINDHOVER

To Christ Our Lord

I caught this morning morning's minion, kingdom of daylight's dauphin,
     dapple-dawn-drawn Falcon, in his riding
Of the rolling level underneath him steady air, and striding
High there, how he rung upon the rein of a wimpling wing
In his ecstasy! then off, off forth on swing,
     As a skate's heel sweeps smooth on a bow-bend: the hurl
     and gliding
     Rebuffed the big wind. My heart in hiding
Stirred for a bird,—the achieve of, the mastery of the thing!

Brute beauty and valour and act, oh, air, pride, plume, here
     Buckle! And the fire that breaks from thee, then a billion
Times told lovelier, more dangerous, O my chevalier!
     No wonder of it: sheer plod makes plough down sillion
Shine, and blue-bleak embers, ah my dear,
     Fall, gall themselves, and gash gold vermillion.

THAT NATURE IS A HERACLITEAN FIRE AND OF THE COMFORT OF THE RESURRECTION

Cloud-puffball, torn tufts, tossed pillows flaunt forth, then
     chevy on an air-
built thoroughfare: heaven-roysterers, in gay-gangs, they throng:
     they glitter in marches.
Down roughcast, down dazzling whitewash, wherever an elm arches,
Shivelights and shadowtackle in long lashes lace, lance, and pair.
Delightfully the bright wind boisterous ropes, wrestles, beats earth bare
Of yestertempest's creases; in pool and rut peel parches
Squandering ooze to squeezed dough, crust, dust; stanches, starches
Squandroned masks and manmarks treadmire toil there
Footfretted in it. Million-fueled, nature's bonfire burns on.
But quench her bonniest, dearest to her, her clearest-selved spark
Man, how fast his firedint, his mark on mind, is gone!
Both are in an unfathomable, all is in an enormous dark
Drowned. O pity and indignation! Manshape, that shone
Sheer off, disseveral, a star, death blots black out; nor mark
          Is any of him at all so stark
But vastness blurs and time beats level. Enough! the Resurrection,
A heart's-clarion! Away grief's gasping, joyless days, dejection.
          Across my foundering deck shone
A beacon, an eternal beam. Flesh fade, and mortal trash
Fall to the residuary worm; world's wildfire, leave but ash:
          In a flash, at a trumpet crash,
I am all at once what Christ is, since he was what I am, and
This Jack, joke, poor potsherd, patch, matchwood, immortal diamond,
          Is immortal diamond.

PIED BEAUTY

Glory be to God for dappled things —
   For skies of couple-colour as a brinded cow;
     For rose-moles all in stipple upon trout that swim;
Fresh-firecoal chestnut-falls; finches' wings;
   Landscape plotted and pieced — fold, fallow, and plough;
     And all trades, their gear and tackle and trim.

All things counter, original, spare, strange;
   Whatever is fickle, freckled, (who knows how?)
     With swift, slow; sweet, sour; adazzle, dim;
He fathers-forth whose beauty is past change;
       Praise him.

SONNET

Thou art indeed just, Lord, if I contend
With thee; but, sir, so what I plead is just.
Why do sinners' ways prosper? and why must
Disappointment all I endeavour end?
   Wert thou my enemy, O thou my friend,
How wouldst thou worse, I wonder, than thou dost
Defeat, thwart me? Oh, the sots and thralls of lust
Do in spare hours more thrive than I that spend,
Sir, life upon thy cause. See, banks and brakes
Now, leaved how thick! laced they are again
With fretty chervil, look, and fresh wind shakes
Them; birds build — but not I build; no, but strain,
Times's eunuch, and not breed one work that wakes.
Mine, O thou lord of life, send my roots rain.

SONNET TO R. B.

The fine delight that fathers thought; the strong
Spur, live and lancing like the blowpipe flame,
Breathes once and, quenches faster than it came,
Leaves yet the mind a mother of immortal song.
Nine months she then, nay years, nine years she long
Within her wears, bears, cares and moulds the same:
The widow of an insight lost she lives, with aim
Now known and hand at work now never wrong.
   Sweet fire the sire of muse, my soul needs this;
I want the one rapture of an inspiration.
O then if in my lagging lines you miss
The roll, the rise, the carol, the creation,
My winter world, that scarcely breathes that bliss
Now, yields you, with some sighs, our explanation.

ALICE MEYNELL
(1847–1922)

AT ONE time the popular choice for the position of poet laureate of England, Alice Christiana Meynell was born at Barnes, near London, in 1847. Her parents, Thomas J. and Christiana Thompson were introduced to each other by Charles Dickens, who remained an intimate friend of the family. Traveling with her nomadic parents between England, France, and Italy, Alice Meynell received her education abroad as well as in England. At an early age she entered the Catholic Church.

In 1877 she married Wilfrid Meynell, a prominent editor and publisher. She was the mother of eight children. The Meynell home, Palace Court, became the haven for some of the leading literary lights of the age. Frequent visitors were Robert Browning, John Ruskin, Coventry Patmore, and Rosetti. Mrs. Meynell proved a great influence on the life and work of George Meredith, who called her the "penciling mamma" — she often sat at a long table writing while four girls and three boys edited the family newspaper under the table. Her sister, Lady Butler, painter of the well-known picture, "Roll Call," illustrated some of her works.

Perhaps the greatest importance of the Meynell house was that it offered shelter and security to a struggling youth named Francis Thompson, whose true genius as a poet remains still to be fully recognized. Through their magazine, *Merrie England,* the Meynells discovered Thompson, and it was in their house that he wrote many of his poems.

Alice Meynell was justly famous for her beauty, her writings, and her good sense. In her exquisite hands the varying impulses of the Catholic Revival were braided into something like a first unity. But if her unusual beauty made her one of the most sought after women of her time, her witty insights, in the essays she wrote, and the deep limpidity of her poetry soon solidly established her in public esteem. *The Rhythm of Life,* a collection of her best essays which she herself edited, 1914, reveals her full mastery of English prose. Her poems have been widely admired. Of her early verse, "Renouncement" has been called a perfect sonnet, and the lovely but tinkly "Shepherdess" is included in almost every anthology of great poetry. A careful examination of her *Collected Poems,* 1923, will prove that she grew in stature with the years. The spare beauty of her lines hardened into genuine revelation, as in the "Threshing Machine," which appeared in the final years of her life. Mrs. Meynell was perhaps the pioneer poet in the work of restoring poetry to classical economy; a movement which in the twentieth century has made great strides under T. S. Eliot and Ezra Pound.

Her *Biography,* 1929, a charming study written by her daughter, Viola, gives a completely intimate picture of her life and surroundings.

ADVENT MEDITATION*

Rorate Coeli desuper, et nubes pluant Justum. Aperiatur Terra, et germinet Salvatorem.

*The above and following poems have been selected from *The Poems of Alice Meynell,* Complete Edition (London: Oxford University Press, 1941–1942).

No sudden thing of glory and fear
Was the Lord's coming; but the dear
Slow Nature's days followed each other
To form the Saviour from His Mother
— One of the children of the year.

The earth, the rain, received the trust,
— The sun and dews, to frame the Just.
He drew His daily life from these,
According to His own decrees
Who makes man from the fertile dust.

Sweet summer and the winter wild.
These brought Him forth, the Undefiled.
The happy Springs renewed again
His daily bread, the growing grain,
The food and raiment of the Child.

RENOUNCEMENT

I must not think of thee; and, tired yet
    strong,
I shun the thought that lurks in all delight —
The thought of thee — and in the blue
    Heaven's height,
And in the sweetest passage of a song.

Oh, just beyond the fairest thoughts that
    throng
This breast, the thought of thee waits, hidden
    yet bright;
But it must never, never come in sight;
I must stop short of thee the whole day
    long.

But when sleep comes to close each difficult
    day,
When night gives pause to the long watch
    I keep,
And all my bonds I needs must loose apart,

Must doff my will as raiment laid away, —
With the first dream that comes with the
    first sleep
I run, I run, I am gathered to thy heart.

A THRUSH BEFORE DAWN

A voice peals in this end of night
    A phrase of notes resembling stars,
Single and spiritual notes of light.
    What call they at my window-bars?
        The South, the past, the day to be,
        An ancient infelicity.

Darkling, deliberate, what sings
    This wonderful one, alone, at peace?
What wilder things than song, what things
    Sweeter than youth, clearer than Greece,
        Dearer than Italy, untold
        Delight, and freshness centuries old?

And first first-loves, a multitude,
    The exaltation of their pain;
Ancestral childhood long renewed;

And midnights of invisible rain;
    And gardens, gardens, night and day,
    Gardens and childhood all the way.

What Middle Ages passionate,
    O passionless voice! What distant bells
Lodged in the hills, what palace state
    Illyrian! For it speaks, it tells,
        Without desire, without dismay,
        Some morrow and some yesterday.

All-natural things! But more — Whence came
    This yet remoter mystery?
How do these starry notes proclaim
    A graver still divinity?
        This hope, this sanctity of fear?
        O innocent throat! O human ear!

A FATHER OF WOMEN

Ad Sororem E. B.

"Thy father was transfused into thy blood."
— DRYDEN, *Ode to Mrs. Anne Killigrew*.

Our father works in us,
The daughters of his manhood. Not undone,
Is he, not wasted, though transmuted thus,
    And though he left no son,

Therefore on him I cry
To arm me: 'For my delicate mind a casque,
A breastplate for my heart, courage to die,
    Of thee, captain, I ask.

'Nor strengthen only; press
A finger on this violent blood and pale,
Over this rash will let thy tenderness
    A while pause, and prevail.

'And shepherd-father, thou
Whose staff folded my thoughts before my
    birth,
Control them now I am of earth, and now
    Thou art no more of earth.

'O liberal, constant, dear!
Crush in my nature the ungenerous art
Of the inferior; set me high, and here,
    Here garner up thy heart.'

Like to him now are they,
The million living fathers of the War —
Mourning the crippled world, the bitter
    day —
    Whose striplings are no more.

The crippled world! Come then,
Fathers of women with your honour in trust;
Approve, accept, know them daughters of
    men,
    Now that your sons are dust.

THE UNKNOWN GOD

One of the crowd went up,
And knelt before the Paten and the Cup,
Received the Lord, returned in peace, and
    prayed
Close to my side; then in my heart I said:

'O Christ, in this man's life —
This stranger who is Thine — in all his strife,
All his felicity, his good and ill,
In the assaulted stronghold of his will,

'I do confess Thee here,
Alive within this life; I know Thee near

Within this lonely conscience, closed away
Within this brother's solitary day.

'Christ in his unknown heart,
His intellect unknown — this love, this art,
This battle and this peace, this destiny
That I shall never know, look upon me!

'Christ in his numbered breath,
Christ in his beating heart and in his death,
Christ in his mystery! From that secret place
And from that separate dwelling, give me
    grace.'

CHIMES

Brief, on a flying night,
From the shaken tower,
A flock of bells take flight,
And go with the hour.

Like birds from the cote to the gales,
Abrupt — O hark!

A fleet of bells set sails,
And go to the dark.

Sudden the cold airs swing.
Alone, aloud,
A verse of bells takes wing
And flies with the cloud.

AT NIGHT

To W. M.

Home, home from the horizon far and clear,
Hither the soft wings sweep;
Flocks of the memories of the day draw near
The dovecote doors of sleep.

Oh, which are they that come through sweet-
est light
Of all these homing birds?
Which with the straightest and the swiftest
flight?
Your words to me, your words!

"I AM THE WAY"

Thou art the Way.
Hadst Thou been nothing but the goal,
I cannot say
If Thou hadst ever met my soul.

I cannot see —
I, child of process — if there lies

An end for me,
Full of repose, full of replies.

I'll not reproach
The road that winds, my feet that err.
Access, approach,
Art Thou, time, way, and wayfarer.

THE SHEPHERDESS

She walks — the lady of my delight —
A shepherdess of sheep.
Her flocks are thoughts. She keeps them
white;
She guards them from the steep;
She feeds them on the fragrant height,
And folds them in for sleep.

She roams maternal hills and bright,
Dark valleys safe and deep.
Into that tender breast at night

The chastest stars may peep.
She walks — the lady of my delight —
A shepherdess of sheep.

She holds her little thoughts in sight,
Through gay they run and leap.
She is so circumspect and right;
She has her soul to keep.
She walks — the lady of my delight —
A shepherdess of sheep.

THE RHYTHM OF LIFE*

I

IF LIFE is not always poetical, it is at least metrical. Periodicity rules over the mental experience of man, according to the path of the orbit of his thoughts. Distances are not gauged, ellipses not measured, velocities not ascertained, times not known. Nevertheless, the recurrence is sure. What the mind suffered last week, or last year, it does not suffer now; but it will suffer again next week or next year. Happiness is not a matter of events; it depends upon the tides of the mind. Disease is metrical, closing in at shorter and shorter periods towards death, sweeping abroad at longer and longer intervals toward recovery. Sorrow for one cause was intolerable yesterday, and will be intolerable to-morrow; today it is easy to bear, but the cause has not passed. Even the burden of a spiritual distress unsolved is bound to leave the heart to a temporary peace; and remorse itself does not remain — it returns. Gaiety takes us by a dear surprise. If we had made a course of notes of its visits, we might have been on the watch, and would have had an expectation instead of a discovery. No one makes such observations; in all the diaries of students of the interior world, there have never come to light the records of the Kepler of such cycles. But Thomas à Kempis knew of the recurrences, if he did not measure them. In his cell alone with the elements — 'What wouldst thou more than these? For out of these were all things made' — he learnt the stay to be found in the depth of the hour of bitterness, and the remembrance that restrains the soul at the coming of the moment of delight, giving it a more conscious welcome, but presaging for it an inexorable flight. And 'rarely, rarely comest thou,' sighed Shelley, not to Delight merely, but to the spirit of Delight. Delight can be compelled beforehand, called, and constrained to our service — Ariel can be bound to a daily task; but such artificial violence throws life out of

metre, and it is not the spirit that is thus compelled. That flits upon an orbit elliptically or parabolically or hyperbolically curved, keeping no man knows what trysts with Time.

It seems fit that Shelley and the author of the *Imitation* should both have been keen and simple enough to perceive these flights, and to guess at the order of this periodicity. Both souls were in close touch with the spirits of their several worlds, and no deliberate human rules, no infractions of the liberty and law of the universal movement, kept, from them the knowledge of recurrences *Eppur si muove*. They knew that presence does not exist without absence; they knew that what is just upon its flight of farewell is already on its long path of return. They knew that what is approaching to the very touch is hastening towards departure. 'O wind,' cried Shelley, in autumn,

'O wind,
If winter comes can spring be far behind?'
They knew that the flux is equal to the reflux; that to interrupt with unlawful recurrences, out of time, is to weaken the impulse of onset and retreat; the sweep and impetus of movement. To live in constant efforts after an equal life, whether the equality be sought in mental production, or in spiritual sweetness, or in the joy of the senses, is to live without either rest or full activity. The souls of certain of the saints, being singularly simple and single, have been in the most complete subjection to the law of periodicity. Ecstasy and desolation visited them by seasons. They endured, during spaces of vacant time, the interior loss of all for which they had sacrificed the world.

They rejoiced in the uncovenanted beatitude of sweetness alight in their hearts. Like them are the poets whom, three times or ten times in the course of a long life, the Muse has approached, touched, and forsaken. And yet hardly like them; not always so docile, nor so wholly prepared for the departure, the brevity, of the golden and irrevocable hour. Few poets have fully rec-

*Meynell, Alice, *The Rhythm of Life* (New York: John Lane Co., 1896), pp. 1–6.

ognized the metrical absence of their Muse. For full recognition is expressed in one only way — silence.

It has been found that several tribes in Africa and in America worship the moon, and not the sun; a great number worship both; but no tribes are known to adore the sun, and not the moon. For the periodicity of the sun is still in part a secret; but that of the moon is modestly apparent, perpetually influential. On her depend the tides; and she is Selene, mother of Herse, bringer of the dews that recurrently irrigate lands where rain is rare. More than any other companion of earth is she the Measurer. Early Indo-Germanic languages knew her by that name. Her metrical phases are the symbol of the order of recurrence. Constancy in approach and in departure is the reason of her inconstancies. Juliet will not receive a vow spoken in invocation of the moon; but Juliet did not live to know that love itself has tidal times — lapses and ebbs which are due to the metrical rule of the interior heart, but which the lover vainly and unkindly attributes to some outward alteration in the beloved. For man — except those elect already named — is hardly aware of periodicity. The individual man either never learns it fully, or learns it late. And he learns it so late, because it is a matter of cumulative experience upon which cumulative evidence is lacking. It is in the after-part of each life that the law is learnt so definitely as to do away with the hope or fear of continuance. That young sorrow comes so near to despair is a result of this young ignorance. So is the early hope of great achievement. Life seems so long, and its capacity so great, to one who knows nothing of all the intervals it needs must hold — intervals between aspirations, between actions, pauses as inevitable as the pauses of sleep. And life looks impossible to the young unfortunate, unaware of the inevitable and unfailing refreshment. It would be for their peace to learn that there is a tide in the affairs of men, in a sense more subtle — if it is not too audacious to add a meaning to Shakespeare — than the phrase was meant to contain. Their joy is flying away from them on its way home; their life will wax and wane; and if they would be wise, they must wake and rest in its phases, knowing that they are ruled by the law that commands all things — a sun's revolutions and the rhythmic pangs of maternity.

WILFRID MEYNELL
(1852–   )

ALICE MEYNELL was truly a great woman. Much of her greatness was buttressed by the strong character of her husband Wilfrid, to whom she dedicated her lovely poems. They made an admirable couple: Mrs. Meynell was quick, emotionally dynamic, brilliantly conversational; Wilfrid Meynell was quiet, amiable in temper, and of profound good judgment.

He was born of Quaker parents in Yorkshire and educated in that country of strong men and sparkling atmosphere. A convert to the Church in 1870, Meynell soon displayed his talents by becoming editor of *The Weekly Register* and *Merrie England,* a literary magazine which played an admirable part in bringing the works of Catholics to public notice. Among the many Catholic writers of the time who met their public through the kindly interest of Meynell was Francis Thompson. To him Meynell became rescuer, father, and guide, and it was chiefly through his care that Thompson was enabled to write his memorable poems.

In addition to his labors as editor, Meynell became a publisher's literary adviser, a role for which he was well fitted by his impeccable judgment, his wide acquaintance with authors, and his truly remarkable faculty for the detection of talent.

With his marriage to Alice Thompson, his home became one of the liveliest literary salons in London. There the Catholic literary Revival flared into full brilliance.

Though long since retired from active work, Meynell has continued to father young authors and has been friend and adviser to many American writers who have loved him for the amiability of his disposition, the richness of his memories, and the shrewdness of his mind.

Meynell has published no works of first intensity. His poems are whimsically charming and display a love of paradox and puns.

Of his works *Who Goes There?,* containing sketches of World War I, has passages of genuine pathos and merit and *John Henry Newman,* a tribute upon the death of the great Cardinal, embodies reminiscences and judgments which are important in completely estimating the character of Newman. Meynell's best monument is his edition of the works of Francis Thompson.

THE OUTER WORLD*

A MAN is entered in a Biographical Dictionary by the date of his birth; but it is really the date of death that ranges him in the memories of mankind. Macaulay and Newman belong to a different epoch, but were born within a month or two of each other. Newman was a baby when Keats, a child of four or five, had not yet even heard of Lemprière. Shelley, just over eight, was already exciting the admiration of his sisters by his declamation of Latin verse. Byron was beginning his tumultuous teens, scribbling his first verses, and being well hated at Harrow. Newman hardly ranks as the contemporary of these, though he was twenty when Keats died, was of age when Shelley died, and when Byron died was twenty-three. With Coleridge, Southey, and Wordsworth, though these were all born between thirty and thirty-five years before him, he lived for thirty-three, forty-two, and forty-nine years. In 1836, Faber, returning to Oxford from the Long, which he had spent at the Lakes, reported that "Wordsworth spoke of Newman's sermons, some of which he had read and liked exceedingly." Walter Scott was thirty when Newman was born, and when Scott died Newman was beginning the Tractarian movement which was to give Abbotsford to Rome.

Newman's literary admirations were in great part those of the period. For Scott he had all Mr. Gladstone's enthusiasm. The tinsel of that mediaevalism did not disconcert him; and he gratefully mentions Scott as having in some sort, by his scenes of chivalry, prepared the path for the Catholic revival; surely a route to the Oratory by the way of Wardour Street! Scott's novels he put into the hands of the boys at the Oratory school at Edgbaston as prizes, and even examined in them. Perhaps he had his happiest holiday when he spent five weeks at Abbotsford at the end of 1852, the guest of Mr. Hope-Scott, who, like his wife, Lockhart's daughter, had become a Catholic. When Newman got the invitation he wrote in reply: "It would be a great pleasure to spend some time with you, and then I have ever had the extremest sympathy for Walter Scott, and it would delight me to see his place. When he was dying, I was saying prayers (whatever they were worth) for him continually, thinking of Keble's words, 'Think on the minstrel as ye kneel.'" Lockhart was still alive, and the visits his daughter and son-in-law paid him in London, he repaid at Abbotsford, whither, finally, he had his books taken. There, in the breakfast-room, because he could not leave the ground-floor, and because he shunned the dining-room where Sir Walter gave up the ghost, the old editor, a stoic amid suffering, a Protestant among Catholics, passed away,

*Meynell, Wilfrid, *John Henry Newman* (London: Kegan Paul, Trench, Trubner and Co., 1890), pp. 88–105.

with Father Lockhart, a distant cousin, at his unresponsive side, and the sound of his daughter's voice, reading prayers from her "Garden of the Soul," in his ears.

One can well imagine the mystification of the old editor of the *Quarterly* in presence of the Popery which sat at his hearth, although he had been willing to give Tractarianism a distant hearing in his Review. In 1837, one of the party at Oxford complacently records that "Lockhart finds he must have an infusion of Oxford principles; it takes with people now — that is, such people as read the *Quarterly;*" and Philip Pusey, the member of Parliament, told his brother Edward that one of Newman's greatest triumphs was his "getting hold of the *Quarterly*." A little later this complacency must have been shaken by the report that Murray had said he would have given a thousand pounds to be able to suppress the article which Sewell had written.

Though the *Quarterly* might turn half an ear timidly towards the arresting preacher of St. Mary the Virgin, such leniency could not be expected from the rival Review. Of course Macaulay was cock-sure, even *before* reading one of Newman's Anglican books, that he could reply to it. Writing to the editor of the *Edinburgh,* Napier, in February, 1843, he says: "I hear much of a defence of the miracles of the third and fourth centuries by Newman. I have not yet read it. I think that I could treat that subject without giving any scandal to any rational person; and I should like it much. The times require a Middleton." There was no weak openness to conviction lurking behind those words; nor yet behind these, written eight months later, also to Napier, and also before he had read the book he was eager to smash: "Newman announces an English hagiology in numbers which is to contain the lives of such blessed saints as Thomas à Becket and Dunstan. I should not dislike to be the devil's advocate on such an occasion." In his essay on the "Comic Dramatists of the Restoration," Macaulay just alludes to the Tractarians, saying that Jeremy Collier's notions touching "the importance of vestments, ceremonies, and solemn days, differed little from those which

are now held by Dr. Pusey and Mr. Newman" — a sentence which suggests to the initiated that the writer wrote once more without having read Newman — who was never a Ritualist, and treasured no husk except it held a kernel.

After all, it was left to Sir James Stephen and to Henry Rogers to pillory Popery in the pages of the *Edinburgh*. The first of these, after confessing in a letter to Napier, in 1841, that whatever comes he "cannot but cherish the good old Protestant feelings of our ancestors," thus conveniently explains away Mr. Newman: "As for Newman himself, I am sorry that his integrity should be impugned. I am convinced that a more upright man does not exist. But his understanding is essentially illogical and inveterately imaginative; and I have reason to fear that he labours under a degree of cerebral excitement, which unfits him for the mastery of his own thoughts and the guidance of his own pen." It is worth noting, that while Newman was being thus described on hearsay as a literary lunatic, Pusey, his constant companion, was writing of him to a friend: "You will be glad to hear that the immediate excitement about Tract 90 is subsiding. It has been a harassing time for N., but he was wonderfully calm."

Macaulay, instead of reading the books he had already prejudged, probably contented himself with reading the *Edinburgh* attack on them (April, 1843), and not all of that. "I have read three or four pages of the article on the Puseyites, which I like very much. I should be glad to know who wrote it." The writer was Henry Rogers, who congratulated himself with the true Whig confidence, when he sent his MS. to the editor, that he had "not spared ridicule" in treating "publications which are having a large sale, and are doing immense mischief amongst the young, the ardent, and the sentimental." But "the young, the ardent, and the sentimental" had grown into men and reviewers by the time the "Apologia" appeared; and Newman, for the first time, found himself seriously considered, whether favourably or not, by secular publications.

Indeed, "the young, the ardent, and the sentimental" of the early forties had made themselves felt in the other walks of life, as well as in literature, before many years were over. They manned the Anglican Church. Rival Cabinet Ministers might be seen sitting under the same Tractarian shepherd in Mayfair. A Lord Chief Justice ranked it as his highest honour to be the host of Cardinal Newman, even after his secession; and there was no house in London where he was more welcome than at the Deanery of St. Paul's. Dean Church was one of that immense body of actual contemporaries or immediate juniors who came under Newman's personal influence, and who, in their turn, spread the principles which have transformed the Anglican Communion. In one sense the *Guardian* expresses the bare truth when it speaks of Newman as "the founder of the Anglican Church as it now is," and says: "Great as his services have been to the Communion in which he died, they are as nothing by the side of those he rendered to the Communion in which the most eventful years of his life were spent. He will be mourned by many in the Roman Church; but their sorrow will be less than ours, because they have not the same paramount reason to be grateful to him." Not in admiration for his mind, nor in reverence for his character, nor in personal devotion yielded him even by strangers, can those to whom he came be outstripped by those whom he left. His life was divided with a strange equality of time between the two Communions; for he lived in each for half of it almost to a month. But he actually changed the face of the Anglican Church, while he could not alter one feature of the immutable other.

Of all his contemporaries, therefore, the Anglican clergy bear most the marks of him. What their predecessors were seventy years ago, when Newman began "to come out of his shell," has ceased to be a memory, but it remains as a tradition. "Decent, easy men, who supremely enjoyed the gifts of the founder, from the toil of reading, thinking, or writing they had absolved their conscience. Their conversation stagnated in a round of college business, Tory politics, personal anecdotes, and private scandal. Their dull and deep potations excused the intemperance of youth." Such were the Oxford dons of an earlier generation, as described by Gibbon, Newman's greatest master in style, and his finger-post to the Fathers. "Whenever you meet a clergyman of my time," said Sydney Smith to Mr. Gladstone about the year 1835, "you may be sure he is a bad clergyman;" and Sydney Smith had as little love as Gibbon himself would have had for "Puseyism."

Vainly was Evangelicalism pitched against "two-bottle orthodoxy." In Wesley, Newman as a Catholic recognized "the shadow of a Catholic saint;" but the name of Wesley worked no wonders in the Oxford of Newman's early days. The Evangelicals entrenched themselves in an obscure college, and their influence never spread beyond St. Edmund's Hall. Mozley says it may have been a common peculiarity of their complexions, but the St. Edmund's men never looked clean. He adds that their mental and moral claims to influence were inconspicuous; and Archbishop Tait of Canterbury admits that there is too much truth in this ugly delineation. Newman and his friends, on the other hand, joined learning with sanctity, and united good-breeding with unworldliness. "We loved the Evangelicals because they loved our Lord," said Pusey—a formula which sums up the Catholic attitude towards the Salvation Army to-day; but that is the beginning and the end of the bond; and Newman saw, even if Keble did not, that liberalism in religion, represented by Whately and the rest, was a force Evangelicalism could not touch; that Evangelicalism was itself only another form of liberalism, though the feelings and prejudices of its adherents were on the side of personal religiousness. The men who had a general idea of the importance of dogma, but who had not the enthusiasm of religion, and the men who had the enthusiasm but no science or coherence, met together under Newman, and supplied to each other the deficiency of each. The leaders themselves—Newman, Pusey, and Keble—united tender personal piety with a zeal for dogmatic exactitude — for truth in thought as well as in conduct.

The reasons why the early leadership seemed to lie with Pusey, and not with Newman, are well known. Equally well known is it that Newman was the mainspring of the movement. "Out of my own head," he says he started the Tracts, and the Tracts became the text-books of the new Anglicanism. The doctrines they expounded, though fresh to the hearers, were old as the Apostles, and were gathered by Newman from the Bible he loved and studied; they had been taught without intermission by the Catholic Church from the first Peter to the last Leo; and the Anglican Church itself, under Archbishop Laud, fitfully received them. The result of Newman's labour as a revivalist is seen to-day in half the rectories of England. The typical Anglican minister trains, conducts, even dresses himself on the model of the Catholic priest; and if externals could make him the real thing, the real thing he would perfectly be. Beautiful were the tributes which Newman's death elicited from the conspicuous pulpits of Anglicanism, and most affecting to Catholics; but surely some of the preachers strangely misunderstood their master when they hinted that he might never have left Anglicanism in 1845 had he foreseen how many Roman collars would be worn, how many beards be shaved off, how many "celebrations" be announced, and confessions heard, in the Establishment in 1890. Why, the Arians in their day had Bishops, and Masses, and organization as perfect as that of the orthodox; but it was with Athanasius that Newman ranged himself while still an Anglican; and it was precisely the parallel he found between Anglicans and Arians or Donatists that brought him at last from Oxford to Birmingham. It was he, in truth, who said to Anglicans such as these —

Look into the matter more steadily; it is very pleasant to decorate your chapels, oratories, and studies now, but you cannot be doing this for ever. It is pleasant to adopt a habit or a vestment; to use your Office-book or your beads; but it is like feeding on flowers unless you have that objective vision in your faith, and that satisfaction in your reason, of which devotional exercises and ecclesiastical appointments are the suitable expression. They will not last in the long run, unless commanded and rewarded on Divine authority; they cannot be made to rest on the influence of individuals. It is well to have rich architecture, curious works of art, and splendid vestments, when you have a present God; but oh, what a mockery if you have not! If your externals surpass what is within, you are so far as hollow as your Evangelical opponents, who baptize, yet expect no grace. Thus your Church becomes not a home, but a sepulchre; like those high cathedrals once Catholic, which you do not know what to do with, which you shut up, and make monuments of, sacred to the memory of what has passed away."

"You are under a destiny," very solemnly said Newman also to the Anglican clergy, after he had become a Catholic; and he was attributing to them what he had always believed in a very special manner of himself. Not the third Napoleon himself had franker conviction of the distinctness of his fate. During the tour in the South of Europe, in 1833 — the tour which produced "Lead, Kindly Light" — "I began," he tells us, "to think that I had a mission." When he paused in Rome and was asked by Monsignor Wiseman to pay a second visit, he replied with great gravity, "I have a work to do in England." In Sicily, after an illness, he sat down on his bed and began to sob violently. "My servant asked what ailed me. I could only answer him, 'I have a work to do in England.'" The record, with the obvious hint, is made by himself; and he evidently believed it to be no mere coincidence that his return home, with its strange adventures of both delay and speed, timed with Keble's sermon on "National Apostasy." It was the first Sunday after his arrival; and he says, "I have ever considered this day as the start of the religious movement of 1833." When he retired to Littlemore, as a sort of half-way house between England and Rome, he turned up an old copy-book, and it took his breath away to find on it a cross drawn between the words "verse" and "book." Moreover, a further device, in which one less smitten with his destiny might have recognized a sister's chain and pendant, he could not make out to be anything but "a set of beads with a little cross." Then there came his reception into the Catholic Church, and thus the man of destiny records it: "I am this night expecting Father Dominic the Passionist, who from his youth has been led to have distinct and direct thoughts, first, of the countries of the north, and then of England. After thirty years' (almost) waiting, he was, without his own act, sent here." This is in the "Apologia;" and in "Loss and Gain," under fictitious names, the story is told in greater detail: —

On the Apennines, near Viterbo, there dwelt a shepherd boy, in the first years of this century, whose mind had early been drawn heavenward; and one day, as he prayed before an image of the Madonna, he felt a vivid intimation that he was to preach the Gospel under the northern sky. There appeared no means by which a Roman peasant should be turned into a missionary; nor did the prospect open, when this youth found himself, first, a lay brother, then a Father, in the Congregation of the Passion. Yet, though no external means appeared, the inward impression did not fade — on the contrary, it became more definite; and, in process of time, instead of the dim north, England was engraven on his heart. And, strange to say, as years went on, without his seeking, for he was simply under obedience, our peasant found himself at length upon the very shore of the stormy Northern Sea, whence Caesar of old looked out for a new world to conquer; yet that he should cross the Strait was still as little likely as before. But the day came, not, however, by any determination of his own, but by the same Providence which, thirty years before, had given him the intimation of it.

The importance which each Christian must of necessity attach to himself — he for whom the Heavens descended to the earth, who has angels for his ministers, who is an heir of Paradise, and who traces the special designs of Providence in the details of his daily life —

might seem to be alien to the humility and to the self-abnegation which Christianity enjoins. Yet he, whose Christian egoism is most sublime, he it is who, paradoxically, abases and annihilates himself most completely. "From a boy I had been led to consider that my Maker and I, His creature, were the two beings, luminously such." And the attitude remained to the end, and determined the disposition of Newman towards all people and things. "It is face to face in all matters between man and his God. He alone creates; He alone has redeemed; before His awful eyes we go in death; and in the vision of Him is our eternal beatitude."

But those who came near to the Sacred Person had reflections of His glory, and as such were held in worship by Newman — the angels and the saints. And the men about himself he frankly regarded in the light of their relations, not with the outer world, but with him and his spiritual being. The record of his Oxford contemporaries is the record of what they were to him. "John Henry Newman." He learnt, for instance, habits of thought and the idea of the Church as a corporate body from Whately; Hurrell Froude "fixed deep in me the idea of devotion to the Blessed Virgin, and led me gradually to believe in the Real Presence;" Keble familiarized him with the sacramental system; and from Dr. Hawkins he learnt the value of tradition. The bond was a close one in all cases; but it had its basis on religion. In the streets of Dublin, long after, Whately as Archbishop, and Newman as Rector of the Catholic University, met without recognition; but the story of his having absented himself, years before, from chapel on purpose to avoid receiving the Sacrament with Dr. Whately, was pure invention. "He made himself dead to me," says Newman of Whately with great simplicity; adding, "My reason told me it was impossible we could have got on together longer had he stayed in Oxford; yet I loved him too much to bid him farewell without pain." When Kingsley said, "Truth for its own sake had never been a virtue with the Roman clergy," and this in a mere magazine with the poor life of a month in it, no one would have bothered his head over it—the charge was too hackneyed to need a new rebuff from Catholics. But "Father Newman" was linked with the passage, fortunately, as he himself afterwards thought. He accuses "me, John Henry Newman," exclaimed the hermit at Birmingham, whose destiny the Heavens had made known to him.

So the "Apologia" was written. Later on, the passages which seemed to have personal resentment were suppressed by the author; who, moreover, gave the Rev. Sir William Cope a most interesting explanation of his adoption of the world's own weapons—hard words—in the unequal duel: the world would not believe him if he spoke calmly. His after-thoughts were that Kingsley should escape resentment because he had become accidentally "the instrument in the good Providence of God, by whom I had an opportunity given me, which otherwise I should not have had, of vindicating my character and conduct in my 'Apologia.'" Not, as he might well have said, "vindicating the Catholic doctrine as to truth, and the sin of lying;" but vindicating, what with Newman was a synonym, "my character and conduct." And Newman adds, in the same letter, that a friend had chanced to hear Kingsley "preaching about me kindly;" and about Athanasius, too, he had been writing less unkindly; so "I said Mass for his soul as soon as I heard of his death."

The old friends he lost and the new friends he made when he became a Catholic were they whom "God gave me when He took every one else away." "And in you, Ambrose St. John," that chief new friend, he says, "I gather up and bear in memory those familiar and affectionate companions and counsellors who in Oxford were given to me to be my daily solace and relief; and all those others, of great name and high example, who were my thorough friends; and also those many younger men, whether I knew them or not, who have never been disloyal to me by word or deed." To Pius IX he paid his homage in a sermon at Birmingham, in which he recalls "his great act towards us here, towards me." "One of his first acts after he was Pope was, in his great condescension, to call me to Rome; then, when I got there, he bade me send for my friends to be with me; and he formed us into an Oratory. . . . Such is the Pope now happily reigning in the Chair of St. Peter; such are our personal obligations to him; such has he been towards us, towards you, my brethren."

It was precisely this pervading personality in Newman that distinguished him from his contemporaries.

COVENTRY PATMORE
(1823-1896)

DESPITE the comparatively insignificant number of his works, Coventry Kearsey Deighton Patmore is considered one of the major poets of the nineteenth century by many critics. Born at Woodford, Essex, in 1823, his early education was of a private nature under the direction of his father, who was a writer of considerable prominence and ability. Specialization in science led him into university life, but he soon abandoned science in favor of a natural tendency toward literature. The death of his father with attendant financial reverses caused a temporary halt in his literary efforts. In 1847 he accepted the position of assistant librarian in the British Museum but was forced to resign because of poor health.

At an early age Patmore married the daughter of a nonconformist clergyman, Emily Augusta Andrews, who was the inspiration of his best loved work, *The Angel in the House*. His next important work, *The Unknown Eros*, was never entirely understood in his own time nor, except among poets, has it achieved wider popularity since his death.

Shortly before the beginning of *The Unknown Eros,* Patmore joined the Catholic Church. He was happily married again to an heiress, and he settled in Sussex with his wife. At her death he moved to Hastings, where in his last years he published *The Rod, the Root and the Flower,* a prose work much in the style of Pascal's *Pensées.* Patmore died in 1896.

In the poems of Patmore, and his prose as well, there is clear evidence that he grew with the years. In *The Angel in the House,* 1854–1862, Patmore captured the Victorian fancy with his somewhat too slippered description of love and married life. With his second marriage and the publication of *The Unknown Eros and Other Odes,* 1877, Patmore adopted an exquisite new conception of the ode form.

Scarcely more amazing than his change in technique was his revelation of a deepened attitude toward both life and love, based on a hurried study of mystical theology. The half-thought-out ecstasies of *The Unknown Eros* became certainties in *The Rod, the Root and the Flower,* 1895, which clearly links human love to the divine and broadens and deepens the concept of love until it has Christian and permanent significance.

Patmore's ideas of prosody had considerable influence in his time; his subtle rhythms were used by Francis Thompson in some of his best work, as even a casual comparison of their poems will demonstrate.

The Memories and Correspondence of Patmore were edited by Basil Champneys and published in 1900.

THE TOYS*

My little Son, who look'd from thoughtful
    eyes
And moved and spoke in quiet grown-
    up wise,
Having my law the seventh time disobey'd,
I struck him, and dismiss'd
With hard word and unkiss'd,
His mother, who was patient, being dead.
Then, fearing lest his grief should hinder
    sleep,
I visited his bed,
But found him slumbering deep,
With darken'd eyelids, and their lashes yet
From his late sobbing wet.
And I, with moan,
Kissing away his tears, left others of my own;
For, on a table drawn beside his head,

He had put, within his reach,
A box of counters and a red-vein'd stone,
A piece of glass abraded by the beach
And six or seven shells,
A bottle with bluebells
And two French copper coins, ranged there
    with careful art,
To comfort his sad heart.
So when that night I pray'd
To God, I wept, and said:
Ah, when at last we lie with tranced breath,
Not vexing Thee in death,
And Thou rememberest of what toys
We made our joys,
How weakly understood,
Thy great commanded good,
Then, fatherly not less
Than I whom Thou hast moulded from
    the clay,
Thou'lt leave Thy wrath, and say,
"I will be sorry for their childishness."

*The above and following poems have been selected from *Poems of Coventry Patmore* (London: G. Bell and Sons, 1915).

A FAREWELL*

With all my will, but much against my heart,
We two now part.
My Very Dear,
Our solace is, the sad road lies so clear.
It needs no art,
With faint, averted feet
And many a tear,
In our opposed paths to persevere.
Go thou to East, I West.
We will not say
There's any hope, it is so far away.
But, O, my Best,

*The Unknown Eros, Book I — XVI.

When the one darling of our widowhead,
The nursling Grief,
Is dead,
And no dews blur our eyes
To see the peach-bloom come in evening
    skies,
Perchance we may,
Where now this night is day,
And even through faith of still averted feet,
Making full circle of our banishment,
Amazed meet;
The bitter journey to the bourne so sweet
Seasoning the termless feast of our content
With tears of recognition never dry.

THE PARAGON*

When I behold the skies aloft
  Passing the pageantry of dreams.
The cloud whose bosom, cygnet-soft,
  A couch for nuptial Juno seems,
The ocean broad, the mountain bright,
  The shadowy vales with feeding herds,
I from my lyre the music smite,
  Nor want for justly matching words.
All forces of the sea and air,
  All interests of hill and plain,
I so can sing, in seasons fair,
  That who hath felt may feel again.
Elated oft by such free songs,
  I think with utterance free to raise
That hymn for which the whole world longs,
  A worthy hymn in woman's praise;
A hymn bright-noted like a bird's,
  Arousing these song-sleepy times
With rhapsodies of perfect words,
  Ruled by returning kiss of rhymes.
But when I look on her and hope
  To tell with joy what I admire,
My thoughts lie cramp'd in narrow scope,
  Or in the feeble birth expire;
No mystery of well-woven speech,
  No simplest phrase of tenderest fall,
No liken'd excellence can reach

*The Angel in the House, Canto II, Mary and
Mildred, Preludes.

Her, the most excellent of all,
The best half of creation's best,
  Its heart to feel, its eye to see,
The crown and complex of the rest,
  Its aim and its epitome.
Nay, might I utter my conceit,
  'Twere after all a vulgar song,
For she's so simply, subtly sweet,
  My deepest rapture does her wrong.
Yet is it now my chosen task
  To sing her worth as Maid and Wife;
Nor happier post than this I ask,
  To live her laureate all my life.
On wings of love uplifted free,
  And by her gentleness made great,
I'll teach how noble man should be
  To match with such a lovely mate;
And then in her may move the more
  The woman's wish to be desired,
(By praise increased), till both shall soar,
  With blissful emulations fired.
And, as geranium, pink, or rose
  Is thrice itself through power of art,
So may my happy skill disclose
  New fairness even in her fair heart;
Until that churl shall nowhere be
  Who bends not, awed, before the throne
Of her affecting majesty,
  So meek, so far unlike our own;

Until (for who may hope too much
  From her who wields the powers of love?)
Our lifted lives at last shall touch
  That happy goal to which they move;

Until we find, as darkness rolls
  Away, and evil mists dissolve,
The nuptial contrasts are the poles
  On which the heavenly spheres revolve.

LOVE AT LARGE

Whene'er I come where ladies are,
  How sad soever I was before,
Though like a ship frost-bound and far
  Withheld in ice from the ocean's roar,
Third-winter'd in that dreadful dock,
  With stiffen'd cordage, sails decay'd,
And crew that care for calm and shock
  Alike, too dull to be dismay'd,
Yet, if I come where ladies are,
  How sad soever I was before,

Then is my sadness banish'd far,
  And I am like that ship no more;
Or like that ship if the ice-field splits,
  Burst by the sudden polar Spring,
And all thank God with their warming wits,
  And kiss each other and dance and sing,
And hoist fresh sails, that make the breeze
  Blow them along the liquid sea,
Out of the North, where life did freeze,
  Into the haven where they would be.

THE LOVER*

He meets, by heavenly chance express,
  The destined maid; some hidden hand
Unveils to him that loveliness
  Which others cannot understand.
His merits in her presence grow,
  To match the promise in her eyes,
And round her happy footsteps blow
  The authentic airs of Paradise.
For joy of her he cannot sleep;
  Her beauty haunts him all the night;
It melts his heart, it makes him weep
  For wonder, worship, and delight.
O, paradox of love, he longs,
  Most humble when he most aspires,
To suffer scorn and cruel wrongs
  From her he honours and desires.
Her graces make him rich, and ask
  No guerdon; this imperial style

Affronts him; he disdains to bask,
  The pensioner of her priceless smile.
He prays for some hard thing to do,
  Some work of fame and labour immense,
To stretch the languid bulk and thew
  Of love's fresh-born magnipotence.
No smallest boon were bought too dear,
  Though barter'd for his love-sick life;
Yet trusts he, with undaunted cheer,
  To vanquish heaven, and call her Wife.
He notes how queens of sweetness still
  Neglect their crowns, and stoop to mate;
How, self-consign'd with lavish will,
  They ask but love proportionate;
How swift pursuit by small degrees,
  Love's tactic, works like miracle;
How valour, clothed in courtesies,
  Brings down the haughtiest citadel;
And therefore, though he merits not
  To kiss the braid upon her skirt,
His hope, discouraged ne'er a jot,
  Out-soars all possible desert.

*The above and following poems have been selected from *The Angel in the House*, Canto III, Honoria, Preludes.

LOVE A VIRTUE

Strong passions mean weak will, and he
    Who truly knows the strength and bliss
Which are in love, will own with me
    No passion but a virtue 'tis.
Few hear my word; it soars above
    The subtlest senses of the swarm
Of wretched things which know not love,
    Their Psyche still a wingless worm.

Ice-cold seems heaven's noble glow
    To spirits whose vital heat is hell;
And to corrupt hearts even so
    The songs I sing, the tale I tell.
These cannot see the robes of white
    In which I sing of love. Alack,
But darkness shows in heavenly light,
    Though whiteness, in the dark, is black!

UNTHRIFT

Ah, wasteful woman, she who may
    On her sweet self set her own price,
Knowing man cannot choose but pay,
    How has she cheapen'd paradise;

How given for nought her priceless gift,
    How spoil'd the bread and spill'd the wine,
Which, spent with due, respective thrift,
    Had made brutes men, and men divine.

THE ATTAINMENT

You love? That's high as you shall go;
    For 'tis as true as Gospel text,

Not noble then is never so,
    Either in this world or the next.

SAINT VALENTINE'S DAY*

Well dost thou, Love, thy solemn Feast
    to hold
In vestal February;
Not rather choosing out some rosy day
From the rich coronet of the coming May,
When all things meet to marry!
    O, quick, praevernal Power
That signall'st punctual through the sleepy
    mould
The Snowdrop's time to flower,
Fair as the rash oath of virginity
Which is first-love's first cry;
O, Baby Spring,
That flutter'st sudden 'neath the breast of
    Earth
A month before the birth;

Whence is the peaceful poignancy,
The joy contrite,
Sadder than sorrow, sweeter than delight,
That burthens now the breath of everything,
Though each one sighs as if to each alone
The Cherish'd pang were known?
At dusk of dawn, on his dark spray apart,
With it the Blackbird breaks the young Day's
    heart;
In evening's hush
About it talks the heavenly-minded Thrush;
The hill with like remorse
Smiles to the Sun's smile in his westering
    course;
The fisher's drooping skiff
In yonder sheltering bay;
The choughs that call about the shining cliff:
The children, noisy in the setting ray;

*The above and following poems are selected from
The Unknown Eros, Bk. I, pp. 281–285.

Own the sweet season, each thing as it may;
Thoughts of strange kindness and forgotten
    peace
In me increase;
And tears arise
Within my happy, happy Mistress' eyes,
And, lo, her lips, averted from my kiss,
Ask from Love's bounty, ah, much more than
    bliss!
  Is't the sequester'd and exceeding sweet
Of dear Desire electing his defeat?
Is't the waked Earth now to yon purpling
    cope
Uttering first-love's first cry,
Vainly renouncing, with a Seraph's sigh,
Love's natural hope?
Fair-meaning Earth, foredoom'd to perjury!
Behold, all amorous May,
With roses heap'd upon her laughing brows,
Avoids thee of thy vows!
Were it for thee, with her warm bosom near,
To abide the sharpness of the Seraph's-
    sphere?
Forget thy foolish words;
Go to her summons gay,
Thy heart with dead, wing'd Innocencies
    fill'd,
Ev'n as a nest with birds
After the old ones by the hawk are kill'd.
  Well dost thou, Love, to celebrate
The noon of thy soft ecstasy,
Or e'er it be too late,

Or e'er the Snowdrop die!
  Know, Dear, these are not mine
But Wisdom's words, confirmed by divine
Doctors and Saints, though fitly seldom heard
Save in their own prepense-occulted word,
Lest fools be fool'd the further by false hope,
And wrest sweet knowledge to their own
    decline;
And (to approve I speak within my scope)
The Mistress of that dateless exile gray
Is named in surpliced Schools *Tristitia*.
  But, O, my Darling, look in thy heart
    and see
How unto me,
Secured of my prime care, thy happy state,
In the most unclean cell
Of sordid Hell,
And worried by the most ingenious hate,
It never could be anything but well,
Nor from my soul, full of thy sanctity,
Such pleasure die
As the poor harlot's, in whose body stirs
The innocent life that is and is not hers:
Unless, alas, this fount of my relief
By thy unheavenly grief
Were closed.
So, with a consecrating kiss
And hearts made one in past all previous
    peace,
And on one hope reposed,
Promise me this!

TRISTITIA

  Darling, with hearts conjoin'd in such a
    peace
That Hope, so not to cease,
Must still gaze back,
And count, along our love's most happy track,
The landmarks of like inconceiv'd increase,
Promise me this:
If thou alone should'st win
God's perfect bliss,
And I, beguiled by gracious-seeming sin,
Say, loving too much thee,
Love's last goal miss,
And any vows may then have memory,

Never, by grief for what I bear or lack,
To mar thy joyance of heav'n's jubilee.
Promise me this;
For else I should be hurl'd,
Beyond just doom
And by the deed, to Death's interior gloom,
From the mild borders of the banish'd world
Wherein they dwell
Who builded not unalterable fate
On pride, fraud, envy, cruel lust, or hate;
Yet loved too laxly sweetness and heart's ease,
And strove the creature more than God to
    please.

For such as these
Loss without measure, sadness without end!
Yet not for this do thou disheaven'd be
With thinking upon me.
Though black, when scann'd from heaven's
    surpassing bright,
This might mean light,
Foil'd with the dim days of mortality.
For God is everywhere.
Go down to deepest Hell, and He is there,
And, as a true but quite estranged Friend,
He works, 'gainst gnashing teeth of devil-
    ish ire,
With love deep hidden lest it be blasphemed,
If possible, to blend
Ease with the pangs of its inveterate fire;
Yea, in the worst
And from His Face most wilfully accurst

Of souls in vain redeem'd,
He does with potions of oblivion kill
Remorse of the lost Love that helps them still.
    Apart from these,
Near the sky-borders of that banish'd world,
Wander pale spirits among willow'd leas,
Lost beyond measure, sadden'd without end,
But since, while erring most, retaining yet
Some ineffectual fervour of regret,
Retaining still such weal
As spurned Lovers feel,
Preferring far to all the world's delight
Their loss so infinite,
Or poets, when they mark
In the clouds dun
A loitering flush of the long sunken sun,
And turn away with tears into the dark.

DEPARTURE

It was not like your great and gracious ways!
Do you, that have nought other to lament,
Never, my Love, repent
Of how, that July afternoon,
You went,
With sudden, unintelligible phrase,
And frighten'd eye,
Upon your journey of so many days,
Without a single kiss, or a good-bye?
I knew, indeed, that you were parting soon;
And so we sate, within the low sun's rays,
You whispering to me, for your voice
    was weak,
Your harrowing praise.
Well, it was well,
To hear you such thing speak,
And I could tell
What made your eyes a growing gloom
    of love,

As a warm South-wind sombres a March
    grove.
And it was like your great and gracious ways
To turn your talk on daily things, my Dear,
Lifting the luminous, pathetic lash
To let the laughter flash,
Whilst I drew near,
Because you spoke so low that I could
    scarcely hear.
But all at once to leave me at the last,
More at the wonder than the loss aghast,
With huddled, unintelligible phrase,
And frighten'd eye,
And go your journey of all days
With not one kiss, or a good-bye,
And the only loveless look the look with
    which you pass'd:
'Twas all unlike your great and gracious
    ways.

DELICIAE SAPIENTIAE DE AMORE*

Love, light for me
Thy ruddiest blazing torch,
That I, albeit a begger by the Porch
Of the glad Palace of Virginity,
May gaze within, and sing the pomp I see;
For, crown'd with roses all,
'Tis there, O Love, they keep thy festival!
But first warn off the beatific spot
Those wretched who have not
Even afar beheld the shining wall
And those who, once beholding, have forgot,
And those, most vile, who dress
The charnel spectre drear
Of utterly dishallow'd nothingness
In that refulgent fame,
And cry, Lo, here!
And name
The Lady whose smiles inflame
The sphere.
Bring, Love, anear,
And bid be not afraid
Young Lover true, and love-foreboding Maid,
And wedded Spouse, if virginal of thought;
For I will sing of nought
Less sweet to hear
Than seems
A music in their half-remember'd dreams.
   The magnet calls the steel:
Answers the iron to the magnet's breath;
What do they feel
But death!
The clouds of summer kiss in flame and rain,
And are not found again;
But the heavens themselves eternal are with
   fire
Of unapproach'd desire,
By the aching heart of Love, which cannot
   rest,
In blissfullest pathos so indeed possess'd.
O, spousals high;
O, doctrine blest,
Unutterable in even the happiest sigh;
This know ye all
Who can recall
With what a welling of indignant tears
Love's simpleness first hears

The meaning of his mortal covenant,
And from what pride comes down
To wear the crown
Of which 'twas very heaven to feel the want.
How envies he the ways
Of yonder hopeless star,
And so would laugh and yearn
With trembling lids eterne,
Ineffably content from infinitely far
Only to gaze
On his bright Mistress's responding rays,
That never know eclipse;
And, once in his long year,
With praeternuptial ecstasy and fear,
By the delicious law of that ellipse
Wherein all citizens of ether move,
With hastening pace to come
Nearer, though never near,
His Love
And always inaccessible sweet Home;
There on his path doubly to burn
Kiss'd by her doubled light
That whispers of its source,
The ardent secret ever clothed with Night,
Then go forth in new force
Towards a new return,
Rejoicing as a Bridegroom on his course!
This know ye all;
Therefore gaze bold,
That so in you be joyful hope increas'd.
Through the Palace portals, and behold
The dainty and unsating Marriage-Feast.
O, hear
Them singing clear
'Cor meum et caro mea' round the 'I am,'
The Husband of the Heavens, and the Lamb
Whom they for ever follow there that kept,
Or losing, never slept
Till they reconquer'd had in mortal fight
The standard white.
O, hear
From the harps they bore from Earth, five-
   strung, what music springs,
While the glad Spirits chide
The wondering strings!
And how the shining sacrificial Choirs,
Offering for aye their dearest hearts' desires,
Which to their hearts come back beatified,

*The Unknown Eros, Bk. II, pp. 330–334.

Hymn, the bright aisles along,
The nuptial song,
Song ever new to us and them, that saith,
'Hail Virgin in Virginity a Spouse!'
Heard first below
Within the little house
At Nazareth;
Heard yet in many a cell where brides of
    Christ
Lie hid, emparadised,
And where, although
By the hour 'tis night,
There's light,
The Day still lingering in the lap of snow.
Gaze and be not afraid
Ye wedded few that honour, in sweet thought
And glittering will,
So freshly from the garden gather still
The lily sacrificed;
For ye, though self-suspected here for nought,
Are highly styled
With the thousands twelve times twelve of
    undefiled.
Gaze and be not afraid
Young Lover true and love-foreboding Maid.
The full noon of deific vision bright
Abashes nor abates
No spark minute of Nature's keen delight.
'Tis there your Hymen waits!

There where in courts afar, all unconfused,
    they crowd,
As fumes the starlight soft
In gulfs of cloud,
And each to the other, well-content,
Sighs oft,
' 'Twas this we meant!'
Gaze without blame
Ye in whom living Love yet blushes for
    dead shame.
There of pure Virgin none
Is fairer seen,
Save One,
Than Mary Magdalene.
Gaze without doubt or fear
Ye to whom generous Love, by any name,
    is dear
Love makes the life to be
A fount perpetual of virginity;
For, lo, the Elect
Of generous Love, how named soe'er, affect
Nothing but God,
Or mediate or direct,
Nothing but God,
The Husband of the Heavens:
And who Him love, in potence great or small,
Are, one and all,
Heirs of the Palace glad,
And inly clad
With the bridal robes of ardour virginal.

MAGNA MORALIA*

VI

IF A man's ways and works are good and great, it is because the man himself is better and greater, and because he cannot help the light of his unique personality showing in them. The greatest skill in composition, the most perfect finish of manners will never equal in value the least touch of that true style or distinction which consists in the manifestation of such a personality. On the other hand, the traits by which individuality is expressed are ordinarily so delicate and intangible that, though it may exist in a high degree in the man himself, its light cannot appear in his works or ways, unless these are purged from all coarseness and eccentricity.

VII

The greatest of contemplatives can only "see in part and know in part," and he is like a child who is learning to distinguish upon an instrument the first notes, which combined, shall make the harmonies of heaven. These notes, indeed, are in themselves

    Sweet as stops
Of planetary music heard in trance,

and are far more than enough to satisfy

*Patmore, Coventry, *The Rod, the Root and the Flower* (London: G. Bell and Sons, 1914), p. 151.

his present capacity for felicity. He does not attempt to combine them; for, if he does, he finds that he is like a child educing confusion by striking his ignorant palm, here and there, upon the scale, instead of touching, with careful finger; its separate tones; for some tones, though all are celestial, jar when joined without intervention of others, and suggest passing doubts and confusions of spirit as to their being really heavenly.

VIII

When God has arduously wrought the six degrees of the Soul's new creation, and she is pronounced *"very* good," He rests from his labour, and bids her also to rest in the Sabbath of contemplation of His love and of His beauty, as mirrored in herself. She "wakes up after His likeness and is satisfied with it"; and greater wonders are wrought in her in one minute of mutual felicity than would be worked by a day of martyrdom, or a year of heroic action.

IX

He who renounces goods, house, wife, etc., for God's sake shall receive a hundredfold in this life, with life everlasting. But he who, having obtained this hundredfold return of all his natural delights transfigured, renounces this also, and acknowledges no consolation but his share in the agony of the Cross, shall shine for ever in heaven as a sun among the stars. Yet even he cannot escape his temporal reward, but hyssop itself, in touching his lips, becomes honey.

Thus irresistibly by Gods embraced
Is she who boasts her more than mortal chaste.

X

"What *reward* shall I give unto the Lord for all He has done to me? I will take the cup of salvation and call upon His Name." A lover does not want presents and services from his Beloved, but only that she should accept *His* presents and services.

XI

In proportion as our obedience, — having been made perfect in obvious things, — be-

comes minute and delicate, it becomes more meritorious and greatly rewarded. The difference between a commonly well-behaved woman and a high-bred lady consists in very small things — but what a difference it is!

XII

When the Tempter can no longer persuade us to our destruction by representing unclean things as clean, he perpetually harasses us, and endeavours to delay our progress by representing clean things as unclean. In the first stage of our advance we are purified by self-denial, in the second by denial, almost equally laborious, of the enemy's false charges.

XIII

Perception is hindered by nothing so much as by impatience and anxiety to attain it, and by trying to recall and dwell upon it when attained. "If the Lord tarry wait for Him," and then "He will not tarry, but will come quickly." To them that wait in quietness, attention, and silence of their own thought, all things reveal themselves, but

None e'er hears twice the same who hears the Songs of Heaven's unanimous spheres,

and, if you would receive new perception, you must, as St. John of the Cross says, "Go forth into regions where nothing is perceived," and seek always, with David, to sing "a *new* song." These perceptions are "treasures laid up in heaven." We need not be anxious about them. "The *heart* will not forget the things the eyes have seen." There was a truly divine epicureanism hidden in the reply of the Greek philosopher to some one who wondered how it was that he seemed to despise the delight of love: "I have tasted that sweetness once." He that would be worthy of the Beatific Vision must fix his thoughts, not on the beatitude, but on the Vision. "The Vision," writes St. Thomas Aquinas, "is a virtue, the beatitude an accident," and the Psalmist says: "So let me behold Thy Presence in *righteousness* that I may wake up after Thy likeness and be satisfied with it."

FRANCIS THOMPSON
(1859–1907)

IT IS doubtful if universal literature has yet come to a full appreciation of the poetic genius that was Francis Thompson. Overshadowing the scant satisfaction that he derived from life is the literary legacy that was left the world upon his death in 1907. He was born at Preston, Lancastershire, England, in 1859, the son of a provincial doctor. A part of his education was received at Ushaw College where the first evidence of his love of creative literature made itself known. There followed his vain attempt to fulfill his vocation for the priesthood. His incurable indolence, physical weakness, and incredible impracticality forced his spiritual adviser to counsel him to abandon the idea of becoming a priest.

Following the wishes of his father, he went to Manchester University to study medicine. Failing at this, he became for a time assistant to a maker of surgical instruments. This was revolting to his nature and, without advising his father, he became a homeless wanderer on the streets of London. After brief employment as book agent and shoemaker's assistant, he became little more than a tramp. Often famished and cold, receiving occasional alms, earning a few pence selling matches or calling cabs, haunting the libraries until driven away because of his unkempt appearance, a helpless victim of consumption and the opium habit, finding his only woman friend in a nameless girl of the streets — such were the three years that Thompson spent in London.

However, he did manage to write a little during this time and some of his poems eventually came into the hands of Wilfrid Meynell, Catholic publisher and editor of *Merrie England*. After some difficulty, Meynell found Thompson and brought him to his own home as friend and guest. Recognized as the discoverer of Thompson, Meynell said, "Let none be named the benefactor of him who gave more to all than any could give him."

Thompson became an intimate of the Meynell circle. Though he never entirely gave up the opium habit, except for intermittent periods, he conquered it sufficiently to apply himself to the writing of great poetry. His shyness and quick sensibility often made his life miserable. He died, 1907, of tuberculosis.

Due to the mounting chorus in praise of Hopkins, and the fashionable instability of much of Catholic criticism, Thompson no longer receives the attention which should be given him. In his great odes Thompson, following the Liturgy, used the signs in nature correctly, as manifestations of the sacramental character of the universe. In a series of daringly flamboyant figures he piles magnificent picture upon picture until the world of beauty stands out clearly as the house of God.

Some critics have censured his tendency toward florid magnificence, but they do it without taking into account Thompson's purpose, which contrary to the vague surface worship of nature indulged to the full by the Romantic poets, was a successful attempt to look behind the glowing façade of nature into the very purpose of the forms of creation. If the outer forms were baroque and florid, God's world, as he made it, stood revealed in a thousand dazzling pictures which were but the façade of revealed glory. Christ walks the murky waters of the Thames, His face looks out, as well, through the frozen bread of the snowflakes, and the fountains of His beauty pour in cascades from the rainbows on the Sussex downs. Eye had not seen, but tongue might declare a purpose and discern a pattern.

Sister Songs, Thompson's first book of poems, was dedicated to the Meynell family. It is a graceful and facile collection of poems, sometimes marred by a confusion of Victorian and Renaissance attitudes toward the Meynell girls and their mother Alice.

Of Thompson's later work his "Hound of

Heaven" is perhaps his most beautifully integrated poem. Because of its universal appeal, it has, unfortunately overshadowed his great odes "To the Setting Sun," "Orient Ode," and the superb but revealing economy of his ode "To the Dead Cardinal of Westminster," written upon the death of Cardinal Manning. Of equal rank with these are the "New Year Chimes," a rhythmical commentary on the eternity of God, and the "Mistress of Vision," a dream treatise on divine wisdom. In "Assumpta Maria" Thompson reached the zenith of his power to combine the natural and the supernatural.

His poems are most easily studied in the excellent edition edited by Terence Connolly, S.J. This edition has adequate textual notes except for "New Year's Chimes" and the "Mistress of Vision."

Thompson's prose is still admired by many critics. Of his critical essays the one on Shelley is perhaps the most complete and artistically balanced. Thompson's love of Shelley fails to dim his critical faculties and though his praise of Shelley's excellences verges on baroque writing, the essay is a critical masterpiece, for "love begets knowledge where the hard mind fails."

His excellent and definitive biography, by Everard Meynell, was published in 1916.

ASSUMPTA MARIA*

"Thou needst not make new songs, but say
the old."   —*Cowley*
'Mortals, that behold a Woman
    Rising 'twixt the Moon and Sun;
    Who am I the heavens assume? an
All am I, and I am one.

'Multitudinous ascend I,
    Dreadful as a battle arrayed,
For I bear you whither tend I;
    Ye are I: be undismayed!
I, the Ark that for the graven
    Tables of the Law was made;
Man's own heart was one; one, Heaven;
    Both within my womb were laid.
        For there Anteros with Eros,
            Heaven with man, conjoined was,—
        Twin-stone of the Law, *Ischyros,*
            Agios Athanatos!

'I, the flesh-girt Paradises
    Gardenered by the Adam new,
Daintied o'er with dear devices
    Which He loved, for He grew.
I, the boundless strict Savannah
    Which God's leaping feet go through;

I, the Heaven whence the Manna,
    Weary Israel, slid on you!
        He the Anteros and Eros,
            I the body, He the Cross;
        He upbeareth me, *Ischyros,*
            Agios Athanatos!

'I am Daniel's mystic Mountain,
    Whence the mighty stone was rolled;
I am the four Rivers' Fountain,
    Watering Paradise of old;
Cloud down-raining the Just One am,
    Danae of the Shower of Gold;
I the Hostel of the Sun am;
    He the Lamb, and I the Fold.
        He the Anteros and Eros,
            I the body, He the Cross;
        He is fast to me, *Ischyros,*
            Agios Athanatos!

'I, the Presence-hall where Angels
    Do enwheel their placèd King—
Even my thoughts which, without change
    else,
    Cyclic burn and cyclic sing.
To the hollow of Heaven transplanted,
    I a breathing Eden spring,
Where with venom all outpanted
    Lies the slimed Curse shrivelling.

---

*The above and following poems have been selected from *Complete Poetical Works of Francis Thompson* (New York: The Modern Library, 1913).

For the brazen Serpent clear on
   That old fangèd knowledge shone;
I to wisdom rise, *Ischyron,*
   Agion Athanaton!

'Then commanded and spake to me
   He who framed all things that be;
And my Maker entered through me,
   In my tent His rest took He.
Lo! He standeth, Spouse and Brother,
   I to Him, and He to me,
Who upraised me where my mother
   Fell, beneath the apple-tree.
     Risen 'twixt Anteros and Eros,
      Blood and Water, Moon and Sun,
     He upbears me, He *Ischyros,*
      I bear Him, the *Athanaton!'*

Where is laid the Lord arisen?
   In the light we walk in gloom;
Though the Sun has burst his prison,
   We know not his biding-room,
Tell us where the Lord sojourneth,
   For we find an empty tomb.
Whence He sprung, there He returneth,
   Mystic Sun,—the Virgin's Womb.
     Hidden Sun, His beams so near us,
      Cloud-empillared as He was
     From of old, there He, *Ischyros,*
      Waits our search, *Athanatos.*

Who is She, in candid vesture,
   Rushing up from out the brine?
Treading with resilient gesture
   Air, and with that Cup divine?
She in us and we in her are,
   Beating Godward: all that pine,
Lo, a wonder and a terror—
   The Sun hath blushed the Sea to Wine!
     He the Anteros and Eros,
      She the Bride and Spirit; for
     Now the days of promise near us,
      And the Sea shall be no more.

Open wide thy gates, O Virgin,
   That the King may enter thee!
At all gates the clangours gurge in,
   God's paludament lightens, see!
Camp of Angels! Well we even
   Of this thing may doubtful be,—
If thou art assumed to Heaven,
   Or is Heaven assumed to thee!
     Consummatum. Christ the promised,
      Thy maiden realm, is won, O Strong!
     Since to such sweet Kingdom comest,
      Remember me, poor Thief of Song!

Cadent fails the stars along:—
   Mortals, that behold a woman
   Rising 'twixt the Moon and Sun;
   Who am I the heavens assume? an
   All am I, and I am one.

TO THE DEAD CARDINAL OF WESTMINSTER

(Henry Edward Manning:

Died January, 1892)

I will not perturbate
Thy Paradisal State
    With praise
    Of thy dead days;

To the new-heavened say,
'Spirit, thou wert fine clay';
    This do,
    Thy praise who knew.

Therefore my spirit clings
Heaven's porter by the wings,
    And holds
    Its gated golds

Apart, with thee to press
A private business;—
    Whence,
    Deign me audience.

Anchorite, who didst dwell
With all the world for cell,
    My soul
    Round me doth roll.

A sequestration bare.
Too far alike we were,
Too far
Dissimilar.

For its burning fruitage I
Do climb the tree o' the sky;
Do prize
Some human eyes.

You smelt the Heaven-blossoms,
And all the sweet embosoms
The dear
Uranian year.

Those Eyes my weak gaze shuns,
Which to the suns are Suns.
Did
Not affray your lid.

The carpet was let down
(With golden moultings strown)
For you
Of the angels' blue.

But I, ex-Paradised,
The shoulder of your Christ
Find high
To lean thereby.

So flaps my helpless sail,
Bellying with neither gale,
Of Heaven
Nor Orcus even.

Life is a coquetry
Of Death, which wearies me,
Too sure
Of the amour;

A tiring-room where I
Death's divers garments try,
Till fit
Some fashion sit.

It seemeth me too much
I do rehearse for such
A mean
And single scene.

The sandy glass hence bear —
Antique remembrancer:
My veins
Do spare its pains.

With secret sympathy
My thoughts repeat in me
Infirm
The turn o' the worm

Beneath my appointed sod;
The grave is in my blood;
I shake
To winds that take

Its grasses by the top;
The rains thereon that drop
Perturb
With drip acerb

My subtly answering soul;
The feet across its knoll
Do jar
Me from afar.

As sap foretastes the spring;
As Earth ere blossoming
Thrills
With far daffodils,

And feels her breast turn sweet
With the unconceivèd wheat;
So doth
My flesh foreloathe

The abhorrèd spring of Dis,
With seething presciences
Affirm
The preparate worm.

I have no thought that I,
When at the last I die,
Shall reach
To gain your speech.

But you, should that be so,
May very well, I know,
May well
To me in hell

With recognizing eyes
Look from your Paradise —
    'God bless
    Thy hopelessness!'

Call, holy soul, O call
The hosts angelical,
    And say, —
    'See, far away

'Lies one I saw on earth;
One stricken from his birth
    With curse
    Of destinate verse.

'What place doth He ye serve
For such sad spirit reserve, —
    Given,
    In dark lieu of Heaven,

'The impitiable Daemon,
Beauty, to adorn and dream on,
    To be
    Perpetually

'Hers, but she never his?
He reapeth miseries;
    Foreknows
    His wages woes;

'He lives detachèd days;
He serveth not for praise;
    For gold
    He is not sold;

'Deaf is he to world's tongue;
He scorneth for his song
    The loud
    Shouts of the crowd;

'He asketh not world's eyes;
Not to world's ears he cries;
    Saith, — "These
    Shut, if ye please!"

'He measureth world's pleasure,
World's ease, as Saints might measure;

For hire
Just love entire.

'He asks, not grudging pain;
And knows his asking vain,
    And cries —
    "Love! Love!" and dies,

'In guerdon of long duty,
Unowned by Love or Beauty;
    And goes —
    Tell, tell, who knows!

'Aliens from Heaven's worth,
Fine beasts who nose i' the earth,
    Do there
    Reward prepare.

'But are *his* great desires
Food but for nether fires?
    Ah me,
    A mystery!

'Can it be his alone,
To find when all is known
    That what
    He solely sought

'Is lost, and thereto lost
All that its seeking cost?
    That he
    Must finally,

'Through sacrificial tears,
And anchoretic years,
    Tryst
    With the sensualist?'

So ask; and if they tell
The secret terrible,
    Good friend,
    I pray thee send

Some high gold embassage
To teach my unripe age.
    Tell!
    Lest my feet walk hell.

LILIUM REGIS

O Lily of the King! low lies thy silver wing,
   And long has been the hour of thine
      unqueening;
And thy scent of Paradise on the night-wind
      spills its sighs,
   Nor any take the secrets of its meaning.
O Lily of the King! I speak a heavy thing,
   O patience, most sorrowful of daughters!
Lo, the hour is at hand for the troubling of
      the land,
   And red shall be the breaking of the
      waters.

Sit fast upon thy stalk, when the blast shall
      with thee talk,
   With the mercies of the King for thine
      awning;
And the just understand that thine hour is
      at hand,
   Thine hour at hand with power in the
      dawning.

When the nations lie in blood, and their
      kings a broken brood,
   Look up, O most sorrowful of daughters!
Lift up thy head and hark what sounds are
      in the dark,
   For His feet are coming to thee on the
      waters!

O Lily of the King! I shall not see, that sing,
   I shall not see the hour of thy queening!
But my Song shall see, and wake like a
      flower that dawn-winds shake,
   And sigh with joy the odours of its
      meaning.
O Lily of the King, remember then the thing
   That this dead mouth sang; and thy
      daughters,
As they dance before His way, sing there on
      the Day
   What I sang when the Night was on the
      waters!

NEW YEAR'S CHIMES

What is the song the stars sing?
   (*And a million songs are as song of one*)
This is the song the stars sing:
   (*Sweeter song's none*)

One to set, and many to sing,
   (*And a million songs are as song of one*)
One to stand, and many to cling,
The many things, and the one Thing,
   The one that runs not, the many that run.

The ever new weaveth the ever old,
   (*And a million songs are as song of one*)
Ever telling the never told;
The silver saith, and the said is gold,
   And done ever the never done.

The Chase that's chased is the Lord o' the
      chase,
   (*And a million songs are as song of one*)
And the Pursued cries on the race;
   And the hounds in leash are the hounds
      that run.

Hidden stars by the shown stars' sheen;
   (*And a million suns are but as one*)
Colours unseen by the colours seen,
And sounds unheard heard sounds between.
   And a night is in the light of the sun.
An ambuscade of light in night,
   (*And a million secrets are but as one*)
And a night is dark in the sun's light,
   And a world in the world man looks upon.

Hidden stars by the shown stars' wings,
   (*And a million cycles are but as one*)
And a world with unapparent strings
Knits the simulant world of things;
   Behold, and vision thereof is none.

The world above in the world below,
   (*And a million worlds are but as one*)
And the One in all; as the sun's strength so
Strives in all strength, glows in all glow
   Of the earth that wits not, and man
      thereon.

Braced in its own fourfold embrace
   (*And a million worlds are but as one*)
And round it all God's arms of grace,
The world, so as the Vision says,
   Doth with its great lightning-tramples run.

And thunder bruiteth into thunder,
   (*And a million sounds are as sound of one*)
From stellate peak to peak is tossed a voice
   of wonder,
And the height stoops down to the depths
   thereunder,
   And sun leans forth to his brother-sun.

And the more ample years unfold
   (*With a million songs as song of one*)

A little new of the ever old,
A little told of the never told,
   Added act of the never done.

Loud the descant, and low the theme,
   (*A million songs are as song of one*)
And the dream of the world is dream in
   dream,
But the one Is is, or nought could seem;
   And the song runs round to the song
   begun.
This is the song the stars sing,
   (*Tunèd all in time*)
Tintinnabulous, tuned to ring
A multitudinous-single thing
   (*Rung all in rhyme*).

ANY SAINT

His shoulder did I hold
Too high that I, o'erbold
      Weak one,
      Should lean thereon.

But He a little hath
Declined His stately path
      And my
      Feet set more high;

That the slack arm may reach
His shoulder, and faint speech
      Stir
      His unwithering hair.

And bolder now and bolder
I lean upon that shoulder,
      So dear
      He is and near:

And with His aureole
The tresses of my soul
      Are blent
      In wished content.

Yea, this too gentle Lover
Hath flattering words to move her
      To pride
      By His sweet side.

Ah, Love! somewhat let be —
Lest my humility
      Grow weak
      When Thou dost speak.

Rebate Thy tender suit,
Lest to herself impute
      Some worth
      Thy bride of earth!

A maid too easily
Conceits herself to be
      Those things
      Her lover sings;

And being straitly wooed,
Believes herself the Good
      And Fair
      He seeks in her.

Turn something of Thy look,
And fear me with rebuke,
      That I
      May timorously

Take tremors in Thy arms,
And with contrived charms
      Allure
      A love unsure.

Not to me, not to me,
Builded so flawfully,
    O God,
      Thy humbling laud!

Not to this man, but Man,—
Universe in a span;
    Point
      Of the spheres conjoint;

In whom eternally
Thou, Light, dost focus Thee!—
    Didst pave
      The way o' the wave;

Rivet with stars the Heaven,
For causeways to Thy driven
    Car
      In its coming far

Unto him, only him;
In Thy deific whim
    Didst bound
      Thy works' great round

In this small ring of flesh;
The sky's gold-knotted mesh
    Thy wrist
      Did only twist

To take him in that net.—
Man! swinging-wicket set
    Between
      The Unseen and Seen;

Lo, God's two worlds immense,
Of spirit and of sense,
    Wed
      In this narrow bed;

Yea, and the midge's hymn
Answers the seraphim
    Athwart
      Thy body's court!

Great arm-fellow of God!
To the ancestral clod
    Kin,
      And to cherubim;

Bread predilectedly
O' the worm and Deity!
    Hark,
      O God's clay-sealed Ark,

To praise that fits thee, clear
To the ear within the ear,
    But dense
      To clay-sealed sense.

All the Omnific made
When, in a word he said,
    (Mystery!)
      He uttered thee;

Thee His great utterance bore
O secret metaphor
    Of what
      Thou dream'st no jot!

Cosmic metonymy;
Weak world-unshuttering key;
    One
      Seal of Solomon!

Trope that itself not scans
Its huge significance,
    Which tries
      Cherubic eyes!

Primer where the angels all
God's grammar spell in small,
    Nor spell
      The highest too well!

Point for the great descants
Of starry disputants;
    Equation
      Of creation!

Thou meaning, couldst thou see,
Of all which dafteth thee;
    So plain,
      It mocks thy pain.

Stone of the Law indeed,
Thine own self couldst thou read
    Thy bliss
      Within thee is.

Compost of Heaven and mire,
Slow foot and swift desire!
    Lo,
      To have Yes, choose No;

Gird, and thou shalt unbind;
Seek not, and thou shalt find;
    To eat
      Deny thy meat;

And thou shalt be fulfilled
With all sweet things unwilled:
    So best
      God loves to jest

With children small — a freak
Of heavenly hide-and-seek
    Fit
      For thy wayward wit,

Who art thyself a thing
Of whim and wavering;
    Free
      When His wings pen thee;

Sole fully blest, to feel
God whistle thee at heel;

    Drunk up
    As a dew-drop,

When He bends down, sun-wise,
Intemperable eyes;
    Most proud,
      When utterly bowed,

To feel thyself and be
His dear nonentity —
    Caught
      Beyond human thought

In the thunder-spout of Him,
Until thy being dim,
    And be
      Dead deathlessly.

Stoop, stoop; for thou dost fear
The nettle's wrathful spear,
    So slight
      Art thou of might!

Rise; for Heaven hath no frown
When thou to thee pluck'st down,
    Strong clod!
      The neck of God.

ALL FLESH

I do not need the skies'
Pomp, when I would be wise;
For pleasaunce nor to use
Heaven's champaign when I muse.
One grass-blade in its veins
Wisdom's whole flood contains:
Thereon my foundering mind
Odyssean fate can find.

O little blade, now vaunt
Thee, and be arrogant!
Tell the proud sun that he
Sweated in shaping thee;
Night, that she did unvest
Her mooned and argent breast
To suckle thee. Heaven fain
Yearned over thee in rain,
And with wide parent wing
Shadowed thee, nested thing,

Fed thee, and slaved for thy
Impotent tyranny.
Nature's broad thews bent
Meek for thy content.
Mastering littleness
Which the wise heavens confess,
The frailty which doth draw
Magnipotence to its law —
These were, O happy one, these
Thy laughing puissances!
Be confident of thought,
Seeing that thou art naught;
And be thy pride thou'rt all
Delectably safe and small.
Epitomized in thee
Was the mystery
Which shakes the spheres conjoint —
God focussed to a point.

All thy fine mouths shout
Scorn upon dull-eyed doubt.
Impenetrable fool
Is he thou canst not school
To the humility
By which the angels see!
Unfathomably framed
Sister, I am not shamed
Before the cherubin

To vaunt my flesh thy kin.
My one hand thine, and one
Imprisoned in God's own,
I am as God; alas,
And such a god of grass!
A little root clay-caught,
A wind, a flame, a thought,
Inestimably naught!

THE HOUND OF HEAVEN

I fled Him, down the nights and down the
    days;
I fled Him, down the arches of the years;
I fled Him, down the labyrinthine ways
Of my own mind; and in the mist of tears
I hid from Him, and under running laugh-
    ter.
    Up vistaed hopes I sped;
    And shot, precipitated,
Adown Titanic glooms of chasmèd fears,
From those strong Feet that followed, fol-
    lowed after.
    But with unhurrying chase,
    And unperturbèd pace,
Deliberate speed, majestic instancy,
    They beat — and a Voice beat
    More instant than the Feet —
'All things betray thee, who betrayest Me.'

I pleaded, outlaw-wise,
By many a hearted casement, curtained red,
Trellised with intertwining charities;
(For, though I knew His love Who fol-
    lowèd,
    Yet was I sore adread
Lest, having Him, I must have naught be-
    side.)
But, if one little casement parted wide,
The gust of His approach would clash it to:
Fear wist not to evade, as Love wist to
    pursue.
Across the margent of the world I fled,
And troubled the gold gateways of the stars,
Smiting for shelter on their clangèd bars:
    Fretted to dulcet jars
And silvern chatter the pale ports o' the
    moon.

I said to Dawn: Be sudden — to Eve: Be
    soon;
With thy young skiey blossoms heap me over
    From this tremendous Lover —
Float thy vague veil about me, lest He see!
I tempted all His servitors, but to find
My own betrayal in their constancy,
In faith to Him their fickleness to me,
Their traitorous trueness, and their loyal
    deceit.
To all swift things for swiftness did I sue;
Clung to the whistling mane of every wind.
    But whether they swept, smoothly fleet,
The long savannahs of the blue;
    Or whether, Thunder-driven,
They clanged his chariot 'thwart a heaven,
Plashy with flying lightnings round the
    spurn 'o their feet: —
Fear wist not to evade as Love wist to pursue.
    Still with unhurrying chase,
    And unperturbèd pace,
Deliberate speed, majestic instancy,
    Came on the following Feet,
    And a Voice above their beat —
'Naught shelters thee, who wilt not shelter
    Me.'

I sought no more that after which I strayed
    In face of man or maid;
But still within the little children's eyes
    Seems something, something that replies,
They at least are for me, surely for me!
I turned me to them very wistfully;
But just as their young eyes grew sudden fair
    With dawning answers there,
Their angel plucked them from me by the
    hair.

'Come then, ye other children, Nature's —
    share
With me' (said I) 'your delicate fellowship;
  Let me greet you lip to lip,
  Let me twine you with caresses,
  Wantoning
  With our Lady-Mother's vagrant tresses,
  Banqueting
  With her in her wind-walled palace,
  Underneath her azured daïs,
  Quaffing, as your taintless way is,
  From a chalice
Lucent-weeping out of the dayspring.'
  So it was done:
I in their delicate fellowship was one —
Drew the bolt of Nature's secrecies.
  I knew all the swift importings
  On the wilful face of skies;
  I knew how the clouds arise
  Spuméd of the wild sea-snortings;
  All that's born or dies
  Rose and drooped with; made them shapers
Of mine own moods, or wailful or divine;
  With them joyed and was bereaven.
  I was heavy with the even,
  When she lit her glimmering tapers
  Round the day's dead sanctities.
  I laughed in the morning's eyes.
I triumphed and I saddened with all weather,
  Heaven and I wept together,
And its sweet tears were salt with mortal
  mine;
Against the red throb of its sunset-heart
  I laid my own to beat,
  And share commingling heat;
But not by that, by that, was eased my
  human smart.
In vain my tears were wet on Heaven's grey
  cheek.
For ah! we know not what each other says,
  These things and I; in sound *I* speak —
Their sound is but their stir, they speak by
  silences.
Nature, poor stepdame, cannot slake my
  drouth;
  Let her, if she would owe me,
Drop yon blue bosom-veil of sky, and show
  me
  The breasts o' her tenderness:
Never did any milk of hers once bless
  My thirsting mouth.

Nigh and nigh draws the chase,
With unperturbèd pace,
Deliberate speed, majestic instancy;
And past those noisèd Feet
A voice comes yet more fleet —
'Lo! naught contents thee, who content'st
  not Me.'

Naked I wait Thy love's uplifted stroke!
My harness piece by piece Thou hast hewn
  from me,
  And smitten me to my knee;
  I am defenceless utterly.
  I slept, methinks, and woke,
And, slowly gazing, find me stripped in sleep.
In the rash lustihead of my young powers,
  I shook the pillaring hours
And pulled my life upon me; grimed with
  smears,
I stand amid the dust o' the mounded years—
My mangled youth lies dead beneath the
  heap.
My days have crackled and gone up in smoke,
Have puffed and burst as sun-starts on a
  stream.
  Yea, faileth now even dream
The dreamer, and the lute the lutanist
Even the linked fantasies, in whose blossomy
  twist
I swung the earth a trinket at my wrist,
Are yielding; cords of all too weak account
For earth with heavy griefs so overplussed.
  Ah! is Thy love indeed
  A weed, albeit an amaranthine weed,
Suffering no flowers except its own to mount?
  Ah! must —
  Designer infinite! —
Ah! must Thou char the wood ere Thou
  canst limn with it?
My freshness spent its wavering shower i' the
  dust;
And now my heart is as a broken fount,
Wherein tear-drippings stagnate, spilt down
  ever
  From the dank thoughts that shiver
Upon the sighful branches of my mind.
  Such is; what is to be?
The pulp so bitter, how shall taste the rind?
I dimly guess what Time in mists confounds;
Yet ever and anon a trumpet sounds
From the hid battlements of Eternity;

Those shaken mists a space unsettle, then
Round the half-glimpséd turrets slowly wash
    again.
  But not ere him who summoneth
  I first have seen, enwound
With glooming robes purpureal, cypress-
    crowned;
His name I know, and what his trumpet
    saith.
Whether man's heart or life it be which
    yields
  Thee harvest, must Thy harvest-fields
  Be dunged with rotten death?
  Now of that long pursuit
  Comes on at hand the bruit;
  That Voice is round me like a bursting sea:
  'And is thy earth so marred,
  Shattered in shard on shard?
  Lo, all things fly thee, for thou fliest Me!
  Strange, piteous, futile thing!
Wherefore should any set thee love apart?
Seeing none but I makes much of naught'
    (He said),

'And human love needs human meriting:
  How hast thou merited —
Of all man's clotted clay the dingiest clot?
  Alack, thou knowest not
How little worthy of any love thou art!
Whom wilt thou find to love ignoble thee,
  Save Me, save only Me?
All which I took from thee I did but take,
  Not for thy harms,
But just that thou might'st seek it in My
    arms.
  All which thy child's mistake
Fancies as lost, I have stored for thee at
    home:
  Rise, clasp My hand, and come!'
Halts by me that footfall:
Is my gloom, after all,
Shade of His hand, outstretched caressingly?
'Ah, fondest, blindest, weakest,
I am He Whom thou seekest!
Thou dravest love from thee, who dravest
  Me.'

THE KINGDOM OF GOD

'In No Strange Land'

O world invisible, we view thee,
O world intangible, we touch thee,
O world unknowable, we know thee,
Inapprehensible, we clutch thee!

Does the fish soar to find the ocean,
The eagle plunge to find the air —
That we ask of the stars in motion
If they have rumour of thee there?

Not where the wheeling systems darken,
And our benumbed conceiving soars! —
The drift of pinions, would we harken,
Beats at our own clay-shuttered doors.

The angels keep their ancient places; —
Turn but a stone, and start a wing!
'Tis ye, 'tis your estrangéd faces,
That miss the many-splendoured thing.

But (when so sad thou canst not sadder)
Cry; — and upon thy so sore loss
Shall shine the traffic of Jacob's ladder
Pitched betwixt Heaven and Charing Cross.

Yea, in the night, my Soul, my daughter,
Cry, — clinging Heaven by the hems;
And lo, Christ walking on the water
Not of Genesareth, but Thames!

SHELLEY*

AFTER all, to finish where we began, perhaps the poems on which the lover of Shelley leans most lovingly, which he has oftenest in his mind, which best represent Shelley to him, and which he instinctively reverts to when Shelley's name is mentioned, are some of the shorter poems and detached lyrics. Here Shelley forgets for a while all that ever makes his verse turbid; forgets that he is anything but a poet, forgets sometimes that he is anything but a child; lies back in his skiff, and looks at the clouds. He plays truant from earth, slips through the wicket of fancy into heaven's meadow, and goes gathering stars. Here we have that absolute virgin-gold of song which is the scarcest among human products, and for which we can go to but three poets — Coleridge, Shelley, Chopin, and perhaps we should add Keats: *Christabel* and *Kubla Khan; The Skylark, The Cloud,* and *The Sensitive Plant* (in its first two parts); *The Eve of Saint Agnes* and *The Nightingale;* certain of the Nocturnes; these things make very quintessentialized loveliness. It is the attar of poetry.

Remark, as a thing worth remarking, that, although Shelley's diction is at other times singularly rich, it ceases in these poems to be rich, or to obtrude itself at all; it is imperceptible; his Muse has become a veritable Echo, whose body has dissolved from her voice. Indeed, when his diction is richest, nevertheless the poetry so dominates the expression that we only feel the latter as an atmosphere until we are satiated with the former; then we discover with surprise to how imperial a vesture we had been so blinded by gazing on the face of his song. A lesson, this, deserving to be conned by a generation so opposite in tendency as our own: a lesson that in poetry, as in the kingdom of God, we should not take thought too greatly wherewith we shall be clothed,

The Works of Francis Thompson, Vol. III, Prose (New York: Charles Scribner and Sons, 1913). pp. 30–37.

but seek first the spirit, and all these things will be added unto us.

On the marvellous music of Shelley's verse we need not dwell, except to note that he avoids that metronomic beat of rhythm which Edgar Poe introduced into modern lyric measures, as Pope introduced it into the rhyming heroics of his day. Our varied metres are becoming as painfully over-polished as Pope's one metre. Shelley could at need sacrifice smoothness to fitness. He could write an anapaest that would send Mr. Swinburne into strong shudders (e.g., 'stream did glide') when he instinctively felt that by so forgoing the more obvious music of melody he would secure the higher music of harmony. If we have to add that in other ways he was far from escaping the defects of his merits, and would sometimes have to acknowledge that his Nilotic flood too often overflowed its banks, what is this but saying that he died young?

It may be thought that in our casual comments on Shelley's life we have been blind to its evil side. That, however, is not the case. We see clearly that he committed grave sins, and one cruel crime; but we remember also that he was an Atheist from his boyhood; we reflect how gross must have been the moral neglect in the training of a child who could be an Atheist from his boyhood: and we decline to judge so unhappy a being by the rules which we should apply to a Catholic. It seems to us that Shelley was struggling — blindly, weakly, stumblingly, but still struggling — towards higher things. His Pantheism is an indication of it. Pantheism is a half-way house, and marks ascent or descent according to the direction from which it is approached. Now Shelley came to it from absolute Atheism; therefore in his case it meant rise. Again, his poetry alone would lead us to the same conclusion, for we do not believe that a truly corrupted spirit can write consistently ethereal poetry. We should believe in nothing if we believed that, for it would be the consecration of a lie. Poetry is a thermometer: by taking its average height you can estimate the normal temperature of its writer's mind. The devil can do many things. But the devil cannot write poetry. He may mar a poet, but he cannot make a poet. Among all the temptations wherewith he tempted St. Anthony, though we have often seen it stated that he howled, we have never seen it stated that he sang.

Shelley's anarchic principles were as a rule held by him with some misdirected view to truth. He disbelieved in kings. And it is not a mere fact — regret it if you will — that in all European countries, except two, monarchs are a mere survival, the obsolete buttons on coat-tails of rule, which serve no purpose but to be continually coming off? It is a miserable thing to note how every little Balkan State, having obtained liberty (save the mark!) by Act of Congress, straightway proceeds to secure the service of a professional king. These gentlemen are plentiful in Europe. They are the 'noble Chairmen' who lend their names for a consideration to any enterprising company which may be speculating in Liberty. When we see these things, we revert to the old lines in which Persius tells how you cannot turn Dama into a freeman by twirling him round your finger and calling him Marcus Dama.

Again Shelley desired a religion of humanity, and that meant, to him, a religion for humanity, a religion which, unlike the spectral Christianity about him, should permeate and regulate the whole organization of men. And the feeling is one with which a Catholic must sympathize, in an age where — if we may say so without irreverence — the Almighty has been made a constitutional Deity, with certain state-grants of worship, but no influence over political affairs. In these matters Shelley's aims were generous, if his methods were perniciously mistaken. In his theory of Free Love alone, borrowed like the rest from the Revolution, his aim was as mischievous as his method. At the same time he was at least logical. His theory was repulsive, but comprehensible. Whereas from our present via media — facilitation of divorce — can only result the era when the young lady in reduced circumstances will no longer turn governess, but will be open to engagement as wife at a reasonable stipend.

We spoke of the purity of Shelley's poetry. We know of but three pages to which exception can be taken. One is happily hidden under a heap of Shellein rubbish. Another is offensive because it presents his theory of Free Love in its most odious form. The third is very much a matter, we think, for the individual conscience. Compare with this the genuinely corrupt Byron, through the cracks and fissures of whose heaving versification steam up perpetually the sulphurous vapours from his central iniquity. We cannot credit that any Christian ever had his faith shaken through reading Shelley, unless his faith were shaken before he read Shelley. Is any safely-havened bark likely to slip its cable, and make for a flag planted on the very reef where the planter himself was wrecked?

Why indeed (one is tempted to ask in concluding) should it be that the poets who have written for us the poetry richest in skiey grain, most free from admixture with the duller things on earth — the Shelleys, the Coleridges, the Keats' — are the very poets whose lives are among the saddest records in literature? Is it that (by some subtle mystery of analogy) sorrow, passion, and fantasy are indissolubly connected, like water, fire, and cloud; that as from sun and dew are born the vapours, so from fire and tears ascend the 'visions of aerial joy'; that the harvest waves richest over the battle-fields of the soul; that the heart, like the earth, smells sweetest after rain; that the spell on which depend such necromatic castles is some spirit of pain charm-prisoned at their base? Such a poet, it may be, mists with sighs the window of his life until the tears run down it; then some air of searching poetry, like an air of searching frost, turns it to a crystal wonder. The god of golden song is the god, too, of the golden sun; so peradventure songlight is like sunlight, and darkens the countenance of the soul. Perhaps the rays are to the stars what thorns are to the flowers; and so the poet, after wandering over heaven, returns with bleeding feet. Less tragic in its merely temporal aspect than the life of Keats or Coleridge, the life of Shelley in its moral aspect is, perhaps, more tragical than that of either; his dying seems a myth, a figure of his living; the material shipwreck a figure of the immaterial.

Enchanted child, born into a world un-childlike; spoiled darling of Nature, playmate of her elemental daughters; 'pard-like spirit, beautiful and swift,' laired amidst the burning fastnesses of his own fervid mind; bold foot along the verges of precipitous dream; light leaper from crag to crag of inaccessible fancies; towering Genius, whose soul rose like a ladder between heaven and earth with the angels of song ascending and descending it; — he is shrunken into the little vessel of death, and sealed with the unshatterable seal of doom, and cast down deep below the rolling tides of Time.

Mighty meat for little guests, when the heart of Shelley was laid in the cemetery of Caius Cestius! Beauty, music, sweetness, tears — the mouth of the worm has fed of them all. Into that sacred bridal-gloom of death where he holds his nuptials with eternity let not our rash speculations follow him; let us hope rather that as, amidst material nature, where our dull eyes see only ruin, the finer eye of science has discovered life in putridity and vigour in decay, seeing dissolution even and disintegration, which in the mouth of man symbolize disorder, to be in the works of God undeviating order, and the manner of our corruption to be no less wonderful than the manner of our health, — so, amidst the supernatural universe, some tender undreamed surprise of life in doom awaited that wild nature, which, worn by warfare with itself, its Maker, and all the world now

Sleeps, and never palates more the dug,
The beggars nurse, and Caesar's.

ERNEST CHRISTOPHER DOWSON
(1867–1900)

THE life of Ernest Christopher Dowson presents a singularly pathetic picture. Born in Kent, England, in 1867, he completed his elementary education at home. Having matriculated at Queens College, Oxford, he contracted tuberculosis in 1887, an eventuality that forced him to leave college without his degree.

Several years later, after a tragic love affair, he traveled in Italy, the Netherlands, and France in a vain search for some alleviation for his afflicted body. Returning to England in a mood approaching despair, he died at Catford February 23, 1900.

His verse, consisting mostly of short poems, is living evidence of Dowson's intense individuality.

NUNS OF THE PERPETUAL ADORATION*

Calm, sad, secure; behind high convent walls,
　These watch the sacred lamp, these watch
　　and pray:

And it is one with them when evening falls,
　And one with them the cold return of day.

These heed not time; their nights and days
　　they make
　Into a long, returning rosary,

---

*The above and following poems have been selected from *The Poems of Ernest Dowson* (New York: Dodd, Mead and Co., 1922).

Whereon their lives are threaded for Christ's
    sake;
Meekness and vigilance and chastity.

A vowed patrol, in silent companies,
    Life-long they keep before the living Christ.
In the dim church, their prayers and penances
    Are fragrant incense to the Sacrificed.

Outside, the world is wild and passionate;
    Man's weary laughter and his sick despair
Entreat at their impenetrable gate:
    They heed no voices in their dream of
        prayer.

They saw the glory of the world displayed;
    They saw the bitter of it, and the sweet;
They knew the roses of the world should
        fade,

And be trod under by the hurrying feet.
Therefore they rather put away desire,
    And crossed their hands and came to sanc-
        tuary
And veiled their heads and put on coarse
        attire:
    Because their comeliness was vanity.

And there they rest; they have serene insight
    Of the illuminating dawn to be:
Mary's sweet Star dispels for them the night,
    The proper darkness of humanity.

Calm, sad, secure; with faces worn and mild:
    Surely their choice of vigil is the best?
Yea! for our roses fade, the world is wild;
    But there, beside the altar, there is rest.

BENEDICTIO DOMINI

Without, the sullen noises of the street!
    The voice of London, inarticulate,
Hoarse and blaspheming, surges in to meet
    The silent blessing of the Immaculate.

Dark is the church, and dim the worshippers,
    Hushed with bowed heads as though by
        some old spell,
While through the incense-laden air there
        stirs
    The admonition of a silver bell.

Dark is the church, save where the altar stands,
    Dressed like a bride, illustrious with light,
Where one old priest exalts with tremulous
        hands
    The one true solace of man's fallen plight.

Strange silence here: without, the sounding
        street
    Heralds the world's swift passage to the fire:
O Benediction, perfect and complete!
    When shall men cease to suffer and desire?

NON SUM QUALIS ERAM BONAE SUB REGNO CYNARAE

Last night, ah, yesternight, betwixt her lips
        and mine
There fell thy shadow, Cynara! thy breath
        was shed
Upon my soul between the kisses and the
        wine;
And I was desolate and sick of an old
        passion,
    Yea, I was desolate and bowed my head:
I have been faithful to thee, Cynara! in my
        fashion.

All night upon mine heart I felt her warm
        heart beat,
Night-long within mine arms in love and
        sleep she lay;
Surely the kisses of her bought red mouth
        were sweet;
But I was desolate and sick of an old passion,
    When I awoke and found the dawn was
        gray:
I have been faithful to thee, Cynara! in my
        fashion.

I have forgot much, Cynara! gone with the
  wind,
Flung roses, roses riotously with the throng,
Dancing, to put thy pale, lost lilies out of
  mind;
But I was desolate and sick of an old passion,
  Yea, all the time, because the dance was
    long:
I have been faithful to thee, Cynara! in my
  fashion.

I cried for madder music and for stronger
  wine,
But when the feast is finished and the lamps
  expire,
Then falls thy shadow, Cynara! the night is
  thine;
And I am desolate and sick of an old passion,
  Yea, hungry for the lips of my desire:
I have been faithful to thee, Cynara! in my
  fashion.

EXTREME UNCTION

Upon the eyes, the lips, the feet,
  On all the passages of sense,
The atoning oil is spread with sweet
  Renewal of lost innocence.

The feet, that lately ran so fast
  To meet desire, are soothly sealed;
The eyes, that were so often cast
  On vanity, are touched and healed.

From troublous sights and sounds set free;
  In such a twilight hour of breath,

Shall one retrace his life, or see,
  Through shadows, the true face of death?

Vials of mercy! Sacring oils!
  I know not where nor when I come,
Nor through what wandering and toils,
  To crave of you Viaticum.

Yet, when the walls of flesh grow weak,
  In such an hour, it well may be,
Through mist and darkness, light will break,
  And each anointed sense will see.

MICHAEL FIELD

Catherine Bradley (*1848–1914*)
Edith Cooper (*1862–1913*)

EDITH COOPER was the niece of Catherine Bradley. Their association began when Edith was three years of age. The elder woman, educated at Newnham College, Cambridge, and the College de France, took complete charge of her niece's education. Both women studied the classics and philosophy and upon settling in seclusion, first at Reigate and later at Richmond in Surrey, they began to collaborate in writing. The first fruits of their collaboration, published under the pseudonym, Michael Field, caused something of a sensation. Browning praised their first work highly and the literary world prepared to receive a new genius. When it was discovered that Michael Field was Miss Bradley and her niece, and when a rather artificial series of closet dramas had appeared as a result of their collaboration, the world lost interest in their work.

Both died of cancer; Edith Cooper in 1913, her aunt in 1914. In 1923 Mary Sturgeon and E. Sturge-Moore collected the best lyrics of the two women and made a brave attempt to rehabilitate their literary fame. The attempt remained such; except for some few lyrics the poetry of Michael Field never reaches the heights achieved by Mrs. Meynell or Christina Rossetti.

The best sketch of the life of Michael Field is that by Mary Sturgeon.

DESCENT FROM THE CROSS*

Come down from the Cross, my soul, and
    save thyself — come down!
Thou wilt be free as wind. None meeting
    thee will know
How thou wert hanging stark, my soul,
    outside the town,
Thou wilt fare to and fro;
Thy feet in grass will smell of faithful thyme;
    thy head. . . .
Think of the thorns, my soul — how thou
    wilt cast them off,
With shudder at the bleeding clench they
    hold!
But on their wounds thou wilt a balsam
    spread,
And over that a verdurous circle rolled
With gathered violets, sweet bright violets,
    sweet
As incense of the thyme on thy free feet;
A wreath thou wilt not give away, nor wilt
    thou doff.

Come down from the Cross, my soul, and
    save thyself; yea, move
As scudding swans pass lithely on a sea-
    ward stream!
Thou wilt have everything thou wert made
    great to love;
Thou wilt have ease for every dream;
No nails with fang will hold thy purpose
    to one aim;
There will be arbours round about thee, not
    one trunk
Against thy shoulders pressed and burning
    them with hate,
Yea, burning with intolerable flame.
O lips, such noxious vinegar have drunk,
There are through valley-woods and
    mountain glades

Rivers where thirst in naked prowess
    wades;
And there are wells in solitude whose chill
    no hour abates!

Come down from the Cross, my soul, and
    save thyself! A sign
Thou wilt become to many as a shooting star.
They will believe thou art ethereal, divine,
When thou art where they are;
They will believe in thee and give thee feasts
    and praise.
They will believe thy power when thou hast
    loosed thy nails;
For power to them is fetterless and grand:
For destiny to them, along their ways,
Is one whose earthly Kingdom never fails.
Thou wilt be as a prophet or a king
In thy tremendous term of flourishing —
And thy hot royalty with acclamations
    fanned.

Come down from the Cross, my soul, and
    save thyself! . . . Beware!
Art thou not crucified with God, who is
    thy breath?
Wilt thou not hang as He while mockers
    laugh and stare?
Wilt thou not die His death?
Wilt thou not stay as He with nails and
    thorns and thirst?
Wilt thou not choose to conquer faith in
    His lone style?
Wilt thou not be with Him and hold
    thee still?
Voices have cried to Him, Come Down!
    Accursed
And vain those voices, striving to beguile!
How heedless, solemn-gray in powerful mass,
Christ droops among the echoes as
    they pass!
O soul, remain with Him, with Him thy
    doom fulfil!

*The above and the following poems have been se-
lected from *Poems of Michael Field* (Boston: Houghton
Mifflin Co.), printed in Great Britain.

THE TRAGIC MARY QUEEN OF SCOTS

I could wish to be dead!
Too quick with life were the tears I shed,
Too sweet for tears is the life I led;
And ah, too lonesome my marriage-bed!
I could wish to be dead.

I could wish to be dead,
For just a word that rings in my head;
Too dear, too dear are the words he said,
They must never be remembered.
I could wish to be dead.

I could wish to be dead:
The wish to be loved is all mis-read,
And to love, one learns when one is wed,
Is to suffer bitter shame; instead
I could wish to be dead.

LIONEL PIGOT JOHNSON
(1867–1902)

LIKE many another author of great promise, an early death marked the end of the gifted but immature literary life of Lionel Pigot Johnson. He died in 1902 at the age of thirty-five, apparently on the threshold of a great career. Born at Broadstairs on the Kentish coast, March 15, 1867, his education was acquired at Winchester College and at New College Oxford.

Within a year after his graduation from the latter institution he was received into the Catholic Church. Literary endeavors completely occupied the next ten years of his life until his death in 1902. During this time he published three books, *The Art of Thomas Hardy,* 1894, and two volumes of poetry, 1897 and 1898. The poetry is the product of careful and sometimes painful workmanship. It is expressive of real emotion, modified by a classical enduring charm, yet is limited in its range.

He published *Ireland and Other Poems* in 1897 and *Poems* in 1898. In his *Post Liminium,* a series of Essays, 1912, is exhibited his sound principles of criticism, his fount of wisdom and humor and his search for literary perfection.

TO MORFYDD*

A voice on the winds,
A voice by the waters,
    Wanders and cries:
  Oh, what are the winds?
And what are the waters?
    Mine are your eyes!

Western the winds are,
And western the waters,
    Where the light lies:

Oh, what are the winds?
And what are the waters?
    Mine are your eyes!

Cold, cold, grow the winds,
And wild grow the waters,
    Where the sun dies:
  Oh! what are the winds?
And what are the waters?
    Mine are your eyes!

And down the night winds,
And down the night waters,
   the music flies:
Oh! what are the winds?

And what are the waters?
Cold be the winds,
And wild be the waters,
   So mine be your eyes!

*The above and following poems have been selected from *Poetical Works of Lionel Johnson* (London: Elkin Matthews. New York: The Macmillan Co., 1917).

THE DARK ANGEL

Dark Angel, with thine aching lust
To rid the world of Penitence:
Malicious Angel, who still dost
My soul such subtile violence!

Because of thee, no thought, no thing,
Abides for me undesecrate:
Dark Angel, ever on the wing,
Who never reachest me too late!

When music sounds, then changest thou
Its silvery to a sultry fire:
Nor will thine envious heart allow
Delight untortured by desire.

Through thee, the gracious Muses turn
To Furies, O mine Enemy!
And all the things of beauty burn
With flames of evil ecstasy.

When sunlight glows upon the flowers,
Or ripples down the dancing sea:
Thou, with thy troop of passionate powers,
Beleagurest, bewilderest, me.

Within the breath of autumn woods,
Within the winter silences:
Thy venomous spirit stirs and broods,
O Master of impieties!

The ardour of red flame is thine,
And thine the steely soul of ice:
Thou poisonest the fair design
Of nature, with unfair device.

Apples of ashes, golden bright;
Waters of bitterness, how sweet!
O banquet of a foul delight,
Prepared by thee, dark Paraclete!

I fight thee, in the Holy Name!
Yet, what thou dost, is what God saith:
Tempter! should I escape thy flame,
Thou wilt have helped my soul from Death:

The second Death, that never dies,
That cannot die, when time is dead:
Live Death, wherein the lost soul cries,
Eternally uncomforted.

Dark Angel, with thine aching lust!
Of two defeats, of two despairs:
Less dread, a change to drifting dust,
Than thine eternity of cares.

Do what thou wilt, thou shalt not so,
Dark Angel! triumph over me:
Lonely, unto the Lone I go:
Divine, to the Divinity.

OUR LADY OF THE SNOWS

Far from the world, far from delight,
Distinguishing not day from night;
Vowed to one sacrifice of all
The happy things, that men befall;
Pleading one sacrifice, before
Whom sun and sea and wind adore;

Far from earth's comfort, far away,
We cry to God, we cry and pray
For men, who have the common day.
Dance, merry world! and sing: but we,
Hearing, remember Calvary:
Get gold, and thrive you! but the sun

Once paled; and the centurion
Said: *This dead man was God's own Son.*
Think you, we shrink from common toil,
Works of the mart, works of the soil;
That, prisoners of strong despair,
We breathe this melancholy air;
Forgetting the dear calls of race,
And bonds of house, and ties of place;
That, cowards, from the field we turn,
And heavenward, in our weakness, yearn?
Unjust! unkind! while you despise
Our lonely years, our mournful cries:
You are the happier for our prayer;
The guerdon of our souls, you share
Not in such feebleness of heart,
We play our solitary part;
Not fugitives of battle, we
Hide from the world, and let things be:
But rather, looking over earth,
Between the bounds of death and birth;
And sad at heart, for sorrow and sin,
We wondered, where might help begin.
And on our wonder came God's choice,
A sudden light, a clarion voice,
Clearing the dark, and sounding clear:
And we obeyed: behold us, here!
In prison bound, but with your chains:
Sufferers, but of alien pains.
Merry the world, and thrives apace,
Each in his customary place:
Sailors upon the carrying sea,
Shepherds upon the pasture lea,
And merchants of the town; and they,
Who march to death, the fighting way;
And there are lovers in the spring,

With those, who dance, and those, who sing:
The commonwealth of every day,
Eastward and westward, far away.
Once the sun paled; once cried aloud
The Roman, from beneath the cloud:
This day the Son of God is dead!
Yet heed men, what the Roman said?
They heed not: we then heed for them,
The mindless of Jerusalem;
Careless, they live and die: but we
Care, in their stead, for Calvary.
O joyous men and women! strong,
To urge the wheel of life along,
With strenuous arm and cheerful strain,
And wisdom of laborious brain:
We give our life, our heart, our breath,
That you may live to conquer death;
That, past your tomb, with souls in health,
Joy may be yours, and blessed wealth;
Through vigils of the painful night,
Our spirits with your tempters fight:
For you, for you, we live alone,
Where no joy comes, where cold winds moan:
Nor friends have we, nor have we foes;
Our Queen is of the lonely Snows.
Ah! and sometimes, our prayers between,
Come sudden thoughts of what hath been:
Dreams! And from dreams, once more
   we fall
To prayer: *God save, Christ keep, them all.*
And thou, who knowest not these things,
Hearken, what news our message brings!
Our toils, thy joy of life forgot:
Our lives of prayer forget thee not.

CHRISTMAS

Sing *Bethlehem!* Sing *Bethlehem!*
You daughters of Jerusalem!
Keep sorrow for Gethsemani,
And mourning for Mount Calvary!

Why are your lids and lashes wet?
Here is no darkling Olivet.
Sing *Bethlehem!* Sing *Bethlehem!*
You daughters of Jerusalem!

How should we sing of Bethlehem,
We, daughters of Jerusalem?
We are the people of the Jews:
Our balms would soothe Him not, but bruise.

Ah, Calvary! ah, Calvary!
We wretched women cry to thee:
We, daughters of Jerusalem;
And enemies of Bethlehem.

With faces cast upon the dust,
We weep those things, which do we must:
Our tears embitter Calvary,
And water thee, Gethsemani!

Nay, *Bethlehem!* Sing *Bethlehem!*
Poor daughters of Jerusalem!
You know not, what you do: but He
Will pardon you on Calvary.

CHRISTMAS—II

The last week before Christmas,
  Hoar lies the orchard grass
From pear tree unto apple tree,
  Where feet well shod must pass:
By dripping trees a woodman's fire
  Burns the last leaves, alas!
And the blue smoke drifts through the air,
  Above the branches bare.

The last week before Christmas,
  The last before the snow:
Stand steaming cattle by the hedge,
  With meek heads bending low
The chattering rivulet flows fast,
  While there is time to flow
And the blue smoke drifts through the air
  Above the branches bare.

The last week before Christmas,
  Red berries few to find:
The brown fir cones upon the bough
  Move to a gentle wind:
Down the gray sky go chilly gleams,
  Bringing the sun to mind:
And the blue smoke drifts through the air,
  Above the branches bare.

Oh! last week before Christmas,
  Second before New Year:
Heap heart of oak upon the hearth,
  And keep you now good cheer:
With *Christus natus* for an health,
  And *Christi Mater* dear:
Then blue's the sky, and bright's the air,
  Above the blossoms fair!

PASCAL*

PASCAL, says Sainte-Beuve, "is at the heart of Christianity itself": Pascal, says Hume, is a Christian Diogenes, the great example of artificial life. Assuredly, he is nothing by halves, be it wordling or convert, sceptic or believer, physicist or Jansenist. Pascal "the stern and sick," as Goethe calls him, was not made for golden mediocrities, but for passions and ardours in their fullest vehemence. His sister and biographer notes well his *humeur bouillante*. Of most men in notable extremes it is commonly not hard to give an exact account, but Pascal must always abide in a twilight. For though Port-Royal be intimately known to us through countless sources, and though portions of Pascal's life be plain enough, yet the work

from which we try to fashion the true image of his soul, remains a thing of shreds and patches. . . . Pascal in his loneliness, agony, ardour, records the cries of his heart, the subtleties of his brain, with painful haste and zeal, sometimes with an incoherence not wholly sane. St. Augustine and Rousseau leave us their *Confessions* in perfect form: the passion is in orderly display. But Pascal's thoughts are like snatches of sudden prayer, like a dream's broken talk, like Hamlet's soliloquies, interspersed with wide passages of methodical reasoning.

His scientific glory crowned him upon the summit of the Puy de Dôme, the scene of his experiments in atmospheric pressure: fame was there, pride and ambition, in the free, exhilarating air. But when he wrote the *Pensées* he saw ever beside him a deep pit

*Johnson, Lionel, *Post Liminium*: Essays and Critical Papers (London: Elkin Mathews, 1912), pp. 155–162.

opening its unfathomed glooms and fears: an hallucination, doubtless, bred of his miraculous escape (as he held it to be), from the accident at the Pont de Neuilly; but the delusion had its intensity of true meaning. Jansenism, that sombre and harsh way of thought, a would-be Catholic Calvinism or Montanism, warped and darkened the world to his eyes. Yet, Jansenism apart, Pascal was one of those Christians who have no possibility of being happy, except through joy of sorrow and the delight of abnegation. To Théophile Gautier Christianity was odious, as the cause of melanchody, mysticism, and self-denial, because it humiliated the natural man, and poisoned pleasure, and induced an infinite longing. Those were its glories and charms for Pascal, who came perilously near to voluptuousness in the rapture of self-torture, the ecstasies of asceticism. One Good Friday, Dr. Johnson, not to be interrupted in his devotions by Boswell, gave him the *Pensées*. That dear and ridiculous gentleman found in them "a truly divine unction." But unction is not the word; Fénelon, Francis of Sales, have unction; Pascal has a prostrate self-abasement magnificently complete, in which "imbecile nature" is bidden to keep silence, and "impotent reason" to humble itself. All of which is simple, logical, orthodox Christianity: the necessary attitude of man in the presence of the ultimate mysteries, in the ante-chamber of realities. But Pascal, brooding over his *Deus absconditus*, cannot conclude with a complacent expression of man's limited faculties, and a few pious words about doing our best with what light we have. He waxes exultant and sonorous, terrible and savage, lyrical and mournful, as he dwells upon the estate of "man the admirable, the pitiable." But never a word of whining pessimism, petulant reproach: only a splendid self-contempt, a scourging of the "hateful I." Nothing, says St. Ambrose, is loftier than humility, which cannot be exalted, being the superior state; and Pascal's self-abjection is his tribute to man's marred greatness and high destiny. The *Pensées* keep up a perpetual harping upon the greatness and littleness of man, as revealed in their greatness by Christianity. "His very infirmities

prove man's greatness: they are the infirmities of a great lord, of a discrowned king." Upon every page we think of Pascal as a baptized Lucretius, whose rolling thunders and swift lightnings come from Sinai and Calvary: he is one of the elect sad souls whose profound severity is heartening.

We cannot judge of what value would have been his *Defence of Christianity*, for which most of the *Pensées* are suggestions and notes; probably, it would have been the supreme masterpiece of French prose, if not of all modern prose, but unconvincing to the unbelieving, and perilous to the faithful. Pyrrhonism, in Pascal's sense a kind of Christian Agnosticism, is a philosophic necessary of life; but Pascal was no metaphysician or theologian, and his reasoned treatise would assuredly have crossed forbidden boundaries. Like his favourite Montaigne, he had no method in the observation of life; his proficiency in mathematics, that precise study, led him to distrust and to decry less narrowly exacting principles of thought. *"Il faut avoir ces trois qualités: pyrrhonien, géomètre, chrétien soumis."* There is no heresy in that, but it does not auger well for a work of professed apologetics. Not his reasoning, but his temperament, not his arguments, but his ideas are what enrich the *Pensées,* making them one of the world's great books. Those to whom the Olympian serenity of Goethe, his "classic equability," seems an intolerable imposture, take instinctively to Pascal: he humbles them and exalts, inspires and saddens; his irony scathes, his compassion salves. His *"profondeur de tristesse et d'éloquence,"* to use Villemain's phrase, sends forth doctrines more commanding and more possible than exhortations to live in "the Whole, the Good, the Beautiful": the straitest sect of the Manichees seems more plausible than that. *"La maladie est l'état naturel des chrétiens"* is Pascal's teaching; and, really, we have read much of the same sort in the Gospels! It is for insisting upon this side of Christianity that Mr. Cotter Morison, a strenuous anti-Christian, calls Catholicism "more Scriptural" than Protestantism.

Not that a Christian life, says Pascal, is *"une vie de tristesse";* but because Christian sorrow is more delightful than all worldly joy. Pascal, author of the *Provincial Letters,* was no dusky, dreary penitent, soured and selfish; he had been an accomplished man of this world, and he became an accomplished man of the next, whose "conversation in heaven" had its gracious dignities. "Oh, what a noble mind is here o'erthrown!" has been quoted of Pascal. "Society" in Jerusalem may have said the same of Paul, after that deplorable delusion upon the way to Damascus. Passion, indeed, is the note of the *Pensées,* an intense, devouring energy of soul and spirit; but there is no sign of any mental degradation. His bodily pains were not those of the crazed fanatic; his style is still trenchant and pure: even what seem to be lapses from perfect sanity may very well be but the hasty phrases of a man in pain, jotting down rough notes, single words, mere indications of a meaning intelligible to himself. The world has not forgiven its deserter. What the world would pardon in an illiterate friar it does not pardon in Pascal the scientific and polite. With Bayle, it calls him a "paradox of the human race." Volumes have been written to prove that he was, and was not, Catholic, Protestant, sceptic, believer: his brain and his MSS. have been examined and forced to yield evidence. Verily, it is dangerous to be a very passionate Christian, trampling on the world's pride — with a greater. "Mediocrity alone is good!" says Pascal in his contempt.

"The heart has its reasons unknown to reason" is one of his familiar, famous sayings; his finer *Pensées* are of that intimate kind. True, he argues much, even to the verge of naked cynicism, about the "chances" of religion being true: the celebrated argument of the wager. But he speaks far more of Christianity as in itself desirable and delightful, as ennobling and dignifying its receiver. We fight inch by inch against conviction if told that a friend has played us false; but we have an immediate longing to believe the truth of some honourable report. Pascal falls in Platonic Love (to use the term correctly for once) with Christianity; he cannot do otherwise. "Who can withold credence and adoration from so divine a light?" And

it was for the honour, as he held, of Christianity in its pure grandeur that he fought his jealous fight with the Jesuit casuistry and for the Jansenist heresy, and became more casuistical than any Jesuit in the process. He was untainted by the sometimes worldly motives which were mixed with the acts of Port-Royal; his pride and scorn and stubbornness were for the sake of a Christianity about, as he thought, to be watered down, and made cheap, and given over to "the crowd, incapable of perfectness." He lacked that mark of the saints, pitilessness for himself, but boundless charity for others; his Puritanism was averse from all softness and indulgence towards the world in little things, that it might be won to the greater things. In that he was absolutely outside the whole tradition of the historical Church, and allied with a goodly number of heretics, perfectionists of many kinds, who have sought to lay burdens not to be borne on the multitude. He professes a full and firm obedience to the divine authority of Rome; and yet: "If my *Letters* are condemned in Rome, still what *I* condemn in my *Letters* is condemned in Heaven!" It smacks of Lucifer and Luther; there is some "hateful *I*" about that. The fervent passion of the man, jealous for the cause he believes divine, drives him into inconsistency; he was not, indeed a Lamennais, but much of a Savonarola or a Sarpi, in fighting for his convictions against his superiors. Reasons of the heart account for the worst in him, as for the best: he would hardly have been pleased to learn that Gibbon read the *Provincial Letters* once a year as a model of theological argument. Not the controversies of his day, but his thoughts on eternal things preserve his glory. Like Wordsworth, but with a more personal and fiery passion, he contemplates the tragedy of life, its "fierce confederate storm" of sorrows, its heights and deeps, turning the light of a restless imagination upon the secular scene, and noting the poignancies of the play. He has made his *"renonciation totale et douce,"* but the burning renunciant sends his thoughts far over the world and its history, appraising the value of things, letting escape him no trace of man's degradation or man's grandeur, eager to show what Christianity can do for both. A lover of superiorities, he has pity for their opposites, but mere contempt for the meagre and the middling; he is capable of making submission to evil, but not a compromise, and, if the heights of sanctity be unattainable, he will still attempt them. France has no writer, certainly no lay writer, who resembles him in his superb austerity: *"on mourra seul,"* he said, and in truth he both was and is a man of isolation, dwelling apart. *"Pensée fait la grandeur de l'homme"*: profoundly, absolutely, is that true of Pascal. He is no phrasemonger, witty, light, clever; "an epigrammatist — a bad man," is one of his rough jottings. Nor is he the elegant and querulous keeper of a sentimental journal. He is one of the voices which at rare intervals come from the heart of a man, and go to the hearts of men: *cor ad cor loquitur,* and deep answers deep.

ROBERT HUGH BENSON
(1871–1914)

ROBERT HUGH BENSON, the son of Edward Benson, Archbishop of Canterbury, was born November 18, 1871. He was educated at Eton and Cambridge and upon the completion of his university career became an Anglican curate. After nine years of labor in London and Kemsing he entered the Catholic Church. As a Catholic, Benson soon revealed his talent as a preacher and novelist. He led a busy life and produced within a short space of time many Catholic novels of great promise. He died at Salford, October, 1914, and was buried in the garden of his home, Hare St. House, Buntingford.

Benson's novels reveal a marvelous grasp of psychology. He has hardly a peer when he describes inner struggles of the mind or attempts to trace out the sources of preternatural or supernatural events. Though it may be said that his work was produced too rapidly to rank him with the great novelists, his books are always interesting, and some of them: *By What Authority,* 1904, *Come Rack, Come Rope,* 1912, and many others, such as *Oddsfish, The King's Achievement,* shed considerable light on the human background of penal days in a way which no mere historian can match. His chief defect lies in character drawing: his male characters are frequently well probed but his women are little more than surface portraits. *Lord of the World,* 1908, is one of his best works. The amazing way in which it sums up our times is a tribute to Benson's analytic powers and the strength of his imagination.

Father Martindale's life of Benson in two volumes, Longmans, 1916, gives an interesting account of his varied career.

CHAPTER VI
THE VICTORY*

II

AN HOUR later the priest toiled back in the hot twilight up the path from the village, followed by half-a-dozen silent men, twenty yards behind, whose curiosity exceeded their credulousness. He had left a few more standing bewildered at the doors of the little mud-houses; and had seen perhaps a hundred families, weighted with domestic articles, pour like a stream down the rocky

*Benson, Robert Hugh, *Lord of the World* (New York: Dodd, Mead and Co., 1940), pp. 342–352.

path that led to Khaifa. He had been cursed by some, even threatened; stared upon by others; mocked by a few. The fanatical said that the Christians had brought God's wrath upon the place, and the darkness upon the sky: the sun was dying, for these hounds were too evil for him to look upon and live. Others again seemed to see nothing remarkable in the state of the weather. . . .

There was no change in that sky from its state an hour before, except that perhaps it had lightened a little as the sun climbed higher behind that impenetrable dusky shroud. Hills, grass, men's faces — all bore to the priest's eyes the look of unreality; they were as things seen in a dream by eyes that roll with sleep through lids weighted with lead. Even to other physical senses that unreality was present; and once more he remembered his dream, thankful that that horror at least was absent. But silence seemed other than a negation of sound, it was a thing in itself, an affirmation, unruffled by the sound of footsteps, the thin barking of dogs, the murmur of voices. It appeared as if the stillness of eternity had descended and embraced the world's activities, and as if that world, in a desperate attempt to assert its own reality, was braced in a set, motionless, noiseless, breathless effort to hold itself in being. What Silvester has said just now was beginning to be true of this man also. The touch of the powdery soil and the warm pebbles beneath the priest's bare feet seemed something apart from the consciousness that usually regards the things of sense as more real and more intimate than the things of spirit. Matter still had a reality, still occupied space, but it was of a subjective nature, the result of internal rather than external powers. He appeared to himself already to be scarcely more than a soul, intent and steady, united by a thread only to the body and the world with which he was yet in relations. He knew that the appalling heat was there; once even, before his eyes a patch of beaten ground cracked and lisped as water that touches hot iron, as he trod upon it. He could feel the heat upon his forehead and hands, his whole body was swathed and soaked in it; yet he regarded it as from an outside standpoint,

as a man with neuritis perceives that the pain is no longer in his hand but in the pillow which supports it. So, too, with what his eyes looked upon and his ears heard; so, too, with that faint bitter taste that lay upon his lips and nostrils. There was no longer in him fear or even hope — he regarded himself, the world, and even the enshrouding and awful Presence of spirit as facts with which he had but little to do. He was scarcely even interested; still less was he distressed. There was Thabor before him — at least what once had been Thabor, now it was no more than a huge and dusky dome-shape which impressed itself upon his retina and informed his passive brain of its existence and outline, though that existence seemed no better than that of a dissolving phantom.

It seemed then almost natural — or at least as natural as all else — as he came in through the passage and opened the chapel-door, to see that the floor was crowded with prostrate motionless figures. There they lay, all alike in the white burnous which he had given out last night; and, with forehead on arms, as during the singing of the Litany of the Saints at an ordination, lay the figure he knew best and loved more than all the world, the shoulders and white hair at a slight elevation upon the single altar step. Above the plain altar itself burned the six tall candles; and in the midst, on the mean little throne, stood the white-metal monstrance, with its White Centre. . . .

Then he, too, dropped, and lay as he was. . . .

He did not know how long it was before the circling observant consciousness, the flow of slow images, the vibration of particular thoughts, ceased and stilled as a pool rocks quietly to peace after the dropped stone has long lain still. But it came at last — that superb tranquillity, possible only when the senses are physically awake, with which God, perhaps once in a lifetime, rewards the aspiring trustful soul — that point of complete rest in the heart of the Fount of all existence with which one day He will reward eternally the spirits of His children. There was no thought in him of articulating this experience, of analysing its elements, or fingering this or that strain of ecstatic joy. The time for self-regarding was passed. It was enough that the experience was there, although he was not even self-reflective enough to tell himself so. He had passed from that circle whence the soul looks within, from that circle, too, whence it looks upon objective glory, to that very centre where it reposes — and the first sign to him that time had passed was the murmur of words, heard distinctly and understood, although with that apartness with which a drowsy man perceives a message from without — heard as through a veil through which nothing but thinnest essence could transpire.

Spiritus Domini replevit orbem terrarum. . . . The Spirit of the Lord hath fulfilled all things, alleluia: and that which contains all things hath knowledge of the voice, alleluia, alleluia, alleluia.

Exsurgat Deus (and the voice rose ever so slightly). *"Let God arise and let His enemies be scattered; and let them who hate Him flee before His face."*

Gloria Patri. . . .

Then he raised his heavy head; and a phantom figure stood there in red vestments, seeming to float rather than to stand, with thin hands outstretched, and white cap on white hair seen in the gleam of the steady candle-flames; another, also in white, kneeled on the step. . . .

Kyrie eleison . . . Gloria in excelsis Deo . . . those things passed like a shadow-show, with movements and rustlings, but he perceived rather the light which cast them. He heard *Deus qui in hodierna die . . .* but his passive mind gave no pulse of reflex action, no stir of understanding until these words. *Cum complerentur dies Pentecostes. . . .*

"When the day of Pentecost was fully come, all the disciples were with one accord in the same place; and there came from heaven suddenly a sound, as of a mighty wind approaching, and it filled the house where they were sitting. . . ."

Then he remembered and understood. . . . It was Pentecost then! And with memory a shred of reflection came back. Where then was the wind, and the flame, and the earth-quake, and the secret voice? Yet the world was silent, rigid in its last effort at self-assertion: there was no tremor to show that God remembered; no actual point of light, yet, breaking the appalling vault of gloom that lay over sea and land to reveal that He burned there in eternity, transcendent and dominant; not even a voice; and at that he understood yet more. He perceived that that world, whose monstrous parody his sleep had presented to him in the night, was other than that he had feared it to be; it was sweet, not terrible; friendly, not hostile; clear, not night. . . . He dropped his head again upon his hands, at once ashamed and content; and again he sank down to depths of glimmering inner peace. . . .

Not again, for a while, did he perceive what he did or thought, or what passed there, five yards away on the low step. Once only a ripple passed across that sea of glass, a ripple of fire and sound like a rising star that flicks a line of light across a sleeping lake, like a thin thread of vibration streaming from a quivering string across the stillness of a deep night — and he perceived for an instant as in a formless mirror that a lower nature was struck into existence and into union with the Divine nature at the same moment. . . . And then no more again but the great encompassing hush, the sense of the innermost heart of reality, till he found himself kneeling at the rail, and knew that That which alone truly existed on earth approached him with the swiftness of thought and the ardour of Divine Love. . . .

Then, as the mass ended, and he raised his passive happy soul to receive the last gift of God, there was a cry, a sudden clamour in the passage, and a man stood in the doorway, gabbling Arabic.

III

Yet even at that sound and sight his soul scarcely tightened the languid threads that united it through every fibre of his body with the world of sense. He saw and heard the tumult in the passage, frantic eyes and mouths crying aloud, and, in strange contrast, the pale ecstatic faces of those princes who turned and looked; even within the tranquil presence-chamber of the spirit where two beings, Incarnate God and all but Discarnate Man, were locked in embrace, a certain mental process went on. Yet all was still as apart from him as a lighted stage and its drama from a self-contained spectator. In the material world, now as attenuated as a mirage, events were at hand; but to his soul, balanced now on reality and awake to facts, these things were but a spectacle. . . .

He turned to the altar again, and there, as he had known it would be, in the midst of clear light, all was at peace: the celebrant, seen as through molten glass, adored as He murmured the mystery of the Word-made-Flesh, and once more passing to the centre, sank upon His knees.

Again the priest understood; for thought was no longer the process of mind, rather it was the glance of a spirit. He knew all now; and by an inevitable impulse, his throat began to sing aloud words that, as he sang, opened for the first time as flowers telling their secret to the sun.

> O Salutaris Hostia
> Qui coeli pandis ostium. . . .

They were all singing now; even the Mohammedan catechumen who had burst in a moment ago sang with the rest, his lean head thrust out and his arms tight across his breast; the tiny chapel rang with the forty voices, and the vast world thrilled to hear it. . . .

Still singing, the priest saw the veil laid as by a phantom upon the Pontiff's shoulders; there was a movement, a surge of figures — shadows only in the midst of substance,

> Uni Trinoque Domino. . . .

— and the Pope stood erect, Himself a pallor in the heart of light, with spectral folds of silk dripping from His shoulders, His hands swathed in them, and His down-bent head hidden by the silver-rayed monstrance and That which it bore. . . .

> Qui vitam sine termino
> Nobis donet in patria. . . .

They were moving now, and the world of life swung with them; of so much was he aware. He was out in the passage, among the white, frenzied faces that with bared teeth stared up at that sight, silenced at last by the thunder of *Pange Lingua,* and the radiance of those who passed out to eternal life. . . . At the corner he turned for an instant to see the six pale flames move along a dozen yards behind, as spear-heads about a King, and in the midst the silver rays and the White Heart of God. . . . Then he was out, and the battle lay in array. . . .

That sky on which he had looked an hour ago had passed from darkness charged with light to light overlaid with darkness — from glimmering night to Wrathful Day — and that light was red. . . .

From behind Thabor on the left to Carmel on the far right, above the hills twenty miles away rested an enormous vault of colour; here were no gradations from zenith to horizon; all was the one deep smoulder of crimson as of the glow of iron. It was such a colour as men have seen at sunsets after rain, while the clouds, more translucent each instant, transmit the glory they cannot contain. Here, too, was the sun, pale as the Host, set like a fragile wafer above the Mount of Transfiguration, and there, far down in the west where men had once cried upon Baal in vain, hung the sickle of the white moon. Yet all was no more than stained light that lies broken across carven work of stone. . . .

> In suprema nocte coena,

sang the myriad voices,

> Recumbens cum fratribus
> Observata lege plena
> Cibis in legalibus
> Cibum turbae duodenae
> Se dat suis manibus. . . .

He saw, too, poised as motes in light, that ring of strange fish-creatures, white as milk, except where the angry glory turned their backs to flame, white-winged like floating moths, from the tiny shape far to the south to the monster at hand scarcely five hundred yards away; and even as he looked, singing as he looked, he understood that the circle was nearer, and perceived that these as yet knew nothing. . . .

> *Verbum caro, panem verum*
> *Verbo carnem efficit.* . . .

They were nearer still, until now even at his feet there slid along the ground the shadow of a monstrous bird, pale and undefined, as between the wan sun and himself moved out the vast shape that a moment ago hung above the Hill. . . . Then again it backed across and waited. . . .

> *Et si sensus deficit*
> *Ad formandum cor sincerum*
> *Sola fides sufficit.* . . .

He had halted and turned, going in the midst of his fellows, hearing, he thought, the thrill of harping and the throb of heavenly drums; and, across the space, moved now the six flames, steady as if cut of steel in that stupendous poise of heaven and earth; and in their centre the silver-rayed glory and the Whiteness of God made Man. . . .

Then, with a roar, came the thunder again, pealing in circle beyond circle of those tremendous Presences — Thrones and Powers — who, themselves to the world as substance to shadow, are but shadows again beneath the apex and within the ring of Absolute Deity. . . . The thunder broke loose, shaking the earth that now cringed on the quivering edge of dissolution. . . .

> *Tantum ergo sacramentum*
> *Veneremur cernui*
> *Et antiquum documentum*
> *Novo cedat ritui.* . . .

Ah! yes; it was He for Whom God waited now — He who far up beneath that trembling shadow of a dome, itself but the piteous core of unimagined splendour, came in His swift chariot, blind to all save that on which He had fixed His eyes so long, unaware that His world corrupted about Him, His shadow moving like a pale cloud across the ghostly plain where Israel had fought and Sennacherib boasted — that plain lighted now with a yet deeper glow, as heaven, kindling to glory beyond glory of yet fiercer spiritual flame, still restrained the power knit at last to the relief of final revelation, and for the last time the voices sang. . . .

> *Praestet fides supplementum*
> *Sensuum defectui.* . . .

He was coming now, swifter than ever, the heir of temporal ages and the Exile of eternity, the final piteous Prince of rebels, the creature against God, blinder than the sun which paled and the earth that shook; and, as He came, passing even then through the last material stage to the thinness of a spirit-fabric, the floating circle swirled behind Him, tossing like phantom birds in the wake of a phantom ship. . . . He was coming, and the earth, rent once again in its allegiance, shrank and reeled in the agony of divided homage. . . .

He was coming — and already the shadow swept off the plain and vanished, and the pale netted wings were rising to the check; and the great bell clanged, and the long sweet chord rang out — not more than whispers heard across the pealing storm of everlasting praise. . . .

> *Genitori genitoque*
> *Laus et jubilatio*
> *Salus honor virtus quoque*
> *Sit et benedictio*
> *Procedenti ab utroque*
> *Compar sit laudatio.* . . .

and once more

> PROCEDENTI AB UTROQUE
> COMPAR SIT LAUDATIO. . . .

Then this world passed, and the glory of it.

WILFRID WARD
(1856–1916)

THE eminent biographer of Newman, Wilfrid Ward, was born at Hempstead, England, 1856. He got his education at Ushaw, Rome, and London University. In 1890 he became professor of Philosophy at Ushaw and was made editor of the *Dublin Review* in 1906. In 1896 Wilfrid Ward founded the Synthetic Society for the discussion of the philosophical bases for Christian belief. Until his death, 1916, Ward was active in the intellectual concerns of the Church. He was one of the most significant laymen of his time and his wide service to the Catholic cause is only now becoming fully apparent.

Ward's life of *Cardinal Newman* and the *Life and Times of Cardinal Wiseman* still rank at his best works. His most interesting and fascinating writing, however, is to be found in his *Journals,* edited by his daughter Maisie Ward.

REMINISCENCES OF CHILDHOOD*
Childhood, 1856–1867

THE Oxford movement brought William George Ward into the Catholic Church, included an energetic attempt at reviving the Christian life of an exclusive and devoted form which almost recalled the days of Apostolic Christianity. My father's tendency to do all he did with intense thoroughness led him for many years, including those of my childhood, to carry this attempt very far. And some of the results are worth recording as contributions to the experimental psychology of religion.

People who in childhood are prepared exclusively for another and a better world, and afterwards find that they have to take their place somehow in this world, go through very curious experiences, and learn a good deal at first hand and roughly, which, for those whose education is directly designed for their life on earth, is part of an accepted groove, and as little reflected on as the air they breathe. My three sisters who became nuns and my youngest brother, who is a priest, continued the way of life we had learned as children. To them life was, on the whole, what they had from the first been taught to expect. But it was not so with those who joined neither the priesthood nor the cloister. For them, nothing could be more different than the world of reality from the world of their childish dreams.

My own experience was, in one respect, especially peculiar; for the rigidly exclusive ecclesiastical atmosphere in which my youth was passed was eventually succeeded by habits of frequent intercourse with persons of all shades of religious beliefs. In some cases I was on terms of familiar intimacy with men who were in my childhood very vaguely thought of by me as part of the outside world of darkness and sin. And among my friends who were not Catholics were people whom I learnt to respect and admire as much as any I have known in the whole course of my life, as will appear in the course of this narrative. Yet this fact has never led me to doubt that the Catholic Church is what it claims to be — the true successor to the early Christian Church, preserving Christianity in its purest form. Had the miscellaneous intellectual company of my later life wholly uprooted the beliefs of my early hot-house years, the story would have had little interest. But, in

*Ward, Wilfrid, *Reminiscences of Childhood* (London: Sheed and Ward, Ltd.), Chapter II.

fact, I learnt much from my "enemies" without ceasing to agree in fundamentals with my early friends.

Two eminent men, both eventually Archbishops and Cardinals, overshadowed our youth and joined with my father in making it what it was — Henry Edward Manning, and Herbert Vaughan. One other — Father Frederick Faber who died when I was only seven — had an equally large share in creating the atmosphere in which we lived, and had much influence on the lives of my elder sisters.

As life went on I was thrown into relations, in some cases close ones, with men of widely different religious views — from the agnosticism of Huxley to the High Anglicanism of Dr. Liddon and Dean Church. Even from some of those who stood furthest apart from me in their actual conclusions, I learnt much that helped to determine my way of looking on life. Nor was the result, so far as I can judge, a medley of inconsistent opinions. It rather illustrated to my mind the fact that views are strongly held mainly in virtue of true elements in them, and that error arises from false perspective, or from closing the mind. I felt with my later friends that each side had a good deal to learn from the other; though many in both camps failed to see this. Bigotry and onesidedness were not at all the monopoly of religious obscurantists. The record of influences so various, and of their outcome has, I hope, an interest quite apart from the individual subjected to them. Yet that individual must tell the story as his own.

I was born on January 2, 1856, at the house in Hertfordshire built by Pugin ten years earlier for my father and mother. After joining the Catholic Church in 1845, they had wished to remove from Oxford to the vicinity of some great Catholic College. Cardinal Wiseman suggested St. Edmund's College, at Old Hall Green, near Ware, the lineal sucessor of Douai, where English Catholics had been educated from the reign of Elizabeth onwards; and the College authorities gave the ground on which our house was built. My father had known Pugin at Oxford when he designed the new buildings (never executed) for Balliol. And the great architect was, more-over, associated with St. Edmund's College itself, for which he designed the beautiful chapel which contains what he considered his finest rood screen.

My father had his full share of unworldliness and wholehearted devotion to the interest of religion which Mr. Mozley has described as characteristic of the Oxford Tractarians. He was a poor man when he went to Old Hall, but when he inherited in 1849 a large family property in the Isle of Wight and Hampshire, which included most of the town of Cowes, he had not the slightest desire to take up the position which it offered him. "If there is anyone who can bear wealth it is you," Newman wrote to him; and certainly his worst enemy never accused him of over-valuing the advantages of a rich man. He remained at Old Hall, and through the good offices of Cardinal Wiseman came to an arrangement with the President to give lectures in theology three times a week to the divinity students of the College. This he ever regarded as the happiest time of his life. The work in England fulfilled completely his ideal of life.

The separation from their relations and from old family friends was marked with many of the converts to Catholicism at that time, but I doubt whether it was as complete in any other instance as with my father. I remember his contrasting his own case in that respect with that of his friend, the late Mr. Phillips de Lisle. To de Lisle the life of a country gentlemen was far more congenial, though he carried it on as a Catholic on lines in which religion was far more prominent than with his predecessors. He built a Cistercian Monastery and promoted Catholic interests; but he lived on his estate in Leicestershire, taking his share in county business, and as a natural consequence, most of his family friendships remained unbroken. With my father it was quite otherwise. All his tastes and pursuits were those of a student and a thinker. The life of a country gentleman and all its ideals were positively distasteful to him. And nine years elapsed after he had inherited his property before he attempted to live at Northwood — his place near Cowes. He tried the experiment in 1858 as a matter of duty, and used to ascribe the breakdown of health which sent him back to Old Hall in 1860 largely to the acute *ennui* caused by a mode of life and duties so uncongenial.

In an essay written to prove the freedom of the will by instances bringing into strong relief the possibility of action heroically opposed to one's natural bent, he once gave the following half-conscious description of his own sentiments in regard to the pleasures and duties of a landed proprietor:

"I am a large landed proprietor, and I rejoice in my thereby assured income as a means of securely prosecuting my physical or literary or philosophical studies. Otherwise I am profoundly uninterested in my estate. I cannot distinguish wheat from barley; I am quite indifferent to field sports. I have no value whatever for my social position. I have no tendency whatever towards personal relations with my agricultural dependants. Information reaches me that my agent has been acting with gross injustice to various of my tenants, and is endeavouring to stifle their complaint. What is my spontaneous impulse? Probably to invent some salve for my conscience as regards the tenants, and to plunge myself afresh in my favourite studies. I have no particular affection for my tenants, any more that I have for any other farmers who may happen to live in my neighbourhood, and pursue their (to me utterly unintelligible) avocations. I can easily persuade myself, if I choose, that I may conscientiously ignore the information I have received, and continue without further inquiry to repose trust in my agent. On the other hand, if I am really conscientious, I am able by means of due thought to see clearly where my duty lies. Accordingly I put forth anti-impulsive effort. With sighing and weariness of heart I bid adieu to my studies for the necessary herculean labour; to interview the complaining tenants; to apprehend (1) the meaning and (2) the merits of the accusation they bring, and finally to take such practical steps as I may judge necessary."

Of his character and that of Frederick Oakeley, their common friend, Archbishop Tait wrote, "Two more single-hearted and devoted men, I believe, never lived"; and this singleness of aim was, after 1845, consecrated to the cause of the Catholic Church. The friends I remember staying with us in my childhood at Old Hall were all men who shared my father's religious tastes, and I do not think he kept up relations with any single old friend of his family. Cardinal Wiseman, Bishop Moriarty of Kerry, Henry Edward Manning, Henry Wilberforce, Father Dalgairns, the Count and Countess de Torre Diaz, Cardinal Reisach, Mr. William Palmer, (Lord Selborne's brother) and, again and again, Father (afterwards Cardinal) Herbert Vaughan, are almost the only names I recall of his guests at Old Hall, beyond one or two close relations between the years 1862 and 1866. Even such visits were rare, and only a momentary break in our curious routine of monastic regularity. The details of that routine have perhaps a general interest as a token of the extraordinary change in English family life which the Oxford Movement sometimes brought about — a change (not, indeed, in the view of life, but in the mode of life) comparable to that which took place in the families which were converted to Christianity in the days of the Roman Empire.

Father Herbert Vaughan was an intimate friend and guide to the family. His frequent visits were the great excitement of our early youth. His beautiful face and presence (quite as handsome as that of his later life and yet more refined) made him the object of almost romantic interest. My mother was especially devoted to him. We regarded him as a saint, and watched his every action looking out for signs for our guidance. We used to hear him take the discipline at night in his room, and observed closely his acts of self-denial in the course of the day. It was he mainly who put it into our heads that we were all to be priests and nuns. Every time he visited us he told us of some exciting scheme of his own for the glory of the Church, and we were profoundly interested in his plan of going to America in order to collect money for founding a college for foreign missions. He was to start at the end of 1863, but before he went he brought to fulfillment the consecration of my eldest sister to the religious life. She entered the Dominican convent of St. Dominic at Stone as a girl of sixteen in July, 1863.

Father Vaughan sailed in December for America, and his note to my mother before starting marks, in one very reserved in the expression of his feelings, the character of their friendship and the ideal which possessed us all of working together for the Church:

"It is impossible to say all that is in one's mind at parting — one's only resource is to be silent, and yet one desires to speak and to write some of those words of affection which it is not so easy to utter. It is a great pain to leave you in your many anxieties. . . . But how good is God! He provides for us all, and He leads one in one way and another in another, by various routes, till at last we shall meet in Him and in the embraces of the Sacred Heart. We shall all be apostles together — you by prayer and I by work."

While he was absent my mother constantly talked of him; and the letters he wrote to her describing his romantic adventures in America, his frequent rebuffs and ultimate success, were listened to by the family eagerly.

Cardinal Wiseman visited us more than once during these years at Old Hall, and his great love of children made us quite devoted to him. As I was the second son, he regarded me as the future churchman, and once he put his biretta on my head saying, "You will be a Cardinal." This was long remembered by the family — but I did not play my part, the prophecy remained unfulfilled.

The Cardinal died in 1865. I was a boy of only nine but I remember the sense of tragedy, and the subsequent excitement about the nomination of his successor. My father could think of nothing else — he regarded Manning's appointment as veritably the great hope for the future of the country. No crisis in the political world seemed to him in the least comparable to this in importance. I have already said that we knew through the reflecting medium of a child's mind that controversies were going on between the party of Newman and the party of Manning and

my father. But more than this, we thought of the world that really mattered somewhat as of a great battlefield with two camps — which we always called "the right side" and "the wrong side," the former consisting of all who took my father's general views on matters ecclesiastical, the latter of those who opposed them. The "wrong side" was a mixed multitude representing varied interests. It included Newman, Sir John Simeon, Mr. Oxenham, Sir John Acton and the President and Vice-President of St. Edmund's. These all represented for my father shades of ecclesiastical "liberalism." Eventually I learnt that the so-called "liberalism" of the authorities at St. Edmund's had only consisted in opposition of the policy of my father and Herbert Vaughan. The latter, when he became Vice-President, seconded by my father as professor of Dogmatic Theology, made a party among the divinity students of zealous young men who became Oblates of St. Charles. They adopted many habits from foreign seminaries, and were regarded by their neighbours as indiscreet and priggish and hostile to the President.

But though somewhat vaguely and indiscriminately conceived, these two ecclesiastical parties or armies were very real to us; and the conflicts, successes and defeats of the "right side" were as keenly interesting to us as the communiques from the front during the war. Looking back now I feel the great aptness of Huxley's comparison of my father to Don Quixote — made by Huxley with such insistence on the true spirit of chivalry which he carried into all his work. Nothing could be more simple and noble than the enthusiasms for which he fought as we all felt at the time. The ideas he opposed were definite and his reasoning in their regard very cogent. But the persons he selected as their champions were often I venture to think not at all accurately understood by him. I cannot help now seeing tilting at windmills in some cases where he and we in those days saw battles with the most doughty and dangerous knights errant. The supposed champions of "liberalism" were — except perhaps Sir John Acton — rather playing the part of practical men who tempered ideas by commonsense, than fighting for any ideal cause.

Cardinal Wiseman, much as we loved him, had been in our eyes a weak champion of the "right side." In dark moments it had been feared that he might prove a wobbler, but his puissant Provost, Dr. Manning, had in critical junctures interpreted him for the best before the world, and his reputation for orthodoxy was never destroyed. Still it was whispered that he had a sneaking weakness for Montalembert (who was on the "wrong side"). He had said rather compromising words about Reunion between England and Rome, which, though repented of when Manning had become his prop and adviser in later years, remained a testimony to a certain want of the true militant spirit and of a clear recognition of the division of all things and all men into an ecclesiastical black and white. Now that he was dead it was all-important that Manning should succeed him. Manning and Vaughan were our two ideal leaders of the "right side." They would bring in Roman vestments and cottas; they would make all the clergy like the Oblates; they would make all the old-fashioned priests Roman and zealous — except perhaps a recalcitrant few whom they would excommunicate. On this question of the succession to Wiseman in our eyes depended the whole future of our ecclesiastical world in England, which to us was the whole world. My father was so anxious that he could not sleep at night. We knew that he was writing urgently to the Vatican on the subject; on the other hand it was well known that nearly all the influence of the Bishops and Canons in England was against the appointment of Manning.

While we were eagerly awaiting the issue, my mother received a letter on the subject from Herbert Vaughan which showed that his thoughts were set in the same direction:

"What sad news on reaching Rio! I cannot get out of mind the death of our dear friend, the Cardinal. . . . Of priests he was, as you know, my great friend and supporter. . . . And now another thought presses — who is to sit in his vacant place? Who is to put on his armour? Who is to continue the work of which he laid the foundations? . . . It will require very delicate and prudent fingers to draw the threads which must bring into closer relationship the Church and the State; and, above all, it will need a very clear head and a very unfaltering hand, and the seven gifts of the Holy Ghost, to meet the disloyal Catholic intellect, which seems to be growing with the luxuriance and the strength of a weed. The only man I see is my Father Superior (Dr. Manning). But what are his chances with all the Bishops and the Chapter and Barnabo against his appointment? The Holy Ghost has hard times of it with us English Catholics. I suspect Rome will choose 'Dignus' or 'Dignior'! Expediency and the Devil hate 'Dignissimus.'"

In the event Pope Pius IX, as is well known, took the election into his own hands, and set aside the recommendations of the Chapter. It was a time of immense excitement; my father had despaired of success. In April (1865) he wrote: "I have given up almost all hopes of Manning's appointment. He says himself there is not the remotest chance of it, nor again of Clifford. He says it will lie entirely between Ullathorne and Grant."

When the appointment actually came, Monsignor Talbot telegraphed the news to my father, and I remember his rushing into the drawing-room, telegram in hand, and jumping over a chair which was in his way as he called out: "Henry Edward, by the Grace of God, Archbishop of Westminster." We went down to the room we used as a chapel, and forthwith sang the *Te Deum*. Such is my own memory. But I have clearly forgotten two jumps, for my sister's contemporary entry for May 8th in her diary, in large printed characters, runs as follows: "Dr. Manning, Archbishop of Westminster!!!! Papa jumped three times." Readers of my father's life may remember Lord Blachford's account of my father's first reading of Froude's Remains, "He literally jumped for joy." In a letter written a few weeks later my father adds a postscript in which he reports that the sleeplessness he had been suffering from had ceased, and adds: "*Te Deum laudamus,* good sleep by night, a good Archbishop by day and a good opera in the evening are adequate for human felicity."

My father's feelings towards Manning were a curious mixture. He had a great regard for him as our great ecclesiastical champion of the Holy See in these latter days. The Roman ideal of the priesthood and of community life was carried out at Bayswater. War was declared on many manners and customs of the old-fashioned English priests whom my father regarded as not sufficiently ascetic or Roman. Manning stood for the rigid enforcement of all the customs of Rome. He was the embodiment of the "good cause" on which my father's enthusiasm was always concentrated. Manning stood for the "right side"; Newman for the "wrong side" in the world of ideals which was to my father the real world — the only world that mattered.

But in the life which to other people is real, the everyday life of this actual world, Manning was by no means entirely congenial to him. The Archbishop's visits were not an unmixed pleasure to my father, and in his outspoken moments we learnt this. My father was devoted to French plays, and eventually prided himself on possessing every French play that had ever been written. Manning disapproved of his taste for the theatre and of the French plays inclusively. It was a trifling difference in itself that my father lived with four windows open in his study, while Manning hated fresh air; but this became a serious source of incompatibility in their intercourse. "Directly Manning comes into my study he shuts all my windows. Then he goes to the bookcase and sniffs at my French plays," my father remarked one day when I noticed that he was awaiting the Archbishop's advent with somewhat mixed feelings. Manning used to become very grave when any remark fell from us which recalled the fact that my father had been to the opera on the preceeding night. This, too, my father somewhat resented. He thought it a trifle sanctimonious, and held that Manning took a somewhat puritanical view of the play or opera, partly because he was incapable of appreciating either. "Manning has no ear for music, and would be simply bored at the opera. The play or opera is to me just the kind of pleasure which attending a debate in the House of Commons is to him," my father used to say.

Though he jumped for joy at the news of Manning's appointment as Archbishop, the Archbishop's bodily presence was not so eagerly received. Once when he told Manning that he had been suffering from great depression, Manning, with the utmost kindness, said: "When you feel like that again, come and spend an evening with me at the Archbishop's House." The inextinguishable laughter with which my father repeated the remark told its own story. His real admiration for Manning was always acknowledged; but he had to brace himself for an interview much as he did for other trying efforts which were demanded in the interests of the work he was doing. On the other hand, though he held that Newman was "on the wrong side," he often told me how his heart used to beat when he heard Newman's step on his staircase at Balliol; and he seemed ever to think that Newman understood him and made allowances for his temperament and his weaknesses as no one else did. His love of vivid contrasts made him reflect with a certain satisfaction on this opposition in both cases between public and private feeling.

My own recollections of Manning go back to my very earliest years. I cannot remember the time when he was not a friend of my father's, and a familiar figure to us. We used often to stay with an aunt close to his residence in Bayswater while he was still Provost of Westminster. His majestic presence and intensely spiritual aspect left on us an indelible impression. Our childish absorption in the pageants of the Church no doubt increased our admiration for this singularly picturesque prelate. As Protonotary Apostolic he had the right, on special occasions, to wear the mitre, in which he looked singularly impressive. We used often to lunch with the community of Oblates of St. Charles of which he was the Father Superior. These occasions completely and absolutely realised our ideal of ecclesiastical life. There was a long Latin grace before and after lunch, spiritual reading during the meal; then followed a short visit to the Blessed Sacrament, and afterwards we assembled in the community room and sat in a circle while the Provost talked to us in impressive tones of matters of interest to the Church. All this left a picture never afterwards effaced. The Oblate Fathers in the Roman clerical dress — with cassock, silk stockings, and buckled shoes — signified to us the true Continental ideal of the priesthood; the careless apparel of the English clergy with unbuttoned cassock showing that they wore ordinary black trousers instead of the Roman knee breeches, indicated in our minds a want in this respect. I or one of my brothers often acted as his trainbearer after he was made Archbishop, and we were at close quarters with the great ceremonial functions of which he was the central figure.

Manning's grace and activity were very noteworthy, and he was an athlete in his college days. I remember walking with him — when he was staying with us at Old Hall — and his taking us all by surprise by vaulting over a five-barred gate which was locked; for the purpose, I think, of picking a flower someone wanted.

When Father Vaughan had gone on his long journey to America, Manning became my mother's spiritual director, and over her and his other penitents he had a very great ascendancy. He had made a close study of such French models of direction as St. Francis de Sales and Fénelon.

My father was very often with Manning in the first year of his appointment. My eldest brother was trainbearer at his consecration. We used occasionally to go and see him at York Place, and he used to come to us in London, not to dine but after dinner — for the "I never eat and I never drink" of Disraeli's Cardinal Grandison was almost literally true of Manning's ascetic habit. On March 3, 1866, I read in my sister's diary: "The two boys and Gertrude were confirmed at the Archbishop's private chapel. We had breakfast with him after. He was very kind and gave us rosaries blessed by the Pope. When he and Mama left the room after breakfast Gertrude went round the room

looking at the pictures of the Bishops and giving them all names . . . Father Vaughan returned in the evening with us."

Both Vaughan and Manning were often our companions in the visits we paid in the same year to Holcombe House near Hendon which Father Vaughan had bought with my father's assistance as the scene of his new College for Foreign Missions. In this enterprise we saw Herbert Vaughan in the mood most characteristic of him, full of keen happiness and varied schemes for the future. The Archbishop took great interest in the project. I find a visit recorded in my sister's diary on July 17, 1866, and two days later Archbishop Manning and Cardinal Reisach visited us for two days at Old Hall. An ecclesiastical dignitary was our ideal of all that is most inspiring, this visit of a Cardinal straight from Rome put us all in the seventh heaven. Reisach had come to England to enquire and report to Rome on the question of Catholics going to Oxford. Newman's correspondence showed that he resented this visit to my father the more because he himself was not consulted by Cardinal Reisach. He was taken by Manning only to a strong partisan on his own side.

In setting down some details of the life we led under the influence of the strong religious atmosphere created by my father's tastes and character, I must guard against being misunderstood. Some incidents are, no doubt, in themselves trivial, some even ludicrous; but they were manifestations of an early devotion to a single ideal which left its stamp on us for life. Of the effects, good and bad, on a set of eager and keen children, some of them — like myself — not naturally very deeply religious, of concentrating the tastes and imagination almost entirely on one class of subjects, something shall be said later. Here I have merely to record faithfully our manner of life.

The Catholic Church was our one serious interest; our dreams and our day-dreams were of its Offices and its hierarchy. It was assumed, as a matter of course, that when we grew up the boys of the family would become priests and the girls nuns. This consummation, moreover, was not to be duly delayed, as a dialogue in one of our stories — we were prolific writers — shows. One interlocutor, evidently tainted by the world, maintains that a girl should wait until she is twenty before becoming a nun. The other, filled with the zeal of the Lord, rebukes him. "What! Would you give your best years to the world, and only the poor remainder to Almighty God?"

Our daily routine was largely moulded on what we read in the Lives of the Saints, and in spiritual books. Meditation, Mass at the parish church adjoining St. Edmund's College, and family prayers, had their appointed hours. In Lent and Advent my mother read a Saint's Life aloud for an hour every evening. Each room in the house had a patron saint, whose name was on a scroll outside; and this record of the past still remains, for the names have not been removed since the house was converted into the junior school for St. Edmund's College. The imitative instinct which leads many boys and girls to play at being soldiers, or sailors, or gypsies, or fairies, led us to play at being priests and nuns, and this, most elaborately and systematically. It was so systematic that it was hardly "playing," and had in it an element of seriousness. When I was a boy of six, unable yet to read Latin, I went through every detail of the ritual of Low Mass almost daily in the full vestments of a priest, reciting the verses of the *"Dixit Dominus"* which I knew by heart from often hearing it, for the Introit, Offertory and Communion. The introductory psalm, "Introibo ad altare Dei," as well as the Kyrie, Gloria and Credo, we also knew by heart. The ceremonies of the Canon were gone through, but not the words. The liturgy was quite perfectly performed at St. Edmund's College, and we were fired with the ambition to reproduce ourselves the beautiful scenes we witnessed, and to sing the High Mass in our chapel. On Easter Sunday, 1863, we first made the experiment — so I see from the diary of one of my sisters, which contains a water colour sketch of the ceremony — I was the deacon, being then seven years old; by brother Bernard, who acted as sub-deacon, was six, and my eldest brother, who was the celebrating priest, nine. In the following year we performed on Holy Saturday the long morning Office and Mass. We first attended the whole service at St. Edmund's College, and then we went through it all at home. It was not a case of a child's faint imitation. We read Dale's *Baldeschi* as our guide in matters ceremonial, and omitted no single ceremony from beginning to end. This must have meant quite five hours devoted to ecclesiastical ceremonial. I still know by heart the Gregorian music and words of St. Augustine's beautiful hymn, the "Exultet," which, as deacon, aged eight years, I was taught to sing for the blessing of our toy Paschal candle. My brother Bernard, as sub-deacon, learnt the short Epistle for Easter Day, when he could hardly read at all. My eldest brother alone could read Latin.

There was nothing histrionic in all this, and there was hardly ever an onlooker present. In the child's desire to realize in action what had fired our imagination as spectators — much as children have been known to wish to be highwaymen after reading Dick Turpin. It was all undertaken with the lively encouragement of Father Herbert Vaughan (who was our spiritual director) and of my mother. My father passively acquiesced, but he was always a little afraid of some of our proceedings degenerating into irreverence, and our realism did, on one occasion, go too far for him. We erected a sanctuary lamp, bought a small gilt monstrance, and gave "Benediction." My mother brought to see the celebration the poor women — most of them Irish Catholics — who came to the house every week to receive various helpful gifts. They naturally uttered prayers and beat their breasts at the Benediction which they took to be the real service. This incident was afterwards referred to as rather a joke in my father's presence, but he took it otherwise. Flushing scarlet, he seized his walking-stick, entered the chapel, knocked down the sanctuary lamp and said: "That must never be lighted again, nor the monstrance used." No further word was ever spoken by anyone on the subject; the monstrance was put away in a cupboard, and the lamp was pulled down.

The constant dwelling on Saint's Lives, books of devotion and chapters of ecclesiastical History, inspired us all to much more than liturgical performances. We often denied ourselves favourite wishes or favourite pleasures, and occasionally tried sterner austerities, attempts which were in my own case, however, evanescent. Our thoughts ran on conflicts with the devil, on the drama of the life of the soul, on vows to do heroic deeds for the Church, and on the problems of moral theology. We were ready to fancy ourselves engaged in this life of spiritual adventure and at the age of eight I got into profound depression from a temptation I believed myself to experience to make not an heroic vow but an impossible one. I had been told that to vow an impossibility was mortally sinful because the vow could not be executed. A voice whispered during my prayers urging me to make such a perverse vow, which took the concrete form of a vow to jump over the moon! After a struggle with the tempter I yielded, and made the vow, and then could not rest until I had been to confession. The priest to whom I confessed was puzzled at being told that I had vowed to do something impossible, and asked if I had vowed to do something very good. I said "No." "Bad?" he asked. "No, something indifferent," I replied.

The two direct inspirers of our religious endeavours were (as I have said) my mother and her director, Father Herbert Vaughan, to whom she was devoted. My father was in early years a dim figure in the background of whom we were in great awe, but whom we seldom saw. There is no doubt that my mother instilled into us the strictest conscientiousness from the dawn of reason, and if any of us did not adequately realize all her hopes it was our own fault. The teaching was all on the pattern of the conventual life. Her imagination ran very much on the founders of religious orders, and I remember seeing her in the habit of the Third Order of St. Francis of which she was a member. I think she regarded herself as the Abbess or Prioress of the Old Hall Community.

My mother's imagination dwelt much on the history of the Church, and anything jarring with her views of the persons and places which specially interested her in this connexion was keenly resented by her. There was a statue of St. Thomas of Canterbury in the ante-chapel at St. Edmund's which had a beard. This angered her extremely, and she pointed out to the President of the College that authentic records showed that the saint was shaven. Going one day to the ante-chapel, to my amazement, I found the statue without a beard and with a slightly prominent chin, closely resembling that of Father Herbert Vaughan. I could hardly believe my eyes, and almost suspected a miracle. But I afterwards learnt that the President had consented to my mother doing as she pleased with the statue provided it was dealt with by a skilful hand, and a competent sculptor had been given *carte blanche* and had effected the desired change.

On another occasion, somewhat later, I remember her being very much depressed for days together at some history she was reading of the reign of Richard II. She said she considered that his position had been most difficult; and that, if his salvation had been in danger, it was largely owing to circumstances, and not to his own fault. A day or two later she told us, with an appearance of relief, that she had sent a pound to an Oblate Father, to say four Masses for the repose of the soul of the dead King.

While the exclusively unworldly ideals of the heads of the family issued in the quasi-monastic life which I have described, and made our deepest interest purely ecclesiastical, I am bound to say that human nature did at times assert itself in other directions. In holiday seasons the novels of Sir Walter Scott were read aloud nightly, and we used to dress up as Front de Boeuf or the Black Knight or Brian du Bois Guilbert and fight with wooden broadswords like other children. And our varied store of paper dolls representing fairies and genii as well as knights and squires, told of an imagination which roamed beyond the ecclesiastical boundaries.

The imitative faculty of which we, like many other children, had a large share, took a somewhat different direction, at the end of 1866 — from which date onwards our life was, I think, decidedly less monastic than it had been. Inspired by the fact that my father had consented at Archbishop Manning's desire to edit *The Dublin Review,* we started a review of our own which we called *The Old Hall Gazette,* which lasted for two years. I still have all the numbers, beginning in January, 1867, and ending in December, 1868. We attempted at first to use a lithograph press which, however, did not prove a success, and therefore we had the great labour of transcribing the twelve copies which were circulated among our subscribers. I quote a few specimens of the articles and poems written by us as children, as instances of the manner in which the strong views of my father and mother were refracted in the childish mind.

Father Ignatius Dudley Ryder, of the Oratory, published in 1867 an attack on my father's stringent views on Papal Infallibility. He wittily characterized the ascription of infallibility to so many of the Pope's utterances as encumbering him with a gift which was inconvenient though very wonderful — "like Midas's touch of gold." His private letters were so humorous and so delightful that my father conceived a great liking for him though, personally, he had only known him slightly in his boyhood. The *Old Hall Gazette* reflected, as in duty bound, the combination of repudiation of his views, with great hopes for the future of so pleasant a young man. All that was evil in his opinions was referred by us to a higher source — Newman himself — whom, at that time, we regarded as dangerous from his kindness to Sir John Acton and Mr. Simpson, the conductors of that very liberal periodical the *Home and Foreign Review.* A marvellous travesty of Father Ryder's views is succeeded in the leading article for March, 1868 (the eldest of the editors being then seventeen), by the following words:

"We need not add that so loyally disposed a Catholic as Father Ryder really is, in spite of the extraordinary lukewarm jumble of theories he has formed for himself, would never for a moment put the matter before himself in so disrespectful a light. We only wish that his doctrinal position was on as high a level as his spiritual one, and indeed we by no means despair of seeing the day

when so promising a mind will perceive its errors, and work as vigorously in God's cause as hitherto it has done, unconsciously against it. But that will not be, we fear, till the aged though majestic tree falls, which, while beautiful and venerable to look on, effectually checks the growth of the young and hopeful grass beneath its unhealthy shade."

This was not the only allusion to Dr. Newman in our pages, which reflected the state of the ecclesiastical atmosphere at that time. A writer in the Chronicle of October, 1867, had reminded Englishmen of the passage in Newman's "Letter to Pusey" in which he denies that the school of Manning and Ward are authoritative exponents of Catholicism. On this the *Old Hall Gazette* comments with some acrimony as follows:

"Why the opinion of a private priest like Dr. Newman concerning who are and who are not exponents of Catholicism should go for more than the Archbishop's known convictions, is hard to say, except that people who are incapable of forming solid judgments themselves must take some infallible guide to direct the current of their thoughts, and a person of unusual genius like Dr. Newman who has, besides, rendered such services to Catholicism, such a gifted individual appears generally to be preferred even to the visible Head of the Church as a mould by which to form opinions."

The view of life which we caught from my father, and which underlay the mode of living which I have above described, will be most convincingly illustrated by an article in the *Old Hall Gazette* written by one of my sisters at the age of fifteen, and almost alarmingly serious in its tone. The essay concerned a subject much in our minds (as we meant to be priests and nuns) — the religious vocation; and its main point was that a really Christian life, even for the laity, is necessarily a hard and elevated one, and that many criticisms on the conventual life really express only the natural human disinclination for the life of self-denial which a Christian is inevitably called upon to undertake. That hard life is made easier and not more difficult by conventual discipline; but "to make virtue easy is just the opposite of making life easy."

"A vocation for the world then does not mean that such and such souls have a Divine patent for getting to Heaven amid pleasure and comfort without any of the privations of the cloister. A vocation for the world does not mean that some souls may go out into society so continually as to diminish frightfully the time they are able to devote to God, to spend lavish sums on dress, jewels, furniture, etc., and to waste time *ad libitum*. This is what a vocation for the world means; it means that some souls would be unable without spiritual detriment instead of advancement to undergo the labours, restraints, solitude, and privations of the religious life. Their spirits are not strong enough to stand these things without becoming sad, discouraged, perhaps scrupulous; and a sad religious is one without a vocation. Consequently, God in His mercy arranged for them a mode of life more suited to their temperament. They are allowed to retain their worldly possessions, but that does not mean that they may become inordinately wedded and attached to them. They are allowed to possess the paraphernalia necessary to their station in life, but that does not mean that they may waste on uselessly expensive baubles, and load themselves with unnecessary splendour. They are allowed to remain free from the restraints of the religious rule, but a well-regulated Christian conscience is no easy matter. Do what you will, if you wish to serve God, you *must* have a hard life of it, and happy are you if God has given you that vocation by which you may escape from the temptations of the external world — the religious vocation."

In 1866 my sister Agnes followed her elder sister's example and became a Benedictine nun at Oulton. We thought her rather degenerate for she was quite old — eighteen years old — when she went. Her sister had gone at sixteen.

We used in these years to pay occasional visits to the Isle of Wight which was then somewhat primitive. We stayed for some weeks in 1866 at the hotel built on my father's property in Alum Bay, and depended, I remember, for our meat supply almost entirely on the rabbits the waiter shot on the warren. We used to drive over to see my father's aunts at West Hill, Cowes, which fifty years ago was a great centre in that part of the Island. My father was always on affectionate terms with his aunts, and it was through our visits to West Hill that, as children, we became aware of the existence of the rest of the family. The Miss Wards in some sense acted as my father's deputies at Cowes, keeping open house and taking a lively interest in the welfare of the town which might otherwise have suffered considerably from the fact that my father was an absentee. My father's eldest aunt, Miss Emma Ward, was a very capable woman with a great deal of character, well known in Cowes, having kept house for her father at Northwood from her mother's death in 1813, until his death in 1829. The late Queen Victoria paid a tribute to her generous charities and her personal popularity in the Court Circular when she died in 1880. At West Hill we encountered a whole tribe of cousins, and cousins' cousins — Beckfords, Farquharsons, Sloanes, Stanleys, Hankeys, Wynyards, Seymours, Durells, and Wards.

While staying at Freshwater about the year 1866 we made the acquaintance of Mrs. Cameron, whose name we did not then know. We were playing on "the Terrace," near Freshwater Bay, and a lady with fighting cocks in her hands, apparelled in a strange dress of various colours, came up and asked, "Are you the children of Squire Ward?" and then asked us to come in to tea. I remember being quite unable to understand the merriment I created at tea by saying, "I want to butter my bread with some jam." "The lady of the fighting cocks" as we called her, often asked us into her house, but I did not learn who she was until we lived in Freshwater some years later when we became great friends.

These sallies into the outer world meant only six weeks of holiday from Old Hall with its potent religious atmosphere. My own theological standpoint was eventually far removed from the early one which I learned from my father; but all these early habits and enthusiasms stamped indelibly on us the main ideals of a Catholic. And this was undoubtedly a personal possession of great value. Even apart from its importance from a Catholic standpoint it helped immensely towards unity of view and — strange as some may think it — it eventually told in my own case for large-mindedness. Anxiety about the fundamentals of faith leads some persons to be nervous of relinquishing any

beliefs hitherto entertained — lest it may prove the first step towards a more general denial. When one has no doubt that in fundamentals one is right and secure, one shrinks the less from complete candour. One does not tremble lest to face a new fact may mean to dissolve one's faith. This feeling of perfect security was engendered by the nature of our life as children. Thus in a sense the very narrowness of my early training told for breadth in the long run — because the narrowness meant the exclusiveness which gives depth and stability to belief.

CARDINAL GASQUET
(1846–1929)

FRANCIS AIDAN CARDINAL GASQUET was born in London, October 5, 1846. He was educated at Downside College by the Benedictines. He later joined the Order and became abbot of Downside. His historical researches and scholarly life brought him to the notice of the Roman Curia. He was created cardinal in 1914 and in 1918 became prefect of the Vatican

Archives. He carried out extensive research in English history from medieval times to the Reformation. He died in Rome April 5, 1929.

Gasquet's best work is *The Eve of the Reformation,* one of his volumes of English Catholic History. This work does much to show that Catholic England was not only "merrie" but vigorously pious.

CHAPTER X

PARISH LIFE IN CATHOLIC ENGLAND*

A VENETIAN traveller at the beginning of the sixteenth century bears witness to the influence of religion upon the English people of that time. His opinion is all the more valuable, inasmuch as he appeals to the experience of his master, who was also the companion of his travels, to confirm his own impressions, and as he was fully alive to the weak points in the English character, of which he thus records his opinion: "The English are great lovers of themselves and of everything belonging to them; they think

that there are no other men but themselves and no other world but England. Whenever they see a handsome foreigner they say that 'he looks like an Englishman,' or that 'it is a great pity that he should not be an Englishman,' and when they partake of any delicacy with a foreigner they ask him whether such a thing is made in his country." In regard to the religious practices of the people, this intelligent foreigner says, "They all attend Mass every day, and say many *Paternosters* in public. The women carry long rosaries in their hands, and any who can read take the Office of Our Lady with them, and with some companion recite it in Church

---

*Gasquet, Francis Aidan, D.D., O.S.B., *The Eve of the Reformation* (New York: G. P. Putnam's Sons, 1901), pp. 285–293.

verse by verse, in a low voice, after the manner of churchmen. On Sundays they always hear Mass in their parish church and give liberal alms, because they may not offer less than a piece of money of which fourteen are equivalent to a golden ducat. Neither do they omit any form incumbent on good Christians."

In these days perhaps the suggestion that the English people commonly in the early sixteenth century were present daily at morning Mass is likely to be received with caution, and classed among the strange tales proverbially told by travellers, then as now. It is, however, confirmed by another Venetian who visited England, some few years later, and who asserts that every morning "at daybreak he went to Mass arm-in-arm with some English nobleman or other." And, indeed, the same desire of the people to be present daily at the Sacrifice of the Mass is attested by Archbishop Cranmer when, after the change had come, he holds up to ridicule the traditional observances previously in vogue. What he specially objected to was the common practice of those who run, as he says, "from altar to altar, and from sacring, as they call it, to sacring, peeping, tooting and gazing at that thing which the priest held up in his hands . . . and saying, 'this day have I seen my Maker,' and 'I cannot be quiet except I see my Maker once a day.'"

If there were no other evidence of the affection of the English people on the eve of the Reformation for their religion, that of the stone walls of the churches would be sufficient to prove the sincerity of their love. In the whole history of English architecture nothing is more remarkable than the activity in church building manifested during the later half of the fifteenth and the early part of the sixteenth century. From one end of England to the other in the Church walls are to be seen the evidences of thought and skill, labour and wealth, spent freely upon the sacred buildings during the period when it might not unnaturally have been thought that the civil dissensions of the Wars of the Roses, and the consequent destruction of life and property, would have been fatal to enterprise in the field of church building and

church decoration and enrichment. It is not in any way an exaggeration to say that wellnigh every village church in England can show signs of this marvellous activity, whilst in many cases there is unmistakeable evidence of personal care and thought in the smallest details.

No less remarkable than the extent of this movement is the source from which the money necessary for all the work upon the cathedrals and parish churches of the country came. In previous centuries, to a great extent churches and monastic buildings owed their existence and embellishment mainly to the individual enterprise of the powerful nobles or rich ecclesiastics; but from the middle of the fifteenth century the numerous, and in many cases, even vast operations, undertaken in regard to ecclesiastical buildings and ornamentation, were the work of the people at large, and were mainly directed by their chosen representatives. At the close of the fifteenth century, church work was in every sense of the word a popular work, and the wills, inventories, and churchwardens' accounts prove beyond question that the people generally contributed generously according to their means, and that theirs was the initiative, and theirs the energetic administration by which the whole was accomplished. Gifts of money and valuables, bequests of all kinds, systematic collections by parish officials, or by directors of guilds, often extending over considerable periods, and the proceeds of parish plays and parish feasts, were the ordinary means by which the sums necessary to carry out these works of building and embellishment were provided. Those who had no money to give brought articles of jewelry, such as rings, brooches, buckles, and the like, or articles of dress or of domestic utility, to be converted into vestments, banners, and altar hangings to adorn the images and shrines, to make the sacred vessels of God's house, or to be sold for like purposes. For the same end, and to secure the perpetuity of lamps before the Blessed Sacrament, or lights before the altars of saints, people gave houses and lands into the care of the parish officials, or made over to them cattle and sheep to be held in trust, which, when let out at a rent, formed a permanent endowment for the furtherence of these sacred purposes.

Undoubtedly, the period with which we are concerned was not merely an age of building, but an age of decoration, and of decoration which may almost be described as "lavish." The very architecture of the time is proof of the wealth of ornament with which men sought to give expression to their enthusiastic love of the Houses of God, which they had come to regard as the centre of their social no less than of their religious life. Flowing lines in tracery and arch moulding gave place to straight lines, groined roofs were enriched by extra ribs, and panels of elaborate work covered the plain surfaces of former times; the very key-stones of the vaulting became pendants, and the springers branched out like palm trees, forming that rich and entirely English variety of groin called "fantracery," such as we see at Sherborne, Eton, King's College, Cambridge, and Henry VII's Chapel at Westminster. "In other respects," says a modern writer, "the architects of the fifteenth century were very successful. Few things can be seen more beautiful than the steeples of Gloucester Cathedral and St. Mary's, Taunton. The open roofs, as for example, that of St. Peter Mancroft, Norwich, are superb, and finally they have left us a large number of enormous parish churches all over the country, full of interesting furniture and decoration."

The fact is, that this was the last expression of Gothic as a living art. The builders and beautifiers of the English churches on the eve of the religious changes spoke still a living language, and their works still tell us of the fulness of the hearts which planned and executed such works. It is somewhat difficult for us to understand this, when living in an age of imitation, and at a time when architecture has no longer a language of its own. "Imitation," writes Mr. Ferguson, "is in fact all we aim at in the architectural art of the present day. We entrust its exercise to a specially educated class, most learned in the details of the style they are called upon to work in, and they produce buildings which delight the scholars and archaeologists of the day, but which the less educated classes neither understand nor appreciate, and which will lose their significance the moment the fashion which produced them has passed away.

"The difference between this artificial state of things and the practice of a true style will not be difficult to understand. When, for instance, Gothic was a living art in England, men expressed themselves in it as in any other part of the vernacular. Whatever was done was a part of the usual, ordinary every-day life, and men had no more difficulty in understanding what others were doing than in comprehending what they were saying. A mason did not require to be a learned man to chisel what he had carved ever since he was a boy, and what alone he had seen being done during his lifetime, and he adapted new forms just in the same manner and as naturally as men adapt new modes of expression in language as they happen to be introduced, without even remarking it. At that time any educated man could design in Gothic Art, just as any man who can read and write can now compose and give utterance to any poetry or prose that may be in him.

"Where art is a true art, it is naturally practised and as easily understood as a vernacular literature of which, indeed, it is an essential and most expressive part, and so it was in Greece and Rome, and so, too, in the Middle Ages. But with us it is little more than a dead corpse, galvanised into spasmodic life by a few selected practitioners for the amusement and delight of a small section of the specially educated classes. It expresses truthfully neither our wants nor our feelings, and we ought not to be surprised how very unsatisfactory every modern building really is, even when executed by the most talented architects as compared with the productions of our village mason or parish priest at an age when men sought only to express clearly what they felt strongly, and sought to do it only in their natural mother tongue, untrammelled by the fetters of a dead or familiar foreign form of speech."

To any one who will examine the churchwardens' accounts of the period previous to the religious changes, the truth of the above quotation will clearly appear. Then, if ever, ecclesiastical art and architecture was the living expression of popular feeling and popular love of religion, and the wholesale destruction of ancient architectural monuments throughout the land, the pulling down of rood and screen and image, the casting down of monuments sacred to the memory of the best and holiest and most venerated names in the long roll of English men of honour, the breaking up of stone-work and metal work upon which the marks of the chisel of the mason and graver were yet fresh, the whitewash daubed over paintings which had helped to make the parish churches objects of beauty and interest to the people, the ruthless smashing of the pictured window lights, and the pillage of the sacred vessels and vestments and hangings, which the people and their fathers had loved to provide for God's service — all this and much more of the same kind, the perhaps inevitable accompaniments of the religious change, was nothing less to the people than proscription by authority of the national language of art and architecture, such as they had hitherto understood it. And never probably had the language been more truly the language of the people at large. For reasons just assigned, the work of church building and church decoration, and the provision of vestments and plate, the care of the fabric and the very details of things necessary for the church services, were in the hands of the people. The period in question had given rise to the great middle class, and here, as in Germany, the burgher folk, the merchants and traders, began literally to lavish their gifts in adornment of their parish churches, and to vie one with another in the profusion of their generosity.

It is somewhat difficult for us, as we look upon the generally bare and unfurnished churches that have been left to us as monuments of the past about which we are concerned, to realise what they must have been before what a modern writer has fitly called "the great pillage" commenced. All, from the great minsters and cathedral churches down to the poorest little village sanctuary, were in those days simply overflowing with wealth and objects of beauty which loving hands had gathered together to adorn God's house, and to make it the best and brightest spot in their little world, and so far as their means would allow, the very pride of their hearts. This is no fancy picture. The inventories of English churches in this period when compared, say, with those of Italy, reveal the fact that the former were in every way incomparably better burnished than the latter. The Venetian traveller in England in 1500 was impressed by this very thing during his journeyings throughout the country. He notes and comments upon the great sums of money regularly given to the church as a matter of course by Englishmen of all sorts. Then after speaking of the important wealth of the country as evidenced by the silver plate possessed by all but the poorest in the land, he continues:

"But above all are their riches displayed in the church treasures, for there is not a parish church in the kingdom so mean as not to possess crucifixes, candlesticks, censers, patens and cups of silver, nor is there a convent of mendicant friars so poor as not to have all these same articles in silver, besides many other ornaments worthy of a cathedral church in the same metal. Your magnificence may therefore imagine what the decorations of these enormously rich Benedictine, Carthusian, and Cistercian monasteries must be . . . . I have been informed that amongst other things many of these monasteries possess unicorns' horns of an extraordinary size. I have also been told that they have some splendid tombs of English saints, such as St. Oswald, St. Edmund, and St. Edward, all kings and martyrs. I saw, one day being with your magnificence, at Westminster, a place out of London, the tomb of that saint, King Edward the Confessor, in the Church of the foresaid place, Westminster; and indeed, neither St. Martin of Tours, a church in France, which I have heard is one of the richest in existence, nor anything else that I have ever seen, can be put into comparison with it. The magnificence of the tomb of St. Thomas The Martyr, Archbishop of Canterbury, surpasses all belief."

Our present concern, however, is not with the greater churches of the kingdom, but with the parish churches which were scattered in such profusion all over the country. An examination of such parochial accounts as are still preserved affords an insight into the working of the parish, and evidences the care taken by the people to maintain and increase the treasures of their churches. What is most remarkable about the accounts that remain, which are, of course, but the scanty survivals from the wreck, is their consistent tenor. They one and all tell the same story of general and intelligent interest taken by the people as a whole in the beautifying and supporting of their parish churches. In a very real sense, that seems strange to us now, it was their church; their life centred in it, and they were intimately concerned in its working and management. The articles of furniture and plate, the vestments and hangings, had a well-known history, and were regarded as — what in truth they were — the common property of every soul in the particular village or district. Such accounts as we are referring to prove that specific gifts and contributions continued to flow in an ample stream to the churches from men and women of every sort and condition up to the very eve of the great religious changes.

PART

I

THE ENGLISH REVIVAL

Section 2 — The Age of Belloc

HILAIRE BELLOC

(1870–   )

PROBABLY the most versatile of all contemporary writers of English, Joseph Hilaire Belloc, was born at La Celle, St. Cloud, France, in 1870, the son of a French barrister, Louis Stanton Belloc. His mother, Bessie Rayner Parkes, was prominent in the early days of the woman suffrage movement. Completing his primary education at the Oratory school, Edgbaston, Belloc as a French citizen served with the artillery at Toul, later entering Balliol College, Oxford. He became a naturalized British subject in 1902 and served as Member of Parliament for Salford from 1906 until 1910, first as a Liberal and later as an Independent.

Already soldier and later a statesman, the publication of *Sonnets and Verses* in 1896, launched Belloc upon the varied and often tempestuous literary career that was to see him at one time or another as journalist, historian, novelist, poet, and critic. His lively historical sense and compelling prose style was evidenced in *Danton,* in 1899, and *Robespierre,* in 1901. Independence of mind in politics had marked his undergraduate days at Oxford and was not long in coming to the fore when he took his seat in Parliament. In his opposition to the South African War, in his radical labor policy, and later in his association with Cecil Chesterton in conducting *The Eye Witness* and in writing *The Party System* and *The Servile State,* this independence was a dominating force.

A cross section of his literary works gives credence to the statement that no one has ever compiled a complete Belloc bibliography. Books of nonsense rhymes, such as *The Bad Child's Book of Beasts* (1896), *The Path to Rome,* a remarkable travel sketch (1902), satires such as *Mr. Clutterbuck's Election* (1908), numerous volumes of essays, collected poems (1924), military and topographical studies, and *The Cruise of the Nora* (1925) — these give an idea of the great variety of fields into which Belloc has gone with astonishing results.

Nor is his style any less varied than his subject matter. He seldom fails to match his diction to his theme. As an upholder of Catholic tradition, Belloc has summed up his attitude best in *Europe and the Faith* (1920), and *How the Reformation Happened* (1928). His works on French history include *Marie Antoinette* (1909), *Richelieu* (1929), and *Joan of Arc* (1929). His four-volume *History of England* (1925–1931) is also significant.

As a prose stylist Belloc is magnificent or austere as his subject demands. His expository prose is so tightly packed and logically organized as to suffer with even the exclusion of a qualifying phrase. Yet he can steep his lines in purple if the occasion demands or make them march with superb rhetoric as in his life of Cranmer.

Perhaps the key to the man is an understanding of his poet's heart. He sees the world Dantesquely and this fires the background of his prose and gives an almost infernal glow to his satire of which the best examples are to be found in his poems.

SONNETS*

XXIX

The World's a stage. The light is in
    one's eyes.
The Auditorium is extremely dark.
The more dishonest get the larger rise;
The more offensive make the greater mark.
The women on it prosper by their shape,
Some few by their vivacity. The men,
By tailoring in breeches and in cape.
The world's a stage — I say it once again.

The scenery is very much the best
Of what the wretched drama has to show,

*The above and following poems have been selected from *Sonnets and Verse,* by Hilaire Belloc (London: Duckworth and Co., 1923).

Also the prompter happens to be dumb,
We drink behind the scenes and pass a jest
On all our folly; then, before we go
Loud   cries   for   "Author" . . . but   he
    doesn't come.

XXX

The world's a stage — and I'm the Super
    man,
And no one seems responsible for salary.
I roar my part as loudly as I can
And all I mouth I mouth it to the gallery.
I haven't got another rhyme in "alery"
It would have made a better job, no doubt
If I had left attempt at Rhyming out,
Like Alfred Tennyson adapting Malory.
The world's a stage, the company of which
Has very little talent and less reading:
But many a waddling heathen painted bitch
And many a standing cad of gutter breeding.
    We sweat to learn our book: for all
        our pains
    We pass. The Chucker-out alone remains.

XXXI

The world's a stage. The trifling entrance fee
Is paid (by proxy) to the registrar.
The Orchestra is very loud and free
But plays no music in particular.
They do not print a programme, that I know.

The cast is large. There isn't any plot.
The acting of the piece is far below
The very worst of modernistic rot.

The only part about it I enjoy
Is what was called in English the Foyay.
There will I stand apart awhile and toy
With thought, and set my cigarette alight;
And then — without returning to the play —
On with my coat and out into the night.

XXXIII

Of meadows drowsy with Trinacrian bees,
Of shapes that moved a rising mist among —
Persephone between the Cypress trees —
Of lengthier shades along the woodland flung,
Of calm upon the hardly whispering seas,
Of cloud that to the distant island clung —
He made of emerald evening and of these
A holier song than ever yet was sung.

But silence and the single-thoughted night,
Hearing such music took him for their own
To that long land, where, men forgotten
    quite
Harpless he errs by Lethe stream alone.
He never more will know that windflower's
    white —
He never more shall hear uneasy autumn
    moan.

LINES TO A DON

Remote and ineffectual Don
That dared attack my Chesterton,
With that poor weapon, half-impelled,
Unlearnt, unsteady, hardly held,
Unworthy for a tilt with men —
Your quavering and corroded pen;
Don poor at Bed and worse at Table,
Don pinched, Don starved, Don miserable;
Don stuttering, Don with roving eyes,
Don nervous, Don of crudities;
Don clerical, Don ordinary,
Don self-absorbed and solitary;
Don here-and-there, Don epileptic;
Don puffed and empty, Don dyspeptic;
Don middle-class, Don sycophantic,
Don dull, Don brutish, Don pedantic;

Don hypocritical, Don bad,
Don furtive, Don three-quarters mad;
Don (since a man must make an end),
Don that shall never be my friend.

Don different from those regal Dons!
With hearts of gold and lungs of bronze,
Who shout and bang and roar and bawl
The Absolute across the hall,
Or sail in amply bellowing gown
Emormous through the Sacred Town,
Bearing from College to their homes
Deep cargoes of gigantic tomes;
Dons admirable! Dons of Might!
Uprising on my inward sight
Compact of ancient tales, and port

And sleep — and learning of a sort.
Dons English, worthy of the land;
Dons rooted; Dons that understand.
Good Dons perpetual that remain
A landmark, walling in the plain —
The horizon of my memories —
Like large and comfortable trees.

Don very much apart from these,
Thou scapegoat Don, thou Don devoted,
Don to thine own damnation quoted,
Perplexed to find thy trivial name
Reared in my verse to lasting shame.
Don dreadful, rasping Don and wearing,
Repulsive Don — Don past all bearing.

Don of the cold and doubtful breath,
Don despicable, Don of death;
Don nasty, skimpy, silent, level;
Don evil; Don that serves the devil.
Don ugly — that makes fifty lines.
There is a canon which confines
A Rhymed Octosyllabic Curse
If written in Iambic Verse
To fifty lines. I never cut;
I far prefer to end it — but
Believe me I shall soon return.
My fires are banked, yet still they burn
To write some more about the Don
That dared attack my Chesterton.

TO DIVES

Dives, when you and I go down to Hell,
Where scriblers end and millionaires as well,
We shall be carrying on our separate backs
Two very large but very different packs;
And as you stagger under yours, my friend,
Down the dull shore where all our jour-
    neys end,
And go before me (as your rank demands)
Towards the infinite flat underlands,
And that dear river of forgetfulness —
Charon, a man of exquisite address
(For, as your wife's progenitors could tell,
They're very strict on etiquette in Hell),
Will, since you are a lord, observe, "My lord,
We cannot take these weighty things aboard!"
Then down they go, my wretched Dives,
    down —
The fifteen sorts of boots you kept for town,
The hat to meet the Devil in; the plain
But costly ties; the cases of champagne;
The solid watch, and seal, and chain, and
    charm;
The working model of a Burning Farm
(To give the little Belials); all the three
Biscuits for Cerberus; the guarantee
From Lambeth that the Rich can never burn,
And even promising a safe return;

The admirable overcoat, designed
To cross Cocytus — very warmly lined:
Sweet Dives, you will leave them all behind ·
And enter Hell as tattered and as bare
As was your father when he took the air
Behind a barrow-load in Leicester Square.
Then turned to me, and noting one thing
    that brings
With careless step a mist of shadowy things:
Laughter and memories, and a few regrets,
Some honour, and a quantity of debts,
A doubt or two of sorts, a trust in God,
And (what will seem to you extremely odd)
His father's granfer's father's father's name,
Unspoilt, untitled, even spelt the same;
Charon, who twenty thousand times before
Has ferried Poets to the ulterior shore,
Will estimate the weight I bear, and cry —
"Comrade!" (He has himself been known
    to try
His hand at Latin and Italian verse,
Much in the style of Virgil — only worse)
"We let such vain imaginaries pass!"
Then tell me, Dives, which will look
    the ass —
You, or myself? Or Charon? Who can tell?
They order things so damnably in Hell.

THE SOUTH COUNTRY

When I am living in the Midlands
That are sodden and unkind,
I light my lamp in the evening:
My work is left behind;
And the great hills of the South Country
Come back into my mind.

The great hills of the South Country
They stand along the sea;
And it's there walking in the high woods
That I could wish to be,
And the men that were boys when I was
    a boy
Walking along with me.

The men that live in North England
I saw them for a day:
Their hearts are set upon the waste fells,
Their skies are fast and grey;
From their castle-walls a man may see
The mountains far away.

The men that live in West England
They see the Severn strong,
A-rolling on rough water brown,
Light aspen leaves along.
They have the secret of the Rocks,
And the oldest kind of song.

But the men that live in the South Country
Are the kindest and most wise,
They get their laughter from the loud surf,
And the faith in their happy eyes
Comes surely from our Sister the Spring
When over the sea she flies;

The violets suddenly bloom at her feet,
She blesses us with surprise.

I never get between the pines
But I smell the Sussex air;
Nor I never come on a belt of sand
But my home is there.
And along the sky the line of the Downs
So noble and so bare.

A lost thing could I never find,
Nor a broken thing mend:
And I fear I shall be all alone
When I get towards the end.
Who will there be to comfort me
Or who will be my friend?

I will gather and carefully make my friends
Of the men of the Sussex Weald;
They watch the stars from silent folds,
They stiffly plough the field.
By them and the God of the South Country
My poor soul shall be healed.

If I ever become a rich man,
Or if ever I grow to be old,
I will build a house with deep thatch
To shelter me from the cold,
And there shall the Sussex songs be sung
And the story of Sussex told.

I will hold my house in the high wood
Within a walk of the sea,
And the men that were boys when I was
    a boy
Shall sit and drink with me.

TARANTELLA

Do you remember an Inn,
Miranda?
Do you remember an Inn?
And the tedding and the spreading
Of the straw for a bedding,
And the fleas that tease in the High Pyrenees,
And the wine that tasted of the tar?
And the cheers and the jeers of the young
    muleteers

(Under the dark of the vine verandah)?
Do you remember an Inn, Miranda,
Do you remember an Inn?
And the cheers and the jeers of the young
    muleteers
Who hadn't got a penny,
And who weren't paying any,
And the hammer at the doors and the Din?
And the Hip! Hop! Hap!

Of the clap
Of the hands to the twirl and the swirl
Of the girl gone chancing,
Glancing,
Dancing,
Backing and advancing,
Snapping of the clapper to the spin
Out and in —
And the Ting, Tong, Tang of the guitar!
Do you remember an Inn,
Miranda?
Do you remember an Inn?

Never more;
Miranda,
Never more.
Only the high peaks hoar:
And Aragon a torrent at the door.
No sound
In the walls of the Halls where falls
The tread
Of the feet of the dead to the ground.
No sound:
Only the boom
Of the far Waterfall like Doom.

CRANMER*

CHAPTER XVI

THE FIRE

THE dawn of the 21st of March broke on the windows of Cranmer's prison room. The rain was falling. Garcina entered. He brought no promise of reprieve, nor any announcement of doom; but a paper briefly summing up the attitude which Cranmer had taken, made public and affirmed with so much vehemence. It was a memorandum of what should be read out when he came before them all in the last hours to meet whatever fate was before him. In it came an appeal imploring those who heard him to pray for him, prayer on his own account; begging of them to live well as he had not lived; a declaration of Queen Mary's right to be Queen indeed of England, and at the end of all, a full confession of the faith.

Thomas Cranmer wrote that paper out and signed it, and kept it upon him for what was to come.

Immediately after, under the rain, a procession formed in great solemnity.

On these high occasions it was customary for the sermon, always preached, to be delivered from a platform in the open air, as it had been when Anne Askew suffered and when Jane Bocher suffered, who so boldly replied to the preacher. But as the rain still fell so steadily on this March morning the arrangements were changed: the sermon was to be preached in St. Mary's Church. There was Cranmer to hear the last exhortation, and perhaps to be told that he had touched the heart of those in power, or their policy, and should go free after all.

Opposite the pulpit whence Cole, the Provost of Eton, was to preach was a sort of stage whereon Cranmer himself was set; and all about him was that congregation of the University and the priests from without, and of the public as well. The rain beat upon the windows, and all men watching Cranmer saw him deep in dejection with the tears upon his face and, as it seemed, repentant of all that in him which they so much abhorred and of which he had so openly and vehemently repented, manifestly, before all men.

Then Cole, that Provost of Eton, began. First he made a recital of all Cranmer's enormous misdeeds: how he stood at the root of all the alteration in this realm of England — the turmoil, the chaos and dispute; how he had permitted himself to be judge in the matter of the divorce (but this, it was admitted, was not of malice but of weakness); how he had then become a great setter-forth of heresy, written upon it, continued it, yea — even to these last weeks till grace had touched him.

So much for the preliminaries; the denunciations which were to be expected showering down on that aged, shorn, humbled — self-humbled-head.

*From *Cranmer*, pp. 320–326. Copyright, 1931, by Hilaire Belloc, published by J. G. Lippincott Co.

But there came something more which struck like a shaft into the heart of that bowed old man who sat listening. For Cole continued by saying this: that never had evils so enormous been excused, never had a man continuing so long in them been pardoned, *and for the sake of example pardon could not now be granted: the Queen and the Council had taken their decision and Cranmer was to die.*

What Cole had to say further mattered no more to Cranmer, though what he had to say further was long enough: how fall from such a height to such depths should be an example to all — how the man now condemned should meet his end — how he should remember as he himself had said in his famous published torrent of regret and penitence, that the penitent thief had been told by Christ Himself: "This day shalt thou be with Me in Paradise," and how he might thus brave himself against the terrors of the fire. And Cranmer heard from those lips before the sermon ended how he had glorified God by doing penance at last and by confessing, how God, in His mercy, had reclaimed him and called him home. So Cole ended on that note of praise, but added that in every Church of Oxford he should be prayed for, and Masses said for his soul and Dirges sung; and every priest that heard was exhorted to say such Masses for Cranmer's soul.

Then, the sermon being ended, Cole begged all that great assembly in the Church of St. Mary's to pray in unison for the man that was to die.

Cranmer knelt down with the rest, forming one of the great company at prayer and a man of the day speaking of what he saw with his own eyes, wrote: "I think there were never such a number so earnestly praying together; for they that hated him before now loved him for his conversion and hope of continuance."

When this praying was over Cranmer rose all in tears. He had wept often enough while Cole was speaking; he did not cease to weep now that he was standing up to answer for himself.

"Good people," he began, "I had intended, indeed, to desire you to pray for me, which, because Mr. Doctor hath desired and you already done, I thank you most heartily for it. And now I will pray for myself as I can best devise for my own comfort, and say the prayer word for word as I have here written it." Whereat he pulled from his sleeve that document he had written in the hours before, early in the morning. He read it, still standing up.

"Oh, Father of Heaven, oh, Son of God, Redeemer of the World, oh, Holy Ghost, proceeding from Them both and Master of the World, have mercy upon me most wretched caitiff and miserable sinner; I, who have offended more grievously than any can express. Whither should I flee for succour! To Heaven I may be unable to lift up mine eyes; and in earth I find no refuge. . . . Oh, Lord God, my sins be great, yet have mercy upon me for Thy great mercy. Oh, God the Son, Thou wast not made Man for few nor small offences. . . . Although my sins be great, yet Thy Mercy is greater, I crave nothing, oh, Lord, for mine own merits, but for Thy Name's sake, that it may be glorified thereby, and for Thy Dear Son Jesus Christ's sake. And now, therefore, Our Father which art in Heaven. . . ."

Then, falling upon his knees, he recited the "Our Father"; but it was noted by some that he added not, as was customary, the Angelic Salutation to Our Lady, and that the "Hail Mary" did not follow from his lips.

Then he rose again, and told them how everyone at the approach of death desires to say something whereby he might be remembered, and implored the Grace of God that by what he was about to say at his departing, God also might be glorified. Next he begged them not to yield in anything for reasons of this world. Next, that they should obey the King and Queen gladly, and that they should love each other, and that the rich should give to the poor. He begged all the rich that might hear him to ponder that, saying that the poor were now so many and food and drink so dear: "For though," he said, "I have been long in prison, yet I have heard of the great penury of the poor. Consider that

that which is given to the poor is given to God, whom we have not otherwise present corporally with us but in the poor."

Now having said so much, he did not add the words in the draft prepared and written out by him early in the morning when it was doubtful whether he should live or die — that Queen Mary was Queen of right, and had just title by the Blood Royal. But he went on: "I see before mine eyes presently either Heaven ready to receive me, or Hell ready to swallow me up. I shall, therefore, to-day show you my very faith; for now is no time to dissemble, whatsoever I have written in times past." And when he had declared his belief in God the Father Almighty, Monarch of Heaven and Earth, and His Articulate Word made manifest to us by Our Saviour Jesus Christ, and His Apostles and Prophets in the Old Testament and the New, he came to something which had not been written in the manner they expected.

"There was one more thing," he told them, "which troubled his conscience more than any other thing he ever did or said in his life — the setting abroad of writings contrary to the truth which he thought in his heart." What writings, not those of the life he had abjured — but these late writings, in which he had abjured it: his Recantations. "They were written contrary to the truth which I thought in my heart, and written for fear of death, to save my life if it might be. . . . All such bills which I have written or signed with mine own hand since my degradation, wherein I have written many things untrue. And forasmuch as I have written many things contrary to what I believe in my heart, my hand shall first be punished; for if I may come to the fire it shall be first burned. And as for the Pope, I refuse him, for Christ's enemy and anti-Christ, with all his false doctrine."

So they would burn him, would they? Then he would speak at last. And he had spoken.

There arose a tumult and hubbub, with men crying out against him and all moving as though they would seize him.

But Cranmer ran out from that Church, over the waste ground northward, past the few houses and past Brasenose College Gate and down narrow Brasenose Lane at full speed — this old, short man still so vigorous; and after him all the crowd of them, keeping pace as best they could under the driving rain: and so on and on under the wall to the North Gate, under the floor above which his old prison was, and so to the stake before him where the hundreds of furze faggots were piled, and the wooden faggots above them.

Even as he went one or two, panting, still begged him to remember and save himself, and to witness to the truth. But he paid no heed to them all.

He put off his outer robe quickly, standing before them in the long shirt which came down to his feet; he was bound to the stake by that iron girdle which is still kept as a relic of that long past day.

There stood by one Edge of Brasenose College, earnest in the Faith, who implored him to bear witness to it before he died. But Cranmer paid no heed, until he answered at last: "But as for that recantation, I repent it right sore because I knew it was against the truth." And as he would still be speaking, Lord Williams of Thame, the Royal Officer who had charge, cried out: "Make short! Make short!" Then did Cranmer take one or two about him by the hand, and Edge left him, still calling on him to repent. But he answered: "This is the hand that wrote it, and therefore it shall suffer first punishment." And men saw and bore witness to this, that he held his hand out steadfastly into the flame.

Also, as the fire rose about him, he made no cry or complaint, which was a marvel, but still held out his hand till flame and smoke hid all.

This is the way in which Cranmer died.

THE SERVILE STATE*

WITH the close of the middle ages the societies of Western Christendom and England among the rest were economically free.

Property was an institution native to the State and enjoyed by the great mass of its citizens. Co-operative institutions, voluntary regulations of labour, restricted the completely independent use of property by its owners only in order to keep that institution intact and to prevent the absorption of small property by great.

This excellent state of affairs which we had reached after many centuries of Christian development, and in which the old institution of slavery had finally been eliminated from Christendom, did not everywhere survive. In England in particular it was ruined. The seeds of the disaster were sown in the sixteenth century. Its first apparent effects came to light in the seventeenth. During the eighteenth century England came to be finally, though insecurely, established upon a proletarian basis, that is, it had already become a society of rich men possessed of the means of production on the one hand, and a majority dispossessed of those means upon the other. With the nineteenth century the evil plant had come to its maturity, and England had become before the close of that period a purely Capitalist State, the type and model of Capitalism for the whole world: with the means of production tightly held by a very small group of citizens, and the whole determining mass of the nation dispossessed of capital and land, and dispossessed, therefore, in all cases of security, and in many of sufficiency as well. The mass of Englishmen, still possessed of political, lacked more and more the elements of economic, freedom, and were in a worse posture than free citizens have been found themselves before in the history of Europe.

By what steps did so enormous a catastrophe fall upon us?

The first step in the process consisted in the mishandling of a great economic revolution which marked the sixteenth century. The lands and the accumulated wealth of the monasteries were taken out of the hands of their old possessors with the intention of vesting them in the Crown — but they passed, as a fact, not into the hands of the Crown, but into the hands of an already wealthy section of the community who, after the change was complete, became in the succeeding hundred years the governing power of England.

This is what happened: —

The England of the early sixteenth century, the England over which Henry VIII inherited his powerful Crown in youth, though it was an England in which the great mass of men owned the land they tilled and the houses in which they dwelt, and the implements with which they worked, was yet an England in which these goods, though widely distributed, were distributed unequally.

Then, as now, the soil and its fixtures were the basis of all wealth, but the proportion between the value of the soil and its fixtures and the value of other means of production (implements, stores of clothing and of subsistence, etc.) was different from what it is now. The land and the fixtures upon it formed a very much larger fraction of the totality of the means of production than they do today. They represent today not one-half the total means of production of this country, and though they are the necessary foundation for all wealth production, yet our great machines, our stores of food and clothing, our coal and oil, our ships and the rest of it, come to more than the true value of the land and of the fixtures upon the land: they come to more than the arable soil and the pasture, the constructional value of the houses, wharves and docks, and so forth. In the early sixteenth century the land and the fixtures upon it came, upon the contrary, to very much more than all other forms of wealth combined.

Now this form of wealth was here, more

---

*Belloc, Hilaire, *The Servile State* (London: Constable and Co., 1927), pp. 57–68.

than in any other Western European country, already in the hands of a wealthy land-owning class at the end of the Middle Ages.

It is impossible to give the exact statistics, because none were gathered, and we can only make general statements based upon inference and research. But, roughly speaking, we may say that of the total value of the land and its fixtures, probably rather more than a quarter, though less than a third, was in the hands of this wealthy class.

The England of that day was mainly agricultural, and consisted of more than four, but less than six million people, and in every agricultural community you would have the Lord, as he was legally called (the squire, as he was already conversationally termed), in possession of more demesne land than in any other country. On the average you found him, I say owning in this absolute fashion rather more than a quarter, perhaps a third of the land of the village: in the towns the distribution was more even. Sometimes it was a private individual who was in this position, sometime a corporation, but in every village you would have found this demesne land absolutely owned by the political head of the village, occupying a considerable proportion of its acreage. The rest, though distributed as property among the less fortunate of the population, and carrying with it houses and implements from which they could not be dispossessed, paid certain dues to the Lord, and, what was more, the Lord exercised local justice. This class of wealthy land-owners had been also for now one hundred years the Justice upon whom local administration depended.

There was no reason why this state of affairs should not gradually have led to the rise of the Peasant and the decay of the Lord. That is what happened in France, and it might perfectly well have happened here. A peasantry eager to purchase might have gradually extended their holdings at the expense of the demesne land, and to the distribution of property, which was already fairly complete, there might have been added another excellent element, namely, the more equal possession of that property. But any such process of gradual buying by the small man

from the great, such as would seem natural to the temper of us European people, and such as has since taken place nearly everywhere in countries which were left free to act upon their popular instincts, was interrupted in this country by an artificial revolution of the most violent kind. This artificial revolution consisted in the seizing of the monastic lands by the Crown.

It is important to grasp clearly the nature of this operation, for the whole economic future of England was to flow from it.

Of the *demesne* lands, and the power of local administration which they carried with them (a very important feature, as we shall see later), rather more than a quarter were in the hands of the Church; the Church was therefore the "Lord" of something over 25 per cent., say 28 per cent., or perhaps nearly 30 per cent., of English agricultural communities, and the overseers of a like proportion of all English agricultural produce. The Church was further the absolute owner in practice of something like 30 per cent. of the demesne land in the villages, and the receiver of something like 30 per cent. of the customary dues, etc., paid by the smaller owners to the greater. All this economic power lay until 1535 in the hand of Cathedral Chapters, communities of monks and nuns, educational establishments conducted by the clergy and so forth.

When the monastic lands were confiscated by Henry VIII., not the whole of this vast economic influence was suddenly extinguished. The secular clergy remained endowed, and most of the educational establishments, though looted, retained some revenue; but though the whole 30 per cent. did not suffer confiscation, something well over 20 per cent. did, and the revolution affected by this vast operation was by far the most complete, the most sudden, and the most momentous of any that has taken place in the economic history of any European people.

It was at first *intended* to retain this great mass of the means of production in the hands of the Crown, that must be clearly remembered by any student of the fortunes of England, and by all who marvel at the contrast between the old England and the new.

Had that intention been firmly maintained, the English State and its government would have been the most powerful in Europe.

The Executive (which in those days meant the *King*) would have had a greater opportunity for crushing the resistance of the wealthy, for backing its political power with economic power, and for ordering the social life of its subjects than any other executive in Christendom.

Had Henry VIII. and his successors kept the land thus confiscated, the power of the French Monarchy, at which we are astonished, would have been nothing to the power of the English.

The King of England would have had in his own hands an instrument of control of the most absolute sort. He would presumably have used it, as a strong central government always does, for the weakening of the wealthier classes, and to the indirect advantage of the mass of the people. At any rate, it would have been a very different England indeed from the England we know, if the King had held fast to his own after the dissolution of the monasteries.

Now it is precisely here that the capital point in this great revolution appears. *The King failed to keep the lands he had seized.* That class of large landowners which already existed and controlled, as I have said, anything from a quarter to a third of the agricultural values of England, were too strong for the monarchy. They insisted upon land being granted to themselves, sometimes freely, sometimes for ridiculously small sums, and they were strong enough in Parliament, **and through** the local administrative power they had, to see that their demands were satisfied. Nothing that the Crown let go ever went back to the Crown, and year after year more and more of what had once been the monastic land became the absolute possession of the large landowners.

Observe the effect of this. All over England men who already held in virtually absolute property from one-quarter to one-third of the soil and the ploughs and the barns of a village, became possessed in a very few years of a further great section of the means of production, which turned the scale wholly in their favour. They added to that third a new and extra fifth. They became at a blow the owners of *half* the land! In many centres of capital importance they had come to own *more* than half of the land. They were in many districts not only the unquestioned superiors, but the economic masters of the rest of the community. They could buy to the greatest advantage. They were strictly **competitive,** getting every shilling of due and of rent where the old clerical landlords had been *customary* — leaving much to the tenant. They began to fill the universities, the judiciary. The Crown less and less decided between great and small. More and more the great could decide in their own favour. They soon possessed by these operations the bulk of the means of production, and they immediately began the process of eating up the small independent men and gradually forming those great estates which, in the course of a few generations, became identical with the village itself. All over England you may notice that the great squires' houses date from this revolution or after it. The manorial house, the house of the local great man as it was in the Middle Ages, survives here and there to show of what immense effect this revolution was. The low-timbered place with its steadings and outbuildings, only a larger farmhouse among the other farmhouses, is turned after the Reformation and thenceforward into a palace. Save where great castles (which were only held of the Crown and not owned) made an exception, the pre-Reformation gentry lived as men richer than, but not the masters of, other farmers around them. *After* the Reformation there began to arise all over England those great "country houses" which rapidly became the typical centres of English agricultural life.

The process was in full swing before Henry died. Unfortunately for England, he left as his heir a sickly child, during the six years of whose reign, from 1547 to 1553, the loot went on at an appalling rate. When he died and Mary came to the throne it was nearly completed. A mass of new families had arisen, wealthy out of all proportion to anything which the older England had known, and bound by a common interest to the older families which had joined in the grab. Every single man who sat in Parliament for a county required his price for voting the dissolution of the monasteries; every single man received it. A list of the members of the Dissolution Parliament is enough to prove this, and, apart from their power in Parliament, this class had a hundred other ways of insisting on their will. The Howards (already of some lineage), the Cavendishes, the Cecils, the Russels, and fifty other new families thus rose upon the ruins of religion; and the process went steadily on until, about one hundred years after its inception, the whole face of England was changed.

In the place of a powerful Crown disposing of revenues far greater than that of any subject, you had a Crown at its wit's end for money, and dominated by subjects some of whom were its equals in wealth, and who could, especially through the action of Parliament (which they now controlled), do much what they willed with Government.

In other words, by the first third of the seventeenth century by 1630–40, the economic revolution was finally accomplished, and the new economic reality thrusting itself upon the old traditions of England was a powerful oligarchy of large owners overshadowing an impoverished and dwindled monarchy.

Other causes had contributed to this de-plorable result. The change in the value of money had hit the Crown very hard; the peculiar history of the Tudor family, their violent passions, their lack of resolution and of any continuous policy, to some extent the character of Charles I, himself, and many another subsidiary cause may be quoted. But the great main fact upon which the whole thing is dependent is the wealth of the country had been transferred to the great landowners, and that this transference had tipped the scale over entirely in their favour as against the peasantry.

The diminished and impoverished Crown could no longer stand. It fought against the new wealth, the struggle of the Civil Wars; it was utterly defeated; and when a final settlement was arrived at in 1660, you have all the realities of power in the hands of a small powerful class of wealthy men, the King still surrounded by the forms and traditions of his old power, but in practice a salaried puppet. And in that social world which underlies all political appearances, the great dominating note was that a few wealthy families had got hold of the bulk of the means of production in England, while the same families exercised all local administrative power and were moreover the Judges, the Higher Education, the Church and the generals. They quite overshadowed what was left of central government in this country.

THERMIDOR*

ROBESPIERRE at that moment was utterly different from all that the older members of the Convention or his friends or France had known for five years. His pedantry dropped off him; hard sentences spoken from the soul, heedless of notes, left his eyes clear of the glasses that had veiled them even during his defence of twenty-four hours before. He did not rise into the tribune, but, stepping out from the bench where he had sat at random into the floor of the hall, he accepted with his eyes the thousand faces whose unity arose to blast him, and he was possessed for a moment of a freedom and energy that were hardly part of himself. He felt. The air was still full of the swarm of "Tyrant! Tyrant!" when he passed right in front of the President's chair, across the tribune and the secretaries, and, folding his arms, he looked straight up at the Mountain.

There was his home. He was a man of

*Belloc, Hilaire, *Robespierre* (New York, London: G. P. Putnam and Sons), pp. 375–396.

subtle temper, overmetaphysical, inclined to posture also: still, he had come out of that band of ardent men who founded the Republic. There he had sat not two years before when the newly elected members for Paris and the pride of the Southern Blood had determined the new career of France. Among these old comrades some hand or some voice would be raised. What face looked out at him thence from the darkness beneath the galleries: Dubois Crancé, that had been a mousquetaire, that was all a noble and that had still a small smile playing about his large mouth. This soldier, cropped-haired, bronze-faced, straight-headed, looked down upon him and made no sound. Robespierre had denounced him once because he, a soldier, dared to give quarter in Lyons; he had recalled him from the west. And with Crancé you may read all the Mountain. Some in that party feared, some despised, some condemned the influence of a single man; but of all the soil whence he had sprung no one moved. Then, because he was hunted and alone, he turned himself round, still outwardly contained, but with the nervous quivering of his jaws working again, and saw the hundreds upon hundreds that went up in tiers and were the plain and the Right; royalists under him, silent men, men who "continued to live" in the Terror. He had never yet depended upon them, they had continually depended upon him. He begged — it was abject, but he was never a fighter — the alliance of those of whom he had once been protector; a mixture of violent cries, of hidden laughs, and of silence foiled him. He called them the "pure men" — that is, the men without politics, a just title — it raised no echo.

To a gulf of silence another wave of intolerable sound succeeded. He sought to dominate it by speech, but in the chair above him, whether distraught by the renewed anarchy or whether deliberate, Collot d'Herbois refused to listen but only called for order, ringing his great bell.

Then Robespierre, quite beside himself now and shouting epithets, turned upon him and called on him for a last time — called him a "Speaker of murderers," but even as he turned, the thing he found was no longer the expected enemy. It was not Collot d'Herbois that he saw above him presiding, but a young man from the valley of the Marne, a man who had come from the poplars and slow rivers, the Pouilleuse; from the place where you may see a long way off on the edges of the sky the great hill of Rheims and the vines, and the forest over all. Thuriot sat above him, and the memory of Danton ran through the hall. That young commander, a smile of the Champagne, had neither time to silence him nor to give him speech, when, as Robespierre exhausted by so violent an effort against a wall of men left an interval of silence, another man from the Marne — from the little Aube — another Danton again returning, the unknown Garnier, cried across the hall: "The blood of Danton chokes you."

Not knowing well what he said, confused by such different adversaries (he had within the hour been accused of defending Danton), Robespierre looked up a moment, cried out, "So, you reproach me with Danton . . ." and then by a movement unique in his life, he ran up the extreme gangway of the Left and faced the Convention. He had leaned more and more away from the pure Republic, more and more back to mysticism and tolerance and alliance with the creeds, but in this supreme moment he stood in the place belonging to the extreme stoics from whom he had drawn his first powers and to whose keeping after death his legend was to return. It was a thing mysterious and crammed with meaning that he who had eschewed all poignancy and all sudden force of gesture, whose very nature was opposed to immediate effects, now stretched out his hands in the attitude which is at once that of appeal and of despair, and cried out, "Vote for my death!" No one answered.

A certain Louchet, an obscure, just man, one that later stood out firmly for the Republic against the muddy flood of the reaction, called out clearly across the silence, "Arrest him!"

The cry determined not only his arrest — that was of course — but was also the cue for as signal an act of heroism and of devotion as our modern history records. Lebas that had consistently loved him, and upon whose clear northern temper no suspicion of un-reason can attach itself, rose in his place and said that if Robespierre was to die, he also demanded death. His friends near him caught his coat to pull him down. Out in the Rue St. Honoré an admirable woman was waiting for his return; a child, rather, and her child. In a noble enthusiasm he threw everything away for honour. Then, shamed by so much virtue, Augustin, that had never done much good to himself not much evil to the public, rose also, saying that what his brother suffered he would suffer. But if one triumvir, then three also of necessity and logic had to pass. Couthon, in spite of his lameness, St. Just, in spite of his con-temptuous silence, suffered the vote. All these three, a little band that had dreamed vain things were put to the judgment of the Assembly; and when Thuriot asked for the Noes, so silent was the Mountain that he could write in the register that yet remains, "Unanimity." So, in a hubbub that declined into repose, the last scene of the Republic was acted.

Some one asked them to leave the Assembly and stand at the bar. They went and stood. Then another asked why no officers had them in custody. It was because the officers could not yet believe that this had happened. When the order was given by the president, the ushers formally laid their hands upon the shoulders of the men that had imagined a new earth. There was nothing more to be done. A few vain remarks and platitudes, a sudden enthusiasm for the Republic which the Convention thought to have saved, the stampede of the public galleries, and the adjournment for two hours ended this memorable victory. It was not yet five of the afternoon; four hours had decided the battle.

When this first part of the work was accomplished the sky gave no relief; an un-natural evening ready for further evil brooded sultry and oppressive above the city.

In the minds of men also a strange mixture of close activity and of reluctance, things moving in silence, filled the remaining hours of daylight. This contrast proceeded from the spirit that lends all its irony to Ther-midor. Paris was confused. To judge by the immediate readiness or fury of the Commune it might have been the great 10th of August, the rising for national existence; it might have been full peace to judge by the quiet certitude of the Convention. Each was de-ceived. The Parliament had no force to meet the populace had the populace armed; the municipal body had no populace to arm. The legal authority of the one, the moral leadership of the other, turned into a smoke of phrases; and, after most inconsequent adventures, the midnight struggle in which the drama ended was but the success of a few dozens over a handful of individuals.

Yet so tenacious was the tradition of the Revolution in the hearts of the politicians, so little did they see how the great victories had calmed political violence, that each group went on, in the air and dissociated from reality, thinking, the one that a city, the other that a nation was behind it. At the Hotel de Ville the full enthusiasm of '93 blazed out; the great words were recovered and the sharp decisions upon which the Revolution had hitherto turned were taken. It was five o'clock when Herman's note, official but very non-committal in its language and in the person of its bearer, came to the Commune. Fleuriot-Lescot received it and the insurrection the municipality had planned took shape im-mediately. The Council-General was sum-moned. Payan did what in a greater moment and for a national purpose Danton had done; he opened the doors to the general crowd; the crowd entered but was silent. With that kneading of direct action and passion which the Revolution had discovered, the Com-mune threw out decree after decree, each in the right order, each so framed that had there been a Paris to answer them, an organ-ised army with its spirit and its plan would have arisen in two hours; but they worked in a void.

The barriers were to be shut, the tocsin rung, the drums were to beat the mobilisa-tion, the cannons were summoned, the sections were to meet to remain in permanence and to arm; Hanriot was given his objective — the Convention; the Convention was "to be freed." But these gates, bells, drums, marches and attacks, were not machines whose levers the Commune held; they depended upon men for their agency or no bells would ring, no drums beat. The very theory of the Commune had dissolved cohesion in the solvent of liberty, and the fatigue of the great wars had drugged spontaneity to sleep. Such few citizens as gathered in the sections, debated on false issues; hesitated, dared not. The Tocsin rang spasmodically here and there; ceased in St. German's, began too late in St. Antoine, was made a quarrel of in St. Roch. Only the thin bell of the Hotel de Ville itself swung continuously in its dainty cupola, as though to show that only the federate band of the municipality felt that the moment was supreme or could maintain a purpose. As for the mother of the city, Notre Dame, it was silent.

To this torrent of active, empty decrees in the Hotel de Ville there was answered another torrent, paper also, in the great room of the Pavillon de Flore. The Convention was not without a head, the Committee of Public Safety lent itself to be the organ and authority of the law. The decrees fell like leaves; to swing the gates open, to ring no peal, to dissolve the sections, none to obey Hanriot, to arrest every man that rebelled. They signed and signed; they called the lower committee in to help them; what authority their names would give was poured out as though the great Committee had never hesitated, and as though the moment were indeed (as some historians have been misled into thinking it) the crisis of a long struggle and the end of a set plan. If they failed they were willing to risk the fate of failure. Carnot gave his name to half the documents, Barrère to nearly all, Prieur to whatever was presented to him. In this decision to throw away the scabbard the Committee were acting as their enemy the Commune also desired to act; but with more thoroughness. For when young Payan had summoned the Council-General of the municipality in the Hotel de Ville there were hesitations; not all consented

to sign the list of insurrection, and there was some attempt to destroy even such signatures as had been given.

What meaning could attach to these opposing battalions of words, these soundless batteries of official papers?

This: the Commune was but half obeyed, but the Committee and the Convention seemed to be obeyed altogether. Every citizen that sat down to his meal, every gate left open, every bell left silent appeared a homage to the Parliament. Had they turned to positive decrees; had they ordered action, Paris would not have moved much more for them than for the Hotel de Ville, but the negative commands of the Committee fell on a neutral Paris, and clothed their authors with an appearance of power. For if to a lethargic man one says, "Do this," another, "Do not do this," the second appears to be the master.

Meanwhile Paris dined. The Convention, while its Committee thus slaved, had adjourned till seven; it mingled with the life of the city, it dined with the rest.

And the five prisoners dined.

There are gaps in the story of Thermidor that are like the inconsequent accidents of a dream. There should have been a pomp and some great force holding these men — Robespierre, Lebas, Couthon, St. Just should have gone off the prisoners of a brigade — they went down the few steps to the rooms of the lower committee with no one but the ushers of the house to guard them. There, attended only by the sergeant's guard that was constantly posted and that had received no accession of strength, they very easily and soberly dined.

What came to rescue them and to affirm the insurrection? A great mob or the organisation of a battalion? Nothing of the kind. Hanriot, heavy with wine, started off with a couple of aides-de-camp and perhaps a half-a-dozen friends. In the Rue St. Honoré Courtois called him names out of window. He passed on. Farther down the street he met a gentleman walking; he heard the gentleman mentioned as opposed to Robespierre; he had him sent off under a corporal and four men to the post of the Palais Royal.

He appeared at the rooms of the lower committee and argued with the guard; they opposed his opinions. He drew his sword as he stood in the doorway. A deputy of the committee got up on the table and ordered the guard to arrest him and his companions. They did so, and as he was a strong and violent man they bound him with cords. Meanwhile Robespierre, not a little disturbed at a man's leaping on the table where he was dining, rose from his plate and napkin and interrupted his meal to advise Hanriot not to resist; saying he desired nothing more than a trial at the bar of the revolutionary tribunal. The others sat on at meat till the scuffle was over.

There is something terrible in this splash of grotesque; the handful that appeared on the great stage of a decisive hour, without audience, in such a small domestic way, and without any one circumstance of tragedy. The incongruity of such unaccented scenes determining so great an event was part of the spirit of Thermidor; it fell with the silence and stillness of the air, with the steady grey sky, the even, growing heat, and the delay of the storm.

Some while yet before seven, their meal over, little detachments of the guard took each of the five separately to separate prisons. Lebas to La Force, along the narrow streets eastwards, past the very doors of the Commune. St. Just to the old Scotch college on the hill of the university. It had been made a rough prison of for the time, and there, encased in lead, the brain of the last Stuart watched in the wall beside him. Robespierre was taken beyond to the Luxembourg: the two others to St. Lazare and to La Bourbe.

All this went easily and well. The note of that dinner table was continued. There was no rebellion or violence, nor even argument. Robespierre was confident of trial; the rest were either silent with pride (as was St. Just), or left their fate to the confidence of Robespierre (as did Lebas and Augustine). None marked their passage, no appeal was made; the astounding silence of Paris left an empty and wide road for their various passages.

Meanwhile the Commune, that had seized reality and was determined on a supreme effort, had all prepared, as it thought, to save the Republic in which it still passionately lived, and for which this man still stood.

The Commune had done much since the first insurrectionary call, though but two hours had been given them in which to act. They had raised the Jacobins; at seven, just as the prisoners reached their prisons, the remnant of the great club met to make a wing of the insurrection. I say "a remnant," yet it was still the Jacobins. A man could stand up in it and say he had voted against Robespierre and the momentary violence that followed such a declaration was succeeded by his recall and by an attempted apology. It sent a deputation to the Commune; it declared a permanent session.

The sections, the primary assemblies whose permanent officials and whose interested leaders were men drilled and chosen by what had been Robespierre's organisation, met also. The common citizens came in small numbers, and such as came were uncertain, leaning if anything towards the Convention. They passed neutral votes. They did not march. The night oppressed them, and the universal falling back into repose. Also the Commune with a strange audacity, being in reality a dead relic but thinking themselves all Paris, declared outlaws all those whom they called conspirators against the deputies. They forbade any man to follow the national authority, saying that till the nation and liberty were saved they alone ruled.

One part of the officials heard them — the jailers. At St. Lazare an excuse was found for refusing to receive Augustine; he was led away to La Force, and there two municipals in arms took him their willing prisoner to the Commune, and brought him back to the Hotel de Ville rescued, the first of the five. So Lebas, refused at La Force and sent on to the Conciergerie on the Island, was freed. Just as he went off, a hired carriage driving up brought him his wife and her sister, who implored his return. He was tender to her and remembered the little child: he told her to wait till the morning. She went home, and he to the gathering crowd of the insurrection at the Hotel de

Ville; but they did not meet again, for in the night this man, whose simple and republican mind compels me to admiration as I write his name, gave himself death.

While the Commune sent out its emissaries to the university to rescue St. Just, and to La Bourbe to rescue Couthon, Robespierre had thrown away the last of the cards fate offered him. They had taken him first to the Luxembourg in a cab. He had gone up the hill of old quarter simply, hardly under a guard. The wide Rue Tournon received the closed carriage in which he drove, and he reached the palace. The porter replied as the porter of every prison had replied that evening, but he, not from a premonition but from an insistent legality, demanded admission. The Convention had arrested him; he would obey it. He desired to stand his trial. Of all this the porter knew nothing, and, half tempted by an apparent safety, he permitted his companions (for they were hardly his enemies) to drive him down the hill again — they scarcely knew whither.

Since all the jailers in the capital showed this same temper, Charnier perhaps, or the gendarme with him, bethought him of a guard-room. The armed force, the sections, were at least doubtful or perhaps loyal to the Parliament, and he was half sick of his mission. The nearest guard-room was that of the Mairie on the Island, through the oldest and darkest streets of the university; therefore he drove his charge down to the river, and across the Pont-Neuf to the Goldsmith's Quay. They left him there less under arrest than among neutrals.

It was still light, more or less, in the street without; the Place de Grève beyond the law courts, across the Seine, was filling with men; the lamps that swung over the narrow streets were being lowered for lighting. The clear noise that comes up from a French town on long summer evenings was the chorus of that little scene.

The militia guard of the Island would neither fight for Robespierre nor detain him. They had paid little heed to the Commune; they had understood little of the Convention. They found Robespierre among them, and were somewhat embarrassed. He sat, powdered, careful and restrained at the rough table which a dozen dirty uniforms, the drippings of one oil-lamp, and the growing darkness infected with squalor. Here was the famous name they had heard so often — perhaps the Republic in person; they were not over sure. They would neither fight for him nor detain him.

Had he remained there steadfast to his first determination, sleeping that night on the planks of the guard-room and demanding his trial next day at the bar of the revolutionary tribunal, he might have left the Island safe to return to freedom; lessened indeed, part only of government, but still alive — he and his theory alive. The river was his bulwark; the great law courts, in whose vaults he sat half a prisoner, were his refuge. He guessed it, but there ran in him that fatal flaw of visionaries, by which in easy times they lose their wealth and in times of tumult their lives; he could not judge upon or mould the things under his hand, but continued to live in the things beyond the world. A sharp accident persuaded him against himself.

Hanriot, released at last, had sought Robespierre at the Luxembourg, and had returned without him. The Commune had again sent out to discover him. There appeared in the doorless arch of his refuge some few figures of the Hotel de Ville. They had come for him and had found him there, almost the last of the Five. He refused to follow them and to step outside the law. The darkness grew. They returned. He suffered himself to be led on by their ardour and their active habit; he came out into the dying light and no hand stopped him nor was any bayonet crossed. He passed through the labyrinth of tall houses, before the porch, where, as a boy, he had remembered the chapter of the cathedral and his cousin the priest that had loved him; over the old bridge of Notre Dame where the river was still broad silver, and came out upon the Place de Grève with his companions, who rejoiced as at a kind of triumph.

Indistinguishable in the heavy darkness a crowd there disputed and eddied. There was a little faint acclamation: he did not heed it. They hurried him through the uncertain hundreds towards the high and delicate façade that showed blacker against the eastward arch of the night, and under the lowering sky of a returning storm. It seemed a creature ready for prey. Its tall, great windows were all lit and menaced the west like eyes; its soul of insurrection moved in it as though with a voice and an intelligence it could drive Paris against the nation and hurl the Convention from the sombre palace that stood up a mile away, a fortress against the last bars of daylight. That living beast was the Commune. It swallowed him up.

The great hall that he entered upon the first floor was filled with men and ablaze with candles. Save Couthon all the rescued had arrived: like Hanriot, bound early in the evening by half-a-dozen enemies and easily cut loose later by a handful of friends. They were surrounded by the Commune vigorous and creating vigour: without, an increasing crowd seemed to support them, and the Commune still gathered. One would have said in this first hour of the night that the Revolt was on the march and already victorious. But with Robespierre himself, their standard of whom they knew so little, there had come in upon them the paralysis that arises from thought. The organisation ceased, the orders failed, his signature was wanting and remained wanting.

There is not in the whole five years a moment in which the man appears more nakedly than in this night which was his last. His unalterable principle, his failure in the face of things, his fixed purpose in morals, his final irresolution in action are the master-keys that read him. For four hours he stopped the advance of time with debate, disputing the strict right of insurrection, doubting it, demanding persuasion. In the heat of despair, of violent appeals, and almost of commands to their own king, time raced by these men for whom time was everything; the hours went furiously on, uselessly, like an unharnessed river.

But in the Convention that same tide of time flowing was harnessed and ground out action in a great mill till every pulse of it produced a decision and completed a force.

They outlawed the municipality, Hanriot, at last the five members themselves. Legendre found wisdom in stress, went with a knot of guards and shut the Jacobins where active Vivier was still in the chair; arrested him. The Convention named leaders for an armed force. They sent throughout the dark streets and to each of the ill-attended, yawning sections a decree to rouse and decide them; they caused to be read at the crossways and shouted by criers their terrible "Hors la Loi!" which has been like the bell of the plague throughout French history and which Buonaparte alone survived.

The men in the Hotel de Ville heard it. At the extreme corner of the Grève where the old Rue de la Vannerie then came in, the outposts of the Convention had lit torches and were trumpeting it out on the stroke of twelve to the mob in the square: conquering their irresolution; deciding them. The tocsin had ceased. There was a silence in the great room among the rebels to hear the criers; some one ran out and seized them, but it was too late, the crowd was shaken, no gun-crew was formed. Then as though to mark the silence and to proclaim doom the tenuous chimes of midnight tinkled from the clocks of the Boucherie, of the Cathedral, and of St. Jean; the 9th Thermidor had ended and the 10th rolled in the end.

The air had been very still in the unnatural heat of the night, but the first breezes before rain stirred with the turn of the morning, and upon the silence which nothing had yet disturbed, save the subdued debate of the crowd, the occasional rallying cry of Hanriot from the windows or the sudden shout of the "Hors la Loi" thunder broke. Revealed in sharp flashes, driven by the terror of the storm, the doubters poured off home under the sheets of rain. Some hauled away their pieces, some abandoned them, until in the second hour of the morning, when the thunder had rolled off along the river-plain and the rain withdrawn had refreshed the city with a new air, there remained but a group here and there gazing to no purpose at the windows, and the half-deserted guns: twin shadows, men and cannon reflected in the pools of the pavement.

Within, the wiser men had already despaired; but the more determined still wrestled with the man in whose quarrel, as they thought, they had challenged death. The wiser called for arms and had them piled upon the table of the inner room; the more determined summoned Robespierre for the last time. He sat at the centre of the great baize table, enthroned, as it were, having on his left the mayor, on his right Payan, and before him the document all signed by his defenders and awaiting his name; the last arm of the defence at bay.

For the appeal to the sections had failed, the messengers had returned to report only confusion, and the Commune bethought them of one section at least to which the mere name of Robespierre should be a shaft of leadership. The grave relic of Mansard which we call the Place Vendôme and in which the bronze pillar of Napoleon recalls at once in its majesty the embodiment of the Revolution in arms and in the marks of its fall the modern parody of insurrection, was a section under the name of "the Pikes." Therein Robespierre had lived and to this the last appeal was made. It was written out by Lerebours who alone survived of all that company; Payan, Louvet, Legrand had put their names to it — they laid it before Robespierre. He held the pen doubtfully and would not sign. A final urging disturbed him but failed to startle him into action. It proceeded from Couthon.

The cripple with large painful eyes came to him, like a reminiscence of his past four months of power; a man upon whose fevered debility far more than upon the creative angers of St. Just Robespierre had been able to impress the sanctity of his system.

Couthon then, just released from prison, came in on the arms of two gendarmes. It was past one o'clock; the columns of the Convention were on the road to the assault, there was not an hour left in which to decide. When Robespierre had thanked the men that supported his friend, and while his mind was yet moved by the reunion of the proscribed, Couthon added his plea to all that St. Just had said more passionately and to the hard phrases of Lebas.

For half-an-hour or more he bore the scene, the crowd of men standing and crying against his principle; then slowly, with the half resolution which had undermined him throughout that night he traced the first letters of his name. He saw forming, in this abandonment of all himself, the first signature that ever he had put to rebellion; an insult to his single dogma and a denial of the general will; he dared not achieve the sacrilege. With that beginning he ended; he refused to complete the signature, and putting down the pen, he laid his head on his left hand and stared at the paper before him. The clock on the façade struck two.

The scene was over. Whether he signed or no, nothing would have come of it save an abdication of the close consistency of his life. Time, which he had refused to consider, now overwhelmed him. Already two slow mobs that the Convention had gathered were converging on the Place de Grève; Barras from the Quays, Leonard Bourdon from the markets had met and joined their forces in front of the Hotel de Ville. No cannon opposed them. If Hanriot ran out to rally a dozen gunners it led to nothing but his own rough handling; he broke away covered with wounds, ran through the archway and hid in the inner yard of the Town Hall. The last remaining cannon of the defence were mingled with those of the assailants and turned against the building. Leonard Bourdon and his following crowded up the great central staircase and the Commune had fallen.

From the windows of the main hall on the first floor Lebas had seen the troops of the Convention fill the square. He walked into the small room adjoining, took a loaded pistol, shot himself and fell dead. With the first light his enemies took him out and buried this soldierly, unlaughing man side by side with Rabelais in the damp narrow yard of the St. Paul. The shot began what was for some a panic, for the rest a stupefaction.

Augustine, never worthy or decided, leapt out upon the cornice of the façade, stood for a moment above the crowd and then dashed himself down upon the steps of the great porch. They picked him up yet living and carried him into the lodge. Lescot stood suddenly up and made a movement as though to defend his leader, but he had done no more than rise when the end came.

For as Robespierre still sat motionless, his elbow on the arm of his chair, his face turned downward and a little away from the door, a boy of nineteen ran up the stair before the rest and stood behind in the entry. It was Merda. Leonard Bourdon followed close behind; but before a sign or an order could be given Merda had raised his pistol and fired. Struck full in the face, his jaw shattered and his blood breaking over the document before him Robespierre fell down; St. Just that had stood by all the while, receiving the inevitable with great dignity and silence, knelt on one knee beside him and tried to staunch the wound. Then in a scene whose details have remained to us but whose impression is but a huge confusion, the conquerors poured in and occupied the room with numbers.

To this, which was the true end of his life, little should be added. The long hours that remained to him were but a confused lethargy; dull pain, the loss of blood, long fasting, lack of sleep drained his life dry before the guillotine could claim it.

They took him on a stretcher to the Tuileries where all the prisoners were gathered, and, in the room of the Pavillon Marsan where he had supped the night before they laid him upon the table, giving him for a pillow a deal box, and some one handed him a pistol-case of cloth with which from time to time he feebly tried to wipe the blood from his face.

When the sun had already risen they sent doctors to him, who, probing his mouth and taking from it his broken teeth, yet drew no sound from him nor any gesture. Only his eyes, which remained bright, were fixed upon them all the while like those of an animal wounded. They bound his jaw with bandages and left him so, for chance visitors to stare at all the long morning; and St. Just sat by his side, his eyes red and swollen perhaps from weeping, certainly from vigil.

During those five interminable hours Robespierre neither moaned nor mumbled a broken word, but lay quite silent, though at rare intervals the guards jested about him and his wound and his coming fate. But to this silence there was one exception, for as he attempted to reach his garter, which cramped and numbed his leg, an assistant, kinder than the rest, stepped forward and loosened it for him. Then Robespierre whispered indistinctly with his swollen lips, "Thank you, sir." Equality was dying.

It was long before noon when the prisoners were taken away to the conciergerie; formalities of a certain length, the reunion of the other outlaws, the identification of each consumed the day, and it was not till past five of the summer afternoon that the tumbrills rolled out of the great gates of wrought iron.

A long and useless agony marked the road to the guillotine. So slowly went the carts, and with such frequent shocks and stoppages from the dense crowd, that the bare two miles of road took up nearly as many hours. On the Quai des Lunettes, where his familiar custom had half-endeared him to the stalls, the opticians and their workers saw him go by, and raised no cries. In the Rue St. Denis, the Rue de la Ferronerie, past the Markets, crowded windows and the reappearance of a luxurious world proclaimed the reaction; but especially in the Rue St. Honoré all that society which, since the victories, was reconquering France, made a parade of enthusiasm — and the people echoed it.

They say that at the western end the soldiers who had lined the whole way could not restrain the flood of the mob; the house fronts were filled; there were flowers and ceaseless acclamations. To one the Terror, to another unclean equality, to another madness, to another the Republic, yet to another the threat of punishment seemed to be passing in the tumbril. But as a fact it was only Robespierre.

He hung limp and exsanguine from the cords that bound him; hatless, his stock lost, his light-blue coat dimmed with the accumulations of the night and the dust of prisons, his white nankeen short-hose muddy and splashed with blood, his head loose at the neck; he looked like a man swooning.

It is not right to watch him thus, for the man had passed. I will not describe the end. Perhaps Carrier shouted behind the cart, perhaps they played some bacchanalian thing before the empty house of Duplay, perhaps a woman struck him in the Rue Royale. In the great square to which the guillotine had returned for his last sacrifice, the twenty-two were poured out in expiation, Robespierre the last. He gave, as they loosened his bandage, a loud cry of pain. The axe fell, and powder shook from his hair.

THE PATH TO ROME*

Part I

WHEN I awoke it was full eight o'clock, and the sun had gained great power. I saw him shining at me through the branches of my trees like a patient enemy outside a city that one watches through the loopholes of a tower, and I began to be afraid of taking the road. I looked below me down the steep bank between the trunks and saw the canal looking like a black marble, and I heard the buzzing of the flies above it, and I noted that all the mist had gone. A very long way off, the noise of its ripples coming clearly along the floor of the water, was a lazy barge and a horse drawing it. From time to time the tow-rope slackened into the still surface, and I heard it dripping as it rose. The rest of the valley was silent except for the underhumming of insects which marks the strength of the sun.

Now I saw clearly how difficult it was to turn night into day, for I found myself condemned either to waste many hours that ought to be consumed on my pilgrimage, or else to march on under the extreme heat; and when I had drunk what was left of my Brule wine (which then seemed delicious), and had eaten a piece of bread, I stiffly jolted down the bank and regained the highway.

In the first village I came to I found that Mass was over, and this justly annoyed me; for what is a pilgrimage in which a man cannot hear Mass every morning? Of all the things I have read about St. Louis which make me wish I had known him to speak to, nothing seems to me more delightful than his habit of getting Mass daily whenever he marched down south, but why this should be so delightful I cannot tell. Of course there is a grace and influence belonging to such a custom, but it is not of that I am speaking but of the pleasing sensation of order and accomplishment which attaches to a day one has opened by Mass: a purely temporal, and, for all I know, what the monks back at the ironworks would have called a carnal feeling, but a source of continual comfort to me. Let them go their way and let me go mine.

This comfort I ascribe to four causes (just above you will find it written that I could not tell why this should be so, but what of that?), and these causes are:

1. That for half-an-hour just at the opening of the day you are silent and recollected, and have to put off cares, interests, and passions in the repetition of a familiar action. This must certainly be a great benefit to the body and give it tone.

2. That the Mass is a careful and rapid ritual. Now it is the function of all ritual (as we see in games, social arrangements and so forth) to relieve the mind by so much of responsibility and initiative and to catch you up (as it were) into itself, leading your life for you during the time it lasts. In this way you experience a singular repose, after which

*Belloc, Hilaire, The Path to Rome (New York: G. P. Putnam's Sons, 1902), pp. 45-53.

fallowness I am sure one is fitter for action and judgment.

3. That the surroundings incline you to good and reasonable thoughts, and for the moment deaden the rasp and jar of that busy wickedness which both working in one's self and received from others is the true source of all human miseries. Thus the time spent at Mass is like a short repose in a deep and well-built library, into which no sounds come and where you feel yourself secure against the outer world.

4. And the most important cause of this feeling of satisfaction is that you are doing what the human race has done for thousands upon thousands of years. This is a matter of such moment that I am astonished people hear it so little. Whatever is buried right into our blood from immemorial habit that we must be certain to do if we are to be fairly happy (of course no grown man or woman can really be happy for long — but I mean reasonably happy), and, what is more important, decent and secure of our souls. Thus one should from time to time hunt animals, or at the very least shoot at a mark; one should always drink some kind of fermented liquor with one's food — and especially deeply upon great feast-days; one should go on the water from time to time; and one should dance on occasions; and one should sing in chorus. For all these things man has done since God put him into a garden and his eyes first became troubled with a soul. Similarly some teacher or ranter or other, whose name I forget, said lately one very wise thing at least, which was that every man should do a little work with his hands.

Oh, what good philosophy this is, and how much better it would be if rich people instead of raining the influence of their rank and spending their money on leagues for this or that exceptional thing, were to spend it in converting the middle-class to ordinary living and to the tradition of the race. Indeed, if I had power for some thirty years I would see to it that people should be allowed to follow their inbred instincts in these matters, and should hunt, drink, sing, dance, sail, and dig, and those that would not should be compelled by force.

Now in the morning Mass you do all that the race needs to do and has done for all these ages where religion was concerned: there you have the sacred and separate Enclosure, the Altar, the Priest in his Vestments, the set ritual, the ancient and hierarchic tongue, and all that your nature cries out for in the matter of worship.

From these considerations it is easy to understand how put out I was to find Mass over on this first morning of my pilgrimage. And I went along the burning road in a very ill-humour till I saw upon my right, beyond a low wall and in a kind of park, a house that seemed built on some artificial raised ground surrounded by a wall, but this may have been an illusion, the house being really only very tall. At any rate I drew it, and in the village just beyond it I learnt something curious about the man that owned it.

For I had gone into a house to take a third meal of bread and wine and to replenish my bottle when the old woman of the house, who was a kindly person, told me she had just then no wine. "But," she said, "Mr. So and So that lives in the big house sells it to any one who cares to buy even in the smallest quantities, and you will see his shed standing by the side of the road."

Everything happened just as she had said. I came to the big shed by the park wall, and there was a kind of counter made of boards, and several big tuns and two men: one in an apron serving, and the other in a little box or compartment writing. I was somewhat timid to ask for so little as a quart, but the apron man in the most business-like way filled my bottle at a tap and asked for fourpence. He was willing to talk, and told me many things: of good years in wine, of the nature of their trade, of the influence of the moon on brewing, of the importance of spigots, and what not; but when I tried to get out of him whether the owner were an eccentric private gentleman or a merchant that had the sense to earn little pennies as well as large ones, I could not make him understand my meaning; for his idea of rank was utterly different from mine and took no account of idleness and luxury and daftness, but was based entirely upon money and clothes. Moreover we were both of us Republicans, so the matter was of no great moment. Courteously saluting ourselves we parted, he remaining to sell wine and I hobbling to Rome, now a little painfully with my sack the heavier by a quart of wine, which as you probably know, weighs almost exactly two pounds and a half.

It was by this time close upon eleven, and I had long reached the stage where some kinds of men begin talking of Dogged Determination, Bull-dog pluck, the stubborn blood of the island race, and so forth, but when those who can boast a little of the sacred French blood are in a mood of set despair (both kinds march on, and the mobility of either infantry is much the same), I say I had long got to this point of exhaustion when it occurred to me that I should need an excellent and thorough meal at midday. But on looking at my map I found that there was nothing nearer than this town of Charmes that was marked on the milestones, and that was the first place I should come to in the department of the Vosges.

It would take much too long to describe the dodges that weary men and stiff have recourse to when they are at the close of a difficult task: how they divide it up in lengths in their minds, how they count numbers, how they begin to solve problems in mental arithmetic: I tried them all. Then I thought of a new one, which is really excellent and which I recommend to the whole world. It is to vary the road, suddenly taking now the fields, now the river, but only occasionally the turnpike. This last lap was very well suited for such a method. The valley had become more like a wide and shallow trench than ever. The hills on either side were low and exactly even. Up the middle of it went the river, the canal and the road, and these two last had only a field between them; now broad, now narrow.

First on the tow-path, then on the road, then on the grass, then back on the tow-path, I pieced out the last baking mile into Charmes that lies at the foot of a rather higher hill, and at last was dragging myself up the street just as the bell was ringing the noon Angelus; nor, however tedious you may have found it to read this final effort of mine, can you have found it a quarter as wearisome as I did to walk it; and surely between writer and reader there should be give and take, now the one furnishing the entertainment and now the other.

GILBERT KEITH CHESTERTON

(1874–1936)

A CAVALIER in the grand manner was Gilbert Keith Chesterton. He was born in London, 1874, and early in his school career demonstrated his talent for literature by taking the Milton Prize at St. Paul's School. In 1891 he abandoned formal education in order to study art at the Slade School, and though he achieved some competence in drawing, literature was in his blood and his original mind and ebullience of spirit led him into free-lance journalism. Publication of the *Wild Knight* (1900) indicated that a new star had arisen in the sky of literature. The title of his first book is symbolic of the man. There was something courteous and knightly about him, and even in the fury of controversy or righteous anger he made his points with radiant good humor. Unlike Don Quixote he only too often saw he was tilting with windmills, in his jousts with Wells and Shaw, but with large laughter he was always polite enough to let such adversaries think he mistook them for men. It flattered them and added point to his jests.

This spurious naïvete made his most telling arguments seem childish and surprised, but upon reflection, the acuteness and subtlety of the man demonstrated themselves and the public found enjoyment in his game of dragon slaying. He looked such an amiable bait in his own traps of paradox. This was not playing the game in the conventional sense, but when he was in it, it was twice as much fun. The publication of the *Defendant* (1901) and *Heretics* (1905) proved his mettle and improved his style, and with the disclosure of a shrewd talent for literary criticism in *Robert Browning* (1903) and *Charles Dickens* (1906) his public became convinced of his wide mind and surprising ability of expression.

His dislike of industrial capitalism and Victorian economists was no greater than his mistrust of socialism and his distaste led to a spate of splendid books: *Orthodoxy* (1906), *What's Wrong With the World* (1910), *The Man Who Was Thursday* (1908), and *The Ball and the Cross* (1909). During this period he produced a quantity of poetry, much of it the best work of his time. *Lepanto* and the *Ballad of the White Horse* are truly great poems, but even Chesterton's comic verse is not negligible. Many men wrote comic verse; Chesterton wrote comic poetry, and his satire was scarifying.

As early as 1913 Chesterton had tried his hand at playwriting in a fanciful play *Magic,* but he lacked the dramatic directness necessary for work of this kind. In another genre, that of detective fiction, he was eminently successful, the four volume Father Brown series being spread over the period between 1911 and 1927.

Although his reception into the Church was an important event of his life, it changed neither his life nor his writings. Like Eric Gill, he had always been a Catholic, a fact amply born out by the Catholic quality of all his books.

Of his later works the most important are: *A Short History of England* (1917), *St. Francis of Assisi* (1923), *The Everlasting Man* (1925), *The Judgment of Dr. Johnson* (1927), and *Generally Speaking* (1929). His *Autobiography,* a summary of his outlook, brings the reader into the mind and heart of the man.

Of the several studies of his life the best is that of Maisie Ward, *Gilbert Keith Chesterton,* Sheed and Ward (1944). It gives a complete and definitive picture of Chesterton.

TRANSLATION FROM DU BELLAY*

Happy, who like Ulysses or that lord
  Who raped the fleece, returning full and sage,
With usage and the world's wide reason stored,
  With his own kin can taste the end of age.
When shall I see, when shall I see, God knows!

  My little village smoke; or pass the door,
The old dear door of that unhappy house
  That is to me a kingdom and much more?
Mightier to me the house my fathers made
  Than your audacious heads, O Halls of Rome!
More than your Tiber is my Loire to me,
  Than Palatine my little Lyré there;
And more than all the winds of all the sea
  The quiet kindness of the Angevin air.

*The above and following poems have been selected from *Collected Poems of G. K. Chesterton* (New York Dodd, Mead and Co., 1932).

A HYMN

O God of earth and altar,
Bow down and hear our cry,
Our earthly rulers falter,
Our people drift and die;
The walls of gold entomb us,
The swords of scorn divide,
Take not thy thunder from us,
But take away our pride.

From all that terror teaches,
From lies of tongue and pen,
From all the easy speeches
That comfort cruel men,

From sale and profanation
Of honour and the sword,
From sleep and from damnation,
Deliver us, Good Lord!

Tie in a living tether
The prince and priest and thrall,
Bind all our lives together,
Smite us and save us all;
In ire and exultation
Aflame with faith, and free,
Lift up a living nation,
A single sword to thee.

ANTICHRIST, OR THE REUNION OF CHRISTENDOM: AN ODE

"A bill which has shocked the conscience of every Christian community in Europe." — *F. E. Smith, on the Welsh Disestablishment Bill.*

Are they clinging to their crosses,
    F. E. Smith,
Where the Breton boat-fleet tosses,
    Are they, Smith?
Do they, fasting, tramping, bleeding,
    Wait the news from this our city?
Groaning "That's the Second Reading!"
    Hissing "There is still Committee!"
If the voice of Cecil falters,
    If McKenna's point has pith,
Do they tremble for their altars?
    Do they, Smith?

Russian peasants round their pope
    Huddled, Smith,
Hear about it all, I hope,
    Don't they, Smith?
In the mountain hamlets clothing
    Peaks beyond Caucasian pales,
Where Establishment means nothing
    And they never heard of Wales,
Do they read it all in Hansard
    With a crib to read it with —

"Welsh Tithes; Dr. Clifford Answered."
    Really, Smith?

In the lands where Christians were,
    F. E. Smith,
In the little lands laid bare,
    Smith, O Smith!
Where the Turkish bands are busy,
    And the Tory name is blessed
Since they hailed the Cross of Dizzy
    On the banners from the West!
Men don't think it half so hard if
    Islam burns their kin and kith,
Since a curate lives in Cardiff
    Saved by Smith.

It would greatly, I must own,
    Soothe me, Smith!
If you left this theme alone,
    Holy Smith!
For your legal cause or civil
    You fight well and get your fee;
For your God or dream or devil
    You will answer, not to me.
Talk about the pews and steeples
    And the Cash that goes therewith!
But the souls of Christian peoples . . .
    Chuck it, Smith!

LEPANTO

White founts falling in the Courts of the sun,
And the Soldan of Byzantium is smiling as they run;
There is laughter like the fountains in that face of all men feared,
It stirs the forest darkness, the darkness of his beard,
It curls the blood-red crescent, the crescent of his lips,
For the inmost sea of all the earth is shaken with his ships.
They have dared the white republics up the capes of Italy,
They have dashed the Adriatic round the Lion of the Sea,
And the Pope has cast his arms abroad for agony and loss,
And called the kings of Christendom for swords about the Cross.
The cold queen of England is looking in the glass;
The shadow of the Valois is yawning at the Mass;
From evening isles fantastical rings faint the Spanish gun,
And the Lord upon the Golden Horn is laughing in the sun.

Dim drums throbbing, in the hills half heard.
Where only on a nameless throne a crownless prince has stirred,
Where, risen from a doubtful seat and half attainted stall,
The last knight of Europe takes weapons from the wall,
The last and lingering troubadour to whom the bird has sung,
That once went singing southward when all the world was young.
In that enormous silence, tiny and unafraid,
Comes up along a winding road the noise of the Crusade.
Strong gongs groaning as the guns boom far,
Don John of Austria is going to the war,
Stiff flags straining in the night-blasts cold
In the gloom black-purple, in the glint old-gold,
Torchlight crimson on the copper kettle-drums,
Then the tuckets, then the trumpets, then the cannon, and he comes.
Don John laughing in the brave beard curled,
Spurning of his stirrups like the thrones of all the world,
Holding his head up for a flag of all the free.
Love-light of Spain—hurrah!
Death-light of Africa!
Don John of Austria
Is riding to the sea.

Mahound is in his paradise above the evening star,
(*Don John of Austria is going to the war.*)
He moves a mighty turban on the timeless houri's knees,
His turban that is woven of the sunsets and the seas,
He shakes the peacock gardens as he rises from his ease,
And he strides among the tree-tops and is taller than the trees,
And his voice through all the garden is a thunder sent to bring
Black Azrael and Ariel and Ammon on the wing.
Giants and the Genii,
Multiplex of wing and eye,
Whose strong obedience broke the sky
When Solomon was king.

They rush in red and purple from the red clouds of the morn,
From temples where the yellow gods shut up their eyes in scorn;
They rise in green robes roaring from the green hells of the sea
Where fallen skies and evil hues and eyeless creatures be;
On them the sea-valves cluster and the grey sea-forests curl,
Splashed with a splendid sickness, the sickness of the pearl;
They swell in sapphire smoke out of the blue cracks of the ground, —
They gather and they wonder and give worship to Mahound.
And he saith, "Break up the mountains where the hermit-folk can hide,
And sift the red and silver sands lest bone of saint abide,
And chase the Giaours flying night and day, not giving rest,
For that which was our trouble comes again out of the west.
We have set the seal of Solomon on all things under sun,
Of knowledge and of sorrow and endurance of things done,
But a noise is in the mountains, in the mountains, and I know
The voice that shook our palaces — four hundred years ago:
It is he that saith not 'Kismet'; it is he that knows not Fate;
It is Richard, it is Raymond, it is Godfrey in the gate!
It is he whose loss is laughter when he counts the wager worth,
Put down your feet upon him, that our peace be on the earth."
For he heard drums groaning and he heard guns far,
(*Don John of Austria is going to the war.*)
Sudden and still — hurrah!
Bolt from Iberia!
Don John of Austria
Is gone by Alcalar.

St. Michael's on his Mountain in the sea-roads of the north
(*Don John of Austria is girt and going forth.*)
Where the grey seas glitter and the sharp tides shift
And the sea-folk labour and the red sails lift.
He shakes his lance of iron and he claps his wings of stone;
The noise is gone through Normandy; the noise is gone alone;
The North is full of tangled things and texts and aching eyes
And dead is all the innocence of anger and surprise,
And Christian killeth Christian in a narrow dusty room,
And Christian dreadeth Christ that hath a newer face of doom,
And Christian hateth Mary that God kissed in Galilee,
But Don John of Austria is riding to the sea.
Don John calling through the blast and the eclipse
Crying with the trumpet, with the trumpet of his lips,
Trumpet that sayeth ha!
Domino gloria!
Don John of Austria
Is shouting to the ships.

King Philip's in his closet with the Fleece about his neck
(*Don John of Austria is armed upon the deck.*)
The walls are hung with velvet that is black and soft as sin,
And little dwarfs creep out of it and little dwarfs creep in.

He holds a crystal phial that has colours like the moon,
He touches, and it tingles, and he trembles very soon,
And his face is as a fungus of a leprous white and grey
Like plants in the high houses that are shuttered from the day,
And death is in the phial and the end of noble work,
But Don John of Austria has fired upon the Turk.
Don John's hunting, and his hounds have bayed —
Booms away past Italy the rumour of his raid.
Gun upon gun, ha! ha!
Gun upon gun, hurrah!
Don John of Austria
Has loosed the cannonade.

The Pope was in his chapel before day or battle broke,
(*Don John of Austria is hidden in the smoke.*)
The hidden room in man's house where God sits all the year,
The secret window whence the world looks small and very dear.
He sees as in a mirror on the monstrous twilight sea
The crescent of his cruel ships whose name is mystery;
They fling great shadows foe-wards, making Cross and Castle dark,
They veil the plumed lions on the galleys of St. Mark;
And above the ships are palaces of brown, black-bearded chiefs,
And below the ships are prisons, where with multitudinous griefs,
Christian captives sick and sunless, all a labouring race repines
Like a race in sunken cities, like a nation in the mines.
They are lost like slaves that swat, and in the skies of morning hung
The stair-ways of the tallest gods when tyranny was young.
They are countless, voiceless, hopeless as those fallen or fleeing on
Before the high Kings' horses in the granite of Babylon.
And many a one grows witless in his quiet room in hell
Where a yellow face looks inward through the lattice of his cell,
And he finds his God forgotten, and he seeks no more a sign —
(*But Don John of Austria has burst the battle-line!*)
Don John pounding from the slaughter-painted poop,
Purpling all the ocean like a bloody pirate's sloop,

Scarlet running over on the silvers and the golds,
Breaking of the hatches up and bursting of the holds,
Thronging of the thousands up that labour under sea
White for bliss and blind for sun and stunned for liberty.
Vivat Hispania!
Domino Gloria!
Don John of Austria
Has set his people free!

Cervantes on his galley sets the sword back in the sheath
(*Don John of Austria rides homeward with a wreath.*)
And he sees across a weary land a straggling road in Spain,
Up which a lean and foolish knight for ever rides in vain,
And he smiles, but not as Sultans smile, and settles back the blade. . . .
(*But Don John of Austria rides home from the Crusade.*)

THE LOGICAL VEGETARIAN

"Why shouldn't I have a purely vegetarian drink? Why shouldn't I take vegetables in their highest form, so to speak? The modest vegetarians ought obviously to stick to wine or beer, plain vegetarian drinks, instead of filling their goblets with the blood of bulls and elephants, as all conventional meat-eaters do, I suppose." — *Dalroy.*

You will find me drinking rum,
Like a sailor in a slum,
You will find me drinking beer like a
    Bavarian.
You will find me drinking gin
In the lowest kind of inn,
Because I am a rigid Vegetarian.

So I cleared the inn of wine,
And I tried to climb the sign,
And I tried to hail the constable as "Marion."
    But he said I couldn't speak,
    And he bowled me to the Beak
Because I was a happy Vegetarian.

Oh, I knew a Doctor Gluck,
And his nose it had a hook,
And his attitudes were anything but Aryan;
    So I gave him all the pork
    That I had, upon a fork
Because I am myself a Vegetarian.

I am silent in the Club,
I am silent in the pub,
I am silent on a bally peak in Darien;
    For I stuff away for life
    Shoving peas in with a knife,
Because I am at heart a Vegetarian.

No more the milk of cows
Shall pollute my private house
Than the milk of the wild mares of the
    Barbarian;
    I will stick to port and sherry,
    For they are so very, very,
So very, very, very Vegetarian.

CHAPTER XII

THE ORTHODOX BARBER*

THOSE thinkers who cannot believe in any gods often assert that the love of humanity would be in itself sufficient for them; and so, perhaps, it would, if they had it. There is a very real thing which may be called the love of humanity; in our time it exists almost entirely among those that are called uneducated people; and it does not exist at all among the people who talk about it.

A positive pleasure in being in the presence of any other human being is chiefly remarkable, for instance, in the masses on Bank Holiday; that is why they are so much nearer Heaven (despite appearances) than any other part of our population.

I remember seeing a crowd of factory girls getting into an empty train at a wayside country station. There were about twenty of them; they all got into one carriage; and they left all the rest of the train entirely empty. That is the real love of humanity. That is the definite pleasure in the immediate proximity of one's own kind. Only this coarse, rank, real love of men seems to be entirely lacking in those who propose the love of humanity as a substitute for all other love; honourable, rationalistic idealists.

I can well remember the explosion of human joy which marked the sudden starting of that train; all the factory girls who could not find seats (and they must have been the majority) relieving their feelings by jumping up and down. Now I have never seen any

*Chesterton, G. K., *Tremendous Trifles* (New York: Dodd, Mead and Co., 1915), pp. 168–175.

rationalistic idealists do this. I have never seen twenty modern philosophers crowd into one third-class carriage for the mere pleasure of being together. I have never seen twenty Mr. McCabes all in one carriage and all jumping up and down.

Some people express a fear that vulgar trippers will overrun all beautiful places, such as Hampstead or Burnham Beeches. But their fear is unreasonable; because trippers always prefer to trip together; they pack as close as they can; they have a suffocating passion of philanthropy.

But among the minor and milder aspects of the same principle, I have no hesitation in placing the problem of the colloquial barber. Before any modern man talks with authority about loving men, I insist (I insist with violence) that he shall always be very much pleased when his barber tries to talk to him. His barber is humanity: let him love that. If he is not pleased at this, I will not accept any substitute in the way of interest in the Congo or in the future of Japan. If a man cannot love his barber whom he has seen, how shall he love the Japanese whom he has not seen?

It is urged against the barber that he begins by talking about the weather; so do all dukes and diplomatists, only that they talk about it with ostentatious fatigue and indifference, whereas the barber talks about it with an astonishing, nay incredible, freshness of interest. It is objected to him that he tells people that they are going bald. That is to say, his very virtues are cast up against him; he is blamed because, being a specialist, he is a sincere specialist, and because, being a tradesman, he is not entirely a slave. But if the reader really objects to the conversation of barbers, there is one method of escape which I can easily recommend and not unfrequently adopt; that is, to do all the talking yourself, as in the following case. The following scene between me and a human (I trust), living barber really took place a few days ago.

I had been invited to some At Home to meet the Colonial Premiers, and lest I should be mistaken for some partly reformed bushranger out of the interior of Australia I went into a shop in the Strand to get shaved. While I was undergoing the torture the man said to me —

"There seems to be a lot in the papers about this new shaving, sir. It seems you can shave yourself with anything — with a stick or a stone or a pole or a poker" (here I began for the first time to detect a sarcastic intonation) "or a shovel or a — ".

Here he hesitated for a word, and I, although I knew nothing about the matter, helped him out with suggestions in the same rhetorical vein.

"Or a button-hook," I said, "or a blunderbuss or a battering-ram or a piston-rod — "

He resumed, refreshed with this assistance, "Or a curtain-rod or a candle-stick or a — "

"Cow-catcher," I suggested eagerly, and we continued in this ecstatic duet for some time. Then I asked him what it was all about, and he told me. He explained the thing eloquently and at length.

"The funny part of it is," he said, "that the thing isn't new at all. It's been talked about ever since I was a boy, and long before. There was always a notion that the razor might be done without somehow. But none of those schemes ever came to anything; and I don't believe myself that this will."

"Why, as to that," I said, rising slowly from the chair and trying to put on my coat inside out, "I don't know how it may be in the case of you and your new shaving. Shaving, with all respect to you, is a trivial and materialistic thing, and in such things startling inventions are sometimes made. But what you say reminds me in some dark and dreamy fashion of something else. I recall it especially when you tell me, with such evident experience and sincerity, that the new shaving is not really new. My friend, the human race is always trying this dodge of making everything entirely easy; but the difficulty which it shifts off one thing it shifts on to another. If one man has not the toil of preparing a man's chin, I suppose that some other man has the toil of preparing something very curious to put on a man's chin. It would be very nice if we could be shaved without troubling anybody. It would be nicer still if we could go unshaved without annoying anybody —

'But, O wise friend, chief Barber of the Strand, Brother, nor you nor I have made the world.'

Whoever made it, who is wiser, and we hope better than we, made it under strange limitations, and with painful conditions of pleasure.

"In the first and darkest of its books it is fiercely written that a man shall not eat his cake and have it; and though all men talked until the stars were old it would still be true that a man who had shaved had lost his beard, and that a man who had lost his razor could not shave with it. But every now and then men jump up with the new something or other and say that everything can be had without sacrifice, that bad is good if you are only enlightened, and that there is no real difference between being shaved and not being shaved. The difference, they say, is only a difference of degree; everything is evolutionary and relative. Shavedness is im-manent in man. Every tenpenny nail is a Potential Razor. The superstitious people of the past (they say) believed that a lot of black bristles standing out at right angles to one's face was a positive affair. But the higher criticism teaches us better. Bristles are merely negative. They are a Shadow where Shaving should be.

"Well, it all goes on, and I suppose it all means something. But a baby is the Kingdom of God, and if you try to kiss a baby he will know whether you are shaved or not. Perhaps I am mixing up being shaved and being saved; my democratic sympathies have always led me to drop my 'h's'. In another moment I may suggest that goats represent the lost because goats have long beards. This is growing altogether too allegorical.

"Nevertheless," I added, as I paid the bill. "I have really been profoundly interested in what you told me about the New Shaving. Have you ever heard of a thing called the New Theology?"

He smiled and said that he had not.

THE EVERLASTING MAN*

Part II–Chapter I

CHRISTMAS for us in Christendom has become one thing, and in one sense even a simple thing. But like all the truths of that tradition, it is in another sense a very complex thing. Its unique note is the simultaneous striking of many notes; of humility, of gaiety, of gratitude, of mystical fear, but also of vigilance and of drama. It is not only an occasion for the peacemakers any more than for the merry-makers; it is not only a Hindu peace conference any more than it is only a Scandinavian winter feast. There is something defiant in it also; something that makes the abrupt bells at midnight sound like the great guns of a battle that has just been won. All this indescribable thing that we call the Christmas atmosphere only hangs in the air as something like a lingering fragrance or fading vapour from the exultant explosion of that one hour in the Judean hills nearly two thousand years ago. But the savour is still unmistakable, and it is something too subtle or too solitary to be covered by our use of the world peace. By the very nature of the story the rejoicings in the cavern were rejoicings in a fortress or an outlaw's den; properly understood it is not unduly flippant to say they were rejoicings in a dug-out. It is not only true that such a subterranean chamber was a hiding-place from enemies; and that the enemies were already scouring the stony plain that lay above it like a sky. It is not only that the very horse-hoofs of Herod might in that sense have passed like thunder over the sunken head of Christ. It is also that there is in that image a true idea of an outpost, of a piercing through the rock and an entrance into an enemy territory. There is in this buried divinity an idea of *undermining*

*Chesterton, G. K., *The Everlasting Man* (New York: Dodd, Mead and Co., 1926), pp. 217–223.

the world; of shaking the towers and palaces from below; even as Herod the great king felt that earthquake under him and swayed with his swaying palace.

That is perhaps the mightiest of the mysteries of the cave. It is already apparent that though men are said to have looked for hell under the earth, in this case it is rather heaven that is under the earth. And there follows in this strange story the idea of an upheaval of heaven. That is the paradox of the whole position; that henceforth the highest thing can only work from below. Royalty can only return to its own by a sort of rebellion. Indeed the Church from its beginnings, and perhaps especially in its beginnings, was not so much a principality as a revolution against the prince of the world. This sense that the world had been conquered by the great usurper, and was in his possession, has been much deplored or derided by those optimists who identify enlightenment with ease. But it was responsible for all that thrill of defiance and a beautiful danger that made the good news seem to be really both good and new. It was in truth against a huge unconscious usurpation that it raised a revolt, and originally so obscure a revolt. Olympus still occupied the sky like a motionless cloud moulded into many mighty forms; philosophy still sat in the high places and even on the thrones of the kings, when Christ was born in the cave and Christianity in the catacombs.

In both cases we may remark the same paradox of revolution; the sense of something despised and of something feared. The cave in one aspect is only a hole or corner into which the outcasts are swept like rubbish; yet in the other aspect it is a hiding-place of something valuable which the tyrants are seeking like treasure. In one sense they are there because the innkeeper would not even remember them, and in another because the king can never forget them. We have already noted that this paradox appeared also in the treatment of the early Church. It was important while it was still insignificant, and certainly while it was still impotent. It was important solely because it was intolerable; and in that sense it is true to say that it was intolerable because it was intolerant. It was resented, because, in its own still and almost secret way, it had declared war. It had risen out of the ground to wreck the heaven and earth of heathenism. It did not try to destroy all that creation of gold and marble; but it contemplated a world without it. It dared to look right through it as though the gold and marble had been glass. Those who charged the Christians with burning down Rome with firebrands were slanderers; but they were at least far nearer to the nature of Christianity than those among the moderns who tell us that the Christians were a sort of ethical society, being martyred in a languid fashion for telling men they had a duty to their neighbours, and only mildly disliked because they were meek and mild.

Herod had his place, therefore, in the miracle play of Bethlehem because he is the menace to the Church Militant and shows it from the first as under persecution and fighting for its life. For those who think this is a discord, it is a discord that sounds simultaneously with the Christmas bells. For those who think the idea of the Crusade is one that spoils the idea of the Cross, we can only say that for them the idea of the Cross is spoiled; the idea of the Cross is spoiled quite literally in the cradle. It is not here to the purpose to argue with them on the abstract ethics of fighting; the purpose in this place is merely to sum up the combination of ideas that make up the Christian and Catholic idea, and to note that all of them are already crystallized in the first Christmas story. They are three distinct and commonly contrasted things which are nevertheless one thing; but this is the only thing which can make them one. The first is the human instinct for a heaven that shall be as literal and almost as local as a home. It is the idea pursued by all poets and pagans making myths; that a particular place must be the shrine of the god or the abode of the blest; that fairyland is a land; or that the return of the ghost must be the resurrection of the body. I do not here reason about the refusal of rationalism to satisfy this need. I only say that if the rationalists refuse to satisfy it, the pagans will not

be satisfied. This is present in the story of
Bethlehem and Jerusalem as it is present in
the story of Delos and Delphi; and as it is
not present in the whole universe of Lucretius or the whole universe of Herbert Spencer. The second element is a philosophy
larger than other philosophies; larger than
that of Lucretius and infinitely larger than
that of Herbert Spencer. It looks at the world
through a hundred windows where the ancient stoic or the modern agnostic only looks
through one. It sees life with thousands of
eyes belonging to thousands of different sorts
of people, where the other is only the individual standpoint of a stoic or an agnostic.
It has something for all moods of man, it
finds work for all kinds of men, it understands secrets of psychology, it is aware of
depths of evil, it is able to distinguish between real and unreal marvels and miraculous exceptions, it trains itself in tact about
hard cases, all with a multiplicity and subtlety and imagination about the varieties of
life which is far beyond the bald or breezy
platitudes of most ancient or modern moral
philosophy. In a word, there is more in it;
it finds more in existence to think about; it
gets more out of life. Masses of this material
about our many-sided life have been added
since the time of St. Thomas Aquinas. But
St. Thomas Aquinas alone would have found
himself limited in the world of Confucius
or of Comte. And the third point is this;
that while it is local enough for poetry and
larger than any other philosophy, it is also
a challenge and a fight. While it is deliberately broadened to embrace every aspect of
truth, it is still stiffly embattled against every
mode of error. It gets every kind of man to
fight for it, it gets every kind of weapon to
fight with, it widens its knowledge of the
things that are fought for and against with
every art of curiosity or sympathy; but it
never forgets that it is fighting. It proclaims
peace on earth and never forgets why there
was war in heaven.

This is the trinity of truths symbolised
here by the three types in the old Christmas
story; the shepherds and the kings and that
other king who warred upon the children.
It is simply not true to say that other reli-

gions and philosophies are in this respect its
rivals. It is not true to say that any one of
them combines these characters; it is not true
to say that any one of them pretends to
combine them. Buddhism may profess to be
equally mystical; it does not even profess to
be equally military. Islam may profess to be
equally military; it does not even profess to
be equally metaphysical and subtle. Confu-
cianism may profess to satisfy the need of the
philosophers for order and reason; it does
not even profess to satisfy the need of the
mystics for miracle and sacrament and the
consecration of concrete things. There are
many evidences of this presence of a spirit
at once universal and unique. One will serve
here which is the symbol of the subject of
this chapter; that no other story, no pagan
legend or philosophical anecdote or historical
event, does in fact affect any of us with that
peculiar and even poignant impression produced on us by the word Bethlehem. No
other birth of a god or childhood of a sage
seems to us to be Christmas or anything like
Christmas. It is either too cold or too frivolous, or too formal and classical, or too simple
and savage, or too occult and complicated.
Not one of us, whatever his opinions, would
ever go to such a scene with the sense that
he was going home. He might admire it
because it was poetical, or because it was
philosophical, or any number of other things
in separation; but not because it was itself.
The truth is that there is a quite peculiar and
individual character about the hold of this
story on human nature; it is not in its psychological substance at all like a mere legend
or the life of a great man. It does not exactly
in the ordinary sense turn our minds to
greatness; to those extensions and exaggerations of humanity which are turned into gods
and heroes, even by the healthiest sort of
hero-worship. It does not exactly work outwards, adventurously, to the wonders to be
found at the ends of the earth. It is rather
something that surprises us from behind,
from the hidden and personal part of our being; like that which can sometimes take us
off our guard in the pathos of small objects
or the blind pieties of the poor. It is rather as
if a man had found an inner room in the

very heart of his own house, which he had never suspected; and seen a light from within. It is as if he found something at the back of his own heart that betrayed him into good. It is not made of what the world would call strong materials; or rather it is made of materials whose strength is in that winged levity with which they brush us and pass. It is all that is in us but a brief tenderness that is there made eternal; all that means no more than a momentary softening that is in some strange fashion become a strengthening and a repose; it is the broken speech and the lost word that are made positive and suspended unbroken; as the strange kings fade into a far country and the mountains resound no more with the feet of the shepherds; and only the night and the cavern lie in fold upon fold over something more human than humanity.

ON DETECTIVE NOVELS*

IT IS now some years since Miss Carolyn Wells, the American lady who has produced many of our most charming stories of murder and mystification, wrote to a magazine to complain of the unsatisfactory sort of review accorded to that sort of book; but not yet has the abuse been corrected. She said it is only too obvious that the task of reviewing detective stories is given to people who do not like detective stories. She says, and I think not unreasonably, that this is very unreasonable: a book of poems is not sent to a man who hates poetry; an ordinary novel is not reviewed by a rigid moralist who regards all novels as immoral. If mystery stories have any right to be reviewed at all, they have a right to be reviewed by the sort of person who understands why they were written. And the lady proceeds to say that, by this neglect, the nature of the technique really required in such a tale is never adequately discussed. I, for one, agree with her that it is a matter well worthy of discussion. There is no better reading, and in the true sense no more serious reading, than the few critical passages which great critics have devoted to this literary question; such as Edgar Allan Poe's disquisition on analysis at the beginning of the beautiful idyll about the murderous ape; or the studies of Andrew Lang on the problem of Edwin Drood; or the remarks of Stevenson on the police novel at the end of The Wrecker. Any such discussion, clearly conducted, will soon show that the rules of art are as much involved in this artistic form as in any other; and it is not any objection to such a form that people can enjoy it who cannot criticize it. The same is true of any good song or any sound romance. By a curious confusion, many modern critics have passed from the proposition that a masterpiece may be unpopular to the other proposition that unless it is unpopular it cannot be a masterpiece. It is as if one were to say that because a clever man may have an impediment in his speech, therefore a man cannot be clever unless he stammers. For all unpopularity is a sort of obscurity; and all obscurity is a defect of expression like a stammer. Anyhow, I am in this matter on the popular side; I am interested in all sorts of sensational fiction, good, bad and indifferent, and would willingly discuss it with a much less capable exponent of it than the author of Vicky Van. And if anyone likes to say that my tastes are vulgar and inartistic and illiterate, I can only say I am quite content to be as vulgar as Poe and as inartistic and illiterate as Andrew Lang.

Now, it is all the more curious that the technique of such tales is not discussed, because they are exactly the sort in which technique is nearly the whole of the trick.

It is all the more odd that such writers have no critical guidance, because it is one of the few forms of art in which they could to some extent be guided. And it is all the

*Chesterton, G. K., Generally Speaking (New York: Dodd, Mead and Co., 1929), pp. 1-7.

more strange that nobody discusses the rules, because it is one of the rare cases in which some rules could be laid down. The very fact that the work is not of the highest order of creation makes it possible to treat it as a question of construction. But while people are willing to teach poets imagination, they seem to think it hopeless to help plotters in a matter of mere ingenuity. There are text-books instructing people in the manufacture of sonnets, as if the visions of bare ruined quires where late sweet birds sang, or of the ground-whirl of the perished leaves of hope, the wind of death's imperishable wing, were things to be explained like a conjuring trick. We have monographs expounding the art of the Short Story, as if the dripping horror of the *House of Usher* or the sunny irony of the *Treasure of Franchard* were recipes out of a cookery book. But in the case of the only kind of story to which the strict laws of logic are in some sense applicable, nobody seems to bother to apply them, or even to ask whether in this or in that case they are applied. Nobody writes the simple book which I expect every day to see on the book-stalls, called *How to Write a Detective Story*.

I myself have got no further than discovering how not to write one. But even from my own failures I have gained stray glimpses of what such a scheme of warnings might be. Of one preliminary principle I am pretty certain. The whole point of a sensational story is that the secret should be simple. The whole story exists for the moment of surprise; and it should be a moment. It should not be something that it takes twenty minutes to explain, and twenty-four hours to learn by heart, for fear of forgetting it. The best way of testing it is to make an imaginative picture in the mind of some such dramatic moment. Imagine a dark garden at twilight, and a terrible voice crying out in the distance, and coming nearer and nearer along the serpentine garden paths until the words become dreadfully distinct; a cry coming from some sinister yet familiar figure in the story, a stranger or a servant from whom we subconsciously expect some such rending revelation. Now, it is clear that the cry which breaks from him must be something short

and simple in itself, as, "The butler is his father," or "The Archdeacon is Bloody Bill," or "The Emperor has cut his throat," or what not. But too many otherwise ingenious romancers seem to think it their duty to discover what is the most complicated and improbable series of events that could be combined to produce a certain result. The result may be logical, but it is not sensational.

The servant cannot rend the silence of the twilight garden by shrieking aloud: "The throat of the Emperor was cut under the following circumstances: his Imperial Majesty was attempting to shave himself and went to sleep in the middle of it, fatigued with the cares of state; the Archdeacon was attempting at first in a Christian spirit to complete the shaving operation on the sleeping monarch, when he was suddenly tempted to a murderous act by the memory of the Disestablishment Bill, but repented after making a mere scratch and flung the razor on the floor; the faithful butler, hearing the commotion, rushed in and snatched up the weapon, but in the confusion of the moment cut the Emperor's throat instead of the Archdeacon's; so everything is satisfactory, and the young man and the girl can leave off suspecting each other of assassination and get married." Now, this explanation, however reasonable and complete, is not one that can be conveniently uttered as an exclamation or can sound suddenly in the twilight garden like the trump of doom. Anyone who will try the experiment of crying aloud the above paragraph in his own twilight garden will realize the difficulty here referred to. It is exactly one of those little technical experiments, illustrated with diagrams, with which our little text-book would abound.

Another truth to which our little text-book would at least tentatively incline is that the *roman policier* should be on the model of the short story rather than the novel.

There are splendid exceptions: *The Moonstone* and one or two Gaboriaus are great works in this style; as are, in our own time, Mr. Bentley's *Trent's Last Case,* and Mr. Milne's *Red House Mystery.* But I think that the difficulties of a long detective novel are real difficulties, though very clever men can by various expedients get over them. The chief difficulty is that the detective story is, after all, a drama of masks and not of faces. It depends on men's false characters rather than their real characters. The author cannot tell us until the last chapter any of the most interesting things about the most interesting people. It is a masquerade ball in which everybody is disguised as somebody else, and there is no true personal interest until the clock strikes twelve. That is, as I have said, we cannot really get at the psychology and philosophy, the morals and the religion, of the thing until we have read the last chapter.

The length of a short story is about the legitimate length for this particular drama of the mere misunderstanding of fact. When all is said and done, there have never been better detective stories than the old series of Sherlock Holmes; and though the name of that magnificent magician has been spread over the whole world, and is perhaps the one great popular legend made in the modern world, I do not think that Sir Arthur Conan Doyle has ever been thanked enough for them. As one of many millions, I offer my own mite of homage.

Chapter XVII

ON THE WIT OF WHISTLER*

THAT capable and ingenious writer, Mr. Arthur Symons, has included in a book of essays recently published, I believe, an apologia for "London Nights," in which he says that morality should be wholly subordinated to art in criticism, and he uses the somewhat singular argument that art of the worship of beauty is the same in all ages, while morality differs in every period and in every respect. He appears to defy his critics or his readers to mention any permanent feature or quality in ethics. This is surely a very curious example of that extravagant bias against morality which makes so many ultra-modern aesthetes as morbid and fanatical as any Eastern hermit. Unquestionably it is a very common phrase of modern intellectualism to say that the morality of one age can be entirely different to the morality of another. And like a great many other phases of modern intellectualism, it means literally nothing at all. If the two moralities are entirely different, why do you call them both moralities? It is as if a man said, "Camels in various places are totally diverse; some have six legs, some have none, some have scales, some have feathers, some have horns, some have wings, some are

green, some are triangular. There is no point which they have in common." The ordinary man of sense would reply, "Then what makes you call them all camels? What do you mean by a camel? How do you know a camel when you see one?" Of course, there is a permanent substance of morality, as much as there is a permanent substance of art; to say that is only to say that morality is morality, and that art is art. An ideal art critic would, no doubt, see the enduring beauty under every school; equally an ideal moralist would see the enduring ethic under every code. But practically some of the best Englishmen that ever lived could see nothing but filth and idolatry in the starry piety of the Brahmin. And it is equally true that practically the greatest group of artists that the world has ever seen, the giants of the Renaissance, could see nothing but barbarism in the ethereal energy of Gothic.

This bias against morality among the modern aesthetes is a thing very much paraded. And yet it is not really a bias against morality; it is a bias against other people's morality. It is generally founded on a very definite moral preference for a certain sort of life, pagan, plausible, humane. The modern aesthete, wishing us to believe that he values beauty more than conduct, reads Mallarme,

*Chesterton, G. K., *Heretics* (New York: Dodd, Mead and Co., 1935), pp. 234–246.

and drinks absinthe in a tavern. But this is not only his favourite kind of beauty; it is also his favourite kind of conduct. If he really wished us to believe that he cared for beauty only, he ought to go to nothing but Wesleyan school treats, and paint the sunlight in the hair of the Wesleyan babies. He ought to read nothing but very eloquent theological sermons by old-fashioned Presbyterian divines. Here the lack of all possible moral sympathy would prove that his interest was purely verbal or pictorial, as it is; in all the books he reads and writes he clings to the skirts of his own morality and his own immorality. The champion of *l'art pour l'art* is always denouncing Ruskin for his moralising. If he were really a champion of *l'art pour l'art,* he would be always insisting on Ruskin for his style.

The doctrine of the distinction between art and morality owes a great part of its success to art and morality being hopelessly mixed up in the persons and performances of its greatest exponents. Of this lucky contradiction the very incarnation was Whistler. No man ever preached the impersonality of art so well; no man ever preached the impersonality of art so personally. For him pictures had nothing to do with the problems of character; but for all his fiercest admirers his character was, as a matter of fact, far more interesting than his pictures. He gloried in standing as an artist apart from right and wrong. But he succeeded by talking from morning till night about his rights and about his wrongs. His talents were many, his virtues, it must be confessed, not many, beyond that kindness to tried friends, on which many of his biographers insist, but which surely is a quality of all sane men, of pirates and pickpockets; beyond this, his outstanding virtues limit themselves chiefly to two admirable ones — courage and an abstract love of good work. Yet I fancy he won at last more by those two virtues than by all his talents. A man must be something of a moralist if he is to preach, even if he is to preach unmorality. Professor Walter Raleigh, in his "In Memoriam: James McNeill Whistler," insists, truly enough, on the strong streak of an eccentric

honesty in matters strictly pictorial, which ran through his complex and slightly confused character. "He would destroy any of his works rather than leave a careless or inexpressive touch within the limits of the frame. He would begin again a hundred times over rather than attempt by patching to make his work seem better than it was."

No one will blame Professor Raleigh, who had to read a sort of funeral oration over Whistler at the opening of the Memorial Exhibition, if, finding himself in that position, he confined himself mostly to the merits and the stronger qualities of his subject. We should naturally go to some other type of composition for a proper consideration of the weaknesses of Whistler. But these must never be omitted from our view of him. Indeed, the truth is that it was not so much a question of the weaknesses of Whistler as of the intrinsic and primary weakness of Whistler. He was one of those people who live up to their emotional incomes, who are always taut and tingling with vanity. Hence he had no strength to spare; hence he had no kindness, no geniality; for geniality is almost definable as strength to spare. He had no godlike carelessness; he never forgot himself; his whole life was, to use his own expression, an arrangement. He went in for "the art of living" — a miserable trick. In a word, he was a great artist; but emphatically not a great man. In this connection I must differ strongly with Professor Raleigh upon what is, from a superficial literary point of view, one of his most effective points. He compares Whistler's laughter to the laughter of another man who was a great man as well as a great artist. "His attitude to the public was exactly the attitude taken up by Robert Browning, who suffered as long a period of neglect and mistake, in those lines of 'The Ring and the Book' —

" ' Well, British Public, ye who like me not,
(God love you!) and will have your proper laugh
At the dark question; laugh it! I'd laugh first.' "

"Mr. Whistler," adds Professor Raleigh,

"always laughed first." The truth is, I believe, that Whistler never laughed at all. There was no laughter in his nature; because there was no thoughtlessness and self-abandonment, no humility. I cannot understand anybody reading "The Gentle Art of Making Enemies" and thinking that there is any laughter in the wit. His wit is a torture to him. He twists himself into arabesques of verbal felicity; he is full of a fierce carefulness; he is inspired with the complete seriousness of sincere malice. He hurts himself to hurt his opponent. Browning did laugh, because Browning did not care; Browning did not care, because Browning was a great man. And when Browning said in brackets to the simple, sensible people who did not like his books, "God love you!" he was not sneering in the least. He was laughing — that is to say, he meant exactly what he said.

There are three distinct classes of great satirists who are also great men — that is to say, three classes of men who can laugh at something without losing their souls. The satirist of the first type is the man who, first of all, enjoys himself, and then enjoys his enemies. In this sense he loves his enemy, and by a kind of exaggeration of Christianity he loves his enemy the more he becomes an enemy. He has a sort of overwhelming and aggressive happiness in his assertion of anger; his curse is as human as a benediction. Of this type of satire the great example is Rabelais. This is the first typical example of satire, the satire which is voluble, which is violent, which is indecent, but which is not malicious. The satire of Whistler was not this. He was never in any of his controversies simply happy; the proof of it is that he never talked absolute nonsense. There is a second type of mind which produces satire with the quality of greatness. That is embodied in the satirist whose passions are released and let go by some intolerable sense of wrong. He is maddened by the sense of men being maddened; his tongue becomes an unruly member, and testifies against all mankind. Such a man was Swift, in whom the *saeva indignatio* was a bitterness to others, because it was a bitterness to

himself. Such a satirist Whistler was not. He did not laugh because he was happy, like Rabelais. But neither did he laugh because he was unhappy, like Swift.

The third type of great satire is that in which the satirist is enabled to rise superior to his victim in the only serious sense which superiority can bear, in that of pitying the sinner and respecting the man even while he satirises both. Such an achievement can be found in a thing like Pope's "Atticus," a poem in which the satirist feels that he is satirising the weaknesses which belong specially to literary genius. Consequently he takes a pleasure in pointing out his enemy's strength before he points out his weakness. That is, perhaps, the highest and most honourable form of satire. That is not the satire of Whistler. He is not full of a great sorrow for the wrong done to human nature; for him the wrong is altogether done to himself.

He was not a great personality, because he thought so much about himself. And the case is stronger even than that. He was sometimes not even a great artist, because he thought so much about art. Any man with a vital knowledge of the human psychology ought to have the most profound suspicion of anybody who claims to be an artist, and talks a great deal about art. Art is a right and human thing, like walking or saying one's prayers; but the moment it begins to be talked about very solemnly, a man may be fairly certain that the thing has come into a congestion and a kind of difficulty.

The artistic temperament is a disease that afflicts amateurs. It is a disease which arises from men not having sufficient power of expression to utter and get rid of the element of art in their being. It is healthful to every sane man to utter the art within him; it is essential to every sane man to get rid of the art within him at all costs. Artists of a large and wholesome vitality get rid of their art easily, as they breathe easily, or perspire easily. But in artists of less force, the thing becomes a pressure, and produces a definite pain, which is called the artistic temperament. Thus, very great artists are able to be ordinary men — men like Shake-speare or Browning. There are many real tragedies of the artistic temperament, trage-dies of vanity or violence or fear. But the great tragedy of the artistic temperament is that it cannot produce any art.

Whistler could produce art; and in so far he was a great man. But he could not forget art; and in so far he was only a man with the artistic temperament. There can be no stronger manifestation of the man who is a really great artist than the fact that he can dismiss the subject of art; that he can, upon due occasion, wish art at the bottom of the sea. Similarly, we should always be much more inclined to trust a solicitor who did not talk about conveyancing over the nuts and wine. What we really desire of any man conducting any business is that the full force of an ordinary man should be put into that particular study. We do not desire that the full force of that study should be put into an ordinary man. We do not in the least wish that our particular law-suit should pour its energy into our barrister's games with his children, or rides on his bicycle, or meditations on the morn-ing star. But we do, as a matter of fact, desire that his games with his children, and his rides on his bicycle, and his meditations on the morning star should pour something of their energy into our law-suit. We do desire that if he has gained any especial lung development from the bicycle, or any bright and pleasing metaphors from the morning star, that they should be placed at our dis-posal in that particular forensic controversy. In a word, we are very glad that he is an ordinary man, since that may help him to be an exceptional lawyer.

Whistler never ceased to be an artist. As Mr. Max Beerbohm pointed out in one of his extraordinary sensible and sincere cri-tiques, Whistler really regarded Whistler as his greatest work of art. The white lock, the single eye-glass, the remark-hat — these were much dearer to him than any nocturnes or arrangements that he ever threw off. He could throw off the nocturnes; for some mysterious reason he could not throw off the hat. He never threw off from himself

that disproportionate accumulation of aesthe-ticism which is the burden of the amateur.

It need hardly be said that this is the real explanation of the thing which has puzzled so many dilettante critics, the problem of the extreme ordinariness of the behaviour of so many great geniuses in history. Their behaviour was so ordinary that it was not recorded; hence it was so ordinary that it seemed mysterious. Hence people say that Bacon wrote Shakespeare. The modern artis-tic temperament cannot understand how a man who could write such lyrics as Shake-speare wrote, could be as keen as Shake-speare was on business transactions in a little town in Warwickshire. The explanation is simple enough; it is that Shakespeare had a real lyrical impulse, wrote a real lyric, and so got rid of the impulse and went about his business. Being an artist did not pre-vent him from being an ordinary man, any more than being a sleeper at night or being a diner at dinner prevented him from being an ordinary man.

All very great teachers and leaders have had this habit of assuming their point of view to be one which was human and casual, one which would readily appeal to every passing man. If a man is genuinely superior to his fellows the first thing that he believes in is the equality of man. We can see this, for instance, in that strange and innocent rationality with which Christ addressed any motley crowd that happened to stand about Him. "What man of you having a hundred sheep, and losing one, would not leave the ninety and nine in the wilderness, and go after that which was lost?" Or, again, "What man of you if his son ask for bread will he give him a stone, or if he ask for a fish will he give him a serpent?" This plainness, this almost prosaic camaraderie, is the note of all very great minds.

To very great minds the things on which men agree are so immeasurably more im-portant than the things on which they differ, that the latter, for all practical purposes, disappear. They have too much in them of an ancient laughter even to endure to dis-cuss the difference between the hats of two men who were both born of a woman, or between the subtly varied cultures of two men who have both to die. The first-rate great man is equal with other men, like Shakespeare. The second-rate great man is on his knees to other men, like Whitman. The third-rate great man is superior to other men, like Whistler.

JOHN AYSCOUGH

(1858–1928)

FRANCIS BICKERSTAFFE - D R E W, who wrote under the pen name of John Ayscough, was born at Headingheeds, England, 1858. An Oxford graduate, he was converted to the Catholic Church in 1878 and was ordained priest 1874. Pius IX created him a Domestic Prelate. In 1902 Monsignor Bickerstaffe-Drew received the medal *Pro Ecclesia et Pontifice*. In World War I, in which Monsignor Bickerstaffe-Drew was a chaplain, he achieved considerable distinction because of his war writings. He died in 1928 and is buried at Winterbourne Gunner.

The novels of John Ayscough, such as *Monksbridge* and *Abbotscourt*, though not of first intensity, reveal Ayscough's soundness as a delineator of character.

ENGLISH*

AN ORCHARD flanking a well-to-do farm-house, itself the last house in a village: the village stone-built, like all the others in that region. The cottages along the street more like farmhouses than the actual one by the orchard, because the latter had smartened itself up, and half villafied itself. The street curving down to its middle-point like a slackly strung rope, and in the hollow of the dip the church, locked and empty, priestless; the priest, a soldier somewhere.

In the street hardly any native life: our lot just arrived, but scarcely any villagers showing: shuttered houses, blind-eyed, perhaps hiding cowering peasants, women, children, old men: the emptiness of the street striking oddly, as though it were midnight and daylight.

Two English officers, very dusty, after a march that had begun at break of dawn, glancing about as they trudged tiredly along to the billet in the orchard. A door gingerly opened and an old face thrust out. "Monsieur! Should we fly?"

"Fly? But no." One of the Englishmen calls out, "What should one fly from?"

"The Germans — one says they are at the next village."

The Englishman does not believe — a mere scare: and says so. "We are stopping here tonight," he argues. "If they were at —— we should not be staying here."

The old grey face, unconvinced, ready for misfortune, haggard, but stonily calm, goes in, and the door shuts: a bolt creaks: and the two Englishmen move on.

"Should you have advised that?" asks the younger of them.

"To stay? Why on earth should they flee when no man pursueth?"

"I don't feel sure of that. There's something in the air — a menace."

They came to the gate into the orchard, rather a narrow gate, not convenient for getting great ambulance-wagons through:

*Ayscough, John, *French Windows* (New York: Longmans, Green and Co., 1918), pp. 52–67.

the orchard itself not very convenient for packing them; some already in, their horses out and being watered, or being taken out, other being got in up the steep, soft slope from the road.

Under the trees, next to the hedge on one side, officer's servants choosing spots for their masters' bedding, and unrolling the blankets. In a corner, the men's cooks making a fire, and piling up their big cooking-pots ("Dixies" they call them) round it, the officers' cooks lighting a much smaller, opposition fire near where the servants are laying out the blankets; another servant "laying the dining-room table," i.e. setting enamelled tin mugs, numb-looking knives and forks, on a waterproof sheet on the grass.

Some officers, washing themselves, out of canvas buckets: one or two shaving, and also walking about. The Ancient decides both to wash and shave, and gathers together the essentials, then walks off to the farm. At the pump, and at a horse-trough, a fierce washing and splashing of men stripped to the waist. He asks, insinuatingly, at the kitchen-door if there is any room where he may go and wash too: the proposition received favourably; and he is escorted to a room on the ground-floor, tiled, and opening on to a walled garden with a few dahlias and a good many high-stepping hens in it. The room contains a big bedstead, almost grandiose, and a chair with three legs and an empty buttertub sustaining the fourth corner; also a table covered with ragged American leather, on which are three used paper collars coloured like meerschaum pipes, an extremely small tin bowl, and a bucket full of water presumably second-hand. On a shelf is a fine old Renaissance crucifix, on a chest of drawers a statue of Our Lady of Lourdes with little pots of cow-medicines at her feet. There is a framed photograph (an enlargement, evidently, and wooley) of the master of the house, in the uniform of a *Marechale Chef de Logis* of a cavalry regiment: the original far, far away. When did he last lie in that hot-looking bed: Will he ever come back to lie in it again? His unknown guest entreats that he may: and tries to take the comfort of a promise from the portrait — not a fateful face, but round, well-satisfied; the figure dapper, stoutish, prosperous. No tragic wistfulness in the big, wide-opened, shrewd eyes. But eh! alas! if only the fateful-faced ones fell, how short would be the roll of the slain. . . .

Outside the window in the garden it seems there is another pump, and three exploring soldiers discover it; and after considerable, if hasty, peeling, pump obligingly on each other. The Ancient hands out his bucket and begs for a clean re-fill.

On the tiled floor he manages almost a bath. Then, a shave; then a return to the orchard, and supper which happens to be dinner also. It is dark now, and the few lights here and there among the crowded trees, show up Rembrandtish groups and faces.

A motor-cyclist dispatch-rider arrives before the cheese.

"Up and off."

In the dark the "beds" are hurriedly rolled up again: fires are kicked out: pots and kettles huddled away into their wagons: horses quickly harnessed, their driver condoling with them over unfinished oats; cracking of boughs as the wagons struggle through the trees, quite invisible now in the moonless dark; in wonderfully few minutes what was a camp is a camp no longer, and the "unit" waits in the road for the order to march. Silent groups of peasants flit by, homeless now: you can hear their shuffling feet, their breathing as they pass close to you, hardly a voice, even in a sob; even the children make no wail, hurry and dread hold them too silent. Whither they go they know not; why, they can scarce know, these babies on whom (as on their fathers gone already whither they know not) the horrible, dull riddle of the war has fallen. One wonders when they will come back — tomorrow? Never? Is the darkness swallowing, assimilating, them? or will the dawn's light see them creeping chilly home, after a nightmare of false alarm? Part of the riddle. In a thousand variants the riddle keeps asking itself all day, all night, always.

One cannot see the village. Not a light in any house of it. Not a glint of moonshine catches belfry or gable anywhere. Swallowed too, in the thick, hot, dusty dark.

One thinks of Keats' village — "emptied of its folk this pious morn," its villagers all gone following the lowing kine to the festal sacrifice: not by association does that bland and lovely picture come leaping into memory — by contrast. No pious eve this — or is it? Of what unfestal sacrifice are these village-folk themselves the victims?

"Quick march."

The cadence of five hundred feet, no sound else. No song whistled or sung. And nothing visible: no doubt each man can see his neighbour, but no eye could pick out of the blackness any shape of the whole marching column. It moves along the bottom of the night as though gulfed in a black and great water. No man of all that march has ever seen the fields that flank this road, nor ever will see them: what they may be like he cannot guess, nor is he guessing: if there be homes here they do not betray their nearness, but huddle into the sombre, stealthy skirts of the night. There may be corn-lands, garden plots, trees, orchards — there may be anything: an army, friendly or hostile. Somewhere hereabouts are two armies, our own, of which this little block of silent-moving men forms a tiny part; perhaps that of our French comrades; we do not know in the least; certainly not far off, that of our swift, alert foe. We do not know: not to know anything is for such as ourselves a note of this early phase of the war.

And no one asks: no questions are heard, no surmise. Perhaps every man wonders, but none asks "Whither?" or "Why?" The Ancient wonders too: not whither, or why: for the name of one place would mean as little to him, if he knew it, as that of another: nor if he could be told the actual purpose of each march would he perhaps understand, for to him all war and strategy are an unlearned language. Only he wonders of what the men are thinking as they go: of what homes, friends, partings?

Sometimes one can tell by the sound of the marching feet that they fall on a narrowed road between high banks; oftener there must be flat ground to left and right.

"Halt!"

Cross-roads, and a momentary pause. Then the way to the left is chosen and the column moves again. Uphill this time. For a bare half-mile.

Then there comes the clatter of a ridden horse galloping after us, and its rider, finding the commanding officer, tells him,

"They are there. At the top of the hill. . . ."

The Ancient, close by, hears him.

Another halt, and a turn about; to turn the wagons, is very difficult: they are not made to turn on narrow roads, and on a narrow road without flat ground on either side would be impossible; who can tell in this smother of darkness whether this road be broad or narrow, what it is like to right and left? They are turned, and it is "Quick march!" again, downhill. Odd to think who was behind; to wonder how near?

For a long way it is downhill, easier going for tired feet, and for a long way the road passes between steep high banks. The silence, and the rhythmic monotone of the marching feet makes one sleepy, deadly sleepy. What luxury if one could lie down among the soft, deep dust of the wayside and be asleep. Can one sleep walking; is there only the somnambulance of disease? Often the Ancient thought he must have slept moving; perhaps only for a few moments, that seemed to have been long.

Another halt at last: a long wait, and then the orders not to camp, but for all to rest where they were. Some lay down at once on the roadside, some clambered up the high banks and lay among the stubble they found at the top. The Ancient scrambled up to the driving-seat of a wagon, intending to sleep there. But the night was cold now, and the sleep that had seemed to swallow him up, to assault him like an obsesion, as he walked, would not come now that it was bidden. Ficklest of friends! So rude to thrust herself on us uninvited at awkard moments, so standing upon punctilio when entreated.

The horses slept: their driver slept: some-one inside the wagon was certainly asleep, as he assured the public most resonantly.

The Ancient tried to sleep by telling him-self a story of matchless pointlessness and banalité about a man called Jones, who had twelve children, and the eldest married Caro-lina Williams and had twelve children, the eldest of whom, etc., etc. But it would not do: he only began to have a monstrous in-terest in the alliances of the Jones family.

The man asleep inside the wagon slept on, but ceased to snore. There was no sound now except the occasional jingle of a harness as a horse shifted in his sleep.

At last there came another sound, very strange and troubling of someone weeping: of someone invisibile behind the curtain of the wagon, but close, close to, crying very low and quietly. There were no women there to weep: and the memory of the Ancient, always errant and vagrant, clapped into his mind that great saying of the old heathen historian, concerning a tribe of the very people now our enemies: "It is for their women, indeed, to weep: for their men to remember."

Was this Englishman who wept remem-bering too?

What more gross than for one man to thrust in and show himself aware of another man's tears? In broad daylight, face to face, the Ancient could not have done it: he must have turned away and hidden the indiscre-tion of having noted.

But in this thick and lonely night, two awake in the midst of a sleeping company, it seemed different: the two watchers so near together, hardly a foot of space between them, for one to hold himself aloof, dis-creetly heedless, from the trouble in some young heart so near his own, seemed but a cold and callous hardness.

"What is it?" he whispered, drawing the curtain aside, and bending towards it.

It was so dark that the whiteness of the curtains barely showed less black than the night herself; so much darker inside that no face became visible.

"Sir, I thought everyone was asleep. I didn't know as you was there." A young voice, with the northland burr in it that to the Ancient, north-country born, always sounds homely, friendly.

"I beg your pardon. . . ."

"Nay, it's me as should. I never thought to trouble no one."

"It only troubles me to think you are in trouble. I'm ashamed to have let you know I heard you, only I couldn't help it. You and I are the only ones awake, and one of us is sad — I couldn't help speaking, though one man's words can't alter another's trouble."

"Sir, I thank you kindly. They're all strange to me yet; I've ne'er a choom; there's bin no time yet, nor yet no chance, o' making any. So I think. And I couldna sleep: and . . . I were thinking of my gal."

"Are you engaged to be married?"

"Nay, I am married. There's the trooble. Married not twelve months. And my wife she was near her time — not full come it wasn't, but near. Then the mobilization order came, and I had to get over to Dublin; and the very day we embarked came a letter, not from her, but from her sister; and it was gave to me on board, and I read it as we was moving down and the folk cheering, and the sirens squealin', and it said how Tessie'd worried o'er me going, and her pains had coom on her: and the child had been born, and she was very ill and all, and the nurse as was Catholic, like yourself, sir, had chris-tened him after me, but he died an hour after. . . ."

A little pause, a struggle too easy to divine, though by hard force inaudible, and the young voice took up its humble plain tale.

"I'd told her, a hoondred times, as soon there'd be the little 'un to comfort her. And she'd listen, an' cooldna say me Nay. She know'd it 'ud comfort her. Yet it troobled her an' all as the child 'ud coom and me not there to give it e'er welcome. 'Eh, Jim, but I niver thought to be left alone *then*,' she said, and I told her nor me eether; but it was just Dooty, and had to be doon; and she couldna say me Nay to that eether; nor she didna try. She didna cry, but her face daunted me. She didna cry not even when I coomed away; p'raps she couldna, p'raps she wouldna — but she fell out o' me arms, and it was like death she looked; and the Irish nurse I told you of ran in, and made me a sign as I had better go, and I had to go."

Another little struggling pause, and then:

"Eh, Sir: when I knew as she hadna the child to think on — we'd both on us bin thinking of it, and plotting for it iver so long — when I couldna say any more, as I'd said to myself o'er and o'er again, 'The child'll coomfort her: it'll force her to think of *it,* i'stid o' think, think, thinking o' me: and all the crowd o' the ship, and all the crowds on the quays, cheering, and the sirens yelling. . . . Eh, Sir, it were bitter 'ard. . . . And just now it all coomed o'er me again: and . . . Sir, ye'd never guess what it is to a young man to know as he can niver see his soon's face as he's longed to see so many long days. The times I've fancied it! And the times I've plotted for it, and said 'I'll do this and that for the child' . . . and I'll *niver* see it: and the poor lass to have but a peep of it, and then to see it no more eether. And she's delicate; p'raps she's gone to seek it . . . and if so our little home's gone wi' her. I could niver fancy tryin' to make another, if that as I brought her back to is gone: niver. I couldna fancy being hoosband to another woman, nor father to another woman's child. . . ."

What can a man say to comfort a pain like that?

He may know what he should say: may know well where the only hope of comfort lies; but to be glib in saying it, how smug and shallow must one be for that! And must God always need an interpreter? If He keeps His own reverent silence, and will not always speak aloud to wounded hearts of His children, *must* it be always that some blundering man may try to be more eloquent than He?

The young voice fell, and the old voice could not trespass on the terrible sacred silence. Silence herself sat between the old man and the young, making friends of them. And the old man could do nothing but keep

saying to that other Young Man of Nazareth, "Do it yourself. You care more than I. It was your wound: heal it."

It was the young sonless father who spoke at last.

"Sir," he said, whispering, "are you asleep?"

"Asleep! God forbid that I could sleep: I'm not so bad as that."

"Bad, eh, boot you're kind."

A big young hand had come out through the curtain, and its owner felt it wet.

"I didn't dare to say anything," said the old man. "I longed to, but I durst not. I'm stupid, but I would not be impertinent."

"I'd like it if you'd talk. You'd niver say a word to hurt me: and I'm lonesome for none to talk to."

Then they did talk: the young man saying as much as the old. Perhaps that way he got most ease. But I am shy to set down all that strange talk here: for it was strange how two men, alone in that darkness, awake in the midst of so many sleepers, with so many dreams perhaps being dreamed so near at hand, two men so divided by age, by religion, by the course of life, could talk of the great real things of life, neither knowing the other's name, one at least not knowing the other's face, and be at home together, in that foreign land, and grow intimate as only sorrow and the sharing of sorrow can make us: one of them very generous in taking for help the mere desire to help, and the other very humble and reverent at the simple, unwitting revelation of a nature very manly, singularly pure and unselfish, marvellously refined, with a refinement that no uncouth fashion of speech, nor rough phrase, could hide or alter: of a nature very brave, for all those tears, most manly and with a plain unbraggart readiness for danger and for duty.

I have spoken, a moment since, of the difference of faith between the two men: but, between them in the night there was God, and at that Divine bridge they met, and stood together, not seeing each other for the darkness, but seeing Him.

Another of these beginnings without an end?

MRS. WILFRID WARD

(1864–1932)

FATED to be one of the incredible Wards, Josephine Mary Hope-Scott was born in London, 1864. Her mother was Lady Victoria Howard, daughter of the Duke of Norfolk. Josephine Mary was educated privately at Abbotsford and Arundel Castle. Married to Wilfrid Ward in 1887, she gave her first married years to her charming family. Her ability to write mature novels was of later growth. She died in London, 1932.

Mrs. Ward's novels are well constructed and psychologically exact. She is an excellent observer of character and her descriptive ability is delightful.

In *Tudor Sunset,* her best work, she has admirably recreated the fears and persecution of the final years of Elizabeth's reign. Though the novel is presumably a love story, Elizabeth is its chief character. It is she who moves enigmatically at the center of the atmosphere of magnificence and intrigue.

TUDOR SUNSET*

CHAPTER VI

NOT many hours later Whitlock saw Topcliffe again. Looking through the open door into the pages' gallery, he espied FitzUrse. The old courtier was sitting on a bench in the window and he beckoned Richard who joined him. It was soon after dinner and the boys were grouped about the refectory table, and at a first glance he thought them to be at play with the dice.

"'Tis a pleasant sight," he said to himself as he crossed the long room, and he cast admiring glances at the youths, who, before long might make or mar the fortunes of the realm. Here they were at ease, but gorgeous in silk and velvet and laced ruffles. Their figures trained by every sport as well as a severe drill, they now with extreme grace lolled listlessly or sat up erect or half lay on the oak benches. Some few dangled their long thin legs as they sat on the ends of the refectory table. Yet at no time, even when on duty, did they really betray to the onlooker the characteristics of the courtier as they did now.

"I like to watch them," said FitzUrse; "they are cautious withal, and they know which way the wind blows. They have as many intrigues as are found in the Queen's Council; they keep their own court of justice, and with them, woe to the vanquished. But they are generous in their generous moods withal. I meddle not with mischief, but no harm is there in being aware of the same. Stay awhile, and if we keep speaking we shall be supposed to be busy with our own matters, and we may gain somewhat."

Richard sat down with his back of a purpose turned towards the boys, and found he had perforce to listen to FitzUrse.

"When I was one of those lads by Her Grace's goodwill I learnt lessons that would have saved many a man who missed the same. See that fair tall fellow, a leader in all revels, it is he who gives the word and the rest follow. If he jibes they jibe, if he applauds they do. Or that strong stout lad at the end of the table whose fists do as much as the other's tongue — think you they will be fortunate?" He shook his head and went on. "Dame Fortune likes not spoilt boys. Those two spoilt by their fellows will not bear well the first kicks — and kicks there must be. Her Grace's kicks first of all!" He laughed. "There was a grand hefty fellow who amused her mightily by his dancing.

*Ward, Mrs. Wilfrid, *Tudor Sunset* (London: Sheed and Ward, Ltd.), pp. 144–150.

'Twas amazing the feats of dancing that fellow performed. But one night when twirling high in the air down he comes, bang all of him, flat on the ground, and the Queen laughed loudly before all her Court and gave him a kick. 'Get up, Sir Ox,' and he, instead of taking the jest, looked like a whipped schoolboy. He broke his heart over that tumble; said it was a bad wicked world; turned recusant, and died on the gallows!" FitzUrse laughed. "Get up, Sir Ox. What a soft fellow!"

"Think you," queried Whitlock, "these be as fine a set of lads as you have seen here in past days?"

FitzUrse sighed heavily. "Say it not in Gath, but I am old, my friend, and am I like to see any better than those of my own youth who achieved greatness or had greatness thrust upon them? But these I grant you are goodly lads to look on, only, sir, what will they see after I am gone? Who will rule over them? At the best a Scot, a cold-hearted Puritanical fellow"—then he stopped and looked annoyed. "But I beckoned you, not to hear me talk, but to make out what is afoot among these pages, for I know the signs of the weather."

Whitlock turned towards the table. "See," went on FitzUrse, "they are plying Topcliffe with drink."

Richard was startled, for he had not seen the chief of pursuivants seated half-way down the table. The boys clustered round the object of his abhorrence, had hidden him from view. Two leaned forward on each side with their elbows on the shining black of the old oak opposite, three fine young figures sprawled half-way across the table. Richard went white to the lips and bit them to keep his tongue from cursing aloud.

"Never till to-day did I set eyes on Topcliffe," he muttered.

"He has laid low now for a long while," said FitzUrse; "after getting himself out of prison he went to the country and there lay quiet in a manor he got from a recusant. But here he is again."

"How came he to prison himself?"

"There are different tales, but the one I credit is that his son having killed a man, a murder not according to law, Topcliffe thought to get him off scot free, and failing, did fall into a rage with the judge in open court. The town, too, had turned against him for his lust of blood and torture. Mr. Secretary was not pleased with his handling of the poet Southwell, which same came out in court, this Southwell with singular courage making a great protestation in court against Topcliffe although being still wholly in Topcliffe's power at the time. Now listen; your ears are younger than mine, but look not as if occupied in listening. These lads want to know why Topcliffe is back and what he is up to. They know Court gossip better than you or I, and we may learn from them."

An old man's voice now dominated the chatterers:

"There are none but traitors in that religion: your English hearts can tell you that!" Topcliffe had started in a deep bass, but his voice quivered as an old man's will.

Two boys spoke at once—a dark boy, the third on Topcliffe's left, and the fine, fair spark FitzUrse had pointed out with golden locks, who leaned across the table.

"But how came it that you, Mr. Topcliffe, conformed under the late Queen?" asked the first; and the other cried out:

"Why then did you last year let the man Page get away while you hanged the old woman Lyne who could not harm Her Grace?"

Topcliffe turned a deaf ear to one challenge, but replied to the other:

"Page is got now, and will be hanged, drawn and quartered while still alive a few days hence. The ladies of the Court can no longer jeer at me for that!" An ironical cheer came from a few of the listeners.

"And why, pray you, was I to blame for the death of Mrs. Lyne? She harboured priests and mass was said in her house."

"No blame, no blame," said the bland voice of a tall, quiet youth; "we know you have a merciful heart and did not make the laws."

There was a pause, and Whitlock said in a low voice: "How can princes endure such tools?"

"An evil necessity. A ruler cannot brook

defiance, or he will soon cease to rule. Some-one must do what has to be done. But this man is of good birth, and yet he has a real taste for his mission, and the taste grows with the satisfaction thereof. He hath a dog-like loyalty to Her Grace, who, like many another owner of a savage beast, does not mislike him for maltreating others. It is a pleasing sensation to have your hand licked by the tongue within cruel jaws."

They were talking louder at the table.

"You were happy as a king when they gave you Robert Southwell."

"I was like a king in that I could punish a traitor according to my pleasure. Mark you, I did not kill my man. That only was not allowed by the Council."

"But you racked him manfully, bravely, did you not?"

The old man turned stiffly and spoke with drunken solemnity:

"Who said I racked him? I did not rack him." He looked round the group. "No man shall say I racked him. He was the most weighty man that ever I did take. I had to get from him the answer to the question of the Countess of Arundel, of Mr. Gerrard and other most desperate men. But in court I made him say I had not racked him."

"In court he said he would liefer have been killed than endure the tortures you put him to."

"Aye, in open court he dared to call me a bad name; me a bad man!"

"That was the bravest fellow of them all," cried a boy standing behind Topcliffe.

The veteran inquisitor turned round.

"Go on, my boys, go on! Wait till you have the Spaniards here, and the Jesuits are in power and Her Grace murdered. Go on, you young fools!"

"But if Southwell was not racked, what was done to him that made so great a stir?"

Topcliffe willingly explained:

"As I wrote Her Grace, it would make tongues wag to practise a new punishment in the common prisons. But in mine own strong chamber I would make him hang against the wall, his hands but as high as he could reach. 'Twas but like a trick in your boisterous dance Trenshemoare."

"Was that all?" This was no great affair, and some young faces looked disappointed. They liked not Topcliffe, but they liked excitement and tales of horror.

Topcliffe felt that he was not saying what was expected. His laugh was exceedingly loud and unpleasant.

"That is what I told Her Grace. But how would you like, my lads, to have iron rings on your wrists and be hung by them against the wall, with your legs trussed up behind? 'Tis crucifixion without the cross. I told Her Grace it would loose his tongue, though I did not tell her all." He gave a little chuckle. Plied with more drink, he answered the next question.

"And did it loose his tongue?"

"Not it; for verily this was the most silent monster I ever dealt with — not one name of plotters, his fellows; not a fact of any sort; not the colour of the horse he rode on, for fear I could thereby trace the owner. And yet at times he appeared to be dying with pain; but we revived him with burnt paper and hung him up again. It was a good trick, that of the wall, but some men turned squeamish and speak of Topcliffian methods. When faithful Topcliffe is gone who will save Her Grace? I have helped more traitors go to Tyburn than all the gentlemen and noblemen of the Court, yet I was put in gaol on false pretexts, and by the same disgrace I was in a fair way and made apt to adventure my life every night to murderers. For when I was committed there was in all prisons re-joicing, and wine was given in Westminster Hall for joy of that news. 'Tis like the then fresh dead bones o' Father Southwell and Father Walpole did dance for joy! when I got loose, I went to the country, to mine own estate, and lay quiet."

"Your own, Mr. Topcliffe?" It was a voice that spoke for the first time, a low bitter voice — that passed unheeded. Richard could not see the speaker.

"But I have given up my happy life as a gentleman in the country to come to town and unmask the traitors who are plotting —" he paused.

"Aye, plotting! a new plot:" cried a boy opposite.

"A devilish plot?" laughed another. "Tell us, tell us, good sir," said a third.

But Topcliffe looked at them all and each, and shook his head so that his white locks fell over his little eyes and the smile of expectant pleasure made the loose old lips tremble.

"I have three of them trussed up in Newgate. Page himself is lying in limbo, in the most noisome cell in London, but there be better in store — we shall strike higher." He began to get up on uncertain legs.

"Come, we have had enough," said FitzUrse; "he grows cautious, and in that mood will betray nothing."

Whitlock, at least, could endure no more. As they walked through the long passages to the main entrance FitzUrse said politely:

"What you murmur hath a sound like poetry. Is it your own verse? May I share it?"

"No, thank God, not mine own. It was writ by the man Topcliffe speaks of who was put to the torture thirteen separate times," and he repeated:

Come, cruell death, why lingerest thou so longe?
What doth withould thy dynte from fatall stroke?
Now prest I am, alas! thou dost me wronge,
To let me live, more anger to provoke:

Thy right is had when thou hast stopt my breathe.
Why dost thou stay to worke my dooble deathe?"

FitzUrse spoke coldly:
"Fortunate are the few who can call thus for pity. How many suffer and die without a plaint that lives after them."

They had passed the pages' quarters. In the distance they could now see an important group — with Sir Robert Cecil in the midst. Richard slipped into a side passage and FitzUrse gave a shrug of relief. Whitlock surely was strangely moved. A faint suspicion in his regard suddenly became definite, and FitzUrse decided on a line of conduct for the future.

Meanwhile Richard escaped to his chambers, where he stood gazing at an unglazed window framing the pale blue of the winter's sky. He covered his face with his hands, and now other words of Southwell's rose to his lips:

"Not where I breathe, but where I love, I live;
Not where I love, but where I am, I die;
The life I wish must future glory give,
The deaths I feele in present daungers lye."

MAURICE BARING

(1874–1945)

MAURICE BARING was born in 1874 and educated, as so many famous writers have been, at Eton and Trinity College, Cambridge. In his student days he became friendly with Belloc and Chesterton. A friendship which grew with the years. In 1898 Baring entered the diplomatic service as attaché to the British Embassy in Paris. In World War I he was a Wing Commander in the R.A.F. He was converted to Catholicism in 1909 and died in December, 1945.

Baring was distinguished for his Christian urbanity rather than for any specifically Catholic note which may be found in his work. Except for some few sonnets and scattered passages in his prose works, Baring seemed to have skirted the deep wells of Catholic life. He seems content to pose as a citizen of the world who saw more and set it down ably because he looked and listened but did not declare himself formally in his work.

THE PUPPET SHOW OF MEMORY*

CHAPTER XII

RUSSIA: THE BEGINNING OF THE REVOLUTION

I SPENT Easter in Moscow, and this was one of the most impressive experiences I ever had.

I have spent Easter in various cities — in Rome, Florence, Athens, and Hildesheim — and although in each of these places the feast has its own peculiar aspect, yet by far the most impressive and the most interesting celebration of the Easter festival I have ever witnessed was that of Moscow. This is not to be wondered at, for Easter is the most important feast of the year in Russia, the season of festivity and holiday-making in a greater degree than Christmas or New Year's Day. Secondly, Easter, which is kept with equal solemnity all over Russia, was especially interesting in Moscow, because Moscow is the stronghold of old traditions and the city of churches. Even more than Cologne, it is

> *"Die Stadt die viele hundert
> Kapellen und Kirchen hat."*

There is a church almost in every street, and the Kremlin is a citadel of cathedrals. During Holy Week, towards the end of which the evidences of the fasting season grow more and more obvious by the closing of restaurants and the impossibility of buying any wine and spirits, there were, of course, services every day. During the first three days of Holy Week there was a curious ceremony to be seen in the Kremlin, which was held every two years. This was the preparation of the chrism or holy oil. While it was slowly stirred and churned in great cauldrons, filling the room with hot fragrance, a deacon read the Gospel without ceasing (he was relieved at intervals by others), and this lasted day and night for three days. On Maundy Thursday the chrism was removed in silver vessels to the Cathedral. The supply had to last the whole of Russia for two years. I went to

the morning service in the Cathedral of the Assumption on Maundy Thursday. The church was crowded to suffocation. Everybody stood up, as there was no room to kneel. The church was lit with countless small wax tapers. The priests were clothed in white and silver. The singing of the noble plain chant without any accompaniment ebbed and flowed in perfect discipline; the bass voices were unequalled in the world. Every class of the population was represented in the church. There were no seats, no pews, no precedence nor privilege. There was a smell of incense and a still stronger smell of poor people, without which, someone said, a church is not a church. On Good Friday there was the service of the Holy Shroud, and besides this a later service in which the Gospel was read out in fourteen different languages, and finally a service beginning at one o'clock in the morning and ending at four, to commemorate the Burial of Our Lord. How the priests endured the strain of these many and exceedingly long services was a thing to be wondered at; for the fast, which was kept strictly during all this period, precluded butter, eggs, and milk, in addition to all the more solid forms of nourishment, and the services were about six times as long as those of the Catholic or other churches.

The most solemn service of the year took place at midnight on Saturday in Easter Week. From eight until ten o'clock the town, which during the day had been crowded with people buying provisions and presents and Easter eggs, seemed to be asleep and dead. At about ten people began to stream towards the Kremlin. At eleven o'clock there was already a dense crowd, many of the people holding lighted tapers, waiting outside in the square, between the Cathedral of the Assumption and that of Ivan Veliki. A little before twelve the cathedrals and palaces on the Kremlin were all lighted up with ribbons of various coloured lights. Twelve o'clock struck, and then the bell of Ivan Veliki began to boom: a beautiful, fullvoiced, immense volume of sound — a sound which Clara

---

*Baring, Maurice, *The Puppet Show of Memory* (Boston: Little Brown and Co.), pp. 334–337.

Schumann said was the most beautiful she had ever heard. It was answered by other bells, and a little later all the bells of all the churches in Moscow were ringing together. Then from the Cathedral came the procession: first, the singers in crimson and gold; the bearers of the gilt banners; the Metropolitan, also in stiff vestments of crimson and gold; and after him the officials in their uniforms. They walked round the Cathedral to look for the Body of Our Lord, and returned to the Cathedral to tell the news that He was risen. The guns went off, rockets were fired, and illuminations were seen across the river, lighting up the distant cupola of the great Church of the Saviour with a cloud of fire.

The crowd began to disperse and to pour into the various churches. I went to the Manège — an enormous riding school, in which the Ekaterinoslav Regiment had its church. Half the building looked like a fair. Long tables, twinkling with hundreds of wax tapers, were loaded with the three articles of food which were eaten at Easter — a huge cake called *kulich;* a kind of sweet cream made of curds and eggs, cream and sugar, called *Paskha* (Easter); and Easter eggs, dipped and dyed in many colours. They were waiting to be blessed. The church itself was a tiny little recess on one side of the building. There the priests were officiating, and down below in the centre of the building the whole regiment was drawn up. There were two services — a service which began at midnight and lasted about half an hour; and Mass, which followed immediately after it, lasting till about three in the morning. At the end of the first service, when the words, "Christ is risen," were sung, the priest kissed the deacon three times, and then the members of the congregation kissed each other, one person saying, "Christ is risen," and the other answering, "He is risen, indeed." The colonel

kissed the sergeant; the sergeant kissed all the men one after another. While this ceremony was proceeding, I left and went to the Church of the Saviour, where the first service was not yet over. Here the crowd was so dense that it was almost impossible to get into the church, although it was immense. The singing in this church was ineffable. I waited until the end of the first service, and then I was borne by the crowd to one of the narrow entrances and hurled through the doorway outside. The crowd was not rough; they were not jostling one another, but with cheerful carelessness people dived into it as you dive into a scrimmage at football, and propelled the unresisting herd towards the entrance, the result being, of course, that a mass of people got wedged into the doorway, and the process of getting out took longer than it need have done; and had there been a panic, nothing could have prevented people being crushed to death. After this I went to a friend's house to break the fast and eat *kulich, Paskha,* and Easter eggs, and finally returned home when the dawn was faintly shining on the dark waters of the Moscow River, whence the ice had only lately disappeared.

In the morning people came to bring me Easter greetings and to give me Easter eggs, and to receive gifts. I was writing in my sitting-room and I heard a faint mutter in the next room, a small voice murmuring, *Gospodi, Gospodi* ("Lord, Lord"). I went to see who it was, and found it was the policeman, sighing for his tip, not wishing to disturb, but at the same time anxious to indicate his presence. He brought me a crimson egg. Then came the doorkeeper and the cook. The policeman must, I think, have been pleased with his tip, because policemen kept on coming all the morning, and there were not more than two who belonged to my street.

CANDLEMAS*

The town is half awake; the nave, the choir,
Are dark, and all is dim, within, without;
But every chapel fringed with the devout,
Is bright with February flowers of fire.

At Mass, a thousand years ago in Rome,
Thus Priest, thus Server at the alter bowed;
Thus knelt, thus blessed itself the kneeling
    crowd,
At Dawn, within the secret catacomb.

Thus shall they meet for Mass, until the day
The glory of the world shall pass away.
And beauty far away from human reach,

And power, and wealth beyond all mortal
    price,
And glory that outsoars all thought, all
    speech,
Speak in the whispered words of sacrifice.

*The above and following poem have been selected
from *Collected Poems of Maurice Baring* (New York:
John Lane Co., 1911).

VITA NUOVA

I

I found the clue I sought not, in the night,
While wandering in a pathless maze of
    gloom;
The sky was hid behind huge shapes of
    doom;
There was no moon, nor any star in sight.

My hopes, my dreams, my faithless creeds
    were slain,
Like corpses on a battlefield they lay;
The world was but a graveyard dark with
    clay;
The stifling cloud denied one drop of rain;

Then from the gibby marge of the abyss,
I cried aloud in agony and fear,
When, suddenly, it seemed my single tear
Stretched and became a shining bridge to
    bliss.

I stood before a topless gate. Within
I guessed the light, I dared not enter in.

II

One day I heard a whisper: "Wherefore wait?
Why linger in a separated porch?
Why nurse the flicker of a severed torch?
The fire is there, ablaze beyond the gate.

Why tremble, foolish soul? Why hesitate?
However faint the knock, it will be heard."

I knocked, and swiftly came the answering
    word,
Which bade me enter to my own estate.

I found myself in a familiar place;
And there my broken soul began to mend;
I knew the smile of every long-lost face —

They whom I had forgot remembered me;
I knelt, I knew — it was too bright to see —
The welcome of a King who was my friend.

III

My treasure and my resting-place are found,
My mother-land, my immemorial home;
Beyond the reefs of treasonable foam,
I know the lights that flash upon the sound.

Lightning may strike, and hurricane may
    blow,
Whatever shall befall, I cannot fear:
Whether the hour be far away or near,
That tranquil harbour shines and waits, I
    know.

I know. There is no mortal word to say;
For what there is to speak is vast and dim;
But haply, if God please, beyond the day,

Delivered from the bars and bonds of speech,
Made strong with language which the angels
    teach,
I'll share my secret with the Seraphim.

C. C. MARTINDALE
(*1879–   *)

THE famous encyclopedists of history would have to look to their laurels in an encounter with Father Martindale. He was born in England May 25, 1879, of titled parents, and his school years were glittered with milestones of medals and prizes. After preparatory years at Harrow, Father Martindale proceeded to Stonyhurst and Campion Hall, Oxford, where he maintained his brilliant record as a student. He was converted to Catholicism, 1897, entered the Society of Jesus, and was ordained priest, 1911. Since that time Father Martindale has spent his time in teaching, writing, and in parish work. He is a beloved figure in many of the poorest sections of London where he has devoted his remarkable talents to the common people.

Father Martindale's published works are a monument to his industry and brilliance. He is a subtle essayist, biographer, travel writer, hagiographer and liturgist, and a sage commentator on world affairs.

The Goddess of Ghosts, one of Father Martindale's early works, is a good example of his style and charm. Though all his biographies are valuable for their insight, that of *Robert Hugh Benson* is perhaps the most complete and intimate.

AN EVENING AT EPHESUS*

EARLIER in the afternoon, a thunderstorm had washed the summer day to freshness, and now the sun was setting in a limpid west. The marble villa, raised above Ephesus, not so high but that the murmur of the city reached it — in fact, at the bottom of the steep garden the street was paved and populous — stood golden among its trees. It was the evening when Anaximander came to visit Diodidaktos, for, each fifth day, one of the two old friends would sup with the other, turn and turn about, and to-night Diodidaktos was host. This had been their custom for quite a number of years, save when Diodidaktos was on his travels, for he travelled much, and asked of his wealth most of all that it should show him the world and the ways of man. Trajan was Emperor at Rome, and the whole scheme of life, in the inhabited earth, might well be challenging a man's philosophy. The friends had agreed upon the fifth day for the whimsical reason that the morrow and the after-morrow of a supper should be spent, the first, in unthoughtful repose upon a pleasant memory, the second, in serene reflection upon what ideas it had provided; then came a neutral day; then, a period of half-felt loneliness growing into desire: the day itself of the next meeting, the fifth day, was spent in joyous anticipation of the evening. Thus did the two old men gently delude themselves, philosophizing over and systematizing an affection which, in truth, was as simple as a schoolboy's.

The Arkadian slave announced supper, and they left the terrace, where they had been making sure that it would be dry enough for them to sit after the meal, and drink their wine beneath the moon. Certainly it would be dry enough. Diodidaktos gave the order. A table should be set out, and low chairs with rugs and footstools.

As they passed through the vestibule Anaximander exclaimed in astonishment:

"But look, Diodidaktos! The horrible little Heraklês is gone! What does that mean? Have you suddenly found it was intolerable, as I always said? What has converted you?"

The little Heraklês was an ancient theme

---

*Martindale, Cyril C., S.J., *The Goddess of Ghosts* (New York: P. J. Kenedy and Sons, 1915).

of affectionate quarrel. The coarse terra-cotta image had been brought there, years before, by the Arkadian slave, whose devotion to the famous hero was profound, and there it had stood, clashing singularly with the graceful appointments of the vestibule (for the philosopher was, too, an artist), and the more irretrievably because of the grotesque practice of the slave, which never ceased to annoy Anaximander. Chremês used to tie little pieces of rag or even wisps of wool or flax to the image, whenever he asked a favour from it; the rags hung there till the favour was granted; and as the kindly hero's refusals were, for all his kindliness, more numerous by far than his favours, the little statue had practically disappeared beneath a mop of discoloured tattered stuffs, quite fantastically out of keeping with the exquisite Asiatic textures which alone diversified the marble.

"He took it away himself," answered Diodidaktos, smiling. "I quite miss it."

"How like you," said the other, almost petulantly. "You weakly give in to a slave's whim in the first instance, and then defend your action, and end by believing your defence!"

"Why should I have disappointed him? It pleased him so much, and made — really! a not unpleasant contrast. And so I grew accustomed to it. Old folks do grow accustomed. And Arkadia I love, and all that comes from it."

"I have never understood your affection for those barbaric mountains. What can they breed but boors?"

"Hush! Chremês will overhear you: and him too I love."

"Why has he taken away his statue?"

"Ah," said the other, his tone altering, "frankly, I cannot understand. He is different, these days."

"Perhaps the good Heraklês has been too obdurate, and he has shifted his homages?"

"No, it is in all his talk, his look, his silences. . . ."

"Tut, he is in love," said Anaximander.

Diodidaktos laughed a little.

"He constantly falls in love," he answered, "and is none the worse for it. At most, a little distracted in his work. Now he has, if anything, more industry, and especially, more foresight."

"Oh, it is love, be sure of it. Don't they call love an inspiration? He is inspired!"

Diodidaktos regretted, in his friend, only a certain tone of cynicism and of raillery. He could allow for it, however, and now, without arguing, altered the subject.

"There are such lovely places in Arkadia! Never shall I forget my autumn there! Could you but see the 'down-dropping water of the Styx,' Anaximander — the terrible sheer red cliff of Chelmos, with the black, glistening streak where the straight waterfall has set it streaming, and the fall itself — like a silver veil as it hangs, motionless, with Iris in its silver, motionless, or just swaying like smoke in the finest zephyr, and lo, a roaring cataract where it reaches the rocks below. Oh, Anaximander, the beautiful blue-green cataract; the grey rocks with the snow in their clefts; the terrible thundering echoes, the baying of the wild dogs that roam there . . . Hekaté wanders there, assuredly; Artemis hunts there: the place is full of daemons."

"Lo, our old quarrel, Diodidaktos. Colours, sounds — melting snows and fleeting waters — what are these to the true philosopher? Why waste time upon the fleeting, the vanishing appearances of the never-the-same, the corruptible and illusory? And why, O you whose whole life should be one warfare against the myths that becloud men's minds, why do you elect to speak of Hekatés and huntresses and what not, and set these monstrous shadows once more to pass and play across the mist of human thought?"

"But the myths of Arkadia are beautiful, and Arkadia is beautiful."

"I am like Sokratês, who said that fields and trees had nothing at all to teach him, and better than Plato, who, though he professed to bid farewell to the starry heavens, and the woes and wailings of stringed instruments, that he might find his joy in the concept of pure number, absolute motion, and sheer relationship, till he should pass behind, into the Ever-the-same, the Unrelated, and the One, — yet did bedeck his philosophy in such human draperies of allegory, that none know what he teaches and what rejects."

"I am like Sophoklês," retorted Diodidaktos, smiling, "who loved the little valleys, and the jonquils, and the nightingales; and I am weaker — ah! than Plato, who, because of the human loveliness of his poetry — for Plato was a poet — has captivated for three whole centuries the thoughts of those even who would be his enemies!"

"But oh — Arkadia! with its river Aroania, where trout sing like thrushes — its Tegea, which a lock of Medusa's hair has made impregnable: Mount Lykaios, where the man who sees the sacrifice becomes a wolf —"

"Hush," cried the other, still smiling, but more gravely, "do not blaspheme that myth at any rate! With my own eyes, before now, I have beheld a mortal, who, too eager to gaze with unveiled face upon the hidden things of the gods, thrust himself, insolently, upon the inmost secret, and turned, on a sudden, into a beast, and lived no more a man's life, but a beast's. . . ."

He said this, trusting utterly to their friendship; for long ago, Anaximander, in his youth, after a period of incredible austerity, philosophic absorption, and contempt of his fellow men, had lapsed suddenly into a life of unmeasured wantonness and riot. Only the unrebuking loyalty of Diodidaktos had suddenly shown him to himself, and restored him. All Anaximander's petulance dropped from him.

"But after nine years," he said, half wistfully, "if the man-wolf has refrained from slaying man as his fellow wolves do, he can return to human shape?"

"Assuredly," said his friend, very gently. "And so to conquer is a triumph better than any at the games."

"It was your help, dear friend —" he began; but his voice broke, and his thought wandered back to the years when fidelity, now so certain, was strained almost to the snapping point.

"There is another myth of the Wolf Mountain," said Diodidaktos, "which too you ought to love. When a man climbs to its summit, there within the Temple precinct, he casts no shadow. Perchance, when we —

when I — shall have truly scaled the heights and entered into that Temple which awaits us, we shall no longer need to cast those human shadows upon things which now we cast, and I shall not even need to contemplate these fair shadows of the God, which all things are, and which I love, for they are lovely, but you reject them, being shadows."

They ceased; and for them sitting there the last twilight died and only the two tall cressets sent wavering dark and brightness round the ceiling and the walls. Outside, they could see that the air was tremulous with moonlight. Cleansing their fingers on fine bread, they went out to the terrace, where the fruit was piled in delicate baskets of ivory, and the wine gleamed black beneath the moon.   ·

"But seriously, my friend," said Anaximander when they were sitting down, "your writing has become, for many people, quite useless, because of its robes of allegory. You hurt your reputation for letters among both true philosophers and ordinary folk."

"I have none," he answered, "and I seek none."

"These think you esoteric, and shun you; those, frivolous, and disregard you."

"Frivolous I am," said Diodidaktos, perversely perhaps; "but not because, with Plato, I write in allegory."

"Only yesterday, talking to a Roman —"

Diodidaktos made an infinitely expressive gesture.

"Oh, yes," Anaximander urged, "a Roman, and you can't neglect the Romans! Vulgar they certainly are, these rich men from overseas, and they cannot create and cannot even understand: yet are they our rulers; and if you do not Hellenize them, they will Romanize us, and are indeed well on already with their vulgarizing work. Speak to them so that they will hear!"

"But am I really, for the sake of these complacent men, who know neither when nor how to laugh, nor how to dress nor eat, am I for them to sacrifice the poet's most delicate methods of all, reticence, subtlety, hint, and, above all, irony? Irony is the Greek's birthright. Irony is employed for the delight of the elect, and for the punishment of self-satisfied barbarians. What else do they deserve?"

"But your subtle thrusts are wasted. They absorb them, unnoticing. Your points are too pointed to be felt."

"There I conquer! They perish, and perceive it not."

"But your victory is meant to be in the mind. Of what avail, to confute, if they whom you confute never guess their own defeat?"

"They do guess it — they stand bewildered. But we — we sit, and smile."

"Ah, no! Diodidaktos! you malign yourself. You, a Hellene, with, as you said, the prerogative of quick wit, to use it so! What better are you, how are you not worse, than the Roman at his gladiatorial show?"

"Dear friend — yes! perhaps in my pique I spoke too fast. Never at all am I really moved to selfish retaliation save when these pompous and portentous Romans, putting forth the placard of Universal Knowledge and Councillors-in-Chief to God, complacently upbraid me with shirking truth, or disguising truth, or masking my own thought because they find my parchments 'ambiguous' or vague, not realizing that that alone can be stated neatly and compactly which is not worth stating at all. But these are very few, and even they are like to have nobler instincts which they depress."

They were silent for a while, and his thoughts flitted backwards and forwards from the solemn offices and class-rooms of the Capital, to the strange dream in which Arkadia still lay. To Arkadia, too, Anaximander's thoughts reverted.

"But Diodidaktos! how are your myths *true?* My astronomy is true: my theories of numbers or of rhythm may be untrue, but from the true they start, and are offered as but hypotheses. How are your tales true? The man does *not* become a wolf; the very Arkadian who tells it, disbelieves it; and no Arkadian would dream of owning to your poetical remodelling of the tale. You take a principle of ethics, of politics, education, what not — and you cast all into doubt by involving it in myth."

"Dear Anaximander, you conceive awry the very nature of a myth, and of its truth. Its truth is not what he who frames it sees, nor what he who narrates it sees. There is, throughout it, an impulse from the Gods. The poet, when he sings, sings without calculation; and when the impulse is gone by, he wakes, and pauses, and perceives he has sung marvels whereof, while singing, he had no knowledge. Nay, and others, brooding over his words, shall show him what they contained, and he knew it not, for not he put it there, but Apollo. He on the man was playing as a master-harpist on his harp, drawing therefrom harp-music, in good sooth, for the harp is a harp and not a flute, — not violence to his instrument does the God work — yet far better than any lesser being might draw from it, and far better than the harp, left to itself, untouched, untried, might have uttered. The poet's task, too, is it to reveal to man what treasures of thoughts noble and divine are really theirs, concealed by Zeus in the shrine of their own soul, which they had never yet unveiled. Though for some, better were it if never they peered within. . . . Truth, O Anaximander, is inexhaustible, and once the poet touches Truth, he strikes a note that echoes to the Infinite, and he can never limit his meaning."

"At times, Diodidaktos, you madden me! Explain me this, that thinking alike on scarcely any subject, we yet stick friends! My argument goes thus: granting that for poets and common-folks allegory is good and licit, yet even for them, surely you should make it clear whether *now* you are speaking allegory, now not! You ought to say: Such is my allegory; now will I explain it. But you speak — oh, like Plato, of 'carpenters, beds, metal-work' and what not, and expect us on a sudden to decry therein whole mysteries. Again, you are indignant if we suspect that *here,* or *here,* you may have some meaning behind the obvious!"

Diodidaktos smiled, and rising, paced the terrace. He looked out over the enormous view which the moonlight flooded. There were the distant mountains, southward, Mount Prion, Mount Paktyas, and beyond, curving round the bay, its point losing itself behind the long island ridge of Samos, the glorious line of Mykalê. So extraordinarily brilliant was the night, that not alone the winding Käster and the channel from the sea into the great harbour shone like silver, but the paler roads, the Magnesian road, the road to Smyrna, were dimly visible. Great masses, too, of buildings might be discerned: the Stadium; even, he fancied, the theatre hollowed out into the Akropolis at the further end of the long market-place; but above all, the enormous temple of the Ephesian Artemis, faint indigo and silver in the vast empty spaces of its sanctuary. He stood listening: imagination succoured him; in the confused murmur of the city, not yet asleep, he fancied he could distinguish the sounds he knew must meet in it — the sailors' cries and the creaking of pulleys: the songs of women; the drunker laughter of youths among the taverns, and especially from the Goddess's sanctuary, where, in the huddled huts along its wall, an army of miscreants dwelt in sordid safety. And lo, confronting one another, the enormous temple and the sea! These gathered up, for Diodidaktos, two vast mysterious choruses, two terrible heavenward outcries, the general prayer of man, and the praise of nature. For untold generations, what passionate crowds had not flocked towards that shrine, built and rebuilt across the ages! What thronging pilgrimages had not flocked to the feet of the many-breasted Mother of them all! Yes, the dreadful ancient Goddess, many-breasted, many-named, Mother of men and Queen of beasts and birds, held there her court; in that strange welcome met student and mendicant, scribe of hymns and prayers, and murderer, harlot, humble devotee and fanatic. She indeed was the Force, in her vast symbol was enrobed the Force that swayed the world, issuing into strife, and love, death, birth and re-creation. . . . And yet the sea and the echoing silver mountains, and the empty sky where the Moon sailed splendid, summed up, they too, the thrust and aspiration of the Life-force: differently, more pure, not less august, they at that moment seemed, and yet less human. But,

the human heart that had sought from them a symbol of the great Expression, the Utterance of God to men, had fallen into grossness, into manifest worship of the ungodlike, no less surely than the idolaters of the weird image of the Goddess. . . .

As he stood there he knew but one thing, namely, that this outspread scene carried with it some vast signification: it stood for something: it pointed further than itself: it conveyed a Thought, and Thought was Light, and a Truth. And Truth was the real; the living, the ultimate real. How he yearned to reach it! But the brilliant moonlit scene for him was darkness. He could not fathom it. Man, he knew, must of a surety be a truer image, a more explicit Utterance of the Ultimate than aught else, yet how so? — how were these drunken revellers, these fantastic worshippers, in every way more vocal of God than the silvery shadowy mountains, and this sea of molten silver? The Image in its Temple, ablaze with lamps, than the lonely Moon?

"The very light is darkness," he muttered.

"Were it so indeed, Master," said Chremês, at his elbow, "great were that darkness. But now the light is shining in the darkness, and the darkness cannot imprison it."

Frightened, it would seem, by his own voice's sound, he stopped, and explained his errand. A friend, Diphilos, had passed by the house, accompanying into the town a very old man who had been supping at a farm above them. Might the two travellers sit for a brief moment and rest? For the aged man was weary.

Willingly they might rest. Did he know the aged man? Yes, he knew him. . . . The slave spoke as though he were a little dazed.

Why, Anaximander asked, had he removed the Heraklês?

"There are stronger than Heraklês," he answered, vaguely.

"On whose name then do you now call, when you need succor? Who is the stronger?"

The slave moved awkwardly, and fingered a little ivory disc, shaped like a theatre ticket, which hung around his neck. He glanced deprecatingly at his master.

"Courage, Chremês," he said, kindly. "Do not fear Anaximander. He shall not laugh at you! Place your light in whatever lamp-stand you will! The darkness, O most sage philosopher, shall indeed not extinguish it. Well said, Chremês! True witness, truly borne, to the true light!"

He nodded, and the slave, still seemingly half-dazed, retired.

"Love-lorn," laughed Anaximander. "Love-lost altogether. I shouldn't trust the trimming of your lamps to him, my friend. But answer me my argument. All science, or all allegory. All clear knowledge, or all poetry, all dream. All or none."

"O worthiest friend, your uncompromising All or None! 'You cannot divide hot and cold with a hatchet.' A wiser than either of us once said that. In life, be sure, Truth is manifold. There is this truth of things we touch and see. Therein, no man, I own it, becomes a wolf. There is the poetical truth of metaphor; and herein man well may be said to become a wolf; and ethically, deeper still, he may sink into the beast. And there are truths of the understanding, un-true forever physically, and neither true nor untrue ethically, as what you delight in dreaming of, the Circle as such, Motion as such, the Infinite, the Unrelated. And there is spiritual truth, which is the life wherein are rooted these true ideas, and right laws, and lovely imaginings, and good and pleasant things. And through ideas and laws and dreams and things, that Life tells itself forth, utters itself more or less perfectly; now more, now less; now intelligibly to me, now not; now too darkly for my wits, per-chance because 'tis *my* wit, perchance, be-cause 'tis human wit at all. So in the world at large, if I do contemplate it, I see now more, now less, of God's great Utterance, perchance a word, perchance a phrase; now, but a letter, or scattered letters, or again, syllables; per-chance I can but feel sure that what I see and hear must spell somewhat of the mighty Proclamation, yet know not what; or again, I may see, for a flash, and then go blind again; hear, and relapse to being deaf. And if then I try to re-utter what I see and hear, or have seen and heard, how shall I do so

save by a throbbing discourse, a pulsing with more knowledge or with less according as my memories contain — nay, as my first per-ceptions contained, and were by me known so to contain, more or less response to the Challenge of that Life. And that which comes to root its existence in that life, is alone in truth existing and alive."

He paused, and from the dark garden arose the murmur of Chremês talking to his two guests. It would appear that the old man was speaking, but the words were inaudible.

"Alas," said Anaximander, "what con-fusion! Confused language, Diodidaktos! yours ever is: and, I fear, beneath it, con-fused thought."

For a moment Diodidaktos showed anger; almost, contempt.

"I have said before," said he, "that only at the cost of slaying the life in that of which you speak, can you move by what you, Anaximander, call clear thoughts, and state them clearly. Life flows, life throbs. In the world and in the soul, somewhat, risen to the surface, plunges anew, and re-emerges different already; and the ripples themselves, in that through which it rises, are re-absorbed — vanished and are not lost. The sea has not a pattern, like a temple cornice; nor the wind a rhythm like a hexameter, though sea and wind are musical most utterly."

"God geometrizes."

"But He hides His geometry. Man's skele-ton is hidden, and man is not his skeleton."

"Ah, man! man! man! Your mind is plunged in matter and in humanity. Your ideas are swaddled up in flesh. For me, the disincarnate!"

"Alas, dear friend," said the other gently; "there indeed is where we, once and for all, do differ. For me, that which a thing is meant to be, is best studied in that poor endeavour towards itself which I see and touch and afterwards grow to understand. *There* is the cognizable utterance: there is the spoken word. The disincarnate! Would you really, Anaximander, claim to study the essence of the thing aloof, separate, living its spiritual life in God's inviolable mind? No, no! God has stamped Himself upon this world of ours; it rises to His likeness as the wax to the seal's: it moulds itself to Him, like the garment to the wearer. It reproduces Him, like son a father — yea, as so many say, this dear world is His one-begotten, His well-beloved, His substantial reflection, His mediator to our minds. Nor will I neglect it nor desert it, nor be ungrateful to it; it brings God to me; it fills me with Him; I eat it, I drink it, and grow inebriate with God."

The other, touched by his friend's fervour, became gentle in his turn, almost sad.

"Dear Diodidaktos," he answered, "remember this; that you and I both own that though the world is a Word from God, yet *is* it not God: you honour it *as* His word, I transcend it, being *but* His word, seeking Himself. In truth, dear friend, the difference between us is but very slight. It is the difference between two human thoughts; but the difference between either of these, and the God they image forth, is infinite."

"Alas, you are too right! And now what shall we do? Men by your way and by mine have, these ages past, sought and sought yet further; and the utmost we can reach is a poor half understanding of one another! But of *Him* . . .! What shall the future bring?"

"The future! What else than the re-arrangement of the past! We have used up all human thinking. We are at the end. Who should contribute further? Not we. Not Rome. Nay, nor the East, nor Egypt: Egypt has mated with Hellas, and we have seen the offspring, that it too is powerless for succour. From India I had half hoped — the Brahmans. . . . But see these travellers! what have they brought back, the best of them? No, dear Diodidaktos, here have we for ever God and this one world and this one thought. He is *in* it, yet because He is not *it,* He is infinitely separate. Our thought, playing over them, yet because it is not they, is severed utterly yet again, and though our ears are echoing dizzily with that great Word, and our eyes dazzled by that Light, yet we go deaf and blind, and very lonely."

They ceased, discouraged.

In this silence were audible the footsteps of the slave and his visitors returning from the paved place in the garden below. Evidently the visitors were departing. The little company, after a moment, emerged from behind a clipped box-hedge, and started to climb the shallow steps leading to the gate. It could be seen that the old man was indeed very old and bowed, with a long silver beard, and a mantle whose hood fell back as he raised his head to look round over the city. He leant on the arm of a disciple, a son perhaps, quite a young man, obviously of the people, enormously strong, and warm-blooded, clearly for he wore but a light tunic. As they stayed thus to look down upon Ephesus the silence was complete. Now no song was heard, no dog barked. Diodidaktos and Anaximander sat watching, holding their breath: the group of three stood as if carved of stone, black against the sea. Over everything alike, sea and town and temple, the moonlight threw its tremulous glory. Then in the silence the old man spoke, very slowly, very quietly, with long pauses, but with an intensity that thrilled the night:

"In the beginning, existed the Word —
And the Word was with God —
And the Word *was* God."

In the pause the spell lapsed.

"A philosopher, too!" whispered Diodidaktos.

"A Stoic?"

"I expect so. But Syrianized. His accent is Syrian."

The aged voice continued:

"All things by means of Him came into being,
And apart from Him came into being naught.
That which in Him came to be, was Life,
And the Life was the Light of men. . . .
The Light is shining in the darkness —"

Chremês broke in upon his voice:

"And the darkness has not prisoned it. . . ."

"Alas," whispered Diodidaktos, "neither I nor he can vouch for that. How can he tell?"

The aged voice resumed:

"That which we have heard, that which

we have seen with our eyes, that which we have gazed upon and our hands have handled it — concerning the Word of Life — yes! the Life has been revealed, and we have seen, and are bearing witness, and are announcing unto you the Life, Eternal Life, which existed with the Father, and was revealed to us — what we have seen and have heard, that we announce to you also, that you also may have common share with us. . . ." The voice died. . . .

"What can this doctrine be?" Diodidaktos whispered.

"At least the philosopher is on your side," his companion answered — "he has seen, he has handled — how so, one fain would ask!"

Standing unaided, now, the old man stretched his hands towards the city, and the temple, and the sea.

"The Word became Flesh, and spread His tent amongst us —"

"Ah, that," the two old men murmured, in unison, "that can never be."

"And we beheld His glory," came the deeper accents of the disciple, "a glory as of One sole-begotten of the Father . . ." his eyes rested on the far horizon, and his voice faltered.

"Full," resumed the old man, — and, on his side, his voice grew stronger till it filled the night — "full of grace and truth."

Chremês bowed his head.

"And from that fullness," he whispered, "we all of us have taken, — ah, favour upon favour. . . ."

The aged hand moved crosswise through the air, over the city, over Chremês.

Then the wicket closed behind the speakers, and the slave turned slowly to the house.

"He is too old to teach," said Anaximander.

"But his disciple is young: the future still is his."

They too went in.

AT HARE STREET HOUSE*

PART III

CHAPTER I

O happie harbor of the Saints,
    O sweete and pleasant soyle,
In thee noe sorrow may be found,
    Noe greefs, noe care, noe toyle!

Thy gardens and thy gallant walkes
    Continually are greene;
There growe such sweete and pleasant flowers
    As noe where else are seene.
    — From Hierusalem, my happie home

I

THE chapters which must describe Hugh Benson's later years, spent by him with Hare Street House as his headquarters, appear to me to be difficult to write, because they have no landmarks. Six years is the longest period, since his childhood, which he spent anywhere; yet as a period it is

*Martindale, C. C., S.J., *The Life of Monsignor Robert Hugh Benson* (New York: Longmans, Green and Co., 1917), pp. 131–138.

amorphous: it is undifferentiated within itself, and, alas, unfinished, for the human historian at least. The journeys to Rome and America are a novel feature, no doubt, and the years are punctuated by the publishing of books; yet in this is marked no progress or development. His elevation to the ecclesiastical rank of papal chamberlain had no importance for his life. His operation in January, 1913, did indeed mark a certain crisis, and at that moment he may definitely be said to have stepped across into middle age. But at that time not two full years were left to him. I have thought it best, then, to try first to make a picture of Hugh's house and of the life he lived in it — and if here I have seemed to dwell upon the trivial and external, I have done so because precisely in these details his personality expressed itself when he was most of all his own master and at his ease; and if I have been tempted to resent my own description of these privacies of another man's life, and feared horribly lest good feeling should again and again be hurt by it, I have remembered that I write direct from the lips, or, at any rate, with the leave, of the innermost of his circle; and somehow Hugh Benson has come to be a man of whom everyone says everything.

Then I have wished to give an account of his exterior activity as a priest — his preaching, his apostolate, and his direction of souls; then, working inwards, of that strange department of his interests which was occupied with the abnormal and preternatural; then, of Hugh Benson as an artist; then, of that preface to his inmost life which was spent, so to say, near Gethsemane and Calvary, and was full of the mystery of pain and fear and loneliness; finally, of that most interior life of all, and of the dawn of death.

In this period letters are far fewer. And if, hitherto, I have asked to be forgiven for constant quotation, I will ask to have it here believed that I do not speak only from surmise. Still, in these pages dealing so much with a more interior world, the part of subjective bias is bound to be greater.

Any of Monsignor Benson's friends who had the good fortune to be asked to Hare Street would witness that the ritual observed on these occasions practically never varied, especially if he himself should travel down with you. You waited for him in the mephitic atmosphere of Liverpool Street Station, till, within a moment or two of the train's departure, Hugh arrived, "very fussed," in his enormous overcoat, his Trilby hat, rather dusty, carrying his own bag. You forgot this film, so to say, upon his flashing personality, the moment he caught sight of you. The charm of his address and his delightful smile and affectionate hand were all you found yourself aware of. In the third-class carriage, after a breathless greeting, he would yawn. "I must pray," he said; "simply loads of Office to say, and, oh! I'm so t-t-tired." His breviary was produced, and he relapsed into mumbling silence. At St. Margaret's you changed; and in the train, starting from another platform, Hugh at least would talk.

At Buntingford a high dog-cart was waiting, driven by Mr. Reeman, his invaluable servant. You drove through undramatic roads, with the gentle undulation of the Hertfordshire country on either side, pasture and ploughed land and some fields where crops are sown. Willows, beeches, and elms make shadowy landmarks, or stand in great masses of firmer colour; and among them a few houses show, and here and there the needle-like Eastern steeple rises from its squat tower. I can imagine this country having its charm and even its romance, but especially in certain autumn lights, when clouds are torn for the sunset, and the strong rays burn on yellow leaves; or even when the air is full of water, and the fields pale, and the leaves whirling in grey winds. It has its peace too, in the golden haze of late summer or a serene and early autumn, when the outlines, always muffled, are still further fused, and only the bees are loud in the cottage gardens. But, frankly, the neighbourhood needs helping out, I think, by glamour of some sort or another; a touch of terror, as in autumn, or of lazy summer splendour will do what the dismal winter and harsh spring cannot.

The village shows itself; you enter its irregular street at right angles, and turn down it to the left; on your right a paling, a gate, and then a wall, with lime trees behind them, are your first glimpse of home. You pass them, turning in beyond, to the yard, while this is what first is reached by one motoring from Cambridge, and for him, the house is almost what he first encounters in the village. Should Hugh Benson not have been with you on your journey, this is where he would have met you, on the doorstep, very much his own master, taking you in at once in every detail, and rather breathless in his welcome. You were shown your room; you were shouted for, in some few minutes, for whatever meal might already be awaiting you.

As for the house, it is described deliciously, rather en grand, in *Oddsfish,* with all Benson's own improvements. There was a village tradition, he says, that a house had stood there for 600 years, "but the oldest work

I can see in it," he adds, "is but Tudor. The foundations, however, may be much older." The lovely gate in front of the house dates from Charles II: the "Fore-Court" gate, with the Hearts of Jesus and Mary in the scroll-work, and a Priest's Hat, was of Benson's own designs, "drawn out" by Mr. Gabriel Pippet, and not erected till 1912. A little paved path leads from the gates to the front door, and round the front and north side of the house. Neither was this put down till 1912. The flagstones came from the House of Commons, parts of which were being repaved. "Aren't they splendid?" he kept inquiring, as pleased as a child. "And every one of them hallowed by the passing footsteps of Lloyd George. . . !" The low brick walls, capped with stone, dividing these walks from the lawn, were put up quite late, in 1914. He was particularly fond of them, and I think he liked the idea that nothing in the shape of a conveyance could quite reach the door. It was inconvenient, but seignorial; and he introduces this feature, on a large scale, in the Medds' house, in *The Coward*. Plants stand there in rough pots, and the lawn goes right and left, between the house and the lime-tree fence and road. The house-front is of Georgian brick, mellow with age; the tiled symmetrical roof rises above it, and two stacks of moulded Tudor chimneys stand on its either angle. For the restoration of these roofs Benson had to pay heavily before the "bare and desolate" place was habitable.

You entered, by the front door, directly into the outer hall, small enough, but not undistinguished, with its antlers carved wood, and pious pictures. To the left is the dining-room; to the right the library; again, to the right, by the side of the stairs, and giving on to what was called the inner hall, hung with a quaint tapestry — Hugh Benson's work — representing Joan of Arc, was the little Parlour of the Grail. The rest of the ground floor was occupied by the kitchen and its offices. It was that way, between kitchen and dining-room, that a passage led to the stable-yard and its coach-house buildings. The stairs are panelled — a piece of work begun in 1912, Monsignor Benson

carving the panels. The emblems on the first flight were personal and historical — monograms, for example, of guests; those on the second flight are of the Passion — many of the pictures hanging here are the originals of Mr. Pippet's illustrations of the Nativity play, and others. A plastered "hiding-place" (as Father Benson would believe it) over the door from the inner to the back hall was found; and gradually the steps were improved, and changed, on the first flight, for old oak. On the first floor, three rooms face the road: a large one, at the southwest corner, called the nursery; a "tapestry" room, over the hall, of which I will describe the tapestry below; and Hugh's own room, over the dining-room. This communicated with an old powder-closet which made for him a tiny dressing-room.

It has its pathos, I think, that George Herbert, once disesteemed, here came into his own; his *Holiness on the Head* hangs, illuminated, over the wash-hand stand. In Benson's own room, the panelling was perfected in 1910, and a Gothic arch of soft church stone was found behind the cheap fireplace. All through the house the fireplaces were altered, though in the room above the library, known as the Captain's room, owing to its prolonged tenancy by Captain Anderson, a friend of Monsignor Benson's (1910 to Easter, 1911), the fine original fireplace needed no improvement. This was the room which ranked as haunted.

In his Chronicle he writes:

. . . Other sayings of the house were (1) that there was a hidden treasure in it; (2) that there was an underground passage leading from it; (3) that it was haunted; (4) that in "old days" it had been a great place for entertainments. . . . As regards (1), I have heard no more. As regards (2), I have seen, when the grass is newly cut on the lawn, what looks like the roof of a tunnel in outline, running as from the southeast corner of the great cellar. And a young man in the town once told me that he had been a child in the house, and remembered stamping in the orchard to hear the hollow sound. As regards (3), two or three ladies told me that they had heard an old man groaning, it seemed, in the long orchard walk. . . . Further, the same young man told me of the ghost, and that the sound of voices talking was often heard between the floor of the Doctor's room and the ceiling of the kitchen. So much for the common talk I heard.

When Benson spent the night, which he did, on and off, for some two years, in the haunted room, "the only trouble I had here was a dream, with an old man's groan in it." Mildly alarmist anecdotes were from time to time forthcoming. In 1911 a servant, sitting on the stairs while we were at dinner, heard the door of "the Captain's" or the "haunted" room open, steps come out, and return.

Also, A—— S——, the artist (once a prizefighter), had, on two nights out of three, while sleeping in that room, heard steps come upstairs, the handle turn, the steps enter, and a voice, as of a "tall old woman," say either "Is that you?" or "Are you there?" He felt no fear, but only an inability to move or speak, and a tingling in every limb, as of electricity. Father ——, to whom I related this, told me that he, in the "nursery" next door, had heard the steps, as if on plain boards, come up one night, enter the haunted room, and come out and downstairs again.

The remaining rooms on the floor above have their quaint interest; through one the rain-water is carried from the roof by a raised leaden channel into the gutter outside. Most of these rooms were panelled, but the panelling process was very slow. Much excellent oak was discovered here and there under painted deal. He made use of all this, and collected odd bits of oak, table-legs and the like, which, all of them, were of service.

VINCENT McNABB
(1868–1943)

MANY an extraordinary Englishman is Irish, as was Father Vincent McNabb, O.P. He was born July 8, 1868, at Portaferry on Strangford Lough, County Down, Ireland. In early boyhood he moved to Belfast with his family and went from that city to Newcastle on Tyne. His vocation to the priesthood was shown at an early age. For a time young Vincent attended the diocesan seminary at Belfast but when he was seventeen years old he entered the Dominican novitiate at Woodchester. After his ordination, September 19, 1891, he went to Louvain where he acquired the degree of Lector of Theology.

With the completion of his studies, Father McNabb taught at Woodchester and Hawksyard. In 1900 he was elected Prior of Woodchester, the beginning of administrative duties which, at various stations, kept him in office until his death, June 17, 1943. Everyone loved Father Vincent: he was as much at home with the intellectual and eminent as with the poor and forsaken. He was a primitive friar observing poverty and charity in a way reminiscent of St. Francis. He mended his habit and shoes until it was difficult to say where patch began and fabric ended. His charity was dramatic in its intensity, never losing a public occasion for self-abasement. Many people considered him eccentric; because he was so real he might have been a contemporary of Jacopone. He showed better than any history what St. Dominic and his friars were like.

This real approach to his vocation did not obscure his sense of fun, his dialectical magnificence, or his practical talent for organization and administration.

Father McNabb played a large part in the work of the Catholic Evidence Guild and he was instrumental in forming the Aquinas Society and the Thomas More Society.

He lectured extensively in the United States and England and spent his boundless energies in collecting funds for churches.

LIBERAL CATHOLICISM*

THE late Bishop Brownlow in forwarding to his clergy the "Joint Pastoral of the English Hierarchy on Liberal Catholicism" added the following words:

"It is possible that the term 'Liberal Catholic' may be misunderstood by some, and be supposed to be equivalent to 'Catholic Liberal'; and the Pastoral may thus be supposed to strike at Catholics who are Liberal in politics. Nothing could be further from the minds of the Bishops; for the Catholic Church has among her most faithful children, persons of every political party; and there are Catholic Liberals who are quite as loyal and devout members of the Church as Catholic Conservatives. There is a propensity in human nature which prompts us to apply ecclesiastical censures to other people; instead of taking the warnings home to ourselves. The faithful cannot be too much on their guard against imbibing the poison of Liberal Catholicism; but they should be equally careful to abstain from stigmatising others as 'Liberal Catholics' who may be as loyal to the Church as themselves." (Jan. 1, 1901)

The wise words of a wise prelate are but a reminder that nowhere more than in ecclesiastical politics and doctrine do words prove themselves the veils of thought. In saying what must be said on the present subject the writer must trust that his readers will go beyond the spoken word to the unspoken thought; and even beyond the thought to the thing if real ambiguity is to be avoided. For on a subject surrounded by undefined frontiers and teeming with unsettled terminology, a writer could hope to avoid ambiguities only by leaving the realm of realities for that of intellectual logarithms. So that though I shall not hope, I shall expect to be somewhat obscure; whilst still expecting and hoping to leave the matter a little less obscure than before.

Thus I shall ask you to allow me to

condemn once for all whatever we find ourselves obliged to condemn by the Joint Pastoral. Yet I need not add that we are not therefore obliged to condemn the whole of Liberal Catholicism merely because we are obliged to condemn it as a whole. Nor are we therefore to anathematise the thing because the word is suspect. Have we not heard warm denunciations of the phrase "Catholic Socialism"? yet in point of fact the Church in her relations to religious orders not only approves but favours a form of Socialism; and not only Socialism but Communism! Thus there may be, and the Joint Pastoral says there is, in ecclesiastical matters a definite intellectual or political atmosphere known as "Liberal Catholicism"; this is indeed reprehensible; and yet a certain tone of Liberalism amongst Catholics is allowable in theory and wise in practice.

It may help us to clear the matter in hand if we begin by distinguishing two spheres of Liberalism, viz.: the speculative and the practical, the sphere of culture and the sphere of politics. A man may be liberal in one; and a reactionary in the other. Thinkers are not necessarily statesmen. Nor are there many Prime Ministers who could write or perhaps appreciate the *Foundations of Belief*. In ecclesiastical affairs a Catholic may be a liberal to excess in matters of thought, and medieval beyond endurance in matters of policy. Again, boldness in ecclesiastical policy is not necessarily the outcome of originality in thought. A safe secretary of the Index might play havoc with the Propaganda. A broad-minded Canon-Penitentiary might almost strangle the Holy Office. St. Thomas Aquinas was never elected Prior. St. Gregory and St. Leo are the only Doctors to wear the Tiara. Plato's ideal of statesmen-philosophers viewed historically has remained one of the most foolish dreams of one of the wisest men; so far removed is the sphere of deed from the sphere of thought.

Another distinction is of hardly less practical importance. Liberal Catholics of the

*McNabb, Father Vincent Joseph, O.P., *From a Friar's Cell* (New York: P. J. Kenedy and Sons, 1923), pp. 139-158.

exaggerated type are not confined to the laity. Just as it is naïve anthropomorphism that adjusts the categories of Church and world by identifying the Church with clerics and the world with laics or with the reigning dynasty, so it is the same immature thinking that identifies liberalism with the lay minds and conservatism with the clerical. For though it may be true to say that that somewhat indefinite thing, the world, cannot flow into the mere abstract Church, still Our Blessed Lord's own gracious parables lead us to expect tares in the broad concrete field, and fruitless branches on the wide-spreading concrete tree of the Church. False liberalism is not a parasite of the mere lay mind. It has no prejudices against clerics. Indeed if we take the heresiarchs such as Arius, Nestorius, Eutyches and the rest to be classical examples of the liberalism we would condemn, it is regrettable to find that they are not laymen. Most of the wrong thinking from which the Church has suffered has come from clerics; and as a class we are tolerable to our Master only because in spite of the grievous hurt we have done, He has commissioned us to be the salt of the earth. The very greatness of our mission and of our powers has brought about the evil we have wrought. For all power wherever found is power for evil as well as for good; and the greater the power, the greater the evil.

A definition of Liberal Catholicism either of the sound or unsound type will hardly be expected from one to whom in both its forms it appears rather as an attitude than an opinion. To the true liberal Catholic false liberalism is something a little less intolerable than heresy and a little more dangerous than schism; for as the Ancren Riwle observes, "a foe that seems a friend is a traitor beyond all traitors." And it not seldom happens that the severe sentence passed by the true liberal upon false liberalism is passed in turn upon the true liberal by those who repudiate both the name and the reality of liberalism.

Liberalism is sometimes so defined as to be synonymous with that definite *mentalité,* to quote a phrase of Fonsegrive — which meas-ures all intellectual propositions or statements, whether dogmas or scientific conclusions, by the principles and standards of experience. So used, Liberalism becomes identical with what the Vatican Council has called Rationalism. Undoubtedly there is some infiltration of Liberalism into Rationalism or vice versa. But a clear distinction may be made between both; and it is no part of a philosopher's duty to ignore or obscure distinctions. Rationalism as a word never bears a good meaning; Liberalism may mean something good or something bad. There are no orthodox rationalists; but there may be orthodox liberals. It is not easy to state wherein the distinction between the two lies, even though we are quite sure that a distinction does lie between them. Perhaps we shall be near the truth if we say that Liberalism is a leaning, and Rationalism is a bent; or that Liberalism is a tone of thought and Rationalism is a dogma; or that Liberalism may be the raw material and Rationalism the finished product. A rationalist is one who looks on himself in theory and practice as everywhere free from the bridle of authority; a liberal Catholic is one who merely acts as though free from the limitations of here and now. A rationalist is a high priest and prophet of reason; a liberal Catholic acknowledges himself the student and even the servant of faith. And if the rationalist has no limitations but those of the mind thinking and the objects thought, the liberal Catholic makes light of the limitations or restrictions of time and place. For, Liberalism not being a dogma but an attitude, the same dogma may today characterize an advanced liberal and tomorrow betoken the most orthodox Catholic. Arianism, Nestorianism, Lutheranism are dogmas or denials subject to no change. But the unsafe liberal Catholic of the twentieth century may anathematise his fellow liberal of the nineteenth; and may deserve a like anathema only by his forgetfulness that to anticipate is often as dangerous as to delay; and that the twentieth century must not too hastily take up the methods of the twenty-first.

This leads us to one of the chief elements of Liberalism, false and true. A true liberal is a true loyalist. But his loyalty is to the Church's future no less than to its past. He does not look on today as the tomb of yesterday but as the womb of tomorrow. Though the Church's past is one of splendor he looks forward to a more splendid future. For him Christianity is indeed the fulfilment of the promises; but still more is it the bringing in of a better hope. Jesus Christ is a midpoint ending and beginning divine promises. The world the Church covets most is a world that is to be. Its daily prayer is "Thy Kingdom Come!" Its eyes in apostolic days were not turned back upon an Eden but forward to a millennium. Thus the true liberal does not look on Christianity as a crucifixion, though it dies daily; but as a resurrection, for behold! it lives. Nor can he see in the Incarnation merely an episode; but an institution. Jesus Christ is the same yesterday, today and forever. A true liberal does not rest his faith on a dead past but on a living present; nor on an historical fact but on an existent reality; nor on an empty tomb but on a Real Presence. Sometimes he seems to disregard history; but this is only his human way of saying that the future is almost more to him than the past. He is impatient when a certain class of Catholics boast of their loyalty, thereby expressing a mere sentiment for what has been, as though loyalty like memory was only retrospective. In Lacordaire's strong phrase, he is "a citizen of the future," and he bows down before the New Era that is to be.

Therein lie his strength and weakness. Because the future is not the past, he is tempted to think that it must be other than the past. Unless closely watched and wisely guided, this feeling may grow to mean that between past and future there must be a break. In his zeal for continuance he may be led on to hold a break of continuity; as if the Church had persistence only at the cost of consciousness. In other spheres this would not matter much, but the Church must be a continuous consciousness. For she has the mind of Christ, and what He was yesterday, He is today and will be forever.

This element of expectation which is the life — and may be the death — of sound liberalism is joined with a certain insistence on doubt and difficulty. If to look into the present state of the economy of Redemption is to peer through a glass darkly, what must it be to look through the added darkness of tomorrow? A true liberal is a man whose face is set eastward. As he journeys onward he is always an hour's march before the rising sun, in that darkest hour before dawn. He will scarcely allow himself the consolation of seeing each day's sun at mid-day, for that would be to rest on the way, and to falter in pressing forward toward the goal; and for him life and especially spiritual life is movement; and "Not to go on is to go back." He lives in an hour of darkness; and makes his dwelling place amidst the clouds.

This again is his strength and weakness. Unless he has the true philosophic attitude of faith he will allow difficulties to usurp the jurisdiction of doubts; ignorance will become error; and, in spite of "malo esse quam videri" things will be taken not to be, because they are not seen to be. In matters of doctrine this attitude leads some men to leave entrenchments and to go out in the open in the hope of cutting off an enemy who has made a feint of flight. How often have lines of defence been abandoned for no better reason than that they were built yesterday, and now it is today; or that they were thrown up in the night and now the sun is shining on them; or that the defenders know better than their foes the weak parts of the defence? Never was a fortress equally strong everywhere; and never was it defended by men who were conscious only of its weakness. But it does not cease to be defensible merely because all its parts are not equally strong; or because no one knows its weakness so well as its defenders. Part strengthens part; nor is it taken until every bastion has been won.

In practical matters the frame of mind which allows difficulties to weigh like doubts, will allow the defects of persons to compromise institutions. But whilst a loyal Catholic may well turn his eyes towards the future, he must not fret his soul because others have the official duty of turning towards the past and looking warily to the Church's steps.

To the elements of Liberalism in general we may now add those of modern Liberalism; which we shall find to take their shape and colour from the modern social and intellectual environment.

Liberalism in ecclesiastical politics would seem to be identical with or begotten of a reaction against medieval feudalism. It is profoundly interesting that in feudalism, i.e., in the first definitely Christian civilisation we have seen, society is found resting on something like a social pact; and labor is associated not with slavery but with free serfs bound by oaths to military service. In pursuance of something like the same principle, the relations between Church and State were fixed by Charters or Concordats, whereby the civil and ecclesiastical powers so bound each other to mutual aid that we find Bishops and Abbots leading troops, and secular judges meddling with theology. In spite of the politic toleration of Jews the common teaching of feudalism was "One Kingdom: One Church." All this reminds us that the age of crusades and charters bore within its heart something of the romantic idealism that had led the Church of Jerusalem into a premature effort after communism. The crisis of feudalism came when Protestantism brought western civilisation face to face with the still more complex problem of dealing with men not in the abstract but in the concrete, not with idealised rational animals but with German monks and English sovereigns. But even after three hundred years of struggle feudalism has not taken leave of Europe. In some states it still serves to embody the relations between civil and ecclesiastical powers. Every year however adds to the frailty of its tenure. Even as we speak its last foothold in a great continental nation is being washed away by the floods of uprising Socialism. Comparing these feudal relations to a dying man, over-cautious conservatism is the child who will not see death approaching, being blinded by the memory of his father's long years and many illnesses; the false liberal is the child who would hasten the father's death by withdrawing the pillow or by a bustling preparation for the funeral. The true loyal liberal is the child who, whilst doing his best to keep life as long as possible, would not prepare for the death which he has so long foreseen and dreaded.

Just as Liberalism in ecclesiastical politics is a counter-current to feudalism, so in ecclesiastical thought it is a counter-current to formalism. Carried beyond its limits this liberal current broadens out into merely destructive criticism. It is significant that Descartes the Gaul and Kant the German, the two most influential thinkers since the sixteenth century, should have given us the practice and theory of criticism. But criticism is naturally if not necessarily formless and amorphous. Its aim is to make debris; it sometimes ends with chaos. It should not end there, if critics were true to the etymology of their name. For if a critic is a judge, his judgments should be decisions and should stand. The true Catholic liberal thinker recognises that though the Church is founded on a rock, men build thereon "gold, silver, precious stones, wood, hay, stubble." From time to time an examination has to be made not of the foundation "which is Christ Jesus" but of the lower courses of masonry laid down by man. This inspection of the lower courses of masonry and rejection of what is old or crumbling is a critical work worthy of the best intellects of the Church. Nowadays much has to be done in the sphere of philosophy and history. Philosophy has to be translated into modern forms of thought or to be revised by a new synthesis of psychological and cosmological data. History has almost to be rewritten. In great part only its outlines remain true to fact; and large regions of eventful history have for the first time to be welcomed within its frontiers. Strangely enough, exaggerated liberalism of thought sometimes flees to philosophy and sometimes to history in its protest against the formalism of the past. For the most dominant current in modern philosophy is singularly amorphous and even nebulous; whilst history has almost shrunk back to a bare index and précis-making of past events, shorn of all the formal and ideal valuations of former ages.

A further element in modern Catholic liberalism is the recognition of rights. It would be straining a threadbare theme to insist on the fact that Christianity has practically created the theory of man's unchartered rights. Medievalism, whether in thought or action, was not altogether freed from the thraldom of petty intellectual and social tyranny. Plato and Aristotle were in the sphere of thought what Constantine and William the Conqueror were in the social sphere. Few, even of the boldest thinkers, dared cast aside the over-lordship of these two "tyrants" of thought. But theirs was a mild Hellenic thraldom, tempered by their graceful καλοκαγθία. And in spite of the subtleties of commentators their philosophy is the nearest approach the world has yet seen to organized good sense.

But the sixteenth century at one stroke broke away from the statutory to the natural rights of man as man. Exaggerated liberalism, which is but an over-development of this birth-throe, is too insistent upon its claims and too unobservant of its duties. Sound liberalism is more concerned to grant freedom than to claim it. And outside these two classes a third class is still found for whom the modern and essentially Christian idea of a human being freighted with duties growing into rights and rights resting on fulfilled duties is a disloyalty to a past Christian civilization.

So far we have assumed that Liberalism is loyalty to the future equally with the past — that it is therefore a keen realisation of difficulty. Moreover in its modern form it concludes a democratic counter-current to feudalism and a critical counter-current to formalism joined to an explicit assertion of the social and intellectual rights of man.

The nineteenth century gave us a notable example of true ecclesiastical liberalism in two men born within a few months of each other, John Henry Lacordaire and John Henry Newman. Both were converts; both had been smitten in different degrees by unbelief. Lacordaire was a liberal in action; Newman, in thought. Lacordaire had few difficulties with the Creed; Newman hardly touched ecclesiastical politics. Lacordaire was neither attracted nor repelled by the dogmatic side of the Church. Of his conversion he could write, "I have reached Catholic belief through social belief; and nothing appears to me better demonstrated than the argument: Society is necessary; therefore the Christian religion is divine, for it is the means of bringing religion to its true perfection." Newman was actually kept back by the political action of the Church at the time when he was being drawn to acknowledge her as the covenanted guarantee and guide of dogmatic developments. Lacordaire called himself a "Citizen of the Future" and found a journal entitled *The New Era;* Newman left behind the outline of a vast scheme of development. Lacordaire sprang from a nation that was breaking the bonds of feudalism in Church and State; Newman belonged to a State-church that hardly felt its feudal fetters in the profession of dogmatic liberalism. Both the Gallic tribune of the Church and the Anglo-Saxon thinker insisted on the rights of action and thought — Lacordaire, in his phrase, "Liberty is not given, it is taken"; Newman in his phrase, "Conscience first, Pope afterwards." Yet both men made their claims for others more than for themselves: Lacordaire thrice bowed to the stern voice of obedience; Newman could write "My own Bishop is my Pope." "A Bishop's lightest word *ex cathedra* is heavy." Lacordaire, although he could say on his death-bed "I hope to live and die a repentant Catholic and an unrepentant liberal," did not recognise that his liberalism energized mostly in his outer life of action; Newman, because he was geographically and ecclesiastically associated with Tory feudalism, detested liberalism in politics to such an extent as not to recognize that he was a Sir Galahad of dogmatic liberalism. Lacordaire was before his age in demanding and employing the three freedoms, of the Press, of Education, and of Church Government; Newman in his *Grammar of Assent, Development of Doctrine,* and *Essay of Inspiration* has laid down liberal lines of thought in the sphere of Philosophy, Theology and Scripture. Lastly, Lamennais, the apostate French Abbé, throws into relief the sound liberalism of Lacordaire; and Darwin, the spoiled priest of the Establishment and author of a purely biological theory of development, is subtly contrasted with Newman, his pioneer in the sphere of theological development.

From the lives of these two great souls and true liberals it would seem that a lesson is taught to us whose path is beset by even greater dangers than those they so fully overcame. Lacordaire the fearless man of action stands in contrast with Newman the quiet thinker. The man who held Notre Dame spell-bound by his eloquence was above all an ascetic; the seer who won England by the story of his change of soul was a mystic. In that, as in so much else, their lives and especially their inner lives are still symbolical. Some of us are beset in the sphere of church government by temptations to an unrestrained political liberalism. Too intent on tomorrow, we are fretful with today. For such of us even the terrors of Lacordaire's inflictive asceticism are not without a stern lesson. The student of St. Sulpice who threw the quaint college-caps behind the fire, and the sub-editor of *L'Avenir* who wrote impassioned pleas for disestablishment had to practice many an hour of rude ἄσκησις before his soul brought itself to its final childlike pliancy in the hands of authority. So steeped in the love of freedom as to allow it no small share in his choice of a religious order, he yet undertook the life of vowed obedience; nor did his life ever lag behind his vow. "Child of an age that knew not how to obey," he felt that it could learn and he could teach no better lesson than that of the Son Who was obedient unto death. The dangers springing from the applause of thousands of his fellow-citizens whom he was leading to faith, he stifled under the feet of some simple lay-brother to whom he poured out the humbling story of his sins. He first lived, then preached, Christ crucified. Social theories and ecclesiastical politics became simple to this passionate wooer of the Cross when he recognised that his Master's divine diplomacy was to live what He preached and to give His life for His foes. Personal rights and privileges came to him colored by the thought that the One Who had all rights and privileges emptied Himself of all save that of claiming to be loved by loving unto

death those who hated unto death. His whole inner life has been summed up in these striking words: "His love for the Cross was exclusive, passionate; not a platonic love, but a fire that led him to copy the pattern shown him on Calvary. All his mysticism was reduced to this simple principle: To suffer: — to suffer in order to satisfy justice — to suffer in order to prove love." He was a true ascetic; and could therefore dare to be a true liberal. For he bore in his soul the marks of Christ crucified; he sought to blot out the handwriting against the world he lived in by nailing it to the cross; and everywhere as he moved amongst men his life and word preached the truth that the Cross of Christ is alone the redemption and enfranchisement of man.

If Lacordaire was an ascetic, Newman was a mystic. As Lacordaire's sound liberalism grew out of his true asceticism, so did Newman's sound liberalism grow out of his true mysticism. For him a vision was the object and the reward of life. Had he been rapt with St. Paul to a sight of the third heaven, had he seen things which even his golden tongue could not utter, he would have spoken of his rapture as "seeing through a glass darkly" in comparison with the vision he was to see. Death, to such a soul, could only seem the swift passage "from shadows and symbols to the Truth." Yet he wasted his life in no vain mood of regret for a vision he could nowhere descry in this world of shadows. He had the seer's gift of seeing beyond and within; and of seeing first of all, the dim frontiers of further fields of light. Nature was sacramental to him; it was the garment of God. It was even liturgical and "chanted to his soul with solemn voice." Things did not therefore cease to belong to nature because they proved to be divine. And as the meanest flower — a spray of snapdragon on a college-wall — had thoughts too deep for tears, so did the simplest revealed truth no matter in what half-forgotten language enshrined, open up vistas of thought along which his great mind ranged to the Infinite. Such a simple phrase as "The Word was made flesh" he could not read without seeing three fathomless mysteries yawning under his feet. To him the formulas of faith were not too shallow but too deep for thought. He had the sensitiveness of those mystics who could not hear the name of God by whomsoever spoken without being borne against their will into high regions of super-conscious thought. Filled with the bliss of the divine cloud he showed no fretfulness under the dim lights of the Credo. There were no mysteries for him; but one all em-bracing mystery — God. And in that light he saw light, and in that shadow he bore meekly with all shadows. Like St. Teresa, whose soul thrilled whilst chanting the Creed at Mass, his whole mind swayed to the bal-anced antitheses of the Creed of Athanasius. He looked upon it almost as the grandest song of faith, for whilst he chanted it, his mind leaped beyond the word to the divine reality and there found itself flooded by the "Blessed Vision of Peace."

Visitors to the Convent of the Carmelites in Paris are shown the cell where Lacordaire prayed; and upon the wall, are still pointed out the blood-marks of his pitiless self-con-quest. You have but to go an hour's walk along the Iffley Road from Oxford to see the brick-floored cell where Newman knelt to see and stood to write the "master light of all his seeing" — the vision that led him on. Such as would dare to tread the way of these two great souls and do some little of the work they left undone, must one day kneel down at least in spirit within those two shrines and learn their lesson. For only when some of the Master's ascetic and mystic self-denial — some of the sorrows or shadows of Golgotha — has mastered our soul may we hope to be true to our freedom and our responsibilities, to our past and our future, to ourselves and to God.

ERIC GILL

(*1882–1941*)

ERIC GILL, born in 1882, was the son of a "Chapel" minister. His childhood was an imaginative interior saga which in 1913 led him into the Catholic Church.

He was educated privately and at the Chi-chester Art School. He became one of the most famous English sculptors of his time, although he always referred to himself with humility as a stonecutter.

Some of his better known works are to be seen in the stations of the cross at West-minster Cathedral, the war memorial in

Leeds, and the ornamental sculptures on the B.B.C. Building in London.

With the publication of his *Autobiography,* all biographical account of the man compared with his own story, seems anaemic. For Gill, in fabricating the story of his life, did so with such gusto and clarity as to place his self-told tale in the top rank of autobiographical writing.

His stimulating theory of art is seen at its best in *Beauty Looks After Herself.*

POSTSCRIPT*

4. JERUSALEM

THE removal from Wales to Pigotts, Speen, Bucks, though not undertaken with any such purpose in view, brought about a return to sculpture. At Capel-y-ffin

*Gill, Eric, *Autobiography* (New York: Devin-Adair Co., 1941), pp. 261–274.

I hadn't had any but small carving jobs, either because architects and people got the idea that I was too far away, or just because there didn't happen to be work for me to do. As I have said, I wasn't worrying, because I had plenty of lettering work and wood en-graving. But no sooner did we get to Pigotts than sculpturing works began pouring in.

From a worldly point of view the most important of these were the carvings at Broadcasting House and the enormous bas reliefs at the League of Nations building at Geneva. The former from my point of view are a failure. I mean simply that I don't much like looking at them. The idea was grand but I was incapable of carrying it out adequately. Prospero and Ariel! Well, you think. *The Tempest* and romance and Shakespeare and all that stuff. Very clever of the B.B.C. to hit on the idea, Ariel and arial. Ha! Ha! And the B.B.C. kidding itself, in the approved manner of all big organizations (British or foreign, public or private), that it represents all that is good and noble and disinterested — like the British Empire or Selfridges (and the U. S. Constitution and the Comité des Forges, not to mention our superb and all powerful and all pure-Nordic race). But wait. Read *The Tempest*. I don't know anything about Shakespeare's intentions, but it didn't seem to me to be unduly straining the poem to see in the figure of Prospero much more than than that of a clever old magician, or in that of Ariel more than that of a silly fairy. Had not Prospero power over the immortal gods? At any rate it seemed to be only right and proper that I should see the matter in as bright a light as possible and so I betook upon me to portray God the Father and God the Son. For even if that were not Shakespeare's meaning it ought to be the B.B.C.'s.

Then I had the amazing honour of the job at Geneva. This was to be the British Government's gift for the adornment of the new building. I don't know who suggested that it should take the form of a work of sculpture — but Anthony Eden seemed to be very keen on it, and I was asked if I would undertake it. So I went to Geneva to see the building and to discuss the project with the politicians and secretaries on the spot. The site chosen (in the foyer of the League Council Hall) was a frieze fifty-five feet long and about eight feet high — and of course, it instantly occurred to me that the most suitable subject in the world, and one which would

go very well in the space, was "The Turning out of the Money Changers." For as I tried to explain to the Secretary General (whom I afterwards discovered to have been formerly in the French Ministry of Finance) and to other people at the party to which I was invited, that more than anything else was what the League of Nations ought to be engaged upon — the ridding of Europe and the World of the stranglehold of finance, both national and international. It seemed obvious to me and in my innocence I thought the League of Nations would jump at the idea. I didn't mean that international bankers were the cause of all evil, but that the money-making motive was paramount in our affairs so that all valuations other than those in £ s. d. were neglected. Consequently commercialism was not only rampant in every little village hut, as it was in every little heart, but also in all government departments and in international affairs. And so on! The idea was received quite coldly. One American financial delegate said that if such a sculpture were put up it would be "the last and greatest hypocrisy of the British Empire." And of course I quite saw that. In the end the idea was turned down because it was "too Christian." . . . It was ruled that nothing specifically Christian must be represented, for fear of giving offence to the Jews and the Turks and others, but that if I liked to suggest a subject from the Old Testament, that would be acceptable as that book was in good odour with all except atheists and "we needn't worry about *them*." So I proceeded on those lines and the result is that there, in the middle of that monstrous exhibition of dead architecture and pseudo-modernity, is a colossal representation of the recreation of Adam with a great text proclaiming the overmastery of God and in smaller side panels children and animals echoing the same sentiment. I fear the American financial delegate still has good cause for jeers. That work took from 1935 to 1938.

But from the point of view from which I am writing this book, the most important sculpturing job I had in these years was the carving of ten panels on the New Museum at Jerusalem — a noble building. This involved my staying in the Holy Land for four months in 1934 and I went again in 1937. Except for our stays at Salies-de-Béarn I have never been away from England so long. I have been to Ireland several times on lecturing business (on one occasion I arrived a week too soon. So I went to Galway and the Aran Islands for the week) and to Scotland on the same business. I had a fortnight in Germany in 1930 when I went to work at Count Kessler's press at Weimar (he took me for drives round the Thuringewald several times, and as we went along the roads under the fruit trees we often saw young men who held out their arms as we passed. I asked Kessler what they did that for. He said: "Oh, they're followers of a man called Hitler and that's their sign. . . ." It seems odd to think that was in June 1930 and now it's only June 1940). I went a lot of times to Paris though never for more than a week at a time and I went several times to Italy though only to Rome and Rapallo, and to Rome only for nine days altogether. So, apart from Salies and Jerusalem, I don't consider that I have come much under the influence of foreign parts or foreign people.

I have tried to say what Salies meant to us. I wish I could properly assess the influence of Jerusalem. I was exceedingly fortunate to have the work there. I'm no particular good at travelling — in fact very bad at it, much too worried about the luggage and the tickets and I can't sleep in trains — I don't like sightseeing or acquiring information and I am no good at foreign languages. So unless I've got a job to do I'd rather stay at home. But at Jerusalem I had work, and a good long job. And it involved my working on the scaffold in the open sun with all the Arab workmen. I wore Arab clothes, which means dressing more splendidly than European kings and princes, and hob-nobbed with Laurie Cribb who came with me in Arab cafés and suqs. It was altogether splendid — surely it must have been influential.

For Palestine is the Holy Land. That was the most notable and even the most noticeable thing about it, and yet there are people who go there who say they don't notice it. They say they think Jerusalem very disap-

pointing. But to me it was like living with the Apostles. It was like living in the Bible. It was the antithesis of everything our England stands for. You can hardly think of anything which the two countries have in common except our common humanity and in England that is overlaid, corrupted and debauched by every kind of inhuman nonsense, whereas in Palestine, among the Arabs, it is uppermost and unspoiled. I am not saying there is nothing wrong in Palestine. Wherever there are men there is sin and violence and selfishness and disease. Moreover there are poor in Palestine poorer than anything we can conceive in our up-to-date towns. In spite of all that it is the Holy Land and they live a holy life, whereas England is unholy and people can only live holy lives in secret.

I think it is no use my writing thus. I cannot prove what I say. I can hardly find anyone to agree. The English in Palestine and the Jews seem to conceive it to be their mission to reform everything and to turn the Arabs into good Europeans. And there is so much that is irresistible in their reforms. The water supply of Jerusalem is now good and plentiful whereas formerly it was scanty and poisoned. Malaria has been abolished. Ophthalmia is being steadily dealt with. Banditry is being suppressed. The wresting of the land from the selfish grasp of absentee landlords. The agricultural, arboricultural and horticultural work of the young Zion colonists, as it seemed to me, superb in itself and of great educational benefit to the Arabs. The work of the Hebrew University, and of the Jewish hospitals and clinics. . . . These things are good. Are they not? But, then, on the other side. . . . Except in the old city of Jerusalem, where the streets are only footways, motor cars and motor omnibuses are everywhere. Everywhere there is importation of the cheap mass products of Europe and Japan. The smart modern Jews are building smart modern towns and introducing smart modern ways, including smart modern prostitution . . . and smart modern factories, and smart modern clothes. Are these things good? They are not.

But the discussion of such judgments is beyond the scope of this book. I only want to, somehow, make it clear that since going to Palestine my mind is pervaded by a different order of living — an order previously only guessed at, but now experienced — an order not only human but essentially holy. "Know ye not that you are the temple of God and that the spirit of God dwelleth in you? But if any man violate the temple of God, him shall God destroy. For the temple of God is holy, which you are." Which you are! that is the point. . . . Oh they are lousy in Palestine. Lousy with disease, lousy with spiritual vermin too. Are we lousy in England? No, no we are not. Are we lousy spiritually? No, no — the words have no meaning any more. Don't think I saw no bad in Palestine. There was bad everywhere. But the good was not yet dead.

I am not going to write about beautiful things (which I should very likely never have seen at all but for the friendship and enthusiasm of Austen Harrison, the architect — on whom be peace) the beauty of the Judean desert, the beauty of Siloam, the beauty of Justinian's church at Bethlehem, not even the beauty of the Haram at Jerusalem, the Moslem holy place, the most beautiful place I have ever seen and the farthest removed from the Bank of England and all its devil worship, and the most civilized, the most cultured, the most quiet and serene, the most spacious, the most spiritually pervaded place now remaining in the whole world. Tell me where there is another. Is it in London, in Trafalgar Square? . . . Is it the Place de la Concorde? . . . Is it on the Acropolis at Athens? They tell me that is very lovely, but at Jerusalem living men worship the living God; at Athens there is but a memory of what was. . . . Is it even in the piazza of St. Peter's? No, not there. That is a grand and solemn place, the gigantic arms inviting the concourse of all the children of men; but it is an impious work — architecture, swagger, human prowess, human greatness. . . . The face of Christ has been more defiled by our praise than by spittle — for we have not praised Him, but ourselves.

Palestine was the last of the revelations vouchsafed to me. It confirmed and enfolded all the others. And it was a twofold revelation. In the Holy Land I saw a holy land indeed; I also saw, as it were eye to eye, the sweating face of Christ. The half-ruinous church of the Holy Sepulchre at Jerusalem, the half-ruinous church of the Nativity at Bethlehem, these things are symbolical; and we are incapable of renovating them. And the fact is more than a symbol. For what could we do? The government of Caesar could employ learned and sympathetic architects and archaeologians and engineers. We could employ a joint-stock limited-liability company of contractors from Khartoum or Stamboul and they could employ a horde of "Hands." And American millionaires could subscribe the money — very good men, I dare say, but very bad money — the proceeds of usury and robbery. And then we should have a nice brand-new Holy Sepulchre — very refined and correct according to the style of the Crusaders, and a nice brand-new Church of the Nativity — very correct and refined according to the style of Justinian and Byzantium.

But I don't believe it will happen. By the inscrutable decree of God the sweat is not thus to be wiped from His face. He suffers less if the Copts and the Greeks and the Romans quarrel among themselves than if, having abandoned the Cross, they hand the whole notion of salvation over to the sanitary authority. That is what our civilization is seeking to do. That has not yet happened at Jerusalem. They have not yet rendered to to Caesar the things that are God's.

Far then from finding disappointment in Palestine I found only good; for I found the divine beauty. And it was a double good; for I saw not only the beauty but the tears and sweat. Illusion fell away. The nonsensical and illusory grandeurs of Rome, Rome, the Holy City, decked out in the finery of Ball Rooms and Banks, the soul-ensnaring magnificence of statistical display, the grand appearance of doctrinal and ethical unity . . . It seemed to me that we should do better to eschew our grandeurs and forget our numbers — and brag less about unity while, to the heathen and the pagans and the infidels, the most conspicuous thing about Christians is their sectarian disunity (and this we symbolize with a diabolical precision by our bloody fights in the Holy Sepulchre itself — fights stopped only by the police and Moslem police at that) and their only unity is a merely secular one. For while we fight among ourselves about doctrine we are united in the common worship of money and material success. Here I do not exaggerate. That is the awful thing.

But let nothing I say be taken as implying disloyalty to the Roman Church, mother and mistress, or to the Holy Father, Vicar indeed of Christ. There is of course a sense in which the Church and her adherents are one and the same, so that what is true of one is true of the others, and when they are guilty, she is condemned. But in another sense it is not so. She wears the garb of time and place, and that garb is subject to corruption. As pride and vain-glory afflict us, so is she afflicted. The natural tendency of all strong institutions to pharisaism cannot be avoided. Governors and administrators must always see things from their professional standpoint. Vested interests spring up, both temporal and spiritual. And how easy it is to deceive ourselves into thinking that the "precious ointment" has been provided for His burial, when perhaps it really has been provided for our own satisfaction and when, moreover, it is only precious in the sense that it has cost money and is not otherwise precious at all, being merely "made in Birmingham."

And one thing has become increasingly clear to me and it is very important. Accusations against the Church can only be substantiated by Church Doctrine! Do the Christian clergy and laity side with the rich against the poor? Many seem to do so. And is it wrong? You may well think so. But how will you prove it but by recourse to Christian teaching? Is not much of our worship both vain and vain-glorious? And is it not vanity reprehensible and vain-glory noxious to the Lord of Hosts? How will you prove these things but from the Holy Writ and the lives of the Saints? And if you are annoyed by the policeman-like frame of mind of many of the clergy and their apparent conviction that the spirit killeth but the letter quickeneth (so that you would think getting to heaven was a business of going "by the book") you must still remember that the opposite doctrine is Christian teaching and that it is the authority to which they themselves appeal who is the judge. And if the Church in Europe and America is full of disease of spirit, lukewarm, pharasaical and subservient to the powers of this world and full of enthusiasm for the material advantages with which science and machinery have seduced us, there is still the Holy Land and, in spite of its poverty, we still think it holy.

What I am struggling to say is that while I never saw or imagined anything more lovely than the Holy Land — whether you think of it as a land or as human habitations, so also I never saw anything less corrupted by human pride and sin. And I understand as never before the virtue of poverty and how peace on earth can have no other basis. I saw a vision of all the peoples of the earth struggling ceaselessly with one another for material possessions and material advantages. And I saw that the greater the material success so much more the frightful must be the struggle. For the competition for riches means a ceaseless spurring of men's powers of invention in weapons and methods of destruction, until in the end, as Pope Pius XII said almost immediately after his election: "In this age of mechanization the human person becomes merely a more perfect tool in industrial-production and . . . a perfected tool for mechanized warfare."

And thus men will perish in the ruins of their disgraced cities, perish with curses in their hearts, curses upon a life which was lived in misery and is ending in frightful fear.

And I saw that the only people who lived in holiness and dignity were those who lived in poverty of spirit. Blessed be ye poor; for yours is the kingdom of God. It was in the Holy Land that that lesson had first been taught. It was in the Holy Land that that lesson could still be learned. And it became clear that it is no use renouncing war unless we first of all renounce riches. That is the awful job before us. A whole world crazy for material riches and the Christians as crazy as anyone else — giving secret love to Christ but in their lives contradicting themselves. A whole world doomed to perpetual fighting — and no remedy but to persuade it to renounce riches. What a forlorn hope!

So I came back from Palestine with my mind made up — or at least on the way to it. But this was not going to make things easy. Henceforward I must take up a position even more antagonistic to my contemporaries than that of a mere critic of the mechanistic system. I must take a position antagonistic to the very basis of their civilization. And I must appear antagonistic even to the Church itself. Of course that is all nonsense but that is how it must appear. For the Christians everywhere have committed themselves to the support of capitalist-industrialism and therefore to the wars in its defence, mechanized war to preserve mechanized living; while I believe that capitalism is robbery, industrialism is blasphemy and war is murder.

I had not realized this. I had been misled by the romanticism of my childhood and youth. And I had been misled by the logic of medieval Christian theology. For according to the theologians war is not always unjustifiable and is therefore not always murder. A war of defence, for instance, the defence of home and country against an unjust aggressor (like the defence of a man's home and family against robbers) provided it be conducted in a just manner and with a reasonable chance of success, is a just war. But nothing can justify actual sin and direct evil may not be done that good may come. You may not mutilate prisoners, or slay non-combatants. And you may not spread false reports of your enemies' evil deeds or promote a propaganda of hate and ill-will. I had assumed that war today was as likely to be just as wars of the past. But now my eyes were opened. And I saw that just as modern capitalism could not justly claim that it merited Christian support because it upheld the sacred rights of property (because for one kind of property it preserved it destroyed a hundred, and the kind of property it chiefly destroyed was the very kind that Christian philosophers were most anxious to

preserve — the personal property of the peasant and small craftsman), so modern war had become a totally different business from that envisaged by the medieval theologians.

And just as capitalists see everything in terms of saleability; thus they must naturally see labour also. Labour is something to be bought and sold at its competitive or market price. We are blind to the monstrous, the devilish inhumanity and therefore blasphemy of this theory and the practice founded upon it. How can a man and his wife feed and clothe their family in a human and holy manner if they are thus treated as mechanisms? We do not treat animals thus. A horse must have his proper food and shelter whatever happens but a motor car needs oil and petrol only when it is being used. The capitalist treatment of human beings is like the treatment of machines. Do not think this revolutionary theory is a new thing. It is stated clearly in the Gospel in the parable of the labourers, and we Christians do not merely deny our humanity in supporting capitalism; we also deny Christ. Whether a man works one or twelve hours he lives the whole day. It is that division of men into wage-earners and others which constitutes the class division and necessitates the "class war." The wage-earners are simply instruments to be exploited for profit, the rest of men are the exploiters. And thus as Christians unjustly hide behind the Christian teaching on war and capitalism, so they unjustly defend the "wage-system." For though some men will always prefer to be wage-earners and some will willingly choose to take wages occasionally, a system which deprives the majority of men of ownership of the means of production and drives them to the irresponsible labour of industrialism, is in its nature ungodly and anti-Christian.

And thinking over these things I saw the hypocrisy of my country and its politicians. I remembered the jingo imperialism of my childhood and youth. The wars of petty conquest which we had been brought up to think heroic. And I remembered the condemnation of the Israelitish landowner who sought to "add field to field," and I saw that the same condemnation was due to the state which sought to add colony to colony. And I saw the hypocrisy of all the blather about "the white man's burden." And I saw how the British were not only responsible for the beginnings of capitalist-industrialism and for its monstrous financial developments, but also for the imperialism which was its inevitable result. And I saw the mad foolishness of our British prophets and their racial pride and swagger — Kipling with his "verily we are the people" and his damned talk about "the lesser breeds without the law" — the "traitor clerks" who won fame and riches by pandering to the ambitions of vulgar money-makers. I had long since learned the truth about South Africa, but I had not seen clearly, until I went to Palestine, the dirty materialism which inspired all modern militarism, nor the impossible ungodliness of modern mechanical war-making.

But one thing is clear: I must keep clear of politics — politics as the word is understood in our time and in what are called democratic countries. And I must keep clear of politicians — the gang of professional parliamentarians and town and country councillors. For in the first place politics is beyond me. Politics is like foreign languages — something outside my scope, something I can't do. Moreover I do not believe political arrangements and re-arrangements are real. It is all a confused business of ramps and rackets — pretended quarrels and dishonest commercial schemings, having no relation to the real interests of peoples, neither to their spiritual nor their material welfare, and conducted upon no principles other than momentary self-interest. The prestige of parliament is an empty fraud and all its grandiose and clumsy procedure is more outworn and even less venerable than the ritual in Anglican cathedrals. And politics is now a profession! Professionalism is a curse in any trade — the defense of anything, without due consideration of its goodness, on account of pecuniary interest or inertia. Public schools, the army, the law, architecture and, most frightful, the Church, all suffer from the curse of professionalism, though all these are served by trained and honestly devoted men. But politicians, as I have remarked before, can make no such claim to our respect. It is not too much to say that they are trained to nothing but vote-catching, and they are not and they never have been anything but agents for the defence of the monetary interests. Such was the origin of parliamentary representation, such is its very soul. This is no place for even the briefest outline of parliamentary history; it is only necessary to note that all its evils have been grossly augmented since the final and decisive victory of finance which the nineteenth century witnessed. There is now no hope of a reform of our society by parliamentary means.

"Religion is politics, politics is brotherhood," said William Blake, and, I may add: "Brotherhood is poverty and poverty is peace." That is where I found myself and that is where I shall remain.

ART AND PRUDENCE*

Art is skill — skill in doing or skill in making.
Whatever else art may be it is always that.
Skill is the body of art.
Deliberation is its soul or "form."
Art is deliberate skill — skill with mind behind it.
"Art abides always on the side of the mind."
There is a thing called the mind of God.
Hence there is a thing called the art of God.

*Gill, Eric, *Beauty Looks After Herself* (New York: Sheed and Ward, 1933), pp. 11–29.

There is a thing called the mind of man.

Hence there is a thing called the art of man.

Only by metaphor do we speak of the art of the spider;

The spider, having no mind, cannot use deliberate skill.

The skill of the spider is directly dependent upon the mind of God.

The art of the spider is the art of God.

The art of the spider is like that of a factory "hand" — directed from outside.
As the owner of a jam factory said to a visitor: "I am God almighty in this place."

But man has a mind of his own and therefore free will.

A rational soul necessarily connotes free will.

Hence there is strictly speaking an art of man as well as an art of God.

But, unlike God, man cannot make out of nothing.

Man's mind, his intelligence and will, can only know the truth that God knows and desire the good that God wills.

Imbecility and ill will are privations.

Skill in making and skill in doing are both loosely called art.

Doing is an activity directed to an end in view — the end in view being man's good, his last good, Heaven.

But when a man's deeds are directed not to his own good simply but to the good of a *thing,* then doing becomes *making.*

An act that is good, or thought to be good, with regard to oneself is called a *prudent* act.

An act that is good, or thought to be good, with regard to a thing to be made is called *art.*

A man whose acts are conformed to his own good is called a *prudent man.*

A man whose acts are conformed to the good of things is called an *artist.*

In both cases skill in doing is required,

Skill in doing good to oneself is called *prudence.*

Skill in doing good to things is called *art.*

Prudence is the means to happiness in oneself.

Art is the means to pleasure in what is not oneself.

To have happiness is the object of prudence.

Happiness in oneself is a good and is the object of the will.

Happiness is subjective.

To have pleasure in things is the object of art.

Pleasure in things is a good and is the object of the intelligence.

Pleasure is objective.

Great intelligence is not necessary for prudence (happiness).

Great prudence is not necessary for intelligence (pleasure).

A fool may be a saint.

A villain may be an artist.

A fool may be a villain.

A saint may be an artist.

But a fool cannot be an artist, nor a villain a saint.

Ethics is the science of happiness in oneself.

Aesthetics is the science of pleasure in things.

Both are departments of philosophy.

Prudence is the application of ethics to practice.

Art is the application of aesthetics to practice.

The practice of prudence is called morals.

The practice of art is called craft or craftsmanship.

Happiness being man's goal, his final goal, it behoves a man to be a prudent man;
for prudence has man's final happiness for its object.

But happiness is a state of mind.

It is that state of mind in which what is desired is known.

Final happiness is the state of mind in which the desired God is the known God.

When what is desired is known it is said to be *seen*.

Final happiness is to see God.

This is called "the Beatific Vision."

Happiness is, therefore, not a state of bliss merely;
It is a state of bliss in knowledge.

But knowledge is necessarily knowledge of something — not of *no* thing.
Happiness is in a knowledge of that thing or those things that are pleasing.
Happiness is in knowledge of those things that are pleasing to the mind.

Those things are pleasing to the mind which are in themselves good.

God alone is good.

So those things are pleasing to the mind which are of God or in God.

Here below we may see God in all things (that is earthly happiness).
We may see through all things to God.

The state of Heaven is that in which we see all things in God.
We see through God to all things.

The prudent man acts so that he may achieve the blissful state of heavenly happiness.

But that state is one in which he has knowledge of all things in God —
Gaudium de veritate.

Happiness is therefore not separable from pleasure in things.

Prudence is therefore not separable from art.

As making has need of doing — so prudence has need of art.

The achieving of happiness in oneself is the business of prudence.

The supplying of pleasure in things is the business of art.

Art and prudence are, as it were, one flesh.
There is a marriage between them.
There is also a lovers' quarrel between them.
Each seeks the perfection of its own.

Now man taken abstractly as the bride of God is female.
Hence the Church is the bride of Christ.
Man and the Church are one.
The clergy alone are not the Church.
The laity alone are not the Church.
Man united to God is the Church.

Man taken abstractly in his collaboration with God, i.e., as maker, is male.
Man the artist is male.
But, unlike God, he is not creator of things out of nothing.
He is creator in the second degree.
He is a channel, a vehicle for God's creative power.
Through man God brings creation to a greater and more poignant degree
of beauty.
Art improves on Nature.
That is what it is for.

Beauty is the splendour of Being.

The beautiful thing is that which, being seen, pleases.

The beautiful is therefore the object of art, for only beautiful things give pleasure to the mind, and the pleasure of the mind is the object of art.

The skill of the artist has for its end the production of things which shall give pleasure being seen.

Being seen means being desired and known.

  But this pleasure is not the pleasure of knowing.

  It is the pleasure of knowing the thing seen.

The Church is man in his aim of achieving happiness.

She is therefore the guardian of faith and morals.

  She is the mouthpiece of Prudence.

  The Church is Prudent Man.

  The Church is man knowing and acting in accordance with his end — happiness in Heaven — the Beatific Vision.

The artist is man in his aim of making what shall give pleasure.

  Happiness feeds on pleasure.

  Pleasant things are the meat and drink of happiness.

The ultimate happiness is heaven: for union with God is union with the source of all good and therefore with all things that are pleasing.

Now the perfectly prudent man is a man of perfectly good will.

The perfect artist is a man of perfectly good sense.

Perfectly good will is, it seems, possible to man.

Perfectly good sense is, it seems, not possible to man.

  His finite condition deprives him of the possibility of perfect knowledge.

Moreover, the perfection of good will is passive: —

  "Grant that I may love thee always: then do with me what thou wilt," and again: "Be it done to me according to thy word."

But perfectly good sense is active.

  "The words of God effect what they signify."

Man can be perfectly passive,

Man cannot be perfectly active

He can do nothing of himself.

"We are not able to please thee by our own acts."

Man can only be a perfectly willing agent.

His free will does not give him creative power.

  It gives him simply perfect power to will what God wills.

  A finite intelligence does not give him perfect knowledge of what God knows.

Hence prudence is superior to art with regard to man, but "art . . . metaphysically is superior to prudence."

Man *taken abstractly* is both female and male.

  He is both man of prudence and artist.

  He is both churchman and statesman.

In the concrete, man is divided.

  Church and State are separated.

  Prudence and art are opposed — not as enemies but as lovers.

In the concrete, Church and prudence take precedence of government over State and art.

  And each seeks the perfection of its own.

But in the modern world this right and proper opposition is obscured.

  It is obscured by the tyranny of commerce — by the tyranny of the middleman, conveniently so called because he stands in the middle obstructing every-thing and obstructing particularly the marriage of art and prudence.

The servant has become the master.

The go-between has become the boss.

In the welter the Church, in the order of doing, seeks to salvage what she can for prudence.

In the order of making, the State salvages what it can for art.

Under these circumstances the prudent man often becomes a prig and the artist often becomes merely a purveyor of setimental trifles.

Under a regime of commercial insubordination the mass of men are neither men of prudence nor artists.

But a semblance of prudence is more in evidence than even a semblance of art.

Worldly prudence makes a better show of virtue than worldly art.

To make money, to achieve material security and prosperity, looks more virtuous than to make what is merely pleasing.

Stock-broking morality and the morality of manufacturers and bankers stinks less in the nostrils of the prudent man, with his eye on Heaven, than does the art of music-halls or of dancing-places.

Such morality seems to be directed to the indubitably legitimate end of making money for the support of families.

There seems no doubt that men must live and must support their families.

On the other hand, music-hall art and such like seems to be directed to no known end but worldly pleasure.

The prudent man looks askance at it.

St. Augustine said: "Love God and do what you will." *Dilige Deum et fac quod vis.*

The artist says: "Love and make what you like."

This is the highest prudence.

But the prudent man thinks them dangerous sayings: for though most men know what they like doing or making, few men know certainly that they love God.

Nevertheless, these rules are the only really safe rules.

It is the business of the prudent man to inculcate the love of God.

The love of God involves acceptance of what God has revealed and obedience to His law.

But "the service of God is perfect freedom."

This is not because love makes the law of no effect but because he who loves God loves what God loves.

"As the eyes of servants are upon the hands of their masters, as the eyes of a maid-servant are upon the hands of her mistress, so are our eyes upon the Lord our God."

So also the obedience of a wife to her husband spells neither sin nor servility.

But in the modern world prudence is rare — though seemingly less rare than art.

Our governors, the men of business, our rich men, are struggling for power.

Our workmen, we poor men, are struggling for worldly pleasure.

The Church is powerless.

Statesmen are at the mercy of financiers.

Saints and artists are but hot-house plants — eccentrics.

But though sanctity be peculiar, prudence has the lip-service of rich men.

Honesty still remains the best policy.

"Safety-first" becomes the best catch-word.

Happiness is still desirable.

And though it be a hot-house plant, art also has the lip-service of rich men.

The appetite for pleasure still requires satisfaction.

But, in a world in which man's last end has been forgotten or denied, the pursuit of worldly happiness seems less dangerous than the pursuit of worldly pleasure.

Therefore worldly happiness seems less an enemy than worldly pleasure.

The man who seeks happiness here below is looked upon more kindly than he who seeks pleasure.

The man of business is looked upon more kindly by the man of prudence than is the artist.

For the man of business ministers to happiness, though only worldly happiness.

But the artist ministers to pleasure, and often the pleasure of the senses merely.

Avarice seems less hideous to the prudent man than *Idolatry*.

Selfishness seems less damnable to him than *Sensuality*.

There is therefore some ill-feeling between the prudent man and the artist.

The lovers' quarrel between art and prudence has become an unloving "scrap."

The opposition has become a conflict.

The man of prudence is shocked by the artist's inclination to value things as ends in themselves —

Worth *making* for their own sakes —

Loved for their beauty.

He sees *idolatry* at the end of that road.

He is also shocked by the artist's acceptance of all things of sense as beautiful and therefore pleasing in themselves —

Worth *having* for their own sakes —

Loved for their pleasantness.

He sees sensuality at the end of that road.

Upon the other hand, the artist is shocked by the prudent man's inclination to see things merely as means to ends —

Not worth anything for their own sakes —

Their beauty neither seen nor loved.

He sees Manchester at the end of that road.

He is also shocked by the prudent man's inclination to see in the pleasures of sense mere filthiness.

To him that is a kind of blasphemy.

The prudent man accuses the artist of sin.

The artist cries "blasphemer" in reply.

They see no good in one another.

It is not for me to speak as a man of prudence — though the artist is a man and should be a prudent man.

I can only speak as artist.

As artists it is for us to see all things as ends in themselves —

To see all things in God and God is the end —

To see all things as beautiful in themselves.

"The beauty of God," says St. Thomas Aquinas, quoting Denis, "is the cause of the being of all that is."

It is for us to see things as worth making for their own sakes, and not merely as means to ends.

We are not "welfare workers."

We do not even seek "to leave the world better than we found it."

We are as children making toys for men and God to play with, and "playing before him at all times."

But this serious view is not taken by many men of prudence.

Theirs is the frivolous view that things are not worth anything in themselves.

Clothes, for instance, are not for us as they seem to be for the prudent man, merely useful protections against cold or unchastity.

Clothes are primarily for dignity and adornment.

Whether men and women go naked, or whether they go clothed as monks and nuns, or whether they go half naked or half clothed like our mothers and sisters — it is all one to us.

It is for them to decide — and their pastors.

We merely ask that they be beautiful — that they be things which give pleasure being seen.

What else should anyone ask?

Trains, for instance: suppose two trains go from Manchester to London; one through a stinking and noisy tunnel all the way, the other silently through green valleys. Which train would a sensible person take?

Your prudent man, it seems, having regard merely to the end of the journey, would ask simply which was the quicker route.

Your artist, your practical man (for art is a virtue of the practical intelligence) would ask which would make the journey better in itself — as a journey.

Let us return to the beginning.

Prudence is concerned with the man.

Art is concerned with the thing.

Man is more important than things.

Prudence is more important than art.

Man's end is happiness.

The end of art is pleasure.

But happiness consists in pleasure.

Happiness is the state of being *pleased* with things, of being pleased with *things*.

Making pleasing things is the business of art.

The pleasure of the senses is good.

Art which aims at pleasing the mind through the senses is good.

The pleasure of the mind is good.

Art which aims at pleasing the mind and in regard to which the senses are disinterested is good.

But man is matter and spirit —

Both are real and both good.

An art which pleases the senses only and does not make its appeal to the whole man is necessarily bad art.

An art which makes its appeal to the mind only and does not please the whole man is necessarily bad art.

That is good art which pleases the senses as they ought to be pleased and the mind as it ought to be pleased.

With good art prudence should have no quarrel;

God gave man senses that man should have pleasant feelings.

The reasonable pleasure of the senses is the God-designed reward of those acts, such as eating and "sleeping," which God wills man to do.

With good art prudence should have no quarrel; God gave men minds wherewith to have pleasant thoughts.

The reasonable pleasure of the mind is the reward of those acts which are called contemplative: that is to say: the vision of Being, the vision of things as ends.

But many prudent men quarrel with art, however good, because many prudent men are prudes.

The prude is afraid of the pleasure of the senses.

And many prudent men quarrel with art, however good, because many prudent men are proud.

The proud man scorns anything not in imitation of himself: that is to say: he scorns anything which has not himself for its end.

These quarrels can never be settled until most men of prudence are also artists and most artists have become men of prudence.

This pleasing state of affairs will not come about until the present civilization has passed away.

D. B. WYNDHAM-LEWIS

(1884–   )

HUMORIST, cosmopolitan, satirist, historian, are symbols which express some of the talents of D. B. Wyndham-Lewis. Of Welsh and Irish extraction, Wyndham-Lewis has given his life to writing.

In World War I he was twice wounded. At the conclusion of the war his column in the *Express* and *Daily Mail* gave evidence of his wide interests and sparkling wit.

Though he is justly celebrated as a wit and a maker of richly humorous essays, his best talent is historical. *Francois Villon,* 1928, leaves us with a definitive picture of the most salty of poets. It does more in giving us insights into the time in which Villon lived. Nothing is hid or extenuated, yet the picture is richly human. *King Spider,* 1929, Lewis' life of Louis XI of France, gives out the same notes of ripeness.

Both volumes are meticulously documented, but never once does the impedimenta of scholarship overwhelm the glowingly human character of the story.

CONTEMPLATION OF A SKULL*

BETWEEN Cosne in the Nivernais and Tours the Loire River, pursuing its way among tufted islands and golden sands towards the Atlantic, takes a wide curving sweep, with Orleans at the midpoint of the bend. Within this arc between Loire and Cher lies the plain of the Sologne, the

*Reprinted by permission from *King Spider: Some aspects of Louis XI of France and His Companions,* by D. B. Wyndham Lewis; Copyright, 1929, by Coward McCann, Inc., pp. 18–30.

Roman *Solitarium,* for so many centuries a desert of marshes, sparse woods, lonely meres, fogs, fevers, brigands, sand and rotten clay, but now drained and fertile. Over the western frontier of this plain, near the waters of the Loire and in its valley, whose serene and gracious air seems always to hold a soft light of its own, not derived from an outer sun, stands the village of Cléry; some ten miles from Orleans on the old road to Blois. On the road, some time before the cobbled village street, with its old roofs and its inns the "Beautiful Ostrich" and the "Image of our Lady" is entered, the eye is glorified with the far-lifted vision of the basilica of Our Lady of Cléry.

The tall church springs above the roofs of Cléry village and stands in its slender grace and luminous pure proportion of stone and glass — triple nave, clerestories, transept, ambulatory, flying-buttresses, high vaulted roof, *moult noble et belle* — like some reliquary fashioned by one of those devout master-craftsmen of the Middle Ages whose ambition Heredia has sung in one of his grave and gorgeous sonnets:

Aussi, voyant mon âge incliner vers le soir
Je veux, ainsi que fir Fray Juan de Ségovie
Mourir en ciselant dans l'or un ostensoir.

Thus, when my life's last beads are almost told,
May I, like Fray Juan of old Segovia
Die chiselling a monstrance in fine gold!
                                    — *Les Trophées*

Flamboyant Gothic has rarely produced more exact and sustained harmony. The sixty noble windows which in Louis XI's time flamed like a conflagration of jewels are now, except those at the end of the choir, filled with clear white glass, and the high walls, once covered with tapestry, are dazzlingly bare in the sun of a late autumn afternoon in 1928. In place of the Royal Chapter of Canons, keeping public prayer rising to heaven like a ceaseless fountain hour after hour, day after day, the children of Cléry village are finishing the psalms of Vespers, and in place of the celebrated motets of Jehan van Ockeghem the Fleming, Master of the King's Music and the greatest European musician of his age, a schoolmistress is extracting the hymn *Lucis Creator* piecemeal from a protesting harmonium. But the beauty of the basilica remains, and its crowds and some of the ancient glory return to it still every September, at the time of the Cléry pilgrimage; and still, enthroned under a lumbering pseudo-Gothic stone canopy of the nineteenth century, Our Lady of Cléry with the Child Jesus, enveloped in a great stiff cope of white embroidered silk, in the mode of Spain, looks down the choir and sees her faithful servant Louis XI of France kneeling in effigy, his hands outstretched and his eyes fixed on her. So Louis ordered his monument to be set, at such an oblique angle to the nave that his bronze counterfeit might kneel and supplicate his Patroness throughout the ages.

But this is not the *pourtraiture du Roy nostre sire,* in hunting costume, horn slung on back, his favorite dog by his side, which Messire Jehan Bourré at the King's command ordered with such careful detail from Master Colin of Amiens, to be cast in bronze by Master Conrad of Cologne and Master Laurens Wrine of Tours, the Royal cannon-founder. The Calvinistic fury of Condé's troops, while they held the Orléanais in 1562, destroyed this statue, as they destroyed — burned, ravished, sacked, looted — so many other memorable and sacred things in France, as they very nearly destroyed the church of Cléry entire. The bronze statue was replaced in 1622 by the present marble, carved by Michael Bourdin of Orleans with (as may be readily perceived) more than one anachronism in the costume and no particular fidelity to tradition as regards the features: yet a sound piece of craftsmanship. This, again, was toppled down in 1792, beheaded by joyous *sansculottes,* broken, rescued by the admirable Lenoir for his museum in Paris, by him restored with considerable skill, replaced at the Restoration, and in 1896, after one or two unfortunate attempts at variation earlier in the century, restored finally — in the absence of original plans — as it now stands. Our Lady's statue is placed today not, as formerly, on an altar in the center of the transept, but above the high altar; but the King's eyes are still fixed on her as they were four centuries ago.

A sacristan clatters down the aisle with keys, stoops and pulls at a ring in an oblong plate of iron, hinged and flush with the floor of the nave. He swings up the plate, and descends a short flight of stone steps, switching on a harsh blaze of electricity. The vault is small, and completely occupied on the right-hand side by a massy stone sepulchre, in which, undisturbed in the year of the fall of the Capetian Monarchy by an envoy of the Revolution who stripped their coffins of lead for guns, lie the bones of Louis XI, King of France, his second wife Charlotte of Savoy, and their second child, Louis.

The afternoon sunshine slants through the high clerestory windows down the steps, paling before the cruder glow underground. From the nave comes the sound of fresh young voices singing the Magnificat.

> *"Deposuit potentes de sede, et exaltavit humiles . . ."*
> *"Et voici,"* says the sacristan, *"le crâne du roi Louis, et celui de sa femme."*

The two skulls lie together in a glass case at the end of their tomb. Both were twice damaged in the last century by falls of the roof of their funeral-chamber provoked by probing archaeologists ignorant of the existence of the staircase. Of the King's skull there remain the lower jaw, stubbornly prognathous, the upper jaw, and, resting on it, the cranial bowl, reddish-brown, sawn through horizontally by the royal embalmers soon after death. This, then, is the crucible in which so much Italian subtlety was brewed, so much foxy ruse and patient calculation, and debate, and dissimulation, shrewd assessment of men and their price, and patriotic fury, and dogged devotion. Through the lump of nervous gray substance which filled this bowl there vibrated a hard, keen, luminous intelligence; from it there radiated a hundred fluid threads and feelers communicating policy to that brooding brain. This is the skull of the master, bearing also the plain marks of that hypertrophy of meningitis which towards the end of his life so quickly struck him into senility.

At the sight of any great skull, such as Swift's, the barriers of the centuries melt suddenly away and a flood of realistic and intimate recollection occupies the mind. This red-brown bulging bowl is the head of a greater man than Swift.

The smaller skull of Queen Charlotte by its side is without its upper half, and of a lighter brown. Between the two lies a fragment of the King's sternum, extracted from his breast when his heart was taken to St. Denis to be buried with his ancestors. In the sarcophagus below, the skeletons are almost complete. Louis' skull dominates all. Power lingers in it, like the scent of wine in an empty jar.

From the high vaulting of the nave echo children's voices in the last longing supplication of the *Salve Regina,* which the owner of this skull had so often repeated in this church, possibly before this same statue, absorbed in his devotion.

"O clemens, O pia, O dulcis!"

Chairs scrape on the stone pavement overhead, feet clatter, doors creak and subside. At the top of the steps the sacristan lets down the lid of the vault again with a faint clang. The white spaces of nave and choir are full of sunlight and of silence. A village boy is extinguishing the altar candles; a tiny bird swoops and loops lightly across the arches.

The history of the shrine of Cléry begins in the thirteenth century, but its magnificence belongs to Louis XI. This church is his monument, and it is impossible to separate it from his memory. His personality pervades it today in death as long ago in life; yet he did but continue and complete the work of others. The finding of the statue of Our Lady of Cléry in 1280 made the village church of that time a place of pilgrimage very soon as famous throughout France as Our Lady of Rocamadour and Our Lady of Chartres. Simon de Melun, Marshal of France and companion of St. Louis, founded five prebends there; Philippe le Bel added five more and drew up plans for a fine new church. Philippe de Valois in 1339 laid the first stone of the new church, which the infidel Salisbury destroyed in the next century during the siege of Orleans. His head was irreparably smashed by a French canon ball shortly afterwards. St. Joan spurred past the ruins on the way from her victory at Orleans. Charles VII attached certain revenues to the restoration work. It was a little later, in 1443, that the Dauphin Louis, at Dieppe, swore the oath which finally raised Cléry from the ground and made it the jewel of Flamboyant Gothic it still remains. The circumstances are as gallant . . . as a page from an illuminated manuscript, and may most fittingly be related here, while we are still contemplating the fane they glorified.

The port of Dieppe is familiar to all who cross by the daily steamers to and from Newhaven in Sussex. After entering the harbor the steamer passes on the port side a tall cliff crowned by the fishermen's church. Underneath, in the cliff-face, are those caves or grottoes called Les Goves, inhabited by the very poor. This broad, steep cliff, which commands the whole town, is (and was) called Le Pollet, and is today the fishermen's quarter of Old Dieppe beloved of so many artists and especially, in the Yellow Book period, of the poet Ernest Dowson. Here in 1443 stood a redoubtable fort or bastille of stone, whose guns could cover the town and the roads entering it — for the town was then very small.

The English commander Talbot had only recently built the bastille of Le Pollet for the purpose of retaking Dieppe from the French corsair Desmarets, who held the town across the harbor. Although the English had a strong footing in Normandy, which had been theirs for some twenty-six years, and had turned Rouen, their headquarters, into a stout fortress, there had been a recent peasant rising in the valley of the Vire and in Caux. This, with Desmarets' seizing of Dieppe, called for strong measures, for the English were not likely to allow the considerable riches of Normandy to be wrested from them without a tough struggle. We have therefore on the one hand Talbot's troops and artillery on the Pollet, and Desmarets in the town of Dieppe, revictualled at intervals from the sea by the French. The Dauphin, a youth of twenty, already annealed in battle, begins his march up from the south; halts in Paris (where he lays a heavy tax — not the first — on the citizens), tours the country round Compiègne, collecting more troops and persuading hesitant nobles; and finally, on August 11, arrives with his force before the walls of Dieppe. With him is the great gallant Dunois, one of the Paladins. Talbot's artillery is doing enormous damage,

and Desmarets is about to give up the unequal struggle. On August 12 Louis formally calls on the English in the bastille to surrender. They answer that they are prepared to fight to the death. Louis places his guns and gives his final order. In the morning of August 14, the Eve of the Assumption, his troops are given a generous wine-ration; and at ten A.M. his trumpets sound the assault.

In a drowsy mid-August afternoon, when the old port of Dieppe is asleep in the sun, when a few fishing boats and one or two tramp steamers only are mirrored in the calm harbor water, before the bustle of the Newhaven steamer's arrival wakes all to life, one may stand on the Pollet and reconstruct the battle of that day. Away across the harbor is the magnificent old Flamboyant church of St. Jacques; behind it, hidden St. Remy; further behind again, on the sea-front, beyond the Casino, is the Château. These witnessed the fight. The moats around Talbot's thick new fortress were wide and profound; above them on the battlements were some five hundred English, with powerful cannon, served by courageous crews. For three hours the Dauphin's men attacked and attacked under the hot sun, manning the ladders, gaining footholds, thrusting and hewing and hacking, now winning a little ground, now shaken off. The English guns were terrible, and in the end the French began to despair.

"Then," says the Canon Médon, historian of Cléry, "the said Dauphin, finding himself in great consternation of mind and being destitute of all human aid, demanded of Jean Comte de Dunois, 'Cousin, in which direction is Notre Dame de Cléry?' and being informed, cast himself down on his knees and vowed to Our Lady that if she would grant him victory he would rebuild the church (of Cléry) after the plans of his predecessor Philippe le Bel, and would enlarge and glorify it with great honor."

As if in answer to his supplication a sweet silvery clamor came floating across the water, clear above the roar of the guns, the clash and shock of arms, the shouts and groans of the combatants. It came from the churches of Dieppe, joyously ringing for First Vespers of the Assumption, which is one of Our Lady's greatest feasts. The Dauphin ordered a fresh assault, and his men broke through the defense. This time it was victory. When all was over Louis, removing his shoes, walked barefoot to the church of St. Jacques to render thanks to God, Our Lady, and St. James, patron of knights. His vow is called the Vow of Dieppe.

Louis was not able to begin work on Cléry at once, being immediately occupied after the victory of Dieppe with leading the army of the Flayers over the Rhine, many leagues away. But in his absence his captain Dunois, that splendid soldier, diplomat, and devout client of Our Lady of Cléry, began the rebuilding, with the encouragement and assistance of Charles VII, himself a benefactor of the church. The work was pushed forward. In 1450 the sculptors began decorating the north door. Henceforth the sanctuary of Cléry and devotion to Her whose statue it held will be one of the two passions of Louis' life, his visits and gifts innumerable, his confidence unshakable. Here in 1470, he implored Our Lady to send the Crown a son and heir, and was granted one. Here in 1471 he established for the first time in France (though it was already a custom in Brittany) the Italian custom of ringing the midday Angelus, extending the order to the whole of his realm. In 1482, the year before his death, he began extending the nave by four more bays. And here, long before his end, he ordered his tomb.

Of the manner, whether regal or simple, in which the man who raised up and enriched this tall casket of stone and glass to the glory of God and the Mother of God entered its portals for the last time, there exists no account. Commynes, who records Louis' last moments at Plessis-les-Tours with such care, is entirely silent upon the funeral, except that, alone among contemporary historians, he remembers that the sacramental Ampulla of Coronation from Rheims, which had stood on the buffet of Louis' chamber at his passing, accompanied the body to Cléry. "It stood on his buffet" (says Commynes) "at the hour of his death; and it had been his intention to receive from

it a similar anointing as that which he received at his coronation; and indeed many believed that his desire was to have his whole body anointed with it, a thing which is scarcely believable, for the said Holy Ampulla is very small, and there is not very much oil in it. I saw it at the hour of which I speak, and also when my said Lord was laid in his grave at Notre Dame de Cléry."

The immediately previous happenings are recorded. On the news of Louis' death on Saturday night, August 31, 1483, taken by a messenger spurring posthaste to Tours, there is mourning and consternation; mourning for the royal Citizen of Tours, who so cherished his city, and consternation at the turn events may take. A strong watch has already been set upon the ramparts, a strong garrison is posted at the Castle and in the town, and the Mayor and aldermen go to and fro in the night posting the guards, escorted by wax torches. Meanwhile the bells of the basilica of St. Martin of Tours begin tolling, and so continue for three days, during which time the Canons set out along the road to Plessis in answerable sad and glorious pomp to bring the body to Tours. They return escorting the bier and the Ampulla, and Louis is carried into the ancient basilica, where the new great silver grille, his gift, encloses the reliquaries of St. Martin; and the Offices begin — the Office of the Dead, the all-night vigil, the unending roll of prayers, and, with the dawn, the first of the Masses of Requiem for his good estate. A solemn Requiem is sung at Amiens also. And then, in the first week of September, 1483, the last stage of the journey begins, according to the King's order, expressed long before:

"Since We have had, since Our youth, among the other churches of Our realm, a very particular devotion to that of Our Lady of Cléry, for the reason that whenever We have had recourse to Her, We have found and perceived that Our Lord Jesus Christ, through the mediation of the glorious Virgin Mary, . . . has come to Our relief and granted Us succor in Our Need; for which reason We have ordered Our burial in this church. . . . "

While away in Paris the authorities, as perturbed as those of Tours, are mounting guard along the walls, the long, slow funeral procession sets out from Tours along the left bank of the Loire, in the September air, all along that luminous valley, with the meadows and cornfields and vineyards — this year 1483, recalls P. Champion, quoting Guillaume Oudin, was marvellous for the vintage and all other crops — on the one side, on the other the wide silver river with its boats; in every hamlet along the road a tolling of bells and a procession of the inhabitants to pay honor to the corpse; in the city of Blois, halfway towards Cléry, a station for the night, no doubt, amid the mournful *tintamarre* of bronze from every church and convent, and all night long the dirge and vigil as before. At length the church of Cléry rises into sight from its fields and before the village is reached the Royal Chapter in procession have met their royal brother-canon's body. The nave and choir, hung with black, are full of tapers, full of mourners, noble and peasant; and just below the transept, on the north side, obliquely turned towards the statue of Our Lady, kneels the bronze king, awaiting the dead; beneath, the new open vault. The bells toll on in the still sweet air, and the rise and fall of plainsong mixes with their liquid throbbing, the torches flame, the procession halts at the western door. In the garden of the little high-roofed house of mellow brick which the King built for himself, facing the south side of the church (it is still there), birds are twittering and flying and perching in the trellis of his vine, which he ordered Bourré to have planted only a year ago.

The bier of King Louis enters the nave, and is sprinkled with holy water; and the consolations of the Liturgy proceed, whether attended by the military ceremonial which marked the funeral of Dunois in this church a few years before, or — as one or two historians have conjectured, seeing that no account has been handed down — in their own noble simplicity. It is impossible to ignore the presence of the Ampulla, which of itself demanded high reverence; on the other hand, once the Ampulla had been escorted to the high altar the funeral rites could proceed plain enough, and are the same for king or peasant. *De Profundis,* sings the choir, and *Miserere,* those psalms. "*Subvenite sancti Dei,*" chants the officiating priest. "Come to his assistance, all ye saints of God, meet him all ye angels of the Lord, receiving his soul, offering it in the sight of the Most High." And the assistants answer: "May Christ receive thee who hath called thee, and may the angels conduct thee to Abraham's bosom." And the body of King Louis descends at length into the tomb. It is prayed finally once more, on behalf of this indefatigable traveler and ceaseless toiler, that he may be forgiven his life's sins and granted eternal rest and light perpetual. Outside the open western door, over the sea of heads, the sky is blue, birds sing, the vineyards are ripe to harvest, the countryside of Touraine is bathed in peace; and the artificer of peace, the man who has pulled France out of the mire, lies where he wished to be.

Requiem aeternam. "Eternal rest give to him, O Lord." He had not known it much during life.

PORTRAIT OF A MASTER OF ARTS*

A LITTLE before nine o'clock of a bitter night in Paris, on the threshold of Christmas, 1456, the sacristan or minor beadle of the University whose duty it was to ring the bell of Sorbonne for the night Angelus climbed into the rope-chamber, grasped his rope and jerked it, and set the tongue in the steeple above him swinging: *Bome. Bome. Bome.*

A pause.

*Reprinted by permission from *Francois Villon: A Documented Survey,* by D. B. Wyndham Lewis; copyright, 1928, by Coward McCann, Inc., pp. 3-11.

Bome. Bome. Bome.

The waves of sound rolled heavily over University, over the sloping huddled roofs, down to the river, reverberating and shaking the air. In a few years onward, when a decree of Louis XI. shall have made national what is now a custom peculiar to University and to the devout Celts of Brittany, the first note of Angelus from Sorbonne will be answered by a brazen salvo, *tintamarre,* and clangour from all the bells of Paris full volley, as it were Ringing Island itself; by the deep bay of St. Germain-des-Prés, St. Sévérin clamouring over the river to St. Merri, a fainter jangle coming down the wind from Notre-Dame and St. Germain l'Auxerrois, St. Peter of the Bulls chiming to St. Gervais and the Celestines by the Bastille, St. Martin's Priory awaking the bells of the Chartreux and the Dominicans of the Rue St. Jacques, and joining all together in a flurry, all the three hundred churches and convents of Paris. This was the holy clamour and tintinnabulation which caused Pontanus the secular poet (as Master Janotus de Bragmardo the Sophist observed in his great Sorbonnical discourse on Bells) very profanely and wantonly to express the wish, while composing his carminiform verses, that all the bells of Paris had been made of feathers and the clappers thereof of foxes' tails. But on this December night of 1456 the University salutes Our Lady alone, and the booming of its solitary bell in the darkness is to be fixed and to echo in men's memory as long as poetry can quicken and enlarge the human spirit. For at the last stroke of the bell of Sorbonne a dark young clerk sitting alone in an upper chamber of a house called the Porte Rouge in the cloister of St. Benoît-le-Bientourné, in the shadow of Sorbonne, lower down the hill towards the river, having paper and inkhorn and candle before him, looks up from his writing and, laying down his pen, with fingers stiff with cold signs himself and begins to recite hastily, half under his breath, the Salutation:

Angelus Domini nuntiavit Mariae, et concepit
   de Spiritu Sancto:
Ave Maria, gratia plena . . .

And so to the end. The night is silent. He pauses, picks up his pen again, and contemplating for a moment his distorted shadow blackening the ceiling, with sudden resolution bends to his manuscript.

Finablement (he writes), *en escripvant,*
Ce soir, seulet, estant en bonne,
Dictant ces laiz et descripvant
F'oïs la cloche de Sorbonne,
Qui tousjours a neuf heures sonne
Le Salut que l'Ange predit;
Si suspendis et y mis bonne
Pour prier comme le cuer dit.

(Lastly, as I describe and set down these bequests in writing to-night, being alone, and in good dispositions, I hear the bell of Sorbonne, which rings every night at nine o'clock the Salutation brought by the Angel: and I pause to pray, as the heart directs.)

He shivers, gathers round him more closely his shabby gown, and continues writing. It is permissible, while the candle-flame ceases for a moment to flicker in the draught and throws his saturnine visage into relief, to study for a moment the appearance of this scholar: François de Montcorbier, *dit* Villon, Master of Arts in the University of Paris.

He is lean and lank, bony of arms and legs, sharp-featured, dark, secret, "dry and black as a maulkin," as he has just described himself in the verse on which he is now engaged: with eyes, as they look up at the shuddering of the flame, that have already a quick sideways glance, instinctively on guard against the leap from the shadows and the hand clapped suddenly on his shoulder. This uneasy roving of the eyes has become his normal habit. His upper lip has a permanent twist, the result of a dagger-slash received a year ago outside the church of St. Benoît-le-Bientourné in the street below. It is impossible to imagine that this improves his features. As he sits writing — he is nearing the end of his manuscript, and his teeth are chattering; the candle is beginning to gutter (he has noted it in a verse) and his ink is beginning to freeze — a chuckle breaks from him. Within the hour a select company at the *Pomme de Pin,* the *Mule,* or the *Grant*

Godet, will be sniggering at some of the rhymed bequests set down in this, his *Lais,* his burlesque will and testament. It is the eve of a journey to Angers in Anjou, where he is withdrawing to ease him of the cruelty of a mistress; probably of his creditors too; and (as will appear in due time) most likely for a practical and sinister purpose also.

He rises, stuffs the papers into his breast, blows out the expiring candle, and with a natural cat-like tread passes out and down the stairs. The outer door closes gently. François Villon's night has begun.

His own works, and a sequence of documents drawn up by the officers of justice, enable the portrait to be faithfully completed. Master François Villon is now, in this year 1456, in his twenty-sixth year, and has already drunk deep of the cup which is to inebriate him almost continuously hence forth. The street, the tavern, and the brothel know and hail him as *ung bon follastre;* his recurring moodiness and lovesickness apart. He has already killed his man in the affair outside St. Benoît, and has only recently returned to Paris after a prudent withdrawel to the neighbourhood of Bourg-la-Reine, on the Orleans road. Of the Seven Deadly Sins known to the Medievals (for they had not yet been abolished by a Viennese Jew) he is already held firmly in bond by at least five: Covetousness, Lust, Sloth, Gluttony, and Anger. Of these Lust most of all, I think, has him captive in her bailiwick. The *pension-naires* of the house of Mistress Overdone, Fat Margot, in the dark street across the river behind the Precinct of Notre-Dame, a procession of Jehanetons and Blanches and Guillemettes (their names are set in his verse), have already enslaved in turn his senses and helped to empty his lean purse: and in return he has begun (or will soon begin) to levy on one or two of them the tribute which in all ages gentlemen of imperious appetite and slender means have levied on the good-natured fair. His own evidence a little later shows him a *souteneur.* No pimp before or since him has ever made a ballade about it.

There is no reason to doubt that during his late journey into the country Villon has affiliated himself to the company called the Coquillards, in whose secret jargon or *jobelin* he will later write half a dozen ballades. In the ranks of the Coquille, whose activities extend over a large part of France, are found the best card-sharpers, brigands, footpads, dice-coggers, crimps, Mohocks, mumpers, pimps, ponces, horse-stealers, confidence-men, bruisers, thugs, lock-pickers, coin-clippers, housebreakers, hired assassins, and all-round desperadoes in Europe, true children of wing-heeled Mercury, patron of thieves and politicians. . . .

. . . But when his recurring heaviness, "allicholy and musing," as Mistress Quickly said, seizes him, like a Quartan Ague, he can be no company, huddled in his black gown and brooding in his corner, with the empty hanap before him and his dark eyes staring into nothing. Nevertheless of the popularity of this scholar there can be no doubt. He has (in his gay and desperate moods) a quick, salt wit, and he can put his friends and enemies into verses which arouse yells of laughter, so biting and so apt they are. He can rhyme drunk or sober; and he is already acknowledged around the Halles quarter the best sneak-thief and *trompeur* of his year: so brilliant that some years hence he will have become a legend and his exploits will be written down in verse, crowning him the hero of more than one trick which rings familiar in the ears of readers of *Tyl Eulenspiegel.* Although this Master of Arts is in the year 1456 fairly well advanced, as we observe, along the road to Montfaucon gibbet, where the pretty gentlemen swing high, keeping their sheep by moonlight. It has been suggested, and with plausibility, that a hundred years later Rabelais drew Panurge from the figure and fame of François Villon: Panurge with his *faulx visaige,* his slim middle stature and his long nose, like a razor-handle, his misfortune of being fond of women yet subject to panic, and his other worse misfortune of being eternally short of money, and his horse-play, and swindling, and trickery, and debauchery, and rude jests — *"pipeur, beuvuer, batteur de pavé, ribleur, s'il en estoit a*

Paris . . . et tousjours machinoit quelque chose contre les sergens et contre le guet."
All this is very Villon.

Finally, to round off this portrait, apologetically, and in the teeth of good taste and modern scruples, I have to suggest that this deboshed ruffian, whose companions are blackguards and trulls, has within him not only filial love and patriotism but also a glowing spark of the faith which he learned from his mother and has never lost: to which he returns, as in his verse, breaking out afterwards and sinning, and repenting with groans, and returning once more to his vomit, like some other sinners and some saints. This faith of his flames out often in the two Testaments, so stuffed with ribaldry and laughter, most of all in the Ballade of the Hanged, in his own Epitaph, and in that great Ballade in which he casts from him for a moment the crapulous years and kneels by his mother's side, stretching out his hands with her to the compassionate Mother of God and uttering that prayer which begins,

> *Dame du ceil, regente terrienne,*
> *Emperiere des infernaux palus,*

[Lady of Heaven and earth, and therewithal, Crowned Empress of the nether clefts of Hell.]
— Rossetti

and is his noblest work. This religion of his — I excuse myself once more: it is imperative to mention it — runs through the drab chronicle of his life like a bright gold thread, and is as much part of the essential Villon as his mocking humour and his sardonic philosophy. On the eve of being led out to be hanged he can compose a quatrain that his neck will shortly discover how much another part of his body weighs: but before his wry grin, as you might say, has completely faded, he is commending himself and his doomed companions (whom he already sees swinging, sundried and blackened, on Montfaucon, with the birds stabbing at their hollow eyes) devoutly to the prayers of men and the mercy of Christ, in words which are written in the blood of his heart.

In the symphony of Medieval Paris which is Villon's poetry, in its rich tumult, its vivid colour, its cruelties and generosities and riotings and obscenities and crimes and dirt and splendour and prevailing largeness — the Middle Ages were sometimes scandalous, but never vulgar — in its strange pathos and preoccupation with Death, in all this there is mixed the brawl of the streets and the laughing loud song of taverns, the screams and giggling of daughters of joy and the everlasting disputations of the Sorbonnical Doctors, the clink of goblets and the clash of steel, the thud of flying feet and the jangle of chains and the creak of ropes on Montfaucon gallows: but under all these noises there runs, with a steady beat, permanent, like ground-bass, the chant of *De Profundis* and the *Salve Regina*.

On this night of December 1456 Master François Villon is already, I think, emptying a cup by the fire in the tavern of his choice and exchanging rude jokes with the ladies and gentlemen there assembled. It is profitable to leave him there for the moment and to turn and contemplate the University which has bred and the Town which nourishes this scholar.

ALFRED NOYES
(1880–   )

THE life of Alfred Noyes has been a lyric pilgrimage. Born in Staffordshire and educated at Oxford, Noyes soon made a name for himself as a master of lyric and narrative poems. His early success did not overwhelm him; rather it sharpened his critical faculties and judgment without obscuring his flair for song.

In 1913 Noyes gave the Lowell Lectures at Boston, and for eight years was visiting professor of English Literature at Princeton University (1914–1922). Always reverent and religiously inclined, Noyes caused little surprise when he became a Catholic (1928).

Alfred Noyes is primarily a poet, as his many volumes of collected poems readily prove. The habit of ecstasy, as one might call it, makes his vision of life intense and discerning. His poetical brilliance transforms his prose into a splendid instrument of communication. It sharpens his critical judgments and adds depth to his philosophical grasp of life and living.

Many of his prose works have been widely read. Among them, *No Other Man,* a story of the end and beginning of the world, has had a wide sale. It sums up much of Noyes' philosophy of life.

His *Pageant of Letters,* which contains his appreciation of poetry, and eighteen essays on some of the major poets in our literary history, is a fine example of Noyes' ability to appreciate and criticize. It is marked by shrewd judgment and objective balance.

His search for God, which culminated in his reception into the Catholic Church, is beautifully set down in the grave lines of *The Unknown God,* a memorable and notable book.

Noyes' *Barrel Organ* and the unforgettable *Highwayman,* which mark his genius as a poet, are part of our great English heritage, but even a casual glance at the list of Noyes' published books will indicate that he has played a distinguished role in almost every field of writing. His diction is of the age or time; as a matter of fact, Noyes is more thoroughly modern than many writers who in style and in the rhythm of St. Vitus strain toward the barren eminence of *Tender Buttons* or *Finnegan's Wake.*

THE UNKNOWN GOD*

CHAPTER VIII

IF I tried to picture the way in which the vast system of law was actually used by the supreme Power, I found that the analogy of music always illuminated the whole matter.

There is a kinship between mathematics and music. But, as an analogy or diagram of the creative process in the universe, music has the advantage of including both the scientific precision, and the depth and richness of life itself. It always seemed to me that music, being itself a creative art, and at the same time detached from particulars, could analogize and thus elucidate many baffling questions. Its answers could not be taken as evidence, of course, but they might indicate the way in which a problem might be solved. The figurative use of one of its technical terms — "the resolution of discords" — has passed into common speech, but every musician knows that in his most intricate and subtle modulations he is doing something which somehow represents the way in which things may really happen. He is working out the golden mathematics of the process of wisdom whereby all things are ordered from end to end. In his recent Romanes Lecture in the Sheldonian Theatre, Sir Henry Hadow remarked that music was "a form of life miraculously born and spreading through a succession of forms which it had itself created. Its office was not to break with tradition, but to extend and interpret it, and gradually to shape whatever was of permanent value."

If this be true, we could hardly find a closer analogy than music offers us for the operations of the Spirit which Hegel saw at work in all history. The analogy suggests a possible (indeed the only "reasonable and acceptable") clue to the "purpose" which Darwin found in his "grand sequence" of evolutionary events, "gradually to shape whatever was of permanent value." It gives point to the otherwise meaningless idea of Schopenhauer that "music exhibits the world-

*Noyes, Alfred, *The Unknown God* (New York: Sheed & Ward, 1934), pp. 103–109.

will in its rising and falling, in its elementary and its complicated forms, and reveals to us its secret history, its rebuffs, its struggles and its torments." It illustrates the intuitive creed of Shelley

".... He doth bear
His part, while the one Spirit's plastic stress
Sweeps through the dull dense world, compelling there
All new successions to the forms they wear."

It touches with a universal significance the old legend of the city built to music. It makes us see, with Abt Vogler, how the whole fabric of the universe, and the walls and spires of the City of God, may be willed into being. It throws its own light on that riddle of the philosophers — the emergence of higher values whereby, as Browning put it, "out of three sounds we frame not a fourth sound, but a star." It tells us that behind those sounds there is a finger and "a flash of the Will that can."

It recognizes that the golden discoveries of music, as one chord leads to another in a logical progress along the road of law, illuminate and help us to interpret the ancient saying of the Word made flesh, *I come not to destroy but to fulfill.*

On these lines, as far back as I can remember, I used to ask myself how music would deal with some of the questions that baffled ordinary thought; and I carried it far beyond the "resolution of discords." The poets had used this kind of argument by musical illustration a thousand times. Some of Browning's profoundest truths were reached in this way as certainly as Kepler arrived at his astronomical laws by reasoning from the analogy of a law in music. The analogy was not evidence. It merely provided a scheme of general principles which aided him to form a mathematical hypothesis. This was tested later, and found to correspond with the facts. And so, of matters upon which mathematics had nothing to say — sorrow, for instance:

"It sounds often well to let
One string, when ye play music, keep at fret
The whole song through."

The merely aesthetic view of the matter expressed in those lines of Swinburne is based on principles that have a wider application. Even as a child I used to wonder what would happen to all the adventure stories if there were no real and terrible risks to be run, and whether pictures could exist if there were no shadows, and the daffodils had to be painted in gold on gold. Later, the question arose as to how we could have the triumphant joy of Beethoven without the tragic despair over which that very triumph takes place. Music illustrated these necessities of the nature of things as nothing else could for me. It also illustrated the possible ways in which a supreme Composer might use even those necessities to enhance the final victory. Great music can do this, moving from point to point, from key to key, with a logical precision too subtle for mathematics, although in the most scientific sense it is a mathematical progression. It illustrates the resources at the disposal of the supreme Composer, and the way in which the creative end may be willed through an organic system of interdependent laws, each holding good, and binding even the Composer, unless and until it be overruled by a higher law, whereof an infinite hierarchy are at his disposal; so that, in his perfection, freedom and law are reconciled. It left room for all the fugues or wanderings of free spirits; and, while it might make sure, by its own laws, that the Composer's will should eventually be done, it worked by infinitely more subtle ways than the deterministic systems of materialism, or even the mathematical systems of quantitative thought. There was room in the universal symphony for intellectual and spiritual persuasion, as opposed to force and "necessity." All the influences of beauty and goodness, tenderness, and affection, could be exerted through it. Even sin and remorse could play their part; and, when all things had failed, there was still room in it for the ultimate appeal which is mightier than all compulsion, the appeal of a perfect self-sacrifice, which might awaken love for the Highest at last, and so draw, without compulsion, all those whom the gift of freedom had led astray, back to their true end, in the heart of their Father and their God.

The necessity indicated in the famous line "we needs must love the highest when we see it," is thus not a necessity that interferes with our freedom in any intelligible sense; but rather a "necessity" that crowns our true freedom by opening the way to its perfect fulfilment. The philosopher throws away his freedom, and the whole of the universe with it, for an idle quibble, if he insists that the gift of sight has subjected him to undue compulsion by enabling him to discover the way out of his prison, and thereby imposing an obvious choice upon him. We can all see his point. Life is short, and the point may be conceded to him, together with a thousand other similar points that philosophers have raised in a thousand volumes during these excessively complicated and analytical days. But we are dealing with what concerns rational human beings. The way of Love is not the way of compulsion or mechanism. Its imperatives, like those of truth, or reason, may be absolute, but they do not imprison, they liberate the spirit within us, which leaps to recognize a reality transcending all its limitations, as the wisdom and spirit of the universe transcend all the caprices of our finite nature.

"Whoso hath felt the spirit of the Highest
    Cannot confound or doubt Him or deny;
Yea, with one voice, O world, though thou
        deniest,
    Stand thou on that side, for on this am I."

Those lines from Myers' great poem on St. Paul represent only the human side of the relation. The divine side is represented by that tremendous saying in which not only death but necessity and compulsion were for ever swallowed up in the victory of a divine act of self-sacrifice: "I, when I am lifted up, will *draw* all men to Me."

This, it seemed to me, was the true secret of the atonement, which had so often been misunderstood and misrepresented. It was not an expiation by a scape-goat to appease the wrath of God. Nor is the word "propitiation," in its modern sense, adequate. Modern writers have often attacked it in terms which show that they have borrowed their ideas of it from undeveloped minds, and have not even considered the central fact upon which everything turns — that the act is one of self-sacrifice, and that the God who offered it is also the God who received it. They need not go to the Christian philosophy to encounter the philosophical problem which only the conception of the supreme Spirit as Triune can solve. Hegel discovered the necessity in the very nature of the relation between subject and object, and their union in the absolute Reality. But it is enough to say here, that, in the divine atonement, the Sender and the Sent, the Priest and the Victim are one. That is why Nicaea decreed its belief in One who was *Deum de Deo, Lumen de lumine, consubstantialem patri.* There may be some profound ethical necessity in the nature of God Himself which exacts a price in suffering from God Himself if the wrong is to be righted without annulling the freedom of His creatures. He may win them, but not compel them. It may be that He must win them by personal sacrifice, not by indulgence, if those ethical requirements are to be fulfilled. But the motive was perfectly stated nineteen hundred years ago, in terms which completely annul the conception of the scapegoat and the angry Judge: "God so loved the world that He sent His only-begotten Son."

ARNOLD LUNN
(*1881–*   )

ARNOLD LUNN, son of Sir Henry Lunn, M.D., was born in Madras, India, April 8, 1881. He was educated at Harrow and at Balliol College, Oxford. In 1937 his inquiring mind led him from Anglicanism to the Catholic Church.

Lunn is one of the best dialecticians of our day. In discussion he holds his opponents to the point at issue with devastating logic. He is also interested in mountain climbing and skiing, and his eminence in the latter field is indicated by the esteem in which he is held by the International Ski Club, of which he is a past-president.

Lunn's interests are accurately mirrored in his many books. He has written several books on skiing, and his descriptive faculty which is highly developed is seen at its best in his travel books: *The Alps, Switzerland, The Italian Lakes,* and *Venice.* He has also written illuminatingly of religion in *Now I See,* and has set down the salient facts of his life in *Come What May.*

CHAPTER XXIX

"DESPITE OF WRINKLES"*

So thou through windows of thine age shalt see
Despite of wrinkles this thy time.
                                        — *Shakespeare*

THE tactful but insistent knocking intruded itself into the texture of my dream. I clung desperately to the illusive vision, but it evaded me, and I awoke regretfully. Turning on the light, I blinked sulkily at the ceiling. Surely I had earned a long and lazy night after four days' consecutive skiing, in the last of which I had climbed some 6,000 feet in powder snow. I padded across the room and looked out the window, hoping to discover some pretext for calling the expedition off, but the uncompromising stars robbed me of all excuses for laziness.

Lena, who still distributes tea and cakes to thirsty ski-ers at the Hotel Central, beamed over our breakfast as hot coffee dispelled the sluggish trail of sleep.

It had just turned five when Fritz and I stepped out into the street, lit by one disconsolate lamp. Passing between houses heavy with sleep, we emerged on to the starlit snows. As we tramped up the path to Hertenbuhl the first hint of colour intruded on the darkness. The Wetterhorn was no longer a shadowy line, but was defined with sharp precision against the velvet darkness of the sky. We recovered our faith in the existence of the sun. The Alps might still be drowsy with sleep, but in the Near East it was day. The Golden Horn was glowing in the dawn, and colour would soon be stirring in the lagoons of Venice. As we climbed higher the stars went out one by one as if touched by an unseen hand, until only the morning star remained. We watched the last phase from a point near Grindelalp. The eastern sky was radiant with Dante's "*splendori antelucani.*" The little wind which goes before the dawn ruffled the silence and the mountains stirred with expectancy. Arrows of light began to radiate from an invisible focus behind the Wetterhorn. The sun slowly climbed above the ramparts of rock. The flat and lifeless snows at our feet, flecked with pearl-gray shadows, sparkled into ten thousand stars, and mind and body relaxed in the flood of colour and warmth.

One day the projected railway will be built and there will perhaps be a restaurant at the point where Fritz and I met the dawn, and

---

*From *Come What May,* by Arnold Lunn. Reprinted by permission of Little, Brown & Co., Boston: 1941, pp. 315–325.

ski-ers will see from their bedroom windows what Fritz and I saw when the sun came out of his eastern chamber and climbed into the sky behind the Wetterhorn. But will they? I think not. The dawns which one has earned by long hours of toil beneath the frosty stars are more wonderful than those which one watches in comfort from a bedroom window. There is a close connection between the ascetic and the aesthetic. It would puzzle a materialist to explain how frequently the reward of beauty is associated with the discipline of toil, as if Nature consciously reserves her noblest effect for those who take some trouble to earn them. There is no reason why powder snow should be lovelier than the beaten snow of a standard course, but you have to earn your powder snow by climbing, whereas you need only buy a ticket to discover beaten snow. A single ski track which is a symbol of a difficulty conquered is far more beautiful than the "tramlines" of a ski-er who has never mastered the technique of keeping his ski together. The sun's relation to the horizon is the same at sunset as at sunrise, but the dawn which the idle never see is lovelier than the sunset which the lazy can enjoy.

If beauty were determined solely by the laws of optics and by the angle of the sun, the last hour before the sunset should be as beautiful as the first hour after the dawn; but this is not the case, as, indeed, the Italian and Flemish primitives were well aware. The painters of the great ages loved the cool and fragrant beauty of the hour which follows the dawn. Art began to decline when artists stayed in bed.

Early risers are often intolerably smug, and Fritz and I certainly felt a glow of complacent satisfaction as we looked down on the sleeping valley far below. There is a quality in the cool little breezes which come with the dawn, and a cleansing virtue in the clean air of the early morning hills, which dissolves the last traces of sluggishness in one's blood. Down there in the valley, in a stuffy atmosphere of tumbled blankets, drowsy folks were blinking at the sunlight which was filtering through the curtains, but we were alert and eager for the unfinished adventure.

Once again we pointed our ski uphill, but without that dragging reluctance with which we had faced the few hundred feet above Grindelwald. Then we had been oppressed by the thought of the 6,300 vertical feet between us and the summit, but the 3,000 feet which we had climbed, so far from draining our strength had recharged our energies. Fatigue is a function of the mind no less than of the body, and second wind is a psychological no less than a physical phenomenon. Our expenditure of physical effort had been partially offset by the lightening of the mental load with which we had started the ascent.

It would be easier to convert Cresta ski-ers into ski-tourers if we could persuade them that a long, steady climb is often less tiring than a short spurt. I enjoy all but the first half-hour of a 5,000-foot peak. But I never cease to resent the 50 feet which separates the top of the Allmendhubel funicular from the Allmendhubel summit. On such short sections the mind is impatient to reach the top; but as one leaves the valley for a big expedition one resigns oneself to the long hours which must pass before the summit is attained, and resignation is followed by enjoyment. For there is a subtle pleasure in the rhythm of a long-continued ascent, a rhythm which is obscured in the staccato of a short spurt. The experienced climber achieves a balanced movement in which ease and comfort are not sacrificed to speed, and which leaves the mind free to enjoy the beauty of slowly widening horizons.

Just below the Krinne Pass we paused once again and glanced back at the long valley up which we had just been climbing. The delicate silver point of the ascending zigzags of our tracks enriched the beauty of the soft glinting snow-fields seen against the low sun. The handiwork of man is not always an unwelcome addition to the handiwork of nature. Thirty years ago two ski-ers whom I had never met traversed the Oberland Glaciers from Meiringen, just before we crossed those same passes from the Lotschen Valley. In those days there was no Jungfrau Railway and the solitude of the Concordia Platz in January was seldom disturbed. We spent six days among glaciers, six days during which the tracks of our unknown ski-ers represented the one fragile link with the world of man. A faint aroma of human companionship still clung to their imprint on the snow. Some afterglow from the emotions which they had experienced still seemed to linger in the pattern of their downward curves. I have never, to my knowledge, met those ski-ers, and if we did meet we should meet as strangers; but when their tracks finally vanished in the shadows of the Grimsel Gorge we felt as though we were parting from friends with whom we had shared the ardours and endurance of a great adventure.

The beauty of ski tracks varies in inverse proportion to their number. An intersecting pattern of "tempo turns" on a canvas undefiled by beginners is among the loveliest of man's contributions to natural beauty. But the mass production of tracks defiles the delicate individuality of snow crystals, whose facets reflect the sun. Humanity, when it gate-crashes into nature's winter shrine, leaves its record in the surface of the standard course, but the lines etched by mountaineers into the remoter snows suggest one of those relationships in which intimacy imposes on the good nature of a friend.

We left our skiis on the Blue Glacier Pass, and scrambled on foot up to the Wildgerst cairn, which we reached six hours after leaving Grindelwald, and there we passed an idle hour of pure content, in the golden warmth of windless sunshine.

"The gods," says Aristotle, "may be honoured but not praised, for we praise things by reference to a standard, and the gods are beyond compare." And that is exactly what I feel about the Oberland; but as this chapter will be read not only by the faithful who need no proof, but by sceptics, I will try, for their sake, and not for mine, to justify my conviction that the North Wall of the Oberland is "beyond compare" for splendour of invention and variety of creative design. There are certain stock mountain types which are repeated indefinitely throughout the Alps. Limestone runs naturally to vertica; "steps" and dolomitical towers, granite to spires and pyramids. A faint suggestion of

mass production intrudes itself into one's enjoyment of ranges in which either granite or limestone predominates, but there are no mountains in the world in the least like the Wetterhorn, or the Eiger, or the Jungfrau. God made them and broke the mould.

The interplay of granite and limestone is perhaps one of the complex causes to which this range owes its variety of form. The Finsteraarhorn is pure Gothic. There is a suggestion of the basilica in the roof of the Dammastock, and of the classic entablature in the broad snow crest of the east face of the Monch. The Jungfrau, on the other hand, is a masterpiece in the Baroque style. The "frozen hurricanes" of her hanging glaciers and the volutes of the Silberhorn and Schneehorn convey much the same impression of exultant movement that the Baroque architects conveyed in stone. And the Jungfrau, like the Salute at Venice, has the serene assurance which no Baroque exuberance can disturb.

Our reaction to mountain scenery is a complex of aesthetic emotion and personal associations. Whether the universe would continue to exist if there were no conscious beings to observe it is a question upon which philosophers have disagreed. Among the mountains these anthropocentric fantasies seem less improbable, for there are moods in which it is easy to believe that the Matterhorn and the Jungfrau are in some sense a creation of man's adoration, and that a mountain such as the Dent Blanche above Zermatt only emerged from the trance of time when it was first discovered by mountaineers. Other mountains, such as Mont Blanc and the Jungfrau, inspired poets long before they challenged mountaineers. Now, the Oberland is associated not only with the beginning of mountaineering, but also with the dawn of the Romantic movement. Byron and Goethe discovered the beauty of these peaks long before Mr. Justice Wills and Leslie Stephen began to climb them. "Leslie Stephen," writes Hugh Kingsmill, "found Byron's Swiss poetry cheap and insincere. As a hard-headed agnostic, suspicious of emotion not founded on fact, he resented no doubt such verse as:

The fish swam by the castle wall,
And they seemed joyous each and all.
The eagle rode the rising blast,
Methought he never flew so fast.

This eagle, flying past Chillon to the mountains of Ouida's Ischl, rode a purely romantic blast, and was visible only to romantic eyes. The orthodox climber, however, does not care for romance. His love of the mountains is based, like domestic love, on knowledge and understanding. It is reasoned, almost respectable. But the visions of Byron and of the German Romantics have the magic of first love, passionately adoring what is unknown and out of reach."

My brother does less than justice to Leslie Stephen, and his strictures apply, not to "orthodox climbers," but only to a minority whom I for one should not describe as orthodox. But his tribute to the Romantics is discerning, perhaps because it is based on "that knowledge and understanding" which he depreciates. He could have strengthened his case had he been familiar with the art produced during the Romantic revival. At a time when the Corsican was making trouble in the foothills, and the Russians were tramping across the Alpine passes, the eccentrics who thought mountains beautiful penetrated into the Oberland Valley and began to paint the Jungfrau and the Wetterhorn. Those old coloured aquatints — a process which seems to have disappeared — have a charm for me which no modern painting possesses, for these period pieces carry the mind back to the days when the mountains had not been climbed or explored.

Instead of attempting to prove that the Oberland is "beyond compare," I might have done better to quote Browning:

Here's my case. Of old I used to love him,

and leave it at that. Certainly that golden hour on the Wildgerst was untroubled by critical dissection of the mountains which were our delight. The serene winter sunshine evoked a mood of unquestioning adoration. The crests were edged by a ribbon of reflected light which mirrored the unseen snows on the invisible southern slope of the range, a bordering of silver-blue which sof-

tened the transition from the concrete line where the mountain ended to the infinite depths of the unfathomable sky. Ruskin, who was not only a superb master of rhetoric, but also an accurate scientific observer, noted this curious and most unusual effect in a famous passage describing the Alps from the south.

"Then, in the luminous air beyond and behind this blue horizon line, stand, as it were, the shadows of mountains, they themselves dark, for the southern slopes of the Alps of the Lago Maggiore and Bellinzona are all without snow; but the light of the unseen snowfields, lying level behind the visible peaks, is sent up with strange reflection upon the clouds; an everlasting light of calm Aurora in the north."

The Alps are, of course, lovelier in spring than in winter. I have seen the May dawn from the Wildgerst and the dull grey foreground of shadowed snow to the north served as a foil to the colour scale ranging from the green-blue of Brienz to the dark gentian of distant Lucerne; but even in January these foothills are pregnant with colour. The Alps are the sentinels of Italy, and her gracious influence softens their asperity. How different the view which we saw from the Wildgerst and the panorama from the Hardanger Jokul above Finse on the Oslo-Bergen line. Even in summer the ice-capped plateau is bleak and inhuman, for the glaciers lie heavy upon the unfertile rock below, a shroud covering a corpse; but the snows which mantle the Alpine foothills are a blanket below which the convalescent is gaining strength.

We scrambled down from the Wildgerst to the Blue Glacier Pass, where our ski awaited us. The physical process of putting on one's ski is the same whether one has climbed 6,000 feet or taken train to a railway station, but the mental reactions are very different.

The Cresta ski-er who enjoys perhaps a dozen downhill runs in a few hours knows nothing of the thrill of the unique moments in the ski-tourer's day, the moments for which the long hours of the climb provide the appropriate preparation. And the ski-er who has a pet name for every bump of his favourite standard course is a stranger to that moment of quickening suspense as the skis dive down the first slope of an unexplored run on untracked snow. Neither Fritz nor I had crossed the Wildgerst or compared notes with anybody who had. But I had studied the Wildgerst from the Great Scheidegg, and had noted that though the slopes between the Blue Glacier Pass and the valley face south, they are intersected by tributary ridges, on the short north slopes of which we might reasonably expect to find powder. My plan was to use these ridges to enjoy powder-snow ski-ing on a slope of sun-crusted snow. No such problems enrich the joys of Cresta ski-ing.

Finally, the very ski themselves seem a thousands times more animated when you buckle them on your feeet on some windy pass thousands of feet above the haunts of gregarious ski-ers. Fight your way through a crowd, disentangle your ski from a hundred others on a railway truck, and you will not find it easy to establish sympathetic co-operation with the inert and lifeless boards. But the ski which have been your companions for hours, the ski which have left a continuous furrow from the valley floor to a mountain crest, seem charged with dynamic energy. They react to your impatience and share your eagerness to be off.

Twenty years have passed since Fritz and I linked our turns down the snows of the Wildgerst, but "time which antiquates antiquity hath yet spared" the memory of our ski-ing partnership. I can still remember the resolve to *schuss* a steep slope leading to a cup-shaped hollow; the sudden terror as the ski dived through wind-driven patchy snow, the urge to lie down, the determination to stand, the struggle to force the ski together, the wind in one's ears which rose to tempest fury, the shock as the ski dived into the heavy snow of the outrun, the relief as their points appeared above the white smother, immense surprise as the uncontrollable demons hurrying through space suddenly sobered into the most docile of slaves, and the glory of the Christiania swing which brought the opening act to its triumphant conclusion.

Fritz was a few seconds late in starting. I watched him as he came over the skyline, and saw him sway as his ski struck the wind-touched powder. He fought for and regained control; he thrust out his leading ski to meet the shock of the outrun, swept past me and swung round with such speed that he faced the slope which he had descended. Fritz looked back at the line of beauty which he had created in the snow. And he saw that it was good. And like the morning stars at the dawn of creation he shouted for joy.

My next vivid memory is of a moment of acute suspense as my ski took control on the southern slope. I had waited too long before turning, and I knew that if I tried to turn in the crust I should be thrown violently outwards; and I was consoled to see that the slope below switched back and up on to the short northern face of the tributary ridge, and there with luck I should strike powder before being carried over the crest on to the next steep slope of sun-crusted snow. . . . Oh, the relief, as the crisp cutting sound of the crust yielded to the velvet touch and soft rustle of powder; but the speed was still uncomfortably high. Could I make the turn or should I be carried over the ridge? It was one of those days when everything goes right and every turn comes off. With a yard to spare my ski swung round to rest.

From the pass to the Schwarzwald we dropped 5,000 feet on the southern slopes, yet by exploiting the friendly aid of the accommodating ridges we had found 4,000 feet of powder-snow ski-ing on these great expanses of crust. Sometimes we followed with long, sinuous curves a winding ribbon of powder only a few yards in breadth, sometimes we could let our ski have their heads, secure in the knowledge that the powder would not change to crust before we could swing to rest. Ski-ing such as this is not for the mentally inert, for there was no point between the pass and the valley which did not call for quick judgement, which did not test the power to diagnose, while still on the move, the ever-changing surface of the snow. This is cross-country ski-ing at its best, a skilled craft, exacting in its demands and generous in its reward.

We paused for a few moments at the frontier between the open slopes and the first of the pines which decorate the last slopes leading down to the valley. The sombre cliffs of the Wetterhorn towered above us, enmeshed in the web of twilight. Every phase of this glorious day seems linked in memory with the changing aspects of the Wetterhorn, from the classic Grindelwald view to the triple-crested peaks which Lory painted from the meadows above Rosenlaui. At every halt our eyes instinctively turned towards our great companion. We had "learned his great language, caught his clear accents," and now as the shadows deepened we paid him the tribute of a grateful farewell.

The last few hundred feet of curving descent through a pattern of pine carried us from the colour and radiance of the high mountains into the kingdom of unchallenged winter. We had reached the sheltered and shadowed valley, where the firs sagged beneath their burden of snow, and where the river-bed was a stranger to the benediction of the sun. We called a short halt beside an inn whose rafters stooped towards and almost met the snow. A group of pines on a western hill suddenly burst into flames as the sun set behind their snow-laden branches.

Easy wood-running and open glades led from Schwarzwald to Rosenlaui. The crystalline flaky snow rustled under our ski like autumn leaves. It is only in the most sheltered of valleys and in the neighborhood of river-banks that one finds this most perfect of all forms of powder snow.

The last hint of daylight had vanished from the west as we started slowly along the plain between Rosenlaui and the steep cliff over which the Reichenbach falls to Meiringen. The thin trickle of the river edged its dispirited way round ice-fretted boulders and beneath smothers of snow, and its icy breath reached us in a frosty trail of mist which stung like a whip. It was bitterly cold. The night had broken that bridge of human associations which man laboriously builds between himself and the mountains. All sense of companionship had disappeared. These shadowy masses fading by slow gradations into the sharper darkness of the star-pointed night had recovered their inhuman aloofness. They had forgotten the brief episode of contact with man, and were dreaming, not of that mere yesterday when mammoths lumbered across the rivers of ice which flow down the valley of the Aar, but of that remoter abyss in past time when the first island summits of the Alps appeared above the silent waters of the central seas.

The darkness and solitude and the lonely stars began to oppress us. *"Le silence éternel de ces espaces infinis m'effraie."* Then suddenly we turned a corner and the valley of Meiringen opened below us, and the inhabited hills sparkled with the cheerful constellations of human lights, evoking friendly pictures of snug interiors, and of the warm welcome which we knew would be awaiting us at the Bear at Meiringen. The Bear is one of those inns which still retain something of the atmosphere of romantic Switzerland. It is the sort of place in which Leslie Stephen or Byron would have felt at home.

CHAPTER XII

THOUGHTS ABOUT CONTROVERSY*

THE depression made things very difficult for the family business indeed. The embargo on foreign travel would have ruined us, had not the usual raven appeared. My friend, Christopher Mackintosh, who takes longer odds than any man I know in a ski race, certainly took a sporting risk when he invested all his resources in a successful attempt to tide our firm through those grim months.

In the weeks that followed, weeks of unending anxiety, I remember with gratitude

*Lunn, Arnold, *Now I See* (New York: Sheed and Ward, 1937), pp. 95–101.

the hours I spent with my brother-in-law and his wife Elizabeth. The Catholic belief in prayer is infectious, and though I have always found it difficult to believe that my own prayers, or other people's prayers, could make the least difference to me, my faith in prayer returned in a Catholic household. I went down to Oxford two or three times, and Father Knox was more than kind, in his own curiously impersonal way. "I hope," he once remarked, "that you won't crack up with all this worry. I've had the greatest difficulty in persuading people that a recent convert is not in a mental home to which Protestants consigned him. If you break down after you are received, your reception will be accounted for on similar lines." "Thank you," I said acidly, "if I am received I will remember that my continued health is important to the Church because my insanity might weaken the effectiveness of my surrender to your arguments." For once in a way I felt that I had scored.

And in this connection I may perhaps interpolate at this point a sentence written just after my reception. On the day before I was received I suggested that Father Knox should read those passages in my manuscript which referred to himself. "Yes, I think I'd better," he said, "just to see that you haven't said anything offensively fulsome about me."

He was inclined to demur at my description of his very unbookish behaviour when I first suggested coming down to Oxford to see him, and when he had finished, he remarked, "Well, I suppose this will perpetuate the legend of me as an aloof, grim person."

"You're difficult to please," I said. "Here am I going to vast trouble to avoid being 'offensively fulsome,' and all you do is to tick me off for not being fulsome enough."

It is, of course, the knowledge that what I write will be read by Father Knox which cramps my style and which has checked my natural expansiveness. I should, however, be sorry if I have failed to convey my very deep sense of gratitude for Father Knox's unwearing patience, continued hospitality and unfailing kindness.

Shortly after *Difficulties* appeared, Mr. Cyril Joad challenged me to defend Christianity. I had met Joad, for after launching a violent attack on one of his books in the *English Review,* I had asked him to lunch. A man will almost always accept an invitation from a critic who has attacked him. Women find it less easy to disassociate personal disagreements from intellectual differences. I remember my pathetic attempt to use the fact that I attacked Mrs. Naomi Mitchison's *Outline for Boys and Girls* as a pretext for making her acquaintance. Like Queen Victoria, she was not amused.

But Joad accepted my invitation with imperturbable good humour. He walked into my very sedate club carrying a rucksack from which a tennis racquet protruded and which contained among other things, tennis balls and his flannel trousers. I was delighted. "You may think I'm pretty untidy," I remarked to my wife that evening, "but at least I'm ten Joad-power." I lured Mr. Joad down to stay with us, hoping that his appearance would make my wife grateful for small mercies. But the blackleg went back on me. He had had his beard trimmed, had apparently bought a new suit of clothes, and looked disgustingly smart.

There is something attractive about Joad. "I can't help liking him," said a well-known priest when discussing some of his more outrageous attacks on Christianity. Unlike most of our modern prophets he still believes in reason, and the third edition of our joint book is now prefaced by a joint manifesto in which we reaffirm the faith in reason which we share. I enjoyed this controversy. I was pleased to discover how easily Christianity can be defended against the modern attack. The only parts of the book in which I felt uncomfortable were those in which Joad confronted me with a fine confused assortment of Protestant doctrine. If I had restricted my defence to Catholicism I should have had an easier time. The difficulty was to adopt a Catholic line of defence throughout without rejecting too vigorously those forms of Christianity in which I no longer believed. *The Freethinker* reluctantly admitted that I had not the worst of the argument.

It is no new thing for controversial letters to be published, but such letters have usually arisen accidentally out of spontaneous controversy. I believe my book with Father Knox marked a new departure, for I believe that this was the first occasion on which a Catholic and non-Catholic agreed to debate the general issue of Catholicism in a series of letters. As I have now completed two such books and am in the process of completing a third, I may perhaps be allowed to comment on a type of controversy which I invented, or at least helped to popularise.

It is clear, as several reviewers pointed out, that this type of controversy has its disadvantages. An orderly presentation of the case is difficult. Digressions and irrelevancies are almost inevitable. It might be possible, of course, to edit such letters, but I believe that the human interest and spontaneity of the letters would be destroyed, if they were carefully re-edited before publication.

Moreover, I believe that this type of book has certain advantages which are lacking in the orderly and coherent statement of a case by a single writer. "How often," wrote Count Michael de la Bedoyere, in the *Catholic Herald,* "do we wish when we read apologetics for or against Christianity that the obvious answer to a certain point was thrown at the head of the apologist. In this book answers obvious and subtle are constantly being hurled at the writers."

But to my mind the main value of a correspondence controversy is the possibility of reaching a public which would never open a book of Christian apologetics. It is difficult to-day for the Christian to reach the non-Christian public, but a straight fight between a Christian and a leading secularist will be read with interest by those who enjoy a scrap, and by secularists who will read a book of this type, in the hope that the Christian will be knocked out in the first round.

As a nation we tend to dislike controversy, particularly in religious matters, a dislike which is due to our national distrust of logic. Our faith in the value of controversy as a means of arriving at the truth, naturally depends on our faith in the power of logic to draw correct conclusions from given premises.

Our mediaeval ancestors believed in con-

troversy because they believed in reason. "It it necessary," wrote St. Thomas Aquinas, "to dispute in public about the Faith provided there be those who are equal and adapted to the task of confuting error, since in this way people are strengthened in the Faith, and unbelievers are deprived of the opportunity to speak, while if those who ought to withstand the perverters of truth are silent, this would tend to strengthen error."

Our mediaeval forefathers not only believed in controversy, but they also regarded with profound respect the great controversialists. Indeed, a champion controversialist enjoyed in the Middle Ages much the same prestige as a champion golfer enjoys to-day.

The distrust of controversy dates from the Reformation. Luther's famous slogan, "Justification by Faith," was nominally aimed at those who were supposed to believe in "Justification by Works," but was, in effect, an attack on the Catholics who believed in justification by reason.

"The dreary syllogisms of the scholastics," said Luther in effect, "lead nowhere. Religion begins not in the brain but in the heart. Don't argue, just feel, and go on feeling. . . ."

I believe that our national distrust of logic is derived from the fact that Protestantism is illogical. There must be something wrong, we feel, about a mode of reasoning which seems to lead to Rome. Though we no longer realise why we distrust logic, since most Englishmen to-day are only Protestants in so far as they are not Catholics, the old distrust still remains, and find expression in phrases which are part and parcel of our national philosophy. Let me ask the reader's indulgence while I examine three such phrases.

It may be true in theory, but it does not work out in practice. If it does not work out in practice it is not true in theory. The theory which does not bear the test of practice should be either revised or rejected.

You can prove anything from statistics. No, you can't. If the statistics are accurate and the argument which is based on the statistics is logical, the conclusion will be true. The conclusion will be false (a) if the statistics are incorrect, (b) if they are incomplete, and (c) if you have ignored other factors which modify the deductions drawn from the statistics.

A mere debating point. Why "mere"? Is an argument to be suspect *merely* because it is effective in debate? The "mere debating point" is either effective or ineffective. If ineffective, it is not a debating point, but a debating lapse. If it is effective, it is effective either because the argument is sound, or because the opposition are too stupid to refute an unsound argument.

No mediaeval thinker would have understood the phrase, "a mere debating point." A debating point, he would have urged in his bewilderment, was either good or bad. It was meaningless to describe it as "mere."

The ardent controversialist, as I know full well, is an object of suspicion in modern England, not only because of doubts of the value of controversy, but because foolish people equate the controversial with the quarrelsome. I have been involved in many controversies, and have enjoyed them all, controversies about public schools, ski-ing controversies, controversies with the Norwegians, and religious controversy. All great fun. But though I have crossed swords with many people, I do not think I have made any enemies in my controversies. I do not see why controversy should develop into a personal quarrel. Chess is a form of controversy, but chess tournaments seldom degenerate into personal brawls. Nor can I see why hard hitting should be a virtue in a controversy between two boxers, and a vice in a controversy between two Christians. I have just received a pained letter from a Modernist who dislikes an article of mine on public school religion which appeared in the *English Review,* and who reproaches me with employing the weapons of sarcasm and irony in my campaign. I think a Christian might be forgiven for using weapons which the Founder of Christianity used with such devastating effect against the Pharisees. The modern theory that you should always treat the religious convictions of other people with profound respect finds no support in the Gospels. Mutual tolerance of religious views is the product not of faith, but of doubt. I have, however, noticed that those who condemn Catholic attacks on Modernists lodge no protest when the Modernist attacks the Catholic.

Hard hitting need not imply personal bitterness. A controversy need not be acrimonious because it is uncompromising in its vigour. Contempt for heresy is consistent with respect for the individual heretic. If Mr. Joad and I proved nothing else by our joint book, at least we have shown that it is possible for a Christian and an anti-Christian to hammer away at each other with the utmost violence without impairing mutual respect and mutual friendship.

BEDE JARRETT
(*1881–1934*)

THE cynic who defined a martyr as "one who has to live with a saint," should have met Father Bede Jarrett, O.P. The experience would have convinced the critic of his own shallowness and it might possibly have taught him to cultivate a critical approach to the "prunes and prisms" school of hagiography.

Balance and sweet temper, remarkable executive ability, and insight into human problems and souls were some of the characteristic marks of Father Jarrett's sanctity. A sweetness came out of the man, but it contained no element of the weak or the saccharine, nor did it detract even faintly from a sense of humor warmly but tenderly aware of the large laughter which lurks in the pretensions of human pride.

Bede Jarrett was the son of an army officer. He received his first schooling at Stonyhurst and completed his formal education at Oxford with the M.A. degree. In 1905 he was ordained priest in the Dominican Order. He was a model son of St. Dominic, loved and admired by his fellow monks. In community life love and admiration beget responsibility, which in the case of Father Jarrett made him provincial of the English Dominicans (1916–1932), prior of Blackfriars, the Oxford house of the Dominicans, and editor of *Blackfriars Magazine* (1932–1934).

These honors indicate but a small part of his remarkable labors. In England Father Jarrett was in constant demand as a lecturer and his popularity at home was as nothing compared with his enthusiastic reception in America where he lectured for five seasons.

Despite his multiplying responsibilities, Father Jarrett found time to write many books. His excellence as a director of souls may be readily seen in *The Abiding Presence of the Holy Ghost in the Soul*, 1918; *Meditations for Layfolk*, 1915; and his meditations for young men, *Space of Life Between*. He was equally at home in biography and history. A fine full-length study of Emperor Charles IV, and his *History of Europe* show something of the rich depths of his spirit; his amiably careful scholarship demonstrates its charm in his forthright *Social Theories of the Middle Ages*, 1926.

In the flood tide of popularity and admiration Fr. Jarrett died suddenly in 1934. Though no biography could do justice to the man, the sketch of his life written by Father Bernard Delaney, O.P., which appeared in both *Blackfriars* and the *Catholic World*, shortly after Father Jarrett's death, is an indication of the abiding impression he made on his fellow priests.

CHAPTER III

THE COMMUNISTS*

THERE have always been religious teachers for whom all material creation was a thing of evil. Through the whole of the Middle Ages, under the various names of Manicheans, Albigensians, Vaudois, &c., they became exceedingly vigourous, though their importance was only fitful. For them property was essentially unclean, something to be avoided as carrying with it the indwelling of the spirit of evil. Etienne de Bourbon, a Dominican preacher of the thirteenth century, who got into communication with one of these strange religionists, has left us a record, exceedingly unprejudiced, of their beliefs. And amongst their other tenets, he mentions this, that they condemned all who held landed property. It will be here noticed that as regards these Vaudois (or Poor Men of Lyons, as he informs us they were called), there could have been no question of communism at all, for a common holding of property would have been as objectionable as private property. To hold material things either in community or severalty was in either case to bind oneself to the evil principle. Yet Etienne tells us that there was a sect among them which did sanction communism; they were called, in fact, the *Communati* (*Tractatus de Diversis Materiis Predicabilibus*, Paris, 1877, p. 281). How they were able to reconcile this social state with their beliefs it is quite impossible to say; but the presumption is that the example of the early Christians was cited as of sufficient authority by some of these teachers. Certain it is that a sect still lingered on into the thirteenth century, called the *Apostolici*, who clung to the system which had been in vogue among the Apostles. St. Thomas Aquinas (*Summa Theologica*, 2a, 2ae, 66, 2) mentions them, and quotes St. Augustine as one who had already refuted them. But these were seemingly a Christian body, whereas the Albigensians could hardly make any such claim, since they repudiated any belief in Christ's humanity, for it conflicted with their most central dogma.

Still it is clear that there were in existence

---

*Jarrett, Bede, O.P., M.A., *Mediaeval Socialism* (New York: Dodge Publishing Co.), pp. 29–41.

certain obscure bodies which clung to communism. The published records of the Inquisition refer incessantly to preachers of this kind who denied private property, asserted that no rich man could get to heaven, and attacked the practice of almsgiving as something utterly immoral.

The relation between these teachers and the Orders of friars has never been adequately investigated. We know that the Dominicans and Franciscans were from their earliest institution sent against them, and must therefore have been well acquainted with their errors. And, as a fact, we find rising among the friars a party which seemed no little infected with the "spiritual" tendency of these very Vaudois. The Franciscan reverence for poverty, which the Poor Man of Assisi had so strenuously advocated, had in fact become almost a superstition. Instead of being, as the saint had intended it to be, merely a means to an end, it had in process of time become looked upon as the essential of religion. When, therefore, the excessive adoption of it made religious life an almost impossible thing, an influential party among the Franciscans endeavoured to have certain modifications made which should limit it within reasonable bounds. But opposed to them was a determined, resolute minority, which vigorously refused to have any part in such "relaxations." The dispute between these two branches of the Order became at last so tempestuous that it was carried to the Pope, who appointed a commission of cardinals and theologians to adjudicate on the rival theories. Their award was naturally in favour of those who, by their reasonable interpretation of the meaning of poverty, were fighting for the efficiency of their Order. But this drove the extreme party into still further extremes. They rejected at once all papal right to interfere with the constitutions of the friars, and declared that only St. Francis could undo what St. Francis himself had bound up. Nor was this all, for in the pursuance of their zeal for poverty they passed quickly from denunciations of the Pope and the wealthy clergy (in which their rhetoric found very effective matter for argument) into abstract reasoning on the whole question of the private possession of property. The treatises which they have left in crabbed Latin and involved methods of argument make wearisome and irritating reading. Most are exceedingly prolix. After pages of profound disquisitions, the conclusions reached seem to have advanced the problem no further. Yet the gist of the whole is certainly an attempt to deny to any Christian the right to temporal possessions. Michael of Cesena, the most logical and most effective of the whole group, who eventually became the Minister-General of this portion of the Order, does not hesitate to affirm the incompatibility of Christianity and private property. From being a question as to the teaching of St. Francis, the matter had grown to one as to the teaching of Christ; and in order to prove satisfactorily that the practice of poverty as inculcated by St. Francis was absolute and inviolable, it was found necessary to hold that it was equally the declared doctrine of Christ.

Even Ockham, a brilliant Oxford Franciscan, who, together with Michael, defended the Emperor, Louis of Bavaria, in his struggle against Pope John XXII, let fall in the heat of controversy some sayings which must have puzzled his august patron; for Louis would have been the very last person for whom communism had any charms. Closely allied in spirit with these "Spiritual Franciscans," as they were called, or Fraticelli, were those curious mediaeval bodies of Beguins and Beghards. Hopelessly pantheistic in their notion of the Divine Being, and following most peculiar methods of reaching on earth the Beatific Vision, they took up with the same doctrine of the religious duty of the communistic life. They declared the practice of holding private property to be contrary to the Divine Law.

Another preacher of communism, and one whose name is well known for the active propaganda of his opinions, and for his share in the English Peasant Revolt of 1381, was John Ball, known to history as "The Mad Priest of Kent." There is some difficulty in finding out what his real theories were, for his chroniclers were his enemies, who took no very elaborate steps to ascertain the exact truth about him. Of course there is the famous couplet which is said to have been the text of all his sermons:

> "Whaune Adam dalf and Eve span,
> Who was thane a gentilman?"

At least, so it is reported of him in the *Chronicon Angliae,* the work of an unknown monk of St. Alban (Roll Series, 1874, London, p. 321). Froissart, that picturesque journalist, who naturally, as a friend of the Court, detested the levelling doctrines of this political rebel, gives what he calls one of John Ball's customary sermons. He is evidently not attempting to report any actual sermon, but rather to give a general summary of what was supposed to be Ball's opinions. As such, it is worth quoting in full.

"My good friends, things cannot go on well in England, nor ever will until everything shall be in common; when there shall be neither vassal nor lord, and all distinctions levelled; when lords shall be no more masters than ourselves. How ill have they used us! And for what reason do they thus hold us in bondage? Are we not all descended from the same parents — Adam and Eve? And what can they show, and what reason give, why they should be more the masters than ourselves? Except, perhaps, in making us labour and work for them to spend." Froissart goes on to say that for speeches of this nature the Archbishop of Canterbury put Ball in prison, and adds that for himself he considers that "it would have been better if he had been confined there all his life, or had been put to death." However, the Archbishop "set him at liberty, for he could not for conscience sake have put him to death" (Froissart's *Chronicle,* 1848, London, book II. cap. 73, pp. 652–653).

From this extract all that can be gathered with certainty is the popular idea of the opinions John Ball held; and it is instructive to find that in the Primate's eyes there was nothing in the doctrine to warrant the extreme penalty of the law. But in reality we have no certainty as to what Ball actually taught, for in another account we find that, preaching on Corpus Christi Day, June 13, 1381, during the last days of the revolt, far fiercer words are ascribed to him. He is made to appeal to the people to destroy the evil lords and unjust judges, who lurked like tares among the wheat. "For when the great ones have been rooted up and cast away, all will enjoy equal freedom — all will have common nobility, rank, and power." Of course it may be that the war-fever of the revolt had affected his language; but the sudden change of tone imputed in the later speeches makes the reader somewhat suspicious of the authenticity.

The same difficulty which is experienced in discovering the real mind of Ball is encountered when dealing with Wat Tyler and Jack Straw, who were with him, the leaders of the revolt. The confession of Jack Straw quoted in the *Chronican Angliae,* like nearly all mediaeval "confessions," cannot be taken seriously. His accusers and judges readily supplied what they considered he should have himself admitted. Without any better evidence we cannot with safety say along what lines he pushed his theories, or whether, indeed, he had any theories at all. Again, Wat Tyler is reported to have spoken threateningly to the King on the morning of his murder by Lord Mayor Walworth; but the evidence is once more entirely one-sided, contributed by those who were only too anxious to produce information which should blacken the rebels in the minds of the educated classes. As a matter of fact, the purely official documents, in which we can probably put much more reliance (such as the petitions that poured in from all parts of the country on behalf of the peasants, and the proclamations issued by Richard II, in which all their demands were granted on condition of their immediate withdrawal from the capital), do not leave the impression that the people really advocated any communistic doctrines; oppression is complained of, the lawyers execrated, the labour laws are denounced, and that is practically all.

It may be, indeed, that the traditional view of Ball and his followers, which makes them one with the contemporaneous revolts of the Jacquerie in France, the Ciompi in Florence, &c., has some basis in fact. But at present we have no means of gauging the precise amount of truth it contains.

But even better known than John Ball is one who is commonly connected with the Peasant Revolt, and whose social opinions are often grouped under the same heading as that of the "Mad Priest of Kent," — John Wycliff, Master of Balliol, and parson of Lutterworth. This Oxford professor has left us a number of works from which to quarry materials to build up afresh the edifice he intended to erect. His chief contribution is contained in his *De Civili Dominio*. But its composition extended over a long period of years, during which time his views were evidently changing; so that the precise meaning of his famous theory on the Dominion of Grace is therefore difficult to ascertain.

But in the opening of his treatise he lays down the two main "truths" upon which his whole system rests:

I. No one in mortal sin has any right to the gifts of God;

II. Whoever is in a state of grace has a right, not indeed to possess the good things of God, but to use them.

He seems to look upon the whole question from a feudal point of view. Sin is treason, involving therefore the forfeiture of all that is held of God. Grace, on the other hand, makes us the liegemen of God, and gives us the only possible right to all His good gifts. But, he would seem to argue, it is incontestable that property and power are from God, for so Scripture plainly assures us. Therefore, he concludes, by grace, and grace alone, are we put in dominion over all things; once we are in loyal subjection to God, we own all things, and hold them by the only sure title. "Dominion by grace" is thus made to lead direct to communism. His conclusion is quite clear: *Omnia debent esse communia.*

In one of his sermons (Oxford, 1869, vol. i. p. 260), when he has proved this point with much complacent argumentation, he poses himself with the obvious difficulty that in point of fact this is not true; for many who are apparently in mortal sin do possess property and have dominion. What, then, is to be done, for "they be commonly mighty, and no man dare take from them"? His answer is not very cheerful, for he has to console his

questioner with the barren scholastic comfort that "nevertheless, he hath them not, but occupieth things that be not his." Emboldened by the virtue of this dry logic, he breaks out into his gospel of plain assertion that "the saints have now all things that they would have." His whole argument, accordingly, does not get very far, for he is still speaking really (though he does not at times very clearly distinguish between the two) much more about the right to a thing than its actual possession. He does not really defend the despoiling of the evil rich at all — in his own graphic phrase, "God must serve the Devil"; and all that the blameless poor can do is to say to themselves that though the rich "possess" or "occupy" the poor "have." It seems strange sort of "having"; but he is careful to note that, "as philosophers say, 'having is in many manners.'"

Wycliff himself, perhaps, had not definitely made up his mind as to the real significance of his teaching; for the system which he sketches does not seem to have been clearly thought out. His words certainly appear to bear a communistic sense; but it is quite plain that this was not the intention of the writer. He defends Plato at some length against the criticism of Aristotle, but only on the ground that the disciple misunderstood the master: "for I do not think Socrates to have so intended, but only to have had the true catholic idea that each should have the use of what belongs to his brother" (*De Civili Dominio*, London, 1884–1904, vol. i. p. 99). And just a few lines farther on he adds, "But whether Socrates understood this or not, I shall not further question. This only I know, that by the law of charity every Christian ought to have the just use of what belongs to his neighbour." What else is this really but the teaching of Aristotle that there should be "private Property and common use"? It is, in fact, the very antithesis of communism.

Some have thought that he was fettered in his language by his academic position; but no Oxford don has ever said such hard things about his Alma Mater as did this master of Balliol. "Universities," says he, "houses of study, colleges, as well as degrees and masterships in them, are vanities introduced by the heathen, and profit the Church as little and as much as does Satan himself." Surely it were impossible to accuse such a man of economy of language, and of being cowed by any University fetish.

His words, we have noted above, certainly can bear the interpretation of a very levelling philosophy. Even in his own generation he was accused through his followers of having had a hand in instigating the revolt. His reply was an angry expostulation (Trevelyan's *England in the Age of Wycliff*, 1909, London, p. 201). Indeed, considering that John of Gaunt was his best friend and protector, it would be foolish to connect Wycliff with the Peasant Rising. The insurgents, in their hatred of Gaunt, whom they looked upon as the cause of their oppression, made all whom they met swear to have no king named John (*Chronicon Angliae*, p. 286). And John Ball, whom the author of the *Fasciculi Zizaniorum* (p. 273, Roll Series, 1856, London) calls the "darling follower" of Wycliff, can only be considered as such in his doctrinal teaching on the dogma of the Real Presence. It must be remembered that to contemporary England Wycliff's fame came from two of his opinions, viz. his denial of a real objective Presence in the Mass (for Christ was there only by "ghostly wit"), and his advice to King and Parliament to confiscate Church lands. But whenever Ball or anyone else is accused of being a follower of Wycliff, nothing else is probably referred to than the professor's well-known opinion on the sacrament of the Eucharist. Hence it is that the *Chronicon Angliae* speaks of John Ball as having been imprisoned earlier in life for his Wycliffite errors, which it calls simply *perversa dogmata*. The "Morning Star of the Reformation" being therefore declared innocent of complicity with the Peasant Revolt, it is interesting to note to whom it is that he ascribes the whole force of the rebellion. For him the head and front of all offending was the hated friars.

Against this imputation the four Orders of friars (the Domincans, Franciscans, Augustinians, and Carmelites) issued a protest. Fortunately in their spirited reply they give the reasons on account of which they are sup-posed to have shared in the rising. These were principally negative. Thus it was stated that their influence with the people was so great that had they ventured to oppose the spirit of revolt their words would have been listened to (*Fasciculi Zizaniorum*, p. 293). The chronicler of St. Albans is equally convinced of their weakness in not preventing it, and declares that the flattery which they used alike on rich and poor had also no mean share in producing the social unrest (*Chronicon Angliae*, p. 312). Langland also, in his "Vision of Piers Plowman," goes out of his way to denounce them for their levelling doctrines:

"Envy heard this and bade friars go to school,
And learn logic and law and eke contemplation,
And preach men of Plato and prove it by Seneca
That all things under Heaven ought to be in common,
And yet he lieth, as I live, and to the lewd so preacheth
For God made to men a law and Moses it taught—
Non concupisces rem proximi tui"
(Thou shalt not covet thy neighbour's goods).

Here then it is distinctly asserted that the spread of communistic doctrines was due to the friars. Moreover, the same popular opinion is reflected in the fabricated confession of Jack Straw, for he is made to declare that had the rebels been successful, all the monastic orders, as well as the secular clergy, would have been put to death, and only the friars would have been allowed to continue. Their numbers would have sufficed for the spiritual needs of the whole kingdom (*Chronicon Angliae*, p. 309). Moreover, it has been noticed that not a few of them actually took part in the revolt, heading some of the bands of countrymen who marched on London.

It will be seen, therefore, that Communism was a favourite rallying-cry throughout the Middle Ages for all those on whom the oppression of the feudal yoke bore heavily. It was partly also a religious ideal for some of the strange gnostic sects which flourished at that era. Moreover, it was an efficient weapon when used as an accusation, for Wycliff and the friars alike both dreaded its imputation. Perhaps of all that period, John Ball alone held it consistently and without shame. Eloquent in the way of popular appeal, he manifestly endeavoured to force it as a social report on the peasantry, who were suffering under the intolerable grievance of the Statutes of Labourers. But though he roused the countryside to his following, and made the people for the first time a thing of dread to nobles and King, it does not appear that his ideas spread much beyond his immediate lieutenants. Just as in their petitions the rebels made no doctrinal statements against Church teaching, nor any capital out of heretical attacks (except, singularly enough, to accuse the Primate, whom they subsequently put to death, of overmuch leniency to Lollards), so, too, they made no reference to the central idea of Ball's social theories. In fact, little abstract matter could well have appealed to them. Concrete oppression was all they knew, and were this done away with, it is evident that they would have been well content.

The case of the friars is curious. For though their superiors made many attempts to prove their hostility to the rebels, it is evident that their actual teaching was suspected by those in high places. It is the exact reversal of the case of Wycliff. His views, which sounded so favourable to communism, are found on examination to be really nothing but a plea to leave things alone, "for the saints have now all they would have"; while on the other hand the theories of the friars, in themselves so logical and consistent, and in appearance obviously conservative to the fullest extent, turn out to contain the germ of revolution.

Said Lord Acton with his sober wit: "Not the devil, but St. Thomas Aquinas, was the first Whig."

COMPTON MACKENZIE

(1883–)

TO RECOUNT the facts of Compton Mackenzie's life would demand the writing of a novel as brilliant as one of his own works. To say that he was born in Hartlepool, January 17, 1883, is the product of Eton and Oxford, a convert, traveler, Royal marine, literary critic, playwright, novelist, clubman, intelligence agent, rector of Glasgow University, and president of the Siamese Cat Club, sets down most of the facts of his life, but little of its luster which must be sought in the distillation of his published works.

As a novelist Mackenzie shows an enormous gusto for living, amiably disciplined by a half-satirical sense of humor which makes his characters delightfully real.

Although he began as a poet, his two-volume novel, *Sinister Street*, 1913–1914, established his reputation as a distinguished novelist. This reputation has grown with the years and his many novels.

THE HEAVENLY LADDER*

MARK, gazing out of the windows of the carriage, made up his mind to journey to Subiaco on foot.

He left Rome very early next morning

---

*Mackenzie, Compton, *The Heavenly Ladder* (New York: Geo. H. Doran Co., 1924), pp. 349–355.

and slept at Tivoli; but he did not stay long amid those enchanted groves and grottos, those temples and tumbling green cascades, for he wished to reach the Abbey of Santa Scolastica by Friday evening, so that he might spend the vigil of Pentecost in Benedict's Sacred Cave. The mountains closed in upon the road, which grew wilder with every step. He hurried faster and faster, his heart beating with the conviction that somehow before he trod this road again he should be at peace.

Mark reached the abbey about dusk; and next day at dawn he climbed the steep mile that separated it from the smaller monastery of the Sacro Speco. As at Monte Cassino, the pilgrim passed through a grove of primeval ilex-trees before he drew near to the object of his pilgrimage. These relics of that fabled Saturnian age must have shaded the footsteps of Benedict when he first came here centuries ago. Did he mark the glinting of the sun's golden patens on the mossy ground, or was his mind already intent on those three years of contemplation that were to fit him for the task he had in hand! Yes, he must have noticed this holy virgin shade and willed that no man should violate it with wedge and axe until the end of time. And when he and his companions were driven to flight by the abominable Florentius, perhaps on Monte Cassino he had spared the holm-oaks of Venus in memory of this grove.

Mark emerged into the sunlight and saw in front of him the monastery of the Sacro Speco, built on huge arches into the face of the cliff. He passed through a Gothic doorway inscribed above with the names of the illustrious pilgrims who had visited this holy spot — twenty saints and fourteen popes besides many princes, queens, and emperors, and entered the highest of the three churches built one on top of the other to enclose the upper and the lower caves of St. Benedict, the oldest Gothic churches in Italy and worthy to enshrine what for long had been the beating heart of Christianity.

Mark spent hour after hour wandering up and down the Holy Stairs from shrine to shrine and from church to church in that dim harmony of multitudinous forms and fancies. Every arch and every ceiling and every wall was a paradise of glowing frescoes, and every smallest bit of space was a jewel of colour or a gleam of gold, except where here and there the naked rock broke into the building and brought home to the pilgrim that this was indeed the cave of Benedict and that all this radiant conception of Christian faith was only made possible by that three years' sojourn among the savage and inhospitable rocks during which he learnt from God the wisdom and the strength to save the world for civilization.

Of all the frescoes that which drew Mark's steps back oftenest to gaze upon it was the contemporary portrait of St. Francis of Assisi, who, in 1218 or 1222, midway between St. Benedict and ourselves, had turned aside to worship here. The fresco must have been painted as nowadays one would take a photograph, for the portrait was of plain Brother Francis without the stigmata, without the saintly nimbus, with nothing but a scroll in his left hand inscribed *Pax huic domui.*

Peace to this house! That long, thin face and sparse beard beneath the high pointed hood, the prominent ears, the fine hands and nose and frail neck, and, beyond all, those eyes at once humorous, ecstatic, grave, and compassionate of God's Little Poor Man of Assisi, had a vitality even in this fresco far greater than the vitality of any living person Mark had ever met. The face of Christ shone out from that Byzantine portraiture; and even as Francis was granted to wear his Saviour's wounds, so might he have been granted the image of his Saviour's countenance. Brother Odo, the diffident little Benedictine monk who painted it, had added a miniature of himself kneeling at the saint's feet, and even in that humble position only daring to show his face and clasped hands. Perhaps he had timidly painted himself in when Francis was canonized ten years later.

Mark went out at last into the *roseto,* a diminutive garden made by terracing the rocks in the angle of the monastery buildings. This place, once a thicket of briers, had been the scene of St. Benedict's great temptation of the flesh, which he had overcome by rolling his body among the thorns until it was covered with wounds. God's Little Poor Man had visited this place hundreds of years afterwards and had grafted on the briers sweet-scented double-roses; and to this day these roses of St. Francis had remained here, and there were no thorns upon them.

Mark sat down and gave himself up to the sweet influences of this ledge in space. The mighty face of the mountain rose behind him, and the little garden came to an end just beyond where he was sitting, in a precipice then ran sheer to the bed of the sounding Anio far below. All else was the vivid blue of the Italian sky. He took from his pocket the Rule of St. Benedict, and began to read:

Of the various kinds of monks.
It is obvious that there are four kinds of monks. The First are the Cenobites, that is those who do their service in a monastery under a rule and an abbot.
The second are the Anchorites, that is Hermits who, not in the first zest of conversion, but by the daily trials of the monastery have already learnt by the help of the many to fight against the devil; and going forth well armed from the ranks of their brethren to the single-handed combat of the solitary place are now able to fight in safety without the help of others and by their own exertions to overcome, under God's aid, the vices of the flesh and their own evil thoughts.

Yet St. Benedict himself fought the solitary fight before he founded his order and won it when still a young man in his twenties. But he feared solitude for others, and he was right to fear it. Such a solitude as his own at Nancepean, Mark thought with a shudder, might easily have brought him to damnation, if he had not fled from it into what had really been a kind of monasticism, the active service of war. Yes, St. Benedict used *militans* in the original Latin to describe the service of monks who lived under a rule and abbot.

A third and truly detestable kind of monks are the Sarabaites, who having been tried by no rule as gold is tried by the fire, and having learnt nothing from experience, and being soft as lead, keep faith with the world in their works while, as their tonsure proves, they lie to God. These men in twos or threes or singly without a shepherd shut themselves up not in the Lord's sheepfolds, but in their own, where they make a law for themselves out of the pleasure of gratifying their own desires. Whatever they think or choose to do, that they call holy, and what they do not like, that they consider unlawful.

The tinkling cowbells of the high Alpine pastures sounded again through the silvery mist.

And other sheep I have, which are not of this fold: them also I must bring, and they shall hear My voice; and there shall be one fold and one shepherd.

A sharp question cut the golden meshes of his fine-spun meditation.
Was not the Church of England a church of Sarabaites?

The fourth kind of monks are those called Gyrovagues, who spend their whole lives in wandering about different provinces, staying in different cells for three or four days at a time, always roaming, never stable, given up to their own pleasures and the snares of gluttony, and worse in every way than the Sarabaites. In regard to their miserable existence silence is better than speech.

A sharper question pierced his soul.
Was not he himself a Gyrovague?
Mark spent that night between sleeping and waking, and always in the darkness the stern face of St. Benedict reproached him and always the eyes of St. Francis pitied him, and prayed for him, and laughed at him; but at Mass the church was filled with a sound from Heaven as of a rushing mighty wind, and Mark heard above that sound Truth speaking with the voice of a little child:

If any man will come after Me, let him deny himself, and take up his cross daily, and follow Me.
For whosoever will save his life shall lose it: but whosoever will lose his life for My sake, the same shall save it.

After Mass he went out into the rose-garden and denied himself, saying: "I am not a priest," and a profound tranquillity fell upon his soul.
He opened the Rule of St. Benedict and read:

Whence, brethren, if we wish to attain the summit of humility and swiftly to reach that heavenly exaltation to which we can only ascend by the humility of this present life, we must by our ever-ascending actions erect such a ladder as that which Jacob saw in his dream, by which the angels appeared descending and ascending. This descent and ascent are to be understood by us not otherwise than that we descend by exaltation and ascend by humility. And the ladder thus erected is our life in the world, which if the heart be humbled is raised by the Lord to Heaven. The sides of this ladder we call our body and soul, and in its sides the Divine Call has inserted the various rungs of humility's discipline by which we may ascend:

THE FEAR OF GOD.

THE SURRENDER OF SELF WILL.

THE OBEDIENCE TO OTHERS FOR THE LOVE OF GOD.

THE DELIGHT IN THE HARDSHIPS OF SUCH OBEDIENCE.

THE CONFESSION OF OUR SINS.

TO BE CONTENT WITH THE WORST AND ESTEEM ONESELF A BAD WORKMAN.

TO CALL ONESELF VILER THAN ALL AND TO BELIEVE IT.

TO KEEP THE RULE AND TO IMITATE ONE'S SENIORS.

TO KEEP ONE'S TONGUE SILENT UNTIL ASKED A QUESTION.

TO BE NOT EASILY MOVED TO LAUGHTER.

TO SPEAK GENTLY, HUMBLY, AND GRAVELY.

TO SHOW THE HUMILITY OF THE HEART IN THE BEARING OF THE BODY.

Mysterious Ladder which St. Thomas Aquinas preferred to put the other way round! There was something that even the angelic Doctor did not know.

Having, therefore, ascended all the rungs of humility, the monk will soon reach the love of God, which being perfect puts fear out of doors whereby he shall begin to keep all precepts, which hitherto he used to observe with some dread, without striving and as it were naturally and habitually, no longer through fear of hell, but for the love of Christ and out of the good habit of virtue and delight in it: which God will deign to show forth by the Holy Ghost dwelling in His workman now cleansed from his vices and his sins.

Mark fell on his knees:

O Holy Ghost, Thou Who in the bosom of the Holy Trinity art the indissoluble bond, the living tie, and the eternal embrace between the Father and the Son, unite me to our Lord Jesus Christ and through Him to the Father. Grant me the temper for that region and that sanctuary where our life is established forever.

Grant me to reach it by the one way which Our Lord traced and Himself followed; the humility of little children.

Mark longed to be received into the Church immediately; but he thought that it would be presumptuous to seek reception here. So, on the feast of St. Anthony of Padua, he came to Crapano and asked the parroco to give him instruction in the Catholic Faith.

The parroco was enchanted by the prospect of receiving an Englishman into the Church, and ascribed it to the gratification of St. Anthony at the lavish way in which his children had just celebrated his feast. He had been starved of fireworks, *poverino*, throughout the war, but they had made up for it this year as Mark would admit. Yes, Mark would be the first Englishman he should have had the privilege of converting.

"Ma il nostro padre Sant' Antonio è buon' assai! Dovrebbe essere molto contento che la guerra sia finita."

The good man set out to look for the penny catechism, and when he had found the little green booklet he suggested that Mark should grapple with its theology a few pages at a time.

"Piano, piano! Forse Lei non capisce, ma sara un poco difficile."

Mark was not to overstrain his memory. When one was no longer a child, it was difficult to learn things by heart.

Mark promised that he would turn himself back into a child so as to learn the catechism by all his heart.

"Bravo!" the parroco cried. *"'E bella, la giovinezza!"*

Mark agreed that youth was very beautiful. And he, like a child, was beginning life all over again.

HELEN PARRY EDEN
(1885–   )

HELEN PARRY, daughter of a judge, married the artist Denis Eden in 1906. She was educated at Manchester University and studied art under Byam Shaw and Rex Cole. She became a Catholic in 1909.

Mrs. Eden excels as a writer of light verse. Her poems are not without touches of delicate humor and they also reveal her mastery of rich and individual rhythms. Her two volumes, *Bread and Circuses* and *Coal and Candlelight,* develop true insights into the holy matter of living, which her *String of Sapphires* enlarges by retelling in verse the simple story of our Lord's life.

SORROW*

Of Sorrow, 'tis as Saints have said —
That his ill-savoured lamp shall shed
A light to Heaven, when, blown about
By the world's vain and windy rout,
The candles of delight burn out.

Then usher Sorrow to thy board,
Give him such fare as may afford
Thy single habitation — best

To met him half-way in his quest,
The importunate and sad-eyed guest.

Yet somewhat should he give who took
Thy hospitality, for look,
His is no random vagrancy,
Beneath his rags what hints there be
Of a celestial livery.

Sweet Sorrow, play a grateful part,
Break me the marble of my heart
And of its fragments pave a street
Where, to my bliss, myself may meet
One hastening with piercèd feet.

*The above and following poems have been selected from *Bread and Circuses*, by Helen Parry Eden (London: John Lane Co.).

LULLABY FOR A LITTLE GIRL

Now Candle-flames disperse the rout
Of shadows and their giant wars;
And though the roof of night without
Be spanned with dusk and set with stars,
'Tis lullaby,
The elm-tops cry,
And lullaby, the leaves that pass
In stealth across the window-glass.

The comb shall sleek your drooping head
And through the darling tangles go
And all your night attire is spread
Before the fire to face the glow,

And lullaby,
The cinders sigh,
For ev'ry rosy palace gone,
Fall'n in their dwarfish Ilion.

Now rest, your prayers said aright
And timely supped your milky bowl,
Your little body all as white
And sweet as your unsoiled soul;
And lullaby,
Her melody,
Who from the quilted bedside goes,
A-tiptoe, when your eyelids close.

POST-COMMUNION

Lord, when to Thine embrace I run
Gathered like waters to the Sun,
Shape me to such celestial mirth
As may go back and glad the earth.
Let Thy rays compass me, and crowd
Into the semblance of a cloud
Mine idle and dispersed powers;
That I, the casket of Thy showers,
May, for my closeness, coloured be
(Howe'er so faintly) like to Thee,

And when Thou loosest me to go
Diffused into Thy world below,
May I, till drip of words shall cease,
Sing of Refreshment, Light and Peace;
And, poured into the Time's abyss,
Revive one blossom for Thy bliss.

THE PETALS

Yourself in bed
(My lovely Drowsy-head)
Your garments lie like petals shed

Upon the floor
Whose carpet is strewn o'er
With little things that late you wore.

For the morrow's wear
I fold them neat and fair
And lay them on the nursery chair;

And round them lie
Airs of the hours that die
With all their stored-up fragrancy.

As a flower might
Give out to the cool night
The warmth it drank in day-long light

So wool and lawn
From your soft skin withdrawn
(Whereon they were assumed at dawn)

Breathe the spent mood,
Lost act and attitude,
Of the small sweetness they endued.

Ere all turn cold
No garment that I hold
But shakes a vision from its fold

Of little feet
That vainly would be fleet,
Tangled about with meadow-sweet,

And of bent knees
When Betsey kneeling sees,
In the parched hedgerow, strawberries.

Such things I see
Folding your clothes, which be
Weeds of the dead day's comedy.

The while I pray
Your part may be alway
So simple and so good to play,

And do desire
Your life may still respire
Such sweetness as your cast attire.

THE ANGELUS-BELL

My night-dress hangs on fire-guard rail
And my cup of milk on the table stands,
The day goes down like a distant sail
And leaves me undressed in my Mother's
    hands.

She has washed me clean of the long day's
    grime
And the pillow is cool for my sleepy head,
For the Angelus-bell with its three-fold
    chime
Has tolled the sun and myself to bed.

CAROL OF A HARD CHRISTMAS*

Winter is come with snow like wool
On all that was so beautiful,
And rime is scattered ashen-grey
On all the grace of yesterday,
In specie hesterna.

The bower most bright of turf and bough
Is but a den of brushwood now,
Yet Jesse's stem,
In Bethlehem,
Its diadem hath re-assumed,
A Flower more sweet than ever bloomed
In die verna.

The world is dark and full of doubt,
The lamps of sin are soon put out,
And they who lit them, in a trice
Departed to their destinies,
In puncto ad inferna;

The stars are dim, the roads are foul
Bewildered strays the weary soul,
Yet see! a ray
Doth show the way,
And mortal clay is made tonight
The lantern of the One True Light,
Carnis lucerna.

Now little wealth is to be won,
And bare goes many a good man's son,
And closed is many a merry door,
And all is scarcer than before
In die hodierna;

But whoso hath the least to spend
May fare the better in the end,
If he but know
That Portal low
Where-through lie open to our eyes
God's bliss and all his braveries,
Vita aeterna.

*The above poem has been selected from *Whistles of Silver and Other Stories* (Milwaukee: Bruce Publishing Co.).

SHANE LESLIE
(1885–   )

JOHN RANDOLPH SHANE LESLIE was born in Dublin, September 29, 1885. He was educated at Eton and Cambridge where he acquired the scholarship and deep appreciation of form distinguishing all his writings. He has been editor of the *Dublin Review*, lecturer, poet, and tramp. His humor is extremely subtle and formed upon no pattern but his own. In 1944 Leslie succeeded to his father's title and became Sir Shane Leslie.

Though his life of *Cardinal Manning*, 1921, written to offset the Purcell's opus on the same subject, is reckoned his finest work, Leslie is actually seen at his best in such works as *The Oxford Movement*, 1933, which gives full play to his humor and delicate sense of the ridiculous.

CHAPTER VIII

THE ROAD TO ROME*

"Tu es Petrus and *Credo in Unam Sanctam Catholicam Ecclesiam* reveal to me a Divine Monarchy claiming a sentiment of loyalty to a Person in Heaven before which all other kingdoms melt away."
— *Manning to Gladstone,* (1848).

LEAVING his friend Dodsworth in charge at Lavington, and armed with an introduction to Döllinger from Gladstone, Manning left England for Malines, where he was shown Relics, and felt that they "awaken and keep alive a high standard of personal devotion." He saw Louvain, Aix, and Cologne, all Catholic hives. Protestant Homburg he found "stripped of outward Christianity." Inquiry gave him to know that the Prussian King was "obstinate, an actor, a humbug." The joyful news of Gladstone's Oxford election caused him to write (August 17, 1847): "And now Saladin must die. It is hard on you to tell you so on the morrow of your successes. But so it is. I do not see how it is possible for questions of religious policy to be postponed." Suddenly he returned home ill: "I am doing no work, but grazing like a Siberian Lamb." In October he set out again to Rome by Paris, Avignon, and Nice. He took notes of Catholic services, and filled his diary with verbal vignettes. "In a garden by the sea a little girl of eight dancing to the chime all alone." A symbol of the English Church, perhaps. "Above Genoa the blue loom of the snow, mountains, and below the rose colour, then the silver of the moon chafing upon the waters."

In Rome friends rose to meet him. At Santa Croce he "saw Newman in his chamber," a sight still awesome to Anglican eyes. They met once in the street. So ill was Manning that Newman did not recognize him. On December 8 Manning set eyes on his future friend and eventual creator, Pius IX. He went about Rome with Sidney Herbert and Florence Nightingale. Until his death the Pope remembered seeing the Archdeacon kneeling in the Piazza di Spagna. These were the days of what Macaulay called Brahminical Government in Rome, of an indulgent despotism tempered by canon law. The great question was whether the Pope would bow to the mob. A half-religious, half-revolutionary crowd cheered for "the democratic Bambino." Manning wrote to Gladstone (January 20, 1848):

"I have been often reminded of you, seeing the same sights and hearing the same litanies we used to hear at St. Luigi. Outwardly Rome is unchanged — the streets, shops, pavements, heaps of dirt not yet taken away. But morally and inwardly there is a vast change: a very visible increase of intelligence and energy, with free, public expression in word and writing. Believing that the unfolding of individual and national character, and therefore of social forces and institutions, is a Divine law and blessing, I cannot but hope more than fear for Italy. It seems to be a law that old countries, if they destroy their organisation, cannot reform and reconstruct themselves — at least, not within a period shorter than a geological era. And I therefore am afraid that anything which upsets an existing order, instead of recalling it to its first idea, only clears a field for confusion. But we have no need to go to Rome. If this upset is not preparing in England, Lord John is at least blameless."

England's only upset was a religious one. At Nice Manning read that the heretical Hampden had been confirmed as Bishop of Hereford, and, when the Dean refused his seal, he wrote to Gladstone: "It is surely an omen that Lord John Russell insulted the Dean of Hereford from Woburn Abbey." To the faithful Dodsworth (January 28, 1848): "Don't tell any soul what I add now, but there is something which has brought you and other days to my mind, and that is the evening Benediction. The sacred beauty with which things are done here is, of course, beyond all places. I am very deeply

*Leslie, Shane, *Henry Edward Manning, His Life and Labours* (London: Burns, Oates & Washbourne, 1921), pp. 81–95.

impressed with what I see of the religious orders here, especially the Passionists. It is impossible not to love Pius IX. His is the most truly English countenance I have seen in Italy."

Pius gave the Constitution to his children. There was more play-acting than revolution, carnival than carnage. Priests wore the tricolor. St. Andrew's head was stolen, and a price put on it! The Austrian Emperor's arms were taken up the Corso by a dwarf mounted on an ass, and burnt. "Alas for the Caesars!" noted Manning; but Francis Joseph's end was not yet. A nobler sight was Pius blessing the Constitution, "with a mixture of majesty, love, and supplication." Manning went into the Church of Perpetual Adoration, "and as the *Tantum Ergo* was sung, the band outside passed playing *Pio Nono.* A strange clash — the world 'so musical and loud,' and the Lorelei of contact between the natural and the supernatural." But Mazzinian steeds were dragging the papal chariot, and the reins were dashed from the Cardinal-charioteer. To Gladstone Manning wrote (April 3, 1848):

"I may say that six weeks has revolutionised Italy and Europe. What are we to read in this? Is it not the moral and popular development, the fruit of 'thirty years of peace, demanding recognition and social power? In this view I am inclined to look at it with hope, especially when I see that after all these sudden and violent movements in advance, England is in all popular freedom and power immeasurably ahead. When I think of our social state, the only account I can give of it (as I often have to do to Italians) is that we are a republic under a hereditary President. It is wonderful to see the Catholic Church in America, France, and Italy distinctly of the progress and popular party — indeed, in many ways at the head of it. It falls in with an old belief of mine in which I think you share. I mean that the Church of the last ages will be as the Church of the first, isolated and separate from the Civil Powers of the World. In the first ages the Church won them by making them Christian; in these days they are renouncing the Church by making themselves again merely secular and material. And in these has long been and is now my fear for the Church of England. I am afraid it will be deceived into trusting the State too long, and thereby secularising itself. I hope I may find some way of interpreting the insularity you confess to. For myself, I know no real sense in which I dare hold it. I never had much of it, and feel that every year has convinced me more deeply that Protestantism is heretical and Nationalism is Judaic. Farewell, my dear friend. I begin to think of home, but the lines of confusion, three deep, are drawn from Hungary to the Pyrenees, and as yet I have not fixed my route. If I can I hope to see Lombardy in its first days of freedom."

Englishmen encouraged revolution in Italy, but were morally shocked at the contemporary Irish rising, which Ventura, Manning's favourite preacher, seemed to justify. Of his pamphlet Mrs. Sidney Herbert wrote: "He cannot resist a hit at us and poor Ireland in every chapter; and still worse, have you read Bishop O'Higgins's answer to Rome? It is too hopeless." As an offset, Sidney Herbert and Manning arranged for Trevelyan's Irish pamphlet to be translated for the Pope. Ventura told Manning that palliatives would not do for Ireland, and that, like Sicily, Ireland must have her own Parliament. Manning recorded Ventura's famous words to the Pope, "Let not your Holiness look to the Sovereigns of Europe, who are shadows which may vanish within the year, but to the peoples, who are realities and last for ever," which sank into his mind as deep as the beauty of Holy Week. On April 9 he was presented to Pius with other English folk. On May 11 private audience was granted to *"Archidiacono* Manning" at Mount Cavallo. He was given his ecclesiastical title on his paper of entry. The Pope was interested in the work of Mrs. Fry, and startled to hear from him that Anglicans received the Cup at Communion against all liturgical hygiene.

Manning started to drive home, visiting the deathchamber of St. Francis. In Perugia he noted, "The bells broke out and reminded me of Harrow and Oxford, under a cloudless sky and yellow moon." Homesickness took shape in all his notes. The Church at Assisi, "like the under-Church of York, painted. The form is a Latin cross with an end like the seven chapels at Durham. Windows like the style of Westminster Abbey. After dinner to St. Damiano; reminded me of Hever and the moat." He delighted in St. Clare's Oratory, "like one of our rude Early English." The refectory "reminded me of the groined roof at Cold Waltham." He came slowly home, scribbling thumb-sketches of pictures and services, sermons and cathedrals, but the home touch never ceased. "The country to Forli like Midland counties." Even the outline of the Apennines "becomes a flat tableland as the South Downs." He went to Benediction in Ravenna, and noted malefactions expiated in Purgatory: "A monk not bowing at the *Gloria,* a preacher making too much of his composition, a virgin careful about her food on Fridays."

He visited the tombs of Dante and Augustine of Hippo, and, greatest of all, of St. Charles Borromeo, his future patron. In after-years he wrote of what occurred at Milan: "I have always felt to be a call from St. Charles. I was thinking in prayer, if only I could know that St. Charles, who represents the Council of Trent, was right and we wrong. The Deacon was singing the Gospel, and the last words, *et erit unum ovile et unus pastor,* came upon me, as if I had never heard them before."

He returned to England with a quiet determination to lead Anglicanism to its conclusions. The Bishops had accepted Hampden, and with almost humorous despair Manning wrote an ingenious Charge, making allowances for Hampden's opinions. It was a possible way out of an impossible situation. It was a legal brief for the Establishment. Rumours of Manning's trend in Rome had alarmed his friends. Pusey, Gladstone, and Noberly had written anxiously. To the latter Manning wrote: "My opinions are what they were when I wrote to you from Rome. My Charge is the case for the Church of England." He ceased the orthodox halloo in order to try running with the heretical

hare. Still he was riding for a fall. To Dodsworth: "I cannot serve what I cannot defend, and if I had failed to find a just defence I am afraid to think of what must have followed." He told Gladstone in St. James's Park that during his illness he had been assured that the English Church (not the Establishment) was a part of the living Church, but to Dodsworth he wrote: "I feel clearer and more ready for all hazards. I have had things to cheer me, great depth and devotion in individuals with no tinge of Anglicanism or any such sham" (August 14, 1848).

When despondency fell upon him he could not lean on Pusey's tired heart or be comforted by the official unbrotherliness of Samuel Wilberforce. He stayed himself on Dodsworth and Robert Wilberforce, to whom he wrote under the seal. To the former he wrote next year (March 23, 1849): "As to the sacrifice, if I believed the Church of England to condemn what the Church of Rome teaches I should be in a strait. But my soul sickens. And I feel that I am defending, not the Church of England against Rome, but my own position against the Church of England. We are in it, are we of it?"

In the autumn he set out for Wales and Scotland, whence Sidney Herbert wrote: "Expect a rather desolate aspect, and respect me, upon whose skill in venery you will be entirely dependent for food, which I will bring, as in Landseer's picture, to you, the fat Abbot of Glastonbury." In Wales Manning preached at the foundation of Lord Feilding's church, which before completion followed its founder into the Catholic Fold. Manning could later only wearily beg Lady Feilding: "Do nothing in haste. I will use no false or worldly persuasions to stay you from anything. But do not act where you are and as you are, and under the impressions now upon you." They were received in Scotland, whither Manning had preceded them. He visited the graves of Paley and John Knox in contrast to the tombs of Dante and St. Francis the previous year. He preached in Glasgow, and sketched Glamis Castle. At St. Andrews he remembered

Cardinal Beaton and Wishart, and at Archbishop Sharpe's monument noted "two deeds of blood and one of sacrilege." He was struck by the "universal drunkenness," and reflected: "I had hoped for a quiet evening in the past, but it is better to have an instructive warning of the present." Elsewhere he tried his pastoral hand by visiting the poor, but "they seemed unused to it." At Dunblane he saw Archbishop Sharpe's Thomas à Kempis, "same edition as mine. At the beginning was written *non magna relinquo magna sequor.* On the last *nec te quaesieris extra,* and on the flyleaf *Honores spret summus honor."* Every word seemed to apply to the wanderer. A year later he wrote of his holidays to Dodsworth: "They were very pleasant, and in memory are to me refreshing and soothing. Glamis Castle and St. Andrews often come up before me. We did not think then where we should be now; nor now, where next September?"

Silence and study, patience and the *Patres,* were all that were left to Manning, as he racked shelf and mind in resolving whether St. Augustine was an Anglican. "I suppose you are up to the chin in that great Suarez which I saw in your rooms. How can you swim in such dry waters?" asked Robert Wilberforce. "I wish I could see you in my study plunging and gambolling on the great waters of Suarez," was the reply. But Anglican Archdeacons can hardly have been in their element.

Manning began to be troubled, not for himself only, but for his followers. Gentle remonstrance took the place of stern anger toward those who passed to Rome. When Henry Wilberforce went he wrote to his wife (Advent, 1849): "Under seal. I do not know whether to be sorry or glad at what has happened. I have intentionally spared you the perplexity of bearing what I was bearing myself. You remember my promise that the day I feel my soul to demand anything for its safety you shall know. I have not forgotten it, and I have never yet felt this demand. But I have felt and do feel an overwhelming fear lest I should be under an illusion. I know of nothing else which weighs with me but this, lest I contradict the will

of my Lord. On St. Andrew's Day I offered myself, as I have again and again, and never so often as in Rome, to follow on the spot if only I can have, not sign or token, but the conviction of a moral agent that it is the will of my Lord. Pray for me sevenfold, for to mistake in such a path as this, is to one who must give account of souls something like death." And a year later: "I tremble continually lest I should fall through pride. And you cannot have escaped the shadow of my faults except by an extraordinary grace." But by this time a new agency had begun to work.

As a witty Frenchman wrote, the revolution reached England in the form of *le père Gorham!* Gorham was a well-read botanist, who was presented to a living in the Diocese of "Henry of Exeter," who declined to institute him as a heretic. Gorham rejected the Grace at Baptism, which did not occur to him to be as necessary to infant souls as dew to the flowers of the field. To the violent distress of the High Churchmen, he wisely put his trust in Princes and appealed successfully to the temporal power against his Bishop, who wrote to Manning (August 7, 1850):

"*Private.* Yesterday afternoon, in virtue of the *fiat* of the Archbishop of Canterbury, Mr. Gorham was instituted to the Vicarage of Brampford Speke by Sir H. J. Fust! His Grace's complicity in this awful work is thus consummated, and I cannot hold communion with him. I cannot communicate *in sacris* with him."

Into this case Manning tilted with all his strength. He carried his Anglican life in his hands, and was prepared to fall. He wrote, he published and petitioned against "this awful work." He applied canon law, it was noted, "like arguments from pure mathematics." He charged gravely that "three hundred years of Statute Law are not to be slipped off in a day." By law and logic he tested "whether the Church of England be a Divine or a human society." As he had written to Bishop Wilberforce (April 24, 1849), "One Gorham case is enough for one day, and the peril of this decision, whether for the truth or against it, is great. I dread the day when such a subject as the other Holy Sacrament shall be brought, not into a Council or Synod, not before the Church in any form in which we may believe the Holy Spirit may guide and preserve us, but into a wrangling Court before an incompetent Judge. Do you remember in our walk at Graffham just before your consecration that I said I am full of fear from our want of true and accurate study and interpretation of our positive doctrines? This is just such a crisis as I feared."

Gladstone was no less alarmed, writing: "If Mr. Gorham be carried through, and that upon the merits, I say not only is there no doctrine of baptismal regeneration in the Church of England as State-interpreted, but there is no doctrine at all!" He found that "there would stand forth clear as day to all who did not shut their eyes the absolute necessity of the living voice of the Church to guard her mute witness against profanation." Manning at least did not shut his eyes, but Gladstone would not sign the declaration prepared by Manning and his friends. "This was the first divergence between him and Hope and myself." Manning preserved a vivid memory, writing to Gladstone (November 13, 1869): "Do you remember the night at your house when the thirteen signed the Resolutions about the Gorham Judgment? And the morning when you were in bed with influenza and I came and told you that the judgment was given in his favour? You will ask me why I should fear that you have gone back from what you were then?"

In after-years Gladstone was indignant because Manning stated "that I would not sign because I was a Privy Councillor," and Lord Morley in his *Life* is at pains to cover the refusal to sign by referring to Gladstone's diary for a note — "March 14. Hope, Badeley, Talbot, Cavendish, Denison, Dr. Pusey, Keble, Bennett here from 9 to 12 on the draft of the Resolutions" — and adding: "This would appear to be the last meeting, and Manning is not named as present," which proves that it was not the last meeting, for Manning and Robert Wilberforce, who is not mentioned either, were both to sign. Hope

wrote to Manning that day (March 14, 1850): "I will see Gladstone and talk matters over with him, but there are worse hindrances than he is likely to prove. Pusey came here with Keble yesterday and remained some hours criticising our Resolutions. Hoping to get matters adjusted, I proposed a meeting of all who could be got together at Gladstone's this morning." Gladstone noted of this meeting, "On the whole I resolved to try some immediate effect," as appears in Hope's further word to Manning, "Gladstone still for delay, but I think all but himself for Resolutions to be immediately put forth." Gladstone simply failed his friends in the day of battle. Manning excused him at the time (April 6, 1850):

"I am well satisfied, much as it cost me, that you did not sign our paper. Your address was very valuable, and was a second witness, and it leaves you freer. Not that freedom can long remain to us. In the last fortnight of quiet my thoughts have been settling down calmly into a conviction which is part of my consciousness that this question is vital. As an article of necessary faith. As involving the Divine authority of the Church. You could not be slower than I to come to this point. But it is a question of gold or life."

When Manning hinted secession from the Church, Gladstone hinted retirement from politics, and proposed a society of mutual restraint, who should bind themselves to take no "step of a decisive character" without consultation. Manning declined "any engagement of the kind" (May 22, 1850): "In such a moral probation as is now upon us I conceive that time is not to be measured by the dial, but by events; that it is not chronological, but moral." What this meant appears in a note to Miss Maurice (August 5, 1850): "I see nothing before me within any horizon my eye can ascertain. I have always said to you, not dial time, but moral time. Principles and their issues, events and facts, are the hours and minutes of moral time." And again, showing his love for concise and scholastic sentences:

"I always felt that the Low Church had no objective Truths, the High Church little subjective religion. Now I see that in the

Catholic System the objective and subjective are the concave and the convex. I do not say that the body and the soul, because these are two, and the objective and subjective become one. God and man are one by Incarnation. A Theology of 300 years is in conflict with a Faith of 1,800 years. I was born in the 300. My mature thoughts transplant me into the 1,800. This is the real balance, but people will not so look at it. I believe a man might hold what he likes in the English Church if he would be quiet and uphold the Church. The dishonesty is to be honest."

A bitter letter from Bishop Wilberforce he described as "good as the vinegar and the gall was good." A week later (October 26, 1850) he asked Miss Maurice, "Ought I to resign before going abroad?" Gladstone he would only promise to let know the news first. Gladstone sparred desperately for time. He went so far as to write that if "the Church of England must be understood really to deny that the Church of Rome is a true Church, because they differ in essential points, I should answer that I know of no such points!" Meantime, Gladstone's pamphlet appeared, and Manning made a point, regarding "the Supremacy as known to the Common Law which the Tudor Statutes profess only to declare. My deep conviction is that they went beyond the Common Law in the vital point, and that Sir Thomas More lost his head between the edges of the old and new Supremacy. But the lapse of time seems to give us advantage for restoring the Common Law supremacy, to which I believe Pius IX would make as little objection as Pius II." (A day came when Manning petitioned the successor of Pius IX to canonise Sir Thomas.)

The confusion was immense. Gladstone wrote of a famous Dean, "I have seen Hook, he drivels," while "He of Exeter seems to have befooled himself." Exeter's chaplain, Maskell, wrote: "Pusey says one thing, Robert Wilberforce another, Gladstone something else, and you, with an openness for which I give God thanks, speak plainly in contradiction of them all!" "The truth seems to me more and more to be that a Church

takes a great deal of killing," pleaded Gladstone, as he denied the rumours affecting Manning, who thought it kindest to state (June 25, 1850): "I dare not say that my conscience will not submit itself to the Church which has its circuits throughout the world and its centre by accident in Rome." He could not help adding: "But I have written too much." Gladstone began to wail: "She nevertheless may be the last compulsory home of all who, in the West at least, intend with God's help to hold by a definite revealed truth; but if it be so, a long and loud alas for Christendom!" Autumn found Manning fencing with the unsympathetic Samuel of Oxford: "I fear our separation from the Church, and even opposition to it, is a self-evident fact. If the authority of the British Empire should cease to flow into Canada it would fall into Civil War. And the restoration of internal peace would be a separation like the United States, unless it should reunite itself with the Empire at large." Secessions rained like leaves. The Henry Wilberforces passed out. William Anderdon, whom Manning wrote he "stayed twice as long as I could," followed. Poor John Anderdon wrote: "I cannot say more of my love for you than that next to the ties of wife and children you bind me closest, nor more of my love for the Church than that I would rather you kept fast hold than even my beloved son." Before the New York Dodsworth had gone, after a minute exchange of notes (December 30, 1850): "Pray for me. At last the decisive step is taken. By God's grace I am to be received tomorrow. I go at 12 o'clock. Remember me then if you can." The answer was (December 31, 1850): "Dearest Friend, — God be with you. Nothing can part us. Pray for me and trust me with God. Ever your loving friend, H.E.M." And the nineteenth century was divided in twain, leaving Manning's heart not otherwise, for by this time he had left Lavington.

Pius had not only given the Romans a Constitution, but the English a Hierarchy, according to the Needs of each. "Can we meet the challenge which comes over the water?" Manning asked Gladstone. The

Gorham Judgment had shown a moral agency fail. The restoration of the Hierarchy exhibited an enduring and unfailing one in operation. An archaic wave of No-Popery swept the country, and when it reached Chichester, Manning allowed it to carry him gently from his moorings. "I believe that it is set for the fall and rising again of many, and that men are parting upon it for life," he told Gladstone, who threw his last shaft by recalling the solemn statement Manning had made to him after his illness. In 1896 Gladstone said he could still take an oath in a court of law that Manning had said substantially, "Dying men, or men within the shadow of death, as I was last year, have a clearer insight into things unseen of others, a deeper knowledge of all that relates to Divine faith. In such a communion with death and the region beyond death I had an absolute assurance in heart and soul, solemn beyond expression, that the English Church (I am not speaking of the Establishment) is a living portion of the Church of Christ." This apparent test of Manning's insincerity Gladstone made in 1850, and again in 1896 after Manning's death, when he understood that Manning's Anglican letters to him had been destroyed. It is interesting to append Manning's original answer, for he never wrote to him from Lavington again (November 17, 1850):

"I have a perfect recollection of the conversation you refer to, and I feel that what I said then is in perfect accordance with my present mind. I have no shame in saying that since then I have seen what I did not see before. I have the deepest anxiety to make clear my integrity before God and man, but to square myself by myself is of no high importance to me. Will you also allow me to appeal to you for such a re-examination of your theological conclusions as you have given to your political opinions? To you I seem what you seem to others."

On November 22, the clergy required him to convene them in order that the Arch-deaconry might protest against the Roman Hierarchy. To Dodsworth he wrote: "I have therefore seen the Bishop and offered to resign my office, or to convene and express my dissent and resignation. Events have greatly brought this to its issue in the way I waited for. I wish to play it out as on a field until the last move of duty is done. Then I shall lay down my weapons." On the day before the meeting he wrote to his Bishop: "Although my resignation was not formally accepted, I consider it to be morally complete." Years later the Rev. H. D. Clarke recalled the "great murmur of intention to charge the Archdeacon with his Roman tendencies, but no one was bold enough to realise the threat." According to the *Brighton Herald* of November 23, "the pale, gentlemanly, quiet and melancholy looking Archdeacon commenced the proceedings by reading several prayers, most of the clergy kneeling during the time." At the close Manning spoke his last charge. His sorrowful dignity won a vote of thanks. "I began to feel as if every man had gone to his own house and left the matter," he wrote to Hope the next day. "Since then events have driven me to a decision." On November 27 the restored church at Lavington was consecrated, Bishop Samuel preaching in the morning and Manning in the evening. "A day of intense sadness, intensified by the dimness of a November evening. All were oppressed with the feeling of the great loss they were to sustain," remembered Dean Randall. On December 3 he departed for good. To Miss Maurice he wrote (December 5, 1850): "I read your kind words as I passed out of Lavington on Tuesday morning. Last Sunday was a time of strange spiritual sorrow, a heaviness of soul such as I dare hardly speak of. Love, tenderness, long and fond memories of home and flock, were around me and upon me. But through all a calm, clear conviction stood unmoved. And now I am here, and all things seem fulfilling themselves as I look on."

THE FIRST PHASE*

THE Oxford Movement sprang like an exotic flower out of fallow and dust. The Movement itself was the tinted dawn of the Victorian Era and symbolised that coming period of strife. The realms of thought, philosophy and belief in England were all uncontested. Intellectual England resembled Africa before being rushed by the rival powers. The Victorians grew less settled and content in their souls. Their social and material fabric stood, as they thought, like the pyramids, but there was no field of creed or intellect over which champions and prophets did not conquer or perish in Homeric warfare. The struggle for Oxford between the new Movement and the old guard in possession resembled the war of Greeks and Trojans.

Before the dawn there fell an exquisite and multicoloured dew, the romance of Sir Walter Scott. The past not only of Scotland but of the mediaeval rose gently from the dead. He loved monkish Latin and caught the scenery if not the soul of the Middle Ages. There were novels dedicated to the *Abbot* or the *Monastery* full of more or less inaccurate Catholicism. The Jesuit as well as the Covenanter passed guilelessly before the reader. The pomp, the beauty, the cruelty, the mystery, the strength associated in his mind with the old religion was flung by a sorcerer's pen into the stately homes of England. In quietly leisured and undistracted days the ink of Scott flowed like roseate lava over honest and enthusiastic souls. Scott no more dreamed that he was reviving Romanism in the Church than that he was persuading the War Office to restore chain armour. Scott moved not as a mitred priest but as a minstrel. He had recalled Crusader and monk and even a creaky old ritual. The thirst which he engendered for Romance led to desires for Rome. His Gothic toy of Abbotsford signalled a revival in the Sacristy. Sir Walter sowed where Newman was to

reap. With the *Stabat Mater* on his lips he died in 1832. In the next year came the Oxford Movement.

Eighteen thirty-two was also marked by the Reform Bill. It was the year which really ended the Eighteenth Century. Centuries did not properly close in double zeros. In English History the Seventeenth Century ended with the Revolution in 1688 and the Sixteenth in 1603 with the death of Elizabeth. The excitement leading to the Reform Bill had stirred the Church. The Bishop of Bristol had his Palace burnt and, sad to say, Archbishop Howley was mobbed in Canterbury. On November 5 the Guys burnt in Cathedral Cities suspiciously resembled Bishops. Government felt that something must be done and uncourageously suppressed ten Anglican Sees in Ireland. On July 14, 1833, this was denounced by Keble in a famous Sermon on National Apostasy, described as "a mixture of the sublime and the insignificant," preached in St. Mary's, Oxford. Thence Newman dated the birthday of the Movement, of which he was to be the life and which in turn was to prove his Anglican death. The Victorian Century, which closed in 1914, had begun.

If the Church of England had been more freely visited by flame, the sign might have been regarded as Pentecostal. It needed firing badly for the supernatural was dead or very dusty. The best Parsons were reflected in the works of Goldsmith, Fielding, and Sterne. But the Vicar of Wakefield was not, in Scott's words, the type "predestined to be a glorified Saint!" They kept dull Diaries and dined upon tithe pig. They enjoyed country life and cherished such crumbs of sport and lees of wine as reached them from the Squire's table. Some hunted and some merited benefices by marrying the cast mistress of a patron. A fishing parson kept his live bait in the font.

The beautiful old Churches were rich with the mouldy deposit of the Middle Ages. They were stuffed with high box pews,

*Leslie, Shane, *The Oxford Movement* 1833–1933 (Milwaukee: Bruce Publishing Co., 1933), pp. 39–45.

"whether to conceal disorder or to proclaim pride." Squires sat round charcoal fires in their cushioned seats, while servants and labourers from high galleries prayed God bless King and Squire and Squire's relations. Three-deckers combining pulpit and desk rose like wooden pagodas, from the lowest tier of which the Parish Clerk supplanted the mediaeval acolyte like a gargoyle. Female pew-openers in town had to be tipped, while beadles smote the poor or ushered the rich with heavy wands. In London fashionable preachers buzzed under soundingboards in private Chapels. Hannah More and Wilberforce toured thirteen Parishes in Gloucestershire ("as sure as God's in Gloucestershire" was the mediaeval proverb) to report that the only discoverable Bible was used to prop a flower-pot. In the country there proceeded from lofts and galleries the sound of fiddles and barrel-organs and all manner of wheezy music. People sat or knelt "balancing between the chest and the end of the back." Gentlemen prayed as though consulting Urim and Thummin, in their top hats.

Doctrine was nowhere. Sacraments, except for formalities, had gone with the Nonjurors. Baptisms were performed in a mass. Cases were known where even water was dispensed with. At Confirmation sponsors were collected on the street for the price of a pint of beer. The wife of a West Country Bishop gave Confirmation Balls. A broad-minded Bishop described Confirmation as "a perfectly unobjectionable Ceremony." Communion was little more than taking wine with the Parson, who handed what remained to the Sexton to drink. When the Manchester Churchwardens complained that weekly Communion was a burden on the rates, the Bishop of Chester politely made it a quarterly proceeding. The Bishops, whose names were as often written in the Peerage as in the Book of Life, were wonderful to record. Shute Barrington of Durham took his foxhounds on visitation. Watson of Llandaff passed a studious life away from his See. He built an elegant Palace on Windermere which unluckily was not in his Diocese. At his Cambridge residence he strengthened an

upper room for parties, which proved useful a century later when used for Mass by the Catholic Chaplain to the University. The chief Bishop whose name survives is Malthus, who wrote his famous Essay on Population, whether he was troubled by agricultural distress or the fecundity of Parsons.

The English Bishops were as disgraceful as many of the French before the Revolution. At the dawn of the Oxford Movement a new type had arisen called "Greek Play Bishops." To have edited a Latin Missal would have been a less qualification. As Disraeli said, Peel sought "successors of the Apostles among third-rate hunters of syllables."

Yet there was no conscious irreverence. The Church was always in the hands of gentlemen. Kegan Paul recalled a Vicar turning to the Communicants with: "Has any lady or gentleman a Corkscrew?" like a Conjuror addressing his audience. At Eton in the Eighteenth Century members of the Sixth Form received Communion once a term or were fined a guinea. Holy Tables, when worn out, were sent to the taproom. Chalices decorated the tables of the rich. A famous racehorse was called Crucifix. Ash Wednesday was so moveable a feast that at Lichfield one year it was postponed a week to suit the Fair of the name. The hunting parsons were a civilised throwback to the fighting Bishops of the Middle Ages. The unwritten code allowed them to hunt but not to race. Pugin recorded that "in Lincoln the son of the late Bishop, who refused to subscribe to the erection of his throne, lost £7,000 at the Lincoln Races." And J. E. C. Bodley told how Archbishop Harcourt contrived to drive past the York Races in coach and six. The upper Clergy were men of the world, but good men of the world. They thought it ungentlemanly to interfere with private life. They only asked for the cloak of respectability against Jacobin and Dissenter. The Jacobin, not the Jacobite, was their real enemy and critic. Benbow's *Crimes of the Clergy* appeared in 1823 and was suppressed. It was a fearful but sometimes amusing Calendar. Crimes of turpitude can be thrown at the black sheep of any Church and are unworthy of citation, but there was something very English in Mr. Wright of Boughton who was accused of singing the Athanasian Creed to a fox-hunting tune! He was preferable to the Clergyman who once apologised for mentioning Christ in a Christmas Sermon!

At the Universities the standards were low. The Articles of Religion were signed with punctilious indifference. At Cambridge the celibate Fellows were accorded unhallowed connections. But Simeon of King's for fifty years had preached and revived religion. A century has passed and the landing halfway to his rooms is still called the Saint's Rest. To this day the Oxford Movement is countered by Simeon's Trustees who purchase Benefices in a manner that makes Simeony akin to Simony. Oxford harboured neither piety nor learning. Lord Chesterfield said that Oxford would only be known to exist owing to the treasonable spirit avowed there. Treason to State had melted. Treason to the established Church was yet to come. The Church at best was philanthropic and only wished her children not to conspire or inspire. She was not dissatisfied since she had no competition. Church and State cohabited in an atmosphere of great security. The Church cringed and the State patronised. They never conflicted and civil Divorce was hardly known. It required an Act of Parliament to break wedlock. Anglican principles had apparently attracted the favour of God and the Empire of the world. To those recalling the fate of Louis XIV, Philip of Spain, and Napoleon it seemed as though Heaven favoured the Book of Common Prayer. Revolution was coming, but in the most unexpected and subtle manner: a Catholic revival in the National Church.

Let us link history. The victor of Waterloo had made a pale and ascetic Student of Christchurch, Professor of Hebrew at Oxford. His name was Edward Bouverie Pusey, of a family so old that they held the manor of Pusey by a horn from Canute. Pusey was an old Etonian and had studied theology in Germany. He became the Anglican anti-Pope. Here are two measurements: Dean Hutton described him as "surpassingly sincere, profoundly erudite, piercingly appellant": Cardinal Manning, as "intellectually contrary, suicidal, ecclesiastically unlawful, foolish."

Meantime a band of choice spirits collected at Oriel College under Provost Hawkins: Whately, the Wilberforce brothers, Keble, Newman. They conversed in a hushed agitation and as a grim innovation the teapot was served instead of College Port. They peered abroad and desired better things. Whately taught Newman Logic and passed on, the first to see and fear the ghost of Mysticism. Newman made a nervous trip in the Mediterranean and on an Orange boat wrote the *Pillar of Cloud* from which the world has since drawn Kindly Light. He felt a task before him which became clearer after Keble's clarion sermon. In September he began to issue *Tracts for the Times*. Oxford was unready for Times or Tracts. Nobody of age or position visioned the dynamic powers flickering in the young men.

MARTIN D'ARCY

(*1888–*   )

BORN of Catholic parents in the lovely city of Bath, 1888, Martin Cyril D'Arcy was educated at Stonyhurst, Oxford, and the Gregorian University at Rome. He was ordained priest in the Society of Jesus in 1921.

For a time he taught at Stonyhurst and was attached to the Jesuit Church in Farm Street.

Father D'Arcy was, for some years before becoming provincial of the English Jesuits, Master of Campion Hall, the Jesuit college in Oxford. It is largely through his efforts that the splendid new hall has been built. Father D'Arcy played a large part in the life of the university where he was as well known for his wit and social talents as he was for his brilliant lectures.

Like so many Jesuits, his interests are wide as any catalogue of his published work will attest. *The Mass and the Redemption* and *Mirage and Truth* are two of his more popular works. For depth of thought and charm of style, however, *The Mind and Heart of Love* stands first among Father D'Arcy's books.

THE CHRISTIAN IDEAL*

IT IS in the Atonement that the Christian religion rises into its dazzling splendour. To the Gentile, as St. Paul said, it was folly, "to the Jews a stumbling-block, but to those who believe, the power and the wisdom of God." By belief here St. Paul does not mean a private emotional experience which the sober heads would name superstition; he means the difference between the Pharisee who saw a man on a cross and the centurion who with the same scene before him saw God, and that it is our "estranged faces that miss the many splendoured thing." On an external and superficial aspect the dogma of the Atonement is the interpretation put upon the story of a man Christ who was crucified by his own people and was reported to have risen from the dead — let us say, therefore, the slaying by the Jews of their greatest prophet and an empty tomb. The traditional religious interpretation of it is that this Christ sacrificed Himself for His people and the world and so made atonement for sin to God. To understand it further we must however fall back on the principle I have already stated, that God's love works through the intentions of man and completes his understanding. Now amongst these intentions or, let us say, ways of looking at things, injury, punishment, satisfaction and forgiveness play an immemorial part. Moreover, in relation to the forces which control life these phases take on the nature of sacrifice. No doubt sacrifice is best explained as the natural expression of homage of a creature in presence of its maker, but the form which

that sacrifice has taken has passed through the whole gamut of emotions of which man is capable. Sacrifice, therefore, being the way we all take when wrongdoing and reparation are in question, the symbol and the reality of God's intercourse with man and man's treatment of Him are embodied and shown forth in sacrifice; and the wisdom, if we may so dare speak, of God is proved by the fact that the crucifix can be understood by everyone, from the most simple to the wisest, that it has always struck home to the religious mind in a unique manner, and that it condenses all that can be thought and desired in one outstanding respresentation.

All this goes to confirm the statement formerly made that man dictates to God the manner in which God will act, the while God's love triumphs through these very limitations, and this truth is seen in shining glory in the Redemption. The human act, like the Holy Grail or the blood of St. Januarius, changes as we look upon it, and what was human in appearance glows red with divinity. The lowest level of understanding is seen in the barbaric notion that God being angry with mankind for its evil doing maltreats the innocent because His lust for punishment must be sated. This travesty of the truth appears occasionally in anti-religious literature. More noble is the view that an innocent and pure victim substitutes himself for the guilty and acts as their ransom.

The idea imbedded in this view is too close to human nature to be altogether wrong. Incident after incident from fable and history shows its appeal to some instinct in us, and indeed there can be no question of the virtue

*D'Arcy, M. C., S.J., *Mirage and Truth* (New York: The Macmillan Co., 1935), pp. 163–179.

of the victim who freely takes the place of his guilty friends. What troubles us in the transaction is not the valour and generosity of the man, but the willingness of God to let an innocent man be punished in place of the guilty. So long as the innocent and the guilty are entirely separate, we are left dissatisfied and God's action remains strange. But the whole action is changed if the sufferer be God Himself become man for the love of men, and if the divine love be so responsive to human demands that God "empties Himself," becoming truly a man. This Son of Man is not a substitute; the assumption of manhood makes Him one with all the guilty, as their representative, their head and perfection and the principle of a new life. Love dominates the whole proceeding, making it unfold a whole new train of divine events. Love identifies the Lord of life with a race which by its refusal and pride had checked the movement of man into a life of absolute truth and goodness. This incarnate Love works out the fatal choice of man, takes all that we have decided to be and expresses it once for all in a cosmic act which sums up the results of our conduct. Each man, we are told, slays the thing he loves, and the better self which God has offered us takes shape in the figure on a cross. But before this shattering spectacle can reduce us to the despair of an Othello, the eye of faith bids us see that it is divine love which is suffering and that this divine love by that very act of self-sacrifice has lifted us into union with itself.

This is the last stage of the mystery. "But God (who is rich in mercy) for his exceeding charity wherewith he loved us even when we were dead in sins, hath quickened us together with Christ." That is to say that just as the death of the God-Man was a representative act, incorporating in it all that we have and are — no mere substitution but identification — so the victory in death, the splendour surrounding the divine humility and love, belongs to all those who now accept this new divine offer. That this is no fanciful interpretation the words of the greatest theologians set forth in their own quiet technical language will show. By the Passion man learns how much God loves man; and by it he is incited to that return of love in which the perfection of our human salvation consists. . . . Secondly, because by it he gave us an example of obedience, humility, constancy, justice and the other virtues displayed in the Passion. . . . Thirdly, because Christ by his Passion not only freed man from sin but merited for him justifying grace and the glory of beatitude as will be explained later. . . .

What that explanation is the simplest Christian child knows, namely, that in the words of the Fourth Gospel, "he came unto his own and his own received him not, but to as many as received him he gave power to be the sons of God." The divine life which was Christ's by natural right he confers on all who become his members and accept his grace. To develop this further would be to begin the theology of grace, and many may be familiar with it or at least think that they know its main assertions. Sufficient therefore will it be to suggest this way of approaching the subject, so often misunderstood, of Catholic teaching. This, at any rate, ought to be clear, that the surface meaning of the Atonement is only a hint of the depths which lie beneath, and if we wish for a clue to the marvellous story of Christ we must begin by remembering that He has lowered Himself to our level and that it is by starting there that we shall be most likely to reach onwards to the inner significance of His life.

I recall this hint for two reasons. The first is that only by such means does it seem possible that a religion could be universal, and the second that by bearing it in mind we shall be able to see the injustice of the criticism which has been brought against Christianity by those who would fly higher. Few of us stop to consider how almost impossible it would appear that a religion should be pure and exalted and at the same time universal. Nevertheless, the difficulty is obvious and has made itself felt fatally in almost all if not all religions except Christianity. As all know the Hindoo belief as developed by its sages is lofty and profound, though to many of us it loses itself in the sands of speculation. On the other hand, the popular cult is accompanied by much that is abhorrent and seems to be a dissolute counterfeit of the inner teaching, and what holds true of this eastern religion is paralleled in the worship of Greece and Rome. The populace and the elite will never agree in their tastes, and whereas the man in the street or in the fields is quickened only by imagery and by an appeal to his emotions, the student and the recluse prefer to discard what they call the deceptive trappings of sense. God who wills the salvation of all men would, it seems, be forced, too, to make the way easy if He is to take into consideration the childishness of so many and the sensual and selfish inclinations of the majority of the human race. And yet if He were to act on this plea how could He face the criticism which would immediately arise to the effect that God's ideal for man is not even as noble as what human beings have been able to invent for themselves? We can then imagine the dilemma of God: either I announce an ideal which is worthy of its divine author, and then I must make it so exalted and arduous that only the few will be able to attempt it, or I must take into account the weakness of the multitudes and ordain a rule of life so easy that it will fall short of the best which man himself can conceive and be unworthy of Me. Moreover, if this ideal is to be universal it must be capable of translation into the idiom of countless races in every age with their changing tastes and desires, their varying cultures and philosophies. The South Sea Islander worshiping before his wooden idol is to have the same religion as the admirer of Hegel, and the girl behind the counter in Woolworth's as Oscar Wildes and Cézannes. Truly, as the prophet said, the wolf is to lie down with the lamb! Thus we are to have a religion which is so graded that without loss to its integrity it can appeal to every type of man, the simple and the profound, the barbarian and the sophisticated, the introvert and the extrovert, the matter-of-fact and the romantic, the conventional and the odd, those who have to see before they can think and those who prefer to think before they will see.

Moreover, this religion must have no chinks in its armour; it must be armed cap-à-pie. This means that it must be the last word in truth and at the same time open out infinite vistas for the mystics to see and rejoice thereat, and in addition it must gather all, these mystics included, into a unity which in its mutual love and singleness of purpose will surpass that of any family gathering. And as if this were not already too much the beauty and truth of that religion must float like a visible banner before all and be capable of transformation into vivid, coloured, sensuous form. A religion which neglects the senses is doomed to failure for the simple reason that men and women in all the major concerns of life, whether it be lovemaking or the formation of city and community life, are stirred by what they can see and feel and touch. A reasoned philosophy without any condiment can never be a universal religion; a revivalist appeal which depends mainly on the emotions dies almost as soon as it is born; the mystic who sings outside all choruses cannot command a company, and the meistersingers who prefer custom and rule to any new inspiration and rely on organization as an end in itself suffocate others and are in time suffocated themselves.

I know of only one religion which even remotely approaches the demands just laid down, and that is the Christian religion. Were this the occasion to make a defence of it I should spend some time trying to show how closely knitted together are the three requisites just named. It is intellectual, in this sense at least, that it never leaves its dogmas covered with wool; it sets them forth and tries to show in theological language taken from the best thought in the world that they are the product of a supreme wisdom and logically flawless. The insistence which this religion places on the truth inscribed in dogma does not prevent it, nevertheless from giving full scope for the mystics who have ever abounded within it, and these dogmas are translated into ever-varying and coloured symbols and rites, which are controlled by the truth to be expressed; and, lastly, the abstractions of the intellect are made living in the Word made flesh, Divinity made visible in the form of a man who was seen and touched. It is in Christ and by Christ that all which otherwise might have seemed impossible is accomplished, and just because He is a man as well as God, able to speak in a human language which nevertheless draws from the unsoundable riches of eternity, His message of truth is not checked by time or space by undue learning or undue simplicity, by changes in custom and culture, by love of the visible image or love of the invisible. If Christ be God, then it is possible for God to manifest Himself through the veil of flesh, and it follows that the highest truth too can be so shaded for the childish mind of man that it can be at the disposal of all. One condition is required, that the sensuous devotions, the emotional appeals, the imagery and the pageantry and all that goes to aid the half-paralysed intellect to raise itself to the spiritual should be controlled by dogma. If once these various mediums become detached from the truth they are there to exhibit, then the images rapidly become idols and the devotion superstition.

Another way of putting this distinction of Christianity is to say that it alone can concentrate and forward life. Christ said that He came to give life and that more abundantly, and however difficult it may be to define what we mean by life, there can be no doubt that all else, thought, artistic or mystic experience, happiness, are to be judged by its increase. We cannot by taking thought add one cubit to our stature, and neither story nor the best thought-out philosophy or conversation can serve as an adequate deputy. That is the reason why people tire of speculation and taking things at second-hand. The life which is ours is manifested in our instincts and in our longings, and it includes all, every part of us, in its growth. This growth is what concerns each one of us individually, and we know not what we are and what we may become. The God we can conceive of must draw near and touch us by His presence. He must be to us not what a cold idea is dwelling in the mind, not the *Deus absconditus* but a God of love who gives increase to our elfin love and life. Such a visitant takes us by surprise and sweeps aside our protestations of strength or weakness in order to envelop both in His understanding of what we are. As Pascal has said, there are two schools of supposed wisdom which would feed the soul and end by leaving it famished and dying; "the one knowing man's duties and ignoring his helplessness, is lost in presumption, whilst the other, knowing his helplessness and not his duty, falls into cowardice. . . . " Neither of these can give life, and I quote these words of Pascal because they illustrate the error of all those who have been mentioned as proposing a more excellent way than that of Christianity.

I have said that the second reason for starting with the "Emptying" or humility of Christ was that it helped us to see the errors of those who proposed this more excellent way. It might be said that their errors can be marked down without any preliminary fuss, and I admit readily that most of the alternatives to the Christian ideal do turn out, when scrutinized carefully, to be vague and mystagogic. They tend to rely on some new power within us, some new experience which draws back the curtains of a dark, undefined mystery. This is the fate of those who would escape all charted regions. They are hypnotized by the night in which all cows are black. The odd result is that one can never tell whether the new heaven and the new experience are at the lowest or highest end of the scale of the values we are accustomed to recognize. It used to be said of an interpretation of Hegel that it left one in doubt whether his system was pure materialism or pure idealism, and that it could not matter as the two were only different sides of one another. The economic materialist has, as we know, made up his mind quite clearly what Hegel ought to have meant. Our great English thinker, Bradley, was also forced to describe the all-embracing experience which consummated life in terms of sensation, and Bergson, having given the cold shoulder to reason, is never able to free his readers from the uncertainty whether "intuition" means a swoon into ecstasy or into unconsciousness. And if the professional philosophers are at a loss, we need not wonder if the literary prophets of the day, like D. H. Lawrence and Middleton Murry, dash from one inconsistency to another.

This is true, and the blindness which their "seeing" has brought upon them might be used as an argument for the old orthodoxy and an illustration of the old belief that no one can presume to look on God and go unscathed. The fact, however, that at various times thinkers and prophets have arisen to tell us of some new and mystic way to happiness seems to imply that they must have had some, at any rate, apparent reason for their belief. And I do not think that we have far to seek for this reason. It is given to us by Brewster and it has been one of the recurrent complaints of man. When we try to map out the spiritual heavens and penetrate into the secret of nature, we find ourselves baffled by the very weapons upon which we had at first merrily relied. We are like a boy who tries to reproduce all the rich coloured life of the countryside with the aid of a pencil or charcoal alone. Our thought seems to be limited by our own weakness, to be an expression of ourselves more than it is of the universe, and so it is that the imaginative artist despises dull reason, that Bergson dismisses it as a mere dummy in a shop window, and the mystic longs to be one with what is around him and above him and to throb in unison with its rhythms and pulsations. They would cast the slough of the reason and get rid of their discontent. Here Lawrence and Modernists of a certain variety join forces and make an odd company; the latter fall back on a religious experience which steeps them, as Thetis protected Achilles, against the assaults of science and its rationalists; and Lawrence longed for a "mystery, the reality of that which can never be known, vital, sensual reality that can never be transmuted into mind content, but remains outside, living body of darkness and silence and subtlety, the mystic body of reality."

Joined by this magic experience is a longing for invulnerability. The here of The Fountain would at all costs reach this happy state and so live beyond good and evil as we divide them, beyond the familiar world of love and hate, excitement and disappointment. It is interesting to recall that some of the quietists in the seventeenth century taught that those who arrived at the stage of perfect quietude could no longer sin at all and that consequently they were free to do what they liked. This illusion, for such I must call it, is not as uncommon as might be expected, and it appears in the illuminism of several sects. It is noteworthy because it is so akin in spirit to the dream of invulnerability, the state of perfection in which one is so master of oneself that nothing can disturb the peace of the soul. Put this unperturbed state and the occult, esoteric experience together and we have the complete contrast with that of the Christian ideal. The language of both may have at times a similar sound, but the meanings intended diverge utterly.

Why then is this alternative so persuasive to many? I have already suggested the answer in mentioning the discontent so many feel at the results achieved by our normal faculties. Is this discontent legitimate? As the Christian saints have been conspicuous for a certain discontent, and as one of the greatest of them has enshrined this attitude in the ever-memorable words, "Thou hast made us for Thyself, and our hearts are uneasy until they shall rest in Thee," it might seem that we should have to answer in the affirmative. Yes, the answer is in the affirmative, but there is one mighty and decisive condition, and it is this condition which is not observed by all those of whom I have written. It is recorded in the principle already stated that God has accommodated His love and His atonement to man and while so handicapping Himself and His power has nevertheless gained His end. It is we, let me repeat, who disturbed the even motion of God's love at the beginning, and it is we who by our desires expressed what we are in the crucifixion of love. We thereby determined how we must proceed if we would be perfect. "The servant is not greater than his master," and if we humiliated God we must have been dishonest and dishonourable, the kind of people who are capable of tearing up promises as scraps of paper, of bestowing the Judas kiss. No wonder the precursor of Christ demanded a change of heart, that the rough ways should be made smooth and the crooked ways straight! The decisive condition, therefore, is that we should first recognize the truth about ourselves, and that, in other words, is the recognition of the need, not as Brewster thought for an auto-da fé of ourselves, but for the virtue of humility.

To consider the ideal of life in the light of this principle of humility is as sure a path to truth as it is to holiness within one. Everything will be found to fit into place. We have the reason why the human character, as we know it in ourselves and in history, can be nicknamed Tantalus. He is for ever tantalized by a vision of greatness which he never achieves. There is in man a divorce between what he should do and what he does, between the vision and the reality, and even within the vision between the glimpses of a land flowing with plenty and the arid desert of his philosophy of it. He is like a deserted lover who was never meant to live alone and beguiles himself for a time with self-love. The story which Christianity puts at the beginning is precisely a choice between the divine love and this self-love, and it explains all that happens subsequently by the doom of a foolish and fatal choice. As man has so mistakenly exaggerated his own worth and determined to rely on himself, God takes man at his word and leaves him to discover by bitter experience that it is not good to be alone and that human dignity despoiled of the supernal love which integrates and elevates it falls apart in an interior conflict, in a scission of concupiscence and duty. The remedy is again humility. God who has taken man at his word and delivered him to his desires now works to his good through those desires. He becomes flesh and blood, "humbles himself, taking the form of a servant," and still obedient to the will of man He is taken outside a city and made into a figure of shame. But because He has so identified Himself with man, His love and His humility become man's propitiation and a new way is opened to the highest of all ideals, union with God. The tree of life was from henceforth to be the tree of Golgotha, and the new message is given in the words from a modern and intensely Christian poem:

I tell you naught for your comfort,
Yea, naught for your desire,
Save that the sky grows darker yet
And the sea rises higher.

Quick-seeing poets like Blake have told us that we can hold infinite space in the palm of our hand. This glimpse of a great truth has however seldom, outside Christianity, been recognized in its universal application. The Christian religion, having the example of its Master before it, assures man that he must begin with littleness if he is to reach infinity, and that the best illustration of littleness is himself. The modern substitutes all ignore that littleness and rely on something which never belonged to man at all; they cry for the moon of ecstasy and complete happiness and they invent a mysterious power to get them what they want. That power is not theirs for the having for the reason that it does not exist. They would spring out of their skin by their own strength and with the same spring reach Nirvana. We all know that the name given to unholy dealings with supernatural forces is black magic, and though pseudo-mysticism does not deserve so bad a name as that, it is of the same family type. The Christian practice is so normal and history has proved it to be life-giving. We must begin with what we are, no matter whether the method prove dull or humiliating. It is, at any rate, common in the sense that it is not reserved for a clique, for "the heaviest hind may easily come silently and suddenly upon me in a lane." Nor need it be dull because our thoughts about the inmost wonder of the universe must be clothed in a language which appears inadequate. The Brewsters and the Middleton Murrys would throw away that thought; the Christian takes it humbly as crumbs at least from the table, and as he tries to profit by what he is given he comes gradually to discover that thought and reason are not to be despised; that there is a connection running up from what is our best to the ideal beyond all ideals; the reason wherewith we have worked as with a talent put at our disposal turns out to be the coinage of God. It is marked with the superscription of truth and goodness, however faint the impression of the latter may be.

CHAPTER VI

LOVE AND THE SELF*

He gave man his desire but sent therewith
　　a lean heart.
Nothing but men of all unvenomed things
Doth work upon itself with inborn stings.
　　　　　　　　　　　　—J. Donne

　That is to say, genius is the power of leaving one's own interests, wishes and aims entirely out of sight; thus of entirely renouncing one's own personality for a time, so as to remain pure knowing subject, clear vision of the world ...
　　　　　　　　　　— Schopenhauer

　All originality is an eaglet which breaks through its shell only in the sublime and fulminating atmosphere of Sinai.
　　　　　　　　　　— Louis Bertrand

IT IS now time to examine more closely the meaning of some of the principal ideas, which have so far been used, ideas such as those of the self, of love and the relation between love and thought, anima and animus. All men have some understanding of what love and the self mean by themselves, though it is not easy to analyse their meaning and free it from ragged edges. The advantage of keeping to literature and common speech in using such ideas is that we are always in touch with the best of all crucibles, experience. Experience does not allow a gross lie to have a long life; it challenges it with constant contradiction. The philosopher, on the other hand, may invent meanings and receive an imprimatur from fellow thinkers; even the scientist, in so far as he separates his branch of study from contact with other branches or general experience, is not so well off as the man who has to live what he knows and test it in everyday experience. Now the notions of love and of the self are universal, and most must have a fair idea of what they mean because they have their own experience to guide them and a long heritage of common

sense and wisdom. All that philosophy can do is to remove ambiguities and so clarify the ideas that arguments drawn from them work together to form a wider and higher conception of the meaning of life.

　In distinguishing living things from non-living we are aware of what may be called an embryonic selfhood in them. That is to say, we realize that they are growing of themselves and by their own effort. There is the beginning of a new unity and inner life, for which the word growth is often used. Most on reflection would say that there is no need to postulate anything beyond the life of the bodily organism to explain what happens. The bodily metabolism, the reflex actions, the instincts and impulses, the formation of habits, the life of the senses, all proceed within a determined end, which is specific and limited and transitory. We can speak of an organic unity and even of individual characteristics, but only by metaphor, of a person. That is to say, the self of an animal has not come into its own kingdom; it cannot take charge of its own being and appoint its own objectives, weigh them, reckon its own powers by reference to its past and its future hopes, retire behind its desires and activities to a deeper self, which has its scouts and patrols in thought and conscience, and suffers loss or gain in all experience. Selfhood, at least, means this, and in the world we know it is the prerogative of human beings alone. Man has been called a tool-bearing animal, but he is far more than this; he has a power to mirror himself and to mirror within himself the length and breadth of reality, and he can stand off from his impulses and thoughts and guide them in a direction which he himself chooses. Moreover, one part of himself, and that the most intimate, does not belong to anything, being or power in the world. There he knows himself morally, and not physically, subject to an absolute, a subjection which is first discerned in the duty of keeping his word, saying what is true and

*D'Arcy, M. C., S.J., *The Mind and Heart of Love* (London: Faber and Faber, Ltd., 1914), pp. 156–168.

choosing what is right. It is on these grounds he claims to be regarded as a moral person with rights and duties, a self in the full and proper sense of the word.

As sharing a body with the animals and possessing mind and a rational will man begins a new order. What is animal will not be destroyed but taken up into the life of the unified self. Freud tends to ignore the new setting in which the instincts and desires are grouped, and even Jung argues as if the spiritual self were only a voyager out of the racial self, who must return to seek health there when he grows impoverished. Taking facts at their surface value they argue that there are several selves, egos and super-egos and ids, but in fact in their very explanation they presuppose a fundamental unity, only they ignore it or misunderstand it. It is true that neither consciousness nor self-consciousness sums up what is meant by being a self and a person; the mind which thinks, the will which is desire in action, are activities of the same self which animates the body. One does not work without the other in this life, and the thoughts which I think, the hopes I have, the memories I cherish, the habits I have grown into, the aches and disappointments, the physical and spiritual scars, are mine in a sense which they can never be to any other. I am their owner, the only being who has suffered them or enjoyed them in the past, who is conscious of that past as being present to me now and to no one else as both past and present; and who now can make them work together to the fulfillment of my personal destiny.

If then the self has an inseparable unity which takes in all the phases of it which we see in the mirror of consciousness, all our desires and what has been called the unconscious, it embraces the animus and the anima and must be sharply distinguished from the ego or empirical self or the other limited meanings assigned to it by many modern psychologists. Much, however, of what they say can be admitted provided that we do not swear by their assumptions and hypotheses. Much, too, can be left open for free speculation so long as that speculation does not impair the integrity of the self.

There are some, for instance, who believe in what has been called, 'the fine point of the soul'. Mystics sometimes refer to this; they seem to feel that in their experience it is as if spiritual fingers had felt their way right down into the depths of the soul and touched a last nerve, which was more tender and alive than any other part of themselves. Here is the lair of their individuality, what has made them to be distinct from all others and most responsive to the touch of their God and Lover. If this be so, the Anima, as for instance as she appears in Claudel's parable, could very rightly be said to stand for this Cinderella, who dwells in the most inner recess of the self, the work-a-day maid who is also the sleeping princess of the fairy tale and most inaccessible to vulgar reporting. Some, dropping the imagery, have recourse to a theory of the self as an hypostatized longing, a love-dynamism with multitudinous desires all flowing out from one ultimate blindfold longing, which is only enlightened when the other desires have been purified or negated and God graces it by His presence and love. Or, again, we may use a favourite distinction of the philosophers, to which we shall have to return later, between essence and existence. All the contents of my being, as human, are common to other human beings. A scientist cataloguing human nature can refer to Tom, Dick or Harry indifferently; they all serve his purpose, because as examples of human nature they are all alike. But Tom as a living, existing being can never be the same as Dick or Harry, and it is this positive and singular perfection of Tom, this having a life and existence of his own, which makes him address other persons as 'Thou' and not as 'It', and give loving homage to God. Still another view has been expressed by the poet, Gerard Hopkins, among others. The version of it, however, by Hopkins is little known and is of such a rare quality that it deserves a special notice.

He starts with the customary, scholastic definition of a person, which is taken from Boethius. A person is 'the individual substance of a rational nature.' In this definition Hopkins distinguishes the self, which is the individual substance, from the nature with which it is clothed or 'overlaid'. A 'self is the intrinsic oneness of a thing', and to bring out, as I think, the importance he attaches to the word 'intrinsic', he sharply separates off the self from those broken fragments of things, like a branch or log of wood, or artificial unities, such as a billiard ball. Both the billiard ball and the branch have an independent existence; they are separate from other things and exist by themselves. But they are not true selves, for their unity is accidental and there is no positive individual character in a billiard ball which makes one different from another. (The very fact that superstitious people do sometimes attribute to a favourite golf ball or a lucky penny a peculiar, intrinsic quality brings out Hopkins' point.) A true self like a baby has a determinate character from the beginning. It is not an artificial unity; it does not result from anything else; it is not completely indifferent, a neutral, which gets all its positive character from the nature of which it is the individual component. Hopkins insists that this self must be prior to all determination, and even before it exists the bare self must be positive and intrinsically different from every other self. 'A bare self, to which no nature has yet been added, which is not yet clothed in or overlaid with a nature, is indeed nothing, a Zero, in the score or account of existence, but as possible it is positive, like a positive infinitesimal, and intrinsically different from every other self.'

In asserting that the self is positive even before it exists Hopkins, as must be observed, separates himself off from those above mentioned who connect up personality with a human being's existence as contrasted with his nature or essence. He argues that the facts cannot be explained satisfactorily in any other way. Suppose, he says, that there are various natures A and B and Y and Z and various selves a and b and y and z. Now if a and b and y are all capable of receiving any of the natures mentioned, and, in fact, we get the combination aA, bA, and yZ, these combinations must be quite arbitrary 'or absolute facts not depending on any essential rela-

tion between a and A, b and A . . . but on the will of the Creator.' Further, a and b are in the same nature A. But a uses it well and is saved, b ill and is damned: these are two facts, two fates, not depending on the relation between a and b on the one hand and A on the other. Now as the difference of the facts or fates does not depend on A, which is the same for both, it must depend on a and b. So that selves are from the first intrinsically different.'

This argument is clear enough, if we keep in mind that he is writing of human nature. An example from a nature below the human will not do. Let us take the example of bird nature to stand for A and two eggs or chicks to stand for a and b. The chicks have both the same nature; that nature, therefore, cannot be responsible for the different lives or fates of the two chicks. The difference must come from the individual and positive differences in the two chicks. But Hopkins does not believe that they have real selfhood. 'Two eggs precisely alike, two birds precisely alike, will behave precisely alike; if they had been exchanged no difference would have been made.' (To prevent a possible objection it should be noticed that Hopkins is not saying that all eggs or all chicks are exactly alike. In wartime we know only too well that eggs are not all alike. His point is that if you start two human beings from scratch they will not breast the tape together, whereas two chicks, from two identical eggs would always be identical.) Only in human beings is the self unique and able to differentiate itself from all other selves. The nature which is ours as human beings 'supplies the exercise', the self supplies the determination. In other words, two eggs are not free, and therefore they are determined by their nature; but a human being is free and so he is always determining himself — and for that freedom to have any meaning the self must, so to speak, have its own say, must contribute something which is peculiarly its own. This kind of freedom Hopkins calls freedom of pitch, and he distinguishes it from freedom of play which is attributable to the nature.

But what is the relation of this freedom of pitch, which belongs to the self, to the personality? Hopkins has declared that the self, *quâ* self, is prior to nature; it is not merely a cipher, the instance of a universal or nature with which the scientist likes to deal. His objection to the scientific account, necessary as it is in its place, as a complete statement, is that then personality would be unimportant and men and women no more different from one another than two pins or peas. Each self must be positive and unique even prior to its being clothed in a nature. But is this self prior also to freedom of pitch? No, he says, that cannot be, for if there 'were something prior even to pitch, of which that pitch would itself be the pitch, then we could suppose that that, like everything else, was subject to God's will and could be pitched, could be determined, this way or that. But this is really saying that a thing is and is not itself, is and is not *A,* is and is not.' The pitch or inclination, the personal way of behaving must be identified with the self or else we should have a process going on *ad infinitum,* the pitch being the pitch of something which itself must have a pitch. Therefore, the self, even in the stage of possibility, before it has become united with the nature so as to be a full existing human person, is positive precisely as having 'pitch, moral pitch, determination of right and wrong.' This pitch is present when nature is added, and then we have freedom of exercise as well. The personal self is presented with a choice; just because it has a self and a pitch it is always inclined towards one of the alternatives, but as it has now a nature it can be so far indifferent as to choose one or the other, and this exercise of freedom is what Hopkins means by freedom of play — and also by a third kind of freedom which he now introduces, that of field. This freedom of field completes his analysis of self and person, and fortunately he gives several examples to illustrate the difference between his three freedoms. That of field, as the word denotes, refers to the field of operation, or choice; that of play is in the execution, and that of pitch in self-determination. 'Thus it is freedom of play to be free of some benevolent man's purse, to have access to it at your will; it is freedom of pitch to be

allowed to take from it what you want, not to be limited by conditions of his imposing; it is freedom of field to find there *more than one coin to choose from.* Or it is freedom of pitch to be able to choose for yourself which of several doors you will go in by; it is freedom of play to go unhindered to it and through the one you choose; but suppose all were false doors or locked but the very one you happened to choose and you do not know it, there is here wanting freedom of field.' All these three freedoms should belong to us in our human and earthly condition, but for the perfection of the self only one is essentially required, and that is freedom of pitch. It is this which belongs most intimately to the self, and the more perfect the personality the less may any other freedom be needed. Choice in the sense of taking one alternative and leaving another implies some imperfection when the choice is between good and evil. There is no field or evil open to one who loves truly, and for this reason theologians teach that God could never have that kind of freedom of field, nor any field where love of Himself is concerned. God's freedom is the perfection of that which is called pitch, and it is true freedom, indeed the plenary freedom. 'It is choice as when in English we say "because I choose", which means no more than (and with precision does mean) I instress my will to so-and-so. And this freedom and no other, no freedom of field, the divine will has towards its own necessary acts. And no freedom is more perfect; for freedom of field is only an accident.' Hopkins's next words sum up his doctrine of self and this freedom of pitch and show what exactly he meant by person or self as opposed to merely artificial and independent or merely natural units. 'So also *pitch* is ultimately simple positiveness, that by which being differs from and is more than nothingness and not-being, and it is with precision expressed by the English *do* (the simple auxiliary), which we employ or emphasize, as "he said it, he did say it", we do not mean that the fact is any more a fact but that we the more state it. . . . So that this pitch might be expressed, if it were good English, the *doing*be, the *doing*choose, the *doing* so-and-so in that sense. Where there was no question of will it would become mere fact; where there is will it is free action, moral action. And such "doing-be", and the thread or chain of such pitches or "doing-be's", prior to nature's being overlaid, is self, personality; but it is not truly self: self or personality then truly comes into being when the self, the person, comes into being with the accession of nature.'

Hopkins seems to think that this self which he has with such diligence unearthed is identical with what Duns Scotus, a thinker he much admired, meant by the 'haecceitas', the 'thisness', which constitutes the inner core of personality. The better-known theories of the self do not allow for this special, positive selfhood which is prior to nature. The upholders of them maintain that human personality can be adequately explained without recourse to this 'infinitesimal.' They, too, do however make a distinction between the individual or person and the nature sufficient to justify the distinctions employed in preceding chapters between two forms of love such as Eros and Agape and that of anima and animus. It does not matter essentially what view of the self is held so long as these distinctions are seen not to be arbitrary but to have a true ground. Nevertheless, a view which explicitly demands a sharp distinction and throws light on it is of interest, and that is why it is well worth while mastering the theory which Hopkins has so carefully thought out, or else adopting one of the views which have been given above. Common sense, joined to some knowledge of the great movements of love as shown in history or recorded in prose or poetry, can find the right answer. But there are behind the answer such great issues connected with man's destiny, his relation to others and to God, that in the following pages the solution will have to take on more and more philosophical character.

Whatever view we take it is clear that the self is more than mere consciousness or even self-consciousness. The self has the power of thinking and , willing; it is real and alive even when it is asleep or robbed by illness or immaturity of thinking; it is independent and unique and has rights and duties. All indeed that is human in us, and that is everything, is of and from and by the self. Some would hold, however, that when we have enumerated the attributes of a human being we have no need to go further to find a self beyond these. The self will be the permanent and subsistent source and unity of all the movements of the body and mind, though it will be expressed more representatively in those higher movements, such as thought and will, which are exclusively human. If that is so, the anima will be this determining form, or again the form or soul with the one exception of the reason, or again the soul at its highest (which could serve as the 'fine point of the soul'), or, lastly, the massed and cryptic potentialities of the self, be they noble or ignoble. Our impressions of human nature do correspond with these divisions. We think of men as able thinkers but without an interesting personality, but at the same time, while we distinguish character from intelligence, intellect and will are the marks of a great personality. And often enough we are in doubt because we feel that there are latent powers in a man which may prove his making or undoing. By means of animus and anima we are able to link together these various aspects of the self.

These distinctions, however, within the self though real must not be so exaggerated as to cause us to lose sight of the radical unity of that self. The caution cannot be too often repeated. It is our misfortune that the divisions we are forced to make are too easily translated into a series of private properties, each with sharp and fast boundaries. We talk of the eye seeing, the mind thinking and the will acting and deciding, and worse still, of the unconscious influencing us; but really it is the self which has eyes and a mind and a will that is the subject of seeing and thinking and willing. Nor can we separate the various powers and activities of the self off from one another so sharply as we should like. Our very instincts and senses are impregnated with soul and thought, and will overlap in a most confusing way. The picture we form of ourselves is convenient, but misleading; it is usually oversimplified and too rigid. The self is set behind or below its different powers; it is supposed to manipulate the body and to delegate its authority to the senses or the mind; it is at one moment confounded with self-consciousness, but on other occasions it is enthroned behind or hidden in the dark cellars of the unconsciousness. The poet shows that the self is living vividly in the imagination, the artist has his soul in his finger tips, the conscious and the 'unconscious' are in constant correspondence, and the mind is a blank without some interest to quicken it, and the will cannot be itself a spiritual power unless in some sense it is itself or, through its intimacy with the soul, awake and aware.

The self, therefore, however retiring a part it may seem to play in many books of psychology, is necessarily the key to all the works of man. Even what is called the 'unconscious' seems to have been dangerously separated off from it. Freud and Jung and Adler and many others have done valuable service in showing us the influence of the non-rational factors of the personality in life. But their theories are defective because of the lack of proper consideration of the self. The various *fonctionnaires,* the policeman, the dissident parties which they have to create for the unconscious realm in order to make it intelligible are at best what Eddington would call in another context, pointer readings. Having been deprived of consciousness they are often reinvested with conscious authority, and their phantom existence usurps the place of real, conscious experience. That is not to say that they have no true message. Perhaps we understate the all-pervading influence of the self which is ours. For a long period psychologists confused it with the mind or the self given in self-consciousness. They seem now to have rebounded from the manifest inadequacy of this idea to a conception of the self which makes it almost totally unconscious. It becomes a materialistic poltergeist. To correct this it would be well to re-emphasize the spiritual nature of the self. Whatever else we may say about it is at least the originator and owner of those activities of mind and will which prove it to be of the spiritual order, and therefore above any materialistic or organic explanation. We do not take this fact of the spirituality of the self sufficiently seriously and press it to its logical conclusions. We are content to admit that in mind we have a power which is immaterial in its essence and commit the rest of the self to the nether regions of matter or organic life. But the unity of the self precludes this and if spirit cannot abdicate and accept an inferior status, we ought to be able to perceive spirit in all that is not completely impervious to its operation. Now we know that much happens in the so-called unconscious which is different from the conscious operations of the reason, and we have enough evidence to conclude that the seeing and hearing, for example, of a human being, the gestalt and the general impression, the fancy and the memory are very different from those which belong to an animal. If this be so, then we can suppose that the soul is alive and operating in all the activities of man, which permit of it, that it makes sensation and feeling protoplastic of mind, turns sight into perception and imagery into imagination, and at times of stress, when its life is threatened or it is full of expectancy of meeting the longed-for Unknown, it even dispenses with normal channels of communication, it makes contact by secret signs, and tokens and telepathy and ecstasy and the beating of the heart. Its relation with the various powers works according to the Communist formula: from each according to his capacity and to each according to his needs. The sensitive and psycho-physical faculties and impulses determine the kind of way the self can work in and through them, and it has to keep step with their capacities and answer to their needs. This holds true even of the mind and will. The mind of man is a function with a definite end, and in interests of the self are to that extent forwarded by it. But as we all know the mind can be an embarrassment; its aim is pretentious, but its bag is disappointing; it has to paralyse the living reality before it can make it its own; philosophy is not the warmest of professions, though its object be truth. The self is deeply implicated in its thinking, but it is more than its thought, and its deepest desires reach beyond it. The will, too, which seems so intimately personal, is so often rebellious and confuses the self by bursting, like a rocket, into a number of divergent desires. Owing no doubt to Original Sin, the self has to spend its time bringing order into its desires, instead of being able to discover and concentrate upon what is the true desire of its heart.

The self, then, works in and· through its various powers, but just because each of them has its own special virtue and perspicacity, it must not be identified with them, and moreover it is troubled because of their very variety and their conflicting appeal and possible domination. The anima is always having to listen to what the reason tells it with intransigeant authority, and if it becomes rebellious it is in grave danger of yielding to the importunate desires, giving up its reason and imperilling its immortal self. The animus, as we have seen, is imperious; it cannot help wanting to grasp reality, to make it its own and so form a body of knowledge. As I have suggested, it is the spiritual and sublimated form of the acquisitive and domineering appetite of the animal; it is the spiritual self acting necessarily to its own best interests, growing to its own perfection, that Eros which Nygren denounced as ego-centrism. The anima, on the other hand, is used to express both this self, and the self with animus left out. As the latter, in its spiritualized and sublimated form, it is the analogue of the yielding, self-sacrificing impulse. As human it is a longing, like to a maid with arms outstretched, expectant and in search for what it may adore. Its only safety, as it would seem, lies in keeping close to animus. No sooner does it part from reason than it begins to sing the song of death and annihilation. At first it is thrilled with the apparent freedom and passes through a period of romance. Such romance, however, feeds on illusion, and as time goes on the anima begins to bend before strange gods and to play with the dark passions until, in the end, it passes into the dark night and succumbs to a wholly irrational craving for oblivion.

I have said that the only seeming way of safety for the anima is to live in close companionship with the animus. But there is another alternative which has been sometimes followed, another turning, to a *terra incerta et invia*. Instead of the descent to the dark regions of the unconscious those who are the priests of this other way call it an ascent through purification and unworldliness to the absolute. In our day Gerald Heard and Aldous Huxley have been active in advocating it, and it has been the immemorial practice of the East. The Dionysiac cult and the mystery religions taught also this mystical way. What judgment should be passed on this mystical flight which takes the anima beyond the understanding of the animus? I do not think that experience or philosophy can give a safe general answer. The reason for this is that we have no means of knowing God's will or man's individual correspondence with grace. Because God is so silent, we are inclined to leave His part out of our explanations, and yet in the final issue all depends upon Him. So far as we can guess, God does work upon souls which have given themselves to this way of self-negation. Whatever the intrinsic value of the choice and of the method, God may make what is deficient good whenever there is a right intention. It may well be, therefore, that many find the true God by becoming initiates of this uncovenanted mysticism. But when this has been said there is need also of caution. No way of life is more open to delusion, and many seem to confuse the means with the end, or, what is worse, to find in the emptiness to which the exercises in self-denial lead a substitute for that supernaturalization of the self and communion with a living and bountiful God. They mistake, that is, a relation which may suit beings other than persons with one between persons. The latter cannot end in any diminishment on either side. A person cannot throw away his unique status and lower himself to a means. He can at most pervert his being, sound its depths and get lost there, and then in the great emptiness enjoy a feeling which may be called atavistic, but is in no sense the glory of a spirit and a person. Nor can the other with whom a person is in love drain out that personality and leave him so crushed as to have no resemblance to himself. Love between persons means that each wants the other to be more himself. Each is unique, and that uniqueness can become so precious that other people may be forgotten or treated merely as servants of that love. In this sense we are jealous for the beloved and long to see the whole world offered up in sacrifice for him or her. And if this be true as between human persons far more is it true in the relation of God to the soul. But so invisible is God and so infinitely removed in point of excellence, that the self is overcome at the comparison and blames its limitations. The only way to find God is by the path of unknowing — and it is here that the danger begins. The spiritual anima has awakened to a life which reason cannot fully understand or supply; it does not want to possess but to give, and in this state of inquietude it is impatient of the golden cage which is what a full human personal life now seems to be. The desire may turn to a frenzy or to a deliberate ascesis; the search is out beyond all that is associated with selfish ambition; and so it may happen that the anima may find methods, a technique for adventuring into immensities and down into abysses without madness; it learns to model itself so as to be receptive of the highest experience a human being can reach, to be in a state of tension and receptivity such that the mystical language used in describing it resembles closely the most authentic divine union. But it does not follow that the divine union has taken place. The language which a genuine mystic uses must always be inadequate; it must give the interior impression, the effect upon the soul rather than a description of the being who has made the impression. He is by nature one whom language cannot describe. It is from indirect evidence and from the context that the acquaintance or reader of the mystic can be fairly sure of the objectivity of the experience. But when the experience is described in terms which seem to exclude a personal God it is possible that the soul has stretched itself out to its highest receptivity and it is this very condition which is being related, as the sound of words can have a magical effect upon the emotions and bring them into accord with their meaning, though the meaning be missed; or as pursed lips can automatically give the response to a note struck. But as the spirit cannot be entirely inactive it sublimates the desire inherent in the anima and conceives itself as lost to itself and fused with some all-comprehensive perfection or Absolute. The grave danger here is that the spirit has borrowed from the lower levels of the anima and, if it be not watchful, it slips down to that level. That this may happen is borne out by the evidence of so much religious experience and the oscillation in many mystery cults and mystical movements between the holy and the obscene, the pure and the savage sacrifice. From the *Varieties of Religious Experience* we have all learnt how easy it is to ape the highest movements and inspiration of the spirit, whether by drugs or suggestion or rhythmical exercises. As sleep gives rest to the body, so can a mood of absorption give repose to the spirit and be mistaken for eternal peace. And there it is, moreover, always the danger of a decline to that animal craving for perpetuity outside its own individual existence, the joy in subjection and belonging to another.

Civilized man tends to build a rampart round his humanity to protect himself from the enemies to his happiness, whether within or without. He likes to be in control, to manage his fate as far as possible, to be a lord within a definite kingdom, however small. In accordance with this desire Coventry Patmore sings of the body as 'creation's crowning good, wall of infinitude.' 'The great immensity of space makes me shudder', said Pascal, and though without the Incarnation the city of man is tiny and closed and may bore and certainly never endures, it is yet a consolation and a protection. This is why the classical ideal never dies, and sets up its tents in the desert and rejects the romantic mirage. Animus and anima come together and form one being. In their unity they are human nature, and they are meant to complement each other. In segregating them and keeping them apart one has to some extent committed oneself to abstractions. They are both movements of the one soul or self; they overlap, and like the intellect and the will belong to each other. There is no mind without interest and no will which is completely blind. Even the mind in its essential activity can be considered as partly passive, though it ends in possessing itself of the object to be known; and the will is active in its desires and the seat of mastery, though it never seeks to possess in the same way as the mind. It is just because they are so blended that we have difficulty in separating out their basic aim, and fail, perhaps, to realize that the possessive mind dictates to the desire what it wants and the desire checks the mind from being totally egocentric. They are, therefore, like the positive and negative, the rise and fall in the rhythm of the body and in the arts; they make up the natural life of the soul; and so long as they are able to play their parts together without frustration or discord they define the humanistic ideal, what Aristotle and many another philosopher would have defined as the happiness of mortal men.

I say 'happiness of mortal men', and there is the rub. Human beings live in time and create civilizations, in which the foolish hope to find an abiding joy. But the joy is mortal and not abiding. Immortality lies elsewhere. Claudel spoke in a parable of the anima having an immortal lover. This it is that enlists our sympathy with the multiform attempts of the anima to play truant to the animus. Firmly as we believe that animus and anima must be reconciled and work harmoniously, it seems that this can only be done if their respective roles are at times changed. The anima must take the lead and the reason be led into a friendly and wise captivity; the egocentric part of man, while surviving, as it must do in all persons, must play second fiddle to the agape of the soul. But is this not to give up all the glory of reason, to relax its control and surrender to the Dionysiac stampede perhaps to the heights, but more likely to the depths? That would indeed be the danger — and has proved in history to be a supreme danger — were there not one chartered way which the anima can take in order to find the true God and the trysting place of divine love. According to the Christian philosophy that way does exist, and it is the way of faith, which, as the definition goes, is an act of the intellect commanded by the will. By this faith the soul commits itself to believe the word of another, the word of God Himself, who has divine news to give. It is the beginning of the new love story, which has its source in the agape of God and the corresponding agape of the soul lifted above itself. Reason remains and is dowered with a new power to help out the anima in its peregrination. There is a darkness to be entered, the darkness of faith and the dark night of the soul, but this darkness is totally unlike the dark passion of romance or the unconscious world of Avernus, to which in the old days it was bidden to descend. It is a darkness which is due to excess of light and neither the human is lost nor the personal. The living God is there, the Shepherd who leads his flock, whose rod and whose staff are there to guide and hold; and the Word made Flesh is 'the truth and the way and the life.'

E. I. WATKIN

(1888–   )

IN 1888 Edwin Ingram Watkin was born at Stand, near Manchester. He attended St. Paul's School and completed his education at New College Oxford with the M.A. degree. Watkin was converted to Catholicism in 1908. He lives a retired life in Norfolk.

Of the many Catholic writers of the late Revival, Watkin is probably the deepest and most important. He has seen, as no other writer of the period, the complete picture of Catholicism with mystical life as its white-hot center and creative core.

The *Philosophy of Mysticism* (Harcourt, 1920), was the first of his important works. In lambent style Watkin analyzes the bases of the mystical life and shows forth its appeal and beauty.

The Bow in the Clouds, one of the *Essays in Order,* enlarged the work of his first volume by explaining under the symbolism of the colours of the rainbow, the immanence of God in all life from the microscopic to the mystical.

In the *Catholic Centre* Watkin explains the proportion and balance of the faith as contrasted with the extremism and lack of balance outside the Church.

With the publication of Catholic *Art and Culture,* Watkin turns from the center of the circle to its periphery. The spirit of the faith is seen molding and informing three cultures: the Romanesque, the springtide of the Church; Gothic, its summer fullness, Baroque, the flamboyance of autumn.

Though Watkins envisages the present age as the winter period of the Church, he sees, just as clearly, the second spring in which the magnificence of Catholic life shall yet inform other cultures until time is no more.

CHAPTER I

THE LITURGY, THE EXPRESSION OF THE CATHOLIC CENTRE*

CHRISTIANITY is often reproached with being a religion of sorrow and life-slaying renunciation. The reaction against this is the secularist insistence on the things of this world, natural and bodily pleasures, the happiness of healthy activity amid beautiful scenes. And in fact Catholic devotion has for centuries emphasized too exclusively the aspect of suffering. Though every altar has fittingly its crucifix, and the church walls are almost covered with the Stations of the Cross, we seldom see representations of the triumphant Christ, the Resurrection and Ascension. Where they are depicted at all, they occupy a subordinate place as panels in a reredos or among the subjects of a stained glass window. The impression received is inevitably that the Passion and generally the sorrowful mysteries are the centre of the Christian religion. In fact, the Liturgy, with its fifty days of Paschal alleluias as against a fortnight of Passiontide, shows the true proportion. The Cross is the way; the Resurrection the goal. The cross is of time; the Resurrection for eternity. And the Cross itself is primarily not the suffering of death, but

the victorious struggle of Life over and through death. Doctrinally and liturgically the central position of the Church is clear. She refuses to blink the fact of suffering and death, and their necessity in a sinful world — facts from which the modern world is trying desperately to turn away its eyes. Nor will she shrink from demanding renunciation, the taking of the Cross. But she does not, like many oriental cults, make renunciation an end in itself. She will not, perversely, value suffering for its own sake, or morbidly fall in love with death. Keeping the *via media* between East and West, optimism and pessimism, the shirking and the cult of pain, she teaches, through her theology and her liturgy, that happiness is man's true good, not sorrow, that he is made, not to suffer but to be happy, and that eternal happiness may, if he will, be his. Also that death is evil, life good, and man destined to life, not death. For Christ came to give abundant life and everlasting life. Thus the Cross, while duly affirmed, is set in its right place in the scheme of salvation.

But, as we have just seen, this is not the case with popular devotion, as evidenced by the adornment of our churches. In the primi-

---

*Watkin, E. I., *The Catholic Centre* (New York: Sheed and Ward, 1939), pp. 7–13.

tive Church popular devotion must have gone to the opposite extreme — perhaps because the Cross was sufficiently preached by the frequent calls to martyrdom. For the crucifix was not permitted, and the idyllic figure of the Good Shepherd dominated Christian iconography. And whereas Easter was kept as early as the Apostolic age, there was as yet no Good Friday.

If the Liturgy were restored to the consciousness of Catholics, its balance would be restored with it, and our churches represent the triumph even more than the Passion of Our Lord.

Akin to this question of suffering and happiness, is the question of bodily health. If we examine the liturgical prayers we shall perhaps be surprised at the emphasis placed upon health: "Grant Thy servants to enjoy constant health of soul and body." Over and over again there recurs a petition for health. Even on Ash Wednesday the ashes of mortification, for all their reminder of death, are blessed, among other purposes, to bestow the health which delays our mortal end. The reception of the Blessed Sacrament is èxpected to promote bodily health, and even the profession of faith in the Blessed Trinity. There is, indeed, a Secret which suggests that obedience to God's moral law will ensure good health: "We beseech Thee, Almighty God, that our sins may be cleansed by this Sacrifice, for then Thou dost bestow upon us true health of mind *and body.*" (Wednesday after Fourth Sunday in Lent.) Moreover, there is the Sacrament of Unction, one of whose objects is to heal. And theologians hold that ill-health was not among the sufferings endured by the Incarnate Word. If He bore our afflictions, He did not literally bear our sicknesses. Evidently the Church believes that a healthy body is the natural concomitant of the healthy soul; that health, not sickness, conduces to a sound spiritual life, whereas physical disease is likely to foster psychological disease. On either side of this centre are two extremes. One is partly represented by a practical valuation of physical fitness above mental and spiritual values. This is the attitude of National Socialism and, to a lesser degree, of Fascism. It is rep-resented most explicitly and completely by Christian Science. Christian Science exaggerates the fact that spiritual integrity, of itself, and *ceteris paribus,* produces physical health —the truth no doubt which the collect just mentioned states — into the obviously false statement that a right spiritual condition inevitably produces bodily health, indeed that disease is unreal, the product of false thinking. And it also exaggerates the fact of spiritual healing, exemplified by recoveries after anointing and by cures at Lourdes, into the demonstrable untruth that every disease is curable by mental treatment. For although even naturally the soul can to a certain extent heal the body, beyond a certain point its power must be increased by a special infusion of supernatural grace to make this possible — as in the cures at Lourdes where, for example, Gabriel Gargam, paralysed and the victim of an incurable gangrene, could be cured only by the powerful infusion of supernatural faith granted him by God, at Mary's intercession, so Catholics believe.

For an excess in the opposite direction, unfortunately we need go no further than popular Catholic spirituality.

Though bodily health is sought at Lourdes, and is generally prayed for, its importance is, or has been till lately, minimised. Holy Communion has not been expected to benefit the health, and even the healing aspect of Unction has been largely lost sight of. Catholics have treated ill-health like other forms of suffering and mortification, ignoring the fact that in view of the intimate union of body and soul, bodily disease must tend to produce some morbid psychical effect. Nor has it entered their minds that holiness in itself tends to good health. They have, on the contrary, associated it rather with sickness. Even the morbid notion of a mystical vocation to illness has taken root, and has in many instances borne practical fruit. St. Lidwine was but one example of these disease victims. It has been forgotten that the supreme Victim was not the victim of ill-health. It may indeed be true, as Baron von Hügel thought, that the tension of mystical life — an extreme supernatural life for which the human organism was not evolved — produces what he termed mystical ill-health from which, in fact, so many of the Saints have suffered. This, however, is not good in itself, but evil, the effect, not of the Divine action in the soul which of itself produces, as at Lourdes, health not disease, but of human weakness. At most, disease can be over-ruled to the profit of the soul. It must not be regarded, as too often it has been, even, I am sorry to say, by St. Bernard, as *of itself* good and spiritually profitable, still less as a direct work and call of God. Catholics should not forget Our Lord's attitude to disease. He said of the paralytic woman that this daughter of Israel had been bound not by God, but by Satan. Is it to be wondered at that so long as Catholics adopt this distorted attitude in respect of disease and health, and do not so much as dream that faith in the Trinity can and should produce health, that Christian Science exaggerates the truth they neglect, into their one-sided and therefore untenable belief which nevertheless, being held with strong conviction, is able in virtue of the truth in it to effect many surprising cures? Yet, as we have seen, all the while the liturgy has taught the full Catholic truth, the *via media* between the popular Catholic view and Christian Science, the exact centre of truth on the relation between health and holiness.

On another question particularly urgent to-day, Catholicism as expressed by the liturgy keeps the *via media* and occupies the centre. It is the relation between the individual and society, between individualism and "sociality," or, if to avoid this barbarism I may be allowed so to style it, "socialism."

An extreme and onesided emphasis on the individual as opposed to society was represented in religion by Protestantism, in politics by traditional Liberalism and its economic expression *laissez faire*. For pure Protestantism the Church is invisible; the visible religious society is without Divine authority or infallible teaching; the individual and his private relations with God, his private salvation, are the substance of Christianity. He is to determine Christian truth by his private interpretation of Scripture and to judge the Church by this private standard. Political Liberalism, largely the product of Protestantism, though rightfully limiting the coercive powers of the state, regarded not only the state but society as an inorganic aggregate of the individuals composing it, a heap of atoms bound together by a purely exterior bond, mutual interests, or a supposed original contract, as an association to achieve some object desired by the associates. And in the economic sphere *laissez faire* expected the conflict of competing individuals, each moved by self-interest, to produce an economic order profitable to the community.

At the other extreme there are Catholics who seem to regard the substance of religion as blind obedience to the clergy, and the refusal to criticise any action they may take. At the same extreme were various state religions of antiquity which consisted exclusively, or almost exclusively, of public ceremonies which were conducted by the official priesthood, sometimes as in ancient Rome, partially identical with the civil authorities, and in which individual religion played no part or at best a very subordinate one.

To-day this extreme of "sociality" is represented by the most complete and massive embodiment it has ever assumed, a manifestation which, though arising in the field of secular politics, has already invaded the sphere of religion. I mean the totalitarian state, whether of National Socialist or Communist complexion, which by its claim to possess the entire man, to be the ultimate authority in every sphere of human life and to be regarded and venerated as the supreme and absolute value, has become the lay church of pseudo-religion. Here the individual has no value as such. He is but the instrument and member of his national society, and his meaning and value are exhausted by. this social relation. The individual is, in short, but a function of society, a subject of the omnipotent state.

Between these extremes of individualism and socialism Catholicism keeps the balance. As Christ's mystical Body, the Church is an organic whole, not simply the aggregate of her members, and the entire religious life of the individual is thus a function of the life of the Church. For it is inspired by the Soul of that social body of Christ, the Holy Spirit, and every act contributes to build up the whole, as the activities of the cell contribute to build up the life of the body. Thus the Catholic Church is not the inorganic society of Liberalism. On the other hand, unlike the totalitarian state, the law of the Church is not imposed from without by the compulsion of force, but freely accepted by the individual conscience. Nor is the individual in his religious life *simply* a function of the Church. For his progressive incorporation into the Church by an increas-

ingly perfect obedience to the law of the Spirit, the organic law of her life, is at the same time his personal sanctification, his progressive union with God, and therefore an increase of his personal good and happiness which are the possession of God. Moreover, the value of the individual, far from being depreciated, receives its highest recognition. For he is treated as an immortal soul whose salvation may not be sacrificed for any society. In fact, the object of the Church is precisely the eternal salvation of her members.

VIOLET*

The Positive Sciences

VIOLET, the first visible colour of the rainbow, represents the knowledge of reality at its lower levels afforded by the physical and biological sciences, that is to say, man's more abstract knowledge of matter and biological life, and union with them — though it is a union which is also separation. All these sciences are based upon the abstraction and analysis by the discursive reason of appropriate data contained in the global intuitions of physical sensation. We cannot, it is true, draw a sharp line of demarcation between scientific abstraction and analysis and the unscientific experience which underlies and precedes formulated science. Only the most rudimentary sensations are pure intuitions of sense. Such, for example, are the sense of light on first awakening from sleep, hearing a noise which might be anything from a thunderclap to the banging of a door, or the apprehension of water by a thirsty traveller. Normally our sense activities, however seemingly instantaneous, include a factor of rational analysis which selects from the complex of sensational significant forms, whereby the object perceived is related to others already known. It is at this point that error may supervene and give rise to false classifications and so called hallucinations of

sense. The sciences do but continue in their more methodical procedure the rudimentary and careless 'science' of unmethodical experience.

Moreover the synthetic achievements of science — indeed the syntheses of ordinary experience — would be impossible without the intervention of a higher faculty or mode of operation, the intellectual intuition which directly apprehends the intelligible forms and values, implicit even in physical and biological reality as the inner principle of its order. Indeed, this intuition plays an important part even in that abstraction of conceptual data upon which the sciences are founded. The soul is one, not manifold; and in normal human knowledge the three epistemological modes — sensible intuition or sensation, discursive and analytic reasoning, spiritual intuition or intellect (aptly so-called, as in truth an 'inward-reading,' *intus legere,* of the significant forms implicit in the more superficial phenomenon) co-operate in varying proportions.

Nevertheless the positive sciences are pre-eminently the work of the analytic and discursive reason. As such they must assume postulates, and can yield no information as to ultimates, e.g., the nature of matter, force, life, mind or the origin and finality of the universe. The remark erroneously said to have been made by Laplace, when asked by Napoleon why in his astronomy he had made

*From: *The Bow in the Clouds,* by E. I. Watkin, by permission of The Macmillan Co., Publishers, New York: 1930, pp. 53–56.

no mention of a Creator — 'I had no need of that hypothesis' — is, therefore, whatever exception may be taken to its tone, excellent science. Astronomy must assume the existence of the sidereal universe. It may indeed trace its history from a state of maximum organisation through successive phases of nebulae, star-clusters and stellar systems to its present condition. And it may even forecast its future development to some hypothetical end of cosmic death. But as to the origin of this evolution or any purpose underlying it astronomy must be silent.

Moreover we must be on our guard against a too hasty acceptance of current scientific hypotheses because they happen to support what is, or is supposed to be, divinely revealed, or more generally to favour religion.

For example, it is tempting to accept as the complete final truth Sir James Jeans's picture of an ageing universe. Does it not bear out the literal truth of that sublime Scripture which contrasts with the eternity of the Word the mortal stars: 'They all shall wax old as doth a garment . . . but Thou art the self-same and Thy years shall not fail'? Perhaps, and yet already Professor Millikan assures us that in the laboratory of interstellar space some process of cosmic chemistry is rejuvenating the universe, which therefore, as far as science can tell us, would seem to have no beginning or end — its life eternally renewed, as cycle follows cycle. Which of these two hypotheses is true only scientific research can decide. Religion and philosophy can await the decision with equanimity. And as for our text — if for the universe as a whole there is no senility — the stars grow old in turn, and the complementary statement, 'like a vesture shalt Thou change them and they shall be changed,' possesses a literal truth which it would not possess under the alternative hypothesis. When in the Middle Ages 'science' as represented by Aristotle appeared to teach the incorruptibility of the heavenly bodies — this indeed in flat contradiction of the Biblical text — Catholic theology did not dispute its verdict in the name of revelation.

Again, Professor Eddington's denial that spatial extension constitutes the essential nature of matter makes it easier to accept St. Thomas's view — essential to his statement of transubstantiation that quantity is not substantial but simply the primary accident of substance. But it would be unwise indeed to regard this as a scientific proof of the Thomistic thesis. Not yet may we hail with a too certain delight the current astronomical hypothesis of a finite universe. A future astronomy may disprove the calculations and arguments by which the universe is at present regarded as a limited, if unimaginably vast, area of time-space. And in any case astronomy can never prove a finite universe. Beyond the universe open to our ken, others may exist cut off from the reach of any human instrument. If we hold the universe to be finite, our only sure ground must be philosophical; the intrinsic self-contradiction of an unlimited creation, a being contingent and relative but nevertheless infinite.

And relativity itself? Here we must carefully distinguish between the relativity of all finite being inherent in its contingence, and at its maximum in the inorganic matter furthest removed from God's Absolute Being — a metaphysical truth established independently of any hypothesis or confirmation by the physical sciences — and relativity as an astronomical hypothesis which may yet be replaced by what I may term with an oxymoron a relative absolutism, that is to say, by the hypothesis that time-space and its measurements are within the physical sphere of reference absolutism. That is to say, by the hypothesis that time-space and its measurements are within the physical sphere of reference absolute, however relative with reference to that spiritual order of which the physical sciences can make no report. Further, we must, if we are to face the facts honestly, admit that the report of physical science is not always so immediately helpful to religion. Astronomy, for example, reveals a universe in which, so far as we can discover, life, and *a fortiori* mind, is confined to a few specks, in an all-but unbounded ocean of inorganic matter. Is this prodigious surplus of blind mechanism, this seemingly purposeless waste, what we should expect in the Creation of Divine Wisdom? No doubt the materialist must face the counter-diffi-culty, why and how, in this ocean of in-organic matter, vital and rational phenomena have made their appearance. But the fact remains that astronomy in its present state does appear to show an unaccountable dys-teleology in the material universe. It may be that spirits can exist where life as we know it cannot.

It may be that solar systems are more fre-quent than science will at present allow. It may be that the measured distances are but relative. Or it may be that God squanders this quasi-infinite waste of matter to show of how little worth are inorganic matter and mere quantity, as compared with life and mind with their qualitative values. In any case, the mind that can measure a universe of matter is self-evidently of greater value than the unintelligent and lifeless vastness it measures.

From all this it is clear that if the physical sciences cannot disprove the data of philoso-phy and religion, they cannot prove them. To look to science to justify and permit reli-gious belief — the attitude of mind that ex-claims with a relieved joy: 'There really is a God, Professor Jeans tells me so; my will is free, Professor Heisenberg detects indeter-minacy among the electrons; I actually can pray, Professor Oliver Lodge has given his sanction' — is not merely undignified and, as we have seen, perilous; it is radically un-philosophical. To base religion on science involves the same illicit extension of the province of the latter as the older rejection of religion as unscientific. Metaphysical rea-soning on the other hand may anticipate a conclusion of physical science.

Relativity, as General Smuts has pointed out in his presidential address to the British Association (1931), 'has replaced the mech-anistic world view' of nineteenth-century sci-ence by 'the mathematician's conception of the universe as a symbolic structure.' But when science was still wholly wedded to mechanism, Newman on metaphysical con-siderations suggested in a sermon preached in 1843 the economic symbolism which has replaced it in the following century. 'What if . . . the laws of physics are themselves

but generalisations of economical exhibitions.' He even concluded almost in the very lan-guage of Professor Whitehead that the Copernican and Ptolemaic astronomies were perhaps mere practical economies, neither true absolutely.

Religion and metaphysics may indeed find in the facts disclosed by science, and even in hypotheses, which however inadequate and incomplete are at least partially true, reflec-tions and analogies of their distinctive truths. And they will always welcome in the results of the sciences a revelation of God's work in the lower plane of His creation. St. Au-gustine, absorbed in the contemplation of God and the soul, would know nothing besides.

"Whoso knoweth both Thee and them (the truths of astronomy) is not the happier for them, but for Thee only. Men go on to search out the hidden powers of nature which to know profits not. Who sees not how content we should be to be ignorant of the hidden mysteries of heaven and earth?" This limita-tion, which defined the province of human thought and interest for centuries to come, was as a temporary restriction invaluable. If the modern preoccupation with the positive sciences and their practical fruits has so largely obscured man's spiritual vision, we can readily understand how disastrous the scientific progress of modern times would have proved before the doctrine of God and the soul, knowledge of the supreme spiritual realities, had been explored by the devotion and speculation of Christian saints and think-ers, and the results securely housed in the teaching and living witness of the Church. Only when that work had been accomplished could physical science develop without blind-ing men entirely to the world of spirit. Even the corresponding restrictions of the temporal and spatial framework of human vision to a universe some six thousand years old, and no more extensive than a compact system of sun, planets and stellar heaven revolving around a central earth was of great service to man's spiritual life and knowledge.

On such an artificially limited stage the mind's eye, which otherwise might have lost itself in those infinites of time and space, whose prospects Pascal would later find so terrific, was concentrated on the supremely important drama of redemption, of man's union, individual and social with God, in a word, his deification. Otherwise, Western thought might have succumbed to the formless pantheism of Indian speculation, whose pendent is the measureless aeons, mahayugas, manvantaras, kalpas, of Hindu and Buddhist cosmology; or, defeated by the material immensities, might have measured the worth of man, not by the intrinsic nobility of his spirit and its capacity for God, but by his physical insignificance. But however salutary this restriction of interest, it could not be and ought not to have been permanent. Knowledge of God and itself once secure, the mind could look directly at the phenomena of physical and biological nature. St. Augustine's argument, if a happy error, was nevertheless fallacious. Could we know God as He is, we should indeed have no need to know creatures as well — not even our own soul. We should know them better in Him.

But on earth, where we cannot see God, we add to our knowledge of God, by knowing sensible phenomena, both in the experience of everyday life and more profoundly in the truths discovered and systematised by the sciences. Every new truth learned, be its object a physical element or some humble form of organic life, is indirectly an addition to our knowledge of the Divine Creator.

Moreover the sciences have an important function to perform in the service of religion; indeed, of metaphysics also. Among the many contributions to religious thought made by the late Baron von Hügel was his powerful purification which the positive sciences might effect for the religious man. Though science cannot, as we have seen, tell us anything directly of God, it can by its disclosure of the reign of impersonal law, cleanse the justifiable and necessary anthropomorphism of religion from the false anthropomorphism which sees in God a magnified man arbitrarily interfering with every detail of the natural processes. Such an attitude, too common hitherto, is radically incompatible with the mentality produced by the study of the positive sciences. But who dare call its dis-

appearance a loss for religion? God is greater, not pettier, than impersonal law.

By bringing home the magnitude of the part played by impersonal and unintelligent forces, physical and biological, the modern development of positive sciences has no doubt emphasized the extent and magnitude of the problem of evil. Where our ancestors were content with a more facile explanation of suffering and evil conduct as always the expression, penalty, or direct consequence of wilful sin, we realise to-day, as never before, how suffering and internecine strife prevailed throughout the vast epochs which preceded the advent of humanity, how heredity and environment, and the subsconscious operation of instincts unrecognised by the agent himself, so enmesh the individual that his will is at every turn overweighted and overborne, how much suffering not merely does not, but in the circumstances cannot, produce a countervailing spiritual good. And men turn in despair to such irreligious pessimism as we find, for example, in the novels of a Thomas Hardy.

Here, too, there is no going back. Because the positivist enlightenment, in showing us the power of unintelligent forces, has too often, by the natural reaction which in our partial and jerky human progress accompanies every advance, become blind to the spiritual Personality behind and beyond, we may not reply by a blindness in the opposite direction.

We must rather find an outlook sufficiently wide to embrace both these complementary aspects of reality. Such an outlook is provided by Catholic theology and philosophy when their implications are boldly worked out and defects of presentation due to the scientific immaturity of an earlier age removed. In his most profound study of the problem of evil, Father Joseph Rickaby, S.J., has argued that the defect of the lower levels of being — physical and even biological intrinsically involves evil. Therefore, since even God cannot effect what is inherently impossible, He could not have created a universe embracing such orders of being without the presence of evil. Nor could He create human free will without sin arising sooner or later. "The element of nothingness enters into every created being. This element means defectibility and consequent proneness to evil. God cannot create a creature free from this element of nothingness and defectibility, for He cannot create a creature that shall not be finite. . . .

We may plausibly conjecture that it would be impossible for God, because against the nature of things, to create a universe . . . with no evil, physical or moral, anywhere. Such an all-blameless universe is an impossibility, as much as a round square triangle is an impossibility.

The element of Nothingness . . . must issue in evil somewhere. This is the necessity of evil, rooted in the very nature of finite and created things, and not to be eliminated thence, even by the wisdom and omnipotence of God." God, though in Himself infinite and absolute, cannot be so in finite and relative creatures. And the more limited and relative they are, the less can He be so in them. Hence physical and even biological laws, while revealing God's will to the extent of their positive being, are so limited and deficient that their order is and must be partial disorder when judged even by the law of human reason. The Divine Face is indeed mirrored in these depths of partial being — but the lineaments grow fainter as we descend. And if the discoveries and methods of modern science were not needed to inform us of this, they have been, and are — such is the limitation of human nature — necessary to make us realise it. A Catholic philosopher like Wust can exaggerate the order of sub-human creation, as though the chaos of matter-energy bordering on sheer nothingness were there wholly subdued to form, whereas it breaks through in an irrationality and evil, an apparent lack of design, in strange contrast with the teleology which even the inorganic in certain aspects displays, and which on the biological plane achieves miracles of adaptation.

And this element of disorder, which led Plato or his master Socrates from an earlier hope that all physical phenomena possess a complete teleological justification, to the realisation that "evils hover of necessity around mortal nature and this earthly sphere," the

element of relatively formless energy yet unconquered by the advance of form, also appears in the grotesque ugliness — sometimes, so close is the intertwining of positive being and its negation, in fantastic conjunction with a bizarre beauty — not only of those primaeval monsters long since extinct, but of many lower forms of life still surviving: loathly parasites, tape-worms, slugs, millipedes, octopuses, jellyfish. To many observers, indeed, these creatures seem beautiful, and that also with truth. No creature is wholly formless, and in so far as a creature expresses form it is beautiful. Nevertheless there is in material creatures an element of formlessness which, if practically negligible in the highest of these, a beautiful human body, is sufficient in many of the lower creatures — as indeed in human deformities — to outweigh for most observers the positive form and its beauty and thus produce in them an apprehension of repulsive ugliness.

In such cases we are conscious of a deformity that appals by its revelation of the primordial chaos insurgent beneath the order superimposed. And if this peculiarly repellent ugliness is absent from inorganic nature, it is because it lacks life. Because it is inorganic, its comparative lack of form does not contrast with the higher degree of formation which an organism implies. A rock or billow is beautiful in its simple contours. Could they come to life they would be hideous, creatures of nightmare. Perhaps the quickest way to realise this disconcerting blend, design and chaos, rationality and irrationality, co-operation and ruthless conflict, in the last resort of being, is to study the behaviour of those insects — bees, wasps, ants and termites — in whom biological instinct, as the principle of a social organisation, has achieved its maximum. Yet here also there is no justification for any radical pessimism, nor even for any disparagement of these lower physical and biological orders and the sciences which study them. Religion need not turn away from these inferior levels of being with disdain or fear.

They are not evil as the Manichees held, nor mere illusion as Vedanta teaches. Everywhere as we climb the ladder of being, the positive, orderly and good increasingly prevails over the negative, chaotic and evil. Life organises the physical elements in its service and bends their mechanical laws to fulfil its inherent teleology. The harmonies become more complex and more subtle, the co-operation more elaborate, unity manifest in and through an increasing multiplicity. No doubt in consequence of inherent limitation, advance and gain in one direction involve regression and loss in another. For example, the cellular complexity essential to all but the simplest organisms involves natural death, unknown to the unicellular organisms that multiply by fission. But death will be followed by the advent of sex — a richer and more intense mode of union than the bonds of gravity or relative position, or the chemical combinations that preceded it. Nor is death a great evil for beings whose value is specific rather than individual. There is a balance of gain and progress, and when the advance of life has reached a blind alley in one direction — for instance, in the production of saurian monsters too bulky for their intelligence — it strikes out in another direction where the achievement will be greater. The scientist thus watches the Spirit moving over the waters to give form and life, that higher and more interior form. And if the work seems slow because these lower types of creature oppose the passive resistance of their deficient being to God's organising, moulding and lifegiving work, our measurements are of no account in the Divine eternity.

AUTUMN: THE AGE OF BAROQUE*

THE religious architecture of Baroque is often regarded as a distinctively Jesuit style. This is a misconception. Had any other style been popular the Jesuits would have employed it. But in truth the Baroque style in its free use of splendid display and forms of earthly beauty was congenial to the spirit of the Society. For the Jesuits, the shock troops of the counter-Reformation, were determined to conquer humanism for Christ. St. Ignatius' life may be divided into three portions. In the first he was a man of the world, in the second a man of God, in the third a man of God and a man of the world and a man of the world to win the world for God. The Society he founded has perpetuated the final phase of its founder's life. The Jesuit has been a man of God and a man of the world for God. The Jesuit ideal is to employ humanism in the service of religion. The Jesuits would take men where they found them that they might not leave them there. To wean them away from sin they would comply with whatever is not actually sinful. The end, the greater glory of God justifies not, as their enemies allege, all means, but all means not immoral. Those who blame the Society for this should at least have the justice to arraign St. Paul, who a millennium and a half before St. Ignatius declared that he would be all things to all men to save some. And the Jesuits were attempting to save nothing less than Christendom, to save it from the disintegration of heresy and a rebellious humanism.

Since the European child was now an adolescent he must receive a suitable education. The Jesuits therefore became the educators of Catholic Europe, imparting an education better than any hitherto available. His tastes must be gratified and given a Godward direction. He loved display. Architecture and painting, pageantry and music, must delight eye and ear — in the worship of God. He was erotic and passionate. He must have a passionate and erotic religion to sublimate and redirect his passion. He loved the theatre and the dance. The Jesuits staged religious or morally edifying dramas with the utmost elaboration of stagecraft. They even fostered the development of the ballet. The Renaissance adolescent was proud of his knowledge. The Jesuits were men of letters and learning, able to play their part in every

*Watkin, E. I., *Catholic Art and Culture* (New York: Sheed and Ward, 1944), pp. 147–157.

field of literature and study. In the seventeenth century he became interested in science and its practical applications. Jesuits were scientists. The Jesuit Lana designed a flying ship whose principle at least was sound (1670). And it was the Jesuits' astronomical knowledge which opened China to them. He was proud of his independent will. The Jesuits championed free-will against an older theology which seemed to deny its rights. But they did it so to win it for the free service of God. In moral theology they demanded the least they could from men little disposed to obedience. But from that minimum of observance they sought by the sacraments, devotional exercises, preaching and ritual to raise men to heights of sanctity. For this they have been and are severely censured, even by Catholics. If the Church were better confined to a devout minority, Christian in every fibre of their being, the censure would be just. If, however, there were to be a Catholic Christendom, that is to say, a society of Catholic peoples, where the universal profession of Catholic faith provided for all a Catholic environment with its religious privileges and possibilities, they could have adopted no other policy. In fact their policy had been decided in principle long since, when the Church baptised societies *en masse,* the Roman Empire first, then the barbarian tribes that conquered it. The decision involved a Church not confined to mature Christians but composed of believers who were in the main but raw material for a long and necessarily very imperfect process of education and sanctification. The Jesuits and the counter Reformation on which they set their seal did not pursue this predetermined policy under novel conditions by extending its application to meet them.

In the end the humanist revolt proved too strong. The counter-Reformation was defeated. Christendom exists no longer. Has its demise proved a benefit to religion? In some respects, no doubt. But on balance? Unless we are prepared to answer with a confident affirmative, we are not entitled to censure the policy pursued by the Society of Jesus.

We have observed that Gothic art employed in its symbolism the natural and human contents of Vincent's mirrors. The Gothic spirit of Baroque enlarged enormously the number and variety of these human and natural symbols. If the Gothic cathedral is a microcosm of the medieval religion-culture, the Baroque religion-culture which continued it offers the student a microcosm far smaller and more accessible. It is the emblem book. Even more than the Church or the formal garden, the emblem book is an epitome of Baroque. There is no quicker way of entering into its spirit than by poring over the illustrations of an emblem book and reading the explanatory text.

The emblems, charming, quaint and more fantastic than anything possible in architecture or topiary, are drawn from every department of nature and human life. The emblem is the symbol, because it is the reflection, on the sensible plane, of a moral or religious fact. As we should expect in the literature of the adolescent, the erotic emblem is the commonest. Images of earthly passion, never coarse or suggestive but conceived according to the mythological fancy of late antiquity, symbolise every phase and aspect of love, sacred and profane. Cupid appears constantly, to represent either the heavenly Eros or the earthly Eros he defeats.

Ingenuity is taxed to the utmost to discover emblems and analogies and for this end searches the entire world of nature and man. The literary counterpart of the emblem is the conceit. It is in fact a verbal emblem, sought with equal ingenuity. It was not, as Doctor Johnson maintained with his too blunt common sense, the perversity of a misapplied erudition that made the Baroque poet strain his wits devising elaborate conceits. It was his appreciation of the truth, believed with equal conviction by the medieval Catholic, that everything below is the symbol of something above, every object of sense the symbol of a spiritual reality. This was as true of the designer of emblems. It was the same principle that fostered in such men as Paracelsus, Boehme, and Thomas Vaughan the belief that in consequence of this analogy between the physical and the spiritual orders knowledge of one would throw light on the other. The transmutation, for example of the spirit of God's grace warranted a corresponding transmutation to the elements, and experimental knowledge of the latter illuminated the former. Mysticism justified alchemy. Alchemy in turn threw light on mysticism. This, indeed, was a mistake. We know too little of the spiritual order to derive from it scientific illumination. And the Church frowned on this "theosophy." It has no place in the teaching of the great Catholic mystics. But the emblem and the conceit, belonging as they do to the order of imagination and of art, not of science, require only knowledge of religious and moral truth and of the visible aspects of the objects that are to symbolise it. That they are out of fashion with modern Catholics is evidence that the latter have lost this powerful conviction of the unity of all knowledge and of all things knowable in the unity of a creation hierarchically ordered towards the supernatural creation of grace.

To be sure, our emblems and conceits could not be those of Seicento. The world from which they must be taken has changed, is incalculably more extensive and more complex. Science has discovered a vast universe of natural knowledge. The world we know is not the world our ancestors knew. But we should not discard their fundamentally Catholic principle, no less in truth than the principle of Divine Incarnation. Meanwhile we could do worse than return for a leisured hour to the emblem book and its companion, the Baroque poem, and enter into the "joyful wisdom" of their elaborate fancies which so often convey profound truth. And if we understand the emblem book, we appreciate Baroque art and culture; we appreciate the counter-Reformation, and we appreciate the Jesuits. For we shall see in all alike a Catholic religion-culture extending to every department of human experience, and relating it to God, the Infinite in and beyond the boundary, the Christian form of a classical matter, the vertical motion of the spirit dominating the horizontal. That is to say, we shall appreciate the entire religion-culture of which the Baroque culture was the vintage, the religion-culture of Catholic Europe as under particular historical conditions it extended the

Incarnation by expressing it in a given cultural material, the inheritance of classical antiquity. Truly there is much to be learned from the emblem book, and, I think, from a teacher of no slight charm.

We shall best understand the Christian humanism at which Baroque culture, continuing the Gothic, aimed, and which at its best it achieved more completely than the latter, if we consider an example studied by Bremond in that volume of his *Histoire du Sentiment Religieux en France* devoted to Christian humanism — *"humanisme dévot"* he termed it — namely, the Platonist Capuchin, Yves de Paris. That his writings are still unobtainable encourages me the more to dwell upon a writer of singular charm and, what is more important, so comprehensive and centrally Catholic in his interests. He seems in fact the human incarnation of those Vincentian mirrors, presented by the decoration of the Gothic cathedral, and later by the emblem book. Nor has Yves merely the interest of the scholar or the dilettante of knowledge. He displays a passionate love of beauty in every form. And the entire range of his interests is unified and rendered an organic whole by his Christian Platonism, which beholds in the objects of sense and in men's secular occupations shadows, and therefore revelations, of the Divine Beauty and Government above them.

This Capuchin might have said with truth, *"Nihil humanum a me alienum."* "Nothing human is foreign to me." Nor any natural beauty. As he describes it, we share his enjoyment of a walk, "Right against the eastern date where the great sun begins his state," as the English poet was writing at this very time. "As soon as you leave the house you are embraced by the west wind that delights you with its freshness and closing the pores of the skin renders the spirits more intent upon the splendours of a spectacle of which the leaves already advertise you by a rustle of admiration. The light which fills the air with its delicious and ever-increasing flood, whose source is as yet invisible, shows us by this dawn of a new day what the dawn of the world was like before the stars were created. Assuredly it seems as though all things were being given their being as they emerge from the indistinction of darkness with their diverse shapes and colours. . . . The pleasure the eye receives as it beholds the vast spaces of the atmosphere whiten with the light and bodies adorned with divers colours incites the wise men to look for the source of these glories and without long reflection he turns, as by a natural sympathy, to the East. What treasures and wonders he sees there! Those little clouds whose rivalry is too weak to obscure the day-star put on his liveries and become the harbinger of his advent. They curl and twine in wavelets of fire, they compose thrones of crystal, long porticoes of rubies and diamonds, streets paved with agate, tapestries embroidered with gold and pearl, and fancy pictures them a throng of luminous dwarfs marching in front of the sun's triumphant chariot.

"At last the sun becomes visible as a zone of burning light which in less than no time has grown into a semi-circle and is soon a perfect orb. Do not lose these moments when for a brief space you may fix your gaze on this fair sun, since the vapours rising from the ground and extending from the horizon to where you stand have woven for him a transparent veil tempering his brilliance to your weak vision. Marvel at this wheel of flame whose borders redder and more supportable by the eye leave in the midst spaces that whiten as they spread out and are lost in remote depths, impenetrable abysses of light." A bed of flowers delights Yves and he is charmed by the sight of violets, "robed in royal purple and richly scented, growing in a wood" or "anemones spread out over the ground whose bright colouring better than the tallest trees represents the orb of the day." And he takes pleasure in watching a bee, a line of ants, two snails meeting. He would like specimens or at least pictures of natural objects from every order. He enjoys the sight of a gallant vessel leaving port. Those were the days before the sailing ship had yielded place to the ungainly monsters of steam and oil. He enjoys travel, in particular his visit to Italy, when he saw the ruins of ancient Rome side by side with the fresh beauties of

the new, emerging from the hands of Bernini, Borromini, and Cortona.

Yves' view of humanity is perhaps too optimistic. He dwells by preference on the goodness in men and is indulgent to their follies. He seems unaware of the hideous cruelty which then as now, made men behave as fiends. In his day soldiers murdered civilians by hand, in our own by bombs dropped from the air. Père Yves contemplates humanity in God and therefore sees rather what God can make of man than what man can become when he revolts against God.

For Yves humanism is Christian, not secular. Every spectacle, human or natural, raises his mind to God. When we contemplate a star-lit sky on a calm night, "All our feelings are above nature. Our thoughts ascend above earth into a boundless expanse of light that holds all our powers in suspense and makes us marvel at something more than we behold and enjoy a bliss we do not understand." And "If we plunge into the solitude of a forest amidst the silence and in sight of those great trees, majestic in the height of their trunks and the wide expanse of their branches, our mind is straightway rapt into itself, our heart is sensible of unwonted emotion and the entire body, trembling with a reverent awe, makes us aware of an infinite greatness that demands the free homage of our will." In his sensitiveness to wild beauty, however, Père Yves is not Baroque. He anticipates Rousseau and the romantic love of nature he inaugurated. But, as Croce has pointed out, the individual is not perfectly and exclusively representative of any aspect of human thought or culture, least of all men of outstanding endowment. But for Yves there is no danger of pantheism, of the romantic substitution of the indefinite for the Infinite. To the Infinite his entire mind and heart, even his very senses, are directed. It is the goal of all his appreciation of man and nature, even of his delight in human beauty and love, considered, however, as objects of contemplation, not of vital union. For he sees plainly the distinction between aesthetic appreciation of human beauty and the desire to possess it by a physical union.

Yves does not contemplate God only through creatures, but directly through contemplative prayer. God is apprehended in "the highest part of the soul without the aid of reasoning. . . . Climb to the furthest point of your intellect and your own unity will make contact with this sovereign Unity and you will understand something of the infinite that embraces you." "It is for Him that our hearts sigh by sudden aspirations whose nature we cannot conceive because they rise to the infinite and the subtle point of our souls approaches this indivisible Being by a concept that exceeds reason" — concept seems hardly the right word for what is in fact a dim intuition — "and by a love which forestalls the search of knowledge." Here is the transcendent Infinity attained by the contemplation of Baroque religion that crowns and unites its wide humanist culture, as in art its representation dominates and pervades the wealth of visible forms and colours. Yves, the humanist and the lover of nature, is a mystic and his knowledge and enjoyment of creatures are directed to the knowledge and the praise of the Creator. He combines the detachment which made him choose the life of a bare-foot friar with an appreciation of creatures as intense as it was comprehensive. In this he exemplified the ideal and the fullest achievement of Catholic religion and culture it has inspired, above all, of the Baroque culture that most extensively combined the two factors, detachment and appreciation, the vertical and the horizontal movements of the human spirit, mysticism and humanism. His singularly attractive figure may well remain with us to justify Christian humanism against the Puritanism, Catholic or Protestant, which looks askance at man and nature, and because God, could we know Him as He is, would suffice all our needs, concludes that on earth, when as yet He is invisible, we can dispense with His mirrored reflections. Specialists of the vertical movement, such, for example, as the Curé d' Ars, whose call and *attrait* are an exclusive devotion to the direct service of God, though they rise to the summit of holiness, are narrower

and less imitable by the majority of Catholics than humanist contemplatives such as Père Yves. Nor were all the saints men of such exclusively vertical *attrait*. St. Venantius Fortunatus has his place among them beside St. John Vianney. "Wisdom is justified in all her children."

In his monograph on Bernini, Max von Boehn speaks of the passion for the drama which possessed the Romans of the seventeenth century. "Clement IX wrote the merriest comedies which Michel Angelo de Rossi and Abbatini set to music": Sullivans to the papal Gilbert! Imagine, if you can, a Victorian Archbishop of Canterbury composing librettos for Sullivan. Gilbert no doubt would have been highly diverted by the spectacle of Archbishop Tait writing the libretto of "Iolanthe." And Boehn tells us of a bloody brawl in a convent occasioned by a confessor who pronounced it sinful for nuns to act.

This love of the theatre is not confined to Rome. It was universal throughout Baroque culture. Drama appealed to the emotional tension of an age when the ecstasies of sense and spirit met in conflict. And it gratified the self-assertive exhibitionism of the adolescent European. Moreover, the stage gave plentiful scope to the Baroque love of pageantry and the tendency to unite several arts in the production of a common effect.

Drama, however, was not confined to the literal stage. The entire Baroque culture and way of living was a drama, religious and secular. And its stage was the church, the street, the public place, the palace of wide rooms richly appointed and reached by princely staircases, and the formal fantastic garden. The elaborate dresses were the costumes of the characters in this perpetual drama, the elaborate etiquette, its book of words. The ranks and precedence observed so meticulously were the parts assigned to the players at their birth. This Baroque drama was polite. It was composed and performed in accordance with strict rules. It observed unities accepted as universally as were those of the French classical stage. For it was not a tragedy, enacted beneath a sky overcast with cloud, in a world open in every direction. Its action was bounded on all sides by the frontiers imposed by the Catholic view of the world. Its infinity was upward only, the infinity of that heaven of light painted on the vaults of churches. Below, it was played in the garden of hedges and topiary, the Baroque culture.

The garden was, in fact, a favourite stage. Most princely gardens were furnished with an open-air theatre whose walls were clipped hedges. And Le Notre designed the gardens of Versailles to be the stage of elaborate dramas, masques and pageants.

Religious worship observes a ritual fixed in every detail. Now for the first time elaborate rubrics are enforced by Rome. Treaties are made and wars waged by rule. For all the ingenuity displayed in devising conceits and surprising effects, literary equivalents of the devices and surprises of the Baroque water-garden, poetry employs a stereotyped vocabulary, and an unvarying material, drawn chiefly from classical myth and history and seeks always the same type of effect. If painting, sculpture and architecture are freer than poetry, the rule is bent rather than broken and we are sensible of the boundary, even when it is transcended. The Gothic spirit must always reckon with the classical forms it employs.

Baroque culture is closed in every direction save one, towards heaven. The knowledge, indeed, was being accumulated and the forces gathering strength which would demolish these boundaries, uproot these trim hedges and throw the garden back into wilderness. Meantime, however, fancy sported in the security of its enclosure. And the drama was played with the decorum of its prescribed movements.

RONALD ARBUTHNOTT KNOX
(*1888*–   )

RONALD KNOX, the youngest son of the Anglican Bishop of Manchester, was born in 1888. He received his education at Eton and Balliol College, Oxford. In 1910 he was elected a fellow of Trinity College. He became a Catholic in 1919, entered the priesthood, and spent several years as chaplain to the Newman Club in Oxford. He has retired from active duty in order to pursue the task of making a new Catholic translation of the Scriptures which is his greatest work.

Father Knox's reputation for humor seldom obscures his scholarly bent. His humorous works, which have made his fame, are quite definitely an outgrowth of his student days in the Oxford Union when he delighted the undergraduates with parodies and witty repartee. His *Spiritual Aeneid,* 1918, shows the scholarly and deeply religious side of his nature.

No praise is too high for his translation of the New Testament. For the first time one can read the Epistles of St. Paul without verbiage. Monsignor Knox has, perhaps, not consciously weeded out the Latinisms, but whether consciously or not he has given us an edition which is basically Anglo-Saxon.

REUNION ALL ROUND*

CHAPTER ONE

IT WAS customary with our Ancestors, to designate *Mahomet* by the title of *The False Prophet.* A more modern and more

*Taken from *Essays In Satire,* by Rev. Ronald Knox, published and copyrighted by E. P. Dutton & Co., Inc., New York: 1930, pp. 53–56.

temperate Judgement will not allow us to contend further, than that he was unduly positive in his Assertions. And there is this to be said for him at least, that he was a good, sound *Protestant;* and that his quarrel with the Debas'd Church of his Time was mainly about its heathenish *Mariolatry,* and the unduly strict views it held about *Marriage;* all which should make us conceive a sympathy and Respect for him, as in some ways the Forerunner of our own *Reformation.* Further, it cannot be deny'd, that the Mahometans admit the historical truth of many of those Facts, upon which the Christian Religion is, or was until the last half-century, suppos'd to be founded. True, they have hitherto failed to invest the Facts with same theological colouring we are accustom'd to put on them, and it must be confest they show a certain Reluctancy to avow the most elementary Articles of our Faith. But is this Difficulty final? Let five *Christian,* and five *Mahometan* Theologians be closeted together for a week to discuss these controverted Doctrines, the Christians explaining to their less enlightened Co-assessors what sense such Doctrines are really meant to convey; and I for one shall be vastly surpriz'd if, at the end of the week, the Mahometans are not prepared to accept the *Athanasian Creed* in the same sense in which it is maintain'd by some of the most highly-plac'd Ecclesiasticks of our own Country.

It is, I apprehend, in Matters of Discipline rather than of Doctrine we shall need a certain amount of *give* and *take* before our Differences can be settled. Christian Men are accustomed to be content with one Wife, and even in *America* with one at a time; Whereas in *Turkey* he would be though a very chicken-hearted Husband who had not endow'd four Ladies simultaneously with his own Surname. This might seem to be an irreconcilable Difference of Principle; but fortunately, where Numbers are concern'd, Mathematicks provides us with a ready Solution of the Difficulty, by the Method of Averages. Nor does it need the brain of a profound Scholar to determine, that in the Church of the future we shall all be conscientious *Bigamists;* thereby avoiding at once the Expence of a *Harem,* and the Monotony of our present European System. We shall also obviate at one blow the difficulty of finding Wives in *Baghdad,* and the difficulty of finding Husbands in *Balham.* We shall, of course, adopt at the same time the Mahometan Rule, by which a Man may at any time turn his Wife out of doors, upon finding her displeasing to himself, and take a new one, modifying it only so far, as to extend the Privilege equally to the Wife, as to the Husband: in this Way we shall meet a long-felt Demand on the part of the lower Classes in our Country, as well as recognizing an existing Practice in the case of their Superiors in Social Rank. At the same time, we shall abolish those accounts of Divorce Court Proceedings in our News-sheets, which are admitted by everyone to be injurious to Publick Morals.

A SPIRITUAL AENEID*

CHAPTER X

ALTHOUGH (I need hardly say) it was not I who set the fashion, it remains true that I was well ahead of the market when I published *Naboth's Vineyard* as a tract. For this year — I mean the summer of 1913 to the summer of 1914 — was one of almost incessant religious controversy; the canons boomed daily against one another in the columns of the *Times,* missionary meetings were distended to an unwonted size by the inspiriting effect of a "crisis in the Church"; Anglican principles were freely discussed in railway carriages and in Senior Common-rooms, and a friend of mine was told at Parker's (The Tractarian bookseller of Oxford) that there had never been such a demand for religious pamphlets in the last forty years. There were giants in the field in those days, and I cannot say of the developments in question *quorum pars magna fui;* but at least *et nos aliquod nomenque descusque gessimus* — both *Naboth's Vineyard and Some Loose Stones* achieved popu-

*Knox, Ronald, *A Spiritual Aeneid* (New York, London: Longmans, Green Co., 1919), pp. 158–171.

larity from the situation which sprang up after them and quite independently of them, and my next literary production became, by force of bitter circumstances, the epilogue to the controversy.

It is necessary to recall the facts that were then common knowledge, since buried, not by distance of time, but by the obliterating effect of a world war. Representatives of the two Anglican dioceses of Uganda and Mombasa took part that summer in a conference at Kikuyu with representatives of various Free Church missions at which problems of co-operation between the various denominations were discussed. A programme was drawn up (subject, of course, to revision by the home authorities) which recognised among other things the "exchange of pulpits" and the admission of non-Anglicans to Communion in Anglican churches. Both the two dioceses involved belonged to the Church Missionary Society, which is evangelical both in its traditions and in its modern atmosphere. But the neighbouring diocese of Zanzibar belonged to the Universities' Mission to Central Africa, founded under Tractarian influence and supported principally by "advanced" churches in England. Naturally this attitude towards the Free Church could not commend itself to such a diocese, and the situation that arose was a complicated one — if the Kikuyu resolutions were carried into effect, Anglicans on one side of a quite artificial boundary would be encouraged to communicate at non-episcopal churches, while Anglicans on the other side of it would be forbidden to enter them. There is a "floating population" even in East Africa, and it seemed as if the emigrant from Zanzibar to Mombasa or vice versa would have some difficulty in seeing the point.

There was thus a quite practical difficulty, but the Kikuyu Conference went further. It closed with a United Communion Service conducted by an Anglican bishop in a non-episcopal church, at which Anglicans and non-Anglicans worshipped and communicated together. This was not altogether a unique occurrence: the revisers of the Bible, for example, communicated together at Westminster Abbey. But the circumstances of the occurrence were exceptional, and Bishop Weston, of Zanzibar, felt it his duty to protest. This was not the only symptom which disturbed him. As an accomplished theologian of orthodox tendencies he had read *Foundations,* and seen more clearly than most people the great departures from orthodox tradition which the book involved — particularly in the matter of the Resurrection. Finally, as one jealous for the honour of the Mother of God, he resented the action of the Bishop of St. Albans against the Catholic league, described in the last chapter. He therefore addressed an open letter to the Bishop of St. Albans, really directed *Urbi et Orbi,* in which he protested against all these three developments, and followed it up by demanding of the Archbishop of Canterbury (as standing in a peculiar relation to the missionary dioceses) that he should convoke a court to pronounce upon the "heretical" proceedings at Kikuyu.

The Corringham incident, where the Evangelicals appeared as persecutors and their opponents as the victims, was conveniently forgotten: the whole British public and the whole British press fell to wrangling about the other two points. On the matter of intercommunion, the Dean of Durham was the protagonist of Protestantism; on the question of doctrinal orthodoxy it was Professor Sanday who chiefly espoused the Foundationist cause; Bishop Weston's most important champion in England was reputed to be the Bishop of Oxford, though he did not greatly involve himself in any newspaper correspondence. The British public, warm-hearted as usual rather than clear-headed, could only see one side to the whole question; persecution of anybody by anybody about anything must be wrong, and when the offence alleged was one of "charity" towards members of another denomination, the issue became even clearer. In Oxford itself the academic world of the Senior Common-rooms, which always reflects faithfully the tendencies of the uneducated public, was almost entirely on the side of free speculation about the faith (for there was talk of inhibiting Mr. Streeter) and of "hospitality" to Nonconformists at Anglican altars.

In fact, nothing was wanting to produce a Church crisis, of the magnitude of the "Jerusalem Bischopric," the Colenso schism, and all the exitements of Tractarian Days. Now, it is a curious thing about these crises that, nowadays, they always occasion the rumour and sometimes the threat that a large body of orthodox people may be expected to "secede," and yet very few people ever do. The curate hurries to and fro, pale-faced and calling for action, but his vicar, inured to scandals in the establishment, shows no intention of budging:

Satis una superque
Vidimus excidia, et captae superavimus urbi:
Sic, o sic positum affati discedite corpus.

Even I and my friends could remember the "United Communion" at Hereford on the occasion of the Coronation; we had survived the "Brighton row," and the loss of Caldey, and, while we were all prepared to support Bishop Weston, we made no motion of packing up our trunks.

I found myself, however, at the age of twenty-five, affected by the influence of people younger than myself. I went that winter to San Remo, with two friends who were in search of rest and health — one of these was B, whom I have referred to above. C was writing to one or other of us as frequently as the nature of the Italian postal service would allow. And both of them, neophytes so far as "my religion" was concerned, plainly took the Kikuyu business more seriously than I did. My only way of soothing them was to suggest that the whole battle had not yet been fought; it was bound to come to a head in 1918, when the next Pan Anglican Congress would meet: till then we must keep our powder dry. I did very seriously anticipate that the effects of these troubles might be to split the Church of England; and if this was to be so I wanted to be in at the funeral. Meanwhile, I set about writing an article on the whole question which afterwards appeared in the *British Review,* and I also prepared a paper about it which I read in Keble the next term.

I do not think that San Remo had much to say to my religious development. We used to hear Benediction there at a convent chapel more exquisitely rendered than I have ever heard it elsewhere, but I was by now sufficiently used to Catholic services not to feel an outsider when I attended them. Not that I ever did on the Continent what I have heard defended as a permissible practice — take Communion from and even confess myself to Catholic priests, who would not realize what I was. The fact that certain priests have been found so ignorant or so wanting in theological principle as to communicate Anglicans deliberately — so one is told — never seemed to me to provide the smallest excuse for presenting oneself, without explanation, for Communion in circumstances where one would naturally be mistaken for a Catholic. The fact that I believe myself to be a Catholic made no difference: I was not going to practice deception — a kind of deception which is fortunately very rare. Nor, conversely, did I agree with that strict school of thought which holds that Anglican chaplaincies in Catholic countries are an abomination: propaganda in Catholic countries was obviously wicked, but to supply the religious needs of Europe residents was natural enough. I celebrated at the chaplaincy every Sunday, and on Christmas Day in the presence of a large and startled congregation: "Thank God, *that's over,*" a gentleman observed audibly as I came down from the altar, unconsciously giving the response to my last Gospel. On Christmas Day I also preached, condemning all ideas of "peace on earth" which rested on confusions of thought in the manner of Kikuyu.

Bishop Weston came back to England in 1914, to prefer his charges in person. He visited Oxford and had dinner in my rooms (he is himself a Trinity man); a small collection of sympathetic college chaplains came to meet him and discuss things. He pointed out to us that it was a far more awkward situation for us than for himself; he was master in his own diocese, and commanded the support of the other Universities' Mission bishops, and the sympathy of the whole synod of South Africa; if the worst came to the worst he could defy the people at home.

In effect, it will be remembered, the Archbishop decided that no competent court was to be found, and referred the whole dispute to an unofficial commission recently constituted. It seemed probable, especially in view of what happened that summer, that the question would be shelved almost indefinitely — what else were commissions appointed for? It was a false calculation.

From the Lent of 1914 to the Easter of 1915 I was more fully engaged than ever in preaching and in lecturing. During that Lent, for example, I paid a visit to St. David's College, Lampeter, to put my own point of view before the students; and so far were the officials of the college from resenting my firebrand activities that Dr. Bebb, the then principal, was kind enough to afford me the hospitality of his own house. I also gave a course of addresses at a church in Worcester under the auspices of the local English Church Union, under the titles "Two Views of the Church," "Two Views of the Faith," "Two Views of the Mass," etc. My object was to prove that if you were prepared to accept views less definite than my own, then you were logically reduced to taking a "Kikuyu" view of the Church, a *Foundations* view of the Faith, and so on. In fact, my efforts were directed not so much to convincing those who held a merely "Liberal" stand-point about ecclesiastical definitions, as to rallying cautious, yet orthodox "High Churchmen" to the standard of sacramentalism. In Holy Week I went down to Plymouth, having obtained leave from the Bishop to preach a series of non-controversial addresses on the Passion, including the devotion of the Three Hours, at St. James's.

It was in an interval of these activities that I went to stay at Cranborne for a reading party. I think I did most of the work, for my sermons kept me hard at it. But now and then, when I was waiting for the finish of an unnecessarily protracted game of billiards, I would prowl round the shelves that lined the walls of the library there, and so came to renew my acquaintance with the admirable satirical vein of Dean Swift. It was in a railway carriage that the idea occurred to

me of utilizing his manner for the conveyance of an ecclesiastical message. The idea slept in my mind, and the very moment I had returned from preaching the Three Hours it claimed me imperiously. The old atmosphere of August, 1913, was round me; Mr. Child and Mr. Baker were still there, though on this occasion I was staying with Mr. Miers, the vicar; B was with me, and Mr. Gurney suddenly arrived from Cologne, where he had meant to spend Holy Week, complaining that they did not "do things properly" at the Cathedral there. I wrote feverishly, as if my hands from their long practice could not be kept off the keys of my typewriter: the result was ready by Easter Tuesday. Thus, whereas *Absolute and Abitofhell* was the work of months, *Reunion All Round* (for so I had labelled my new pasquinade) was all completed in four days. Completed, that is, as far as writing went, for the production was a matter of anxious care both to Mr. Gurney and to myself; the type and the spelling of Swift's day had to be carefully imitated, as well as the rubrication of the title-page: even the paper was of a brownish cream colour, that gave the impression of having been soiled by age. I dedicated the book to Mr. and Mrs. Henry Head, friends whom I had met with Mr. Lyon at Middlecot, and discovered to be devoted admirers of Swift.

The argument of the book was a simple *reductio ad absurdum*. If (as the British public seemed to think) it was the duty of all *Christian* bodies to unite for worship, sinking their differences on each side, why should the movement be confined to Christians? What about the Jews, from whom we were only separated by the Council of Jerusalem? And if the Jews, why not the Moḥommedans? We could always split the difference between monogamy and tetragamy by having two wives all round. The Brahmins presented few difficulties; the worshippers of Mumbo-jumbo only needed a passing reference. At this point the spirit of satire carried me away, and I suggested with every appearance of misgiving that perhaps after all, given proper precautions, charity should demand of us that we should accept the submission of the Pope. After making arrangements for the suitable degradation of the Roman hierarchy, I went boldly forward to the case of the atheists, and suggested that we might join with them in a common definition of the Divine Nature, which should assert it to be such as to involve Existence and Non-existence simultaneously. Here, with a few exhortations to the public, I left my argument to my readers.

Now, a *reductio ad absurdum* argument may be used merely for fun, and without any serious purpose of satire behind it. But I did not write in this vein of good-tempered exaggeration: I meant what I said — or rather, of course, I meant the opposite of what I said. If you are to do this, your logical developments must depend upon a valid reasoning process — in satire, no less than in a mathematical treatise. Thus, although it was possible to regard *Reunion All Round* as merely a graceful *jeu d'esprit,* I meant it for much more than this: I meant that, if the principles of Kikuyu were right, something like this (discounting, of course, the casual absurdities) did really follow as a logical consequence. If, in the name of charity, it was the duty of the Church to aim at the inclusion of all good men who were professing Christians, and herself make sacrifices in order to do so, why should she not have the same duty in connection with all good men simply because they were good? Why should a belief, often of the shadowiest, in the undefined "Divinity" of Christ be a touchstone of Church membership? For the life of me I could never see why we had to regret being out of communion with a good man like Dr. Horton, more than being out of communion with a good man like Professor Gilbert Murray, who repudiates Theism. If the Church, without being called "uncharitable," is to have tests and definitions at all, why should you draw the line at this test or that definition, and cry out in horror, "No, no, that would be uncharitable?"

I know that some of my Anglican readers think all this very preposterous; but we must wait till Theosophy has come out a little more into the light of day. I have read a manual of theosophical belief which declares confidently that the religion of the future lies in a combination of all that is best in Christianity and Brahminism — that very combination that tickled us so when we read it in *Reunion All Round.* And Mr. Wells, who is an adept at the logical carrying out of implied principles, has already provided us with a religion in which a personal God, not an Incarnate God, is asserted as a basis of doctrine.

Once again the secular press was more kind to me than the ecclesiastical, and the advertisement of the book in the S.S.P.P. catalogue still, I think, contains the following press comment: "The turn of Swift's sentences is admirably caught." *Spectator.* "A foolish flippant skit." *Cambridge Christian Life.*

But the book enjoyed a wider popularity than its press notices might have warranted; it was short, readable, and eminently topical. If reports were true, it was read by a community of Catholic nuns, who supposed the suggestions to be quite serious; it was read in refectory at the English College, under the impression that I was a Catholic, and caused great doubts of my salvation when it proved that I was not; it was read to the Prime Minister as he sat in bathing costume on the river-bank in that hottest of summers. I was even told that it gained the hearts of the episcopate, chiefly owing to an undesigned allusion in the sub-title — but stay, even the Anglican episcopate has its secrets. It won, in cold print, the commendation of my earliest master and model, Mr. G. K. Chesterton.

During this year I increased my circle of Catholic friends. I had already the hospitality of Father Lang while he was chaplain at Oxford, but his successor, Father Maturin, was a man with whom (in spite of the obvious sanctity of his life) I felt an unusual degree of human contact. By origin he was one of my own Cowley Fathers; in the controversies of the moment he took an interest which hardly pretended to be dispassionate. From his surprise at the calmness with which the Kikuyu incident was regarded you might have thought him an Anglican still. I was always rather afraid of Catholic priests at this time, feeling that they might be "getting at me," but Father Maturin always treated you with the openness of a friend. I made another acquaintance, slight at the time, but destined to develop, with the Catholic priesthood when, at one of Miss Anderson's "evenings" at 4 Broad Street, I met the friend of more than one of my friends, Father Martindale. Mr. and Mrs. Wilfrid Ward paid a visit to Oxford, and I met them both at Mr. Urquhart's table and at Mr. Raper's; Mrs. Ward took me to task over a heresy in *Some Loose Stones,* which I afterwards tried to defend in the preface to the second edition; I freely admit that she has St. Thomas on her side, and I have no doubt that she is right, but I was pleased to be able to quote St. Leo in contradiction of her. To Mr. Urquhart also I owed the privilege of sitting at the same table with the Cardinal Archbishop. I did not, however, like some of my school, make a point of meeting Catholics and exchanging views with them; their existence in the abstract I welcomed, and felt every setback to Catholicism as a personal loss, but in the presence of Catholics, except my old friends, I seldom failed to feel uneasy.

In the summer vacation I was at work again. Messrs. Longmans had suggested an orthodox substitute for *Foundations.* For various reasons this work, which was to be of joint authorship, never saw the light, at least in the form contemplated; but all July I was with Mr. Williams, first at Brighton and then at Plymouth, alternately hammering at my own subject (the Incarnation) and debating with him acrimoniously on the views he meant to express about authority. To me an

authority which could not be traced back to the mediaeval Roman Church, without admixture of Eastern Orthodoxy, was still impossible. From Brighton I fulfilled a preaching engagement which made me feel that my recent writings had given me a standing even in prudent Anglo-Catholic circles — I delivered the sermon at the annual festival of the St. Margaret's Sisterhood, East Grinstead, where the most unimpeachable bulwarks of the Tractarian tradition are liable to appear. An address to the Oxford E.C.U. about the need of an authority which could say to the unorthodox theologian not merely "Resign!" but "Recant!" — I did not, of course, suggest thumbscrews or faggots, but merely a voice speaking with the certainty of divine guidance — was published about this time, and commended me afresh to my old Mentor, Mr. Coles. I no longer felt myself an Ishmael and an outlaw. Another of my closest friends at Oxford had begun to make his confessions; yet another had (so to speak) put himself under instruction, and I looked forward with bright hopes to a reading party in August.

History will revere the name of one of our present statesmen, whose *obiter dictum* used often to be quoted, "I never read the papers." I never read the papers at this time, and it was only in casual conversation I learned that all was not well with Europe. Then the bugles went round to call up the Naval Reserve; a big German cargo ship sulkily submitted to be towed across the Sound into its long resting-place, and as I travelled north to stay with B in the Midlands, I read the Foreign Secretary's speech.

THE HOLY GOSPEL OF JESUS CHRIST
ACCORDING TO ST. LUKE*

Chapter Two

IT HAPPENED that a decree went out at this time from the emperor Augustus, enjoining that the whole world should be

*Knox, Msgr. Ronald A., *The New Testament in English* (New York: Sheed and Ward, 1944), pp. 115-116.

registered: this register was the one first made during the time when Cyrinus was governor of Syria. All must go and give in their names, each in his own city; and Joseph, being of David's clan and family, came up from the town of Nazareth, in Galilee, to David's city in Judea, the city called Bethlehem, to give in his name there. With him was his espoused wife Mary, who was then in her pregnancy; and it was while they were still there that the time came for her delivery. She brought forth her son, her first-born, whom she wrapped in his swaddling-clothes, and laid in a manger, because there was no room for them in the inn.

In the same country there were shepherds awake in the fields, keeping night-watches over their flocks. And all at once an angel of the Lord came and stood by them, and the glory of the Lord shone about them, so that they were overcome with fear. But the angel said to them. Do not be afraid; behold, the news I bring you is good news of a great rejoicing for the whole people. This day, in the city of David, a Saviour has been born for you, no other than the Lord Christ. This is the sign by which you are to know him; you will find a child still in swaddling-clothes, lying in a manger. Then, on a sudden, a multitude of the heavenly army appeared to them at the angel's side, giving praise to God, and saying, Glory to God in high heaven, and peace on earth to men that are God's friends.

When the angels had left them and gone back into heaven, the shepherds said to one another, Come let us make our way to Bethlehem, and see for ourselves this happening which God has made known to us. And so they went with all haste, and found Mary and Joseph there, with the child lying in the manger. On seeing him, they discovered the truth of what had been told them about this child. All those who heard it were full of amazement at the story which the shepherds told them; but Mary treasured up all these sayings, and reflected on them in her heart. And the shepherds went home giving praise and glory to God, at seeing and hearing that all was as it had been told them.

THE HOLY GOSPEL OF JESUS CHRIST ACCORDING TO ST. JOHN*

Chapter Fifteen

I AM the true vine, and it is my Father who tends it. The branch that yields no fruit in me, he cuts away; the branch that does yield fruit, he trims clean, so that it may yield more fruit. You, through the message I have preached to you, are clean already; you have only to live on in me, and I will live on in you. The branch that does not live on in the vine can yield no fruit of itself; no more can you, if you do not live on in me. I am the vine, you are its branches; if a man lives on in me, and I in him, then he will yield abundant fruit; separated from me, you have no power to do anything. If a man does not live on in me, he can only be like the branch that is cast off and withers away; such a branch is picked up and thrown into the fire, to burn there. As long as you live on in me, and my words live on in you, you will be able to make what request you will, and have it granted. My Father's name has been glorified, if you yield abundant fruit, and prove yourselves my disciples. I have bestowed my love upon you, just as my Father has bestowed his love upon me; live on, then, in my love. You will live on in my love, if you keep my commandments, just as it is by keeping my Father's commandments that I live on in his love.

All this I have told you, so that my joy may be yours, and the measure of your joy may be filled up. This is my commandment, that you should love one another, as I have loved you. This is the greatest love a man can show, that he should lay down his life for his friends; and you, if you do all that I command you, are my friends. I do not speak of you any more as my servants; a servant is one who does not understand what his master is about, whereas I have made known to you all that my Father has told me; and so I have called you my friends. It was not you that chose me, it was I that

Ibid., pp. 219–221.

chose you. The task I have appointed you is to go out and bear fruit, fruit which will endure; so that every request you make to the Father in my name may be granted to you. These are the directions I give you, that you should love one another.

If the world hates you, be sure that it hated me before it learned to hate you. If you belonged to the world, the world would know you for its own and love you; it is because you do not belong to the world, because I have singled you out from the midst of the world, that the world hates you. Do not forget what I said to you, No servant can be greater than his master. They will persecute you just as they have persecuted me; they will pay the same attention to your words as to mine. And they will treat you thus because you bear my name; they have no knowledge of him who sent me. If I had not come and given them my message, they would not have been in fault; as it is, their fault can find no excuse. To hate me is to hate my Father too. If I had not done what no one else could have done in their midst they would not have been in fault; as it is, they have hated, with open eyes, both me and my Father. And all this, in fullfilment of the saying which is written in their law, They hated me without cause. Well, when the truth-giving Spirit, which proceeds from the Father, has come to befriend you, he whom I will send to you from the Father's side, he will bear witness of what I was; and you too are to be my witnesses, you who from the first have been in my company.

ST. PAUL'S FIRST LETTER TO THE CORINTHIANS*

CHAPTER THIRTEEN

I MAY speak with every tongue that men and angels use; yet if I lack charity, I am no better than echoing bronze, or the clash of cymbals. I may have powers of prophecy, no secret hidden from me, no knowledge too deep for me; I may have utter faith, so that I can move mountains; yet if I lack charity, I count for nothing. I may give away all that I have, to feed the poor; I may give myself up to be burnt at the stake; if I lack charity, it goes for nothing.

Charity is patient, is kind; charity feels no envy; charity is never perverse or proud, never insolent; has no selfish aims, cannot be provoked, does not brood over an injury; takes no pleasure in wrongdoing, but rejoices at the victory of truth; sustains, believes, hopes, endures, to the last. The time will come when we shall outgrow prophecy, when speaking with tongues will come to an end, when knowledge will be swept away; we shall never have finished with charity. Our knowledge, our prophecy, are only glimpses of the truth; and these glimpses will be swept away when the time of fulfillment comes. (Just so, when I was a child, I talked like a child, I had the intelligence, the thoughts of a child; since I became a man, I have outgrown childish ways.) At present, we are looking at a confused reflection in a mirror; then, we shall see face to face; now, I have only glimpses of knowledge; then, I shall recognize God as he has recognized me. Meanwhile, faith, hope and charity persist, all three; but the greatest of them all is charity.

*Ibid., pp. 365–66.

J. B. MORTON
(*1893–*   )

UNDER the title "Beachcomber," J. B. Morton writes a column in the *Daily Express,* and though the *Express* is anathema to cultured Englishmen, because of the flashy character of its journalism, there are few Englishmen, cultured or otherwise, who fail to appreciate Beachcomber's satires on life and manners. If the "Pukka Sahib" and the "rather-rather" type of Britisher are disappearing from English life, Beachcomber is largely responsible for their disappearance.

His humor is hilarious and at its best is fun for the sake of fun. It has a "zany" quality which few writers, other than Rabelais, find it possible to maintain.

Hag's Harvest and *Morton's Folly* display Morton at his best. His sly but cultivated thrusts at modern complacency and manners, or lack of them, his creation of a world of oddities more real than life, make his satire as compelling as it is individual.

PRE-CAMBRIAN MAN*

COME now! Let us have a little popular science. Let me tell you, for instance, of the epoch-making discovery of Professor Piffl, who has dug up, in the great Baba desert, the little finger (of the left hand) of what was beyond all doubt our ancestor. It is obvious from photographs of this finger that the possessor was Short of stature, Low-browed, Frightfully Hairy, Utterly Stupid, Dorsocephalic, Nambipambidexterous, Bibrachial, Esurient, Cretinous, Polypituitary, Glandular, Subendocrine, Jumbic, Polygamous, Pterobolic, Dalloid, Cutaneous, Transmelliferous, and, to all intents and

*Morton, J. B., *Morton's Folly* (New York: Doubleday, Doran and Co.), pp. 145–147.

purposes, probably, Penumbric. In the face of such staggering evidence, the whole history of the human race, as hitherto understood, fades to nothing.

This far-away ancestor of ours probably ate mud and crawled on his hands and knees. Nobody knows what he wanted a little finger for. It was perhaps, merely an example of retrogressive evolution, being a degeneration from the Pranx of the Lemur, or, again, from the prawn's foot. That this man had webbing between his toes and furry ears is now generally accepted.

You have learned enough for to-day.

N.B. — He was awfully pre-Cambrian. *October 14*

RUSSIA AS IT REALLY IS*

I

EVERYONE in Moscow was most kind to us. I asked one of the guides if there was any scarcity of food. He laughed at the mere idea, so that disposes once for all of the wicked propaganda of those at home in England who do not understand this great and noble experiment.

Ibid., pp. 258–264.

We visited a school, and were amazed to find the children as clean as pins and very alert. The guide suggested that we should ask some of them about England. At once a chorus of voices repeated the names of the leading politicians and writers of England. We were quite embarrassed to find our own names in the list. What intelligent children!

Mrs. Thunderstroke, the Socialist worker, strayed from our party, and explored some of the narrow streets. She thought she had discovered a bread queue, and was most indignant, until it was explained to her that it was only a Russian outdoor game. They stand in single file for quite a long time, muttering and shouting various sentences. So utterly Russian!

II

October 15

We attended a cultural lecture in a large building. The lecturer was a prominent official of the Party, and his subject was the New Consciousness of the Worker-State.

The audience was composed of workers who were brought in from one of the rest-homes.

We could not understand the lecture, as it was in Russian, but it was interesting to note that there was not a single interruption or adverse criticism.

At the end of the lecture our guide brought up a man and suggested that we should question him through an interpreter. Mrs. Thunderstroke asked him if he was happy. He mumbled something which the interpreter said meant, "I am deliriously happy. The Soviet regime has freed the workers. On to World Revolution!"

Before we left England we were told by reactionaries that the workers were, in some cases, discontented with their lot. I would like to make it clear that we have discovered none of this discontent. The wireless programmes contain nothing hostile to the Soviet, nor do the loudspeakers at street-corners criticise the regime adversely.

When we asked our guide about it, he said that all this talk of discontent was capitalist propaganda.

One of our party very indiscreetly repeated a story about a small town in which all the churches were burnt down and the priests massacred, and pointed out that this led people to say that religion was persecuted.

"It is not encouraged," said the guide, "because it is the opium of the people. But how can you say it is persecuted in a place where there is nothing to persecute? If the churches do not exist and the priests are dead, there can be no religion going on. Therefore it cannot be persecuted."

III

October 16

On our way to visit the old summer palaces of the Czars, on the Black Sea, we called at a collective farm.

The guide explained that under the Czar the peasants were slaves, and that many of them were forced to till their own land instead of tilling communal land for the State. Each family lived separately in a very primitive dwelling, instead of having so many cubic metres of space allotted to it in a communal barrack.

He said that those peasants who did not like working on State farms were given a chance of taking a long journey, often as far at the Arctic regions.

We asked a man on the State farm, through an interpreter, whether he enjoyed his work. He said that he did, and that Lenin had freed the Workers. We asked him how much money he was allowed to earn, and he replied that money was not everything, and that Lenin had freed the Workers. We asked him about his religion. He said that religion was the opium of the people and that it was a good thing it had been done away with by the will of the people, and that Lenin had freed the Workers.

IV

October 17

We have visited one of the old summer palaces on the Black Sea coast.

It had been turned into a rest-home for the workers.

In what was once the banqueting hall, the workers were being lectured on the capitalist tendency of the pictures and the furniture —both of which remained.

The interpreter told us that all art before the Revolution had been propaganda for the capitalist classes. He said that the idea of families living in their own homes, instead of in communal flats or barracks, was an invention of the capitalists to emphasize the gulf between one man and another.

The guide said that many of the workers resting here could not read or write, but that, in order to remedy this state of affairs, a certain sum was docked from their pay as an annual subscription to a newspaper, and further sums as subscriptions to the various Workers' societies.

We asked if we might question some of the workers, but the guide said that tomorrow would be a better day, after he would have had time to prepare them for the shock of meeting such distinguished visitors.

V

October 18

Our party was taken to see a play to-day.

The guide said it dealt with the capitalist exploitation of surplus value, the democratisation of social processes, labour-power, and the dictatorship of the proletariat. Mrs. Thunderstroke said, "If every member of the proletariat has equal rights, and there are no capitalists, to whom do the proletariat dictate?" But the guide held up his hand for silence, as the big scene was beginning.

It showed a family of aristocrats at dinner. A servant spilt some soup over a lady's dress. Whereupon the host seized a knout which lay beside him on the table and beat the servant to death. The guest roared with laughter.

Next day we went to a lecture on bourgeois art in Europe. The audience included a Mingrelian tobacco-grower, two mechanics from a steel-cable factory in the Urals, a savage from the Obi basin, a Sart, a Mohammedan bandit from Daghestan, Samoieds from Arctic creeks, Yakuts, Buriats, Bashkirs, an Usbeg from Khiva, a Mongol from Kamchatka, a party of operatives on leave from Cheliabinsk, and some Kalmucks from the Sarpa hills. "All this," said the guide, "is representative of the new Russia, where art is part of the life of the worker."

VI

October 19

Our guide secured us an interview with a prominent official of the Communist Party from the Altai. We asked a number of questions, but the interpreter said that the dialect this man spoke consisted only of some hundred and thirty words. "It is best," he said, "to let him tell you about his work." The interpreter made a sign, and the man at once spoke a sentence or two with great rapidity. What he said was translated for us as follows: "Before the revolution the exploiter stole surplus value from the exploited, but now nobody is exploited, because the State is in supreme control of the means of production, and all the workers have to do is to put the fruits of their labour at the disposal of the State. World revolution will free the proletariat of the world."

We asked our guide about the shops, of which there seemed to be so few. He said that if a worker could secure a permit he could buy what he wanted within reason, unless the shop had not got enough of it. He said that the spare parts for radios sold best because it was easy to get a permit to buy them, and every one wanted to listen to the Soviet programmes.

VII

October 20

We had almost made up our minds that the Soviet system was flawless, and that the world must adopt it wholesale in order to survive, when we saw an official, a burly man in a leather jacket and peaked cap, maltreating a skinny horse. Such a sight brought a cry of anger from Mrs. Thunderstroke, and Mr. Milk protested to the guide. The incident has considerably modified our opinion of Soviet Russia.

We had to wait two days for a train. The guide explained that in capitalist countries every one is so eager to amass money and to exploit the proletariat that trains have to be punctual whereas in Russia other things are considered more important.

The train, when it arrived had not enough fuel to go to the place we had intended to visit, so we had to get out after twenty minutes, and walk a long way to the nearest town.

CHRISTOPHER DAWSON
(1889–   )

THE distinguished historian of culture, Christopher Dawson, was born at Yorks, England, 1889. The foundations of his education were laid at Winchester, its fabric erected at Trinity College, Oxford.

Dawson became a convert in 1914. Since that time Dawson's researches in cultural history have completed the movement begun by Lingard in the nineteenth century. With cool precision and scholarly detachment Dawson has revealed the main roots of Western culture. His conclusions have done much to buttress the Catholic thesis. Dawson was lecturer in the Philosophy of Religion at Liverpool University, 1933–1934, and became lecturer in the History of Culture at University College, Exeter, 1935. He is at the present time editor of the *Dublin Review*.

Dawson was a prime mover in the *Essays in Order* which did much to revitalize the intellectual outlook of Catholics in England and America. His books have materially fostered a more mature approach to the riches of the faith.

His essays on culture from the *Age of the Gods,* which examines the origins of culture in prehistoric Europe and the ancient East, to his last published work, *The Judgment of the Nations,* are all penetrating analyses of the various factors which make European culture understandable and implicitly progressive. Dawson is not only concerned with analyses. He exposes as well the aberrations which have brought about the decline of the West and he quite fearlessly indicates the reintegration which is necessary if peace and vitality are to return to the world and the European Continent.

HUMANISM AND THE NEW ORDER*

FOR centuries a civilisation will follow the same path, worshipping the same gods, cherishing the same ideals, acknowledging the same moral and intellectual standards. And then all at once a change will come, the springs of the old life run dry, and men suddenly awake to a new world, in which the ruling principles of the former age seem to lose their validity and to become inapplicable or meaningless.

This is what occurred in the time of the Roman Empire, when the ancient world, which had lived for centuries on the inherited capital of the Hellenistic culture, seemed suddenly to come to the end of its resources and to realise its need of something entirely new. For four hundred years the civilised world had been reading the same books, admiring the same works of art, and cultivating the same types of social and personal expression. Then came the change of the third and fourth centuries, A.D., when the forms of the Hellenistic culture suddenly lost their vitality and men turned to a new art, a new thought and a new way of life — from philosophy to theology, from the Greek statue to the Byzantine mosaic, from the gymnasium to the monastery.

This species of cultural discontinuity is not unknown in other civilisations — for example in China in the third and fourth centuries A.D. — but it seems specially characteristic of the West. It took place once more in the fifteenth and sixteenth centuries at the close of the Middle Ages, and we seem to be experiencing something of the kind in Europe to-day. During the last period of the nineteenth century and the first years of the twentieth century a further phase of Western civilisation came to an end. The old capital was exhausted and there was nothing to take its place. Liberalism and Nationalism had

Essays in Order (New York: Macmillan Co., 1931), pp. 155–165.

won their long fight with the old order, but they had lost their own ideals. In Italy the Risorgimento had given place to the age of Crispi and the Triple Alliance, and in France the centenary of the Republic was being celebrated by the Panama scandals. It was a dark age — dark not as in the early Middle Ages with the honest night of barbarism, but with the close uneasy gloom that comes before a storm. In the past, the periods of climax, as a rule, have been ages of material distress and economic decline, but the terrifying thing about that age was its prosperity, its confidence, its material success. "There has never," wrote Péguy, "been an age in which money was to such a degree the only master and God. And never have the rich been so protected against the poor and the poor so unprotected against the rich. . . .

"And never has the temporal been so protected against the spiritual; and never has the spiritual been so unprotected against the temporal."

The goal of the Liberal Enlightenment and Revolution had been reached, and Europe at last possessed a completely secularised culture. The old religion had not been destroyed; in fact throughout Protestant Europe the Churches still possessed a position of established privilege. But they held this position only on the condition that they did not interfere with the reign of Mammon. In reality they had been pushed aside into a backwater where they were free to stagnate in peace and to brood over the memory of dead controversies which had moved the mind of Europe three centuries before.

On the other hand the intellectuals who had contributed so much to the victory of the new order of things were in a somewhat similar plight. They found themselves powerless to influence the movement of civilisation, which had cut itself free, not only from tradition, but also from art and thought. The spiritual leadership that was possessed by Voltaire and Rousseau, by Goethe and Fichte, was now a thing of the past. The men of letters were expected to follow society, not to lead it. And this is what many of them did, whether with the professional servility of the journalist or with the disinterested

fanaticism of the realist, who affirmed his artistic integrity by the creation of an imaginary world no less devoid of spiritual significance than was the social world in which he lived. But a large number, probably the majority, found neither of these alternatives satisfactory. They turned to literature and art as a means of escape from reality. That was the meaning to many of the catchword, "Art for Art's sake." Symbolism and aestheticism, the Ivory Tower and the Celtic Twilight, Satanism and the cult of "Evil," hashish and absinthe; all of them were ways by which the last survivors of Romanticism made their escape, leaving the enemy in possession of the field.

There was, however, one exception, one man who refused to surrender.

Whatever his weakness Friedrich Nietzsche was neither a time-server nor a coward. He at least stood for the supremacy of spirit, when so many of those whose office it was to defend it had fallen asleep or had gone over to the enemy. He remained faithful to the old ideals of the Renaissance culture, the ideals of creative genius and of the self-affirmation of the free personality, and he revolted against the blasphemies of an age which degraded the personality and denied the power of the spirit in the name of humanity and liberty.

Nevertheless, Nietzsche himself was far from being a humanist. Humanism is essentially a *via media,* and in the nineteenth century the *via media* had become identical with mediocrity. In Nietzsche's eyes humanity had become something either ridiculous or shameful, and the attempt to pass beyond humanity led him to the negation of humanism and the destruction of his own personality; as he said, the way of the creator is to burn himself in his own fire. Yet the tragedy of Nietzsche is the tragedy of the end of humanism, since it only reveals with exceptional clearness the ultimate consequences of the antinomy that was inherent in the humanist tradition from the beginning.

The essentially transitory character of the humanist culture has been obscured by the dominance of the belief in Progress and by the shallow and dogmatic optimism which characterised nineteenth-century Liberalism. It was only an exceptionally original mind, like that of the late T. F. Hulme, that could free itself from the influence of Liberal dogma and could recognise *the signs of the times* — the passing of the ideals that had dominated European civilisation for four centuries, and the dawn of a new order.

In the years that followed the war this consciousness has become general, at least on the Continent, owing largely to the popularity of Spengler's well-known book, *The Decline of the West*. But Spengler's arbitrary and subjective theorising threw no light upon the inner meaning of the change. A much more profound analysis of the modern situation is to be found in the works of the modern Russian thinkers of the school of Solovyov, above all Nicholas Berdyaev. In his book *Der Sinn der Geschichte* and in his later essays on "The New Middle Ages," Berdyaev has dealt with the passing of humanism not as an instance of historical fatality, but in its ultimate significance for the spiritual life of humanity, and has shown how the disintegration of the Renaissance culture was the result of a spiritual disunity and conflict which it was never able to overcome.

In spite of its ideal of a purely human perfection and its cult of classical form, there was in humanism something excessive, a kind of *hubris* which led it to destruction. We see this already in the brilliant culture of the fifteenth-century Italy, where the unbridled individualism of princes and cities led to the loss of national independence. But that is only a superficial instance of the instability of the new order. It is not in any obvious material failure, but in its very triumphs and successes, that the real weakness of the movement is to be found. For each fresh victory of the humanistic spirit undermined the foundations of its own vitality.

The Renaissance has its beginning in the self-discovery, the self-realization and the self-exaltation of Man. Mediaeval man has attempted to base his life on the supernatural. His ideal of knowledge was not the adventurous quest of the human mind exploring its own kingdom; it was an intuition of the eternal verities which is itself an emanation from the Divine Intellect — *irradiatio et participatio primae lucis*. The men of the Renaissance, on the other hand, turned away from the eternal and the absolute to the world of nature and human experience. They rejected their dependence on the supernatural, and vindicated their independence and supremacy in the temporal order. But thereby they were gradually led by an internal process of logic to criticise the principles of their own knowledge and to lose confidence in their own freedom. The self-affirmation of man gradually led to the denial of the spiritual foundations of his freedom and knowledge. This tendency shows itself in every department of modern thought. In philosophy, it leads from the dogmatic rationalism of Descartes and the dogmatic empiricism of Locke to the radical scepticism of Hume and the subjectivism of later German thought. Reason is gradually stripped of its prerogatives until nothing is left to it but the bare "as if" of Vaihinger.

In science, the growth of man's knowledge and his control over nature is accompanied by a growing sense of man's dependence on material forces. He gradually loses his position of exception and superiority and sinks back into nature. He becomes a subordinate part of the great mechanical system that his scientific genius has created. In the same way, the economic process, which led to the exploitation of the world by man and the vast increase of his material resources, ends in the subjection of man to the rule of the machine and the mechanisation of human life. Finally, in the political and social sphere, the revolt against the mediaeval principle of hierarchy and the reassertion of the rights of the secular power led to the absolutism of the modern national state. This again was followed by a second revolt — the assertion of the rights of man against secular authority which culminated in the French Revolution. But this second revolt also led to disillusion. It led, on the one hand, to the disintegration of the organic principle in society into an individualistic atomism, which leaves the individual isolated and helpless before the new economic forces, and, on the other, to the growth of the new bureaucratic state, that "coldest of cold monsters," which exerts a more irresistible and far-reaching control over the individual life than was ever possessed by the absolute monarchies of the old *régime*.

So we have the paradox that at the beginning of the Renaissance, when the conquest of nature and the creation of modern science are still unrealised, man appears in godlike freedom with a sense of unbounded power and greatness; while at the end of the nineteenth century, when nature has been conquered and there seem no limits to the powers of science, man is once more conscious of his misery and weakness as the slave of material circumstance and physical appetite and death. Instead of the heroic exaltation of humanity which was characteristic of the naturalism of the Renaissance, we see the humiliation of humanity in the anti-human naturalism of Zola. Man is stripped of his glory and freedom and left as a naked human animal shivering in an inhuman universe.

Thus humanism by its own inner development is eventually brought to deny itself and to pass away into its opposite. For Nietzsche, who refused to surrender the spiritual element in the Renaissance tradition, humanism is transcended in an effort to attain to the superhuman without abandoning the self-assertion and the rebellious freedom of the individual will — an attempt which inevitably ends in self-destruction. But modern civilisation as a whole could not follow this path. It naturally chose to live as best it could, rather than to commit a spectacular suicide. And so, in order to adapt itself to the new conditions, it was forced to throw over the humanist tradition.

Hence the increasing acceptance of the mechanisation of life that has characterised the last thirty years. Above all, in the period since the war there has been a growing tendency towards the de-intellectualisation and exteriorisation of European life. The old fixed canons of social and moral conduct have been abandoned, and society has given itself up to the current of external change without any attempt towards self-direction or the preservation of spiritual continuity. But this acceptance of new conditions is in itself negative, and possesses no creative quality. It points to the dying-down and stagnation of culture rather than its renewal. Nor is this surprising. For centuries, Western civilisation has received its impetus from the humanist tradition, and the dying-away of that tradition naturally involves the temporary cessation of cultural creativeness.

From this point of view it is very significant that almost the only original element in the thought of the new age should be the work of Jews. In physical science the dominant figure is Einstein, in psychology it is Freud, in economics and sociology it is Marx — and each of them has exerted an influence on the thought of the age that far transcends the limits of his particular subject. And it is easy to understand the reasons of this. The Jewish mind alone in the West has its own sources of life which are independent of the Hellenic and the Renaissance traditions. It has seen too many civilisations rise and fall to be discouraged by the failure of humanism. On the contrary it thrives in an atmosphere of determinism and historical destiny, which seems fatal to the humanist spirit.

This holds good especially of the Marxian attitude, which is characteristic of the new conditions, although it originated at a time when liberalism and romanticism were still flourishing. But Marx addressed himself to those elements in the modern world which were already deprived of any share in the heritage of humanist culture. He found the proletariat enslaved to the machine, and he sought, not to destroy this servitude, but to equalise and rationalise it by extending it to the whole social organism.

DEMOCRACY*

OF ALL the elements of the European tradition democracy is the one that is most difficult to appreciate in an objective and impartial spirit. It has been surrounded by an atmosphere of loose thinking which has obscured its true nature and has degraded it until it has become an empty catchword that covers every kind of political sentimentality and falsehood.

And yet it stands, none the less, for an element in European life that is of a permanent value and importance. It is the most characteristic expression of European political ideals, and if we attempt to separate it from its historical roots in European culture and to identify it with an abstract ideal that had its first conception in the mind of Rousseau, we shall inevitably misunderstand both democracy and Europe. There are two mistaken views of democracy, both of which have caused infinite misunderstandings in the past and which even today are not altogether extinct. One of these regards democracy as a crude destructive force that cares nothing for the finer values of civilised life, that is indifferent to culture and scientific knowledge and seeks only to satisfy the vanity and greed of the masses. This is the fallacy of the reactionaries. And, on the other hand, there is the ideal of democracy that is founded on false belief in the perfectibility of human nature. It regards all the evils of society as due to the misdeeds of kings and governments and believes that if once the power is put into the hands of the common people everything will go well, every one will be happy, and the world will be transformed into a Utopia.

In reality, democracy is neither the enemy of culture, nor a cure for all the ills of humanity. It is simply the culmination of the old European tradition of social and political freedom that has always been one of the essential elements of Western culture.

The basis of democracy is the ideal of public law and civic rights which Europe inherited from Greece and Rome, and which

*Dawson, Christopher, The Modern Dilemma (London: (Sheed and Ward, 1932), pp. 52–69.

is almost absent in Oriental societies however advanced they may be in civilisation. Consequently the fundamental opposition is not that between democracy and aristocracy, but that between citizenship and despotism. In the East the individual is nothing and the state is everything. It is a divine power — the Shadow of God on Earth, as the Sultan of Turkey used to call himself — and any claim to independent rights against that power on the part of the individual is inconceivable.

But in the West a man has his rights, even against the state. The whole history of Europe is the story of the vindication of these rights and the affirmation of human freedom, whether by classes or communities or individuals, from the English Barons at Runnymede, the free cities of the Middle Ages, the Swiss peasants and the English House of Commons, down to the final affirmation of the Rights of Man by the fathers of the United States and the founders of the French Republic. It was inevitable that these rights should begin as the rights of a privileged class, and gradually be extended to the rest of the community. For unfortunately, they are not the natural birthright of the human race, as the early Liberals used to believe. They are the culmination of a long process of social development — the flower of an advanced civilisation. The free man who was the ideal of the eighteenth-century democrats was not a mere nobody; he was an ideal type — no less ideal than the mediaeval knight or the Renaissance gentleman, and in the same line of descent. In fact, the ideal was first launched by aristocrats of the type of Alfieri and Mirabeau, and the English Whigs and the Virginian planters. The famous lines of Burns: "The rank is but the guinea stamp, a man's a man for a' that," do not mean that *quality* doesn't matter; on the contrary, they mean that quality is so important that it far outweighs the conventional labels that society has substituted for it.

Thus, paradoxical as it may appear, the democratic ideal has its origin in the aristocratic principle. In fact, Western democracy is essentially *aristocracy for all*. It was just the same with the Greeks. Greek democracy was not a proletariat; it had its origin in the extension to the majority of the civic rights that had originally been the jealously guarded privilege of a small body of patricians. Athens, the greatest of Greek democracies, was in reality one of the most aristocratic communities that has ever existed.

And this ideal, whether ancient Greek or modern European, has nothing in common with the Oriental ideal of the absolute state. The free man has no place in the latter; it is the impersonal power of the community, whether embodied in an absolute monarch, or a priesthood or a democracy, that is all in all. Of course, this ideal is also capable of acquiring a popular form. The absolute state may represent the interests of the whole people rather than of a privileged class; it may even, as in Communist Russia, become the instrument of a dictatorship of the proletariat. But this does not make it democratic in the Western sense. Bolshevism is a popular version of Tsarism, just as democracy is aristocracy for all. The essential note of democracy is the recognition of the dignity and the rights of the individual citizen. And thus it is very closely associated with the traditions of humanism and humanitarianism, of which I have spoken above. In fact, apart from humanitarianism democracy becomes an empty and meaningless form. The political rights of democracy presuppose the moral rights of humanity, and if the humanitarian movement had not inspired Western society with an enthusiasm for social justice and for the cause of the weak and the oppressed, modern democracy would never have come into existence.

But in spite of the superiority of the democratic idea — at least to the Western mind — we must admit that it is much harder to realise than the ideal of the absolute state. The despotic *régime* is the one that has succeeded, at least in the past. And even today, the vast and rapid advance of democracy should not blind us to the fact that the opposite ideal is still vigorous and that in some respects it is once more gaining ground at the expense of democracy.

The chief cause of this is not political but economic. As Mr. Leonard Woolf has pointed out, it is the problem of economic equality that is the real crux of democracy. You can give nominal political rights to every citizen without much difficulty, but when you attempt to put into practice the full programme of real democracy — that is to say, to give every citizen equal opportunities of happiness and an equal share in the good things of life — you are faced with a serious dilemma. Complete economic equality seems attainable only by state socialism, and any thoroughgoing system of socialism seems to involve, as in Russia, the omnipotence of the state and all the dangers of a return to despotism and the negation of individual rights which that implies. The democratic ideal in its economic aspect is neither that of pure individualism nor that of pure state socialism; it is the ideal of a free co-operative economy in which every man has control over his own life and possesses an economic foundation for his social liberty. In other words, economic democracy means capitalism for all: it means an extension of the rights of property to every citizen rather than the abolition of private property in the interests of the state. It is inconsistent with the individualistic society in which a small number of very rich men control the lives of the great masses of their fellow citizens; but it is also inconsistent with the communist society in which the economic life of the individual is even more completely controlled by the machinery of an all-powerful state.

We must, in fact, recognise (and it is very seldom recognised) that the idea of equality is not necessarily or exclusively democratic. Pure democracy leads to equality, but so does pure despotism. And as a matter of fact, it is easier to attain the negative ideal of a dead level of equality in equal servitude than to achieve the positive ideal of equality in freedom and fulness of life.

But, as I have said, democracy is aristocracy for all; it is levelling up, not levelling down. The true democrat does not wish to attain equality by lowering the cultural standard of society and by reducing everyone to a drab uniformity of existence. He desires the richest and fullest life that is possible. In the communist Utopia, there is no room for a Wordsworth or a Beethoven. The artist, no less than the engineer or the bureaucrat, is the servant of the economic machine, and his highest aim is to be a kind of publicity agent for the communist state. But in the democratic Utopia, the state would be the servant and not the absolute master of the human personality, and the development of individual genius would be encouraged as much as possible, for one Mozart adds more to the real wealth of society than a hundred millionaires or political organisers.

All that the democrat demands in the name of equality is that no man shall be debarred by economic or social privileges from developing his own genius or from enjoying the results of the genius of others.

Every society must have its *élite;* the only question is what kind of an *élite* it desires to have. In a despotic society the *élite* are the picked servants of the state, like the Communist Party in Russia, the later Roman bureaucracy, or the priests and officials of the old Oriental despotism. We find the extreme development of this ideal in those Oriental states, like mediaeval Egypt or Turkey under the Ottoman Sultans, in which the country was governed by picked slaves and members of the subject races who owed everything to the sovereign power and had no rights of their own. But in the civic type of society, whether it is democracy or an aristocracy, the *élite* are not bound to the service of the state. They are free men with the right to live their own life and develop their own personalities under the most advantageous conditions.

The only difference between the aristocracy and the democracy is that in the one case the *élite* forms a hereditary class which tends to monopolise political power and social privilege, while in the other they are the leaders of their fellow citizens, who set the standard of culture for the rest of the community and use their opportunities for the enrichment of the common social life.

This was the secret of the achievements of Greek democracy. The *élite* at Athens had no monopoly of political power, but they possessed a cultural leadership. Their aristocrats, like Pericles, were great democratic leaders, and their rich men were expected to use their wealth to provide for the public amusements of the citizens. And thus the brilliant achievements of Greek art and literature were not the selfish monopoly of the few, but the common possession of the whole body of citizens; as we see, above all, in the case of the Greek drama, perhaps the greatest civic art that has ever existed.

It may be objected that this is not real democracy, and that the Athenians would have done better to abolish their *élite* and to use their wealth for the increase of the ordinary man's income. But though it is true that you cannot enjoy the higher goods of culture if you have not enough to eat, it is also true that you cannot get twice as much culture by doubling the amount you eat. The truly rich society is not the one that goes on piling up economic wealth as an end in itself, but the one that uses its wealth as the foundation on which to build a rich and many-sided culture. From this point of view, a country like ancient Greece, in which hardly anybody could afford more than one good meal a day, was richer than the United States at the height of its prosperity.

The great fault of modern democracy — a fault that is common to the capitalist and the socialist — is that it accepts economic wealth as the end of society and the standard of personal happiness. We have made the increase of wealth the one criterion of social improvement, and consequently our aristocracy is an aristocracy of money-makers, and our democratic ideal is mainly an ideal of more money for everyone. But the standard of life is really not an economic but a vital thing; it is a question of how you live rather than how much you live on. Just as a man who buys one's house does not buy one's family and friends and interests — all the things that made up the life that was lived in that house — so two men may possess the same money income, and yet have totally different standards of life.

Even if we could guarantee every unemployed person an income of £400 a year, we should not have solved the vital problem of unemployment, which is the problem of social maladjustment. St. Francis of Assisi possessed no income at all, and his material standard of life was below that of a modern tramp. But for all that he was infinitely better off than the modern unemployed, because he had achieved a complete measure of social adjustment. To take a less extreme instance; during the happiest and most productive part of his life, Wordsworth had, I believe, an income of about £70 a year, and he would have been no better off with a million, because he had found the way of life that suited him. If he had lived in a different kind of society, for instance in modern America, he would have needed twelve times that income and he would still have been cramped and unsatisfied.

The great curse of our modern society is not so much the lack of money as the fact that the lack of money condemns a man to a squalid and incomplete existence. But even if he has money, and a great deal of it, he is still in danger of leading an incomplete life, because our whole social order is directed to economic instead of spiritual ends. The economic view of life regards money as equivalent of satisfaction. Get money, and if you get enough of it you will get everything else that is worth having. The Christian view of life, on the other hand, puts economic things in the second place. First seek the Kingdom and God, and everything else will be added to you. And this is not so absurd as it sounds, for we have only to think for a moment to realise that the ills of modern society do not spring from poverty; in fact society today is probably richer in material wealth than any society that has ever existed. What we are suffering from is lack of social adjustment and the failure to subordinate material and economic goods to human and spiritual ones.

To take a concrete example. The difficulties of our present situation are largely due to the fact that England sacrificed her agriculture and her agricultural population in the last century in order to become the workshop of the world. The preservation of our agrarian foundation was perfectly possible, but it would have involved a loss of immediate profit, a simpler standard of life, and a lower national money income, and consequently it was sacrificed to our industrial supremacy. We got the money, but we have paid the price in the loss of national stability and of a balanced social economy. But the most serious loss is not the loss of economic self-sufficiency; it is the loss of the rural class which has destroyed the old foundation of our national life and dried up the stream of British colonial expansion at its source.

And even more serious are the spiritual consequences of economic materialism.

Europe gained the leadership in world culture, not by its material wealth, but by its pre-eminence in the things of the mind — in science and literature and ideas. It created the ideals which the rest of the world followed. If modern democracy were to involve giving up this mission and abandoning spiritual leadership for material satisfaction, then it would justly mean the decline of Western culture. But as we have seen, democracy is by no means essentially materialistic; the democratic movement was founded on idealism, and if it is losing its ideals that is not the fault of the people as a whole. One of the most acute critics of modern tendencies, M. Lucien Romier, has written as follows:

The modern masses are not closed to ideas, but they want them and understand them only within the limits of their own experience and their own most constant and vital preoccupations. The problem is not to level all thought down to mass tendencies, but to answer the questions put by the masses. If the pure scientist or the philosopher who is capable of originality and leadership refuses to answer — then some slave of the crowd, some low journalist or venal politician, anxious for popularity and profit, will answer instead.

This is the vital problem of democracy, the problem of spiritual leadership. We need men who are something more than cunning manipulators of the political and economic machine, men who stand not for success or material efficiency, but for the old Christian ideals of faith, hope and charity.

And it is not only religious people who feel this. Even a thorough sceptic and modernist like Bertrand Russell is just as convinced as we are that if modern society goes on putting power and economic efficiency above spiritual values, it will end in disaster. This is what he says:

Our world has a heritage of culture and beauty, but unfortunately we have been handing on this heritage only to the less active and important members of each generation. The government of the world (by which I do not mean its ministerial posts, but its key positions of power) has been allowed to fall into the hands of men ignorant of the past, without tenderness to what is traditional, without understanding of what they are destroying.

And consequently the new society that is arising, based on pure economic and scientific technology, is a society that is

incompatible with the pursuit of truth, with love, with art, with spontaneous delight with every ideal that men have cherished with the sole exception of ascetic renunciation.

It is impossible to state the issue more clearly. The society that exists for wealth and power alone may attain a kind of greatness, but it is the greatness of despotism, not that of a democracy.

Democracy in the last resort rests on a spiritual community. It arose in the West because European society was based on a religious foundation. Even before the common man acquired political rights, he possessed a real kind of spiritual citizenship as a member of the universal Christian society. This was the fundamental citizenship in comparison with which a man's membership of the state was a secondary and relative matter. And consequently, the state was not the absolute master of the destinies of the individual. It could not treat him merely as an instrument for the attainment of its ends. For every man, even the poorest and the weakest, only belonged in part to the state. His personality was free and possessed an absolute spiritual value which was incomparably higher than anything in the economic or the political order. The state existed for man and not man for the state.

This is the principle which humanitarianism owed to the Christian tradition and which it handed on to modern democracy.

As soon as this principle is abandoned, the moral foundations of democracy are destroyed and we are faced with the alternative of a return to some new form of state absolutism or mass dictatorship.

And thus we come back to the fundamental issue of the modern dilemma, an issue that may be expressed as the choice between religious and secular ideals or between the spiritual and the materialistic view of life. The new forces of science and material organisation have endowed modern man and the modern state with powers and resources that far exceed anything mankind has hitherto known. But these forces can be used alike for destruction and for creation, for life and death, to the glory of God or in the service of Satan.

The nineteenth century did not face the issue. It allowed the new forces to be exploited in a haphazard way for selfish and material and temporary ends, without any constructive plan or any vision of life as a whole. It kept religion for Sundays and it left culture to the upper classes. But we have come to see that this individualistic and sectional solution is no solution at all. Either religion and spiritual culture must inspire the whole of life, or they will be thrown out of social life altogether. Either we must accept the materialistic view of life, which substitutes the worship of the machine and the absolutism of mass civilisation for the ideals of the Christian and the humanitarian traditions, or else we must return to the spiritual foundations on which European civilisation has been built and attempt to make the new material forces the instruments of a spiritual purpose.

There is no real reason for believing that the ideals of European science and democracy and of the humanitarian tradition have been destroyed by the forces of change. But if they are to be preserved, we need something more than a vague idealism based on our personal desires. We must recognise the existence of an objective spiritual order that transcends the sphere of politics and economics; that is to say, we must return to a religious view of life.

RISE OF WESTERN CIVILIZATION*

CHAPTER VII

THE Jewish affirmation of the significance and value of history found a yet wider development in Christianity. The world process was conceived not as an unchanging order governed by the fatal law of necessity, but as a divine drama whose successive acts were the Creation and Fall of Man, his Redemption, and his glorious restoration.

Hence, in spite of the Christian opposition between "This World" and "The World to Come," there can be no tampering with the reality and uniqueness of the historical process. The irreconcilibility of Christianity with the dominant theory of cosmic cycles is obvious, and was stated uncompromisingly by the early Fathers. "If we accept that theory," says Origen, "then Adam and Eve will do in a second world exactly as they have done in this: the same deluge will be repeated; the same Moses will bring the same people out of Egypt, Judas will a second time betray his Lord, and again Paul will keep the garments of those who will stone Stephen."

And it was on this very ground that the Church had to fight its earliest battles, for Gnosticism was essentially an attempt to combine the belief in spiritual redemption with the theory of world-aeons and of the illusory nature of earthly change, and consequently the whole anti-Gnostic apologia of St. Irenaeus is directed to the defence of the value and reality of the historical development. "Since men are real, theirs must be a real establishment. They do not vanish into non-existence, but progress among existent things." "There is one Son who performs the Father's will, and one human race in which the mysteries of God are realised." "God arranged everything from the first with a view to the perfection of man, in order to deify him and reveal His own dispensations, so that goodness may be made manifest, justice made perfect, and the Church may be fashioned after the image of His Son. Thus

man may eventually reach maturity, and, being ripened by such privileges, may see and comprehend God."

It was to this consciousness of its unique character and mission that Christianity owes its extraordinary powers of expansion and conquest which revolutionized the whole development of Western civilization. For it cannot be too strongly insisted that the victory of the Church in the 4th century was not, as many modern critics would have us believe, the natural culmination of the religious evolution of the ancient world. It was, on the contrary, a violent interruption of that process which forced European civilization out of its old orbit into a path which it would never have followed by its own momentum. It is true that the classical culture and the religion of the city state with which it was associated were losing their vitality, and that nothing could have arrested the movement of orientalization which ultimately conquered the Roman world. But this movement found its normal expression either in the undiluted form which is represented by the different Gnostic and Manichaean sects, or in a bastard Hellenistic syncretism. The religion of the Emperor Julian and his Neoplatonist teachers, in spite of their devotion to the Hellenic past was actually more impregnated with oriental elements than was that of the Christian Fathers, such as Eusebius of Caesarea, Theodore of Mopsuestia, Theodoret, Basil and the two Gregories.

For the writings of the latter, in spite of their avowed hostility to the Greek religious tradition, were characterized by a genuine spirit of humanism, for which there was little room in the spiritualistic theosophy of Julian and Maximus of Tyre. Their whole apologetic is dominated by the conception of Man as the center and crown of the created universe. The first book of the *Theophany* of Eusebius is a long panegyric of humanity, — man the craftsman and artist, the builder of cities and the sailor of ships, — man the scientist and philosopher who alone can foretell the changes of the heavenly bodies and knows the hidden causes of things, — man a

---

*Dawson, Christopher, *Progress and Religion* (New York: Sheed & Ward, 1938), pp. 162–184.

god upon earth, "the dear child of the Divine Word."

So, too, St. Gregory of Nyssa sees in man not only "the god-like image of the archetypal beauty," but the channel through which the whole material creation acquires consciousness and becomes spiritualized and united to God. Just as in the material world itself, he says, there is an inner organic harmony of creation, so, too, there is, by the Divine wisdom, a certain commingling of the intelligible world with the sensible creation, so that no part of creation might be rejected or deprived of Divine fellowship. And the bond of this mixture and communion is to be found in human nature. Man was created by God "in order that the earthly element might be raised by union with the Divine, and so the Divine Grace in one even course, as it were, might uniformly extend through all creation, the lower nature being mingled with that which is above the world." This created nature, however, is essentially changeable. It continually passes through a process of evolution, which so long as it acts in accordance with nature will always be progressive, but which, on the other hand, may become a movement of degeneration and decline, if once the will should become perverted.

This is what has happened in the actual history of humanity, and therefore it has been necessary for the Divine Nature to unite itself with mankind in a second creation which will restore and still further develop the original function of humanity. Thus the Incarnation is the source of a new movement of regeneration and progress which leads ultimately to the deification of human nature by its participation in the Divine Life. The life of the Divine Trinity externalizes itself in the Church as the restored humanity, and the purpose of creation finds its complete fulfillment in the Incarnate Word, "Who unites the universe to Himself, bringing in His own Person the different kinds of existing things to one accord and harmony."

This presentation of the Christian doctrine of man and the Incarnation is a conscious attempt to express the new Christian world view in a form accessible to the Greek mind.

It is a genuine synthesis of the Christian and the Platonic traditions, and one which, in spite of Harnack's criticism, is in entire agreement with the spirit of St. Paul himself. Nevertheless, the Hellenic tradition to which Eusebius and St. Gregory addressed themselves was not the dominant force in the world of the day. At the same time that the Church was successfully carrying on its apostolate in the Graeco-Roman world, it was itself being assailed in the rear by the orientalizing heresies which sought to convert Christianity into a religion of pure spirit, and asserted that the body and the material world were essentially evil. This force not only manifested itself in forms such as Manichaeanism and Gnosticism, which were the open enemies of orthodox Christianity, but also made itself felt within the Church by the influence of Encratite works such as the apocryphal Gospels and Acta, as well as by the Monophysite tendency which denied the orthodox doctrine of the full humanity of Christ, and which saw in the Incarnation only the appearance upon earth of the divinity in bodily form.

Consequently the Byzantine culture does not simply represent the fusion of the Hellenistic-Roman tradition with Christianity. It contains a third element of oriental origin which is, in fact, the preponderant influence in Byzantine civilization. It is to be seen in social and political organization of the Empire which borrowed from Sassanian Persia all the external forms of the oriental sacred monarchy. The rigid hierarchy of the Byzantine state which centres in the Sacred Palace and the quasi-divine person of the Holy Emperor is neither Roman nor Christian, but purely oriental. And the same influence is to be seen in Byzantine religion in its tendency to neglect the historical and dynamic element in the Christian tradition, and to become absorbed in theological speculations regarding the nature of the Godhead. This tendency reaches its climax in the writings of the so-called Dionysius the Areopagite, which probably date from the close of the 5th century, and have exerted an incalculable influence on the religious life of the Byzantine world. Here we may see the most extreme assertion of the Divine Transcendence and the negation of all finite modes of being.

"As intelligible things are not to be comprehended by the senses . . . so, too, the infinite Super-Being transcends Being, the Super-intelligible unity transcends Intelligences, the One that is beyond thought transcends comprehension, and the Good which is beyond speech transcends expression. For it is a Monad which unifies every unity, a Super-essential Essence, an Unintelligible Mind, an Ineffable word, or rather the negation of Reason, Intelligence, Word, and every particular form of existence."

Consequently in order to attain to the knowledge of this Divine Negation "man must plunge into the mystical darkness of Unknowing in which he lays aside all rational knowledge and becomes absorbed in that which is wholly intangible and invisible . . . so that he is united to that which is wholly unknowable by the highest part of the mind in the complete cessation of rational knowledge and knows in a manner beyond mind by knowing nothing."

But this way of absolute negation is not the whole of the Dionysian teaching. It is supplemeted by the theory of a mystical hierarchy, by which the initiate is gradually led upwards by a series of ritual acts and sacramental symbols from the Sensible to the Intelligible and from the Intelligible to the Divine.

Thus abstract mysticism is linked up with a fixed ritual and ceremonial order which is its earthly and sensible counterpart: in his own words "the Theurgy is the completion of the Theology."

Similarly the moral ideal of the Byzantine world found its expression in the uncompromising other-worldliness of the monks of the desert which represents the extreme development of the oriental spirit of asceticism and world-denial within the boundaries of orthodox Christianity. For the naked fasting ascetics of Nitria and the Thebaid, the state and the world of social duties had ceased to exist. They had cut themselves off from all social ties; they recognised no political obligation. They lived entirely for the spirit, and

left the body nothing save the right to bare existence.

Nevertheless, even this radically oriental version of Christianity did not satisfy the Eastern world. With the coming of Islam it reverted to a simple type of religion, which felt no need for any incarnation of the divine or any progressive transformation of human nature. The bridge between God and Man was broken, and the Divine Omnipotence once more reigned in lonely splendour, like the sun over the desert.

In the Roman West, in spite of its lower standard of civilization, the conditions were more favourable for the development of an original and creative Christian culture. For here the Church did not become incorporated in a fixed social and political order which it was powerless to modify; it found itself abandoned to its own resources in a world of chaos and destruction. It had to contend, not with the influence of an alien spiritual tradition but with the forces of barbarism and social disorder. But long before the fall of the Empire, Western Catholicism had already acquired the distinctive characteristics that were to mark its future development. The oldest document of Western Christianity —the First Epistle of Clement—already shows the Latin sense of order and its practical ideal of social duty. Even the Western heresies from the days of Novatian and the Donatists to Pelagius and Priscillian are not concerned with speculative theology, but with the concrete matters of Church order or with the problems of moral conduct and moral responsibility.

Moreover the emphasis on the social aspect of the Christian tradition led the Western Church to assume a much more independent attitude to the state than that of the Byzantine Church. Hilary of Poitiers in the reign of Constantine, attacks the interference of the state in religious matters with a vehemence that is hardly surpassed by the champions of the mediaeval Papacy, and St. Ambrose, in his relations with the Christian Emperors, affirms the authority of the spiritual power in the spirit of a mediaeval pontiff rather than a Byzantine prelate. The Emperor, he says, is within the Church, not above it, and consequently it is the duty of the Christian ruler to subordinate his action to the Church's decrees in all matters that concern the faith.

But it was St. Augustine who first gave a more profound philosophical and theological orientation to the genius of the Western Church. It is true that his thought was by no means free of oriental elements. It was not for nothing that he had been for years a disciple of the Manicheans, and that his mind had also been permeated by the influence of Neoplatonism. He was dominated by that nostalgia of the infinite which led the thinkers of the oriental world to turn away from the world of experience towards the eternal vision of transcendent Being. Nevertheless he was also a Latin, and his Latin sense of social and historical reality led him to do justice to the social and historical elements that are implicit in the Christian tradition. His ideal was not an impersonal Nirvana, but the City of God, and he saw the spiritual order not as a static metaphysical principle, but as a dynamic force which manifests itself in human society. Two loves, he says, built two cities. The love of Self builds up Babylon to the contempt of God, and the love of God builds up Jerusalem to the contempt of Self. All history consists of the evolution of these principles embodied in two societies, "blended one with another and moving on in all changes of times from the beginning of the human race even to the end of the world."

Consequently the present world is neither a complete static order nor an unmeaning and illusory appearance. It is the birth process of a spiritual creation, the seminal or embryonic activity of a new life. And the actuating principle in this process is the Divine Spirit which manifests itself in the world, outwardly through the sacramental order of the Church, and inwardly in the soul by the operation of the spiritual will. For St. Augustine's emphasis on the weakness of human nature and the omnipotence of divine grace does not imply any undervaluing of the ethical aspect of life. On the contrary, paradoxical as it may seem, it was the importance that he attached to the moral will that led him to depreciate its freedom.

The human will is the engine that God employs for the creation of a new world.

Thus while Christianity in the East tended to become a speculative mysticism embodied in a system of ritual — a $\mu\nu\sigma\tau\alpha\gamma\omega\gamma\iota\alpha$ in the technical sense — in the West, under the influence of Augustine, it became a dynamic moral and social force. This is the distinction which Ritschl stated so forcibly in his comparison of St. Augustine with the Pseudo-Areopagite. The latter he says, was the founder of a ritual ecclesiasticism, the former of an ecclesiasticism of moral tasks in the service of a world-wide Christianity. It is true that this aspect of Western Christianity can easily be exaggerated. St. Augustine was not an Americanist. He did not value the active moral life as an end in itself. He realized as fully as any oriental the supremacy of the transcendent and the ideal of mystical contemplation. But while the East concentrated itself on this aspect of religion to the exclusion of all else, the spirit of the Western Church is expressed in the great words of the dying St. Martin: *"Domine si populo tuo adhuc sum necessarius, non recuso laborem."*

This is the spirit which inspired the Western Church in the age of darkness and anarchy which followed the downfall of the Empire. It is to be seen in the work of the Papacy, as represented above all by St. Gregory, who laboured amidst the ruins of a dying civilization to serve the cause of social justice and humanity. It is to be seen no less in the new Benedictine monasticism which converted the purely ascetic tradition of the monks of the desert into a disciplined social institution in the service of the Universal Church. These two powers were the chief and almost the only constructive forces in Western Europe during the Dark Ages. It was they who reunited England to Christendom and created a new centre of Christian and Latin culture in the North. And it was the Saxon monks, such as Willibrord and Boniface and Alcuin who, in close alliance with the Papacy, converted heathen Germany, reformed the Frankish church, and laid the foundations for the Carolingian culture.

Hence the new civilization which slowly

and painfully began to emerge in the early middle ages was in a very special sense a religious creation, for it was based on an ecclesiastical not a political unity. While in the East, the imperial unity was still all inclusive and the Church was essentially the Church of the Empire, in the West it was the Church that was the universal society and the state that was weak, barbarous and divided. The only true citizenship that remained to the common man was his membership of the Church, and it involved a far deeper and wider loyalty than his allegiance to the secular state. It was the fundamental social relation which overrode all distinctions of class and nationality. The Church was a world in itself, with its own culture, its own organization and its own law. In so far as civilization survived, it was directly dependent on the Church, whether in the great Carolingian monasteries, such as St. Gall or Fulda, which were the chief centres of cultural and economic life, or in the cities which came to depend on the bishops and the ecclesiastical element for their very existence. The state, on the other hand, had become divorced from the city and the civic culture and reverted more and more to the warlike traditions of a barbarous tribal aristocracy.

For mediaeval Europe no longer possessed a homogeneous material culture, such as we find, for example, in China or India. It was a loose federation of the most diverse types of race and culture under the hegemony of a common religious and ecclesiastical tradition. This explains the contradictions and disunity of mediaeval culture — the contrast of its cruelty and its charity, its beauty and squalor, its spiritual vitality and its material barbarism. For the element of higher culture did not spring naturally from the traditions of the social organism itself, but came in from outside as a spiritual power which had to remould and transform the social material in which it attempted to embody itself.

And so in the 11th and 12th centuries, when the social revival of Western Europe began, the new development was inspired by religious motives, and proceeded directly from the tradition of the spiritual society. The struggle of the Investitures and the in-

ternational supremacy of the reformed Papacy were the visible signs of the victory of the spiritual power over the feudal and barbaric elements in European society. Everywhere men became conscious of their common citizenship in the great spiritual commonwealth of Christendom. And this spiritual citizenship was the foundation of a new society. As members of the feudal state, men were separated by the countless divisions of allegiance and jurisdiction. They were parcelled out like sheep with the land, on which they lived, among different lordships. But as members of the Church, they met on a common ground. "Before Christ," writes St. Ivo of Chartres, "there is neither free man nor serf, all who participate in the same sacraments are equal."

And, in fact, a new democratic spirit of brotherhood and social co-operation begins to make itself felt in Europe at this epoch. In every walk of life men leagued themselves together in voluntary associations for social objects under religious auspices. The main types of association were three in number: the sworn "peace" for the enforcement of the Truce of God and the suppression of brigandage; the fellowship of the road, which pilgrims or merchants entered into for mutual protection; and the confraternity or "Charite," a local union for charitable or social objects under the patronage of some popular saint. From these origins there sprang the great movement of communal activity which transformed the social life of mediaeval Europe. It was no longer based exclusively on military service and feudal subordination. It was a vast complex of social organisms, a federation of corporate bodies, each of which possessed an independent activity, and made its own contribution to the common weal. The national kingdom itself was conceived as a federation of different orders, each with its own social function — the Estates of the Realm.

And the same tendency is equally active in the ecclesiastical sphere. The socialization of monasticism in the service of the universal Church which had been begun by the Benedictines, was carried still further in the new period. The reform of the Church in the 11th century was to a great extent a monastic movement, in which, for the first time, the monks were impelled by the force of their own ideals to leave the peace of the cloister and to throw themselves into a semi-political struggle. And in the following century the life of St. Bernard shows how the strictest ideals of monastic asceticism were not inconsistent with a social activity which embraced every aspect of the international life of Christendom. Henceforward the monastery is no longer a self-contained society with no relations to the outer world. It forms part of a wider unity, the Order, which in turn is an organ of the universal Church. And the new ideal finds a still more complete expression in the mendicant orders which arose in the 13th century, such as the Franciscans and the Dominicans. Here the ideal of service entirely replaces the old aim of retirement from the world. The friars are no longer bound to the rigid uniformity of cloistered life: they are free to go anywhere and do anything which the needs of the Church require. They answer to the needs of the new civic life, with its communal activity, as the fixed territorial abbey did to those of the old feudal agrarian state.

Thus by the 13th century Christendom had organized itself as a vast international unity founded on an ecclesiastical rather than a political basis. This unity, moreover, was not confined to purely religious matters, it embraced the whole of social life. All education and literary culture, all art, all matters of social welfare, such as the relief of the poor and the care of the sick, fell within the Church's sphere of influence. It even exercised a direct influence on war and politics, since the 'Papacy was the supreme arbiter in any question in which the interests of religion or justice were at state, and since it could launch the armies of Christendom in a crusade against the enemies of the faith or those who disregarded the rights of the Church.

It might seem as though Europe was destined to become a theocratic Church-state, after the manner of Islam, with the Pope as the Commander of the Faithful. And, indeed, there was a real danger that as the Church succeeded in dominating the state, it would itself be secularized by the growth of wealth and political power, until it became a legal rather than a spiritual organization. This danger was, however, counteracted by the spiritual revival which accompanied the social and intellectual renaissance of the 12th century. The dynamic moral energy of the Augustinian tradition continued to characterize Western Catholicism, and found expression in a new and more personal type of piety. The humanity of Christ became the centre of the religious life in a sense in which it had never been before. In place of the severe figure of the Byzantine Christ, throned in awful majesty as ruler and judge of men, there appears the figure of the Saviour in His human weakness and passibility. This attempt to enter into a close personal relationship with the Divine Humanity gives birth to a kind of religious realism which is very different from the abstract theological piety of the patristic and Byzantine types. We see this already in the writings of St. Bernard, but it is in the life and teaching of St. Francis that the new spirit finds its fullest development. The ideal of St. Francis is to relive the life of Christ in the experience of daily life. There is no longer any separation between faith and life, or between the spiritual and the material, since the two worlds have become fused together in the living reality of practical experience. And so, too, the asceticism of St. Francis no longer involves the rejection of the natural world and the turning away of the mind from the created to the Absolute. The rule of Poverty is a means of liberation, not a movement of negation. It brings man back to the fellowship of God's creation which had been lost or vitiated by self-will.

The powers of nature which had been first divinized and worshipped, and then in turn rejected by man as he realized the transcendence of the spiritual, are now brought back into the world of religion, and in his great canticle of the sun, St. Francis once more celebrates the praises of Mother Earth, the bearer of fruit, who keeps and sustains us, Brother Fire, who is "fair and joyous and mighty and strong," and all the other holy creatures of God. Thus the Franciscan attitude to nature and human life marks a turning point in the religious history of the West. It is the end of the long period during which human nature and the present world had been dwarfed and immobilized by the shadow of eternity, and the beginning of a new epoch of humanism and interest in nature. As Karl Burdach has shown, its importance is not limited to the religious field, but it has a wider significance for the whole development of European culture. Its influence is to be seen both in the new art of the 13th and 14th century Italy, which already contains the germs of the Renaissance, and in the social movements of the 14th century, in which for the first time the poorest and most oppressed elements of mediaeval society asserted their claims to justice.

But it is in the region of thought that the new realization of the reality and value of humanity and the whole order of nature had the most important results. The great intellectual synthesis of the 13th century has often been regarded as the triumph of theological dogmatism. It was in reality the assertion of the rights of the human reason and the foundation of European science. As Harnack has said, "Scholasticism is nothing else but scientific thought," and its weakness in the sphere of natural science is simply due to the fact that there was as yet no body of observed facts upon which it could exercise itself. Greek science, as embodied in the writings of Aristotle, represented a level of scientific achievement far higher than anything which the mediaeval world could attain to by its unaided powers, and consequently it was taken over *en bloc* by the scholastic movement. It was, however, no small achievement to succeed in bringing this mass of knowledge into living relation with mediaeval culture. Greek science belonged to the Greek world, and it is not easy to transplant it into another world ruled by a different vital rhythm, and inspired by different moral and religious principles. This was the experience of the Islamic world where the same experiment was made with no less enthusiasm and with a considerably higher endowment of cultural tradition than in the West. In Islam, however, the internal conflict between the scientific and the religious traditions proved incapable of solution. The Moslem thinker who in genius and influence most resembles St. Thomas — Ghazali — devoted his powers to "the destruction of philosophy" rather than to its reconciliation with faith, and this not because he was a mere obscurantist, but because he saw more clearly than his opponents the fundamental incompatibility of the central Moslem doctrine of the divine omnipotence with the Hellenic conception of the universe as an intelligible order which is transparent to the human reason.

In the West the relations between religion and philosophy were different because the former was based on an historical rather than a metaphysical relation. The provinces of faith and reason did not coincide, they were complementary and not contradictory. Each had its own *raison d'être* and its own sphere of activity. Against the oriental religions of absolute being and pure spirit, with their tendency to deny the reality or the value of the material world, Christianity had undeviatingly maintained the dignity of humanity, and the value of the material element in man's nature.

Hitherto, however, Christian thought had not fully realized the implications of this doctrine. The predominance of oriental influences had led to a concentration on the spiritual side of man's nature; its ideal was "to pass beyond sensible things and to become united to the divine and the intelligible by the power of the intelligence." It was the work of the new philosophy, as represented above all by St. Thomas, for the first time to break with the old established tradition of oriental spiritualism and Neoplatonic idealism, and to bring man back into the order of nature. He taught that the human intelligence is not that of a pure spirit, it is consubstantial with matter, and finds its natural activity in the sphere of the sensible and the particular.

Consequently man cannot attain in this life to the direct intuition of truth and spiritual reality. He must build up an intelligible world slowly and painfully from the data of the senses, ordered and systematized by science, until at last the intelligible order which is inherent in created things is disengaged from the envelope of matter and contemplated in its relation to the absolute Being by the light of higher intelligence.

Thus, looked at from one point of view, man is so low in the scale of creation, so deeply sunk in animality as hardly to deserve the title of an intellectual being. Even the rational activity of which he is so proud, is a distinctively animal form of intellect, and can only arise where the higher intelligence is veiled and impeded by the conditions of space and time. On the other hand man occupies a unique position in the universe precisely because he is the lowest of all spiritual natures. He is the point at which the world of spirit touches the world of sense, and it is through him and in him that the material creation attains to intelligibility and becomes enlightened and spiritualized.

Man is, as it were, a God upon earth, since it is his function to reduce the unintelligible chaos of the world of phenomena to reason and order. But he is so bound to matter that he is himself in continual danger of being dragged down to the purely animal life of the senses and passions. And since he cannot free himself by transcending the conditions of his nature in an intellectual approach to the world of pure spirit, the Divine Word has manifested itself to man through the sensible and the concrete in a form which is appropriate to the limitations of his intellectual powers. Thus the Incarnation does not destroy or supersede nature. It is analogous and complementary to it, since it restores and extends man's natural function as the bond of union between the material and the spiritual worlds. This is the fundamental principle of the synthesis of St. Thomas. His whole work is governed by the desire to show the concordance in difference of the two orders. Alike in his epistemology, his ethics and his politics, St. Thomas emphasizes the rights and the autonomous character of natural activity, the province of Reason as distinct from that of Faith, the moral law

of Nature as distinct from that of Grace, the rights of the State as distinct from those of the Church.

It is true that St. Thomas had no intention of turning men's minds away from the spiritual world to the study of particular and contingent being. His philosophic ideal, as Père Rousselot has shown, is emphatically an absolute intellectualism, and he regards the science of the sensible world merely as the lowest rung in a ladder which leads the mind step by step to the contemplation of eternal truth. Nevertheless the new appreciation of the rights of nature and reason which his philosophy involved marked a turning point in the history of European thought. The human mind was no longer absorbed in the contemplation of the eternal and the unchanging, it was set free to take up once more its natural task of the material organization of the world by science and law.

But it is obvious that St. Thomas himself and the men of his generation had no conception of the vastness and complexity of the problem. Their synthesis was regarded as final and complete, since they could not foresee that the advance of scientific knowledge would lead to the entire reconstruction of Aristotelian physics. As soon as the European mind began to exploit the riches of knowledge and power that the world contained, it began to turn away from the intellectualism of St. Thomas towards a purely rational or empirical ideal of knowledge.

In every department of life the later Middle Ages witnessed a reaction from the idealism of the old religious culture. In philosophy, nominalism and criticism were triumphant, in art, realism took the place of abstract symbolism. In politics and social life, the unity of mediaeval Christendom was being broken up by the growing forces of nationalism and secular culture. The new peoples of the West in the pride and vigour of youth were preparing to emancipate themselves from ecclesiastical tutelage and to set about creating an independent cultural life of their own.

THE AGE OF EMPIRE IN THE NEAR EAST*

CHAPTER XIII

THE age of Amenophis III was of exceptional importance for the development of architecture and art. It saw the rise of the classical types of temple which were to remain characteristic of the Egyptian culture as long as the latter survived. The smaller type of its base and pillared portico recalls in its simplicity of form the peripteral Greek temple of classical times, while the vast temples of Karnak and Luxor, with their monumental gateways flanked by towering pylons, their colonnaded courts, and their great pillared halls, sometimes consisting of a central nave, lit by a clerestory, and two lower aisles, are comparable rather to the mediaeval cathedrals of the west, with which they are indeed ultimately connected through the tradition of the Hellenistic and Roman basilica.

The decoration of these buildings was as magnificent as their design. The walls and pylons were covered with painting and sculpture, the gates and pillars were overlaid with gold and the floors with silver, which to the Egyptians was a metal hardly less precious than gold itself.

The same luxury characterized the court life of the age. The contents of the royal tombs, such as that of Tutenkhamon, have shown us the splendour of the jewellery and ornaments, the wonderful inlaid furniture, the carved ivory, the glazed pottery, and the beautiful opaque polychrome glass which was a special invention of the period. The bodies of the kings were no longer laid to rest in pyramids, but in the great rock-cut corridor tombs which line the cliffs of the Valley of the Kings on the edge of the desert west of Thebes. Nevertheless, the cult of the dead remained no less elaborate than in the days of the Old Kingdom. Indeed, it was in this period that the cult of Osiris and the religion of the celestial hereafter attained its full development, and became the common heritage of the whole Egyptian people.

But the most remarkable religious development of the imperial age was the attempt of Amenophis IV to create a new state religion and to replace the official cultus of the old royal god Amon Re of Thebes by the worship of the Aton or Sun Disk. Even at this time the priesthood of Amon was the wealthiest and most powerful corporation in the state, and in order to free himself from its influence the young king took the drastic step of abandoning the old capital of Thebes, and founding a new city, dedicated to the new worship, at Akhetaton, "The Splendour of the Aton," the modern Tell el Amarna. In conformity with the same idea he changed his own name from Amonhotep, "Amon rests," to Ikhnaton, "the Aton is satisfied," and encouraged his family and his courtiers to do the same.

Nor was he content with this formal recognition of the supremacy of the new divinity. He did all that was in his power to overthrow the old cults, and above all that of Amon, by the disendowment of their temples and priesthoods, and even by erasing the name of Amon from the monuments.

The iconoclastic violence of these proceedings shows that something more was at stake than the addition of a new divinity of the old type to the Egyption pantheon. It was a religious revolution which differed from anything that had gone before in its exclusive and monotheistic spirit. The Aton was not a sun god of the type of Re and Horus and Amon. It was conceived by Ikhnaton as the one vital principle, creating and informing the whole universe.

"Creator of the germ in woman,
Maker of seed in man,
Giving life to the son in the body of his mother,
Soothing him that he may not weep,
Nurse even in the womb,
Giver of breath to animate everyone that he maketh!
When he comest forth from the body on the day of his birth,
Thou openest his mouth in speech,
Thou suppliest his necessities.

"When the fledgling in the egg chirps in the shell,

*Dawson, Christopher, *The Age of the Gods* (New York: Sheed and Ward, 1934), pp. 295–299.

Thou givest him breath therein to preserve
    him alive.
He cometh forth from the egg to chirp with
    all his might,
He goeth about upon his two feet
When he hath come forth therefrom.

"How manifold are thy works!
They are hidden from before us,
O sole God whose power no other possesseth.
Thou didst create the earth according to thy
    heart
While thou wast alone.

"Thou alone shining in thy form as living Aton,
Dawning, glittering, going afar and returning.
Thou makest millions of forms
Through thyself alone;
Cities, towns and tribes, highways and rivers.
All eyes see thee before them,
For thou art Aton of the day over the earth."[1]

In these utterances we can see the beginnings of a wider and more spiritual type
of religion than the Archaic Culture had
ever known. The pessimism and intellectual
distress of the preceding age had prepared
the way for a more profound conception of
life, which was to find its full expression
in the great world religions and philosophies
of the following millennium. It is true that
the cult of the Aton had its more material
aspect. Professor Breasted has said that "in
the Ancient East monotheism was but imperialism in religion," and the Aton cult with
its three sacred cities in Egypt, in Syria, and
in Nubia, was the spiritual counterpart of
the Egyptian imperial expansion — one God
in heaven, as there was one king on earth.
Nevertheless, the religious element in Ikhnaton's policy far outweighed the political. He
was profoundly convinced of his personal
mission and inspiration, and the power and
prosperity of the Egyptian Empire was a
secondary consideration with him.

"Thou art in my heart (says the great hymn),
There is none that knoweth thee
Save thy son Ikhnaton,
Thou has made him wise
In thy designs and in thy might."

And the manifestation of "the Truth" to
his chosen followers and his subjects seems
always to have been the principal preoccupa-

[1] Tr. J. H. Breasted, *Development of Religion and Thought in Ancient Egypt*, pp. 324–328.

tion of his life. He was in fact a contemplative and an artist rather than a politician.
The beautiful naturalistic art of the new
capital at Tell el Amarna seems to have been
due to his personal inspiration and to his
desire for the visible embodiment of "the
Truth." Nothing can give us a clearer idea
of the contrast between the spirit of the new
movement and that of the old imperial tradition than the portraits of the king and his
family, which in their morbid refinement and
their exotic charm resemble the creations of
the Buddhist art of Ajanta and Sigiri far
more than the powerful and virile figures
of the old warrior kings.

III. The Decline of the Egyptian Empire

As a personality Ikhnaton is certainly the
most interesting and significant character
among the rulers of Egypt, but from a material standpoint his reign was disastrous for
Egypt. He thoroughly offended the traditional feeling both of priests and people, he
neglected the military organisation of the
empire, and left the distant provinces to their
own devices. The Tell el Amarna archives
are full of the pressing appeals of the faithful
vassals and governors of Egypt in Syria for
reinforcements and help. The whole country
was in confusion. The Hittite power of
Eastern Asia Minor was advancing into
North Syria, and the Amorite ruler Abdas-
shirta threw off his allegiance to Pharaoh
and made war upon the faithful cities. In
the south a horde of Semitic tribes from
the desert — Habiru — burst into Palestine,
plundering and burning in all directions.
Thus the Asiatic Empire of Egypt fell to
pieces even during the lifetime of Ikhnaton,
and on his death in 1362 B.C. his work of religious reform was equally undone. His son-
in-law Tutenkhaton — for he left no son —
returned to Thebes, changed his name to
Tutenkhamon, and restored the supremacy
of the priests of Amon, and the old traditional cults. In its turn the name of the new
deity was erased from all the monuments,
and the dead king Ikhnaton was condemned
as a heretic and an enemy of the gods. The
great reformer went down to posterity under
the name of "the criminal of Akhetaton."

SHEILA KAYE-SMITH
(1888–   )

IN HER childhood days Sheila Kaye-Smith had three ambitions: to live in the country, to be a celebrated novelist, and to be extremely high church. She has achieved her goals beyond expectation. In the quiet of her Sussex home she writes well and her novels have had an enthusiastic reception. In 1929 she was received into the Church with her husband, the Rev. Penrose Fry.

Though her novels are deep in their problems of personality and well written, except for the last two, *Gallybird*, 1934, *Rose Deeprose*, 1936, they show no specifically Catholic consciousness. Calvert Alexander has correctly explained that "Religion and things of the spirit have never been absent in any of her work"; it is, however to be expected that the riches of the Catholic religion have deepened her sense of life and values.

PART V

PEDAL POINT AND CODA*

FROM my window as I write I look up every few moments and gaze across a stretch of what once was lawn. It is yellow with buttercups and patched with purple hearts of clover. The oxeyes, which Joe Boorman calls Margaret daisies, are wide open above it on their bronze stalks; the smaller daisies (sewed-a-button daisies) are hidden among spears of waving grass. In my eyes it is all more beautiful than when it was a lawn, than when we scorched the flowers with lawnsand, and cut the grass to the length of a Victorian convict's hair, and set out friends to work with daisy cutters when they unsuspectingly came to tea.

To most people it is dereliction — "Oh, what a pity you've had to let it go" — and there was a moment, just before it happened, when I too regretted that we had so much grass in our garden plan, so much more than could be mown by an old heavy, obstinate hand mower. Our idea had been to make our garden merge as smoothly as possible into the surrounding countryside. We did not want to gash the fields with civilization, even with the civilization of Eden.

So we made our hedge of "quick" and of the hornbeam which in this part of England is called beech, just as if it were the hedge of a field; and we planted tall Lombardy poplars and ash trees where we wanted shade, and arranged for our flowers to grow in and about stretches of unbroken grass. The lawn, when newly mown, was like a green lake under lovely shadows. There was a strange thrill in stepping on to it from the fields, over the garden stile — a primitive thrill running back to man's first joys of cultivation, when from the exterior roughness he entered the smooth garth of his homesteading.

But it had to go, because we had neither the labor nor the petrol to keep it mown and soon I found that its going was to be no robbery but a new gift. The flowers that had been our enemies became our friends, and all the foreground now is a carpet of them, as lovely in its colors as the grass was in its green. Our scheme, however, for blending with the fieldscape around us has not been improved, because though we are successively a daisy field, a buttercup field, a clover field, a hayfield standing and a hayfield mown, the fields outside have been so incredibly smartened up that we look shaggy by contrast. The step over the stile brings the same change from rough to smooth, but now it is in the opposite direction.

This is not a chapter on gardening. I have no intention of leading any reader up any garden path, for on the subject of gardening, I am a heretic. Everything I might be ex-

---
*Kaye-Smith, Sheila, *Kitchen Fugue* (New York and London: Harper & Brothers, 1945), pp. 172–179.

pected to feel in a garden, I feel instead in the kitchen. There I feel happy, confident, interested and interested and soothed — I feel useful and creative. I have never felt anything like this while gardening; planting, weeding, digging, all give me sensations of inefficiency and frustration, to which is added an acute bodily discomfort.

Possibly I might enjoy gardening more if it could be done in a vertical position, but there seems no way of remaining upright unless one's garden were to be designed like a mountain vineyard, in a series of terraces. In the garden I kneel, stoop or crouch; in the kitchen I sit or stand, except for those few moments when a man-made oven brings me to my knees. In the garden, too, my mind never seems to be really engaged, nor is it ever really free. It moves in circles of irritation round the body's struggle, whereas in the kitchen it is fully and gently absorbed in the body's activity as butter in a good sauce.

I do not like gardening, nor am I particularly interested in gardens — in country gardens, that is to say. A town garden is a very different thing. It breaks up the bricks and mortar and provides a refuge from them for the town dweller. It allows him to grow a certain amount of his own goodness and beauty — green peas and sweet peas, leeks and lilies. Its multiplication also makes the beauty of the town. In May and June I am always struck anew by the loveliness of our London suburbs, a loveliness which is almost entirely due to their gardens, for the building and layout as a rule are hideous. A village, too, gains in beauty from the little floral trays which the cottages hold out before them, from the hollyhock and tall delphinium reaching for the thatch. Even a modern bungalow has been redeemed from ugliness by the flowers and trees and bushes that have, while adorning, veiled its ultimate brutalities.

But a well-built house among fields and woods needs no such setting. It must have its kitchen garden and its orchard, and its beds of favorite flowers. But it seems to me that here the complications and elaborations of the British middle-class garden are out of place, and any undue insistence on them will spoil the surrounding beauty only in a smaller degree than agressive bricks and mortar. For your garden needs to be absorbed by the countryside as well as your house, and a hedge of cupressus — even if alive, and in my experience it is more often dead — looks nearly as awkward beside a chestnut shaw as a pink asbestos roof or a stained-glass window.

I have used the term "middle-class," not in disdain but because the constant talk about gardens and gardening that you hear or used to hear seems to me essentially a middle-class indulgence. I never hear cottage people talking about their gardens — at least not in the same way. Joe Boorman will announce that his potatoes were "freezed" last night or that the mice have "terrified" the spinach, and Mrs. Boorman will point proudly to her spiklus — a solitary specimen of salpiglossus — but neither holds forth on plans or alterations or tells you how fine their cannas were or are going to be. Also they never move things about — they are far too wise. At the other end of the scale, I do not imagine that dukes and millionaires gossip much together about schemes for replanting the orangery or for transferring the Italian garden from the east to the west side of the lake. It is the people midway between these two groups of garden owners who discuss them so incessantly, and so incessantly emulate and imitate one another that in the end all their gardens seem to be very much alike.

This may sound captious, and I daresay it is; but I have suffered much in the past from garden purists. Once at a luncheon party I sat next an elderly gentleman who spoke of the daisies on my lawn in much the same tone as a district visitor might speak of the bugs in a slum tenement. Another enthusiast had a way of translating into Latin the name of any flower I mentioned and handing it back to me like a schoolmistress returning a corrected exercise. There was also the party in the "Himalayan" garden where a friend hoarsely whispered to me to hold my tongue because I was upsetting my host by admitting all the wrong things. And even now — after five years of total war — I am still greeted by those whose first wild cry is — "How is the garden? Looking lovely, of course!"

It is looking lovely, but not in the way they mean — nor is it the way I should mean for peaceful permanence. I like wild gardens, but not untidy ones; there is a distinction. A wild garden follows the lines of nature, with broad spaces and planting, flowers and trees growing without formal arrangement but in groups conditioned by such natural considerations as soil and slopes and shade. An untidy garden, however, has less of nature in it than of art run to seed. It cries out, like all true art, for elimination, for pruning. My garden, as I see it now, is like one of those vast interminable novels in which nothing is either set in order or left out. The wild flowers in the grass are beautiful in themselves, but they have no artistic unity with the rest; and the flowers in the flower beds wear that air of dereliction which all civilized flowers, especially roses, wear when invaded by the wild.

In a few weeks they will look better. Old Mr. Moon and old Ted Guiver (nobody knows why one is "Mr." and the other just Ted) will come with their scythes and sweep the wild weedy hay into swatches as regular as if a machine had made them, and nearly as quickly as a machine. They will tell me stories of how this place looked in days far bygone and then they will bring their little old pony to fetch away his winter fodder. At least I hope all this will happen, but from year to year it is precarious; for in a drought our hay may not be worth the carrying, and a wet, springy year means so much hay everywhere that the little old pony may not need ours; and every year Mr. Moon and Ted Guiver a little older, a little nearer being reaped instead of reaping.

If they do not come we shall look worse than ever, and if they do we shall not look too good; for a scythed lawn is very different from a mown lawn, and we certainly should not have planned so much green space around us if we had known we should have

to depend on the same method as Father Time. . . . Yet how modern and artificial is this distinction. A hundred years ago there were no lawn-mowers in England and every lawn was scythed. The lawns of Buckingham Palace were scythed — the lawns of Pemberley were scythed and the lawns of Mansfield Park; and the lawns (though this will surprise us less) of Brambleton and Booby Hall. We are only going back to the eighteenth century, a time very much more advanced than the barbarism which has necessitated our retreat.

But for better, for worse, the petrol lawn-mower is here, and already I am planning how our desolate places can be restored. For though I do not love gardening I love flowers — indeed, my love of flowers is one reason why I dislike gardening. One reads and hears of the green thumb, the thumb which brings life to every plant it moves and touches. My thumb is a black thumb, and every plant I handle shows its resentment by dying at once. So because I love flowers I have given up handling them. I will rescue them from assaulting weeds and I like arranging them in vases; but I will never interfere with their private, growing lives.

When I was a child my love of flowers was fanatical. Had their beauty been less transient, I should have preferred them to toys. I would do almost anything to obtain the gift of one and my scanty supplies of pocket money often went in their purchase, for we had no garden worthy of the name. We used to pick a certain number of wild flowers in the country; primrosing picnics were among the greatest of the year's treats. But the greatest treat of all was our annual visit to a parsonage garden, where the flowers were not wild, yet free for my plucking.

To this parsonage every June two elderly ladies came as paying guests. They were patients of my father's, and when he called on them I always drove out with him. They were not particularly attractive old ladies. The elder was very, very old indeed, and the younger, her companion, had no roof to her mouth. I took very little interest in them when they were in their own home;

but about them for a single summer month hung all the perfumed glamour of lilac and roses, of jasmine and syringa, irises, peonies, poppies, sweet William and Canterbury bells.

While my father attended the employer, the companion would take the doctor's little girl into the garden, where I was allowed freely and uniquely to pick anything I chose. I remember particularly the little creamy bankshire roses that covered the wall. They were a new experience for me — I had seen them nowhere else; and now when I want them for my own walls they seem to have disappeared from gardeners' catalogues and I am fobbed off with substitutes which are not at all the same thing. The thought arises that they may be very much better, that my bankshire roses are a graft on memory, which no nursery man ever created. Creamy roses with golden hearts, pressed tight in sweet-smelling trusses . . . it is possible that my white Dorothy Perkins, while no improvement on what I remember, may be a great improvement on what I actually saw.

I think it must be my memory which has made me such a lover of cheerful, easy flowers — the kind that grow in cottage gardens, always the most generous to a craving child. When we came here I filled the beds with old favorites and bright colors, so that our garden is little more than an extended version of the cottage gardens round us. Uninteresting and unenterprising, says the garden purist; but somehow I cannot bring myself to grow at infinite trouble and expense in half a ton of special manure a tiny blossom the size of a pin's head — even if it be the only speciman outside Afghanistan.

But though I am no gardener, I honor the vocation, which seems to carry with it the relics of man's unfallen state. In the garden he is not only assisting the Creator, but actually developing and improving on His work. As he patiently improves the wild rose with its faint hues and fugitive scent into the glowing colors and heady perfume of a Dame Edith Helen, a Reverend Page Roberts, or an Etoile de Hollande, it looks to me as if he were doing a share of the divine work, a work for which he was originally intended and should now be doing on an infinitely wider, more fruitful, more significant scale.

It is as if God had given man certain ideas and then asked him to improve upon them, as a kindergarten teacher gives a child a mat to embroider with colored wools. I shall be told that wild flowers are lovely as cultivated flowers, and so no doubt they are in bulk, but not in detail. For their full effect of beauty they depend on masses — sheets of asphodel, carpets of bluebells, clumps of primroses. Is a single bluebell as beautiful as a single hyacinth? Can a single wild lupin, taken from the purple carpet of some Orkney field, compete with a single cultivated spike of Golden Russell? The original wild rhododendron is small and sparsley flowered in comparison with the varieties that man has conceived. In fact every wild flower seems susceptible, by cultivation, fertilization, or grafting, of improvements on its first design.

In this work man has been more honorably successful than in his similar work with the beasts, where he has often followed strange fancies of his own. He has bred horses into nerves and folly, dogs into adenoids and difficult whelpings, cats in and out of squints. With flowers, he has been less irresponsible, and a garden is still in some measure Eden which bears all too plainly the marks of fallen estate.

I see now that my garden must be made smaller; some of it must be given back to the meadow from which it was originally taken. For though petrol will return to the lawn-mower, I do not expect, or indeed hope for, any adequate return of the labor that pushed that mower over the grass for twelve hours every week. It would be a sorry scandal if the agricultural laborer were once more to be driven out of the fields into gardens. Nor should I attempt to persuade him — it would be in vain. For the war would have shown me, if I did not know already, how infinitely the countryman prefers field work to garden work, and how reluctantly, and for economic reasons only, he must in those prewar years have given us his collaboration in our long fuss about things-that-do-not-really-matter.

Part V*

6

"LORD, speak to my sister."

That prayer is often in my heart, but the sister concerned is Martha. I pray to be delivered from Martha, from her interruptions and irruptions, from her bursting into my moments of recollection. The Mass is not yet half over, but Martha is already telling me that it is time I mixed the batter for the Yorkshire pudding — "It ought to stand at least an hour." Or she suddenly shouts: "Have you remembered to write that list for the Army and Navy Stores: . . . No? . . . Well, there's a pencil in your handbag. You had better do it now, or you will forget it entirely." Mary tries hard to cling to her "better part," but there is, for some reason, about Martha the bustling voice of conscience, and the distractions she provides have a moral urgency lacking in the normal run of distractions during Mass.

"Lord, speak to my sister."

These two sisters have become symbols. In actual fact they are saints of the Church, inspired by different though not contrary virtues; but symbolically they divide the human race. I write as a child of Mary, voicing my complaint against the children of Martha, whom Kipling has championed on grounds that seem to me mistaken. Certainly he has misunderstood her story. When she interrupted the conversation between her Guest and her sister with the demand that it should cease forthwith and Mary devote herself instead to her assistance, she was showing herself, it seems to me, an indifferent hostess — one of the type which will not allow her company to enjoy itself in its own way.

For her, no doubt, the meal she was preparing was the most important part of the entertainment, and she could not allow for a different taste. We are told that she was "cumbered about" — a graphic phrase — and "careful about many things." But it would be wrong to picture her as an overworked housewife in the modern British style, drudging and struggling while her sister loafed. An

oriental household such as hers would have been full of servants and her activities mainly those of supervision and organization. No, it seems to me that she was being fussy and overanxious, and perhaps a little resentful of the detachment of her sister and her Guest. Her halo is not made of the stuff of that awkward moment.

Mary, on the other hand, has not had her due from those who take no account of official halos. They regard her as a pious dreamer, too selfish and lazy to do her plain duty. I have even heard her reproached for waiting in the house when Christ came to visit it on the death of Lazarus, and Martha characteristically rushed out to meet Him, "but Mary sat at home." They ignore the fact that it was Mary, not Martha, who attended her Lord through all the dangers and horrors of the Crucifixion. She sat at home when the welcoming crowd ran out to meet Him, but when the mob cried, "Crucify him!" she ran to be at His side. I can picture Martha comforting the bereaved Apostles with her hospitality, but Mary who once sat at home is now among the soldiers and the mob at the foot of the Cross. This timid, spineless creature is exposing her body to danger and her soul to the utmost grief. It is she, too, and not Martha, who is to be engaged in the unpleasantly practical business of embalming the body which had been hastily put into the grave on the eve of the last Sabbath.

Of course to those whose ideas of holiness are still Victorian in shape, the traditional identification of Mary of Bethany with Mary of Magdala is something almost shocking. Yet there is nothing wrong with it in psychology or in experience. It is an error to think that it is always the good girl of the family who becomes a nun — it is just as likely to be her "difficult" sister. The contemplative life needs qualities of concentration and self-donation which, if turned in the wrong direction, might well lead to the streets of Magdala. Useful, bustling Martha has an outlet for her temperament in every small concern, in every pasing moment of the day, but the Mary type — reflective, interior, in-

*Ibid., pp. 193–202.

active, introverted — call it what you will — cannot escape through these small archways. It demands a wider exit into love or into religion, and we can imagine Martha's sister making her first escape into love. It is just as easy to imagine the disillusion, the growing disgust of such a nature with its own choice — the conflict, the revulsion, and the final liberation when seven devils are cast out.

History is full of similar examples, from St. Augustine to Charles de Foucauld, from Lais of Corinth through Teresa of Avila to Eve de Lavallière. No, I cannot see any psychological difficulty, but I certainly see a social one. I find it difficult to picture a converted harlot in a Jewish household of the first century. According to tradition, Martha and Mary belonged to a rich and noble family, and they seem to have been respected citizens of Bethany. When Lazarus died their home was full of mourning neighbors and there does not appear to be any sign of social ostracism and only one individual expression of Pharisaic contempt.

On the other hand, the constitution of the family is peculiar by the standards of its age and race. Two unmarried sisters living with an unmarried brother must surely have been a remarkable phenomenon in early Palestine. It belongs rather to our own times, and its existence in those suggests some unusual circumstance. Have I leave to conjecture Bethany as a sort of Little Gidding, where a brother and two sisters live a semi-conventual life, sharing all three in the repentance and reparation of the "woman who was a sinner" but now has "chosen that better part?"

Certainly the household of Bethany loses much of its life if we exclude Mary Magdalen and reduce it to two flat opposites. Only a second-rate novelist will mold a character as a consistent type. Most of us are compounded just as antithetically as those two Marys. Indeed most of us have Martha thrown in as well, and life is one long conflict between the three.

"Lord, speak to my sister." . . .

7

It is noticeable that the Lord did nothing of the kind. Nor, if I may reverently make such a conjecture, would He have "spoken" to Martha, had the protest been on Mary's side, had she complained that the fuss and clatter of Martha's serving interfered with her spiritual concentration. My conjecture is based on His earlier pronouncement that "wisdom is justified of all her children."

This phrase surely expressed the whole secret of toleration. Or rather it gives it a much wider base than toleration usually has. Nowadays at its best it stands for little more than putting up with the other man's deficiencies because it would be bad manners to interfere, and at its worst a mere indifference.

We pride ourselves on being more tolerant than our fathers, but I doubt if we are any such thing. It is only the grounds of our intolerance that have shifted. We are just as intolerant in the political field as our ancestors were in matters of religion. Religion no longer shines so brightly that we are dazzled, and blind to any light save that which blinds us; but politics — or rather, ideologies — do. Three hundred years ago it would have required all the moral courage I possess and probably much more, to avow myself a Catholic, whereas now it would require the same quality to avow myself a Fascist — which I nervously add that I am not. I am as anxious to escape any undeserved suspicion of that kind as a decent sixteenth century citizen would be to avoid the suspicion of popery. The results in each case would probably be the same — contempt, distrust, social ostracism, if not imprisonment without trial.

All this makes me feel a little out of place, for I have no political or ideological emotions. Fascism and Communism both affect me in the same way. They both seem equally to consist in the diversion of the religious instinct into social and political channels. In each case the state takes the place of God and the Kingdom of Heaven falls to earth with a sickening thud. I see in neither any real chance for freedom, individuality, art or inspiration. The whole world becomes metallic and set in a mold. Humanity no longer walks or runs, still less skips or dances — in spite of people's parks and Strength through Joy — but marches, marches . . . left, right — left, right . . . the jungle drum is back again, beating a new version of its old rhythm but no tune.

At home our politics are less sinister, but not more inspiring. And again they are all the same. What is the difference between a Labor and a Conservative government in power? Bureaucracy comes down on each like a rubber stamp and obliterates anything individual it may have written on the parliamentary page when it was out of office. Just as well, says the cynic; that is the way we keep this country quiet and comfortable when every other country is burning and blowing up. But it is very difficult to feel intolerant under such conditions.

But perhaps it would not matter so much if one did not also feel uninterested. For any large proportion of a country to be uninterested in politics amounts to a national disaster. It was mainly because so many good and intelligent people in France had held aloof from politics, or rather from *ces sales politiciens qui nous empoisonnent la vie* (as I once heard them described by a responsible citizen), that the country came to grief in 1940. For too long good and intelligent people had stood apart from the mess, shrugging their shoulders and letting it seep into the Army, the Navy, and all the main departments of national life except the Church. In Britain our politics are not dirty, but they are dull, because so often burning questions are quenched into a compromise that pleases nobody. There is also the fact — at least I am prepared to argue that it is a fact — that our present electoral system is not truly representative. It expresses only in the vaguest way the real wishes and opinions of the man and woman in the street.

I have had a vote ever since votes were given to women, but I have never voted wholeheartedly, because never have I felt at any time that any candidate represented me. My present member of Parliament is without doubt an excellent and worthy man. But he is not likely ever to say or do anything that I would say or do in his place. He does not

appear to care twopence for my real interests, which are not so very unlike those of the thousands of other women who have voted for him and then longed to kick him in the pants. If I write to him, either in protest or petition, he sends me a printed postcard telling me that the matter is receiving his attention, which means that it has gone into his wastepaper basket.

I have been told that the only way to have a grievance noticed is to write to the *Times,* upon which the Ministry concerned will come tumbling over your M.P's head to get the matter hushed up. But in that case, why bother about a vote?

The fact is that I should have an author to represent me, a farmer should have a farmer, and doctors a doctor, and engineers an engineer, till the House of Commons becomes a vast Rotary Club. Somebody sniffs and says that would be the corporative state . . . Fascism . . . Fe, Fi, Fo, Fum . . . to which I reply that it seems a pity that such a truly democratic plan should hitherto have been tried out in Fascist countries only. Geographical representation is all very well if the part of the country represented is self-contained and the member a genuine inhabitant. It is a farce for a stranger to come down to Little Muddlecombe from London and ask for the division's vote on the sole strength of his being a Socialist — or a Liberal — or a Conservative, while having at best only an acquired and sketchy knowledge of his constituency's needs.

I am not suggesting that petty local interests should take precedence of national planning (as happened in an early Rye election, when the program of both candidates centered on the question of repairs to the Landgate clock), but I suggest that the representative of a trade, profession or guild is more genuinely representative of his constituency than the representative of a set of people held together only by the arbitrary politico-geographical boundaries.

There is no use arguing with me, for I am convinced beforehand that the system would not work. Canvassing and elections would both have to be conducted through the post, and once Parliament was assembled the party system would be at an end, because one day the dentists and the doctors might vote against them.

It would always be a case of individual responsibility, of weighing each question on its own merits, of personal initiative and private information. It would work only in a country where everybody thinks or where nobody thinks at all. In this country, where the art of herd thinking has reached such perfection, it would be a setback to democracy. We should find ourselves compelled to think separately, and the loss of interest in politics would become a general instead of an exceptional discontent. As a nation we have always loved party politics — loved them so dearly that it matters little if the parties under their war paint are really all the same. In countries where the parties are fundamentally opposed, the situation is different, and I only hope that our zeal for party government will not turn us into its missionaries throughout an already sufficiently unquiet world.

But, as I have said, this is not a subject on which I can bring myself to think or feel very strongly. I am wrong, because I make myself like those Frenchmen of the 1930's who when the floods were rising turned their backs and puffed smoke rings. Nor am I really a tolerant person. Like many people, I am intolerant in small matters. I can agree with my adversary very well on grand affairs of politics and religion, but I find it much more difficult to get on with him if he wants to shut the window when I want it open.

In this I think I am behaving in an especially female manner. I have noticed that many women have a tendency to invest the smaller issues of life with a sort of moral significance which is invisible to the average male. I have heard a woman speak of friends who expected (in peacetime) what she called a "meat breakfast" in tones that could not have been more damning had they expected gin instead of early tea. A friend who dislikes onions always conveys the idea that onions are morally reprehensible, and I know another woman whose contempt of lentils has

produced in me such a guilt complex that I have made them, as far as she is concerned, a private addiction. The controversy between tea and coffee, too, sometimes echoes former asperities between unionists and home-rulers.

As for myself, I find my main intolerance to lie in matters of temperament. I fall too easily into an attitude of moral indignation against those who differ from my personal tastes in their emotional and mental make-up. I like people who are capable without being energetic, I like people whose affections are strong, but sentimentality makes me feel sick and sadistic. I like people to have wit and humour, but I hate them to be merry and bright. I am ill at ease with those whose life has no religious depth, but equally ill at ease with those whose life is all depths, without any temporal surface to skip on. I am shy of those who have no "nerves" but are afraid only of legitimate perils. I flee in terror from those who would be mentally or physically intimate.

These are my personal tastes and distastes and I have a right to them. Where I am wrong is in attaching blame and contempt to those who gush or sparkle, slop or flop, or who entertain the fish queue with their own private solution of the riddle of the universe. We are all guilty. Those of us who are quick in thought and action grow impatient with the careful, deliberate steps of the slow-minded, while these believe that our failures are one and all due to the speed of our undertakings. The introvert chills and repels the extrovert, who in his turn fills the introvert with embarrassed boredom. The intellectual is only too ready to despise the simple-minded, who counters with a heavy derision of all highbrows. Nervous people think nerveless people are either swanking or made of leather, and the nerveless people are all agreed that the nervous could "help it if only they tried." From all of us rises the prayer — "Lord, speak to my sister — change her spots to my stripes," ignoring the fact that the Lord who made the tiger made the leopard too.

If there is one beauty which the divine Artist seems to have spread more widely than another in His creation it is the beauty of variety. *Circumdata de Varietate,* says the Vulgate of the robe of the King's daughter — "surrounded with variety." And certainly (if I may so express myself) there is no more uncommon thing in nature than two things which are the same. Sameness, regimentation, mass production, these are all manifestations of the enemy — of Satanic interference with mankind and his development. Any sort of totalitarian civilization, whether the state be represented by a dictator or more insidiously by a bureaucracy, produces, systematizes and establishes these evils, crushing together Martha and Mary in one soulless identity. The Lord will not speak to your sister, but the Führer will.

A. J. CRONIN
(*1896–*)

DR. CRONIN finds himself very much at home in an age of crusades and the weave of his life makes his own crusading understandable. Born in Cardross, Scotland, Cronin lost both his father and mother while he was only a boy and he savored want and even neglect by close and bitter experience. He was finally adopted by his uncle, a priest, and by dint of his own shrewdness and sharp mind managed to finish his education as a doctor at Glasgow University. Dr. Cronin first practiced medicine in South Wales and finally transferred to London. He was an unqualified success as a doctor and was admitted to membership in the Royal College of Physicians.

Dr. Cronin's crusading spirit has shown itself in many of his works, such as the *Citadel* and *Hatter's Castle,* both of which were successful novels. With the publication of *The Keys of the Kingdom,* a Catholic novel of sorts, Cronin aroused both the spirit of condemnation and praise. Being primarily a novelist of plots rather than character, Dr. Cronin quite naturally painted his characters in high lights, black and white, good and bad. It does tighten the plot and accelerate its pace, but sensitive people who look upon Cronin as a novelist of character, were hurt by an honest attempt to create in Father Chisholm the type of *Christianity in action* which is so dear to the heart of a crusader.

Crusaders are not often theologians and few of them have ever taken logic. On the whole, Dr. Cronin's *Keys of the Kingdom* was of marked advantage to the Church. Inability to see into his technique of plot construction, alone, made a controversial issue of something which was negligible.

The Green Years, which followed *The Keys of the Kingdom,* is a study of a boy's sorrows seen against the humorously harsh background of Scotch life. Kindness and Avarice meet in the lists, and when the fight is over Kindness has won, but through trickery.

Dr. Cronin is indeed a master of plots as the movie tycoons know only too well. As a character writer, however, he often lacks depth and finesse. It is his valid sense of humor and his crusading love for the underdog which lift his novels to the margins of greatness.

STRANGE VOCATION*

I MUST, I must get back to this morning and Rusty Mac. This being a holiday of obligation, I had the forenoon on my hands. On my way down to post a letter at the lodge I ran into the Headmaster coming up from the Stinchar with his rod and without fish. He stopped, supporting his short burly form on the gaff, his ruddy face screwed up, rather put out, beneath his blaze of red hair. I do love Rusty Mac. I think he has some fondness for me and perhaps the simplest explanation is that we are both so dourly Scottish and both of us fishers . . . the only two in the school. When Lady Frazer endowed the College from her Stinchar properties, Rusty claimed the river as his own. The jingo in the *Holywell Monitor* beginning.

> I'll not have my pools
> Whipped to ribbons by fools . . .

neatly takes off his attitude — for he's a mad fisher. There's a story of him, in the middle of mass at Frazer Castle, which Holywell serves, when his staunch friend, the Presbyterian Gillie, stuck his head through the window of the oratory, bursting with suppressed excitement. 'Your reverence! They're rising like fury in Lochaber Pool!' Never was a mass more quickly completed. The stupefied congregation, including Her Ladyship, was pattered over, blessed at breakneck speed; then a dark streak, not unlike the local concept of the Devil, was seen flying from the sacristy. 'Jock! Jock! What flee are they taking?'

"Now, he looked at me disgustedly. 'Not a fish in sight. Just when I wanted one for the notables!' The Bishop of the diocese and the retiring principal of our English Seminary at San Morales were coming to lunch at Holywell that day.

"I said, 'There's a fish in the Glebe Pool, sir.'

" 'There's no fish in the river at all, not even a grilse . . . I've been out since six.'

" 'It's a big one.'

*Cronin, A. J., *The Keys of the Kingdom*, (Boston: Little, Brown and Co., 1941), pp. 61–64.

" 'Imaginary!'

" 'I saw it there yesterday, under the weir, but of course I didn't dare try for it.'

"From beneath his sandy brows he gave me his dour smile. 'You're a perverse demon, Chisholm. If you want to waste your time — you've my dispensation.' He handed me his rod and walked off.

"I went down to the Glebe Pool, my heart leaping as it always does at the sound of running water. The fly on the leader was a Silver Doctor, perfect for the size and colour of the river. I began to fish the pool. I fished it for an hour. Salmon are painfully scarce this season. Once I thought I saw the movement of a dark fin in the shadows of the opposite bank. But I touched nothing. Suddenly I heard a discreet cough. I swung round. Rusty Mac, dressed in his best blacks, wearing gloves and his ceremonial top hat, had stopped on his way to meet his guests at Doune Station, to condole with me.

" 'It's these large ones, Chisholm —' he said with a sepulchral grin — 'they're always the hardest!'

"As he spoke, I made a final cast thirty yards across the pool. The fly fell exactly on the spume eddying beneath the far edge of weir. The next instant I felt the fish, struck, and was fast in it.

" 'Ye have one!' Rusty cried. Then the salmon jumped — four feet in the air. Though for my own part I nearly dropped, the effect on Rusty was stupendous. I could feel him stiffen beside me. 'In the name of God!' he muttered in stricken awe. The salmon was the biggest I had ever seen, here, in the Stinchar, or in my father's Tweedside bothy. 'Keep his head up!' Rusty suddenly shouted. 'Man, man — give him the butt!'

"I was doing my best. But now the fish was in control. It set off, downstream, in a mad tearing rush. I followed. And Rusty followed me.

"The Stinchar, at Holywell, is not like the Tweed. It runs in a brown torrent through pines and gorges, making not inconsiderable somersaults over slippery boulders and high shaley ledges. At the end of ten minutes, Rusty Mac and I were half a mile downstream, somewhat the worse for wear. But we still stayed with the fish.

" 'Hold him, hold him!' Mac was hoarse from shouting. 'You fool, you fool, don't let him get in that slack!' The brute, of course, was already in the slack, sulking in a deep hole, with the leader ensnared in a mess of sunken roots.

" 'Ease him, ease him!' Mac hopped in anguish. 'Just ease him while I give him a stone.'

"Gingerly, breathlessly, he began flipping stones, trying to start out the fish without snapping the cast. The game continued for an agony of time. Then Whirr! — off went the fish, to the scream of the reel. And off again went Rusty and I.

"An hour later, or thereabouts, in the slow wide flats opposite Doune village, the salmon at last showed signs of defeat. Exhausted, panting, torn by a hundred agonizing and entrancing hazards, Rusty gave a final command.

" 'Now, now! On this sand!' He croaked: 'We've no gaff. If he takes you down farther, he's gone for good.'

"My mouth was gulpy and dry. Nervously, I stood the fish close. It came, quiet, then suddenly made a last frantic scuttle. Rusty let out a hollow groan. 'Lightly . . . lightly! If you lose him now I'll never forgive you!'

"In the shallows the fish seemed incredible. I could see the frayed gut of the leader. If I lost him! — an icy lump came under my shirt. I slid him gently to the little flat of sand. In an absolute tense silence Mac bent over, whipped his hand in the gills and heaved the fish, monstrous, onto the grass.

" 'A record, a record!' Mac chanted, swept, as was I, by a wave of heavenly joy. We had joined hands and were dancing the fandango.

'Forty-two pounds if it's an ounce . . . we'll put it in the book.' He actually embraced me. 'Man, man — You're a bonny, bonny fisher.'

"At that moment, from the single railway lines across the river, came the faint whistle of an engine. Rusty paused, gazed in bewildered fashion at the plume of smoke, at the toylike red-and-white-signal which had suddenly dipped over Doune village station. Recollection flooded him. He dug in consternation for his watch. 'Good Heavens, Chisholm!' His tone was that of the Holywell Headmaster. 'That's the Bishop's train.'

"His dilemma was apparent: he had five minutes to meet his distinguished visitors and five miles of roundabout road to reach the station — visible, only two fields away, across the Stinchar.

"I could see him slowly make up his mind. 'Take the fish back, Chisholm, and have them boil it whole for luncheon. Go quickly now. And remember Lot's wife and the Pillar of salt. Whatever you do, don't look back.'

"I couldn't help it. Once I reached the first bend of the stream, from behind a bush, I risked a salty ending. Father Mac had already stripped to the buff and tied his clothing in a bundle. Wearing his top hat firmly on his head, with the bundle uplifted like a crozier, he stepped stark naked into the river. Wading and swimming, he reached the other side, scrambled into his suit and sprinted manfully towards the approaching train.

"I lay on the grass, rolling, in a kind of ecstasy. It was not the vision — which would live with me forever — of the top hat planted dauntlessly upon the nubile brow, but the moral pluck which lay behind the escapade. I thought: He too must hate our pious prudery, which shudders at the sight of human flesh, and cloaks the female form as though it were an infamy."

DOUGLAS WOODRUFF
(*1897–*   )

THE present editor of the *London Tablet,* John Douglas Woodruff, was born in England, 1897. He acquired his education at Downside and New College, Oxford. While at Oxford, Woodruff's skill in dialectics led to his inclusion in the Oxford debating team which toured the United States in the twenties. As a result of these tours Woodruff produced a hilarious satire, *Plato's American Republic,* a series of Socratic dialogues which satirize American mores. The success of this volume led to the publication of a companion piece, *Plato's Brittania,* and once again Woodruff demonstrated his ability to pillory the illogical and ridiculous at home, as he had abroad.

Woodruff's writing is excellent and there is nothing malicious in his satire.

As editor of the *Tablet* since 1926, Woodruff has shown an awareness of international affairs which has enabled him to forecast events with considerable accuracy. This quality has given to the *Tablet* a prominent role in shaping Catholic opinion in England and in the United States.

BOOK THE EIGHTH*

YOU remember," I said, "how it is argued in that dialogue of Plato which he has called the Laws, that the proper life for the ordinary citizen is not to live in a city, but on his own plot of land, commanding property enough for his own modest wants?"

"Yes," they said, "for though we were not present to take part in the discussion, we know the argument well."

"I wish the English knew it," I said, "but I could find very few of them who had read the Laws, although it is, of course, translated into their tongue. But in their popular schools it is wholly unknown, as are all Plato's writings, for they do not encourage the young to ask fundamental questions or to ask what the life of a State or an individual ought to be."

"They are afraid, I suppose," said Agathon.

"In part it is fear," I agreed, "but they are also convinced that such discussions are a waste of time. They would say that such proposals are all very well in theory, and when they have said that about anything, they consider they have disposed of it for good and all. They would say that they are a city

people and must learn to put to best advantage the lives that have to be lived in their great cities."

"They are proud of those great cities," exclaimed Lysis.

"Yes," I said, "and they take them for granted and have already forgotten that they are but the growth of yesterday. Now, would you not say that it was particularly important for those who have to live in such places to try to develop their powers of criticizing and judging when they are young? For the mere fact of living in a large city and being one of a large crowd deadens the power of reflection and choice. Does it seem to you at all difficult to understand how men who are forever availing themselves of organization provided by unseen organizers, catching buses and visiting great shops and taking for granted the supply of light and warmth, will come insensibly to believe that they are in safe hands and that somebody is in charge of the whole life of the people who will see that they never lose their trade or come to lasting hurt?"

"I thought the guardians were in charge," said Lysis.

"Alas!" I said, "the guardians are quite

*From *Plato's Brittania,* Book VIII, pp. 197–211, Copyright, 1931, by Douglas Woodruff. Courtesy of G. P. Putnam's Sons.

ready to attempt anything and to make all sorts of regulations, but they have no more idea than anyone else what is going to happen to these great agglomerations of people in these modern cities of the English. For the truth is that the ordinary English derive from their surroundings an illusory sense of security, and although they feel keenly and naturally the insecurity of their individual positions, they believe that as a community they cannot fail to move forward all the time."

"Move forward to what, Socrates?"

"To greater comfort and longer life and more pleasures for all."

"It must be a great consolation to them," said Lysis, "to have that thought as they walk their dull and crowded streets."

"Yes," I said, "for men are sustained by faith, and those who are fond of their young, as the English are, rejoice to think that there is a good time coming even if they are not to enjoy it themselves."

"I suppose, Socrates," said Lysis meditatively, "that there is a great difference between the outlook of the richer English, who are forever looking to the past and thinking of the great Queen, and that of the artisans, who look all the time to the future?"

"Yes," I said, "for the richer sort readily agree that progress is by no means inevitable and the things are, in fact, growing worse, and are ready to identify their own history and their failure to increase their real comfort over that which the great Queen provided with the general history of the human race; while the artisans make just the same mistake and think that, because they have been able to obtain many comforts which the great Queen made them do without, things will continue to improve forever provided that artisans enjoy more and more influence. And those who grumble most loudly are those who are most convinced that it is the natural order of events for everything to improve."

Here Agathon said:

"It is not so unreasonable, Socrates, if you remember the type of mind which is theirs, forever seeking to find out and improve practical inventions. For they make a real progress there all the time, and so increase their ability to produce."

"Yes," I agreed; "and as they have achieved a slightly better distribution of their riches than was achieved when they first grew rich, it is natural for them to be sanguine and to think that, as their science is going to enrich them so will their political constitution enable them to see that the increased wealth is shared among them all. Such is, at any rate, their hope, and they have ceased to place their faith in the gods and have begun to place it in electricity, for they rely upon electricity to solve all their problems in a short time."

"Does electricity help them much to-day?"

"Yes," I said, "though they do not appreciate it as the Americans do, who rush eagerly to every new thing, and could hardly wait for the use of electricity to be understood before hurrying to employ it to execute their criminals."

"From humane feeling, Socrates?" asked Agathon, "since they know that nothing could console a condemned American more than the knowledge that he was to die in the latest and most up-to-date manner, however painful it might prove to be."

"No," I said, "for Americans show little humanity to those whom their strange and multifarious laws condemn, but because they believed that eletricity would save them, and they like to feel that they will be able at a pinch to execute the whole nation without delaying business, should the necessity arise, for they know they are not good at keeping laws. But the English, not recognizing any similar great boon in electricity, have come more slowly to an appreciation of all that it can do for them, nor were they greatly interested till they heard somebody say it would do all their household work. Then they became full of attention, foreseeing the day when they would all be able to live like ladies and gentlemen."

"And when will that great day dawn, Socrates?" asked Phaelon.

"The English," I said, "are schooled to patience and know that there is a great difficulty to be surmounted first. For they do not see their way to prevent a few rich men from controlling the electricity as they control so much else, and doling it out to the mass of citizens for as much as they can make them pay; so that they cannot be certain they will not have always to work for wages as hard as ever, in order to pay for the use of electricity at home."

"Not as hard as ever, Socrates," said Agathon, "for the work itself will be performed by electricity, and all the English will have to do will be to turn on switches in factories in order to earn the money to turn on switches at home."

"Yes," I said, "but they are a little uneasy, and rightly, lest no one will agree to pay them more than a pittance for turning on factory switches; and it is even possible that artisans will be considered quite superfluous and that rich men will own all the switches and all the land, so that the poor will not be able to earn anything, not even enough to pay rent for the land they stand on, and will have to beg, as a favor for which they cannot pay, for the electric shock which will send them out of the world."

"Would the rich give them a powerful electric shock without payment?" asked Lysis.

"I doubt it gravely," I answered, "for they would reply that it was not business, and that it was equally uneconomic to employ the poor or to execute them free."

"What would happen then?"

"The State would keep all the poor, I suppose," I said, "perhaps putting them in prison as vagrants lacking any visible means of subsistence, for that is the phrase in their criminal law by which they describe what is the greatest of all offenses according to their view."

"It is easy to understand why the poor rely so much upon the State," said Lysis, "even if those who act in its name are not particularly wise or good, for the State alone can save them from the uncertain mercies of the rich."

"Yes," I said, "not the individual rich whom they used to know in the countryside, but great corporations not even living in their island, but collecting power for no

sound reason in every country of the world that does not keep a vigilant watch."

"That is why they have so many news-sheets," said Lysis, "to keep a vigilant watch and see what is happening to themselves?"

"No," I said, "we cannot credit the English with anything so sensible as that. Although they have one or two grave news-sheets from which they can learn about events if they are prepared to take the trouble, yet the most part of their news-sheets and the ones they devour most greedily, are intended as distractions, and they do not look in them for truth, but for entertainment."

"And what, Socrates, can be more entertaining than the truth?"

"Lies," said Agathon, before I could answer, "for lies can take many shapes and suit themselves to the secret desires of those that are to hear them, but the truth is what it is and nothing else. So that the owners of these news-sheets are kind as well as prudent when they make a point of printing lies instead of the truth."

"They do not seem to find the matter quite so simple," I said, "but no doubt they will learn that there is really no need for them to spend the money that they do in gathering tidings of what has happened, and that it will be quite sufficient if they will agree among themselves what tales to make up; for the mass of the English have no means of testing what they say except by comparing one news-sheet with another, and must accept as true anything that all the papers agree to assert. Now the great things that the people desire to read about are of two kinds — crimes and accidents. For wickedness carries its own strong appeal with it, and accidents they love partly because the misfortunes of others are always good reading, but chiefly because many of them have a special reason for desiring to think that accidents are exceedingly common and may happen to any of them any day."

"Why on earth should they wish to think that?"

"Because these news-sheets will insure them and give them large sums for becoming good news-stories in this way, and the more overwhelming the catastrophe that visits them the more will the papers pay them."

"Truly the act of a guardian, to offset calamity with gold."

"Yes," I said, "and the bulk of the English can see no other way of obtaining much money except by having a bad accident, and will not willingly give up hope. For that reason many of them applaud the invention of flying machines, which is otherwise plainly a great misfortune for their country, exposing them to the hostile bombs of foreigners and making them no longer an island free from attack.

"But the proprietors of these popular news-sheets have a special reason for telling all the lies they can," I resumed, "for they live by those who buy the right to praise their own goods in the news-sheets, and these manufacturers desire naturally to praise their goods in the hearing of the most gullible people they can find. So that they look eagerly to see which paper has the most gullible public and pay the largest sums to advertise there."

"It must be good fun owning a news-sheet," said Phaelon, "and thinking of new tales to beguile the populace all the time."

"Yes," I said, "and all the more because so many of the English regard the owners of these sheets as their moral leaders and as entitled to influence them all they can in the gravest matters, thinking those to be of necessity good men who pay so much for accidents and take such pains to entertain their fellows. So that it does not seem odd to allow these men to arrange discussions on the nature of the gods, and to choose the people whose views ought, in their opinion, to be heard with reverence."

"Even these proprietors," suggested Lysis, "could discover with a little trouble the names of wise and good men, in Greece or some other part of the Mediterranean."

"No," I said, "you forget that even when the discussion is on the most important matters, their chief aim is still to entertain and amuse. Whether from a sly malice or for some other reason, they love to persuade actors, and makers of feigned tales, and drivers of cars and aeroplanes, and athletes to describe in print what they imagine the nature of the gods to be."

"Truly," said Agropatus heartily, "they understand their business of entertaining the people."

"Yes," I said, "but it is not quite as you suppose, for what these people write or sign their names to is read with eagerness, because of their notoriety, and with agreement, because they are in no wise more sensible than those who read them, and for the most part praise up the country and generation to which they belong and look forward to a coming rosy dawn. And nothing flatters the bulk of the people more than to read contemptuous remarks about the darkness of the minds of their forefathers, and they are particularly pleased to be told that their determination only to believe that to be evil which they feel no inclination to do, is a new and admirable thing and not a permanent temptation which men in every age have had to meet."

"After all," said Agathon, "I believe these news-sheets cost very little."

"A penny," I answered, "and twopence on Sundays when the thoughts are extra deep; and the English say that they cannot expect much truth for such sums, especially as they are not prepared to take any trouble over their reading. If they find what pleases them it is as much as they expect, and they refuse to pay even so much as a penny for views with which they do not already agree."

"That makes it easy for the masters of the news-sheets to show which sophists to employ," said Lysis.

"Yes," I said, "it is perfectly simple, and the first rule for those who write about moral questions in these papers is to assume that morals are invented by men for their own convenience, and that the only question is what moral principles it is convenient and pleasurable to hold."

"They should study the Dialogues of Plato," said Agropatus, "and they would learn not only how false but also how ancient is any such view."

"Yes," I said, "their complacency would

be much disturbed if they could not go on thinking that they were searching out these matters for the first time and that nobody began to know anything at all till the time of the great Queen. They are full — if we may apply to them a sentence from that dialogue called the Laws, of which we spoke a little while ago — of a very grievous sort of ignorance which is imagined to be the greatest wisdom, as the Athenian there says when he is rightly denouncing those who say there is no God or that he takes no heed of men, or, again, that he can be propitiated to look with favor upon unjust men by means of offerings and does not require men to live justly. But most of all the English need to understand about the soul and how nature and the things they see around them are its works, and they must learn to avoid using the word 'nature' as though they meant to say that nature and not soul is the first creative power."

"You cannot expect them to do so for a penny," said Agathon.

"No," I said, "and as long as they derive their chief impressions about the most important questions from casual readings in news-sheets they will sink deeper in their impious muddles, imagining that the nature of the gods can be whatever they or their favorite novelists choose. Nor are they more muddled on any matter than on this of the soul."

"After all these centuries?" said Agropatus.

"Yes," I said, "for they are troubled by the phrases they pick up from the lips of physical investigators, and it is the delight of many of these men to pose as theologians and to startle the populace with unfamiliar doctrines and to cut fine capers, knowing that the multitude cannot distinguish between a chemist and a philosopher, and will easily believe them to be profound and good men."

"So that they are often vexed as well as entertained?"

"Yes," I said, "and do not know what to make of themselves at all. For the condition of their minds is such that they are ruled by their imaginations and jump to all sorts of conclusions. So that when those who study the human body explain to them the effect of different substances in inducing them to act in this way or in that, or the students of human behavior explain to them the ways in which they act, they feel that anything that can be described and analyzed cannot be of any great importance. So that they are troubled on their Sunday, or Day of Rest, for when they have read that their characters result from nothing but the way in which their nurse spoke to them in their infancy or the chemicals in their body, they do not feel able to go out on to the golf links with the same clear resolve to improve their moral characters, and can do no more than sit in the golf clubhouse with wrinkled brows and evil tempers."

"What is this that they do on their Sundays, Socrates?"

"Why," I said, "they read these news-sheets and play this game of golf, but only if they are sufficiently well-to-do, for the English have contrived to make it very expensive even to hit a little ball about in green fields. Now, with the more prosperous English this golf has displaced the old worship of the gods, for they believe that if there are any gods at all they are only pleased with the actions and not with the prayers of men. So they have devised this test or torment and have set apart these hours every week for this stern moral gymnastic which they term 'golf.' They say it is more pleasing to the gods if they learn self-restraint under conditions of trial more severe than those used by the Spartans in the training of their youth; and whether they are studying patience by searching for balls they have lost or fortitude and dogged persistence by striving to hit balls from impossible positions, which have been constructed for no other purpose, they appoint themselves this round of trials and disappointments and emerge, as they believe, healthier and nobler men. So do they stir themselves to their depths, as these ball games have a unique power of doing, and then they are ready for all the trials and encounters of the following week."

FRANK SHEED
(1897–)

IN 1897 Francis Joseph Sheed was born in Sydney, Australia. He received his A.B. and LL.B. from the University of Sydney. While living in London, through a mutual interest in apologetics, Sheed met and married Maisie Ward. As copartners they organized the Catholic Evidence Guild. Its purpose is the apostolic work of spreading the faith by the preparation of speakers, who in Hyde Park and elsewhere speak for the Church in accents logical and sweetly reasonable. The movement has brought many converts to the Church and has done yeoman service in moderating bigotry. Branches of the guild were later organized in Sydney and the United States.

In 1925 Sheed and his wife formed the publishing company of Sheed and Ward. An American branch of the firm was opened in 1933.

As publishers, Sheed and Ward have spared no pains in making available to the Catholic reading public the best works of Catholic authors.

The talents of Frank Sheed are not all poured out in the publishing business. He is in much demand as a lecturer and his own published works are a tribute to his lucid mind and Christian energy.

He has also translated several of the works of Henri Ghéon, notably *The Secret of St. John Bosco.*

Sheed's prose is clear and eminently readable. *Communism and Man, Ground Plan for Catholic Reading,* and *Map of Life* are some of his best known works.

MARX AND THE FUTURE*

IF WE are to grasp the significance of Marx's theory of the inevitable advent of the Socialist society, we must look a little more closely at his view of the progress of Capitalism. We have already seen that for him Capitalism was following that inescapable dialectical law by which each dominant class raises up that which will destroy it. Big industry by a necessity of its own nature gathers the workers into larger and larger units, thus putting them into a strategic position for Capitalism's ultimate overthrow. Further, again by a necessity of its own nature, Capitalism makes the lot of its employees harder and harder to bear, so that Marx can say in the *Communist Manifesto*: "The workers have nothing to lose but their chains." In the previous chapter we saw in essence Marx's theory of the way in which Capitalism must obey the law of the dialectic and produce the class which should destroy it. Here it is in his own words:

"Along with the constantly diminishing number of the magnates of capital, who usurp and monopolize all advantages of this process of transformation, grows the mass of misery, oppression, slavery, degradation, exploitation; but with this, too, grows the revolt of the working class, a class always increasing in numbers, and disciplined, united, organized by the very mechanism of the process of Capitalist production itself. The monopoly of capital becomes a fetter on the mode of production, which has sprung up and flourished along with it and under it. Centralization of the means of production and socialization of labor at last reach a point where they become incompatible with their Capitalist integument. This integument is burst asunder. The knell of Capitalist private property sounds. The expropriators are expropriated."

*Sheed, F. J., *Communism and Man* (New York: Sheed and Ward, 1945), pp. 50–64.

It follows from all this that the progress to the next stage, wherein the proletariat are to take over, is dependent upon the lot of the proletariat getting harder and harder. Therefore, anyone who tries to improve the lot of the workers is an enemy of progress. There is no limit to Marx's hatred of the philanthropist who tries to improve things within the present system. Marx indeed will take part in agitation for the improvement of the workers' lot, not because he wishes the improvement to take place but because the agitation gives the workers some preliminary training in common action and thus helps to train them into an effective revolutionary force. The Christian, moved by love of God and his neighbor, who tries to remedy the suffering of the poor, is a hindrance to the necessary revolt of the masses, while the most ruthless Capitalist is a help to that revolt. But hindrance or help, the revolt must come, *must* come.

Marx however arrives at the certainty of the destruction of the Capitalist system by another road altogether, which has no essential connection with anything the proletariat may do or suffer. He argues — and very powerfully—that Capitalism will destroy itself by a defect in its own nature. Means of production become more and more efficient: but markets dwindle as all nations are industrialized. More is produced than consumers can buy, hence comes crises. "And how does the bourgeoisie get over these crises? On the one hand by enforced destruction of a mass of productive forces, on the other, by the conquest of new markets, and by the more thorough exploitation of the old ones. That is to say, by paving the way for more extensive and more destructive crises, and by diminishing the means whereby crises are prevented.

"The weapons with which the bourgeoisie felled feudalism to the ground are now turned against the bourgeoisie itself."

Obviously these two explanations — the increasing misery and power of the proletariat, and the inability of Capitalism to survive the crises its own nature produces — are not the same explanation, nor does Marx harmonize

them in such a way as to bring them into one picture. The result is that Capitalism is doomed to die by two equally inevitable but independent deaths. At any rate, it *is* doomed to die.

And here we must notice the reason why Capitalism is significant not as simply one more stage in the endless movement of human history, but as the stage before the last. The reason is that under a Capitalist system the whole conflict has now been simplified down to two classes. The Capitalist and the Proletariat, the haves and the have-nots, at last face each other in a clear conflict with no third parties to provide an alternative issue. "Of all the classes that stand face to face with the bourgeoisie today, the proletariat alone is a really revolutionary class. The other classes decay and finally disappear in the face of modern industry; the proletariat is its special and essential product."

For the fullest statement as to the nature of the Proletarian State and its development into the true Communist Society, we must go to Marx's *Critique of the Gotha Programme.* "Between the Capitalist and the Communist systems of society lies the period of the revolutionary transformation of the one into the other. This corresponds to a political transition period whose state can be nothing else but the revolutionary dictatorship of the proletariat." Thus, this dictatorship will be only a transitional stage: and in the beginning it will be very far from the perfect Communist ideal. For in the first place, as Marx explains, the necessity of overcoming hostile elements will lead to the very strictest control of all. And in the second place the proletariat themselves will not be capable of the true Communist standard of action "in the first phase of Communist society as it has issued from Capitalist society after long travail. Right can never be superior to the economic development and the stage of civilization conditioned thereby." Or, as Marx writes a few pages earlier: "What we are dealing with here is a Communist society, not as it has *developed on its own basis* but on the contrary as it is just issuing out of Capitalist society:

a society that still retains in every respect economic, moral and intellectual, the birthmarks of the old society from whose womb it is issuing."

The main practical result will be that men are remunerated equally for equal work — so that the more skilled workman will receive more than the less skilled. Thus a first measure of justice is established — in that those who do not work will not receive any share of the products and that among workers the share of the product will be graded according to the quality of the work. Men are not yet ready for the highest ideal of all — when they work according to their capacity and receive according to their needs: but at least they receive according to the value of their work and not according to privilege.

"In the higher phase of Communist society, after the enslaving subordination of the individual under the division of labor has disappeared, and therewith also the opposition between manual and intellectual labor; after labor has become not only a means of life, but also the highest want in life; when, with the development of all the faculties of the individual, the productive forces have correspondingly increased, and all the springs of social wealth flow more abundantly — only then may the limited horizon of Capitalist right be left behind entirely, and society inscribe on its banners: 'From everyone according to his faculties, to everyone according to his needs.'"

But in the transition stage, because there are still hostile elements to be coerced, and because proletarian men are not yet at the level required of them, the State will remain — for the State's proper function is coercion.

Meanwhile the Proletarian Dictatorship will be marked by profound changes affecting Property, the Family and Religion.

First as to Property. The *Communist Manifesto* makes it clear that some kind of property will remain.

"We by no means intend to abolish this personal appropriation of the products of labor, an appropriation that is made for the maintenance and reproduction of human life, and that leaves no surplus wherewith to command the labor of others. All that we want to do away with is the miserable character of this appropriation, under which the laborer lives merely to increase capital, and is allowed to live only in so far as the interest of the ruling class requires it."

"Communism deprives no man of the power to appropriate the products of society; all that it does is to deprive him of the power to subjugate the labor of others by means of such appropriation."

This is repeated in the *Critique of the Gotha Programme:* during the Dictatorship differences in wealth will still exist but these cannot lead to exploitation because the means of production (factories, machines, land and such-like) will be forever removed from private ownership. Thus, there will be no classes — for, as Lenin comments, classes arise from the "difference between the members of society in their relation to the social means of production."

The family also is to undergo some great change. Modern industry, Marx tells us, has created a new economic foundation "for a higher form of the family and of the relations between the sexes." But the nature of this change remains a little vague: all that is clear is that the sexual code will in some way be different. Does Communism mean sexual promiscuity? The *Communist Manifesto* does not deny this, but retorts by saying that the present marriage system is no better:

"Bourgeois marriage is in reality a system of wives in common and thus, at the most, what the Communists might possibly be reproached with is that they desire to introduce, in substitution for a hypocritically concealed, an openly legalized community of women. For the rest, it is self-evident that the abolition of the present system of production must bring with it the abolition of the community of women springing from that system, i.e., of prostitution both public and private."

This is a little rhetorical but seems clear enough, and in his Property and the Family (p. 97) Engels says the same thing without rhetoric: "We are at this moment moving towards a social revolution in which the present economic bases of monogamy will disappear. . . . Once the means of production have passed into common ownership, the individual family ceases to be the economic unit of society. The care and education of children will become a public concern."

Religion, too, will vanish. We have seen the sense in which Marx calls religion the opium of the people. (Lenin improves on the phrase by calling religion "a crude sort of spiritual vodka.") Engels writes that all the chatter about the immortality of the soul has lost its meaning.

There is an interesting sentence in a letter of Marx to Engels (September 25, 1869): "During this journey across Belgium, the stay at Aix-la-Chapelle and the voyage up the Rhine, I have become convinced that it is necessary to struggle energetically against the priests, especially in Catholic regions." But this *need* not mean a direct attack upon religion. Lenin tells us that Engels "commenting on the famous manifesto of the Blanquists . . . treated their noisy proclamation of war on religion as foolishness, and stated that such a declaration of war was the best means of reviving interest in religion, and of hindering its dying out. Engels blamed the Blanquists for failing to understand that only the mass working-class struggle, drawing the widest sections of the proletariat into all forms of conscious and revolutionary social *work,* will as a matter of fact free the oppressed masses from the yoke of religion."

Nor is all this — as some Christian sympathizers with Communism explain — merely a praiseworthy rejection of false conceptions of religion. It is a total rejection, lock, stock and barrel, of any possible idea of a Being higher than man and a life after death. Lenin is expressing the mind of Marx and Engels when, speaking of those who agree with the Communist rejection of religion as it is and then proceed to urge some rarefied "religious" view of their own, he says: "These representatives of the educated bourgeoisie nearly always supplement their own refutations of religious prejudice with such arguments as at once expose them as the ideological slaves of the bourgeoisie, as the 'graduated flunkeys

of clericalism.'" Those who would proceed to invest Socialism with religious values receive equally short shrift. For some the statement "Socialism is my religion" is a step from religion to Socialism, for others it is a step from Socialism to religion. Only in the first sense can the Communist allow it as even tolerable.

The proletarian state will be, for all practical purposes, classless in that there will be only the one class. But as the dialectical process of history has in the past always arisen from the strife of classes, and cannot now arise since there is no alternative class history as we now know it will have come to an end. The proletarian state will be merely a transitional thing developing painlessly into the classless society. There being no private property, and no privilege, the very roots of conflict will have gone. The motive of private gain will no more appear. There will be only one rule; from each according to his capacity, to each according to his needs. The State, says Engels, will not be abolished, it will gradually "wither away." Upon this Lenin comments: "Only in a Communist society when the resistance of the Capitalists has been completely broken, when the Capitalists have disappeared, when there are no classes (i.e., when there is no difference between the members of society in their relation to the social means of production), only *then* 'the State ceases to exist,' and *'it becomes possible to speak of freedom.'* Only then will democracy itself begin to *wither away* owing to the simple fact that, freed from capitalist slavery, from the untold horrors, savagery, absurdities and infamies of capitalist exploitation, people will gradually *become accustomed* to the observation of the elementary rules of social life that have been known for centuries and repeated for thousands of years in all precepts of common life; they will become accustomed to observing them without force, without coercion, without subordination, without the *special apparatus* of coercion which is called the State."

As to the length of time this process will take, there is no certainty. Lenin observes that on this matter Marx made no prophecy.

"We have a right to speak solely of the inevitable withering away of the state, emphasizing the protracted nature of this process and its dependence upon the rapidity of development of the *higher phase* of Communism, leaving quite open the question of lengths of time, or the concrete forms of withering away, since material for the solution of such questions is not available." But sooner or later the perfect Communist society will certainly come, and it will last for ever, for the cause of change will have vanished.

Society being now perfectly organized for production and for the distribution of what is produced, all man's needs will be met. Religion will, therefore, simply vanish, since in the past it has been invented by man to console himself for needs unsatisfied under the older system. There will be no need for force, since every member of society will conceive of himself only as a member of society and will be quite incapable of pursuing (because quite incapable of conceiving) individual ends as distinct from the collective purpose. In this new society there will be no need for force, indeed for anything which we now understand as government, any more than in a beehive. Man will have been completely socialized and will be incapable of any action other than social action. Thus, according to the point of view, one might say that history will have ended or that history will have begun. In plain words, the Millennium will have arrived.

That Marx regarded the Dictatorship of the Proletariat and its development into the classless society as inevitable, there is no doubt whatever. "The fall of Capitalism and the victory of the Proletariat are equally inevitable," says the *Communist Manifesto;* and we have seen him writing to Weydemeyer that "the class-struggle leads necessarily to the Dictatorship of the Proletariat (and) that this dictatorship is but the transition to the abolition of all classes and to the creation of a society of free equal men." And Engels states as one of the basic truths underlying the *Manifesto* that the proletariat cannot attain its emancipation "without at the same time, *and once for all* emancipating

society at large from all exploitation, oppression, class-distinction and class-struggles." G. D. H. Cole (who is a little embarrassed by the fact) admits that "Marx did think that Socialism would be the next phase in the history of Western Civilization. Undoubtedly he often spoke as if he regarded the coming of Socialism as inevitable, and only the time and manner of coming as open to doubt."

But if the coming of the Classless Society is inevitable, need anything be done about it? What is the need of a revolutionary class and revolutionary activity to bring about something that cannot help happening? The question became a major issue in the early twentieth century with Lenin urging revolutionary action and Kautsky relying on inevitability; and we see the same thing emerging in the present condemnation of Bukharin's Mechanist Materialism for stressing the passivity of nature and man in their reaction to environment and thus blunting the edge of revolutionary ardor. But there is no doubt about Marx's answer to the question.

"The materialist doctrine that men are products of circumstances and upbringing and that, therefore, changed men are products of other circumstances and changed upbringing, forgets that *circumstances are changed precisely by man* and that the educator must himself be educated."

Men are not simply acted upon; they act; and their action is part of that dialectical law which will bring reality to its inevitable goal. Men cannot prevent reality reaching its goal but they can hasten or slow down its movements. This point emerges in a letter of Marx to Kugelmann (of April 17, 1871) as to the harmonization of inevitability with the obviously accidental character of much that happens:

"These accidents themselves fall naturally into the general course of development and are compensated by other accidents. But acceleration and delay are very dependent upon 'accidents,' which include the 'accident' of the character of those who at first stand at the head of the movement."

For one who has seen Marx as the ruthless

realist, the idyllic ending of the classless society which shall know no end comes with a curious shock. There is nothing in the principle of dialectic which can allow any such happy family. It is all very well for Marx to say that under the present system the issue has been simplified down to two classes and that under the system that is to follow there will be but the one class and that, therefore, class war will be impossible. Certain obvious objections to this simplification will be considered later; but even the greatest sentimentalist can see the certainty of the development of antagonisms (and even class antagonisms) strong enough to disrupt the proletarian state. And Marx was not normally a sentimentalist.

We are faced with a contradiction here. And this may remind us of another contradiction. In the last chapter we saw Marx's view of morality: that there is no such thing as a good man or a bad man, but only a good or bad member of his class. Bukharin has expressed this Marxian principal in the statement that morality simply means the rules of conduct dictated by class. In Marx's theory what we call the bad element in any society plays as necessary a part in the dialectical process as the good element. He condemned any effort to draw up a category of absolutely good and absolutely bad as bourgeois fetishism. Considering all this, the last thing one would expect from Marx is moral indignation. But moral indignation literally rages in him. No one has looked deeper into the causes of these two separate contradictions than Christopher Dawson. His solution has a brilliant simplicity of its own. Marx was a materialist philosopher. But Marx was a Jew.

"Karl Marx was of the seed of the prophets, in spite of his contempt for anything that savored of mysticism or religious idealism. . . . The Messianic hope, the belief in the coming destruction of the Gentile power and the deliverance of Israel were to the Jew not mere echoes of Biblical tradition; they were burnt into the very fibre of his being by centuries of thwarted social impulse in the squalid Ghettoes of Germany and Poland. And in the same way the social dualism be-

tween the elect and the reprobate, between the people of God and the Gentile world-power, was a fact of bitter personal experience of which even the most insensitive was made conscious, in the hundred petty annoyances of Ghetto life. . . .

"Now the Revolution and the coming of Liberalism had put an end to this state of things. . . . (But Karl Marx) could not deny his Jewish heredity and his Jewish spirit . . . the only way of escape that remained open to him was by the revolutionary tradition, which was then at the height of its prestige and popularity. In this he found satisfaction at once for his conscious hostility to bourgeois civilization and for the deeper revolt of his repressed religious instincts.

"The three fundamental elements in the Jewish historical attitude — the opposition between the chosen people and the Gentile world, the inexorable Divine judgment on the latter and the restoration of the former in the Messianic kingdom — all found their corresponding principles in the revolutionary faith of Karl Marx. Thus the bourgeois took the place of the Gentiles, and the economic poor took the place of the spiritual poor of the Old Testament . . . while the Messianic kingdom finds an obvious parallel in the dictatorship of the proletariat which will reign until it has put down all rule and authority and power and in the end will deliver up its kingdom to the classless and stateless society of the future which will be all in all."

This, as it seems to me, is the obvious solution of our two problems. The materialist philosopher laughing scornfully at Hegel for his dream of a finality that will one day be reached, the determinist calmly seeing all the actions of men as necessary for the realization of human progress and so not to be judged by the outworn categories of good and bad, these are united in the one person with the Jewish inheritor of the tradition of the Millennium, of the race of the prophets who had so rigorously cried out their condemnation of moral evil. Exploitation has been the great original sin of humanity; of that sin the proletariat has been innocent; and its innocence shall bring it to reign in a kingdom of happiness without end.

Not only does this seem to me to be the solution of the personal problem of Karl Marx; it seems also to be the explanation of the power of Marx's doctrine to appeal to men's minds. Not German materialist philosophy but passionate Jewish idealism has winged his message. And it is, perhaps, not for nothing that Marx's doctrine has been adopted and put into practice by Russia — the home of the one apocalyptic people of the modern world.

MAISIE WARD
(*1889–*)

ALL her life Maisie Ward has moved in a world of writers. Daughter of a novelist mother and Wilfrid Ward, whose biography of Newman is a definitive work, it is not astonishing that Maisie Ward should become one of the noted women writers of her time.

With her husband, Frank Sheed, Maisie Ward organized the Catholic Evidence Guild and later formed the Sheed and Ward Company which has done so much for Catholic writing.

Mrs. Sheed, like her husband, is a de-lightful lecturer. She has made many tours of the American continent and still is in great demand with audiences in both the United States and Canada.

Though she has several books to her credit, she has followed in the footsteps of her father by writing the definitive life of Chesterton, *Gilbert Keith Chesterton*. In this work Maisie Ward has examined every facet in the life and works of Chesterton and has set down a record of the great man which is both scholarly and delightful.

CHAPTER XIII

ORTHODOXY*

BECAUSE *Orthodoxy* is supremely Chesterton's own history of his mind more must be said of it than of his other published works. For "This book is the life of a man. And a man is his mind." The Notebook shows him thinking and feeling in his youth exactly on the lines that he recalls — but they were only lines — in fact an outline. The richness of life was needed, the richness of thought, to turn the outline into the masterpiece. No man, not even Chesterton, could have written *Orthodoxy* at the age of twenty. It was sufficiently remarkable that he should have written it at thirty-five; but only a man who had been thinking along those lines at twenty and much earlier could have written it at all. For the book is as he says "a sort of slovenly autobiography." It is not so much an argument for Orthodoxy as the story of how one man discovered Orthodoxy as the only answer to the riddle of the universe.

In an interview, given shortly after its publication, Gilbert told of a temptation that had once been his and which he had overcome almost before he realized that he had been tempted. That temptation was to become a prophet like all the men in *Heretics,* by emphasizing one aspect of truth and ignoring the others. To do this would, he knew, bring him a great crowd of disciples. He had a vision — which constantly grew wider and deeper — of the many-sided unity of Truth, but he saw that all the

Ward, Maisie, *Gilbert Keith Chesterton*, (New York: Sheed and Ward, 1943), pp. 208–219.

prophets of the age, from Walt Whitman and Schopenhauer to Wells and Shaw, had become so by taking one side of truth and making it all of truth. It is so much easier to see and magnify a part than laboriously to strive to embrace the whole:

> . . . a sage feels too small for life
> And a fool too large for it.

Not that he condemned as fools the able men of his generation. For Wells he had a great esteem, for Shaw a greater. Whitman he had in his youth almost idolized. But increasingly he recognized even Whitman as representing an idea that was too narrow because it was only an aspect. There was not room in Whitman's philosophy for some of the facts he had already discovered and he felt he had not yet completed his journey. He must not, for the sake of being a prophet and of having a following, sacrifice — I will not say a truth already found, but a truth that might still be lurking somewhere. He could not be the architect of his own intellectual universe any more that he had been the creator of sun, moon and earth. "God and humanity made it," he said of the philosophy he discovered, "and it made me."

He had begun in boyhood, as we have seen, by realizing that the world as depicted in fairy tales was saner and more sensible than the world as seen by the intellectuals of his own day. These men had lost the sense of life's value. They spoke of the world as a vast place governed by iron laws of necessity. Chesterton felt in it the presence of will, while the mere thought of vastness was to him about as cheerful a conception as that of a jail that should with its cold empty passages cover half the country. "These expanders of the universe had nothing to show us except more and more infinite corridors of space lit by ghastly suns and empty of all that was divine.

"These people professed that the universe was one coherent thing; but they were not fond of the universe. But I was frightfully fond of the universe and wanted to address it by a diminutive. I often did so; and it never seemed to mind. Actually and

in truth I did feel that these dim dogmas of vitality were better expressed by calling the world small than by calling it large. For about infinity there was a sort of carelessness which was the reverse of the fierce and pious care which I felt touching the pricelessness and the peril of life. They showed only a dreary waste; but I felt a sort of sacred thrift. For economy is far more romantic than extravagance. To them stars were an unending income of halfpence; but I felt about the golden sun and the silver moon as a schoolboy feels if he has one sovereign and one shilling.

"These subconscious convictions are best hit off by the colour and tone of certain tales. Thus I have said that stories of magic alone can express my sense that life is not only a pleasure but a kind of eccentric privilege. I may express this other feeling of cosmic cosiness by allusion to another book always read in boyhood, "Robinson Crusoe," which I read about this time, and which owes its eternal vivacity to the fact that it celebrates the poetry of limits, nay, even the wild romance of prudence. Crusoe is a man on a small rock with a few comforts just snatched from the sea; the best thing in the book is simply the list of things saved from the wreck. The greatest of poems is an inventory. . . .

"I really felt (the fancy may seem foolish) as if all the order and number of things were the romantic remnant of Crusoe's ship. That there are two sexes and one sun, was like the fact that there were two guns and one ax. It was poignantly urgent that none should be lost; but somehow, it was rather fun that none could be added. The trees and the plants seemed like things saved from the wreck: and when I saw the Matterhorn I was glad that it had not been overlooked in the confusion. I felt economical about the stars as if they were sapphires (they are called so in Milton's Eden): I hoarded the hills. For the universe is a single jewel, and while it is a natural cant to talk of a jewel as peerless and priceless, of this jewel it is literally true. This cosmos is indeed without peer and without price: for there cannot be another one."

A fragment of an essay on Hans Anderson that cannot be later than the age of seventeen shows Gilbert trying to shape part of what he calls here, "The Ethics of Elfland," but a large part was, as he says, "subconscious." In this chapter he sums up the results of musings about the universe begun so long ago — small wonder that he had seemed to sleep over his lessons while he was seeing these visions and dreaming these dreams which after every effort to tell them he still knows remains half untold:

". . . the attempt to utter the unutterable things. These are my ultimate attitudes towards life; the soils for the seeds of doctrine. These in some dark way I thought before I could write, and felt before I could think; that we may proceed more easily afterwards, I will roughly recapitulate them now. I felt in my bones; first, that this world does not explain itself. It may be a miracle with a supernatural explanation; it may be a conjuring trick, with a natural explanation. But the explanation of the conjuring trick, if it is to satisfy me, will have to be better than the natural explanations I have heard. The thing is magic, true or false. Second, I came to feel as if magic must have a meaning, and meaning must have some one to mean it. There was something personal in the world, as in a work of art; whatever it meant it meant violently. Third, I thought this purpose beautiful in its old design, in spite of its defects, such as dragons. Fourth, that the proper form of thanks to it is some form of humility and restraint; we should thank God for beer and Burgundy by not drinking too much of them. We owed, also, an obedience to whatever made us. And last, and strangest, there had come into my mind a vague and vast impression that in some way all good was a remnant to be stored and held sacred out of some primordial ruin. Man had saved his good as Crusoe saved his goods; he had saved them from a wreck. All this I felt and the age gave me no encouragement to feel it. And all the time I had not even thought of Christian theology."

This theology came with the answers to all the tremendous questions asked by life. Here the convert has one great advantage over the Catholic brought up in the Faith. Most of us hear the answers before we have asked the questions: hence intellectually we lack what G. K. calls "the soil for the seeds of doctrine." It is nearly impossible to understand an answer to a question you have not formulated. And without the sense of urgency that an insistent question brings, many people do not even try. All the years of his boyhood and early manhood Chesterton was facing the fundamental questions and hammering out his answers. At first he had no thought of Christianity as even a possible answer. Growing up in a world called Christian, he fancied it a philosophy that had been tried and found wanting. It was only as he realized that the answers he was finding for himself always fitted into, were always confirmed by, the Christian view of things that he began to turn towards it. He sees a great deal of humour in the way he strained his voice in a painfully juvenile attempt to utter his new truths, only to find that they were not his and were not new, but were part of an eternal philosophy.

In the chapter called "The Flag of the World" he tells of the moment when he discovered the confirmation and reinforcing of his own speculations by the Christian theology. The point at which this came concerned his feelings about the men of his youth who labelled themselves Optimist and Pessimist. Both, he felt, were wrong. It must be possible at once to love and to hate the world, to love it more than enough to get on with it, to hate it enough to get it on. And the Church solved this difficulty by her doctrine of creation and of Original Sin. "God had written not so much a poem, but rather a play; a play he had planned as perfect, but which had necessarily been left to human actors and stage-managers who had since made a great mess of it."

As to that mess the Christian could be as pessimistic as he liked, as to the original design he must be optimistic, for it was his work to restore it. "St. George could still fight the dragon . . . if he were as big as the world he could yet be killed in the name of the world.

"And then followed an experience impossible to describe. It was as if I had been blundering about since my birth with two huge and unmanageable machines, of different shapes and without apparent connection — the world and the Christian tradition. I had found this hole in the world: the fact that one must somehow find a way of loving the world without trusting it; somehow one must love the world without being worldly. I found this projecting feature of Christian theology, like a sort of hard spike, the dogmatic insistence that God was personal, and had made a world separate from Himself. The spike of dogma fitted exactly into the hole in the world — it had evidently been meant to go there — and then the strange thing began to happen. When once these two parts of the two machines had come together, one after another, all the other parts fitted and fell in with an eerie exactitude. I could hear bolt after bolt over all the machinery falling into its place with a kind of click of relief. Having got one part right, all the other parts were repeating that rectitude, as clock after clock strikes noon. Instinct after instinct was answered by doctrine after doctrine. Or, to vary the metaphor, I was like one who had advanced into a hostile country to take one high fortress. And when that fort had fallen the whole country surrendered and turned solid behind me. The whole land was lit up, as it were, back to the first fields of my childhood. All those blind fancies of boyhood which in the fourth chapter I have tried in vain to trace on the darkness, became suddenly transparent and sane. I was right when I felt that I would almost rather say that grass was the wrong colour than say that it must by necessity have been that colour; it might verily have been any other. My sense that happiness hung on the crazy thread of a condition did mean something when all was said: it meant the whole doctrine of the Fall. Even those dim and shapeless monsters of notions which I have not been able to describe, much less defend, stepped quietly into their places like colossal caryatides of the creed. The fancy that the cosmos were not vast and void, but small and cosy, had a fulfilled significance

now, for anything that is a work of art must be small in the sight of the artist; to God the stars might be only small and dear, like diamonds. And my haunting instinct that somehow good was not merely a tool to be used, but a relic to be guarded, like the goods from Crusoe's ship — even that had been the wild whisper of something originally wise, for, according to Christianity, we were indeed the survivors of a wreck, the crew of a golden ship that had gone down before the beginning of the world."

In a chapter called "The Paradoxes of Christianity," the richness of his mind is most manifest; and in that chapter can best be seen what Mr. Belloc meant when he told me Chesterton's style reminded him of St. Augustine's. Talking over with an old schoolfellow of his the list of books he had, as we have seen, drawn up for T. P.'s *Weekly,* I discovered deep doubt as to whether Gilbert would really read these books, as most of us understand reading, combined with a conviction that he would have got out of them at a glance more than most of us by prolonged study. I have certainly never known anyone his equal at what the schoolboy calls "degutting" a book. He did not seem to study an author, yet he certainly knew him.

But it remained that his own mind, reflecting and experiencing, made of his own life his greatest storehouse, so that in all this book there was, as my father pointed out in the *Dublin Review* at the time, an intensely original new light cast on the eternal philosophy about which so much had already been written. The discovery specially needed, perhaps, for his own age was that Christianity represented a new balance that constituted a liberation. The ancient Greek or Roman had aimed at equilibrium by enforcing moderation and getting rid of extremes. Christianity "made moderation out of the still crash of two impetuous emotions." It "got over the difficulty of combining furious opposites by keeping them both, and keeping them both furious." "The more I considered Christianity, the more I felt that while it had established a rule and order, the chief aim of that order was to give room for good things to run wild." Thus inside Christianity the pacifist could become a monk, and the warrior a Crusader, St. Francis could praise good more loudly than Walt Whitman, and St. Jerome denounce evil more darkly than Schopenhauer — but both emotions must be kept in their place. I remember how George Wyndham laughed as he recited to us the paragraph where this idea reached its climax.

"And sometimes this pure gentleness and this pure fierceness met and justified their juncture; the paradox of all the prophets was fulfilled, and, in the soul of St. Louis, the lion lay down with the lamb. But remember that this text is too lightly interpreted. It is constantly assumed, especially in our Tolstoyan tendencies, that when the lion lies down with the lamb the lion becomes lamb-like. But that is a brutal annexation and imperialism on the part of the lamb. That is simply the lamb absorbing the lion instead of the lion eating the lamb. The real problem is — Can the lion lie down with the lamb and still retain his royal ferocity? *That* is the problem the Church attempted; that is the miracle she achieved.

"All this applied not only to the release of the emotions, the development of all the elements that go to make up humanity, but even more to the truths of Revelation. A heresy always means lopping off a part of the truth and, therefore, ultimately a loss of liberty. Orthodoxy, in keeping the whole truth, safeguarded freedom and prevented any one of the great and devouring ideas she was teaching from swallowing any other truth. This was the justification of councils, of definitions, even of persecutions and wars of religion: that they had stood for the defence of reason as well as of faith. They had stood to prevent the suicide of thought which must result if the exciting but difficult balance were lost that had replaced the classical moderation.

"The Church could not afford to swerve a hair's breadth on some things if she was to continue her great and daring experiment of the irregular equilibrium. Once let one idea become less powerful and some other idea would become too powerful. It was no flock of sheep the Christian shepherd was leading, but a herd of bulls and tigers, of terrible ideals and devouring doctrines, each one of them strong enough to turn to a false religion and lay waste the world. Remember that the Church went in specifically for dangerous ideas; she was a lion tamer. The idea of birth through a Holy Spirit, of the death of a divine being, of the forgiveness of sins, or the fulfillment of prophecies, are ideas which, any one can see, need but a touch to turn them into something blasphemous or ferocious. . . . A sentence phrased wrong about the nature of symbolism would have broken all the best statues in Europe. A slip in the definitions might stop all of the dances; might wither all the Christmas trees or break all the Easter eggs. Doctrines had to be defined within strict limits, even in order that man might enjoy general human liberties. The Church had to be careful, if only that the world might be careless.

This is the thrilling romance of Orthodoxy. People have fallen into a foolish habit of speaking of orthodoxy as something heavy, humdrum, and safe. There never was anything so perilous or so exciting as orthodoxy. It was sanity; and to be sane is more dramatic than to be mad. It was the equilibrium of a man behind madly rushing horses, seeming to stoop this way and to sway that, yet in every attitude having the grace of statuary and the accuracy of arithmetic. The Church in its early days went fierce and fast with any warhorse; yet it is utterly unhistoric to say that she merely went mad along one idea, like a vulgar fanaticism. She swerved to left and right, so as exactly to avoid enormous obstacles. She left on one hand the huge bulk of Arianism, buttressed by all the worldly powers to make Christianity too worldly. The next instant she was swerving to avoid an orientalism, which would have made it too unworldly. The orthodox Church never took the tame course or accepted the conventions; the orthodox Church was never respectable. It would have been easier to have accepted the earthly power of the Arians. It would have been easy, in the Calvinistic seventeenth century, to fall into the bottomless pit of predestination. It is easy to be a madman; it is easy to be a heretic. It is always easy to let the age have its head; the difficult thing is to keep one's own. It is always easy to be a modernist; as it is easy to be a snob. To have fallen into any of those open traps of error and exaggeration which fashion after fashion and sect after sect set along the historic path of Christendom — that would indeed have been simple. It is always simple to fall; there are an infinity of angles at which one falls, only one at which one stands. To have fallen into any one of the fads from Gnosticism to Christian Science would indeed have been obvious and tame. But to have avoided them all has been one whirling adventure; and in my vision the heavenly chariot flies thundering through the ages, the dull heresies sprawling and prostrate, the wild truth reeling but erect."

No quotation can adequately convey the wealth of thought in the book. Yet amazingly, the *Times* reviewer rebuked G. K. for substituting emotion for intellect, partly on the strength of a sentence in the chapter called "The Maniac." "The madman is the man who has lost everything except his reason." The reviews, when one reads them as a whole, exactly confirm what Wilfred Ward said in the *Dublin Review:* that whereas he had regarded *Orthodoxy* as a triumphant vindication of his own view that G. K. was a really profound thinker, he found to his amazement that those who had thought him superficial, hailed it as a proof of theirs.

Obviously with a man so much concerned with ultimates the place accorded him in letters will depend upon whether one agrees or disagrees with his conclusions. In a country that is not Catholic this consideration must affect the standing of any Catholic thinker. Thus Newman was considered by Carlyle to have "the brain of a moderate sized rabbit," yet by others his is counted the greatest mind of the century. Similarly Arnold Bennett could credit Chesterton with only a second-class intellectual apparatus — because he was a dogmatist. To this Chesterton replied (in Fancies versus Fads): "In truth there are only two kinds of people, those who accept dogmas and know it and those who accept dogmas and don't know it. My only advan-

tage over the gifted novelist lies in my belonging to the former class." If one grasps the Catholic view of dogma the answer is satisfying; if not the objector is left with his original objection — as against Chesterton, as against Newman. And Chesterton had the extra disadvantage of being a journalist famous for his jokes now moving in Newman's unquestioned field of philosophy and theology. It was in part the difficulty of convincing a man against his will. These critics, as Wilfred Ward pointed out, read superficially and looked only at the fooling, the fantastic puns and comparisons, ignoring the underlying deep seriousness and lines of thought that made him, as it then seemed boldly, rank Chesterton with such writers as Butler, Coleridge and Newman. Taking as his text the saying, "Truth can understand error, but error cannot understand truth," Wilfred Ward called his article, "Mr. Chesterton among the Prophets."

He showed especially the curious confusion made in such comments as the one I have quoted from the *Times*, and made clearer what Chesterton was really saying by a comparison with the "illative sense" of Cardinal Newman. It is the usual difficulty of trying to express a partly new idea. Newman had coined an expression, but it did not express all he meant, still less all that Chesterton meant. Yet it was difficult to use the word "reason" in this particular discussion, without giving to it two different meanings. For in two chapters, "The Maniac" and "The Suicide of Thought," Chesterton was concerned to show that Authority was needed for the defence of reason (in the larger sense) against its own power of self-destruction. Yet the maniac commits this suicide by an excessive use of reason (in the narrower sense). "He is not hampered by a sense of humour or by charity, or by the dumb certainties of experience. He is the more logical for losing certain sane affections. . . . He is in the clean and well-lit prison of one idea: he is sharpened to one painful point."

To Chesterton it seemed that most of the modern religions and philosophies were like the argument by which a madman suffering from persecution mania proves that he is in a world of enemies: it is complete, it is un-answerable, yet it is false. The madman's mind "moves in a perfect but narrow circle. . . . The insane explanation is quite as com-plete as the sane one, only it is not so large. . . . There is such a thing as a narrow universality; there is such a thing as a small and cramped eternity; you may see it in many modern religions." Philosophies such as Materialism, Idealism, Monism, all have in their explanations of the universe this quality of the madman's argument of "cov-ering everything and leaving everything out." The Materialist, like the Madman is "un-conscious of the alien energies and the large indifference of the earth; he is not thinking of the real things of the earth, of fighting peoples or proud mothers or first love or fear upon the sea. The earth is so very large and the cosmos is so very small."

People sometimes say, "life is larger than logic," when they want to dismiss logic, but that was not Chesterton's way. He wanted

logic, he needed logic, as part of the abun-dance of the mind's life, as part of a much larger whole. What was the word — we are looking for it still — for a use of the mind that included all these things; logic and imagination, mysticism and ecstasy and po-etry and joy; a use of the mind that could embrace the universe and reach upwards to God without losing its balance. The mind must work in time, yet it can reach out into Eternity: it is conditioned by space but it can glimpse infinity. The modern world has im-prisoned the mind. Far more than the body it needed great open spaces. And Chesterton, breaking violently out of prison, looked around and saw how the Church had given health to the mind by giving it the space to move in and great ideas to move among. Chesterton, the poet, saw too that man is a poet and must therefore, "get his head into the heavens." He needs mysticism and among Her great ideas, the Church gives him mysteries.

BRUCE MARSHALL

(1899–   )

ONE who describes himself as "writing novels if regarded as a chartered ac-countant; accountancy if regarded as a novel-ist" could only be the Bruce Marshall of *Father Malachy's Miracle.*

Born in the Royal City of Edinburgh, June 24, 1899, Bruce Marshall went to school there, finishing his education at the University of Edinburgh. He went into the army in World War I, and was wounded in action a few days before the armistice. Marshall became a convert to Catholicism in 1918.

His first "Catholic" novel, *Father Mala-chy's Miracle,* was so brilliantly humorous that it appeared to be a *tour de force.* That it was not is obvious in the publication of a second novel, *The World, the Flesh, and Father Smith,* in which the humor, though it has lost some of its hilarity, displays itself salubriously with the unfolding of character. This is a gain, for there is a sharpness in objective wit which much more adequately and naturally serves the purpose of a novelist when it has become characteristic.

FATHER MALACHY'S MIRACLE*

CHAPTER X

SATURDAY, the seventeenth of December, was the octave of the miracle; and, as though to celebrate the fact, the more shrieking of the great dailies published summaries of all the opinions expressed thereon by prominent people during the week. The most metropolitan of deans came, of course, an easy first with a hundred or so public condemnations of magic masquerading as religion and as an outworn sophistry, credited only by Irishmen and Spaniards, which was making a last grotesque struggle to justify itself in the eyes of thinking men. A very eminent female writer on contraceptives was also quoted as stating that the miracle was just "one more instance of latent Freudianism becoming patent," though how she had arrived at this conclusion was not reported. *Punch* was represented by two hearty cartoons: one of the goalkeepers of a much-pressed association football team beseeching the shade of Father Malachy to translate his goal a few hundred yards farther down the field; and another of a drunken reveller prodding to find the keyhole of his front door and blaming Father Malachy for having stolen it. The *Church Times,* that gentleman in a chasuble and a top hat, had written: "While remaining perfectly open to conviction of the supernatural character of the recent extraordinary happenings by the Firth of Forth, we would state quite clearly that, even if the alleged miracle turns out to have been an actual miracle, we cannot accept these events, however remarkable in themselves, as constituting in any way a definite proof of the Petrine claims; and we would remind our readers that miracles are not the especial prerogative of the Roman Church as is instanced by the little-known fact that one of the early Oxford Tractarians, within the memory of the writer's grandfather, once caused a decapitated frog to become alive again by invoking the aid of St. Charles the

First." The *Tablet,* the glory of English Romanism, did not gulp the miracle any more gluttonishly than its Anglican contemporary but stated that, while miracles were, and had always been, possible, it would be as well to await the expression of competent hierarchical opinion; and the *Universe,* the *Daily Mail* of the Faith, had come out with photographs of the Bass Rock and of the bishop of Midlothian pontificating the *Te Deum* in front of the quondam site of the Garden of Eden but, like its more sedate aunt, had cautioned: "Don't believe until you have to." The Brighton *Baptist* and the Liverpool *Eugenist* had been equally vituperative.

But, as the shrieking dailies informed their millions, the hit of the week had been the verse sung at Newcastle by the leading lady of the *Whose Baby Are You?* company:

"Malachy, your mericle,
Has made us all hysterical,
    For we had to fly
    Right through the sky
Until we reached North Berwickle."

Father Malachy saddened as he read these summaries. The thing was so evidently of God, and yet even those of the Household of the Faith were cautious about accepting it as such. What hope was there for a world which insisted on preferring Barabbas to Christ, Barabbas with a saxophone, Barabbas with a wireless set, Barabbas with his ladies who thought it intellectual to be light. Barabbas who couldn't believe in God because he believed so much in himself?

Tears gathered in his eyes as he gazed, mentally, out over the world. Everywhere faith seemed to be dying, in Andalucia as in Clackmannan, in Brittany as in Los Angeles. And Scotland, bonnie, darling Scotland which had always cared for the things of God, bonnie, darling Scotland was going the same way as France and South America. No God; no worship, no true love; just investment companies and cinemas and hotel lounges. Oh, for the days when there was a mitred abbot at Dunfermline and a cardinal

*Marshall, Bruce, *Father Malachy's Miracle* (New York: Doubleday, Doran and Co., 1931), pp. 254–259.

archbishop of St. Andrews who rode in scarlet and ermine. Oh, for the days when faith was faith and love was love and the altar was the trysting place of heaven and earth. Oh, for the days when the incense rose in Melrose and the sacring bell was heard in Jedburgh. Oh, for the days when the Church of God was the Church of God in gold and silver for all men to see and not a despised remnant slouching along back streets in ungainly coats and bagging trousers.

And yet they could come again, those dead days. They could come again, like flowers after a long winter. They could come again, John Henry Newman's Second Spring in Scotland. They could come again, those days when St. Andrews should ring as Sevilla and Dunkeld as Bologna, those days when the Blessed Sacrament should be carried again through the tired streets and men and women would know It for God-with-us. Yes, they would come again if men would only humble themselves and believe, they could come again, those days when Scotland was Scotland and not just a strident suburb of New York.

His eyes dried as his heart cheered and he got up and moved to the window. Yes, there was a crowd outside the site of the miracle. Some kneeling, some gaping, some looking as though they didn't know whether to gape or to kneel. No, no, all was not yet lost. Lourdes didn't get itself believed in in a day. His miracle might yet convert the world.

Reassured, he was about to turn back when a sudden burst of song crashed itself upon his ears:

> "Malachy, your mericle,
> Has made us all hysterical,
>   For we had to fly
>   Right through the sky
> Until we reached North Berwickle."

A band of urchins, probably. He didn't want to see. The tears came again, streaming this time. "O Blessed Jesus," he prayed, "make them see, make them see. Bring the world back, bring Scotland back; be met on the road to Rannoch as You were once met on the road to Emmaus." And the tears went on streaming, spreading out into tributaries as they flowed.

THE WORLD, THE FLESH, AND FATHER SMITH*

II

THE Bishop liked a sausage for his lunch, and maintained that nobody in the whole diocese could cook one as well as he himself did, not even the Jesuits, who had a lay brother who was a real dab at the job. Father Smith explained this tactfully to the landlady on the day that his lordship was due to lunch at the priest's lodgings, prior to accompanying him to the station to meet the Sacred Heart nuns who had been expelled from France. At first Mrs. Walsh said that she had never heard of such an idea, a holy bishop, who could consecrate and ordain, cooking his own sausage; but she gave in when the Bishop himself arrived in his worn old overcoat with the top button almost off

and smiled at her out of his clear twinkling eyes so blue beneath his thatch of white hair. She said that, faith, if his lordship would allow her to sew the button on his overcoat, she would allow his lordship to cook the sausage, only it wasn't to be just one sausage, but three at the very least, because an important man like a bishop needed to eat a lot and be strong so that he could carry out his great and wonderful work. So they all went into the kitchen together, and Mrs. Walsh sat down and sewed the button tight on his lordship's overcoat and the Bishop stood over the frying pan and explained to them both that the reason most people didn't cook sausages properly was that they forgot to keep turning them round.

The Bishop and Father Smith did not talk much during lunch because the sausages were so good and because they had not much time

*Marshall, Bruce, *The World, the Flesh, and Father Smith* (Boston: Houghton Mifflin Co., 1945), pp. 24–37.

if they were to be at the station in time to meet the French nuns when they arrived at two-fifteen. The Bishop was forty-seven years old and he had been a bishop for the past three years, because the Pope liked having young bishops in that part of Scotland, where the parishes were scattered and separated by sea, mountain, and loch. The Bishop liked Father Smith and Father Smith liked the Bishop, but they did not often meet, because his lordship was always travelling about in trains and boats, preaching and administering confirmation in distant valleys and dells.

They had decided to take a tram to the station because the diocesan funds wouldn't run to cabs both ways, and anyway, it was a different matter ordering cabs for holy nuns, but our Lord was fully justified in expecting hale and hearty priests to travel less luxuriously, if not to walk on their legs. As they waited by the lamp-post which said 'CARS STOP BY REQUEST' and 'FIRE PLUG 50 YDS.' and 'PLEASE DO NOT SPIT ON THE PAVEMENT,' the Bishop asked Father Smith if he had heard the rumour that King Edward VII had been to Lourdes and knelt during the procession of the Blessed Sacrament. Father Smith said that he had heard all sorts of rumours about King Edward VII, but never one quite like that, and the Bishop said that he knew what Father Smith meant, but they must both remember that kings and princes were exposed to much severer temptations than ordinary men and that it would be very wonderful indeed if Almighty God were to convert King Edward to the Catholic religion, because it would certainly do a lot of good.

When their tram came swaying along, the Bishop stepped by mistake on a metal plug which the driver had forgotten to remove when he changed ends at the terminus and there was a lovely inconsequent sound, just like the sacring bell at Mass and really quite appropriate, Father Smith said. They went inside because it wasn't worth while going up on top for so short a distance. Father Smith was pleased to find that it was James Scott who was the conductor and he introduced him to the Bishop, explaining all about the new baby and about how Mr. Scott went to the dépôt every morning very early so that he might sprinkle his tram from end to end with holy water before the day's work began. Mr. Scott blushed a little when Father Smith said this and Father Smith supposed that this must be because there were Protestants listening who wouldn't understand, and thought, what with human respect and one thing and another, how very much more merit a layman like James Scott must gain for leading a good life than himself and the Bishop.

But Mr. Scott couldn't stand talking for long, because he had to be handing out his white and blue and red tickets. As he moved away down the aisle, punching and ping-ing, the Bishop began to talk about liturgical and formal prayer, Father Smith sat with his hat on his knees, because he did not think it polite to sit in front of a bishop with his head covered, even in a tram car.

People were wrong to condemn liturgical and formal prayer, the Bishop said, because it was only courteous to God to think about what you were going to say to Him before you said it. Whereupon Father Smith said that he thought the critics of liturgical prayer condemned it, because repetition tended to make it meaningless, with the result that sinners could murmur Hail Marys with their lips while planning further misdemeanours in their minds.

'I wonder, though, if they are quite right,' the Bishop said out above the booming and the zooming of the tram. 'It seems to me that even the hardiest sinner cannot utter the sheer poetry of the Church's prayers without having his soul in some way ennobled by their lovely sound. Moreover, the Pater and the Ave are earth's sweetest greeting to heaven, and only a vain man would imagine that he could frame a more beautiful. And whenever I look out on the hideousness and harshness of our industrial cities, I thank Almighty God deep down in my heart for having given His Church so many exquisite rites and ceremonies. For it is not bread and circuses which the people require, but poetry and prayer.'

' "Poetry is the phrase which the young

man murmurs in his heart; all the rest is only literature." I remember reading that in a magazine once,' Father Smith said.

'That's true as far as it goes, but it does not go far enough,' the Bishop said. 'When young men murmur poetry in their hearts, they are looking for God even although they may not know it. It is poetry which is a reflection of religion, not religion of poetry.'

Father Smith could see that people were beginning to stare at the Bishop and himself, popping at them hard glittering hating eyes, like the soda-water bottle stoppers you pressed down with your thumb. He knew, however, that they were staring only because they were so accustomed to hearing people say things which didn't matter that they were shocked when they heard people say things which did. If the Bishop and himself had been talking about steel shares or the price of jute, nobody would have looked at them at all, but because they were talking about the things which alone gave meaning to life, their words aroused hatred, anger, and contempt. The priest thought sadly about all the talking that there was in the world each day — about the wind and the rain and golf and Aunt Maggie's new dress — and he thought, too, about all the important things that never seemed to get said.

'Probably your lordship is right,' he said, more loudly than was necessary, because he wasn't going to be shamed out of talking about the things of God just because a tramload of worldlings was staring at him. 'After all, our Lord and the saints have hammered out and chastened the holy phrases, so perhaps there is a grace to be found even in their echo.'

The Right Reverend Monsignor Canon O'Duffy, administrator of the pro-Cathedral, was already on the platform when they arrived at the station. He had been invited to meet the French nuns too, but because he was making a bee line for the gentlemen's lavatory, the Bishop and Father Smith pretended not to see him, but stood and examined the literature exposed on the bookstall, which seemed to be very very worldly, although the Bishop was pleased to remark that there were cheap editions of books by Robert Hugh Benson. There was also a new novel out by a young man called Hugh Walpole, and while the Bishop and Father Smith were wondering who he could be, Monsignor O'Duffy came back from the gentlemen's lavatory and joined them. Monsignor O'Duffy was a great ape of a priest with coarse hair and a great hunk of face like a miner's, who poured his tea into his saucer to cool it and blew his nose on a red handkerchief at chapter meetings.

'Having a wee free read at the books, I see?' the monsignore greeted as he joined the Bishop and Father Smith. 'Afternoon, your lordship.'

'Father Smith and I have just been having a most interesting discussion on poetry,' the Bishop said.

'Poetry's all blether,' the monsignore said. 'A lot of nonsense about "love" and "dove" and I don't know all what and often it's downright sinful. Give me football for the lads any day of the week. And as for the lassies, they can sit by the fireside and do a bit sewing and be very much better for not bothering their heads about all yon highfalutin' rubbish.'

The Bishop and Father Smith saw that it was no use pressing the subject of poetry any further with Monsignor Canon O'Duffy, so Father Smith said that he wondered whether any of the nuns spoke English and hoped that they did, because his French was beginning to get rather rusty, which wasn't quite true because he rather prided himself on his French. Monsignor O'Duffy said right out that it was no use counting on him for any of the parlez-voo business, but the Bishop said that he had spoken quite a lot of French in his day, because he had been at Saint Sulpice before he had been at Valladolid and had had to read aloud in the refectory. Father Smith was rather disappointed to hear this, because he wouldn't have minded being the only one able to do the talking, but he mastered his dissatisfaction quickly, because he knew that it was unchristian.

Far away out along the bend of the railway line, at the junction of the golf course and Sir Dugald Ippecacuanha's estate, a puff of smoke appeared above the trees, and a miniature worm of train rolled tinily along the embankment. Father Smith had often seen the puff of smoke at the same time and in the same place, and each time that he saw it he sent a spiral of thanks up to God, for having ruled even the world with the rhythm of liturgy and for keeping all the other safe old trees on earth still in their same safe places. 'J'ai, tu as, il a,' Monsignor O'Duffy began to recite with heavy humour. 'Avez-vous vu la plume de ma tante,' but the Bishop interrupted him by reminding him that it was the first-class carriages which always stopped in front of the bookstall, and that they had better move further along the platform, because the good and holy French nuns would be sure to be travelling third.

The Bishop was right. The nuns were travelling third-class and at the very end of the train, next the guard's van. Monsignor O'Duffy, as he grunted along to meet them, said that he had noticed that nuns always travelled in the back of trains, and Father Smith said that that was perhaps because they were so mindful of our Lord's saying that the last in this world should be the first in the next. The nuns smiled when they saw the three priests and the three priests smiled back. The Bishop took off his hat and uttered the little speech which he had been rehearsing since Septuagesima: 'Bon jour, ma Révérende Mère. Je suis enchanté de faire votre connaissance. Permettez-moi de vous souhaiter, ainsi qu'à toute votre communauté, la bienvenue sur la terre d'Écosse.' Father Smith said, 'Je suppose que vos bagages se trouveront dans le fourgon,' and Monsignor O'Duffy said, 'Oo là, là, oui, oui,' at which the Reverend Mother laughed.

There were eight nuns in all and they stood with the wind blowing pretty pillows of pattern into their habits while Reverend Mother introduced herself and them. Father Smith didn't catch all the names, because they were French and Reverend Mother said them so quickly, and because he was too busy admiring the nuns' sweet happy holy faces to pay much attention. Two or three of the nuns were young, with such lovely rosy cheeks and strong white teeth and bright blue eyes that Father Smith wondered why on earth the French had wanted to get rid of them, because they must have looked so lovely walking along old cobbled streets.

The nuns apologized for having brought so much luggage with them, but they said that they couldn't have borne to have left all their beautiful candlesticks and vestments behind, especially the red chasuble that had once been worn by the Curé d'Ars. The Bishop said that he quite understood this and that they had done quite rightly because Almighty God would be more honoured by beautiful things being used in His service in Scotland than by having them left behind in France, only he didn't say it very quickly, because he hadn't had since Septuagesima Sunday to practise it over in French. A bevy of large-striped stockbrokers in blown-out plus fours with brassies and cleeks glared at the nuns as they passed, but Monsignor O'Duffy glared back even harder, and the stockbrokers moved on, staunch Protestants who were willing to do anything for their religion except go to church.

While Monsignor O'Duffy and Father Smith were seeing about the luggage, the Bishop explained to the nuns that they must expect to find their religion hated just as much in Scotland as in France, although less accurately. The reason for this, he said, was that the enemies of the Church in France had had the Gospel preached to them, but had rejected it, whereas in Scotland men scoffed and reviled through prejudice and ignorance. Reverend Mother said that she quite understood this and that she was sure that the other nuns understood it, too, and that they would all pray a lot for Scotland, that God might give it back the blessing of Faith.

The Bishop and Father Smith had ordered only two cabs for the nuns, because they hadn't known that there was going to be so much luggage, but Monsignor O'Duffy managed to collar a third, because the driver was a member of the pro-Cathedral parish, although he hadn't made his Easter duties for the last five years, at least so the monsignore said. Reverend Mother and the Bishop and Monsignor O'Duffy all got into the first cab and four of the nuns into the second and only three into the last, because they had to take the box containing the red chasuble which had once been worn by the Curé d'Ars inside with them, as they couldn't very well trust it up front with the cabman on top, especially when he hadn't been to holy communion for so long. As the cabs moved off, a gang of hooligans who had been standing watching in front of a railway poster for Devon, Glorious Devon, started to jeer; but the Bishop told Reverend Mother that she mustn't worry about that sort of thing, as the oafs and loungers who were yelling didn't really hate the doctrines of the Church about our Lord and the Blessed Sacrament, but only the garbled distortions which ignorant men had represented to them.

As they rolled down through the town, the Bishop asked Reverend Mother if she had ever been to Rome and Reverend Mother said that she had, but that she hadn't been as impressed as she had imagined and that she was sorry to say that some of the princes and high prelates of the Church hadn't seemed to have very spiritual faces and had hurried through even the holy mysteries of the Mass in a distraught and irreverent manner. The Bishop said that that was perhaps because the Saxon mind could think of only one thing at once, whereas the Latin mind could think of several, so that it was possible that an Italian cardinal's eyes and face might reflect the worldly thoughts of half his mind, whereas the other half was really and truly thinking about our Lord and all that He had done for us. He said that he had noticed the same thing about British and continental soldiers; British soldiers looked as though they meant their drill, whereas continental soldiers slopped about in a most unmilitary manner, so that there was, curiously enough, a psychological connection between two such entirely dissimilar ceremonies as a High Mass in Westminster Cathedral and a full-dress parade of the Argyll and Sutherland Highlanders. Reverend Mother said that there was perhaps something in what the Bishop said, but that his lordship must not forget that she herself was a Latin and no Saxon and that in spite

of that fact she had been considerably shocked by the scurried ceremonial and the slothful thought of some of the higher clergy in Rome. Monsignor O'Duffy said, 'Oo, là, là, oui, oui,' and everybody laughed a lot, although deep down within themselves they were all quite pained that the higher clergy in Rome didn't look more spiritual.

Father Smith said that what they had just been talking about reminded him of a story about a Frenchman who had gone to confession and accused himself of not having been impressed by what he had seen in the holy city. 'Ah, mon enfant,' his confessor had said, 'il vaut toujours mieux ne pas visiter la cuisine du Bon Dieu.' The Bishop laughed so much at this story that Monsignor O'Duffy wondered if he was ever going to stop, and was rather irritated when his lordship went on for so long because he himself hadn't understood a word, although he had said, 'ou là, là, oui, oui.'

But if Monsignor O'Duffy didn't know French, he knew Italian which he had learnt at the Scots College in Rome. For although he had an Irish name, the monsignore had been born at Tobermory. There was once, he said, when the Bishop had finished laughing, an Italian priest who had to preach a sermon on the feast of the patron saint of his native town, San Pietro di Buonarotti. 'San Pietro Damiano fu un buon' santo,' he began, 'San Pietro di Roma fu un excellentissimo santo, ma San Pietro di Buonarotti, phew, che santo, amici miei?'

They were all still laughing at Monsignor O'Duffy's story when the cab drew up in front of the house which the nuns had had bought for them while they were still in France and which they were later going to convert into a school. Father Bonnyboat, of the Church of Our Lady, Mirror of Justice, Gormnevis, who had been entrusted by the Bishop with the purchase of the new convent, was on the doorstep to greet them. He held in his hand a parrot in a cage, which he presented to Reverend Mother with a stiff little bow, saying 'oiseau, oiseau,' and explaining that he had had the bird for five years and that it could say both 'Dominus vobiscum' and 'per omnia saecula saeculorum,' but that it was with the greatest pleasure in the world that he presented it to Reverend Mother. Reverend Mother seemed rather embarrassed by the gift, and for a moment or two Father Smith was afraid that she was going to say that the rule of her order forbade herself or her nuns to keep parrots however holy their cluckings, but in the end she thanked Father Bonnyboat prettily enough, and then they all went in to tea.

The nuns sat at a long table in the bare room which Father Bonnyboat had had prepared as a refectory. Reverend Mother did the pouring-out and the Bishop insisted on handing round the scones, even to the priests, because he knew that the highest title of the highest of bishops was Servus Servorum Dei, the Servant of the Servants of God. Father Bonnyboat had wanted to provide a little holy reading aloud during the meal, but the only French books he had been able to lay hands on were by Anatole France and Emile Zola. The Bishop had said that they weren't quite suitable and that Father Bonnyboat could make up for this lack of edification in his sermon in the chapel afterwards.

'Aiméz-vous les scones écossais?' Father Bonnyboat asked a young nun.

'Oui, ils sont délicieux, mais je crois qu'à l'avenir il va falloir nous contenter d'une alimentation plus austère.'

'Quelquefois en Écosse on a des kippers à son thé,' Father Bonnyboat said.

'Oo là, là, oui, oui,' Monsignor O'Duffy said with his mouth full.

As soon as tea was over, they all went into the chapel, which Father Bonnyboat had installed in the old billiard room. A small wooden altar had been erected and the Blessed Sacrament was reserved, with a red lamp burning in front. The Bishop had previously blessed the billiard room quite thoroughly, saying that he thought this specially necessary, because the house had previously belonged to a chartered accountant. When they had all prayed a little, Monsignor O'Duffy sat down at the harmonium and wheezed out 'Je suis Chrétien,' which the nuns all sang with low clear voices and the

priests didn't sing at all because the nuns sang so beautifully.

When Father Bonnyboat stood up to preach, the Bishop was afraid that the priest was going to yell out the customary rant which he kept for big occasions, 'My dear brethren in Jesus Christ, none of you will ever wake up in heaven wondering how on earth you've got there,' because such a sermon would not have been kind to nuns, who had every reason to hope for salvation. Instead, the priest preached a sensible little sermon on sanctity, and in English too, because he couldn't get his subjunctives right in French, so he said. The world was wrong to laugh at saints, Father Bonnyboat said, because the production of a saint was God's highest handiwork. To be a saint didn't mean being a weak namby-pamby creature who couldn't say boo to a goose; to be a saint meant loving God with one's whole heart and one's whole mind and doing, thinking, and saying all things to His greater glory. That was the only philosophy which could save the world, but it would never save the world because God Himself had said that his kingdom was not of this world, but that did not mean that monks and nuns and priests were wrong in trying to be saints themselves and in encouraging others to try to be saints too. Our Lord Himself had said that many were called but that few were chosen, and that the vast supernatural machinery of the Church would have been worth while if in all time and space it had succeeded in producing only one saint. In the eyes of God it was the invisible victories in the human soul which mattered and not the great splashing news in the papers about politics and Sir Thomas Lipton's yachts. When Father Bonnyboat had finished, Monsignor O'Duffy began to play the organ again and the Bishop, Father Smith, and Father Bonnyboat went out to vest for Solemn Benediction of the Blessed Sacrament.

Father Smith always loved the service of Benediction, because it was so beautiful with our Lord there all white in the centre of the monstrance, and he sometimes wondered why lay-people wanted to go to concerts and theatres at all, when they could have so much more pleasure praising and adoring God this way. It was beginning to get dark when, as deacon, he took the Host out of the tabernacle, and the only lights in the chapel were the candles on the altar which glowed like stars. In the tender smudge of darkness the nuns knelt and sang lovely words so that even Monsignor O'Duffy's chunk of face looked holy as it hung like a raw red moon above the keys of the harmonium. The nuns sang the *O Salutaris* and the Litany of Our Lady and Father Smith thought that he had never heard any sound more exquisite than the syllables of 'speculum justitiae' as they came clear and sweet from those invisible French lips. Then the nuns sang *Salve Regina* and the *Tantum Ergo,* and the Bishop raised the Blessed Sacrament in the monstrance and made the sign of the cross high up over the kneeling nuns, stretching his arms away out, as though he were trying to bless all the sinners that there were in the world as well. The nuns sang the *Laudate Dominum* at a pious little gallop while Father Smith put the Blessed Sacrament back in the tabernacle. Then they all sang over again, 'Adoremus in aeternum Sanctissimum Sacramentum' among the wreaths of incense, and the Bishop and Father Smith and Father Bonnyboat left the chapel in their rich white vestments.

Reverend Mother and the nuns all wanted to come to the door with the Bishop and the priests to see them off and to thank them for their kindness, but the Bishop pointed out that the climate of Scotland was much more rigorous than that of France and that their good-byes could be said just as well in the hall. Reverend Mother said that it was très, très, gentil de la part de monseigneur l'évêque et de messieurs les curés de s'être donné tant de mal pour de pauvres religieuses refugiées, and the Bishop said that it had been no trouble at all and the nuns said, 'Mais si, mais si,' and Monsignor O'Duffy said, 'Oo là, là, oui, oui,' and everybody laughed a lot including his lordship the Bishop.

Father Smith realized that there was trouble afoot as soon as the door of the convent had closed behind them, but he pretended not to see, as he walked with the Bishop and the other priests, the blobs of hating faces strung like bladders along the outer railing. He tried also not to hear the ugly things that they were shouting because he knew that our Lord wanted Catholics to be brave and to suffer for His Name's sake as well as to adore Him in beautiful chants and because he knew that he wasn't brave and didn't want to suffer the least bit.

Then he looked at the Bishop's serene face and Father Bonnyboat's surprised frown and Monsignor O'Duffy's jutting jowl, and he remembered all the saints, virgins, confessors, and martyrs who had endured so much for the love of Christ. 'Passio Domini Nostri Jesu Christi,' he murmured and knew no more as the sharp stone hit him on the temple and he fell, unconscious, to the ground.

CHRISTOPHER HOLLIS
(*1902–*   )

AXEBRIDGE in Somerset was the birthplace of Christopher Hollis, March, 1902. He was educated at Eton and Balliol College, Oxford. While at Oxford, Hollis made a considerable reputation as a debater which led to his inclusion in the Oxford University debating team which toured America. This American experience gave rise to Hollis' *American Heresy,* an analysis of our philosophy of "bigger and better elephants."

At the conclusion of his university career

and the reception of the A.B. degree Hollis entered the Church. He was one of the Masters at Stonyhurst for a time, spent a year in economic research at Notre Dame University, is at present a director and editor of *The London Tablet*.

Hollis' biographies: *Erasmus, Dryden,* and *St. Thomas More* are intelligent studies which show his ability to delineate character as well as a competent grasp of history. *Monstrous Regiment* is a well-balanced analysis of the English Reformation.

CHAPTER V

THE OPEN WAR*

THE chief persecutor of the Catholics was a certain Richard Topcliffe. He first took to his trade after the Northern Rebellion through his anxiety to get hold of the lands of one Richard Norton, of Norton Conyers, in Yorkshire. Soon afterwards we find him quarrelling with Sir Christopher Wray, the Chief Justice who afterwards condemned Blessed Edmund Campion to death, over the appropriation of a prebendal stall in Lichfield Cathedral. The evidence for his atrocities comes not from his enemies or victims but from his own boasts. "Because the often exercise of the rack in the Tower was so odious and so much spoken of by the people, Topcliffe had authority to torment priests in his own house in such sort as he shall think good," and he himself boasted that, in comparison with his private machine, the official racks were mere child's play. After his torturing of Robert Southwell, public opinion was so disgusted that Cecil had to pretend to arrest him for having exceeded his powers. It was but a pretense and he was soon out and at work again. In 1594 he brought against one Fitzherbert an action which throws a curious light upon the state of public morality among the governing class at that time. Topcliffe sued Fitzherbert for five thousand pounds, on the ground that Fitzherbert had promised to pay him that sum if he would get Fitzherbert's father and uncle and a certain Mr. Bassett condemned for recusancy and then torture them to death. Both sides admitted the contract. Topcliffe

maintained that he had fulfilled the conditions: Fitzherbert denied it. Mr. Bassett, he said, was still alive, and, though the father and uncle had, it is true, been tortured and were now dead, yet it could not be proved that torture was the cause of death. Fitzherbert maintained that they had died from gaol-fever. Even the Elizabethan court felt that there were some limits beyond which baseness should not be publicly advertised and "the matter was put over for secret hearing." Yet nine years later we find that Topcliffe has somehow managed to annex the estate of the Fitzherberts to his other possessions.

One other story in illustration must suffice. There was a certain gentleman of Warwickshire, a Mr. Arden, a cousin of some sort, it seems, of Shakespeare. He had been so foolhardy as to refuse to sell some land which he possessed to Elizabeth's favourite, the Earl of Leicester. Arden had a son-in-law called Somerville, a Catholic and a lunatic. In one of his fits of insanity Somerville asserted, or was said to have asserted, that he would murder all Protestants and the Queen at the head of them. On this excuse Arden was arrested, though he had, it seems, had nothing to do with his son-in-law's eccentricities. With Arden was arrested Hall, a missionary priest, whom Arden had kept in his house disguised as a gardener. Both Arden and Hall were put to torture, and on the rack Hall was induced to admit that he had once heard Arden express a wish that the Queen was in Heaven. On this evidence Arden was convicted of a conspiracy to kill the Queen and executed, and his lands were seized by Leicester. An authority as little op-

*From *The Monstrous Regiment,* by Christopher Hollis, Copyright, 1930. Courtesy of Minton, Balch & Co.; pp. 114–125.

posed to the powers that be as Camden wrote: "The woeful end of this gentleman . . . was generally imputed to Leicester's malice. Certain it is that he had incurred Leicester's heavy displeasure, and not without cause, for he had rashly opposed him in all he could, reproaching him as an adulterer and defaming him as a new upstart."

There was then about the Elizabethan persecution every one of those features by which every persecution is necessarily made so very unpleasant. Blackmail and espionage were rife to an almost incredible degree, and, employed at first for the purpose of the persecution, soon spread, as is their custom, into every department of life, until Cecil, the Queen's Secretary of State, dare not write to Lord Shrewsbury, of the Queen's Council, because he knows that spies will seize the letter and take it to the Queen. "A father," reports the Spanish ambassador, "dares not trust his own son." To be a spy became an international profession. Scoundrels, taking the money both of Elizabeth and Philip, sold the secrets of each to the other and invented secrets where they were not able to discover them.

Yet the Elizabethan persecution had about it also an additional unpleasantness from which most religious persecutions have been free. Lord Arundel, the Elizabethan courtier, was convinced of the truth of the Catholic faith by watching the trial of Campion and by listening to the staged debates between him and his Anglican adversaries. He became a convert and was therefore arrested for treason. He wrote before his arrest to complain that the people who surrounded the Queen were atheists at heart. Leicester, it seems, was almost confessedly atheist. Walsingham, the patron of the free-thinking Marlowe, was suspected of being so, though the language of Protestantism was always ready to his tongue. Elizabeth and Cecil had been Catholics yesterday and would be Catholics again tomorrow if it should be found necessary in order to save their skins. In Mary's reign, when the burnings were on, Cecil had made himself quite ridiculous by going about everywhere with a rosary, mumbling away at his prayers, and to show

his zeal he had crossed over to Brussels in order to escort Cardinal Pole to England. He was now, of course, as vigorous in his outward professions of Protestantism, but, if he believed in anything, it was probably in magic and witchcraft.

Sir Walter Raleigh, too, though he was not at that time of the Council, was widely believed to be atheist and this reputation clung to him right up to the time of his calamitous but well deserved death, which Archbishop Abbot, though he admitted that Raleigh died "a religious and Christian death," yet ascribed to insolence brought on by his "questioning of God's being and omnipotence." At this date in "Sir Walter Raleigh's School of Atheism," according to *An Advertisement Written to a Secretary of my Lord Treasurers of England by an English Intelligencer,* "much diligence was said to be used to get young gentlemen to this school, wherein both Moses and our Saviour, the Old and the New Testaments, are jested at and the scholars taught among other things to spell God backwards."

For the predominance of atheism in Elizabethan society evidence comes from writers varying as widely in opinion and motives as Thomas Nashe at one end and Robert Persons at the other. It is to the honour of the Church of England that very few of those who persecuted in her name believed in her tenets. As Cardinal Allen wrote with the bitterness of an *émigré,* but yet with much truth, the contest is "not for religion of which our enemies have not had a bit, but for the stability of the empire and worldly prosperity."

In modern times the controversy over the Elizabethan persecution is sometimes carried on in very peculiar terms. One side is apt to complain that all the Catholics were traitors, the other side loudly to protest that but a disreputable minority had anything to do with treason. As if they were a sort of Labour Members who obediently paid their income tax though Cecil and the Conservatives happened to be in power! It is impossible to make head or tail of the story if you speak as if treason or loyalty to Elizabeth meant the same thing as treason or loyalty to George V, or use the word "Traitor" as a mere term of abuse. It is always to the interest of those in power to give the word an ugly sound. Yet, as Elizabeth's own godson, John Harrington, wrote,

Treason doth never prosper. What's the reason?
That, if it prosper, none dare call it treason.

The parallel is not with the government of George V, but with such governments as those of Lenin or Calles. A queen with a claim more than doubtful at the first — a perjured queen, who only received her throne on the express condition that she would maintain the Catholic religion and had broken that promise — a queen who was a puppet in the hands of those whose policy was the destruction of English life — such was the Elizabeth to whom English Catholics were asked to be loyal. As for her masters, they were rich men and it is not for us to judge them. As Anatole France has said, *"La miséricorde de Dieu est infinie; il sauvera même un riche."*

It is true that even during the later years of Elizabeth's reign there were many loyal Catholics. In spite of the papal Bull, the Catholics, in the petition presented by Richard Shelley in 1585, protested their loyalty and reminded Elizabeth of the important theological truth that even the Pope cannot justly command what is sinful. The Armada was to arouse no Catholic revolt. Yet Catholic loyalty was a loyalty of despair, and there is no doubt that from the death of Campion and the time of the adoption of the official aggressive policy up to the defeat of the Armada — that middle period during which the Government was tyrannous and not yet national — an enormous proportion of the Catholics, though perhaps willing to bear in submission so long as there was no hope of remedy, would yet have declared against Elizabeth if there had appeared to be a reasonable hope of overturning her.

People are too apt to think of Elizabethan England as they find it depicted in such books as Charles Kingsley's *Westward Ho.* It is necessary to banish from the mind all this talk of Gloriana and the birth of England, of Elizabeth as if she were a sixteenth-century Queen Victoria, only slightly less German, and the ludicrous pretense that no one ever thought of intriguing with a foreigner until the wicked Jesuits put them up to it in the days of good Queen Bess. The error is to transfer to these earlier years that romantic feeling for the old queen which the later Spanish menace created and which lasted until she was drowned beneath the great unpopularity which she earned from the execution of Essex. Kingsley's Elizabethans walk through the English streets, conscious that they live at the dawn of a new era of freedom and adventure, that they have broken with the old and shackled past. "We owe the great writers of the golden age of our literature," Shelley tells us in the Introduction to *Prometheus Unbound,* "to that fervid awakening of the public mind which shook to dust the oldest and most oppressive form of the Christian religion." If it be so, the Elizabethans themselves seem to have been quite unaware of it. We search the real Elizabethan literature in vain for a trace that the Elizabethans had any such feelings about themselves. Rather did they feel — and they were quite right — that they lived in an evil and violent time. They did not especially look forward to the future; rather did many of them, like Shakespeare, look back with a regret, perhaps a merely sentimental regret, to good old times before the universal scramble, to the life of status and to

The constant service of the antique world,
When service sweats for duty, not for meed.

As Carlyle said, Shakespeare's poetry is "the last sunset glory of the Middle Ages."

To what would you have had a Catholic be loyal in this second period of Queen Elizabeth's reign? Governments, it is true, have certain rights simply because they are *de facto* governments. When we recollect that the much quoted line

There's such divinity doth hedge a king,

was put into the mouth of Hamlet's uncle, the usurping regicide, who made such a very bloody beginning and was to come to an equally bloody end, we may suspect that the sixteenth-century monarch-worship was perhaps mixed with a slightly larger dose of quizzical irony than is sometimes understood. Nevertheless, the age certainly did possess this particular vice which was strong to reinforce the legitimate respect for authority. Yet, unless you would have the subject the slave of an Oriental despot, the duty of obedience, as has been already said, is not absolute. A Catholic lived in those days under perpetual sentence of death. At any moment of the night or day he knew that his house might be suddenly broken into and he himself carried off to prison and perhaps to death. If he owned any property, he was at the mercy of any neighbor who wished to delate him. False priests, hirelings of Walsingham and Cecil, had come to him, heard his confession and then betrayed its secrets to the Government. He had perhaps been called to the rack and there tortured for no offence of his own, but simply to induce him to say something that would incriminate a friend or a co-religionist. Nicholas Saunders writes:

"Sometimes when we were sitting merrily at table, conversing familiarly on matters of faith and devotion (for our talk is generally of such things,) there comes a hurried knock at the door, that of a pursuivant. All start up and listen like deer when they hear the huntsman; we leave our food and commend ourselves to God in a brief ejaculation; nor is word or sound heard till the servants come to say what the matter is. If it is nothing we laugh at our fright."

Even if such a Catholic fled abroad, the spies of the Government would follow him, watch his movements, and, if he were a person of importance like Cardinal Allen, perhaps even attempt to remove him by poison or assassination.

For a time the Catholic had perhaps thought it wise to tolerate this reign of terror because it could not last for ever and after it saner times would return with the accession of the Queen's cousin. He now saw that there was little doubt that, in order to prevent the return of those saner times,

somehow or other, sooner or later, the Queen's cousin was going to be done to death. The murder of Campion had shown that a Catholic could not save his life by merely keeping out of politics. It is to be seriously argued that the Catholic who saw a chance of delivery from such a tyranny should refuse that chance simply because the deliverer happened to be a foreigner. As Maurice Clennock wrote with obvious sense, "Better to attain eternal blessedness under a foreign lord than to be cast into the nethermost hell by an enemy at home." You might as well have told the Patriarch Tikhon that he had a duty of loyalty to Lenin because Lenin happened to be living in the Kremlin. The wonder is not that there was so much, but that there was so little Catholic disloyalty. Nor is it remarkable if some considered the use of what was at that day the common weapon of Scotch and French politics, the assassin's knife.

It is most important that this question should not be discussed in the terms of modern Liberalism. The importance of the point must excuse a repetition. To the Catholic the first and most essential concern is that he should be able to get the Sacraments. Yet the life of the Church is more than the isolated lives of the individuals who make it up, and the Catholic can only live his full life in a Catholic community; for his religion does not stop at the church-door; it infects every activity of life. It is right that English Catholics to-day should recognise that they live in a non-Catholic community and they are foolish if they waste too much time in complaining at the necessary disadvantages which such a life imposed upon them. At what exact date did it become proper for the Catholic to admit that England was no longer a Catholic country and so to adjust his policy is debatable. He could hardly be blamed for refusing to recognise it in the early years of Elizabeth's reign. The Elizabethan Catholic, living in the first years of the Counter-Reformation when in every country but England the new Protestantism was losing all along the line, could not have been expected thus complacently to sit down to England's loss of the Faith.

"For men to kill each other about a piece of bread appears, when so stated, the supreme culmination of human folly," writes Froude. Precisely; but, as he goes on to admit, when so stated the problem is stated as falsely as it possibly could be. Neither on the one side nor on the other was it thought that the issue was simply whether Tom and Dick and Harry should have Mass. The issue was whether England should or should not continue to be a Catholic country. No man could have been more loyal to Elizabeth than Blessed Edmund Campion. His loyalty was quite extravagant, and of all the perversions of justice of those times there was none more shameless than that by which he was done to death. Yet there was a certain shrewdness in his persecutors.

The Jesuit ambition, though honorable, was apart from reality. The Jesuits had got the Pope to agree that *"rebus sic stantibus"* Catholics were not under obligation to obey the Bull. But the loyalty which only agrees not to rebel so long as rebellion is hopeless is a dangerous and qualified loyalty. The papal policy in Ireland, where the Vatican was open in its support of rebellion, showed very clearly what the papal policy in England would be, if only an opportunity could be found. And, Bull or no Bull, no power on earth could have persuaded Catholics to tolerate permanently the supremacy of Cecil and his party. Cecil knew very well that an England which was taught to demand the Mass would be an England which, whatever its leaders might advise, would yet certainly demand a radical change in the country's property system and would not for long tolerate the rule of those whose power was founded merely upon successful sacrilege. For the Catholic there is a temporal as well as a spiritual obligation. But it is a very muddled confusion which thinks that, for that reason, the Church either has, or ought to have, nothing to say upon temporal or political problems. There is a Catholic social order and such an order a Catholic population will inevitably demand from its rulers. Cecil was determined to de-catholicize by persecution.

The teachings of Luther, on the other hand, had included a defence of the rights of the landed classes that was almost lunatic in its violence. In his pamphlet *Against the Murderous Robbers Hordes of Peasants,* he had written: "It is not only princes and magistrates who should make an end of them. Every honest man had the right to be judge and executioner of such scoundrels and to slay them as one would kill a mad dog." In his sermons he had spoken of the desirability of slavery. "There was good scripture warrant for it. . . . It was the lack of strong government that created discontent among the rabble and the workers." Erasmus had accused the Lutherans of being "men with but two objects at heart, women and money." And to Cecil and the Elizabethans, while to commit oneself to such a theology would be perhaps a trifle narrow-minded, it was at least most important to "comprehend" it.

Luther, the man of straw, played into the hands of the enemies of all religion. Up to this time all but a small minority in England still shrank both from the violence and from the lucidity of Calvin. The issue was still left between Paganism and the Church. That issue was whether Catholic freedom should survive or whether there should be established the dominance of the Pagan State, omnipotent alike over the conduct and over the consciences of men.

EVELYN WAUGH

(1902–   )

EVELYN WAUGH was born in Hampstead in 1902, and was educated at Lancing and at Hertford College, Oxford. Even in his college days he was admired, and this admiration has widened and grown with the publication of his satirical novels, *Black Mischief, A Handful of Dust, Vile Bodies,* and *Scoop. Black Mischief* satirizes modern machine civilization, *A Handful of Dust* and *Vile Bodies* arraign modern lust masquerading under the name of love, and *Scoop* is a hilarious satire on foreign correspondents and all their works and pomps.

Though Waugh's satirical novels have reached a wide audience, mainly for the wrong reasons, all too few readers know his excellent travel sketches or his scholarly life of Edmund Campion.

In *Brideshead Revisited* Waugh has written a superbly imaginative novel. In its style it fixes forever an age and a magnificence which even in its passing away retains its grand manner. Although this work of Waugh's has been termed a *Catholic novel,* it does not fall into any narrow limits of that term. But it is ultimately Catholic because it shows Catholics, Protestants, and unbelievers against the background of *the thing* against which the "gates of hell" cannot prevail. In this sense it is both Catholic and satirical, but the satire is softened by the human tenderness not found in Waugh's early novels.

CHAPTER ONE

DU COTÉ DE CHEZ BEAVER*

WAS anyone hurt?"

"No one I am thankful to say," said Mrs. Beaver, "except two housemaids who lost their heads and jumped through a glass roof into the paved court. They were in no danger. The fire never properly reached the bedrooms I am afraid. Still they are bound to need doing up, everything black with smoke and drenched in water and luckily they had that old-fashioned sort of extinguisher that ruins *everything.* One really cannot complain. The chief rooms were *completely* gutted and everything was insured. Sylvia Newport knows the people. I must get on to them this morning before that ghoul Mrs. Shutter snaps them up."

Mrs. Beaver stood with her back to the fire, eating her morning yoghort. She held the carton close under her chin and gobbled with a spoon.

"Heavens, how nasty this stuff is. I wish you'd take it, John. You're looking so tired lately. I don't know how I should get through my day without it."

"But, mumsey, I haven't as much to do as you have."

"That's true, my son."

John Beaver lived with his mother at the house in Sussex Gardens where they had moved after his father's death. There was little in it to suggest the austerely elegant interiors which Mrs. Beaver planned for her customers. It was crowded with the unsaleable furniture of two larger houses, without pretension to any period, least of all to the present. The best pieces and those which had sentimental interest for Mrs. Beaver were in the L-shaped drawing room upstairs.

Beaver had a dark little sitting room on the ground floor behind the dining room, and his own telephone. The elderly parlour-maid looked after his clothes. She also dusted, polished and maintained in symmetrical order

---

*Waugh, Evelyn, *A Handful of Dust* (Boston: Little, Brown and Co., 1944), pp. 3–12. Reprinted by permission of the publishers.

on his dressing-table and on the top of his chest of drawers, the collection of sombre and bulky objects that had stood in his father's dressing room; indestructible presents for his wedding and twenty-first birthday, ivory brass bound, covered in pigskin, crested and gold mounted, suggestive of expensive Edwardian masculinity — racing flasks and hunting flasks, cigar cases, tobacco jars, jockeys, elaborate meerschaum pipes, button hooks and hat brushes.

There were four servants, all female and all, save one, elderly.

When anyone asked Beaver why he stayed there instead of setting up on his own, he sometimes said that he thought his mother liked having him there (in spite of her business she was lonely); sometimes that it saved him at least five pounds a week.

His total income varied around six pounds a week, so this was an important saving.

He was twenty-five years old. From leaving Oxford until the beginning of the slump he had worked in an advertising agency. Since then no one had been able to find anything for him to do. So he got up late and sat near his telephone most of the day, hoping to be called up.

Whenever it was possible, Mrs. Beaver took an hour off in the middle of the morning. She was always at her shop punctually at nine, and by half past eleven she needed a break. Then, if no important customer was imminent, she would get into her two-seater and drive home to Sussex Gardens. Beaver was usually dressed by then and she had grown to value their morning interchange of gossip.

"What was your evening?"

"Audrey rang me up at eight and asked me to dinner. Ten of us at the Embassy, rather dreary. Afterwards we all went on to a party by a woman called de Trommet."

"I know who you mean. American. She hasn't paid for the toile-de-jouy chaircovers we made her last April. I had a dull time too; didn't hold a card all the evening and came away with four pounds ten to the bad."

"Poor mumsey."

"I'm lunching at Viola Chasm's. What are you doing? I didn't order anything here, I'm afraid."

"Nothing so far. But I can always go round to Brat's."

"But that's so expensive. I'm sure if we ask Chambers she'll be able to get you something in. I thought you were certain to be out."

"Well I still may be. It isn't twelve yet."

Most of Beaver's invitations came to him at the last moment; occasionally even later, when he had already begun to eat a solitary meal from a tray (". . . John, darling, there's been a muddle and Sonia has arrived without Reggie. Could you be an angel and help me out. Only be quick, because we're going in now"). Then he would go precipitately for a taxi and arrive, with apologies, after the first course. . . . One of his few recent quarrels with his mother had occurred when he left a luncheon party of hers in this way.

"Where are you going for the week-end?"

"Hetton."

"Who's that? I forget?"

"Tony Last."

"Yes, of course. She's lovely, he's rather a stick. I didn't know you knew them."

"Well I don't really. Tony asked me in Brat's the other night. He may have forgotten."

"Send a telegram and remind them. It is far better than ringing up. It gives them less chance to make excuses. Send it tomorrow just before you start. They owe me for a table."

"What's their dossier?"

"I used to see her quite a lot before she married. She was Brenda Rex, Lord St. Cloud's daughter, very fair, under-water look. People used to be mad about her when she was a girl. Everyone thought she would marry Jock Grant-Menzies at one time. Wasted on Tony Last, he's a prig. I should say it was time she began to be bored. They've been married five or six years. Quite well off but everything goes in keeping up the house. I've never seen it but I've an idea it's huge and quite hideous. They've got one child at least, perhaps more."

"Mumsey, you are wonderful. I believe you know about everyone."

"It's a great help. All a matter of paying attention while people are talking."

Mrs. Beaver smoked a cigarette and then

drove back to her shop. An American woman bought two patch-work quilts at thirty guineas each, Lady Metroland telephoned about a bathroom ceiling, an unknown young man paid cash for a cushion; in the intervals between these events, Mrs. Beaver was able to descend to the basement where two dispirited girls were packing lampshades. It was cold down there in spite of a little oil stove and the walls were always damp. The girls were becoming quite deft, she noticed with pleasure, particularly the shorter one who was handling crates like a man.

"That's the way," she said, "you are doing very nicely, Joyce. I'll soon get you on to something more interesting."

"Thank you, Mrs. Beaver."

They had better stay in the packing department for a bit, Mrs. Beaver decided; as long as they would stand it. They had neither of them enough chic to work upstairs. Both had paid good premiums to learn Mrs. Beaver's art.

Beaver sat on beside his telephone. Once it rang and a voice said, "Mr. Beaver: Will you please hold the line, sir, Lady Tipping would like to speak to you."

The intervening silence was full of pleasant expectation. Lady Tipping had a luncheon party that day, he knew; they had spent some time together the evening before and he had been particularly successful with her. Someone had chucked . . .

"Oh, Mr. Beaver, I *am* so sorry to trouble you. I was wondering, could you *possibly* tell me the name of the young man you introduced to me last night at Madame de Trommet's? The one with the reddish moustache. I think he was in Parliament."

"I expect you mean Jock Grant-Menzies."

"Yes, that's the name. You don't by any chance know where I can find him, do you?"

"He's in the book, but I don't suppose he'll be at home now. You might to able to get him at Brat's at about one. He's almost always there."

"Jock Grant-Menzies, Brat Club. Thank you so *very* much. It *is* kind of you. I hope you will come and see me some time. *Goodbye.*"

After that the telephone was silent. At one o'clock Beaver despaired. He put on his overcoat, his gloves, his bowler hat and with neatly rolled umbrella set off to his club, taking a penny bus as far as the corner of Bond Street.

The air of antiquity pervading Brat's, derived from its elegant Georgian façade and finely panelled rooms, was entirely spurious, for it was a club of recent origin, founded in the burst of bonhommie immediately after the war. It was intended for young men, to be a place where they could straddle across the fire and be jolly in the card room without incurring scowls from older members. But now these founders themselves were passing into middle age; they were heavier, balder and redder in the face than when they had been demobilized, but their joviality persisted and it was their turn now to embarrass their successors, deploring their lack of manly and gentlemanly qualities.

Six broad backs shut Beaver from the bar. He settled in one of the armchairs in the outer room and turned over the pages of the *New Yorker,* waiting until someone he knew should turn up.

Jock Grant-Menzies came upstairs. The men at the bar greeted him saying, "Hullo, Jock old boy, what are you drinking?" or simply, "Well, old boy?" He was too young to have fought in the war but these men thought he was all right; they liked him far more than they did Beaver, who, they thought, ought never to have got into the club at all. But Jock stopped to talk to Beaver. "Well, old boy," he said. "What are you drinking?"

"Nothing so far." Beaver looked at his watch. "But I think it's time I had one. Brandy and ginger ale." Jock called to the barman and then said:

"Who was the old girl you wished on me at that party last night?"

"She's called Lady Tipping."

"I thought she might be. That explains it. They gave me a message downstairs that someone with a name like that wanted me to lunch with her."

"Are you going?"

"No, I'm no good at lunch parties. Besides

I decided when I got up that I'd have oysters here."

The barman came with the drinks.

"Mr. Beaver, sir, there's ten shillings against you in my books for last month."

"Ah, thank you, Macdougal, remind me some time, will you?"

"Very good, sir."

Beaver said, "I'm going to Hetton to-morrow."

"Are you now? Give Tony and Brenda my love."

"What's the form?"

"Very quiet and enjoyable."

"No paper games?"

"Oh, no, nothing like that. A certain amount of bridge and backgammon and low poker with the neighbours."

"Comfortable?"

"Not bad. Plenty to drink. Rather a short-age of bathrooms. You can stay in bed all morning."

"I've never met Brenda."

"You'll like her, she's a grand girl. I often think Tony Last's one of the happiest men I know. He's got just enough money, loves the place, one son he's crazy about, devoted wife, not a worry in the world."

"Most enviable. You don't know anyone else who's going, do you? I was wondering if I could get a lift down there."

"I don't, I'm afraid. It's quite easy by train."

"Yes, but it's more pleasant by road."

"And cheaper."

"Yes, and cheaper I suppose . . . well, I'm going down to lunch. You won't have another?"

Beaver rose to go.

"Yes, I think I will."

"Oh, all right. Macdougal. Two more please."

Macdougal said, "Shall I book them to you, sir?"

"Yes, if you will."

Later, at the bar, Jock said, "I made Beaver pay for a drink."

"He can't have liked that."

"He nearly died of it. Know anything about pigs?"

"No. Why?"

"Only that they keep writing to me about them from my constituency."

Beaver went downstairs but before going into the dining room he told the porter to ring up his home and see if there was any message for him.

"Lady Tipping rang up a few minutes ago and asked whether you could come to luncheon with her today."

"Will you ring her up and say that I shall be delighted to but that I may be a few min-utes late."

It was just after half past one when he left Brat's and walked at a good pace towards Hill Street.

BRIDESHEAD REVISITED*

CHAPTER THREE

I RETURNED home for the Long Vaca-tion without plans and without money. To cover end-of-term expenses I had sold my Omega screen to Collins for ten pounds, of which I now kept four; my last cheque overdrew my account by a few shillings, and I had been told that, without my father's authority, I must draw no more. My next

*Waugh, Evelyn, *Brideshead Revisited* (Boston: Little, Brown and Co., 1946), pp. 61–72. Reprinted by per-mission of the publishers.

allowance was not due until October. I was thus faced with a bleak prospect and, turning the matter over in my mind, I felt something not far off remorse for the prodigality of the preceding weeks.

I had started the term with my battels paid and over a hundred pounds in hand. All that had gone, and not a penny paid out where I could get credit. There had been no reason for it, no great pleasure unattainable else; it had gone in ducks and drakes. Sebas-tian often chid me with extravagance, but I resented his censure for a large part of my money went on and with him. His own finances were perpetually, vaguely distressed. "It's all done by lawyers," he said helplessly, "and I suppose they embezzle a lot. Anyway, I never seem to get much. Of course, Mummy would give me anything I asked for."

"Then why don't you ask her for a proper allowance?"

"Oh, Mummy likes everything to be a present. She's so sweet," he said, adding one more line to the picture I was forming of her.

Now Sebastian had disappeared into that other life of his where I was not asked to follow, and I was left, instead, forlorn and regretful.

How ungenerously in later life we disclaim the virtuous moods of our youth, living in retrospect long, summer days of unreflecting dissipation, Dresden figures of pastoral gaiety! Our wisdom, we prefer to think, is all of our own gathering, while, if the truth be told, it is, most of it, the last coin of a legacy that dwindles with time. There is no candour in a story of early manhood which leaves out of account the homesickness for nursery morality, the regrets and resolution of amendment, the black hours which, like zero on the roulette table, turn up with roughly calculable regularity.

Thus I spent the first afternoon at home, wandering from room to room, looking from the plate-glass windows in turn on the garden and the street, in a mood of vehement self-reproach.

My father, I knew, was in the house, but his library was inviolable, and it was not until just before dinner that he appeared to greet me. He was then in his late fifties, but it was his idiosyncrasy to seem much older that his years; to see him one might have put him at seventy, to hear him speak at nearly eighty. He came to me now, with the shuffling mandarin-tread which he affected, and a shy smile of welcome. When he dined at home — and he seldom dined elsewhere — he wore a frogged velvet smoking suit of the kind which had been fashionable many years before and was to be so again, but, at that time, was a deliberate archaism.

"My dear boy, they never told me you were here. Did you have a very exhausting journey? They gave you tea? You are well? I have just made a somewhat audacious purchase from Sonerschein's — a terra-cotta bull of the fifth century. I was examining it and forgot your arrival. Was the carriage very full: You had a corner seat? (He travelled so rarely himself that to hear of others doing so always excited his solicitude.) "Hayter brought you the evening paper? There is no news, of course — such a lot of nonsense."

Dinner was announced. My father from long habit took a book with him to the table and then, remembering my presence, furtively dropped it under his chair. "What do you like to drink? Hayter, what have we for Mr. Charles to drink?"

"There's some whiskey."

"There's whiskey. Perhaps you like something else? What else have we?"

"There isn't anything else in the house, sir."

"There's nothing else. You must tell Hayter what you would like and he will get it. I never keep any wine now. I am forbidden it and no one comes to see me. But while you are here, you must have what you like. You are here for long?"

"I'm not quite sure, Father."

"It's a *very* long vacation," he said wistfully. "In my day we used to go on what were called 'reading parties,' always in mountainous areas. Why? Why," he repeated petulantly, "should alpine scenery be thought conducive to study?"

"I thought of putting in some time at an art school — in the life class."

"My dear boy, you'll find them all shut. The students go to Barbison or such places and paint in the open air. There was an institution in my day called a 'sketching club' — mixed sexes" (snuffle) "bicycles" (snuffle), "pepper-and-salt knickerbockers, holland umbrellas and, it was popularly thought, free love." (Snuffle) "Such a lot of nonsense. I expect they still go on. You might try that."

"One of the problems of the vacation is money, Father."

"Oh, I shouldn't worry about a thing like that at your age."

"You see, I'm rather short."

"Yes?" said my father without any sound of interest.

"In fact I don't quite know how I'm going to get through the next two months."

"Well, I'm the worst person to come to for advice. I've never been 'short,' as you so painfully call it. And yet what else could you say? Hard up? Penurious? Distressed? Embarrassed? Stony-broke" (Snuffle) "On the rocks? In Queer Street? Let us say you are in Queer Street and leave it at that. Your grandfather once said to me, 'Live within your means, but if you do get into difficulties, come to me. Don't go to the Jews.' Such a lot of nonsense. You try. Go to those gentlemen in Jermyn Street who offer advances on note of hand only. My dear boy, they won't give you a sovereign."

"Then what do you suggest my doing?"

"Your cousin Melchior was imprudent with his investments and got into a very queer street. *He* went to Australia."

I had not seen my father so gleeful since he found two pages of second-century papyrus between the leaves of a Lombardic breviary.

"Hayter, I've dropped my book."

It was recovered for him from under his feet and propped against the epergne. For the rest of dinner he was silent save for an occasional snuffle of merriment which could not, I thought, be provoked by the work he read.

Presently we left the table and sat in the garden-room; and there, plainly, he put me out of his mind; his thoughts, I knew, were far away, in those distant ages where he moved at ease, where time passed in centuries and all the figures were defaced and the names of his companions were corrupt readings of words of quite other meaning. He sat in an attitude which to anyone else would have been one of extreme discomfort, askew in his upright armchair, with his book held high and obliquely to the light. Now and then he took a gold pencil case from his watchchain and made an entry in the margin. The windows were open to the summer night; the ticking of the clocks, the distant murmur of traffic on the Bayswater Road, and my father's regular turning of the pages

were the only sounds. I had thought it impolite to smoke a cigar while pleading poverty; now in desperation I went to my room and fetched one. My father did not look up. I pierced it, lit it, and with renewed confidence said, "Father, you surely don't want me to spend the whole vacation here with you?"

"Eh?"

"Won't you find it rather a bore having me at home for so long?"

"I trust I should not betray such an emotion even if I felt it," said my father mildly and turned back to his book.

The evening passed. Eventually all over the room clocks of diverse pattern musically chimed eleven. My father closed his book and removed his spectacles. "You are very welcome, my dear boy," he said. "Stay as long as you find it convenient." At the door he paused and turned back. "Your cousin Melchior worked his passage to Australia before the mast." (Snuffle) "What, I wonder, is 'before the mast'?"

During the sultry week that followed my relations with my father deteriorated sharply. I saw little of him during the day; he spent hours on end in the library; now and then he emerged and I would hear him calling over the banisters: "Hayter. Call me a cab." Then he would be away, sometimes for half an hour or less, sometimes for a whole day; his errands were never explained. Often I saw trays going up to him at odd hours, laden with meagre nursery snacks — rusks, glasses of milk, bananas and so forth. If we met in a passage or on the stairs he would look at me vacantly and say "Ah-ha" or "Very warm," or "Splendid, splendid," but in the evening, when he came to the garden-room in his velvet smoking suit, he always greeted me formally.

The dinner table was our battlefield.

On the second evening I took my book with me to the dining room. His mild and wandering eye fastened on it with sudden attention, and as we passed through the hall he surreptitiously left his own at a side table. When we sat down he said plaintively: "I do think, Charles, you might talk to me. I've had a very exhausting day. I was looking forward to a little conversation."

"Of course, Father. What shall we talk about?"

"Cheer me up. Take me out of myself"; (petulantly) "tell me all about the new plays."

"But I haven't been to any."

"You should, you know, you really should. It's not natural in a young man to spend all his evenings at home."

"Well, Father, as I told you, I haven't much money to spare for theatre-going."

"My dear boy, you must not let money become your master in this way. Why, at your age, your cousin Melchior was part owner of a musical piece. It was one of his few happy ventures. You should go to the play as part of your education. If you read the lives of eminent men you will find that quite half of them made their first acquaintance with drama from the gallery. I am told there is no pleasure like it. It is there that you find the real critics and devotees. It is called 'sitting with the gods.' The expense is nugatory, and even while you wait for admission in the street you are diverted by 'buskers.' We will sit with the gods together one night. How do you find Mrs. Abel's cooking?"

"Rather insipid."

"It was inspired by my sister Philippa. She gave Mrs. Abel ten menus, and they have never been varied. When I am alone I do not notice what I eat, but now you are here, we must have a change. What would you like? What is in season? Are you fond of lobsters? Hayter, tell Mrs. Abel to give us lobsters to-morrow night."

Dinner that evening consisted of a white, tasteless soup, over-fried fillets of sole with a pink sauce, lamb cutlets propped against a cone of mashed potato, stewed pears in jelly standing on a kind of sponge cake.

"It is purely out of respect for your Aunt Philippa that I dine at this length. She laid it down that a three-course dinner was middle-class. 'If you once let the servants get their way,' she said, 'you will find yourself dining nightly off a single chop.' There is nothing I should like more. In fact, that is exactly what I do when I go to my club on Mrs. Abel's

evening out. But your aunt ordained that at home I must have soup and three courses; some nights it is fish, meant and savoury, on others it is meat, sweet, savoury — there are a number of possible permutations.

"It is remarkable how some people are able to put their opinions in lapidary form; your aunt had that gift.

"It is odd to think that she and I once dined together nightly — just as you and I do, my boy. Now *she* made unremitting efforts to take me out of myself. She used to tell me about her reading. It was in *her* mind to make a home with me, you know. She thought I should get into funny ways if I was left on my own. Perhaps I *have* got into funny ways. Have I? But it didn't do. I got her out in the end."

There was an unmistakable note of menace in his voice as he said this.

It was largely by reason of Aunt Philippa that I now found myself so much a stranger in my father's house. After my mother's death she came to live with my father and me, no doubt, as he said, with the idea of making her home with us. I knew nothing, then, of the nightly agonies at the dinner table. My aunt made herself my companion, and I accepted her without question. That was for a year. The first change was that she re-opened her house in Surrey which she had meant to sell, and lived there during my school terms, coming to London only for a few days' shopping and entertainment. In the summer we went to lodgings together at the seaside. Then in my last year at school she left England. *"I got her out in the end,"* he said with derision and triumph of that kindly lady, and he knew that I heard in the words a challenge to myself.

As we left the dining-room my father said, "Hayter, have you said anything yet to Mrs. Abel about the lobsters I ordered for to-morrow?"

"No, sir."

"Do not do so."

"Very good, sir."

And when we reached our chairs in the garden-room he said:

"I wonder whether Hayter had any intention of mentioning lobsters. I rather think not. Do you know, I believe he thought I was joking?"

Next day by chance, a weapon came to hand. I met an old acquaintance of school days, a contemporary of mine named Jorkins. I had never had much liking for Jorkins. Once, in my Aunt Philippa's day, he had come to tea, and she had condemned him as being probably charming at heart, but unattractive at first sight. Now I greeted him with enthusiasm and asked him to dinner. He came and showed little alteration. My father must have been warned by Hayter that there was a guest, for instead of his velvet suit he wore a tail coat; this, with a black waistcoat, very high collar, and very narrow white tie, was his evening dress; he wore it with an air of melancholy as though it were court mourning, which he had assumed in early youth and, finding the style sympathetic, had retained. He never possessed a dinner jacket.

"Good evening, good evening. So nice of you to come all this way."

"Oh, it wasn't far," said Jorkins, who lived in Sussex Square.

"Science annihilates distance," said my father disconcertingly. "You are over here on business?"

"Well, I'm *in* business, if that's what you mean."

"I had a cousin who was in business — you wouldn't know him; it was before your time. I was telling Charles about him only the other night. He has been much in my mind. He came," my father paused to give full weight to the bizarre word — "a cropper."

Jorkins giggled nervously. My father fixed him with a look of reproach.

"You find his misfortune the subject of mirth: Or perhaps the word I used was unfamiliar; you no doubt would say that he 'folded up.'"

My father was master of the situation. He had made a little fantasy for himself, that Jorkins should be an American, and through-out the evening he played a delicate, one-sided parlour-game with him, explaining any peculiarly English terms that occurred in the conversation, translating pounds into dollars,

and courteously deferring to him with such phrases as "Of course, by *your* standards...";
"All this must seem very parochial to Mr. Jorkins"; "In the vast spaces to which *you* are accustomed. . ."; so that my guest was left with the vague sense that there was a misconception somewhere as to his identity, which he never got the chance of explaining. Again and again during dinner he sought my father's eye, thinking to read there the simple statement that this form of address was an elaborate joke, but met instead a look of such mild benignity that he was left baffled.

Once I thought my father had gone too far, when he said: "I am afraid that, living in London, you must sadly miss your national game."

"My national game?" asked Jorkins, slow in the uptake, but scenting that here, at last, was the opportunity for clearing the matter up.

My father glanced from him to me and his expression changed from kindness to malice; then back to kindness again as he turned once more to Jorkins. It was the look of a gambler who lays down fours against a full house. "Your national game," he said gently, *"cricket,"* and he snuffled un-controllably, shaking all over and wiping his eyes with his napkin. "Surely, working in the City, you find your time on the cricket-field greatly curtailed?"

At the door of the dining-room he left us. "Good night, Mr. Jorkins," he said. "I hope you will pay us another visit when you next 'cross the herring pond.'"

"I say, what did your governor mean by that? He seemed almost to think I was an American."

"He's rather odd at times."

"I mean all that about advising me to visit Westminster Abbey. It seemed rum."

"Yes. I can't quite explain."

"I almost thought he was pulling my leg," said Jorkins in puzzled tones.

My father's counter-attack was delivered a few days later. He sought me out and said, "Mr. Jorkins is still here?"

"No, Father, of course not. He only came to dinner."

"Oh, I hoped he was staying with us. Such a versatile young man. But you will be dining in?"

"Yes."

"I am giving a little party to diversify the rather monotonous series of your evenings at home. You think Mrs. Abel is up to it? No. But our guests are not exacting. Sir Cuthbert and Lady Orme-Herrick are what might be called the nucleus. I hope for a little music afterwards. I have included in the invitations some young people for you."

My presentiments of my father's plan were surpassed by the actuality. As the guests assembled in the room which my father, without self-consciousness, called "the Gallery," it was plain to me that they had been carefully chosen for my discomfort. The "young people" were Miss Gloria Orme-Herrick, a student of the cello; her fiancé, a bald young man from the British Museum; and a monoglot Munich publisher. I saw my father snuffing at me from behind a case of ceramics as he stood with them. That evening he wore, like a chivalric badge of battle, a small red rose in his button-hole.

Dinner was long and chosen, like the guests, in a spirit of careful mockery. It was not of Aunt Philippa's choosing, but had been reconstructed from a much earlier period, long before he was of an age to dine downstairs. The dishes were ornamental in appearance and regularly alternated in colour between red and white. They and the wine were equally tasteless. After dinner my father led the German publisher to the piano, and then, while he played, left the dining-room to show Sir Cuthbert Orme-Herrick the Etruscan bull in the gallery.

It was a gruesome evening, and I was astonished to find, when at last the party broke up, that it was only a few minutes after eleven. My father helped himself to a glass of barley-water and said: "What very dull friends I have! You know, without the spur of your presence I should never have roused myself to invite them. I have been very negligent about entertaining lately. Now that you are paying me such a long visit, I will have many such evenings. You liked Miss Gloria Orme-Herrick?"

"No."

"No? Was it her little moustache you objected to or her very large feet? Do you think she enjoyed herself?"

"No."

"That was my impression also. I doubt if any of our guests will count this as one of their happiest evenings. That young foreigner played atrociously, I thought. Where can I have met him? And Miss Constantia Smethwick — where can I have met *her?* But the obligations of hospitality must be observed. As long as you are here, you shall not be dull."

Strife was internecine during the next fortnight, but I suffered the more, for my father had greater reserves to draw on and a wider territory for maneouvre, while I was pinned to my bridgehead between the uplands and the sea. He never declared his war aims, and I do not to this day know whether they were purely punitive — whether he had really at the back of his mind some geopolitical idea of getting me out of the country, as Aunt Philippa had been driven to Bordighera and my cousin Melchior to Darwin, or whether, as seems most likely, he fought for the sheer love of a battle, in which indeed he shone.

THE MARTYR*

CAMPION lay in irons for eleven days between his trial and his execution. Hitherto his family have made no appearance

*Waugh, Evelyn, *Edmund Campion* (Boston: Little, Brown and Co., 1946), pp. 223–232. Reprinted by permission of the publisher.

in the story; now a sister, of whom we know nothing, came to visit him, empowered to make him a last offer of freedom and a benefice, if he would renounce his Faith. There may have been other visitors — for certain details of his life in prison, such as his statement, quoted above, that in his last racking he thought they intended to kill him, can only have reached Bombinus through the report of friends — but the only one of whom we have record is George Eliot.

"If I had thought that you would have had to suffer aught but imprisonment through my accusing of you, I would never have done it," he said, "however I might have lost by it."

"If that is the case," replied Campion, "I beseech you, in God's name, to do penance, and confess your crime, to God's glory and your own salvation."

But it was fear for his life rather than for his soul that had brought the informer to the Tower; ever since the journey from Lyford, when the people had called him "Judas," he had been haunted by the specter of Catholic reprisal.

"You are much deceived," said Campion, "if you think the Catholics push their detestation and wrath as far as revenge; yet to make you quite safe, I will, if you please, recommend you to a Catholic duke in Germany, where you may live in perfect security."

But it was another man who was saved by the offer. Eliot went back to his trade of spy; Delahays, Campion's gaoler, who was present at the interview, was so moved by Campion's generosity that he became a Catholic.

London was very gay that winter. Anjou was there with his suite and the Court was wholly given over to their entertainment. Sidney, out of favour with the Queen, was engaged with the *Apologie for Poetrie*. The "little frog" was the man of the moment, and to him various friends of Campion resorted in the hope of gaining his intercession. They found him skipping about the tennis court. It was the day before Campion's execution and, by the aid of the French abbé who acted as the Duke's confessor, they were able to obtain an interview. The little man listened to what they had to say; he looked at them stupidly, as though he were just awakened from a deep sleep, scratched his beard and then, turning on his heel, with the one word "Play," resumed the interrupted service.

Campion's last days were occupied entirely with his preparation for death; even in the cell he was able to practice mortifications; he fasted and remained sleepless on his knees for two nights in prayer and meditation.

Sherwin and Briant had been chosen as his companions at the scaffold. They met at the Colearboux Tower, early in the morning of December 1st, and were left together while a search was made for the clothes in which Campion had been arrested; it had been decided to execute him in the buff leather jerkin and velvet venetians which had been so ridiculed at his trial. But the garments had already been misappropriated, and he was finally led out in the gown of Irish frieze which he had worn in prison.

It was raining; it had been raining for some days, and the roads of the city were foul with mud. A great crowd had collected at the gates. "God save you all, gentlemen," Campion greeted them. "God bless you, and make you good Catholics." There were two horses, each with a hurdle at his tail. Campion was bound to one of them, Briant and Sherwin together on the other.

Then they were slowly dragged through the mud and rain, up Cheapside, past St. Martin le Grand and Newgate, along Holborn to Tyburn. Clarke plodded along beside the hurdle, still eager to thrash out to the last word the question of Justification by Faith alone, but Campion seemed not to notice him; over Newgate Arch stood a figure of Our Lady which had so far survived the Anglican hammers. Campion saluted her as he passed. Here and there along the road a Catholic would push himself through the crowd and ask Campion's blessing. One witness, who supplied Bombinus with many details of this last morning, followed close at hand and stood by the scaffold. He records how one gentleman, "either for pity or affection, most courteously wiped" Campion's "face, all spattered with mire and dirt, as he was drawn most miserably through thick and thin; for which charity or haply some sudden moved affection, God reward him and bless him."

The scene at Tyburn was tumultuous. Sir Thomas More had stepped out into the summer sunshine, to meet death quietly and politely at a single stroke of the axe. Every circumstance of Campion's execution was vile and gross.

Sir Francis Knollys, Lord Howard, Sir Henry Lee and other gentlemen of fashion were already waiting beside the scaffold. When the procession arrived, they were disputing whether the motion of the sun from east to west was violent or natural; they postponed the discussion to watch Campion, bedraggled and mudstained, mount the cart which stood below the gallows. The noose was put over his neck. The noise of the crowd was continuous, and only those in his immediate neighbourhood could hear him as he began to speak. He had it in mind to make some religious exhortation.

"*Spectaculum facti sumus Deo, angelis et hominibus,*" he began. "These are the words of St. Paul, Englished thus, 'We are made a spectacle unto God, unto His angels and unto men,' verified this day in me, who am here a spectacle unto my Lord God, a spectacle unto his angels and unto you men."

But he was not allowed to continue. Sir Francis Knollys interrupted, shouting up at him to confess his treason.

"As to the treasons which have been laid to my charge," he said, "and for which I am come here to suffer, I desire you all to bear witness with me that I am thereof altogether innocent."

One of the Council cried that it was too late to deny what had been proved in the court.

"Well, my Lord," he replied, "I am a Catholic man and a priest; in that faith have I lived and in that faith I intend to die. If you esteem my religion treason, then am I guilty; as for the other treason I never committed any, God is my judge. But you have now what you desire. I beseech you to have patience, and suffer me to speak a word or two for discharge of my conscience."

But the gentlemen round the gallows would not let him go forward; they still heckled him about his letter to Pounde, about the invasion by the Pope and the Duke of Florence.

In a few halting sentences he made himself heard above the clamour. He forgave the jury and asked forgiveness of any whose names he might have compromised during his examination; he addressed himself to Sir Francis Knollys on Richardson's behalf, saying that, to his knowledge, that man had never in his possession a copy of the book, which the informers declared they had found in his baggage.

Then a schoolmaster named Hearne stood forward and read a proclamation in the Queen's name, that the execution they were to witness that morning was for treason and not for religion. Campion stood in prayer. The Lords of the Council still shouted up questions to him about the Bull of Excommunication, but now Campion would not answer and stood with his head bowed and his hands folded on his breast. An Anglican clergyman attempted to direct his prayers, but he answered gently, "Sir, you and I are not one in religion, wherefore I pray you content yourself. I bar none of prayer; but I only desire them that are of the household of faith to pray with me, and in mine agony to say one creed."

They called to him to pray in English, but he replied with great mildness that "he would pray God in a language which they both well understood."

There was more noise; the Councillors demanded that he should ask the Queen's forgiveness.

"Wherein have I offended her? In this I am innocent. This is my last speech; in this give me credit — I have and do pray for her."

Still the courtiers were not satisfied. Lord Howard demanded to know what Queen he prayed for.

"Yea, for Elizabeth your Queen and my Queen, unto whom I wish a long quiet reign with all prosperity."

The cart was then driven from under him, the eager crowd swayed forward, and Campion was left hanging, until, unconscious, perhaps already dead, he was cut down and the butcher began his work.

When the spectacle was over the crowd dispersed. An emotional witness records that several thousand were turned to the Faith by the events of that day. Many thousands there have been, but they were not in that assembly. The Elizabethan mob dearly loved a bloody execution, and any felon was the hero of a few hours, whatever his crimes. If any felt uneasy about the Queen's justice, there were gentler pleasures to attract their minds; in particular two Dutchmen, who were the rage of the moment; the one was seven feet seven inches in height, *"comelie of person but lame of the legs (for he had broken them of lifting a barrel of beer)"*; his companion was a midget who could walk between the giant's legs, wearing a feather in his cap; he had *"never a good foot nor any knee at all and yet could dance a gallard, no arm but a stump on which he could dance a cup and after toss it about three or four times and every time receive the same on the said stump."* With distractions of this kind the fate of the three priests was soon forgotten. One man, however, returned from Tyburn to Grays Inn profoundly changed; Henry Walpole, Cambridge wit, minor poet, satirist, flaneur, a young man of birth, popular, intelligent, slightly romantic. He came of a Catholic family and occasionally expressed Catholic sentiments, but until that day had kept at a discreet distance from Gilbert and his circle, and was on good terms with authority. He was a typical member of that easy-going majority, on whom the success of the Elizabethan settlement depended, who would have preferred to live under a Catholic *régime* but accepted the change without very serious regret. He had an interest in theology and had attended Campion's conferences with the Anglican clergy. He secured a front place at Tyburn; so close that when Campion's entrails were torn out by the butcher and thrown into the cauldron of boiling water, a spot of blood splashed upon his coat. In that moment he was caught into a new life; he crossed the sea, became a priest, and, thirteen years later, after very terrible sufferings, died the same death as Campion's on the gallows at York.

And so the work of Campion continued; so it continues. He was one of a host of martyrs, each, in their several ways, gallant and venerable; some performed more sensational feats of adventure, some sacrificed more conspicuous positions in the world, many suffered crueller tortures, but to his own and to each succeeding generation, Campion's fame has burned with unique warmth and brilliance; it was his genius to express, in sentences that have resounded across the centuries, the spirit of chivalry in which they suffered, to typify in his zeal, his innocence, his inflexible purpose, the pattern which they followed.

Years later, in the sombre, sceptical atmosphere of the eighteenth century, Bishop Challoner set himself to sift out and collect the English martyrology. The Catholic cause was very near to extinction in England. Families who had resisted the onset of persecution were quietly conforming under neglect. The Church survived here and there in scattered households, regarded by the world as, at the best, something Gothic and slightly absurd, like a ghost or a family curse. Emancipation still lay in the distant future; no career was open to the Catholics; their only ambition was to live quietly in their houses, send their children to school abroad, pay the double land taxes, and, as best they could, avoid antagonising their neighbours. It was then, when the whole gallant sacrifice appeared to have been prodigal and vain, that the story of the martyrs lent them strength.

We are the heirs of their conquest, and enjoy, at our ease, the plenty which they died to win.

To-day a chapel stands by the site of Tyburn; in Oxford, the city he loved best, a noble college is rising dedicated in Campion's honour. *"There will never want in England men that will have care of their own salvation, nor such as shall advance other men's; neither shall this Church here ever fail so long as priests and pastors shall be found for their sheep, rage man or devil never so much."*

ROBERT SPEAIGHT

(1904–   )

ROBERT SPEAIGHT was born in 1904 at Dover, England. He was educated at Oxford, where he was secretary of the Oxford University Dramatic Society. From College he went into the Liverpool Repertory Theatre and after a considerable apprenticeship appeared on the London stage, notably as Hibbert in the original production of *Journeys' End* and á Becket in *Murder In The Cathedral*. He has also played with brilliance many Shakespearean roles at the "Old Vic."

Speaight's second novel, *The Unbroken Heart,* is a fine piece of character drawing. Though it pretends to be a psychological novel, it achieves its telling effect from Speaight's mastery of classic novel writing. It is Miss Macnamara who emerges from the novel as a monumental character of evil worthy of inclusion with Hunecker's "three disagreeable girls."

V

THE ARENA*

I

MISS MACNAMARA had a small apartment in one of the old houses of Aix. It was a sad, grey building, closely entangled with its past. Over the portal a coat of arms was engraved in stone — a reminder of the family to which it had belonged before the Revolution. The Marquis de Savigny had perished in the September massacres, and his fate was an active goad to Miss Macnamara's political temper. It was a springboard for her argument and dogmatism.

"The Revolution!" she exclaimed in answer to one of Desmond's questions the night after their arrival. "The Revolution was one of the major disasters of history. I am not a religious woman, but it almost makes me believe in the devil. There is everything to be said for a civilization based on religion, especially in its more theocratic forms; but for a civilization based on religious atheism there is nothing to be said whatever. The modern world — and particularly modern Ireland — is still suffering from the revolutionary malaise. The denial of original sin which is implicit in the affirmation of liberty began by being a philosophic and psychological error, and had ended by being a political canard. It is the prime temptation of politicians to flatter people, and flattery begets itself. The people who were canonized by the Revolution themselves canonized its greatest son — and Napoleon canonized himself. From democracy to Caesarism is a logical step — but when Caesar falls in the Capitol —" She spread out her hands so that the shawl, which she always wore in the evening, fell from her shoulders on to the arms of her splendid chair.

"This chair now," she continued, fingering its brocade, "is the effect of an age of privilege. It justifies inequality. It is a certificate of taste. Civilization can never be a widespread thing for the simple reason that man is a brutish creature. The Revolution which was made in the name of humanity, reacted like a boomerang on the sanguinary moralists who made it. It dehumanized its own optimists, and replaced the potential fraternity of degree by the impossible fraternity of competition. The France of Louis Seize was an organism which could have been oiled to work. Its necessary discipline and control

*Speaight, Robert, *The Unbroken Heart* (Detroit: The Basilian Press, 1946), pp. 90–103.

were still dormant within it. But modern France is a masterpiece of disorganization. The ordinary Frenchman of to-day does not know who his master is, and would be surprised to learn that it was money — and his ignorance is the price of his freedom. His modern liberty is a delusion, even if his ancient slavery was a fact. But few men have a genuine appetite for reality. Democracy is a lie, and culture is sterilized beneath it. The Revolution could produce an army; it could not produce an armchair."

Again Miss Macnamara let her fingers run over the frayed edges of brocade. They might have been sitting in Merrion Square, Desmond thought. The shadow of the past overhung their conversation; in both places his aunt seemed to be taking refuge in its lamented elegance. It was symptomatic of his new relationship to her that the idea of refuge could even have entered his mind. Miss Macnamara had always seemed to him on top of her chosen world. She rode it bravely and buoyantly. Her sovereignty was habitual. But since she could stoop to deceive, it was possible that she might stoop to surrender. She had something — she might have more — to hide. The power of her intellect was formidable, but it might be merely the instrument of her compensation. Desmond wondered if she thought so intensely because she was not able to love.

She had perhaps loved his father, but the obscure twist of her temperament prevented her from loving himself. She gave him her intellect, or rather she rammed it down his throat; but she gave him nothing else. Yet in a way he was necessary to her. He had, in some hidden interest of hers, to be there. She seemed herself to depend upon his own dependence. He could not even get her to discuss his future, and his future became important in proportion as his confidence grew. He wanted, spiritually, to walk, and he found a symbol of this desire in the thought of Dr. Gautier and Grasse, and the mountain which they would climb together. Also his mind was obsessed with another, more disturbing image. He remembered what he had seen in the train. He wanted, quite passionately, to walk. But Miss Macna-

mara was content to see him crawl; or if he went on his feet, he must go with the steps that she would teach him.

The days passed easily enough. He would spend some hours in study, and in the warmth of the spring afternoons he would prowl about the streets of Aix, admiring and sometimes loving its antiquities. He would halt under the great trees in the Cours Mirabeau, lean against the fountains, explore the churches. He was beginning to learn French, and now and then he would pluck up the courage to speak it to a passer-by. He would ask the time, or the way to some place he was visiting. But he was shy and nervous of his effect. Miss Macnamara had told him that all the Latin languages — and these, she added, were the only languages worth knowing — were easy enough if you knew classical Latin. Rome, she would say, was the mother of tongues as she was the mistress of manners and arts. The Roman intellect had never tried to outsoar its own limitations, and therein was the secret of its power. *Nox est perpetua,* she would repeat grimly. No Platonic idealism had clouded that essential acquiescence.

She was now busy with her great work on Gaul. For this she had not only the stimulus of a place so rich in memories of order destroyed by revolution, but she had the monuments of antiquity at hand. There were the amphitheaters of Arles and Nimes, and the museums of Arles and Vienne. Once a year, during her visit, she would hire a car and drive for a whole day around the neighborhood where the present belongs so happily to the past. There were certainly museums, but there were no museum pieces. Antiquity had never died out in this haunted landscape. The smooth hills had something in common with the Pont de Gard which spanned them; even the women had a sculptured grace and the men a bronzed magnificence. One day she took Desmond to Orange where the actors from the *Comédie Française* were giving Racine's *Bérènice* in the Roman Theatre. It was a brilliant afternoon in April — a Sunday — and the performance was a single one. People from many miles around attended it.

Miss Macnamara fairly glowed in the car as they raced along the dusty roads. It was an occasion after her own heart. She was one of those people who preferred Racine to Shakespeare, and had a sound Voltairean reason for her prejudice.

"Racine," she was saying, "is the supreme expression of his epoch. He had the genius of the great classical artists to create infinity in a nutshell. Mozart did it too. So, in a smaller way, did Vermeer. I suppose it is the secret of life, as it is certainly the secret of Art, to recognize one's limitations. The limitations of not only oneself but of one's kind. The greatest writer and the most enlightened ruler is only an *espèce d'animal*. He is born to disease and death, and apprenticed to misery. He rebels against order. He is only a child in the nursery. Racine and Mozart never went outside the nursery. Consider what Mozart will do with a single motif — the pattery, the precision, the truth! Then compare him with Wagner, and behold the Swastika enthroned. The conceit, the arrogance, the lie! The Teutonic genius, for all its swagger, has never had the courage of humanism. It has not even had the courage of religion. It will not recognize its heroes until its heroes have dethroned its gods. You will find every figment of the human fancy in Wagner — the whole pantomime of fairyland. You will find everything except men and women."

"Tristan and Isolde?" Desmond suggested nervously.

"Tristan and Isolde are among the mistranslations of genius. Their story is meaningless because their tragedy was a mistake. This afternoon you will see a much greater love story — I think it is the greatest of human love stories because it shows the triumph of human reason. The two lovers are very unhappy, but their story is a success." And then Miss Macnamara added: "I hate failure."

The triumphal arch which dwarfs the little town of Orange into insignificance, loomed ahead of them at the end of the Roman road. The sudden vision of it seemed to Desmond to have given his aunt her cue. It was, indeed, the antonym of failure.

"There!" she exclaimed, "doesn't that make a mockery of the modern world?"

It was immediately before them, majestic, imperial, marvelously intact, and Miss Macnamara ordered the car to halt so that they could regard it more closely. She got out and, with Desmond walked round it viewing it from every side. "The frontispiece of antiquity," she concluded.

The amphitheatre was rapidly filling when they arrived and the streets of Orange were congested with cars, bringing an audience from many miles around. At the entrance to the block where their seats were reserved, Miss Macnamara bought two cushions to mitigate the hardness of the stone. It was her sole concession to modernity. They were well placed in the middle of the amphitheatre, which she swept with her lorgnettes.

"Forty thousand people," she said, "could assemble here on a Roman holiday: there will be perhaps twenty thousand this afternoon. Possibly more. They used to give these performances only in August, but now they are trying to attract the spring visitors from the south. A lot of people from England come down here at Easter — I dare say. . . ." Here she broke off with an exclamation of happy surprise, as a middle-aged man and a young girl moved along their row to the two vacant seats beside them.

"Dr. Charles," she said, "this is delightful!" And when her acquaintance had settled down she continued with some animation. "Oxford five years ago was the last time, wasn't it? We wrangled about Tacitus, and you silenced me with the great passage about Poppaea. I acknowledged you were in the right and I have been smarting from the confession ever since. I have an awful habit of only really liking people against whom I bear a grudge." And she laughed a little hoarsely.

"I think it was three lines that took the trick," he replied. *"Rarus in publicum egressus, idque relata parte oris, re satiaret aspectum, vel quia sic dicebat.* You agreed, if I remember rightly, that here was the core of a modern psychological novel."

"Stendhal!" she exclaimed. "How Stendhal would have understood that woman!"

"Ah! I'm afraid I don't read Stendhal."

"Won't they let you — at Oriel?"

"I'm not sure they'd like it," the Professor replied, with a smile. "A famous son of ours once wrote a book called *The Essay on the Development of Christian Doctrine,* which has never seemed to me a subject of very great importance. Now you, Miss Macnamara, should write an Essay on the Development of Classical Tradition."

"It's a good idea. From Tacitus to Stendhal is a very small step. They both speak the language of reality."

"I wish we spoke it at Oriel," the Professor rejoined. "Oxford is a very provincial place."

"That's what. . . ." But Miss Macnamara checked herself. It was not often she tripped up over that obsessing thought. "I don't think you know my nephew," she continued, in a lighter tone. "Desmond, this is an old friend of mine, Dr. Charles."

"Ah! the Wykehamist!" And he rose to shake Desmond by the hand. I forgot, Miss Macnamara, did you meet my daughter?"

The Professor's young companion, who was sitting on the farther side of him, was now introduced to Desmond and his aunt. Neither had been able to see her very clearly as she moved into the row behind her father, but now Desmond was struck with her height. He thought again — the poplar trees and the long roads.

"Rhoda!" Dr. Charles continued, "Supposing we do a little Musical Chairs, if Miss Macnamara doesn't mind. Why don't you sit on the other side of her, and let her and me move up one. She knows much more French and much more about Racine than I do, and you can pick her brains between the acts."

Miss Macnamara betrayed by an involuntary movement of her eyebrow an objection of this plan. The Professor was blind to it, but Desmond caught it quickly enough. The Professor was one of those who enjoy the small social machinations.

"Why not change places with your daughter?" Miss Macnamara replied to him. "Then I shall have the young, and perhaps the ignorant, on either side of me."

"Except the most ignorant of all. No, I won't be parted from an old acquaintance. After all, it is only the middle-aged who have a real thirst for knowledge. It is among the few things left to us."

"Nonsense, Professor," Miss Macnamara rejoined sharply. "Knowledge is the only thing worth having, and we only come to it, in our weakness, when we have explored the illusions which intervene."

Dr. Charles laughed in his hearty, donnish way, and turned to his daughter.

"Go along, Rhoda, and sit at the feet of Gamaliel, but you must change places with him first. Am I right, Miss Macnamara, in thinking that wisdom knows no difference of sex?"

Miss Macnamara had risen irritably to her full height, and gathering her light cape around her was preparing to fall in with the Professor's insistent caprice. Rhoda, who was standing with some embarrassment between them, hid from him the expression on her face. The girl herself, even, was too fussed to notice it, but Desmond who was a silent spectator of the scene, caught the flush of angry humiliation on his aunt's cheeks. A month ago Miss Macnamara would have taken such a moment in her stride, but his own discovery had brought many stones in her path. There was a sense in which she had always seemed to hate him for what he was; she would hate him more for what he knew.

Yet her present annoyance was a sign of her strange need of him. She had wanted to tell him about Racine and draw the moral of Bérénice, but now this raw girl had been interposed between them. The Professor's mind was like a corkscrew; its penetration was invisible. But he always seemed to get his way. He had succeeded in spoiling her afternoon.

Miss Macnamara composed herself afresh, and asked the Professor, with a studied disregard of Rhoda, whether she was at Oxford.

"Oh, yes. She is in her fourth year at Lady Margaret Hall — Greats, of course."

"That 'of course' is very brave, Professor, but you've no right to pay any such compliment to a member of our miserable sex. Not even your own daughter. We usually waste our time with English Literature, as if anyone at a University shouldn't read that anyhow, and I am told we are particularly smart at Anglo-Saxon. The pedantry of you professors! Why do you teach the *jeunesse dorée* of English womanhood the barbarous accents of their original ignorance? I've tried to read the stuff myself. I imagine the Visigoths, who sacked our Roman heritage, spoke a variant of that tongue." And her eye ranged round the amphitheatre, which was now nearly full, and included Rhoda in its contempt. "Think of them — the brutes — charging down the valley of the Rhone from their disgusting forests, their bullet heads aflame with the ardour of destruction. What have they ever given to us, but a score of romantic fallacies? Luther, Wagner, and the Third Reich."

"Beethoven!" It was the first time that Rhoda had spoken, or perhaps it was the first time that any of them had heard her speak. Miss Macnamara swung round at her objection, regarding her very closely. Then she turned, smiling, to the Professor, and asked him:

"Is she very fond of music?"

"Rhoda plays beautifully. Once she is through her Greats, I think she will take it up."

"I see," Miss Macnamara exclaimed largely, bending her eye again upon the girl. "A very Protean young woman! And so you like Beethoven?"

Before Rhoda could reply or extend her original remark, a trumpet sounded through the amphitheatre, Miss Macnamara sat erect, and the eyes of all four were directed to the great antique portico where the actors would presently appear.

"My Racine is very rusty, very rusty indeed," the Professor complained.

"Later, Professor, later." And Miss Macnamara's tone had an authority and an impatience which could not then be gainsaid.

II

Desmond could not remember the last time that he had been to a theatre, and the present performance might have compared, for novelty, with his first pantomime. But there was something in the rhythm and sonority of the verse as it came up to him from below, that made him imagine he was in church. The actors not only spoke with a fine, quiet clarity, but they moved in a hieratic way. They seemed to be less the interpreters of dramatic roles than the votaries of an immense tradition. His aunt had warned him of this. "You are going to see a ritual rather than a play," she had said, and his interest was drugged a little by the method of its presentation.

But then his understanding of French was still imperfect, and the limpid Alexandrines which were quite intelligible to him on paper lost their meaning through the advocacy of the human voice. He knew the story and could follow its phases; but he felt as if he were listening to classical music rather than classical verse. Just as the formal rhythm of a Haydn Quartet will evoke in the listener associations, memories, and longings which have no musical relevance, so the bare cadences of Racine fell upon Desmond's ear, bereft of their argument and emotion, and merely excited a sensibility already quickened by the strangeness of the world about him.

Now it was the perfume, wafted up from the handkerchief of a woman sitting immediately below him; now it was the general, unfamiliar aspect of the crowd; now the majestic relic of imperial architecture; now the caressing warmth of the afternoon which distracted him. More, perhaps, it was the recent impressions of which these were the continuance and the reminder. The smell of Paris, as they had passed through the Gare du Nord to the Gare de Lyon; the energy and the unrest of the train; the strange food, the quick voices; the grey elegance of Aix; the solitary arch before Orange; the casual swiftness of their car and his aunt's motoring veil protecting her face against the dust — all these images succeeded one another in Desmond's mind and were fused into a single, disturbing impression.

Then they received a new accent of novelty. Turning his head, he became sharply aware of the girl beside him. Now that he came to think of it — and he had not thought of it before — it was the first time that he could remember sitting next to a girl. It was the first time that he had even noticed a girl in the sense of looking at her in a critical and admiring way. She was clearly following the play with a greater attention than himself. Probably she spoke French fluently; perhaps he, too, would speak it fluently if he remained for long enough in the South of France. It would be good practice for him, he thought, if they were to speak it together. Dr. Charles and his daughter might come to tea one afternoon; if his aunt failed to invite them, he would invite them himself.

Rhoda seemed to be aware that Desmond was looking at her, for she turned her head nervously in his direction. She was evidently embarrassed, for her cheeks flushed a little and her eyelids fluttered, as if startled by a bright light. Desmond felt he might have done wrong to stare at her, and he dropped his head. But he raised it again presently and from now onward he stole occasional, timid glances at her profile.

She was quite intent in her absorption with the play, and the abruptness which gave an edge to her movement and speech was softened in her repose. There was a resemblance — or so it appeared to Desmond — between the classical cut of her features and the features of the woman now acting Bérènice on the stage. Both had a high dignity, but the actress had a control which was clearly beyond Rhoda's capacity, and there was nothing in Rhoda's sudden intervention on Beethoven's behalf which suggested the varied tones which robbed the great bare lines of Racine of any possible monotony. Their nuances were clearly provoking Rhoda to a delight, which Desmond could not share, and her eyes would every now and again dilate with satisfaction. On the farther side of her Miss Macnamara followed the play with an equal intensity, only looking aside to see how Desmond was receiving it. And beyond her again Dr. Charles sat, as it were, in the shade of her indifference.

Whenever Desmond looked round in their direction, he saw their three profiles, given up to a secret beauty and splendour which he could not understand. They were initiates

where he was a novice. Yet he was glad to be separated from Miss Macnamara, who would have advised him of the drama's progress at every turn, and he preferred to take a momentary glance at Rhoda's reactions than to have his own dictated to him. It was during one of these that he caught his aunt's eye for the first time. He was, at that moment quite given over to reverie, and the faint scent of Rhoda's dark red hair, coiled underneath her wide-brimmed hat, filled his nostrils. But his thought was not with Rhoda or Racine or any part of his present circumstance, but with a recent, and, at times, a scarcely tolerable memory.

"Desmond!" Miss Macnamara's peremptory whisper recalled him to himself and conveyed the wide extent of her rebuke. He had been dreaming and gazing where she would have had him think and listen; and he had been dreaming of what she did not know and gazing at what she did not approve. Indeed, they were all included in her displeasure — Rhoda because she was there, and Dr. Charles because he had interfered. "Listen, Desmond. My heavens, what lines!"

The play, which had been given without an interval, was now nearing its conclusion. The serenity and grandeur of the final speeches were nobly matched by the voices which were admirably contrasted in tone and beautifully controlled in pitch and rhythm, whatever they may have lacked in individual, dramatic intensity. Titus, Antiochus, and Bérènice, stood confronting the necessary sacrifice of happiness. They were facing a loneliness which could only be mitigated by their own nobility and to which they could see no future alleviation. Kings or queens in their own right, they were left with nothing but their kingdoms, and to these inheritances they must be true. Bérènice would return to Palestine, Antiochus to Commagéne, and Titus, who had sacrificed his love for Rome, would remain the prisoner of his political divinity. Yet this, Miss Macnamara had told Desmond, was the law, not only of Rome, but of love itself — and it was a law more immutable that the laws of the Medes and Persians — that love must eternally be crucified.

GRAHAM GREENE
(1904–   )

THE biography of any great man tells both little and much. Out of the public school world with its mannered background and green playing fields came Graham Greene, whose complete understanding of the past made him more alive to the present than any other Catholic novelist of the English Revival.

Son of the headmaster of Birkhamsted, Graham Greene was born in 1904, a true child of the twentieth century. Like many famous men before him he went to Balliol College at Oxford. On coming down from the university, Greene was on the staff of the *London Times,* 1935–1937.

From this complete apprenticeship he graduated to the task of film critic for the *London Spectator* and later became the literary editor of *Night and Day.*

As writer of mystery thrillers, Graham Greene is a master. In *Stamboul Train* and the *Ministry of Fear,* he fabricated stories which, because of their tension and fast pace, have cried aloud to the films and have been eminently successful when produced on the screen.

But Greene is more than a clever writer. In *Brighton Rock* he has increased the dimensions of the "thriller" to admit the full presentation of character and the horrifying monstrosity of our modern world and its inhuman fringes. *Brighton Rock* is not a book for sensitive souls. Its hard realism poses a problem which only living Christian charity and the mercy of God could solve.

Greene points up this problem in *The Labyrinthine Ways,* his best work. It is an amazingly revealing story. In it Greene intensifies his technique of flight, but the movement is vertical as well as horizontal. The final steps of this Christian drama lift it to the level of Greek tragedy. In the glory of martyrdom is found more than the outward trappings of saccharine sanctity: the humility of the willing instrument shines with the refracted rays of Him who asked nothing and gave all to His creatures. Even the young boy in the book feels the thrill of true insight and genuine reality, often so far removed from the precious mannerisms of the hagiographer.

BRIGHTON ROCK*

A MAN in plus fours and a striped tie came to the bar. "Hullo, Ida," he called.

"Hullo, Harry," she said sadly, staring at the paper.

"Have a drink."

"I've got a drink, thank you."

"Swallow it down and have another."

"No, I don't want any more, thank you," she said. "If I'd been there — "

"What'd have been the good?" the sombre man said.

"I could've asked questions."

"Questions, questions," he said irritably. "You keep on saying questions. What about, beats me."

"Why he said he wasn't Fred."

"He wasn't Fred. He was Charles."

"It's not natural." The more she thought about it the more she wished she had been there; it was like a pain in the heart, the thought that no one at the inquest was interested, the second cousin stayed in Middlesbrough, his counsel asked no questions, and Fred's own paper gave him only half a column. On the front page was another photograph: the new Kolley Kibber; he was going to be at Bournemouth tomorrow. They might have waited, she thought, a week. It would have shown respect.

"I'd like to have asked them why he left me like that, to go scampering down the front in that sun."

"He had his job to do. He had to leave those cards."

"Why did he tell me he'd wait?"

"Ah," the sombre man said, "you'd have to ask him that," and at the words it was almost as if he was trying to answer her, answer her in his own kind of hieroglyphics, in the obscure pain, speaking in her nerves as a ghost would have to speak. Ida believed in ghosts.

"There's a lot he'd say if he could," she said. She took up the paper again and read slowly. "He did his job to the end," she said tenderly; she liked men who did their jobs: there was a kind of vitality about it. He'd dropped his cards all the way down the front; they'd come back to the office: from under a boat, from a litter basket, a child's pail. He had only a few left when "Mr. Alfred Jefferson, described as a chief clerk, of Clapham," found him. "If he did kill himself," she said (she was the only counsel to represent the dead), "he did his job first."

"But he didn't kill himself," Clarence said. "You've only got to read. They cut him up and they say he died natural."

"That's queer," Ida said. "He went and left one in a restaurant. I knew he was hungry. He kept on wanting to eat, but whatever made him slip away like that all by himself and leave me waiting? It sounds crazy."

"I suppose he changed his mind about you, Ida."

"I don't like it," Ida said. "It sounds strange to me. I wish I'd been there. I'd have asked 'em a few questions."

"What about you and me going across to the flickers, Ida?"

"I'm not in the mood," Ida said. "It's not every day you lose a friend. And you oughtn't to be in the mood either, with your wife just dead."

"She's been gone a month now," Clarence said; "you can't expect anyone to go on mourning for ever."

"A month's not so long," Ida said sadly, brooding over the paper. A day, she thought, that's all he's been gone, and I dare say there's not another soul but me thinking about him: just someone he picked up for a drink and a cuddle, and again the easy pathos touched her friendly and popular heart. She wouldn't have given it all another thought if there had been other relations besides the second cousin in Middlesbrough, if he hadn't been so alone as well as dead. But there was something fishy to her nose, though there was nothing she could put her finger on except that "Fred" — and everyone would say the same: "He wasn't Fred. You've only to read. Charles Hale."

"You oughtn't to fuss about that, Ida. It's none of your business."

"I know," she said, "it's none of mine." But it's none of anybody's, her heart repeated to her; that was the trouble: no one but her to ask questions. She knew a woman once who'd seen her husband, after he was dead, standing by the wireless set trying to twiddle the knob: she twiddled the way he wanted and he disappeared and immediately she heard an announcer say on Midland Regional: Gale warning on the Channel." She had been thinking of taking one of the Sunday trips to Calais, that was the point. It just showed: you couldn't laugh at the idea of ghosts. And if Fred, she thought, wanted to tell someone something, it wouldn't be to his second cousin in Middlesbrough that he'd go; why shouldn't he come to me? He had left her waiting there; she had waited nearly half an hour: perhaps he wanted to tell her why. "He was a gentleman," she said aloud, and with bolder resolution she cocked her hat and smoothed her hair and rose from the wine barrel. "I've got to be going," she said. "So long."

"Where to? I've never known you in such a hurry, Ida," he complained bitterly.

Ida put her finger on the paper. "Someone ought to be there," she said, "even if second cousins aren't."

"He won't care who's putting him in the ground."

"You never know," Ida said, remembering the ghost by the radio set. "It shows respect. Besides — I like a funeral."

But he wasn't exactly being put in the ground in the bright new flowery suburb where he had lodged. There were no unhygienic buryings in that place. Two stately brick towers, like those of a Scandinavian town hall, cloisters with little plaques along the walls like war memorials, a bare cold secular chapel which could be adapted quietly and conveniently to any creed: no cemetery, wax flowers, impoverished jampots of wilting wild flowers. Ida was late. Hesitating a moment outside the door for fear the place might be full of Fred's friends, she thought someone had turned on the National Programme. She knew that cultured inexpressive heartless voice, but when she opened the door, a man, not a machine, stood up in a black cassock, saying: "Heaven." There was nobody there but someone like a landlady, a servant who had parked her pram outside, two men impatiently whispering.

"Our belief in heaven," the clergyman went on, "is not qualified by our disbelief in the old medieval hell. We believe," he said, glancing swiftly along the smooth polished slipway towards the New Art doors through which the coffin would be launched into the flames, "we believe that this our brother is already at one with the One." He stamped his words, like little pats of butter, with his personal remark. "He has attained unity. We do not know what that One is with whom (or with which) he is now one. We do not retain the old medieval beliefs in glassy seas and golden crowns. Truth is beauty and there is more beauty for us, a truth-loving generation, in the certainty that our brother is at this moment reabsorbed in the universal spirit." He touched a little buzzer, the New Art doors opened, the flames flapped, and the coffin slid smoothly down into the fiery sea. The doors closed, the nurse rose and made for the door, the clergyman smiled gently from behind the slipway, like a conjurer who has produced his nine hundred and fortieth rabbit without a hitch.

It was all over. Ida squeezed out with difficulty a last tear into a handkerchief scented with California Poppy. She liked a funeral — but it was with horror — as other people like a ghost story. Death shocked her, life was so important. She wasn't religious. She didn't believe in heaven or hell, only in ghosts, ouija boards, tables that rapped and little inept voices speaking plaintively of flowers. Let Papists treat death with flippancy: life wasn't so important perhaps to them as what came after; but to her death was the end of everything. At one with the One, it didn't mean a thing beside a glass of Guinness on a sunny day. She believed in ghosts, but you couldn't call that thin transparent existence life eternal: the squeak of a board, a piece of ectoplasm in a glass cupboard at the psychical research headquarters, a voice she'd heard once at a seance saying: "Everything is very beautiful in the upper place. There are flowers everywhere."

Flowers, Ida thought scornfully; that wasn't life. Life was sunlight on brass bedposts, ruby port, the leap of the heart when the outsider you have backed passes the post and the colours go bobbing up. Life was poor Fred's mouth pressed down on hers in the taxi, vibrating with the engine along the parade. What was the sense of dying if it made you babble of flowers? Fred didn't want flowers, he wanted — and the enjoyable distress she had felt in Henneky's returned. She took life with a deadly seriousness: she was prepared to cause any amount of unhappiness to anyone in order to defend the only thing she believed in. To lose your lover — "broken hearts," she would say, "always mend" — to be maimed or blinded — "lucky," she'd tell you, "to be alive at all." There was something dangerous and remorseless in her optimism, whether she was laughing in Henneky's or weeping at a funeral or a marriage.

She came out of the crematorium, and there from the twin towers above her head fumed the very last of Fred, a thin stream of grey smoke from the ovens. People passing up the flowery suburban road looked up and noted the smoke; it had been a busy day at the furnaces. Fred dropped in indistinguishable grey ash on the pink blossoms: he became part of the smoke nuisance over London, and Ida wept.

But while she wept a determination grew: it grew all the way to the tram lines which would lead her back to her familiar territory, to the bars and the electric signs and the variety theatres. Man is made by the places in which he lives, and Ida's mind worked with the simplicity and the regularity of a sky sign: the ever-tipping glass, the ever-revolving wheel, the plain question flashing on and off: "Do You Use Forhan's for the Gums?" I'd do as much for Tom, she thought, for Clarence, that old deceitful ghost in Hennecky's, for Harry. It's the least you can do for anyone — ask questions, questions at inquests, questions at seances. Somebody had made Fred unhappy, and somebody was going to be made unhappy in turn. An eye for an eye. If you believed in God, you might leave vengeance to Him, but you couldn't trust the One, the universal spirit. Vengeance was Ida's, just as much as reward was Ida's, the soft gluey mouth affixed in taxis, the warm handclasp in cinemas, the only reward there was. And vengeance and reward — they were both fun.

The tram tingled and sparked down the Embankment. If it was a woman who had made Fred unhappy, she'd tell her what she thought. If Fred had killed himself, she'd find it out, the papers would print the news, someone would suffer. Ida was going to begin at the beginning and work right on. She was a sticker.

The first stage (she had held the paper in her hand all through the service) was Molly Pink, "described as a private secretary," employed by Messrs. Carter and Galloway.

Ida came up from Charing Cross Station into the hot and windy light in the Strand flickering on the carburetors; in an upper room of Stanley Gibbons's a man with a long grey Edwardian moustache sat in a window examining a postage stamp through a magnifying glass; a great dray laden with barrels stamped by, and the fountains played in Trafalgar Square, a cool translucent flower blooming and dropping into the drab sooty basins. It'll cost money, Ida repeated to herself, it always costs money if you want to know the truth, and she walked slowly up St. Martin's Lane, calculating, while all the time beneath the melancholy and the resolution, her heart beat faster to the refrain: it's exciting, it's fun, it's living. In Seven Dials the Negroes were hanging round the Royal Oak doors in tight natty suitings and old school ties, and Ida recognized one of them and passed the time of day. "How's business, Joe?" The great white teeth went on like a row of lights in the darkness above the bright striped shirt. "Fine, Ida, fine."

"And the hay fever?"

"Tur'ble, Ida, tur'ble."

"So long, Joe."

"So long, Ida."

It was a quarter of an hour's walk to Messrs. Carter & Galloway's, who were at the very top of a tall building on the outskirts of Gray's Inn. She had to economize now: she wouldn't even take a bus; and when she got to the dusty antiquated building, there wasn't a lift. The long flights of stone stairs wearied Ida. She'd had a long day and nothing to eat but a bun at the station. She sat down on a window sill and took off her shoes. Her feet were hot, she wiggled her toes. An old gentleman came down. He had a long moustache and a sidelong raffish look. He wore a check coat, a yellow waistcoat, and a grey bowler. He took off his bowler. "In distress, madam?" he said, peering down at Ida with little bleary eyes. "Be of assistance?"

"I don't allow anyone else to scratch my toes," Ida said.

"Ha, ha," the old gentleman said, "a card. After my own heart. Up or down?"

"Up. All the way to the top."

"Carter & Galloway. Good firm. Tell 'em I sent you."

"What's your name?"

"Moyne, Charlie Moyne. Seen you here before."

"Never."

"Some place else. Never forget fine figure of a woman. Tell 'em Moyne sent you."

"Why don't they have a lift in this place?"

"Old-fashioned people. Old-fashioned myself. Seen you at Epsom."

"You might have."

"Always tell a sporting-woman. Ask you round the corner to split a bottle of fizz if those beggars hadn't taken the last fiver I came out with. Wanted to go and lay a couple. Have to go home first. Odds'll go down while I'm doing it. You'll see. You wouldn't oblige me, I suppose? Two quid, Charlie Moyne." The bloodshot eyes watched her without hope, a little aloof and careless; the buttons on the yellow waistcoat stirred as the old heart hammered.

"Here," Ida said, "you can have a quid; now run along."

"Awfully kind of you. Give me your card. Post you a cheque tonight."

"I haven't got a card," Ida said.

"Came out without mine too. Never mind. Charlie Moyne. Care of Carter & Galloway. All know me here."

"That's all right," Ida said. "I'll see you again. I've got to be going on up."

"Take my arm," he helped her up. "Tell 'em Moyne sent you. Special terms." She looked back at the turn of the stairs. He was tucking the pound note away in his waistcoat, smoothing the moustache which was still golden at the tips, like a cigarette smoker's fingers, setting his bowler at an angle. Poor old geezer, Ida thought, he never expected to get that, watching him go off down the stairs in his jaunty and ancient despair.

There were only two doors on the top landing. She opened one marked "Inquiries," and there without a doubt was Molly Pink. In a little room hardly larger than a broom cupboard she sat beside a gas ring sucking a sweet. A kettle hissed at Ida as she entered. A swollen spotty face glared back at her without a word.

"Excuse me," Ida said.

"The partners is out."

"I came to see you."

The mouth fell a little open, a lump of toffee stirred on the tongue, the kettle whistled.

"Me?"

"Yes," Ida said. "You'd better look out. The kettle'll boil over. You *are* Molly Pink?"

"You want a cup?" The room was lined from floor to ceiling with files. A little window disclosed through the undisturbed dust of many years another block of buildings with the same arrangement of windows staring dustily back like a reflection. A dead fly hung in a broken web.

"I don't like tea," Ida said.

"That's lucky. There's only one cup," Molly said, filling a thick brown teapot with a chipped spout.

"A friend of mine called Moyne . . ." Ida began.

"Oh, him!" Molly said. "We just turned him out of house and home." A copy of *Woman and Beauty* was propped open on her typewriter, and her eyes slid continually back to it.

"Out of house and home?"

"House and home. He came to see the partners. He tried to blarney."

"Did he see them?"

"The partners is out. Have a toffee?"

"It's bad for the figure," Ida said.

"I make up for it. I don't eat breakfast."

Over Molly's head Ida could see the labels on the files: "Rents of 1–6 Mud Lane." "Rents of Wainage Estate, Balham." "Rents of. . . ." They were surrounded by the pride of ownership, property. . . .

"I came here," Ida said, "because you met a friend of mine."

"Sit down," Molly said. "That's the clients' chair. I has to entertain 'em. Mr. Moyne's not a friend."

"Not Moyne. Someone called Hale."

"I don't want any more to do with that business. You ought to 'ave seen the partners. They was furious. I had to have a day off for the inquest. They kept me hours late next day."

"I just want to hear what happened."

"What happened. The partners is awful when roused."

"I mean about Fred — Hale."

"I didn't exactly know him."

"That man you said at the inquest came up — "

"He wasn't a man. He was just a kid. He knew Mr. Hale."

"But in the paper it said — "

"Oh, Mr. Hale *said* he didn't know him.

I didn't tell them different. They didn't ask me. Except was there anything odd in his manner. Well, there wasn't anything you'd call odd. He was just scared, that's all. We get lots like that in here."

"But you didn't tell them that?"

"That's nothing uncommon. I knew what it was at once. He owed the kid money. We get lots like that. Like Charlie Moyne."

"He was scared, was he? Poor old Fred."

"'I'm not Fred,'" he said, "sharp as you please. But I could tell all right. So could my girl friend."

"What was the kid like?"

"Oh, just a kid."

"Tall?"

"Not particularly."

"Fair?"

"I couldn't say that."

"How old was he?"

"'Bout my age, I dessay."

"What's that?"

"Eighteen," Molly said, staring defiantly across the typewriter and the steaming kettle, sucking a toffee.

"Did he ask for money?"

"He didn't have time to ask for money."

"You didn't notice anything else?"

"He was awful anxious for me to go along with him. But I couldn't, not with my girl friend there."

"Thanks," Ida said, "it's something learnt."

"You a woman detective?" Molly asked.

"Oh, no, I'm just a friend of his."

There *was* something fishy: she was convinced of it now. She remembered again how scared he'd been in the taxi, and going down Holborn towards her digs behind Russell Square, in the late afternoon sun, she thought again of the way in which he had handed her the ten shillings before she went down into the Ladies'. He was a real gentleman; perhaps it was the last few shillings he had; and those people — that boy — dunning him for money. Perhaps he was another one ruined like Charlie Moyne, and now that her memory of his face was getting a bit dim, she couldn't help lending him a few of Charlie Moyne's features, the bloodshot eyes if nothing else. Sporting gentlemen, freehanded gentlemen, real gen-

tlemen. The commercials dropped their dewlaps in the hall of the Imperial, the sun lay flat across the plane trees, and a bell rang for tea in a boarding house in Coram Street.

I'll try the Board, Ida thought.

When she got in, there was a card on the hall table, a card of Brighton Pier; if I was superstitious, she thought, if I was superstitious. She turned it over. It was only from Phil Corkery, asking her to come down. She had the same every year from Eastbourne, Hastings, and once from Aberystwyth. But she never went. He wasn't someone she liked to encourage. Too quiet. Not what she called a man.

She went to the basement stairs and called Old Crowe. She needed two sets of fingers for the board and she knew it would give the old man pleasure. "Old Crowe," she called, peering down the stone stairs. "Old Crowe."

"What is it, Ida?"

"I'm going to have a turn at the Board."

She didn't wait for him, but went up to her bed-sitting-room to make ready. The room faced east and the sun was gone. It was cold and dusk. Ida turned on the gas fire and drew the old scarlet velvet curtains to shut out the grey skies and chimney pots. Then she patted the divan bed into shape and drew two chairs to the table. In a glass-fronted cupboard her life stared back at her, a good life: pieces of china bought at the seaside, a photograph of Tom, an Edgar Wallace, a Netta Syrett from a second-hand stall, some sheets of music, *The Good Companions,* her mother's picture, more china, a few jointed animals made of wood and elastic, trinkets given her by this, that, and the other, *Sorrell and Son,* the board.

She took the board gently down and locked the cupboard. A flat oval piece of polished wood on tiny wheels, it looked like something that had crept out of a drawer in a basement kitchen. But in fact it was Old Crowe who had done that, knocking gently on the door, sidling in, white hair, grey face, short-sighted pit-pony eyes, blinking at the bare globe in Ida's reading lamp. Ida tossed a pink netty scarf over the light and dimmed it for him.

"You got something to ask it, Ida?" Old Crowe said. He shivered a little, frightened and fascinated. Ida sharpened a pencil and inserted it in the prow of the little board.

"Sit down, Old Crowe. What have you been doing all day?"

"They had a funeral at twenty-seven. One of those Indian students."

"I been to a funeral too. Was yours a good one?"

"There aren't any good funerals these days. Not with plumes."

Ida gave the little board a push. It slid sideways across the polished table more than ever like a beetle. "The pencil's too long," Old Crowe said. He sat, hugging his hands between his knees, bent forward watching the board. Ida screwed the pencil a little higher. "Past or future?" Old Crowe said, panting a little.

"I want to get into touch today," Ida said.

"Dead or alive?" Old Crowe said.

"Dead. I seen him burnt this afternoon. Cremated. Come on, Old Crowe, put your fingers on."

"Better take off your rings," Old Crowe said. "Gold confuses it."

Ida unclothed her fingers, laid the tips on the board, which squeaked away from her across the sheet of foolscap. "Come on, Old Crowe," she said.

Old Crowe giggled. He said: "It's naughty," and placed his bony digits on the very rim, where they throbbed a nervous tattoo. "What are you going to ask it, Ida?"

"Are you there, Fred?"

The board squeaked away under their fingers, drawing long lines across the paper this way and that. "It's got a will of its own," Ida said.

"Hush," said Old Crowe.

The board bucked a little with its hind wheel and came to a stop. "We might look now," Ida said. She pushed the board to one side, and they stared together at the network of pencilling.

"You might make out a Y there," Ida said.

"Or it might be an N."

"Anyway something's there. We'll try again." She put her fingers firmly on the board. "What happened to you, Fred?" and immediately the board was off and away. All her indomitable will worked through her fingers: she wasn't going to have any nonsense this time, and across the board the grey face of Old Crowe frowned with concentration.

"It's writing — real letters," Ida said with triumph, and as her fingers momentarily loosened their grip she could feel the board slide firmly away as if on another's errand.

"Hush," said Old Crowe, but it bucked and stopped. They pushed the board away, and there unmistakable, in large thin letters was a word, but not a word they knew: "SUKILL."

"It looks like a name," Old Crowe said.

"It must mean something," Ida said. "The Board always means something. We'll try again," and again the little wooden beetle scampered off, drawing its tortuous trail. The globe burnt red under the scarf, and Old Crowe whistled between his teeth. "Now," Ida said and lifted the board. A long ragged word ran diagonally across the paper: "FRESUICILLEYE."

"Well," Old Crowe said, "that's a mouthful. You can't make anything out of that, Ida."

"Can't I though?" Ida said. "Why, it's clear as clear. *Fre* is short for Fred and *Suici* for Suicide and Eye: that's what I always say — an eye for an eye and a tooth for a tooth."

"What about those two L's?"

"I don't know yet, but I'll bear them in mind." She leant back in her chair with a sense of power and triumph. "I'm not superstitious," she said, "but you can't get over that. The Board knows."

"She knows," Old Crowe said, sucking his teeth.

"One more try?" The board slid and squeaked and abruptly stopped. Clear as clear the name stared up at her: "PHIL."

"Well," Ida said, "well." She blushed a little "like a sugar biscuit?"

"Thank you, Ida, thank you."

Ida took a tin out of the cupboard drawer and pushed it over to Old Crowe. "They drove him to death," Ida said happily. "I knew there was something fishy. See that

Eye. That as good as tells me what to do." Her eye lingered on *PHIL.* "I'm going to make those people sorry they were ever born." She drew her breath luxuriously and stretched her monumental legs. "Right and wrong," she said, "I believe in right and wrong," and delving a little deeper, with a sigh of happy satiety, she said: "It's going to be exciting, it's going to be fun, it's going to be a bit of life, Old Crowe," giving him the highest praise she could give to anything, while the old man sucked his tooth and the pink light wavered on the Warwick Deeping.

THE LABYRINTHINE WAYS*

CHAPTER TWO

THE squad of police made their way back to the station: they walked raggedly with rifles slung anyhow: ends of cotton where buttons should have been: a puttee slipping down over the ankle: small men with black secret Indian eyes. The small plaza on the hill-top was lighted with globes strung together in threes and joined by trailing overhead wires. The Treasury, the Presidencia, a dentist's, the prison — a low white colonnaded building which dated back three hundred years, and then the steep street down — the back wall of a ruined church: whichever way you went you came ultimately to water and to river. Pink classical façades peeled off and showed mud beneath, and the mud slowly reverted to mud. Round the plaza the evening parade went on: women in one direction, men in the other: young men in red shirts milled boisterously round the gaseosa stalls.

The lieutenant walked in front of his men with an air of bitter distaste. He might have been chained to them unwillingly: perhaps the scar on his jaw was a relic of an escape. His gaiters were polished, and his pistol-holster: his buttons were all sewn on. He had a sharp crooked nose jutting out of a lean dancer's face: his neatness gave an effect of inordinate ambition in the shabby city. A sour smell came up to the plaza from the river and the vultures were bedded on the roofs, under the tent of their rough black wings. Sometimes a little moron head peered out

and down and a claw shifted. At nine-thirty exactly, all the lights in the plaza went out.

A policeman clumsily presented arms and the squad marched into barracks; they waited for no order, hanging up their rifles by the officers' room, lurching on into the courtyard, to their hammocks, or the excusado. Some of them kicked off their boots and lay down. Plaster was peeling off the mud walls: a generation of policemen had scrawled messages on the whitewash. A few peasants waited on a bench, hands between their knees. Nobody paid them any attention. Two men were fighting in the lavatory.

"Where is the jefe?" the lieutenant asked. No one knew: they thought he was playing billiards somewhere in the town. The lieutenant sat down with dapper irritation at the chief's table: behind his head two hearts were entwined in pencil on the whitewash. "All right," he said, "what are you waiting for? Bring in the prisoners." They came in bowing, hat in hand, one behind the other. "So-and-so. Drunk and disorderly." "Fined five pesos." "But I can't pay, your Excellency." "Let him clean out the lavatory and the cells then." "So-and-so. Defaced an election poster." "Fined five pesos." "So-and-so. Found wearing a holy medal under his shirt." "Fined five pesos." The duty drew to a close: there was nothing of importance. Through the open door the mosquitoes came whirring in.

Outside, the sentry could be heard presenting arms: it was the Chief of Police. He came breezily in, a stout man with a pink fat face, dressed in white flannels, with a wide-awake hat and a cartridge-belt and a big pistol clapping his thigh. He held a handkerchief to his mouth: he was in distress. "Toothache again," he said, "toothache."

"Nothing to report," the lieutenant said with contempt.

"The Governor was at me again today," the chief complained.

"Liquor?"

"No, a priest."

"The last was shot weeks ago."

"He doesn't think so."

"The devil of it is," the lieutenant said, "we haven't photographs." He glanced along the wall to the picture of James Calver, wanted in the United States for bank robbery and homicide: a tough uneven face taken at two angles: description circulated to every station in Central America: the low forehead and the fanatic bent-on-one-thing eyes. He looked at it with regret: there was so little chance that he would ever get south: he would be picked up in some dive at the border—in Juarez or Piedras Negras or Nogales.

"He says we have," the chief complained. "My tooth, oh, my tooth!" He tried to find something in his hip-pocket, but the holster got in the way. The lieutenant tapped his polished boot impatiently. "There," the chief said. A large number of people sat round a table: young girls in white muslin: older women with untidy hair and harassed expressions: a few men peered shyly and solicitously out of the background. All the faces were made up of small dots: it was a newspaper photograph of a first communion party taken years ago: a youngish man in a Roman collar sat among the women. You can imagine him petted with small delicacies, preserved for their use in the stifling atmosphere of intimacy and respect. He sat there, plump, with protuberant eyes, bubbling with harmless feminine jokes. "It was taken years ago."

"He looks like all the rest," the lieutenant said. It was obscure, but you could read into the smudgy photograph a well-shaved, well-powdered jowl much too developed for his age. The good things of life had come to him too early—the respect of his contemporaries, a safe livelihood. The trite religious word upon the tongue, the joke to ease the way, the ready acceptance of other people's homage . . . a happy man. A natural hatred as between dog and dog stirred in the lieutenant's bowels. "We've shot him half a dozen times," he said.

"The Governor has had a report . . . he tried to get away last week to Vera Cruz."

"What are the Red Shirts doing that he comes to *us?*"

"Oh, they missed him, of course. It was just luck that he didn't catch the boat."

"What happened to him?"

"They found his mule. The Governor says he must have him this month. Before the rains come."

"Where was his parish?"

"Concepción and the villages around. But he left there years ago."

"Is anything known?"

"He can pass as a gringo. He spent six years at some American Seminary. I don't know what else. He was born in Carmen—the son of a storekeeper. Not that that helps."

"They all look alike to me," the lieutenant said. Something you could almost have called horror moved him when he looked at the white muslin dresses—he remembered the smell of incense in the churches of his boyhood, the candles and the laciness and the self-esteem, the immense demands made from the altar steps by men who didn't know the meaning of sacrifice. The old peasants knelt there before the holy images with their arms held out in the attitude of the cross: tired by the long day's labour in the plantations, they squeezed out a further mortification. And the priest came round with the collecting-bag taking their centavos, abusing them for their small comforting sins, and sacrificing nothing at all in return—except a little sexual indulgence. And that was easy, the lieutenant thought. He himself felt no need of women. He said: "We will catch him. It is only a question of time."

"My tooth," the chief wailed again. He said: "It poisons the whole of life. Today my biggest break was twenty-five."

"You will have to change your dentist."

"They are all the same."

The lieutenant took the photograph and pinned it on the wall. James Calver, bank robber and homicide, stared in harsh profile towards the first communion party. "He is a man at any rate," the lieutenant said, with approval.

"Who?"

"The gringo."

The chief said: "You heard what he did in Houston. Got away with ten thousand dollars. Two C-men were shot."

"G-men."

"It's an honour — in a way — to deal with such people." He slapped furiously out at a mosquito.

"A man like that," the lieutenant said, "does no real harm. A few men dead. We all have to die. The money — somebody has to spend it. We do more good when we catch one of these." He had the dignity of an idea, standing in the little whitewashed room in his polished boots and his venom. There was something disinterested in his ambition: a kind of virtue in his desire to catch the sleek respected guest of the first communion party.

The chief said mournfully: "He must be devilishly cunning if he's been going on for years."

"Anybody could do it," the lieutenant said. "We haven't really troubled about them — unless they put themselves in our hands. Why, I could guarantee to fetch this man in, inside a month if. . . ."

"If what?"

"If I had the power."

"It's easy to talk," the chief said. "What would you do?"

"This is a small state. Mountains on the north, the sea on the south, I'd beat it as you beat a street, house by house."

"Oh, it sounds easy," the chief wailed indistinctly with his handkerchief against his mouth.

The lieutenant said suddenly: "I will tell you what I'd do. I would take a man from every village in the state as a hostage. If the villagers didn't report the man when he came, the hostages would be shot — and ᵗhen we'd take more."

"A lot of them would die, of course."

"Wouldn't it be worth it?" the lieutenant ˢaid with a kind of exultation. "To be rid ᵒf those people for ever."

"You know," the chief said, "you've got something there."

The lieutenant walked home through the shuttered town. All his life had lain here: the Syndicate of Workers and Peasants had been once a school. He had helped to wipe out the unhappy memory. The whole town was changed: the cement playground up the hill near the cemetery where iron swings stood out like gallows in the moony darkness where was the site of the cathedral. The new children would have new memories: nothing would ever be as it was. There was something of a priest in his intent observant walk — a theologian going back over the errors of the past to destroy them again.

He reached his own lodging. The houses were all one storied, whitewashed, built around small patios, with a well and a few flowers. The windows on the street were barred. Inside the lieutenant's room there was a bed made of old packing-cases with a straw mat laid on top, a cushion and a sheet. There was a picture of the President on the wall, a calendar, and on the tile floor a table and a rocking chair. In the light of a candle it looked as comfortless as a prison or a monastic cell.

The lieutenant sat down upon his bed and began to take off his boots. It was the hour of prayer. Black beetles exploded against the walls like crackers. More than a dozen crawled over the tiles with injured wings. It infuriated him to think that there were still people in the state who believed in a loving and merciful God. There are mystics who are said to have experienced God directly. He was a mystic, too, and what he had experienced was vacancy — a complete certainty in the existence of a dying, cooling world, of human beings who had evolved from animals for no purpose at all. He knew.

He lay down in his shirt and breeches on the bed and blew out the candle. Heat stood in the room like an enemy. But he believed against the evidence of his senses in the cold empty ether spaces. A radio was playing somewhere: music from Mexico City, or perhaps even from London or New York, filtered into this obscure neglected state. It seemed to him like a weakness: this was his own land, and he would have walled it in with steel if he could, until he had eradicated from it everything which reminded him of how it had once appeared to a miserable child. He wanted to destroy everything: to be alone without any memories at all. Life began five years ago.

The lieutenant lay on his back with his eyes open while the beetles detonated on the ceiling. He remembered the priest the Red Shirts had shot against the wall of the cemetery up the hill, another little fat man with popping eyes. He was a monsignor, and he thought that would protect him: he had a sort of contempt for the lower clergy, and right up to the last he was explaining his rank. Only at the very end had he remembered his prayers. He knelt down and

they had given him time for a short act of contrition. The lieutenant had watched him: he wasn't directly concerned. Altogether they had shot about five priests — two or three had escaped, the bishop was safely in Mexico City, and one man had conformed to the Governor's law that all priests must marry. He lived now near the river with his house-keeper. That, of course, was the best solution of all, to leave the living witness to the weakness of their faith. It showed the deception they had practiced all these years. For if they really believed in heaven or hell, they wouldn't mind a little pain now, in return for what immensities. . . . The lieutenant, lying on his hard bed, in the damp hot dark, felt no sympathy at all with the weakness of the flesh.

GERALD VANN

(1906–   )

FATHER GERALD VANN, O.P., publicist and preacher, was born August 24, 1906, at St. Mary Cray, Kent, England. He attended the preparatory school of the English Dominicans, took his S.T.L. at the Angelico in Rome and his M.A. at Oxford. Since 1934 he has been a member of the faculty at Blackfriars School, Laxton, England.

Before World War II, Father Vann was an ardent worker in the cause of peace. Toward this end he labored tirelessly at the Continental meetings of the Catholic Council for International Relations and founded, 1937, The Union of Prayer for Peace.

Father Vann has written several books which were well received by the critics and the general public.

His style is fresh and easy and his books contain many memorable and quotable passages. Like Maritain he has demonstrated the perennial quality of St. Thomas by applying his principles to current problems.

Father Vann's best work is to be seen in the following volumes: *On Being Human, Of His Fulness, St. Thomas Aquinas,* all published by Sheed and Ward, and in *Morals Makyth Man* (Longmans), and *Morality and War* (Burns, Oates).

THE VISION OF MAN*

NOWHERE is the degradation of the grasping, utilizing attitude to created things more terrible nor the loneliness that

follows from it more profound than in the relationship between human beings. We are roused to fury when we see a barbarian destroying or insulting a work of art, still more if he ill-treats an animal; infinitely more if

*Vann, Gerald, O.P., *The Heart of Man* (New York: Longmans, Green and Co.), pp. 47–66.

he ill-treats a child. Yet we seem to find it hard to see the same brutality in its less dramatic forms. We recognize the brutality of cruelty and we recognize the brutality which is blind to beauty; we do not always recognize the brutality of treating ends as means. We can see that the industrial magnate who treats his "hands" as though they were cattle is a disgrace to humanity; we do not always see so readily that to treat them as "hands" at all it a disgrace to humanity. We know that to ravish a woman is the act of a brute; but do we ever stop to wonder just how much that passes for love-making is also the act of a brute?

In both cases the sin is in essence the same. Begin by asking what a human being is. You will be led to answer first of all in terms of a sort of infinity. We have learnt much in recent years of the way in which the individual recapitulates the history of the race and of the world; not an isolated atom with nothing but his own personal history, but a storehouse of the age-old thoughts and desires and experiences of created things. Then there is the infinity of the mind's power to know, its power to "become in a manner all things." Above all, there is the divine destiny: to become one, not with all things merely, but with the Maker of all things. Secondly, you will be led to the quality of uniqueness. No two human beings are exactly alike; each is this particular body-spirit and not another, each has his own particular gifts and powers and qualities, his own heredity, his own partly inherited, partly self-determined character and temperament, his own particular experience and way of reacting to experience. Because unique, he cannot without violence and degradation be regimented or dragooned; because infinite, he cannot be regarded simply as part of the finite world, still less of a finite social system, still less again of an economic structure. He is these things, indeed, as we shall see; but he is much more. In his infinity he overtops the world. It was the opinion of St. Thomas that the secrets of men's hearts are not part of the universe; not even the angels can know them: they stand in a direct relationship to God alone.

In the Middle Ages they had a maxim, *corruptio optimi pessima,* the greater the thing the deeper the degredation if it is corrupted. To treat men as economic "hands" or as political "units" in defiance of their uniqueness and infinity is a unique and infinite degradation: you are treating the greatest thing in the world as a means. To treat a human being as a means to pleasure and to call it love is the greatest degradation of all.

There are some people (the scientifically minded) who will not have the activities of hormones romanticized: for them, falling in love is just a bio-chemical reaction to appropriate stimuli, and should be treated with scientific freedom and detachment. Then there is the joyous pagan: he does, in a sense, love and worship beauty, but he interprets worship in a somewhat activist sense, and beauty in terms of corruption rather than production; he believes in gathering rosebuds, and though he weep as they droop and wither, he makes no attempt to stop the rot; like Herrick, he

> co'd never love indeed;
> Never see mine own heart bleed:
> Never crucifie my life
> Or for Widow, Maid, or Wife —
so that they for their part
> By and by
> . . . do lie
> Poor girls, neglected.

These two types both forget that man lives a many-levelled life, but that it is the *man* who lives it. We are not just body, we are not just mind; we are not just body *and* mind either; we are body-mind. You cannot, once within the sphere of conscious activity, say that this or that affects the body but not the mind, the mind but not the body: everything that is done or experienced is done or experienced by the body-mind.

And, therefore, there is an essential difference between sex in man and sex in animals. Sex in man is all that the biologist says it is; but it is infinitely more, and more precious, than that. For in the union of two bodies, it is the union of two persons that can be achieved. That is why sex is a mystery. If you view sex simply as a biological function or a physical plaything you miss its whole meaning, and the deep human realities it could disclose to you will remain hidden. Nothing could be more inaccurate than to speak of Casanova as one of the world's greatest lovers: there can have been few men who knew less of love than Casanova, for he never, as far as one can see, touched reality at all, never emerged from the narrow, brittle shell of his own little ego.

But to be a Casanova is something worse than being only half a man: it is to treat other human beings as less than human too. The only possible human way in which we can approach human beings is with awe and reverence as towards a mystery, though admittedly the mystery is not without its humour. If we forget the mystery, we are brutish, even though we may not be brutal. It may be the blind animal brutishness that has never known the spirit, or it may be the shallow commercialized brutishness that exploits the body and ignores the mind; in either case it is a destruction of humanity because it cannot adore, it can only grab. We hate the tripper who cannot even contemplate a bluebell but has to tear and maul and destroy it; but how much worse to be unable to contemplate the human being, and to maul and destroy that!

Why is it that our world has exchanged art in its daily life for ugliness if not because it has lost its reverence for things? And why do we find ourselves condemned to live in a world that has exchanged love for hatred and enmity and rivalry if not because it has lost its reverence for men and women? There is a degradation worse than the carnage of the battlefield and the bombed city: you find it in the commercial exploitation which uses men as featureless economic units, you find it in concentration camps which treat them as specimens for the sadist, and you find it in the private exploitation which treats them as pleasure-machines.

The soul of love-making is humility. Indeed, you must have a double reverence and humility; first because there is no art without reverence, and love-making is an art in the simple sense of making what is true and good and beautiful; and secondly, because its material is not stone or paint, nor merely flesh, but the mysterious infinity of the person. Those teachers are very wise who tell us that humility is the ground of all the virtues; we are in evil case if we forget it, for it will mean that the false self and not the true is enthroned. We shall want to possess and domineer over truth and turn it to our own purposes instead of wanting it to take possession of us; and so we shall lose wisdom and prudence which are the humility of the mind. We shall want to domineer over things and be absolute owners and masters and treat them as mere utilities instead of remembering that we are only God's stewards and that things are to be loved and reverenced because they are the work of His hands; and so we shall not have the poverty of spirit and we shall not have justice, for to have these is to be humble (in theory and in practice) about our possessions. We shall turn our aggressive instinct, our desire for mastery and power, to self-assertion and selfishness instead of harnessing our energies to the service of the Light; and so we shall love fortitude, which is humility in strength and courage. And finally, we shall want to grab and domineer over bodily beauty and be arbitrary masters of our own bodily powers instead of accepting on our knees the gift of wholeness which love brings us; and so we shall lose temperateness, the humility of the flesh.

Temperateness is not the denial of passion; on the contrary.

Shall I compare thee to a summer's day?
Thou art more lovely and more temperate.

Spring is more temperate than summer; it is also more passionate. Temperateness is not the absence of passion, it is the transfiguring of passion into wholeness. Without it, you will have the chaos that follows the primal sin: you will have the senses usurping sovereignty and excluding the spirit; you will have them deciding good and evil and excluding God; you will have the destruction of the integrity of the person where you should have an immense enhancement of life. But is not temperateness always trying to tell us what not to do, trying to exclude and deny?

No, it excludes only as a sculptor or an etcher excludes, in order to create form; it denies only in order to affirm. It is positive as the temperateness of spring is positive; but it is positive also as art is positive. Look at its opposite, the grasping mauling autonomy of dehumanized passion, if you want to see what it means to destroy.

We can learn a lesson from one of the great love-stories of our European heritage. Abelard wrote a treatise on the meaning of love, and much that was in it he owed to Cicero; but he owed more to Héloïse and to the wisdom with which she interpreted their tragedy. "It was desire more than love, *amicitia,* that bound you to me," she wrote to him; but of herself she said, *"Nihil unquam in te nisi te exquisivi:* Never did I seek anything in you save you yourself: you alone I wanted, not what you could give me." What the true lover loves is the beloved person, not just his own pleasure in her. He may ask gifts indeed; but the gifts on both sides are equally a receiving. He that loseth his life shall find it. The false self speaks of love, but it is a false love which is only a form of grabbing; there is no escape from the loneliness of the ego there. In real love we can hardly distinguish giving from getting: each is indistinguishably both. The lover's giving is his getting: that his gift should be lovingly accepted is itself a gift to him, and the gift he values most.

From reverence and humility we come to the understanding of love. With reverence we are already far from vulgarity and violence; with humility we leave behind us the shallows of selfish pleasure-seeking; it is with the love that comes of them that we shall find we have enlarged our life and immeasurably enriched it because in poverty of spirit we shall at last have enlarged our hearts. "With my body I thee *worship*," we say in the liturgy of marriage; without worship there is disaster as well as sin. At the height of passion especially it is easy to forget the person, to forget the breadth and depth of love, to let the hard-won unity of the self be split up again into fragments, and passion in autonomy become a preying brute. It is only by a habitual reverence and humility

and worship that the danger can be forestalled. And always love-making demands patience and gentleness and sometimes heroic generosity if there is not to be the proud snatching of a selfish pleasure where there should be the deep oneness of a shared joy. Sexual pleasure is not a king in its own right; it is one element in a whole, and being one element only, it may not rule. It is one element in the totality of the oneness of two *persons;* if it is not that, if it is a dictator, it ceases to be human at all.

There is something very attractive about the joyous pagan gathering his rosebuds; but it is because we allow ourselves to forget the wholeness of the human situation and fix our attention on one element within it. Do you find it hard to *feel* that this is so? Think of the immensity of the total love of two human beings. At the height of passion, love produces ecstasy. The word means being outside the self: it means "I live, now not I," it means "It is thyself." A man and a woman are each unique and infinite: "I have said, Ye are gods." Here you have two infinities that are one: not a drab assuagement of tumescence, not a slick exercise of a biological function, not the feckless gathering of rosebuds, but the marriage of gods. Ecstasy means living in another. Here, you are living in the being you love; you are living in the race whose history you summarize, whose function you fulfill, whose life you gather in your hands and pass on to the future ages; you are living (if you have eyes to see) in God, to whose life and love you thus do homage, whose infinite mighty art waits upon you to work with you — you making the body, He the spirit — to fashion another infinity. This is the immensity that sex can open out to you; and will you isolate it and turn it into a toy? For here if anywhere it must be clear that you are not the master of heaven and earth, and that you must go down on your knees to receive a gift greater than yourself. It is the snatcher and the mauler who destroy; the temperate man adores.

You cannot grab at the infinite; you can only wait and worship. Christian temperateness is a form of worship first of all because every act of virtue is also, and primarily, an act of religion, but also in a special sense because its main purpose is to humble the senses and make ecstasy possible. It begins with a sort of loving fear: modesty in the modern sense and a kind of shyness and a sense of awe, and at the same time a fear of the ugliness of violence and of the power of passion to destroy integrity. And therefore, as complement to this initial reverence, there is the love of beauty, which is clarity and integrity; the spirit of nobility, of *gentilezza,* as opposed to the vulgarity of a personality in disintegration. Read the treatise of St. Thomas on temperateness in the *Summa Theologica* and you will find these two ideas constantly recurring; you will find some modes of virtue mentioned which do not immediately refer to physical love but which, nevertheless, because they go to make up the whole picture of the temperate man, help to make up the whole picture of the lover. You will find chastity described precisely as guarding the integrity of the body-spirit against disintegration; then you will find gentleness, which is an element in the worship of the lovely and the sacred; you will find clemency, which is opposed to cruelty, and, therefore, to the cruelty of using a human being as a means to pleasure. There is a vice of *curiositas,* which is not healthy curiosity but a desire for knowledge or experience which for one reason or another is disordered and destructive — and in this case would describe the dilettante who flits from one human being to another in search of novelty and so destroys the integrity of each, and always misses the deeps of reality. There is *modestia,* which guards against the violation of that privacy and intimacy of the body-spirit to which love alone can give access, and then ensures that love-play shall not be robbed of its integrity by being turned into an experiment in selfish localized pleasure instead of the sharing of a deep personal joy.

And then you find a discussion of humility and the primal sin of pride. It is the root of the whole matter. The other virtues, too, are grounded in humility and destroyed by pride; but the death of the false self day by day, the challenging of the false self where

its brutality and the effects of its arrogance can be most marked, is especially the task of temperateness. You will find, too, a discussion of death as the wages of sin, of this primal sin; and of the servility of intemperance because especially it is destructive of beauty. The chaste man is free, not because he is passionless, but because his passion does not destroy but expresses and enlarges the spirit; and chastity brings not death but life because, just as in the aesthetic vision it is in and through the senses that the whole being is enlarged, so here too, and to an infinitely deeper and wider extent, it is in and through the senses that the two infinities meet and are made one.

Corruptio optimi pessima. You have to be so careful when you hold in your hands a thing of great loveliness and value. Think how tenderly we treat a glass of wine of rare vintage, and rightly; yet that is not infinite, that is not a person, that cannot be hurt as a man or a woman can be hurt. You can hurt love and yourself and the other, if you wrench the physical from its human totality; or if you are selfish and use the other as a means; or if you are proud in the primal sense of denying the mystery and excluding God. Christian temperateness is not the tempered possessive enjoyment of things, but rather a worshipping union *with* things *in* God; it is saying to another human being, "It is thyself," so that both together in their oneness may make the final affirmation to the Infinite Love, "It is Thyself."

This gentleness is not just an external thing. It is not primarily an external thing. It is primarily a gentleness of mind. How terrible when people are led to believe, or left to believe, that once they are in love they have nothing to do but live happy ever after, they have nothing further to learn. Love is an endless creative process; the oneness of the two is not born but made. Do you think that two people, however much in love, will love each other in exactly the same way? Do you think they will never differ in the way they want to express their love? Do you think that because they are living in love they cease to be individuals, or that the false self is wholly dead? There is always the tension; there is always the temptation to sink back into the separate selfhood, there is always the danger that passion may destroy the unity of the person; it is only by long, patient labour that you can hope to forge the unity of the deep personal will which can govern separate superficial desire.

So, when you make love you must be gentle and humble, because it is to the mystery of a human being that you are making love. Love is an endless creative process; it is also an endless voyage of discovery. Because you are in love with each other do you think you know each other? Perhaps when you are both old you will have learnt a little — but only if all the time you have loved deeply and been deeply aware of your ignorance. And if you are proud and refuse to accept your ignorance, if you are proud and try to dictate to this shared life which is so much greater than your own, then you will kill your real self though no doubt you will not notice it, and you will kill the heart it should have been your glory to serve. If you accept your ignorance and know your smallness in face of this mystery, then you will make many mistakes, you will find your passion imperfect because of its ability to make you forget love, you will know pain and disappointment and repentance, but you will be able to be reborn and be a child. Here especially the grain of wheat must fall into the ground lest itself remain alone.

If you degrade love by brutality or selfishness or pride, you destroy it; and you will find its wholeness broken up into two fragments, each of them ugly; you will find passion twisted into lust, and emotion twisted into sentimentality. Both of them are superficial, both of them are unreal, both of them are disruptive; and their fruit is loneliness. When passion breaks away from the deep life of a man it can never enlarge him, it has nothing to say to the heart; it can never be a marriage of gods, only an animal mauling its prey. When emotion breaks away from the deep will of a man it runs away from reality; it makes for itself a fantasy-object which obscures the real; endlessly agitated over the superficial well-being of its object it never goes down to the depths to find the

real good and the real evil; there is no meeting, it can never help.

We live a many-levelled life, and real love is a sharing of life on all these levels, but a sharing of them in their integrity, a sharing of the whole being; and that is why the fullness of love is not likely to be given us this side the grave for we are not likely this side the grave to be completely whole. But though the fullness of love is something that must wait upon our wholeness, love itself is precisely what makes us whole; when we have the fullness to say, "It is Thyself," but it is love that makes us begin to say it.

Lust and sentimentality separate, but love unites; and God who is Love Redemptive gives us love with its joys and sorrows to restore our wholeness, to bring us again out of the cold. He gives us love with its joys and especially its sorrows because it can lead us to rebirth. If you skim along the surface of life, you will never know the need of a Saviour except by hearsay, for you will never know the depths of the human heart. If love were an endless idyll unflecked by sorrow you would be endlessly happy, but you would not know the intensity of happiness as you might, for you would still not know the depths of the human heart. But if you know the love that can lead you near to heartbreak, if you know not only the heights of ecstasy but the depths of pain, then you will know you stand before a mystery and you will be silenced, you will have seen the abyss of the human heart which only infinity can fill, and perhaps you will find yourself forced to look beyond the barriers of the finite for the Love in which all other loves are fulfilled.

To say "I love you in God" may be an insult; but not if we say it aright. Created things live only by and in the Uncreated; to see them apart from Him is to see them out of their true element. It is not seeing them in God that does violence to them or diminishes their reality, it is seeing them apart from Him; for just as passion is destroyed when it ceases to live in the wholeness of the person, so things are destroyed when they are abstracted from the eternal Whole. To see and love in God is not to see and love a shadow; it is to see and love the real where it is most real. The daffodils haste away and are lost to us; but they are for ever present in the eternal "now." If you love the daffodil in the isolation of idolatry, your love dies when it fades and is gone; if you love it in the Eternal, you love it for ever. And the human being? You do not love aright unless you love in humility and worship, and will you be more humble and reverent or less when you know that the being you love and God are one? Will you be more gentle or less, more afraid of selfish domineering and violence or less? With all your strength you will be temperate, for you will know that your hands hold the temple of God.

You want to be master and maker, and you are right; but you cannot be these things unless you have learnt to love, and to love as we ought is hard. So God, whose love makes things lovely, gives you this particular human love to make things easier for you. If you want to see what real tenderness is, look at the love of God: You will not find in Him any sentimentality, you will find no weak humanitarian mildness in the infinite consuming Fire, no shielding us from the pain that can show us what life means; but you will find the tenderness that tempers the wind for the shorn lamb, that will do anything, short of violence to its own gift of free will, to lead us back in spite of ourselves to wholeness, that will run the risk of defeat by a finite rival rather than leave us without this best and greatest signpost to itself. God is Lover and Maker; he made us in His image, to know Him and love Him and serve Him and be happy; and we serve Him by being lovers and makers in our turn, but lovers first and then makers, for His creation is the expression of His love. He made us to know and love Him and to be makers; it is the same journey that leads us to both ends: to find the vision of the One and to be makers we must learn to love, and to love we must learn to accept the gift of pain.

You want to be master and maker; but for that you must learn the reality of love and not its romanticized shadow. You can, if you like, close your eyes to the pain and toil and tension that love involves and build instead a fantasy world from which difficulties and conflicts are excluded and the days pass by in a haze of cloudless happiness and it is always spring; but the wages of this sin is death. The sort of making which does not spring from worship is brutality; but the sort of making which does not spring from worship of reality is a sham. If you romanticize the harshness of reality, you hitch your waggon to a tinsel star; you may deceive yourself all your life long, you may find pleasure which will pass muster as happiness; but sooner or later reality will obtrude itself, and the whole fabric will dissolve, and perhaps it will be too late then to build again with solid bricks and stones. We are not children in a feckless limbo but men and women in a world of travail, where loveliness is flecked with sorrow, and ecstasy is often begotten of pain; and we can be lovers and makers only when our hearts have been battered and broken on reality, and so have learnt to make our whole life a whisper of worship like the murmur of the sea.

Love, like prayer, has its moments of ecstasy; but it is made up not of these but of the simplicities, the common joys and burdens, of every day. It is a long and laborious process, though its drudgeries are suffused with joy. We are led to it because of our incompleteness, because the heart is a hunger, because we are always seeking for fulfilment of body, mind and will. Man and woman complete one another, but the demands of passion will not always coincide: there is the labour and sometimes the agony of approaching, touching, entering, another mind, there is the long labour of forging the unity of the deep personal will. We live in a world where the realities of love are often obscured, for love itself is largely disintegrated into lust and sentiment. In a world that is grasping, greedy, self-seeking, the reality of worship needs to be explained to us. In a world that speaks of love as a romanticized passion, we need to be shown the labour it involves.

The young especially need to be told that love is not a glamorous fairy tale, but a life-work which involves all the patient toil that no great life-work, no great art, can avoid.

But they need to be told, too, that it is a divine destiny, which the life of God within us can make both easier and more glorious.

They need to be told that in order to open their eyes and hearts, God may lead them near to heartbreak; but they need to be told, too, of the deep abiding happiness and the moments of dazzling glory, of the joys that will come to them, not in the next world only when their troubles are over, but in this world too.

They need to be told of the greatness of the love of man and woman as ministers of God's omnipotence, as makers with God of what will not pass away. They need to be told to expect failures and misunderstandings, for the perfect work is not made in a day; but they need to be told, too, that the failures need never be final but, on the contrary, like every evil, can be made the material of a deeper awareness and a more perfect love.

They need to be told that there may be times when they will cry their eyes out with fright or with sorrow; but they need to be told, too, that there will be times when they will cry their eyes out for joy. They need to be told not to be afraid of idolatry or of God's rivalry provided they love Him faithfully; for their love is His will and their worship of Him, and is only deepened and strengthened by their prayer if they pray, as they should, hand in hand.

You want to be a maker, and you cannot make unless you have learnt to love; but if you are a lover, then indeed you are inescapably a maker, for loving is itself making. By their love the two are made one; the long, laborious process is itself happiness because it is the making of life; the daily sharing of joys and burdens, of work and play, of deepening vision and of worship — all this is love-making, and making of love is the making of life. But love is endlessly self-diffusive: the two are made one most completely in and through their common making of the family; and the family in its turn, if it is living in love, will not rest in a private, enclosed beatitude, but will shed its light and warmth in an ever-widening arc of love and service upon the world.

The love of humanity can be romanticized as the love of man and woman can be romanticized: it is possible to feel sentimentally devoted to humanity and to hate and despise men and women. But the family that is living in love will be one of those lovely homes where the doors seem always to be open and the rooms always full — full of all sorts of oddities as well as all sorts of loveliness, full of the waifs and strays of society as well as the immediate circle of friends, full because you find there at all times the unassuming glory of charity, which is love and reverence for every human being and the warmth and welcome of home.

It is with our love as with our material possessions and all our gifts: we are only stewards. The love that is given us is meant to serve others besides ourselves; it is meant to lead us to the labour of helping to heal humanity and the stricken world. Here, above all, it is a terrible thing to bury our talent in a napkin. It is Love that mediates and makes atonement between God and men. If you are given the gift of love, it is not least in order that you, too, may mediate. Love is power; to love in God is to love in the power of God and to act with the power of God; if you are faithful to the love and the power, you will mediate because you will bear God's blessing and holiness to the world and so help restore it to Him; you will help to bring back creation to its fullest in the life of man, and the life of man and the world together to its fullness in the infinity of the life of God.

But the wicket swings "between the Unseen and Seen." Human love can be doubly our teacher: it can lead us to the threshold of God's throne, and then returning filled with His life it can illuminate the world for us, teach us to love the whole of God's handiwork and so to heal and strengthen and console. But the wicket swings; there is an imperiousness and a power to absorb us in this love of another human being which may lead us to refuse the double lesson. We may want to say, "This is all, and everything else a distraction"; or we want to say, "Later I will worship, but not now." There were some in the Gospel parable who would not come to the banquet because of their business concerns — they were the men of power, condemned to remain alone. But there was another who had married a wife. . . .

This is the greatest tragedy: when two who are one, who have been reborn in one another, who have, therefore, gone infinitely beyond the empty unreality of the man who remains alone, and stand as it were at the gates of paradise, nevertheless turn away — because they, too, have great possessions. This is the greatest tragedy: that you can repeat in company with another the lonely disintegration of the primal sin; that even though you are living in love you can turn away from Love. And then the original disruption is repeated: just as pride tears man from God and robs his nature of its wholeness, so this pride, too, tears love from its eternity and robs it even of its temporary wholeness.

Is this last untrue? Because the wicket shuts against the Infinite must love become intemperate? No, it can be temperate, it can worship, it can be irreproachable — but can it be these things except at the expense of something else? In one of two ways I think it must fail of perfect wholeness. It can be temperate at the expense of depth, it can be temperate because the horizon is foreshortened, the mystery reduced to clear and distinct proportions with which reason can be competent to deal; perhaps we are back in the eighteenth century? Or, like the great Romantics, it can cling to the depth and the mystery; it can cling to the immensity of living in love, and then, though like them it will have its liturgy of worship, I wonder whether the forces it unleashes will not be sometimes beyond its control. Apollo or Dionysius: it must invoke the one or the other; yet we can follow neither alone if we want reality, for each is only a fragment of the whole.

The love of the one we love can lead us to the love of the One, though our way is surer if we have first seen Him and learnt to live in eternity and then are given His gift of human love. It remains to turn, or to turn again, to the many; and the love of God gives us the power, the love of man gives us the experience of the pattern; we should not now treat things as means. How can you help thinking when you see a society in which human beings are treated as "hands" or political units that it must be a society which has forgotten how to love? How can you help thinking when you see a society in which there is much lust and a welter of sentiment that it must be a society which has destroyed love? And if so, then why bother to make blueprints for a world society — the first thing is to rebuild the home. We are all a family. You cannot build a world society by reason alone; imagine a home which was run by reason alone — it would be not a home but a hell. We shall not be rid of injustice and hatred and war until we have learnt how to love. It is so obvious that it seems a platitude; but we forget that to love is to say, "It is thyself"; to love is to reverence and worship, to be temperate and tender.

But am I really expected to love every one and everything like this? Am I really expected to reverence and worship the washerwoman, the dustman, the man who brings the milk? Yes, you are; and the mongrel dog and the stray cat, too. But you are expected to love them, not to be sentimental. If you have seen worship interpreted in terms of simpering statues with little lace frills, if you have seen brotherhood interpreted in terms of oily smirks and the sort of conversation that is kind to be cruel, if you have seen temperateness interpreted in terms of a mealy-mouthed horror at the joys and realities of life, then, indeed, you might well recoil.

But only look at the opposite of worship and reverence, look at the opposite of the temperate and the tender. You have seen a thing in these days whereby the whole world is degraded and the whole race of man; you have seen two million Jews torn from their homes, transported, massacred. No need to idealize them, no need to romanticize; some of them no doubt were great and noble, many were charming, but many also were no doubt unattractive and perhaps repulsive, the sort of man or woman you might avoid in the street. But they were human beings. They were human beings, each unique and with a sort of infinity about them, each capable of sharing the life of God.

And now look at your own life and your own surroundings. You may have authority over many, you may be in an exalted position, you may be counted among the great, and there is no need to sentimentalize and so embarrass other people. But if ever you use your authority to treat men as featureless units, your position to look through people as though they were not there, if ever your greatness induces you to think of the failures as beneath contempt, then you are doing to them what was done to these Jews. There is a difference of degree, not of kind.

If you treat men as units, you treat them as cattle. Humility is not maudlin; it is only truth. Our Lord did not hesitate to call evil men (and they were evil because they were proud) a brood of vipers; the saints have not been accustomed to mince their words; but beneath the evil there is still the uniqueness and the infinity, and it is this, you find, that the saints will never forget. We take our sides in the struggle of good with evil; but if we fight for good, we labour to love and to heal. Even where there is obvious wickedness, we must protect and fight against the external crime, indeed, but we may never judge of sin because we can never know the human heart. There was one woman who was thought wicked, and men were preparing to stone her; but our Lord who did know the heart sent her away in peace. Perhaps she is now high in glory.

Our task is to love and to heal and so to follow remotely in His footsteps. But you cannot love without reverence; you cannot heal unless you are tender — for it is loneliness that we have to heal.

And the dog and the cat? They too are our responsibility. In Rome, there is a little forum which used to be a sort of home for stray cats; the pomp and tinsel efficiency of Fascism have long since swept them away. On the other hand, there are some who would pass unmoved by a starving beggar, but are white with fury if they see an animal insufficiently cared for. Temperateness gives us, among other things, proportion: sentimentality becomes most outrageous when passion, which should be fulfilled in the love of human beings, is driven underground and repressed. We must put things in their right order.

In the beginning, God planted a garden. We cannot return to it, but we can do something to recover what was lost. We come from the Good, who is our home; but we come into evil, for "there passed away a glory from the earth"; we have to try with toil and tears to make our way back, and the way back is the way of love and worship. All our life is meant to be that: the love and worship of the one we love and the many we love and the earth we love, within the love and worship of the God who is Love. And if we try to keep to that way, we shall do more than receive the healing power of God into ourselves: we shall walk not alone but together with these others we love, helped and helping; and as we come gradually nearer to God, our love will deepen and widen and grow stronger, we shall share more and more in Christ's healing love and power, and so, because our lives in themselves will be an affirmation of the reality to be restored, we shall be among the company of those who lead humanity and the whole earth back, a family, to its home.

PART

II

THE FRENCH INFLUENCE

THE influence of French thought upon the English has been very considerable ever since the Norman Conquest. The historical interlinking of the two nations had its constant reflex in the literary sphere up to the time of the Reformation in England. For almost a century after that event the influence of France was negligible. When it revived, however, in the seventeenth century and grew during the eighteenth, it was not only the skepticism of Montaigne and the large laughter of Rabelais which were reflected in England. Pascal's *Penseés* were translated by Bishop Kennett and the lucid works of Fénelon were read and admired by Anglican divines. It is true that Pascal and Fénelon were popular, more often than not, because they were considered rebels against "popish pretension." Their works did have a definite influence on English writers as is clear from a critical study of the sources of Pope's *Essay on Man.* In the nineteenth century the French influence widened and is seen at its best and worst in such authors as Ruskin, Wilde, Pater, Swinburne, and Dowson.

With the rebirth of Catholic letters in England, the Catholic Movement was largely affected by French writers. The French influence, never wholly divorced from either mysticism or true doctrine, aided greatly in the reappraisal of reformation history. Catholic poets and novelists achieved a new distillation in their work through their acquaintance with Huysmans, Rimbaud, Laforgue, and Baudelaire. That acquaintance deepened with the appearance of Claudel, Bazin, Bloy, Maritain, and Gilson.

There is still one aspect of the French influence which has been too little appreciated in both England and America. It is the Catholic Movement in poetry which owes its present ideo-realism to Baudelaire and his followers. Only a generation ago the very name of Baudelaire was heard with suspicion in Catholic circles. A surface view of the *Flowers of Evil* made it convenient for Catholic critics to forget Baudelaire. When they remembered his name at all it was to lash at him with disapproving phrases, or to attach to him the term hedonist. There is a type of hedonism, however, which, in the mercy of God, produces something closely akin to sanctity. In a sense those who love and serve unintegrated beauty may be said to arrive at upside-down holiness. From the very brink of hell they are enabled to look up to paradise with the longing of Dives. Because they also, and at the same time, look down into the deeps of the nether horror, seership descends upon them whenever they examine the world and the works of man.

Such was Baudelaire. During that part of the nineteenth century in which he lived and exerted his greatest influence, English poetry showed a tendency toward becoming an end in itself. In the early part of the century Wordsworth and the Lake Poets set up a sort of Pan-literaryism. By the end of the century, poets like Tennyson and Browning were more than half prepared for the belief that through the mercy of evolution, the time was ripe to substitute poetry and art for religion. While the major poets of the nineteenth century were, unconsciously, preparing to do away with God and religion, Baudelaire was building, in France, the first flimsy sticks of a bridge which was to cross both temptations.

With green, dyed hair and hollow eyes he walked the French salons, galvanizing the disintegrated world with a mad laugh. He, too, went to beauty, but he went with a sword. He tore aside the veils in the glittering temples of Astarte, revealing no naked beauty except the naked beauty of the last horror. In the agonies of the *Flowers of Evil* his friends and followers found the first living materials and the humble wisdom for recreating French poetry in the pattern of traditionalist thought. On the surface the enlightenment went on; underneath decay proceeded apace, but the voice of Baudelaire was not stilled; an echo crying aloud for God and spirit became a living voice in Rimbaud's *Bateau Ivre* and *Saison en Enfer*. It was as if an ivory boat proceeded through the flaming beauties of imagination and distance, and though, indeed, no hound of heaven followed on the shore, it was only because God walked the vertiginous canyons or the waters of the sea-wide eternities.

The influence of Baudelaire and his followers has been enormous. In France it sounded the note for Huysmans and Claudel, its echoes in England provided both the gold and the scorpions for such writers as Swinburne, Pater, Wilde, and Dowson. Today it is clear to those historians of literature with even the least sensibility that Baudelaire and his followers were true precursors of the full return to traditionalist thought. They provided the arsenal for the reduction to absurdity of the eccentric poses of both the liberals and materialists. They took poetry out of her literary prison and returned her to life. They provided also the humble beginnings of that ardent spirituality and passionate conviction which makes it possible for men like Bloy and Claudel and Maritain to speak to our age in its own tongue; a tongue which tells, only too clearly, both the old that stands and the new that recreates itself.

As the sun's strength so
Strives in all strength, glows in all glow
Of the earth that wits not, and man thereon.

CHARLES BAUDELAIRE

(*1821–1867*)

BY THE middle of the nineteenth century the enlightenment seemed successful in France. Taine, Renan, and their followers had established a materialism complete and triumphant. The soul had expired: science and knowledge were to carry man toward a new dawn of life and love. Then Charles Baudelaire appeared on the scene.

He had been born in 1821 of distinguished parents. A voyage to the East Indies had inflamed his imagination. He might have been a happy poet had his mother not contracted a second marriage. Inordinately attached to her as he was, Baudelaire hated his new father and looked upon the marriage with the eye of a Hamlet. His life became a long attempt to shock the world, but opium and moral depravity brought no surcease. In the literary world Baudelaire cultivated a glacial dandyism which had brought him notoriety if not repute. Some of his early poems were published in *Revue des Deux Mondes*.

The collected works of Edgar Allan Poe were a powerful influence on Baudelaire. In them he found a mirror of his own mind and theories. Out of gratitude he made a splendid translation of Poe, 1856–1865, and in his diary elevated Poe to a plane which, up to that time, had been occupied by God and his old nurse, Marianne.

Les Fleurs du Mal, Baudelaire's great book of poems, appeared in 1857. Its publication occasioned a scandal. The police seized the edition and it was not allowed to appear until it had been expurgated.

Baudelaire continued on his shocking course. His *Little Prose Poems,* which begot a new movement in French literature, were well received. They contained no "new shudder." Stimulating his jaded senses with drugs and moral degradation Baudelaire at last sank into madness and died, 1867.

No completely adequate translation of his works has yet appeared. Arthur Symon's translation, as T. S. Eliot has pointed out, is a Swinburnian superficiality which contains little or nothing of Baudelaire's depth or anguish of heart.

Les Fleurs du Mal created modern French poetry. It became the bible of the Symbolists, and the *Little Poems In Prose* gave the movement new rhythms which broke the primacy of the Alexandrine and made modern French poetry the rich music which it is today.

Baudelaire did more than this. His poems follow in the true line that stems from Villon. They are basically spiritual and far from being satanic in character, except for a few which are theatrical and fleshy, they do a good work in exposing the incompleteness and hollow shams of a purely materialistic world, which in its blind progress from the countinghouse to the factory, from the bar and the night club to the bordello and the unhappy home, sees only rotten death as the end of all.

The bourgeois conception of life, even in its idea of religion as a pleasing and necessary formalism, buttresses the materialistic thesis. It kills the spiritual and abolishes the mystic. Over this stifling conception of the end of man flow the scoriac measures of Baudelaire, burying it as deep as Pompeii. Baudelaire is on the side of the angels, an apostle of immortality.

His poems are personalized messages. He does not ask his readers to escape into an imaginary world where characters from history or literature posture in the grand manner. The world he draws is our world of sin, tears, anguish, and death. Above its horror, however, glitters a rainbow of the spirit world which like "the desire of the moth for the star" bespeaks our true destiny and end.

THE FANG*

No man that's worthy of the name
But in his helpless heart alive
Harbours a yellow, talkative
Serpent, he cannot hush nor tame.

Gaze if you like into the eyes
Of dryads . . . Just before you drown,
The Fang says, "You've a date in town."

Beget your children, plant your trees,
Chisel your marble, build your song. . . .
The Fang says, "Well, — it's not for long."

Hope — if you're hopeful — or despair;
Nothing's to hinder you; but hark! —
Always the hissing head is there,
The insupportable remark.

— Edna St. Vincent Millay

*The above and following poems are taken from
Flowers of Evil (New York: Harper and Brothers, 1936).

THE ANGELIC ONE

Spirit of happiness, hast thou heard tell of woe?
Hast thou heard tell of anguish, and remorse, and care —
Of those long nights when in the black fist of Despair
The heart is crumpled up like paper? Dost thou know,
Spirit of happiness? Hast thou heard tell of woe?

Spirit of kindliness, hast thou heard tell of hate,
The clenched hands in the darkness, the silent bitter tears,
With Vengeance beating in the arteries of our ears
Its dogged tom-tom, irresistible as fate?
Spirit of kindliness, hast thou heard tell of hate?

Spirit of health, hast thou heard whisper of Disease,
Whose pallid children, in the courtyard grey with soot
Of the bleak hospital, go dragging a slow foot
To find a patch of sunlight? Hast thou heard of these?
Spirit of health, has thou heard whisper of Disease?

Spirit of beauty, hast thou heard of ugliness,
Of the long secret torment of growing old — above
All else, the pain of reading in the eyes we love
A wordless horror, even while the lips say "yes"?
Spirit of beauty, hast thou heard of ugliness?

Spirit of joy, spirit of beauty, spirit of light,
David, grown old, would have thought nothing to implore
Thy healing touch, thy warm young presence in the night;
But, spirit, I only ask of thee thy prayers, no more —
Spirit of joy, spirit of beauty, spirit of light!

— George Dillon

LANDSCAPE

I want to write a book of chaste and simple verse,
Sleep in an attic, like the old astrologers,
Up near the sky, and hear upon the morning air
The tolling of the bells. I want to sit and stare,
My chin in my two hands, out on the humming shops,
The weathervanes, the chimneys, and the steepletops
That rise like masts above the city, straight and tall,
And the mysterious big heavens over all.

I want to watch the blue mist of the night come on,
The windows and the stars illumined, one by one,
The rivers of dark smoke pour upward lazily,
And the moon rise and turn them silver. I shall see
The springs, the summers, and the autumns slowly pass;
And when old Winter puts his blank face to the glass,
I shall close all my shutters, pull the curtains tight,
And build me stately palaces by candlelight.

And I shall dream of luxuries beyond surmise,
Gardens that are a stairway into azure skies,
Fountains that weep in alabaster, birds that sing
All day — of every childish and idyllic thing.
A revolution thundering in the street below
Will never lure me from my task, I shall be so
Lost in that quiet ecstasy, the keenest still,
Of calling back the springtime at my own free will,
Of feeling a sun rise within me, fierce and hot,
And make a whole bright landscape of my burning thought.

— George Dillon

DE PROFUNDIS CLAMAVI

I do implore thy pity, Thou whom alone I love,
Deep in this mournful vale wherein my heart is fallen.
It is a world completely sad, where the low sullen
Skies seem about to rain pure horror from above.

A fireless sun swims over six months of every year;
Six months of every year the earth is lost in shadow.
It is a bleaker land than any Arctic meadow:
Nor streams, nor flowers, nor fruits, nor birds, nor forest here!

Surely there is no evil imaginable to compare
With the cruelty of that cold sun in the cold air
And that enormous night, like the first chaos of things;

I envy the very animals, to whom slumber brings
Over and over the gift of being thoughtless and blind,
So slowly does the thread of these dark years unwind.

— George Dillon

INTOXICATION*

ONE must be for ever drunken: that is the sole question of importance. If you would not feel the horrible burden of Time that bruises your shoulders and bends you to the earth, you must be drunken without cease. But how? With wine, with poetry, with virtue, with what you please. But be drunken. And if sometimes, on the steps of a palace, on the green grass by a moat, or in the dull loneliness of your chamber, you should waken up, your intoxication already lessened or gone, ask of the wind, of the wave, of the star, of the bird, of the time-piece; ask of all that flees, all that sighs, all that revolves, all that sings, all that speaks, ask of these the hour; and wind and wave and star and bird and timepiece will answer you: "It is the hour to be drunken! Lest you be the martyred slaves of Time, intoxicate yourselves, be drunken without cease! With wine, with poetry, with virtue, or with what you will."

*The above and following selections are from *The Poems and Prose Poems of Charles Baudelaire* (New York: Brentano's, 1919).

THE CONFITEOR OF THE ARTIST

HOW penetrating is the end of an autumn day! Ah, yes, penetrating enough to be painful even; for there are certain delicious sensations whose vagueness does not prevent them from being intense; and none more keen than the perception of the Infinite. He has a great delight who drowns his gaze in the immensity of sky and sea. Solitude, silence, the incomparable chastity of the azure — a little sail trembling upon the horizon, by its very littleness and isolation imitating my irremediable existence — the melodious monotone of the surge — all these things thinking through me and I through them (for in the grandeur of the reverie the Ego is swiftly lost); they think, I say, but musically and picturesquely, without quibbles, without syllogisms, without deductions.

These thoughts, as they arise in me or spring forth from external objects, soon become always too intense. The energy working within pleasure creates an uneasiness, a positive suffering. My nerves are too tense to give other than clamouring and dolorous vibrations.

THE MARKSMAN

AS THE carriage traversed the wood he bade the driver draw up in the neighborhood of a shooting gallery, saying that he would like to have a few shots to kill time. Is not the slaying of the monster Time the most ordinary and legitimate occupation of man? — So he gallantly offered his hand to his dear, adorable, and execrable wife; the mysterious woman to whom he owed so many pleasures, so many pains, and perhaps also a great part of his genius.

Several bullets went wide of the proposed mark, one of them flew far into the heavens, and as the charming creature laughted deliriously, mocking the clumsiness of her husband, he turned to her brusquely and said: "Observe that doll yonder, to the right, with its nose in the air, and with so haughty an appearance. Very well, dear angel, I will imagine to myself that it is you!"

He closed both eyes and pulled the trigger. The doll was neatly decapitated.

Then, bending towards his dear, adorable, and execrable wife, his inevitable and pitiless muse, he kissed her respectfully upon the hand, and added, "Ah, dear angel, how I thank you for my skill!"

AT ONE O'CLOCK IN THE MORNING

ALONE at last! Nothing is to be heard but the rattle of a few tardy and tired-out cabs. There will be silence now, if not repose, for several hours at least. At last the tyranny of the human face has disappeared — I shall not suffer except alone. At last it is permitted me to refresh myself in a bath of shadows. But first a double turn of the key in the lock. It seems to me that this turn of the key will deepen my solitude and strengthen the barriers which actually separate me from the world.

A horrible life and a horrible city! Let us run over the events of the day. I have seen several literary men; one of them wished to know if he could get to Russia by land (he seemed to have an idea that Russia was a island); I have disputed generously enough with the editor of a review, who to each objection replied: "We take the part of respectable people," which implies that every other paper but his own is edited by a knave; I have saluted some twenty people, fifteen of them unknown to me; and shaken hands with a like number, without having taken the precaution of first buying gloves; I have been driven to kill time, during a shower, with a mountebank, who wanted me to design for her a costume as Venusta; I have made my bow to a theatre manager, who said: "You will do well, perhaps, to interview Z; he is the heaviest, foolishest, and most celebrated of all my authors; with him perhaps you will be able to come to something. See him, and then we'll see." I have boasted (why?) of several villainous deeds I never committed, and indignantly denied certain shameful things I accomplished with joy, certain misdeeds of fanfaronade, crimes of human respect; I have refused an easy favour to a friend and given a written recommendation to a perfect fool. Heavens! it's well ended.

Discontented with myself and with everything and everybody else, I should be glad enough to redeem myself and regain my self-respect in the silence and solitude.

Souls of those whom I have loved, whom I have sung, fortify me; sustain me; drive away the lies and the corrupting vapours of this world; and Thou, Lord my God, accord me so much grace as shall produce some beautiful verse to prove to myself that I am not the least of men, that I am not inferior to those I despise.

ALREADY!

A HUNDRED times already the sun had leaped, radiant or saddened, from the immense cup of the sea whose rim could scarcely be seen; a hundred times it had again sunk, glittering or morose, into its mighty bath of twilight. For many days we had contemplated the other side of the firmament, and deciphered the celestial alphabet of the antipodes. And each of the passengers sighed and complained. One had said that the approach of land only exasperated their sufferings. "When, then," they said, "shall we cease to sleep a sleep broken by the surge, troubled by a wind that snores louder than we? When shall we be able to eat at an unmoving table?"

There were those who thought of their own firesides, who regretted their sullen, faithless wives, and their noisy progeny. All so doted upon the image of the absent land, that I believe they would have eaten grass with as much enthusiasm as the beasts.

At length a coast was signalled, and on approaching we saw a magnificent and dazzling land. It seemed as though the music of life flowed therefrom in a vague murmur, and the banks, rich with all kinds of growths, breathed, for leagues around, a delicious odour of flowers and fruits.

Each one therefore was joyful; his evil humour left him. Quarrels were forgotten, reciprocal wrongs forgiven, the thought of duels was blotted out of the memory, and rancour fled away like smoke.

I alone was sad, inconceivably sad. Like a priest from whom one has torn his divinity, I could not, without heartbreaking bitterness, leave this so monstrously seductive ocean, this sea so infinitely various in its terrifying simplicity, which seemed to contain in itself and represent by its joys, and attractions, and angers, and smiles, the moods and agonies and ecstasies of all souls that have lived, that live, and that shall yet live.

In saying good-bye to this incomparable beauty I felt as though I had been smitten to death; and that is why when each of my companions said: "At last!" I could only cry "Already!"

Here meanwhile was the land, the land with its noises, its passions, its commodities, its festivals: a land rich and magnificent, full of promises, that sent to us a mysterious perfume of rose and musk, and from whence the music of life flowed in an amorous murmuring.

PAUL VERLAINE
(1844–1896)

PAUL VERLAINE was born at Metz, March 30, 1844. He was the only child of his parents and was consequently spoiled and very carefully brought up. He was educated at the Laudry Institute and the Lycée Bonaparte. He took his bachelor of letters degree in 1862. After taking this degree he worked for the Paris Insurance Company, and later was a clerk in the Hotel de Ville. He joined the Parnassian group and at 22 published his first book of verse, *Poèmes Saturniens.* These poems reveal the influence of Baudelaire but they also clearly indicate Verlaine's feeling for word harmonies which became the source of his enduring fame.

His married life was of short duration. Under the spell of his own instability, drink, and his friendship with Arthur Rimbaud, Verlaine became a tramp and a wanderer. When Rimbaud forsook the unsavory friendship, Verlaine returned for a time to the Church. During this period of sanity and quiet he published his best and perhaps only fully Catholic work, *Sagesse,* 1881.

He was not long at peace. Through drink and evil living his life became a fabric of misery. In the midst of the cold of winter and the deeper cold of abandonment, Verlaine died January 8, 1896.

Except for *Sagesse* and *Romance sans Paroles,* his poems are distinguished for their delicate paganism. As a master of words, however, he has few equals in French poetry. Those of his verses which deal with his faith overflow with tenderness and simplicity.

FROM SAGESSE*

I

The little hands that once were mine,
The hands I loved, the lovely hands,
After the roadways and the strands,
And realms and kingdoms once divine,

And mortal loss of all that seems
Lost with the old sad pagan things
Royal as in the days of kings
The dear hands open to my dreams.

Hands of dream, hands of holy flame
Upon my soul in blessing laid,
What is it that these hands have said
That my soul hears and swoons to them?

*The above and following poem are selected from *Modern Book of French Verse* (New York: Boni and Liveright, 1920).

Is it a phantom, this pure sight
Of mother's love made tenderer,
Of spirit with spirit linked to share
The mutual kinship of delight?

Good sorrow, dear remorse, and ye,
Blest dreams, O hands ordained of heaven
To tell me if I am forgiven
Make but the sign that pardons me!

—Arthur Symons

II

O My God, thou hast wounded me with love
Behold the wound that's still vibrating,
O my God, thou hast wounded me with love.

O my God, thy fear has fallen upon me,
Behold the burn is there, and it throbs aloud,
O my God, thy fear has fallen upon me.

O my God, I have known that all is vile
And that thy glory hath stationed itself in me
O my God, I have known that all is vile.

Drown my soul in floods, floods of thy wine,
Mingle my life with the body of thy bread
Drown my soul in flood, floods of thy wine.

Take my blood that I have not poured out,
Take my flesh unworthy of suffering,
Take my blood that I have not poured out.

Take my brow, that has only learned to blush
To be the footstool of thine adorable feet
Take my brow, that has only learned to blush.

Take my hands, because they have laboured
     not
For coals of fire and for rare frankincense,

Take my hands, because they have laboured
     not.

Take my heart that has beaten for vain
     things,
To throb under the thorn of Calvary,
Take my heart that has beaten for vain
     things.

Take my feet, frivolous travelers,
That they may run to the crying of thy grace,
Take my feet, frivolous travelers.

Take my voice, a harsh and lying noise,
For the reproaches of thy Penitence,
Take my voice, a harsh and lying noise.

Take mine eyes, luminaries of deceit,
That they may be extinguished in the tears of
     prayer,
Take mine eyes, luminaries of deceit.

Alas, thou, God of pardon and promises,
What is the pit of mine ingratitude,
Alas, thou, God of pardon and promises.

God of terror and God of holiness,
Alas, my sinfulness is a black abyss,
God of terror and God of holiness.

Thou God of peace, of joy and delight
All my tears, all my ignorances,
Thou God of peace, of joy and delight.

Thou, O God, knowest all this, all this,
How poor I am, poorer than any man,
Thou, O God, knowest all this, all this.

And what I have, my God, I give to thee.

— Arthur Symons

WHAT HAVE YOU DONE ?*

The sky above the roof,
Is so blue and so calm
The tree above the roof
Cradles its palm.

The bell in the sky we watch
Quietly rings;

A bird on the tree we watch,
Mournfully sings.

Lord, O Lord, life is here
Gently fluttering down
That peaceful stir we hear
Comes from the town.

What have you done, you there
Endlessly weeping; in sooth
What have you done, you there,
With your youth?

*The above and following poem are selected from
Modern French Poetry, An Anthology, translated by
Joseph T. Shipley, (New York: Greenberg Publishers).

AUTUMN SONG

The heavy thrall
Of the sobbing call
Of the fall
Weighs, nor departs,
Like my heart's
Pall

Overcome
And dumb
As the hours creep

I see the haze
Of olden days
And weep.

And I go away
The winds prey,
In barren, brief
Whirl hither and yon
Like a wan
Dead leaf.

SON THOU MUST LOVE ME*

"Son, thou must love me! See — " my Saviour said,
"My heart that glows and bleeds, my wounded side,
My hurt feet that the Magdalene, wet-eyed,
Clasps kneeling, and my tortured arms outspread

"To bear thy sins. Look on the cross, stained red!
The nails, the sponge, that, all, thy soul shall guide

To love on earth where flesh thrones in its pride,
My Body and Blood alone, thy Wine and Bread.

"Have I not loved thee even unto death,
O brother mine, son in the Holy Ghost?
Have I not suffered, as was writ I must,

"And with thine agony sobbed out my breath?
Hath not thy nightly sweat bedewed my brow,
O lamentable friend that seeks me now?"

*The above and following poems have been selected from: *Poems of Paul Verlaine*, translated by Gertrude Hall (Chicago: Stone and Kimbal, 1895).

GIVE EAR UNTO THE GENTLE LAY

It says how glorious to be
Like children, without more delay,
The tender gladness it doth say
Of peace not bought with victory.

Accept the voice, — ah, hear the whole
Of its persistent, artless strain:

Naught so can soothe a soul's own pain,
As making glad another soul!

It pines in bonds but for a day,
The soul that without murmur bears. . . .
How unperplexed, how free it fares!
Oh, listen to the gentle lay!

I'VE SEEN AGAIN

I've seen again the One child: verily,
I felt the last wound open in my breast,
The last, whose perfect torture doth attest
That on some happy day I too shall die!

Good icy arrow, piercing thoroughly!
Most timely came it from their dreams to wrest
The sluggish scruples laid too long to rest, —
And all my Christian blood hymned fervently.

I still hear; still I see! O worshipped rule
Of God! I know at last how comfortful
To hear and see! I see, I hear always!

O innocence, O hope! Lowly and mild,
How I shall love you, sweet hands of my
    child,
Whose task shall be to close our eyes one day!

ARTHUR RIMBAUD
(1854–1891)

THE life of Arthur Rimbaud is an amazing chronicle. He was born at Charleville in the Ardennes, October 20, 1854. His father was an Infantry captain, his mother a determined woman of the bourgeois class. Arthur was a pious, docile child but extremely intelligent. His mother created in him her will to dominate and his school years were a procession of prizes. In the heat of full adolescence he suddenly revealed a flair for creating glittering but realistic poetry. Secretly he was smothered by the provincial atmosphere and the pious platitudes of his class and town. In 1870 he ran away to Paris twice, and in 1871 he met the poet Verlaine in the City of Light. The insane individualism of Rimbaud completely captured Verlaine. He left his wife and in contempt of the public the two friends began a life of vagabondage in France, England, and Belgium. It was a short life. After two years, which were alternately a time of creative thought and debauched living, Rimbaud decided to free himself. Verlaine, angered at the desertion, shot Rimbaud as he was preparing to leave Brussels. Verlaine went to prison, Rimbaud returned to his mother's house.

Though the two years of Rimbaud's association with Verlaine had produced his greatest poems, *Illuminations,* Rimbaud analyzed this madness of creation in the unforgettable lines of his *Saison en Enfer,* 1873. Rimbaud also completely turned his back on literature and after an adventurous career on the Continent became a gun runner and a trader in Abyssinia, 1880–1891. Stricken by a horrible malady, he returned to Marseilles to die. Within sight of death he returned to the Church. Fortified with the sacraments and flooded with the joy of his return to peace with God, Rimbaud died November 10, 1891.

His early poems were distinctive but derivative. In *Illuminations* and *Saison en Enfer,* however, he broke the ground for a new type of poetry which concerned itself with interior states rather than with words and the outer world. The excellence of these works lies not alone in their psychological acuity and imaginative brilliance but chiefly, for us, in their spiritual overtones and in the confused hunger they display for spiritual reality and simplicity. Truly Rimbaud is, like Baudelaire, the ancestor of Claudel and Jammes as well as the father of modern poetry. His blasphemy of God and his hatred of religion stemmed from his confusion of mind and his defective religious training. Behind the gamin face he showed the world, his soul agonized and thirsted for the serene and the beautiful.

Paul Claudel's introduction to Rimbaud's collected works is an excellent study of the man. A competent English account of his worth may be found in Bernard Fäy's *Since Victor Hugo* — Boston: Little Brown and Co., 1927.

MYSTIC*

ON THE slope of the knoll angels whirl their woolen robes in pastures of emerald and steel.

From the meadows flames leap up to the summit of the little hill. At the left, the mould is trampled by all the homicides and all the battles, and all the disastrous noises

describe their curve. Behind the right-hand ridge the line of Orients and of progress.

And while the band at the top of the picture is formed of the revolving and rushing hum of seashells and of human nights,

The following sweetness of the stars, and of the night, and all the rest, descends opposite the knoll like a basket before our face, and makes the abyss perfumed and blue below.

*The above and following three poems have been selected from: *Prose Poems From The Illuminations,* by Arthur Rimbaud, translated by Louise Varese (Norfolk, Conn.: New Directions Press, 1946).

FLOWERS

FROM golden stairs, — among silk cords, green velvets, gray gauzes, and crystal discs that turn black as bronze in the sun, I see the digitalis opening on a carpet of silver filigree, of eyes and tresses.

Yellow gold-pieces strewn over agate, ma-

hogany columns supporting emerald domes, bouquets of white satin and delicate sprays of rubies, surround the water-rose.

Like a god with huge blue eyes and limbs of snow, the sea and sky attract to the marble terraces the throng or roses, young and strong.

DAWN

I HAVE embraced the summer dawn.

Nothing yet stirred in front of the palaces. The water was dead. The shadows still camped in the woodland road. I walked, taking quick warm breaths; and gems looked on, and wings rose without a sound.

The first venture was, in a path already filled with fresh, pale glints, a flower who told me her name.

I laughed at the waterfall that tousled through the pines; on the silver summit ⁻ecognized the goddess.

Then, one by one, I lifted up her veils. In the lane, waving my arms. Across the plain, where I denounced her to the cock. To the city she fled among the steeples and the domes; running like a beggar on the marble quays, I chased her.

Far up the road near a laurel wood, I wrapped her round with her gathered veils, and I felt a little her immense form. Dawn and the child sank down at the border of the wood.

Waking, it was noon.

CHILDHOOD

I AM the saint at prayer on the terrace like beasts grazing down to the sea of Palestine.

I am the scholar of the dark armchair. Branches and rain beat against the casements of the library.

I am the pedestrian of the highroad by way of the dwarf woods; the roar of the sluices covers my steps. I see for a long time the melancholy golden wash of the setting sun.

I might well be the child abandoned on the jetty gone out to the high sea, the little farm-boy following the lane whose forehead touches the sky.

The paths are rough. The hillocks are covered with broom. The air is motionless. How far the birds and the springs are! This can only be the end of the world, going forward.

A SEASON IN HELL*

It is recovered!
What? Eternity!
It is the sun in motion
    Upon the ocean.

My eternal soul,
Observe your vow
Through the night's solitude
And the day on fire.

Thus you free yourself
Of human supports,
Of vulgar transports!
You fly thus . . .

No hope ever,
No *orietur.*
Science and patience,
The torture is sure.

No more yesterday,
Embers of satin,
Your ardor
Is Order.
It is recovered!
— What? — Eternity.
It is the sun in motion
    Upon the ocean.

I became a fabulous opera: I saw that all

beings have a fatality for happiness: action is not life, but a way of softening some power, an enervation. Morality is the weakness of the skull.

To each being, several *other* lives seemed to me to be due. This gentleman does not know what he is doing: he is an angel. This family is a litter of dogs. In front of some men, I spoke out loud with one moment of one of their other lives.

None of the sophistries of madness, — madness which shuts one up inside oneself, — have been forgotten by me: I can relate them all, I possess the system.

My health was menaced. Terror came. I fell into a sleep lasting several days, and, waking, I continued the saddest dreams. I was ripe for death, and by a route of dangers my weakness led me to the ends of the world, to Kimmeria, the fatherland of shadow and of whirlwinds.

I had to travel, to distract the magics assembled in my skull. On the sea, which I loved as if it had cleansed me of defilement, I saw the consoling Cross arise. I had been damned by the rainbow. Happiness was my fatality, my remorse, my worm; my life would always be much too immense to be devoted to power and to beauty.

Happiness! Its tooth, sweet as death, warned me at cock-crow, — *ad matutinum,* at *Christus Venit,* — in the most sombre cities:

---

*The above and following poem have been selected from *A Season In Hell,* by Arthur Rimbaud, translated by Delmore Schwartz (Norfolk, Conn.: New Directions Press).

O seasons, O castles!
What soul is faultless?

I have made the magic study
Of happiness, which none evades.

Hurrah for it each time
That the Gallic cock crows.

Ah! I shall have no more want:
It has taken charge of my life.

This charm has taken soul and flesh
And dispelled their struggles.

O seasons, O castles!

The hour of flight, alas!
Will be the hour of decease.

O seasons, O castles!

That is past. I know today how to greet beauty.

THE LIGHTNING

HUMAN toil! That is the explosion which lights up my abyss from time to time.

"Nothing is vanity; science, and forward!" cries the modern Ecclesiastes, that is to say, *Everybody*. And yet the cadavers of the wicked and slothful fall upon the hearts of the others. . . . Ah, hurry, hurry a little; down there, beyond the night, those rewards, future, everlasting . . . shall they escape us? . . .

— What can I do? I know toil; and science is too slow. Let prayers gallop and let the light roar . . . I see it clearly. It is too simple, and the weather will be too warm; they will pass me by. I have my duty, I shall show my pride in it as some others do, by putting it aside.

My life is worn out. Come! Let us make believe, let us idle, O pity! And we shall exist by our own amusement, dreaming of monstrous loves, and fantastic universes, complaining and finding fault with the appearances of the world, acrobat, beggar, artist, bandit, — priest! On my bed in the hospital, the smell of incense has returned to me so strongly: Guardian of the holy perfumes, confessor, martyr. . . .

There I recognize the filthy education of my childhood. Then, what! . . . Go my twenty years, if others go twenty years. . . .

No! No! at present I revolt against death! Work seems too trivial to my pride; my betrayal to the world would be too brief a punishment. At the last moment I would strike out right and left. . . .

Then — oh! — dear, poor soul, eternity would not be lost to us!

JORIS KARL HUYSMANS
(*1848–1907*)

ONE of the most amazingly sensitive writers of the nineteenth century, Joris Karl Huysmans, was born at Paris, February 5, 1848. Due to his sensitive nervous organization, Huysmans had a miserable childhood. At the Lycée St. Louis, Huysmans proved only an average student. For a time he contemplated law as a career, but in 1868 entered the Ministry of the Interior. From this time forward Huysmans parceled out his time between his official duties and writing.

Shortly after the appearance of his remarkable book, *Against the Grain*, Huysmans returned to the Church. Though he was by nature petulant and critical and found it difficult to tolerate fools gladly, Huysmans turned toward the spiritual life with devotedness.

In 1897 Huysmans was elected president of the Goncourt Academy, and the French government recognized his eminence by decorating him with the Legion of Honor, 1905.

Soon after his election as president of the Goncourt Academy, Huysmans retired from the Department of the Interior. Until the Benedictines were driven from France Huysmans lived with them at the Villa Notre Dame in Ligugé. With their departure he returned to Paris.

He was attacked with a malignant cancer of the throat which caused his death May 12, 1907. During his last illness, Huysmans refused all opiates which might dull his pain and bore his sufferings with truly Christian joy. He was buried in the Montparnasse Cemetery in the habit of a Benedictine Oblate.

Huysmans was a true disciple of Poe and Baudelaire. His learning was encyclopedic, his ability to express himself so wide that it overflowed the French language into the slang of Paris, the argot of gamins and beggars and the Paris underworld.

The first works of Huysmans were liberally salted with naturalistic realism and coarseness, but they are not his great works, which were to bring him lasting fame.

In *Against the Grain,* that source book of the aesthete, Huysmans revealed for the first time an interest in the Church. This experiment in the sensuous led Huysmans to develop his aesthetic doctrine in other novels: *En Route, The Oblate,* and *Down There,* an ugly study of Satanism and the black mass as practiced by sadists of his time.

The Cathedral is Huysman's greatest work. Not properly a novel but a history of the cathedral at Chartres, it sums up the glory of the Middle Ages in language sensitively exalted.

The complete works of Huysmans were published in France in 1930.

THE OBLATE*

CHAPTER VII

D URTAL shook hands with his confessor and went down the stair-way leading to the cloister. Under the arches he saw a light moving ahead of him; it was little Brother Blanche, the acolyte, with his candle. He was walking in front of Father d'Auberoche who was on his way to the church bearing relics on a tray covered with a veil. The apse was like a hive; novices were busy putting the last touch to everything, and the dimly-lit choir was black with them. Dom d'Auberoche passed, the buzzing ceased and all the novices moved aside; he laid his salver with the relics on the altar; he removed the linen cloth and, taking the brass and bronze gilt reliquaries, he put them between the candlesticks; to honour the relics and to apprise the faithful of their presence, novices lighted two gold lamps at each end of the altar. Father d'Auberoche made due obeisance to those holy remains, genuflected before the tabernacle, and retired; the Father sacristan proceeded to light the lamps and the candles. Very soon the far end of the sanctuary was one blaze of light.

An oriental carpet had been laid down, covering the altar-steps and the pavement of the choir. The altar was adorned with candles and evergreens, and on it were placed the priestly vestments of the Abbot and the two mitres, the gold mitre and the precious mitre, one on the Epistle side and the other on the Gospel side.

The choir was draped with white, fringed hangings and on the left, with three steps leading up to it, stood the Abbot's throne. The seat of red velvet, with a canopy overhead, stood out in relief against the white drapery; behind the throne was the Abbot's

*Huysmans, Joris Karl, *The Oblate,* pp. 128–138. Translated by Edward Perceval, published and copyrighted 1924, by E. P. Dutton and Co., Inc., New York.

coat of arms painted on a board. The Abbot's usual seat, somewhat in front of the monks' stalls, was covered with red velvet with a gold fringe, like the throne; there was also a prie-dieu, covered with green baize, placed before the altar.

"Oh, oh!" said Durtal to himself, "the Smyrna carpet and the green prie-dieu are always the signs of a first-class feast!"

The bells began to ring. In single file, wearing albs and headed by the Prior, the monks now came out of the sacristy and approached the door of the church that opened on to the cloister to receive the abbot, and present him with the holy water. The nave was filling with village folk, the monk who acted as parish priest put the children in their proper places amid a loud clatter of clogs and boots. Pushing his way through the crowd, M. Lampre took his seat next to Durtal. The Most Noble Baron des Atours, with his family, also made his entry. With an air of patronage he glanced round at his menials as they made way for him; he knelt down in the front row of chairs and buried his face in his hands; but only for a moment, for soon one hand was needed to twist his stubbly moustache and the other to pat the smooth ball-like surface of his skull. The distinction of his wife was somewhat problematic, but the ugliness of his daughter painfully plain; she was not unlike her mother, but even more provincial and common-looking; as for the son, a worthy enough young man who had been brought up in the most fashionable pious schools, he remained standing, his gloved hands grasping the knob of his cane, while the other end dug its way into the rotten straw of the chair in front of him.

One felt inclined to wonder whether these people knew how to read; at any rate they had not a book among them, but, whether at Mass, or at Matins, or at Vespers, did nothing but finger their costly, silver-stringed rosaries, that made a jingling noise like that of a horse champing its bit.

Suddenly the organ burst into a triumphal march; the Abbot entered the nave, preceded by two masters of ceremonies; between them walked the crosier-bearer, wearing an alb and on his shoulders the *vimpa,* a scarf of white satin lined with cherry-coloured silk, in the ends of which he clasped the stem of the crosier. The Abbot, whose long black train was borne by a novice, gave his blessing right and left as he passed to the kneeling throng of worshippers who crossed themselves.

He knelt at the prie-dieu, and his whole court of attendants, cope-men, and religious vested in albs, likewise knelt, so that all one saw was a golden note of interrogation overlooking a field of dead moons, the crosier dominating the big white tonsures.

At a signal from Father d'Auberoche all arose and the Abbot went to his throne, on each side of which his assistant deacons took their place; whereupon the prie-dieu was removed.

The choir was full, two upper rows of stalls being occupied by the professed and the novices in their black cowls, while in the lower ones were the lay-brothers in brown cowls. Below them again, on benches, were the choir boys in bright red cassocks; and in the empty space between, limited though this was, the servers deployed with absolute precision, crosier-bearer and candle-bearer and mitre-bearer all performing their duties without the slightest hitch.

The Abbot began the Office.

As Father Felletin had foreseen, Durtal was at once fascinated by the *Invitatorium.* It was the usual Psalm, *Venite, exultemus,* summoning Christians to adore their Lord with its refrain, sometimes short, "Christ is born to us"; sometimes long, "Christ is born to us; O, come, let us worship."

This splendid psalm, with its tender half mournful melody, tells of Creation, and of God's rights; the wondrous works of God are set forth and His lament at the ingratitude of His people.

The voice of the cantors recounted measuredly His marvels: "The sea is His and He made it, and His hands prepared the dry land. O, come let us worship and fall down and kneel before the Lord, our Maker, for He is the Lord our God, and we are the people of His pasture and the sheep of His hand." Then the choir took up the refrain, "Christ is born to us, O come, let us worship."

Then, after the glorious hymn of St. Ambrose, *Christe Redemptor,* the Office proper began. It was divided into three "vigils" or nocturns, composed of psalms, lessons and responses. These nocturns had a meaning. Durandus, the thirteenth-century Bishop of Mende, explained them clearly in his *Rationale.* The first nocturn deals allegorically with the period before the Law given to Moses; and, in the Middle Ages, whilst it was sung, the altar was hidden by a black veil to symbolize the gloom of the Mosaic Law and the sentence pronounced on man in Eden. The second nocturn shows the time that elapsed since the written Law, and then the altar was hidden with a white veil because the prophecies of the Old Testament already shed a sort of furtive light on fallen mankind. The third nocturn sets forth the love of the Church and the mercies of the Comforter, and the altar was draped with purple, as emblem of the Holy Ghost and of the Blood of our Saviour.

The service proceeded with alternate psalmody and chanting. The whole was splendid, but the finest was found in the Lessons and their Responses. A monk, led by a master of ceremonies, came down from his stall and took his place at the lectern in the middle of the choir; there he chanted or recited, for it was not exactly the one nor yet the other. The tone was even, the melody slow and somewhat plaintive, sounding like a lullaby of the soul, and breaking off abruptly on a mournful note, like a tear that falls.

"Ah! Dom Felletin was right," thought Durtal. "It is a grand service for a grand night. While the old world is sinning or sleeping, the Messiah is born and the shepherds, dazzled, come to adore Him; and at the same moment those men of mystery, those dream-figures foretold long before St. Matthew by Isaiah and the Psalmist, set out from one knows not where and race on dromedaries through the night, led by a star, to adore in their turn a Child, and then to disappear along a road other than that by which they came.

"To what a mass of controversy has this star given rise! But to all the blundering hypotheses of our astronomers I prefer the view the Middle Ages borrowed from the Apocryphal Book of Seth and which we find in St. Epiphanius and in the Imperfect Commentary on St. Matthew. They thought that the Star of Bethlehem that appeared to the Magi showed the Child seated beneath a Cross in a glowing sphere and most of the early masters depict the star thus, for instance, Roger Van der Weyden, in one of the panels of his marvelous *Nativity* in the museum of Berlin."

Durtal's reflections were cut short by monks moving to and fro in the choir. The Abbot was being vested. A master of ceremonies, standing in front of the altar, removed one by one the vestments placed on it, the alb, the girdle, the stole and the cope, and handed them to novices who one after another presented them to the deacons at the throne, first bending the knee to the Abbot.

When his long black cappa had been removed and he was robed in his white alb, Dom Anthime Bernard looked taller still, as from the steps of his throne he overlooked the entire church and, after he had put on the girdle, as he moved his arm to adjust the pectoral cross, the ring on his finger sparkled in the light of the tapers. At a sign from Pere d'Auberoche the mitre-bearer, covered with a shawl similar to that of the crosier-bearer, approached the throne, and, having donned the stole and cope, the Abbot intoned the *Te Deum.*

Here Durtal was obliged to moderate his enthusiasm, for he remembered other *Te Deums* heard in the great Paris churches; he said to himself that, for instance at St. Sulpice, the hymn sounds far grander, sung to the blare of a great organ by a full choir reinforced by the whole body of the seminarists. The "Royal" *Magnificat,* also, had a majesty and a fullness lacking to the jejune and feeble settings used by Solesmes. But, indeed, to give such splendid pieces their full significance, it would need hundreds of voices, and in what monastery could one hope to find so large a choir?

His disenchantment, however, did not last long, for the Abbot, surrounded by cope-men, thurifer and candle-bearer, began to chant the genealogy of Christ from a Gospel-book held by a monk in his two hands and resting against his forehead; the strange, sad monotonous cadences seemed to evoke a procession of the Patriarchs who each at the mention of his name flashed past, and then sank back into the gloom.

When the reading was at an end and whilst the Abbot was changing his cope for a chasuble the choir sang the short hymn, Greek in origin, the *Te Decet Laus* and the Office closed with the prayer of the day and the *Benedicamus Domino.*

The four principal cantors who had gone to robe themselves in the sacristy now re-turned and Dom Ramondoux, the Precentor, had stuck in a ring near his seat surmounted by a statuette of St. Benigna the copper rod which was his sign of office.

He and the others were now seated on low-backed benches, just inside the communion rails at the entrance to the choir and op-posite the altar. Thus their coped backs were turned to the public, backs splendid in shim-mering velvet, interwoven with silver and with cherry-silk, on which the Gothic mono-grams of Christ and our Lady were em-broidered in gold.

Leaving their benches and standing in the middle of the choir, they chanted the Introit, whilst the Abbot, attended by his court, began Mass.

When they had reached the *Kyrie Eleison,* the congregation joined in, the girls and boys of the village being led by the parish-priest. The same happened at the Creed.

Durtal, for a moment, seemed to get a clear glimpse into the past, and to see and hear villagers singing the melodies of St. Gregory in the Middle Ages. Obviously such chanting was not as perfect as that at Solesmes, but it was something different. It lacked art, but it had vim; it was an out-burst, an effusion of the soul of the people, the fervour of a mob that for a moment is touched. It was as if, for a few minutes, an early Church had come to life, in which the people, throbbing in unison with its

priests, were truly taking a part in the ceremonies and praying with them and using the same tongue and the same musical dialect, and this, for this to happen in our own times seemed so utterly unlooked-for that Durtal thought that he must once more be dreaming.

Thus the Mass went on while the organ flooded the church with sound. The Abbot stood before the altar, or took his seat on the throne; he was shod and gloved in white; he was now bare-headed, then wear-ing the gold mitre and then the precious mitre all edged with gems; his hands were now clasped, now held the crosier, then re-stored it to the kneeling novice who kissed his ring. The smoke of incense hid the altar-lights and the two lamps on either side of the relics each looked like a topaz glowing in the blue mist. Through this perfumed haze which was rising to the roof could be seen a motionless figure in gold at the foot of the altar steps; of the sub-deacon holding up before his eyes the paten veiled, waiting for the end of the *Pater Noster;* he was the symbol of the Old Testament, of the Synagogue which had not eyes to see the accomplishment of the mysteries. And the Mass went on, all the serving boys kneeling in a row with lighted torches in their hands during the Elevation, which the sound of bells proclaimed to the night out-side; finally, after the *Agnus Dei,* the Abbot gave the Pax to the deacon, who went down the steps and gave it in turn to the sub-deacon, who, preceded by the master of cere-monies, went to the stalls and there embraced the senior monk, who transmitted it to the others, each leaning over each other's shoulders and then bowing to each other with hands joined.

And now Durtal watched no longer; the moment of Communion was at hand and in the apse the little bell was ringing loudly; there was a stir among the novices and the lay-brothers who began to range themselves in double file; the deacon chanted the *Confiteor* in a tone hardly expressive of con-trition, and, while two monks held an out-stretched long white cloth, all knelt down to communicate. Then the Abbot came down the altar steps with all his following and gave the Blessed Sacrament to the faithful, while behind him stood the serving boys, each holding a torch.

A noise of rough boots and clogs filled the church, making the Abbot's voice almost inaudible; one could catch the words *"Corpus Domini,"* but the rest was lost in the clatter of feet; coming back to his place, Durtal forgot the Liturgy and the Mass, caring only to implore God to forgive him his sins and deliver him from evil. He came back to the world when he heard the Abbot chanting the Pontifical blessing.

"Sit nomen Domini benedictum."

And all the monks responded:

"Ex hoc nunc et usque in saeculum."

"Adjutorium nostrum in nomine Domini."

"Qui fecit caelum et terram."

And the Abbot, staff in hand, gave the blessing:

"Benedicat vos omnipotens Deus, Pater et Filius et Spiritus Sanctus."

And at each invocation of the three Persons he made the sign of the cross over the people, to his left, towards the centre, and to his right.

As Lauds began Durtal went out. His feet were frozen. Madame Bavoil met him at the porch with the lanterns, which they lighted. It was freezing hard and snow was falling.

"Wait for us," cried Mlle. de Garambois, who, muffled up in furs and accompanied by her uncle, was just behind them.

"I must take you home," she said, "not to supper; that would hardly do, but to have a glass of hot punch in front of a good fire."

They set off along a path already half hidden by snow; lights were to be seen, hurrying in all directions, while the window-panes of the inns glowed in the darkness.

Under the pretext of giving them punch, their kind hostess had loaded a table in the dining-room with pastry and cold meat.

It was a quiet homely room; the sideboard and chairs were in the style of Henry II; the pine cones blazed and crackled on the hearth, giving forth their odour of resin, and Durtal sat toasting his shoe-soles.

"We have fallen into a trap," said Mme. Bavoil, laughing, "it is a regular supper that we are threatened with. But I suppose that, on Christmas Day, a little greediness is allowed."

But, in spite of all persuasion, she herself would only swallow a morsel of bread and cheese.

The snow was still falling and the lantern lights along the roads had disappeared. Drunken shouts were heard in every direction; the peasants were all getting tipsy in the shelter of the inns.

"What a pity! They were behaving so nicely just now when they were singing with the monks," said Madame Bavoil.

"Oh!" exclaimed Durtal, "we musn't mind that. Those who sang in church are employees of the monks. They go to Mass to please the Fathers, but wait till the monks have gone. . . ."

"In any case," said M. Lampre, "even admitting that these fellows are in earnest, they do but conform with mediaeval tradition, for piety in olden days among our ancestors did not preclude a certain coarse jollity, especially in Burgundy. Whatever fools may say about the Middle Ages, that period was not one of prudery. Would you believe it, Madame Bavoil, that in olden times, before the Mass of this day, in certain churches they solemnly celebrated the Feast of the Ass and, what is more, that the author of the service, of both words and music, was no other than the Right Reverend Lord Archbishop of Sens, Pierre de Corbeil? So you see that from the thirteenth to the fifteenth century the poor Ass shared in the triumphs of the Redeemer."

"When I think that he bore on his back Jesus," murmured Madame Bavoil, "I long to caress his muzzle."

"There was also the Feast of Fools," continued M. Lampre. "The performers elected a Bishop whom they enthroned with many laughable ceremonies, and this buffoon gave his blessing to the people gathered in the church, while peasants, smeared with must and dressed up as clowns, and harridans swung censers around him, the incense being made of old shoe-leather."

"I fail to see anything religious about such drunken revelry," observed Madame Bavoil.

"And yet they were. These parodies had a Biblical origin. The Ass was honoured because of the one that spoke, and by its remonstrances called forth Balaam's famous prophecy about the coming of the Messiah. The ass was thus, in a way, one of the prophets of Christ. The ass, too, was present near the cradle when He was born; and it was again an ass that carried Him in triumph on Palm Sunday; hence the ass well deserved to have a place in the Christmas festival.

"As for the Feast of Fools, its real name was Feast of the 'Deposuit,' with a reference to *Deposuit potentes de sede* from the *Magnificat*. It aimed at humbling pride and at exalting humility. On that day Bishops and priests counted for nothing, were, in fact, deposed. It was the common people, the menials and serving-lads of the monasteries who were the masters, and they received and used their right to twit the monks and prelates with their hypocrisy, their simony, their favoritism, and occasionally with other sins. It was a topsy-turvy world; yet, by tolerating such occasions of harmless retaliation — until, indeed, they degenerated into pure farce — the Church surely showed her condescension and broadmindedness; by smiling on such follies she proved her indulgence towards the small and lowly, and her readiness to let them vent their grievances."

"Suppose we go to bed," said Madame Bavoil, "it's rather late, and, after all, we shall have to get up tomorrow."

"Today, if you please, for three o'clock is striking," replied Durtal as he re-lit the lanterns.

"That M. Lampre is a very learned man," said Madame Bavoil, as they trudged through the snow; "I am sure he is kind-hearted, but he always seems to be too critical of others and not critical enough of himself."

"Ah, you too, you always expect everybody to be a saint. Alas! I fear the stamp that coined the saints is broken and the Great Master of the Mint now strikes no more coins; here and there, perhaps, in provincial retreats, or in obscure corners of towns, you may yet find some. There are certainly some in the cloisters; I personally have known a few at La Trappe de Notre Dame de L'Atre; but they fly the outside world and, living unseen, how can one ever hope to know them?

"Such a saint, however, who enjoyed a certain notoriety, died lately in a Benedictine monastery in Belgium; but the information I have about him is contradictory and I give it to you for what it is worth.

"This monk, Father Paul de Moll, is said to have been one of the most extraordinary wonder-workers of our time. He healed all ills with a touch; nothing came amiss; toothache and headache vanished like consumption and cancer; incurable diseases were dealt with as easily as indispositions; men and animals, he healed them both; his one simple prescription being the use of water in which a medal of St. Benedict had been dipped.

"This monk, who was our contemporary, for he was born in 1824 and died in 1896, belonged to the Abbey of Termond. He himself re-established the Abbey of Afflighem, and founded the Priory of Steenbrugge. He was a great ascetic and loved self-sacrifice in all its forms, though, to look at him, a kindly jovial man, quietly smoking his pipe, one would never have suspected it.

"But among the hundreds of miracles that he is supposed to have wrought in Flanders, how many are true? Some seem supported by good evidence, others require further examination, for they seem to rest on mere hearsay.

"His life, written in all good faith by a gentleman named Van Speybrouck, is so incoherent and, historically, so faulty that it cannot be relied upon. For the honour of the Order, let us hope that this Father de Moll was not a simple wizard, but a real saint. But it is for the Holy Church to enlighten us."

THE CATHEDRAL*

CHAPTER XII

"WHAT a wind!" muttered Durtal, hastening back to the west front, where he went up the steps and pushed the door open.

The entrance to this immense and obscure church is always coercive; we instinctively bend the head and advance cautiously under the oppressive majesty of its vault. Durtal stopped when he had gone a few steps, dazzled by the illumination of the choir in contrast with the dark alley of the nave, which only gained a little light where it joined the transepts. The Christ had the legs and feet in shadow, the body in subdued light, and the head bathed in a torrent of glory; Durtal gazed up in the air at the motionless ranks of Patriarchs, and Apostles, and Bishops, and Saints in a glow as of dying fires, dimly lighted glass, guarding the Sacred Body at their feet, below them; they stood in rows along the upper storey in huge pointed settings, with wheels above them, showing to Jesus, nailed to earth, His army of faithful soldiers, His legions as enumerated in the Scriptures, the Legends, the Martyrology; Durtal could identify in the armed throng of the painted windows St. Laurence, St. Stephen, St. Giles, St. Nicholas of Myra, St. Martin, St. George of Cappadocia, St. Symphorian, St. Philip, St. Foix, St. Laumer, and how many more whose names he could not recollect — and paused in admiration near the transept, in front of a figure of Abraham fixed for ever in a threatening gesture, holding a sword over a crouching Isaac, the blade shining brightly against the infinite blue.

He stood admiring the conceptions and the craftsmanship of those thirteenth century glass-workers, their emphatic language, necessary at such great heights, the way in which they had made the pictures legible from a distance by introducing a single figure in each, whenever that was possible, and paint-

ing it in massive outline, with contrasting colours, so as to be easily taken in at a glance when seen from below.

But the triumph of this art was neither in the choir, nor in the transepts of the church, nor in the nave; it was at the entrance, on the inner side of the wall, where on the outside stood the statues of the nameless queens. Durtal delighted in this glorious show, but he always postponed it a little to excite himself by expectancy, and revel in the leap of joy it gave him, repetition of the sensation not having yet availed to weaken it.

On this particular day, under a sunny sky, these three windows of the twelfth century blazed with splendour with their broad short blades, the blade of a claymore, flat wide panels of glass under the rose that held the most prominent place over the west door.

It was a twinkling sheet of cornflowers and sparks, a shifting maze of blue flames — a paler blue than that in which Abraham, at the end of the nave, brandished his knife; this pale limpid blue resembled the flames of burning punch and of the ignited powder of sulphur, and the lightning flash of sapphires, but of quite young sapphires, as it were, still infantine and tremulous. And in the right hand pointed window he could distinguish in burning red the Stem of Jesse — figures piled up espalier fashion, in the flue fire of the sky; while to the left and in the middle, scenes were shown from the Life of Jesus — the Annunciation, Palm Sunday, the Transfiguration, the Last Supper, and the Supper at Emmaus; and above these three windows Christ hurled thunder from the heart of the great rose, the dead emerged from their graves at the trumpetcall, and St. Michael weighed souls.

"How did the glass-makers discover and compound that twelfth century blue?" wondered Durtal. "And why have their successors so long lost it, as well as their red?

"In the twelfth century glass-painters made use chiefly of three colours; first, blue — that ineffable, uncertain skyblue which is the glory of the Chartres windows; then red —

*Huysmans, Joris Karl, *The Cathedral*, translated by Clara Bell (New York: New Amsterdam Book Co., 1898), pp. 270–285.

a purplish red, full and important; and green — inferior in quality to the two others. For white they preferred a greenish tinge.

"In the following century the palette is more extensive but the stain is darker; the glass, too, is thicker. And yet, what a glowing blue of pure, bold sapphire tone the artists of the furnace had at their command, and what a fine red they used, the colour of fresh blood! Yellow, of which they were less lavish, was, if I may judge from the robe of a king near the Abraham, in a window by the transept, a daring hue of bright lemon. But apart from these three colours, which have a sort of resonance, and burst forth like songs of joy in these transparent pictures, others grow more sober; the violets are like Orleans plums or purple egg-fruit, the browns are of the hue of burnt sugar, the chive-coloured greens turn dark.

"But what masterpieces of colour they achieved by the harmony and contrast of these tones, and with what skill did they handle the lead-lines, emphasizing certain details, punctuating and dividing these paragraphs of flame as if with lines of ink.

"And another thing which is amazing is the perfect agreement of all these various crafts, practised side by side, treating the same subjects, or supplementing each other — each, by its own mode of expression, under one guiding mind, contributing to the whole; with what a sense of fitness, with what skill were the posts distributed, the places assigned to each as beseemed the purpose of his craft, the requirements of his art.

"Architecture having finished the lower portion of the edifice, retires into the background to make way for Sculpture, giving it the fine opportunity of the doorways; and Sculpture, hitherto invisible at excessive heights, as a mere accessory, suddenly finds itself supreme. With due sense of justice it now comes forward where it can be seen, and the sister art retires, leaving it to address the multitude, giving it the noblest framework in those arched doorways, imitating a deeper perspective by their concentric arches, diminishing and retreating to the doorframes.

"In other instances Architecture does not give everything to one art, but divides the bounty of her great *façade* between sculpture and painting; reserving to the former the hollows and nooks where statues may find niches, and giving to glass-painters the tympanum of the great door, where at Chartres the image-maker has displayed the Triumph of Christ. This we see in the great west doors of Tours and of Reims.

"This plan of substituting glass for bas-reliefs had its disadvantages; seen from outside — their wrong side — these diaphanous pictures look like spiders' nets on an enormous scale and thick with dust. With the light on them the windows are, in fact, grey or black; it is only by going inside and looking back that their fire can be seen flashing; the outside is here sacrificed to the inside. Why?

"Perhaps," said Durtal, answering himself, "it is symbolical of the soul having light inwardly, an allegory of the spiritual life —"

He took in all the windows of the nave with a rapid glance, and it struck him that their effect was a combination of the prison and the grave, with their coals of fire burning behind iron bars, some crossed like the windows of a gaol, and others twisting like black twigs and branches. Is not glass painting of all arts that in which God does most to help the artist, the art which man, unaided, can never make perfect, since the sky alone can give life to the colours by a beam of sunshine, and lend movement to the lines? In short, man fashions the form, prepares the body, and must wait till God infuses the soul.

"It is to-day a high-day of light and the Sun of Justice is visiting His Mother," he went on, as he walked to where the pillared thicket of the choir ended at the south transept, to look at the window known as Notre Dame de la belle Verrière, the figure, in blue, relieved against a mingled background of deadleaf olive, brown, iris violet, plum-green; She gazed out with her sad and pensive pout — a pout very cleverly restored by a modern glass-painter; and Durtal remembered that people had come to pray to Her, as he now went to pray to the Virgin of the Pillar and Notre Dame de Sous Terre.

Such devotion was a thing of the past; the men of our time needed, it would seem, a more tangible, a more material Virgin than this slender, fragile image, hardly visible in dark weather; nevertheless, a few peasants still kept up the habit of kneeling and offering a taper before Her, and Durtal, who loved these old neglected Madonnas, joined them and invoked Her too.

Two other windows also appealed to him by the singularity of the figures, perched very high up, in the depths of the apse, and serving as attendant pages, at a distance, to the Virgin holding Her Son in the centre light commanding the whole perspective of the cathedral; these each contained in a light-toned lancet, a barbarous and grotesque seraph, with sharply-marked features, white wings full of eyes, and robes with jagged, strap-like edges of a pale green colour; their legs were bare, and they were represented as floating. These two angels had jujube yellow aureoles tilted to the back like sailors' hats; and this ragged attire, the feathers folded over the breast, the hat of glory, with their general expression of refractory wilfulness, suggested the idea that these beings were at once paupers, Apaches or Mohicans, and seamen.

As to the remaining windows, especially those which included several figures and were divided into several pictures, it would have needed a telescope and have taken many days of study only to make out the story they told, and discover the details; and months would not have sufficed for the task, since the glass had been in many cases repaired and often replaced without regard to order, so that it was especially difficult to decipher it.

An attempt had been made to count the number of figures represented in the cathedral windows; they were as many as 3889; in the mediaeval times everybody had been eager to present a glass picture to the Virgin. Not cardinals only, kings, bishops and princes, canons and nobles, but the corporations of the town had also contributed these panels of fire; the richest, such as the Guilds of Drapers and Furriers, of Goldsmiths and Money-changers, had each presented five to Our Lady, while the poorer companies of the Master Scavengers and Water-carriers, the Porters and Rag-pickers, each gave one.

Pondering on these things, Durtal wandered round the ambulatory and paused in front of a small stone Virgin ensconced at the foot of the stairs leading up to the chapel of Saint Piat, constructed in the fourteenth century as a sort of outbuilding behind the apse. This Virgin, dating from the same period, had shrunk into the shade, effacing Herself, deferentially leaving the more important places to the senior Madonnas.

She carried an Infant playing with a bird, in allusion, no doubt, to the passage in the apocryphal Gospels of the Infancy, and of Thomas the Israelite, which shows us the Child Jesus amusing Himself by modelling birds out of clay, and giving them life by breathing upon them.

Then Durtal continued his walk through the chapels; stopping only to look at one which contained relics of opposite utility and double purpose; the shrines of Saint Piat and Saint Taurinus. The bones of the former saint were displayed to secure dry weather in times of rain, and those of the second to invoke rain in times of drought. But what was far less comforting and more irritating even than this array of side chapels, with their wretched adornment — with names that had been changed since their first dedication so that the tutelary protection earned by centuries of service had ceased to exist — was the choir, battered, dirty, degraded as if on purpose.

In 1763 the old Chapter had thought fit to deface the Gothic columns, and to have them colour-washed by a Milanese lime-washer, of a yellowish pink specked with grey; then they had abandoned to the town museum some magnificent pieces of Flemish tapestry that screened the inner circuit of the choir aisles, and had put in their place bas-reliefs in marble executed by the dreadful bungler who had crushed the altar under the gigantic group of the Virgin. And mischance had helped. In 1789 the Sansculottes were intending to destroy this mountainous

Assumption, and some ill-starred idiot saved it by placing a cap of liberty on the Virgin's head!

To think that some beautiful windows were knocked out in order to get a better light for this mass of lard! If only there were the slightest hope of ever getting rid of it; but alas! all such hopes are vain. Some years ago, when Monseigneur Regnault was Bishop, the idea was indeed suggested — not of making away with this petrified lump of tallow, but at least of getting rid of the bas-reliefs.

Then the prelate — who stuffed his ears with cotton for fear of taking cold — set his face against it; and for reasons of equal importance, no doubt, the sacrilegious hideousness of this Assumption must be for ever endured, and the marble screens as well.

But though the interior of this choir was a disgrace, the groups round the ambulatory of the apse and the outer wall of the choir were well worth lingering over.

These figures under canopies and tabernacles carved by Jehan de Beauce began on the right by the south transept, went round the horse-shoe behind the altar, and ended at the north transept where the Black Virgin of the Pillar stands.

The subjects were the same as those treated in the small capitols of the royal doorway, outside the church, above the panegyric of the kings, saints, and queens. They were taken from the Apocryphal legends, the Gospel of the Childhood of Mary, and the Protoevangelist James the Less.

The first of these groups was executed by an artist named Jehan Soulas. The contract, dated January 2nd, 1518, between this sculptor and the delegates of the authorities conducting the works of the church, still existed. It set forth that Jehan Soulas, a master image-maker, dwelling in Paris at the cemetery of Saint Jehan in the parish of Saint Jehan en Grève, pledged himself to execute in good stone of the Tonnerre quarry, and better than the images that are found about the choir of Notre Dame de Paris, the four first groups, of which the subjects were prescribed and explained; in consideration of the sum of two hundred and eighty *livres Tournois*,

which the Chapter of Chartres undertook to pay him as he might require.

Soulas, who had undoubtedly learned his craft from some Flemish artist, produced certain little *genre* pictures well adapted, by their spirit and liveliness, to cheer the soul that the solemnity of the windows might have depressed; for in this aisle they really seemed to let the light filter through Indian shawl-stuff, admitting only a few dull sparks and smoky gleams.

The second group, representing Saint Anna receiving from an unseen angel an order to go to meet Joachim at the Golden Gate, was a marvel of grace and subtle observation; the saint stood listening attentive in front of her faldstool, by which lay a little dog; and a waiting-maid, seen in profile, carrying an empty pitcher, smiled with a knowing air and a wink in her eye. And in the next scene, where the husband and wife were embracing each other with the trepidation of a worthy old couple, stammering with joy and clasping trembling hands, the same woman, seen fullface this time, was so delighted at their happiness that she could not keep still, but, holding up her skirts, was almost in the act of dancing.

A little further on, the image-maker had represented the birth of Mary, a thoroughly Flemish scene; in the background, a bed with curtains, on which Saint Anna reclines, watched by a maid, while the midwife and her attendant washed the infant in a basin.

But another of these bas-reliefs, close to the Renaissance clock, which interrupts the series of this history told in the choir-aisle, was even more astonishing. In this Mary was sewing at baby-clothes while reading, and Saint Joseph, asleep in a chair, his head resting on his hand, was instructed in a dream of the Immaculate Conception of the Virgin. And he not only had his eyes shut, he was sleeping so soundly, so really, that one could see him breathe, one felt his body stretching, relaxing, in the perfect abandonment of his whole being. And how diligently the young mother stitched while she was absorbed in prayers, her nose in her book! Never, certainly, was life more closely apprehended, or expressed with greater certainty and truth to life caught in the act, at the instant, ere it moved.

Next to this domestic scene, and the Adoration of the Shepherds and Angels, came the Circumcision of Jesus, with a white paper apron pasted on by some low jester; then the Adoration of the Magi; and Jehan de Soulas and pupils of his studio had finished the work on their side. They were succeeded by inferior craftsmen, François Marchant of Orleans, and Nicolas Guybert of Chartres; and after them art went on sinking lower and lower, down to one Sieur Boudin, who had dared to sign his miserable puppets, down to the stupid conventionality of Jean de Dieu, Legros, Tuby, and Mazières, to the cold and pagan work of the seventeenth and eighteenth centuries. But there was an improvement in the eight last groups opposite the Virgin of the Pillar — some simple figures carved by the pupils of Soulas; these, however, were to some extent wasted, since they stood in the shadow, and it was almost impossible to judge of them in that half-dead light.

In reviewing this ambulatory, in parts so pleasing and in others so unseemly, Durtal could not help recalling the details of a similar but more complete work — one that had not been wrought in succeeding ages and disfigured by discrepancies of talent and date. This work was at Amiens, and it, likewise, was the decoration of the outer aisle of a cathedral choir.

The story of the life of Saint Firmin, the first Bishop and patron saint of the city, and of the discovery and translation of his relics by Saint Salvo, was told in a series of groups that had been gilt and painted; then, to complete the circuit of the sanctuary, the life of the second patron of Amiens had been added, Saint John the Baptist; and in the scene of the Baptism of Christ a fair-haired angel was represented holding a napkin, an ingenuous and arch being, one of the most adorable seraphic faces ever carved or painted by Flemish art in France.

This legend of Saint Firmin was set forth, like that of the Birth of the Virgin at Chartres, in separate chapters of stone, surmounted in the same way with gothic canopies or tabernacles; and in the compartment where Saint Salvo, surrounded by the multitude, discerns the beams which radiate from a cloud to indicate the spot where the lost body of the Martyr had been buried, a man on his knees with clasped hands, seems to pant, uplifted in prayer, burning, projected by the leap of his soul, his face transfigured, turning a mere rustic into a saint in ecstasy, already dwelling in God far above the earth.

This worshipper was the masterpiece of the ambulatory at Amiens, as the sleeping Saint Joseph was of the bas-reliefs at Chartres.

"Take it for all in all," said Durtal to himself, "that work in the Picardy Cathedral is more explicit, more complete, more various, more eloquent even than that of the church in La Beauce. Irrespective of the fact that the unknown image-maker who created it was as highly gifted as Soulas with acute observation, and persuasive and of decided simple-mindedness and spirit, he had besides a peculiar and more noble vein of feeling. And then his subjects were not restricted to the presentment of two or three personages; he frequently grouped a swarming crowd, in which each man, woman, or child differed in individual character and feature from every other, and was conspicuously marked by that unlikeness, so clear and living was the realism of each small figure!

"After all, " thought Durtal, looking once more at the choir aisles, "though Soulas may be inferior to the sculptor of Amiens, he is none the less a delightful artist and a true master, and his groups may console us for the ignominious work of Bridan and the atrocious decoration of the choir."

He then went to kneel before the Black Virgin, and returning to the North transept near which She stands, he gazed once more in amazement at the incandescent flowers of the windows; again he was captivated and moved by the five pointed windows under the rose, in which, on each side of the Mauresque Saint Anna, stood David and Solomon, a forbidding pair, in a furnace of purple, and Melchisedec and Aaron with Tawny complexions and hairy faces, with enormous colourless eyes standing out passionless in a blaze of daylight.

The radiating rose-window above them was not of the vast diameter of those in Notre Dame de Paris, nor of the incomparable elegance of the star-patterned rose at Amiens. It was smaller and heavier, sparkling with flowers like saxifrages of flame, opening in the pierced wall.

Durtal turned on his heel to look at the South transept, where five great windows faced those on the North. There he saw, blazing like torches on each side of the Virgin placed exactly opposite Saint Anna, the four Evangelists borne on the shoulders of the four greater Prophets — Saint Matthew on Isaiah, Saint Luke on Jeremiah, Saint John on Ezekiel, Saint Mark on Daniel — each stranger than the other, with their eyes like the lenses of opera-glasses, their hair in ripples, their beards like the up-torn roots of trees; excepting Saint John, who was always represented as a beardless youth in the Latin Mediaeval Church, to symbolize his virginity; but the most grotesque of these giants was perhaps Saint Luke, who perched on Jeremiah's back, gently scratches the prophet's head, as if he were a parrot, while turning woeful, meditative eyes up to Heaven.

Durtal went down the nave, darker than the choir; the pavement sloped gently to the door, for in the Middle Ages it was washed every morning after the departure of the crowds who slept on it; and he looked down, in the middle, on the labyrinth marked out on the ground in lines of white stone and ribbons of blue stone, twisting in a spiral, like a watch-spring. This path our fathers devoutly paced, repeating special prayers during the hour they spent in doing so, and thus performing an imaginary pilgrimage to the Holy Land to earn indulgences.

When he was out in the square once more, he turned back to take in the splendid effect of the whole before going home.

He felt at once happy and awe-stricken, carried out of himself by the tremendous and yet beautiful aspect of the church.

How grandiose and how aerial was this cathedral, sprung like a jet from the soul of a man who had formed it in his own image, to record his ascent in mystic paths, up and up by degrees in the light; passing through the contemplative life in the transept, soaring in the choir into the full glory of the unitive life, far away now from the purgatorial life, the dark passage of the nave.

And this assumption of a soul was attended, supported, by the bands of angels, the apostles, the prophets, and the righteous, all arrayed in their glorified bodies of flame, an escort of honour to the Cross lying low on the stones, and the image of the Mother enthroned in all the high places of this vast reliquary, opening the walls, as it seemed, to present to Her, as for a perpetual festival, their posies of gems that had blossomed in the fiery heat of the glass windows.

Nowhere else was the Virgin so well cared for, so cherished, so emphatically proclaimed the absolute mistress of the realm thus offered to Her; and one detail proved this. In every other cathedral kings, saints, bishops, and benefactors lay buried in the depths of the soil; not so at Chartres. Not a body had ever been buried there; this church had never been made a sarcophagus, because, as one of its historians — old Rouillard — says, "it has the preeminent distinction of being the couch or bed of the Virgin."

Thus it was Her home; here She was supreme amid the court of Her Elect, watching over the sacramental Body of Her Son in the sanctuary of the inmost chapel, where lamps were ever burning, guarding Him as She had done in His infancy; holding Him on Her knee in every carving, every painted window; seen in every storey of the building, between the ranks of saints, and sitting at last on a pillar, revealing herself to the poor and lowly, under the humble aspect of a sunburnt woman, scorched by the dog-days, tanned by wind and rain. Nay, She went lower still, down to the cellars of Her palace, waiting in the crypt to give audience to the waverers, the timid souls who were abashed by the sunlit splendour of Her Court.

How completely does this sanctuary — where the sweet and awful presence is ever felt of the Child who never leaves His Mother — lift the spirit above all realities, into the secret rapture of pure beauty!

"And how good must They both be," Durtal said to himself, as he looked round and found himself alone, "never to abandon this desert, never to weary of waiting for worshippers! But for the honest country folk who come at all hours to kiss the pillar, what a solitude it would be, even on Sunday, for this cathedral is never full. However, to be just, at the nine o'clock mass on Sundays the lower end of the nave is thronged," and he smiled, remembering that end of the church packed with little girls brought in schools by Sisters, and with peasant women who, not being able to see there to read their prayers, would light ends of taper and crowd together closely, several looking over one book.

This familiarity, this childlike simplicity of piety, which the dreadful sacristans of Paris would never endure in a church, were so natural at Chartres, so thoroughly in harmony with the homely and unceremonious welcome of Our Lady!

"A thing to be ascertained," said Durtal, starting on a new line of thought, "is whether this church has preserved its surface uninjured, or whether it may not have been coloured in the thirteenth century. Some writers assert that, in Mediaeval times, the interiors of cathedrals were always painted. Is that the fact? Or, admitting that the statement is correct as to all Romanesque churches, is it equally so with regard to Gothic churches?

"For my part, I like to believe that the sanctuary of Chartres was never befooled with gaudiness, such as we have to endure at Saint Germain des Prés, in Paris, and Notre Dame la Grande at Poitiers. In fact such colour can only be conceived of — if at all — as used in small chapels; why stain the walls of a cathedral with motley? For this tattooing, so to speak, reduces the sense of space, brings down the roof, and makes the pillars clumsy; in short, it eliminates the mysterious soul of the nave, and destroys the sober majesty of the aisle with its feebly vulgar fret or guilloche, lozenges or crosses, scattered over the pillars and walls, in a paste of treacly yellow, endive-green, vinous purple, lava drab, brick red — a whole range of dull and dirty colours; to say nothing of the horror of a vault dotted with stars that look as if they had been cut out of gilt paper and stuck against a smalt background, a sky of washing blue!

"It is endurable — if it must be — in the Sainte-Chapelle, because it is very small, an oratory, a shrine; it might even be intelligible in that wonderful church at Brou, which is a boudoir; its vaulting and pendants are in polychrome and gold, and the ground has been paved with enamelled tiles, of which visible traces remain round the tombs. This gaudiness of the roof and floor was in harmony with the filagree tracery of the walls, the heraldic glass, and the clear windows, the profusion of lace-like carving and coats of arms in the stone-work, blossoming with bunches of daisies mingling with labels, mottoes, monograms, Saint Francis' girdles and knots. The colouring was in keeping with the alabaster retables, the black marble tombs, the pinnacled tabernacles with their crockets of curled and dentate foliage. We can then quite easily imagine the columns and walls painted, the ribs and bosses washed with gold, and making a harmonious whole of this *bonbonnière,* which indeed is a piece of jewelry rather than of architecture.

This building at Brou was the last effort of mediaeval times, the last rocket flung up by the flamboyant Gothic style — a Gothic which though fallen from its glory struggled against death, fought against returning paganism and the invading Renaissance. The era of the great cathedrals ended in the production of this exquisite abortion, which was in its way a masterpiece, a gem of prettiness, of ingenuity, of tormented and coquettish taste.

"It was emblematic of the soul of the sixteenth century, already devoid of reserve; the sanctuary, too brightly lighted, was secularized; we here see it fully blown, and it never folded up or veiled itself again. We discern in this a lady's bower, all paint and gold; the little chapels (or pews) with chimney-places where Margaret of Austria could warm herself as she heard Mass, furnished with scented cushions, provided with sweetmeats and toys and dogs.

"Brou is a fine lady's drawing-room, not the house for all comers. Then, naturally, with its screen-work, and the carving of the rood-loft stretching like a lace portal across the entrance to the choir, it invites, it almost requires some skilful tinting of the details, the touches of colour that complete it, and harmonize it finally with the elegance of the founder, the Princess Marguerite, whose presence is far more conspicuous in this little church than is that of the Virgin.

"Even then it would be satisfactory to know whether the walls and pillars at Brou ever were really painted; the contrary seems proven. But in any case, though a touch of *rouge* might not ill beseem this curious sanctum, it would not be so at Chartres, for the only suitable hue is the shining, greasy patina, grey turning to silver, stone-colour turning buff — the colouring given by age, by time helped by accumulated vapours of prayer and the fumes of incense and tapers!"

And Durtal, arguing over his own reflections, ended by reverting, as he always did, to his own person, saying to himself, —

"Who knows that I may not some day bitterly regret this cathedral and all the sweet meditations it suggests; for, after all, I shall have no more opportunities for such long loitering, such relaxation of mind, since I shall be subject to the discipline of bells ringing for conventual drill if I suffer myself to be locked up in a cloister!

"Who knows whether, in the silence of a cell, I should not miss even the foolish cawing of those black jackdaws that croak without pause," he went on, looking up with a smile at the cloud of birds that settled on the towers; and he recalled a legend which tells that since the fire in 1836 these birds quit the cathedral every evening at the very hour when the conflagration began, and do not return till dawn, after spending the night in a wood at three leagues from Chartres.

This tale is as absurd as another, also dear to the old wives of the city, and which tells that if you spit on a certain square of stone, set with black cement into the pavement behind the choir, blood will exude.

"Hah, it is you, Madame Bavoil."

"Yes, our friend, I myself. I have just been on an errand for the Father, and am going home again to make the soup. And you, are you packing your trunks?"

"My trunks?"

"Why, are not you going off to a convent?" said she, laughing.

"Would not you like to see it?" exclaimed Durtal. "Catch me at that! Enlisting as a private subject to a pious drill, one of a poor squad, whose every movement must mark time, and who, though he is not expected to keep his hands over the seam of his trousers, is required to hide them under his scapulary —"

"Ta, ta, ta," interrupted the housekeeper, "I tell you once more, you are grudging, bargaining with God —"

"But before coming to so serious a decision it is quite necessary that I should argue all the pros and cons; in such a case some mental litigation is clearly permissible."

She shrugged her shoulders; and there was such peace in her face, such a glow of flame lurked behind the liquid blackness of her eyes, that Durtal stood looking at her, admiring the honesty and purity of a soul which could thus rise to the threshold of her eyes and come forth in her look.

"How happy you are!" he exclaimed.

A cloud dimmed her eyes, and she looked down.

"Envy no one, our friend," said she, "for each has his own struggles and griefs."

And when he had parted from her, Durtal, as he went home, thought of the disasters she had confessed, the cessation of her intercourse with Heaven, the fall of a soul that had been wont to soar above the clouds. How she must suffer!

"No, no," he said, "the service of the Lord is not all roses. If we study the lives of the Saints we see these Elect tormented by dreadful maladies, and the most painful trials. No, holiness on earth is no child's play, life is not amusement. To Saints, indeed, even on earth excessive suffering finds compensation in excessive joys; but to other Christians, such small fry as we are, what distress and trouble! We question the everlasting silence and none answers; we wait and none comes. In vain do we proclaim

Him as Illimitable, Incomprehensible, Unthinkable, and confess that every effort of our reason is vain, we cannot cease to wonder, and still less cease to suffer! And yet — and yet if we consider, the darkness about us is not absolutely impenetrable, there is light in places and we can discern some truths, such as this:

"God treats us as He treats plants. He is, in a certain sense, the soul's year; but a year in which the order of the seasons is reversed; for the spiritual seasons begin with spring, followed by winter, and then autumn comes, followed by summer.

"The moment of conversion is the spring, the soul is joyful and Christ sows the good seed; then comes the cold and all is dark, the terror-stricken soul believes itself forsaken and bewails itself; but without its feeling it during the trials of the purgatorial life, the seed germinates in the contemplative peace of autumn and flourishes in the summer life of Union.

"Aye; but each one must be the helping gardener of his own soul, listening to the instructions of the Master who plans the task and directs the work. Alas, we are no more the humble labourers of the Middle Ages, who toiled, giving God thanks, who submitted without discussion to the Master's orders.

"We, by our little faith, have exhausted the value of prayer, the panacea of aspirations; consequently many things seem to us unjust and cruel, and we rebel, we ask for pledges; we hesitate to begin our task, we want to be paid in advance, and our distrust makes us vile! — O Lord, give us grace to pray, and never dream of demanding an earnest of Thy favours! Give us grace to obey and be silent!

"And I may add," said Durtal to himself as he smiled on Madame Mesurat, who opened the door in answer to his ring, "Grant me, Lord, the grace not to be too much irritated by the buzzing of this great fly, the inexhaustible flow of this good woman's tongue!"

HENRI BREMOND
(1865–1933)

FRANCE has many learned priests who have made their mark in the world of letters. Learning among the French clergy is an old story, but the story took on a new luster when Abbé Henri Bremond was honored by a government which was anticlerical if not irreligious.

Bremond had an extraordinary life. Born of a family of lawyers at Aix-en-Provence, he joined the Society of Jesus at 18, studied for ten years in Wales, and was ordained priest in 1892. He did not remain with the Jesuits but became one of the most influential priests of his time as a scholar, writer, and spiritual director.

His great work, *Literary History of Religious Thought,* is a work of enormous erudition and subtle thought. This work brought Abbé Bremond many honors: the

Grand Prize of the French Academy, 1922, election to the French Academy itself in 1923, and an honorary degree (D. Litt.) from Oxford University, 1928.

His *History* is more than an inquiry into religious thought. It meticulously sets down the progress and changes in mystical orientation as seen in the experiences of even the obscure mystics in their hidden lives in the convents of France.

Bremond's *Prayer and Poetry* is an illuminating example of his excellence as a writer and the analytical magnificence of his mind. It is of great help in defining the difference between the activity of the poet and the mystic. Bremond has, at least, stated the basic source of their difference and Catholic criticism would gain stature and clarity if Bremond's work were better known.

CHAPTER XVIII

THE POET AND THE MYSTIC*

SO, IN order to solve the enigma of the Aristotelian Catharsis, we have to have recourse to the psychology of the mystics. Which brings us back to our point of departure: it is not the poet who illuminates the mystery of the mystics; on the contrary, it is the mystic, and the mystic in his most sublime states, who helps us to penetrate the mystery of the poet. How should it be otherwise, since, on the one hand, poetic and mystical experience belong by their psychological mechanism to the same order of knowledge — real knowledge — not immediately conceptual, but unitive . . . ; and that, on the other, mystical experience is the highest degree and the supreme development here below of all real knowledge; indeed the most perfect kind of real knowledge, not only an account of the supernatural character which all believers attribute to it, and which assures its transcendence, but, further, because it alone sets in movement the whole psychological mechanism, all the springs which actuate real knowledge.

We said with Père de Grandmaison that poetic activity was a profane, natural sort of preliminary sketch of mystical activity — profane and natural, surely, we have just repeated it; but, what is more, confused, clumsy, full of holes or blanks, so that the poet in the last resort is but an evanescent mystic whose mysticism breaks down.

I beg the poets not to be angry. The splendid gift that they have received demands that they should be like this. The more they realise the idea of the poet as such, the further they are from the idea of the mystic as such. The infirmity which we are about to study does not originate in some definite poetic or artistic shortcoming, but exists in the very nature of things; it is, indeed, a sort of metaphysical perfection. The poet whose specifically poetical activitity should be identified with mystical activity properly so called

*Bremond, Henri, *Prayer and Poetry*, translated by Algar Thorold (London: Burns, Oates and Washbourne, Ltd., 1927), pp. 187–200.

would violate the order of the world; it would be as impossible for a lame man to walk straight.

The more of a poet any particular poet is, the more he is tormented by the need of comunicating his experience; the more of a poet he is, the easier and the more inevitable he finds that magic transmuting power of words by means of which something of his poetical experience passes from his deeper soul to ours. The more of a mystic any particular mystic is, the less he feels this need of self-communication, and the more such communication seems to him impossible, should he have the desire to make it, as, indeed, in point of fact it is, all mystical grace supposes, "an absolutely gratuitous and free intervention on the part of God." Well, you will say, does not that alone prove the inferiority of the mystic and the superiority of the poet? Yes, without any doubt, if it is a question of the communication of ideas, images, sentiments; no, if it is a question of a piece of real unitive knowledge. What can be clearly conceived can be clearly expressed; what one possesses, that to which one is united by the apex of the soul, cannot be given out. In both cases there is a certain apprehension, a possession of the real, without which there can be neither poetry nor mysticism; but in the case of the poet the apprehension is more superficial than is that of the mystic, less solid, less unifying. But surely, you will say again, by what right do you forbid the poet to make his apprehension, his possession, as close and deep as he may choose? It is not I who forbid him; it is poetic inspiration itself in its hurry to find words in which to communicate its message to the world. The poet *qua* poet can do nothing but speak. That is at once his glory and his irremediable weakness. He receives and appropriates a treasure which becomes partly ours through the effect of his magic of words; there is his glory. But the poet, in his haste to exploit and transmit this treasure, handles it badly, and only gets hold of it superficially; that is his weakness. As this point may seem a little subtle, may I be allowed to explain it in dry technical terms, which will give us an opportunity to analyse more profoundly than we have been able to do up to the present, the fundamental parable of Animus and Anima, the distinction between the I and the Me?

We define both the activities, with the comparison of which this whole work is concerned, as real and unitive knowledge. There is apprehension, possession of the real in both cases, that of the poet and that of the mystic. Now, we must remember that, although this experience requires first of all the awakening and *entrée en scène* of *Anima* set free by the Catharsis, it cannot be carried out without the collaboration of *Animus*. That the union thus commenced should grow complete and produce all its fruit, it is necessary that at least two of our faculties, the reason and the will, at first more or less suspended and reduced to a repose which is never total; that these two faculties, I say, refreshed by that very repose and stimulated by the intense activity of the apex of the soul, should take a hand in the game. That presence which *Anima* alone can touch, and which she has just touched in the first phase of the experience, but only obscurely and indistinctly, must be "thought," interpreted, named, classed as well as he can, in his ordinary categories by *Animus*. He must freely accept and will this experience, which has imposed itself on the centre of the soul, and be ready to pay whatever price may be exacted in return for this gratuitous gift. The possession of the real, union with God, only becomes truly human and fully fertile at this double price: the active adhesion of the reason and the active adhesion of the will.

Which is the most necessary of the two to the perfection of the experience? Manifestly, the adhesion of the will. This becomes at once intelligible from a glance at the map of the soul. The will is nearer the centre of the soul than the discursive reason — so near, indeed, that it can only be distinguished from it with difficulty — and numerous mystics identify the two, in which, however, I think they are mistaken, since every act of the will

in the proper sense of the word, every exercise of free choice, supposes a previous intervention of rational knowledge: *Nil volitum nisi cognitum*. However, without entering into these distinctions, we clearly perceive that the union which offers itself, which already begins to effect itself in real knowledge, the union of *Anima* with the real, the commencement of love not yet meriting the name of love, awaits, implores, and calls for the firm adhesion of *Animus* — that is, an integral act of free-will. The soul should open itself entirely to the gift which is made to it, drawing it in, breathing it in, permitting it to reach, to penetrate, to electrify, so to say, all the fibres of the will. And it is just here that the infirmity of the poet is displayed; the love which is asked of him, and easy for him to give, *qua* poet, he cannot give, although in the course of normal mystical experience *Animus* unites himself with all his voluntary energy to the presence felt in the depths of *Anima*. Whence comes this necessary difference? Once more, from the special character belonging to poetic activity, the sole object of the poet being, not like that of the mystic, to appropriate to himself the divine gift, but to discover the suitable incantations by means of which the poetic current may pass to the *Anima* of the reader. Poetic experience does not permit the union of love which follows every normal mystic experience to take place. The poet *qua* poet only unites himself to the real in order to separate himself immediately from it. This is not, I beg of you to believe, a paradox; or, rather, it is a paradox, but not invented by me; it is the paradox of the poet. For the poet is, as we said, a broken-down mystic, the same as ourselves in the moral order (by which I mean mediocre), while the gift that he has received ought to enrich him, lift him above average humanity, make him equal to the saints. His paradox is that of a force which urges to the sublime life the subject on which it seizes, and which yet, at the same time, distracts him, in spite of himself, from these magnificent ambitions, and concentrates him, exhausting itself by doing so, on such trifling matters as "a happy choice of harmonious words." It is the paradox of the spring dispersed at its source. "One would say," writes Vinet, "that poets have been sent to speak, and not to be. When they have done their poem, there remains nothing in them of that great thought rather of that force, as if they had lost it by giving it expression." And he adds with his marvellous insight: "Too strong a moral life is often an obstacle to poetic creation." From which comes our attitude towards the poet; we place nothing above poetry but prayer, but as for the majority, at least, of poets, we have some difficulty in taking them tragically. A strange race, said Coventry Patmore, who knew them well. They are like half-saints; they have the most exquisite spiritual sense and the most cowardly conscience. Their genius seems to confer on them a sort of sanctity independent of all virtue. So they prophesy without incurring any responsibility. The saint does not dare say aloud what he has in his heart; he would be judged himself by his words. He would betray the personal sanctity which has made of him a seer. Contrariwise with the poet. He can say anything; he knows quite well that, however beautiful his visions may be, no one will take him for a saint. Hear Patmore, himself a poet:

The poet occupies a singular position in the hierarchy of beings: half-way between a saint and Balaam's ass.

These ideas, which are not new, but which philosophers, with the exception of Maurice Blondel, have not yet, perhaps, deliberately confronted, would demand an infinite development. I will content myself with summing them up in two lines: in every mystical experience worthy of the name, *Animus* and *Anima* collaborate in an act of love, of love in the perfect sense of the word; that is the end appointed by Providence, and also psychologically necessary to this experience. In the poetic experience this act of love, of the complete union with the real, touched and confusedly possessed, miscarries fatally, the *Animus* or the will of the poet being absorbed by other activities which do not tend to realise, to draw closer, to perfect that union.

And note the consequence, equally inevitable, of the inhibition we have just observed: the almost complete paralysis of *Animus* (the will) involves a partial paralysis of *Anima* (the reason). In passionate pursuit of the conceptual symbols, ideas and images on which he has to graft, so to speak, his incantations, and without which he will have no means of making the magic current pass. the poet — that is, the *Animus* of the poet — at first summoned to the centre of the soul, flies from it almost immediately, brought back to the zone of notions and words by the need he has of self-communication. A lamentable breakdown, with which we do not reproach the poet, because it is the ransom of his genius. His reason turns away from the Real when he has but scarcely seized it, and cannot do otherwise. His reason has no means of appropriating that Real by interpretation; for that another gift would be required, that of mystical grace. And it is here, I think, that we find the essential difference between the poet and the mystic. God being the Reality of Realities, they are both united to God, but the God thus possessed is not named by the *Animus* of the poet, while the *Animus* of the mystic names him. It is very certain that we have to pass through God in order to reach effectively the smallest reality, but it is no less certain that we can only pass through God by means of God. Now to pass through the living and hidden God is to enter the mystical order; it is to accept detachment, the night of the senses and of the understanding, the gratuitous initiative of the heavenly Father, the docile response to the grace of charity, the effective union of our will with the divine will. Without this initiative, without this superhuman and special infusion of light and love, and without the active response of *Animus* to this God whom he has recognised and named, there may no doubt sometimes occur simple mimetisms, and also preliminary sketches, preparations, and hypothetical anticipations of the soul, but there is no mysticism in the proper and sacred sense of the word.

There is, therefore, heterogeneity, without any possible confusion; an impassable barrier between the two experiences with which we are occupied. Mysticism is absolutely transcendent; poetic experience is, indeed, a preliminary sketch of mystical experience, but a sketch which, on the one hand, calls for the brush to complete it, and, on the other, rejects it. A curious fact, which has not perhaps been sufficiently noted, is that this is only strictly true of the higher poetic states — of those, I mean, which crystallise in true poems. In the case of ourselves, inferior poets, nothing prevents the experience provoked by the view of a landscape or the reading of the poets being enriching to us, insensibly transforming itself into a religious or even a specifically mystical experience; not only does nothing prevent this, but, on the contrary, the order of nature and the order of Providence wish the sketch, in our case, to become a portrait. The reason is always the same: the poet *qua* poet cannot prevent himself speaking; the reader can, and ought to remain silent, because the shock communicated to our deeper soul by the magic of the verse is not intense enough to impose on us this effort of artistic creation which takes entire hold of the poet, and only lets him go with difficulty. We are free to let the current mount to our surface faculties, to apply our reason to the one task of the interpretation of the mystery which invades us, and our will to that of drawing closer the union begun. In order to give its real name to the reality which offers itself to our apprehension, and to possess it fully, we no doubt require a new and better grace, a free gift which the reading of the most sublime poet will not impart to us, but for which it invites us to ask. In the case of the perfect poet himself, the poetic experience tends to turn into prayer, but never actually does so; in our case, it does so without difficulty, and thanks to the poet. Strange and paradoxical nature of poetry; a prayer which does not itself pray, but which makes others pray.

There are, of course, metaphysical precisions to be made. Not very subtle ones for those, at least, who have not been at odds with the play of ideas from their birth. It is therefore useless to remind me that Racine used to go to Mass. The pure poet never existed; pure poetic experience is a myth. A great poet may also be a pious man; indeed,

an authentic contemplative like St. Augustine or the author of the *Imitation*. But even in their case poetic activity disengaged by an effort of analysis and isolated from the thousand activities which accompany it, block it, and turn by turn help and obstruct it, is not a formal act either of love or of faith. It has nothing specifically religious or meritorious about it. I am, naturally, speaking only of those pages of the *Confessions,* equivalent in their verbal magic to the most beautiful lines of Virgil. The more poetically perfect these pages are, the further they are from prayer; and the further they are from prayer, the more they are productive of prayer. And that, too, directly: automatically, so to speak; not in the manner of sermons or of pious effusions in prose. For, once more, we are not here concerned with the ideas presented by the poet or with the sentiments which he awakes in our minds; we are concerned with the movement which he imprints on the centre of our souls, releasing by doing so a whole psychological mechanism, the springs of which require nothing but a supernatural impulse to be adapted to the specific activities, and serve the special ends of true prayer. From which the reader may see that it would be equally unintelligent to remind me that Lucretius was a blasphemer. The man, the philosopher who expresses such and such ideas and sentiments, certainly. The poet *qua* poet, no. Poetic experience knows not blasphemy any more than prayer, but while it is absolutely impossible for it to provoke to blasphemy, it cannot help starting the psychological mechanism of prayer. The chapter on Lucretius in Keble's *Praelectiones Academicae* is nothing but a long hymn. And now, whether we have been too subtle or not, we come back to something more commonplace."

"It is at once by poetry and by penetrating beyond it," writes Baudelaire, "by music and by penetrating beyond it, that the soul catches a glimpse of the splendour on the other side of the grave; and when an exquisite poem brings tears to the eyes, these tears are no proof of excessive pleasure. Poetry, as such, is never the pleasure of the senses.

"They are, rather, the witness of an irritated sensibility, a demand of the nerves, no!

of *Anima,* of a nature exiled in the imperfect which longs to *seize immediately* on this very earth the paradise revealed to it."

This is true of all poetic experience, whatever may be the "subject" treated by the poet. Beauty, says Maritain, all beauty, tends of itself to unite us to God. The reason and the manner of this tendency is what I have been trying to show in these pages, and which I repeat in a few words: *primo,* there is another thought besides abstract and discursive thought, another knowledge as well as conceptual and rational knowledge; *secundo,* neither real knowledge nor rational knowledge, each of which, moreover, requires the other for its development, can reach completion without implying the exercise of faculties divinely set in motion by the

mystical life. Whence come both the excellence and the essential imperfection of poetical experience, the stepping-stone to a higher experience, which in some way it calls out for, but to which, of itself, it would never lead; rather would it block approach.

A fine passage of M. Hamon sums up admirably what I have tried to say in this last chapter: "It is incomparably easier to love *if one remains silent than if one talks.* The care of searching for words greatly obstructs the movement of the heart, which always loses something by doing so, unless it is recompensed for its loss by the gain that others may make. If the result is a little less love and a little more distraction and danger, the soul suffers a great loss if she knows the price of love and of prayer."

RENÉ BAZIN
(*1853–1932*)

NOVELIST of the family and family life, René Bazin was born in Angers, France, 1853. Thinking he had a vocation, Bazin went to the seminary for a time but gave up the clerical life to study law, which he later taught for many years at the University of Angers.

His novels soon attracted the attention of the French literary world and Bazin was elected to the French Academy, 1904. Further honors came to him when he was made a Knight Commander of St. Gregory and an officer in the Legion of Honor.

As a novelist Bazin is not of first rank. He lacks the insight which make the novelist a true dissector of character. Without achieving complete eminence in his field, Bazin

has done an excellent work in showing that Catholic family life is not without its problems, which only grace and common sense can solve.

Bazin's importance to the Catholic Revival is not to be dismissed lightly. The moderate realism of his writing has influenced several generations of Catholic writers, who for too many years, before the translation of Bazin's novels, dedicated their talents to sentimental and superficial writing.

Magnificat is usually considered Bazin's best work, but *The Nun* is far more realistic and dramatic. Bazin also gave an excellent example to Catholic biographers in his fine life of *Charles Foucauld.*

III

VIA DOLOROSA*

ON THE morrow, which was the 20th of June, and a Friday, the Sisters were definitely informed of the day which was to be their last together, and of the treatment they were to receive. Ursula Magre had sent the required report to the chief of police, who was satisfied that with a little diplomacy he would be spared the unpleasant necessity of violence against women, with the spectacle of shattered doors, of forcible entry into bolted cells, with the noise, the protests, the whole display of house-breaking which the spectators are apt to take ill. A timely word on behalf of the Mother-House had made all smooth. A *commissaire* called on the Superior. He was a jovial-looking man, who at the first glance seemed more than good-natured — familiar, and on acquaintance proved to be so. He took the tone appropriate to his character, and as he thought, to the occasion. Sister Justine received him, standing in the corridor, a few steps within the door.

"My poor lady," he said, "my business is not always a joke for me — "

"Mine never is to me," interrupted the Superior. "You have come to expel me?"

"No, Madame. Compose yourself, and let us have our talk without losing our tempers. I have called with the order for closing the school and for vacating the premises — "

"Which are our own property."

"That is not my business. They have to be vacated. I am not an unkind man, and I am willing that you should choose your own day, but on condition that there shall be no disturbance, no kind of demonstration whatever. The matter is in your hands."

"I know it is."

"Then we understand each other?"

Deeply humiliated, her hands idle at her side, very careful of her words, so that she might in no way compromise that dear house at Clermont, in which the race of saintly women might yet be suffered to survive, yet

keeping her eyes level and abating none of the dignity of her defeat by any word or tone of entreaty or of fear, Sister Justine informed the police emissary of her resolution. She desired a delay of a week in order to prepare for departure. She desired to hold the prize-giving as usual. She wished that last gathering to be on Friday, the weekly day of the Passion. She asked that a police agent should lay hands upon her shoulders, as on those of an arrested criminal. She would leave on the evening of the same day. On her part she engaged not to spread the tidings of the expulsion, and not to allow the hour of departure to be known to any but the Sisters themselves.

The man made a show of quarrelling with the terms, but finally agreed. He had obtained precisely what he had been sent to secure.

The week that followed was much like the last week of all other scholastic years. When the mistresses announced to the classes that the prize-giving would take place on the usual date of the 27th there was much surprise. On the morrow the parents protested. Some of them threatened to take away their girls if the holidays were to be made so intolerably long; a few suspected or understood, and the clamour subsided. Within the school the examinations proceeded, the lists were made, and the Sisters were up late at work on the correction of exercises. They tried to talk of the "fête" as they used to do. Sister Pascale and Sister Edwige had orders to make the garlands of green box wherewith the schoolroom had always been hung. Until the last moment, order and tradition governed the life of the convent. A young girl of the district helped them in this last labour — Louise Casale, an ironer, obliged by anaemia to forgo the labour and the atmosphere of the ironing-room. She had not been a pupil of the convent, but had been educated at a lay-school in total ignorance of all religion, in spite of which the thing they had not taught

*Bazin, René, *The Nun* (New York: Charles Scribner's Sons, 1908), pp. 122–142.

her had strongly attracted her heart, so that for many months past she had watched for opportunities of speaking to the Sisters, of offering them such small services as she had to give, and of showing them her ingenuous sympathy. When bringing linen to the house she had made acquaintance, one by one, with all the five; and having heard that the prize-giving was near, she asked permission to help in the "decorations."

"I know a garden," she said, with her southern accent, "where there is a great deal of box to spare. The gardener is a friend of mine — only just a friend, mind you. Though I have been brought up in the *laïque,* I am an honest girl all the same."

"You have the eyes of one, Louise," Sister Justine had answered her. "No one will ever make a mistake about that. Shall I show you how I believe in you? I am going to lend you Sister Léonide for half a day."

Louise Casale clapped her hands.

"Just half a day. You will cut the box together, and perhaps you will find another friend of yours who will carry it home."

She had returned to the convent with a barrow full of "green," and now in the largest room — which was a play-room in bad weather and a theatre once a year, when the Shrove Tuesday play was acted by the little girls — three women, standing in drifts and piles of leaves, tied the sprigs in bunches to long ropes for festoons and wreaths. They carried the box about in their gowns, held up by the hems. They were Sister Edwige, Sister Pascale, and Louise Casale. This girl, tall, brown, well built and broad of shoulder, lacked nothing for the bloom of beauty except a richer flow of blood, and of this nothing but her work had robbed her. Her thin cheeks, of extreme pallor, and her narrow nose looked too small for her wide white brows and her great eyes, over-long, and dwelling in perpetual shadow.

It was the eve of the exhibition-day. Louise and the Sisters fastened paper roses at intervals on the garlands, from the stock used already in ten successive years. They required a considerable distance in order to be recognised as flowers, even of paper.

"Here are at least twenty metres," said Louise. "Two metres more, and we have done. What time is it?"

"Half past five," said Sister Pascale. "My hands are all green. I am glad we have not to put up the wreaths till the morning." She added in another tone, "It will be pretty, won't it?'

There was no answer. A noise of wheels outside mingled with the rustling of the foliage within. Then Louise spoke to her in a resolute low voice:

"Sister Pascale, please tell me — don't keep me in the dark."

"What am I to tell you?"

"Why, that you are going. You are going, are you not? Something has happened? Am I right? Have I guessed?"

They were close to one another, like two rope-spinners meeting. They had ceased working. Even Sister Edwige caught the words. She did not look round, but her hands too paused. Sister Pascale could not answer. But she looked at the girl whom chance, and something more, had brought to her side in that supreme hour. And hardly had their eyes met when the two young creatures opened their arms and gathered each other heart against heart, weeping. O mournful and hopeless friendship! Strangers a while ago, met from afar, they would have loved one another, but they were to part forever.

"Forgive me, Sister Pascale," said Louise, "I am sorry. I like you so!"

Sister Pascale took from the fold of her dress a last few sprigs of box, but she seemed to see nothing more of her wreath-making; her little fingers mechanically smoothed the leaves as though they had been millinery feathers that she was putting into shape. Her breast heaved, and her head sank. Louise, taller than she, bent close to the black veil and whispered:

"I am not really pious, as you are, but I love coming here. I have thought about ever so many things. And only six months ago I didn't know you; I used to talk against the Sisters — I did. And now when I think of getting married —. Did you ever think about getting married before you were a Sister?"

"Why, yes," said Pascale, "like all girls."

"Well, sometimes I think I should like the kind of marriage that one would never be sorry for afterwards. Sometimes I think I should — not always."

"Ah! that is not an easy matter."

"You don't understand. I mean a marriage like yours, that one would never be sorry for in one's own soul."

"Oh, my little girl," said Pascale; "what a time to tell me such a thing!"

"Yes," said Louise "What a time! I ought to have kept my silliness to myself. Well, it's all over. When you are gone I shall go back and be like all the others."

Sister Edwige had turned. A stout figure, active and short-legged, had entered.

"Come, my children, in two minutes you must wind up. It's recreation time. I am not turning you out, Louise. Why! what is the matter? What is this tragic look about?"

Louise scattered on the floor the box she had carried in her skirt.

"I am going," she said. "Good-bye, Sisters."

"Does she know?" asked Sister Justine; and Sister Edwige answered, "Yes."

The Superior called down the passage, hoping that her voice would overtake the girl:

"Say nothing, Louise, say nothing, for our sakes."

An uncertain answer was sent back, broken by the echoes, and unintelligible.

"Come to recreation, my children," commanded the Superior.

Sister Edwige and Sister Pascale let go the wreath they had fastened off, and said with one voice:

"It is the last recreation."

And seeing that Sister Justine was already on her way to the terrace, they followed her, keeping together, holding each other by the hand — a thing they had never done before — and walked thus to the end of the alley, where the other three awaited them.

Again they were ranged, three on one side, two on the other, and the two were Edwige and Pascale. But to-night they did not keep under the shed; they walked in the courtyard. The law, the rule of their vocation called and controlled them. As lovers return to the scene of their loves, and tread again their own vestiges and walk in the paths of the beloved past, these women spent the last hours of their liberty in the place where their children had lived with them a full and happy life — their children to whom they had devoted themselves, who had been the cause and end of their self-sacrifice, as they were now the innocent cause of their trouble. After recreation, they knew, there would be prayer in church, and no silent meeting to follow, for on this night, they must be busy preparing for the morrow's journey.

The sun, very low, illuminated the dust of the air, and there was not the least particle or atom that did not carry light in the golden atmosphere. A summer day like so many of its fellows was coming to an end amid the labour, the sweat, the pain of the city. Workmen were still at their post, employers in their offices, at their tables, at their telephones. And meanwhile, a loss immeasurable was about to befall them; for five women were together for the last time amongst them. When these were dispersed and gone, innumerable lives would be made poorer, would be altered, would be lowered. One kind of riches, less honoured, than another in the world, had come to an end. A grief, pitied by few, had locked in a last clasp of farewell five human creatures of whom the world was not worthy.

Sister Léonide had let her fire go out, and would never light it again. All alike controlled their grief. Sister Justine, her face drawn, was resolute to keep up the old tone of motherly jollity that had put heart into her nuns and into a thousand women in trouble. Sister Danielle endured her crucifixion, clinging with all her will to her cross of sacrifice, never cruel to her until today. Within her heart she repressed a tempest of indignation and revolt. She ordered words of peace to her lips; she set a smile there, like a knot of ribbon on the cross of a sword. Sister Edwige had lost her serenity, and looked much older; in one night her beautiful eyes, her delicate cheeks, had gathered a setting of slight wrinkles. Sister Léonide kept her customary air, cheerful and alert; her nickel watch, like a great onion, had slipped below her waist-belt, and she consulted it as though her office as time-keeper was the chief thing in her mind. Sister Pascale stood in tears, looking at each of her companions. To-morrow Sister Danielle and Sister Edwige would be gone to their relations, far away and far apart. To-morrow Sister Léonide would set off for the village, where, at the last hour, a position as assistant teacher in a free school had been found for her. To-morrow she, the Lyons girl, would have left her city for Nimes, and the roof of her aunt.

The five women paced the court-yard between one wall and another.

"My children," said Sister Justine, "you must think, as I do, of the generations of little girls we have known here. We have watched them at play where we are standing."

They trod the dust trampled by those little feet. One cast her eyes upon the sand, with its intricate and innumerable foot-marks; another looked at the schoolroom windows; another followed with her eyes the flight of a flock of sparrows that came to take their customary possession of the place towards night-fall. They thought of the little daughters of working men for whose benefit all had been done — the stones built up into walls, the roof-tiles set, the ground levelled, the cement floor laid, and their own lives spent; half of one life, a little less of another, the greater part of a third. Soft voices, sweet looks, deep reaching words, dear confidences, faults and falsehoods reproved, ardours and passions that alarmed these watchful mistresses, fervours that delighted them — all, all those childhoods were remembered.

"We must pray for them all every day, every day as long as we live; that will be our perpetual presence in this dear place. Promise!"

Bowed heads replied. Sister Justine held in leash the emotions of these four younger women. Her soldier blood, aware of the moment for command and the moment for relaxation of discipline, told her that there was no danger of coldness or forgetfulness among these daughters of her heart, but that she had now rather to harden them against too painful a tenderness towards their lost children.

"To-morrow, Sister Léonide," she said, "reveille at five minutes to five. We shall begin the day of trial by hearing Mass. After that you will nail up the wreaths. I want the children to keep a pleasant recollection of their last term. Let them see cheerful things about us, as it will be difficult for us to show them cheerful faces. At ten minutes to nine you will put the parents and the children in their places. You, Sister Pascale, will have charge of the little girls; you, Sister Edwige, of the grown-ups."

"And when do we go?"

"I shall give you the time."

"By what street? Are we to go together? Where are we to turn, Mother?"

The sun went down. Sister Léonide pulled up her watch, anxious that the evening should not overtake her with her task unfinished. They were silent; and a single thought that had not been far from each now took possession of them all. They had not yet suffered the utmost. The moment, the brief moment of real parting had come, for to-morrow no one must weep. The five women stopped in the corner of the court-yard, to the east. They drew together. Hardly, from any window of an overlooking house, could the little group of homespun gowns and black veils be perceived in the twilight. And if they were seen, what mattered it? The Superior held out her arms.

"Come," she said, "my children, and let me kiss you. And now if you have any last requests to make, the time is short."

The four nuns, successively in the order of their age, came to her heart and took the kiss of peace. Their Mother having kissed them on either cheek, traced on their brows the sign of the Cross. All her tenderness, human and religious, was in her action. When she took into her arms the youngest of her daughters — Pascale — she held her, unable to let her go, or to say any more than those weeping words:

"O dearest! O dearest!"

Then she turned towards the house, and Sister Léonide followed her; for the last time the night bell was to be rung. The three others lingered. The grave, the wise Danielle took by the arm the youngest of the Sisters.

"I loved you dearly, dearly. I shall love you in my prayers. I should never have told you, if the end of our life together had not come. Good-bye, little Pascale. Keep yourself for God."

She pressed the arm of the young Sister, who was weeping, and who answered in broken phrases:

"And I — I always had a great affection, a great admiration — I shall never hear your name without finding it a support to my weakness. I shall never think of you without feeling a better woman — because of the example — "

But already the slender figure had withdrawn; that soul of sacrifice denied itself a useless emotion; she went away, leaving the young Sister, whom another joined. This was one who was not quite able to restrain her tears, one of less iron courage, one who had never ceased, for two and a half years past, to show Pascale how much she loved her.

"If we are not too poor, and I should ever be able to call you near me, I will send for you," said Sister Edwige.

"You are uneasy about me?"

"Ah, yes, I am uneasy," said Edwige's touching voice.

"Don't be too anxious. I shall be all right — I hope, I hope — "

"Not as you are here."

"But where shall I ever be as I am here? I am very unhappy. I had all my peace at Saint Hildegarde's because I always said to myself, 'It is for life!' And now, and now — "

The bell rang, and the two young figures, drooping, passed into the house, apart, speaking no more to one another, their feet effacing the footsteps of their children.

The night came, and she who for five-and-twenty years had directed the Sisters, the classes, the children, the former pupils, and the many clients of the school and the convent, withdrew to her cell — a servant's garret, furnished with a small bed, two chairs, and a black table. At more than sixty years of age she was to leave — no doubt for ever — the scene of her long and willing sacrifice. Before she unpinned her veil, she stood before her plaster crucifix and examined herself.

"Have I allowed the Rule of our Order to grow lax, to grow stale? Have I lessened the time of prayer? Lengthened the time of leisure? Broken without strict necessity the evening and the morning silence? No, I believe in my conscience, I have done none of these things. Have I held the balance of my soul level amongst my Sisters, and amongst my children? My God, I remember the dead I have loved, I know the living I love. And surely I have felt attractions and affections, and particular sympathies. But where this personal love was not, Thou, O Lord, hast put charity into my heart in its place. I think I was not unjust. I have been disgusted by hypocrisies, by dirt, by evil odours, by the insistent claims of poverty; perhaps I have shown my loathing.

"Have I safeguarded the virgins entrusted to my fostering care, and to the shelter of this Order? Well, there is Sister Léonide, who runs about the town at her work. There is Sister Danielle, who has often visited with me the houses of the poor. These two might walk through fire unsinged. The other two have known here nothing of the world except the children, and the wind that blows in at the doors. Their eyes are frank, their gaiety is innocent and young. Even Sister Danielle is a joyous creature, and if she does not speak of her joy, she cherishes it in silence. Even Pascale, who is steadfast only because she is propped and stayed by others, has had a free spirit and a light heart. She has been happy, I think, until these last days. Many of my daughters have kept the absolute sinlessness of their baptism, and carried it to the grave. As for me, I am old, I have never been afraid of plain speaking, and I have had the grace to forget nearly all the evil I have seen, in the hard work of trying to put it right. My Sisters have had the safety of this enclosure, of perpetual occupation, of their fatigue with tiresome children, of the Rule, of their prayers, of my constant maternal presence; above all, of the continual sense of Thy Presence, my God.

"Have I failed in my duty as a teacher? I have had my pride — my vanity — in the examinations. I have been keen about certificates, and well-written pages, and exercises without a mistake, and correct answers. It is possible that my little girls thought these things more important than they are. There was nothing important but Thou alone. It is of Thee they will have need, in their homes, in their griefs, and in their death. Ah, I fear I did not show plainly that I was first of all a teacher of divine things. My little girls have so much need of Thee. They die so young — often of the second child; and after they have left school they seldom hear a word to lift them up or strengthen their souls. They have so much good will, such a secret sense of honour, so much love of God hidden away — it comes out now and then, they remember their home here, and all they were taught that is good; they are loyal at heart. What, what will become of me? If I am to teach, I shall certainly have less human vanity about it. I entreat Thy pardon. It is so difficult not to have preferences for people. I shall try to do better."

She interrupted her simple prayer.

"Twenty-five years," she said. "I thought I should die here. I have examined myself. I have found human weakness, but my God has not been offended. This is only a trial, and I accept it."

At a few minutes before nine, Sister Pascale and Sister Edwige, standing on ladders, hammer in hand, were fastening up the long green wreaths, giving symmetry to arches and festoons, replacing fallen paper roses. The last nail driven in, they came down. Three little girls of some twelve years old — two poor, spare figures and one fat — were sent to open the doors. And at once began the sound of shuffling feet and of voices in every tone of excitement: "Don't push so!" "Take care of your dress — you are tearing it!" "Where is the hurry — what are you crowding for?" "What a lot of wreaths! And such nice box — I should never have the patience." "What about the prizes? Are you going to have one? Well, not a very big one?" "Go up, there's your place. Don't you see Sister Pascale? She beckoned to you."

Sister Pascale stood on the right of the platform with the prizes — books, bound in red, blue, and gold — on a table at her side. The older girls were to be on the left. Fami-

lies and friends sat together, and all talked. Mothers, grandmothers, grown-up sisters, aunts, great-aunts, neighbours, and even — notwithstanding that it was Friday — two or three men filled the seats within a few minutes. The school-children left their family groups, and the sound of kisses was audible among other noises, and wishes of "Good luck!" But among the crowd some were attentive and observant; a rumour had reached them. "They say something has happened. Have you heard anything about the school?" "Why, no." "It would be a pity." "Just look at Sister Pascale's face — there at the end, where the little ones are sitting." "She got quite red. Who was it spoke to her?" "The little Burel girl — no, Aurielia Dubrugeot, and she brought her a present." "What was it — a cushion?" "No, something that opened; it looks like a valise." "Is it true, Mère Chupin, that the Sisters are going?" "No, my good man; they say so, just to get up a feeling against the Government." "All the same, Sister Pascale looks very unhappy. Poor little Sister Pascale! There's a soft heart for you!" "Look, now she has put the valise in a corner with a cover over it. Aurelia is crying. If you ask me, I don't believe the Sisters are going to be turned out at all. What should they be turned out for?"

The man who had spoken, Goubaud by name, kept a wooden face, with bent brows, and a hand twisting his beard. He looked steadily towards the corner to the right, where Sister Pascale was ranging thirty little heads, dark and fair, and drawing her hands from the clasp of the children trying to kiss them.

"Don't go, don't go away, Sister, little Sister."

The golden eyes, the tender eyes of Pascale were wet with tears. It was true that Aurelia had brought a box — a cardboard box covered with American cloth, for which her family had no use. Another, a pale child of six, who had one blind, blank eye, and one as blue as heaven, came up with her two hands concealing something precious. She called louder than the rest, "Here, Sister Pascale, I brought this for you. I took it off the mantlepiece." Sister Pascale put out her hand, and the beaming child laid in it a pink shell with many spikes. "It's for you, because I like you." She too knew of the parting at hand; she too had heard. Others laughed. Goubaud said to those about him: "We shall know in a moment. There's the Superior. She, at any rate, doesn't look unhappy. But she never does, and looks don't count. She is the stout one."

"She hasn't got stout by taking care of herself," said his neighbour, who missed his meaning. "It's not fat, Père Goubaud, it's her age." The speaker was sixty, but she had "kept her figure," inasmuch as she was as flat as a board and looked like a weasel. "Why, there's none of the clergy on the platform. That never happened before."

There was no priest. Sister Justine, with a mighty effort, mounted that eminence. The audience coughed, and some chairs scraped. Sister Danielle, pale, and looking like Justice appearing among men, entered and sat straight against the wall; the Superior, much eclipsed by the tables and the prizes, raised her hand to speak; Sister Pascale quelled the last two or three little girls clinging to her skirt; Sister Edwige, slender, sad, graceful, obviously a lady in spite of her self-abasements, moved up from her work of arranging places, took her stand to the left of the platform, and pulled from her pocket a paper covered with admirable copper-plate writing — the prize-list, a single copy. Sister Léonide was probably nailing up boxes or closing doors, and was not to be seen.

"I wish to explain to the parents of pupils," said Sister Justine, whose authoritative voice imposed silence, "that it is not by our own wish that we changed the date of breaking-up. The exhibition to-day will not be as formal as usual. We shall have no singing. We are very sorry to have to send home your children so soon; but we were requested to do so, on account of circumstances — "

There was an interruption. Some irrepressible voices called, "They are evicting you. You may as well tell us."

"Be quiet, Goubaud, can't you?"

"Of course they are not going at all."

"I tell you they are."

"Do listen to the Sister; she can't speak with the noise."

"You are an ignorant man, and no mistake!" Sister Justine imposed silence again.

"No noise!" she cried. "All who are our friends will listen quietly to the reading of the prize-list, and will then go home. As for us, I am glad to think that we have done our best to serve you."

"That you have, Sister."

"Then you are really going?"

"No, can't you understand?"

"Hush! Silence!"

Children were crying aloud.

"Read the prize-list, Sister Edwige," said the Superior.

They were as silent as though called upon to listen to soft music. The music was the voice of Edwige reading out the names. And they were silent also as the prize-winners, by threes and fours, rose and went forward to receive a book, or a green paper wreath, and left little trails of excitement behind them in the crowd.

This lasted until half-past eleven. Then the deafening noise of talk and movement arose again into the atmosphere, now close and heavy with the odours of poverty. The people were going; they had paid their last visit to the school; the district was gathering back its little girls. No doubt these people did not forget the Sisters; but the haste of departure, the crowd, the desire for fresh air, the attraction of the street, the thought of the wine-shop, the mere example of the rest — all these poor trivial motives, with the addition of their shyness and their awkward lack of all initiative, left very few indeed to take leave of the school-mistresses where they stood close to the platform, in a little group of children that were the most affectionate, the vainest of their prizes, or the most forlorn and friendless of the school.

"Good-bye — au revoir — Sister Justine, Sister Danielle, Sister Edwige, Sister Pascale."

The nuns bent to kiss the children, pressed the hands of the few mothers, made vague replies to embarrassing questions. And soon they were alone. Mechanically they had retreated to the wall, and it propped their weary figures; they stood there motionless with idle hands, released from the necessity of the ceremonial smile, and watching the backs of fathers, mothers, relatives, and little girls of all sizes, going away for ever: their friends going away, the clients of their charity, who had needed them, to whom they had ministered — their only treasure, their only riches.

They knew many of those backs by the clothes that the wearer never changed. Each Sister felt the cruel price at which human gratitude is won; so much patience, so much self-forgetfulness, so much persevering effort, in the differing cases of so many children, to buy a kiss, a softened manner, a friendly thought, from but one of those who were going by threes and fours along the school corridor and out of a door they would never cross again. There, before their very eyes, their work was falling to pieces.

A slight caress drew Pascale from that sorrowful vision. Close to the platform the young parentless child who had one dead eye was still standing. There had been no one to beckon her out, and she lurked near those who had been kind to her.

Guessing them to be unhappy, seeing them silent and motionless, she stroked with her little fingers the hanging hand of Pascale.

"It is Marie," said the young Sister. "If I could only take her with me!"

The child was clasped in the arms of them all, and then she went alone, with the noise of her wooden shoes, looking back at intervals, as though to say, "I can see you still." The door closed behind her, and she was the last.

CHAPTER IV

HIS CONVERSION*

THE first months, after the return from Morocco, were almost entirely spent in Algeria. Charles de Foucauld did not at once begin to compile and write the book for which he brought back the materials: he verified his notes, deciphered them if necessary, consulted his friends — in a word, prepared the work that he was to do a little later in Paris. He made a few stops in France, some visiting tours and looking people up, but his "headquarters," his papers, library, and habits continued to be what they were before the great journey. At one moment, it might even be thought that the explorer was going to get married in Algeria. A young girl had taken his fancy. She was of good family, and he came from far. He wrote to Paris, where he found little encouragement. I don't know whether he was badly smitten and what opposition he had. But when he had made another excursion to France, in the summer of 1885, and lived some time near Bordeaux, at his aunt's, Madame

Moitessier, in the Chateau du Tuguet, he gave up the idea. He was called to quite other destinies; he thus helped them forward without knowing it.

A higher will has him in its grip. It urges him on to action, lashes him, and leads him on towards a hidden goal. The call of the desert makes itself heard once more. From the beginning of September, Charles has been at Nice, at his brother-in-law's, M. de Blic, the confidant of his thoughts. What are they? Do you not guess? He is going to set out again: naturally, he is going South. He wants to visit the oases and the *shotts* of Algeria and Tunis. It may be only the prelude to a greater journey. I know an intimate friend of his who believes that the explorer's secret intention was to investigate the means and find the best starting-point for crossing the Sahara. Henceforth who can tell? Foucauld hardly gave any intimation of his plans and did not talk about his recollections. On the eve of undertaking this "excursion," as he used to say, in the regions of the *shotts*, he now and then saw his sister's uneasy looks directed towards

*Bazin, René, *Charles de Foucauld, Hermit and Explorer*, translated by Peter Keelan (New York: Benziger Bros., 1923), pp. 61–71.

him. "Fear nothing," he used to reply, "no harm will happen to me: with care one can go anywhere."

On September 14, he embarked at Port-Vendres for Algiers. A few weeks earlier he had written to his friend de Vassal, who was at El-Golea, begging him to get two camels and two horses, and to engage an Arab servant for the expedition.

The route in all its parts is not known to us. We only know that Foucauld, passing through the south of the province of Oran, visited Laghuat, then, going still more to the south, the oasis of Ghardaia and the inhospitable Mzab, where he was one day to return in the habit of a monk, and to win the sympathy of a people hostile beyond all others to Christians: then El-Golea, Wargla, where Lieutenant Cauvet was officer in charge (at the end of November, 1885); Tuggurt: the region of Jerid, between the *shott* El-Gharsa and the *shott* El-Jerid. An immense journey through desolate countries, where one must travel many days and sleep many nights, before perceiving, paled by the blinding light, a palm-grove's dash of green. If you try to follow it on the atlas, you will find few names printed between the above-mentioned. But what do they indicate? Not villages, as in Europe, or running rivers, but dunes, stony expanses, fossil rivers, dried-up quagmires where, among the salt deposits of the evaporated waters, a few tufts of reddened or grey grass live with difficulty; a well; the uncertain habitat of a wandering tribe. We know, moreover, that Charles de Foucauld, in love with solitude, already affianced to her, often leaves his native servant and baggage behind, and steals off, until he no longer sees anything around him but the desert. He thus more than once went two days ahead. He used to eat what he had in his pockets. At night he lay down on the ground, and gazed for a long time at the stars. Perhaps training himself to do without sleep. Perhaps the religious crisis which I am going to relate kept him awake, questioning, waiting for the breath of God, which fills the heart better in darkness and silence. He loved scenery, and therefore the starry heavens, the grandest

of all. In the morning he saddled his tethered horse, joined his Arab servant, took food enough for a day or two, and went off again.

Having crossed Southern Algeria, from west to east, he must naturally end on the Tunisian coast. The last oasis he visited was, in fact, the warm and hidden oasis of Gabes, quite close to the shore, where barley and vegetables grow under the bushes, and the bushes beneath the shade of high palms. From there he embarked for France.

Back in Nice, on January 23, 1886, after more than four months' absence, Charles rested until February 19. At that date he left his brother-in-law and sister, came and settled down in Paris, where he took a small apartment at No. 50, Rue de Miromesnil. The period which opens belongs to work and the family circle. The family, far from which he had lived for a long time, received him intelligently and delightfully. There was nothing but joy: no sermons or reproaches, and no wish put forward. He was fêted and they were proud of him; he saw the most select and thoughtful society of Paris. Men, whose ascent to power had made them famous without compromising them, conversed in his presence of the religious and political affairs of France. They were Christians who made no mystery of their Faith. Charles met them every week. Gentle feminine influences were all about him; he lived in the intimacy of relations who reminded him of his mother, and from whom he received, without their knowing it, a perpetual example of wit, grace, and wholesome gaiety and piety. They were the Countess Armand de Foucauld, mother of Louis de Foucauld, the future military attaché in Berlin; and Madame Moitessier and her two daughters, the Countess de Flavigny and the Countess de Bondy.

Inés de Foucauld, Charles's aunt, a person of great beauty, painted twice by Ingres, had married M. Moitessier, a native of Mirecourt, who had made a considerable fortune as an importer of tobacco. She lived in a fine mansion, 42 Rue d'Anjou, at the corner of Boulevard Malesherbes, where she received a great deal of company. Very intelligent, endowed with a will of the Foucaulds, which goes where it wants to go; very much a woman of the world; marvellously skilled in the art of making others appreciated and desired, of appearing interested in discussions she did not quite understand, of starting them again if they languished, marking by a word or smile what she did not approve, without ever offending — she had held the political salon of one of the youngest ministers we have had, Louis Buffet, her husband's nephew, who was minister at the age of thirty. Louis Buffet; Aimé Buffet, his brother, an inspector of bridges and roads; Estancelin, duc de Broglie, had remained the intimates of the house. Some were invited of right, and there were others. Charles was one of those at all Madame Moitessier's "Sunday at homes." In addition to that, he used to go to the Rue d'Anjou several times a week to dine at 6 o'clock, of course always in evening dress. When he got home to the Rue de Miromesnil, he undressed, put on a *gandourah,* soft leather slippers, enfolded himself in a burnous, put a cushion under his head, and lay on a carpet. One of the remarkable particularities of Charles de Foucauld's room was that no bed was seen there. There was none. The furniture was that of a man of taste, who had had ancestors in the history of France, and who dreams of the East. On the walls water-colours and pen sketches of landscapes in Morocco hung beside family portraits painted by Largilliere: here and there were suspended arms and stuffs, brought back from Algeria. The book-case did not contain a great number of books, but the greater number were rare ones or elegant editions. Shut up all day, Charles used to write, delete or correct, consult his notes and put together the solid and magnificent book which was to make his name known to all the geographers in the world and even in other circles. If he was puzzled or had to look up something, he left his work-table and went to a public library, or to Duveyrier's. Duveyrier was celebrated at the age of twenty: since then he had lived in the glory of his past, incapable of renewing it. In 1860, when young men are still but B.A.'s, uncertain of the road to choose, already a botanist, geologist, versed in Oriental languages, thoroughly civilized, marvellously endowed for meeting and winning barbarians, he made the then perilous journey from Laghuat to El-Golea. Imprisoned by the inhabitants of El-Golea, then delivered, he only made use of his liberty to plunge into the dread unknown of the Sahara, to visit the South of Tunis, a part of Tripoli and the territory of the Azjers, the most Oriental, and also the most hostile of all the Tuareg tribes. The book he then wrote very justly made him famous; but prostrated by illness, and hence condemned to be no more than an adviser on the Sahara, Duveyrier suffered, not only from being unable to start afresh and make new discoveries and increase his reputation, but from seeing France lessened in 1871, and as it were diffident of her powers. He never lost his recollection of the work he had done, but could not continue it. He received his rival, the explorer of Morocco, affectionately, and began to travel again, but in a way he did not like: on maps, in books, in his memories, and in those of others.

Slowly, the innumerable documents brought back by Foucauld turned into science and life. Not without some astonishment can one witness this transformation in the habits of the former lieutenant of Pont-a-Mousson and Setif. Whence does it come? Principally from an ambition that had taken possession of him, and which he served with that tense and restless will which was the original mark of Charles de Foucauld, and, it may be said, of his race.

After the publication of the book which he wrote after the excursion to the *shotts,* he had resolved to undertake other great journeys. He did not speak of his plans to anybody, but his mind was often busy with them. Another thought haunted and disturbed it.

I said that Charles de Foucauld had been deeply moved, during his sojourn in Algeria and Morocco, by the perpetual invocation of God among those around him. Their calls to prayer, the prostrations five times a day towards the East, the name of Allah unceasingly repeated in conversations or writings, all the religious pomp of Musulman life, led him to say to himself: "And here am I without religion!" For the Jews prayed also, and to the same God as the Arabs or the Moroccans. The vices which had corrupted the mind or heart of these men had not prevented their meditative witness from feeling the grandeur of faith. Again in Algeria, he had even said to a few of his friends: "I am thinking of becoming a Musulman." Words of feeling, which reason had not ratified. On the first examination, it appeared to him, as he confided to one of his intimate friends, that the religion of Mahomet could not be the true one, "being too material." But the uneasiness remained. Blessed be it! For it is a proof of superiority in him who experiences it, a great event in the order of grace, the blessed sign that a soul is going to find the way again. This young man, born in Catholicism, lacked a good understanding of this magnificent, divine and sound religion, and any such sense of its transcendence to return to it without hesitation as soon as the tyranny of matter weighed too heavily upon him. He was, in truth, sad at the bottom of his heart, with an old sadness. Live a life of pleasure as he would, it had only increased. It had held him, as he confessed when he wrote: "silent and overwhelmed at so-called fêtes." Since then, it had neither been dispelled by man's science, nor by action, nor by success and fame. Now he had certainly submitted to the discipline of work, and hence felt better than in the past, but not disburdened of his faults, not what he ought to be, morally very far from those dear ones whom he saw living in his own united and happy family.

He read a great deal. But a great secret cowardice is in us when it is a question of taking up a rule of life which we know to be strict and repressive. We seek approximations in order not to have to come to the ideal of perfection, and trembling nature makes us take counsel with men rather than with God, because we know that God is exacting. It was thus that Charles de Foucauld, in the intervals of writing the *Reconnaissance au Maroc,* used to consult pagan philosophers, and question them upon duty, the soul, and the life to come. He thought their answers were poor. They are necessarily

so. Unguided reason does not go far in the problem of creation and destiny. Charles's mind was too clear to be satisfied with the noise of words and the brilliancy of images. He also knew that the philosophy of ancient times had purified nothing, softened nothing, brought no consolation, and doubtless he would have returned to the maxim of absolute scepticism he had learnt at college: "Man cannot know the truth," if the sight of the chosen little society in which he again found himself had not each day shaken the fragile authority of this inference.

The probity, delicacy, and charity which had become habitual and in a manner natural, the joy also of the consciences around him which were not hidden from him, but which he could read, constantly forced him to return to himself. "Here are," he said to himself, "men and women, all cultivated, some of quite superior intelligence, and since they entirely accept the Catholic Faith, may it not be true? They had studied it, they live it fully. And what do I, indeed, know of it? Honestly, do I know Catholicism?"

Mere anxiety about such things is itself prayer, and God was hearkening to it. A few pages of a Christian book which he had opened after so many others, in a moment of anguish — I do not know what it was — began to enlighten this unbeliever, who had sought perfect beauty and infinite tenderness wherever they were not.

Probably his aunt, cousins, and sister, who came several times to see him in Paris, and whom he loved tenderly, had some suspicion of the interior work which was leading a stray heart and mind to the truth. They did not hurry it on by any human means. They were good and kind, they followed the straight path, they prayed. It was by chance that one evening, at Madame Moitessier's, Charles met Abbé Huvelin, who had long been a friend of many of the de Foucaulds. Being very humble, very simple, very much a man of prayer and mysticism, this old Normal scholar made a great impression on the man who was one day to resemble him. What did he say that evening?

It is quite certain he did not try to be smart. If he had wit, it was because he could not help having it. Friendships like that about to spring up between Charles de Foucauld and him have not their origin in words, nor in the brilliancy of talent, nor in the will to conquer. An unbeliever, who had also lived badly, finds himself in presence of another man, not only believing and chaste, but now a man of prayer, and the essence of pity for man's immense frailty and suffering; perhaps even more, perhaps one of the victims who are said to offer themselves in secret to God, suffering to make reparation for the evil, and to alleviate the punishment of others. These two men may only have exchanged commonplace remarks; may only have bowed, then looked at each other five or six times that evening. That was enough: they recognized and waited for one another; in their hearts henceforth they called this meeting a great event. The one thought: "You are religion itself"; the other: "Brother, unhappy brother, I am but a poor man, but God is very kind. He is seeking your soul's salvation." They never forgot one another.

Abbé Huvelin, born in 1838, was therefore, in 1886, still a young man, although he hardly appeared so; the penitent life which he led from his youth, and which had made his comrades of the École Normale smile or stirred them; the fatigue of being and of having been at the mercy of all sorrows in quest of easing, of all human restlessness seeking a decision; illness also, a sort of general rheumatism which already afflicted him, left him little but the youth of a quick mind and a very tender heart. His head leant upon his shoulder, and his face was full of wrinkles; walking was often a torture to him. In Paris, this curate at Saint Augustine's had a tremendous clientele of penitents, innumerable friends, and, what further singularly added to the complications of his life, a reputation for sanctity.

Holiness is the most powerful attraction for drawing souls together. His had promptly revealed itself in the conferences which he gave to young men, from 1875, on the History of the Church. In spite of his protestations, he had seen women in great numbers, and men whose youth was over, mix with the public for which his conferences in the crypt were first arranged. He spoke also, in the parish pulpit, and they thronged to hear the talks of one who did not make a recitation, did not seek to astonish, but improvised on a theme always thoroughly prepared, pouring forth an exuberant wit in living and natural language, prudent in doctrine, bold in what he had to say, abundant in reminiscences of literature or history, a man of digressions, parentheses, exclamations, and unexpected flashes — above all, a man with a long experience of the world and of mercy. Hence he was near each of his hearers: hence he was their sure and wished-for friend. His pity for sinners, one may say his tenderness for them, touched the most indifferent. They felt that he wished them better so that they might be happier, and that he was always thinking, for those who hardly reflected about it, of the definite hour at which they would appear before God, when they would be judged, condemned in their unhappiness without hope of dying, for death does not exist, even for a moment; all we have is two lives.

The extreme zeal of Abbé Huvelin, the steps he took, the visits he paid and those he received, his immense correspondence — short, affectionate, and clear notes — the increase of austerity, proof of which is forthcoming at certain periods, though we cannot exactly tell why: all this is explained by his love for souls in danger.

For yet another reason, and a very powerful one, he was a counsellor to whom people resorted at once: he understood human suffering. He sympathized with it; whatever it was, he had already met and heard and helped it. For him no aspect of it was unknown. Of it he said, simplifying a phrase of Bossuet's and stripping off its seventeenth-century majesty: "We get a charm from sorrow." In the same spirit he thus defined the Church: "The Church is a widow." This saying to a society woman is also his:

"Long ago I found out how to be happy."
"How?"
"By abstaining from pleasures."
But to give a better understanding of how far such words go, I must quote others, and

shall do so from one of his hearers. At the same time we shall hear the orator speak. It will be no hors-d'oeuvre, since we are speaking with the priest who is to convert Charles de Foucauld and turn him into Father de Foucauld.

"Jesus is the Man of Sorrows, because He is the Son of Man, and man is but sorrow. Sorrow accompanies us from birth to death; it purifies and ennobles us, it gives us charm. It is because it is our inseparable companion that Jesus wished it to be His.

"Great souls — for the honour of humanity, we must have some to follow in the footsteps of Christ — have called for and desired sorrow. They have said the *Fac me tecum plangere* of the *Stabat Mater*. We have no such ambition; we only ask to accept sorrow with compunction and resignation, when it is offered.

"Far from us, above all, be those little sorrows, less easy to endure than the great ones, those wounds so paltry, so peevish, so venomous, wrought by the passions, and by self-love! It is the shame of mankind to suffer so much for so little.

"Jesus in the Garden of Olives. He is sorrowful even unto death. The apostles do not understand His sorrow; this divine sorrow is too far beyond them. To understand it, one must know what sin is. They knew it not, nor can we know it.

"His attitude is not a Greek attitude. He does not dominate His sadnesss, does not say, as a stoic would: 'Sorrow, thou art but a word!' Far from it! Sorrow invaded Him through every pore; it inundated His soul; it rose like a tide and submerged all the heights.

"He prays, but His prayer is not the natural movement, the happy breathing of His soul; nor is it a flow of beautiful thoughts; it is a sob, a sob dying down into an amen. 'So be it!' is His whole prayer. His will, united, identified hitherto with that of the Father, now for the first time seems something distinct. The load is too heavy: 'Thou canst do all things: take away this chalice from Me.'

"He seeks help from the Apostles and finds them asleep. One is alone in sadness when yearning for a word from the heart. Friends come only in our hours of calm, or if they drop in during the storm, they don't want to say what should be said, or they wound by their want of tact or silliness. Such were Job's friends.

"At last an angel comes to strengthen Him: *Angelus confortavit eum*. To strengthen, not to console Him. Grace is essentially strengthening, not consoling. . . ."

I cannot quote more at length without going beyond my purpose. The above quotation and what I have said are enough to make us understand why all human miseries, all doubts, and all repentance went naturally to Abbé Huvelin. He heard confessions at Saint Augustine's, he received many people at home. What a robust and agile mind must this invalid and cripple have had, to form one idea after another of all the moral problems submitted to him, so as to study and solve them in a moment! But he was gifted with so sure a judgment that he unravelled all the cases, and with a vision so penetrating of the intimate dispositions of the persons who consulted him, that several attributed it to a singular grace of God. Even circumstances are quoted in which he alluded to past and secret events in the life of his penitents. His advice was clear, simple, full of good sense, and he did not change it. He varied it according to persons. He did not treat bears as if they were swallows. More than once he was heard to say: "To some, one has to say: 'You must submit to that!' In canonical decisions there is a force with which those who despise them have to reckon more fully than they think." This great specialist in spiritual direction was generally at home in the afternoon. People of all ages and classes, Parisians and passing travellers, were to be met in his little antechamber. By turns they entered the next room, filled with books and papers, in which M. Huvelin was sitting with a cat on his knees, and as resigned to the crowd as to illness. The visitors who had been introduced to him, even in the distant past, were sure to be recognized. He listened with all his faculties. As he was brief, he required them to be the same. His office was a hard one. He, though naturally

gay, was very often seen to weep; he suffered with all the sorrows brought to him,
with all the sins acknowledged to him, or
that he divined in men's hearts.

Such was the priest eminent in holiness —
that is to say, in the science of God and
man — whom Charles de Foucauld had met
late one summer's evening. They did not
immediately see each other again. But in
Charles's soul the tide of grace was rising.
One does not know whence it first comes. It
is promised to men of good-will, or rather
it is already given to them, and their good-
will itself is its work. Just when it looked
a long way off, it has already covered the
muddy background; it is cool; it brings the
birds with it, and its waves, breaking one
after another, all say: "You must believe, be
pure, be joyous with the great joy of God,
and get the light on the living waters." This
dim stirring, this desire for illumination, he
felt more and more strongly within him.
Between two walks or at nightfall, he might
now be seen to go into a church; he would
sit far from the altar, understanding neither
what had drawn him in, nor what held him
there; and he would say none of his prayers
of former days, but this, which went straight
up to heaven: "My God, if You exist, make
me know it!"

One October evening, in one of those
family talks, in which the mind and heart
speak freely and without trying to find the
way, when the children were playing round
the table before going to bed, one of his
cousins said to Charles:

"It appears that Abbé Huvelin will not go
on with his conferences again; I regret it
very much."

"So do I," replied Charles, "for I intended
to follow them."

The reply was not noticed. Some days later
he gravely said to his cousin:

"You are fortunate to believe; I am seeking the light and do not find it."

Between October 27 and 30, the next day
after this conversation, Abbé Huvelin saw a
young man enter his confessional without
kneeling down. He simply bent forward and
said:

"Abbé, I have not the faith, I have come
to ask you to instruct me."

M. Huvelin looked at him.

"Kneel down, confess to God; you will
believe."

"But I did not come for that."

"Confess."

The man who wanted to believe felt that
pardon was for him the condition of light.
He knelt down, and made a confession of all
his life.

When he saw the absolved penitent get up,
the Abbé added:

"Are you fasting?"

"Yes."

"Go to communion!"

And Charles de Foucauld at once approached the holy table, and made his "second first communion."

He did not speak of his conversion. It
was by certain acts that it was gradually seen
that the depths of his soul were changed.
His life continued to be laborious; peace
had returned to it, and was always trans-
parently visible in his eyes, smile, voice or
words. His letters, which never had ceased
being affectionate, became grateful. The
name of God often occurs in them. His life
is silently remoulded on the recovered ideal.
In this renewal all is profound, discreet, and
simple.

LÉON BLOY
(1846–1917)

MANY of the great French Catholics of our day are deeply indebted to Léon Bloy for the gift of faith. Bloy's life remains a mystery of grace, for with all his great gifts he was largely unhappy except in the long hours he spent in prayer.

Bloy was born in Perigeux, 1846, and he had an unhappy childhood without belief or real comfort. His artistic career began with an interest in painting, but as secretary to Barbey d'Aurevilly he turned his talents into the field of literature.

The Woman Who Was Poor is generally considered his best work. It indicates something of his mastery of invective and spiritual depth, though its action often verges on melodrama.

In the *Letters to His Fiancée* Bloy tells his future wife of his anguish and loneliness and exposes his devotion to religion and the science of the soul.

His influence was not confined to his books. Those who knew him loved him and listened to his advice. From the lectures of Bergson many ardent souls took the next step toward the Church by becoming friends of Bloy, who in a sense represented the Church in action as did no other French Catholic of his time. Among his noted converts are Jacques and Räissa Maritain.

OCTOBER 31, 1889.*

JEANNE, MY DEAR LOVE,

I adore you and my whole heart is yours. I am always at your feet, my little queen of the north, and your beautiful fine hair has given me a child-like joy. I have kissed it with an ardour of love that can drive such a man as I to suffering and to suffocation. It is impossible that you should not understand that, my darling love, you who pretend not to understand the Roman veneration for the relics of saints.

The fault, perhaps the only fault, in your education, is to have given you too great a confidence in the speculations of the mind, and I must confess that this disturbs me and grieves me when I think of it. I would like you to live more by the heart than by the mind because that is how I have always lived, and thus we should be more united.

Since you are going to be my wife, and since you are so already by my choice and by our irrevocable formal wish, it is necessary that you should understand me and know exactly what manner of man I am. It would be a very grave and tragic error — since it would hinder you from being completely united to me — if you thought that I was a thinker, an intellectual man. In reality I know very little, and I have never understood but what God has caused me to understand when I have become like a little child.

I am *above all* — never forget it — an *adorer*, and I have always seen myself as lower than the animals whenever I have tried to act otherwise than by love and the workings of love. God has given me imagination and memory, nothing else. But my reason is very dull, more or less what the reason of an ox must be, and the faculty of analysis as philosophers understand it is completely lacking in me.

My mother, whom I resemble, applied to me a famous remark which was once made about a great doctor of the Church: "My dear child, it is true that you are an ox, but an ox whose bellowing will one day astonish Christianity." Poor, sad and dear mother! she preferred me to all my brothers because she thought that God had endowed me with great things. I don't know whether my bellowings will finally have power, but I do know that the faculty of loving is developed in your friend to an unheard-of extent. I assure you that this is enough for me, and I ask nothing else since I am perfectly sure that the rest will be given me in addition. Philosophy wearies me, theology bores me to

---

*Bloy, Léon, *Letters To His Fiancée* (New York: Sheed and Ward, 1937), pp. 46–64.

death, words without love are unintelligible to me, the reasonings of the wise seem like a cloak of darkness, and the conceit of the human mind makes me sick.

I implore you to remember the expression of Our Lord in the eleventh chapter of St. Matthew, verse 25: "I confess to thee, O Father, Lord of heaven and earth, because thou hast hid these things from the wise and prudent, and hast revealed them to the little ones."

Do you think that the superb reformers who dared to take it upon themselves to turn the eyes of millions of souls away from their Mother, remembered those words?

I once knew a very poor girl — Véronique — devoid of learning as much as anyone could be but whose heart shone like all the stars and constellations. She knew nothing, except her own nothingness and the *unreasoning obedience* that love demanded. Because of that she was raised to the contemplation of the glory of God and received such light that I cannot think of it without dying of admiration and awe.

My dear Jeanne, if you thought that by an effort of reason you would arrive at religious truths, you were as cruelly mistaken as if you thought you should go to the North Pole to get to India. The people who have tried to do this have always been frozen to death.

You tell me that you are more of a *heretic* than I realise. I realise that you are very much of one, alas! and it is a thought that fills me with grief, my poor child. *I am a heretic* has always meant: I am separated from God, the enemy of God, I have no Mother, no Father, no brothers, I am without faith, hope and love and my desolate soul is in terrifying solitude. Only with you, dear friend of my heart, you repeat the lessons of your childhood and do not really know what you are saying. If you did know, I should be pierced with despair and should have to renounce you.

The veneration of the Relics of saints — a custom as old as the Church — worries you, my darling. At the same time the things that belonged to your father, for example, are precious to you. If you possessed a fraction of his bones you would carefully enclose it in a padded casket and you would sometimes look at the poor relic with tenderness. Why should you think that God, Who is Love itself, should take no pleasure in the mortal remains of those who were His greatest friends on earth and who are now sharing His glory? The Roman Church — whatever the heretical calumnies may say in this respect — teaches simply that the Spirit of God, that is to say the Third Divine Person, lives in the relics of the saints in the way a powerful scent cannot be detached from the things that it has pervaded; and, because of this, the relics of the saints merit not adoration but honour and veneration. That is all. I fail to understand how such a natural thing can be the cause of so much wonder. I would give my life to kiss the bones of Joseph as he is spoken of in Exodus xiii. 19, and I believe on the testimony of God that very great miracles can be worked by the relics of saints. I recommend to you the text in the fourth book of Kings xiii. 21, and also the book of Ecclesiastes xlviii. 14.

It pains me very much to think of you as a heretic, but, my dear love, I am not really worried. It is obvious to me that God wants you and is calling you. That is why He has given you love for me. Your heart had to be sweetened and softened and made humble by human love. Some day you will think the same as me, or rather you will *feel* like me, and the objections that you have today will seem very small.

I think I shall always remember my visit of about ten years ago to Lyons, the town of martyrs. I went to the crypt where Saint Blandine and Saint Pothin died after receiving cruel punishments for their love of Jesus in the reign of the *gentle* philosopher, Marcus-Aurelius. There I received one of the strongest impressions that the human soul is capable of. I melted with love and I sobbed with joy, and that impression stayed with me for a long time. I then had a further light upon the saints, upon the love of the living God dwelling in the midst of His beloved dead, and I am convinced that no doubts nor difficulties of this world will ever be able to weaken that light from heaven.

Dear Jeanne, a thousand times loved, have confidence in your soul, in the beautiful soul that God has given you, and do not mistrust your heart. It will always be greater, stronger, and more generous than your mind — your mind, which will infallibly lead you astray if you have the misfortune to depend on it. If you knew how much I despise mine, how I scoff at it and flog it every time it tries to dictate to my heart of which, *according to nature,* it should be the humble and obedient servant. We have been made in the likeness of God, of God Who is Three in One, the Father and the Son in the unity of Love. What in us corresponds to the Father is the marvellous *ensemble* of our physical and intellectual organs; the Son is represented by our faculty of knowing, that is to say the human Reason; but all that would be as nothing without the gift of love which surpasses everything, which is greater than everything and which gives us a supreme harmony. Those who obey the first two only are brutes of flesh and pride. Those who follow the Third will one day shine like the sun — be they monsters of ugliness, idiots, or full of all the dirt of humanity.

Beloved, one day I shall write for you and for others what I think about love, because this letter is too short and too hastily written for me to express such sublime thoughts.

Remember that to-morrow is one of the greatest feast-days of Love. It is the feast-day of all those who loved Jesus Christ, who gave Him their souls and their blood for pure *Love,* who were without pride, without confidence in themselves, and who, because of that, shine with the greatest imaginable splendour.

Till to-morrow, then, my darling Jeanne. I adore you and I implore Our Lord Jesus and His Mother to bless you and to ravish your dear soul with joy. I love you with such a great love that I would consent *never* to be happy if I could, at such a cost, cause you to enter into the light.

Your
LÉON BLOY.

Sunday, November 3, '89.

How beautiful your letter is, my beloved Jeanne; and how moving! How admirable are the workings of God in your dear soul! O, you have made me happy to-day, I assure you, very happy and very proud of you, my generous and perfect friend. It is intoxicating for me to have been the occasion of your seeing the light and to have obtained so soon what I hardly dared to hope. Blessed be the saints, blessed be the dead, blessed be the pure Virgin Mary *whose name I possess* and whose all-powerful intercession has achieved this prodigy.

I longed for it so much, my love, and I hardly dared talk to you about it on account of the freedom of your soul, and for fear of frightening you! You will see, my sweet angel of mercy and of light, how we shall be even more perfectly united now that no important disagreement can exist between us; and our conversations which have already been so sweet, will become ravishingly lovely! And when our Father Jesus, so full of tenderness and forgiveness, gives us to each other in the sacrament of marriage which He has instituted, our happiness will be so great and so pure that it seems the inhabitants of paradise will envy us. My dear beloved Jeanne, you will then be, as you already are, my paradise of delight; and observe, my love, that that word is not merely a caress of language — one of those tender exaggerations by which loving hearts try to put something of the infinite into their sentiments. It is rare, as you will see, that I speak without meaning profoundly what I say. The second chapter of Genesis in which the earthly paradise is described is, as I see it, a symbolic picture of *Woman.* That is one of the discoveries of which I am very proud and I assure you that this description is incomparably beautiful. O! Lord Jesus! how happy we shall be when we are in solitude, occupied solely in loving each other in God and in working for our brothers while studying the Scriptures! Sometimes, when I think of that, my heart is so oppressed with desire and so stirred with almost painful flutterings that I feel I shall faint.

God loves you very much, my chosen one, my beautiful conquest, my exquisite and ravishing promised land. God is showing you His love in an exceptional way. Although conversions are not very rare events, yours most certainly is of an extraordinary brand. See how swift have been the movements of grace in you. You cannot judge now, but later on you will see this magnificent sight clearly; you will really know the gift of God and your gratitude to Him will be boundless. What a beautiful future is ours, my darling! Because I want to accept and believe utterly what you have written to me, I want to be certain that you are right in announcing that my suffering is nearly ended and that Jesus, in calling you to His service, has given you conviction. Evidently it must be so. All this that is happening to us is too wonderful, too supernatural, too stamped with the divine Hand for us to be able to suppose that this Hand is going to abandon us half-way; that is to say, before it has let us rest in the light for a while.

You are aware, my dear predestined one, that you are being treated with great love, but if you knew the joy that awaits you! If you knew the delights of the Holy Ghost which will come upon you as soon as you are acquainted with the sacraments of the holy, infallible Church! You see, these joys are such that the whole world seems a heap of mud and one would give up one's limbs to an executioner with transports of joy. I tell you this from experience, as it is impossible to understand or imagine these things when one has not experienced them. You will be drunk with happiness, and at the same time very lucid, and saturated with light. Your heart will be full of Jesus, and you will find Him as heavy as a world and yet so gentle, so exquisitely sweet to carry that you will ask avidly for other burdens to prove your strength. O my beautiful and sweet friend, my adored Jeanne, how enviable you are and how happy I am to have been chosen as the companion of your marvellous pilgrimage — my little wife of goodwill whom the love of God will make one of His saints!

I am happy to-day and very hopeful.

I shall have seen Father Sylvester by Wednesday.

The men who claimed to be wiser than their Mother 300 years ago, and who in fact deprived many peoples and many generations of these delights — which are unknown to Protestant pride — these supposed reformers were really very cruel homicides, and who can measure their terrifying responsibility?

As you know, England was once called Merry England, but since she has refused to obey the prince of Apostles in order to bow down to an infamous Tudor who was a monster of lust and cruelty, she has become — poor nation — a hell of melancholy. I suppose that it is more or less the same with all the nations who have separated themselves from the true Church. It is possible that intellectual speculation has gained, but at what price, great God? For the people who know the Bible and Tradition and the complete history of humanity, Joy is the most infallible sign of the presence of God and that is why the Northern peoples, eaten up with sadness, come and visit the Latin countries where alone there is something of the wonderful joy of the first Christians who died of love rather than by the tooth of lions or the nail of persecutors.

I was thinking, my darling. Will you tell your mother about this *straight away*? Perhaps I am wrong, but I think that it would not be the most prudent course. Take great care. It is not your duty to tell her in advance, and the result of taking that step would be objections and reproaches — in fact a painful correspondence from which your soul would suffer, and it is necessary that you should be serene. I depend on your wisdom, my darling love, and I depend even more on God who will inspire you.

I have been writing for two or three hours now, my good angel, as I am very slow. So I shall stop. I should have liked to write you a sublime letter which would have been like fire and light to you, but I am feeling very stupid to-day and can think of nothing, except that I love you more and more, and shall die of grief if we are not married soon.

Good-bye, then, until Wednesday evening.

Your

Marie-Léon Bloy.

Tuesday evening (November 5).

Jeanne, my beloved wife, my sweetest angel, your letters make me die of happiness and love. I have had two cruel days — yesterday especially — but don't be worried, I am not without hope. I am desolated not to have been able to answer your second blessed letter to-day. I want to write to you quickly here in this café where I am awaiting a friend who, alas, does not seem to be coming. Even if I have neither time nor ability to co-ordinate my ideas, I want to tell you at least that I love you infinitely, that I am mad with love of you and that what hurts me most cruelly is not to be able to share my life with you, sweet dove of the flood of my sufferings who has come carrying the divine olive branch of reconciliation. You speak of your conversion, but, my darling queen, you will understand sometime what a wonderful change has come over me since I have known you.

Well, we shall meet to-morrow, Wednesday, at those nice and faithful friends' who love you already. I tremble with joy at the thought.

My beloved, do not be anxious. The answer from your Danish friend does not surprise me. I had a foreboding that it would not succeed, especially as you mentioned me — which would incline her to criticise you and would make her obstinate.

I am afflicted *for you,* because you have taken a useless step, but it is good for you to have made an experiment. You thought this person was your friend and she is not. It is useful to know these things even if they cause pain.

You know, my dear love, that I have some ideas about *money,* the absence of which has caused me so much suffering. One of my ideas is that this mysterious metal, in virtue of a divine secret, is the *sign of friendship.* I mentioned this once to some imbeciles who thought I was saying something low and cynical, so I gave them a transcendant insight into what I meant: "I recognise a *friend* by this sign — that he gives me money." You, my darling, my beautiful forehead of light, you will understand I am

sure. I have some poor friends who have never been able to help me with their purses, but I *know* that they suffer for me; it is absolutely as though they had given me millions with the blood of their veins. You will see later, my adored, how great this idea is; it lights up this sad and wonderful world where Jesus, the Son of God, was able to be bought and sold for money.

In your dear letter there is a word that troubles me. You say that you want to sacrifice your time to pray. I fear that there is an illusion there. What God demands from each of us is the sacrifice of our *will,* nothing else, and that includes everything.

If circumstances demand that you spend the time when you might be praying in doing trivial things, then you should look on that as an order from God and believe that this sacrifice is more pleasing to Him than prayer, in fact that it is itself a better prayer.

As to my sufferings, my beloved Jeanne, accept them generously as being willed by God, and I beg of you not to pay too much attention to my complaints. If I have got to be unhappy, very unhappy, for a long time yet — which I do not believe — so much the better for you. It is necessary to pay your debt. When we receive a divine grace we ought to realise that someone has paid for it for us. Such is the law. God is infinitely good, but at the same time He is infinitely just and, as such, an infinitely rigorous creditor. About fifteen years ago, when you were still a small girl, I spent months beseeching God, in prayers that resembled tempests, that He should make me suffer as much as a man can suffer so that my friends, my brothers, and all the souls unknown to me who lived in darkness, should receive help; and I assure you, my love, that my prayer was granted in a terrible way. Well, then, I am convinced that it was thus that I conquered you, and that by the harrowing sufferings of fifteen years I have paid for the wonderful joys that are going to be yours.

I tell you that, my dear adored wife, because I want to tell you everything. But I also think that I shall soon have paid everything, and who knows whether your happy conversion is not the signal for my deliverance.

I must stop now. Until to-morrow, my dear love.

Your

LÉON BLOY.

Wednesday morning, November 6, '89.

MY BELOVED,

Last night I wrote you a wretched letter which you will have received this morning, at the moment when I received yours which has made me, as always, very joyful and a little sad. It is very painful to have to be so fearful of the eyes of the world.

I would like to have written you a long and interesting letter, as that is the only resource left to us. But dreadful necessity forces me to go out. I am still suffering, my beloved angel, and my chief consolation is the thought that my sufferings, accepted for your sake, will be useful to you.

May God bless you above all His creatures and may He have pity on us *soon*. . . .

The useless efforts that you have made for me, my most gentle Jeanne, are only another proof of what I have noticed for years and years. Until the unknown hour of my liberation, *I shall have no success,* not even such as the rest of the world has. But I cannot perish. I am upheld in a wonderful and incomprehensible way, but only enough to ensure that I shall not perish, only enough to ensure my living with unconquerable hope and unceasing suffering. This is what I explained to you last night.

The reason for my thinking that the end of the long trial is approaching, and that soon all will be paid that must be paid — is that my strength is giving out. If this life went on for much longer I should die, and that is not possible because I have *certainly* a great work to accomplish.

I am hoping, my only love, that your reputation will not be harmed. I have, however, many enemies and the malice of man is great. It is possible that until that day when I can call you my wife out loud, there will be suspicion and gossip from which I cannot defend you, my poor child. But listen, we must persuade ourselves that we are like the first Christians *given to the beasts.* We must be contemptuous and endure everything for the love of God. You belong to the Lord of Heaven and you are mine for life and eternity. You must be very valiant, courageous, and deaf to uncharitable and cruel remarks.

For myself, I hold the world (for which Jesus said He would not pray) as being so vile that its outrages no longer affect me. If I am not mistaken, I am truly called to do what I was told in days gone by: I have got to expect every kind of malediction, every kind of calumny, and a mountain of mud on my head, and that, I assure you, does not trouble me.

I must stop now, my beloved, to go and suffer for another day. God treats me with great sternness; may His holy name be praised!

My adored, whatever things I may say to you from day to day, never doubt my love, which is great enough to accept everything. I am bound to you in an invincible way and if by a miracle of hell — excuse this absurd supposition — you could fail and yourself lose yourself, you would not lose me. I would still be your husband, your most loving friend and companion in the light of the throne of God, whither I would lead you by the hand, gently.

Until to-night, my beloved. I adore you.

LÉON BLOY.

LÉON BLOY 457

PART I*

CHAPTER XXVI

A BIG evening party at Gacougnol's. Except for Clotilde, all present are men. A half-score of men, counting as man a certain half-fledged snake of the most venomous type who crawled habitually in the spittoons of various editorial offices, and had achieved fame by his ferocious tongue. He is designated only by the descriptive epithet or nickname of Apimanthus. He was once given a crippling cudgelling with a walking-stick—and ever since had trailed himself round. He devoted himself to studied insolence, for all the world like a still in which deadly poisons were prepared.

A queer gathering, if without superficiality one can call anything queer. It was sometimes Gacougnol's whim thus to group together the most ill-assorted individuals.

For instance, who would not gaze in wonder at the droll exterior of the old engraver, Klatz, when he was seen in the company of Leopold and Marchenoir—a dirty and ill-smelling Jew, but incurably untalented, whose babble of apophthegms, like the chattering of an Alsatian second-hand dealer, was valued as an unrivalled medicine against all forms of melancholia?

He was once handsome, people said. When, in Heaven's name? For he looked every minute of a hundred years old! The first time of meeting him, one could fancy one was looking at Ahasuerus, the Wandering Jew. His long beard, of an earthly, dingy white, that outvied the ashes of the dead, looked as if it had dragged for nineteen centuries through all the highways and tombs of the world. Despite their obvious vivacity, his eyes seemed so far off that a telescope, one might almost think, would have been useful for studying them. With that, possibly, one might have discerned, far back in their depths, the morose countenance of the "good" Titus watching the destruction of Jerusalem.

Of a surety such eyes must once have bewitched the foolish daughters of Tyre or Mesopotamia, who came to play upon the citherum or the tympanon beneath the very walls of the impregnable tower of Hippicos, for the damnation of God's people. But since those distant ages how many layers of dust! How many rains upon that dust! How many winds, burning or frozen, all-withering, all-dispersing, all-destroying!

In fine, this personage, with an air of being still in search of the Ark of the Covenant carried away by the Philistines, whenever he entered any place, was for keen ethnologists the definitive result of the most irrefutable Jewish selective breeding.

His Levitical nose in itself implied, inevitably, the *Ve'elle Shemoth*, the *Shophetim,* the *Shir-Hasirim,* or the Lamentations of the Prophet; and the decay of sixty venerable generations, pulverised by planetary ruins, clung to him.

Zephyrin Delumiere was not excluded. A mystagogue bearing no malice, he had certainly forgotten the ungracious welcome accorded to him by Pélopidas on an occasion described earlier in these pages. The magi have memories that lack the knack of retaining anything not occult. This one, moreover, had for some time been clinging closely to the coat-tails of old man Klatz, whose semitic scent fascinated him, and from whom, too, he had picked up a few Hebrew words.

But Gacougnol's eclecticism was especially demonstrated by the presence of Folantin, the naturalist and futurist painter, whose success, long withheld, had just come to him.

It would be difficult to find anything more instructive than the chronological catalogue of his works.

After an initiatory series of unpleasant little landscapes laboriously scratched in the sterile suburbs, after the semi-triumph of a "genre-picture" in which the indecisive love-making of a young mason and a crafty-eyed sempstress, in the privacy of a "furnished bed-sitting room," coagulated beneath the eyes

*Bloy, Léon, *The Woman Who Was Poor* (New York: Sheed and Ward, 1939), pp. 160–172.

of the spectator into livid mastic, like a cheese that had been cut into — Folantin, wearying of not appearing as a Thinker, decided to dispense a modicum of philosophical moralising in his output.

Then there rose on the horizon, to the inexpressible discouragement of a number of manikins of the mahlstick, the starling picture of a complaisant or betrayed husband, made of sugar, carrying a candlestick, and showing out, with the most frigid politeness, a dried-up looking creature whom he has surprised in the arms of his wife. This was entitled, "Domestic Life!" But it evoked less praise than the furnished bed-sitting room, the vogue of which, alas, was beginning to be threatened, and it became necessary to think of something else.

With a complete change of weapons, he painted, with emphasis, a Great Gentleman, a Scion of lofty lineage, whose type he studied in the person of a genuine specimen of the Gentry who had adopted the career of collecting the unlabelled cigar-ends of modern poetry.

The aristocrat was depicted, entirely without his own consent, straddled on a bidet, reading verses with twenty-five feet in the line. And, contrary to all possible human expectation, it so happened that this allegorical portrait became a minor sort of masterpiece, and the nobility of France — once the foremost in the world — once more proved themselves so low that the caricature conceived by Folantin, when confronted with the original, created for a moment an illusion of strength.

The fortunate painter held his head high among the stars, and managed to annex a few disciples. There was no getting away from it. However much opposed one might be to Folantin and his hateful painting documented like a novel of the Moron School, his personality surmounted its pillory, which had become a pedestal, with something of the grandeur of an equestrian statue.

From that moment the new Master spurned small frames, and plunged into huge canvases on the heroic scale.

Crowds jostled one another round his Black Mass and his Trappists at Prayer —

enormous rought-cast compositions, daubed with little niggling brushes, that had to be scrutinised by the square centimetre, with a geologist's or numismatist's magnifying-glass, with no hope of ever attaining the beatific vision of any general whole.

The first of these monstrosities was apparently calculated for the moving and firing of a recent brood of Philistines consumed with a longing for the lubricities of Hell. Nevertheless since our great man felt that in spite of everything it was his mission to instruct his contemporaries, it is at the same time a supreme achievement in a sort of clowning in paint, elaborated and finedrawn till it becomes a whirlpool of detail — but a black whirlpool, unspeakably foetid and profaning!

The Trappists at Prayer aimed at being an antithesis, the obverse of the preceding revelation. Folantin, more triumphantly and blatantly complacent every day, set out to demonstrate how an artist daring enough to kiss the Devil's saddle, was able on the other hand to exploit spiritual ecstasies.

Folantin, with sudden wizardry, discovered Catholicism!

His vision was but poorly rewarded. The bigoted religiosity of St. Sulpice, challenged to a duel, pierced his heart with its aspergillum. Once more, however, he profited by the revival of credit which religious interests seemed to be enjoying, towards the end of the century, and his mantle as an innovator did not shrink to the humble jacket one might have supposed after such an achievement.

The outward appearance of this pontiff might have been compared to one of those very poor trees, the American Walnut, or the Japanese Gum, that bear poisonous or illusory fruit, and give but a pallid shadow. He was specially proud of his hands, which he regarded as extra-ordinary, "the hands of a very thin baby, with thin, tapering fingers," was how he described them, in his kindly way — for he bore himself no grudge.

"I see myself," he declared, to a reporter, "as a courteous cat, very polite, almost affectionate, but touchy — ready to bare my claws at the least word."

The cat, indeed, seemed to be *his animal,* but without its gracefulness. He was capable of lying in wait for his prey, indefinitely; and even for the prey of others. And this with a ferocious gentleness that no insult could disconcert. He welcomed all with a feigned half-smile just showing, letting fall, every now and then, a few delicate, metallic, wire-drawn sentences that sometimes left his hearers wondering if they were listening to a living being.

He was the man who "never got worked up." The scornful tilt of his upper lip was assured, for everlasting, against all lyricism, all enthusiasm, all vehemence of the emotions, and his most apparent passion was to seem like a razor-sharp current beneath a flooded river.

"That fellow is Envy Personified!" Barbey D'Aurevilly one day exclaimed, with precision, and with that word slew him.

All the same, his malignancy was not without circumspection. Exceedingly careful of his celebrity, which he cultivated in secret as if it had been a rare and sensitive cactus, he lost no opportunity of mingling with journalists whom he considered himself entitled to despise, or with certain fellow-painters of frank unreticence, whose ideas he refined on. The nasty story about the original sketch for the Black Mass is considered to be authentic — how he got it for a few louis from an artist dying of want — a superb rough outline which he lost no time in debasing with the brush, after ignominiously dismissing the wretched man who had presented him with such a godsend.

It will seem difficult to believe that the independent Gacougnol should have received at his home a character so perfectly calculated to exasperate him. But, as we have seen, this good man recognized no rule but his good pleasure, and it was undoubtedly in the hope of some clash occurring that he had drawn together under the same roof those whose antagonisms were so inevitable.

In any case, apart from Leopold, Marchenoir, or himself, were there not present Bohémond de l' Isle-de-France, and Lazare Druide, and could the extreme repulsion inspired by Folantin fail to be outweighed by these two radiantly sympathetic personalities?

The former was known all over the world, that is to say, known by the few hundred scattered contemplatives, for whom a true poet sings, and Bohémond, named among the greatest, scarcely sang even for himself. Persuaded that silence was his real spiritual home, he liked to borrow the cry of the eagle, sometimes even the rumble of the wounded rhinoceros, to tell all the stars that he was in exile.

Accoutred, for the derision of the literary public, with a lofty name in which he was dying, his whole efforts were strained to project himself out of the ghastly world in which a savage fate had imprisoned him.

One might liken him to one of those brilliant insects, the brighter coloured dipterans, shut in, as it were, by the bed of a river of light, dashing itself to death with a quivering, undying optimism, against the clear, pitiless glass that separated it from its heaven. A woodlouse, surely would have found some other way out. He did not even look for one. He strove wildly for the one impossible way of escape, precisely because he knew its impossibility, and because it was against the law of his nature to attempt anything not out of all reason.

One knew his Arch-angel-like hatred for the Philistine, the Knight-Templar ferocity that he held in reserve for the confusion, when opportunity arose, of that respectable member of the Reprobated, that "slayer of swans," as he dubbed him, for whom Satan himself in his Hell must blush. It went so far that he could imagine no other way of sanctifying himself.

"Ah! I am compelled to endure your propinquity," he told himself, "I am condemned to listen to your riff-raff's voice, the absurd expression of your debased ideas, your miser's mottoes and the sententious baseness of your loathsome astuteness! Well, then, let's have some fun! You won't get away from my sarcasm!"

So he made himself, for the moment, the Philistine's friend, his dear friend, his nearest of kin, his disciple, his admirer. Affectionately he invited him to open up his heart, to display his innermost emotions before him, Bohémond; led him step by step to full confession and self-revelation, then, unmasking his glittering armoury, he would transfix with one avenging word.

The white-hot mockery of this collateral descendant of the fallen Principalities and Powers sometimes reached such depths of subtlety that his victims were not even aware of it. No matter, it sufficed that it should be recorded by the Unseen Witnesses.

Another painter, Lazare Druide, accompanied him. But Druide was still very little known to fame, and as different from Folantin as a censor swung before the altar is different from a pot of mustard powder in a tradesman's dining room.

Here was one who was a painter as he might have been a lion or a shark, an earthquake or a flood — because it was absolutely inevitable to be what God made one and to be naught else. Only, it would need more than any human language to express how unarguably God had willed him to be a painter, poor man! For it seemed that all that was in him was calculated to rebel against that vocation.

Ah, let him do what he would — let him rouse to a frenzy of admiration or of terror a whole host of intellectuals or devotees; it might well happen that one day soon he would burst upon the notice of the general public by some tremendous discovery; let him! That would still not be he.

One could picture him as a vagabond, a brigand chief, an incendiary, a merciless pirate — fighting with both hands, like that night-mare filibuster who never bounded over the decks of the galleys of Vera Cruz or Maracaibo till he had lit a burning brand in every lock of his infinitely abundant swarthy hair. It is even easier to imagine him placidly guarding the herds of swine beneath the oaks of some ancient monastery, in a stained-glass landscape, his head crowned with a halo of the shepherd-saints, for his was a soul of lovable simplicity.

But painting — or, if you prefer it, the laws of that idiom that consists in the painter's technique — its rules, its methods, its syntax, its canons, its rubrics, its dogmas, its liturgy, its traditions — were never able to cross his threshold.

And in reality, might that not be a truly lofty way of conceiving and practicing the art of painting, comparable to the Evangelical perfection which consisted in stripping oneself of all things?

He was, like Delacroix, reproached for the poverty of his drawing, the frenzy of his colouring. Above all, he was reproved for existing — for he existed too intensely, indeed. Those of his fellow-painters, whose imagination was a muddy and slow-welling spring, could not understand so impetuous a bubbling forth of vitality. How could he tarry for a rigorous accuracy, even if it were really necessary, in the execution of his pictures? Could they not see that he would imperil his chance of ever catching up with his soul, which sped for ever ahead of him . . . ?

Ay, exactly! He had only that — his soul; the noblest and most princely of souls! He seized it, plunged it, saturated it, in a subject worthy of it, and flung it, all shimmering, upon the canvas. Therein lay the whole of his "art," the whole of his "method," his only "trick"; but it was so powerful that it made men cry aloud, and weep, and sob, and raise defensive hands, and flee!

Did we not see this miracle come true at the exhibition of his Andronicus Delivered to the Populace of Byzantium? Such a work can never be forgotten, once it has been seen, even though a man should drag his body for a hundred years through all the miry highways beneath the sun!

Here is the outline of this picture, the work that made him known. Andronicus, the brutal tyrant of the Empire, suddenly hurled from his throne, is abandoned to the mercy of the rabble of Constantinople. And what a rabble! All the scum of the Mediterranean: bandits drawn from Carthage, from Syracusa, from Thessaly, from Alexandria, from Ascalon, from Caesarea, from Antioch; sailors from Genoa or Pisa; Cypriot, Cretan, Armenian, Cilician and Turkoman adventurers; not to speak of the mongrel horde of barbarians, from that delta valley of the Danube, which made Greece stink even to the confines of Bulgaria.

The infamous prince has been thrown into the midst of this chaos, this terrible confusion of savagery, like a worm thrown into an ant-heap. The populace were told, "Here is your emperor — devour him, but share fairly. Every cur must have his morsel." And that foul populace, executioners of a justice of which they knew nothing, tore their emperor to pieces and gnawed at him for a space of three days.

Andronicus, it is said, suffered quietly to the end, content to sigh, every now and then, *"Lord have pity upon me. Why wilt thou break the bruised reed yet further?"*

The misery of this man steeped in cruelties, the gouging out of eyes, parricide, and sacrilege, is so intense, his solitude so perfect, that one would really think that, as if he were a Redeemer, he was taking upon himself the abominations of the multitude who were rending him. The monster is so alone that he suggests the picture of a dying God. His blood-filled countenance provides an orientation for the insults and outrages of a whole world, and he is draped with the pain of the universe as with a mantle.

Let the crowd, their work finished, find their eyes dazzled with the sun of torture that has left history amazed! Doubtless, the expiatory sublimity of such a horror was needed, that the collapse of the ancient empire should be delayed for another three hundred years.

What is to be said of a painter able to suggest such thoughts? And the suggestion, once more, is so powerful, so spontaneous, so triumphantly irresistible in its force, that the composition, vast as its scale is, bursts with its content, and the breathless drama overflows it, and surges out, like a dragon, into the midst of the terrified spectators themselves.

The man's appearance, still youthful, was as vehement as his work. There was never an artist who expressed more completely than he did every trait of his art in his features.

In them could be read a sustained, a continous, enthusiasm, such an enthusiasm as is a rare thing; a marvellous nobility of mind, a devouring zeal for Beauty, which — to his vision — was the raiment worn by holy Justice; intuition flashing lighting-like over the pomps and trappings of Pain; an indignation like that of a river against the folly that obstructs its rolling flood; and all in soaring, tower-like capitals.

As swift as a volcano, and no less sonorous, when some boor was disrespectful, his fury, instantly pathetic, would burst forth, to the confusion of the Philistine, from the heart of a politeness so exquisite that, by comparison with him the Master of Ceremonies of the Escurial would have fallen at once to the level of a stevedore.

PART II

CHAPTER XXXVI*

"THE poor you have always with you." In the whole abyss of time since that Word no man has ever been able to say what poverty is.

The Saints who wedded Poverty from love of her, and begot many children by her, assure us that she is infinitely lovely. Those who will have none of such a mate, die sometimes from terror or despair, at her kiss, and the multitude pass "from the womb

to the grave" without knowing what to make of such an anomalous entity.

When we inquire of God, He replies that it is He who is the Poor One — *Ego sum pauper.* When we inquire not of Him, He displays the glory of His riches.

Creation appears as a flower of Infinite Poverty; and the supreme work of Him Who is called the Almighty was to cause Himself to be crucified like a thief in the most absolute and ignominious destitution.

Ibid., pp. 217–220.

The Angels are silent, and the trembling Devils tear out their tongues rather than speak. Only the idiots of our own generation have taken upon themselves to elucidate this mystery. Meanwhile, till the deep shall swallow them up, Poverty walks tranquilly in her mask, bearing her *sieve*.

How aptly these words of the Gospel according to St. John apply to *her!* "That was the true light which illumines every man that cometh into the world. It was in the world, and the world was made by It, and the world did not know It. It came into Its Kingdom, and Its own received It not.

"Its own!" Yes, certainly. Does not mankind belong to Poverty? There is no beast of the field so naked as man, and it should be a commonplace to declare that the rich are "bad poor."

When the chaos of this fallen world is sorted out, when the stars are begging their bread, and only the most despised dust of the earth is permitted to reflect the Glory; when men know that *nothing was in its place,* and that the rational species lived only on enigmas and illusions; it may well be that the torments of unhappy, unfortunate man, may reveal and display the wretched poverty of soul of a millionaire, corresponding with his rags, on the mysterious Register of Redistribution of Universal Solidarity.

"I don't give a rap for the poor!" cries a Mandarin.

"Very well then, my fine fellow!" says Poverty, under her veil, "then come home with me — I have a good fire, and a good bed —" And she leads him in, to sleep in a charnel-house.

Indeed, it would be enough to disgust one with the ideas of immortality, were it not for the surprises there are, even *before* what is conventionally called "death," and if the pastry that Duchess feeds her dogs with, that they vomit up again, were not destined one day to be the only hope of her eternally famished stomach!

"I am your Father Abraham, Lazarus, my dear dead child, my little child whom I nurse in my Bosom till the joyful Day of Resurrection. You see that great Chaos there, that stretches between us and the cruel rich man.

It is the Abyss that cannot be crossed — the misunderstandings, the illusions, the invincible ignorances. None knows his own *name,* none is acquainted with his own *features.* All faces and all hearts are veiled, like the brow of the parricide, beneath the impenetrable tissue of the elaborate scheme of Penitence. The sufferer knows not for whom he suffers, the happy knows not on whose account he is in joy. The pitiless man whose crumbs you envied, and who is now imploring a drop of Water from the tip of your finger, could not perceive his destitution, except by the illuminating light of the flames in which he is tortured; but it was necessary that I should take you from the hands of the Angels in order that your own wealth might be revealed to you in the eternal mirror of that front of fire. The permanent joys on which that cursed man had counted will, in fact, really never cease, and neither will your poverty ever come to an end. Only, now that Order has been restored, you have changed places. For between you and him there was an affinity so hidden, so completely unknown, that there was none but the Holy Ghost, Who visits the bones of the dead, able to make it spring forth thus into manifest light while you and he are made to confront one another endlessly!"

The rich have a horror of Poverty because they have a dim premonition of the expiatory compact implied by her existence. She terrifies them like the gloomy visage of a creditor who knows no forgiveness of debtors. It seems to them, and not groundlessly, that the terrible poverty they conceal within themselves might well suddenly break through its shackles of gold and its wrappings of iniquity, and run weeping to Her who was the chosen Bride of the Son of God!

At the same time, an instinct inspired from Below warns them against *contagion.* These detestable creatures sense the fact that Poverty is the very Face of Christ, the Face that was spat upon, that put to flight the Prince of this world, and in the presence of which it is not possible to devour the hearts of the poor to the sound of flutes and oboes. They feel that the propinquity of Poverty is dangerous, that the lamps smoke when she draws near, that the candles on their banqueting tables take on the appearance of funeral tapers, and that all pleasure succumbs — that is the contagion of the Divine Sorrows. . . .

To use a trite platitude disconcerting in its profundity, the poor *bring bad luck,* in the same sense in which the King of the Poor declared that He came "to bring a sword." An imminent and inevitably terrible tribulation is incurred by the man of pleasure the fringe of whose garment a poor man has touched, who has looked into a poor man's eye, face to face.

That is why the world is so filled with walls, from the Tower in the Bible that was to have reached up to Heaven — a Tower so famous that the Lord "came down" to see it more closely — and which was doubtless being built to keep away, to all eternity, those naked and homeless Angels who were already wandering about on the earth.

PAUL CLAUDEL

(*1868–*)

A MBASSADOR of the Church and the Third French Republic, Paul-Louis-Charles Marie Claudel was born October 6, 1868, at Ville-Neuve-sur-Fère in Tardenois. In order that his sister might study sculpture with Rodin, the family removed to Paris in 1882. Claudel made his course of studies at the Lycée of Louis Le Grand and was revolted by the rampant materialism which at this time dominated all French studies. At the close of his college career it was Renan himself who crowned Claudel, the man who was to undo much of the mischief Renan had done.

Not long after Claudel had finished his studies, the death of his grandfather and some passages in Rimbaud's *Illuminations* turned his mind toward the Church. On Christmas Day, 1886, while at Mass in Notre Dame, Claudel felt the first impulse of grace. He returned to Vespers in the evening. Suddenly he knew the truth of Christianity and recaptured the world of the spirit which the enlightenment had tried to banish.

Claudel's return to the faith was no let to his genius for poetry or affairs. He entered the consular service of France and has held diplomatic posts in China, Austria, Germany, Italy, Denmark, South America, and Japan. From 1933–1936 he was ambassador to the United States, and later, with the same rank, represented his country at the Court of Belgium.

His writings are as wide as his travels, comprising some twelve dramas, many lyric poems, and several volumes of philosophical and critical essays.

Claudel's plays are the chief source of his fame. They are written in a magnificent, individual rhythm which carries their great ideas with the reverberations of thunder.

Tête d'or, Claudel's first drama, which Madaule, his official interpreter, calls the "triumph of death" is very probably a tribute to Arthur Rimbaud and a symbolic drama of the poet's life. Because of its tight organization and clotted richness of language, reminiscent of King Lear, *Tête d'or* is probably the most easily playable of all Claudel's dramas. It is a massive tragedy and even without knowledge of its inner symbolist meaning, the action of the play holds the interest of the audience to its amazing conclusion.

The City, Claudel's second play, demonstrates the hideous atmosphere of a modern city and those forces which add to and maintain its horror. With the destruction of the old city and the emergence of a poet-priest to guide its rebuilding, the dawn of the millenium shows its first faint promise.

Of Claudel's other dramas, the two most important are *The Tidings Brought to Mary,* a study of atonement, and *The Satin Slipper* which is a superbly massive illustration of the Providence of God in history.

The Satin Slipper is considered the greatest of all Claudel's work. It sums up many of the points in his philosophy of history, his approach to religious truth, and his critical theories. With its length and many scenes it seems an impossible play to produce; but with a few changes in direction and a judicious cutting, such as attend the productions of Shakespearean drama, it might be entirely suitable for the stage.

Claudel's lyric poems are as original as his dramas. They show his ability to see into life coupled with a realistic approach to it which maintains Claudel in his solitary eminence as the greatest poet of our time.

THE TIDINGS BROUGHT TO MARY*

Prologue

The barn at Combernon. It is a lofty edifice, with square pillars that support a vaulted roof. It is empty except for the right wing, which is still filled with straw; and straws are scattered about on the floor, which is of well-trampled earth. At the back is a large double door in the thick wall, with complicated bars and bolts. On the valves of the door are painted rude images of St. Peter and St. Paul, one holding the keys, the other the sword. The scene is lighted by a large yellow wax candle in an iron socket fastened to one of the pillars.

The scenes of the drama take place at the close of the Middle Ages, seen conventionally, as mediaeval poets might have imagined classic antiquity.

The time is night, merging into the hours of dawn.

Enter on a heavy horse, a man wearing a black cloak, and with a leathern bag on the horse's croup behind him, Pierre De Craon. His gigantic shadow moves across the wall, the floor, the pillars.

Suddenly, from behind a pillar, Violaine steps out to meet him. She is tall and slender, and her feet are bare. Her gown is of coarse woollen stuff, and upon her head is a linen coif at once peasant-like and monastic.

VIOLAINE (laughingly raising her hands toward him, with the forefingers crossed):
Halt, my lord cavalier! Dismount!

PIERRE DE CRAON: Violaine! (He gets off the horse.)

VIOLAINE: Softly, Master Pierre! Is that the way one leaves the house, like a thief without an honest greeting to the ladies?

PIERRE DE CRAON: Violaine, take yourself off. It is the dead of night, and we are here alone, the two of us. And you know that I am not such a very safe man.

VIOLAINE: I am not afraid of you, mason! A man is not wicked merely because he wants to be!

And a man doesn't do with me just as he wills!

Poor Pierre! You did not even succeed in killing me with your wretched knife! Nothing but a little snick on my arm which nobody has seen.

PIERRE DE CRAON: Violaine, you must forgive me.

VIOLAINE: It is for that I came.

PIERRE DE CRAON: You are the first woman I ever laid hands on.

The devil, who always seizes his chance, took possession of me.

VIOLAINE: But you found me stronger than him.

PIERRE DE CRAON: Violaine, I am even more dangerous now than I was then.

VIOLAINE: Must we then fight once more?

PIERRE DE CRAON: Even my very presence here is baleful. (Silence.)

VIOLAINE: I don't know what you mean.

PIERRE DE CRAON: Had I not my work? Stones enough to choose and gather, wood enough to join, and metals to melt and mould.

My own work, that suddenly I should lay an impious and lustful hand on the work of another, a living being?

---

*Claudel, Paul, *The Tidings Brought To Mary*, translated by Louise Morgan Sill (New Haven, Conn.: Yale University Press, 1916), pp. 1–13.

VIOLANE: In my father's house, the house of your host! Lord! what would they have said if they had known? But I concealed it well.

And they all take you for a sincere and blameless man, just as they did before.

PIERRE DE CRAON: Under appearances, God judges the heart.

VIOLAINE: We three then will guard the secret.

PIERRE DE CRAON: Violaine!

VIOLAINE: Master Pierre?

PIERRE DE CRAON: Stand there near the candle that I may see you well.

(She stands, smiling, under the candle. He looks a long while at her.)

VIOLAINE: Have you looked at me long enough?

PIERRE DE CRAON: Who are you, young girl, and what part in you has God reserved to himself.

That the hand which touches you with fleshly desire should in that same instant be thus

Withered, as if it had approached too near the mystery of his dwelling-place?

VIOLAINE: What has happened to you, then, since last year?

PIERRE DE CRAON: The very next day after that one you remember. . . .

VIOLAINE: Well — ?

PIERRE DE CRAON: I discovered in my side the horrible scourge.

VIOLAINE: The scourge, you say? what scourge?

PIERRE DE CRAON: Leprosy, the same we read of in the book of Moses.

VIOLAINE: What is leprosy?

PIERRE DE CRAON: Have you never heard of the women who lived alone among the rocks of the Geyn.

Veiled from head to foot, and with a rattle in her hand?

VIOLAINE: That malady, Master Pierre?

PIERRE DE CRAON: Such a scourge it is

That he who has it in its most malicious form

Must be set apart at once,

For there is no living man so healthy that leprosy cannot taint him.

VIOLAINE: Why, then, are you still at liberty among us?

PIERRE DE CRAON: The Bishop gave me a dispensation, and you must know how few people I see,

Except my workmen to give them orders, and my malady is as yet secret and concealed.

And, were I not there, who would give away those new-born churches whom God has confided to my care, on their wedding day?

VIOLAINE: Is that why nobody has seen you this time at Combernon?

PIERRE DE CRAON: I could not avoid returning here,

Because it is my duty to open the side of Monsanvierge

And to unseal the wall for each new flight of doves that seek entrance into the high Ark whose gates may only open toward Heaven!

And this time we led to the altar an illustrious victim, a solemn censer,

The Queen herself, mother of the King, ascending in her own person,

For her son deprived of his kingdom.

And now I return to Rheims.

VIOLAINE: Maker of doors, let me open this one for you.

PIERRE DE CRAON: Was there no one else at the farm to do me this service?

VIOLAINE: The servant likes to sleep, and willingly gave me the keys.

PIERRE DE CRAON: Have you no fear or horror of the leper?

VIOLAINE: There is God, He knows how to protect me.

PIERRE DE CRAON: Give me the key, then.

VIOLAINE: No. Let me. You do not understand the working of these old doors.

Indeed! Do you take me for a dainty damsel

Whose taper fingers are used to nothing rougher than the spur, light as the bone of a bird, that arms the heel of her new knight?

You shall see!

(She turns the keys in the two grinding locks and draws the bolts.)

PIERRE DE CRAON: This iron is very rusty.

VIOLAINE: The door is no longer used. But the road is shorter this way.

(She strains at the bar.)

I have opened the door!

PIERRE DE CRAON: What could resist such an assailant?

What a dust! the old valve from top to bottom creaks and moves,

The black spiders run away, the old nests crumble, and the door at last opens from the centre.

(The door opens; through the darkness can be seen the meadows and the harvest. A feeble glimmer in the east.)

VIOLAINE: This little rain has done everybody good.

PIERRE DE CRAON: The dust in the road will be well laid.

VIOLAINE (in a low voice, affectionately): Peace to you, Pierre!

(Silence. And, suddenly, sonorous and clear and very high in the heaven, the first tolling of the Angelus. Pierre takes off his hat, and both make the sign of the cross.)

VIOLAINE (Her hands clasped and her face raised to heaven, in a voice beautifully clear and touching):

REGINA CAELI, LAETARE, ALLELUIA!

(Second tolling.)

PIERRE DE CRAON (In a hollow voice): QUIA QUEM MERUISTI PORTARE, ALLELUIA!

VIOLAINE: RESURREXIT SICUT DIXIT, ALLELUIA!

(Third tolling.)

PIERRE DE CRAON: ORA PRO NOBIS DEUM.

(Pause.)

VIOLAINE: GAUDE ET LAETARE, VIRGO MARIA, ALLELUIA!

PIERRE DE CRAON: QUIA RESURREXIT DOMINUS VERE, ALLELUIA!

(Peal of the Angelus.)

PIERRE DE CRAON (very low): OREMUS, DEUS QUI PER RESURRECTIONEM FILII TUI DOMINI NOSTRI JESU CHRISTI MUNDUM LAETIFICARE DIGNATUS ES, PRAESTA, QUAESUMUS, UT PER EJUS GENITRICEM VIRGINEM MARIAM PERPETUAE CAPIAMUS GAUDIA VITAE. PER EUNDEM DOMINUM NOSTRUM JESUM CHRISTUM FILIUM TUUM QUI TECUM VIVIT ET REGNAT IN UNITATE SPIRITUS SANCTI DEUS PER OMNIA SAECULA SAECULORUM.

VIOLAINE: AMEN.

(Both cross themselves.)

PIERRE DE CRAON: How early the Angelus rings!

VIOLAINE: They say matins up there at midnight like the Carthusians.

PIERRE DE CARON: I shall be at Rheims this evening.

VIOLAINE: Know you well the road?

First along this hedge,

And then by that low house in the grove of elder bushes, under which you will see five or six beehives.

And a hundred paces further on you reach the King's Highway.

(A pause.)

PIERRE DE CRAON: PAX TIBI.

How all creation seems to rest with God in a profound mystery!

That which was hidden grows visible again with Him, and I feel on my face a breath as fresh as roses.

Praise they God, blessed earth, in tears and darkness!

The fruit is for man, but the flower is for God and the sweet fragrance of all things born.

Thus the virtue of the holy soul that is hidden is subtly revealed, as the mint leaf by its odour.

Violaine, who have opened the door for me, farewell!

I shall never return again to you.

O young tree of the knowledge of God and Evil, behold how my dissolution begins because I have laid my hands upon you,

And already my soul and body are being divided, as the wine in the vat from the crushed grape!

What matters it? I had no need of woman.

I have never possessed a corruptible woman.

The man who in his heart has preferred God, sees when he dies his guardian Angel.

The time will soon come when another door opens,

When he who in this life has pleased but few, having finished his work, falls asleep in the arms of the eternal Bird:

When through translucent walls looms on all sides the sombre Paradise,

And the censers of the night mingle their scent with the odour of the noisome wick as it sputters out.

VIOLAINE: Pierre de Craon, I know that you do not expect to hear from me any false sighs, "Poor fellow!" or "Poor Pierre."

Because to him who suffers the consolation of a joyous comforter is not of much worth, for his anguish is not to us what it is to him.

Suffer with our Lord.

But know that your evil act is forgotten.

So far as it concerns me, and that I am at peace with you,

And that I do not scorn or abhor you because you are stricken with the pest and malady,

But I shall treat you like a healthy man, and like Pierre de Craon, our old friend, whom I respect and love and fear.

What I say to you is true.

PIERRE DE CRAON: Thank you, Violaine.

VIOLAINE: And now I have something to ask you.

PIERRE DE CRAON: Speak.

VIOLAINE: What is this beautiful story that my father has told us? What is this "Justice" that you are building at Rheims, and that will be more beautiful than Saint-Remy and Notre-Dame?

PIERRE DE CRAON: It is the church which the guilds of Rheims gave me to build on the site of the old Parc-aux-Ouilles,

There where the old Marc-de-l'Eveque was burned down yesteryear.

Firstly, as a thank-offering to God for seven fat summers while distress reigned everywhere else in the kingdom.

For abundant grain and fruit, for cheap and beautiful wool,

For cloth and parchment profitably sold to the merchants of Paris and Germany.

Secondly, for the liberties acquired, the privileges conferred by our Lord the King,

The old order issued against us by Bishops Felix II and Abondant de Cramail

Rescinded by the Pope,

And all that by the aid of the bright sword and Champenois coins.

For such is the Christian commonwealth, without servile fear,

But that each should have his right, according to justice, in marvellous diversity,

That charity may be fulfilled.

VIOLAINE: But of which King and of which Pope do you speak?

For there are two, and one does not know which is the good one.

PIERRE DE CRAON: The good one is he who is good to us.

VIOLAINE: You do not speak rightly.

PIERRE DE CRAON: Forgive me. I am only an ignorant man.

VIOLAINE: And whence comes this name given to the new parish?

PIERRE DE CRAON: Have you never heard of Saint Justice who was martyred in an anise field in the time of the Emperor Julian?

(The anise seeds which they put in our gingerbread at the Easter fair.)

As we were trying to divert the waters of a subterranean spring, to make way for our foundations,

We discovered her tomb, with this inscription on a slab of stone, broken in two: JUSTITIA ANCILLA DOMINI IN PACE.

The fragile little skull was broken like a nut — she was a child of eight years —

And a few milk teeth still adhere to the jaw.

For which all Rheims is filled with admiration, and many signs and miracles follow the body

Which we have laid in a chapel, to await the completion of our work.

But under the great foundation stone we have left, like seed, the little teeth.

VIOLAINE: What a beautiful story! And father also told us that all the ladies of Rheims gave their jewels for the building of the Justice.

PIERRE DE CRAON: We have a great heap of them, and many Jews around them like flies.

(Violaine has been looking down and turning hesitatingly a massive gold ring which she wears on her fourth finger.)

PIERRE DE CRAON: What ring is that, Violaine?

VIOLAINE: A ring that Jacques gave me.
(Silence.)

PIERRE DE CRAON: I congratulate you.
(She holds out the ring to him.)

VIOLAINE: It is not yet settled. My father has said nothing.

Well! That is what I wanted to tell you.

Take my beautiful ring, which is all I have, and Jacques gave it to me secretly.

PIERRE DE CRAON: But I do not want it!

VIOLAINE: Take it quickly, or I shall no longer have the strength to part with it.
(He takes the ring.)

TÊTE D'OR*

Act II

(TÊTE-D'OR enters.)

THE KING (advancing to meet him): You have preserved this kingdom.

The men that work, the women that bear children, and the fields that yield food.

You have given a second birth to everything.

Young man, I greet you with the name of the Father.

May blessings gather on your belovèd head.

Enter, conquering hero,

Welcome to this hearth and to this shadowy hall almost bereft of light.

And first I salute you as is fitting.
(He bows before him.)
(All come and one after the other bow before him.)

Hail!

TÊTE-D'OR: I thank you, Sire.

I thank you all. Who am I? What have I done?

That which must be already exists. From whom is this knowledge hidden?
(To Cébès) And you, will you not give me a word of welcome, thus happily returned?

CÉBÈS: O Tête-d'or!

TÊTE-D'OR: Find an excuse! Pretend that you still are sick!

CÉBÈS: Stay here with me. I want to talk to you.

TÊTE-D'OR: He wants to talk to me.

THE KING: Do you wish us to withdraw?

TÊTE-D'OR: Do this for me.

Do this for me, my friends! I ask your pardon.

You shall hear what I have to say to you presently.
(They all go out.)

TÊTE-D'OR: Well, Cébès, here I am. The same as ever!

I come again, having conquered!

CÉBÈS: By these victorious hands, dear friend!

TÊTE-D'OR: Give me a brotherly welcome.
(They embrace.)

CÉBÈS: O man with the power to conquer.

TÊTE-D'OR: I bayed at their heels! I made them rise from the dung in which they sat.

Then I saw that what I wished for was.

CÉBÈS: But how?

TÊTE-D'OR: I am telling you! I was more firm on my horse than on a rock.

—But I wanted to talk with you and there you are still in your bed.

CÉBÈS: Do not pity me.

TÊTE-D'OR: Are you feeling better?

CÉBÈS: Because I am not worth your trouble, hero!

TÊTE-D'OR: You do not render me a true account.

Am I not your tutor? Do you think that all I have done can go for naught? Was it in vain, that adoption that bound us so close together on that night of sorrow?

And are you not mine?
(Silence.)

Eh?

CÉBÈS: Well?

TÊTE-D'OR: What?

CÉBÈS: Nothing.

TÊTE-D'OR: You twist the chain of my sword but do not speak.

---

*Claudel, Paul, *Tête D'Or* (New Haven, Conn.: Yale University Press, 1919), pp. 65–83.

CÉBÈS: Tête d'or . . .

TÊTE-D'OR: Well?

(Silence.)

CÉBÈS: Did you bring back your army with you?

TÊTE-D'OR: Yes, it is close behind me.

CÉBÈS: You have gained the victory! You knew how to command all these men according to their corps and their battalion, and they obeyed you!

TÊTE-D'OR: Yes, for what I saw and knew.

CÉBÈS: What?

TÊTE-D'OR: My opportunity and how to seize it.

The eyes and the brain cry at the selfsame instant:

"This thing must be!" I take that which is due me.

CÉBÈS: And I, I do not see and do not know! What could I have done?

Yet I am wise though in one thing only.

TÊTE-D'OR: Which is?

CÉBÈS: Will it bore you if I tell you everything? or shall I speak freely

As to the man in whom

I have put my trust?

TÊTE-D'OR: In what thing?

CÉBÈS: (very low): To give

Myself

But to give myself to whom? Not

To one as weak as I am.

Nothing imperfect can satisfy me for I do not satisfy myself.

So I seek a man who is perfectly just and true,

That he may be perfectly good and I may love him.

I am only a child, Tête d'or, but I tell you I have within me

A thing older than I,

And it has its own secret source and seeks its own end, in spite of my sodden intellect and unsure senses, and it makes my life bitter.

But I open my eyes and see the sun as it rises and sets,

And nature, and I find no happiness there. And I see other men and they are like myself.

To which of them shall I speak? I shall speak to him and he will make reply.

Each cries, "Like us you must pay for the right to be alive!" But as I say I have no handicraft.

I can only pay with myself.

And all men are full of faults,

—But you, do you think that such a man exists?

TÊTE-D'OR: You lay your hand on an old wound! — He exists.

CÉBÈS: He exists then.

But which of us speaks and is not understood?

Has he rejected me, or am I in any way to blame?

I bear witness to the Truth

That there is nothing here I am not ready to leave behind as one rises from a chair.

But I see a fly, a plant, a stone, yet him I do not see.

And if I do not find him why have my eyes been dowered with the faculty of seeing, my hands with fingers as if they saw!

For I raise my hands and move them here and there!

And will someone speak of self-control and of works of betterment by which the noble man consecrates himself like a temple?

I do not care to be loved. But I know how to love and I would see and have!

And against these sure desires there is only a vague perhaps.

And why will it later be otherwise? For I am made of flesh and blood, as my mother made me.

TÊTE-D'OR: What is it? You look at me strangely and there is something in you that I do not recognise.

CÉBÈS: You have come, O Conqueror,

To all the rest like the promise of a future of happy days!

For me alone you bring no rescue!

TÊTE-D'OR: What do you mean?

CÉBÈS: (lying down again): I am dying.

TÊTE-D'OR: What did you say?

CÉBÈS: What the doctors told me, and it is the truth.

TÊTE-D'OR: No!

CÉBÈS: I shall not live through another night. I shall not live till noon.

Tête-d'or: No! No!

Cébès: It is not the pain that I fear, and the cramps, and the horrible struggle to vomit,

When my mouth is filled with bile and blood and the sweat pours out of my body like water from a sponge.

This I can bear, for my heart is stout, and I shall look in your face, my brother, in the hour of my torture.

Why was I born? For I die and then I shall exist no more.

The shadows had closed about me so that I slept in darkness and woke in darkness. And I saw nothing: and I was deaf and heard no sound.

For I am like a man buried alive, and I am confined as in an oven!

Give me light! Give me light! Give me light! Give me light! For I would see!

Give me air, for I stifle!

Give me to drink, for I do not want the water that they bring me.

But you, give me water to drink, that I may die in peace, for I am consumed with thirst.

O brother! I have put my trust in you! Will you not help me? I beg you, soldier, head of gold, O my bright-haired brother!

Tête-d'or: Oh! That I could do as does the eagle,

Who, letting fall a useless prey, perishes in his ravaged eyrie!

Why did you cross my path?

Why, like pride, having kneeled before me, did you clasp me in your arms like a tree or a fountain?

On my heart, he pressed his face against this throbbing regret!

And again he asks my help in the hour of his death!

And I do not understand! I have done my best

And I have turned my steps towards that house of sin,

And I thought that, having renounced all selfish hope,

Today I would work with my hands.

You speak of desire, the necessity of the present hour constrains me!

The rapacious desire drags me forward through this place of horror.

And he asks, and I cannot reply to this poor luckless child, and he is dying before my eyes!

Cébès: You weep? Is that your only answer?

Tête-d'or: I beg you

To leave me alone and not to question me. What do you want of me? Shall I hide you in my belly and give birth to you again?

It is most horrible

That you should draw these woman's tear-drops from me.

You question me, and like a brutish thing, I can reply only by these vain waters!

Cébès: You shall not escape me thus. Answer and I will question you. For you are my teacher and must answer me.

Answer! When a man dies does something still survive?

Tête-d'or: Be still, and try me no more.

Cébès: Answer! Is there an end of the personality?

For as for the bodily form we know that it disappears.

Tête-d'or: I answer that man has been conceived according to the flesh.

Cébès: And to die is not to escape?

Tête-d'or: This world was made for man and a limit was set about him,

That he might not escape and that no one might enter in.

Cébès: Then I shall die and shall no longer exist?

Tête-d'or: I will tell you what I know when I do not know it.

And my answer is silence, and the breath that blows from the open and black abyss.

You did not breathe in the days when you lay in the womb of your mother,

But her blood entered into your body and flowed in you and your heart was moored to her heart through the middle of your belly,

And having come out of her you breathed and uttered a cry!

I also have uttered a cry,

A cry like a babe new-born, and I have drawn the keen and burning sword, and have beheld

Humanity divide before me like the separation of the waters!

And now I return to you and find you in the lassitude of death!

Must everyone that I love die and leave me alone?

Must you wither in my hands like a flower of the stream before I had asked "Who are you?" and you had answered me?

Pit of weariness! Horror in which I stand! Is there someone here?

Is there something stable here? Who will carve a letter upon the face of the Mountain?

We can eat; we can lay a dish before ourselves and feed;

But the gravel sets our teeth on edge and ever from our eyes there flow invisible tears.

Then go to the common home! And now I say to you,

Hope not to still survive, being dead,

For how can any man see without his eyes, and how else will he be able

To grasp them with his hands?

CÉBÈS: If this is so,

O my body, you have been of little worth,

For you die, and I must die along with you.

I shall die like a four-footed beast, and shall exist no more.

Why then has it been given to me to know this?

(He begins to scream.) Ah! Ah!

TÊTE-D'OR: Yes, cry!

CÉBÈS: Night! O Night!

TÊTE-D'OR: The night is vast and wide, and the sun is lost in it,

And the silence, that no voice breaks nor any word endures.

CÉBÈS: Forever and ever!

TÊTE-D'OR: Cry! Cry!

CÉBÈS: As for you, you live. You live and you watch me dying at your feet.

O Tête-d'or, can't you do something for me? For I suffer!

TÊTE-D'OR (changing his tone): Do not be afraid! I am here! do not be afraid

To die. All is vanity and nothingness.

CÉBÈS: Do not go! Be my nurse! Stay here. Let me be with you

A little longer. Do not be disgusted with me because

I die.

TÊTE-D'OR: Look, I hold your hand. What was it I said just now?

Come! Death is nothing. Smile! Won't you smile for me?

CÉBÈS: Alone!

TÊTE-D'OR: What's that?

CÉBÈS: Alone . . .

TÊTE-D'OR: Alone? What are you saying?

CÉBÈS: I die!

TÊTE-D'OR: Am I not with you?

CÉBÈS: Alone I die!

For I do not know who I am and I flee away and vanish like a spring that disappears!

Then why do you say that you love me? Why do you lie?

For who can love me

Since I cease to be when my body dies?

A bitter indignation boils within me!

My bowels bloat! I am racked with fearful retchings

That strive to rive apart the fastening of my bones!

Alone I die! And I pant in vain for breath and there is something in me that is not satisfied;

More alone than the strangled babe that its murderous mother buries at the bottom of a dunghill,

Among the broken dishes and dead cats, in earth that is full of fat pink worms!

(He tries to get up.)

TÊTE-D'OR: What are you doing? Stay where you are!

Come, you cannot get out of bed!

(He holds him back.)

CÉBÈS: I want to get up, to walk again! Oh! I can live!

Leave me alone! Let go of me!

TÊTE-D'OR: Stay where you are! Are you mad? Don't you recognise me?

What would you do?

CÉBÈS: Will you not let me go, wretched man! O coward!

I hate you — O great beast, he holds me! — Will you not let me go!

(He bites his hand, frees himself, struggles to his feet and falls. Tête-d'or puts him back on his bed.)

TÊTE-D'OR: You see!

CÉBÈS: (screaming): Ho, ho, ho!

TÊTE-D'OR: Be quiet! Calm yourself!

CÉBÈ (screaming): Ho!

TÊTE-D'OR: You turn my heart to ice! Do not howl like a wolf in this unholy night!

CÉBÈS: Oh! O God!

TÊTE-D'OR: Cébès!

CÉBÈS: Let me alone!

TÊTE-D'OR: Have you forgotten . . .

CÉBÈS: Leave me!

(His mouth still open, he slowly lays his head on his pillow. Then he begins to smile. Pause.)

Tête-d'or, there are many kinds of men, the weak and the strong, the sick and the well.

I pity them; the incompetent and the stammering, the poor of spirit and those that ask for alms

With the deprecating smile that masks the shudder of shame behind.

And those that are mocked and cannot make reply, and cowards,

And those who from the darkness of their souls exhale a prayer devoid of savor!

And you, do you not pity me?

And I say to you like that woman

When she lay at the roadside in the shadow of death:

"Why do you let me die?"

TÊTE-D'OR: Take me with you if you wish! Do you think that I am not weary?

Groaning, I strove to tear myself from those strong and bony hands.

And now you weep and would bring me again to that terrible repose!

The wind ruffles my hair and the heartbreak of the earth lies stark and bare before my despairing eyes! And I look and am filled with shame!

O the fate of the bee and the fly whose life lasts only a season and endures but a single day!

And the birds of the wood are also alive; and the caterpillar that crawls on the leaf and the broom that roots in the sand,

And the ravening beast and the thistle with purple flowers!

And you, who are dying, you counsel me to die!

I cannot loose my limbs from these tough ligatures!

O world! O self! O shameful destiny!

Let me be iron and like a thing of wood!

CÉBÈS: What hope . . .

TÊTE-D'OR: I look at you and it is thus you lie!

CÉBÈS: Come, let's not talk of it. Things are better than you think. But, tell me . . .

I do not understand . . . you follow me . . . eh? What inner pride, what secret flame . . .

TÊTE-D'OR: Neither do I understand! I am tired!

You speak of hidden things that the thick tongue shudders to say,

Tales with no basis of reason, blood that flows like saliva!

A little word of consolation watches beneath all wretchedness,

Sweet forget-me-not of fire that lights us mournfully with its faithful gleam!

—Beyond the silence a voice like the human voice

Spoke to my soul and it melted and flowed like iron in the foundry!

Still it resounds! That fervent hope warms us again like coffee!

O glowing geranium! O clot of sunlight! It throbs! It bleeds like a fragment of living flesh!

For there is a force and a spirit in me

Like the bellows blowing on iron in the fire.

I beg of you, do not ask me anything more!

CÉBÈS: Yet it must be.

—Mother, my brother! O nurse with sides caparisoned in steel!

TÊTE-D'OR: Well?

CÉBÈS: O brother, so at last you have found no word to tell me! Ah well,

I, I have something to tell to you.

TÊTE-D'OR: What?

CÉBÈS: It has not been permitted that I should die in such despair! And now I am beyond all pain,

And it troubles me no more. Tête-d'or!

TÊTE-D'OR: What, brother?

Cébès: Take me in your arms and hold me, for there is no longer any strength in me. And put me on your shoulder like an armful of leafy branches.

O Tête-d'or! you have baptised me with your blood. Now like a babe I lie upon your breast and pour forth on your bosom all myself,

For every tie is dissolved and I am like a severed branch.

(Tête-d'or takes Cébès in his arms.)

Tête-d'or: Thus in my turn I take you in my arms.

Cébès: They say

That if in the midst of his path through a dreary solitude,

Of a sudden the wanderer halts at the summons of his heart,

It is love, that locks the man and woman in agonised embrace.

They do not recognise themselves and the lover feels a pang like the stab of a knife beneath his ribs,

And invents those phrases that begin with O,

Imitating the piercing cries of sea-birds, for their silence is like the peace of the waters.

Tête-d'or: What have you to say to me?

Cébès: O Tête-d'or! I am not a woman and neither am I a man,

For I am not of age, and I am already as if I were no more.

Tête-d'or: Who are you then?

Cébès: O Tête-d'or, all pain is past!

The snare is broken and I am free! I am the plant that has been uprooted from the earth!

There is a joy that comes with man's last hour. That joy am I and the secret that can no longer be told.

O Tête-d'or, I give myself to you and deliver myself into your hands. So hold me while I am with you.

Tête-d'or: O Cébès, whom thus I have taken in my arms, I will question you in my turn. Hand yearns to hand

And mouth to mouth, yet never do they meet, for an invisible barrier lies between.

That is the pang of love through which it is like the water that boils and disappears.

Cébès: Then love me more for I scarcely can be called a living man.

And I am like a bird that one seizes on the wing.

Tête-d'or: O brother, I have jealously taken from you the woman you loved. And you would have been happy with her. But it was destined that your love should be given to none but me.

Brother! Child!

O all the tenderness of my heart, I have taken you between my hands!

O burden! O sacrifice that I bear in my arms like a sheep whose feet are bound together!

Shall I call you my child or my brother? For I am more mindful of you

Than a father would have been of that pallid little face. And my heart is attached to yours by a stronger and sweeter tie

Than that which binds a brother to his little brother in the nursery when he plays with him in the evening, and lulls him to sleep with stories and helps in taking off his shoes.

O my friend that I have found in the gloom, are you going to abandon me and leave me all alone?

Cébès: O Tête-d'or, as you gave yourself to me

Even so I give myself to you,

And as you did not trust your secret to me,

Neither shall I entrust to you mine.

I am strangely light and like a thing that can no longer be held.

(He kisses him on the cheek.)

Good-bye!

And now put me back on my bed.

(Meanwhile the first faint signs of dawn appear.)

Tête-d'or: The day!

Cébès: The chilly violet of dawn

Glances across the distant plains, tinting each track and rut with its glamour!

And in the silent farms the roosters cry Cock-a-adoodle-do!

It is the hour when the traveller, huddled among the cushions of his coach,

Awakes, and peers through the pane, and
　　coughs, and sighs,
And souls new-born in the shadows of
　　walls and forests,
Uttering feeble cries like little naked birds,
Fly back again, guided by flaring meteors,
　　into the regions of obscurity.
— what is the hour?

TÊTE-D'OR: The night is over.

CÉBÈS: It is over! — And the daybreak that
　　kindles the sea to flame and with far
　　reaching fires
Colors the roofs and the towered gateways
　　once again is born.
I feel the freshness of the breeze. Open the
　　window!

(Tête-d'or opens it. Prolonged silence.)

TÊTE-D'OR: Can you hear me?

(Pause. Cébès turns his eyes towards him
　　and faintly smiles.)

TÊTE-D'OR: Can you hear me still?

"Put the table under the tree for we shall
　　eat out of doors." — How beautiful the
　　night is!
O Cébès, everything is hushed and there is
　　no voice to break the stillness.
And like the smell of the cupboard in
　　which the bread is kept and like the
　　breath of the oven when the door of it
　　is opened,
There lies before us the plenty of the fields.
It is night. The meadow is thick with har-
　　vest and far away one can almost hear
The swish of the scythe in the lush grass.
Already the fires of the routed stars are
　　paling.
And the nightingale who sings at intervals
When the ascension of the starry heavens
　　above the earth begins . . .

(He stops. — Cébès is dead.)

(Tête-d'or remains motionless for an in-
　　stant, then he lays down the body,
　　shuddering.)

Oh, horrible!

(He sits down.)

I am alone. I am cold.
What difference does it make?
Indeed it matters little that he is dead.
Why should we mourn? Why should we
　　be disconcerted by anything that may
　　happen?
What man of sense would lend himself to
　　such buffoonery?
He who bursts into tears and whose head
　　is bowed with his sobbing
Will pucker his face into the same wrinkles
　　when he is roaring with laughter. Thus
　　they bawl and contort their mouths.
　　Puppets!
— He is dead and I am alone. —
Am I of stone? The leaves of the trees
　　seem made of cloth of iron
And all outdoors is a painted scene to be
　　looked at or not at one's pleasure.
And this sun, whose earliest rays formerly
　　made me resound
Like a stone that clangs against bronze,
　　why, let it rise!
I would as soon see the lung of a cow that
　　floats at the door of a slaughter-house!
Yes, and like an insensible trunk of coral,
I should see my limbs drop from me.
Why should I live? I have no concern with
　　life. I find no pleasure in existence. This
　　is not good for me!
Today!
Today has come and I must show who I
　　am! There is myself to think of! It must
　　be done!
Alone against them all! I will march for-
　　ward and I will maim with the blow of
　　an armored fist the slimy muzzle of
　　bestiality!
I will speak before this assembly of slovens
　　and cowards. And either I will perish at
　　their hands or I will found my appointed
　　empire!
Hola! Hola! Hola!

FRANCIS JAMMES
(*1868–1938*)

THE little creatures of the forest and the limpid loveliness of nature at dawn found a painter worthy of their excellences in Francis Jammes.

He was born December 2 at Tournay. Jammes' father was a government official. His mother was of good family.

As a student Francis was unsuccessful, except in his love of natural history and botany. These subjects engrossed his mind and made his solitary rambles delightful, filling his memory with a wealth of observed beauty.

Jammes was apprenticed to a notary for a short period. For him this was a life without salt and he forsook it to become a poet. Some of the greatest writers encouraged him to publish his work. Their judgment was borne out in the sensation caused by his first books of poems. The directness of his approach, the aptness of his observation, made Jammes seem artless and enchanting in an age hag-ridden by styles and attitudes.

Among the new friends of the budding poet, Paul Claudel was instrumental in bringing Jammes back to the knowledge and practice of religion.

The poems of Jammes are delightful in their Franciscan simplicity; a dawn-lustred love of things colors every line. Though the superficial or hasty may see in this a lack of depth, is it not, in a prattling sort of way, the shortest way to the vision of a world "charged with the grandeur of God"?

Jammes wrote his prose tales with the same loving simplicity found in the expression of his verse. His *Story of the Rabbit* and *My Daughter Bernadette* are telling examples of his artlessness and autobiographical tendencies.

THE ALPHABET OF THE FLOWERS*

THE first days that she was taken to walk in the garden three months ago, Bernadette was like the white heart of nature in August, the spendid flower with a green and blue corolla. Each thing has for a heart the center that desire chooses.

When we raised our eyes above my child to look into the distance, the outline of the flower was the Pyrenees with indented petals.

Autumn has yellowed the corolla while the heart is still white.

You must realize then, O you who care for this little girl! that you sustain all the countryside that she brings with her and that if she had not existed in the universe, the universe would not have existed without her, since God has created it for her.

What? All the earth? And all the star dust that she scarcely notices any more! Do you really think so?

Yes, it is the alphabet invented by the Eternal to teach Bernadette to read. Already, pressed close to the heart of the flower, she is learning to spell the daylight.

THE FAMILY

I WANT to paint our three portraits here for you, mine as I am at forty years, in the shadow thrown by a modest lamp, in March 1909. Under the unruly eyebrows my somewhat heavy face is hollow around the eyes which look like cat's eyes shining with the opaque brilliance of embossed window panes in old country houses. Near-sightedness is evident through eye-glasses balanced across a rather large arched nose whose end is flattened sometimes as the nose swells to breathe the irony expelled from the sensual mouth. The eyes are sometimes very harsh and sometimes very tender. They pass from anger to tranquillity without transition and their moods wrinkle or smooth the slightly receding forehead, more inclined to reflect impressions than to shape thoughts. The average ears have a simple curve. The hair, turning gray and growing thin, and the tangled growth of the black and white beard have no beauty; only the eyes and the hands. Recently the body has grown quite large; a man at last accepting himself as he has become. He has loved enough, suffered enough and prayed enough to renounce little by little all grace that is not divine, the father of Bernadette.

Your mother, at twenty-six, is a large rose whose cheeks hold up her eyes that are like two red-brown beetles seeming to buzz and fly away. Her little double chin, seen in profile, is quite like Louis the Fourteenth's and her mouth, under a large but well-formed nose, is shaped like a fool's cap. Her smile discloses little shining teeth. Two narrower ones have been pushed forward and from each side. She loves and laughs with all her heart, which is of gold and is swayed by the smallest zephyr like that of the rose. No drop of dew welcomes the sun as quickly as one of her tears does a smile. A ribbon is posed on her hair, brother of the Brazilian butterfly over the fire-place which shines like an azure mirror. She is wearing a light waist and a dark skirt this evening. She is sitting on a low chair opposite the fire and I say to her: "Ginette, it is time to take your tonic." She goes out a minute and then returns, leans over this paper tenderly and then sits down again. Now hidden in the darkness she hums in a vibrant voice grown passionate in song. I hear her saying: "The little forget-me-not . . . how fine and delicate she looks." What is she talking about? . . . meantime you are sleeping, O Bernadette! you whom she fastens like a rose on the bosom that nourishes you.

Very near your mother there is a deep shadow, the darkest of the room, and the fire illuminates the face of this shadow, the eternal snow of the hair and, on this long, yellow, very protruding nose rest the gold circles formerly worn around other eyes making a frame for people and things in the Antilles.

O Bernadette! It is your paternal grandmother, it is the living night on her knees before you and she presses you against her somber dress as the evening holds fast a star.

HOLY THURSDAY AND GOOD FRIDAY

YOUR friend, the Child Jesus, has earned with the sweat of his brow in his father's work-shop a piece of bread which he is keeping for you when you are hungry.

And he has said:

"My father, if you are willing, with the rest of the wood let us make a cradle." He has made so many cradles, the poor child Jesus, that there are only two planks left for him to stretch out on. . . . So many cradles have been made in the Carpenter's shop! and yours too, Bernadette!

Ah! The people stopping sometimes in the small workshops of this father and this Son to say "Good evening" did not know that there, at Joseph's, all the cradles of the world to come must be made.

One day it seemed that the wood was short,

that there was only exactly what was necessary for the Cross of Our Lord. And the Mother, pierced to her heart, cries: "O my Son! what place is left for you to die on this wood?"

But the child Jesus smiles and does not give up his cross.

And, in our room your cradle has been made, O my Bernadette!

So I mark here, in a special way, your first Holy Thursday and Good Friday.

Did I not write at the beginning of this book that your guardian angel will protect you, that he will shield you from the runaway horse? For Thursday, when you might have been crushed in your little carriage by a team of horses running without a driver, the animals swerved all at once of their own accord as they grazed you.

And the next day Our Lord died in your place.

THE LITTLE FARM NAMED THE CABBAGE

UNDER a sky azure as the feather of a blue-jay, when the sun sheds its honey on the leaves of the alders and when the wheatfields are like the inside of a lily, the little farm is cool. It is like the kennel of the dog of the Good God. Perhaps it is situated in the middle of the Earth and that it is there fidelity is found. What a wild place it is! About two kilometers away, on the road which is a continuation of the Rue Moncade, you turn to the left. From there a rough road, sometimes miry, sometimes broken, leads you to the farm three hundred meters away. The fields are on the side of a hill sloping from East to West. Below, they are bordered by a little stream where tiny insects skate about, casting on its clear depths their shadows like three-leaved clovers. They are called shoemakers because of the movements they make. Find the summer shadows where you can lunch on the grass, hearing the rustling of the maize. Above, the stream plunges down to the moist ground where the balsam grows abundantly, that tough shrub with the odor of incense, and one also finds sun-dew here and there. When I shall be there no more, remember that I hunted the wood-cock there and that sometimes the solitude seemed slowly to enlarge and contract when my gun was fired. The land rising in the West, above the river, is flanked with thin woods. A farm, opposite ours, overlooks it among the vines. It is the property of Dabitou who, glass in hand, invokes the cordial friendship of old neighbors.

On the opposite crest winds the uneven road reminding one of the torrid fable of The Coach and the Fly. It overhangs the prickly-broom full of humming bees in the sleepy afternoon.

Toward the South a clear fan-shaped vista refreshes the spirit. A ruined tower and splendid mountains seem to speak of a pilgrimage to the Sky.

Think of this pilgrim, pray for him, O my Bernadette, when you hear the sweetness of the breathing cattle in the poverty of the stable.

LIFE

Life is like a little house, built
on the edge of the road, O my Bernadette,
a house quite simple with thick seemly walls.
In the garden we gather grapes and nuts.
Then we leave it.

See the little house
with its flight of steps.
It is there as we are there,
and the fullness of time comes quickly.

What remains of it all when the last hour
    has struck,
when a shadow on its knees weeps like
    a tiny streamlet?
God.

God remains, that is to say the house
from whence we shall never go out,
the house where the angel in prayer at
    the entrance
closes our eyes.

But you must learn, Bernadette, while you
    are living,
what it is, this life; learn it like a lesson,
conned at the end of your fingers, one which
    will charm you
to the very end.

And when your soft, rounded forehead
is raised from the great book where you
    will spell
the bread that comes from wheat
and the wine from grapes,

You will understand that the little house
is dear,
the house by the road, in which there is
    nothing strange,
but four souls live there: Your father,
your mother, your grandmother and you.
See how the heaven
golden as honey
after we waken
covers our dwelling.

PRAYER THAT AN INFANT MAY NOT DIE*

Lord spare to them this very little child
as you preserve a grass-blade in the wind.
What will it cost You, since the mother
    weeps,
Not to have it die there in a brief while,
as a matter that cannot be avoided.

---

*The above and following poems have been selected
from *The Poets of Modern France* by Ludwig Lewisohn.
Copyright 1918 by B. W. Huebsch, Inc. By permission
of The Viking Press Inc., N. Y.

If You grant it life, it will go next year
to toss roses in the Lord's day festival!
But You are too good! 'Twould not be You
    good Lord,
Who place blue death upon the rosy cheek
while there are still fine places where You
    can set
sons beside their mothers at the window.
But why not here? Ah! since the hour calls,
remember, Lord, before the dying child,
You live forever at Your mother's side!

THE CHILD READS THE ALMANAC

Near her egg basket, the child is reading
    the almanac
Beside the saints and the weather phenomena,
She can look at the signs of the zodiac:
Goat, Bull, Ram, Fish, etcetera.

So she can think, the little country lass,
That far above where the constellations float
There are markets, too, like here, with many
    an ass,
or bull, or ram, or fish, or fine she-goat.

    Doubtless it's the sky's market that she is
        reading.
    And when the page turns where the
        balance is
    She fancies in heaven as at a grocery,
    They're weighing coffee, salt, and consciences.

WE SEE WHEN AUTUMN COMES

When Autumn comes we see on the
    telegraph wires
Long lines of swallows shivering.
We can tell that their troubled hearts are cold
and wonder why,
Without having seen it, even the new
    fledgling
Yearns for Africa's warm and cloudless sky.

Without ever having seen it! It is just as we
desire heaven in our moments of fright.
They are there, atilt, perched to observe
    the air;
Then off in a sudden, easy, circled flight
back to their starting point to wander there.

It's hard to leave the portals of the church!
hard; it's no longer so warm as in months
    gone by!
How sad they grow! and why has the nut
    tree, tall
and strong, deceived them, let its leaves
    droop and die?
The year's brood doesn't know it at all,
This springtime clad in the cerements of fall.
And the soul that is worn with suffering
before it crosses the ultimate, holy shore
to gain the haven of eternal spring
tries, pauses, and, ere leaving turns once more.

XXXVIII

THAT THOU ART POOR . . .*

That thou art poor I see:
So plain thy little dress.
Dear heart of gentleness,
My grief I offer thee.

But thou art lovelier
Than others; very sweet
Thy fragrant lips to meet
That my slow pulses stir.

And thou art poor and true
And kind as the poor be,
Wouldst have me give to thee
Kisses and roses too.

For but a lass thou art,
And books have made thee dream,
And olden stories deem
That arbors charm the heart,

Roses and mulberries
And flowers of the plain,
Of which the poets feign,
And boughs of rustling trees.

Yes, thou art poor, I see:
So plain thy little dress.
Dear heart of gentleness,
My grief I offer thee.

*The above and following poem of Francis Jammes
have been selected from *The Poets Of Modern France*,
compiled by Ludwig Lewisohn (New York: B. W.
Huebsch, 1919).

XXXIX

THE TRAINED ASS

I'm the trained ass, the very ass who can
Startle the learned, counting like a man.
With whip in hand my master makes me climb
An old, cracked tub and balance for a time.
The plaudits of the crowd his zeal enhance.
So down I step and next am forced to dance.
"Where's Paris?" someone asks. My foot I place
O'er the right spot upon the map of France.
Next: "Ass, survey the circle, face by face,
And stop and with your nodding head point out

Among the audience the most stupid lout."
. . . I obey, quite sure that I make no mistake . . .
My mind, each time he wants to teach me, knows
How the man daily in his ignorance grows.
At night, in the old tent that flaps and jars
Sadly I sleep under the windy sky.
The obsession of knowledge haunts me. And I try
In my nightmare to count the very stars.

CHARLES PÉGUY

(1873–1914)

DO AS I say, might well have been the motto of Charles Péguy, for in him there is no discrepancy between his thought and his life. He said what he thought and lived it; something of a scandal to an age skilled in hypocrisy.

The events of his life help us to understand Péguy, but not entirely. He was born in Orleans, January 7, 1873. His mother and grandmother cared for him and gave his education its direction and inspiration. His grandmother, especially, remained the great influence of his life. She could neither read nor write, but was a magnificent storyteller. Her tales set the mind of Charles afire, and gave him a fundamental appreciation of forceful expression which is the mark of his writing.

Péguy had been brought up a Catholic, but he lost his faith in his college years and, though he returned to it in mind, he never became a practicing Catholic. This is one of the mysteries of his life. In his words and his moral conduct he *was* a Catholic. He influenced others and brought them to the love of the Church.

During his college years Péguy became a socialist. His socialism was practical and he served in the soup kitchens and went among the poor with the zeal of a religious.

Péguy first became prominent in the Dreyfus affair and, as should be expected, he turned his talents and influence toward the vindication of Dreyfus.

In 1900 Péguy founded the *Cahiers de la Quinzaine* and finally established his shop at 8 Rue de la Sorbonne. His time, henceforth, was devoted to his publication, which made him one of the most influential voices in France.

Péguy entered World War I with the violent conviction of a crusader. He gave a splendid example to his men, who loved and respected him as brave beyond the call of duty. He was killed in action in the Battle of the Marne, September 5, 1914.

In his writings, both poetry and prose, Péguy is a masculine writer, forceful and forthright. His poems are written in primitive rhythms and the thought is charged with a violence of conviction. His prose is equally impressive: the ideas throng and jostle each other and there seems no end to the force and mental magnificence of the man.

THE SUPPLICANTS AND THE SUPPLICATED*

WITH the moderns, a supplication is an act of abasement, a manifestation of platitude; prosternation becomes physical and moral prostration. To sum up in a word, the supplicant is an applicant. Such has been the infiltration of our political morals into the whole of life, into the whole of our social relations and such has been its coloration of it. Supplication in antiquity was an infinitely deeper thing, I might almost say, incomparably, infinitely truer, wholly different, wholly wise, wholly informed. In Homer, in the tragic authors, the supplicant is not an applicant; he is not a petitioner; he is not a man who abases himself, who humbles himself, even in a Christian sense. I need hardly say that he is not a modern who cringes. The ancient supplication, alone worthy of the word supplication and as such the only one worthy of holding our attention, the ancient supplication is in no sense, under no form, an act of platitude. Quite the contrary. On the contrary, read attentively one of those admirable ancient supplications, that supplication of the whole people at the feet of Oedipus, or what surely is even more admirable, what is perhaps the most admirable of all, the supplication of old Priam at the feet of Achilles. Read them over attentively: it is not the supplicated but, on the contrary, the supplicant who, at bottom, carries off the situation, the dialogue with a high hand. In all ancient supplication, — the supplicated is a man who appears to have a fine position; he is even a man who, as we say, has a fine position, who has what is called a fine position. He is a king; he is a tyrant; he is a chief of a kind. In a war, he is a victor; he is a man of some preponderance, visible preponderance. Real preponderance? He is one of the mighty of the earth. In peace he is a rich man, a mighty man, a man who owns a lot of oxen. Let us describe him in a word: he is a happy man,

a man who appears to be, who is happy. — He is a happy man. So, for the Greeks he is a man to be commiserated. The supplicated can speak only in the name of his happiness, at most in the name of happiness in general. This is little. This is nothing. This is less than nothing. This is even the contrary of all advantage. Happiness, understood in this sense as the success of an event, the rather insolent and almost abusive success, is for the Greeks the most infallible sign that a man is marked out for Fate, — by Fate. — Innumerable Greeks, like the modern, have desired, coveted, pursued with all their might the goods of this world, as much as have the innumerable modern and by every kind of means; gold, power, the enjoyment of all pleasures. They were men such as we are. They preferred happiness to misfortune and, commonly, fine weather to rain. But nevertheless it remains and it remains entirely true, that happiness understood technically as the success of an event is for the Greeks the most infallible sign that a man is marked by Fate. So that in this encounter, in this dialogue between the supplicant and the supplicated, which makes up the whole of an ancient supplication, it is the supplicant, no matter what he be, who he be, whether he be the beggar wandering along the highways, whether he be the wretched blind man, whether he be the outlaw, the exterminated, the citizen banished from the city, guilty or not guilty, the child expelled from his family, guilty or not guilty, this in the order of politics and in the order of peace, or, in the order of war, the prisoner, the vanquished, the feeble old man, whether it be the orphan or, on the contrary, the man who has been orphaned, the old man deprived of his descendants, it is always the supplicant who really has the advantage, who carries off the dialogue, who carries off the situation with a high hand.

As to the supplicated, he occupies a great, a high human position. But it is never more than a perfectly wretched human position. — And that is all. It is nothing. Particularly in

*Péguy, Charles, *Men and Saints,* compiled by Anne and Julian Green (New York: Pantheon Books, Inc., 1944).

comparison with other grandeurs. — What makes the weakness, the smallness of the supplicated is that he is only himself and his small portion of the human position. He does not represent.

The supplicant represents. He is no longer himself alone. He is not even himself any longer. He no longer exists. It is no longer he who matters. And that is why the other, the supplicated, must be on his guard. Despoiled of everything by the same event which precisely has made the dangerous happiness of the supplicated: a citizen without a city, an eyeless head, a fatherless child, a childless father, a stomach without bread, a pillowless neck, a roofless head, a man without possessions, the supplicant no longer exists as himself. And it is from that moment that he becomes formidable. He represents.

Because he has been handled, kneaded, manipulated by the human, superhuman fingers of the gods, suddenly he has become dear to the human, superhuman heart of the gods. Because he has been wax in the divine, superdivine fingers of fate he has become mysteriously dear to the divine, superdivine heart of fate. Because the hand of the powers above has weighed heavily upon him, by a singular reversal — not by a compensation — by a sort of filiation, rather, a superior childbirth, a particular adoption, the supplicant has become their protégé, their son. The gods and above them, behind them, fate, have taken away his father. But the gods have become his father. The gods and behind them, fate, the gods have taken away from him the city. But in a way the gods have conferred upon him their own city. The gods, subordinates of fate, have taken away his worldly goods. But those same gods have given him that good which no other good could replace, the gods have given him the first among all goods: he has become a representative of the gods.

There is no idea of compensation or even of justice: such an idea would be a Christian idea, at least a relatively recent idea, in a certain sense a modern idea. — There is a much deeper idea, a sentiment much deeper and far truer, as far as it is permissible to feel one's way a little among these mysterious, deep, true sentiments — a sentiment of life, of art, of creation: that these men have proven themselves malleable men in the shaping hands of fate. —

Hence, without a doubt, comes the fact that the gods are so closely unified with man, that fate is so closely behind the man on whom she has once acted. When we read in the texts that Zeus is hospitable, that he is the god of guests, that guests come from Zeus, that a stranger comes from the gods, that the beggar, that the supplicant, that the poor wretch is an emissary of the gods, let us above all things refrain from believing that these merely are metaphors and embellishments. The moderns treat these grave questions with metaphors and embellishments. The ancients took these expressions literally. Quite truly. These wretched men, the supplicants, were like the ambulant witnesses of fate, doubly the works (let us not say doubly the creatures) of the gods.

That is why in ancient supplication the supplicant has the better part of the supplication. The other, the supplicated, is quite alone, quite naked and represents nothing. He, the supplicant, has behind him all of Olympus and what dominates Olympus itself. He represents a whole world of gods and even represents that which will bury the gods.

He represents destitution, woe, all misfortune, illness, death, the fate which will strike the gods themselves.

In all ancient supplication it is the supplicant that is master, it is the supplicant who dominates. Please note that what he asks can be refused him. If the other, the supplicated, wishes to aggravate his own case he is free to do so. But it is he, the supplicant, the man bowed at the feet of the supplicated who dominates the supplication, the act, the business of the supplication; he it is who is the master, who speaks a grand language, a masterly language and one which has come from afar, which has come from a quite other world. —

They are all of them ambassadors. And the ambassadors of a great king. —

In the face of such an elevation, what do the Greeks make of the meanwhile most important contrast between the just and the unjust, between innocence and crime? What becomes of the category of the just? What becomes of justice? What human honor or dishonor — or if this is too modern a term — what human advantage or disadvantage can compare with the advantage of having been chosen to become the plastic material of the gods and of Her who dominates and who will model the gods themselves, and govern them in the slumber of death? And that is why the criminal supplicant, or to speak exactly, the former criminal — for, since he is a supplicant he can no longer be a criminal — that is why the supplicant termed criminal is for the Greeks a man infinitely wiser, nearer the gods, more innocent than the wisest and the most innocent of happy men.

To the happy man he can always give lessons, lessons in wisdom and innocence. The happy man is always guilty. At least guilty of being happy. But that is the greatest of crimes.

We do not run after the new; we do not run after the unknown; we do not run after the extraordinary; we look for the right and the fitting, and much that is right and much that is fitting was said before us, better than we ourselves would know how to say it.

We are as stupid as Saint Augustine and as Saint Paul, as Saint Louis and as Saint Francis and as Joan of Arc, and why not say it, as stupid as Pascal and as Corneille. —

We others, we make no progress. It is the moderns who make progress. We are stupid once and for all.

MORTAL SIN AND LEPROSY*

[Joinville once declared to St. Louis that his horror of leprosy was so great that he would prefer committing thirty mortal sins rather than become a leper. In gentle reproof St. Louis said it were better to be a leper than to commit one mortal sin.]

GOD SPEAKS:

Having once known what it is to be loved freely, one no longer finds any flavor in
    submissions.
When one has known what it means to be loved by free men, the prostrations of slaves no
    longer please.
When one has seen Saint Louis on his knees, one no longer wishes to see
Those Oriental slaves lying prone on the ground
At body's length, on their stomachs, on the ground. To be loved freely,
Nothing weighs as much as that weighty thing, nothing weighs as much as that thing of
    great price.
It is certainly my greatest invention.
Once one has tasted
What it is to be loved freely
All the rest is no more than submissions.
That is why, says God, we are so fond of those Frenchmen,
And why, among all other people, we love them in an unparalleled way,
And why they will always be my eldest sons.
They have freedom in their blood. Everything they do, they do freely.
They are less slavish and freer in sin itself
Than the others in their exercises. Through them we have tasted,
Through them we have invented, through them we have created
This thing: to be loved by free men. When Saint Louis says that he loves me,

---

*Péguy, *Men and Saints,* pp. 212–231.

I know that he loves me,
At least I know that that one loves me, because he is a French baron.
  Through them we have known
What it is to be loved by free men. All the prostrations in the world
Are not worth the beautiful upright kneeling of a free man.
  All the submissions, all the self-abasements in the world
Are not worth a beautiful prayer, an upright, kneeling prayer of those free men. All the
    submissions in the world
Are not worth the soaring point
The beautiful straight soaring of a single invocation
Of a free love. When Saint Louis loves me, says God, I am sure,
I know what is meant. He is a free man, he is a free baron of the Ile de France. When
    Saint Louis loves me
I am aware, I know what it is to be loved.
(Now that is everything). No doubt he fears God,
But with a noble fear, all filled, all swollen,
All replete with love, like a fruit swollen with juice.
In no wise cowardly, a base fear, a nasty funk
Which claws at the stomach, but a great, but a lofty, but a noble fear,
The fear of displeasing me, because he loves me, and of disobeying me, because he loves me.
And because he loves me, the fear
Of not being found agreeable
And loving and loved under my gaze. No infiltration in that noble fear,
Of an evil funk and of a pernicious and vile cowardice.
And when he loves me, it is true. And when he says that he loves me, it is true. And when
    he says that he would prefer
To be a leper than to fall into mortal sin (so much does he love me), it is true.
When he says it, I know it is true.
It isn't only true that he says it. It is true because it is true. He doesn't say it because it
    sounds well.
He doesn't say that because he saw it in books nor because someone told him to say it.
    He says it because it is so.
He loves me to that extent. He loves me thus. Freely. A proof of it I have in the same race
And that is the Sire de Joinville (whom I love so very much, just the same), another
    French baron,
Who would on the contrary have committed thirty mortal sins rather than become a leper.
(Thirty, poor man, how little he knows what he is talking about)
Doesn't mind saying what he thinks
That is, saying the opposite
In the presence of even so great a king
And of so great a saint
Whom he nevertheless knew to be such,
That is, displeasing such a great king and such a great saint. The freedom of speech
Of one who doesn't wish to run the risk
Of being a leper rather than falling into mortal sin,
Insures for me the freedom of speech of him who prefers being a leper
To falling into mortal sin.
If one says what he thinks the other too says what he thinks.
One proves the other . . .
In their rigmarole about leprosy and mortal sin, this is how I figure, says God.
When Joinville had rather committed thirty mortal sins than to be a leper,

And when Saint Louis had rather be a leper than to fall into one single mortal sin,
I do not conclude, says God, that Saint Louis loves me in an ordinary way
And that Joinville loves me thirty times less than the ordinary way.
That Saint Louis loves me according to measure, in just the wanted measure,
And that Joinville loves me thirty times less than the measure.
I reckon, on the contrary, says God, this is how I figure, this is how I conclude.
I conclude, on the contrary, that Joinville loves me in the ordinary way,
Honestly, just as a poor man is capable of loving me,
Must love me;
And that Saint Louis, on the contrary, loves me thirty times above the ordinary,
Thirty times more than honorably;
That Joinville loves me according to measure,
And that Saint Louis loves me thirty times more than according to measure.
(And if I put that one in my heaven, at least I know why).
That is how I reckon, says God. And so my reckoning is fair, because that leprosy which
     they had in mind,
That leprosy of which they talked, and about being a leper,
Was anything but an imaginary leprosy and a make believe leprosy and an exercise leprosy,
It wasn't a leprosy which they had seen in books and heard talked about
More or less vaguely,
It wasn't a leprosy to talk about, nor a leprosy to frighten people in conversation and in
     figures of speech,
But this was the real leprosy, and they talked about having it themselves, in very sooth,
They knew it well, they had seen it twenty times
In France and in Holy Land,
That disgusting mealy disease, that filthy itch, that evil mange,
That repellent scabby disease which makes man
The horror and shame of man,
That ulcer, that dry rot, in a word that definitive leprosy
Which eats into the skin and the face and the arm and the hand
And the thigh and the leg and the foot
And the stomach and the skin and the bones and the nerves and the veins,
That dry white mold which spreads little by little
And bites as if with a mouse's teeth,
And makes a man the refuse and the flight of man,
And destroys a body like a granulous mold,
And grows on the body those awful white lips,
Those awful dry lips of wounds,
And which always advances and never draws back,
And always wins and never loses,
And goes to the end,
And makes of a man a walking corpse.
It was that leprosy they were talking about and of none other.
It was that leprosy they had in mind and none other,
A real leprosy, in no way a leprosy of exercise.
It was that leprosy which he preferred to have, none other.
Well, I think it is thirty times more startling
And that it means loving me thirty times and that it means thirty times love.

Ah, to be sure, if Joinville with the eyes of the soul had seen

What manner of thing is that leprosy of the soul
Which we not in vain call mortal sin,
If with the eyes of the soul he had seen
That dry rot of the soul infinitely more evil,
Infinitely more ugly, infinitely more pernicious,
Infinitely more malignant, infinitely more odious,
He himself would immediately have understood how absurd his remark was,
And that the question cannot be raised. But all do not see with the eyes of the soul.
I understand that, says God. All are not saints, such is my Christendom.
There are sinners too, there have to be some, it is thus.
He was a good christian, nevertheless, all in all, he was a sinner, there have to be some in
    Christendom.
He was a good Frenchman, Jean, sire de Joinville, a baron of Saint Louis! At least he
    spoke his mind.
Those people make up the bulk of the army. There have to be troops. It is not sufficient to
    have leaders who march ahead.
Those people start most honestly on a crusade, at least once every other time, and very
    honestly go on a crusade,
They fight very well and are very properly killed and win the kingdom of Heaven
    Just like any other kingdom . . .
But there you are, they think: I have only one body (fools, they forget the principal thing,
They forget not only the soul but the body of their eternity,
The body of the resurrection of the bodies),
Only one body have I, they think (thinking only of their earthly body);
If that nasty leprosy takes hold of me, I am lost.
(They mean that their temporal body is temporally lost) . . .
Now they cling to their body. One would think that they believed it was the only thing
    they had.
Yet they know that they have a soul. Life is the union of soul and body.
Death lies in their sundering. But their body seems to them
A strong and jolly fellow.
They are under the impression that leprosy will annihilate their whole body and that it
    will hold them unto the end (they do not consider that at the end of that end begins the
    real beginning)
And so they would prefer to have something else than leprosy.
I suppose they would prefer to catch
A disease of their liking. It is always the same business.
They don't mind facing the most terrible ordeals
And offering me the most awe-inspiring exercises,
So long as they themselves have beforehand
Chosen them. Thereupon the Pharisees cry out and exclaim
And shout and make faces, and those execrable Pharisees
Above all pray, saying: Lord, we thank Thee
That Thou hast not made us like unto that man
Who feareth to catch leprosy. Now I say, on the contrary, says God,
I myself do say: it is something to catch leprosy.
I know what leprosy is. I made it.
I know it. I say: it is something to catch leprosy.
Nor did I ever say that the ordeals and the exercises of their lives,
And the diseases and the miseries of their lives,
And the distresses of their lives were nothing.

I have always said, on the contrary, and I have always thought
And I have always weighed that it was something,
And indeed it must be believed that it was something
Since my Son performed so many miracles on the sick
And since I gave the king of France the power
To heal the king's evil.
The Pharisees raise a hue and cry over the one who doesn't want to catch leprosy,
And they are scandalized, those virtuous ones.
But I who am not virtuous,
Says God,
I do not shout neither am I scandalized.
I do not figure, I do not conclude that Joinville is thirty times below the ordinary.
But I conclude, but I figure on the contrary
That it is that Saint Louis who is out of the ordinary, thirty times out of the ordinary,
    thirty times extraordinary, thirty times above the ordinary.

I do not figure, I do not conclude
That Joinville is thirty times a coward.
But on the contrary, I conclude and I figure
That it is that Saint Louis who is brave thirty times,
Brave thirty times above the ordinary and more than the measure.

I do not figure, I do not conclude
That Joinville is thirty times lower,
But on the contrary I conclude and I figure
That it is that Saint Louis who is thirty times higher,
Thirty times high above the ordinary and more than the measure.

I do not figure, I do not conclude
That Joinville is thirty times small,
But I just know that he is a man
And on the contrary I conclude and I figure,
This is how I figure,
And it is so.
I conclude and I figure that it is that Saint Louis, king of France,
Who is thirty times great, thirty times above the ordinary and more than the measure.

And who is thirty times close to my heart and thirty times my son's brother.
The Pharisees raise a hue and cry over the one who does not wish to catch leprosy,
But the saint does not raise a hue and cry and is not scandalized.
He knows human nature too well, and man's infirmity, and he is only profoundly grieved.

The Pharisees raise a hue and cry over that man who does not wish to catch leprosy.
See on the contrary how gently the Saint speaks to him,
Firmly but gently.
And that firmness is all the more sure and gives me all the more certainty, all the more
    assurance and all the more guaranty since it is gentle.
The hearts of sinners are not taken by violence.
They are not pure enough. Only the kingdom of heaven is taken by violence.

FREEDOM*

GOD SPEAKS:
When you love someone, you love him as he is.
I alone am perfect.
It is probably for that reason
That I know what perfection is
And that I demand less perfection of those poor people.
I know how difficult it is.
And how often, when they are struggling in their trials,
How often do I wish and am I tempted to put my hand under their stomachs
In order to hold them up with my big hand
Just like a father teaching his son how to swim
In the current of the river
And who is divided between two ways of thinking.
For on the one hand, if he holds him up all the time and if he holds him up too much,
The child will depend on this and will never learn how to swim.
But if he doesn't hold him up just at the right moment
That child is bound to swallow more water than is healthy for him.
In the same way, when I teach them how to swim amid their trials
I too am divided by two ways of thinking.
Because if I am always holding them up, if I hold them up too often,
They will never learn to swim by themselves.
But if I don't hold them up just at the right moment,
Perhaps those poor children will swallow more water than is healthy for them.
Such is the difficulty, and it is a great one.
And such as the doubleness itself, the two faces of the problem.
On the one hand, they must work out their salvation for themselves. That is the rule.
It allows of no exception. Otherwise it would not be interesting. They would not be men.
Now I want them to be manly, to be men, and to win by themselves
Their spurs of knighthood.
On the other hand, they must not swallow more water than is healthy for them,
Having made a dive into the ingratitude of sin.
Such is the mystery of man's freedom, says God,
And the mystery of my government towards him and towards his freedom.
If I hold him up too much, he is no longer free
And if I don't hold him up sufficiently, I am endangering his salvation.
Two goods in a sense almost equally precious.
For salvation is of infinite price.
But what kind of salvation would a salvation be that was not free?
What would you call it?
We want that salvation to be acquired by himself,
Himself, man. To be procured by himself.
To come, in a sense, from himself. Such is the secret,
Such is the mystery of man's freedom.
Such is the price we set on man's freedom.
Because I myself am free, says God, and I have created man in my own image and likeness.
Such is the mystery, such the secret, such the price
Of all freedom.

---

*Péguy, Charles, *Basic Verities*, Prose and Poetry (New York: Pantheon Books, Inc., 1943), pp. 201–206.

That freedom of that creature is the most beautiful reflection in this world
Of the Creator's freedom. That is why we are so attached to it,
And set a proper price on it.
A salvation that was not free, that was not, that did not come from a free man could in no wise be attractive to us. What would it amount to?
What would it mean?
What interest would such a salvation have to offer?
A beatitude of slaves, a salvation of slaves, a slavish beatitude, how do you expect me to be interested in that kind of thing? Does one care to be loved by slaves?
If it were only a matter of proving my might, my might has no need of those slaves, my might is well enough known, it is sufficiently known that I am the Almighty.
My might is manifest enough in all matter and in all events.
My might is manifest enough in the sands of the sea and in the stars of heaven.
It is not questioned, it is known, it is manifest enough in inanimate creation.
It is manifest enough in the government,
In the very event that is man.
But in my creation which is endued with life, says God, I wanted something better, I wanted something more.
Infinitely better. Infinitely more. For I wanted that freedom.
I created that very freedom. There are several degrees to my throne.
When you once have known what it is to be loved freely, submission no longer has any taste.
All the prostrations in the world
Are not worth the beautiful upright attitude of a free man as he kneels. All the submission, all the dejection in the world
Are not equal in value to the soaring up point,
The beautiful straight soaring up of one single invocation
From a love that is free.

WAR AND PEACE*

I CLAIM that peace is neither valid nor firm unless the war which preceded it was not only unavoidable but loyally fought. Now I know of at least two loyalties and the second is no less indispensable than the first. The first loyalty consists in treating our adversaries and enemies as men, in respecting their moral persons, in respecting through our behavior towards them the obligations of moral law and, throughout the heat of battle and the animosity of the struggle, in keeping to cleanliness, probity, justice, loyalty, in remaining honest and abstaining from falsehood. This first loyalty is mainly moral. I will call it personal loyalty. I admit a second

*Péguy, *Basic Verities*, pp. 151–155.

loyalty on which the attention of moralists centers far less. This second loyalty is mental as well as moral and consists in treating war itself — once war has become inevitable — as war and not as peace. It consists plainly in this: when one fights, to fight in good earnest. It consists in waging war earnestly, according to its own fashion, as all work must be done, earnestly, according to its own fashion. It consists in fighting hand to hand. It consists in not committing the falsehood of waging war as though it were peace, this being a moral falsehood, like all falsehoods and also a mental falsehood, like all wilful mistakes of judgement and attitude. I call this real loyalty.

I claim that peace is not firm, after its own fashion, unless the preceding war has been firm, after its own fashion. Bitterness is healthy here. Lukewarmness, tameness, quietude and the dampness of mildewed compliances are pernicious. — Bitterness is healthy and fruitful. Bitter battles leave the field clear for healthy work.

Tyranny is always better organized than freedom.

History does not go where one would wish. History goes where it wishes. Innumerable men, peoples, promotions, races would have made unheard-of sacrifices to be inscribed in the temporally eternal book. History always passes them by. And to those who wanted nothing, she gives everything. It is always those who do not expect, who do not think of it, who do not know what it is all about, they it is who are grazed, who are touched, who are mowed down by the great wing. It was those boatmen, those fishermen, those toll-gatherers who were waylaid, torn away, swept off, carried up, shouldered up, kidnapped, as it were, by the Son of God.

One has not the right to betray even a traitor. Traitors must be fought and not betrayed.

THE RIGHTS OF MAN*

THE man who uses prayer and sacrament as an excuse to refrain from work and action, that is, in war times to refrain from fighting, goes against the order of God Himself and against the most ancient commandment, and he breaks it by three monstrous breaks; for in doing so he turns prayer and sacrament against the law of work, against the commandment of work. Prayer and sacrament were not given us, I think, to encourage, to prepare us to disobedience. — Whereas it is permissible, beautiful and deep to ask by prayer, to ask in prayer for the coronation of fortune and that fate of battles which does not reside in the event, it is stupid and disobedient to wish the Good Lord to work in our place and to have the nerve to ask this of Him. To ask for victory and not to feel like fighting, I consider that ill-bred. — This is a well-known system which has always been called the system of peace at any price. This is a scale of value where honor is cheaper than life. —

This is pacifism at any price, a system of peace at any price. I consent to this, but what is absurd and untenable is to place pacifism and if I may say so, complete pacifism under the shield and under the invocation of the Declaration of the Rights of Man. — The Declaration of the Rights of Man was precisely made, precisely introduced into the world to explain that right passed before everything and consequently, before peace. —

It is madness to wish to bind a Declaration of Peace to the Declaration of the Rights of Man. As though a Declaration of Justice were not in itself and instantaneously a declaration of war. There is only one Lady in the world who has caused more wars than injustice: and that is justice. —

I come not to send peace, but a sword. —

Not only justice but charity itself is full of war. Or rather, it should be said: Without going as far as justice even, as far as claims, as far as reparations, as far as exactions of right and of strict justice, beginning with charity itself we know very well that charity is a source of war. Precisely such is the temporal lot. Such is the lot of man and of the world. —

The idea of peace at any price, — the central idea of pacificism, is that peace is an absolute, that peace is even the first of absolutes, that peace has a price unique to this point that a peace in injustice is better than a war for justice. This is the diametrical opposite of the system of the Rights of Man where it is better to have a war for justice than peace in injustice.

*Ibid., pp. 165-171.

HENRI GHÉON

(1875-1944)

THE early years of Henri Vangeon, who writes under the name of Ghéon, were protected and happy. He was born a Catholic and was carefully educated in the faith. Shortly after his First Communion, in emulation of his father, he turned away from the Church and became indifferent. That indifference became a fancied hatred of God with his mother's death in a tragic accident.

In World War I Ghéon, a doctor with the Red Cross, met briefly Dominique Pierre Dupouey, lieutenant-commander of a battalion of marines. The serene faith of Dupouey turned Ghéon once more toward the Church. His state of indecision was resolved by the good advice of Andre Gide, and Ghéon returned to his Father's house on Christmas Day, 1915.

Since his return he has been a tremendous force in Catholic life. His lives of the saints, in the form of biographies or plays, have charmed a wide audience and have infused warmth and depth into the communication of holiness, making it possible for all to see the truth of St. Paul's assertion, we are "all called to be saints."

Ghéon's style is simple and popular, but good. In his plays, which unlike Claudel's are meant to be played, he gives a minimum of stage direction. When his dramas are simply played, they portray a realistic approach to sanctity which genuinely reveals character and a glimpse of the riches of the knowledge of God.

CHAPTER II*

FIRST DIGRESSION: THE FACE OF SALZBURG
THE ARRIVAL — A ROMAN TOWN — THE PRINCE-
BISHOP WOLF DIETRICH VON RAITENAU: HIS
SPLENDOUR AND FALL — HIS SUCCESSORS — A
MOUNTAIN CEMETERY — ST. RUPERT, BISHOP —
THE MARTYR ST. MAXIMUS

PERFECTION

I

THOSE who love Salzburg love Mozart. Those who understand his town must understand him. And Mozart, who perhaps did not love it, little knew how much it resembled him!

If the country explains the man, there is no truer case than this. Neither Schobert nor Paris, nor even Italy, where he was to spend months, towards which his love of light was always to draw him, went so deep. Whatever he thought, I cannot imagine him born or centred anywhere else.

Mozart is explained by Salzburg. To tell the truth I never doubted it for a moment.

Those who go to Salzburg in the summer go there meaning to gorge themselves with music. Nor will they be disappointed: the best orchestra of Vienna, its best singers, the most famous conductors, some unique voices, an excellent Conservatoire, serenades in the open air. . . . One closes one's eyes almost, to hear better or, like the God of Love who is a little Mozart's God, goes blindfold.

"A town in the Austrian Tyrol, 400 metres above sea level, situated on the banks of the Salzach, with four bridges, and dominated on the left bank by the castle of Hohen-Salzburg; 40,000 inhabitants; no industry. . . ."

So much for the guide book.

A small town of bourgeois that becomes a tourist centre as soon as the season opens. A few monuments left over from the days of the prince-bishops. Hardly anything worth

---

*Ghéon, Henri, *In Search of Mozart*, translated by Alexander Dru (New York: Sheed and Ward, 1934), pp. 39–49.

visiting except the surrounding country; fields, woods and mountains with Tyrolese chalets. . . .

I was told that it rained often. As I never carry an umbrella I was prepared to rush from the theatre to the concert, and between times shelter in a cafe, ignoring the outside world.

Well, I was deceived! The morning of my arrival the weather was brilliantly fine. The modern town, near the station, has no charm, but my hotel was a real palace painted ochre colour, with a superb courtyard, vaulted passages and to the south a miracle of a garden.

What a beautiful garden! But I put off visiting it for the present. The first item on my list was to get tickets for the concerts. So I imprisoned myself in a queue of Austrians, Bavarians, Americans and English, Swedes, Italians and Dalmatians. After an hour's wait I was told there was not even standing room.

I went out cursing. Had I gone to Salzburg to see the town? — I was forgetting that Mozart was born there. He even lived for a time in the house opposite the office where I had been waiting. An ordinary looking house that is not visited: a placard politely asks you not to disturb the new owner and I took care not to.

Yet the small gently sloping square with its flower-beds leading up to a 17th century church at one end, all yellow, with green copper cupolas — in spite of its new hotel, new theatre and post office — is laid out with great moderation: the church is its centre point. An old town that is not spoilt by the present is so rare nowadays that it is worth noting and appreciating.

An iron bridge leads to the old town on the other side of the Salzach. Perched up on a rock stands the castle, a Walhalla without heaviness or severity; above and beyond the high Italian roofs of the houses bordering the river, innumerable spires and domes, gay and light, are bathed in sunshine. . . . Where in the world are we?

I crossed the river that seemed suddenly to have become the Arno or the Tiber, and plunged into the streets, so narrow as to be mere lanes, full of a southern shade. Vaulted passages, little balconied courtyards and everywhere magnificent wrought-iron work . . . lost one moment and back again the next. The general effect is bourgeois and sympathetic, though not without a certain distinction. . . . There is his house! Wolfgang must have walked about here . . . and to think that this evening I shall be missing his music. I tried to console myself by humming the incomparable adagio of the *Concerto in A* that I was not to hear. . . . At any rate I could go to the Festspielhaus where Max Reinhardt was giving Goldoni's play — *The Servant and Two Masters* — that Mozart ought to have put to music.

I wandered about the town — there must be any number of small towns in Germany with the same charm, the same appearance — when suddenly without any warning — though contrast is a preparation as Mozart knew well — the narrow street I was in opened on to a square.

I stood still, dazzled. Not dazzled, perhaps, because I saw everything, the very shade was transparent, and everything perfectly clear. . . . Here was the highest peak of Mozart's art. Leaving his humility behind me I stepped out into his light, into the sphere of his gentleness, grandeur and perfection.

The quadrangle, with almost equal sides, is composed of three adjoining palaces, and on the fourth side is a church. Though it really is big it looks enormous, and the proportions take one's breath away. It is built in the grand Roman style of the 16th and 17th centuries that began with Palladio and ended with Bernini, not to everyone's taste though at last receiving its due. Fault may be found with it for excessive decoration but no one can deny its solidity, power and purity of line. At any rate it is the last style that really lived and that presented a new form of grandeur independent of Romanesque, Gothic or Classical models (in the sense in which David understood it). Under the names of Jesuit, Baroque and Rococo it took root in all countries, and particularly in Austria where it was really understood.

And here perhaps is its masterpiece: the cathedral square, a square that is both cathedral close and palace courtyard opening out on to yet others. . . . Were it alone, lost in the midst of lanes and bye-streets, it would only be an incongruous or happy accident, according to the vistor's mood. But hardly has one had time to enjoy the beauty of the square and its silence (for it seems shut in and motors rarely pass that way) than through two porticos one sees two other squares even more open and built in the same grand style. The porticos themselves are such as are only found in the Vatican, with rounded arcades and long windows, surmounted by a balustrade, joining the two palaces to the Cathedral on a level with the third floor. On the right is the square of the chapter, and on the left the square of the Residence: the spiritual and the temporal.

Nor are those the only ones. The cathedral square is prolific. It was the model and inspiration of an entire town that sprang up at about the same time. Only one enclave has survived: the Romanesque and Gothic Church of the Franciscans and their monastery buildings. Everywhere else churches, palaces and abbeys planned on the geometrical idea of the square, but at the same time lifting up to heaven the craziest of shapes, imitate one another and form a single domain both monastic and princely. And the tripper going from court to court, from cloister to cloister is astonished by the repetition that is never without novelty and by passing a dozen times along the same road perpetually renews and increases his own delight.

The mark of a *chef d'oeuvre* is that it may be viewed in any light and from any angle, and though always the same is yet always different. Let me enjoy the calm of noon during which the happiest of chances revealed such marvels. Here are the Residence where Mozart gave concerts to the prince, the cathedral with its two towers and St. Peter's Abbey where between his tenth and twentieth year he conducted so many Masses; the wonderful fountains in which perhaps he bathed his hands. Enormous fountains whose florid and serried basins rise up and seem to top the houses. Their curving dolphins and rampant horses of marble, blackened and polished by the water, shine like seals. As in Venice flights of coloured pigeons

settle in hundreds. The campaniles with their bulbous tops look as though they were ringing. The copper green domes add a delicate shade of colouring to the ochre walls, even those of the little cafe with its virginia creeper terrace hiding under a tiny chapel with an ingeniously complicated little bell tower. An ochre wash reigns everywhere, renewed each year for our delight: on the palaces, on the monasteries, on the houses: from orange to red, from yellow to green; the whole scale of ochres, of gold almost, as it shines from Naples to Genoa. The cathedral alone has a façade of marble, gilded by time, thrown into relief by the dark grey stone of the rest of the fabric. Once again I ask myself: where are we?

There are two recognizable factors.

Salzburg is a little Rome. Salzburg is a composition.

Like a Roman palace or a Mozart masterpiece.

Here is the story as I was told it.

II

The prince-bishops had reigned for centuries, but in time had become more princes than bishops. On the Mönchsberg, the rock beneath which lies the old Salzburg, they had built the *Festung,* the castle that dominates the whole valley. One can still see in it the traces of their former luxury: magnificent halls with gilded beams, cloisonnes and painted ceilings supported on gigantic spiral pillars of wine-coloured marble. For a long time they were semi-barbarous overlords, more occupied with the chase than with art: the Lutheran crisis gave them back their Roman feelings. They withstood the Reformation; the Renaissance swallowed them at a gulp.

Of them all, the one most soaked in Italian taste was Wolf Dietrich von Raitenau, for he was related both to the Medici and the Borromei. He had something of each of them in him. Such portraits as we have of him do not exactly breathe forth sanctity. Hard and severe in his surtout or bright-eyed and smiling with his biretta over one ear, he alternates between brutality and cunning, between the cultivated politeness of a humanist and avidity. Elected in 1587 and not yet twenty when he ascended the double throne, this remarkable man, equipped with as many defects as with qualities, scandalized his people and his flock, opposed the Pope and the Emperor in a quarrel with his Bavarian neighbour over salt, and was finally deposed and imprisoned (in 1612) in his own castle. There he became, so his chronicler tells us, "a mirror of virtue and penitence" — it only remained for him to die.

Arriving in the little town of twisted streets and unsymmetrical façades, of enclosed squares and dark churches, Wolf Dietrich grew indignant. "What barbarism!" For him there was only Rome. From one day to the next he calmly tore down the confusion of mediaeval buildings, Romanesque, Gothic, post-Gothic — masterpieces perhaps — so as to rebuild his capital according to his own taste. And thus there sprang up, as though by magic, a miniature Rome of the Popes in a green valley of the Tyrol. And, intrigued no doubt by the game, the Italian sun followed the architecture: but on that point history is silent.

It is only a story, but like so many stories it rings true. The truth is that Wolf Dietrich could not bear having a Residence that did not conform to the fashion of the day, that he pulled down everything he could, straightened the streets, enlarged the squares, built himself a palace worthy of Julius II and Leo X, ordered enormous monasteries for his monks, sumptuous stables for his horses and could never resign himself to pontificating in a Romanesque basilica. Fortunately it was burnt and he was accused of setting fire to it; but that would have been too much. He sent at once for his Italian architect Scamozzi and ordered him to reproduce, on a smaller scale, the plan of St. Peter's — which was done. God, however, did not let him triumph with his *chef d'oeuvre;* it was his successor who finished it. . . . His immediate successors imitated him in almost everything; at any rate in his magnificence and his mania for building. The first was his nephew, Mark Sittich von Hohenems — Marcus Sitticus in the la-

tinized form — to whom we owe the palace of Hellbrunn; the second, Paris, Count Lodron, who embellished the Mirabelle; then come the two Count Thuns, the counts of Harrach, Firmian and Lichtenstein, whose portraits may be seen in the cathedral, ranged along the walls of the transept, each different in the same purple: pious, sceptical, formidable or florid, with coats-of-arms in beautiful stone bulging on every pediment.

The abbey church restored, the churches of the University and St. Sebastian built, the castles of Aigen and Leopoldskron . . . that is their title to glory. And so on down to Graf Schrattenbach, Sigismund III, Mozart's protector until 1772 — a man of prayer — who drove a tunnel, over a hundred yards long, through the Mönchsberg so as to give Salzburg a replica of the Pausilippo. The inscription engraved under his effigy applies to the whole line, of which he was the last but one: *Te saxa loquuntur.* The stones will indeed talk long of those strange prince-bishops! If for lack of a prison they did not all make amends like Wolf Dietrich, perhaps the stones will have pleaded for them in heaven and a merciful God have accounted them as good works.

The merit of all of them was to have respected the initial idea of the builder, submitting to his plan, modifying only the decorative detail according to changing fashion. And thus the fantasy, the affectations, the pathos and contortions, all that goes to make the charm and ridiculousness of Austrian baroque or rococo, fell obediently into the original plan without destroying or even altering it. And in point of fact it is wonderful to see how cheap and gaudy the stucco, the garlands of cupids, cascades of clouds, shells and volutes, for all their superfluity, are swallowed up and absorbed by the broad lines. We should miss them if they weren't there. Like the arpeggios and *gruppettos* of the period they weigh no more on the cornice or the vaulting than the flourishes on a Mozart melody. Even if all the ornaments of Salzburg seemed to us laughable and odious, the Salzburg of the prince-bishops would remain as pure and great as the day it was born.

Such is the strength of order and style.

How can one think that the young musician passing daily through the streets, courts and squares, short-sighted though he was, blind to all arts but his own, should not have felt one day — or indeed every day — the power of rhythm, the infallible power of true proportion, engraved itself upon him? He could hardly take a step without something being added to his formation. The prince-bishop was sent from Rome with the express purpose of building a classical town . . . for Mozart.

III

Nature had furnished him with an eminently propitious site. A wide valley, bounded by the distant mountains; two beautiful rocks to frame the town, the one bearing the symbol of force, the other rounded like a hillock and destined to the service of God: the Mönchsberg with its Festung and the Kapuzinerberg with its little monastery hiding the poverty of St. Francis. Between the two the S of the river with the same curve as the Seine in Paris . . . a composition in the grand style worthy of Poussin.

Looking at the old pictures so charmingly arranged in the museum, one can see that the face of the town has hardly altered in the last hundred and fifty years; except for the ramparts along the river side that have been pulled down since. Mozart, in fact, saw it almost as we see it now. Not only the sumptuous part of the town but even its surroundings, with its many different charms, springing from the very soil. Wherever he went, whether to Maria Plain, or only on to the terrace commanding a view of the gardens of the Mirabelle, he was met by some harmonious view in which God and man collaborated. What could be more finished than the terraced garden, where unicorns and lions greet the visitor; with its flowered alley-ways, gods and goddesses, and giant vases overflowing with flowers and its little theatre of ewe hedges? Above it all stand the two white towers of the cathedral, and higher still the *barbarous castle* all golden in the setting sun. The whole of Salzburg at a glance: for it owes all its grandeur to its very smallness. The town rises up to heaven without extending beyond man's vision.

He was sensitive to everything, I hope (I am speaking of Mozart); even to the sombre past of Salzburg. He cannot be imprisoned in one century or a single formula . . . not even in light. For here we turn our steps into paths whose charm is in no sense Italian.

First of all comes the Franciscan Church, just before the cathedral square, with its cinder-coloured tower and its roof of steel and jade. Poor, seemingly poor, beside such opulence, it makes no such great contrast with the spirit of the town. The Norman nave, dark as a cellar, narrow and high as a pass, opens, through its one arch, into a Gothic choir devoured by the light of day. The vaulting of the choir looks as though it were supported on a single central column, spreading out like a palm tree. The thrust is so pure and so powerful that the whole edifice seems borne on that one pillar. It looks like the simplest solution of a daring question, the only one that gives the key: the basic key of a symphony, the dominant colour of a picture. Yet without spoiling it or breaking its line, there is half-way up it, a baroque retable above the high altar: the 17th century hanging on the 14th; it is ravishing. The rococo decoration of the chapels round the choir is less fortunate; there is always danger in such marriages.

At the abbey of St. Peter another surprise awaits one. At the end of a sort of narthex the door of the old church offers a grave welcome to the visters to the new church: a few beautiful figures grouped in a tympanum astonished at still seeing the light of day; for with that exception the whole church has been dressed in stucco. . . . The Romanesque Virgin says to the faithful "Enter in, it is still the house of my Father" — and they go in fearlessly, under a superb opera house ceiling.

Finally, going through the open-air passage separating the church from the former cellars of the abbey (for half a shilling one can buy an excellent dry white wine, served in iced glasses), you come upon a perfect little cemetery, so Alpine and Tyrolese that it may be called romantic; and what is more, it is as moving as it is amusing: it is here that the really old Salzburg is buried.

It is a hundred miles from the cathedral square and the Italian sun. Caught in between the abrupt cliff of the Mönchsberg and the naked wall of St. Peter's shorn of all its furbelows, it seems shut in right up to the sky and filled with a watery light. Covering the uneven ground are innumerable grave mounds, gravestones eaten away by moss, and waving stunted pine trees, wrought-iron crosses as delicate as lace work. . . . On the right is the Chapel of the Cross, in the middle the small pointed spire of the Gothic Chapel of St. Marguerite. A large willow, the very type of the weeping willow, drips with all the tears of Germanic sentimentality. The heavy fawn-coloured walls are covered with the recumbent figures that formerly marked graves. In vain an arcade of chapels clings to the rocks; its curve cannot Romanize the scene. It is barbarous, primitive and charming. Half-way up the rocks, hardly visible, cut in the side of the hill and lost in it, is a tiny hermitage with its little roof, cloister and miniature bell tower (doubtless with a bell) watching over the dead.

I was told that a saint, Bishop Rupert, came from Worms in the 6th century; that he founded a monastery on the Mönchsberg and a nunnery on the Nonnberg, and that on this very spot he built the first chapel of

St. Marguerite and from that day on honoured among these rocks the memory of Saint Maximus who, a hundred years earlier, had suffered the violent death of a martyr.

There the picturesque vanishes. Only the sanctity and antiquity of the spot remain. A staircase cut in the stone leads up to the hermitage of St. Maximus, the first Christian of Salzburg. A cavernous passage, chapels that are grottos, one of them dedicated to St. Giles, the other to St. Gertrude, and at the very end a hollowed rock, the bed, so it said, of the saint. It was from one of these windows, at which he used to breathe the evening air, that Maximus was hurled by the Barbarians in 476 when they took the ancient Salzburg by storm. Rupert and Maximus. A confessor and a martyr. No less was required to bring Wolf Dietrich to repentance. Perhaps no less was needed to keep Mozart, his whole life long, the friend of God.

It was not chance alone that directed my steps across the perfect city to the shapeless hole where there lies the secret perfection of love. Without the tomb of the apostles Peter and Paul the Rome of the Renaissance Popes would not have lasted six weeks. Here, in the poor retreat of St. Maximus, I found the corner stone on which rests the destiny of the town of the prince-bishops and of the most marvellous of its children.

THE MARRIAGE OF ST. FRANCIS*

Act III

A pleasant valley some miles from Assisi. Clumps of trees: a village campanile in the distance.

Br. Leo and Br. Juniper are seated Left on a slope. Right, reading upright against a tree, Br. Masseo. Back, Francis, pacing to and fro in meditation. The village bells are ringing as for some festival. Swallows wheeling

round. A symphony of morning. Enter Two Peasants, one very old, one quite young. They enter cautiously, in front of the tree where Masseo is leaning.

OLD PEASANT. Look — but don't go too far. Quite right to make use of them — but don't commit yourself. One never knows where it mayn't lead. With a man like him. . . .

YOUNG PEASANT. Which is he?

OLD PEASANT. I don't know.

YOUNG PEASANT. Well — one might ask.

OLD PEASANT. Don't go — don't go. Listen to what they are saying.

*Ghéon, Henri, The Marriage of St. Francis, a translation by C. C. Martindale, S.J., of La Vie Profonde de St. François (London and New York: Sheed and Ward, 1933).

YOUNG PEASANT. They aren't saying a word — not a syllable.

OLD PEASANT. Ah. They think before they speak.

YOUNG PEASANT. Hush! (They keep quiet to listen.)

LEO. It must make our Father very happy to come back to his native home and find all the bells ringing. God's good bells! When he left they treated him as mad, and he only just escaped having stones thrown at him when he got away. And now he can't so much as get in sight of a steeple, without the bells beginning to dance and stirring up all the populace — they come out to meet our good Father with boughs and flowers.

JUNIPER. We shan't have to do much begging. We shall have more pudding than we can eat.

LEO. You're always thinking about eating.

JUNIPER. Food is my job. If Martha didn't feed Mary, Mary wouldn't have much strength for praying.

LEO. True. I beg your pardon, brother Juniper. (Pause. Juniper laughs.)

LEO. You laugh all on your own?

JUNIPER. Sometimes. (He laughs again.)

LEO. That's uncharitable!

JUNIPER. You're right. One ought to go shares in one's laughter too.

LEO. Well, let's go shares. What are you laughing at?

JUNIPER. I'll tell you. But perhaps it won't make you laugh. I often laugh at things that don't make other people laugh.

LEO. Even so, I'd laugh, just to be laughing along with you.

JUNIPER. Well, then, this is it. I'm thinking of what happened when those inquisitive folks thought I would tell them something . . . remarkable. They hadn't come to be converted. They came to see . . . and the proof is, the fine silk dresses of the ladies. I'm not the bear-leader . . .

LEO. Nor even the bear.

JUNIPER. I pretended not to notice the crowd. But I saw two boys who were playing see-saw not far off, on a plank . . . then, then . . . (he laughs).

LEO. Well?

JUNIPER. Then I made them both get on one end and I got on the other myself. And we played see-saw for a good half-hour. The lookers-on were tired before we were. I got this at least from it, that they thought me perfectly mad. And so I am (he laughs).

LEO. Good . . . good . . . it deserves a good laugh. I hope they learnt the lesson of the see-saw.

JUNIPER (surprised). What was it, Brother Leo?

LEO. You know as well as I do. He who exalts himself shall be made low, he who makes himself low. (Juniper laughs. The Peasants, who were listening, have come gradually closer, and laugh too.)

OLD PEASANT. That's a good lesson!

YOUNG PEASANT. And one that can make you laugh.

JUNIPER. And even laugh much more than I thought myself. He who exalts himself. . . .

LEO. Now that you've had your laugh, what do you want? (to the Peasants).

OLD PEASANT. We want — but then we don't exactly want. . . . We come from the village.

YOUNG PEASANT. To see the Saint.

OLD PEASANT. Hold your tongue. Yes, it's true. . . . But from a certain distance. You must understand that we don't come to "have a little talk with him." We're Christians — good Christians — good Christians — and we don't want to become any better.

LEO. Congratulations, my dear sirs! I wish I could say the same of myself. Well?

OLD PEASANT. You aren't the Saint?

LEO. Great heavens, No!

OLD PEASANT. Nor you, I'm sure?

JUNIPER. Still less me.

LEO. That's impossible.

OLD PEASANT. Couldn't you show him to us? From a distance?

LEO. From a distance, if you prefer. But near or far, he'll be able to catch you, my brothers.

OLD PEASANT. I'm off.

YOUNG PEASANT (holding him). I'm stopping.

OLD PEASANT. Stand in front of me. (He hides behind him. Pointing to Masseo —) That wouldn't be him, just there, by that tree? He frightens me.

LEO. No.

OLD PEASANT. So much the better.

LEO. The one that's walking up and down over there.

OLD PEASANT. Hush! (But Brother John has come down left, and seeing Francis walking up and down, imitates him, from a distance, in all that he does.) Which?

LEO. How do you mean, Which? The one that's lifting up his arms.

OLD PEASANT. But they both are.

LEO. The one who's clasping his hands.

OLD PEASANT. But so they both are.

LEO. The one that's taking his hood off.

OLD PEASANT. But they're both taking it off.

LEO. And now he's putting it on again.

OLD PEASANT. But it's just the same. (To the Young Peasant.) Look, but look, my lad. I see two saints . . . yet I've not gone dithery —

YOUNG PEASANT. I see two saints too.

OLD PEASANT. Is there one saint twice over?

LEO (sees Brother John). Ah — it's Brother John!

JUNIPER. Brother John!

OLD PEASANT. But which is Brother John?

LEO. The tougher of the two.

OLD PEASANT. But which is the Saint?

JUNIPER. The other — the one who's just knelt down.

OLD PEASANT. But the other's kneeling too. . . .

LEO. The one who knelt down first.

OLD PEASANT. But why does the other do all he did?

JUNIPER. To be sure of doing what's right. He acts like that all day long, ever since our blessed Father converted him with the broom.

OLD PEASANT. With the broom? by whacking him? Aha, he takes strong measures. Better be off, my boy.

LEO. Cheer up. He has lots of little ways of hooking people. But as for whacks — the only person he whacks is himself. Our Father Francis was sweeping out a Church. He hates to see the House of God in bad condition.

OLD PEASANT. And quite right too.

LEO. Brother John saw him. He left his oxen at the door, and took the broom from him. Next day, he gave him his oxen — and himself. The broom had converted him.

OLD PEASANT. Oh . . . oh . . . well, but after all a broom — a broom.

LEO. That was how he took the lot of us.

OLD PEASANT. With a broom?

LEO. Or with something of the sort. Brother Juniper, by cooking. I was a parish priest before I followed him. He took me, by bringing me what he called his sins.

OLD PEASANT. Well I wouldn't trust him. If he catches the priests too, I'm off. I'm quite good enough.

YOUNG PEASANT. He's coming. He's coming here.

OLD PEASANT. All the more reason for going. Let's give him a cheer and be off.

OLD AND YOUNG PEASANT. Long live the Saint! (Exeunt. The bells ring louder. Francis comes down forward, with Brother John behind him.)

MASSEO (shuts his book). Why for you? Why you?

FRANCIS. Yes indeed, Brother Masseo — why for me? why these shouts for me? these bells for me? why not for you, Brother, or for Brother Leo? For Brother Juniper, or Brother John, who imitates my every gesture and in consequence is worth just as much as I? "Why you, Francis?" Yes, Masseo, I can read your thoughts! "Why for you, Francis, who are not good to look at — not a man of learning — not noble? Why does all the world run after you? want to see you, listen to you, obey you?" Now I will tell you why. You will be as glad as I am. Because of the piercing eye of God, because of His holy eyes, that went looking through the world, and found even among sinners no worse, or viler, or more wretched sinner than I am. And so me among all did He choose, to confound greatness, strength, the beauty and the wisdom of the world, and to prove to us the more conclusively that from Him it all comes. (Pause.) And also, Brother Masseo, most certainly, because Brother Ass lives ever within me, not well enough shod yet, and saddled, and bridled, and because he might wax vain in the rays of this glory that only my demerit sanctions — therefore do I wish to return to my first plan, to bury myself in some rocky cave like Brother Silvester and like Brother Bernard, and I have decided to preach no more, so as no more to risk yielding to a temptation of vain glory. But since I have lost all confidence in my own judgment, I beg you to go forthwith to that same Brother Silvester and to our Sister Clare, and bid them ask God to enlighten them on the matter. You, Brother John, go down into the village, and beg the villagers to respect our solitude for to-day. I have sinned too gravely against humility for my words to be of any use to them. Unless God commands the opposite, I shall without doubt speak no more henceforward. Meanwhile Brother Juniper shall go and get you your food, and I will stand behind with you, my dear Brother Leo, for you to question me, and examine me, and correct me. Be off, my children.

(They all, save Leo, prostrate themselves and kiss the hem of his tunic. Then, save Leo, they go off in various directions.)

FRANCIS. This would be the proper time for saying Prime and Terce, Brother Lamb . . . but, you remember, we had to give our breviaries in payment for the visits of the doctor to that poor old woman whose both legs are bad. . . . So till the good province of God provides us with some more, this is how we shall talk — turn and turn about: I shall say to myself — "O Brother Francis, you committed so many sins, when you were in the world, that you ought to go to hell." And then you answer, Leo, "It is perfectly true that you deserve hell." And we shall say this over and over again so that I may get deep, deep down into my worthlessness.

LEO. Very well, Father. In the Lord's Name. Begin. (They walk to and fro side by side.)

FRANCIS. O Brother Francis, you committed so many sins when you were in the world that you are only fit for hell.

LEO. O Brother Francis, God will assuredly work so many marvels by means of you, that you will enter paradise.

FRANCIS. But — But — that isn't what you've got to say. I will say: "O Brother Francis, you have committed so many of-fences before God, that you deserve to be accursed for evermore." And you will take care to answer: "Yes, you are certainly fit to be placed among the lost."

LEO. Very well.

FRANCIS. O God of heaven and earth, I have committed so many offences before Thee, that I deserve to be for ever damned.

LEO. God shall make thee such an one among the saved as to be blessed beyond others.

FRANCIS. What is the matter, Brother Leo? Why do you not answer as I told you to? In the name of the most holy virtue of Obedience, I order you to answer exactly as I shall bid you. So I will say first: "Ah wretched creature, dreamest thou that God will have pity upon thee, and knowest thou not that thou deservest no mercy?" And you, Brother Sheep, must answer: "Yes, yes — without doubt you are utterly unworthy of mercy."

LEO. Very well, very well: begin again.

FRANCIS. Ah wretched creature, dost thou dream that God shall have pity upon thee?

LEO. I know that God the Father, whose mercy is infinite and is far far greater than any sin, will have compassion upon thee and overwhelm thee with his grace.

FRANCIS. But, Brother Leo, that's quite wrong. Why are you going against obedience and why do you always answer the opposite of what I told you to?

LEO. God knows, my dearest Father. Each time, I meant to answer as you bade me. But it must have been God who made me answer as He chose, and not according to what I intended.

FRANCIS (kneeling). My dear dear child, when I accuse myself again, I beg you on both knees, say what I tell you to, that I deserve no pardon.

LEO. Say it again, Father, and I will try to answer as you bid me.

FRANCIS. O wretched wretched Francis, do you really think that God will have pity on your tears?

LEO. But of course, Father — God will have mercy on His servant. He will glorify him in eternity, since he who humbles himself shall be exalted. . . . And I shall never be able to say anything else, since it is God Himself who speak through my mouth. (Pause.) Don't be too annoyed with me, Father.

FRANCIS (rising). I thank you, Brother Leo. I will not say it again. (He lets himself sink onto the slope and hides his face in his hands. Brother Leo remains standing by him. A long silence. Then, heavily . . .) Brother Leo, write. You've got your tablets.

LEO. I think so.

FRANCIS. Now write this carefully. "Even though the Brothers Minor gave all the world over a perfect example of sanctity and good edification, that would not yet be the perfect joy." (Pause.) Write, Brother Leo. "Even though a Brother Minor gave sight to the blind, made straight the cripples, cast out devils, restored hearing to the deaf and speech to the dumb, and life to men four days dead, not in that consists the perfect joy." (Pause.) "Though a Brother Minor knew every tongue, prophesied the future, tore each secret from each soul — write that not in that is the perfect joy." (Pause.) "And even though" — yes, write it — "he talked the language of the angels, deciphered the goings of the stars, knew the virtue of each herb, of birds, of fish, of men, of trees, of stones, O little sheep of God, the perfect joy is not yet in any way of it." (Without pausing.) No, nor even, Brother Leo, "if by the spell of his eloquence, with the grace of God he converted every infidel to the Faith." Have you written that?

LEO. Yes, Father. But then, where is the perfect joy? In God's name, I beg you tell me.

FRANCIS. Suppose we came this night to St. Mary of the Angels, or where you will, soaked with rain, frozen with cold, filthy with mud and racked with hunger, and that we rang at the door, and the porter came out and said: "Who are you"? and we answered: "We are two of your brothers," and he retorted: "You are two scallywags, bamboozling everyone and filching the alms of the poor." And suppose he refused to open the door and made us stop in the rain and the cold. And suppose that we succeeded in supporting patiently his insults, without

a murmur, without distress of soul, and suppose we saw that this porter was knowing us for what we are, — really saw that! — and that it was God Himself who was guiding his tongue against us — now write this down well, Brother Leo — Therein consists the Perfect Joy. (Pause.) And if we knocked again, and then he fell into a rage against us, and thrashed us well, and said everything he could against us . . . and then, with cold and hunger gnawing at us, we knocked yet again, praying and weeping, and then armed with a bludgeon he knocked us down into the mire and snow, and beat us till we were black and blue with bruises. . . . And if we accepted with joy all this violent treatment, reflecting that it is our duty to support patiently every anguish that Christ inflicts upon us — then and then only, Brother Leo, should we know what is the perfect joy. For among all the graces of the Spirit that Christ gives to His friends, none is more precious than the grace that enables us to support every insult for Christ and for the Love of God. (The bells begin once more.) Now, there are the bells ringing again, and there are the villagers, despite my forbidding them, beginning to carry out branches in front of God's most worthless servant. And here am I, Brother Leo, a sinner who ought to hold his tongue and swore he would, making you a sermon as if he were in the pulpit of the Gospel. Away, Brother Lamb, and keep the crowd off. You, myself, the whole world, are for me an occasion of doing wrong.

(Brother Leo goes away quietly. St. Francis kneels down before the hillside. The bells ring louder than ever and interwoven with their music you can hear the song of birds. Gradually, from all sides, you can see entering singly or in groups, little children representing birds. Many are in grey, with the Friars Minors' hoods: others are gray and variegated. They speak to music.)

BIRDS. He's alone. . . . He's alone . . . come, come, come.

AN OLD WOODPECKER. Well, well! I haven't seen a man so close for ever so long. One always has to look out for stones — for arrows — for bird-lime!

BIRDS. Lovely, lovely, lovely. . . .

A JAY. I don't know why it's lovely, but lovely it is. . . .

WOODPECKER. This one is, anyway.

BIRDS. It's like nothing on earth. It's not like a tom-tit, nor a redbreast, nor a linnet, nor a swallow. . . .

JAY. It isn't even like a bird at all: but for all that, it's lovely.

WILD PIGEON. But this one especially, brothers.

OLD SPARROW. Shall I tell you whom he's like? Like us, the sparrows. He's grey, he's lack-lustre, he has no glitter, he has no colours.

BIRDS. True, true. . . .

PIGEON. And shall I tell you why we think him so much more beautiful than the rest?

WOODPECKER. Because we can go near him.

PIGEON. Of course. But why can we go near him. Because he is gentle.

BIRDS. Gentle, gentle — see how gentle he is.

SPARROW. One would like to talk to him. (They assent.)

BIRDS. Let's talk to him — talk to him.

WOODPECKER. Little sparrow, what nonsense! One can't talk to men.

OLD CROW. I beg your pardon. The uncle of the great-grandfather of my parents' great-great-grandfather used to tell — it's my parents who told me — that in the days of the great-great-uncle of the great-grandfather of his parents' great-great-grandfather — it was they who told him — all the birds used to talk with men, even birds of prey. And when I say with "men," I mean with the man, for there was only one then, who lived with his wife and was king on land and sea.

BIRDS. Is that true? Is that really true?

MAGPIE. And did the birds talk to his wife too?

CROW. More even than with him, because she liked talking more than he did.

WREN. And weren't they frightened of the man?

CROW. Not a bit. In those days no one was frightened of anybody. For, so they say, no one wished any harm to anyone.

BIRDS. What? what wonderful! . . .

CROW. Oh, that was long ago. Things changed all of a sudden. And all of a sudden everyone started fighting everyone else. We never understood why; but there is a reason. . . .

SPARROW. Will those fine days come again?

CROW. Maybe, maybe. If this man here produces a number of others like himself — who knows?

BIRDS. Who knows?

WREN. What is he doing with his hands up like that?

CROW. I couldn't tell you.

FRANCIS. O loving Lord. . . .

MAGPIE. What is he saying?

FRANCIS. O Creator of all things — of all good things.

SPARROW. What is he saying? what is he saying?

CROW. Oh, we can't understand. Else we should have understood at once.

FRANCIS. Creator of the sun, Creator of life, Creator of Grace. . . .

NIGHTINGALE. It makes one want to sing. . . .

BIRDS. Let's sing! let's sing.

LINNET. Our sweetest song.

BIRDS. Our sweetest, sweetest song. . . .

SPARROW. What shall our song say?

NIGHTINGALE. You know your song doesn't mean anything. Or if it does, we don't know what.

BIRDS. True . . . true. . . .

CROW. Our first parents must have known. As for us, we sing . . . because we do — by tradition.

LINNET. Because we've got the habit. . . .

NIGHTINGALE. And because we like it. . . .

BIRDS. Because we like it. . . .

LINNET. Because it gives us pleasure. . . .

NIGHTINGALE. And perhaps because *he* likes it, linnet.

BIRDS. Perhaps, perhaps.

NIGHTINGALE. So let's sing!

BIRDS. Sing!

NIGHTINGALE. I hardly ever sing except at night . . . but still, for this once. . . .

(The birds all come together like a choir and the bird-music rises. It must be both instrumental and vocal. After a space, it pauses.)

BIRDS. Again! again!

(The melody begins again, and as often, in fact, as the conductor pleases. They call out "Again" before each new burst of song. Francis rises as if suddenly in ecstasy, and, when the music stops, or is sufficiently quiet for him to be heard —)

FRANCIS. Oh — my dear little brothers, little birds, how well you sing! I really must thank you — and congratulate you. I must tell you that since the sacred song of the Three Children in the burning fiery furnace, and the hymn of Mary Magnified, I have never heard anything sung which has gone so straight to my heart. O my little troubadours of birds, at least you don't admire me, you don't flatter me — you aren't like the others. I used to think that the nightingale and the linnet and the — and even the least musical of you all had been created for my sake — my glory — But no, it isn't so, and you don't conceal the fact! So by way of thanking you, I am going to preach you a sort of sermon, I haven't any more the right to preach to men, until indeed our Creator shall have declared His will. But preaching to little birds — that's a very different thing. If you understand me, so much the better. If you find me tedious, you must fly away. (He takes a step forward. The Birds throng round him). O my little brothers the birds, since Sin has darkened God's creation, here you are on the earth without knowing what you're there for. And you sing songs without any words. And there you live, without knowing what you're living for. Well, I'm going to tell you. I am going to translate for you the music that you keep sending up into the sky, in the woods, through the plain. I'm going to improvise myself the poet of your songs! Now listen to me: —

We sing the air that upbears us, the forest that gives us shelter, the down that dresses us, the grain that feeds us. . . .

The spray that sways beneath us, the dew that gives us drink, the sun that warms us, the bright blue sky that dazzles us. . . .

And the dusk that hushes us and the dawn that wakens us, and the fierce fire of noon. . . .

And that we may properly praise the air, the woods, the down and the grain, the bough, the dew, the sun and the blue, blue sky, and dusk and dawn and day . . . let us not faint in saying —

Air of God, woods of God, feathers that God gave us, grain that God gives us —

Leaves of God, dews of God, sunlight of God, and O blue skies of God —

Night of God, noon of God, and God's dear dawn —

And again, and again —

O all God's gifts so good and fair, all from God, and all for the little birds of God. . . .

And that's what you're singing without knowing it, my little brothers, because of this your freedom whereby you fly free everywhere, because of your dress so warm and thick, because of your feathers so wonderfully coloured and adorned. Because of the food that without toil of yours is given you, because of your very song itself that the Creator's self has taught you, because you are so many, and because your very nature, your nature of birds, was mercifully preserved by God within the ark, and by Him multiplied ever since; because, in fine, of this element of air, that you do use as God doth please.

For you sow not neither do you reap, but God provideth for your needs, and gives you rivers that you may drink there, and rocks, that you may seek refuge there, and trees that you may build your nests there — and though you weave nor sew not, yet, from Him too, you have your raiment.

And you see well how the Creator loves you, since He has done you so many loving kindnesses.

So you will be careful, if you have understood me so perfectly as you've been listening to me, never to be ungrateful, my little feathered troubadours, and always diligently to praise God in your songs. (Pause.) Do you agree?

BLACK BIRD. Yes, yes, yes.

FRANCIS. I want to tell you another thing. The Creator has given no less to man, but even more. Yet man sings Him no songs. . . .

But I would like the Friars Minor, becoming just like you, like the least of all you little ones, like the tiny sparrow in his grey dress, to become many, like you, through the in-pouring of the Holy Spirit, and, abandoning themselves to Providence for food and drink and vesture, to fly away through the world just as if they had wings, and cover the earth with the uninterrupted praise of God. Now say three times what I am going to say, to the glory of the Most Holy Trinity — Blessed be the Lord!

BIRDS. Blessed be the Lord.

(*And forthwith a song of birds uprises, like one great Alleluia of instruments and voices, which breaks off at its highest for Francis and the birds to say again: Blessed be the Lord: and after the same music, they say it the third time. Then the same music, but enriched and more ecstatic. During the sermon, there have arrived one after the other, Brother Leo from the back; from the left, the two Peasants, of whom the younger is carrying a cage in his hand. By the right Brother Juniper and Brother John. They all crouch down, kneeling, behind the bushes to watch what is going on. As the song finishes, Brother Masseo finally appears on the right.*)

FRANCIS. Someone's coming . . . be off with you! (*He makes a great sign of the cross over the birds. They go out backwards, whispering —*)

BLACKBIRD. Goodbye, Brother Francis. . . .

(*A great whirr of wings is heard in the music, and they all stand up looking at the sky in amazement.*)

YOUNG PEASANT. Look — look.

OLD PEASANT. Marvellous — Ho! They're all flying away together.

YOUNG PEASANT. They're massed like an army.

OLD PEASANT. But they're making four battalions.

YOUNG PEASANT. They're dividing up —

LEO. One's going north —

JUNIPER. One south —

LEO. One towards the sunrise —

JUNIPER. And one to sunset.

YOUNG PEASANT. A cross! a cross — they're making a cross.

OLD PEASANT. True.

MASSEO. And the four arms of the cross reach all horizons.

LEO. They will reach from world's end to world's end.

JOHN. And they're singing —

YOUNG AND OLD PEASANT. Oh, hark at them singing. . . .

(*The song begins again, triumphant, in the distance. All bow. Then Francis to Masseo.*)

FRANCIS. Tell me, Brother Masseo — what does our Lord, Jesus Christ, bid me do?

MASSEO. I began by asking Brother Silvester in his cave, and then Sister Clare in her convent. Without saying anything to one another, they answered me alike — the same words exactly. (*Francis kneels to receive the word of God, his head bared and his arms stretched out like a cross.*) The Lord wills that Brother Francis should be told that it is not for his salvation alone that he has been called, but that he may reap an abundant harvest of souls, by prayer, and by example, by his presence and his voice.

LEO. To the four winds of heaven, like the birds, my dear Father.

OLD PEASANT. Yes. The birds think the same. (*Francis, after remaining bowed for a moment rises*).

FRANCIS. On, then, in God's Name.

YOUNG PEASANT. Couldn't you stay yet a moment, Father?

FRANCIS. I have received word to go. . . .

YOUNG PEASANT. We could talk as we went. . . . I will go as far as need be.

OLD PEASANT. As far as need be? with the hay not brought in. . . ?

FRANCIS. Let him speak.

YOUNG PEASANT. There. I'm caught. Properly caught. And not with the broomstick, like the brother there (he points to John). Nor by cooking, like that one. I'm a bird-catcher — I know how to set traps better than anyone. I've got a golden crested wren here in my cage — I caught it last night with bird-lime. But look — I'll let it go. (*He opens the cage and the bird flies off.*) I'd step into its place, if I weren't too big. There I used to think I was quite as good a

Christian as God asked of me: the Father could have preached to me for all he's worth and have got nothing from me. But I heard him talking to the birds and all of a sudden I was ashamed to find I was less of a Christian than a magpie was. . . . Suddenly I resolved to make peace with them. And with all the creatures of God, man included. And so I will follow the Saint.

OLD PEASANT. But my boy —

YOUNG PEASANT. You won't come, too?

OLD PEASANT. The hay isn't in.

YOUNG PEASANT. You have no one now to leave it to. What use is it now?

JUNIPER. I will get it in, if you like.

YOUNG PEASANT. And the Brothers shall lie upon it when they come back through the village.

LEO. Good. It shall serve the vagabonds of God. . . .

OLD PEASANT. Very well — very well. I'll come in spite of all. I was right to be on my guard, my boy! I shan't be caught twice.

LEO. You are caught! (Pause).

FRANCIS. God be praised, who has need of no more than a bird that sings, or a sinner like me, to convert a soul! Let us go and preach the Cross of Christ if we carry it not yet. . . .

LEO. Can't we both preach and carry it?

FRANCIS. May God grant it! Come.

(The sound of bells, louder and louder. Noise of the approaching crowd.)

CROWD. The Saint! the Saint, Hurrah for the Saint!

(Francis exit followed by the Brothers.)

FRANÇOIS MAURIAC
(1885–   )

FRANÇOIS MAURIAC was born October 11, 1885, in the city of Bordeaux. His father died when Mauriac was still an infant, and he grew up in the pious atmosphere dominated by his mother and grandmother. It was a lonely childhood except for the voice of nature speaking in hills and trees: a world of bourgeois piety in which the voice of God, resounding in a sensitive soul, tempered sometimes the externalism and stuffiness of purely habitual religion.

Mauriac attended the school of the Marianites, and when he had completed his course went up to Paris to study. With some of his friends he made great plans for a confraternity of Catholic artists, but the plans came to nothing.

Two books of poems brought him the favorable attention of Bourget and Barres, but Mauriac, despite this flattering beginning, turned to prose and the novel. He served with distinction in World War I and at its conclusion returned to his task of writing.

His books, too numerous to mention, are excellently written in a prose which is strong though often poetic in flavor. Mauriac is a psychologist of the first rank, unraveling with tender care the finest skeins of human motive and conduct.

Many critics consider *The Vipers' Tangle* his finest work. It is a study of a man's growth in knowledge of himself which, because that is truly a participation in the knowledge of God, gives to the reader insights and illuminations which are helpful in the life of grace. This study of avarice and hatred is, like Thompson's *Hound of Heaven*, proof of the dogged love of God who waits hopefully even in the forest of our misunderstandings.

XIII
THE BLESSED SACRAMENT AND THE BLESSED VIRGIN*

During that agony of Jesus, I saw the Holy Virgin overwhelmed with sorrow and anguish, in the house of Mary, mother of Mark. . . . She fainted several times, for she saw distinctly several phases of the agony of Jesus. She had already sent messengers for news, but, unable to wait for their return, she went, full of anxiety, with Magdalen and Salome as far as the valley of Josaphat. She was wearing a veil and as she proceeded, she would often stretch her arms towards the Mount of Olives, because she saw in spirit Jesus bathed in a sweat of blood, and it seemed as if she were trying to wipe the face of her Son with her outstretched hands. I witnessed the soaring of her soul towards Jesus who thought of her and who cast a glance at her as if looking for help. . . .

— *Anne Catherine Emmerich.* (*The Sorrowful Passion of Our Lord.*)

SAINT FRANCIS OF ASSISI loved France because the sacred Host was more venerated there than in any other country in the world. It is remarkable that, in spite of the spread of worldliness and irreligion, the Eucharist has been more and more glorified and honored from century to century. The Eucharistic life of Christ has developed in the world as did His human life on earth. Jesus began to breathe in the seclusion of an obscure workshop and rose gradually to infinite glory. Likewise, the first Christians fed on the Bread of Life, but they did so in darkness.

But, even when It is hidden, the Host gives life to the humblest church. Neither hymns nor lights are necessary to let us know that It is there. The small lamp only attests Its presence. The temples of those who deny the real Presence are like corpses. The Lord was taken away and we do not know where they have laid Him. We can feel the gloominess of those churches, and especially of those which were formerly dedicated to the Catholic religion. Now,

they resemble tombs sealed upon nothingness.

A Catholic church remains always open, like the Heart forever open.

Corpus Christi . . . this body of Christ was brought forth by the Blessed Virgin and this is why the veneration paid to the Virgin Mary goes side by side with the cult of the Eucharist, without rivaling it and, *a fortiori,* without rising above it. But we do not separate the Mother from the Son. Lourdes, where non-Catholics imagine that we accord Mary undue eminence, is no doubt the place in the world where Christ in the Eucharist is most glorified. It is the only place in the world where, under the veil of the Host, Christ mingles in the midst of so many sick people, and is as closely pressed by them as He was during His mortal life. His mother prays for these bodies and these souls, and Christ cures them. The procession of the Blessed Sacrament in Lourdes starts from the Grotto to show that Jesus was given to us by the Virgin. And she who stood on Golgotha, at the foot of the Cross of the condemned Man, stands here by the side of the King of eternal glory.

On that Holy Thursday night, where did the Blessed Virgin take refuge? Did she know what was coming? Did she know that the time had come for her to suffer the blow she had been expecting for so many years? She was away from her Son, because it was necessary that she be absent. Had the Mother been with Him, the Son would not have experienced complete abandonment; hardly would He have felt Judas' betrayal. If His Mother had been there, she would have followed her Son to the Garden; she would have watched with Him, and He would not have suffered from the desertion of His friends. He would no longer have been left alone to bear the sins of the world. She would have wiped the bloody sweat from her Son's brow. The cup would not have been drunk to the dregs.

*Mauriac, François, *The Eucharist* (New York and Toronto: Longmans, Green and Co., 1944), pp. 71–75.

The Virgin Mother does not appear in the drama of Calvary until her crucified Son, lifted up between heaven and earth, can no longer receive any help from her. Perhaps the feet were nailed low enough so that she could press her lips against them?

Conversely, we learn through the Acts that the day after the Ascension of Our Lord she was seated in the cenacle with the Apostles (1,14). And as we read in the same Acts (11,42) the new disciples were persevering "in the communion of the breaking of the bread and in the prayers." The faithful console themselves over the sorrows of the Blessed Virgin when meditating on the unfathomable joy that the Eucharist must have given her. The Virgin Mary is the only Mother who was granted the privilege of bearing her Son a second time. Who then dared to draw this parallel between the presence of Christ in the Virgin's bosom and His presence in the heart of the faithful communicant? When Saint Gertrude, about to receive the Host, asked, "O Lord, what gift are you going to grant me?" Jesus Himself answered, "The gift of my whole being with My divine nature as formerly My Virgin Mother received it."

The Lord's Supper to which the Virgin leads us in order that we may partake of her joy, is renewed every morning. The table is always set, the bread always offered. The Christian makes his way to eternity from communion to communion. At each stage in the journey, Christ is waiting for him in order that he may renew his strength and take heart again. But let us take care not to allow too much time to elapse between these stages. Long before the silence and peace which emanate from a communion have been dispelled by nature and by the world, we must make our way into the radiant sphere of another communion. Let there be no opportunity between two communions for a period of darkness in which we would run the risk of falling into snares. We have nothing to fear if Christ marks out our life. Hardly have we had time to lose Him when already we have found Him again.

A contemporary pagan poet speaks of this God with whom no excess is forbidden. How difficult it is to abuse communion! The only requisite to sit down at that table is the nuptial garment, that is to say the state of grace and love. But the Eucharistic life shapes our lives even in the world. Everything matters; every idle thought; every diversion that we indulge in curtails our ability to communicate. We learn from personal experience that after attending a party where we committed no other sin but to dissipate our energies, we no longer dare to approach the Holy Table. How significant this word dissipation is here. We have been dissipating a treasure — our very being, re-created by the Eucharist, our very being that the world has imperceptibly deteriorated and corrupted.

Sometimes the devout soul, dissatisfied with himself and uneasy, examines his conscience and does not find anything definite to be censured; however, he knows he has lost something. The Eucharist confers on any life an atmosphere of its own. For those who do not live sheltered by a cloister, the fight is circumscribed between the peaceful silence of the Eucharist and worldly, noisy excitement. According to the rule of Saint Benedict, the monks should refrain from talking too much. They should not indulge in idle talk or in conversation which leads only to laughter; they should refrain from laughing immoderately.

This rule which is good for monks is good for the layman as well. The Eucharist obliges the faithful in the world to build for themselves an inner citadel, an underground cathedral. Whenever we spend time volubly talking in a parlor, becoming excited, we get away from this tabernacle; we do not know it then, but we find out when we are left alone again; we have been drifting. How much ground we have lost! We must retrace our steps, we must walk again the whole length of the road.

During the thanksgiving after communion, every futile word we say, every excitement we indulge in, separates us from Christ. We build with our hands that wall which estranges us from him. Christ is no longer so near us; His word reaches us from a

greater distance. But such is His merciful-
ness that the slightest impulse of humility
and repentance suffices to overcome every
barrier.

We become worldly through the habit of
frequenting worldly people; likewise, frequent communion shapes the soul. The Eagle
digs into our being a fitting nest for Himself; impresses thereon the shape of the
nest He likes to rest in, the shape of His
own body. Remodeled, or rather transformed,
our hearts will grow less and less amenable
to the lure of worldly things. But, cowardly
as he may be, he who has known the ardent
and creative silence of the Eucharist, will
he not end by leaving the last word to
God? . . .

CHAPTER III*

RIMBAUD

NOW imagine a human being who has
great powers of resistance, who is much
more masterful than I am, and who hates
this servitude. [of the Cross] Imagine a
nature irritated and exasperated to distraction
by this mysterious servitude and finally delivered over to an abandoned hatred of the
cross. He spits on this sign which he drags
after him and assures himself that the bonds
which attach him to it could never stand
out against a methodical and planned degradation of his soul and spirit. Thus he
cultivates blasphemy and perfects it as an
art and fortifies his hatred of sacred things
with an armour of scornful contempt. Then
suddenly, above this stupendous defilement,
a voice rises, complainingly, appealingly; it
is hardly so much as a cry, and no sooner
has the sky received it than the echo is
smothered by frightful jeers and by the laugh
of the devil. As long as this man is strong
enough, he will drag this cross as a prisoner
his ball-chain, never accepting it. He will
obstinately insist on wearing this wood
along all the paths of the world. He will
choose the lands of fire and ashes most
suited to consume it. However heavy the
cross becomes, it will not exhaust his hatred
— until the fateful day, the turning-point in
his destiny, when he sinks down at last under
the weight of the tree and under its agonizing embrace. He still writhes, pulls himself
together and then sinks down again, hurling out a last blasphemy. From his hospital
bed he brings abominable accusations against
the nuns who are tending him; he treats
the angelic sister as a fool and an idiot and
then, at last, he breaks off. This is the
moment marked from all eternity. The cross
which has dragged after him for thirty-seven
years and which he has denied and covered
with spittle offers its arms to him: the dying
man throws himself upon it, presses it to
him, clings to it, embraces it; he is serenely
sad and heaven is in his eyes. His voice
is heard: "Everything must be prepared in
my room, everything must be arranged. The
chaplain will come back with the Sacraments. You will see. They're going to bring
the candles and the lace. There must be
white linen everywhere. . . ."

That is the mystery of Arthur Rimbaud.
He was not only that wild-looking mystic
seen by Claudel nor yet that gutter-snipe
genius who is taken up by the young
sensualists of to-day. He was a man crucified
in spite of himself, who hated his cross and
was tormented by it; and he suffered anguish
in allowing it to win.

If we want to understand Rimbaud we
must understand his terrible mother, "mother
Rimb." She was a Christian and she willed,
with a will of iron, that her children should
be Christians. Arthur, for better or for worse,
was one. He sweated obedience, as he said.
Every Sunday, pomaded and good as gold,
the little boy sat at a mahogany loo-table
reading the Bible. Was he a hypocrite?

*Mauriac, François, *God and Mammon* (New York:
Sheed and Ward, 1936), pp. 41–46.

Remember his holy fury when he saw some college boys laughing round a holy-water font: he threw himself on them with all the force of his young being. But certainly he would have been glad to escape from the rule of the Church which he had not chosen and which he therefore cursed. *Une Saison en Enfer* shows both his subjection and his hatred. He hates the yoke and yet the yoke is upon him. Rimbaud's blasphemy exceeds all bounds because it is deliberate yet torn from his throat as if with difficulty. The note that springs from his very essence, naturally and inevitably, is the note which is, as Claudel says, "of the purity of Paradise, of infinite sweetness, of heart-breaking sadness." What he fails to say is that Rimbaud's heart has received the imprint of grace and that he hears the rational singing of the angels: "Reason is born in me, the world is good, I will bless life and love my sons. . . ." Then stupified by this unknown purity which presents itself in him — as if coming from someone else — he revolts against it and blasphemes Christ terribly. Remember how he walked about London, drunken and criminal-looking. And after having scared Verlaine mortally he declaims, and speaks to him in tender *patois* "of death which brings repentance, of wretched people who certainly exist, of painful toil and of separations which tear hearts in two. In the dens where we got drunk he cried thinking of the people around us, human cattle of misery. He picked up the drunkards in the dark streets. . . ."

Nevertheless, it was Christ Himself that he pursued with such hatred in Verlaine who had returned to God. When Verlaine arranged to meet him in Germany, Rimbaud saw him coming "with a rosary in his claws" in order to convert him. Thus he derived infinite pleasure in getting poor Verlaine drunk and making him renounce God, Our Lady and the saints. And on another occasion he threw himself on him and hit him like a madman. But beyond Ver-

laine's lamentable face which he bruised and wounded, did not he discern Another? Did not he recognise the sweat of blood and the expression of suffering and love? Similarly, was not it a voice other than Verlaine's which he heard in the poems of *Sagesse* — sent to him by his friend when he was at Roche? But it was in the lavatory that Isabelle found the manuscript. Rimbaud was determined to dishonour in Verlaine the living Christ.

From the youthful day when, ashamed at having spoken and having betrayed himself, he vowed himself to silence, until his death agony, when he was surrounded by angels, can we find one single sign of the presence and of the unconquerable possession of Christ? Only one phrase, a single phrase in a letter to his mother from Harrar on May 25th, 1881: "If I am forced to go on wearying myself as at present, and to feed myself on chagrins which are as violent as they are absurd, in vile climates, I fear I may cut short my existence. . . . Could we but enjoy a few years of real rest in this life! Happily this life is the only one: which is obvious because one cannot imagine another life with more boredom in it than this one."

Young Rimbaud had burnt his manuscripts and chosen to remain silent for always. But this little phrase in a hasty letter is enough for one to hear the groaning of an entrapped soul. If ever human words meant the opposite of what they appear to mean, this furious affirmation does: "Happily this life is the only one. . . ."

Then the current of grace was lost once again and only burst forth in the last days of his life, on his hospital bed. You may say that terror removes all importance from these death-bed conversions. But one must remember the astonishment of the chaplain after he had confessed Rimbaud: not only had the dying man the faith, but, according to the chaplain, this faith was of a very rare quality — a quality which he had hardly ever met with before.

CHAPTER XVIII*

THE meadow is brighter than the sky. Smoke goes up from the earth, gorged with water, and the cart-ruts, full of rain, reflect a muddy blue. Everything still interests me just as it did in the days when Calèse belonged to me. Nothing is mine any more, and I do not feel my poverty.

The sound of the rain, at night, on the rotting grape-harvest gives me no less concern than when I was the master of this threatened crop. The fact is that what I took for a sign of attachment to the property is merely the carnal instinct of the peasant, son of peasants, born of those who, for centuries, have anxiously scanned the sky.

The income which I am supposed to get every month will go on accumulating at the lawyer's. I have never had any need of it. I have been a prisoner all my life long to a passion which did not possess me. As a dog barks at the moon, so I was fascinated by a reflection.

Imagine waking up at sixty-eight — being born again on the point of dying! May I be given a few years more, a few months, a few weeks! . . .

The nurse has gone. I feel much better. Amelie and Ernest, who looked after Isa, now look after me. They know how to make injections. Everything is ready at hand: bottles of morphine, nitrate.

The children are so busy that they scarcely ever leave the town, and reappear here only when they need my opinion about a valuation. . . . Everything is passing off without too many disputes. Their terror of being "disadvantaged" has made them take the comic decision to divide the complete sets of damask linen and glassware. They would cut a tapestry in two rather than let any one of them have the benefit of it. They would spoil everything rather than let one share be greater than another.

This is what they call "having a passion for justice." They have spent their lives masking the lowest instincts under fine

names. . . . No, I ought to strike that out. Who knows whether they are not prisoners, as I was myself, to a passion which does not belong to the part of their nature that is deepest?

What do they think about me? That I have been beaten, no doubt, that I have surrendered. They have "got me." Still, at every visit they show me great respect and gratitude. All the same, I surprise them. Hubert especially keeps me under observation; he distrusts me, he is not sure that I am disarmed.

Reassure yourself, my poor boy. I was not very formidable even that day when I came back convalescent to Calèse. But now. . . .

The elms along the roads and the poplars in the meadows make up two broad surfaces, one above the other, and between their sombre lines the mist gathers — the mist and the smoke of bonfires, and that immense breath of earth after it has drunk. For we find ourselves suddenly in the middle of the autumn; and the grapes, on which a little moisture remains caught and shining, will never recover that of which the August rains robbed them.

But for us, perhaps, it is never too late. I have to keep on telling myself that it is never too late.

It was not out of devotion that, the day after my return here, I went into Isa's room. Mere idleness, that complete lack of occupation which I never know whether I like or dislike in the country — that alone moved me to push open the unlatched door, the first at the top of the staircase, to the left. Not only was the window wide open, but so, too, were the wardrobe and the cupboard. The servants had swept the place clean, and the sun devoured, even in the remotest corners, the impalpable remains of a destiny that was finished.

The September afternoon buzzed with awakened flies. The thick, round lime-trees looked like damaged fruit. The blue, deep at the zenith, paled towards the sleeping hills. A trill of laughter burst from a girl whom I could not see; sun-hats moved about at

*Mauriac, François, *Viper's Tangle,* translated by W. B. Wells (New York: Sheed and Ward, 1933), pp. 243–257.

the level of the vines; the grape-harvest had begun.

But the miracle of life had departed from Isa's room; and at the back of the cupboard a pair of gloves, an umbrella, had the air of dead things. I looked at the old stone chimney-piece which carries, sculptured on its tympan, a rake, a spade, a sickle and an ear of corn. These old-time chimneys, in which great logs can burn, are blocked during the summer by big screens of painted canvas. This one represented a yoke of labouring oxen. One day, when I was a little boy, I had slashed it with a pen-knife in a fit of temper.

It was only leaning against the chimney. As I was trying to settle it in its proper place, it fell forward and revealed the black square of the hearth, full of ashes. Then I remembered what the children had told me about that last day of Isa's at Calèse. "She was burning papers; we thought there was a fire. . . ."

I realized, at that moment, that she had felt death coming. One cannot think about his own death and other people's at one and the same time. Obsessed by the fixed idea of my approaching end, how could I have worried about Isa's high blood pressure? "It's nothing — just old age," those fools of children kept on saying.

But she, that day when she made that big fire, knew that her hour was at hand. She had wanted to disappear entirely. She had effaced the least vestiges of herself. I stared, in the hearth, at those grey embers, that the draught barely stirred. The tongs that she used were still there, between the hearth and the wall. I seized them, and foraged in that heap of dust, in that nothingness.

I dug into it, as though it concealed the secret of my life, of our two lives. In proportion as the tongs penetrated into them, the ashes became harder. I assembled a few fragments of paper which the thickness of the leaves had protected; but I rescued only odd words, broken phrases, whose meaning was impenetrable.

They were all in the same handwriting, which I barely recognised. My trembling hands applied themselves to the task. On a tiny fragment, dirtied with soot, I was able to make out this word: *PAX*. Beneath a little cross was a date: "February 23, 1913," and: "my dear daughter. . . ."

Out of other fragments I attempted to reconstitute the characters that were written on the margin of the burned page; but all that I obtained was this: "You are not responsible for the hatred which this child inspires in you. You would be to blame only if you yielded to it. But on the contrary you drive yourself. . . ."

After repeated efforts, I succeeded in reading this much more: ". . . judge the dead harshly . . . the affection that he has for Luc does not prove. . . ." Soot covered the rest, except these sentences: "Forgive without knowing what you have to forgive. Offer for him your. . . ."

I should have time to think it over later. I had no other thought but that of finding something more. I went on foraging, bending over, in a position which stopped my breathing. At one moment the discovery of a moleskin note-book, which appeared to be intact, excited me; but none of its leaves had been spared. On the verso of the cover, I could make out only these few words in Isa's handwriting: *Spiritual Nosegay;* and, underneath: "I am not called He Who condemns, My name is Jesus." (*Christ to Saint Francis de Sales*).

Other quotations followed, but they were illegible. In vain did I bend for long over that dust; I could obtain nothing more. I straightened myself up and looked at my blackened hands. I saw, in the glass, my brow smeared with ashes. A desire for walking took possession of me, as in the days when I was young. I went downstairs forgetful of my heart.

For the first time for weeks, I made my way towards the vines, half-stripped of their fruits, which were nodding into sleep. The country-side was volatile, limpid, airy as those bluish balloons that Marie once used to blow up at the end of a straw. Already the wind and the sun were hardening the cart-ruts, the deep imprints of the oxen.

I walked on, bearing with me the image of that unknown Isa, a prey to strong passions which God alone had possessed the power to master. That housewife had been a sister eaten up by jealousy. Little Luc had been hateful to her . . . a woman capable of hating a little boy . . . jealous because of her own children? Because I preferred Luc to them? But she had hated Marinette. . . .

Yes, yes, she had suffered through me. I had possessed the power to torture her. What madness this was! Marinette was dead, Luc was dead, Isa was dead — dead, dead! And I, an old man still on my feet, but on the brink of that grave into which they had gone down — I rejoiced in the fact that a woman had not been indifferent to me, that I had stirred these depths in her.

It was laughable; and, indeed, laugh I did, all to myself, leaning against a vine stake, face to face with the wan waste of mist in which villages with their churches, roads and all their poplars, were swallowed up. The light of the setting sun blazed a difficult trail through that buried world.

I felt, I saw, I had it in my hands — that crime of mine. It did not consist entirely in that hideous nest of vipers — hatred of my children, desire for revenge, love of money; but also in my refusal to seek beyond those entangled vipers. I had held fast to that loathsome tangle as though it were my very heart — as though the beatings of that heart had merged into those writhing reptiles.

It had not been enough for me, throughout half a century, to recognise nothing in myself except that which was not I. I had done the same thing in the case of other people. Those miserable greeds visible in my children's faces had fascinated me. Robert's stupidity had been what struck me about him, and I had confined myself to that superficial feature. Never had the appearance of other people presented itself to me as something that must be broken through, something that must be penetrated, before one could reach them.

It was at the age of thirty, or at the age of forty, that I should have made this discovery. But to-day I am an old man with a heart that beats too slowly, and I watch the last autumn of my life putting the vines to sleep,

stupefying them with smoke and sunshine.

Those whom I should have loved are dead. Dead are those who might have loved me. As for the survivors, I no longer have the time, or the strength, to set out on a voyage towards them, to discover them. There is nothing in me, down to my voice, my gestures, my laugh, which does not belong to the monster whom I set up against the world, and to whom I gave my name.

Was it exactly these thoughts that I was going over in my mind, as I leant against that vine stake, at the end of a vineyard, opposite the slopes resplendent with Yquem, on which the declining sun rested? An incident, which I must record here, doubtless made them· clearer to me; but they were in me already, that evening, while I made my way back to the house, steeped in my very heart in the peace that filled the earth.

The shadows lengthened. The whole world was nothing but an acceptation. In the distance, hills lost in the gloaming looked liked bowed shoulders. They were awaiting the mist and the night, perhaps to lie down, and stretch themselves, and fall into a human sleep.

I hoped to find Genevieve and Hubert in the house. They had promised to have dinner with me. It was the first time in my life that I looked forward to seeing them, that I found enjoyment in it. I was impatient to show them my new heart.

I must not lose a moment in getting to know them, in making myself known to them. Should I have time to put my discovery to the test before I died? I would go straight to the hearts of my children, I would pass through everything that had separated us. The tangle of vipers was at last cut through. I should advance so quickly into their love that they would weep when they closed my eyes.

They had not arrived. I sat down on a bench, near the road, listening for the sound of a car. The longer they delayed, the more I wanted them to come. I had a return of my old bad temper. Little they cared about keeping me waiting! What did it matter to them if I suffered on their account? They did it on purpose. . . .

I pulled myself up. Their lateness might be due to some reason which I did not know, and it was not likely that it was the precise reason whereby, through force of habit, I nurtured my resentment. The bell rang for dinner. I went to the kitchen to tell Amelie that we had better wait a little longer.

It was very rare for me to be seen under those blackened rafters from which hams hung. I sat down beside the fire, in a wicker chair. Amelie, her husband and Cazau, the handy man, whose loud laughter I had heard in the distance, had fallen silent as soon as I came in. An atmosphere of respect and terror surrounded me.

I never talk to servants. It is not that I am a difficult or exacting master; they simply do not exist in my eyes, I never even notice them. But this evening their presence comforted me. Because my children had not come, I was quite ready to have my meal at a corner of the kitchen table, where the cook was carving the joint.

Cazau took himself off, and Ernest put on a white jacket to wait on me. His silence oppressed me. I tried to find something to say. But I knew nothing about these two people who had devoted themselves to us for the past twenty years. Finally I remembered that their daughter, married at Sauveterre in Guyenne, used to come and see them, and that Isa did not pay her for the rabbit she brought, because she had some meals in the house. I spoke rather quickly, without turning my head.

"Well, Amelie, how is your daughter? Still at Sauveterre?"

She bent her weather-beaten face towards me and stared at me.

"Monsieur knows that she is dead. . . . It will be ten years on the 29th, Saint Michael's Day. Surely Monsieur remembers?"

Her husband, for his part, said nothing, but he looked at me sternly. He thought that I was pretending to have forgotten. I stammered: "I beg your pardon . . . my old head. . . ." But, as always when I am shy and embarrassed, I chuckled a little — I could not help chuckling. The man announced, in his usual voice: "Dinner is served."

I got up at once, and went and sat down in the dining-room, opposite the shade of Isa. Here was Genevieve, then Abbé Ardouin, then Hubert. . . . I looked, between the window and the sideboard, for Marie's high chair, which had served for Janine and for Janine's daughter. I endeavored to swallow a few mouthfuls. The stare of that man who waited on me was horrible to me.

In the drawing-room they had lit a fire of vine-branch faggots. In that room every generation as it withdrew had left, as a tide leaves its shells, albums, caskets, daguerreotypes, astral lamps. Dead knick-knacks littered the tables. The heavy stamp of a horse in the darkness, the sound of the wine-press that adjoins the house, almost broke my heart.

"My little ones, why didn't you come?" The moan rose to my lips. If the servants had heard me through the door, they must have believed that there was a stranger in the drawing-room; for this could not be the voice, or the words, of the old wretch who, they imagined, had pretended on purpose not to know that their daughter was dead.

All of them, wife, children, masters and servants, had formed a conspiracy against my soul. They had dictated this hateful role to me. I had painfully adopted the attitude which they demanded of me. I had conformed to the model which their hatred laid down for me.

What madness, at sixty-eight, to hope to swim against the stream, to impose upon them a new idea of the man that, nevertheless, I am, that I always have been! We only see what we are accustomed to seeing. You, too, my poor children, I do not see you either.

If I were younger, the lines would be less marked, the habits less deeply rooted; but I doubt whether, even in my youth, I could have broken the spell of this enchantment. One needed some strength, I said to myself. What kind of strength? Someone.

Yes, Someone in Whom we are all one, Who would be the guarantor of my victory over myself, in the eyes of my family; Someone Who would bear witness for me, Who would have relieved me of my foul burden, Who would have assumed it. . . .

Even the elect do not learn to love all by

themselves. To get beyond the absurdities, the failings, and above all the stupidity of people, one must possess a secret of love which the world has forgotten. So long as this secret is not rediscovered, you will change human conditions in vain.

I thought that it was selfishness which made me aloof from everything that concerns the economic and the social; and it is true that I was a monster of solitude and indifference; but there was also in me a feeling, an obscure certitude, that all this serves for nothing to revolutionise the face of the world. The world must be touched at its heart. I seek Him Who alone can achieve that victory; and He must Himself be the Heart of hearts, the burning centre of all love.

I felt a desire which perhaps was in itself a prayer. I was on the point, this evening, of falling on my knees, with my arms on the back of a chair, as Isa used to do, in those summers of long ago, with the three children pressing against her skirts. I used to come back from the terrace towards that illuminated window, walking silently and, invisible in the dark garden, look at that group at prayer. "Prostrate before You, O my God," Isa would recite, "I give You thanks that You have given me a heart capable of knowing You and loving You. . . ."

I remained standing in the middle of the room, hesitating, as though I had been hit. I thought of my life; I contemplated my life.

No, one could not swim against such a stream of mud. I had been a man so horrible that I had never had a single friend.

But, I said to myself, was it not because I had always been incapable of disguising myself? If all men went through life as unmasked as I had done for half a century, perhaps one would be astonished to find how little difference in degree there was among them.

In fact, nobody goes through life with his face uncovered — nobody at all. Most people ape highmindedness, nobility. Unknown to themselves, they are conforming to types, literary or otherwise. The saints know this: they hate and despise themselves because they see themselves as they really are. I should not have been so despised if I had not been so frank, so open, so naked.

Such were the thoughts that pursued me, this evening, as I wandered about the dimly lit room, where I stumbled against a heavy piece of furniture of mahogany and rosewood, a piece of jetsam sanded up in the past of a family, where so many bodies, today returned to dust, had sat and lain stretched. Children's boots had dirtied the divan when they buried themselves in it to look at the *Monde Illustré* in 1870. The stuff was still black at the same place. The wind prowled round the house, laying flat the dead leaves of the limetrees. They had forgotten to close the shutters of a bedroom.

HENRI BORDEAUX
(1870–   )

NOVELIST of family life, Henry Bordeaux was born in 1870 at Thonon on the shores of beautiful Lake Geneva. He came of a distinguished family of Haute-Savoie, and his childhood education, under the watchful eyes of a stern but loving father, was composed of tasks rigidly enforced, and lazy hours devoted to omnivorous reading. After attending the college at Thonon, Bordeaux studied law at the Sorbonne and Faculté de Droit in Paris.

In his first years in practice in Savoy he devoted more time to writing than he did to his professional duties. His critical articles were first collected in a volume *Âmes Modernes* which was successful enough to draw Bordeaux to Paris. He was recalled to Savoy upon the death of his father. For four years he filled his father's post as mayor of Thonon.

With the completion of his second work, *Les Écrevains et les Moeurs*, Bordeaux abandoned the law and gave himself entirely to literature. He married in 1901 and devoted himself entirely to writing, except for the years of World War I in which he served in the army and was twice decorated for bravery.

In 1919 he became a member of the French Academy, the youngest of the "Immortals."

Bordeaux remains one of the most prolific writers of his time and divides his year between Savoy and Paris.

Though he has maintained his interest in criticism, his first love, Bordeaux is known best as a novelist. His novels are a defense of family life and they preach the sacredness of marriage, the power of Christian tradition, the strength to be found in vigorous family unity, and the punishment which inevitably follows sin.

The Fear of Living is probably his best work, an astonishing fact, since his heroine is a tired old lady who retains her indomitable courage in the face of tragedy and defection.

All his characters give evidence of Bordeaux's loving study and shrewd mind, and there is a tonic force in his firm adhesion to Christian principle.

CHAPTER X

MARCEL'S DEPARTURE*

A FAMILY meal before a departure reminds us in its sadness of the first meal we have together after the final disappearance of an habitual guest. If no one is missing as yet, still joy has fled. Everyone tries vainly to brighten it, and of this touching, fruitless effort is born a deeper sadness.

Thus the dining-room at Le Maupas, in spite of the October sun which shone into it, was silent and mournful. Marcel was going away at nightfall in Trélaz's carriage to catch the six o'clock train at the station. When the conversation languished nobody thought of taking it up again. With a few unimportant words, spoken without enthusiasm, it would falter back to life, only to die out once more. Marie, the old servant, had prepared Marcel's favorite dishes. Carrying them back to the kitchen almost untouched, she murmured in a cross voice which expressed her own sorrow:

"It isn't right — it isn't right. They want to starve themselves to death!"

After lunch, Marcel went out with his sister.

"I want to see our old walks again," he said.

Through the vineyards on the hill they climbed up to the chestnut-trees at Vimines, under the shade of which grows thick moss where as children they used to gather mushrooms. From the border of the woods they looked out on Lake Bourget in its mountain basin. To appreciate its wild beauty at its best one must see it in the evening.

"Now let's go and see the waterfall," said Marcel.

He wanted to assure himself, as it were, before leaving, of the existence of all those quiet and lonely places which had helped to form his character. From Vimines, whose pointed steeple commands the hill, one comes down through the vineyards and orchards to the waterfall at Coux by a zig-zag path from which are to be seen several very fine views. Opposite lies a chaos of mountains, boldly scaled by rows of pines; on the left, the Nivolet with rocky peaks bathed in a bluish light; on the right, the openings of the valley of the Echelles and La Chartreuse. Marcel stopped short when he saw, between two golden-leaved beeches which framed a picture of savage loveliness, the long waterfall, slender and white, which fell a hundred feet and shone again in a silvery dust in the sunshine. He smiled happily.

"It is beautiful in its lonely surroundings," he said. "Don't let us go down any further. We have still to go to the Montcharvin woods and the ravine of Forezan."

These were some of the old possessions of

*Taken from *The Fear of Living*, by Henry Bordeaux, published and copyrighted by E. P. Dutton & Co., Inc., New York: 1913, pp. 177–190.

Le Maupas, which had been given up when the crash came. Because they were nearer home and, from time immemorial, familiar sights to him, he loved them best. And now though they were sold, they had not lost their charm for him. The beauty of the earth is not to be bought and sold. It belongs to the discoverer who can understand it and enjoy it.

Le Forezan is a deep valley whose steep sides are covered with a ragged growth of brushwood. Here and there the sides are less abrupt, and it is possible to climb down to the stream which runs at the bottom. There, under a far-stretching arch of greenery, are peace, silence, and forgetfulness.

Marcel, who was walking ahead, turned back and saw that his sister was caught in the creepers which crossed the path. Before coming to help her he cried:

"How pretty you look in those bushes."

"Come and help me instead of talking nonsense," said Paule. But he did not hurry. The girl's natural grace harmonised wonderfully with this fresh virgin landscape. He could not help admiring the suppleness of the movements she made to disentangle herself, and the bright flush of health that the exercise brought to her cheeks. When he came up to her, she was quite free from the snare which had held her. "Too late!" she cried.

"Bravo, Paule! You wouldn't be afraid in Cochin-China or the Tonkin forests. You will see them some day. You belong to the same race as your brothers."

"What, I?" she said, the fire in her eyes dying out. "I shall live and die at Le Maupas."

They came back from the valley through the ash wood. These trees with their light trunks reared their heads proudly on high, wearing as a crown the mass of branches from which the autumn wind was tearing the leaves. Half stripped, they showed their shapeliness in all their youthful health and strength, and thousands of uplifted arms waved peacefully. Like naked hamadryads they betrayed the secret of their forms. The scanty leaves which still adorned them were ruddy gold, almost as rich as the fallen ones which thickly carpeted the soil below. Eve-

ning came on and all the wood was bathed in a violet mist, which gave to it the mysterious aspect of a sacred grove.

Turned to the west on one side, on the other looking over meadows and vineyards, the farm of Montcharvin reflected in its windows the glow of the setting sun. This spacious house was built amid the ruins of an old castle, of which one dismantled tower and a Romanesque portico were all that remained. This portico, unprovided with a door and now quite useless, looked on to a roofless shed where old plough-shares were kept, and beyond, by reason of an abrupt descent, to a distant landscape which was framed in its arch. This arrangement called to mind the pictures of the old Italian masters, who, in order, doubtless, to sum up the multiform beauty of the world, used to supplement their human figures with a scene from nature, glimpsed between the columns of a palace or under the arches of a cloister.

Marcel and Paule skirted the old building and, following a screen of trees at the edge of a field which hid the deep valley of Forezan, they stopped in front of a fallen trunk, a natural bench which had been left there for years. Of one accord they sat down.

They saw the shades of evening falling over the land. They saw the path which they had followed and the dead leaves of the woods turning pink and violet. Two bullocks drawing a cart full of milk-cans passed in front of them, and, as they crossed a band of sunshine, a light haze could be plainly seen rising from their nostrils at every breath and mounting upwards. Peace filled the countryside, which was preparing for its winter rest with all the sadness of its shorn meadows and despoiled woods.

Marcel took his sister's hand. Suddenly at his touch she burst into tears. They had too many sensations in their hearts at this moment of leave-taking. He was thinking of Alice and her weakness, Paule was thinking of him. For a moment he waited till the tears he had caused her to shed were dried.

"Listen," he said at last. "You must watch over mother. I shall be away for a long time perhaps."

Uneasily she felt a foreboding of some new

misfortune, but immediately she mastered herself.

"You will come home next year from Algiers, won't you?"

He looked at her tenderly. "I don't know, Paule dear, I am taking part in an expedition which is preparing to cross the Sahara."

"Oh," she cried, "I was sure of it. You ask too much of our courage, Marcel. Mother is old and very worn. She feels our troubles as much as we do ourselves. We must make it easy for her."

Looking at the peaceful fields, he thought how sweet it would be to stay near his mother and sister. But it was only a passing regret, and he went on:

"Are you not there, you, our sister of charity? I have to go far away. I must forget. Don't talk about it now. The Moureau expedition is not yet ready. It won't set out for a year, or more perhaps. I am telling you, because I have no secrets from you. Mother will know about it soon enough."

"Will this expedition take long?" she asked simply.

"No one can say exactly. Probably eighteen months."

She tried to master her sorrow, but overwhelmed she burst into tears.

"You don't know how much Mother and I love you. Oh, if only we could have given our hearts to her who didn't dare to assert her will, she at least might have been able to do what we cannot to keep you here."

He took her in his arms and pressed her to his heart. Sure of this love, whose strength gave him courage, he waited till her despair had passed. But he did not mention Alice. That name should never cross his lips again. He only made a contemptuous allusion to his love.

"Don't let us speak of that, dear. Such a marriage would only have hampered me. A woman has no right to cramp her husband's career. What is a love worth that is not strong enough to bear separation and sorrow and to make a sacrifice? You will stay with Mother. My destiny was to be a globe-trotter — worse luck!"

He felt his sister's form grow stiff in his arms.

"I was not thinking of myself," she said, and in this phrase lay a whole world of inward rebellion, which he divined and understood.

She had known sorrow too young, at an age when life was opening with all its charm, and since her father's death she had experienced much base ingratitude and much insulting patronage to both her mother and herself. From these experiences, she had gained the strength of a stoic, but a bitter pride as well. She had already lost all hope for the future. She tried to forget herself, as she believed herself to be forgotten. The love for her mother and brother satisfied her passion for devotion. Uplifted by her dignity and her contempt for society, she did not seek to analyse the vague feelings which were surging in her ardent heart.

Marcel knew she had the same nature as he, little inclined to talk about self or to worry about her own affairs. He only tried to distract her and spoke with deep affection.

"Paule, don't despair. One of these days you will be happy. You deserve it so much!"

But she turned the conversation:

"Your trip to Paris was about the expedition, wasn't it? You never told me about it," said Paule.

"I did not keep you in the dark long, Paule, not long. I had to fight against all kinds of intrigues and competition. At last I got permission, both for Jean Berlier and myself, to join the expedition."

"Oh, so M. Berlier is going too?"

"Yes, and he will come back a captain and with the Legion of Honour. It will certainly develop him. The desert widens one's heart and brain, as the sea does. You don't think of love-making any more! But why have you left off calling him Jean?"

She made no reply. He looked at her, and then getting up said:

"Let us go back. It is growing dark. We must not leave Mother alone any longer."

Madame Guibert was seated at the door, waiting for them. With her old hands she was knitting some woollen stockings for a farmer's little girl. She had put on her spectacles to see her needles. She often lifted her eyes towards the avenue. This side of the house was covered with the five-leaved ivy whose scarlet color was deepened by the rays of the dying sun.

As soon as she saw Marcel and Paule she smiled at them. But as they were coming up the staircase she quickly took off her spectacles to wipe her eyes.

"At last!" she cried.

Her son kissed her.

"We stayed too long in the Montcharvin woods. But here we are, Mother. Are you not afraid of the cold? It is getting late to be out of doors."

And as they went into the house, the young man turned to look at the neighboring meadows, the chestnut avenue, and the open gate. Knowing how things stood with his family, he was aware that they would have to think of selling Le Maupas, unless his brother Étienne made a fortune in Tonkin. Here he had spent his childhood, and formed his soul. From this country — now all pink and violet — his memories came back to him at his call. They came to him from all sides, like a flight of birds clearly defined in the setting sun. Marcel shut the door. In the drawing-room he went and sat beside his mother on a low seat, leaned on her shoulder, and took her hand.

"I am so comfortable here," he said in a caressing voice which was a contrast to his determined face.

For the first time he noticed the hand that he was holding in his own, a poor, worn, rough hand with fingers swollen and ringless, which betrayed a life of toil and old age. Madame Guibert followed her son's eyes — and understood.

"I was obliged to leave off wearing my wedding ring, it hurt me. I wore your father's for a long time, but the gold grew so thin that one day it broke in two like glass." And she added, as if talking to herself:

"It did not matter. Only our feelings matter. And even death cannot alter them."

Marcel looked at the portrait of his mother, that he knew so well. It represented a woman, pretty and slender, looking like a shy young girl, whose tiny, tapering fingers held a flower, in the quaint old-fashioned way. Then he bent down and put his lips to the withered hand.

In memory he saw again the old lady, worn out and humiliated, coming home from La Chênaie after the refusal, and he thought of the rough way he had received her. Then with the rather haughty grace which lent so much value to his words of love, he said:

"My dear Mother, I have sometimes spoken rudely to you."

She drew her hand gently away and stroked his cheek, smiling a sad yet bright smile, which told the whole story of a soul purified by suffering.

"Be quiet," she murmured brokenly. "I forbid you to blame yourself. Every day I thank God for the children He has given me."

They were silent. Minutes passed, swiftly, irrevocably.

The approaching separation drew nearer, and they enjoyed to the full the happiness of their last moments together.

Nothing brings two lives closer than having suffered in common. When would they ever be together again as they were now in the golden charm of autumn, facing the fading trees, whose dying beauty could be seen through the window? Of these three souls, two had the presentiment that these hours would never come back. Madame Guibert sought in vain her usual bravery in farewell moments. Marcel was thinking of the solitudes of Africa which sometimes keep those who visit them; but, ashamed of his weakness, he banished with cheery words of hope these dark forebodings which cast shadows over the little country drawing-room.

And now Farmer Trélaz came to tell them that the carriage was at the door. The luggage was stowed away in it — a lunch basket not being forgotten for the long journey to Marseilles.

It was quite dark before the ancient vehicle started.

At Chambéry Paule noticed Madame Dulaurens and her daughter under an arcade. She saw Alice grow deadly pale; but turning to her brother, she was surprised to see him quite unmoved. He seemed indifferent. She felt intuitively, however, that he, too, had seen her.

At the station the three had a long wait. They had the little waiting-room to themselves. Madame Guibert never tired of looking at the son who was about to leave her. Suddenly she said:

"You are more like your father than any of the others."

"I have not his faith in life," said Marcel. "I never saw him discouraged. Whenever he failed in anything, he used to lift his head and laugh and say, 'As long as there's life there's hope.'"

"Since his death," said the old lady, "I have lost all my courage."

"He lives again in you, Mother. He still lives for us."

"Through you too. And he is waiting for me."

Marcel kissed her.

"No, Mother, you know we need you," he said.

They were no longer alone, and a short time after, at the porter's call they went out on the platform. There they saw in the darkness the two headlights of the express flash as it sped on towards them. The moment of farewell had come. Never had Madame Guibert shown so much emotion. Again and again she cried, "My son, my dear son," while she embraced him. He smiled to reassure her.

Her last words were a prayer:

"May God bless you and keep you."

All bent and bowed to the earth which was drawing her towards it, she went back on Paule's arm to Trélaz's carriage.

"Don't be unhappy, Mother dear," said Paule, comforting her. "It is only for a year. You used to be so much braver."

All the time she herself was in torture because of the secret that had been entrusted to her.

On the way home they were silent. During the evening at Le Maupas Madame Guibert suddenly burst into tears.

"I am so afraid I shall never see him again," she murmured, when she could give voice to her grief.

"But he is running no risks," Paule assured her, surprised and alarmed at this strange presentiment of a danger of which she alone was aware.

"I don't know. I am as sad as I was the year your father died."

With a great effort she managed to control herself so as not to frighten her daughter. Then, taking the hand of her last child with that gracious gentleness which remained to her from her youth, she said to Paule, thinking of the many separations in the past, some for a long time and others for ever:

"Dear little girl, you are the last flower of my deserted garden."

ÉTIENNE GILSON
(*1884*–   )

THE ripe scholarship of Étienne Gilson has been one of the chief factors in the renaissance of Catholic ideas in France and on the continent.

Gilson was born in France in 1884. All his life he has been devoted to studious pursuits. At the ancient shrine of learning, the Sorbonne, he made his course. It was there he found that wide knowledge of medieval philosophy which has become the particular field of his labors. Much *degreed* (he is a

Doctor of Letters, Law, and Philosophy), Gilson has lost none of his wit or urbanity in the process of becoming learned.

His social talents as well as his scholarship have endeared him to the English-speaking world. He has lectured extensively on the American continent and has been director of the Institute of Medieval Studies in Toronto, visiting lecturer at Harvard, and Gifford lecturer at the University of Aberdeen in Scotland. In his own country he has lectured on Medieval Philosophy at the Sorbonne and the Collège de France.

While Maritain has employed his enlightened mind in the propagation of Thomism, Étienne Gilson has written illuminatingly on the whole field of Medieval Philosophy. Gilson's synthetic view of the mysticism of St. Bernard, *Mystical Theology of St. Bernard* (Sheed and Ward, 1940), and his comprehensive study of the philosophy of Bonaventure, *Philosophy of St. Bonaventure* (Sheed and Ward, 1934), have been of inestimable worth in evaluating St. Thomas realistically against the true background of his own age.

CHAPTER XIX

THE MIDDLE AGES AND HISTORY*

IN ORIENTING nature, and man who is but a part of nature, towards a supernatural end, Christianity necessarily modified the received historical outlook, and even indeed the very conception of history. It is commonly asserted, however, that the Middle Ages remained a complete stranger to every kind of historical preoccupation, and indeed, to use a well-worn expression, was altogether lacking in historical sense. Illustrious scholars have vouched for the fact. The age we call "middle," which we regard, that is to say, as essentially transitional, is supposed, by a queer paradox, to have had no feeling at all for the transitory character of human affairs. Quite the contrary: "Its deepest characteristic is a faith in the immutability of things. Antiquity, especially later antiquity in its last centuries, was dominated by the idea of a perpetual decadence; modern times since their dawn are no less animated by a faith in indefinite progress; the Middle Ages knew neither this discouragement nor this hope. For the men of that time the world had always been such as they saw it — and that, by the way, is why their paintings of scenes from antiquity seem so naïve — and it would doubtless be the same at the last judgment." We might perhaps feel a little surprised at these massive affirmations did we not know how thoroughly indifferent some philologists are when it comes to dealing with ideas. They seem to regard them as insufficiently real to be regarded as facts calling for genuine historical treatment, and manage sometimes to combine with a most exacting scientific rigour about what the mediaevals wrote, a perfectly unscrupulous arbitrariness about what they thought.

The truth here, as elsewhere, is that if we seek our modern conception of history in the Middle Ages we may make up our minds at once that we shall not find it there; and if the absence of this modern conception amounts to the absence of any conception, then we may as well admit that the Middle Ages had none. We might just as easily prove, by the same process, that the Middle Ages had no poetry, or again, as it used to be thought, even in the face of the cathedrals, that it had no art, and, as is still maintained in the presence of all its thinkers, that it had no philosophy. The true question is, on the contrary, whether there was not a specifically mediaeval conception of history, other than that of the Greeks, and other than that of the moderns, but nevertheless real.

We might well have guessed *a priori* that this was the case when we deal with a time when all minds lived on the memory of an historical fact, of an event to which all previous history led up, from which was dated the beginning of a new era; a unique event, which might almost be said to mark a date for God Himself; the Incarnation of the Word and the birth of Jesus Christ. The men of the Middle Ages were possibly unaware that the Greeks dressed otherwise than they did themselves; more probably they

*Gilson, Étienne, *The Spirit of Medieval Philosophy*, translated by A. H. C. Downes (New York: Charles Scribner's Sons, 1940), pp. 383–402.

knew it well enough and cared very little; what they did care about was what the Greeks knew and what the Greeks believed, and still more what they were able neither to know nor to believe. In the distant past, after the history of the creation and the fall, there was just a multitude of men without faith or law; somewhat later the Chosen People, living under the Law, went through their long series of adventures; still more recently came the birth of Christianity, in-augurating a new era, already marked with many great events, the fall of the Roman Empire, for instance, and the foundation of Charlemagne's. How could a civilization believe in the fixity and permanence of things when its own sacred books — that is to say the Bible and the Gospel — were history books? It would be simply a waste of time to enquire of such a society whether it was changing and was aware of the change; nevertheless, we might well enquire how it conceived itself to be changing, that is, whence it came, whither it was going, what exact point it imagined itself to occupy on the road that runs from the past to the future.

Christianity had put the end of man beyond the limits of this earthly life; it had affirmed at the same time that a creative God allows nothing to fall outside the designs of His providence; it therefore had to admit also that everything, both in the life of individuals and in the life of societies of which individuals form a part, is ordered to this supraterrestrial end. Now the first condition of any such ordering is that there should be a regular unfolding of events in time, and first of all, of course, that there should be a time. This time is no abstract framework within which things endure, or, at any rate, it is not only that. Essentially it is a certain mode of existence proper to contingent things, unable to realize themselves all at once in the permanence of a stable present. God is Being, and there is nothing which He can become because there is nothing which He is not; change and duration have therefore no existence for Him. Created things, on the contrary, are finite participations of Being; fragmentary so to speak,

always incomplete, they act in order to ful-fil their own being, and therefore they change and consequently endure. That is why St. Augustine considers the universe as a kind of unfolding, a *distensio,* which imitates in its flowing forth the eternal present and total simultaneity of the life of God.

Man's state, indeed, is neither that of God nor that of things. He is not simply carried forward on an ordered stream of becoming like the rest of the physical world; he is aware that he stands in the midst of it and grasps in thought the flux of becoming itself. Successive instants, that would otherwise simply arrive and pass away into the void, are gathered up and held in his memory, which thus constructs a duration, just as the sense of sight gathers up dispersed matter into a framework of space. By the mere fact that he remembers, man partially redeems the world from the stream of becoming that sweeps it along, and redeems himself along with it. In thinking the universe, and in thinking ourselves, we give birth to an order of being which is a kind of inter-mediary between the mere instantaneity of the being of bodies and the eternal perma-nence of God. But beneath the frail stability of his memory, which would founder into nothingness in its turn did not God support and stabilize it, man himself passes away. Wherefore, far from ignoring the fact that all things change, Christian thought felt almost to anguish the tragic character of the instant. For the instant alone is real; here it is that thought gathers up the debris saved from the shipwreck of the past, herein live all its anticipations of the future; nay, it is here that it simultaneously constructs this past and this future, so that this precarious image of a true permanence that memory extends over the flux of matter, is itself borne on by that flux, and with it all that it would save from collapse into pure nought. Thus the past escapes death only in the instant of a thought that endures, but the in-stans is something that at once stands in the present and presses on toward the future where like-wise it will find no resting-place; and at last an abrupt interruption will close a history and fix a destiny for ever.

Thus for all mediaeval thinkers there existed men that pass in view of an end that does not pass. But this was not all. In proclaiming the "good news" the Gospel not only promised the just an individual beatitude, but also announced their entry into a Kingdom, that is to say, a society of the righteous, united by the bonds of their common beatitude. The preaching of Christ was early understood as the promise of a perfect social life, and the constitution of this society came to be looked upon as the last end of the Incarnation. Every Christian realized therefore that he was called to enter as a member into a far vaster community than any human one to which he belonged already. A stranger to every nation, but recruiting its members from all nations, the City of God will gradually build itself up while the world lasts, and the world itself has no other reason for lasting than the expectation of its final fulfilment. In this celestial, that is to say invisible and mystical, city, men are the stones, and God is the Architect. Under His direction it grows, towards it tend all the laws of His providence, to assure its advent He made Himself Legislator, expressly promulgating the divine law He had already written on men's hearts, and carrying that law beyond what the due order of a merely human society would require, but which would be an insufficient basis for a society in which man should dwell with God. If there were certain Christian virtues, humility for example, not easily to be found a place in the catalogue of Greek virtues, it was precisely because ancient morals were ruled above all by the exigencies of human social life considered as the last end, while Christian morals, on the other hand, were ruled by a society higher than that which subsists between man and man, the society of intelligent creatures with their Creator. What did not exist at all for the Greeks became the necessary foundation of all Christian life; humility is the recognition of the divine sovereignty and the absolute dependence of creatures, and there you have the fundamental law of what St. Thomas so forcibly calls "the republic of men under God." How much was owing to this notion in the "republic

of minds," the "eternal society," or even the "humanity" and the "realm of ends" in the philosophies of Leibnitz, Malebranche, Comte and Kant, we may easily guess; the dream of a universal society of purely spiritual essence is nought but the phantom of the City of God haunting the ruins of metaphysic. For the moment, however, we have only to consider what we can learn from this concerning the Middle Ages, and the place it conceived itself to occupy in history of civilization.

Its first consequence, if we look at it from this standpoint, is the substitution of a new sense of duration, quite other than that of the cycle and eternal return to which Greek necessitarianism so readily lent itself. Man has an individual history, a true "natural history" unfolding itself in linear and foreseen sequence from stage to stage, until at last death comes and cuts it short. This regular process of growth and growing old is also a constant progress from infancy to age, limited, however, by the span of human life. As he advances in age each man accumulates a certain intellectual capital, perfects the cognitive faculties whereby he acquires it, and augments his being, so to speak, as long as his powers permit. When eventually he vanishes from the scene his efforts are not on that account lost, for what is true of individuals is true also of societies that survive them, and of intellectual and mortal disciplines which survive the societies themselves. For this reason, as St. Thomas often notes, there is a progress in the political and social order, just as there is in the intellectual order of science and philosophy, each new generation becoming the beneficiary of all the truths accumulated by its predecessors, profiting even by their very errors, and transmitting a growing heritage to posterity. But then, for Christians, it does not suffice to consider the results acquired by individuals, societies or sciences. Since there exists an end promulgated by God Himself, towards which, as we know, His will directs all men, how should we not gather them all up under one and the same idea, and order the whole sum-total of their progress towards this single end? How should such progress be measured save in relation to such an end? Apart from an end what meaning would "progress" have? For this reason the Christian thinkers would naturally come to conceive, with St. Augustine and Pascal, that the entire human race, whose life resembles that of a single man, passes from Adam till the end of the world through a series of successive states, grows old in regular sequence, laying up meanwhile a store of natural and supernatural knowledge until it shall attain the perfect age, which shall be that of its future glory.

So, if we are to conceive it as the Middle Ages conceived it, must we represent the history of mankind. It is no history of a continuous decadence, since, on the contrary, it affirms a regular collective progress of humanity as such; nor is it the history of an indefinite progress, since, on the contrary, it affirms that progress tends towards its perfection as towards an end; rather is it the history of a progress oriented towards a definite term. There is nothing here in any event to authorize the view that the mediaevals thought that all things had always been what they then were, and so would remain till the day of judgment. The idea of progressive change, as just defined, was formulated in the most forcible manner by St. Augustine and those Christian thinkers he inspired. It was new; neither in Plato nor in Aristotle, not even in the Stoics, do we find the now so familiar notion of humanity conceived as an unique collective being, made up more of dead than living, always in progress towards a perfection, drawing ever nearer and nearer. Ordered and penetrated through and through by an internal finality, almost we might say by an unique intention, the succession of generations in time has not only a real unity, but, being now offered to thought as something more than an accidental succession of events, it acquires an intelligible meaning; and therefore, even if the Middle Ages is to be fixed with a lack of historical sense, we must at least grant it the merit of assisting at the birth of a philosophy of history. Nay, more, let us say that it had one, and that in so far as it still exists, our own is more penetrated with mediaeval

and Christitn principles than we usually imagine.

One might very well conceive a philosophic history in the manner of Voltaire and Hume, that is to say altogether free — or almost so — from Christian influence, and nothing would forbid us to call its conclusions a philosophy of history. It may perhaps be doubted whether, in this sense, there was ever any great historian who had no philosophy of history of his own; even if no effort were made to make it explicit, it would be none the less real, and possibly the more effective as less conscious of itself. The Christians, for their part, were obliged to make their philosophy explicit, and to give it a determinate orientation. They differed, in the first place, from other historians inasmuch as they conceived themselves to be well informed about the beginning and end of history — ignorance of these two essential factors would make it impossible for any infidel to grasp the meaning of history, or even so much as to suspect that it had one. Because they put faith in the Bible and the Gospel, in the story of creation and in the announcement of the Kingdom of God, Christians were able to venture on a synthesis of the totality of history. All subsequent attempts of the same kind merely replaced the transcendent end that assured the unity of the mediaeval synthesis, by various immanent forces that served as substitutes for God; but the enterprise remained substantially the same, and it was the Christians who first of all conceived it: namely, to provide the totality of history with an intelligible explanation, which shall account for the origin of humanity and assign its end.

However ambitious it be, the mere design is insufficient in itself; if we are going to realize it we shall have to accept the necessary conditions. If we are well assured that a God Who cares for the least blade of grass will not leave the rise and fall of empires to chance, if He forewarns us of the designs of His wisdom in ruling them, then we shall feel ourselves competent to discern the hand of Providence in detailed historical facts and explain them accordingly. It will be one and the same thing then to construct history and disentangle its philosophy; all events will fall of themselves into the place assigned them by the divine plan. Such and such a people will live in a particular territorial setting, with such and such a character, such and such virtues and vices; it will appear at a given moment in history, and endure for a determinate time as the economy of the providential order may demand. And not merely such a people, but such an individual, or religion, or philosophy. Following St. Augustine's lead, the Middle Ages therefore represented the history of the world as a great poem, which takes on a complete and intelligible meaning as soon as we know the beginning and the end. Doubtless at many points the hidden sense will escape us; we may suppose that the "ineffable musician" would often keep his secret back; however, we shall decipher enough to be sure that all has a meaning, and to be able to conjecture how each event stands to the unique law that rules the whole. The task is doubtless arduous and full of pitfalls, but it is neither mistaken in principle nor altogether impossible. And so among Christian philosophers there appeared historical works of an amplitude hitherto undreamt of, embracing the totality of accessible facts and systematizing them all in the light of a single principle. St. Augustine's *City of God,* with its sequel in Paul Orosius' *History,* makes no secret of an ambition which, indeed, it could hardly hide, since it was the *raison d'être* of the whole. Looking back on it at the time of the *Retractations,* St. Augustine sums up its aim and plan in a few words: "The first four of these twelve books describe the birth of two Cities, that of God and that of the world, the next four set forth their progress, and the last four their ends." The same design is manifest in the *Discours sur l'Histoire universelle,* wherein Bossuet takes up Augustine's work for the use of a future king of France. It has not escaped the attention of an excellent historian of Bossuet that the idea of this work is closely akin to Pascal's notion of humanity conceived as an unique man, and thereby, through St. Au-

gustine, to the Christian conception of history: "The idea of the *Histoire universelle* was not only to be found in Pascal, but since the early days of the Church it was everywhere, in St. Augustine, in Paul Orosius, in Salvian; it is even to be found in Balzac's declamations. The chief difficulty did not lie in the conception, but in the execution; for it demands an incredible mass of knowledge, intellectual power, logic and skill. To have this outlook on human affairs one only needs to be a Christian, but to build up such a work on the idea one would have to be a Bossuet." The thing could not be better put; let us simply add that the conclusion may be turned the other way about: to build such a work on the idea one only needs to be a Bossuet, but to achieve the idea itself one would have to be a Christian.

So durable has been the influence of Christianity on the conception of history that it is still discernible, after the seventeenth century, in thinkers who appeal to it no longer or even oppose it. It was not Scripture, to be sure, that guided the thought of Condorcet, but none the less he conceives the idea of drawing a "comprehensive picture of the progress of the human mind"; his philosophy of history has been run through a Christian mould of *tempora et aetates,* as if the succession of "epochs" was now the work of "progress" without the Christian God Who assures the progress. It is a typical case of a philosophic conception issuing from a revelation, appropriated by a reason that imagines itself to be the sole and true inventor, and then turned as a weapon against the revelation whence it came. Comte and his "three states," leading up to the religion of humanity, almost makes one think of an Augustine turned atheist, and a City of God brought down from heaven to earth. Schelling's "pantheism," setting out to assure a determinate succession of world-ages — *die Weltalter* — from within, posits a divine immanence at the metaphysical heart of things, and all that history does is to explicitate its development through time. Hegel goes still farther. This bold genius saw clearly that a philosophy of history involves a philosophy of geography; he therefore includes it in his powerful synthesis, which rules the whole dialectical movement of reason. The Greeks had early felt that even the physical world was ruled by a mind; Hegel does them justice here, but neither does he fail to perceive that the application of the same idea to history only took place later on and was the work of Christianity. He twists the Christian idea of providence, in the first place, as essentially theological, as something put forward as a truth of which the proofs do not lie in the rational order; and also as too indeterminate to be really useful even to those who accept it as such: mere certitude that events are ruled by a divine plan that escapes us in no way helps us to link up those events in intelligible relations. It is none the less true that if the Hegelian philosophy of history refuses to vouch for the truth — *die Wahrheit* — of the dogma of providence, it undertakes nevertheless to demonstrate its correctness — *die Richtigkeit*. It could do nothing else, let us add, for it was simply by this that it lived. What Hegel here offers us is once more a *Discourse on Universal History* in which the dialectic of reason has taken the place of God. His ambition to provide us with an intelligible interpretation of history as a whole bears the evident mark of a time in which reason is so profoundly saturated with Christianity that what, without Christianity, it would never have even dreamed of undertaking, it imagines itself able to effect, and to effect from its own sources.

The study of the mediaeval conception of history leads us naturally to ask how the Christian thinkers themselves conceived of their own position with respect to those who had preceded them and those who would come after. When it attained this degree of systematization the philosophy of history would necessarily be wide enough to embrace the history of philosophy. Here, then, the circle of our enquiry begins to close upon itself. Coming back to our starting point, and putting the question with respect to the doctrines that have formed the object of these studies, I would enquire of the Christian thinkers whether the relation in which they stood to Greek philosophy seemed to them to be purely accidental, or whether they conceived it to respond to intelligible necessities, and as occupying a definite place in the unfolding of a divine plan.

The Middle Ages has left us no *Discourse on the Universal History of Philosophy,* but it produced a few fragments, and above all it marked its own position within the totality of this possible history with much more care than might be imagined. These men would not have been in the least astonished to hear that they were living in an age that would be called "middle," that is, an age of transition. The Renaissance, that early invented the term, was also a "middle" age. The same may be said of our own; and indeed the only one that could be conceived otherwise would belong less to history than to eschatology. Nor would they have been in any way mortified to be told they were a generation of heirs. Neither in religion, nor in metaphysics, nor in ethics, did they suppose they had invented everything; their own conception of the unity of all human progress would have stood in the way of that. Quite the contrary; even in their capacity as Christians, and in the supernatural order itself, they recognized the whole Old Testament in the New, and so felt themselves ruled by the providential economy of revelation. The result is that when we speak of Christian philosophy it is impossible to separate the Bible from the Gospel, for the latter incorporates the former, appeals to it everywhere even for the "great commandment," giving it completion at the same time. We could not possibly base a Christian philosophy on the Gospel alone, for even where it does not cite the Old Testament it everywhere presupposes it. And so in the providential plan, as the men of those times conceived it, the preaching of the Gospel inaugurated an "age" of the world which carried on the work of preceding ages, gathered up their fruits and added to them; and this was the age in which they felt themselves placed. Was it not, moreover, on the religious plane, the final age? Could any other follow save the eternal Kingdom of God?

No less did the mediaeval philosophers avow themselves to be heirs in the field of natural knowledge; and, moreover, they knew why they were such. None of them doubted but that from generation to generation there is progress in philosophy. One might apologize for mentioning that they did not overlook this fairly evident fact had they not been accused of doing so. There was quite enough of the history of philosophy in Aristotle, to teach them that the Presocratics, "like children just trying to talk and only succeeding in babbling," had left their successors merely formless attempts at the explanation of things. St. Thomas himself recalls it, and delighted to retrace the history of philosophical problems and to show how men, occupying the ground step by step — pedetentim — came slowly nearer to the truth. The mediaevals felt it incumbent upon them to gather up the spoils of this always incomplete success and push on the advance. They saw themselves providentially placed at the crucial point where the whole heritage of ancient thought, absorbed by Christian revelation, was now to multiply a hundredfold. The age of Charlemagne struck men's minds as the coming of an era of enlightenment: *hoc tempore fuit claritas doctrinae,* wrote St. Bonaventure in the full thirteenth century. Then was effected that *translatio studii* which, handing on to France the learning of Rome and Athens, entrusted to Reims and Chartres and Paris the task of adapting this heritage to, and integrating it with, Christian Wisdom. None better than the poet Chrétien de Troyes has uttered the pride felt by the men of the Middle Age in being the guardians and transmitters of the civilization of the Ancients (Cligès, 27-39). The glory of his native land, which a French poet of the thirteenth century thus delighted to express, was none of his own imagining. The old tradition of the anonymous chronicler of St. Gall preceded him, Vincent of Beauvais followed him, a cloud of witnesses surrounded him. When an Englishman, John of Salisbury, saw Paris in 1164, that is to say before the extra-ordinary doctrinal flowering-season of the future University, he had no hesitation about the providential character of the work

that there went forward: *vere Dominus est in loco isto, et ego nesciebam;* the Lord is surely in this place and I knew it not.

Thus by its own philosophy of history the Middle Ages was led to conceive itself placed at a decisive moment of the drama that opened with the creation of the world. It never imagined that learning had always been what it had become since Charlemagne, nor that further progress was impossible. Nor did it believe that the world, having progressed as far as the thirteenth century, would progress indefinitely by the play of purely natural forces and in virtue of a kind of acquired momentum. In accordance with its own proper outlook it considered rather that humanity had never ceased to change from the days of its infancy, that it would still go on changing, but also that it was on the eve of the great final transformation. Joachim of Flora might announce the new Gospel of the Holy Spirit; those who followed him for a while soon came to recognize that after the Gospel of Jesus Christ there will never be another. Long prepared by the Ancients, the true philosophy had just attained, in all essentials, its definitive form. It was neither Plato's nor Aristotle's, but rather that which had been evolved from both by integration with the body of Christian Wisdom. And many another was there incorporated along with them! The philosophy of Christians was not alone in invoking the Bible and the Greeks: a Jewish philosopher like Maimonides, a Mussulman like Avicenna, had carried out, on their own side, a work that was parallel to that of the Christians themselves. How, then, should there not be close analogies, a genuine kinship even, between doctrines that worked on the same philosophic materials, and appealed to the same religious sources? Thus it is not with Greek philosophy alone that Christian philosophy was bound up in the Middle Ages; like the Ancients, the Jew and the Mussulman also did it service. Nevertheless, the work is about to attain a form which, in all essentials, will be definitive. Roger Bacon himself, all unsatisfied as he was, thought that the "great work" would soon be accomplished. Then the Christian thinker looked forward to nothing but an age of light, in which society, more and more thoroughly Christianized, would become more and more completely itself in the bosom of Christian Wisdom. How long would that time last? No one pretended to know, but all knew that it would be the penultimate act of the great drama that went forward. Afterwards would come the catastrophic reign of Antichrist. Whether the Emperor Charles was to be the last defender of the Church, or whether another was to come after him, none could guess at all. The only thing certain was that after the advent of the supreme champion, whoever he had been or might be, the great tribulations would begin: *post quem fit obscuritas tribulationum*. But they would endure only for the appointed time. Just as the Passion of Christ was as a darkness between two days, so the last assault of evil on good would meet with its defeat. Soon would open the seventh age of humanity, like the seventh day of creation, a prelude to the eternal repose of a day that should have no end: "Then shall descend from Heaven this city — not yet the city that shall be on high, but the city here below — the militant city, as conformable to the triumphant city as may be in this life. It will be reconstructed and restored as it was in the beginning, and then also shall reign peace. How long that peace will endure is known to God."

Apocalyptic considerations these, and less important in their detail than in their spirit and in the promise that concludes and crowns them. *Pax,* the peace from the shadow of the Cross; God's own promise — *pacem relinquo vobis, pacem meam do vobis* — a peace that philosophy is wholly incapable of giving, but whose triumph at least it can promote in integrating itself with Christian Wisdom. Thus, in its own way, it works for the fulfilment of the divine plan, and, as much as in it lies, makes smooth the path for the City of God. For it teaches Justice and opens the way for Charity. In this sense mediaeval philosophy appears to do something more than merely occupy a place in history; in establishing itself in the axis of the divine plan, it works to forward it. There, where social justice reigns, it is pos-

sible to have an order and a factual accord of wills. Let us even say, if you like, that it is possible to have a sort of concord; but peace is something much more, for where there is peace there is concord, but concord does not suffice for the reign of peace. What men call peace is never anything but a space between two wars; a precarious equilibrium that lasts as long as mutual fear prevents dissension from declaring itself. This parody of true peace, this armed fear, which there is no need to denounce to our contemporaries, may very well support a kind of order, but never can it bring mankind tranquillity. Not until the social order becomes the spontaneous expression of an interior peace in men's hearts shall we have tranquillity. Were all men's minds in accord with themselves, all wills interiorly unified by love of the supreme good, then they would know the absence of internal dissension, unity, order from within, a peace, finally, made of the tranquillity born of this order: *pax est tranquillitas ordinis*. But if each will were in accord with itself all wills would be in mutual accord, each would find peace in willing what the others will. Then also we should have a true society, based on union in love of one and the same end. For to love the good is to possess the good; to love it with undivided will is to possess it in peace, in the tranquillity of a stable joy that nothing can disturb. Mediaeval philosophy put forth all its powers to prepare the reign of a peace which of itself it could not give. In labouring for the unification of minds by the constitution of a body of doctrine acceptable by every man's reason it set out to assure the interior unity of souls, and their accord with one another. In teaching that all things desire God, and in asking men to look beneath the infinite multiplicity of their actions for the secret spring that puts them all in motion, Christian philosophy prepares their minds to welcome the order of charity in themselves and to long for the extension of its reign over all the earth. Where is true peace? In the common love of the true good: *vera quidem pax non potest esse nisi circa appetitum veri boni.*

If mediaeval philosophy worked for peace it was because it was itself the workmanship of Peace. All history tends towards the supreme tranquillity of the divine republic as towards its term, because God, the Creator of human beings who move towards Him through time, is Himself Peace. No trembling precarious concord like our peace; not acquired at the price of any internal unification, however perfect it may be supposed to be: He is Peace because He is One, and He is One because He is Being. As, therefore, He has created the finite being and the finite unity, so also He has created the finite peace. In ordering intelligence and wills towards Himself by knowledge and by love, of which, as we have seen, He is the supreme Object, God bestows on consciences the tranquillity that unifies and, in unifying unites. This tranquillity, as a created effect of the divine peace —*quod divina pax effective in rebus producit*— attests therefore in its own way the creative efficacy of a supreme and subsistent Peace whence its own existence derives: *causalitatem effectivam divinae pacis.* Doubtless the divine peace itself escapes our gaze, as God Himself with Whom it is altogether one, but we behold its finite participations in the unity of essences, in the harmony of the laws that link up physical things with each other, and the harmony which social laws would produce rationally amongst men. For Peace reaches through all things from end to end, uniting them with might, and ordering all things sweetly.

So to regard Christian philosophy is not simply to take it at its own valuation, to see it as historically it saw itself, but to see it at work in history, for indeed it went to work. It did not accomplish all it would, nor always even all it ought, for after all it was but a philosophy, that is to say a human effort labouring at a superhuman task. But at any rate all the greatness of which it can legitimately boast came from whatever fidelity it showed to its own proper essence. The spirit of mediaeval philosophy was one with the spirit of Christian philosophy. It was fruitful and creative in so far as it was willing to be incorporated with a Wisdom that lived itself by faith and charity. The Christian thinkers felt almost to anguish the narrow limits of mediaeval Christendom: *boni igitur paucissimi respectu malorum Christianorum, et nulli sunt respectu eorum qui sunt extra statum salutis.* However, even in these narrow bounds, Christian philosophy could live. It died, primarily, of its own dissensions, and these dissensions multiplied as soon as it began to take itself for an end, instead of serving the Wisdom which was at once its end and source. Albertists, Thomists, Scotists, Occamists, all contributed to the ruin of mediaeval philosophy in the exact measure in which they neglected the search for truth to exhaust themselves in barren controversies about the formulae in which it was to be expressed. The multiplicity of these formulae would have constituted no drawback, rather the reverse, if the Christian spirit that kept them in unity had not been too often obscured, sometimes lost. When this happened mediaeval philosophy became no more than a corpse encumbering the soil it had dug and on which alone it could build. For it was the great workman of a Christendom that could not live without it, and without which it could not live. Failing to maintain the organic unity of a philosophy at once truly rational and truly Christian, Scholasticism and Christendom crumbled together under their own weight.

Let us at least hope that the lesson will not be thrown away. It was not modern science, that grand uniter of minds that destroyed Christian philosophy. When modern science was born there was no longer any living Christian philosophy there to welcome and assimilate it. The architect of peace had died of war; the war came of the revolt of national egotisms against Christendom, and this revolt itself, which Christian philosophy should have prevented, came of the internal dissensions that afflicted it because it had forgotten its essence, which was to be Christian. Divided against itself, the house fell. Perhaps it is not too late to attempt its reconstruction; but if Christian philosophy is to start on a new career, a new Christian spirit will have to be everywhere diffused, and philosophy too will have to learn to absorb and retain it. That is the only atmosphere in which it can breathe.

PAUL BOURGET
(1852–1935)

PAUL BOURGET had a theory of life. He wrote it into many of his novels, for he firmly believed the sins of fathers are punished in their children. Had he lived a few years longer he would have seen his theory demonstrated to the hilt in France.

Born September 2, 1852, Paul showed an interest in books and writing while he was very young. His father was a civil engineer, and the education of his son was without roots as the family traveled about from city to city. A smattering of medicine at the Paris Clinic and his long continued interest in the classics did much to prepare Bourget for his life as a novelist and critic.

His first attempts to make a name in letters were in the field of poetry, with *La Vie Inquiète, Édel,* and *Les Aveux.* His poems caused but little stir, and Bourget turned to prose. His *Essays in Contemporary Psychology* and *New Essays* revealed his subtlety as writer and critic. Several books of studies and sketches succeeded his first prose works.

With the advent of his first novel, *L'Irréparable,* Bourget jumped into the spotlight of enduring fame. He gave up his teaching and tutoring that he might devote himself completely to literature. As novel succeeded novel the world delighted to honor him.

In 1919 he became one of the "Forty Immortals" of the French Academy. The French government made him a commander in the Legion of Honor and also curator of the Palace of Chantilly. Spared the anguish of World War II and the debacle of the Third Republic, Bourget died quietly on Christmas Day, 1935.

Though Bourget has excellences as a dramatist and critic, his best work is to be found in his novels.

The Disciple, his greatest work, which marks Bourget's return to the faith, has been quite generally acclaimed. It is a story which tortuously delineates the immorality and futility of the materialistic approach to life.

Bourget returned to the subject in later novels but never again with the same freshness and painstaking thoroughness.

In *L'Émigré* Bourget first expounded his idea of the sufferings which fall upon children because of the sins of their parents. The constant repetition of the same plot in time assumed the proportions of a fixed idea, though Bourget's work in general displayed, until his death, a genuine growth in character drawing and social awareness.

IV. CONFESSION OF A YOUNG MAN OF THE PERIOD*

Transplantation

I HAVE not described this first evening at the château because it had any immediate consequences, for I retired after assuring Count André that I was entirely of his opinion in regard to his young brother, and, having reached my room, I confined myself to consigning these words to my notebook, with comments more or less disdainful; but these first impressions will help you to understand some analogous impressions which followed, and the unexpected crisis which resulted from them.

It is one of those submarine chains of which you speak, and which I find to-day when I throw the sound to the very bottom of my heart. Under the influence of your books, and of your example, I became more and more intellectualized, and I believed that I had definitely renounced the morbid curiosity **of the passions** which had made me find

---

*Bourget, Paul, *The Disciple* (London and New York: F. Tennyson Neely, 1898), pp. 168–179.

exquisite pleasure in my guilty readings. Thus we retain portions of the soul which were very much alive, and which we believe to be dead, but which are only drowsing.

And so little by little, after an acquaintance of only fifteen days with this man, my elder by nine or ten years, and who was, all reality, all energy, this purely speculative existence of which I had so sincerely dreamed, began to seem — how shall I express it? Inferior? Oh, no, for I would not have consented, at the price of an empire, to become Count André, even with his name, his fortune, his physical superiority, and his ideas. Discolored? Not even that. The word incomplete appears to me the only one which expresses the singular disfavor which the sudden comparison between the count and myself diffused over my own convictions.

It is in this feeling of incompleteness that the principal temptation of which I was the victim resides. There is nothing very original, I believe, in the state of mind of a man who, having cultivated to excess the faculty of thought, meets another man having cultivated to the same degree the faculty of action and who feels himself tormented with nostalgia in presence of this action, however despised.

Goethe has drawn the whole of his Faust from this nostalgia. I was not a Faust. I had not, like the old doctor, drained the cup of Science; and yet, I must believe that my studies of these last years, by overexciting me in one direction, had left in me unemployed powers, which trembled with emulation at the approach of this representative of another race of men.

While admiring him, envying and despising him at the same time, during the days which followed, I could not prevent my mind from thinking. And I thought: "That man who would value him for his activity and me for my thought, would truly be the superior man that I have desired to become."

But do not action and thought exclude one another? They were not incompatible at the Renaissance and later, Goethe has incarnated in himself the double destiny of Faust, by turns philosopher and courtier, poet and minister; Stendahl was the romancer and lieu-tenant of dragoons; Constant was the author of "Adolphe" and a fiery orator, as well as duelist, actor and libertine.

This finished culture of the "I," which I had made the final result, the supreme end of my doctrines, was it without this double play of the faculties, this parallelism of the life lived and the life thought?

Probably my first regret at feeling myself thus dispossessed of a whole world, that of fact, was only pride. But with me, and by the essentially philosophic nature of my being, sensations are immediately transformed into ideas.

The smallest accidents appear in my mind to state general problems. Every event of my destiny leads me to some theory on the destiny of all. Here, where another man would have said: "It is a pity that fate should have permitted a single kind of development," I took it on myself to ask if I were not deceived in the law of all development.

Since I had, thanks to your admirable books, freed my soul and cast to earth my vain religious terrors, I had retained only one of my old, pious practices, the habit of daily examining my conscience, under the form of a journal, and from time to time I made what I called an orison. I transported, with a singular enjoyment, the terms of religion into the realm of my personal sensibility. I called that again the liturgy of the "I."

One evening of the second week of my stay at the château, I employed several hours in writing out a general confession, that is to say, in drawing a picture of my diverse instincts since the first awakening of my consciousness. I arrived at this conclusion, that the essential trait of my nature, the characteristic of my inmost being, had always been the faculty of duplication. That means that I had always felt a tendency to be at once passionate and reflective, to live and to see myself live. But by imprisoning myself, as I wished, in pure reflection, by neglecting to live and to have only one eye open upon life, did I not risk resembling that Amiel whose dolorous journal appeared at that time, and sterilizing myself by the abuse of analysis to emptiness?

In vain did your image return to me to

reinforce me in my resolution to live an abstract existence. I recall the phrases on love in the "Theory of the Passion," and I saw you, at my age, abandoning yourself to the culpable experiences which already obscurely tempted me. I do not know if this chemistry of soul, so very complex and very sincere, will seem sufficiently lucid. The work by which an emotion is elaborated in us, and ends by resolving itself into an idea, remains so obscure that the idea is, sometimes, exactly contrary to that which simple reason could have foreseen!

Would it not have been natural, for example, that the kind of admiring antipathy roused in me by my encounter with Count André should have ended either in a declared repulsion, or in a definite admiration? In the first case, I should have thrown myself more into science, and in the other, have desired a more active morality, a more practical virility in my own actions. But the natural for each one, is his own nature. Mine willed that the admiring antipathy for the count should become a principle of criticism, in regard to myself, that this criticism should produce a new theory of life, that this theory should reveal my native disposition for passional curiosity, that the whole should dissolve itself into a nostalgia of sentimental experiences and that, just at this moment, a young girl should enter into my life whose presence alone would have sufficed to provoke the desire to please in any young man of my age.

But I was too intellectual for this desire to be born in my heart without passing through my head. At least, if I felt the charm of grace and delicacy which emanated from this child of twenty years, I felt it while believing that I reasoned about it. There are times when I ask myself if it was so, times when all my history appears more simple, and I say:

"I was honestly in love with Charlotte, because she was pretty, refined and tender, and I was young; then I gave some pretexts of the brain because I was a man proud of ideas and did not wish to love like other men."

Ah! what a comfort when I persuade myself to speak in this way! I can pity myself instead of being a horror to myself, as happens when I recall the cold resolution, which I cherished in my mind, consigned to my notebook, and verified alas! by the event, the resolution, to injure this girl without loving her, from motives of purely psychological curiosity, from the pleasure of acting, of governing a living soul, of contemplating at will and directly this mechanism of passion which I had until then only studied in books, from the vanity of enriching my mind by a new experience.

But it is well, I could not have wished otherwise, impelled as I was by my heredities and my education, removed into the new medium where I was thrown by chance, and bitten, as I was by this ferocious spirit of rivalry against the insolent young man who was my opposite?

But this pure and tender girl was worthy of meeting a man who was not a cold and murderous calculating machine. Only to think of her melts and rends my heart.

I did not notice at first sight that perfection of the lines of the face, that brilliance of complexion, the royalty of bearing which distinguishes the very beautiful woman. Everything in her physiognomy was a delicate demi-tint, from the shade of her chestnut hair to the misty gray of her eyes and to her complexion which was neither pale nor rosy. One thought of modesty when studying her expression, and of fragility when remarking her feet, and hands, and the almost too minute grace of her movements.

Although she was rather short, she appeared tall because of the noble way in which her head was set on her slender neck. If Count André reproduced one of their common ancestors by an evident avatism, she resembled her father, but with so charming an ideality of lines that one could not admit the resemblance unless they were side by side. It was easy, however, to recognize in her the nervous disposition which produced hypochondria in her father.

Charlotte had a sensibility which was almost morbid, which was revealed at times by a slight tremulousness of hands and lips, those beautiful sinuous lips where dwelt a goodness almost divine. Her firm chin showed a rare strength of will in so frail an envelope, and I now understand that the depth of her eyes, sometimes motionless as if fixed on some object visible to herself alone, betrayed a fatal tendency to a fixed idea.

The first trait that I specially observed was her extreme kindness, and this was brought to my notice by little Lucien. The child told me that his sister had several times wished him to ask me if there was anything lacking in my room.

This is a very puerile detail, but it touched me because I felt very lonely in this great house where no person, since my arrival, had seemed to pay the least attention to me. The marquis appeared only at dinner, wrapped in a *robe-de-chambre* and groaning over his health or politics. The marquise was occupied in making the château comfortable, and held long conferences with an upholsterer from Clermont. Count André rode in the morning, hunted in the afternoon, and, in the evening, smoked his cigars without ever addressing a word to me. The governess and the *religieuse* looked at one another and looked at me with a discretion which froze me.

My pupil was an idle and dull boy, who had the redeeming quality of being very simple, very confiding, and of telling me all that I wished to know of himself and the rest of his family. I learned in this way that their stay in the country this year was the work of Count André, which did not astonish me in the least, for I felt more and more that he was the real head of the family; I learned that the year preceding he had wished to marry his sister to one of his comrades, a M. de Plane, whom Charlotte had refused, and who had gone to Tonquin.

In our two daily classes, one in the morning from eight o'clock to half-past nine, the other in the afternoon from three o'clock until half-past four, I had a great deal of trouble to fix the attention of the little idler. Seated on his chair, opposite me on the other side of the table, and rolling his tongue against his cheek, while he covered the paper with his big awkward writing, he would now and then glance up at me.

He noticed on my face the least sign of abstraction. With the animal and sure instinct of children, he soon saw that I would make him go on with his lessons less quickly when he talked to me of his brother or sister, and so this innocent mouth revealed to me that there was, in this cold, strange house, some one who thought of me and of my comfort.

My mother had failed so much in this regard, although I might not wish to confess it! And it was this act of simple politeness which made me regard Mlle. de Jussat with more attention.

The second trait that I discovered in her was a taste for the romantic, not that she had read many romances, but as I have already told you, her sensibility was extreme, and this had given her an apprehension of the real.

Without herself suspecting it she was very different from her father, her mother and her brothers; and she could neither show herself to them in the truth of her nature, nor see them in the truth of theirs without suffering. So she did show herself, and she forced herself not to see them. She formed, spontaneously and ingeniously, opinions of those she loved which were in harmony with her own heart and so directly contrary to the evidence that they would have seemed false or flattering in the eyes of a malevolent observer. She would say to her mother, who was so ordinary and material: "Mamma, you are so quick to see"; to her father so cruelly egotistical: "You are so kind, papa," and to her brother who was so positive, so self-sufficient: "You understand everything," and she believed it. But the delusion in which this gentle creature imprisoned herself, left her a prey to the most complete moral solitude, and deprived her, to a very dangerous degree, of all judgment of character.

She was as ignorant of herself as of others. She languished, unknown to herself, for the society of some one who should have sentiments in harmony with her own. For example, I observed in the first walks that we took together, that she was the only one who could really feel the beauty of the landscape formed by the lake, the woods that surround it, the distant volcanoes and the autumn sky, often more blue than the sky of summer because of the contrast of its azure with the gold of the leaves, and which was sometimes so veiled, so sadly vaporous and distant.

She would fall into silence without any apparent reason, but really because her whole being became dissolved into the charm of things about her. She possessed in the state of pure instinct and unconscious sensation the faculty which makes the great poets and the great lovers, namely, the faculty of forgetting oneself, of dispelling oneself, of losing oneself entirely in whatever touches the heart, whether it be a veiled horizon, a silent and yellow-tinted forest, a piece of music or a touching story.

I did not, at the beginning of our acquaintance, formulate the contrast between that combative animal her brother and this creature of sweetness and grace who ran up the stone staircases of the château with a step so light that it seemed scarcely poised, and whose smile was so welcoming and yet so timid.

I will dare to tell all, since I repeat it, I am not writing in order to paint myself in beautiful colors, but to show myself as I am. I will not say that the desire to make myself beloved by this adorable child, in whose atmosphere I began to feel so much pleasure, was not caused by this contrast between her and her brother.

Perhaps the soul of this young girl became as a field of battle for the secret, the obscure antipathy which two weeks had transformed into hate? Perhaps there was concealed the cruel pleasure of humiliating the soldier, the gentleman, by outraging him in what he held most precious? I know that this is horrible, but I should not be worthy of being your pupil if I did not disclose the lowest depth of my heart. And, after all, this odious cloud of sensations may be only a necessary phenomenon, like the others, like the romantic grace of Charlotte, like the simple energy of her brother, and like my own complexities — so obscure even to myself.

GEORGES BERNANOS
(*1888–*)

IN HIS monograph on *St. Joan of Arc,* 1934, Bernanos wrote, "Sanctity is an adventure, it is truly the only adventure." This sentence sums up his philosophy and makes his life and works somewhat more easily understandable.

There are many critics and philosophers who fail to comprehend his irreconcilable idealism; they see in him something Jansenistic and there are some who would even go so far as to call Bernanos' conception of life Manichean. A complete study of the man puts both theories to flight, revealing Bernanos as a Catholic idealist. The intransigence of his idealism is the factor which gives rise to misunderstandings of the man and his purpose.

Bernanos was born in 1888. His talent for writing revealed itself when he was quite young. After his studies with the Jesuits in the College of Veaugirard, Bernanos became editor of the royalist weekly of Normandy. Though his early views were traditional he soon widened them and accused the Catholic party in France of pursuing a policy which was driving the workers and the peasants into the arms of the Communists.

His accusation touched off a long and acrimonious verbal battle, which so disgusted Bernanos that he left France and retired to Brazil. From his refuge, he drew up a bitter indictment of Hitlerism and was one of the first of the French writers to condemn the men of Vichy.

Bernanos' great novels, *Sous le Soleil de Satan,* 1926, *L'Imposture,* 1927, *La Joie,* 1939, and *Journal d'un Curé de Campagne* are tortuous examinations of the life of grace and mysticism, the first of their kind to appear since Bloy wrote his astonishing book, *The Woman Who Was Poor*. In Bernanos' great novels we behold the powers of darkness arrayed against a humanity shown in many instances as strengthened by grace and triumphant, and in a great many others as weak, mendacious, and evil. That critics find in these works only the domination of evil is partly due to the author's method of leaving to God the final judgment of the battle. Those who fail to put God into the picture may be easily deceived into thinking that Bernanos is setting down an unrelieved picture of an evil world, under the sway of the prince of darkness.

It is a weakness in Bernanos that the mystical joy and resurrected quality of Catholicism are given too little emphasis. The dark night of the soul engrosses his attention and

he sets down its anguish with fidelity: the joy of illumination and the serenity of intuitive union are absent in his portraits, which, in spite of these lacks, are as valid for our education as the gallery of tortured souls which Dostoevsky painted.

It is true that the "adventure of Sanctity" calls for nothing less than perfection, but from the taut and strained will goes up a note of triumph which God hears in the melodious silence of the Trinity. And when the completed record is in, it is God who will cast the score, and assess the credit, a fact which makes any objective catalogue of the struggle an incomplete record, such as are the novels of Bernanos.

For those who require a defense of Bernanos, the monograph by Frank O'Malley in "The Review of Politics" (Vol. 6, No. 4, pp. 403–421. October, 1944) offers a splendid apologia.

THE SAINT OF LUMBRES*

CHAPTER I

HE OPENED the window. He was still awaiting something indefinite. Through a gulf of shadow glistening and dripping with rain, the church, the only live thing, still shone dimly. "Here I am," he said, as though in a dream.

Downstairs old Martha was bolting the doors. The smithy anvil rang far off. But he had already ceased to listen. It was that hour of the night when this man of intrepid courage, sustainer of so many souls, staggered under the weight of his glorious burden. "Poor curé de Lumbres," he said with a smile, "he does nothing well, he can't even sleep now." He also said: "Do you know, I'm afraid of the dark?"

Little by little the sanctuary lamp revealed in the darkness the pointed shapes of tall three-niched windows. The ancient tower,

built between choir and center aisle, raised its massive belfry, its pointed spire immediately over them. He no longer saw them. There he stood alone facing the blackness, as though at a ship's prow. The huge waves of dark, with superhuman noise, surged round him. Invisible fields and woods were rushing in on him from the four corners of the horizon . . . and behind the fields and woods lay other villages, all alike, all perishing with plenty, hating the poor, full of crouching misers, frigid as shrouds. And further still the cities which know no sleep.

"Oh, God! Oh, God!" he kept repeating, unable either to weep or pray. Each minute, as time dies with a dying man, fell into the gulf, irreparable. Short as are the nights, day is always late in coming. Célimène has already rouged her face, the sot has already slept off his liquor. The witch is back from the sabbath still hot with her lusts and has slipped between the white sheets. Day comes too late. But the one and only justice from pole to pole shall astound the world.

*From *The Star of Satan*, Book III, pp. 235–242, by Georges Bernanos. By permission of The Macmillan Company, publishers, 1940.

In the end he sank to his knees, as a ship founders. He did not look so far for that justice which a generous people awaits from its minister of finance — it was far more likely to be over there, below the horizon, all ready and waiting, kneaded with the rising dawn, irresistible, amid darkness flying in smithereens. The open hand shall not close its fingers. The word shall shrivel upon the lips. The monster Evolution, transfixed for all time, shall suddenly cease to sprawl and writhe. That terrible dawn which rises in a man's deep consciousness shall give its form and eternal volume even to his most hidden thoughts, so that the furtive and mendacious heart will no longer be able to perjure itself. *Consummatum est:* that is to say — all has been eternally defined.

Monsieur Loyolet, inspector of schools (by virtue of his degree in literature), expressed a desire to see the saint of Lumbres, whose name was in everybody's mouth. He had come to visit him in secret, along with his daughter and his good lady. He was rather touched. "I had imagined him as quite an imposing sort of man," he said, "a man of distinction, with perfect manners. But this little curé has no dignity, he munches in the open street, like a beggar." "What a pity it is," he also said, "that such a man should believe in the devil."

The curé de Lumbres believes in the devil, and even tonight he felt afraid of him. "For weeks," he said later, "I had been tormented by an agony I had never known before. All my life has been spent in the confessional. Suddenly I was overwhelmed by the sense of my own helplessness: a feeling more of disgust than pity. Only a poor foolish priest like men can really know the horrible monotony of sin. I had nothing to say. I could do no more than give absolution, and weep. . . ."

The clouds above him dissolved in tatters. One, ten, a hundred stars were reborn, singly, at the summit of night. A drizzle of rain fell like liquid dust from a cloud rent by the wind. He breathed the fresh air which the storm had released. Tonight, he would no longer defend himself, there was nothing left for him to defend, he had given everything, he was empty. . . . The human heart! He knew all about it. He, in his heavy boots and shabby cassock, had gained access to the human heart.

That tough old heart of all humanity, inhabited by the enigmatic enemy of souls, the vile and powerful enemy of man, vile and magnificent. The perjured morning star: Lucifer, the false dawn.

He knew so much, poor curé de Lumbres — so much unknown to the Sorbonne. So many things which never get written are scarcely said, avowals which must be torn out as one tears open a scabbed wound — so many things! And he knew what man is in reality: a big child, full of boredom and vice.

Was there anything new the old priest could learn? He who had lived a thousand lives — lives all alike. Nothing could surprise him again. He could die. There are brand new systems of morality but sin can never be new!

For the first time in his life he doubted, not God but man. A thousand memories pressed in upon him — he heard confused complaints, moanings full of shame, the agonized cry of passion hiding from the light, pinned down and revealed by a single word, turned inside out, stripped and displayed in all its nakedness by clear definition. He saw again the miserable shattered faces, the eyes which would and yet would not, the sagging lips which admit defeat, the bitter mouths which answer, No. So many sham rebels, so eloquent before the world, now at his feet, ridiculous! So many proud hearts with a secret rotting in them! So many old men like horrible children! And above them all, their frigid eyes fixed on the world, the mean-hearted young who never forgive.

Today or yesterday, or on the very first day of his priesthood, the same as ever. He had come to the end of his striving; suddenly the obstacle was no more. Those whom he had wanted to free were the very ones who refused all freedom as a burden, and the enemy he had hunted for in heaven laughed below him, illusive and invulnerable.

They had all made game of him. "We seek peace," they said. Not really peace but a short breathing space, a halt in the dark. They came to rid themselves of their venom kneeling at the hermit's feet, and so went back to their dismal pleasures, their joyless lives. (He sometimes compared himself to those ancient walls, insulted by the smut scribbled over them by passers-by, walls which crumble slowly, full of idiotic secrets.)

Those whom he had comforted so often would know him no more. At that moment, one of the most tragic in all his life, he felt that he was assailed on all sides, everything was again in doubt. Certain more perfidious thoughts, long thrust aside, were suddenly there again, and he knew them no longer. He sensed a kind of new meaning in everything, a new savor as it were. . . . For the first time he viewed without love and yet without compassion, the lamentable herd, born to browse and perish. He relished the bitterness of defeat, the bitter sense of his own greatness. The intrepid will, at the confines of agony, would not admit itself defeated, but struggled to regain its balance, at any cost.

Now he was on his feet; he gazed inflexibly out before him. . . . How many nights like tonight, till the last night! But Divine grace will eternally strike into the midst of crowds, will always set its seal on a few of those for whom justice rises like a star, glittering through time. The obedient star comes hurrying to their call.

He had ceased to look at the little church, he looked above it. He was vibrant with joyless exultation. He had almost ceased to suffer, was fixed for all time. He wanted nothing; he was defeated. Pride flooded in through the open breach in his heart.

"I was losing my soul without even thinking about it," he said later on. "I could feel myself hardening like a stone."

The project he had formed so often of hiding himself to die, withdrawn from the world, in some Chartreuse or Trappist monastery, came back to him, but this time it came as a new image, with a sharp sweet shriveling of his heart, a mysterious numbness. Formerly in such instants as these the Shepherd would not leave his flock; he dreamed of taking it even to his place of penance, so that he might still live and merit on its behalf. But now even that memory

faded out of him, the last of all. The tireless fighter for souls asked only for rest, and for one other thing, the secret thought of which slackened every fiber of his being — his need to be allowed to die was like the need to burst into tears. . . . Since indeed his eyes were wet with tears, but they were tears which did not ease his heart, and so the old man in his simplicity no longer knew them for what they were; he was amazed and found no name for his pleasant giddiness; he was on the point of giving way, without opening his eyes, to that supreme temptation in which so many ardent souls who fight their way straight through pleasure and find emptiness, which they grasp to themselves in one strong embrace, had been engulfed before him. Fatigue, at the limit of his huge effort, conquered, spurned off again and again, came flooding out of him, as though his very blood were being shed. No remorse. His most cunning enemy rolled him in the mire of that desperate lassitude, as in a shroud, with infinite skill, in horrible mocking imitation of a mother's care. It was in vain that the distraught old man gazed through the fading darkness with eyes alight for the last time, eyes which would never reflect the brightness of dawn. He could find nothing within himself, no image in which to define this temptation, no sign of this work which was slowly destroying him under the eyes of an impassive monster. Now he no longer craved for his monastery, but for something more secret even than solitude, the swooning fall, enclosed in darkness, through all eternity. To him whose flesh had so long been his slave, lasciviousness at last showed her true face, all one quiet smile. And yet not even such an image nor any other could trouble the senses of this lonely old man, now since another lust had been aroused in his obstinate childlike heart, the delirious hankering after knowledge which drove to perdition the mother of men, when she stood erect and wondering on the very verge of good and evil. To know in order to destroy and, in destruction, to renew knowledge and desire — oh, Light of Satan! — the craving for the void sought for its own sake, abominable effusion of the heart! The saint of Lumbres had no longer the strength to do more than invoke this fearful repose; divine grace cast a veil before these eyes which only a little while ago had still been filled with divine mystery. And now the clear gaze had become hesitant, it had lost the knowledge of where to look. . . . A strange youthfulness, a simple avidity, something like the first wound of the senses, warmed his old blood, beat within his bony chest. He sought hesitantly, he caressed death, through so many veils, with a dying hand.

Had his life had any meaning till that solemn moment? He could not tell. Behind him he could see only arid landscape and the crowds through which he had passed, as he blessed them. And even now! The herd was still ambling at his heels, pressing in on him, granting him no rest, insatiable, with its wide uneasy muttering, the stampede of wounded animals. . . . No! he would not look round, he refused. They had pushed him where he was, to the very edge and beyond it. . . . O miracle! Silence exists, real silence, incomparable silence — rest.

"Let me die," he muttered, "die!" He spelt the word to steep himself in its meaning, to let his heart absorb its sense. Truly he felt it now in his very depths, in his veins, this word, this subtle poison. He persists, redoubles his efforts, with rising feverishness; he longs to swallow it at a draught, hasten

his end. His impatience had in it the sinner's need to delve on and on into the heart of his sin, on and on, to conceal himself from his judge; at such a time Satan weighs down with all his strength on us, and every power of hell is concentrated in a single downward thrust at the one point.

And yet his eyes were still turned upwards towards the square of graying sky from which night was fading away in mists. Never yet had he prayed with such stern tenacity or in such a voice. Never yet had his voice come forth so strongly from his lips, no more than a murmur to other ears, but loud within as the crash of thunder, like a rumble of imprisoned sound in a block of brass. Never before had the humble magician of whom so many tales are told felt himself so close to a miracle, face to face with wonder. It seemed to him that his will was put forth for the first time now, irresistible, and that a single word, spoken in the quiet, would destroy him forever. Yes, nothing kept him from rest but a last movement of sovereign will. He no longer dared to see the church nor the houses of his little flock, in the mists of daybreak; a kind of shame which he hastened to put to flight by irreparable action still held him back. Why be encumbered with unnecessary care? He looked down at the earth, his sanctuary.

THE DIARY OF A COUNTRY PRIEST*

PART 4

ANOTHER horrible night, sleep interspersed with evil dreams. It was raining so hard that I couldn't venture into church. Never have I made such efforts to pray, at first calmly and steadily, then with a kind of savage, concentrated violence, till at last, having struggled back into calm with a huge effort, I persisted, almost desperately

(desperately! how horrible it sounds!) in a sheer transport of will which set me shuddering with anguish. Yet — nothing.

I know, of course, that the wish to pray is a prayer in itself, that God can ask no more than that of us. But this was no duty which I discharged. At that moment I needed prayer as much as I needed air to draw my breath or oxygen to fill my blood. What lay behind me was no longer any normal, familiar life, that everyday life out of which the impulse to pray raises us, with still at the back of our minds the certainty that

*From *The Diary Of A Country Priest*, pp. 103–109. By permission of The Macmillan Company, publishers, 1938.

whensoever we wish we can return. A void was behind me. And in front a wall, a wall of darkness.

The usual notion of prayer is so absurd. How can those who know nothing about it, who pray little or not at all, dare speak so frivolously of prayer? A Carthusian, a Trappist will work for years to make of himself a man of prayer, and then any fool who comes along sets himself up as judge of this lifelong effort. If it were really what they suppose, a kind of chatter, the dialogue of a madman with his shadow, or even less — a vain and superstitious sort of petition to be given the good things of this world, how could innumerable people find until their dying day, I won't even say such great 'comfort' — since they put no faith in the solace of the senses — but sheer, robust, vigorous, abundant joy in prayer? Oh, of course, 'suggestion,' say the scientists. Certainly they can never have known old monks, wise, shrewd, unerring in judgment, and yet aglow with passionate insight, so very tender in their humanity. What miracle enables these semi-lunatics, these prisoners of their own dreams, these sleep-walkers, apparently to enter more deeply each day into the pain of others? An odd sort of dream, an unusual opiate which, far from turning him back into himself and isolating him from his fellows, united the individual with mankind in the spirit of universal charity!

This seems a very daring comparison. I apologize for having advanced it, yet perhaps it might satisfy many people who find it hard to think for themselves, unless the thought has first been halted by some unexpected, surprising image. Could a sane man set himself up as a judge of music because he sometimes touched a keyboard with the tips of his fingers? And surely if a Bach fugue, a Beethoven symphony leave him cold, if he has to content himself with watching on the face of another listener the reflected pleasure of supreme, inaccessible delight, such a man has only himself to blame.

But alas! We take the psychiatrist's word for it. The unanimous testimony of saints is held as of little or no account. They may all affirm that this kind of deepening of spirit is unlike any other experience, that instead of showing us more and more of our own complexity it ends in sudden total illumination, opening out upon azure light — they can be dismissed with a few shrugs. Yet when has any man of prayer told us that prayer had failed him?

Literally I can scarcely stand up this morning. Those hours which seemed to me so long have left me with no precise recollection — nothing but the sensation of a blow, directed from nowhere, its force striking me full in the chest, leaving me mercifully half stunned, so that I can still not gauge its seriousness.

We never pray alone. Doubtless my sorrow was too great. I wanted to have God to myself. He did not come to me.

I read these lines again on awaking this morning. Since then —

Can it only have been an illusion? . . . Or perhaps — The saints experienced those hours of failure and loss. But most certainly never this dull revolt, this spiteful silence of the spirit which almost brings to hate. . . .

One o'clock: the last lamp is out in the village. Wind and rain.

The same solitude, the same silence. And no hope this time of forcing or turning away the obstacle. Besides, there isn't any obstacle. Nothing. God! I breathe, I inhale the night, the night is entering into me by some inconceivable, unimaginable gap in my soul. I, myself, am the night.

Let me force myself to think of other agonies like mine. I can feel no compassion for these strangers. My solitude is complete and hateful. I can feel no pity for myself.

Supposing I were never to love again!

I lay at the foot of my bed, face downwards. Oh, no! I'm certainly not such a fool as to fancy that such methods do any good. I only wanted to make the true gesture of complete acceptance, self-abandonment. I was stretched at the edge of a gulf, a void, like a beggar, a drunkard, like a corpse. I waited there to be picked up.

From the first second, even before my lips had touched the floor, this lie filled me with its shame. For I wasn't expecting anything. What wouldn't I give to be able to suffer!

Even pain holds aloof. Even the most usual, the most humble, the ordinary pain in my inside. I feel horribly well.

No fear of death, it is just as indifferent to me as life: they can't be put into words. I feel as though I had gone right back all the way I've come since God first drew me out of the void.

First I was no more than a spark, an atom of the glowing dust of divine charity. I am that again, and nothing more, lost in unfathomable night. But now the dust-spark has almost ceased to glow, it is nearly extinguished.

Awoke very late. Sleep must have come upon me suddenly, on the floor where I'd thrown myself down. It's already time to begin my mass. But before I go I must record this: That whatsoever happens I will never mention this to anyone and especially not to M. le Curé de Torcy.

This day is so limpid, the air so sweet, of miraculous lightness. . . . When I was a tiny boy, I remember how in the early morning I sometimes used to crouch down in a hedge, dripping with dew, and run back home wet to the skin, shivering, and full of happiness to get a good smack from my poor mother, and a big bowl of steaming hot milk.

All day I've kept recalling my childhood. I think of myself as of one dead.

(N.B. — The next few pages of the exercise-book in which this diary is written have been torn out. A few words still left in the margin have been carefully erased.)

This morning Dr. Delbende was found lying at the edge of Bazancourt wood with his skull blown out, and his body already stiff. It had rolled down into a ditch thickly lined with hazel-trees. They think that his shotgun went off by accident when he tried to disentangle it from the branches.

I had meant to destroy this diary but on thinking it over have decided to get rid of those pages which seemed useless; in any case I know them by heart, having repeated them so many times. It's like a voice always speaking to me, never silent day or night. I suppose this voice will cease when I do? Or else —

For several days I have been thinking a great deal about sin. In defining sin as a failure to obey God's law, I feel there is a risk of conveying too abstract an idea of it. People say such foolish things about sin, and as usual they never take the trouble to think. For centuries now doctors have been discussing disease. If they had been content to define it as a failure to obey the rules of health, they would long since have been in agreement. But they study it in the individual patient in the hope of curing him. And that is just what we priests are also attempting. So that really we aren't very impressed by sneers and smiles and jokes about sin.

And of course people always refuse to see beyond the individual fault. But after all the transgression itself is only the eruption. And the symptoms which most impress outsiders aren't always the gravest and most disquieting.

I believe, in fact I am certain, that many men never give out the whole of themselves, their deepest truth. They live on the surface, and yet, so rich is the soil of humanity that even this thin outer layer is able to yield a kind of meagre harvest which gives the illusion of real living. I've heard that during the last war timid little clerks would turn out to be real leaders; without knowing it, they had in them the passion to command. There is, to be sure, no resemblance there with what we mean when we use the beautiful word 'conversion' — *convertere* — but still it had sufficed that these poor creatures should experience the most primitive sort of heroism, heroism devoid of all purity. How many men will never have the least idea of what is meant by supernatural heroism, without which there can be no inner life! Yet by that very same inner life shall they be judged: after a little thought the thing becomes certain, quite obvious. Therefore? . . . Therefore when death has bereft them of all the artificial props with which society provides people, they will find themselves as they really are, as they were without even knowing it — horrible undeveloped monsters, the stumps of men.

Fashioned thus, what can they say of sin?

What do they know about it? The cancer which is eating into them is painless—like so many tumors. Probably at some period in their lives most of them felt only a vague discomfort, and it soon passed off. It is rare for a child not to have known any inner life, as Christianity understands it, however embryonic the form. One day or another all young lives are stirred by an urge which seems to compel; every pure young breast has depths which are raised to heroism. Not very urgently perhaps, but just strongly enough to show the little creature a glimpse which sometimes half-consciously he accepts, of the huge risk that salvation entails, and gives to human life all of its divinity. He has sensed something of good and evil, has seen them both in their pristine essence unalloyed by notions of social discipline and habit. But of course his reactions are those of a child, and of such a decisive solemn moment the grown-up man will keep no more than the memory of something rather childishly dramatic, something mischievously quaint, whose true meaning he will never realize, yet of which he may talk to the end of his days with a soft, rather too soft a smile, the almost lewd smile of old men. . . .

It is hard to measure the depths of puerility of those the word describes as 'serious men'! An inexplicable, truly supernatural puerility! Although I am only a young priest, I can't help smiling, sometimes. . . . And how kind, how indulgent they are to us! An Arras solicitor to whom I ministered on his death-bed, a man of considerable standing, a former senator, one of the richest men in the whole country, said to me once—apparently by way of some apology for the touch of a quite benevolent scepticism with which he received my exhortations:

'Yes, yes, father, I quite understand. I used to feel just as you do yourself. I was very pious. Why, when I was a lad of eleven nothing on earth would have pursuaded me to go to sleep without having said my three "Hail Marys"—and I even made myself say them all in one breath. Otherwise it might have been unlucky. That's how I felt about it.'

He supposed that was the point at which I had stuck, that we poor priests all stick at eleven years old. Finally, on the day before he died, I heard his confession. What could be said of it? Nothing much. A 'solicitor's life' could most times be expressed in very few words. . . .

The sin against hope—the deadliest sin and perhaps also the most cherished, the most indulged. It takes a long time to become aware of it, and the sadness which precedes and heralds its advent is so delicious! The richest of all the devil's elixers, his ambrosia. Since the agony—

(The next page has been torn out.)

This morning—a surprising discovery. As a rule Mlle. Louise leaves her prayer-book by her seat in church, on the small shelf placed there to hold them. It is a large book, and this morning I discovered it lying in the aisle; the many pictures of saints with which it is stuffed lay scattered. So I was obliged to turn over the leaves, though without much wanting to. Some writing on the back of the fly-leaf caught my eye—the name and address of mademoiselle—probably an old address—at Charleville in the Ardennes. The same writing as that of the anonymous letter. At least I think so.

What difference can that make now?

The great ones of this earth can dismiss all things unanswered, with a gesture, a glance, with even less. But God—

I have lost neither Faith, Hope nor Charity. . . . But in this life, what use to mortal men are eternal goods? What counts is the longing to possess them. I feel I have ceased to long for them.

I saw M. le Curé de Torcy at the funeral of his old friend. I can say this: that the thought of Dr. Delbende never leaves me. But even an agonizing thought is not, can never be, a prayer.

God sees and judges me.

I have decided to go on with this diary because one day I may find it useful to have kept a sincere, scrupulously exact account of what is happening to me in this time of trial. Who knows—useful to me or others? For though my heart has hardened within me (it seems I can no longer pity anyone, to pity has become as difficult as to pray: I realized this again to-night while I was sitting with Adeline Soupault, although I was doing my best to help her) I still think with friendship of some future reader of this diary who probably will never exist. . . . A tenderness I am bound to censure since doubtless in the course of all this writing it is directed towards myself, and nobody else. I have 'turned author' or 'po-ate' as the Dean of Blangermont has it. . . . And yet— Let me set it down here, in all sincerity, that I have not grown slack in my work. Quite the contrary. The unbelievable improvement in my health is of great advantage to my job. And it is not quite accurate to say that I don't pray for Dr. Delbende. I do that, together with all my other duties. I've even knocked off wine during the last few days, but it left me dangerously weak.

A short talk with the Curé de Torcy. This wholly admirable priest is obviously intensely self-controlled. This strikes me instantly, and yet it would be very hard indeed to distinguish any outward sign; no gesture, no particular words, nothing betraying the least suggestion of will or effort. His face frankly displays his suffering, expressing it with a truly royal simplicity. At such moments even the very best people are apt to give themselves away with the kind of look which says to you more or less directly: 'You see how I'm sticking it out; don't praise me, it's my nature; thanks all the same.' But the Curé de Torcy looks straight at you, guilelessly. His eyes beg your compassion and sympathy. But with what nobility they beg! A king might beg in just that way. He had watched for two nights beside the body, and his soutane, as a rule so trim, so scrupulously neat, was rumpled in wide fan-shaped creases and all stained. He had forgotten to shave, perhaps for the first time in his life.

But by this one sign you could see his mastery over himself; that supernatural strength which he gives out was in no way diminished. Though obviously tortured with grief (people are saying that Dr. Delbende committed suicide) he could still create around him a feeling of calm, of peace, of certainty. This morning I acted as his deacon.

I seem to remember how usually at the consecration his finely shaped hands above the chalice would tremble slightly. To-day, not a tremor! They even had an authority, a majesty. It is truly impossible to describe the contrast with a face hollowed by insomnia, fatigue, and some agonizing vision —at which I can guess. . . .

He left at once, refusing to stay for the funeral lunch given by the doctor's niece— very much like Mme. Pegroit in appearance, though even stouter. I went to the station with him, and since we had half an hour to wait for the train, we sat down together on a bench. He was very tired, and when I saw his face in full daylight it looked more haggard than ever. I had not yet noticed two wrinkles down the corners of his mouth, surprisingly sad and bitter lines. I think it was these which made me decide. I suddenly asked:

'Aren't you afraid the doctor may have—'

He cut me short, his imperious eyes seemed to nail the last words to my lips. It was very hard not to look away, but I know how he hates a shifty look. 'Flinching eyes' is what he calls it. Then his expression softened by degrees, he almost smiled.

I won't record all our conversation. Or was it really a conversation? Perhaps it didn't even last twenty minutes. . . . The little empty station-square with its double row of poplars looked even more deserted than usual. I remember a flight of wheeling pigeons, circling round and round as fast as they could, and so low that I could hear the beat of their wings.

I was right. He fears his old friend committed suicide. It seems the doctor had been letting depression get the better of him, having counted to the last moment on inheriting from a very old aunt who recently, in exchange for an annuity, placed her entire fortune in the hands of a certain well-known business man, agent to His Grace the Bishop of S———. In his time the doctor had earned a great deal of money and had spent it lavishly in acts of rather eccentric generosity which were not always kept secret, so that people began to suspect him of wanting to go into politics. Then his younger colleagues encroached on his practice, but he never would consent to change his ways.

'You see, lad, he was never a man to make the best of a bad job. He was always telling me that it was unreasonable to fight what he was pleased to call human savagery and the general idiocy of life. He said that society could never be cured of its injustice, that whoever ended the one would end the other. He compared the illusions of social reformers to those of Pasteur's first disciples, who dreamed of an aseptic world. Really he considered himself an outlaw, no more than that — the survivor of a race long since extinct, even supposing it ever existed — still struggling on without hope of mercy against an invader who, in the course of centuries, had ended by becoming the lawful owner. "I only avenge myself," he'd say. He did not believe in a regular army — you understand? "When I happen to come across an injustice walking alone and unprotected, and I find it about my own weight, not too strong or too weak for me, I jump on its back and twist its neck." It came expensive though! Why, no later than last autumn, for instance, he paid all old Mother Gachevaume's debts, eleven thousand francs, because M. Duponsot who runs the flour mills, had an eye on her land and was meaning to bid for it. Obviously the death of his damned old aunt was the last straw. But after all —! Three or four hundred thousand francs! He'd have squandered that much in next to no time! Because the poor dear fellow was becoming quite impossible in his old age! Why, he'd even got it into his head to keep — yes keep! that old soaker Rebattut, an ex-poacher as lazy as a skunk, who lives in a charcoal-seller's hut stuck on the edge of the Goubault estate. They say he's always running after little cow-girls, is never sober and didn't give two hoots for Dr. Delbende. Mind you, the doctor knew all about that. But he had his reasons. His own extra special reasons as usual!'

'What were they?'

'Well, he said this Rebattut was the best poacher he'd ever known, that you could no more keep him out of the woods than forbid him to eat and drink, and that if the police

didn't leave him alone they'd only end by turning a poor harmless maniac into a dangerous brute. Poor old chap! He'd got all that mixed up in his brain with a lot more cranky notions, real obsessions they were! He used to say to me: "Giving men passions which they're not allowed to satisfy — that's a bit too thick for me. I'm not God, you know!" Of course he loathed the Marquis de Bolbec, and the Marquis had sworn he'd make his gamekeepers goad Rebattut into doing something really serious for which he could be transported. Well, there you have it!'

I think I've already said in this diary that real sadness found no home with M. le Curé de Torcy. His soul is gay. At this very moment, now that I no longer observed his face — he was sitting with his head held very high and looking straight out — a certain note in his voice surprised me. Though grave, it never could be called a sad voice; it vibrates with imperceptible inner joy; so profound a joy that nothing in this world could shake it, like the vast, calm waters under storms.

He went on to tell me many more things, almost mad, unbelievable things. At fourteen Dr. Delbende had intended to be a missionary; he lost his faith in the course of medical studies. He was the favourite student of a certain very famous doctor — I forget the name — and all his teachers prophesied a brilliant future for him. Everyone was amazed when he started a practice in this out-of-the-way place. At that time he said he hadn't the money to take his final degrees and in any case, he was in a bad state of health, due to overwork. But he was inconsolable at not being able to believe. He had some extraordinary ways. He would hurl questions at a crucifix hanging on his bedroom wall. Sometimes he would sob at its feet with his head in his hands, or he would even defy it, shaking his fist.

No doubt I could have listened more calmly to all this a few days previously. But just then I hadn't the courage. It was like a stream of molten lead being poured into an open wound. Never have I suffered like that, and I shall probably never suffer again, not even in death. All I could do was to sit there staring at the ground. If I had raised my eyes to the Curé de Torcy, I really think I should have cried out. Unluckily at such moments as these, it is harder to control your tongue than your eyes.

'If he really did kill himself, do you think —?'

The Curé de Torcy started, as though my question had raised him suddenly from a dream. Indeed, for the last five minutes his voice had sounded a little dreamy; I could feel that he was looking into my mind, and he must have guessed a good deal!

'If anyone else had asked me that!'

A long pause. The little square looked as bright, as empty as ever; at regular intervals the heavy birds, wheeling monotonously, seemed to swoop upon us from a great height. I sat stupidly waiting till they were over us, with their whistling like the swish of a great scythe.

'God is the sole judge,' he said at last, calmly. 'And Maxence' (this was the first time I had heard him use his old friend's Christian name) 'was a just man. God judges the just. Do you think I ever bothered my head much about fools, or mere knaves? What'ud be the use of saints then? They pay to redeem that sort of trash. They're strong enough, whereas —'

His hands were on his knees, his shoulders spread a broad shadow before him.

'We're at war, you see. We've got to keep facing the enemy. Face up to it, he said, you remember? That was his motto. Well in war, does it make all that difference if a third- or fourth-liner, some idiot with a cushy job at the base, happens to get cold feet? Or a putrid old civilian with nothing to do but read his paper, what does that matter at headquarters? But the picked front-liners! A chest is a chest when you get to the trenches. And one less counts! There are always saints. And by saints I mean those who have been given more than others. Rich men! I've always had a secret kind of a notion that if we could take a God's-eye view of human societies, we'd have the key to a good many things we can't understand. After all, God made man in His image:

when man tries to build a social order to suit himself he's bound to make a clumsy copy of the other, the true society. . . . Our division into rich and poor must be based on some great law of the universe. In the eyes of the church the rich man is here to shield the poor, like his elder brother. Well, of course, he often does it without even wanting to, by the sheer action of economic force, as they say. A millionaire goes smash and thousands are chucked out into the streets. So you can just imagine what happens in the invisible world when one of those rich men I've just been talking about, a steward of divine grace, turns tail! The solvency of the mediocre is nothing. Whereas the solvency of a saint! What a scandal if he should happen to fail! You've got to be crazy to refuse to see that the sole justification of inequality in the supernatural order is its risk. Our risk! Both yours and mine.'

Throughout all this he remained bolt upright, and never moved. Anyone seeing him sitting there on that cold, sunny winter afternoon, would have taken him for some worthy country priest, gossiping of parish trivialities, boasting good-naturedly to a young, deferential colleague.

'Now remember what I am going to say to you: perhaps all the harm really came from his loathing of mediocre people: "You hate mediocrities," I kept telling him. He rarely denied it, because I say again, he was a just man. Mediocrities are a trap set by the devil. Mean-spirited people are far too complex for us; they're God's business, not ours; but in the meantime we should shelter mediocrity, take it under our wing. Poor devils, they need some keeping warm! "If you really sought Our Lord you'd end by finding Him," I used to say. He always answered: "I'm looking for God among the poor, where I've the best chance of ever finding Him." But the trouble was that his "poor" were chaps of his own sort. They weren't really poor at all, they were rebels, masters! I said to him one day: "And suppose Jesus were really waiting for you in the guise of one of these worthy people you despise so? Because apart from sin, He takes on Himself and sanctifies all our wretchedness. A coward may be only some poor creature crushed down by overwhelming social forces like a rat caught under a beam; a miser may be miserably anxious, deeply convinced of his impotence and racked with fear of not "making good." Some people who seem brutally heartless may suffer from a kind of "poverty-phobia" — one often meets it — a terror as difficult to explain as the nervous fear of mice or spiders. "Do you ever look for Christ among people of that kind?" I asked him. "And if you don't, then what are you grousing about? You've missed Christ, yourself."

'And perhaps, after all, he did miss Him. . . .'

JACQUES MARITAIN
(*1882–*   )

IF THERE is a man of our time who has set his light upon a tall candlestick, that man is Jacques Maritain. In him the man of thought and the man of prayer are one. This happy combination gives Maritain his illuminated outlook which sees the philosophy of St. Thomas as a genuinely perennial system: at a point in time synthesizing all knowledge, but because of its completeness and truth capable of being applied to life and living in any age; as young today as when the Angelic Doctor laid down his pen for the pursuit of the unitive life with God.

Paris was the birthplace of Maritain. The humanistic and intellectual lad took his questioning mind to both the Sorbonne and Heidelberg before he was satisfied with his thirst for education. At the Sorbonne Maritain and his wife, Raïssa, came under the spell of Bergson. His idealistic and genuinely spiritual mind opened to them the wide horizons of the faith. The warm mysticism of Léon Bloy also played an important role in the conversion to Catholicism of Raïssa and Jacques Maritain in 1905.

In 1908 Maritain began an intensive study of St. Thomas under Pére Clérissac, O.P. The result of this study was a living concept of St. Thomas which gave Maritain the ability to explain Thomism in relation to every crisis and need of our time. The world was quick to respond, and Maritain became a prophet to many who had seen the living light as a system to be studied, or as riches for which some apology had to be made.

Maritain has been in perpetual demand as a lecturer, at the Institute of Medieval Studies in Toronto, in all the great American universities, and at the Institut Catholique in Paris where he was for years a professor of philosophy. The lovable character of the man, his illuminated and living certitudes made him, with the passage of time, the foremost figure in neo-Thomism, and a commanding figure in the Catholic revival of letters. Maritain's words unified Catholic thinkers in the early struggle against Fascism and Hitlerism and his influence was significant in heartening the resistance movement in France.

With the triumph of the movement, Maritain became ambassador to the Holy See.

The introduction to the mind and writing of Maritain is best approached by his life of St. Thomas, *The Angelic Doctor*, which is a glowing analysis of the life and works of St. Thomas. It suggests, in an unforgettable manner, the practical application of Thomistic thought to the very roots of life and progressive living.

With this as a beginning, it will be a labor of love to follow Maritain as he applies the principles of St. Thomas to art and poetry, to morals and thought, through the whole complexity of our modern life.

CHAPTER IV

CATHOLIC THOUGHT AND ITS MISSION*

THE intellectual task confronting the Catholic is a difficult task, as difficult as it is important. As a man, he is in time, and subject to all the vicissitudes of becoming; as a member of the mystical Body of Christ, he is joined to eternity; his most fundamental life has its roots where there is no change nor shadow of alteration, his mind is fixed in primal Truth, loyalty to which is the foundation of the whole edifice of grace in him and the primary benefit which every creature expects from him. This sort of mediation between time and the eternal is for the Christian mind at once a sort of painful cross and a sort of redemptive mission. It must at every moment think the passing, changing world in the light of eternity.

Our problem to-day is so to think the modern world; not only to think the eternal outside the world, which is the first precept of contemplative thought, but also by a second precept similar to the first, to think the world and the present moment in the eternal and by the eternal. And this problem is all the more pressing in that all around us we see the temporal forms in which the world of culture had for centuries received, however haphazardly, the imprint of eternal truths for the most part in a state of collapse and dissolution; this is undoubtedly a grave misfortune, for man is thereby deprived of a multitude of supports which helped him to maintain within himself the life of the spirit; but it is also in certain respects, an incalculable advantage, for, at the same time, that life — and the very life of the Church of Christ — is disencumbered of the terrible human deadweight with which so many abuses and prevarications had burdened the old once Christian world. A new world is emerging from the obscure chrysalis of history with new temporal forms; it may be, all things considered, less habitable than the old; but it is certain that some good and some

truth are immanent in those new forms, and that they manifest in some way the will of God, which is absent from nothing that exists. They may to the same extent serve eternal interests on this earth. The question is to understand this state of the world; and to regulate accordingly our loves and hatreds and our activity.

A double danger, a double error, must here be avoided. We might be tempted to abandon, if not theoretically, at any rate in practice, to lose sight more or less completely of the eternal, to the advantage of time, and allow ourselves to be carried away by the flux of becoming instead of mastering it by the spirit; the truth is that those who do so rather suffer the world than think it; they are acted upon by the world and do not act upon it otherwise than as instruments of the very forces of the world; they glide like fluttering leaves or sodden tree trunks on the water down the stream of history. They are often generous and forewarned of the exigencies of the moment by the intuitions of the heart, but in their hurry to pursue practical efficacy itself, which are of the spiritual order and presuppose the intellectual courage to strip appearances bare, to grapple with principles and to keep thought centred at all cost upon the immutable.

Upon the plea of fidelity to the eternal, the other error, quite the opposite, consists in remaining attached not to the eternal, but to fragments of the past, to moments of history immovably fixed and as it were embalmed in memory, moments upon which we rest our heads to go to sleep; those who do so do not despise the world like the saints, they despise it like the ignorant and the arrogant; they do not think the world, they refuse it; they compromise divine truths with dying forms; and should they happen to possess a higher intelligence than the former of principles which are unchanging and the most acute perception of the errors, aberrations and deficiencies of the present moment, their learning remains barren, in-

*Maritain, Jacques, *Essays In Order: Religion and Culture,* translated by J. F. Scanlon (New York: The Macmillan Co., 1931), pp. 50–55.

complete and negativist, because a certain narrowness of heart prevents them from "knowing the work of men" and doing justice to the work of God in time and history.

The former error is as it were a misconception of the Word by Whom all things are made, and by Whose Cross the world is conquered; it would reduce Christian thought to impotence and mere versatility in the eyes of the world. The latter is as it were a misconception of the Spirit Who hovers above the waters and renews the face of the earth; it would make Christian thought repugnant and hostile in the eyes of the world.

It is difficult to remain absolutely unaffected by one or other of these two errors, not to decline more or less to one side or the other. For it is not a question of an eclectic dosage or finding an equilibrium to balance two weights; exact proportion in this sphere as in general in the sphere of the virtues, is to be obtained only by eminence, by rising far above opposite excesses. Man achieves it only with the utmost difficulty. The Church, however, goes her way in divine fashion amid the too human thoughts and opposite errors of some of her children; the exact measure of virtue is realised in her in full perfection and the superior unity of divers extremes, more particularly of absolute fidelity to eternal things and sedulous attention to the things of time. However difficult the attainment of such an eminent harmony may be for each of us, we must yet strive to achieve it and there, in our time, for the reasons urged above, is a task of manifest urgency. Every delay opposed to the accomplishment thereof is liable to involve irreparable catastrophes, if not for the Church, who has the promises of eternal life, at any rate for the world and culture. To guide us in our task we have the teachings of the Popes and the wisdom of the common Doctor of the Church.

By recovering its spirit of conquest and advancing boldly to grapple with fresh problems and to occupy new positions, the philosophy of St. Thomas will help us to transcend an apparent antinomy which presents itself to-day in its regard. On the one hand, we realise that the Church, in recommending that philosophy with insistence, proposes in the first place to recommend her common Doctor precisely as common Doctor, rather than to revive quarrels dividing the schools. On the other hand, we also realise that the doctrine of the Angelic Doctor is so lofty, and so solidly coherent that it cannot suffer the slightest diminution of its specific determinants without losing its efficacy to penetrate reality. The common Doctor is not the commonplace Doctor in whom there is to be found merely what all the others are agreed upon; he teaches us to assume in the principles of a superior unity every truth uttered by the others, and often manifests a peculiar grace in enhancing the value of particular aspects of things.

Well then! The schools will continue to dispute until the end of time; but let us shift our positions and move forward, let us grapple with fresh difficulties, and by those very aspects in which reality is most starkly apparent: then we shall best realise the necessity — under pain of lapsing into an impotent mediocrity — of maintaining in all their rigour the principles of the greatest assembler of truth the world has ever known and above the opportunity of seeing spontaneously united in the radiance of his pure doctrine minds hailing from the four corners of the earth.

Let there be no mistake. It is the most arduous and serious problems, problems most closely affecting the heart and flesh of humanity, which now press for solution on the Christian mind, as though they had long been kept in reserve for a general assault; what that mind has to face and conquer or assimilate is philosophies, scientific or artistic researches, fashions of thought and culture of a rare technical nature and a precious human quality. It will succeed in its task only if it equips itself with the most formed wisdom, the most exacting science, the most perfect and reliable intellectual harness, the most vigorous and comprehensive doctrine and method. So furnished, it will be able to fulfill its mission, which as I suggested a moment ago, by the very fact of being a Christian mission is in some sort a crucifying mission. *Quis scandalizatur, et ego non uror?* Catholic thought must be raised with Christ between Heaven and earth, and it is by living the painful paradox of an abso-lute fidelity to the eternal closely united to the most sedulous comprehension of the anguish of the time that it is invited to work for the reconciliation of the world and truth.

DIALOGUES*

A LITERARY period betrays itself by the lexicon of its admirations. Most of the time the lexicon signifies less what the period attains than what it lacks; what it succeeds above all in counterfeiting and in spoiling.

Today, in literature, all is for spirit, for purity.

"I beheld Satan as lightning fall from heaven." The spectacle continues. In the past century two great disasters threw their fire into the night. Nietzsche fallen from the heaven of liberty, Wilde from the heaven of art.

A long and slow bookish work of the school and the university, the romantic German metaphysics and a certain Greek English purism emptying into the heart and flesh of man. Schopenhauer and Walter Pater are hidden in the shadow of the drama.

Beauty has not come to the end of its submission to the shameful ascendancy of the god Aesthetics taken as the ultimate end of human life. The interminable, incoercible, appaling laugh of Oscar Wilde consigning a man to sin, still passes like a voluble cry over our arts. It is this that freezes them in their frenzy.

The Angels, perfect natures, cannot turn aside naturally from nature; it is at the supernatural stage that their evil begins; the devil has a supernatural hatred of nature. He uses art to teach it to us.

Contraries cannot unite themselves in the truth; but in error? The modern spirit is at once Rousseauist and Manichean. The adoration of nature and the hatred of nature together outrage the Gospel. The dogma of grace reconciles at the height of the Cross what in the regions of dissemblance is only contradiction tearing the heart.

To put in his life, not in his work, his genius as an artist, nothing more absurd than this design of Wilde; it is to carry over into a flute the art of the cithera, into a bird the law of the snow. His life was only a useless phrase.

It was not the hard labor that broke him. Frank Harris remarks that he came out of prison in a better state than when he entered it. His art itself profited by the prison diet; as witness *De Profundis* and the *Ballad of Reading Gaol.* It was Lord Douglas who broke him. Sin kills poetry also.

In Paris, the priest arrived in time to save his soul, too late to save his art. Art is confined in the terrestrial duration; for it no mercy *in extremis.*

The poets complain of moralists. They themselves constantly confound art and morality to the detriment of both. A confusion of aesthetic values and ethical values, one of the scourges of our time.

Purity. Of this word itself an impure use has been made. It has become an equivocal word, dragged about everywhere. At the Marquis of Sade's, at the Tcheka, etc.

A human act that no moral value affects, that the distinction between good and evil does not even graze, that which no measure, human or divine, can come to touch, except the numbers of sensation, that is "pure." A crime, a vice, a lie, a soiling, malice, blasphemy, all this is "pure" if it is intact, if it is well made, if no turn of reason judges it and interrupts its movement. Always Jean-

*Maritain, Jacques, *Art and Poetry* (New York: Philosophical Library, 1943), pp. 41–48.

Jacques Rousseau: the man who meditates is a depraved animal. Hence the culmination of impurity is decency. A *sincere* priest would mount naked to the altar, as in the black mass.

To clothe in one's self animality with humanity, the senses with reason and wisdom, and humanity itself with the merits of Christ and of His charity, to cover one's hands with the grace of God in order to touch God, as Jacob approaching Isaac with the hands of Esau, this is duplicity, hypocrisy. Sincerity exacts that you should be only what you are in the lowest depth of your being; and purity requires you to show it.

The surrealist dialogue on love.

I know that it is by the example of a lie that the history of Jacob and Rebecca instructs us. The vocabulary of images that God makes for us uses everything to suggest divine things. But of what verity this lie is the figure! To get to the bottom of sincerity, to avow truly what we are and at the same time what God is, it is needful to disguise us — without falsehood this time, and thanks to a gift that transfigures being — in Another Who is more we than we ourselves, and Who vivifies us with a life better than ours. And His blood colors my cheeks, said St. Agnes.

The plants, said Aristotle, live in a perpetual sleep; because they have only a vegetative soul, all their aim is in the flower. They have their mouth in the earth, and it is their hermaphroditic corolla that they expose to the birds of heaven, without the least repression.

Literature, today, would be that plant.

One imagines that in paradise innocence was to ignore good and evil. Purity consists then in behaving as if evil did not exist. I say that is a lie: — the purity of the human being is to recognize the law not of the plant, but of man. In paradise all was not permitted; innocence was not to do good or evil without constraint, but to do only good without suffering conflict. The desire for the knowledge of good and evil was the desire to become, like a god, the rule for good and

evil, and also to scrutinize what the taste of evil contains of knowledge.

Since that time there is no purity save under another tree, where God extended his arms to die.

Poetic purity is a mineral purity. Purity is a human virtue.

Art is not a caricature of creation, it *continues* creation, "creates as it were in the second stage." Morality is not a code of respectability, it is the code of the tests of love.

Because art (that which is true) reflects morality, to declare that art exacts a life morally dangerous, and new experiments in morality as in aesthetics (that is to say experiments to render innocent, thanks to the sorcery of the heart, the very things that God forbids) that means, if you like, subordinating art to morality, but to a morality that art has violated. Under the pretext of taking in art the place of aesthetics, it becomes itself the prey and victim of art.

"One does not stop a bird from singing." But if thy right eye offend thee, pluck it out, said the Saviour.

An author is not a bird. And a bird's song is never anything but the song of the eternal law, in an obedient creature.

To live dangerously. The only way that is free of bravado and deception is to live as a Christian; to steal nothing from love and yet to subtract nothing from the law.

It is easy to practice the law without loving, and easy to love while scorning the law. But he who practices the law without loving does not practice the law, because the first commandment is love. And he who loves while scorning the law does not love, because the law is the first will of Him Who loves us, and Whom we love. The Christian gives up his life every day, he embraces both the law and love; which, joined together, form the cross.

Hardness. Nothing is softer than a gratuitous act, that cheap outburst of irresponsibility preached by the disciples of André Gide. It is the ultimate form of obsequiousness, a cringing before nothingness.

"Love is as hard as hell." Make your choice. You will find only in one or the other an authentic hardness.

Hardness, ellipsis, horror of sentimentalism and of transition, of convention, of roundness, of abundance, these the young men have immediately understood and utilized; there are as many recipes for style, better doubtless, and as easy, alas, as some others. But when these pass into their heart, lead them to hate pity, to cherish envy, malice, villainy, to insult their mothers ritually, to link themselves by pacts of sorcery, they are once more and without even knowing it, the victims of aestheticism. The last Dandies.

Spirit. It is in the flesh itself that modern heresy seeks the spirit. It plants therein all the sins of the spirit, pride, the disdain of God. What it fears above all is truth.

To love only to seek — on condition of never finding — to want only disquietude, that is to hate truth.

The sins against the Spirit are those which destroy in man just that which places him at the disposal of mercy: repentance, hope, consent to the truth. . . . If many of those who have nothing but the spirit in their speech appear to apply themselves to these sins, it is that another Spirit exerts himself to make them imitate his obstinacy.

A good part of current literature is positively possessed. In it could be verified some of the signs used by priests to detect possession: the horror of holy things, pseudo-prophecy, the use of unknown tongues, even levitation; it may be seen circulating upside down, along the vaults of thought.

"Psychic" or natural man receives through the senses all that comes to him from without; it is through them that his ideas come to him, by means of the activity of the intellect. Reason, which transcends the senses, labors however in their work-yard. Philosophy, even the best, remains tributary to their materials.

That is why mystical language knows only two terms: life according to the senses and life according to the spirit; those who sleep in their senses and those who wake in the Holy Spirit. Because there are for us only two fountain-heads: the senses and the Spirit of God.

Man has a spiritual soul, but which informs a body. If it be a question of passing to a life wholly spiritual, his reason does not suffice; his tentatives toward angelism always fail. His only authentic spirituality is bound to grace and to the Holy Spirit.

"The 'psychic' or natural man receiveth not the things of the Spirit of God; for they are foolishness unto him: neither can he know them, because they are spiritually discerned. But he that is spiritual judgeth all things, yet he himself is judged of no man. For who hath known the mind of the Lord, that he may instruct Him? But we have the mind of Christ." Saint Paul judges all the philosophers. He is not judged by them.

A PARADOX OF HISTORY*

ONE of the paradoxes of history is the connexion which at a certain period of Western culture existed for a time (we have already noticed it) between bourgeois society and something which was not re-

*Maritain, Jacques, *Freedom In The Modern World*, translated by Richard O'Sullivan, K.C. (London: Sheed and Ward, 1935), pp. 116–125.

ligion but which may be called the sociological 'projection' or the sociological 'phenomenon' of religion. The expression 'bourgeois society' or 'capitalist society' which is used in current speech (and which is anyhow inadequate) denotes but one aspect of the world of anthropocentric humanism. And truly the mere idea of any bond or fellowship between Christianity and such a society is itself the height of paradox. The fact that many of our contemporaries are able in good faith to believe that religion and the Church are, as the most telling piece of atheist propaganda puts it, pledged to defend the interests of a class and the 'eminent dignity' of capitalism and militarism and the rest, is a sign that good faith is not synonymous with intelligence, and that the opinions of men move among shadows where things appear inverted.

The world which issued from the two great revolutions of the Renaissance and the Reformation is in its leading ideas in the spiritual and the cultural sphere downright anti-Catholic. On every occasion on which it has been able freely to follow its instinctive inclination it has persecuted Catholicism; its philosophy is utilitarian, materialist, or a hypocritical idealism; its politics are Machiavellian; its economics liberal and mechanist. The Fathers of bourgeois society are not exactly Fathers of the Church, whether one seeks them with Max Weber in the company of Calvin, or with M. Seilliere among the followers of Rousseau; nor must we omit to mention the Angel of Descartes and his *ideés claires*. The modern world sprang out of a great aspiration of the heart of man for the blessing of worldly goods, which is the source of captialism and mercantilism and industrialism in the economic order, as it is the source of naturalism and rationalism in philosophy. The successive condemnations of usury by the Church stand at the threshold of modern times like a burning interrogatory as to the lawfulness of its economy.

The Church is in the world but is not of the world. If she invites men to be faithful to social institutions that have been tested by time this does not mean that she is tied to one or other of these institutions; it signifies her recognition that the stability of law is an important element in the welfare of mankind. The Church has constantly shown in the course of history that political and social changes have no terrors for her and that she has a sense singularly free from illusion of the contingent character of human institutions. She teaches obedience to temporal authority and to just laws since all legitimate rule of man over man comes from God; but (saving the case of a temporal power having a ministerial rule in regard to the spiritual authority, as happened with the Empire in the Middle Ages) the Church does not institute the temporal authority, she sanctions the rule of him who is in office — without forbidding efforts to effect a change of government, and without forbidding resistance, by force if need be, to tyrannical rule. With a view to the advancement of her work for the salvation of souls, and so that States also shall respect the ends that are proper to the spiritual nature of man, the Church seeks to act in harmony with the secular power. But she is not unaware that at most times — since the world which turns away from God is subject to a Prince who is not God (*totus in maligno positus est mundus*) —to deal with the temporal power is a little like dealing with the devil. And on the whole one devil is as good as another. A new ruler who establishes his authority cancels out the rights of his predecessor. In truth the Catholic Church took a long time to adjust itself to the bourgeois regime, perhaps because the medieval order which was framed under her protection continued to occupy a place in her memory as it had so long occupied her guardian care. M. Groethuysen has gone so far as to write a book in which he makes this slow adjustment a matter of reproach. The Church has never been tied to the existing regime, and to whatsoever persecutions she may be exposed in those regimes that follow (she is used to persecutions — *supra dorsum meum fabricaverunt peccatores*) we may well believe she will not regret its passing. She has no bond with it.

Bankruptcy of a World in Appearance Christian

To understand the paradox of which we have just been speaking and the way in which men came to believe that religion was tied by its principles to 'bourgeois' or 'capitalist' society, we must penetrate into a world of appearance and of confusion. This illusory belief has its origin in the fundamental confusion (to which attention has already been drawn) between the Church and the Christian world; or between the Catholic religion and the social behaviour of the common run of the Catholics of the ruling classes — in short between the spiritual and the temporal orders. The Church as such has the promise of eternal life, and the Prince of this world has no part with her. He has his place, as we have said, in the Christian world.

The Christian world which issued from the dissolution of medieval Christendom condoned many iniquities — I refer here to a sort of collective failure in the course of history, for which it is senseless to seek to attach responsibility to individuals. This is the world which God is allowing to sink under its burden of death, while new life is forming in the womb of time.

The mission of such a one as Léon Bloy was to herald these things and to cry them from the roof tops. It is strange to observe to what a degree an avowal of this kind seems indecent to many Christians even to-day. They seem to be apprehensive lest they should embarrass apologetic. They judge it better to lay the blame on the craft of wicked men and to treat history after the manner of the Manicheans, arguing as if wicked men were not subject to the government of God but only to that of the devil. The Jews of old and even the Ninevites did not stand on so much ceremony.

The failure of which we speak is that of the social or cultural mass taken in its (imperfect) unity, in its corporate institutions and its 'objective' spirit rather than as a series of individuals taken one by one, and thus it refers primarily to the social order or rather to the spiritual order incarnate in it. It is, we may say, the failure of the civilisation that is called Christian and of each of us to the extent to which we are identified with that civilization.

"Those to blame are the Christians themselves; the old Christian world; not the Christian religion to be sure, but its adepts who very often have shown themselves to be poor Christians. The gospel which, instead of being translated into terms of life, passes into a conventional form of rhetoric and

takes shelter behind actual evil and real injustice, that gospel cannot but arouse revolt against it. . . . The posture of Christian society in face of communism is not only the posture of one who carries in his heart eternal and absolute truth; it is also the posture of the culprit who had failed to live this truth; who has betrayed it." Nicholas Berdyaev, whose metaphysics are to us unacceptable but whose views on human life and history are often profound, here speaks capital truths that cannot be disputed. We prefer to try and fathom the reasons for this fact of history.

A first reason is general in character. It springs from the universal truth that evil is more common than good among men. It is therefore natural that there should be more 'bad Christians' than 'good Christians' in a Christian society and especially in the higher (and therefore more exposed) strata of that society. From the moment when such a society loses its essential spirit and the institutions that were linked to it (as happened to Christendom from the onset of the Renaissance and the Reformation) a new collective consciousness arises whose spirit grows more heavy and sombre the more it deviates from the vital centre of the faith and of the Church. And thus one reaches the 'naturalisation' of religion of which we have written elsewhere, and the exploitation of Christianity by deist or atheist (there is no practical difference) for temporal ends. The thesis that religion is 'good for the people' had developed mightily in the period of enlightened despotism and seems to have been given a political direction (and to have been turned to the advantage of the Prince) before it was given an economic direction (and turned to the advantage of the Rich). "This cult of the marvellous seems positively made for the people," wrote Frederick the Second; and again, "I cannot imagine anyone exercising his mind about the question: is it lawful to deceive the people? I am going to see that it is done." The Academy of Berlin put the question up to competition in 1780. "To this question," replied Johann Freidrich Gillet, one of the prize-men in the competition: "Yes, in my opinion it may be done if weighty and sufficient reasons exist. The people are merely folk. They will ever so remain and ought so to remain. And besides, the history of every age and of our own proves by a multitude of instances that the deception of the people has always brought much benefit to the people and to their leaders."

The weakness of human nature thus affords a simple and natural explanation why so many Christians, lay and ecclesiastic, went so far to excuse and honour and flatter the owners of moneybags in a period when the possession of money was coming to be the principal source of power in society, just as there are those who are ready to pay their respect to military or popular power or power of any other species when it becomes predominant. These truths are too current to merit more detailed examination.

But of the historical failure of which we are speaking there are causes of a more special kind that have a closer relation to the problem under examination. We shall attempt, however imperfectly, to indicate these causes.

In medieval Christendom civilisation, living so to say in *utero Ecclesiae,* sought under the spontaneous impulse of the Faith and almost without reflecting to translate the precepts of the Gospel not only in the spiritual life of citizens but also in the institutions of the temporal and the social order. When with the 'reflective age' the inner differentiation of culture became a leading feature of life, and art and science and philosophy and the State began each to be conscious (with what an awful conscience) of itself, it is perhaps not inaccurate to say that there was no similar study of the social order as such or of the essential nature of its being. How indeed could such a study happen in a world which was to grow to greatness under the ascendancy of Descartes?

Through the voluntary and most praiseworthy manifestations of corporal and spiritual mercy the Christian spirit of love sought in the course of these last centuries to remedy the injustice and the shortcomings of the social order. It may fairly be said nevertheless that there was wanting an instrument

of the philosophical and cultural order, an awareness, a discernment of the essential character of the temporal order and of the life of man on earth, which would enable the Christian mind in opposition to the intellectual currents of the time (for it was the period of the dissolution of Christian ideas) to assess in the order of speculative and of practical knowledge the value of the institutions of economic and social life from the point of view of the realisation of the Gospel precepts in the social and temporal order. During this period the spirit of the Gospels was not wanting to the living and saintly members of the Christian world, but there was wanting an explicit and proper awareness of one of the areas of life in which this Spirit was to be applied. And though the claim of Auguste Comte to be the inventor of social science may be largely inadmissible, it may fairly be argued that the 'scientific' illusions of sociology — and likewise of socialism — have assisted the children of light by obliging them to explore with the aid of philosophic reflection these areas of human life and activity.

These reflexions make it evident that, from the point of view of the social possibilities of Christianity and of the full appreciation of the demands of the Gospel precepts in relation to the temporal institutions of the State, the culture of Christian peoples is even now in an extremely backward condition. They also help us to see how it happened that good and pious souls who practise the maxims of Christianity in their private lives and in their individual relations with others seem suddenly, as soon as they encounter the special order of relations and the moral system *sui generis* that appertain to social life as such to pass to a different plane and to follow the principles of naturalism. And finally these reflexions help us to understand how the change which by slow degrees displaced the economic regime of the Middle Ages and substituted the regime of moneylending and of capitalism (though from the beginning it raised among Christian folk many questions that touch the conscience of individuals and the confessional) was not for such a length of time appreciated and adjudged by the Christian mind (which had in truth been educated on Cartesian lines) from the point of view of its social significance and worth. And so the capitalist regime became established throughout the world, · with passive resistance and secret hostility on the part of Catholic social bodies, but without provoking any active, deliberate or effective opposition from Christian folk or from organized Christian or even Catholic communities.

One ought however to observe that the Catholic conscience did not fail to make its protest heard. In the nineteenth century in particular, at the very time when Capitalism was about to reach maturity and was taking possession of the world, men like Ozanam and Vogelsang and La Tour de Pin raised up their voices. And above all the Church itself made good the shortcomings of Christian society by formulating the principles and the essential truths that govern the whole field of economic affairs and that the established order of modern societies largely fails to recognise. The formulation of these truths and principles is to be found in the doctrinal declarations of Pope Leo XIII on the social order and in the encyclicals of Pope Pius XI that echo these declarations. It is indisputable that these interventions of the Popes and the Catholic activities that they have stimulated and directed have already had a profound effect on legislation and on public opinion.

ART AND BEAUTY*

V

ST. THOMAS, who was as simple as he was wise, defined the beautiful as that which being seen pleases, *id quod visum placet.* These four words say all that is needed: vision, that is to say, *intuitive knowledge,* and *joy.* The Beautiful is that which gives joy, not all joy, but joy in knowing; not the joy proper to the act of knowing, but a joy abounding and overflowing from this act because of the object known. If a thing uplifts and delights the Soul by the very fact of being granted to its intuition, it is good to lay hold of, it is beautiful.

Beauty is essentially an object of the intelligence, for that which *knows* in the full sense of the word is the intelligence, which alone is open to the infinity of Being. The birthplace of Beauty is the intellectual world wherefrom it comes down. But in a certain manner also it falls under the grasp of the senses, in the measure in which with man they serve the intelligence, and are themselves capable of enjoying knowledge: "among all the senses it is only with sight and hearing that beauty has relations, because these two senses are above others *maxime cognoscitivi,* most knowledgeable." The share of the senses in the perception of beauty is even made unmeasurable with us by the fact that our understanding is not intuitive like that of the angels; it sees doubtless but on condition of abstracting and discursing; in man sensitive knowledge alone possesses in perfection the intuitiveness necessary to the perception of the beautiful. Thus man may doubtless enjoy purely intellectual beauty, but the beauty *connatural* to man is that which touches the understanding with delight through the senses and their intuition. Such also is the beauty proper to Art, which works upon sensible material so as to give joy to the mind. Thus would it persuade itself that paradise is not lost. It has the relish of the earthly paradise because it restores, for an instant, the peace and delectation at once of understanding and of sense.

If beauty delights the understanding it is because it is in essence a certain excellence or perfection in the proportion of things to the understanding. Hence the three conditions laid down for it by St. Thomas: integrity, because the understanding loves being; proportion, because the understanding loves order and unity; last and above all,

*Maritain, Jacques, *The Philosophy of Art,* translated by Rev. John O'Connor, S.T.P. (Ditchling, Sussex: St. Dominic's Press, 1923), pp. 32–55.

splendour or clarity, because the understanding loves light and intelligibility. A certain shining quality is in fact according to all the ancients the essential character of beauty — *claritas est de ratione pulchritudinis, lux pulchrificat, quia sine luce omnia sunt turpia* — but it is a sunburst of intelligibility: *splendor veri* said the Platonists, *splendor ordinis* said St. Augustine, who adds that "unity is the form of all beauty," *splendor formae,* said St. Thomas in his precise metaphysical language: for the "forma," that is to say, the principle which makes the proper perfection of all that is, which upbuilds and completes things in their essence and in their qualities, which is, in a word, if one may so say, Being, purely such, or the spiritual essence of all reality, is above all the proper principle of intelligibility, the proper clarity of all things. Thus we may well say every *form* is a footprint or a ray of the Creative Intelligence impressed upon the heart of the created being. Besides all order and all proportion is for the rest a work of intelligence. Therefore, to say with the Schoolmen that beauty is the *shining out of form over the well-proportioned parts of matter* is equal to saying that it is the lightening of intelligence over matter intelligently arranged. The understanding enjoys the beautiful because in it it finds and recognises itself, and gets contact with its own light. And this is so true, that those — such as Francis of Assisi — most note and relish the beauty of things, who know that they come forth from an intelligence, and refer them back to their Author. Without doubt all sensuous beauty demands a certain delectation of the eye itself or of the ear or of the imagination; but there is no beauty unless the intelligence also in some way rejoices. A beautiful colour "baptises the eye" as a strong perfume dilates the nostril; but of these two "forms" or qualities colour alone is called *beautiful,* because being received, as the perfume is not, through a sense capable of disinterested knowledge, it can be, even by its purely sensuous lustre, a matter of joy for the understanding. For the rest, the higher man raises his culture, the more spiritual becomes the glory of the form which transports him.

All the same, it behoves us to note that in the beautiful which we have called connatural to man, and which is proper to human art, this splendour of the form, however purely intelligible it may be in itself, is grasped *in the sensitive, and by the sensitive,* and not apart from it. Intuition of artistic beauty thus stands at the opposite pole from the abstraction of scientific truth. For it is through the very apprehension of sense that here below the light of being pierces to the understanding.

The understanding then, absolved from all effort at abstraction, enjoys without labour and without discursion. It is dispensed from its ordinary toil, it has not to disentangle the intelligible from the material in which it is buried, in order to go, step by step, over its different attributes; as the stag at the wellspring it has nothing to do but drink; it drinks the clarity of Being. Set in the intuition of sense, it is flooded with intellectual light given to it in a flash, in the very sensuous in which it basks and which it does not grasp *sub ratione veri,* but rather *sub ratione delectabilis,* but the blissful impregnation which the light produces in it, and by the ensuing joy in the appetite, which springs out, as to its proper object, towards every well-being of the soul. Only in second intention will it analyze, more or less well, by reflection the causes of this joy.

Thus, although beauty belongs to the metaphysic truth in this sense, that every burst of intelligibility in things takes for granted some conformity with the intelligence which is the cause of things, nevertheless the beautiful is not a sort of truth but a sort of good; the perception of the beautiful is related to knowledge, but so as to contribute itself "as bloom is added unto youth"; it is less a kind of knowledge than a kind of delectation. Beauty is essentially delectable. That is why, by its very nature and *qua* beautiful, it moves desire and produces love, it has a unitive force, whereas truth as such only enlightens. *"Omnibus igitur est pulchrum et bonum desiderabile et amabile et diligibile"* (to all therefore is the beautiful and good desirable and lovable and delectable). It is for her beauty that Wisdom 'is beloved, and it is for itself that all beauty is loved at first, even if thereafter the infirm flesh is caught in the snare. Love in its turn produces ecstasy, that is to say, it puts the lover outside his ego; ecstasy which the soul experiences, in lesser degree, when it is smitten with the beauty of a work of art, and in its plenitude, when it is drunk up like the dew by the beauty of God. And concerning God Himself, according to Denys the Areopagite, one must be bold to say that He in some sort suffers the ecstasy of love because of the abundance of His bounty, which impels Him to shed throughout all things a share of His splendour. But His own love causes the beauty of what He loves, while our own love is caused by the beauty of what we love.

What the ancients said about the beautiful ought to be taken in the most formal sense so as to avoid materialising their thought into any over-narrow specification. There is not only one way but a thousand and ten thousand ways in which the notion of *integrity,* or perfection, or achievement can be realized. The absence of head or arm is a lack of integrity very noticeable in a woman, and very slightly noticeable in a statue, no matter how disappointed M. Ravaisson may have been at not being able to complete the Venus de Milo. The least sketch of da Vinci, let alone of Rodin, is more final than the most finished Bouguereau. And if a Futurist thinks fit to give only one eye, or a quarter of an eye, to the lady whom he is portraying, no one denies his right to do so, one only asks — that is the whole crux — that this quarter eye be all the eye needed by the said lady *in the given case.*

It is the same with proportion, fitness, or harmony. They vary according to their objects or their aims. The right proportion of a man is not the same as that of the child. Figures built up according to the Greek or the Egyptian Canon are perfectly proportioned in their kind. But Rouault's jolly fellows are also perfectly proportioned in their kind. Integrity and proportion have no absolute significance, and must be understood solely in relation to the aim of the work, which is to induce the splendour of form upon the matter.

Lastly and especially, this lustre of the form itself, which is the essential of beauty, has an infinity of different ways of shining on the material. It is the sensuous lustre of the colour or of the modelling, the intelligible clarity of an arabesque, or of balance of masses, of activity or of movement; it is the glint upon things of a human thought or of a divine thought; it is above all the deep splendour of the soul that shines through, of the soul, the principle of animal life and strength or the principle of spiritual life, of sorrow, and of passion. There is yet a loftier splendour, that of grace, but the Greeks knew it not.

Beauty then is by no means conformity with a certain ideal and unchangeable type, in the sense understood by those who confuse the true and the beautiful, knowledge and delectation; who will have it, that in order to apprehend beauty man discovers "through the vision of ideas," "through the material wrappings," "the unseen essence of things," and their "necessary type." St. Thomas was as far removed from this pseudo-Platonism as he was from the idealist ragfair of Winckelmann and of David. There is beauty for him as soon as the shining of any form whatsoever upon properly proportioned material results in the well-being of the intelligence, and he takes care to warn us that in a certain way beauty is *relative* — relative not to the dispositions of the subject in the sense in which the moderns understand relativity, but to the peculiar nature and end of the thing, and to the formal conditions under which it is grasped. *Pulchritudo quodammodo dicitur per respectum ad aliquid . . .* (beauty is in some ways predicated with regard to something else); *alia enim est pulchritudo spiritus et alia corporis, atque alia hujus et illius corporis* (for one is the beauty of spirit, and another the beauty of body, and one of this and another of that body); and beautiful as may be a created thing, it may appear beautiful to some and not to others, because it is not beautiful except under certain aspects, which some discern and others see not at all; it is thus "beautiful in one place and not in another."

If this be so, it is because beauty belongs to the order of *transcendentals,* that is to say, of concepts which overpass every limit of kind or category, and do not allow themselves to be enclosed in any classification, because they suck up everything and reappear everywhere. Like the one, the true, and the good, beauty is Being itself taken from a certain point of view, it is a property of Being; it is not an accident super-added to Being, it only adds to Being a relation of reason, it is Being, inasmuch as Being delights an intellectual nature by its mere intuition.

Thus everything is beautiful, as everything is good, at least in certain relationships. And as Being is everywhere present and everywhere different, so Beauty is scattered everywhere and varies in every place. Like Being and the other transcendentals, it is essentially *analogical,* that is to say, it calls itself by different names, *sub diversa ratione,* of the different subjects of which it is predicated: each sort of being is in its own way, is *good* in its own way, is *beautiful* in its own way.

Analogical concepts are spoken properly of God, in Whom the perfection which they designate exists in a 'formal eminent' fashion, in a pure and infinite condition. God is their "sovereign analogue," and they are found in things only as a broken prismatic glimpse of the face of God. So Beauty is one of the divine names.

God is beautiful. He is the most beautiful of all beings, because, as set forth by Denys the Areopagite and St. Thomas, His Beauty is without change or vicissitude, without increase or diminution; and because it is not like that of things, which all have a particularised beauty, *particulatam pulchritudinem, sicut et particulatam naturam* (a particularised beauty as also a particularised nature). He is beautiful by Himself and in Himself, beautiful absolutely.

He is surpassingly beautiful (*superpulcher*) because in the perfectly simple unity of His nature pre-exists in a manner passing excellent the wellspring of all beauty.

He is Beauty itself, because he gives beauty to all created being, according to the property of each, and because He is the cause of all

unison and all clarity. Indeed every form, that is to say every light, is "a certain irradiation coming out of the primal clarity," "a sharing in the divine clarity." And every unison, or every harmony, every concord, every friendship and every union whatsoever between beings comes forth from the divine Beauty, the primitive and supereminent type of all unison, which likens all things to one another, and calls them all unto itself, well deserving therein "the name of καλός which derives from calling." Thus the "beauty of the creature is none other than a similitude of the divine Beauty shared among things," and, moreover, every form being a principle of being and every unison or harmony being a preserver of being, we can say that the Beauty of God is the cause of the Being of all that is. *Ex divina pulchritudine esse omnium derivatur.*

In the Trinity, St. Thomas adds, the name of Beauty is properly attributed to the Son. As to effective integrity or perfection, He has truly and perfectly in Himself, without any diminution, the nature of the Father. As to due proportion or consonance, He is the express and perfect likeness of the Father; and that is the proportion which belongs to the image as such. Lastly, as to clarity, He is the Word, which is the light and splendour of intelligence, "perfect word, nothing lacking, and so to say the art of God Almighty."

Beauty then belongs to the transcendental and metaphysical order. That is why it tends to carry the soul beyond created things. Speaking of the instinct for Beauty, "it is this," writes the *poet accursed,* to whom modern art owes that it recovered the consciousness of the essentially metaphysical character and despotic spirituality of Beauty, "it is this undying instinct for the beautiful which makes us look upon the Earth and it shows as a hint, as a confidential message from Heaven. The unquenchable thirst for all that lies beyond what life reveals is the most living proof of our immortality. It is at once through poetry and beyond poetry, through and beyond music, that the soul catches sight of the splendours which reign behind the tomb; and when an exquisite poem brings the tears to the eyelids, these tears are not the proof of excessive enjoyment, they are far rather the sign of an irritated melancholy, of an importunity of the nerves, of a nature exiled in the imperfect, which would jump all intervention, and snatch, even here on earth, an unveiled paradise."

As soon as one touches a transcendental, one touches Being itself, a likeness of God, an absolute, the nobility and joy of our life; one enters the domain of the spirit. It is remarkable how men do not really communicate with one another except by passing through Being or one of its properties. In that way alone can they escape from the individuality in which matter encloses them. If they stay on the plane of their sensual needs and their sentimental self, they may tell one another what tales they like, they do not understand one another. They watch without seeing one another, each one infinitely solitary, for all that labour or pleasure fastens them together. But touch Good or Love, like the Saints, touch Truth, like Aristotle, touch Beauty, like Dante or Bach or Giotto, then contact is set up, souls commingle. Men are not really united save by the spirit, light alone brings them together, *"intellectualia et rationalia omnia congregans, et indestructibilia faciens."*

Art in general tends to make a work. But certain arts tend to make a beautiful work, and there they differ essentially from all the others. The work at which all the other arts labour is itself ordered to man's utility, it is therefore a mere means; and it is altogether inside a determined material kind. The work at which the fine arts labour is ordered unto Beauty; inasmuch as it is beautiful, it is an end, an absolute, self-sufficing; and if, in so far as it is a work to be made, it is material and bonded to a kind, inasmuch as it is beautiful it belongs to the kingdom of the mind, and is swallowed up in transcendence and the infinity of Being.

The fine arts thus stand out in the *genus* art as man stands out in the *genus* animal. And like man himself they resemble an horizon where matter and spirit meet. They have a spiritual soul. Hence their many distinctive properties. Their contact with the beautiful modifies in them certain character-istics of art in general, notably in what concerns the rules of art, as we shall try to show; on the other hand, it betrays and carries to a kind of excess other generic marks of artistic virtue, above all its character of intellectuality and its likeness to the speculative virtues.

There is a singular analogy between the fine arts and wisdom. They, like it, are ordained to an object which goes beyond man, and is valuable in itself, unlimited in its amplitude; for Beauty like Being is infinite. They are disinterested, desired for their own sake, truly noble, because their work taken in itself is not done to be used as a means, but to be enjoyed as an end, being a veritable fruit, *aliquid ultimum et delectabile.* Their whole worth is spiritual, and their mode of being is contemplative. For if contemplation is not their act, as it is the act of wisdom, still the fine arts aim at producing a delight of the understanding, that is to say, a sort of contemplation, and they imply also in the artist a sort of contemplation, wherefrom the beauty of the work should redound. That is why it is possible to apply to them, with all due proportion, what St. Thomas says of wisdom, when he compares it to play: "The contemplation of wisdom is readily compared to play, because of two things which are found in play. The first is that play is delectable, and the contemplation of wisdom hath the greatest delightfulness, according to what Wisdom says of herself in Ecclesiasticus: *My breath is sweeter than honey.* The second is that the operations of play are not ordained to anything else, but are sought after for their own sake. It is the same with the delightfulness of wisdom. This is why Divine Wisdom compares her delightfulness to play: *My delight was every day playing in His sight through the round of the earth.*

But Art always abides essentially in the order of Making, and it is by *slave* work on a material that it glimpses the joy of the spirit. Thence for the artist a strange and pathetic condition, itself the image of man's condition in the world, where he must go in and out among bodies, and live with spirits. Though blaming the old poets who made the godhead envious, Aristotle owns that they were right in saying that to it alone is reserved the right and proper ownership of wisdom. "It is not a human possession, for in many ways the nature of man is servile." To produce beauty belongs in the same way to God alone by true ownership, and if the condition of the artist is more human and less lofty than that of the metaphysician, it is also more discordant and more sorrowful because his activity does not abide altogether in the pure immanence of spiritual operations, and does not in itself consist in contemplation, but in making. Without having either the light or the nourishment of wisdom, it is beset with the hard exigencies of the intelligence and the speculative life, and condemned to all the servile miseries of temporal practice and production.

"O brother Leo, little sheep of God, even though a friar minor should speak the tongue of angels and should raise up a man four days dead, write down that that is not the perfect joy. . . . "

Were the Artist to enclose in his work the whole light of heaven and the whole grace of the primal Garden, he would not have perfect joy; because he is on the track of wisdom and runs after the fragrance of its perfumes, but possesses it not. Were the Philosopher to know all the intelligible reasons and all the virtues of Being, he would not have perfect joy; because his wisdom is human. Were the Theologian to know all the analogies of the divine processions and all the reasons for the actions of Christ, he would not have the perfect joy; because his wisdom has a divine origin, but a human measure, and a human voice.

"Ah, voices! die then, dying that you be!"[1]

The Poor and Peacemakers alone have perfect joy, because they possess wisdom and contemplation par excellence, in the silence of creatures and in the voice of Love; united without intermediary to self-existing Truth, they know "the sweetness which God gives, and the delightful taste of the Holy Spirit." This is what made St. Thomas say, speaking sometime before his death about his un-

---

[1]Ruysbroek.

finished *Summa*: 'It seems to me like straw — *mihi videtur ut palea.*' Human straw are the Parthenon and Notre Dame of Chartres, the Sistine Chapel and the Mass in D, which will be burned at the last day. "There is no relish in creatures." The Middle Ages knew this order of things. The Renaissance shattered it. After three centuries of unbelief, prodigal art has made it her aim to be the last end of man, his Bread and Wine, the consubstantial mirror of beatific Beauty. In reality it has only wasted its substance. And the Poet starving for beatitude, who kept asking from art the mystical fullness which God alone can give, has merely emptied himself into the Stigean abyss. The silence of Rimbaud probably marks the end of a secular apostasy. In any case, it clearly means that it is folly to seek in art the words of life eternal and rest for the heart of man; and that the artist, so as not to break in pieces his art or his soul, must simply be, *qua* artist, what art wants him to be — a good workman.

But lo, the modern world, which had promised everything to the artist, will presently leave him no more than the bare means of livelihood. Founded on the two principles *against nature* of the *fertility of money* and of the *finality of the useful,* multiplying without any possible limit both needs and servitude, destroying the leisure of the soul, withdrawing the material *factibile* from the ruling which proportioned it to the ends of the human entity, and imposing on man the panting of the machine and the accelerated movement of matter, the modern world stamps upon human activity a measure genuinely inhuman and a direction genuinely diabolical: for the final end of all this delirium is to keep man from remembering his God,

> *Dum nil perenne cogitat,*
> *Seseque culpis illigat.*

By logical consequence he ought to treat as useless, and therefore as reprobate, all that on any title whatsoever bears the imprint of the spirit.

"A Patrician order in deeds, but a truly democratic barbarism of thought, behold the inheritance of the times that be upon us; the dreamer, the speculative mind, may manage to keep themselves afloat at the cost of their security or well-being; place, success, or glory shall reward the suppleness of the mountebank: more than ever, to a degree unknown to the iron age, poverty and loneliness shall be the wages of the prowess of hero or saint."

Persecuted like the seer and almost like the saint, perhaps at last the artist will come to know his brethren, and find again his true vocation; for in a certain way of speaking he is not of this world, being, the moment he works for beauty, in the way which leads right souls to God and manifests to them unseen things through the seen. Rare then as may be those who shall not will to please the Beast and shift with the wind, it shall be in them, from the sole fact of their exercising a disinterested activity, that the human race will live.

THE WISE ARCHITECT*

LEIBNITZ already in his day lamented the lost unity of Christian culture, a unity which has been in process of dissolution for the past four centuries.

It has often been observed that in three great spiritual crises, the humanist Renaissance, the Protestant Reformation, and the rationalist *Aufklärung,* man achieved a historical revolution of absolutely unparalleled importance, at the end of which he conceived himself as the centre of his history and the ultimate end of his activity on earth, and arrogated to himself the peculiarly divine privilege of absolute independence or all-sufficiency which theologians term *aseitas*. The immense deployment of brute force over the surface of the globe and the industrial enslavement of matter to which Europe gave itself up in the nineteenth century are merely the expression in the sensible order of that spiritual usurpation.

A sort of fictitious unity of the human spirit then arose like a great mirage under the optimistic trappings of positivist pseudo-science, and men believed that they were in sight of the goal, that they were about to become masters and owners of themselves, of all nature and history: it was catastrophe which was imminent, and while matter, apparently vanquished and subdued, imposed its rhythm and the endlessly multiplied exigencies of such satisfactions as it procures upon human life, men found themselves more divided than ever, in disunion with other men, in disunion with themselves; matter is a principle of disunion and can only beget division. Nation against nation, class against class, passion against passion, it is human personality in the end which dissolves, and man tries in vain to find himself in the dissociated fragments of his unconscious velleities and inconsistent sincerities — and yet God knows to what diligent scrutiny each is subjected! — while a sort of fever of despair takes hold of the world.

What are the conditions on which this lost unity can be recovered, not as it once was, for time is irreversible, but reconstituted once more in new forms? One truth seems to me to dominate the whole discussion. Man cannot find his unity in himself; he finds it outside himself, above himself.

It was his determination to be self-sufficient which ruined him. He will find himself again only by becoming attached to his first principle and to the order transcending it. Pure subjectivity, like pure materiality, disperses. It was because their attention was fixed upon being and God with an objectivity at once ingenuous and pious, an objectivity transported with love, that the Christian ages had such a clear and precise appreciation of human and moral things — and unity no less. There is no greater delusion than to seek

*Maritain, Jacques, *The Angelic Doctor*, the life and thought of St. Thomas Aquinas, translated by J. F. Scanlan (New York: Sheed and Ward, 1931), pp. 70–86.

in immanentism the reconciliation of man with himself. Man becomes reconciled with himself only on the cross, which is hard and exterior to him: the cross upon which he is nailed. Objectivity is the first condition of unity.

There are, to be sure, other conditions in the material order and they must not be neglected. But objectivity is primordial because it affects the two activities most worthy of man—the activity of the mind, so far as it is faithful to the object and therefore to the first Being, and the activity of love, so far as it unites us to the principle of our being and our veritable Whole.

The resurrection of metaphysics and a fresh expansion of charity are the essential presuppositions of a return to human unity—to that unity which was perfect only in the Garden of Eden and in Gethsemane in the heart of Christ, the longing for which will never cease to haunt us.

If we cut sections, so to speak, in the tissue of human events, we shall find two very different elements at the various moments of history, especially at moments of major transformation; on the one hand, an element of great importance in matter and volume, which represents the massive result, the residue, as it were, of past effort, an element which may be described as the static factor or the resistance factor, signifying above all something done, concluded, finished.

The other element is nothing as regards volume and appearance, but is ever so much more important as regards energy, an element which may be described as the dynamic factor or the factor of living force signifying above all something in the making or about to be made, something in active preparation, with the formal part to play in the generation of the future.

As far as the former element, the static factor, is concerned, what strikes us in the contemporary world, in the world ravaged by capitalism and positivism, in the world dominated by antitheological and anti-metaphysical civilization, is that pitiful product which goes by the name of the modern man, a being cut off from all his ontological roots and transcendental objects who, because he

sought to find his centre in himself, has become, in Hermann Hesse's phrase, merely a wolf howling in despair towards eternity. But that very fact also shows us that the world has made and finished with the experiment of positivism, pseudo-scientific scepticism, subjectivist idealism, and that the experiment has been sufficiently demonstrative. Such things are dead: though they may still encumber us for a long time, like cadaverous products, they are finished.

If we consider the other historical element, the dynamic factor in the present-day world, what we perceive on the contrary is a profound, an immense need of metaphysics, a great impulse towards metaphysics, towards the restoration of ontological values. The world which is struggling to be, struggling to emerge in the future, is not a world of positivism but a world of metaphysics.

It is not, sufficient to say: the resurrection of metaphysics. The metaphysics in question must be a real metaphysics. I do not overlook all the services which the Bergsonian movement may, as a matter of fact, have rendered in France, the neo-Hegelian and pluralist movements in England, the phenomenologist movement in Germany. But it must nevertheless be admitted that a metaphysics whose conclusion is pure change and a more or less monist evolutionism, or a polytheist moralism or an atheistic ontology, would be no remedy for humanity. The resurrection of metaphysics means in the first place that we are on the threshold of an age of great metaphysical conflicts, great battles of the spirit; and the combatants will not be systems envolved by European speculation only, but Asiatic systems also rejuvenated by modern thinkers of great acumen and distinction, such as are already to be found in Japan and India.

What guide can we appeal to to lead us through the maze of all these metaphysical conflicts? Thomas Aquinas teaches us to distinguish in the intellectual sphere between good and evil, truth and falsehood, a process of angelic sifting, as it were; teaches us how to preserve every true intention contained in the diversity of systems and to correct the rest in a synthesis poised upon reality.

For one of the peculiar characteristics of his philosophy, as has often been observed, is that, so far from being a flabby eclecticism devoid of principles, it is on the contrary a system with principles so exalted and rigid that it reconciles at its elevation, by transcending them, the most antinomous theories, which then appear to be merely the opposite inclines to one same altitude.

St. Thomas, by probing deeply into the intimate nature of knowledge and the peculiar life of the mind, founds upon reason more securely than any other philosopher — as against positivism but yet making the fullest allowance for experience and as against idealism but yet making the fullest allowance for the immanent and constructive activity of the spirit — the objectivity of knowledge, the rights and value of the science of being. But also, as against the false metaphysical systems that threaten to assail us, as against the pantheist immanentism which some philosophers would impose upon us in the name of the East, as against the pragmatism of the Far West, as against the atheistic intellectualism apparent in Europe, he establishes the transcendence of Him Whom we know through His creatures, but Who has no common standard of comparison with them; Who is Being, Intelligence, Goodness, Life and Beatitude, but Who surpasses and transcends infinitely our ideas of being, goodness, and all the other perfections; Whose nature, in short, our concepts grasp by analogy but are powerless to comprehend.

Metaphysics, therefore, in his hands rises above agnosticism and rationalism; it starts out from experience on its ascent to the uncreated Being and restores in the human spirit the proper hierarchy of the speculative values, inaugurates in us the order of wisdom.

If it be a question thereafter of ethical values and the conduct of human life, then it is only too easy to see to what an extent the modern world is the world of selfishness, meanness and insensibility. Once man understood to be self-sufficient, what was there to prevent everything in him becoming dissociated and desiccated in irremediable antagonisms? Such at any rate appears to be the case as regards the residue of the near past.

And, in truth, love lives only by God and by what it deifies, and when it perceives that what it has deified is but a mere fragment of nothing it turns to contempt and hatred. For this reason the love of humanity without God could not end otherwise than in a state in which the last resource of everyone is merely self-worship or suicide.

As far as the second historical element, the dynamic element above referred to, is concerned, what the contemporary world reveals to us precisely by reason of the kind of impossibility to live which anthropocentric egotism creates, is the need and presentiment of a vast effusion of love. Here again we must be on our guard against counterfeits; as we must be on our guard against false systems of metaphysics, so we must also be on our guard against the delusive forms of love.

A false humanitarian mysticism, pseudo-buddhist, theosophical or anthroposophical, a false reign of the heart which claimed to install itself at the expense of the mind, in content of the Word which creates and forms Its laws, a sort of quietist heresy which reduced us to a condition below the level of man, because we should have lost the very idea of truth, and dissolved us in an equivocal poetic sensuality, unworthy of the name of truth, are a few of the evils which threaten us from that point of view. We are far removed from the materialism of the nineteenth century: it is from a pseudo-spiritualism and a pseudo-mysticism that we may expect the greatest dangers of the deviation in our time.

The Angelic Doctor shows us the direct road, reminds us that order dwells in the heart of holy love, and that if in God subsisting Love proceeds from the Father and the increated Word, love in our case also must proceed from truth and pass through the lake of the Word; otherwise its diffusion only means destruction.

He reminds us also that there is only one effective and authentic way of loving our brethren and that is to love them with that same charity which makes us first love God above all. Thus — according to the admirable order of charity described in the second part of the *Summa*, which embraces all men without injuring the native privileges of any — love which unites us, above being, to the principle of being, descends again upon the creature with a divine force, shatters every obstacle and rekindles every coldness, opens up a new world which reveals the divine attributes in a more profound, unsuspected way, a world in which beings not only know one another but also recognize one another, and makes us wish well to our enemies. So we must assert against the deliquescences of sentimentality and the naturalist worship of the human race the true nature of the divine love.

And against the hardening due to the worship of force, the naturalist worship of the individual, the class, the race or the nation, it is the primacy of that love which must be asserted. *Caritas major omnium.* Need it be observed that the whole ethical theory of St. Thomas is based upon that doctrine which he derives from the Gospel and St. Paul? He has erected upon that teaching of the Gospel an infrangible theological synthesis, in which he shows how Love, which makes us undeviatingly desire our last end, enjoys an absolute practical primacy over the whole of our individual and social life and constitutes the very bond of perfection, how it is better for us to love God than to know Him, and how no virtue, lacking such love, is truly virtuous or attains its perfect form, not even justice. And St. Thomas knows that such love really dominates human life, is effective love of God above all things and of one's neighbour as of one's self, only if it is supernatural, rooted in faith, proceeding from the grace of Christ, which makes us in the image of the Crucified, sons and heirs of the God Who is Love. If we follow the Angelic Doctor, we shall realize that peace in man and among men (the direct work of charity, *opus charitatis,* "for love is a unifying force and the efficient cause of unity") descends from that superessential Peace and from that eternal Love which resides in the heart of the Trinity.

The distress of modern times, it was observed in the beginning of this essay, derives from the fact that culture, which is a certain perfection of man, has come to consider itself an ultimate end. It began by despising in its Cartesian or philosophical phase everything above the level of reason; it ends by despising reason itself, suffers both the law of the flesh and the spiritual vertigo which irrationality inevitably precipitates in the case of man. "The error of the modern world consists in its claim to ensure the dominance of supernature over reason." This is the reason why, even in the order of knowledge, the metaphysics referred to a moment ago remains an inadequate remedy. Another wisdom, more exalted and more divine, is born of love itself, through the gifts of the Holy Ghost. And it is for that mystical wisdom in the first place that our misery hungers and thirsts, because it alone is capable of satisfying our hunger and our thirst, being union in experience with divine things and a beginning of beatitude. And yet it still leaves us hungry and thirsty, because vision alone can fully satiate our desire with God.

St. John of the Cross is the great experimental doctor of such wisdom; St. Thomas Aquinas is its great theologian. And because he has defined more accurately than any other doctor the central truth which cannot be disregarded without dealing a mortal blow to contemplation, and Christianity itself — I mean the distinction between nature and grace, and their active compenetration, and the whole organism of the infused gifts — he provides a better explanation than any other of the true nature of mystical wisdom, and defends it better than any other against every counterfeit.

That is the greatest benefit we may expect from him from the point of view of the restoration of Christian culture; for, in the last resort, it is upon that wisdom and contemplation that the whole Christian order on this earth depends.

The unity of a culture is determined in the first place and above all by a certain common philosophical structure, a certain metaphysical and moral attitude, a certain common scale of values, in a word, a certain common conception of the universe, of man and human life, of which social, linguistic, and juridical structures are, so to speak, the embodiment.

This metaphysical unity has long been broken — not certainly completely destroyed, but broken and as it were obliterated in the West. The drama of Western culture consists in the fact that its stock of common metaphysics has been reduced to an utterly inadequate minimum, so that only matter now holds it together. The drama is all the more tragic for us because everything at the moment has to be recreated, everything to be put in place again in our European house. If a common philosophy succeeded in securing acceptance by an elite in Europe, it would be the beginning of the cure of the Western world.

As Thomas Aquinas united in his marvellously tempered constitution the talents of the men of the North and South, of Norman and Lombard, as he integrated in his doctor's mission the Italy of the Popes, the Germany of Albert the Great, the France of St. Louis and the University of Paris, as he combined the treasures of the Greeks and the Latins, the Arabs and the Jews, with the inheritance bequeathed by the Fathers and Christian wisdom, in a word the entire contribution of the known world of his time, so his marvellously synthetic and organic theology, open to every aspect of reality, offers to the intellectual tendencies peculiar to the various nations, and more particularly to the three just mentioned, the means of exercising themselves freely, not in mutual destruction, but in mutual completion and consolidation.

The reason is that St. Thomas succeeded in constructing a philosophical and theological wisdom so elevated in immateriality that it is really free of every particularization of race or environment. Alas! what we have witnessed during the past few centuries is an absolutely opposite phenomenon, a kind of racial materialization of philosophy. Descartes is one of the glories of France, but he hypostasizes certain defects, certain temptations peculiar to the French intellectual temperament. Hegel does the same for Germany; William James, the pragmatists and the pluralists, for the Anglo-Saxon countries. It is time to turn to truth itself, which belongs to no particular country, time to turn to the universality of human reason and supernatu-

ral wisdom. The necessity is all the more urgent because it appears as though the advent of a new era in philosophy were imminent.

Imagine for a moment that Catholics in the various countries realized the primordial importance of intellectual questions, of metaphysics and theology, that they discarded senseless prejudices against scholasticism, that they considered it, not as a mediaeval mummy to be examined with archaeological curiosity, but as a living armour of the mind and the indispensable equipment for the boldest enterprises of discovery; imagine that they fulfilled in practice the ardent aspiration of the Church, which is not to conquer adherents as though Catholicism were a human undertaking, but to serve divine Truth everywhere in the souls of men and the universe; imagine that they transcended intestine divisions and the petty rivalries of schools which everywhere sterilize their activity, finally, that they became conscious of the necessity of a seriousness and sustained intellectual co-operation among Catholics of all nations.

The common Doctor of the Church would then become in all truth their common master; with him to lead them, they might work effectively for the restoration of the West and its unity. Then there would be workers for the harvest. Then in the speculative sphere, Thomist metaphysics might assimilate into a true intellectual order the immense body of the individual sciences, abandoned at the moment to chaos and in danger of having their admirable progress exploited by aberrant philosophies. In the moral sphere, Thomist metaphysics and theology might architectonically preside over the elaboration of the new social order, the Christian economy, the Christian politics which the present state of the world so urgently requires. Finally, to revert to the great primitive symptoms and the great primitive causes of the divisions afflicting us, humanism, protestantism, rationalism, at the end of their tether, having had time to suffer to the extreme the process of self-destruction developed by their initial error, and to experience also the value of many a reality which that error fails to take into account, would be astonished to find in the treasury of the

Angelic Doctor the very truths which they coveted with no clear perception of their nature and which they have only been able to ruin.

I would add that Greek and Russian piety, which differs apparently from Catholic piety not so much in divergences of dogma as in certain characteristics of spirituality, is much less hostile, in my opinion, to the philosophy of St. Thomas than might at first be supposed. It approaches the problems from another angle and the scholastic presentation as a rule irritates and offends it. These are merely questions of modality; and I am convinced that a proper understanding of the Thomist system would dispel innumerable misunderstandings and facilitate many unexpected encounters. I am also convinced that when our separated brethren are driven, under pressure of contemporary errors, to a more systematic and developed theological defence, they will be constrained to seek in the principles elaborated by St. Thomas trusty weapons against vain philosophy.

In all this St. Thomas appears to us as the great intellectual renovator of the West.

Need it be added that it would argue a very imperfect acquaintance with human nature to believe in the possibility of such a Utopia? Nevertheless, if a serious effort is not made in such a direction, one may as well proclaim that culture in the West is doomed. It may be hoped, in spite of everything, that such an effort will be made.

ST. THÉRÈSE OF LISIEUX

(1873-1897)

THE most important French book of our time was not written by any of the resounding names of literary history. It was the work of a young girl who lived her short life in the enclosed garden of the Carmelite Convent at Lisieux in France. In writing the story of her life and "little way," the Little Flower rebuked the wise and the witty and opened up an avenue toward vision and sanctity which brought hope to all, even the fainthearted. For her, any biography but her own work is superfluous.

CHAPTER X

THE NEW COMMANDMENT*

AMONG the numberless graces I have received this year, not the least is a deeper insight into the precept of charity. I had never before fathomed the words of Our Lord: *"The second commandment is like to the first: Thou shalt love thy neighbour as thyself."* I had laboured above all to love God, and it was in loving Him that I discovered the hidden meaning of these other words: *"Not every one that saith to me: Lord! Lord! shall enter into the Kingdom of Heaven, but he that doth the will of My Father."* This will Our Lord revealed to me through the words of His new Commandment addressed to His Apostles at the Last Supper, when He told them *"to love one another as He had loved them."* I set myself to find out how He had loved His Apostles, and I saw that it was not for their natural qualities, seeing they were but ignorant men, whose minds dwelt chiefly on earthly things. Yet He calls them His friends, His brethren; He desires to see them near Him in the Kingdom of His Father; and to open His

*Saint Thérèse of Lisieux, an autobiography, (New York: P. J. Kenedy and Sons,), pp. 162–172.

Kingdom to them He wills to die on the cross, saying: *"Greater love than this no man hath, that a man lay down his life for his friends."*

As I meditated on these divine words, I understood how imperfect was the love I bore my Sisters in religion, and that I did not love them as Our Lord does. Now I know that true charity consists in bearing all my neighbour's defects, in not being surprised at mistakes, but in being edified at the smallest virtues.

Above all else I have learnt that charity must not remain shut up in the heart, for *"No man lighteth a candle and putteth it in a hidden place, nor under a bushel; but upon a candlestick, that they who come in may see the light."* This candle, it seems to me, Mother, represents that charity which enlightens and gladdens, not only those who are dearest to us, but likewise all those who are of the household.

In the Old Law, when God told His people to love their neighbours as themselves, He had not yet come down upon earth; and knowing full well man's strong love of self, He could not ask anything greater. But when Our Lord gave His Apostles a new Commandment—*"His own Commandment"*—He not only required us to love our neighbour as ourselves, but would have us love even as He does, and as He will do until the end of time.

O my Jesus! Thou dost never ask what is impossible; Thou knowest better that I how frail and imperfect I am; Thou knowest that I shall never love my Sisters as Thou hast loved them, unless Thou lovest them Thyself within me, my dearest Master. It is because Thou dost desire to grant me this grace, that Thou hast given a new Commandment, and dearly do I cherish it, since it proves to me that it is Thy Will *to love in me* all those Thou dost bid me love.

When I show charity towards others I know that it is Jesus who is acting within me, and the more closely I am united to Him, the more dearly I love my Sisters. Should I wish to increase this love, and should the devil bring before me the defects of a Sister, I hasten to look for her virtues

and good motives. I call to mind that though I may have seen her fall once, she may have gained many victories over herself which in her humility she conceals, and also that what appears to be a fault may very well, owing to the good intention that prompted it, be an act of virtue. I have all the less difficulty in persuading myself that this is so, because of my own experience.

One day, during recreation, the portress came to ask for a Sister to help her in some particular task which she mentioned. Now I had the eager desire of a child to do this very thing, and as it happened, the choice fell upon me. I began immediately to fold up our needle-work, slowly enough, however, to allow my neighbour to fold hers before me, for I knew it would please her to take my place. Noticing how deliberate I was, the portress said laughingly: "Ah, I thought you would not add this pearl to your crown, you were too slow." And all the community were left under the impression that I had acted according to nature.

I cannot tell you what profit I derived from this incident, and how indulgent it has made me towards others. It still keeps in check any feeling of vanity when I receive praise, for I reflect that since my small acts of virtue can be mistaken for imperfections, why should not imperfection be mistaken for virtue? And I repeat with St. Paul: *"To me it is a very small thing to be judged by you, or by man's day. But neither I judge myself. He that judgeth me is the Lord."* Since, therefore, the Lord is my Judge, I will try always to think leniently of others, that He may judge me leniently—or not at all, since He says: *"Judge not and ye shall not be judged."*

Returning to the Holy Gospels where Our Lord explains to me clearly in what His new Commandment consists, I read in St. Matthew: *"You have heard that it hath been said, Thou shalt love thy neighbour, and hate thy enemy: but I say unto you, Love your enemies and pray for them that persecute you."*

There are, of course, no enemies in Carmel: but, after all, we have our natural likes and dislikes. We may feel drawn towards one Sister and may be tempted to go a long way round to avoid meeting another. Well, Our Lord tells me that this last is the Sister I must love and pray for, even though her manners might lead me to believe that she does not care for me. *"If you love them that love you, what thanks are to you? For sinners also love those that love them"* Nor is it enough to love; we must prove our love. We take a natural delight in pleasing friends, but that is not charity; even sinners do the same.

Elsewhere Our Lord teaches me: *"Give to everyone that asketh thee; and of him that taketh away thy goods, ask them not again."* To give to everyone who asks is less pleasant than to give spontaneously and of one's own accord. Again, if a thing be asked in a courteous way consent is easy, but if, unhappily, tactless words have been used, there is an inward rebellion unless we are perfect in charity. We discover no end of excuses for refusing, and it is only after having made clear to the guilty Sister how rude was her behaviour, that we grant *as a favour* what she requires, or render a slight service which takes perhaps, one-half of the time we have lost in setting forth the difficulties and our own imaginary rights.

If it be difficult to give to anyone who asks, it is still more difficult to let what belongs to us be taken without asking to have it back. I say this is difficult, but I would rather say that it seems so, for *"The yoke of the Lord is sweet and His burden light."* And when we submit to that yoke we at once feel its sweetness.

I said just now that Jesus does not wish me to reclaim what belongs to me. This ought to appear quite natural, since in reality I own nothing, and ought to rejoice when an occasion brings home to me the poverty to which I am solemnly vowed. Formerly, I used to think myself detached from everything, but since Our Lord's words have become clear, I see how imperfect I am. When starting to paint, for instance, if I happen to find the brushes in confusion, if a ruler or a penknife be missing, I am sorely tempted to lose patience, and have strongly to resist the impulse to demand, and sharply demand, the articles required.

I may, of course, ask for them, but if I do so humbly I am not disobeying Our Lord's command. On the contrary, I am like the poor who hold out their hands for the necessaries of life and who if refused are not surprised, because no one owes them anything. To soar above all natural sentiment brings the deepest peace, nor is there any joy equal to that which is felt by the truly poor in spirit. Sometimes they ask with detachment for what is really needful: not only are they refused, but an attempt is made to deprive them of what they already possess. Yet they follow the Master's advice: *"If any man take away thy coat, let go thy cloak also unto him."*

It seems to me that to give up one's cloak is to renounce every right, and look upon oneself as the servant, the slave of all. Divested of a cloak, however, it is easier to walk or run, so the Master adds: *"And whosoever will force thee one mile, go with him other two."* Hence it is not enough for me to give to the one who asks, I ought to anticipate the wish; I should show myself honoured by the request for service, and if anything set apart for my use be taken away I should appear glad to be rid of it.

I cannot always, indeed, carry out to the letter the words of the Gospel, for occasions arise when I am compelled to refuse a request. Yet, when charity has taken deep root in the soul, it shows itself outwardly, and there is always a way of refusing so graciously what one cannot give, that the refusal affords as much pleasure as the gift itself. It is true that people are more ready to beg from those who are most ready to give; still, on the pretext that I shall be forced to refuse, I ought not to avoid an importunate Sister, since the Divine Master has said: "From him that would borrow of thee turn not away." Neither should I be kind for the sake of being considered so, nor in the hope that the Sister will return the service, for once again it is written: *"If you lend to them of whom you hope to receive, what thanks are to you? For sinners lend to sinners, for to receive as much. But you, do good and lend, hoping for nothing thereby, and your reward shall be great."*

Along this path it is but the first step that costs—even on earth the reward will be great. To lend without hope of return may seem hard; one would rather give outright, for a thing once given is no longer ours. When a Sister comes to you and says: "I have our Mother's leave to borrow your help for a few hours, and you may rest assured that later on I will do as much for you," we may be practically certain that the time so lent will never be repaid, and therefore feel sorely tempted to say: "I will give you what you ask!" The remark would gratify self-love, it being more generous to give than to lend, and in addition it would let the Sister feel how little reliance you put in her promise.

The divine precepts do assuredly run counter to our natural inclinations, and without the help of grace it would be impossible to understand them, far less put them in practice.

I fear, dear Mother, that I have expressed myself more confusedly than usual, and I cannot think what you will find to interest you in these rambling pages. However, I am not writing a literary work, and if I have wearied you by this discourse on charity you will at least find in it a proof of your child's good will. I have to confess that I am far from living up to the lights I have received, yet the mere desire of doing so brings me peace. If I happen to stumble in the matter of charity, I rise again immediately, and for some months past I have not even had to struggle. With our Father, St. John of the Cross, I have been able to say: "My house is entirely at peace," and that peace I attribute to a certain victory which I gained over myself. Ever since then, the hosts of Heaven have hastened to my aid, not wishing me to be wounded after my valiant fight on the occasion I am about to describe.

Formerly, a holy nun of our community was a constant source of annoyance to me: the devil must have had something to do with the trial, for undoubtedly it was he who made me see so many disagreeable points in her. Unwilling to yield to my natural antipathy, I remembered that charity ought not merely to exist in the heart but also to show itself in deeds; so I endeavoured to treat this Sister as I should my most cherished friend. Whenever I met her I prayed for her, at the same time offering to God her virtues and her merits. I knew this would delight Our Lord exceedingly, for there is no artist who is not gratified when his works are praised, and the Divine Artist of souls is therefore well pleased when we do not stop at the exterior, but penetrate to the inner sanctuary He has chosen for His abode and admire its beauty.

I did not rest satisfied with praying earnestly for the Sister who gave me such occasions for self-mastery, but I tried also to render her as many services as I could; and when tempted to make a disagreeable answer, I made haste to smile and change the subject of conversation. The *Imitation* says: "It is more profitable to leave to everyone his way of thinking than to give way to contentious discourses," and sometimes when the temptation was particularly violent, if I could slip away without her suspecting my inward struggle, I would run like a deserter from the battlefield. The outcome of all this was that she said to me one day, with a beaming countenance: "Tell me, Soeur Thérèse, what it is that attracts you to me so strongly? I never meet you without being welcomed with your most gracious smile?" Ah! What attracted me was Jesus hidden in the depth of her soul, Jesus who makes sweet even that which is most bitter.

I spoke just now, Mother, of my last resource for escaping defeat,—namely . . . flight. It was scarcely an honourable method, I confess, but whenever I had recourse to it during my novitiate, it was always successful. Here is a striking example which I think will amuse you.

For several days you had been ill with bronchitis and we were all very anxious. One morning in discharge of my office of sacristan I entered your infirmary, very gently, to put back the keys of the Communion grating. Though I took care not to show it, I was inwardly rejoicing at the opportunity of seeing you. One of the Sisters, however, feared that I should wake you, and discreetly wished to take the keys from me.

I told her, with all possible politeness, that I was as anxious as she that there should be no noise, adding that it was my duty to return them. I see now it would have been more perfect to yield, but I did not think so then and consequently tried to enter the room.

What she feared came to pass — the noise we made awoke you, and the blame was cast upon me. The Sister made a lengthy discourse, the point of which was that I was the guilty person. I was burning to defend myself when happily it occurred to me that if I began to do so, I should certainly lose my peace of mind, and that as I had not sufficient virtue to keep silence when accused, my only chance of safety lay in flight. No sooner thought than done, and I fled. . . . But my heart beat so violently, that I could not go far and had to sit down on the stairs to taste in peace and quiet the fruits of my victory. This is without doubt an odd kind of courage, yet I think it better not to expose oneself in the face of certain defeat.

When I think over my novitiate days I see clearly how far removed I was from perfection; some things there are that make me laugh. How good God has been to have trained my soul and lent it wings! All the nets of the hunter can no longer frighten me, for *"A net is set in vain before the eyes of them that have wings."*

It may be that at some future day my present state will appear to me full of defects, but nothing now surprises me. Nor does my utter helplessness distress me; I even glory in it, and expect each day to reveal some fresh imperfection. Indeed these lights on my own nothingness do me more good than lights on matters of faith. Remembering that *"Charity covereth a multitude of sins,"* I draw from the rich mine which Our Saviour has opened up to us in the Gospels; I search the depths of His adorable words, and I cry out with the Psalmist: *"I have run in the way of Thy commandments since Thou hast enlarged my heart."* And charity alone can widen my heart. O Jesus! ever since its sweet flame consumes me, I run with delight in the way of Thy *new Commandment,* and I desire so to run until that glorious day when with Thy retinue of vir-

gins, I shall follow Thee through Thy boundless realm, singing Thy new canticle — the Canticle of Love.

God in His infinite goodness has given me, dear Mother, a clear insight into the deep mysteries of Charity. If only I could express what I know, you would hear a heavenly music; but alas! I can only stammer like a child, and if the words of Jesus were not my support, I should be tempted to beg leave to hold my peace.

When the Divine Master tells me to give to anyone who asks of me, and to allow what is mine to be taken without asking for it back, it seems to me that He speaks not only of the things of earth but also of the goods of Heaven. Neither the one nor the other are really mine; I renounced the first by the vow of poverty and the others are gifts which are simply lent. If God withdraw them, I have no right to complain. But our own ideas, the fruit of our mind and heart, we regard as a sacred and personal treasury upon which none may lay hands. For instance, if I communicate to a Sister some light given me in prayer and she afterwards reveals it as though it were her own, it would seem she is appropriating what is mine. Or if during recreation someone makes a witty remark which her neighbour repeats to the community without acknowledging whence it came, its originator will look on this as a sort of theft. At the time, she preserves an unwilling silence, but on the first opportunity she will insinuate delicately that her thoughts have been borrowed.

Had I not experienced all these human weaknesses, Mother, I could not so well explain them. I should have preferred to believe myself the one who endured such petty temptations, had you not bidden me listen to the novice's difficulties and give them suitable advice. In the discharge of this duty I have learnt much, and above all I have found myself forced to practise what I preached. I can say with all truth that now, by God's grace, I am no more attached to the gifts of the intellect than I am to material things. Should any thought of mine please my Sisters, I find it quite easy to let them regard it as their own. It belongs to the Holy Ghost, not to me, for St. Paul assures us that *"without the Spirit of Love we cannot call God our Father,"* and is not the same Holy Spirit free to use me as a channel to convey a good thought to a soul, without my daring to look on that thought as my private property?

Besides, while I am far from depreciating beautiful thoughts which bring us nearer to God, I have long been of opinion that we must guard against overestimating their worth. Even the highest inspirations are of no value without good works. Others may derive profit from these lights, provided they be duly grateful to Our Lord for allowing them to share in the abundance of one of His more privileged souls; but should that privileged soul take pride in her spiritual wealth and imitate the Pharisee, she becomes like a person dying of starvation before a well-spread table, while his guests enjoy the richest fare, and cast envious glances, perhaps, at the possessor of so many treasures.

How true it is that God alone can sound the heart! How short-sighted are His creatures! When they find a soul whose lights surpass their own, they conclude that the Divine Master loves them less. Yet when did He lose the right to make use of one of His children to provide others with the nourishment they need? That right was not lost in the days of Pharaoh, for God said unto him: *"And therefore I have raised thee, that I may show My power in thee, and My name may be spoken of throughout all the earth."* Centuries have passed since these words were spoken by the Most High, but His ways have remained unchanged — He has ever chosen human agents to accomplish His work among souls.

PART

III

THE IRISH REVIVAL

THE "Island of Saints and Scholars" participated in the Catholic Revival but not on her own terms. The Anglo-Irish dominated the field of literature and though in time they became more Irish than English, their roots were in the English speech, and even when they participated violently in the Celtic Revival they surrounded their participation with so much moonshine that the world found them rather quaint than forceful.

The written records of Ireland were Christian and Catholic, and so were her lovely ruins at Muckross and on the rock of Cashel. Without rationalizing it, perhaps, a revival of nationalism was not to be thought if it was to be a Christian revival as well. There was a way out. Largely ignoring the Christian record, Yeats and A. E. and their followers went beyond it to the pagan period which still lingered in the legends of storytellers. Maeve and Cucuhullain monopolized the scene and the fairies and the leprechauns danced in the hills while the pagans met for annual sacrifice, it is said, on some of the enchanting islands. It was all "lovely, lovely," but it just wasn't Irish. The result of all this posturing and play acting was perhaps the most totally escape literature in all the history of the world.

As a result, the twilight group contributed little or nothing to the early Catholic Revival. In the middle period a tinge of the Catholic spirit manifested itself in some of the works of Douglas Hyde and Catherine Tynan, more magnificently in the novels of Canon Sheehan. James Joyce mirrored this advance in his beautiful short story, *The Dead,* and much more plainly in his remembered love of the Liturgy and the Little Office which set the tone for his most lyric prose in *The Portrait of the Artist as a Young Man.*

As resurgent rationalism forced a measure of freedom in the years preceding 1914, religion flamed out with it in the short lives of three men who were to be leaders in the "Easter Rebellion": Pearse, MacDonagh, and Plunkett. It was not difficult to detect their Catholic spirit: It shone in their deeds and took on added brilliance in their poems, essays, and plays. Unfortunately this promise was cut off in 1916, and Irish Catholic literature has not yet fully recovered from the hard blow.

Those contemporaries of the "martyrs" who remain show only too little of their Catholic background. The wit of Gogarty has always been more Gallic than Gaelic; it excludes him, even in his truly brilliant verse, from that kingdom where men are commanded to retain a child's simplicity.

Among the younger writers there is a renaissance of poetry. Fallon, Daiken, Patrick MacDonagh, Greacen, and Kavanagh show distinct promise but, except for an occasional poem such as Fallon's "Virgin," the high romance, the depth of Catholic culture which distinguished their fathers is missing. Perhaps a too parochial censorship lies at the root of the matter; Catholicism can get nowhere as long as it is seen as *repressive* rather than *expressive*. This is all too clearly evident in the Catholic literature of the Irish *diaspora* which glitters in the work of the D'Arcys, the Walshes, the Feeneys, and the Duggans.

The situation is far from hopeless. The massive excellence of the work of Kate O'Brien and Robert Farren gives evidence that the day will not be long in coming until the example of Pearse, MacDonagh, and Plunkett inspires a new growth in literature, with no twilight in it but only the bright texture of the dawn.

JAMES CLARENCE MANGAN

(1803–1849)

JAMES CLARENCE MANGAN, the Irish Poe, was born and died in Dublin. His parents were poor and, because of their poverty, Mangan was forced to leave school at an early age in order to labor for their support. As a scrivener's clerk and an attorney's helper Mangan spent ten bitter years. It is said that Mangan, during this time, had an unhappy love affair which lent a satirical note to his verse and goaded him into that intemperance which overshadowed his work and later life. Though proof of this assertion is not absolute, the drunkenness and eccentricity of the man are well established. Despite this evidence of weakness, Mangan was a contributor to all the great Irish magazines of his day, and left some eight to nine hundred poems as a legacy to his people.

His verse is not all of first rank. At its best, however, it is passionate and exalted, and on the patriotic level is of the highest order.

Mangan died of cholera in 1849 and was buried in Glasnevin cemetery.

MY DARK ROSALEEN*

O my Dark Rosaleen,
Do not sigh, do not weep!
The priests are on the ocean green,
They march along the deep.
There's wine from the royal Pope
Upon the ocean green;
And Spanish ale shall give you hope,
My Dark Rosaleen!
My own Rosaleen!
Shall glad your heart, shall give you hope,
Shall give you health, and help, and hope,
My Dark Rosaleen!

Over hills and thro' dales,
Have I roamed for your sake;
All yesterday I sailed with sails
On river and on lake.
The Erne at its highest flood
I dashed across unseen,
For there was lightning in my blood,
My Dark Rosaleen!
My own Rosaleen!
O there was lightning in my blood,
Red lightning lightened thro' my blood,
My Dark Rosaleen!

All day long, in unrest,
To and fro, do I move.
The very soul within my breast
Is wasted for you, love!
The heart in my bosom faints
To think of you, my queen,
My life of life, my saint of saints,
My Dark Rosaleen!
My own Rosaleen!
To hear your sweet and sad complaints,
My life, my love, my saint of saints,
My Dark Rosaleen!

Woe and pain, pain and woe,
Are my lot, night and noon,
To see your bright face clouded so,
Like to the mournful moon.
But yet will I rear your throne
Again in golden sheen;
'Tis you shall reign, shall reign alone,
My Dark Rosaleen!
My own Rosaleen!
'Tis you shall have the golden throne,
'Tis you shall reign, and reign alone,
My Dark Rosaleen!

Over dews, over sands,
Will I fly for your weal:

*The above and following poems have been selected from *Selected Poems of James Clarence Mangan*, edited by Imogen Guiney (New York: Lamson Wolffe & Co., 1897).

571

Your holy delicate white hands
Shall girdle me with steel.
At home in your emerald bowers,
From morning's dawn till e'en,
You'll pray for me, my flower of flowers,
My Dark Rosaleen!
My fond Rosaleen!
You'll think of me thro' daylight hours,
My virgin flower, my flower of flowers,
My Dark Rosaleen!

I could scale the blue air,
I could plough the high hills,
O I could kneel all night in prayer,
To heal your many ills!
And one beamy smile from you
Would float like light between
My toils and me, my own, my true,

My Dark Rosaleen!
My fond Rosaleen!
Would give me life and soul anew,
A second life, a soul anew,
My Dark Rosaleen!

O the Erne shall run red
With redundance of blood,
The earth shall rock beneath our tread,
And flames wrap hill and wood,
And gun-peal and slogan-cry
Wake many a glen serene,
Ere you shall fade, ere you shall die,
My Dark Rosaleen!
My own Rosaleen!
The Judgment Hour must first be nigh,
Ere you can fade, ere you can die,
My Dark Rosaleen!

ST. PATRICK'S HYMN BEFORE TARA*

At Tara to-day, in this awful hour,
I call on the Holy Trinity!
Glory to Him who reigneth in power,
The God of the elements, Father, and Son,
And Paraclete Spirit, which Three are
　　the One,
The ever-existing Divinity!

At Tara to-day I call on the Lord,
On Christ, the Omnipotent Word,
Who came to redeem from death and sin
Our fallen race;
And I put and I place
The virtue that lieth and liveth in
His Incarnation lowly,
His Baptism pure and holy,
His Life of toil, and tears, and affliction,
His dolorous Death, his Crucifixion,
His Burial, sacred and sad and lone,
His Resurrection to life again,

His glorious Ascension to Heaven's high
　　throne,
And, lastly, his future dread
And terrible Coming to judge all men,
Both the living and dead;

At Tara to-day I put and I place
The virtue that dwells in the Seraphim's love,
And the virtue and grace
That are in the obedience
And unshaken allegiance
Of all the Archangels and Angels above,
And in the hope of the Resurrection
To everlasting reward and election,
And in the prayers of the Fathers of old,
And in the truths the Prophets foretold,
And in the Apostles' manifold preachings,
And in the Confessors' faith and teachings,
And in the purity ever dwelling
Within the immaculate Virgin's breast,
And in the actions bright and excelling
Of all good men, the just and the blest; —

At Tara to-day, in this fateful hour,
I place all Heaven with its power,
And the sun with its brightness,
And the snow with its whiteness,
And fire with all the strength it hath,

*The original Irish of this hymn was published by
Dr. Petrie, in Vol. xviii, "Transactions of the Royal
Irish Academy." It is in the Bearla Feine, the most
ancient dialect of the Irish, the same in which the
Brehon laws were written. It was printed from the
Liber Hymnorum, preserved in the Library of Trinity
College, Dublin, a manuscript, which, as Dr. Petrie
proves by the authority of Usher and others, must be
nearly twelve hundred and fifty years old.

And lightning with its rapid wrath,
And the winds with their swiftness along
    their path,
And the sea with its deepness,
And the rocks with their steepness,
And the earth with its starkness;
All these I place,
By God's almighty help and grace,
Between myself and the Powers of Darkness!

At Tara to-day
May God be my stay!
May the strength of God now nerve me!
May the power of God preserve me!
May God the Almighty be near me!
May God the Almighty espy me!
May God the Almighty hear me!
May God give me eloquent speech!
May the arm of God protect me!
May the wisdom of God direct me!
May God give me power to teach and
    to preach!
May the shield of God defend me!
May the host of God attend me,
And ward me,
And guard me
Against the wiles of demons and devils,
Against the temptations of vices and evils,
Against the bad passions and wrathful will
Of the reckless mind and the wicked heart;
Against every man who designs me ill,
Whether leagued with others or plotting
    apart!

In this hour of hours,
I place all those powers
Between myself and every foe
Who threatens my body and soul
With danger or dole,
To protect me against the evils that flow
From lying soothsayers' incantations,
From the gloomy laws of the Gentile nations,
From heresy's hateful innovations,

From idolatry's rites and invocations;
Be those my defenders,
My guards against every ban,
And spells of smiths, and Druids, and
    women;
In fine, against every knowledge that renders
The light Heaven sends us dim in
The spirit and soul of man!

May Christ, I pray,
Protect me to-day
Against poison and fire,
Against drowning and wounding,
That so, in His grace abounding,
I may earn the preacher's hire!
Christ, as a light,
Illumine and guide me!
Christ as a shield, o'ershadow and cover me!
Christ be under me! Christ be over me!
Christ be beside me
On left hand and right!
Christ be before me, behind me, about me!
Christ this day be within and without me!

Christ, the lowly and meek,
Christ, the All-Powerful, be
In the heart of each to whom I speak,
In the mouth of each who speaks to me!
In all who draw near me,
Or see me or hear me!

At Tara to-day, in this awful hour,
I call on the Holy Trinity!
Glory to Him who reigneth in power,
The God of the Elements, Father, and Son,
And Paraclete Spirit, which Three are
    the One,
The ever-existing Divinity!

Salvation dwells with the Lord,
With Christ, the Omnipotent Word:
From generation to generation
Grant us, O Lord, thy grace and salvation!

SOUL AND COUNTRY

Arise, my slumbering soul, arise!
And learn what yet remains for thee
To dree or do!
The signs are flaming in the skies;
A struggling world would yet be free,
And live anew.
The earthquake hath not yet been born
That soon shall rock the lands around,
Beneath their base.
Immortal freedom's thunder-horn,
As yet, yields but a doleful sound
to Europe's race.

Look round, my soul, and see and say
If those about thee understand
Their mission here;
The will to smite, the power to slay,
Abound in every heart and hand,
Afar, anear.
But, God! must yet the conqueror's sword
Pierce mind, as heart, in this proud year?
O dream it not!
It sounds a false blaspheming word,
Begot and born of moral fear,
And ill-begot!

To leave the world a name is naught;
To leave a name for glorious deeds
And works of love,
A name to waken lightning thought,
And fire the soul of him who reads,
This tells above.
Napoleon sinks to-day before
The ungilded shrine, the single soul
Of Washington;
Truth's name, alone, shall man adore,
Long as the waves of time shall roll
Henceforward on!

My countrymen! my words are weak,
My health is gone, my soul is dark,
My heart is chill;
Yet would I fain and fondly seek
To see you borne in freedom's bark
O'er ocean still.
Beseech your God, and bide your hour:
He cannot, will not, long be dumb;
Even now His tread
Is heard o'er earth with coming power;
And coming, trust me, it will come,
Else were He dead!

CANON SHEEHAN

(1852–1913)

THE Irish priest is known around the world. Often adulated, frequently disliked, he is a lonely creature and seldom is known from within or properly appreciated for his quicksilver qualities and solid worth. For those who do not understand the Irish priest, the clerical novels of Canon Sheehan are at once witty psychology and astonishing revelation.

Patrick Augustine Sheehan was born at Mallow in 1852, educated at St. Colman's and Maynooth, ordained to the priesthood in 1875. He spent a year on the English mission and was parish priest at Doneraile, Ireland, from 1895–1913. In 1903 Pope Leo XIII conferred upon him an honorary Doctorate and he became a Canon in the same year. He continued to write novels of clerical life until his death in 1913.

Canon Sheehan had great talent as a literary critic and essayist, but his most enduring work is to be found in his analysis of clerical life in Ireland: *My New Curate, Luke Delmege,* and *The Blindness of Dr. Gray.* With profound insight and great humor, Canon Sheehan sketches the inner life of the Irish cleric with all its joys, weaknesses, and struggles. These are no stage Irishmen, but the stuff of great souls who found in quiet vicarages among the trees problems as great as those conquered by their predecessors in the hills and hedges.

UNDER THE CEDARS AND THE STARS*

CVIII

I COULD not help feeling this evening, as the great red shield of the moon rose solemnly above the trees, and Jupiter hung like a dewdrop in the purpled sky, that it should be a great consolation for us to know, that whatever may befall us, little creatures of God, — death, life, sorrow, joy, — the great wheel of existence swings in its beautiful and perfect equilibrium before the face of God; and that even when we shall have departed hence, and our place shall know us no more, there never shall be rift nor break in that cosmical perfection of sun, and star, and season, that seems to know its own beauty, and to exult in it before the face of its Maker. "When the morning stars sang together," may be more than a figure of speech; and it is something to know that, above this little globe of sorrow, which we so strangely call "the valley of tears," the great universe is swinging softly and majestically; and that neither Time, nor Death, the two great solvents, can wither the beauty, or tarnish the lustre of all those other creatures of Omnipotence that are so far beyond the reach of our powers to comprehend; but not beyond the scope of reason to imagine, or interpret.

CIX

Then I began to consider, why did that thought strike me just then, and not at any other time: I had seen burning noons and glorious sunsets without number; I had watched the faint sickle of the new moon in the West, and thanked her for her benevolence, when, gibbous and hunchbacked and unbeautiful, she made all things beneath her beautiful. But this idea of the symmetry and perfection and harmony of Creation had not struck me so forcibly before. Then I remembered that it was but imperfect moons and declining suns that I had seen. The former excluded all ideas of rounded and perfect beauty; the latter, with all their splendours, were the funereal accompaniments of the

death of day. But this great, red moon, burning through the latticed trees, and then paling away as it mounted higher and higher in heaven, was a symbol of the perfect beauty to which all things tend; and it rose in the night-dawn, young and beautiful, and with all the promise of uninterrupted empire all through the silent but eloquent watches of the night, until the white dawn came, and it would fade away, silent as a ghost, down the long avenues of paling stars, towards its grave in the West.

CX

You see then, to be an optimist you must have two associations — youth and the idea of ultimate perfection. Hence every child is an optimist, believing that all things are fair and beautiful; and absolutely idealizing the ugliest things until they put on the wings and outlines of perfect and immaculate loveliness. It is the glorious exaggeration of imagination without experience to clip its wings and bring it down to earth. It is only when the wheels of life begin to move more slowly, as they get clogged and debilitated, that we begin to take analytical views of life; and as our shadows lengthen in the sunset, we allow the past to project its gloom athwart our life-path, until it ends in the near perspective of the tomb. Then, we begin to reason, and shake our heads mournfully, and speculate, and haply become merely resigned. But the full tide of life creeps slowly through our veins; and we begin to pity our far-off selves, who in the imprudence and inexperience of youth, we remember to have been intoxicated with the delirium of life, and to have said aloud, or to our own hearts: All is fair and beautiful; and all is well!

CXI

Then, too, we must have the idea, so uncommon, so slippery, so often confuted, and as often revived, that all things round to final perfection. It needs a healthy brain, or well-defined religious principles, to comprehend it. The whole of literature seems to be a wail of protest against it. Now and again, a great

*Sheehan, Rev. P. A., D.D., *Under the Cedars and the Stars* (New York: Benziger Bros., 1904), pp. 145–149.

optimist, bravely cheers us onward with an expression of faith, like the song of Pippa; or the lines:

There never shall be one lost good! What was shall live as before; The evil is null — is naught — is silence implying sound;
What was good, shall be good, with, for evil, so much good more;
On the earth, the broken arcs; in heaven, a perfect round.

But this is rare! Even when Tennyson seeks to lift his verse on the wings of hope, he finds they are broken, and he falls to earth and sorrow again. And yet, there is no word so detested by men as that word "pessimism"; nor is there any verdict so dreaded by those teachers called philosophers and poets, as the sentence that their teaching is pessimistic. How is this? With so strong a tendency towards the evil thing, how is it that men so much dread the evil reputation? Yet, when you come to consider it, you will find that these writers, one and all, fall into that dreadful category of St. Paul: "Without God, and with no hope in this world."

CXII

On the other hand, you will find that the teachers who point with hope to this final perfection, even though they do not belong to the household of the faith, seem to be carried, almost in spite of themselves, along the current of pure, intellectual thought, towards it. All the terrible contradictions of life seem to merge in one great unification; and that is, that the great positives of life, — virtue, holiness, happiness, health, — are the realities that abide, and continue with a perpetual and seemingly unconscious bias, or rather destiny, towards final perfection; and that the negatives, — sin, vice, disease, death, — although obstructions, can never pass beyond their negative form; and finally fade away, or are merged in their positives, until Evil disappears; and there only remain the Beautiful and the Good. These thinkers, whom some call *Ensemblists,* those who view Life and the Universe as a whole, come very close to the poet who sings:

for somehow good
Shall be the final goal of ill;

and very near the Apostle of the *Gaudetes,* who assures us "that the sorrows of this life are not to be compared with the glory to come that shall be revealed in us."

CXIII

But this dream of final perfection and loveliness, after all, is it a forecast of what shall be in the final evolution of our species; or rather is it not the noble and cherished tradition of a race that once possessed it, and lost it? It would be difficult for the Hegelian school to construct a scheme where all things would round to perfection, considering that they place their theories on the finite and limited nature of things, which therefore are necessarily imperfect; and from whose very essence arise the concomitants of imperfection — sin, disease, death. Hegel denies the immortality of the soul, except in the restricted and unsatisfactory sense of an absorption in the Universal of the individual. But how are we to pass the bounds of imperfection, that is limitation, and reach to the Unlimited, the Perfect, he cannot say. And with the more modern evolutionist theory, the idea is still more intangible and difficult to seize. The slow process of the suns have not brought us far on the road to final perfection. There is evil — disease, vice, death. Has the horizon of human hope a gleam of a better land beyond it; or do not rather the shadows darken as we approach, without the lamp of faith, that bourn of all human sufferiings and joys, where the shadows of death encompass us, and the perils of hell may find us?

CXIV

On the other hand, how noble is the tradition, that we did possess that perfection to which all things tend, but fell from it; that, therefore, final perfection is not the lurid dream of insensate beasts, so much as the far foreshadowing of what must be, because it once was; that, therefore, being fallen, we have the power of rising again to the heights whence we were precipitated; and, above all, we are not a race, moving on to the goal, and sifting itself of all its weaker elements, so that in the survival of the fittest, its dreams of ambition may be attained. But the majesty of the individual soul shines out conspicuous in the lofty scheme of rehabilitation and resurrection; and race-abstractions, race-destinations, etc., give place to the supreme importance that attaches to each single creation of the Almighty in His scheme of universal redemption. When we speak, therefore, of the tendency of all things to final perfection, we mean the recovery of lost rights and happenings, lost dignities and glory; and these not incommensurate with our state; but our righteous privileges and prerogatives, which the sin of our ancestors forfeited; but which we may, through the sacrifice of our Elder Brother, laboriously win back again.

CHAPTER XVII

A LOWLY SAINT*

WHEN Dr. William Gray reached his home that afternoon, he was in one of those moods of agitated thought that were so frequent in him, and in which he had to walk up and down his room to regain composure. He was one of those serious and lofty thinkers that looked down upon literature and art as only fit for children dancing around a Maypole. He could not conceive how any priest could find an interest in such things, which he regarded as belonging so exclusively to a godless world that he regarded it as high treason for any of the captains of the Great Army to be attracted or drawn to them. He felt exactly towards the literary or accomplished priest, as a grim and wrinkled old field-marshal would feel if he had heard that a young subaltern had stolen out of camp at midnight and gone over to the enemy's lines to listen to the strains of some Waldteufel waltz. He would accept no hint or suggestion of compromise with the mysterious "world," which, with all its wiles and magic has been to the imagination of such ruthless logicians something like the vampire witches of mediaeval romance, from whose diabolic charms there was no escape but in instant flight. The meditation of "The Two Standards," and its terrific significance, was always before his eyes. Here was the Church, stretching back in apparently limitless cycles and illimitable, if variable power,

to the very dawn of civilization. Here was the mighty fabric of theology, unshakable and unassailable, and founded on the metaphysic of the subtlest mind that had ever pondered over the vast abysses of human thought. Here were its churches, built not to music, but to the sound of prayer — great poems and orisons that had welled out of the heart of Faith, and grown congealed in eternal forms. Here was its music solemn, grave, majestic, as if it fell from the viols of seraphs into the hearts of saints. Here was its mighty hierarchy of doctors and confessors, — pale, slight figures in dark robes, but more powerful and more aggressive than if they carried the knightly sword, or moved in the ranks of armoured conquerors. Here was its Art breathing of Heaven and the celestial forms that peopled the dreams of saints. Its literature was one poem and only one; but it lighted up Heaven, Earth, and Hell.

And there in the opposite camp was the "world" — that strange, mysterious, undefinable enemy, taking its Protean forms from climate, race, and language. There were its theatres, coliseums, forums, opera-houses with all their pinchbeck and meretricious splendour, where all the vicious propensities of the human heart towards lust and cruelty were fanned and fostered by suggestive pictures or erotic verses or voluptuous music. There, too, were its philosophic systems, vaporous, fantastic, unreal as the smoke that wreathes itself above a witch's caldron, or the

*Sheehan, Canon, D.D., *The Blindness of Dr. Gray* (New York: Longmans, Green & Co., 1909), pp. 168–175.

ashes that lie entombed in the urns of dead gods. There again is its Art, fascinating, beautiful, but picturing only the dead commonplaces of a sordid existence, or the fatal and fated loveliness of a Laïs or a Phryne. And there is its main prop and support — this literature, aping a wisdom which it does not understand, or dealing with subjects that reveal the deformities and baseness, instead of the sacredness and nobility, of the race.

"And here is this curate of mine dabbling with this infernal business; wasting his hours in subjects that would make a statue blush for modesty, or an idiot smile at their puerility. I'll stop that. He is here to do God's work and to save souls; and he must do it, or — go!"

He took up his Breviary to read; and the splendour and beauty and tenderness of its imagery made the world's literature look more tawdry and thoughtless than ever. When he came to the *Te Deum* in the office of Matins, he found that instead of saying:

Sanctus, *sanctus, sanctus* Dominus Deus Sabaoth!

the words of Goethe's song:

Röslein, Röslein, Röslein roth,

would come to his lips. He put down the well-thumbed volume in disgust.

"Serves me right!" he said. "When the devil gets his rhymes into your brain, the Spirit will depart. There is no room for Him!"

And lo! as he considered these things, the Spirit breathed upon him — a gentle and almost imperceptible breath; and his conscience woke up beneath it. The thought occurred to him for the first time that he had also undertaken the immediate charge of an immortal soul in the person of his niece. And what had he done hitherto for her? Nothing. He had amused her; put her in the way of pursuing her studies. But her soul!

He touched the bell; and bade the housekeeper send Annie to him.

"The day is fine, Annie," he said, when she appeared. "Had your luncheon? Well, then, put on your hat, and we'll have a stroll."

The day was fine and bracing; a pallid sun shed some lustre on the landscape; and there was a healthy sting of cold in the clear air, for the light frost lay in the furrows of the fields, and the ground was steeled near the ditches where the shadows fell. Annie in her tight warm jacket, with a little sealskin cap, decorated by one solitary bird, and the red flame of one feather, looked bright and beautiful, as she strove with the spring of youth to keep pace with the long, firm strides of her uncle. He strode along, buried in thought, rather heedless, as old men are, of the efforts his niece was making to keep abreast with him, until they came in view of the sea, that looked cold and joyless in its vast expanses, sailless and shadowless in its gray and lovely solitude.

When they reached the loose sand, which lay piled up near the road, he relaxed a little, and then he said abruptly:

"Can you play? Do you know anything of music?"

"Oh, yes!" she said, panting and gasping a little. "I know something of music. But I am not an experienced player. I hadn't the time."

"You won't have many opportunities of improving here," he said. "There's only one piano, that I know of, in the parish."

"Indeed? And who owns that? The Wycherlys?"

"No! They wouldn't be so absurd. It's this new curate of mine, if you please!"

"Father Liston? Oh, I'm so glad," she said with enthusiasm. "I hope 'tis a good one!"

"I believe so," he said grimly. "He gave as much for the thing as would buy a whole set of the Benedictine edition of the Fathers."

"That's delightful," said Annie. "Won't we have little concerts — but can Father Liston play?"

"I believe so. He played something for me that he called a prelude. And it was — a prelude to as good a sermon on his outrageous nonsense as he ever heard. I've seen a monkey on a barrel-organ; but it wasn't half so ridiculous as a priest sitting at a piano!"

"But, Uncle dear," said Annie, "isn't it a nice accomplishment for a young priest? I can't imagine you now sitting on a piano-stool, and playing symphonies from Bach or Beethoven —"

"Yes, Bach! That's the fellow that got him into the prelude and — the sequence. But, go on! You can't imagine me sitting on a piano-stool. Why?"

"Because you are old, and venerable, and solemn. But I can imagine you sitting at an organ, like the lovely picture of the Franciscan monk, his bare feet touching the pedals, his sandals hanging loose, and the two angels with their music-sheets in the air floating above his head."

"H'm! That's intelligible enough, although I think, that monk would be better employed praying or studing in his cell. But an organ is not a piano."

"No! But still I think 'tis lovely to see a young priest acquainted with all the masters in music and literature."

"You do? Wouldn't it be better for them to be acquainted with their Breviaries, and their Moral Theologies and the *Imitation of Christ?*"

"Well, the two can go together," said Annie, boldly.

"No!" he said, with an emphasis that startled the girl. "The two can't go together by any means. A priest is a fighter, not a play-actor. Do you suppose the devil and his legion of angels are strumming pianos — or snaring souls?"

"That's true!" said his niece musingly. "I suppose not. And I suppose the devil is very busy, Uncle!"

"He is," said her uncle — "very busy, in particular, in trying to get people to forget him."

They had crossed a long stretch of firm sand, and now emerged again into the high road, that ran under fern-laden cliffs, whence little rills of water ran down to swell the small dimensions of a stream that was ever hastening, hastening towards the great sea. Here and there, little ash-trees projected between the rocks that lined the cliff-side, their withered fronds hanging loosely in the air, pushed out by the tiny black buds that, with all the insolence of youth, were urgent for development. And far up in the air, the sharp ledges of the cliffs were fledged with pines

and infant elms; the heavy fronds of bracken, that had escaped the winter frosts, hung down and festooned the black, wet stones that seemed detached from the soft earth, and were only caught by the roots that stretched from the trees above. The road here was firm and hard, for the wintry sun never touched it; but the rime lay near the edges of the rivulet that sang and sparkled to the sea.

After a walk of about half a mile along this shaded road, they suddenly came in front of a cottage, whose gabled roof and diamond-paned windows marked it as something quite different from the ordinary white-walled cabins that form such a distinctive, if unpicturesque, characteristic of an Irish landscape.

Here the pastor stopped, and opening a little, rickety gate, crossed a narrow, gravelled path; and, without ceremony, entered the kitchen of the cottage. His niece followed; and their senses were greeted by a pungent odor of soap-suds and wet linen, whilst the air was so thick with steam that for a long time Annie O'Farrell could see nothing but the vast array of white sheets and other linen that hung in a line across the room.

"Here, Nancy," said the priest, "I have brought my niece, Miss O'Farrell, to see all your shrines and altars."

The girl rose from her bent position over her washtub; and rubbing her wet hands in her apron, she held them out, pale, and flabby and moist from her work.

"She's very welcome," she said. "But you must give me time, your reverence, to light up the statues."

"Of course, of course," he replied. "Run upstairs, and we'll look around here."

There was nothing very sightly to be seen. Great baskets of soiled clothes awaited their turn to be renovated; great tubs held the great masses that were undergoing renovation; and a great boiler hissed and steamed above the range. But yet, it was a pretty thing to see the white dainty tablecloths, napkins, handkerchiefs, cuffs, collars, lingerie of every kind, spotless and folded, and ready for human use again. It was in reality a triumph of human skill, the daily and hourly conquering of difficulties, the beautiful and fragrant ablution of all the sordidness that humanity will contract through all its daily necessities.

Annie took up a handkerchief and a collar; and with feminine instinct — for it appears to be an instinct of woman's nature to cleanse and to heal — she turned them round and round in her dainty fingers, and said to her uncle:

"They are beautifully finished. I have seen nothing like that in the steam-laundries of America."

"It is a noble life," he said, "if we could understand its significance. It is typical of the sacramental power of cleansing and purifying. And, when I add that all that work is consecrated by daily and constant prayer, for all the day long that poor girl is singing hyms or praying to the Sacred Heart, and to the Blessed Virgin, whilst she is scrubbing, and wringing and ironing and folding, you can imagine what a perfect life it is!"

"But she's paid well for all this?" queried Annie.

"H'm," he said, grimly, "there's the commercial spirit of America again. The great god, Mammon, sole ruler and final end of all mankind."

"No! I didn't mean that," she said, somewhat nettled. "But I can't imagine her giving her time and labour without being well paid!"

"Well, and what do you think she charges now, say for that collar and cuff?"

"I should say three or fourpence each at least."

"One half-penny!" he replied, "and she is very glad when she can get it."

Here Nancy came downstairs and announced that her spiritual grottoes and shrines were now fit for inspection. They mounted the narrow stairs, and entered a small bedroom with a coped ceiling, and Annie had to put her hands over her eyes to shade them from the blaze of light that now shone around statue and picture, and every holy emblem and insignia of the great Unseen, that revealed itself by faith every hour of the day to this humble and pious girl. The old man knelt down humbly, great theologian and powerful disquisitionist as he was of all the arcana which it pleases the Eternal Mind to keep veiled from the eyes of Humanity. Here, in the presence of Divine Faith so keen that it had become daily vision, all these terrible abstract questions about the secrets of Godhead, or the intervention of the Diety with human beings, seemed to fade away, as morning mists before the face of the rising sun; and he saw the stately landscape of Faith, each article clearly outlined and defined, by the light of those wax tapers purchased by the sweat and toil of that humble woman.

Refreshed in spirit, and strengthened in faith, he rose up, and after a few murmurs of admiration for the beautiful things they had seen, they descended the stairs again into the workroom; and when Annie had praised and duly honoured the dainty workmanship of the tub and mangle, they passed out into the sweet air of Heaven again.

They had gone down the road towards home a good distance, and the westering sun was casting his dying radiance across the winter landscape, and western windows were gleaming in the yellow splendour, and the tree tops were pale with colour, when, noticing the silence of his niece, her uncle said:

"Why, Annie, what's this — crying?"

She wiped her eyes, and said with a little sob:

"It's the holy Ireland of which I so often heard my mother speak!"

KATHERINE TYNAN HINKSON
(1861–1931)

WHAT Mrs. Meynell did for the Catholic Revival in England toward the end of the past century, was duplicated in the work and character of Katherine Tynan in Ireland. A witty hostess, clever novelist, and facile poet Katherine Tynan was Irish to the core and Catholic as well.

She was born in Dublin, 1861; her school days were spent at the Dominican convent in Drogheda, where her talent for writing was fostered.

Her novels are colorfully Irish but, it must be confessed, explore the surface of things more than the depths which lie beneath.

Her poetry is of a higher order: simple and tender and abounding in insight.

SHEEP AND LAMBS*

All in the April evening,
  April airs were abroad,
The sheep with their little lambs
  Passed me by on the road.

The sheep with their little lambs
  Passed me by on the road
All in the April evening
  I thought on the Lamb of God.

The lambs were weary, and crying
  With a weak, human cry.
I thought on the Lamb of God
  Going meekly to die.

Up in the blue, blue mountains
  Dewy pastures are sweet
Rest for the little bodies,
  Rest for the little feet.

But for the Lamb of God,
  Up on the hill-top green,
Only a Cross of shame
  Two stark crosses between.

All in the April evening,
  April airs were abroad,
I saw the sheep with their lambs,
  And thought on the Lamb of God.

*The above and following poems have been selected from *Ballads and Lyrics,* by Katherine Tynan (London: Kegan Paul, Trench, Trubner & Co., Ltd., 1891).

LUX IN TENEBRIS

At night what things will stalk abroad,
  What veiléd shapes, and eyes of dread!
With phantoms in a lonely road
  And visions of the dead.

The kindly room when day is here,
  At night takes ghostly terrors on;
And every shadow hath its fear,
  And every wind its moan.

Lord Jesus, Day-Star of the world,
  Rise Thou, and bid this dark depart,
And all the east, a rose uncurled,
  Grow golden at the heart!

Lord in the watches of the night,
  Keep Thou my soul! a trembling thing
As any moth that in daylight
  Will spread a rainbow wing.

GOLDEN WEED

Buttercup is golden,
  Gold is a star,
But the yellow bindweed
  Is goldener far.

Gold was the crocus,
  Like a gold cup
That the King's handmaiden
  Stately lifts up.

Gold was the daffodil
  When the winds blow;
And the white daisy
  Gold heart will show.

Gold is the reaping,
  And the great moon:

Gold was the yellow-bill
  Singing in June.

Though all the west sky
  Is flecked to gold flame,
Still my brave yellow weed
  Puts it to shame.

Dappling the wayside
  Burnt up and brown,
Till it is cloth of gold
  For the Queen's gown.

Queen you have gold hair
  Like a gold veil,
But the gold bindweed
  Turns your gold pale.

A DAY-DREAMER

Since coming from the land of dreams is
    lonely,
  And the world's daylight very cold and
    grey,
I will return beyond the sun's rim only,
  Into the gold dusk of my yesterday,

I will return through yonder purple
    coppice, —
  But O, thou love-worn nightingale, be
    still! —
Into a world of silken, scarlet poppies,
  Wherein who loveth dreams shall have his
    fill.

THE SUMMONS*

(*V. L., 14th September, 1914*)
Straight to his death he went,
  A smile on his lips,
All his life's joy unspent
  Into eclipse.

The song of the shell he heard
  Cleaving the dark,
As though 'twere the song of a bird,
  Linnet or lark.

Why would he go so fast
  Out to the dead,
All in a heavenly haste
  Not to be stayed?

What did he see afar
  That drew him after?
Light from a merry star,
  Singing and laughter?

Nay, but a face was his
  Only in dreams,
Only in dreams of bliss
  In the star-gleams.

---

*The above and following poems have been selected
from *Flower of Youth: Poems in War Time,* by
Katherine Tynan (London: Sidgwick & Jackson, Ltd.,
1915).

Nay, but a face that watched
  Long years to see
Who came by the door unlatched,
  If it were he.

What was the voice before
  That lured him on?

"Oh, thou long-hungered for,
  My son, my son!"

Lo, he hath heard, hath seen,
  He hath slipped over
Where the great days begin
  For friend and lover.

THE GREAT MERCY

Betwixt the saddle and the ground
Was mercy sought and mercy found.

Yea, in the twinkling of an eye,
He cried; and thou hast heard his cry.

Between the bullet and its mark
Thy face made morning in his dark.

And while the shell sang on its path
Thou hast run, Thou hast run, preventing
   death.

Thou hast run before and reached the goal,
Gathered to Thee the unhoused soul.

Thou art not bound by Time or Space:
So fast Death runs: Thou hast won the race.

Thou hast said to beaten Death: *Go tell*
Of victories thou once hadst. All's well!

Death, here none die but thee and Sin
Now the great days of Life begin.

And to the Soul: This day I rise
And thee with Me to Paradise.

Betwixt the saddle and the ground
Was Mercy sought and Mercy found.

THE PRAYER

(For Those Who Shall Return)

Lord, when they come back again
  From the dreadful battlefield
To the common ways of men,
  By Thy mercy, Lord, revealed!
Make them to forget the dread
Fields of dying and the dead!

Let them go unhaunted, Lord,
  By the sights that they have seen:
Guard their dreams from shell and sword;
  Lead them by the pastures green,
That they wander all night long
In the fields where they were young.

Grant no charnel horrors slip
  Twixt them and their child's soft face.
Breast to breast and lip to lip,
  Let the lovers meet, embrace!
Be they innocent of all
Memories that affright, appal.

Let their ears love music still,
  And their eyes rejoice to see
Glory on the sea and hill,
  Beauty in the flower and tree.
Drop a veil that none may raise
Over dreadful nights and days.

THOMAS MACDONAGH
(1875-1916)

THE Irish patriot was often a poet and an idealist; he had to be if he were to escape the blandishments of the "Twilight" and the flattery of government sops. Thomas MacDonagh was both idealist and poet, he was even more — a Catholic.

He was born in Ireland in 1875, and was already a writer of some eminence when he went to the National University. After taking a degree he returned to the university as an assistant professor of English Literature in which position he was closely associated with Padraic Pearse. His endeavors met a harsh termination when he was executed in 1916 for his participation in the Easter Week Rising.

MacDonagh is a fine poet. His work is characterized by simplicity and idealism not without a touch of whimsical humor.

LITANY OF BEAUTY*

Joy, if the soul or aught immortal be,
How may this Beauty know mortality?

O Beauty, perfect child of Light,
Sempiternal spirit of delight!
White and set with gold like the gold of the
    night,
The gold of the stars in quiet weather, —
White and shapely and pure! —
O lily-flower from stain secure,
With life and virginity dying together!

One lily liveth so,
Liveth for ever unstained, immortal, a mystic
    flower:
Perfectly wrought its frame,
Gold inwrought and eternal white,
White more white than cold of the snow,
For never, never, near it came,
Never shall come till the end of all,
Hurtful thing in wind or shower,
Worm or stain or blight;
But ever, ever, gently fall
The dews elysian of years that flow
Where it doth live secure
In flawless comeliness mature,
Golden and white and pure,
In the fair far-shining glow
Of eternal and holy Light.

Beauty of earthly things
Wrought by God and with hands of men!
Beauty of Nature and Art,
Fashioned anew for each life Time brings,
For each new soul and living heart!
Beauty of Beauty that fills the ken
Till the soul is swooning, faint with delight!
Beauty of human form and voice,
Of eyes and ears and lips! —
O golden hair and brow of white! —
Wine of beauty that whoso sips
Doth die to a spirit free, and rejoice,
Living with God and living with men,
Rapt rejoice in eternal bliss,
Raising his face to meet the kiss
Of the Beauty seraphic he sees above
In figure of his love.

O Beauty of Wisdom unsought
That in trance to poet is taught,
Uttered in secret lay,
Singing the heart from earth away,
Cunning the soul from care to lure, —
O mystic lily, from stain and death secure,
Till the end of all to stay!
O shapely flower that must for ever endure!

O voice of God that every heart must hear!
O hymn of purest souls that dost unsphere
The ravished soul that hears! O white, white
    gem!

*The above and following poems have been selected from *The Poetical Works of Thomas MacDonagh* (Dublin: The Talbot Press).

O rose that dost the senses drown in bliss:
No thought shall stay the wing, or stem
The song or win the heart to miss
Thy love, thy joy, thy rapture divine!
O Beauty, Beauty, ever thine
The soul, the heart, the brain,
To own thee in a loud perpetual strain,
Shriller and sweeter than song of wine,
Than song of sorrow or love or war!

Beauty of heaven and sun and day,
Beauty of water and frost and star,
Beauty of dusk-tide, narrowing, grey!

Beauty of silver light,
Beauty of purple night,
Beauty of solemn breath,
Beauty of closed eye, and sleep, and death!

Beauty of dawn and dew,
Beauty of morning peace,
Ever ancient and ever new,
Ever renewed till waking cease
Or sleep for ever, when loud the angel's word
Through all the world is heard!

Beauty of brute and bird,
Beauty of earthly creatures
Whose hearts by the hand of God are stirred!

Beauty of the soul,
Beauty informing forms and features,
Fairest to God's eye, —
Beauty that cannot fade or die
Though atoms to ruin roll!

Beauty of blinded Trust,
Led by the hand of God
To a heaven where Cherub hath never trod!

Austere Beauty of Truth
Lighting the way of the just!

Splendid Beauty of Youth,
Staying when Youth is sped,
Living when Life is dead,
Burning in funeral dust!

The glory of form doth pale and pall,
Beauty endures to the end of all.

I HEARD A MUSIC SWEET TO-DAY

I heard a music sweet to-day,
  A simple olden tune,
And thought of yellow leaves of May
  And bursting buds of June,
Of dewdrops sparkling on a spray
  Until the thirst of noon.

A golden primrose in the rain
  Out of the green did grow —
Ah! sweet of life in Winter's wane
  When airs of April blow! —
Then drifted with the changing strain
  Into a dream of snow.

WISHES FOR MY SON

(Born on Saint Cecilia's Day, 1912.)

Now, my son, is life for you,
And I wish you joy of it, —
Joy of power in all you do,
Deeper passion, better wit
Than I had who had enough,
Quicker life and length thereof,
More of every gift but love.

Love I have beyond all men,
Love that now you share with me —
What have I to wish you then
But that you be good and free,
And that God to you may give
Grace in stronger days to live?

For I wish you more than I
Ever knew of glorious deed,
Though no rapture passed me by
That an eager heart could heed,
Though I followed heights and sought
Things the sequel never brought.

Wild and perilous holy things
Flaming with a martyr's blood,
And the joy that laughs and sings
Where a foe must be withstood,
Joy of headlong happy chance
Leading on the battle dance.

But I found no enemy,
No man in a world of wrong,
That Christ's word of charity
Did not render clean and strong —

Who was I to judge my kind,
Blindest groper of the blind?

God to you may give the sight
And the clear undoubting strength
Wars to knit for single right,
Freedom's war to knit at length,
And to win, through wrath and strife,
To the sequel of my life.

But for you, so small and young,
Born on Saint Cecilia's Day,
I in more harmonious song
Now for nearer joys should pray —
Simpler joys: the natural growth
Of your childhood and your youth,
Courage, innocence, and truth:
These for you, so small and young,
In your hand and heart and tongue.

THE POET SAINT

Sphere thee in Confidence
  Singing God's Word,
Led by His Providence,
  Girt with His Sword;

Bartering all for Faith,
  Following e'er
That others deem a wraith,
  Fleeting and fair.

Walk thou no ample way
  Wisdom doth mark;
Seek thou where Folly's day
  Setteth to dark.

Darkness in Clarity
  Wisdom doth find,
Folly in Charity
  Doubting the Kind,

Folly in Piety,
  Folly in Trust,
Heav'n in Satiety,
  Death in Death's dust.

Thou from the dust shall rise
  Over all Fame,
Angels of Paradise
  Singing is thy name.

PADRAIC H. PEARSE
(1880–1916)

ONE of those who made the supreme sacrifice for the cause of Ireland's freedom was Padraic H. Pearse, born in Dublin in 1880. The son of an English father and an Irish mother, he completed his education at the Royal University and soon plunged into writing poetry and studying every phase of the Gaelic language and Irish literature.

He learned Gaelic from peasants who spoke it exclusively, and soon became fluent in the tongue. He lectured in the language at the Catholic University and became editor of the organ of the Gaelic League, *The Sword of Light*. Two schools, St. Enda's for boys and St. Ita's for girls, were founded by Pearse to teach the language by use of the bilingual system. It was among the teachers of these two schools who later became leaders of the cause that the practical idea of the Irish Republic was conceived.

He published a book of verse, *Songs of Slumber and Sorrow,* in Gaelic, and began work on an anthology of Irish verse with translations of his own. To collect funds for his schools he visited the United States. Later Pearse gave himself entirely to the Irish cause, and on May 3, 1916, paid the death penalty for his part in the Easter Uprising.

More a patriot than a poet, Pearse nevertheless has a definite place in English literature. Most critics consider his poem, *Ideal,* a masterpiece.

A WOMAN OF THE MOUNTAIN KEENS HER SON*

Grief on the death, it has blackened my
    heart:
It has snatched my love and left me desolate,
Without friend or companion under the roof
    of my house
But this sorrow in the midst of me, and I
    keening.

As I walked the mountain in the evening
The birds spoke to me sorrowfully,
The sweet snipe spoke and the voiceful
    curlew
Relating to me that my darling was dead.

*The above and following poems have been selected from *Collected Works of Padraic H. Pearse* (New York: Frederick A. Stokes Co.).

I called to you and your voice I heard not,
I called again and I got no answer,
I kissed your mouth, and O God how cold
    it was!
Ah, cold is your bed in the lonely churchyard.

O green-sodded grave in which my child is,
Little narrow grave, since you are his bed,
My blessing on you, and thousands of
    blessings
On the green sods that are over my treasure.

Grief on the death, it cannot be denied,
It lays low, green and withered together,—
And O gentle little son, what tortures me is
That your fair body should be making clay!

I HAVE NOT GARNERED GOLD

I have not garnered gold;
The fame I found hath perished;
In love I got but grief
That withered my life.

Of riches or of store
I shall not leave behind me
(Yet I deem it, O God, sufficient)
But my name in the heart of a child.

IDEAL

Naked I saw thee,
O beauty of beauty,
And I blinded my eyes
For fear I should fail.

I heard thy music,
O melody of melody,
And I closed my ears,
For fear I should falter.

I tasted thy mouth,
O sweetness of sweetness
And I hardened my heart
For fear of my slaying.

I blinded my eyes,
And I closed my ears,
I hardened my heart
And I smothered my desire.

I turned my back
On the vision I had shaped,
And to this road before me
I turned my face.

I have turned my face
To this road before me,
To the deed that I see
And the death I shall die.

CHRIST'S COMING

I have made my heart clean to-night
As a woman might clean her house
Ere her lover come to visit her:
O Lover, pass not by!

I have opened the door of my heart
Like a man that would make a feast
For his son's coming home from afar:
Lovely Thy coming, O Son!

THE FOOL

Since the wise men have not spoken, I speak that am only a fool;
A fool that hath loved his folly,
Yea, more than the wise men in their books or their counting houses, or their quiet homes,
Or their fame in men's mouths;
A fool that in all his days hath done never a prudent thing,
Never hath counted the cost, nor recked if another reaped
The fruit of his mighty sowing, content to scatter the seed;
A fool that is unrepentant, and that soon at the end of all
Shall laugh in his lonely heart as the ripe ears fall to the reaping-hooks
And the poor are filled that were empty,
Tho' he go hungry.

I have squandered the splendid years that the Lord God gave to my youth
In attempting impossible things, deeming them alone worth the toil.
Was it folly or grace? Not men shall judge me, but God.

I have squandered the splendid years:
Lord, if I had the years I would squander them over again,
Aye, fling them from me!
For this I have heard in my heart, that a man shall scatter, not hoard,
Shall do the deed of to-day, nor take thought of to-morrow's teen,
Shall not bargain or huxter with God; or was it a jest of Christ's
And is this my sin before men, to have taken Him at His word?

The lawyers have sat in council, the men with the keen, long faces,
And said, "This man is a fool," and others have said, "He blasphemeth;"
And the wise have pitied the fool that hath striven to give a life
In the world of time and space among the bulks of actual things,
To a dream that was dreamed in the heart, and that only the heart could hold.
O wise men, riddle me this: what if the dream come true?
What if the dream come true? and if millions unborn shall dwell
In the house that I shaped in my heart, the noble house of my thought?
Lord, I have staked my soul, I have staked the lives of my kin
On the truth of Thy dreadful word. Do not remember my failures,
But remember this my faith.

And so I speak.
Yea, ere my hot youth pass, I speak to my people and say:
Ye shall be foolish as I; ye shall scatter, not save;
Ye shall venture your all, lest ye lose what is more than all;
Ye shall call for a miracle, taking Christ at His word.
And for this I will answer, O people, answer here and hereafter,
O people that I have loved shall we not answer together?

THE WAYFARER

The beauty of the world hath made me sad,
This beauty that will pass;
Sometimes my heart hath shaken with great joy
To see a leaping squirrel in a tree,
Or a red lady-bird upon a stalk,
Or little rabbits in a field at evening,
Lit by a slanting sun,
Or some green hill where shadows drifted by
Some quiet hill where mountainy man hath sown
And soon would reap near to the gate of Heaven;
Or children with bare feet upon the sands
Of some ebbed sea, or playing on the streets
Of little towns in Connacht,
Things young and happy.
And then my heart hath told me:
These will pass,
Will pass and change, will die and be no more,
Things bright and green, things young and happy;
And I have gone upon my way
Sorrowful.

THE MOTHER

I do not grudge them: Lord, I do not grudge
My two strong sons that I have seen go out
To break their strength and die, they and a few,
In bloody protest for a glorious thing,
They shall be spoken of among their people,
The generations shall remember them,
And call them blessed;
But I will speak their names to my own heart
In the long nights;
The little names that were familiar once
Round my dead hearth.
Lord, thou art hard on mothers:
We suffer in their coming and their going;
And tho' I grudge them not, I weary, weary
Of the long sorrow — And yet I have my joy:
My sons were faithful, and they fought.

JOSEPH MARY PLUNKETT
(1887–1916)

THE poet and the saint seldom meet in one person as they did in Joseph Mary Plunkett, who was born in Dublin and educated at the Belvidere and Stonyhurst. Plunkett was an ardent patriot and a leader in the Easter Week Rising, which, though called abortive, lit the lamp for the eventual struggle which gave Ireland independence. With joy in his sacrifice, Plunkett was executed for his part in the Rising, 1916.

Plunkett's verse is a soldierly mysticism. He sees the necessity for life to be both aggressive and militant, but not at a sacrifice of the serenity of spirit in which all life is transfigured and made holy. As a writer of exalted lyrics flaming with emotion, Plunkett had had few equals in Ireland or elsewhere. His militant Christianity, so rich in spiritual overtones, makes the age of the heroes which had inspired most of the men in the rebellion look archaic and even anemic. Irish literature suffered a severe blow in the untimely death of Pearse and MacDonagh, but in the death of Joseph Mary Plunkett something rare and beautiful departed from Irish letters which will long wait for as deep a tone, as rare an accent.

THE GLORIES OF THE WORLD SINK DOWN IN GLOOM*

The glories of the world sink down in gloom,
And Babylon and Nineveh and all
Of Hell's high strongholds answer to the call,
The silent waving of a sable plume.
But there shall break a day when Death shall loom
For thee, and thine own panoply appal
Thee, like a stallion in a burning stall,
While blood-red stars blaze out in skies of doom.

Lord of sarcophagus and catacomb,
Blood-drunken Death! Within the columned hall
Of time, thou diest when its pillars fall.
Death of all deaths! Thou diggest thine own tomb,
Makest thy mound of Earth's soon-shattered dome,
And pullest the heavens upon thee for a pall.

*The above and following poems by Joseph Mary Plunkett have been selected from *Poems of the Irish Revolutionary Brotherhood,* compiled by Padraic Colum and Edward J. O'Brien (Boston: Small, Maynard & Co., 1916).

WHEN ALL THE STARS BECOME A MEMORY

When all the stars become a memory
Hid in the heart of Heaven: when the sun
At last is resting from his weary run,
Sinking to glorious silence in the sea
Of God's own glory: when the immensity
Of nature's universe its fate has won
And its reward: when Death to death is done
And deathless Being's all that is to be —
Your praise shall 'scape the grinding of the mills:
My songs shall live to drive their blinding cars
Through fiery apocalypse to Heaven's bars!
When God's loosed might the prophet's word fulfills,
My songs shall see the ruin of the hills,
My songs shall sing the dirges of the stars.

I SEE HIS BLOOD UPON THE ROSE

I see his blood upon the rose
And in the stars the glory of his eyes,
His body gleams amid eternal snows,
His tears fall from the skies.

I see his face in every flower;
The thunder and the singing of the birds

Are but his voice — and carven by his power
Rocks are his written words.

All pathways by his feet are worn,
His strong heart stirs the ever-beating sea,
His crown of thorns is twined with every
      thorn,
His cross is every tree.

THE STARS SANG IN GOD'S GARDEN

The stars sang in God's garden,
The stars are the birds of God;
The night-time is God's harvest,
Its fruits are the words of God.

God ploughed his fields in the morning,
God sowed his seed at noon,
God reaped and gathered in his corn
With the rising of the moon.

The sun rose up at midnight,
The sun rose red as blood,
It showed the Reaper, the dead Christ,
Upon his cross of wood.

For many live that one may die,
And one must die that many live —
The stars are silent in the sky
Lest my poor songs be fugitive.

STRIFE

Because I used to shun
Death and the mouth of Hell,
And count my battle won
When I shall see the sun
The blood and smoke dispel;

Because I used to pray
That, living, I might see
The dawning light of day
Set me up on my way
And from my fetters free;

Because I used to seek
Your answer to my prayer,
And that your soul should speak
For strengthening of the weak
To struggle with despair;

Now I have seen my shame
That I should thus deny
My soul's divinest flame;

Now shall I shout your name,
Now shall I seek to die
By any hands but these;

In battle or in flood
On any lands or seas
No more shall I share ease,
No more shall I spare blood;

When I have need to fight
For Heaven or for your heart,
Against the powers of light,
Or darkness, I shall smite
Until their might depart;

Because I know the spark
Of God has no eclipse,
Now death and I embark
And sail into the dark
With laughter on our lips.

FRANCIS LEDWIDGE

(1891–1917)

FRANCIS LEDWIDGE had little reason to be a poet; his father was an evicted farmer and Francis led a hard life as a vagabond and road mender. But sing he did, and having attracted the attention of Lord Dunsany, his first poems opened the way for a fair future in the field of literature. With the advent of World War I, Ledwidge joined Lord Dunsany's brigade. He was wounded several times and finally died in action in Flanders, July 31, 1917.

There is little formal Catholicism in Ledwidge's verses. However, he does show in the presence of nature the same wild ecstasy which distinguishes the best lyric poems of Aubrey De Vere, an indication, perhaps, of the natural mystic.

WHEN LOVE AND BEAUTY WANDER AWAY*

When Love and Beauty wander away,
And there's no more hearts to be sought and won,
When the old earth limps thro' the dreary day,
And the work of the Seasons cry undone:
Ah! what shall we do for a song to sing,
Who have known Beauty, and Love, and Spring?

When Love and Beauty wander away,
And a pale fear lies on the cheeks of youth,
When there's no more goal to strive for and pray,
And we live at the end of the world's untruth:
Ah! what shall we do for a heart to prove,
Who have known Beauty, and Spring, and Love?

The above and following poems have been reprinted by permission of Coward-McCann, Inc., from *The Complete Poems of Francis Ledwidge* (New York: Brentano's, 1919).

MY MOTHER

God made my mother on an April day,
From sorrow and the mist along the sea,
Lost bird's and wanderers' songs and ocean spray,
And the moon loved her wandering jealously.

Beside the ocean's din she combed her hair,
Singing the nocturne of the passing ships,
Before her earthly lover found her there
And kissed away the music from her lips.

She came unto the hills and saw the change
That brings the swallow and the geese in turns.
But there was not a grief she deemed strange,
For there is that in her which always mourns.

Kind heart she has for all on hill or wave
Whose hopes grew wings like ants to fly away.
I bless the God Who such a mother gave
This poor bird-hearted singer of a day.

HOME

A burst of sudden wings at dawn,
Faint voices in a dreamy noon,
Evenings of mist and murmurings,
And nights with rainbows of the moon.

And through these things a wood-way dim,
And waters dim, and slow sheep seen

On uphill paths that wind away
Through summer sounds and harvest green.

This is a song a robin sang
This morning on a broken tree,
It was about the little fields
That call across the world to me.

IN SEPTEMBER

Still are the meadowlands, and still
Ripens the upland corn,
And over the brown gradual hill
The moon has dipped a horn.

The voices of the dear unknown
With silent hearts now call,

My rose of youth is overblown
And trembles to the fall.

My song forsakes me like the birds
That leave the rain and grey,
I hear the music of the words
My lute can never say.

PADRAIC COLUM

(1881–)

INTIMATE and contemporary of the great men in the Irish revival of letters and national consciousness, Padraic Colum was born at Longford, Ireland, 1881. He was an eclectic, as he himself indicates, being as much at home with Yeats and A. E. as he was with MacDonagh, Pearse, and the two great radicals Moore and Joyce, who had a scorn of groups but loved literature.

Colum participated in all the ardent movements of his time in Ireland: in the theater, the school, and the literary salons in which the "twilighters" spun their theories and evoked their materializations of pre-Christian Ireland.

The genii of Fleet Street beckoned to Colum in the years preceding World War I, and for some time he wrote articles for Dublin and London liberal papers.

In 1914 Padraic Colum and his wife went to America. Circumstances there soon made Colum famous as a writer of children's stories: *The King of Ireland's Son* and *Legends of Hawaii* are two of his best.

Padraic Colum's fame, however, is securely established by his poetry. As a poet he is a master of lyric song which in addition to its intuitive qualities shows an awareness of sensuous beauty and mental magnificence which marks him as one of the important poets of the period.

THE PLOUGHER*

Sunset and silence! A man; around him
    earth savage, earth broken;
Beside him two horses, a plough!

Earth savage, earth broken, the brutes, the
    dawn-man there in the sunset,
And the plough that is twin to the sword,
    that is founder of cities!

"Brute-tamer, plough-maker, earth-breaker!
    Canst hear? There are ages between
    us —
Is it praying you are as you stand there alone
    in the sunset?

Surely our sky-born gods can be nought to
    you, earth-child and earth-master —
Surely your thoughts are of Pan, or of Wotan,
    or Dana?

Yet why give thought to the gods? Has Pan
    led your brutes where they stumble?
Has Dana numbed pain of the child-bed, or
    Wotan put hands to your plough?

What matter your foolish reply! O man
    standing lone and bowed earthward,
Your task is a day near its close. Give thanks
    to the night-giving god."

Slowly the darkness falls, the broken lands
    blend with the savage;
The brute-tamer stands by the brutes, a
    head's breadth only above them.

A head's breadth? Aye, but therein is hell's
    depth and the height up to heaven,
And the thrones of the gods and their halls,
    their chariots, purples, and splendours.

*The above and following poems have been selected
from *Poems*, by Padraic Colum, 1932. By permission of
The Macmillan Company, publishers.

AN OLD WOMAN OF THE ROADS

Oh, to have a little house!
To own the hearth and stool and all!
The heaped-up sods upon the fire,
The pile of turf against the wall!

To have a clock with weights and chains
And pendulum swinging up and down,
A dresser filled with shining delph,
Speckled and white and blue and brown!

I could be busy all the day
Clearing and sweeping hearth and floor,
And fixing on their shelf again
My white and blue and speckled store!

I could be quiet there at night
Besides the fire and by myself,
Sure of a bed and loth to leave
The ticking clock and the shining delph!

Och! but I'm weary of mist and dark,
And roads where there's never a house nor
    bush,
And tired I am of bog and road,
And the crying wind and the lonesome hush!

And I am praying to God on high,
And I am praying him night and day,
For a little house, a house of my own —
Out of the wind's and the rain's way.

A SAINT

The stir of children with fresh dresses on,
And men who meet and say unguarded
    words,
And women from the coops
Of drudgeries released;

And standing at their doors to watch go by
Small pomps with pennons and with first
    spring-flowers,
And, lifted over them,
Your name that sanctifies.

But you, when you came here, it was to front
Hard-handed men, and trouble them for dues
To stay the fatherless —
Portion of what they ploughed.

To claim resource from them whose own
    resource
Was pittance — this you came here to do,
And gave for what you gained
Your season of bright youth:

The hunt upon the mountain-side; the dance
Down in the vale; the whisper at the door;
Kiss on unstaying lips
That afterwards would stay;

Music you could have made would make our
    land
Of noble note and join our different breeds,
And make your name endeared
On roadside and in hall.

All this was changed, as when the warm
    stream
Setting through ocean toward vine-bearing
    isles,
Turns its flow toward capes
Where heather only thrives.

That day that was of battles and hard pledges
Has all been changed into this whitened
    morn —
Music and holiday,
And benediction bells.

FUCHSIA HEDGES IN CONNACHT

I think some saint of Eirinn wandering far
Found you and brought you here —
Demoiselles!
For so I greet you in this alien air!

And like those maidens who were only
    known
In their own land as daughters of the King,
Children of Charlemagne —
You have, by following that pilgrim-saint,
Become high vot'resses —
You have made your palace-beauty dedicate,
And your pomp serviceable:

You stand beside our folds!

I think you came from some old Roman
    land —
Most alien, but most Catholic are you:
Your purpose is the purple that enfolds,
In Passion Week, the Shrine,
Your scarlet is the scarlet of the wounds:
You bring before our walls, before our doors
Lamps of the Sanctuary;
And in this stony place
The time the robin sings,
Through your bells rings the Angelus!

KATE O'BRIEN
(*1898–*   )

SINCE James Joyce emerged on the scene of letters, Ireland has produced no novelist of first rank, except Kate O'Brien. She is of the South; born at Limerick and educated in Dublin. Her first journalistic experience was with the *Manchester Guardian*.

Miss O'Brien's novels have aroused considerable controversy. It is said that she writes shocking novels about characters who are Catholics. This is obviously untrue of the *Land of Spices,* which in its subtle pro-bing of charity drops a bombshell in the midst of bourgeois complacency and smugness. It is a deeply tender study of the anatomy of love which might have been written by a master of the spiritual life.

In the *End of Summer* Miss O'Brien displays her ability to portray character and suggest atmosphere. The tone is deft and light, but the implications of this local drama are searching and deep.

MOLLY REDMOND*

NIGHT recreation was usually taken out of doors in the summer term. The school was divided for playtime into three "recreations." Girls of the senior classes belonged to first recreation; those of honours junior, second junior and first preparatory to second recreation; and second preparatories formed a small band with the courtesy title of third recreation. At midday these groups played, on their own playgrounds, the orthodox games: hockey, basketball, tennis. But after supper they danced or took whatever exercise they felt inclined for, in winter — and in summer they loafed at their ease or sewed or played desultory rounders under the great trees. A nun took charge of each group or "recreation" and kept its members within sight and loosely in order.

Mother Agatha was mistress of second recreation during this summer term. She was fussy and incompetent, and, particularly out of doors, it was easy to hoodwink her, to enjoy tête-à-têtes with one's special friend or to talk in little groups on forbidden topics.

On this Sunday evening of May the sky, open and infinite, renewed its glory in the radiant breast of the lake; the hills had the dark bloom of grapes and seemed to breathe and sigh; the impassioned, flaming garden, held in as it was by conventual order and design, seemed for that all the more at breaking point most feverishly poised — oblated. The perfume of wallflowers was palpable, troubling the air. Fuchsia and sweet geranium foamed along the terrace, and pleasure cries, the distant songs of bathers and of boaters, rang sadly to the children from the far shore of the water.

But the trees of the convent spread their wide and tranquillising arms, and the great house stood deep-based in reproachful calm, secure in its rule, secure in Christ against the brief assaults of evening or of roses. Girls about to leave, awaiting life, felt this dismissal by the spirit of the house of the unanswered, lovely conflict implicit in the hour; heard the same victory in the voices; beyond the lawn, of nuns, taking recreation in Bishop's Walk. And so decided perhaps, tearfully, but in some outlet of relief and holding each other's hands, that Mère Marie-Félice Gravons de St. Roche was calling them.

Younger children also felt this assault from all that lay before their senses — but less conclusively, more naturally. It excited them, made imperative an immediate expression, in no matter what irrelevant direction, of ex-

*O'Brien, Kate, *The Land of Spices* (New York: Doubleday, Doran and Co., 1941), pp. 131–148.

citement. So that it was impossible this evening for Mother Agatha to gather them into a safe and docile ring. They spread away from her, sitting on the shallow steps above their playground, sitting under the chestnut tree, sitting in forbidden twos on the low window sills of the playrooms.

Anna walked by the holly hedge with Norrie O'Dowd and Katey Sheehan. These two were thirteen and therefore might sit for intermediate preparatory in June. They were foretelling their own results now on the points of holly leaves. "Honours, Pass, Fail; Honours, Pass, Fail." Anna was still ineligible for the public examination — she was twelve — so she did "Nun, Married, Old Maid" on her holly leaf.

She noticed that Molly Redmond was sitting alone with Mother Agatha at the other side of the playground; this was even more odd than her air of trouble noted at supper. Someone always had to be dutiful and hang around the mistress at recreation — but that person was *never* Molly Redmond.

"Is Molly in a row or something?" she asked Norrie O'Dowd.

"I don't know. Why? Her marks were all right, I think."

"Ursula de la Pole is 'black out' with her," said Katey. "Jenny Meldon told me during night prayers that Ursula heard something in the parlour today — and she can't be friends with Molly any more."

"Well, that's no great loss," said Norrie. "Ursula de la Pole is nothing but a stuck-up notice box."

"But what did she hear?" asked Anna.

"I don't know. Jenny said she'd find out at rec."

Ursula de la Pole stood near by, under the chestnut tree, with a group of girls around her. She was tall and thin and had bright coppery hair. She still wore a wire band on her teeth, which made her spit when she laughed, and she was still bad at her lessons. But she was a social power in second rec., as was her elder sister Barbara in first. She was snobbish and self-confident and could be amusing sometimes. Although seeming brainless, she could twist and turn the intelligent Mother Mary Andrew in any necessary di-

rection. She and Molly Redmond had had, from second-preparatory days, a cat-and-mouse attraction for each other — for Ursula liked wealth, audacity and a well-bred air, which Molly had, and Molly liked Ursula's undeveloped suggestion of glamour, her impudence and her worldly knowledge. It was a friendship of violent quarrels and giggling reconcilliations and was more an expression of frivolty in each than of heart. Molly did Ursula's algebra, and Ursula collected postcards of Gladys Cooper for Molly; they shared a passion for the king of Spain.

"It's something about Molly's father and mother, Jenny says," said Katey Sheehan.

Anna stirred uneasily. Questions of people's fathers and mothers often made serious trouble, and lately she was not sure how her own parents would stand up to the tests of second rec. Today, in spite of the all-covering happiness of being with Charlie for his birthday, she had noted with anxiety that Daddy did not wear spats on Sunday or stand up every time Mother did — which Colette Bermingham said were two proofs of being a gentleman. Also it was probable that a gentleman wouldn't fall asleep at dessert in the middle of the day.

In fact long ago Ursula de la Pole had been much impressed to learn that Anna's home was called Castle Tory, and often since then her letters, laid in the post basket on Mother Mary Andrew's table, had excited awe among her friends. "Anna Murphy lives in a castle. Did you know?" The De la Poles, generous before such a correct address, had said patronisingly that that was only natural, since Anna was a lady. "Her *grandmother* was at Saint Famille, you know — not just her mother!"

Anna had been relieved by this judgment when it was pronounced and glad that there was no fault to be found with Castle Tory. And being sealed as a lady by the De la Poles saved her from the closer assaults of the snobs.

But of late, from reading the novels of Florence Montgomery and Rosa Mulholland, she saw that the life lived in Castle Tory was not castle life, nor was it even as grand as that led by quite ordinary children of "misters" and "missuses" in those books. Mother didn't wear a tea gown in the afternoon, and she didn't ring a bell if coal had to be put on the fire, and dinner was at two o'clock, and there was no such lovely thing as "schoolroom tea." Besides, you simply couldn't call Delia a "parlourmaid," and Mrs. Rorke wasn't exactly a cook either — she was always out with the chickens or milking a cow. And as for Daddy — well, he just didn't wear spats, the fact had to be faced. And Castle Tory was really only a house, Anna told herself with anxious love — and hadn't even a conservatory.

In fact, Castle Tory was a solid stone farmhouse of good design, built in 1850 by Anna's great-grandfather, who was lucky enough to hold his land and eventually to be able to buy it from a reasonable landlord. It was placed felicitously in the shelter of an old ruined tower from which it took its name, and its owners, the Murphys, were gentlemen farmers or "squireens," with a traditional flair for the breeding of bloodstock. Anna's mother, nee Condon, was the daughter of a successful country-town ironmonger and timber merchant. So lately, from her reading and from observation of school troubles, Anna had begun to fear that the true facts about her pedigree and her address could not possibly satisfy the De la Poles.

But Molly Redmond — surely she had all the requisite splendours? She lived in a place called Monkstown, near Dublin, and her home was called Rosedene and had a tennis court and a croquet lawn. And she was always grumbling because she couldn't have a bath every day at school, and she had bangles and eau de cologne hidden in her desk, and her petticoats were pleated and made of moiré silk and were bought at Switzer's. She had been to London twice for Christmas and always spent the summer holidays at a place called Knocke. Her mother often sent her angel cake and sometimes truffles from Mitchell's, and her father had lately come to see her in a motorcar, a Mercedes, she said it was.

Besides, one day when Colette Bermingham asked her very coolly, "What *is* your father, Molly?" she said he was a turf commissioner. This was a calling no one had ever heard of, and it appeared to be very grand indeed. Norrie O'Dowd thought it was something at Dublin Castle, but the De la Poles said it had to do with the Curragh, they thought, and was an important thing to be. So what could be wrong with Molly's father and mother?

Jenny Meldon came over to them, arm in arm with Colette Bermingham.

"Isn't it awful about Molly Redmond?" said Colette.

"But what has happened?" Anna asked.

"Ursula says she'll have to leave —"

"Be expelled?"

"Well, no — but just be asked to leave. Her father and mother — you know. Do you know what her father really is?"

Norrie, Katey and Anna looked grave, all fearing that their own fathers and mothers were not proof against a De la Pole inquisition.

"No," they said together uneasily.

"He's a bookie," she whispered vigorously.

Anna winced. She did not know what a bookie was, but it sounded peculiar, and she feared that Jenny's whisper must have carried across to where Molly sat. She did not dare to look in that direction now.

"What's a bookie?" asked Katey Sheehan.

"Ursula says he's a man who takes your money at the races when you bet — and that he stands on a chair on the race course and shouts and roars. She says it's an *impossible* thing to be. Worse than having a public house even."

Norrie O'Dowd winced. Her father was in the wine and spirit trade, though he didn't have a public house.

"But she *said* he is a turf commissioner," said Katey.

"Well, he may be that too — I don't know — but anyway, he is a bookie — and it all came out in the *Irish Times* the other day —"

"Oh, it's simply terribly," said Colette in giggles of nervousness. "He is in the law courts, of all things! He won't pay for a fur coat Mrs. Redmond ordered, Ursula says

—and—but really, one oughtn't to say— ought one, Jenny?"

"Considering Ursula says that Lady de la Pole says she'll remove her and Barbara unless Molly is removed—"

"What was in the *Irish Times?*" Anna asked very anxiously.

"It said that someone said in the Four Courts that Mrs. Redmond ordered the fur coat when she was under the influence— you know—drunk!"

Jenny's eyes danced with horror and delight. The three younger girls huddled together.

"You mean—it said *in the papers* that Molly's mother was *drunk?*"

"Oh, much worse. It let out, you see, that Mr. Redmond is just a very common man— a bookie. That's what Ursula says her mother is so wild about—"

"But isn't it worse to be drunk?" asked Anna.

"It's more of a *sin,*" said Colette.

"Yes—but being a bookie is *common.* And Lady de la Pole can't bear there being such a common girl at school with Barbara and Ursula.

"Oh, but wait till you hear this—Lady de la Pole told Mother Eugenia—Barbara and Ursula heard it all, and I must say I think it was exciting for them—Lady de la Pole told old Eugenia that Sir Arthur heard some men talking about the case in the Kildare Street Club—and these men knew Mr. Redmond—he does their bets for them, or whatever it is—and they said that Mr. Redmond is sick of it all—the way Mrs. Redmond drinks, I mean—and that he said to one of them that it was high time he had a legal separation."

The three children to whom this was news, both in fact and in abstract, fell apart now, terribly shocked.

"No, Colette," said Jenny. "Ursula said that Sir Arthur said that Mr. Redmond said that he was going to have a legal separation —even if it *was* a bit late. I heard that distinctly."

Anna's heart was bursting. She saw her mother again as she was this very afternoon

under the chestnut tree, saw her drying her sad eyes and heard her say to Father Doolin: "It's too late now for a legal separation." She had wondered then only for a second what she meant. Now she stared in alarm at the phrase as it issued in Colette's violent whisper. "Drunk" too—that was a word which once or twice in the last year had sought admittance to her emotional understanding and had been thrown back by her defences of dreaminess and reluctance. During the Easter holidays she had heard Joe say to Mrs. Rorke, neither knowing she was near them, "and the master, poor man, as drunk as the divil himself." Jamesy Meagher, too, once told Charlie that Daddy was a drunkard, Charlie didn't exactly know what that was at the time, but he blackened Jamesy's two eyes for him all the same.

But Molly Redmond's mother was drunk when she bought a fur coat and her father wanted a legal separation. Two very frightening, shocking things—so bad that Ursula de la Pole couldn't speak to Molly, and Molly would have to leave Sainte Famille, Lady de la Pole said. But they were both in her family; both these things were known, and mentioned, in Castle Tory.

A girl called Alice Randolph came away from Ursula's group and put her arm round Colette's neck.

"What is a legal separation?" Katey Sheehan was asking timidly.

"It's when married people get permission not to live together any more."

"But do they have to have *permission* for that?"

"Of course they do. Marriage is a sacrament."

"It says somewhere that when people are married they are one flesh," whispered Jenny. "What does that mean?"

Norrie O'Dowd had some literary talent.

"I think it's only a figure of speech," she said.

"Do you, Norrie?" said Alice Randolph with a curious smile.

"Listen—do your father and mother sleep in the same bed?"

Norrie's cheeks reddened.

"Yes," she said slowly. And then: "Shut up, Alice Randolph," she added as she turned and walked away.

"No need to be insulted, Norrie," said Alice blandly; "So do mine."

Anna turned away too, not to follow Norrie but taking an uneasy line of her own about the playground.

Alice Randolph spoke softly to Colette.

"Do you know what it means, Colette — about being one flesh?"

Mother Agatha clapped her hands suddenly and commanded a game of rounders.

"No more of this foolish huddling together," she said. "I can't imagine what you're all whispering about! Come along now, young ladies — a nice quick game."

Most of the rec. came round her, reluctantly — only Ursula and one or two of her friends remaining under the chestnut tree as if they had not heard. Molly Redmond stood near Mother Agatha, lonely and at a loss. It seemed very strange to see her unsure of herself.

"I'll be captain of one side," said Mother Agatha, "and you, Anna Murphy, you're very good at rounders, you be captain of the other. Come on, young ladies — you must stop supporting that tree — we're choosing sides. Quickly, Anna. You choose your first man."

Anna looked round the rec. and at Molly, usually its restless queen, standing apart from it.

"Molly Redmond," she chose.

Molly smiled at her, a good attempt at the friendly, mocking smile which she gave the "little ones," and crossed to her side.

The choosing went on, and as it came near an end Ursula and her last adherent strolled over lazily, submitting themselves in boredom for selection.

It was Anna's turn to choose between the two, who alone were left. Ursula was a good runner and always quickly snapped up by a rounders captain.

"Agnes Moran," Anna chose, and the heavy, lazy girl crossed to join her side, which groaned at the captain's folly.

Anna's choosing of Molly first for her side had been an impulse of love and sympathy, which Molly's smile had suggested she understood; but her rejection of Ursula was not an expression of chivalry but only diplomatic, for she saw that it would be awkward to have the two on the same side. But as Molly glanced quickly at her again, as if searching her thoughts, Anna felt uneasy. She feared she was accidentally suggesting that she had enough courage to defend the underdog, but in truth she felt that she had not. She reflected uncomfortably that if she were socially secure, like Ursula, she would spring to fight for Molly now — but since, after all, Castle Tory was only a house, since Daddy never wore spats and got drunk sometimes, since Mother this very day had spoken of that awful thing, "a legal separation" — oh, how could anyone so shakily placed as she take up the cudgels for a *common* person? On the other hand, if what had just been said showed one to be flying false colours, if one was actually getting away with the very drawbacks which were about to ruin Molly — Anna felt guilty and anxious indeed as she called for lumbering Agnes Moran and saw the sneer of astonishment and enmity which flashed to her at once from Ursula de la Pole.

The latter was chosen by Mother Agatha, and the game began.

Anna's side went in and she batted first. On an easy long stroke she got to second den, and Molly followed her to bat.

Ursula de la Pole could field, but Molly knew how to drive a ball on a long twist. Inspirited by the general nervousness and catching for one second Ursula's contemptuous eye, she sent a fast and savage shot straight down her line.

Ursula flew like a possessed thing to field it; it was a lovely stroke and gave Anna easy time to get the whole way home and make a run. It also stirred Molly to try for third den in one without getting "burned"; this was always a difficult thing to do and was usually only attempted as an insult to bad fielding. As Ursula sped for the ball she saw her enemy's arrogant intention. Frenziedly she fielded and hurled herself back, turning quite superbly without losing a second, to run within aiming distance of

Molly. She hurled the ball with precision. It struck Molly's shoulder as the latter's hand touched the beechtree trunk which was third den. Ursula tripped in her onrush after the ball and fell headlong and flat at Molly's feet.

"Burned! Burned!" yelled Ursula's side.

"Oh no! She's in!" yelled Molly's.

During the community's evening recreation Reverend Mother and one or two other nuns had left Bishop's Walk and gone with Sister Simeon to the poultry yard to admire some chickens which she thought well of in their "foster mother." Sister Simeon had, with the years, grown devoted to incubation, and she tended now to despise the natural ways of hens.

Returning from the inspection which it had delighted the old lay sister to conduct, the nuns decided to rejoin their companions, not by the shrubberies and the lawn field but by Rosary Walk and the playgrounds.

"Since the Lord gives you such success, Sister Simeon," Reverend Mother said, praising her gently, "we must take it that He approves of your methods. But myself I feel, very cruelly perhaps, that chickens, like the rest of us, should take nature's chances."

"And leave us without a pullet to our name, is it, Reverend Mother, in the heel of the hunt?"

Reverend Mother was preoccupied, although she played her part in the recreation talk.

Just after marks, while she was writing a postscript to her monthly letter to her father, Mother Eugenia had come to her study and gossipped.

She had been in the parlour with Lady de la Pole. She was amused by the latter's agitation but also sympathetic; she had seen the *Irish Times* cutting about the Redmond lawsuit, and she thought that from the point of view of the De la Poles and the school, it constituted a situation.

Reverend Mother disagreed.

"We knew who Molly was when we accepted her. We also knew, from Mr. Redmond's own lips, of her mother's occasional — weakness. That, you may remember, was the only reason why he sent the child to school when she was only eight."

"To be sure. Being a turf commissioner is embarrassing, I suppose, but I quite see we can't all be dukes. Only getting yourself into the papers is another thing — being written about as a *bookie* who won't pay for his drunken wife's fur coat."

"He pays full fees for his daughter, Mother Eugenia — which, may I be so crude as to point out, is twice as much as Sir Arthur de la Pole does for his."

"*Touché.* But you have to pay, you know, for being the first generation to get into a school like this. Praise be to God, I often wonder what my poor father would have said if he found that his daughters were at school with his bookie's children!"

"Was Sainte Famille exclusively peerage, then, in your day?"

"Faith, no. Many's the common article was squeezed in even then. But we did draw the line at shopkeepers — and as for *bookies!* But jokes apart, my dear Reverend Mother — Lady de la Pole is in a state. She says — and I agree with her — that this Redmond thing is most unsavoury and that it is very unfortunate that Ursula has always been so friendly with Molly and that she must consult Sir Arthur again but she really thinks of removing her girls."

Reverend Mother smiled.

"So be it. At the risk of being mistaken for a shopkeeper, I must mention that, as between losing two de la Poles and one Redmond, the school accounts will not register any difference."

"You're a hard nut to crack, Reverend Mother. But don't you see it isn't the two silly de la Poles that matter, but the effect of their removal on people like them, people of their own class: Of course, if you really want to settle down to being a national school —"

"I very much want us to be a national school, in the exact sense of the word. I only wish my community would seek to understand it." They both smiled with caution. "Seriously, though, I agree that 'the Redmond thing' is unsavoury, but the unsavoriness is Molly's trouble, *not* Ursula de la

Pole's! It's a very unfortunate state of affairs for any child to have to endure through her parents. Poor Mr. Redmond! He's such a kind, affectionate man."

"Then why in God's name doesn't he pay for the fur coat and keep out of the papers?"

"Oh — one can get maddened. I imagine—"

"Jane de la Pole tells me that her husband heard at the Kildare Street Club that Mr. Redmond is going to have a legal separation, if you please!"

"It might be the best thing —"

"But a man of that class, Reverend Mother? To have the impudence to make such a show of himself! As Jane said — and she doesn't often speak sense — it really does take breeding to live down that kind of thing! But praise be — if we're going to have the bookies going in for it!"

Reverend Mother laughed outright.

"I don't think I need to point out to you the irony of that line of attack, Mother Eugenia, because I know that you do in fact put the laws of God before the assumptions of privilege. And in any case, since when have *you* allowed breeding to Jane de la Pole?"

"On my deathbed I'll deny it to the poor, climbing fool, and may God forgive me! But what are we to do with this Redmond scandal?"

"Close our eyes to it, say our prayers and let the De la Poles go. One Molly Redmond is worth six of them to any school — and if she weren't — still, let the De la Poles go."

"Well, I'm old enough to call you a caution to your face, I suppose. But there'll be trouble in the school, believe me."

"When is there not, about one thing or another? It will pass, Mother Eugenia."

"Aye, child — you're right. And so will the De la Poles — and the Fitzmichaels."

Reverend Mother was touched.

"The Redmonds too," she conceded with a smile.

But although she would not make a mountain of a vulgar little molehill, she was sorry for the sordid gossip that must by now inevitably be sweeping through the school — and she was very much troubled for its victim. And, ascending Rosary Walk, she pondered on how best to protect Molly in the coming weeks and how to guard the school against its own *nostalgie de la boue*. As she turned into the open by the great chestnut tree she saw at once, by the disposition of figures on second-recreation playground, that the baiting had begun and was at its climax. She stood, unobserved, with her nuns under the chestnut tree.

Molly leaned against a beech-tree trunk, her rigid body proclaiming her right to be there, "in den." Ursula, dirty and bedraggled as if from a fall, stood facing her some feet away. Fielders near by looked uneasy, and many of the batting side, including Anna Murphy, Reverend Mother noticed, had crossed the home line, the better to hear whatever was going forward. Mother Agatha, the ball in her hand, looked on from some distance up the field with an irritated expression on her spotty face.

"I 'burned' you," said Ursula.

"Not you!" said Molly. "I was 'in.'"

"That's a lie!"

"But honestly, Ursula, she *was* 'in,'" said a fielder.

"Shut up," said Ursula. "I 'burned' you, Molly Redmond. Are you going to admit it and get out of that 'den'?"

"Who on earth do you think you're talking to?"

"I'm talking to a *bookie's* daughter — I'm ashamed to say!"

Molly's face was as white now as the death mask of the foundress. She closed her eyes and spoke through her teeth.

"I'd hit you — only I'm too strong, and you've just had a fall, trying to field me."

"Trying to field you! As if you could play any game, you cheat!"

"I am *not* a cheat!"

Mother Agatha rang her little pocket bell and called out nervously:

"What is going on down there, young ladies? No quarrelling, if you please! Do let's get on with the game."

Neither Molly nor Ursula heard her. The girls around stood fascinated.

"You *are* a cheat — but you can't help it, of course. All bookies are cheats, my mother says! But at least you'd think he'd pay for the fur coats your mother buys when she gets — drunk."

The nuns with Reverend Mother stirred uneasily, but she did not move.

Molly had no answer now. She covered her white face with her hands but held her body straight and untrembling by pressure of her spine against the beech tree. Reverend Mother thought that she looked very beautiful and piteous then, almost as if crucified.

"Well, why doesn't he pay her bills? Does he even pay for her whiskey? Will he pay for his legal separation?"

Anna, drawing nearer, understood that Molly could not take her hands from her face while these things were being said, and it struck her that perhaps she was the only one in second rec. who was in a position to understand the true painfulness of this quarrel. She could see how startled the others were. And she thought, like Reverend Mother but more vaguely, that Molly looked very beautiful, so stiff and hard against the tree. Also her nerves remembered painfully a great kindness of four years ago.

With a last great effort she came and stood between Ursula and Molly.

"Don't, Ursula," she said very shakily. "What you're saying is private, I think."

"Private! It's in the *Irish Times!*"

Anna could not answer this. She felt she had made a bad beginning.

"Oh well — people get drunk, you know. My daddy does. Honestly."

Ursula was staring at her as if she were some kind of worm. She could hear Molly sobbing now behind her hands. She could hear Mother Agatha jingling toward them. "What is this fuss, young ladies?" She felt unnerved, she felt a fool and very small. She turned with a cowardly wail to Molly and flung her arms about her waist. She spoke to her loudly, through tears:

"He does — he gets drunk, really! And Castle Tory isn't a castle at all! And Molly, listen! Mother said today it was too late for a legal separation! I heard her! I know! Things happen we don't know about! Oh, Molly, don't mind Ursula! Don't cry!"

Mother Agatha did not interfere now because Reverend Mother stood, as if by a miracle, in the strange group by the beech tree. Her eyes were very bright, and Mother Agatha thought, with bewilderment, that she seemed as if pleased by this appalling situation.

She laid her hand on Anna's head.

"Hush, don't cry," she said very gently. "And, Molly, you have nothing to cry for at this minute, my dear child."

Molly, taken from her own rigidity by the assault of Anna, was bent above her now, in the sweet comfort and escape of comforting her.

"It is you, Ursula, who have tears to shed for all this that I have overheard, and you will shed them, my poor child — believe me." The level English voice rang deeper and more strongly than usual, and all the children listened with fast beating hearts. "For you are here at Sainte Famille to learn to live among your fellows as a Christian and a lady, and that cannot be learned by any of us without tears and humiliations. You have learned a little about that just now — by your own yielding to impulses of cruelty and vulgarity which far outstrip our usual temptations. But you have so deeply humiliated yourself before us all that I can for the moment imagine no further punishment. I shall speak to you in private, for your own sake, of the details of your dreadful fit of self-indulgence. For the moment, since I am sure you could not bear to face your companions, I suggest that you return to the house and go to bed — but on your way upstairs you will go into the chapel and ask Our Lord to purify your heart and your lips."

Reverend Mother paused. Ursula flung a wild look of misery at her and then turned quickly, with bent head, toward the house.

Reverend Mother turned to Molly.

"I am very sorry for this," she said simply and distinctly for all to hear. "I can only ask you to be so generous as to forgive us all, and perhaps, out of love of Sainte Famille, you will do me the honour of not hurting your parents by telling them of this disgraceful episode. Will you do that for us, Molly, although you have been so terribly hurt?"

Molly bowed her head and sobbed, tears streaming.

"Oh yes, Reverend Mother — oh yes, of course."

The children were surprised there had been no attempt to argue social codes, to preach equality or to investigate once again what was so rawly exposed — but only grief for Ursula's dreadfulness and this plea for Molly's pardon. They listened in wonder. "Good night now, children," Reverend Mother said. "Enjoy your rounders, all of you."

She moved away but turned again.

"Good night, Anna. No more crying."

As she rejoined the nuns Sister Simeon saw tears in her eyes although she was smiling. On the way back to Bishop's Walk a verse from Vespers came into her head, and she spoke it aloud with pleasure.

"Laudate pueri Dominum: laudate nomen Domini. Sit nomen Domini benedictum ex hoc nunc et usque in saeculum."

The nuns took up the antiphon:

"A solis ortu usque ad occasum . . ."

JAMES LEEN
(*1885–1944*)

FATHER JAMES LEEN was born in County Limerick August 17, 1885. His early education was obtained at Rockwell College in Cashel, an excellent boys' school conducted by the Holy Ghost Fathers. Father Leen later studied at the National University of Ireland and pursued graduate studies at the Gregorian University in Rome, where he received the D.D. In further preparation for his work of teaching, Father Leen rounded off his higher studies with an M.A. on Kant's Theory of Duty.

Father Leen was loved and admired by his fellow priests in the Community of the Holy Ghost. After a short period as director of the house of studies, he was sent to the missions of Southern Nigeria for two years. Upon his return to Ireland he became dean of Blackrock College and later was made president of the same college, a position which he held for ten years.

In 1931 Father Leen was appointed professor of Ethics and Philosophy in the Senior Scholasticate. A long and painful illness gave him the time for thought and prayer which resulted in his first book, *Progress Through Mental Prayer.* Having once set pen to paper, Father Leen produced in quick succession *In the Likeness of Christ, The Holy Ghost, Why the Cross,* and *The True Vine and Its Branches.* His books, published by Sheed and Ward, made him instantly popular, especially in America where he made a sweeping lecture tour in 1939. After a short illness, Father Leen died November 10, 1944.

Father Leen's treatise on the Holy Ghost is perhaps the most complete work of its kind in the English language. Of his other books, *Why the Cross,* a magnificent analysis of suffering, is his best work.

His style is lucid, his approach to human and divine problems subtly complete.

CHAPTER VII*

EDUCATION AND RELIGIOUS INSTRUCTION

THE purpose of a Christian education is to set man right in mind and will in

*Leen, Rev. Edward, C.S.Sp., M.A., D.D., D.Litt., *What Is Education?* (New York: Sheed and Ward, 1944), pp. 164–181.

relation to God, to the material world in which he lives, to his fellow-men and to himself. This rightness or wholeness of relationship to all aspects of reality must express itself in his daily actions as well as in the exercise of those activities that belong to his calling and win for him the means of subsistence. The process of education must, if it is practical — and it is defective if it is not so — whilst establishing him in *rightness,* train and prepare him for the career that will secure for him a living. Unless the training for a living is lifted to the plane of training for rightness, the living runs risk of not being a living at all, but only a subsisting. If a man is to be a man, he cannot be so by halves, or in sections of his existence. In exercising his calling he must be acting as a man. He is not doing so unless he is doing the work that is his in the spirit of one who calls God his Father. The motive that moves him must be one that derives its dynamism not solely from the livelihood that his work yields, but also from the ultimate ideal, to the attainment of which all man's deliberate actions must tend. That ideal is complete manhood as planned by God. Another name for it is personality based on supernatural life.

It is plain that for a Christian education as thorough an initiation as possible into the discipline that sets forth in full the nature of the relations established between God and man by Sanctifying Grace is of supreme importance. To live rightly a man must know what is implied by his adoptive sonship of God, and what practical consequences flow from that sonship. That relationship demands something more than simple rightness in act. It gives an elevated character to that rightness. If it is realized and acted upon, it imparts an elevation to a person's views, judgments, appreciations, bearing, manners; in a word, to a person's whole outlook upon life and things. The religion of God, that is, the religion framed by God, is necessarily calculated to forge a complete personality. It contains within itself all the resources to compass that. If in any individual case it fails to do so, it is man's subjective holding of his religion that is at fault. It may be that he possesses the right religion, but he possesses it inadequately. Its clear light undergoes refraction, distortion, diminution and dimming as it penetrates his mind and will. Grasping God's religion imperfectly, and failing to prize it at its worth, he fails to exploit its resources for the purposes of a noble life.

As has been pointed out, certain elements of a Christian formation aim at educating a man by addressing themselves to the intellect; certain others play their part by working on the will; others again direct themselves to the emotions and feelings. The formative purpose of Christian doctrine, as distinct from all the other disciplines, comprehends the whole man. It aims at forming not the intellect only, but the will and emotions as well. It must, therefore, occupy a central position in the plan of a Christian education. All the other courses must get their inspiration from it. The healthiness of their formative effect corresponds to their dependence on it. It is the hinge on which turns the whole intellectual and moral life of the pupil. On it largely depends what a student is to become.

It is scarcely to be denied that, in the adolescence of those who have now reached the half century, instruction in Christian doctrine did not receive a care and attention corresponding to the importance of that subject. The time devoted to it, the methods employed in teaching it, and the textbooks made use of, left much to be desired. The effects of this were not as bad as they might have been. The drawbacks were neutralised by a number of favourable influences that played upon the souls of the young. Life was simple and its horizons were limited; the channels of publicity were few; books were of a fairly wholesome tone; there were few points of contact with the irreligious thought working corruption elsewhere; and above all, there was an all-pervading supernatural atmosphere that favoured the growth of Christian habits of thought, in spite of the scant attention given to their cultivation. But things have undergone a considerable change in the intervening years. Now the horizons of the country parish have been shifted to all the great capitals of the world. The printing presses are pouring out, year by year, what it is no metaphor to call, a torrent of publications. A vast proportion of these is given to anti-Christian propaganda, open or veiled. The laws of morality are flouted or derided in the novels; the supernatural is left out of account, and a pseudo-science pretends to explain the universe without any need of postulating the existence of God. Not one percent, merely a tiny fraction, of all this output of printed matter, presents a view of things consistent with the Christian faith. All the specious reasoning, all the flattering of restive human passions, all the suggestions of a life freed from galling restraints, makes strong appeal to the rebellious instincts of human nature. These instincts, in Christians as in others, are always in a state of unwilling subjection to the faith. There is in them a smouldering rebellion ever ready to burst into flame. The innuendo, the gibe, the fallacious reasoning and the bland assumptions of haters and of unbelievers, come to apply the torch to the inflammable mass. The defences of the faith are forced, and the results are seen in the decline of Catholic faith and practice in great numbers who, some thirty or forty years ago, would have been dutiful and docile children of the Church.

Before the onslaught of modern life and literature, the defences of the faith revealed an alarming weakness in the case of many who seemed to have had a satisfactory Christian upbringing. The doctrine they learned at school failed either to direct or restrain them. The faith that was in them proved feeble in its resistance to the seductions of life. This caused serious anxiety to those charged with the formation of Christian youth. Anxiety led to investigations of the causes of lamentable failures that were met with in the most unexpected quarters. Blame for what was happening was laid upon defective teaching of Christian doctrine. Reform was called for on all sides. For the past thirty years quite a considerable amount of intelligent discussion has taken place concerning this matter. It has been made the object of widespread and serious study. Articles, pamphlets and books have been written dealing with systems and methods and tests. It was pointed out that the pedagogical methods used in imparting knowledge in other subjects were not employed in the classes of Christian doctrine. An accurate repetition of the words of the catechism was all that was demanded on the part of the children. The language of the catechism was criticised as too technical and too difficult. On the lips of the young people it became a confusion of sounds that could convey very little meaning to their minds. There were demands on all sides for a more simple manner of expressing the truths of the creed.

The faults found with the teaching of Christian doctrine in the secondary schools were of a graver nature still. Instruction in the faith did not keep pace with instruction in the other branches of study. There was no provision made to secure a progressive advance in such knowledge of religion as the students brought from the primary schools. There was no graded course, and there were no textbooks to make such grading possible. The teachers had in their hands nothing more than the elementary catechism, or at best, amplifications or explanations of the text with which the students were familiar from their early years. The time given to religious instruction was very inadequate. The perpetual repetition of the same text made catechism class the dullest and most monotonous of all the classes. It was not surprising that the time allotted to it was frequently encroached on by subjects more interesting and of examination value. In the university, matters were necessarily worse still. The curriculum could not, because of the constitution of the university, make provision for a course in theology obligatory on all students. It is easy to understand that a boy or girl, who had passed through a primary, a secondary and a university course in which, in each case, there was so little provision made for an ever-deepening knowledge of the faith received at baptism, was flung, very imperfectly equipped, into a world where a thousand influences worked steadily against the very idea of God.

The clamours for reform have borne fruit. There has been drafted a national progamme of religious instruction for secondary schools. This programme is arranged to suit the intellectual development of students. Admirable and interesting textbooks have been provided. In each school quite a sufficient number of hours per week are assigned to the doctrinal classes. A student who passes through the five or six years of the present secondary course enters life, or enters the university, with quite a sound knowledge of apologetics, Catholic dogma, scripture, Church history, social science and even of the liturgy and music of the Church. For the university students, lectures in theology have been made accessible; those who attend them for several years in succession can acquire a popular knowledge of theology that would compare not unfavourably with that acquired by seminarists during their four or five years of divinity studies.

Much has been done for secondary and university students, but dissatisfaction with the textbooks available for the primary schools shows no signs of abatement. By far the greater number of pupils who attend school have to face life without having had the advantages of a course of secondary studies. Those of them who are forced by circumstances to withdraw from their formative surroundings and have to practise their faith in an indifferent or hostile milieu do not, in too many instances, stand up too well to the test. Ignorance or imperfect instruction in the faith is blamed for the failure. And this ignorance or want of enlightenment is charged against the catechism itself and the methods of teaching it. It is believed that an improved text and better pedagogical methods would prove an adequate remedy for the evils that modern times have brought into light. Quite a considerable amount of talent, energy and good-will have been given, in the past twenty years, to a study of the various catechisms in use and of catechetical methods. Efforts that have not yet ended have been made to procure a simple and satisfactory text. Various pedagogical methods have been studied, applied and modified according to the dictates of experience. Experts in catechetics, and students of catechetical science have travelled abroad and investigated the systems in operation in various centres, evaluating them by the results these systems were thought to give. The idea inspiring all this enterprise was that a suitable book and a good method of teaching combined together would give to the child's

mind a knowledge, and to the child's will a love of his religion that would ensure a steadfastly good Catholic life.

Now, it seems to me, that this expectation is not justified. What follows will, most likely, meet with some contradiction, and it is put forward with all due deference to the opinion of others. It is not, at any rate, the fruit of either inexperience or hasty consideration. Twenty years ago the duties assigned to me by authority made it incumbent to submit to investigation an analysis the teaching of religion in the primary schools of a British Protectorate. The work proved absorbing; what is more, it aroused an interest in the catechetical enquiries that were then astir, and have been pursued since, with great keenness in all parts of the Catholic world. To the study of writings dealing with catechetical work has been added practical experience in primary and secondary schools. The conclusions that have been formed are the result, therefore, of long thought given both to the theory and to the practice of catechetical teaching.

It is of importance to have better textbooks and improved methods of teaching. But a book no matter how excellent, and a method no matter how sound — where method is concerned with the means employed to give the minds of the pupils facility in absorbing the doctrine taught — will never of themselves achieve, though they may help to achieve, the object aimed at by those who plan catechetical reforms. Many efforts spent on the simplification of the catechism are inspired by the belief that it is possible to produce a book which, when studied, will make of the student a convinced and reliable Catholic, devoted to his religion and a faithful observer of God's laws. This is placing altogether too much reliance on knowledge. It is another instance of the fallacy of the book, that is, the fallacy that a book can form to virtue and holiness. Such a formative power was attributed to the Bible by the Protestants. It looks as if the Catholics were going to fall into the same error with regard to catechism. It is not by the dead letter of the printed text that souls are formed to good, but by the living voice of a teacher who lives and loves the truth he imparts. Faith, now as ever, comes through hearing — but not through the mere hearing of lessons. In this connection the printed word does not supply for, it only crystallises, instruction already given. It preserves that instruction in a convenient form. The simplification of the terms of the catechism is not a matter of such importance as it is deemed to be, and it certainly does not repay all the labour spent on it.

The catechism is a simple compendium of theology in a convenient, correct and condensed form. It is hard to see why, being but this, it is expected to produce such great effects on souls. In seminaries, students in their theological course make an intensive study of all the matter contained in brief in the catechism. Theology can exert a spiritualising effect on the soul — but it does not necessarily do so. Ordinarily it is not expected to have this effect. The students, as a rule, do not seek in theological science the inspiration of their spiritual life. For them theology is something to learn and to know. It is approached as a science. The best theologians are not necessarily the most spiritual men. It is possible, in fact, that a man could have a profound knowledge of theology and yet have very little love of God. He could know much about God, and yet not know God with the knowledge given by intimacy. In school it not infrequently happens that those who carry off the prizes in the examinations in Christian doctrine are not the most distinguished amongst the students for their spirit of religion. Jewish children have been known to eclipse their Christian fellow-students in knowledge of the catechism when they have given their minds to the study of it.

For the past fifteen years the course of Christian doctrine in the secondary schools has left little to be desired for thoroughness. The examinations held every year reveal, in the excellence of the results, that the pupils have, in quite considerable numbers, acquired a good knowledge of Catholic doctrine. But the little interest in religion that follows from this proficiency is shown by the fewness in numbers of those who attend the theology lectures held for the benefit of the university

students. The indifference of our 'educated' classes to acquiring an enlightened and advanced knowledge of the faith in which they have been reared is one of the few disheartening features of our native Catholicity. With few exceptions they take little interest in works devoted to the exposition of Catholic dogma and Catholic philosophy. They are content to go through life with the meagre and rather jejune instruction they have had at school. They do not take the trouble to read the Papal Encyclicals. At heart they tend to regard them as a pious theorising that has little practical significance. They look upon them as containing just those statements which the Pope from his position is expected to pronounce at regular intervals. The Papal pronouncements on social questions, it is true, attracted some attention because it was impossible to shut one's eyes to the fact that they were extremely topical. But what little heed is given to the warning words of the Popes of the last hundred years as they analysed the philosophic errors of their days and gave warning that these errors would be the fertile source of the evils that have actually come upon the world! How few of our 'educated' Catholics are conversant with the Syllabus of Pius IX! The truth is, that as a direct consequence of our schooling, those who pass through secondary and university and professional courses attach little importance to ideas and much to facts. The positive trend of our instruction produced this mentality. All this should make one seriously doubt of the value of the knowledge acquired, and make one fairly certain that it does not serve to make a perfect Christian.

If a course in theology does not necessarily make a man a good Christian, it is hard to see why a course in the catechism should be expected to prove more effective. The wording of the catechism is not the real difficulty, however difficult that wording may be. The truths of the faith must be expressed in technical terms. It cannot be otherwise, seeing that catechism is theology in miniature. The effort to avoid these technical terms in the interests of simplification may easily lead to incorrectness. It is true that these hard words are unmeaning for the child. But the child's knowledge should not consist in knowing these words by rote. It is the duty of the teacher to take each of these terms, and by illustration and by words familiar to his hearers, explain their meaning. As a man using a hammer breaks a stone into a multitude of fragments, so the good teacher should break up the hard, incomprehensible word into a multitude of small words. After that is done the child easily associates with the word in the catechism the meaning that has been gathered from the explanation of the teacher. Good teaching could, and should, do much to obviate the necessity for reforming any of the excellent existing catechisms.

The only practical way of securing that those who are instructed in Christian schools shall be proof against the prevailing naturalism of the world is not only to inform their mind with knowledge, but also to penetrate the will and imagination with the spirit of Christianity. *To be immunized they must be Christianized through and through.* Religion is not of the intellect alone, but of the whole soul. A simplification of the catechism is not as imperative as the whole manner of approach to this question of Christian doctrine. What is needed is not so much a change in the catechism as a change in the catechists. The growing child in its character reflects not a book, but the person under whose ascendency the child comes. If the young person is to acquire a strong Christian temper, it will be done not through the dead letter of the printed page, but through a person whose own mind and will and emotional nature are attuned to the spirit of Christianity. It is not enough that the catechist know accurately the truth he teaches and the morality he expounds. He must have a love of and an enthusiasm for that truth. In his life there must be an endeavour to shape manner and conduct to the Christian moral ideal. The teaching of Christian doctrine is not mere instruction. It is an apostolic work and must be approached in an apostolic spirit. The catechist must aim at inflaming the minds and the hearts and the emotions of his pupils with an enthusiasm for their religion. This is what the first teachers of Christianity set out to do, and

succeeded in doing. The method that availed to plant the faith in pagan hearts, and to strengthen these hearts to face the loss of life rather than renounce it, must be the one that will cause that faith to flourish and extend its influence over the decisions, evaluations, and ideals of the one who is a born Christian. A virtue is strengthened by the same acts as gave it birth.

Enthusiasm for a system is difficult for the average man: enthusiasm for a Person who, perhaps, incarnates a system, comes easier. Man is not a creature of pure intellect. His imagination and feelings play their part in fashioning his life. This the first catechists understood. They gave the pagans not a system, but a personality. The whole effort of their catechesis was to present to their auditors the life and works and character of Jesus. Christianity was belief in, acceptance of, and devoted loyalty to the Person of whom the Apostles spoke. These men made it their whole object to get pagans and Jews to understand, to appreciate, to admire and to imitate Jesus, because He was what He was. Their catechism was Jesus. They spoke of His nature, His manhood, His divinity, His works, His moral teaching, His conflicts, His sufferings, His death, and above all, of the wondrous supernatural life that He offered to men. Their catechesis was a narrative. True, they synthesised it in the symbol, but that was later, a mere convenience for mind and memory, when the work of Christianizing the individual had already taken place. It was not their instrument of Christianizing. For that they relied on words that sprang warm and eloquent from minds that knew and hearts that loved the Saviour. From the Person of Jesus, true God and true Man, radiated the whole system of the religion He taught. He was like the sun, the radiant centre whence streamed forth on all sides the bright rays of divine truths that constitute the complete revelation of God to man. Each of these rays is a dogma that at once illuminates the mind and warms the heart. Jesus is the source from which man is meant to derive all his knowledge of what God is, of God's purposes, of God's relations to himself and of his relations to God: and, finally, it is through Jesus that man comes to realise what he himself is, his origin, his worth and his destiny.

It is only when mind and will and imagination are, as it were steeped in the Person of Jesus, His life, His works, His sayings, His views, His principles, His ideals, that one is strong to resist the seduction of what competes with the Saviour for the loyalty of the human heart. As things now are, as soon as a young man passes from school into the arena of life, he is assailed on all sides by the appeals of values that pretend to be truly human and that are, at the same time, in conflict with those values to which he holds by his faith. Apart from what he hears in his contacts with the Church, there is little that offers itself to his reason and his sensibility that is not to some degree, greater or less, subversive of the world of thought constructed on his faith. These false views are put forward in a very insinuating manner. They are supported by specious arguments, shallow in themselves, but having great persuasiveness for a mind unequipped with philosophy, and untrained in reasoning. His feelings, emotions, weaknesses, prejudices, in fact his whole sensitive and emotional nature, responds warmly to what promises a life fully satisfying to his instincts. The implication always is that life cannot be satisfying until the restrictions imposed by a mediaeval faith are removed.

What is the equipment of the average educated Catholic to meet this onslaught? The most completely instructed has a certain knowledge of his faith. This knowledge is very abstract. It touches his intellect, but has little *psychological* relation to his inner experience as a person whose soul is a theatre where thoughts and passions are working out the drama of his real existence. The faith scarcely touches this drama, except perhaps, on the moral issue. To how many is religion little more than a rule of morality, and the dutiful practice of religion a conformity to law! To live a good life for many is but an observance of regulations: God is for them a legislator conceived after the manner of a state ruler who punishes infringements of, and rewards fidelity to, the laws of the realm.

It is seen to be advantageous to obey, extremely hazardous to rebel. But there is little in all this that responds to man's thirst for a full life, for what will satisfy all his aspirations as a being of sense as well as of spirit. On the one hand he is solicited by a life painted in the colours that appeal to his whole nature. On the other hand he hears only the cold impersonal voice of law, announcing remote rewards and punishments. And as for the reward itself, how does it appear to him? A shadowy existence, the chief attraction of which consists in a negation, that is the absence of labour, trials, and mourning. It is an unequal struggle for the faith. There is, to be sure, always the grace of God always working secretly to nullify the advantages of the hostile forces. But in spite of that the dice are heavily loaded against the faith. Men look for life, and our teaching offers them a system.

It should be the aim of our catechetical efforts so to present the faith to the minds and hearts of the young, that it will open out to them an avenue to vital experience responding to the soul's instinctive aspirations. The life which the faith offers must outrival in attractiveness of appeal the life offered by the opposing theories of human existence. The Saviour proclaimed that He came to give life and abundant life, not merely to offer to man a system of laws. To understand His message one must understand the life that He undertakes to give. He accompanies His offer with the assurance that in that life men will find eminent satisfaction even in this world. It is strange that, though this is so, comparatively little effort is made in Catholic instruction to unveil the splendours and develop the attractiveness of this most appealing life which is given by Sanctifying Grace. One is safe in saying that to very many, to the vast majority, sanctifying grace is the equivalent of moral purity. Comparatively few realise that it is a divine energy that puts them in relations of social intimacy with God. Appeal must be answered by appeal. The analysis and development and illustration of the vital experience that divine grace opens to man, should form the central theme in religious instruction. There can be no love of what is not known. If grace is not known, what it signifies cannot be either appreciated or loved. Since it is the *thing* that supernatural religion offers, if it is not valued, religion cannot be valued. It is hard to see how God can be loved, if the life of God, as offered to us in participation, is neither known, nor in consequence, valued and loved.

Initiation into this knowledge and love is through Jesus Christ. Children should be formed to Christianity by the story of the Saviour. A story always appeals to children. The story of Jesus is a divine wonder-tale of which all fairy tales are but a feeble echo. The first contact of the child-mind with the religion of God should be through this story. After briefly explaining that God is the Supreme Being, Maker and Lord of all things, God became a baby, etc. should be the child's first introduction to the knowing of God. Then the teacher should unfold to the child, already attracted to God by the babyhood of God, what this child was. He was a baby. He had a mother, Mary. Yet, He was God. At one and the same time He was a helpless infant, and yet He was omnipotent. The word omnipotent, of course, should not be used without explanation. The child eager for wonder will not rebel at this. The child-mind rejects the contradictory but not the marvellous. It is marvellous that the Child, as man, is helpless, and as God, is all-powerful. It is not contradictory. He was God's Son — His humanity was formed by God, the Holy Ghost. This introduces the Trinity. Then comes the question of why the Son of God came on earth. There is unfolded the sad tale of the primeval fall. Man broke with God, and would no longer have God's life in him. He went his own way and left God and ceased to be intimate with Him. God sent His son to restore friendship and to give back to man's soul that life without which the friendship was impossible. Here to the child's wondering mind should be unfolded all the splendours of the life of grace. Then comes the story of the life on earth of God's Son. Vividly should be set before the young person the words, the works, and especially the kind of life Jesus wished man to live. The spiritual beauty of

that moral life taught by Christ should be painted in glowing colours to recommend the asceticism without which it cannot be. The child should be taught that this good way of acting is necessary, otherwise the soul cannot get the beautiful life of God which the soul of Jesus had and which He was anxious to share with men. This life He would give by the sacraments. This introduces Baptism and the Eucharist, with a simple explanation of each.

God's Son told men what they should do to please God. He was ordered to tell them this. But men were like Adam and wanted their own way, not God's way. They did not like what Jesus said, and so they killed Him. Jesus died because He would be obedient to what God, His Father, commanded, even though it brought Him into conflict with men and made men hate Him, and finally, kill Him. It was as man that Jesus was obedient. God was very pleased with the obedience of Jesus, and it more than made up for the disobedience of Adam. Because of it, God forgave all the wicked disobedience of all men, even of those who killed Jesus, and He willed to give them back the divine life and the friendship which that life made possible. But then they could not have it unless they were willing to act like Jesus, to be obedient like Him, to be devoted to God with Him and to love God with Him. A little might be said about the fact that the sacraments (by the grace they give) make us in a mysterious way one with Jesus. Finally, there is the end to which all this leads — going home to God, our Father, to love Him and be loved by Him for all eternity. Heaven is to be with God and live His beautiful life. In this simple way could be unfolded a summary of the whole Christian religion with a warmth of appeal that would be calculated to give the child an idea of religion far other than that derived from learning a catechism, no matter how simple the language in which it could be couched. If the catechism enters at all, it should enter at the end only, and as an adjunct to the teaching. It should come only after the mind, will, and imagination, have been captivated by the story of God on earth and the reasons why

He came. Instruction should be mainly through vivid and appealing narrative.

All religion is to know and love and understand God through Jesus Christ as Jesus is revealed in the story of His life. *To understand God is to know His Character.* And, too often, from the catechism children get from the beginning an erroneous idea of God's character. This bad start will always complicate their relations with their Creator and make religion an irksome thing. If their first introduction to God is to Him as a child coming down to earth to woo them back to His love, they cannot ever after think of Him as being but a stern, just, and inflexible judge, weighing out rewards and punishments with passionless aloofness. God is love, says Saint John. Before the child learns the stern realities of life and the terrible issues which depend on the moral struggle, he must be wholly formed to this notion of God stressed by Saint John. Nothing is so revealing of the *beautiful character* of God as the babyhood of God. When God could be a child, what is not to be expected of Him in the way of all that is gracious, loving and tender! The child learns that God is winsome before it learns of any of His other attributes. Religion must be made to appeal to feeling, emotion, sensitiveness, — to tenderness as well as to intellect, if it is to retain a firm grip on the heart and mind of man.

PART III

CHAPTER ONE

THE RESURRECTION*

"Know ye not that all we, who are baptised in Christ Jesus, are baptised in His death? For we are buried together with Him by Baptism into death: that as Christ is risen from the dead by the glory of the Father so we also may walk in newness of life." — Rom. vi. 3–4.

THE resurrection is the central dogma of Catholicism — and it is not obvious why it should be so. The Acts of the Apostles show it to be the fact in the history of Christ that is the most energetically proposed to the belief of those to whom the Apostles preached. This insistence on the resurrection in the apostolic preaching strikes us with some surprise. It is true that its value from an apologetic point of view might be sufficient explanation of its importance in the eyes of the first preachers of the Gospel. In rising from the dead, Christ proved Himself God and therefore could claim the subjection of every human intelligence to all the religious and moral truths that He had propounded to men during the three years of His public life. His Resurrection stamped all that teaching with the approval of God. It was proved true with the truth of God. It established the validity of His claim to be truly God. This reason, though it is true as far as it goes, is not quite satisfying. And it is because we see no other explanation for this passionate and reiterated proclamation of Christ's life after having been crucified, that the instructions of the first heralds of Christianity, such as they have come down to us in the sacred writings, strike us as being singularly cold and ineffective. They stir us scarcely at all. To us, accustomed to a different line of approach to the life of Christ, the preaching of the pioneers of the Gospel message appears to miss or, at least, to stress very insufficiently what is the chief appeal in the life of the Saviour. We instinctively look for a more eloquent and enthusiastic predication of the truths that Jesus came to reveal to men, especially as the Apostles had, by the light from on high received at Pentecost, obtained a vast and deep comprehension of these truths. To their minds, enlightened by the "Spirit of Jesus," what they had dimly and imperfectly understood as it had been spoken to them by the Lord became clear

*Leen, Rev. Edward, C.S.Sp., M.A., D.D., *In The Likeness Of Christ* (New York: Sheed and Ward, 1936), pp. 287–310.

and luminous. After the descent of the Holy Ghost they acquired a grasp of the whole of Christ's revelation in all its truths, in the details of these truths, and in the marvellous unity which bound all these dogmas into one vast, harmonious and dazzling system. Many a Catholic student feels a thrill which is akin to ecstasy when, having mastered in detail the different treatises of Catholic theology, the perfect unity and the inexhaustible riches of the whole system are presented for the first time in his intelligence, in one comprehensive synthetic view. Such light is but darkness compared to the effulgence that irradiated the minds of the Apostles. Is it possible that under the first ecstasy of that effulgence, their preaching could be coldly apologetic? Scarcely. Their boldness, their fire, their enthusiasm was such that those who heard them believed that they were beside themselves owing to the fumes of strong wine. They were, of a truth, delirious — but delirious with the intoxication of the new understanding of things that they had received. They were drunk, not with wine, but with wisdom and knowledge. They flung themselves forth from the upper room, under the violent impulse of the Holy Spirit, to preach Catholicity — and they proclaimed the Resurrection. This being so, it needs must be that in some way or other this dogma must embrace the whole economy of redemption — must be a compendium of the Faith. St. Paul, indeed, in his words to the Corinthians implies that for him it is such. "If Christ," he says, "be not risen again, then is our preaching vain and your faith is also vain." If we understood that mystery as did the Apostles, if we could see it in the light in which it was revealed to them and in which they must have set it before the hearers in their instructions, we would realize that this must needs be so.

The mysteries of Christ's life are something more than mere historical events. If we consider these mysteries exclusively in their historical aspect, the life of Our Lord, as related to us by the Evangelists, will be to us much the same as would be the meagre record of the acts and words of a great and good man, whose fate excites our pity and whose heroism stirs our imagination. It would be that and nothing more. But the incidents narrated by the Evangelists are something more than the lifeless facts of history. They have a life-giving potency that does not and cannot belong to the ordinary contingent incidents committed to the pages of human records. They are not something transient, having no other reality than an aptitude to furnish materials on which to build up an argument or from which to construct a theory.

The events which make up the history of Christ's mortal life are much more than all this. Far from being "dead" facts they are a perpetually energising force in the world. They are, as it were, a typical and dramatic representation of the experiences that the Christian soul must go through in the process of "divinisation." To be for us what it was for the Evangelists, the life of Christ must not be solely an external experience which we undergo. The phases of that life are to be reproduced in our personal experiences if we are to be faithful to our Christian vocation — that is, if we are to correspond to God's designs in our regard and follow the spiritual path that He has traced out for us. This is the constant theme of St. Paul's teaching.

As the Church is ever re-enacting, during all the ages, the life story of her Divine Spouse — undergoing in the Mystical Body what He suffered in His Natural Body, so it must be, too, in some measure, for every individual Christian that lives in real unity with Christ. It was thus that the saints understood the life of the Divine Master. *They not merely contemplate it, they lived it.* This was the source of the immense sympathy they were capable of experiencing for Him in His different states. They felt in a certain measure what He felt, and what is true of Our Lord's life considered as a whole must be true in no imperfect or limited manner of that which was the supreme and crowning mystery in that life — namely, the Resurrection. *This must be, not merely a fact in Christian history, but a phase of Christian experience.*

And yet it is not easy to establish the vital connection between Christ's Resurrection from the dead and our inner spiritual life. The mode of application is not readily discovered: the relation is far from being obvious. This is the reason that meditation on the Resurrection is somewhat vague and unsatisfactory, and to ordinary souls not helpful. It does not yield as fruitful results in imparting spiritual impulse as does meditation on any of the other mysteries of the life of Jesus up to and including the death on the Cross. We know that the contemplation proper to Easter Morning should give us something of great and special import spiritually, and we have a secret feeling that it has *not* been for us what the Church evidently means it to be. We do experience a certain kind of joy — but the emotion that brushes the surface of our soul is in no way comparable in depth or in intensity to the gladness we experience as we bend over the manger in the stable of Bethlehem and gaze on the face of the newly born Babe. There is something inspiriting, too, in the ascetic discipline of Lent. Conscious of our sinfulness we recognise the necessity of expiating our faults and reducing our rebellious flesh to subjection. The Offices of Lent give us courage to undergo these voluntary sufferings, and in the thrill of combat with ourselves we feel that we are doing something definite towards the sanctification of our souls. The tragedy of the Passion, the terrific drama of Calvary, cannot fail to inspire us with horror of sin, which has been the cause of it, and with love of the Incarnate God, whose tenderness for us has driven Him to undergo the torments of the Cross for our sake. This compunction for sin and gratitude to Him Who saved us from it and expiated our guilt are a sustaining force for us in our struggles with our nature. We should, therefore, reasonably expect to find, in the crowning mystery of Our Lord's life, a vigorous impetus towards perfection — and ordinarily speaking, we fail to find it. For many — even spiritual persons — the Paschal time is not one of progress, but rather the contrary. The efforts maintained during Lent are relaxed with a corresponding decline in fervour and interior recollection. During the Infancy, the Hidden Life, the Public Life and the Passion one feels near to Our Lord. His risen life seems to make Him somewhat remote from us. The "Noli me tangere," addressed by Our Risen Lord to Magdalen, haunts our minds and seems to imply an aloofness on the part of Jesus that was not exhibited before His death. We cannot enter into union with Him in His impassible condition as readily as we can do so in His passible condition. The Resurrection is for us, effectively, a withdrawal of Jesus from us; whereas according to everything in the words of Jesus on the eve of His death, it ought to be a more perfect approach of Him to us.

There is certainly something amiss in this somewhat common spiritual attitude. Things should surely not be so. If Our Lord continued to dwell on earth for some time after He triumphed over death, that portion of His life must be meant to have its own purpose and its own meaning for the spiritual life of all those who aim at assimilating themselves to Christ. It is significant that this strange but quite common mental disarray experienced by even pious souls, in their efforts to derive from the mystery of Easter its appropriate spiritual effects, is a reflection of the confusion of mind shown by the disciples when the Risen Lord appeared to them. They simply failed to adjust themselves to the situation. They could not reconcile the thoughts of their mind with the evidence of their senses. They doubted, they feared, they did not know what to believe. We should expect them to be overwhelmed with joy, but we find their joy strongly tempered by fear and perplexity. The reason is found in this, that their understanding of the significance and purpose of the life that Christ led amongst them in His passible state was extremely inadequate. Their dullness of comprehension was due to this, that they shared with their compatriots a very imperfect concept of the spiritual life and consequently of the relations that were meant to exist between them and the Saviour. They were tainted with the prevailing formalism and were probably only just a little less puzzled than Nicodemus as to what the inner transformation and rebirth mentioned by Jesus Christ could signify. They had enjoyed a close union and intimacy with Jesus during the three years together: they had little idea of a kind of union with Him other than that. Hence the Resurrection found them somewhat a loss. They experienced a mode of contact with Jesus that was both new to them and unexpected. Their view of what a spiritual life really meant had to undergo a profound modification.

The death of Christ had come as a dolorous surprise and a cruel disappointment to them; it upset all the hopes they had built on Him. So now, although the fact of the Resurrection established conclusively His claims to the Divinity, it brought them little comfort and less enlightenment. It threw no light, for them, on their own interior or exterior life. The circumstances and manner of the risen life left them little room for hope that the Resurrection would prepare the way for the reconstruction of their shattered earthly dreams. Their dreams had not been entirely dispelled by what should have been the rude awakening of the Crucifixion! But, nevertheless, with a certain sinking of the heart they vaguely surmised that the return from the tomb, though a work of such astonishing power, could not mean the undoing of what they regarded as the great defeat of the Passion. It had not yet clearly dawned on them that there was no defeat to reverse — that, in fact, what appeared to be a defeat was a final and crushing victory. Not as yet having been able to see the forces that were actually locked in combat on Calvary's hill, they did not behold the rout. Hence it was that their joy at seeing Jesus again was tempered by a certain bewilderment and disappointment. They felt that it would not mean all for them that they desired. Presuming that His life's purpose was the restoration of the temporal kingdom of Israel — and they presumed that this was His object — why, if He were able to come back from the dead, had He allowed Himself to be done to death? Had He escaped dying, a thing which was much easier in itself than coming back to life, He would, they reflected, have prevented that utter overthrow of their hopes that, for them, necessarily followed the catastrophe of Calvary. It was incomprehensible

to them that He should be able to come back to life and yet that He should permit Himself to be slain. They rejoiced to see Him again, for they loved Him. The Resurrection was a stupendous and wholly unexpected event, but remained in some sense unsatisfactory. It led nowhere as far as they could see. It did not make possible the realisation of the hopes and ambitions they had based on His leadership. It left the main problem of existence apparently unsolved.

Now all that was due to the fact that their whole outlook on the life of Christ was imperfect — which is another way of saying that their theory of the spiritual life was found wanting. They thought that union with Christ would end in a certain manner: when it did not so end they were utterly at a loss. They judged that His leaving them through death was the greatest misfortune that could befall them, although He had told them that it was expedient for them that He should go. Union with Christ was understood by them in a purely physical and material sense; they did not grasp that it was a union of mystical and spiritual kind that would bring them the advantages that Christ destined for them. They persisted in regarding His life as an epoch in the political and national history of their people; they did not understand that it was the central event in the religious and spiritual life of the race. They were very slow to realise that the life of the Master that they loved was meant to be a force in the spiritual and not in the temporal order. This realisation began to dawn on them only by degrees as they saw that the days following the Resurrection were spent by Our Lord *not in bringing about a political revolution amongst the people, but a mental revolution in themselves.* The last shadows were dispelled from their mind only on the day of Pentecost. It was only then for the first time that they understood the place of Calvary in the scheme of things.

We also have our Messianic drama when we launch forth into the adventure of close intimacy with Jesus. At first we follow Him eagerly: we look to Him expectantly to realise for us the ideal of life on earth. We outline that life for ourselves in imagination. We picture a state of things in which we shall live close by His side and in the enjoyment of a happy existence in a world bathed in sunshine — a world which He will create for us by action on men and things. Then, when He begins to drop dark hints of a cross to be endured as a means to the realisation of our ideal, doubts and hesitations arise within. The cross, far from being a stepping stone to the ideal, appears to us to bar all access to it. We cannot get the cross into our dreams of a happy existence with Christ. The cross seems to us to lie across the path to happiness, like an insurmountable obstacle. To the apostles a progress, development and improvement in the conditions of life they enjoyed with the Master prior to the crucifixion seemed something much to be preferred to the conditions of a life conditioned by death. The life they knew and enjoyed had much more appeal to them than the Risen Life with its strange and somewhat unearthly conditions. As in the case of the apostles, our difficulties with regard to a proper spiritual apprehension of the Resurrection arise from a failure to understand Calvary. We miss the true import of the Resurrection and fail in consequence to assign to it its proper place in the world of spiritual realities. For us, as for the apostles, the Cross has a certain finality, though the finality assigned to it in each case is somewhat different. For them it meant the death-knell of all their political hopes: for us it is something ultimate in the spiritual life, with nothing beyond or behind it in the present world. Absorbed in the contemplation of the Passion as an expiatory sacrifice, we see in it the destruction of our sins, and our rescue from the eternal death. If our meditations on the Passion have as their effect to inspire us with a great hatred of sin, which demanded that cruel expiation; to give us the consoling realisation of the Saviour's love which constrained Him to endure such agony for our sake; to excite in our hearts an affection which should be some response to this great love of God for us, and finally, to give us the strength to bear our crosses with the courage of which Our Lord has given us the example, it would seem that there is noth-

ing else that we should look for in these meditations. If there is anything else that we should look for from the Cross it is to be found — so we judge — in the world beyond the grave — in the happiness of heaven whose gates it has opened for us. And the Resurrection means little else to us than a pledge of our own future rising from the dead when the soul shall be united to a glorified body, to enjoy, in union with it, the happiness God has prepared for His elect. The Cross has its meaning for us in this life, the Resurrection in the life to come. We do not readily perceive that, in God's plan, not only the Cross, but the Risen Life that followed it, is meant to be part of our terrestrial existence. Christ did not pass from the Cross straight to heaven: the Christian is not meant to do so either. In the case of Jesus the cross preceded, prepared and prefaced a risen life on earth: in the case of the Christian the cross is meant to play a somewhat similar role — that is, to be the prelude to a risen life, even here below. The cross cannot be completely understood except it is viewed in the full light of the splendour of the Resurrection. It is the latter, not the former, that is the ultimate mystery for us. God is a God of the Living, not of the Dead. He is a God of Life, not of Death. In any order of things, therefore, established by Him, Life, not Death, must be ultimate. So it is that it is the Resurrection, not the Crucifixion, which must be made the object of Christian endeavour. Our rising from the dead must, in a spiritual sense, be accomplished after the pattern of Christ's whilst we are still on earth. And it is to this that we must direct all our efforts. The Cross is a means, not an end; it finds its explanation only in the empty tomb; it is an entrance into life, not a mode of death. Any death that enters into God's plan must necessarily issue forth in life. If He lays upon us the necessity of dying it is in order that we may live. In God's plan death cannot, even in a modified form, be ultimate. What is or appears to be death in the scheme of things must be, with God, nothing else than a necessary stage in the evolution of life. Life is the end of death, and not death the end of life. With Him death must issue in life.

In the spiritual order of things, which is the one towards which are directed all the operations of God's eternal plan regarding creatures, it is from our dead selves that we must rise to newness of life. This newness of life is the resurrection that is consequent on the death of revolted nature in us, that is, of that life in us which seeks its expression and development at the expense of the divine life of the soul. There is a death which is nothing else but death — and there is a death which leads to a free untrammelled existence. It is to this latter species of mortality that we are united by the Saviour on the Cross, in order that we may rise with Him to the perfect freedom of the life of Easter Morn. What in us is opposed to God must die, in order that God's life, being free from the bonds of mortality that impede it in us, may develop itself without restraint. "Know you not," says St. Paul, "that all we who are baptised in Christ Jesus are baptised in His death? For we are buried together with Him by baptism until death: that as Christ is risen from the dead by the glory of the Father so we also may walk in newness of life."

We rise to this newness of life when we are no longer under the domination of our concupiscences. When we move at the behest of our sinful inclinations we are developing in ourselves the seeds of spiritual mortality. The action of the Cross is to destroy the vitality not of the soul but of the concupiscences which constitute the dangerous disease of the soul. In order that we may live as we ought, our rebellious nature must be crucified. Crucifixion always remains the only mode of salvation.

God sends trials and crosses simply to deaden in us the activity of the forces that make for the decay of the spiritual life, in order that that spiritual life may develop and expand unimpeded. According as the life of perverse nature ebbs away from us on our Cross united with Christ's, the Divine Life that God has placed in all whom He has called begins to make itself more manifest and to display increased vigour and vitality. Our Resurrection to the newness of life, the life wholly controlled by the impulses of God's graces, comes, without any interval, straight on our death to self. It is to that Resurrection, that life in death, that God directs all the circumstances of our life — it is the object He aims at in His dealing with us. We, in our blindness, in our utter incomprehension of that rising from the dead which Our Lord speaks of to us, oppose His designs, thwart His purposes, and cling desperately to the life of self which knows no Resurrection. It is strange how history does repeat itself. Frequently, without our being aware of it, we shall be found re-echoing the words of St. Peter in which he dared to expostulate with our Lord. The Saviour spoke to him of His death and of the restoration to life that was to follow hard upon it. Peter, seeing nothing in the sufferings foretold but something abhorrent; discerning no connection whatsoever between them and the state of glory to which Christ referred; and feeling no attraction for a condition of life which, however good in itself, did not seem to hold out any prospect of greatness in the world where his ambitions were centred, quarrelled with his Master's freely chosen destiny. The risen joys to follow the passion and death had for the apostle but a very cold appeal and did not seem to him a compensation for the sufferings and ignominy and rejection which paved the way for these joys.

The difficulties which the apostles experienced on Easter Morn in adjusting their minds to the fact that the Christ Whom they knew, with Whom they had lived, and Who had died by a death that was made unmistakable by the soldier's lance, was actually before them in flesh and blood, with life coursing through the Body still showing all the marks of the terrible crucifixion, point to the conclusion that, when our Lord had spoken to them of His Rising from the dead, they always understood His words in an eschatological sense. They deemed that the Resurrection had reference to a post-terrestrial life: in a vague kind of a way they assumed it to be something that was to take place when the present world should be at an end. They had not grasped that it had a bearing on man's earthly destiny. Their beliefs in this connection were, very likely, those voiced by Martha, the sister of Lazarus, when on receiving the assurance from the Lord that her brother would rise again she immediately understood Him to refer to the resurrection at the last day. They had scarcely a conception of any other rising from the dead — still less had their minds entertained any idea of a newness of life to be attained through suffering.

And yet it is to lead us to this newness of life that God orders all the sufferings and trials He sends us in our earthly pilgrimage. Our Lord draws us towards this risen life by His example after having merited it for us by His Passion. He teaches us that to arrive at the term it is necessary that the concupiscences in us be crucified, and that it is God's love for us that orders and directs the execution. That tendency in us which makes us cleave to the creature to the prejudice of the Creator, which makes us elect perishable things in preference to eternal, must die. To reach the perfect freedom of this life that is all for God, there must be effected in us a detachment from all that is not of God. Pain and sorrow are the instruments of this detachment. It is through them that sinful desires are dulled and concupiscence reduced to a state of quiescence.

The attraction to evil that is in us, in consequence of original sin, cannot be made to disappear completely in this life. It continues to exist even in the saints. The repugnance we experience in ourselves to what God's laws desire of us, and to what our own will aspires to, retains us in humility and allows us to distinguish clearly between what we can do of ourselves and what God can accomplish in us by His Holy Spirit. The experience of our own powerlessness in the fight against the evil tendencies in our nature teaches us not to attribute to our own strength, but to God's grace, the victories we may achieve in the struggle. The ever-renewed conflict in us convinces us of the necessity of the crucifixion of our wicked nature in order that we may be able to serve God without offending Him.

To live to God we must die to sin, and this death to sin cannot be achieved without its own passion. It was through the Cross that the world was redeemed — it remains that by the Cross and the Cross only, personally borne and endured, each individual enters fully into the redemption and is sanctified. Self must die in order that God may reign in undisputed sway in us. In that lies the whole explanation of suffering in life. It is only over the hilltop of Calvary that we make our way into the brightness and splendour and glowing life of the Garden of the Resurrection. The beauty of a body, free from the corruption of sin, and the radiance of a soul filled with God's life is that in which our Calvary finds its explanation and the term in which it issues. The Cross is the way or the means to the Resurrection. Without the one we cannot have the other. If God makes the path of our life converge on Calvary it is only in order that it may lead us into the calm and peace and light of the Resurrection — of a life in which the germ of mortality, namely, concupiscence, has been successfully combated by the virtue of the grace of Christ, working through sufferings patiently accepted.

But of course, not all sufferings effect in us this wonderful transformation, which is at once an image of Christ's glorious life, and a pledge of future immortality. There were three who underwent crucifixion together on the Hill of Calvary. One of them suffered and blasphemed. Guilty though he was, he rebelled against his fate. He dared to abuse God for the tortures he had brought on himself by his own misdeeds. He railed at and cursed Divine Providence for the evil that had come upon him. "And one of those robbers who were hanged blasphemed Him saying: 'If Thou are Christ, save Thyself and us.'" So there are many, who, when crushed upon the cross of life, instead of entering into themselves, acknowledging their sinfulness and humbling themselves under the Hand of God, revile their Maker for allowing suffering to exist, or at least, for allowing it to befall them. Such men, far from being purified by their passion, plunge themselves into a worse death than that of the body. They sink from one death into one yet more profound.

There are those who when they suffer accept what comes to them in a spirit of expiation. They recognize their sinfulness and acknowledge that by reason of it they deserve chastisement at the Hands of God. Like the good thief, they cast their eyes upon Jesus and consider the fearful tortures that He endured — though sinless. Contrasting His Innocence with their own guilt, they strive not to repine at the cross to which they are nailed; they simply humble themselves under the powerful Hand of God, appeal for mercy and pardon, and beg their offended Master to accept their sufferings as an expiation of their guilt. They ask the suffering Christ to sanctify their crucifixion by applying to it the virtue of His, and they thus merit to hear from the Saviour's lips the promise that from the Cross they shall ascend into the Kingdom of Heaven. In the Cross they find that detachment from earth, that unworldliness by which their salvation is secured. Were it not for the Cross they could never have been severed from the life of earth and brought to the side of Christ.

There is still another class of sufferers. They are those who enter into a voluntary participation in the Passion of Christ — through love of Him and zeal for souls. They have passed the stage where the Cross has been active in promoting in them the love of Christ; it is now that very love which creates the Cross for them. These souls do not merely support with patience such trials as befall them; they will to suffer in order to be more like their Divine Master. They aspire to be united with Christ on the Cross not only that His life may reign in them, but also that, by their own sufferings united with those of the Saviour, effects of salvation may flow out on others. This is the highest and most sublime mode of suffering, and it is only the chosen few that enter on it.

Death implies the cessation of activity. The death through which we are to reach newness of life is the cessation of the activity of the principles of sin in us. Though, as a penalty of the First Transgression, the roots of sin itself cannot be torn out from our being, the vitality of sin can be destroyed.

The apostle does not ask us not to be sinners, but he commands us not to be the slaves of sin. He requires that its domination over us should cease: "Let not sin *reign* in your mortal bodies." The Christian who has passed through the crucible of suffering to a purification of soul is not exempt from the assaults of sin. The newness of life which he has reached cannot be retained without effort. Even the saints are not free from solicitude and anxiety. In spite of their sanctity they remain sinners, but they are not the slaves of sin. The reign of sin has ceased in them, in that they have ceased to obey its lusts. They maintain a constant struggle against their concupiscences, and when they suffer a momentary defeat they do not acquiesce in or take pleasure in the evil to which they have succumbed. They deplore their weakness, exercise themselves in humility because of it, and animate themselves with a still greater desire of union with God as a protection against it. They continue to defeat sin in its very successes.

What is true of the saints in this respect is true of ourselves in a more pronounced fashion. Even when we have experienced the Passion of Christ in our limited manner there remains a hostile force within us, and if we cease to combat it we shall not remain at peace with God nor in tranquil possession of our "risen life." The old evil inclinations, though suppressed, have not been entirely destroyed. The energy of the evil habits has diminished but has not disappeared. Even after long years of inactivity they remain ready to resume their vitality if only the occasions by which they are called into play present themselves. Things which formerly attracted us retain their power of attraction still, in some measure, and will exercise it once more unless we are vigilant and careful in protecting ourselves against their appeal. We must keep ourselves outside the range of their influence. If we, relying on our strength, place ourselves in the circumstances that once were a stumbling block to us, if we make any concession to the ways of acting that were associated with our failures in God's service, if we return to the associations that proved harmful, if there is any resumption of the old conditions of life that witnessed our betrayals of God, then there is grave danger that the smouldering passions will blaze up anew from their ashes.

If we are to preserve our new life intact we must resolutely renounce everything that once proved a temptation to us, and uncompromisingly turn our back on the old ways. We sometimes think that we can safely indulge in an innocent manner an inclination which we formerly indulged in with guilt. This is an error. If we yield in any way to anything evil in ourselves, we shall drift back, little by little, into the channels of sin. To die with Christ and to rise with Him we must push our detachment to the very root of these inclinations in us which if at any time indulged in set us at variance with God.

We must not temporise with the things which make a strong appeal to our sensitive nature. No matter how strong we may feel, we have our strength in weakness. We can never afford to relax in our war with concupiscence. This enemy, in ourselves, cannot be fought without risk, controlled without effort, restrained without anxiety. This strength of our weakness, this energy of what is death-dealing in us should make us humble, vigilant and constantly mortified.

Our conversion must then be wholehearted and must mean the paralysis, if not the death of the tendencies to evil in us. It is our affections that lead us astray by attaching us to what draws us from God. Having once broken these attachments we must on no pretext (and our nature will allege many a specious one) allow them to resume their mastery over us even in a very mild and modified form. Any affection that can draw us away from God or stand between us and God must be combated without truce.

The most successful way to overcome these dangerous attractions is to set up a counter-attraction. Life is not a negative process. It is positive. The new life must not consist in the mere cessation of loving what is evil; it must express itself in the love of what is good. Newness of life does not consist merely in the efforts to avoid sin — it means the positive endeavour to live for God. We die

to sin in order to live to God. The destination of our faculties to the interests of God is the characteristic of that resurrection of the soul that follows on its dying in union with Christ. The aim of the soul that has once been purified (or converted) should be not merely to have an aversion to what is evil, but to conceive a strong love for what is good. Love of God, not mere aversion from sin, should be the controlling motive in its new life. Renovation or Resurrection must mean a new love. When at our being broken on the cross, all the false idols which we worshipped in our hearts tumble into dust before our eyes, we must not allow ourselves to be still and motionless in the tomb of our dead selves. We must, by laying hold on Christ, rise to a new object of love and worship in our hearts. Devotedness to God and His interests is the exercise of the vitality of the life that comes of the death on the Cross.

It is inevitable that suffering should sooner or later present itself in the life of each individual and mingle its bitter savour with every kind of pleasure, even the purest, that one wishes to extract from existence. It did not enter into God's original plan. It is through man's act that it made its way into human life. Owing its origin to human perversity, it is evident that it is an evil thing. It is a foretaste and a beginning of death. God's power and goodness is shown in making this evil thing, this result of man's wrongdoing, an instrument of good. He permits us to suffer. He does not choose to destroy the consequences of the use of our free wills. He prefers to repair these evil consequences. It does not become Him to undo what He has once done — it would be on His part a confession of miscalculation, error, want of prevision. He created, foreseeing the entry into the world of sin and suffering in the train, and as the logical issue of sin, and He takes that evil thing and makes it productive of good. He permits us to suffer, not because He takes pleasure in our suffering, but because He sees that as things now are it is only by suffering that are burned away in our souls the obstacles to the free operations of grace. He does not take away sufferings, but He gives us the power and the means to turn our sufferings to good account. He makes that which is the fruit of sin itself effect the destruction of sin in our souls. He shows us His Divine Son suffering and He invites us to endure our sufferings with the like dispositions, promising us that if we be like Him in His death, we shall be like Him in His Resurrection from death. God exhibited to us in the risen life of the Saviour the type and example of what our life on earth shall be, if we willingly undergo the trials and hardships that are its condition and its preparation. Not all sufferings are salutary: it is only those that are endured in union with Christ. Suffer we must whatever be the spirit in which we endure suffering. It we look upon the pains of this life as an evil thing only and, therefore, as something which we must struggle against desperately we shall not assuage but intensify the bitterness of life. If,

on the other hand, we look upon sufferings as the necessary instrument in the purification of our souls, if we accept them from the Hands of God as such, and if we draw from Christ's passion the strength to bear them in humble submission to God's providence, we through them, free our souls from the contagion of mortality, and heal in our souls the wounds inflicted on them by sin. Through sufferings endured in conformity with Christ we work our way steadily back towards the condition of original justice in which sense was perfectly subject to the spirit, and the spirit to God. Through sufferings, endured supernaturally, we clothe ourselves with the justice of Christ, the new Adam. When nature is dead in us and its rebellious stirrings are quieted we walk in newness of life and in the peace of the Resurrection. If we consent to die with Christ, then also we shall rise from the tomb of our dead selves to live with Christ.

ROBERT FARREN

(*1909–   *)

ROBERT FARREN is a native of Dublin and descendant of Dubliners, with the quicksilver qualities such living and ancestry implies. He attended the primary schools of the Christian Brothers, was trained as a teacher at St. Patrick's College, Drumcondra, and took his master's degree in Scholastic Philosophy at the National University of Ireland.

He was a primary school teacher for ten years before he became director of Gaelic broadcasts at Radio Eirann, principal broadcasting house of Eire. In 1940 Farren was appointed to the board of directors of the Abbey Theatre which, with his work as a writer and his duties at Radio Eirann, gives him a full life.

His poetry is masculine, ardent, direct. From his first book of poems, *Thronging Feet* (1936), to his epic, *This Man Was Ireland,* he shows a consistent development both in techniques and the particular manly qualities which mark him as one of the significant poets of our time.

TWO POETS*

There's a poet from Kiltimagh
and a poet from Gougane Barra;
one has the head of a hawk,
the other the head of a sparrow.

Now the poet from Kiltimagh
and the poet from Gougane Barra
both know that the pitiless hawk
eats the pitiful poor cocksparrow.

And mebbe that's why they don't talk,
not even to say Good-morrow,
the poet from Kiltimagh
and the poet from Gougane Barra.

*The above and following poems have been selected from *Rime, Gentlemen, Please*, by Robert Farren (New York: Sheed and Ward, 1945).

MARTYR'S SON

Everyone else had toys from his father.
Everyone else played "Lions" with his father.
Everyone else has diary and picture
in memory's print on the page of his brain.

Everyone's father's a private inheritance.
But a Public Father, Father of a Glory,
with no private image or character behind
    him
spied by one's personal eyes or brain,
is a title to live up to, deprived of the means.

Then, everyone you see, sees only your father:
you talk — they attend to his talk, not yours —
making you ever the seance medium,
to be heard-through, not to be heard.

Everyone else had toys from his father.
Everyone else played "Lions" with his father.
Everyone else inherits your father,
while you —
have not even a separate grave to see.

NO WOMAN BORN

Young head in sunlight! Not a woman born
has lifted head like her head; plenty's horn
poured no alight abundance like her hair.
Wonder is on her lids like the bright air.

She wakes to worship, and draws-on dull
    mouths to prayer.
There is, to be named one with her, no
    woman born.

PAPAL LEGATE, 1932

*(In Memory of Cardinal Lauri and the
Eucharistic Congress, Dublin.)*

If we had been a little less au fait
with rudimentary theology,
we might have thought the Church Tri-
    umphant 'twas,
landed from Rome upon Dunleary Pier.
These were no living spaldings of the Mass-
    Rock,
no pitchcaps' legatees — their cardinal red,
their monseignorial purple, and the ruff,
the silk sock and the sword
of the lay suite, had other history.

O when I saw them walk,
with all the guessed-at, groped-for atmosphere
of two millennia of Pontiffs' Rome

in vested bodies and in beards' uptilt,
it was as though the Cardinal's Chamberlain
flourished his sword and pierced me — into
    life!
We were familiar with perfervid faith,
with martyrdom, and Christ's Wounds in
    His Bride's
stigmatic body: we had never seen
His Bride's Body answering as the moon
to the sun-splendour of the Risen Christ.
The Church Militant, Petrine, proud,
walked on an Irish street for the first hour
since, in the tower-crammed Kilkenny town,
Il Grande Legato
Giovan Batista
Rinnucini trod,
with Owen Roe.

WINTER WORDS

I

I said to God, "The trees are thin as bones
picked by some jungle beast, the fields are
    stones,
the waters withered into bleak, blue ice,
the sky silenced, without birdbill cries —
the things Thou madest Thou has stricken
    dead."
"Thou fool, look round thee; nothing dies,"
    God said.

I looked around me; and I saw a tree
nuzzling earth's nipples; and a seeded field;
a sky certain of the rolling sun,
waters like whippets tingling for the run. . .
I felt in all my flesh and all my blood
the rearing world, held, by the wrist of God.

II

I had not seen till then
a lawn like a lathered chin;
or guessed that long frost could
make fields froth like tubs;
conceived the meek-faced grass,
violent-willed, hid force
like Furies' heads.
But then, that sud, that spray,
that wild green under gray!

III

The bursting-out of buds in spring rang the
    power of the sun;
I saw the sea walk up the road on the fierce
    hooves of rain;
the wind was its own bellman and struck an
    enormous tongue;
but frost ruled worlds in silence like some
    tremendous brain.

SLEEP

While now I lay me down to sleep
I pray to God my soul to keep,
that, riding out with sleep to-night,
it may turn back with morning's light.

Or, if in sleep it slip my clay,
may it blaze back to that High Day
it left behind to make me man
out of the thing that flesh began. . .

Though flesh and flesh together go
and man beget and woman grow,
yet is there nothing human made
till the new spirit start its trade.

Aye, flesh can sow in flesh, and can
raise crop, but not the crop of man:
until the down-sent soul is come
no human hand or head's begun;
until the ripeness feel the soul
entice it to contrive man-bone
the passion-sown, womb-stemming plant,
bid to turn human, cannot start;

and God makes freshly each new soul,
God, the all-making God, alone.

Then, ghostly-begun by Holy Ghost,
soul to its groping man-thing gropes
and soul and thing make man. Man, born,
walks the wild, haunted world in storm,
in head's and heart's and hand's bright force;
till head, heart, hand each failing goes
earth under haunted earth to turn
down being's steps to stem and worm.
But back the perpetual soul, impelled,
hurtles to Christ, the Lustrous Head.

There then's the map, the world's design
which all forms fit — man, sleep and time.

By hand's and heart's and head's bright force
the living man through earth's life goes;
but force of hand in soul begins,
and souls have force beyond hearts' brims;
so, thought for wing, soul levitates
loose of limbs' plot of time and space;

it beats light wings through time that was,
it spans the silken seas of God,
it tips the aevum's endless start,
eternity's live, stirless heart.

Soul can conceive a thought like God's,
body its thought in verse or bronze,
rib it, add limb — of note, of stone —
just as God gives clay limb to soul:
old thing into unknown thing turned
soul can exalt, expand, the world.

And yet, with this high-searching soul,
man has the death-drift in the bone.
Man's spirit (breath of body's breath,
still heart of beating heart, fine weft
of fleshy weave), alive in sense,
sups on the sensuous universe.
It fans the fiery, clay-blood heart,
drifts with the senses' drift to dark,
cold to that Lustrous Head that lights
or strikes souls dark, with Paradise.

Man, the wild bee of Time, will try
to sip the world and blind an eye
and say there seems no call to die. . .

And so God makes the body sleep
to save the soul for modesty,
rehearsing man with nightly death

to bear the frightful stop of breath.
And so God takes my soul away
and makes my world end every day;
and I, there, with shuttered eye,
a mere breathing body lie,
all-but returned to lightless womb,
all-but inhabitant of tomb:
while God upholds me in His Hand,
and if He fasten fingers hard
O I am lost or lapped in bliss
for all the endless centuries!

While now I lay me down to sleep
I pray to God my soul to keep:
never to let my body die
till Christ's Body in me lie,
till Christ's Blood behind the oil
leaving anointing hand assoil
lid, and limb, and lip, and ear,
and nostril, till the spirit's clear.
Ah then I'll lay me down to sleep
and Father, Son and Spirit keep
my soul until my body leap.

Until my body leap from clay
on all mankind's Uprising Day,
and down-sent soul and body sprung
shall rise together, rung by rung,
and I that was with worm and clod
in my own flesh shall see my God.

LINEAGE*

Had *I* had an inn at Bethlehem
I should have shut my door on them.

Had *I* hanged for theft on Calvary
I'd been deft with mockery.

Even if I'd been on Olivet
I'd have hidden it.

I *am* the boor of Bethlehem,
the hoist Calvary clown,
I was aloft on Olivet
and cringe in the town.

*The above and following poems have been selected
from *Time's Wall Asunder,* by Roibeárd O' Faracháin
(New York: Sheed and Ward, 1939).

MANCHILD

To think God learned to walk,
in Nazareth.
Later ther'd be hard
walking to do,
with heavier falls.

And talking: in Nazareth
God played Adam's game —
naming things,
bringing out words:
and saw His own begetting

imaged, in the word's spring
from the intent regard.

A grave infant world
studied for Calvary,
studied for Genesareth,
prepared to say thrice;
Simon Peter, lovest thou me?

Mary was never asked
if she loved God.

MARY

Thou art God's sky,
in which the Sun arose:
Thou art His moon,
the window of His light.

Thou art God's earth,
God in thee taking root;
God's seed: He was thy tree;
God's tree . . . thy fruit.

Thou art God's spring
jetting out Life;
God's river-bed

through which His torrent rushed;
God's sea
in which He spawned His sacred fish;
God's oyster
secreting the pearl of Christ.
God's lake His cloud rose from
to rain on earth;
God's cloud:
by Him from thee was lightning struck;
God's lightning
blazing the encumbered Heaven;
God's Heaven,
for Heaven's where's God.

GOD CONQUERED

METAPHYSICIAN,
matter has conquered God,
has, grandiloquently,
gainsaid a word
he said once to angels,
grave-faced.

He said:
'Angels, I All-powerful
will shape desire itself unto a creature
which shall be sated with made being,
which shall be satisfied
with less than me.'

And he made matter. No,
not apart.
Want must have tenement,
potency principal:
God concreated matter, creating water;
bended his might to form
a filled desire.

Though angels sang
at the splendour of water,
matter yearned still.
God smiled,
made light.

Forestalling the panting voice
he made dry land.
Spread order in new things.
Added life, life-bearing.
Said 'They are good.'

The Orders craned.
Could the gage hold?
Could the All-desirable
halt desire?
Flight
hem wings?

Above their heads
was a thing like laughter,
but wheeling eyes
saw it not.

Before they spoke
he said 'Drouth still?
Importunate!
Is God, my Thrones,
defeated? Look
in this insatiable I plunge,
between itself and you,
rungs.
I thrust in this gorge
spirit!'
The tiers blaze,
and nine choirs applaud
strange genesis.

Raphael to God:
'O Jester!
Spirit and not desire thee?
Laugh, Man!
Matter, laugh out with God!'

THE CRAFT OF LITERARY CONVERSATION

Conversation
for delectation
turns to *belles lettres:*
don't fret —
with very few
pointers you
may shine with any,
dazzle many
in a crowd
various-browed.

Point one
(good fun):
should someone praise
book by Hayes,
titter: 'Willie
looks so silly
when one knows
how arose
his strife
with his wife
in her meandering
philandering.'

Juxtapose
thumb and nose
with fable

straight from table.
The bigger
the figure
the quicker
the snigger:
Get that
rule pat.

Not talents
not balance
not criticism:
WITTICISM.

Point two
mark you:
anecdote
of the mote
in the eye
of the high
told with verve
breaks the nerve
of the few
heckling you;

tittle-tattle
is half battle,
will handle

ripe scandal,
turn the talk
from the work
to the author —
never bother
what the fact,
when you've cracked
one good name
do the same
for the lot —
like a shot
you'll be their
raconteur.

Not learning,
not discerning,
not painstaking:
LITTLE-MAKING.

Then the play
of the day

by El Ree —
you and he
in your youth
were in truth
hook and eye:
bye-and-bye
you fell out:
not a doubt
Ree's a rogue
a cabog.
Please describe
with a gibe
his orations,
his libations,
Rabelaise
his *malaise.*
Not reading
not breeding
not vision
DERISON.

PART

IV

THE AMERICAN REVIVAL

THE growth of the Church in the United States has been much more swift than the growth in Catholic literature. This is entirely understandable. The immigrants who made up the great body of Catholics in the United States came here, mostly from peasant cultures, mostly with empty pockets. Success and education glittered in the future of their children, but unlulled by dreams, with shrewd foresight and horny hands they took up the job of the moment with one eye always open for the turn of the card, one ear turned to the peremptory summons of opportunity. They sweated under the sun, laying the great steel ribbons of the railroads, they toiled in sculleries, in sewers, in ditches, bakeshops, and fish markets; they swept the floors and carried the hods, but they did not forget God. The "housemaid's cathedral" lifted its twin spires to the Lord and, however small the pay envelope or large the family, something was squeezed out for religion. They lived hard and their vices sometimes were gross, their rages roaring, but their emotions were those of children, and you could have driven a dray through the doors of their hearts. "Micks," "Wops," "Hunkies," "Spicks," "Polacks," the patronizing insolence of the Anglo-Saxons called them, but they went their way undisturbed and saved their souls.

They needed churches and schools and they built them. They needed priests and nuns and they begot them of clean loins and ardent faith; they required instruction in the catechism and apologetics, in a brash world of No-Popery and No-Nothingism. Through a miracle these, too, materialized and religious repartee was something more immediately available than "What yez remembered on the way home from the pharty." One thing they did not yet require and that was literature, unless one happened to be "lace-curtain Irish" or a "tony" convert.

There was a little or no demand for literature. As a consequence the authors who rose up were rare birds, protected by a fond father or mother or by the aura of strangeness which came with them out of the religions from which they had been converted. Neither in the Church nor outside it were there many American models on which one might form a style or pitch a song, and as a consequence, the writers of the time formed themselves on English models, still more intensifying the gulf which separated them from the great body of American Catholics. There could be no Renaissance until Catholic sensibility and Catholic education had reached a higher level. Because of antecedent and more pressing needs, the improvement in sensibility and educational growth waited two or three generations.

Brownson fought for the faith and was followed, perhaps because everyone loved a good fight, perhaps because many detected the American weave of his writing. And in a way they were proud of Dr. Egan, and their eyes lit up at the elegant thought of Bishop Spaulding and Bishop Shanahan and they took pride in the Celtic effusions of Father Abram Ryan and the spirited writing of John Boyle O'Reilly.

It was only at the turn of the century, when education improved and there was leisure and space in the house for a bookcase, that authors of some note arrived on the scene and found a public. John Bannister Tabb, Henry Harland, and F. Marion Crawford, all converts, were welcomed by a large following who probably debated their merits in lyric accents and considered them the greatest authors in the world. And they were all proud of Imogene Guiney, a genuinely talented poet, although her thought was a shade metaphysical for their tastes, and her lines smacked of something seventeenth century and of the England to which she eventually retired.

With the conversion of Joyce and Aline Kilmer, a distinctively American school of Catholic writers began to emerge: Katherine Bregy, Theodore Maynard, Benjamin Musser, Charles Phillips, J. Corson Miller, Father Charles O'Donnell, Agnes Repplier, and many others. Father James M. Gillis and Father Francis Talbot inspired the movement which in its enthusiasm and general level of craftsmanship gave indications that the revival of Catholic letters was well under way in America.

It is more than "an emergence" today. Though Father Leonard Feeney, S.J., and Dr. William Walsh are the only two prose writers who stand comparison with men of the stamp of E. I. Watkins and Maurice Baring, yet Thomas Merton, Robert Lowell, Jessica Powers, Sister Maura, and Sister Maris Stella are writing distinguished and original poems, and the woods are filled with the good song of the lesser poets. In the field of fiction we still lag, perhaps because our public is not yet sufficiently mature to accept without qualms such writing as is found in the works of Sigrid Undset, Kate O'Brien, Evelyn Waugh, or Graham Greene. But the feeling for mature and artistic fiction is growing, and when it has grown sufficiently to provide a wide audience and to pay dividends the writers will appear.

The American Church and the American Catholic started from scratch in a new land. The Churches, schools, and colleges are the first fruits of long and arduous labor. Literature was the last need, and it, too, within a few generations should demonstrate its ability to overcome its handicaps of a slow beginning and the thousand extraneous labors which immediately fall to those who show promise in letters. At least such is the hope. It would seem nearer to fulfillment if our Catholic writers were protected and given the leisure, quiet, and support which are the necessary background for deep thought and artistic excellence.

At the present time the American Revival is in its Meynell period. Creative and distinguished poetry is its chief note, but the signs are multiplying which would indicate that novelists and great prose writers will not be long delayed in appearing. This is not merely a dream. Its reality is forecast by the fine character of our literary journalism as observed in *The Catholic World, America, The Commonweal,* and *Spirit.* Excellent and mature criticisms, discussion of standards, and the angry debate regarding the novel, are sure signs that the public is beginning to learn and ultimately will support authors who can produce mature and careful work. The poet is the instructor in beauty and insight, and the eyes and the youth of poets make the later prose of Bellocs and Chestertons. If John Gilland Brunini's *Whereon to Stand* is meant to take the place of Cardinal Gibbon's *Faith of Our Fathers* as the newspapers announced, then it is possible to see at once just how far we have advanced in fifty years and what solid reasons we have for pride. This book is no *tour de force,* but a blazing sign which shows only too clearly that we are entering into a new period of the revival which promises maturity and completely competent writing.

ORESTES A. BROWNSON

(*1803–1876*)

ORESTES BROWNSON was born at Stockbridge, Vermont. His early years were plagued by poverty. In spite of this handicap, Brownson, like Lincoln, educated himself by wide reading. The texture of his mind was religious, which led him first into the Protestant ministry and finally into the Catholic Church. In 1844 he became editor of *Brownson's Review*. Though he spent his talents on the Catholic cause his final years were marred by acrimonious controversy.

Everything he said touched off quarrels, chiefly because Catholics were sensitive and Brownson was forthright. He died in 1876.

Brownson was a brilliant controversialist. The lucidity of his mind reveals itself in everything he wrote. An excellent study of his critical principles was produced by Virgil Michel. His collected works (25V) were edited by his son, Henry F. Brownson, who also wrote the most satisfactory sketch of his father's life.

CIVIL AND RELIGIOUS LIBERTY*

WE ARE Americans, American born, American bred, and we love our country and will, when called upon, defend it against any and every enemy to the best of our feeble ability; but though we by no means rate American virtue and intelligence so low as do those who will abuse us for not rating it higher, we cannot consent to hoodwink ourselves or to claim for our countrymen a degree of virtue and intelligence they do not possess. We are acquainted with no salutary errors and are forbidden to seek even a good end by any but honest means. The virtue and intelligence of the American people are not sufficient to secure the free, orderly, and wholesome action of the government, for they do not secure it. The government commits every now and then a sad blunder, and the general policy it adopts must prove in the long run suicidal. It has adopted a most iniquitous policy, and its most unjust measures are its most popular measures, such as it would be fatal to any man's political success directly and openly to oppose; and we think we hazard nothing in saying our free institutions cannot be sustained without an augmentation

of popular virtue and intelligence. We do not say the people are not capable of a sufficient degree of virtue and intelligence to sustain a democracy; all we say is they cannot do it without virtue and intelligence, nor without a higher degree of virtue and intelligence than they have as yet attained to. We do not apprehend that many of our countrymen, and we are sure no one whose own virtue and intelligence entitle his opinion to any weight, will dispute this. Then the question of the means of sustaining our democracy resolves itself into the question of augmenting the virtue and intelligence of the people.

The press makes readers, but does little to make virtuous and intelligent readers. The newspaper press is, for the most part, under the control of men of very ordinary abilities, lax principles, and limited acquirements. It echoes and exaggerates popular errors and does little or nothing to create a sound public opinion. Your popular literature caters to popular taste, passions, prejudices, ignorance, and errors; it is by no means above the average degree of virtue and intelligence which already obtains, and can do nothing to create a higher standard of virtue or tone of thought. On what, then, are we to rely?

"On education," answer Frances Wright,

---

*Brownson, Henry F., *Brownson's Views* (New York: Benziger Brothers, 1893), pp. 276–288.

Abner Kneeland, Horace Mann, and the educationists generally. But we must remember that we must have virtue *and* intelligence. Virtue without intelligence will only fit the mass to be duped by the artful and designing, and intelligence without virtue only makes one the abler and more successful villain. Education must be of the right sort if it is to answer our purpose, for a bad education is worse than none. The Mahometans are great sticklers for education, and if we recollect aright it is laid down in the Koran that every believer must at least be taught to read; but we do not find their education does much to advance them in virtue and intelligence. Education, moreover, demands educators, and educators of the right sort. Where are these to be obtained? Who is to select them, judge of their qualifications, sustain or dismiss them? The people? Then you place education in the same category with democracy. You make the people, through their representatives, the educators. The people will select and sustain only such educators as represent their own virtues, vices, intelligence, prejudices, and errors. Whether they educate mediately or immediately, they can impart only what they have and are. Consequently, with them for educators we can, by means even of universal education, get no increase of virtue and intelligence to bear on the government. The people may educate, but where is that which takes care that they educate in a proper manner? Here is the very difficulty we began by pointing out. The people take care of the government and education; but who or what is to take care of the people, who need taking care of quite as much as either education or government? — for, rightly considered, neither government nor education has any other legitimate end than to take care of the people.

The great danger in our country is from the predominance of material interests. Democracy has a direct tendency to favor inequality and injustice. The government must obey the people; that is, it must follow the passions and interests of the people, and of course the stronger passions and interests. These with us are material, such as pertain solely to this life and this world. What our people demand of government is that it adopt and sustain such measures as tend most directly to facilitate the acquisition of wealth. It must, then, follow the passion for wealth and labor especially to promote wordly interests.

But among these worldly interests some are stronger than others and can command the government. These will take possession of the government and wield it for their own special advantage. They will make it the instrument of taxing all the other interests of the country for the special advancement of themselves. This leads to inequality and injustice, which are incompatible with the free, orderly, and wholesome working of the government.

Now, what is wanted is some power to prevent this, to moderate the passion for wealth, and to inspire the people with such a true and firm sense of justice as will prevent any one interest from struggling to advance itself at the expense of another. Without this the stronger material interests predominate, make the government the means of securing their predominance, and of extending it by the burdens which, through the government, they are able to impose on the weaker interests of the country.

The framers of our government foresaw this evil and thought to guard against it by a written constitution. But they intrusted the preservation of the constitution to the care of the people, which was as wise as to lock up your culprit in prison and intrust him with the key. The constitution as a restraint on the will of the people or the governing majority is already a dead letter. It answers to talk about, to declaim about, in electioneering speeches, and even as a theme of newspaper leaders and political essays in reviews; but its effective power is a morning vapor after the sun is well up.

We may be told that enlightened self-interest will suffice — that only instruct the people what is for their interest and they will do it. This is plausible, but all experience to the contrary. Who does not know that it is for his real interest, both for time and eternity, to be a devout Christian? And yet are all devout Christians? The wisdom and prudence of men's conduct cannot be measured by their intelligence. A corrupt man uses his intelligence only as the minister of his corruption. The more you extend intelligence, unless you extend the moral restraints and influences of the gospel at the same time, the more do you sharpen the intellect for evil. The people of the United States are far more instructed than they were fifty years ago, and yet have not half so much of the virtue necessary to sustain a republican government. We are never to expect men to act virtuously simply because their understandings are convinced that virtue is the best calculation. You must make them act from a higher motive. They must be governed by religion; act from the love and the fear of God — from a deep sense of duty; be meek, humble, self-denying; morally brave and heroic; choosing rather to die a thousand deaths than swerve from right principle or disobey the will of God; or they will not practise the virtues without which liberty is an empty name — a mere illusion.

Now, Protestantism never has produced and never can produce the virtues without which a republican government can have no solid foundation. It may have good words; it may say wise and even just things, but it wants the unction of the spirit. It does not reach and regenerate the heart, subdue the passions, and renew the spirit. It has never produced a single saint, and the virtues it calls forth are of the sort exhibited by the old heathen moralists. It praises the Bible, but studies the Greek and Roman classics; boasts of spirituality, but expires in a vain formalism. For the three hundred years it has existed it has proved itself powerful to destroy, but impotent to found; ready to begin, but never able to complete. Whatever it claims that is positive, abiding, it has inherited or borrowed from the ages and the lands of faith. Its own creations rise and vanish as the soap-bubbles blown by our children in their sports. It has never yet shown itself able to command human nature or to say to the roused waves of passion, Peace, be still. It lulls the conscience with the forms of faith and piety; soothes vanity

and fosters pride by its professions of freedom; but leaves the passions all their natural force and permits the man to remain a slave to all his natural lusts. It never subdues or regenerates nature. Hence, throughout all Protestantdom the tendency is to reproduce heathen antiquity with all its cant, hollowness, hypocrisy, slavery, and wretchedness — to narrow men's views down to this transitory life and the fleeting shows of sense, and to make them live and labor for the meat that perisheth. We appeal to England, Sweden, Denmark, Protestant Germany, Holland, and our own country for the truth of what we say. They were Protestant traders who trampled on the cross of Christ to gain the lucrative trade of Japan. It is in no spirit of exultation we allude to Protestant worldly-mindedness and spiritual impotency. Would to God the sketch were from fancy or our own diseased imagination!

We do not mean to deny that in words Protestantism teaches many, perhaps most, of the Christian virtues. It has even some good books on morals and practical religion. Its clergy give good exhortations and labor, no doubt in good faith, for the spiritual culture of their flocks. No doubt much truth, much valuable instruction, is given from Protestant pulpits. The Protestant clergy take no delight in the state of things they see around them. They would gladly see Christ reign in the hearts of men; they no doubt would joyfully dispense the bread of life to their famished people; and they do dispense the best they have. But alas! how can they dispense what they have not received? The living bread is not on their communion table. They communicate, according to their own confession, only a figure, a shadow; and how shall the divine life be nourished with shadows? What we mean to say is, not that Protestantism does not aim to bring men to Christ, to make them pure and holy, but that it has no power to do it. It does not control human nature and produce the fruits of a supernatural faith, hope, and charity. Its faith is merely an opinion or persuasion, its hope a wish, and its charity natural philanthropy. It necessarily leaves human nature as it finds it, and no pruning of that corrupt tree can make it bring forth good fruit. It is of the earth — earthy; and it will bear fruit only for the earth. With unregenerated nature in full activity, we can have only sensuality and mammon-worship.

Hundreds and thousands among us who are by no means favorably disposed to Catholicity see this and deplore it. They say the age has no faith. They see the impotency of Protestantism; that under it all the vices are sheltered; that in spite of it, all the dangerous passions rage unchecked; and they turn away in disgust from its empty forms and vain words. Witness the response the biting sarcasms and withering irony of Carlyle bring from thousands of hearts in this republic, the echoes which the chiselled words and marble sentences of Emerson also bring. Witness, also, the movements of the Come-outers, the Socialists, Fourierists, Communists. All these see that Protestantism has nothing but words, while they want life, realities, not vain *simulacra*. They err most egregiously, no doubt; they go from the dying to the dead; but their error proves the truth of what we advance.

Now, assuming our view of Protestantism to be correct, we demand how it is to sustain, or we, with it alone, are to sustain our republican government. Do we not see, in this growing love of place and plunder, with this growing devotion to wealth, luxury, and pleasure, with these fierce electioneering contests, one no sooner ended than another begins, each to be fiercer and more absorbing and more destructive than the last, and each drawing within its vortex nearly the whole industrial interest of the country and touching almost every man in his honor and his purse, that we want the moral elements without which a republic cannot stand? A republic can stand only as it rests upon the virtues of the people; and these are not the mere natural virtues of worldly prudence and social decency, but those loftier virtues which are possible to human nature only as elevated above itself by the infused habit of supernatural grace. This is a solemn fact to which it is in vain for us to close our eyes. Human nature left to itself tends to dissolution, to destruction, decay, death. So does

every society that rests only on those virtues which have their origin, growth, and maturity in nature alone. This is the case with our own society. We have really no social bond; we have no true patriotism; none of that patience, that self-denial, that loyalty of soul which is necessary to bind man to man, each to each and each to all. Each is for himself. Save who can (Sauve qui peut), we exclaim. Hence a universal scramble. Man overthrows man, brother brother, the father the child and the child the father, the demagogue all; while the devil stands at a distance, looks on, and enjoys the sport. Tell us, ye who boast of the glorious reformation, if a republican form of government is compatible with this moral state of the people?

Even in matters of education we can do little but sharpen the wit and render brother more skilful and successful in plundering brother. With our multitude of sects we may instruct, but not educate. Our children can have no moral training, for morality rests on theology and theology on faith. But faith is expelled from our schools because it is sectarian, and there is no one faith in the country which can be taught without exciting the jealousy of the followers of a rival faith. Cut up into such a multitude of sects, there is and can be no common moral culture in the country, no true religious training. We give a little instruction in reading, writing, arithmetic, grammar, geography, perhaps history, the Greek and Roman classics, and in the physical sciences; and send our children out into the world to form their morals and their religion without other guide or assistant than their own short-sighted reason and perverted passions. How can we expect anything from such a sowing but what we reap? and how, under Protestantism, which broaches everything and settles nothing, raises all questions and answers none, and therefore necessarily giving birth to a perpetual succession of sects, each declaiming with equal reason and justice to have the truth, and the claims of all equally respected, as they must be, by the government, is this terrible evil to be remedied?

But with Catholicity the republic may be sustained, not because the Catholic Church enjoins this form of government or that, but because she nourishes in the hearts of her children the virtues which render popular liberty both desirable and practicable. The Catholic Church meddles *directly* with no form of government. She leaves each people free to adopt such form of government as seems to themselves good, and to administer it in their own way. Her chief concern is to fit men for beatitude, and this she can do under any or all forms of government. But the spirit she breathes into men, the graces she communicates, the dispositions she cultivates, and the virtues she produces, are such that, while they render even arbitrary forms of government tolerable, fit a people for asserting and maintaining freedom. In countries where there are no constitutional checks on power she remedies the evil by imposing moral restraints on its exercise, by inspiring rulers with a sense of justice and the public good. Where such checks do exist, she hallows them and renders them inviolable. In a republic she restrains the passions of the people, teaches them obedience to the laws of God, moderates their desires, weans their affections from the world, frees them from the dominion of their own lusts, and, by the meekness, humility, loyalty of heart which she cherishes, disposes them to the practice of those public virtues which render a republic secure. She also creates by her divine charity a true equality. No republic can stand where the dominant feeling is pride, which finds its expression in the assertion, "I am as good as you." It must be based on love; not on the determination to defend' our own rights and interests, but on the fear to encroach on the rights and interests of others. But this love must be more than the mere sentiment of philanthropy. This sentiment of philanthropy is a very unsubstantial affair. Talk as we will about its excellence, it never goes beyond love to those who love us. We love our friends and neighbors, but hate our enemies. This is all we do as philanthropists. All the fine speeches we make beyond — about the love of humanity and all that — are fine speeches. Philanthropy must be exalted into the supernatural virtue of charity before it can be-

come that love which leads us to honor all men and makes us shrink from encroaching upon the interests of any man, no matter how low or how vile. We must love our neighbor, not for his own sake, but for God's sake — the child, for the sake of the Father; then we can love all and joyfully make the most painful sacrifices for them. It is only in the bosom of the Catholic Church that this sublime charity has ever been found or can be found.

The Catholic Church also cherishes a spirit of independence, a loftiness and dignity of soul, favorable to the maintenance of popular freedom. It ennobles every one of its members. The lowest, the humblest Catholic is a member of that church which was founded by Jesus Christ himself; which has subsisted for eighteen hundred years; which has in every age been blessed with signal tokens of the Redeemer's love; which counts its saints by millions; and the blood of whose martyrs has made all earth hallowed ground. He is admitted into the goodly fellowship of the faithful of all ages and climes, and every day, throughout all the earth, the universal church sends up her prayers for him, and all the church above receives them, and, with her own, bears them as sweet incense up before the throne of the almighty and eternal God. He is a true nobleman, more than the peer of kings or Caesars; for he is a child of the King of kings, and, if faithful unto death, heir of a crown of life, eternal in the heavens, that fadeth not away. Such a man is no slave. His soul is free; he looks into the perfect law of liberty. Can tyrants enslave him? No, indeed; not because he will turn on the tyrant and kill, but because he can die and reign forever. What were a mere human tyrant before a nation of such men? Who could establish arbitrary government over them or subject them to unwholesome or iniquitous laws?

Here is our hope for our republic. We look for our safety to the spread of Catholicity. We render solid and imperishable our free institutions just in proportion as we extend the kingdom of God among our people and establish in their hearts the reign of justice and charity. And here, then, is our answer to all those who tell us Catholicity is incompatible with free institutions. *We tell them that they cannot maintain free institutions without it.* It is not a free government that makes a free people, but a free people that makes a free government; and we know no freedom but that wherewith the Son makes free. You must be free within before you can be free without. They who war against the church because they fancy it hostile to their civil freedom are as mad as those wicked Jews who nailed their Redeemer to the cross. But even now, as then, God be thanked, from the cross ascends the prayer, not in vain, "Father, forgive them, for they know not what they do."

ABRAM J. RYAN
(*1838–1886*)

THE missionary condition of the Church in America during the nineteenth century left to her priests little time for the writing of poetry. An exception to the rule was the life of Father Ryan, who became the poet of the Confederacy and a luminous light to the Irish immigrant.

Father Ryan was born at Norfolk, Virginia, 1838. In 1854 he joined the Vincentians, but left the community in 1862. He became a Confederate chaplain in the Civil War, and at its close was a prisoner for some time, along with Sidney Lanier and many of the southern luminaries.

Father Ryan's poems are emotional and didactic, but at the time in which they were written they had a vogue which many better poets might well envy.

THE CONQUERED BANNER*

Furl that Banner, for 'tis weary;
Round its staff 'tis drooping dreary;
  Furl it, fold it, it is best;
For there's not a man to wave it,
And there's not a sword to save it,
And there's not one left to lave it
In the blood which heroes gave it;
And its foes now scorn and brave it;
  Furl it, hide it — let it rest!

Take that Banner down! 'tis tattered;
Broken is its staff and shattered;
And the valiant hosts are scattered
  Over whom it floated high.
Oh! 'tis hard for us to fold it;
Hard to think there's none to hold it;
Hard that those who once unrolled it
  Now must furl it with a sigh.

Furl that Banner! furl it sadly!
Once ten thousands hailed it gladly,
And ten thousands wildly, madly,
  Swore it should forever wave;
Swore that foeman's sword should never
Hearts like theirs entwined dissever,
Till that flag should float forever
  O'er their freedom or their grave!

Furl it! for the hands that grasped it,
And the hearts that fondly clasped it,
  Cold and dead are lying low;
And that Banner — it is trailing!
While around it sounds the wailing
  Of its people in their woe.

For, though conquered, they adore it!
Love the cold, dead hands that bore it!
Weep for those who fell before it!
Pardon those who trailed and tore it!

*The above and following poems have been selected from *Poems*, by Abram J. Ryan (New York: P. J. Kenedy, 1899).

But, oh! wildly they deplore it,
Now who furl and fold it so.

Furl that Banner! True, 'tis gory
Yet 'tis wreathed around with glory,
And 'twill live in song and story,
Though its folds are in the dust;
For its fame on brightest pages,
Penned by poets and by sages,

Shall go sounding down the ages —
Furl its folds though now we must.

Furl that Banner, softly, slowly!
Treat it gently — it is holy —
    For it droops above the dead.
Touch it not — unfold it never,
Let it droop there, furled forever,
    For its people's hopes are dead!

AFTER SEEING PIUS IX

I saw his face today; he looks a chief
    Who fears nor human rage, nor human
        guile;
Upon his cheeks the twilight of a grief,
    But in that grief the starlight of a smile.
Deep, gentle eyes, with drooping lids that tell
They are the homes where tears of sorrow
        dwell;
A low voice — strangely sweet — whose very
    tone

Tells how those lips speak oft with God
    alone.
I kissed his hand, I fain would kiss his feet;
"No, no," he said; and then, in accents sweet,
His blessing fell upon my bended head.
He bade me rise; a few more words he said,
Then took me by the hand — the while he
        smiled —
And, going, whispered: "Pray for me, my
    child."

SONG OF THE MYSTIC

I walk down the Valley of Silence —
    Down the dim, voiceless valley — alone!
And I hear not the fall of a footstep
    Around me, save God's and my own;
And the hush of my heart is as holy
    As hovers where angels have flown!

Long ago was I weary of voices
    Whose music my heart could not win;
Long ago was I weary of noises
    That fretted my soul with their din;
Long ago was I weary of places
    Where I met but the human — and sin.

I walked in the world with the worldly;
    I craved what the world never gave;
And I said: "In the world each Ideal,
    That shines like a star on life's wave,
Is wrecked on the shores of the Real,
    And sleeps like a dream in a grave."

And still did I pine for the Perfect
    And still found the False with the True;
I sought 'mid the Human for Heaven,
    But caught a mere glimpse of its Blue:
And I wept when the clouds of the Mortal
    Veiled even that glimpse from my view.

And I toiled on, heart-tired of the Human,
    And I moaned 'mid the mazes of men,
Till I knelt, long ago, at an altar
    And I heard a voice call me. Since then
I walk down the Valley of Silence
    That lies far beyond mortal ken.

Do you ask what I found in the Valley?
    'Tis my Trysting Place with the Divine.
And I fell at the feet of the Holy,
    And above me a voice said: "Be mine."
And there arose from the depths of my spirit
    An echo — "My heart shall be thine."

Do you ask how I live in the Valley?
  I weep — and I dream — and I pray.
But my tears are as sweet as the dew-drops
  That fall on the roses in May;
And my prayer, like a perfume from Censers,
  Ascendeth to God night and day.

In the hush of the Valley of Silence
  I dream all the songs that I sing;
And the music floats down the dim Valley,
  Till each finds a word for a wing,
That to hearts, like the Dove of the Deluge,
  A message of Peace they may bring.

But far on the deep there are billows
  That never shall break on the beach;
And I have heard songs in the Silence

That never shall float into speech;
And I have had dreams in the Valley
  Too lofty for language to reach.

And I have seen Thoughts in the Valley —
  Ah! me, how my spirit was stirred!
And they wear holy veils on their faces,
  Their footsteps can scarcely be heard.
They pass through the Valley like Virgins.
  Too pure for the touch of a word!

Do you ask me the place of the Valley,
  Ye hearts that are harrowed by Care?
It lieth afar between mountains,
  And God and His angels are there:
And one is the dark mount of Sorrow,
  And one the bright mountain of Prayer.

JOEL CHANDLER HARRIS
(1848–1908)

AMERICAN literature was made richer in the birth of Joel Chandler Harris at Eatonton, Georgia, 1848. Joel's parents were humble folk. His formal education was meager but his knowledge of "Fields animals and folk" superbly deep. Working on his own, he prepared himself for journalism and served on the staff of several southern papers with distinction until 1890.

Though he had long been a convinced Catholic, Harris delayed his reception into the Church until a few weeks before his death in 1908.

His invention of Uncle Remus, Brer Rabbit the hero, Brer Fox the villain, and all the other lovely characters of his stories, is a work of positive genius. There is much wit and humble wisdom in his tales, all the more telling in the salty accent of the Negro in which his ideas are clothed. With his advent, a distinctly American accent had come into American letters, an accent not superficial, but uttering the deepest note in the American consciousness. Harris remains one of the few American writers undated by the passage of time or changing fashions in literature.

HOW MR. RABBIT WAS TOO SHARP FOR MR. FOX*

UNCLE REMUS," said the little boy one evening, when he had found the old man with little or nothing to do, "did the fox kill and eat the rabbit when he caught him with the Tar-Baby?"

*Harris, Joel Chandler, *Uncle Remus — His Songs and His Sayings* (New York: D. Appleton Co., 1905), pp. 16–19.

"Law, honey, ain't I tell you 'bout dat?" replied the old darkey, chuckling slyly. "I clar ter grashus I ought er tole you dat, but old man Nod wuz ridin' on my eyeleds 'twel a leetle mon'n I'd a dis'member'd my own name, en den on to dat here come yo' mammy hollerin' atter you.

"W'at I tell you w'en I fus' begin? I told

you Brer Rabbit wuz a monstus soon beas'; leas'ways dat's w'at I laid out fer ter tell you. Well, den, honey, don't you go en make no udder kalkalashuns, kaze in dem days Brer Rabbit en his fambly wuz at de head er de gang w'en anny racket wuz on han', en dar dey stayed. 'Fo' you begins fer ter wipe yo' eyes 'bout Brer Rabbit, you wait en see whar' bouts Brer Rabbit gwineter fetch up at. But dat's needer yer ner dar.

"W'en Brer Fox fine Brer Rabbit mixt up wid de Tar-Baby, he feel mighty good, en he roll on de groun' en laff. Bimeby, he up'n say, sezee:

"'Well, I speck I got you dis time, Brer Rabbit,' sezee; 'maybe I ain't, but I speck I is. You been runnin' roun' here sassin' atter me a mighty long time, but I speck you done come ter de een'er de row. You bin cuttin' up yo' capers en bouncin' roun' in dis naberhood ontwel you cum ter b'leeve yo'se'f de boss er de whole gang. En den youer allers som'rs what you got no bizness' sez Brer Fox, sezee. 'Who ax you fer ter come en strike up a 'quaintence wid dish yer Tar-Baby? En who stuck you up dar what you iz? No body in de roun' worril. You des tuck en jam yo'se'f on dat Tar-Baby widout waitin' fer enny invite,' sez Brer Fox, sezee, 'en dar you is, en dar you'll stay twell I fixes up a bresh-pile and fires her up, kaze I'm gwineter bobbycue you dis day, sho,' sez Brer Fox, sezee.

"Den Brer Rabbit talk might 'umble.

"'I don't keer w'at you do wid me, Brer Fox,' sezee, 'so you don't fling me in dat brier-patch. Roas' me, Brer Fox,' sezee, 'but don't fling me in dat brier-patch,' sezee.

"'Hit's so much trouble fer ter kindle a fier,' sez Brer Fox, sezee, 'dat I speck I'll hatter hang you,' sezee.

"'Hang me des ez high as you please, Brer Foz,' sez Brer Rabbit sezee, 'but do fer de Lord's sake don't fling me in dat brier-patch,' sezee.

"'I ain't got no string,' sez Brer Fox, sezee, 'en now I speck I'll hatter drown you,' sezee.

"'Drown me des ez deep ez you please, Brer Fox,' sez Brer Rabbit, sezee, 'but do don't fling me in dat brier-patch,' sezee.

"'Dey ain't no water nigh,' sez Brer Fox, sezee, 'en now I speck I'll hatter skin you,' sezee.

"'Skin me, Brer Fox,' sez Brer Rabbit, sezee, 'snatch out my eyeballs, t'ar out my years by de roots, en cut off my legs,' sezee, 'but do please, Brer Fox, don't fling me in dat brier-patch,' sezee.

"Co'se Brer Fox wanter hurt Brer Rabbit bad ez he kin, so he cotch 'em by de behine legs en slung 'im right in de middle er de brier-patch. Dar wuz a considerbul flutter whar Brer Rabbit struck de bushes, en Brer Fox sorter hang 'roun' for ter see w'at wuz gwinter happen. Bimeby he hear somebody call 'im en way up de hill he see Brer Rabbit settin' cross-legged on a chinkapin log, koamin' de pitch outen his har wid a chip. Den Brer Fox know dat he bin swop off mighty bad. Brer Rabbit wuz bleedzed for ter fling back some er his sass, en he holler out:

"'Bred en bawn in a brier-patch, Brer Fox—bred en bawn in a brier-patch!' en wid dat he skip out des ez lively ez a cricket in de embers."

JOHN LANCASTER SPALDING
(*1840–1916*)

JOHN LANCASTER SPALDING was born at Lebanon, Kentucky, 1840, of distinguished Maryland stock. He had a passion for travel and study which took him abroad to Louvain and Rome, where he completed his extensive education. Upon his return to the United States Father Spalding soon amply demonstrated his talents, especially at the Third Plenary Council of Baltimore. As secretary to his uncle, Archbishop Spalding, he astonished the hierarchy with both learning and eloquence.

In 1877 Father Spalding became Bishop of Peoria. In spite of the heavy burdens of his office, he continued to write and lecture until his death.

Bishop Spalding's essays received enormous praise in his lifetime and there are some critics today, notably Father Gillis, who would compare Bishop Spalding's essays favorably with those of Emerson. Bishop Spalding writes well, it is true; his essays abound with colorful illustrations, genuine wisdom, and an individual approach to life and living. But while Emerson is intuitive and poetical Bishop Spalding remains essentially the logician, elaborating ideas without illuminating them completely. For all his knowledge of the arts and the riches of Western culture, Bishop Spalding's *Essays* lack that small pinch of poetical insight which might have made him a great essayist instead of a good one.

GLIMPSES OF TRUTH*

III

THE love of repose, of order, of a uniform and even course of life would seem to spring from a rational and virtuous disposition, but it is often a result of sloth and selfishness, or of timidity and cowardice; and it may therefore be found in those who seek their ease and comfort at whatever cost, who if they are too indifferent to hate, are too indolent to help. They will not trouble themselves to right wrongs or prevent ills, but suffer things to take their way. They little care what happens if only they be not disturbed. They are incapable of generous emotions and are without noble impulses. If they are clothed with authority they correct no abuses, oppose no obstacles to the downward tendency of the many when left to themselves. They ignore the corruption which gives them no annoyance; and if it be urged on their attention, they consider those who denounce it as officious or impertinent. They would be thought wise and able for doing nothing, and they hold in slight esteem the active, energetic, and zealous, whose example is a rebuke to their own lethargy and inertness. This self-indulgent weakness and love of ease in the men who govern, whether in Church or State, has wrought greater ruin than the scoffings of infidels and the scandals of the vicious: for all understand that unbelievers will mock and that scandals must be; but that they who are placed as guardians over treasures of infinite price should fall asleep and slumber on while thieves break in and steal seems a thing monstrous and incredible to those who have faith in God and the soul. When the weak and careless are appointed to do what only the strong and vigilant can perform, confusion or ruin is inevitable.

When work has become a habit one is lost without it, as the drunkard without his dram, the gambler without his game.

The divinest things — religion, love, truth, beauty, justice — seem to lose their meaning and value when we sink into lassitude and indifference. In such mental state we, together with what is not ourselves, verge in consciousness toward the confines where all that is or has been or can be appears shadowy and unsubstantial. It is a state altogether different from that of the callous and dull, who have no perception of spiritual truth, no definite notions of anything. It is in fact not a state, but a passing obscuration, a moral syncope, a temporary inability to think or love or hope or take delight in aught. It is a signal that we should quit meditation and books, and go out into the open air, into the presence of nature, into the company of flocks and children, where we may drink new health and vigor from the clear and full-flowing fountains of life, afar from the arid wastes of theory and speculation; where we may learn again that it is not by intellectual questionings, but by believing, hoping, loving, and doing that man finds joy and peace.

*Spalding, Rt. Rev. J. L., *Glimpses of Truth* (Chicago: A. C. McClurg, 1903), pp. 67–81.

What a man is he has become. He is born wholly helpless, incapable of surviving for even a brief space without the aid and assistance of beings in whom intelligence has been developed; and what we consider his natural endowments are for the most part products of art. Nothing, for instance, plays a greater role in life and literature than the love of man for woman—the mysterious and all-absorbing passion which bribes or overpowers reason, which thrusts aside the usual motives that influence conduct, which compels those whom it subdues to forget religion, country, parents, and friends; driving heroes to forego honor and glory, sages to forsake wisdom, saints to abandon God. This strange fascination, this marvellous attraction, is not, as one might suppose, a thing of sex and the senses: it is romantic, imaginative, poetic; it is all compact of revery and fancy; it is a product of art, not of nature; a result of civilization, not of instinct. It could not exist among savages who go naked. With them it is simply sexual desire little different from that found in brutes. It arises only when the body is clothed and adorned, habited in mystery, and converted into a thing hidden and sacred, which appeals to the imagination and leads it to build, for the divinity which itself has created, a sanctuary wherein it may worship until the winning of the favor of the goddess becomes the supreme end of life, wherein to fail is to be doomed to misery. So the beloved becomes at once an ideal and an idol. But the divine frenzy is born of vesture, of manner, of artifice, of concealment and of mystery. Take these away and the madness is cured.

> Loosed the girdle and the veil,
> All the heavenly dream grows pale.

They who are drawn together by sexual passion or by interest are not attracted by love, but by instinct or selfishness, and when desire has been satiated or the advantage sought has been gained, they separate, not without loathing or contempt; for it is natural to despise or hate those whom we have made use of whether for gain or lust.

The most blissful moments are those we pass in adoration, or in writing the thoughts that blossom from the roots of our being, which dip into infinite and everduring worlds.

From nature we receive little more than dispositions. For the rest, what we become is the result of circumstances and the co-operation of the will, which is generally determined by environment and chance happenings. All depends on God's providence and grace, but the ways along which He guides us are mysterious and hidden, even after we have passed over them. A mere nothing, whose import we could not have understood, would have changed the whole course of life for any one of us. Things light as straws shape our purposes. If experience teaches anything, it is that we should keep ourselves free of conceit and be slow to judge our fellows.

How many submit to the restraints of society and comply with its requirements for no other reason than because such a course is safer, more respectable, and more certain to lead to success. Much of our virtue, indeed, is as little part of ourselves as are our clothes, and is as easily divested when the social atmosphere or the moral climate changes.

However eager men be for the contest, victors and vanquished alike quickly grow indifferent once it is over. In the triumph there is less joy, in the defeat less disappointment than either could have believed possible. It is so in trials of strength and skill; it is so in the great struggles on which the fates of armies and of nations hang. The keenest delight is anticipatory. When the issue is decided, when what had been a possibility becomes a fact, our interest relaxes, and we turn to the undetermined, which gives free play to the imagination and an open field to hope. So too we find that the death of our dearest friends, the vanishing of our most cherished illusions, without which life had seemed to be meaningless, are not unbearable. However great the loss, in a boundless universe there is always something left to believe, to strive for, and to love.

Whatever may be true of the uneducated, they whose pursuits are intellectual should need no other diversion or relaxation than they find in their studies; and they whose vocation obliges them to deal with religious truth can consent to pass their time at games and other entertainments only when they have lost faith in the reality of the spiritual world.

Strength, physical, intellectual, and moral, is desirable, if for no other reason, than that only the strong can be generous, helpful, and magnanimous. The weak shrink into themselves, nurse their sorrows, emphasize their sufferings and wrongs, and so become complaining, selfish, and exacting. They are the center of their own thoughts and are indifferent to the interest of others. They understand no ills but their own. If they listen to pitiful stories, they do so to get a keener relish for their proper miseries, with which they seem to be in love. They are without gratitude and are incapable of appreciating kindnesses. The strong, on the contrary, if they are not brutal, find happiness in sharing their strength and joy. Their sympathies are deep, and they are eager to make others partakers of the blessings bestowed so largely on themselves.

Self-love, in the true sense, is the love of one's real good — of truth, of virtue, of beauty, of God. It is strongest in those who are most alive in their higher nature. It is the opposite of selfish love, of the love which places the chief good in the things which minister to the senses or nourish conceit and pride, and not in what constitutes the proper worth and joy of life.

Why should I desire that others think as I, that they take interest in what interests me? If all were of one mind, if all had the same tastes, life would be less interesting than it is; and then it is plain that they who have not my experience cannot have my thoughts, that they who have not my character cannot have my tastes. Nevertheless, I would bring others to accept the truth I know, to admire and follow the beauty and goodness which I see; and this yearning springs from what is best within me, from God's presence in my soul, impelling me to reveal to my brothers Him who is truth, beauty, and goodness.

The power which habit has over us is shown in the fact that the things we become accustomed to in our earliest years, — the scenes, the songs, the beliefs, the prejudices even, — however much we may recognize that the value we attributed to them was due chiefly to our own ignorance and crudeness, never cease to be dear.

Having done all thou canst do, await the event with a calm mind. Whatever it be, thou art blameless, and safe therefore from harm.

If we except the present instant, which is gone before we can call attention to it, all time is past, since the future does not exist. What is past has ceased to be; and the whole of life, therefore, is summed in an instant, which — if we try to think of it — vanishes. It is this that gives insight into the illusiveness, the evanescence, the emptiness, the futility of temporal existence, driving the soul back on itself and impelling it to seek escape from annihilation in the bosom of the Eternal, in which, and not in time, it truly lives. Hence the old, though they clearly see that they have but a little while to remain on earth, still continue to plan, to provide, to prolong hope, and to cherish expectation. Though they know it not, they are already dwellers in eternity.

Only the greatest minds greatly influence us, and not even they unless with much toil and patience we work our way into the heart of their thought and love.

The good are cautious and irresolute, and therefore the affairs of the world are delivered over to the bold and unscrupulous, who have neither the will nor the ability to accomplish anything of enduring worth.

The child lives wholly in the present and is influenced solely by what is to happen now. The youth begins to look to the future but does not labor with joy for rewards which are distant. It is a mark of maturity when we grow able to live by hope, to toil on through whatever difficulties and obstacles, strengthened by the thought and expectation of what we shall be or have when years will have passed by. But the wisest and the strongest alone understand that right action is its own sufficient blessing, that to do day by day the best one can do is the highest and sweetest life, whatever may come hereafter.

The welfare and happiness of those around us as servants and neighbors give us small concern, and yet we persuade ourselves that we love our country and all mankind; are foolish enough even to imagine that we are capable of making sacrifices to promote the good of those who shall be born a hundred years hence.

The rich and the office-holders receive greater benefits from society and the institutions by which it is maintained than the multitude; and hence they are voluble in professions of patriotism and of respect for law, though in truth they generally love their country less and are more willing to evade the duties of citizenship than the masses of the people, being corrupted by money and by office.

The wholly sincere are bewildered and lost in the midst of a world of pretence, and would flee from the monstrous all-pervading lie to solitude and the presence of God.

The most perfect beauty, that which bears the divinest charm and is clothed with the sweetest grace, eludes our utmost endeavor to understand its nature. We feel its presence, are subdued by its power, worship at its shrine, but whether it be found in the human countenance or in a poem or a painting, in a statue or a musical composition, we know not what it is; and could the veil of mystery be lifted, the spell would be broken.

Men are followed and flattered for their money, their position, their power to confer honor or office, for their titles and social distinctions; and when they are sought for themselves, it is not for their natural, but for their acquired qualities, — for their skill in law or medicine, in oratory or music, for their fine manners, their knowledge of polite usages, or their ability to entertain. What is inborn, — as a healthful and vigorous constitution or physical beauty, — however much it may be cherished by its possessors, has of itself small social value. A man is not esteemed or rewarded for his strength, but for the uses he has taught himself to put it to; not for what nature has given him, but for what art has made him. Physical beauty may attract individuals of opposite sex, but it is held to be a danger or a doubtful good unless it be associated with intelligence, refinement, and moral worth. One's value,

then, as a social being depends not on what he has received from nature, but on what education has made of him.

That man should be able to know and realize his own insignificance; that he, a being of a day, an atom swallowed in immensity, should be capable of thoughts which wander through eternity, of hopes and loves which touch on infinity, is the most indisputable evidence of his heavenly descent and nature; and we are prepared to find that the profoundest minds have the best insight into the essential littleness of human life, the deepest sentiment of its utter vanity, when it is considered merely as a fact of time.

They who lead the life of meditation and aspiration find such peace and joy therein that they little by little lose the power to take interest in the ambitions, struggles, and intrigues which are the substance of history. It all becomes for them but as the meaningless agitations of the mobile and noisy crowd.

The ancient philosophers theorized, speculated, and argued: the modern observe, experiment, and induce conclusions. This method they apply to everything from matter to sensation and thought; but the farther they advance the wider and deeper the realms of nescience open before them. So their larger knowledge clamors for a larger faith.

They who make us laugh make themselves ridiculous; and therefore, we have a secret contempt for jesters, mimics, comedians, and clowns. It is difficult to take seriously those who amuse us. In the courts of feudal lords and kings the providers of merriment were accounted fools. However willing we may be to pay for such entertainment, we do not respect the individuals by whom it is furnished. Laughter is at the expense of others, and is generally provoked by what makes them appear awkward, absurd, or inferior. A smile may be full of approval, encouragement, and love; but laughter is more apt to be unfeeling, mocking, and bitter; or if not so, it bespeaks a vacant mind, and is loudest and most frequent in the company of the rude. The malice there is often found in it is insinuated in the proverb, he laughs best who laughs last. It is senseless to be provoked to merriment by a mishap or a blunder, and to remain serious when we see men forgetting to live, that they may give all their time to the accumulating and hoarding of money. One may find it ridiculous too that a man should be thought superior because he lives in a great house or drives in a showy equipage, while another is contemned for the marks toil has put on him; and if the wise may ever mock and jeer, they should be allowed this privilege when they behold the servile crowd fawning on successful thieves or applauding lying demagogues.

Resignation is a virtue which religion and philosophy alike inculcate; but there is need of watchfulness lest it degenerate into indifference, sloth, negligence, and insensibility; and this danger hides also in humility, obedience, and patience — in all the passive virtues, which if cultivated overmuch beget an indolent and sluggish temper that is easily mistaken for piety. Virtue is essentially strength; and strength becomes weakness unless it exercise itself.

The stoics teach that the wise man finds his happiness, not in the things that lie without or which are subject to another's will, but within his own mind. It is objected that the disposition which makes this possible is dependent on the causes that affect health of body, and may be lost through the unbalancing of reason or the accidents which inflict such pain as to make one incapable of philosophy. This we shall admit, and yet we hold that to fix one's heart on what cannot be taken from him while he remains himself is the best wisdom.

The sense of responsibility — duty, implying, as it does, moral freedom — is the deepest and holiest thing in us. It is God's witness that at the heart of all there lies, not matter and fate, but spirit and liberty. It is born of the consciousness of a Power within the soul, whose judgments are absolute, whose approval or reprobation is on all the thoughts and words and deeds of men. The supreme interests are moral. They are whatever fosters reverence and obedience, hope and courage, love and devotion; whatever lifts man above the law of physical necessity and places him in a world of freedom and joy, where if evil befall, it can only be through his failure to be true to his best insight.

JOHN BANNISTER TABB

(1845–1909)

THE mid-Victorian period which begot the lengthy ruminations of the "Lords of Language" also fostered John Bannister Tabb, the apostle of brevity. He was born of wealthy Virginian parents at their plantation, The Forest, 1845. His early years were under the supervision of private tutors who gave him an excellent background in literature. After the Civil War, in which he served in the Confederate Navy, Tabb trained himself to teach music and literature. While teaching at St. Paul's School, Tabb fell under the influence of the Rev. Alfred Curtis, an Episcopal clergyman. It was Curtis who led Tabb to the Catholic Church in 1872.

Upon his conversion, Tabb prepared himself for the priesthood. He was ordained in 1884 and continued to teach grammar at St. Charles' College until his death at Ellicot City, Maryland, 1909.

Father Tabb's poems are delightful. In an age devoted to wordy excursions in verse, his poetry is brief but penetrating. It is marked with more than precision in language. Puckish humor and sincere faith make it memorable and perennial.

OUT OF BOUNDS*

A little Boy of heavenly birth,
But far from home to-day,

*The above and following poems are from *The Poetry of Father Tabb*, John Bannister Tabb (New York: Dodd, Mead and Co., 1928).

Comes down to find His ball, the earth,
That sin has cast away.
O comrades, let us one and all
Join in to get Him back his ball!

EVOLUTION

Out of the dusk a shadow,
Then, a spark;
Out of the cloud a silence,
Then, a lark;

Out of the heart a rapture,
Then, a pain;
Out of the dead, cold ashes,
Life again.

ANONYMOUS

Anonymous — nor needs a name
To tell the secret whence the flame,
With light, and warmth, and incense, came
A new creation to proclaim.

So was it when, His labor done,
God saw His work, and smiled thereon:
His glory in the picture shone,
But name upon the canvas, none.

CLOVER

Little masters, hat in hand
Let me in your presence stand,
Till your silence solve for me
This your threefold mystery.

Tell me — for I long to know —
How, in darkness there below,
Was your fairy fabric spun,
Spread and fashioned, three in one.

Did your gossips gold and blue,
Sky and Sunshine, choose for you,

Ere your triple forms were seen,
Suited liveries of green?

Can ye, — if ye dwelt indeed
Captives of a prison seed, —
Like the Genie, once again
Get you back into the grain?

Little masters, may I stand
In your presence, hat in hand,
Waiting till you solve for me
This your threefold mystery?

A CHILD'S PRAYER

Make me, dear Lord, polite and kind
To every one, I pray.

And may I ask you how you find
Yourself, dear Lord, today?

F. MARION CRAWFORD
(1854–1909)

THE life of Marion Crawford is an American saga of success. He was born in Tuscany, 1854, and received a magnificent education at Cambridge, Heidelberg, and Rome. His years as newspaper editor, lecturer, and critic admirably prepared him to become one of the most popular novelists of his time. After his conversion to the Catholic Church, 1880, he produced an amazing number of facile works which, though not of first class intensity, caught the fancy of the time. His romantic novels of Roman life such as *Saracinesca* were eagerly awaited and widely read.

Although Crawford had a complete and remarkable knowledge of every phase of continental life, his books are more to be commended for their sound craftsmanship of plot than for character drawing. He often skirts the edge of melodrama, but he does so with a deftness which makes his situations plausible. His novels, published in an endless stream until his death (1909), are eminently readable.

Crawford's complete works have been published by the Macmillan Company in thirty volumes, and a charming biography of the author, *My Cousin Marion Crawford*, has been written by Maude Elliot.

SARACINESCA*

CHAPTER II

THE hour was six o'clock, and the rooms of the Embassy were as full as they were likely to be that day. There would doubtless have been more people had the weather been fine; but it was raining heavily, and below, in the vast court that formed the centre of the palace, the lamps of fifty carriages gleamed through the water and the darkness, and the coachmen, of all dimensions and characters, sat beneath their huge umbrellas and growled to each other, envying the lot of the footmen who were congregated in the ante-chamber up-stairs around the great bronze braziers. But in the reception-rooms there was much light and warmth; there were bright fires and softly shaded lamps, velvet-footed servants stealing softly among the guests, with immense burdens of tea and cake; men of more or less celebrity chatting about politics in corners; women of more or less beauty gossiping over their tea, or flirting, or wishing they had somebody to flirt with; people

of many nations and ideas, with a goodly leaven of Romans. They all seemed endeavoring to get away from the men and women of their own nationality, in order to amuse themselves with the difficulties of conversation in languages not their own. Whether they amused themselves or not is of small importance; but as they were all willing to find themselves together twice a-day for the five months of the Roman season — from the first improvised dance before Christmas, to the last set ball in the warm April weather after Easter — it may be argued that they did not dislike each other's society. In case the afternoon should seem dull, his Excellency had engaged the services of Signor Strillone, the singer. From time to time he struck a few chords upon the grand piano, and gave forth a song of his own composition in loud and passionate tones, varied with very sudden effects of extreme pianissimo, which occasionally surprised some one who was trying to make his conversation heard above the music.

There was a little knot of people standing about the door of the great drawing-room.

*By permission of The Macmillan Company, Publishers, New York: 1893, pp. 12–26.

Some of them were watching their opportunity to slip away unperceived; others had just arrived, and were making a survey of the scene to ascertain the exact position of their Excellencies, and of the persons they most desired to avoid, before coming forward. Suddenly, just as Signor Strillone had reached a high note and was preparing to bellow upon it before letting his voice die away to a pathetic falsetto, the crowd at the door parted a little. A lady entered the room alone, and stood out before the rest, pausing till the singer should have passed the climax of his song, before she proceeded upon her way. She was a very striking woman; every one knew who she was, every one looked towards her, and the little murmur that went round the room was due to her entrance rather than to Signor Strillone's high note.

The Duchessa d'Astrardente stood still, and quietly looked about her. A minister, two secretaries, and three or four princes sprang towards her, each with a chair in hand; but she declined each offer, nodding to one, thanking another by name, and exchanging a few words with a third. She would not sit down; she had not yet spoken to the ambassadress.

Two men followed her closely as she crossed the room when the song was finished. One was a fair man of five-and-thirty, rather stout, and elaborately dressed. He trod softly and carried his hat behind him, while he leaned a little forward in his walk. There was something unpleasant about his face, caused perhaps by his pale complexion and almost colourless moustache; his blue eyes were small and near together, and had a watery, undecided look; his thin fair hair was parted in the middle over his low forehead; there was a scornful look about his mouth, though half concealed by the moustache; and his chin retreated rather abruptly from his lower lip. On the other hand, he was dressed with extreme care, and his manner showed no small confidence in himself as he pushed forwards, keeping as close as he could to the Duchessa. He had the air of being thoroughly at home in his surroundings.

Ugo del Ferice was indeed rarely discon-

certed, and his self-reliance was most probably one chief cause of his success. He was a man who performed the daily miracle of creating everything for himself out of nothing. His father had barely been considered a member of the lower nobility, although he always called himself "dei conti del Ferice" —of the family of the counts of his name; but where or when the Conti del Ferice had lived, was a question he never was able to answer satisfactorily. He had made a little money, and had squandered most of it before he died, leaving the small remainder to his only son, who had spent every scudo of it in the first year. But to make up for the exiguity of his financial resources, Ugo had from his youth obtained social success. He had begun life by boldly calling himself "Il conte del Ferice." No one had ever thought it worth while to dispute him the title; and as he had hitherto not succeeded in conferring it upon any dowered damsel, the question of his countship was left unchallenged. He had made many acquaintances in the college where he had been educated; for his father had paid for his schooling in the Collegio dei Nobili, and that in itself was a passport — for as the lad grew to the young man, he zealously cultivated the society of his old schoolfellows, and by wisely avoiding all other company, acquired a right to be considered one of themselves. He was very civil and obliging in his youth, and had in that way acquired a certain reputation for being indispensable, which had stood him in good stead. No one asked whether he had paid his tailor's bill; or whether, upon certain conditions, his tailor supplied him with raiment gratis. He was always elaborately dressed, he was always ready to take a hand at cards, and he was always invited to every party in the season. He had cultivated with success the science of amusing, and people asked him to dinner in the winter, and to their country houses in the summer. He had been seen in Paris, and was often seen at Monte Carlo; but his real home and hunting-ground was Rome, where he knew every one, and every one knew him. He had made one or two fruitless attempts to marry young women of

American extraction and large fortune; he had not succeeded in satisfying the paternal mind in regard to guarantees, and had consequently been worsted in his endeavours. Last summer, however, it appeared that he had been favoured with an increase of fortune. He gave out that an old uncle of his, who had settled in the south of Italy, had died, leaving him a modest competence; and while assuming a narrow band of *crêpe* upon his hat, he had adopted also a somewhat more luxurious mode of living. Instead of going on foot or in cabs, he kept a very small coupé, with a very small horse and a diminutive coachman: the whole turn-out was very quiet in appearance, but very serviceable withal. Ugo sometimes wore too much jewellery; but his bad taste, if so it could be called, did not extend to the modest equipage. People accepted the story of the deceased uncle, and congratulated Ugo, whose pale face assumed on such occasions a somewhat deprecating smile. "A few scudi," he would answer — "a very small competence; but what would you have? I need so little — it is enough for me." Nevertheless people who knew him well warned him that he was growing stout.

The other man who followed the Duchessa d'Astrardente across the drawing-room was of a different type. Don Giovanni Saracinesca was neither very tall nor remarkably handsome, though in the matter of his beauty opinion varied greatly. He was very dark — almost as dark for a man as the Duchessa was for a woman. He was strongly built, but very lean, and his features stood out in bold and sharp relief from the setting of his short black hair and pointed beard. His nose was perhaps a little large for his face, and the unusual brilliancy of his eyes gave him an expression of restless energy; there was something noble in the shaping of his high square forehead and in the turn of his sinewy throat. His hands were broad and brown, but nervous and well knit, with straight long fingers and squarely cut nails. Many women said Don Giovanni was the handsomest man in Rome; others said he was too dark or too thin, and that his face was hard and his features ugly. There was

a great difference of opinion in regard to his appearance. Don Giovanni was not married, but there were few marriageable women in Rome who would not have been overjoyed to become his wife. But hitherto he had hesitated — or, to speak more accurately, he had not hesitated at all in his celibacy. His conduct in refusing to marry had elicited much criticism, little of which had reached his ears. He cared not much for what his friends said to him, and not at all for the opinion of the world at large, in consequence of which state of mind people often said he was selfish — a view taken extensively by elderly princesses with unmarried daughters, and even by Don Giovanni's father and only near relation, the old Prince Saracinesca, who earnestly desired to see his name perpetuated. Indeed Giovanni would have made a good husband, for he was honest and constant by nature, courteous by disposition, and considerate by habit and experience. His reputation for wildness rested rather upon his taste for dangerous amusements than upon such scandalous adventures as made up the lives of many of his contemporaries. But to all matrimonial proposals he answered that he was barely thirty years of age, that he had plenty of time before him, that he had not yet seen the woman whom he would be willing to marry, and that he intended to please himself.

The Duchessa d'Astrardente made her speech to her hostess and passed on, still followed by the two men; but they now approached her, one on each side, and endeavoured to engage her attention. Apparently she intended to be impartial, for she sat down in the middle one of three chairs, and motioned to her two companions to seat themselves also, which they immediately did, whereby they became for the moment the two most important men in the room.

Corona d'Astrardente was a very dark woman. In all the Southern land there were no eyes so black as hers, no cheeks of such a warm dark-olive tint, no tresses of such raven hue. But if she was not fair, she was very beautiful; there was a delicacy in her regular features that artists said was matchless; her mouth, not small, but generous and nobly cut, showed perhaps more strength, more even determination, than most men like to see in women's faces; but in the exquisitely moulded nostrils there lurked much sensitiveness and the expression of much courage; and the level brow and straight-cut nose were in their clearness as an earnest of the noble thoughts that were within, and that so often spoke from the depths of her splendid eyes. She was not a scornful beauty, though her face could express scorn well enough. Where another woman would have shown disdain, she needed but to look grave, and her silence did the rest. She wielded magnificent weapons, and wielded them nobly, as she did all things. She needed all her strength, too, for her position from the first was not easy. She had few troubles, but they were great ones, and she bore them bravely.

One may well ask why Corona del Carmine had married the old man who was her husband — the broken-down and worn-out dandy of sixty, whose career was so well known, and whose doings had been as scandalous as his ancient name was famous in the history of his country. Her marriage was in itself almost a tragedy. It matters little to know how it came about; she accepted Astrardente with his dukedom, his great wealth, and his evil past, on the day when she left the convent where she had been educated; she did it to save her father from ruin, almost from starvation; she was seventeen years of age; she was told that the world was bad, and she resolved to begin her life by a heroic sacrifice; she took the step heroically, and no human being had ever heard her complain. Five years had elapsed since then, and her father — for whom she had given all she had, herself, her beauty, her brave heart, and her hopes of happiness — her old father, whom she so loved, was dead, the last of his race, saving only this beautiful but childless daughter. What she suffered now — whether she suffered at all — no man knew. There had been a wild burst of enthusiasm when she appeared first in society, a universal cry that it was a sin and a shame. But the cynics who had said she would console herself had been obliged to own their worldly wisdom at fault; the men of all sorts who had lost their hearts to her were ignominiously driven in course of time to find them again elsewhere. Amid all the excitement of the first two years of her life in the world, Corona had moved calmly upon her way, wrapped in the perfect dignity of her character; and the old Duca d'Astrardente had smiled and played with the curled locks of his wonderful wig, and had told every one that his wife was the one woman in the universe who was above suspicion. People had laughed incredulously at first; but as time wore on they held their peace, tacitly acknowledging that the aged fop was right as usual, but swearing in their hearts that it was the shame of shames to see the noblest woman in their midst tied to such a wretched remnant of dissipated humanity as the Duca d'Astrardente. Corona went everywhere, like other people; she received in her own house a vast number of acquaintances; there were a few friends who came and went much as they pleased, and some of them were young; but there was never a breath of scandal breathed about the Duchessa. She was indeed above suspicion.

She sat now between two men who were evidently anxious to please her. The position was not new; she was, as usual, to talk to both, and yet to show no preference for either. And yet she had a preference, and in her heart she knew it was a strong one. It was by no means indifferent to her which of those two men left her side and which remained. She was above suspicion — yes, above the suspicion of any human being besides herself, as she had been for five long years. She knew that had her husband entered the room and passed that way, he would have nodded to Giovanni Saracinesca as carelessly as though Giovanni had been his wife's brother — as carelessly as he would have noticed Ugo del Ferice upon her other side. But in her own heart she knew that there was but one face in all Rome she loved to see, but one voice she loved, and dreaded too, for it had the power to make her life seem unreal, till she wondered how long it would last, and whether there would ever be any change. The difference between Giovanni and other men had always been apparent. Others would sit beside her and make conversation, and then occasionally would make speeches she did not care to hear, would talk to her of love — some praising it as the only thing worth living for, some with affected cynicism scoffing at it as the greatest of unrealities, contradicting themselves a moment later in some passionate declaration to herself. When they were foolish she laughed at them; when they went too far, she quietly rose and left them. Such experiences had grown rare of late, for she had earned the reputation of being cold and unmoved, and that protected her. But Giovanni had never talked like the rest of them. He never mentioned the old, worn subjects that the others harped upon. She would not have found it easy to say what he talked about, for he talked indifferently about many subjects. She was not sure whether he spent more time with her when in society than with other women; she reflected that he was not so brilliant as many men she knew, not so talkative as the majority of men she met; she knew only — and it was the thing she most bitterly reproached herself with — that she preferred his face above all other faces, and his voice beyond all voices. It never entered her head to think that she loved him; it was bad enough in her simple creed that there should be any man whom she would rather see than not, and whom she missed when he did not approach her. She was a very strong and loyal woman, who had sacrificed herself to a man who knew the world very thoroughly, who in the thoroughness of his knowledge was able to see that the world is not all bad, and who, in spite of all his evil deeds, was proud of his wife's loyalty. Astrardente had made a bargain when he married Corona; but he was a wise man in his generation, and he knew and valued her when he had got her. He knew the precise dangers to which she was exposed, and he was not so cruel as to expose her to them willingly. He had at first watched keenly the effect produced upon her by conversing with men of all

sorts in the world, and among others he had noticed Giovanni; but he had come to the conclusion that his wife was equal to any situation in which she might be placed. Moreover, Giovanni was not an *habitué* at the Palazzo Astrardente, and showed none of the usual signs of anxiety to please the Duchessa.

From the time when Corona began to notice her own predilection for Saracinesca, she had been angry with herself for it, and she tried to avoid him; at all events, she gave him no idea that she liked him especially. Her husband, who at first had delivered many lectures on the subject of behaviour in the world, had especially warned her against showing any marked coldness to a man she wished to shun. "Men," said he, "are accustomed to that; they regard it as the first indication that a woman is really interested; when you want to get rid of a man, treat him systematically as you treat everybody, and he will be wounded at your indifference and go away." But Giovanni did not go, and Corona began to wonder whether she ought not to do something to break the interest she felt in him.

At the present moment she wanted a cup of tea. She would have liked to send Ugo del Ferice for it; she did what she thought least pleasant to herself, and she sent Giovanni. The servants who were serving the refreshments had all left the room, and Saracinesca went in pursuit of them. As soon as he was gone Del Ferice spoke. His voice was soft, and had an insinuating tone in it.

"They are saying that Don Giovanni is to be married," he remarked, watching the Duchessa from the corners of his eyes as he indifferently delivered himself of his news.

The Duchessa was too dark a woman to show emotion easily. Perhaps she did not believe the story; her eyes fixed themselves on some distant object in the room, as though she were intensely interested in something she saw, and she paused before she answered.

"That is news indeed, if it is true. And whom is he going to marry?"

"Donna Tullia Mayer, the widow of the

financier. She is immensely rich, and is some kind of cousin of the Saracinesca."

"How strange!" exclaimed Corona. "I was just looking at her. Is not that she over there, with the green feathers?"

"Yes," answered Del Ferice, looking in the direction the Duchessa indicated. "That is she. One may know her at a vast distance by her dress. But it is not all settled yet."

"Then one cannot congratulate Don Giovanni to-day?" asked the Duchessa, facing her interlocutor rather suddenly.

"No," he answered; "it is perhaps better not to speak to him about it."

"It is as well that you warned me, for I would certainly have spoken."

"I do not imagine that Saracinesca likes to talk of his affairs of the heart," said Del Ferice, with considerable gravity. "But here he comes. I had hoped he would have taken even longer to get that cup of tea."

"It was long enough for you to tell your news," answered Corona quietly, as Don Giovanni came up.

"What is the news?" asked he, as he sat down beside her.

"Only an engagement that is not yet announced," answered the Duchessa. "Del Ferice has the secret; perhaps he will tell you."

Giovanni glanced across her at the fair pale man, whose fat face, however, expressed nothing. Seeing he was not enlightened, Saracinesca civilly turned the subject.

"Are you going to the meet to-morrow, Duchessa?" he asked.

"That depends upon the weather and upon the Duke," she answered. "Are you going to follow?"

"Of course. What a pity it is that you do not ride!"

"It seems such an unnatural thing to see a woman hunting," remarked Del Ferice, who remembered to have heard the Duchessa say something of the kind, and was consequently sure that she would agree with him.

"You do not ride yourself," said Don Giovanni, shortly. "That is the reason you do not approve of it for ladies."

"I am not rich enough to hunt," said Ugo, modestly. "Besides the other reason is a good one; for when ladies hunt I am deprived of their society."

The Duchessa laughed slightly. She never felt less like laughing in her life, and yet it was necessary to encourage the conversation. Giovanni did not abandon the subject.

"It will be a beautiful meet," he said. "Many people are going out for the first time this year. There is a man here who has brought his horses from England. I forget his name — a rich Englishman."

"I have met him," said Del Ferice, who was proud of knowing everybody. "He is a type — enormously rich — a lord — I cannot pronounce his name — not married either. He will make a sensation in society. He won races in Paris last year, and they say he will enter one of his hunters for the steeplechases here at Easter."

"That is a great inducement to go to the meet, to see this Englishman," said the Duchessa rather wearily, as she leaned back in her chair. Giovanni was silent, but showed no intention of going. Del Ferice, with an equal determination to stay, chattered vivaciously.

"Don Giovanni is quite right," he continued. "Every one is going. There will be two or three drags. Madame Mayer has induced Valdarno to have out his four-in-hand, and to take her and a large party."

The Duchessa did not hear the remainder of Del Ferice's speech, for at the mention of Donna Tullia — now commonly called Madame Mayer — she instinctively turned and looked at Giovanni. He, too, had caught the name, though he was not listening in the least to Ugo's chatter; and as he met Corona's eyes he moved uneasily, as much as to say he wished the fellow would stop talking. A moment later, Del Ferice rose from his seat; he had seen Donna Tullia passing near, and thought the opportunity favourable for obtaining an invitation to join the party on the drag. With a murmured excuse which Corona did not hear, he went in pursuit of his game.

"I thought he was never going," said

Giovanni, moodily. He was not in the habit of posing as the rival of any one who happened to be talking to the Duchessa. He had never said anything of the kind before, and Corona experienced a new sensation, not altogether unpleasant. She looked at him in some surprise.

"Do you not like Del Ferice?" she inquired, gravely.

"Do you like him yourself?" he asked in reply.

"What a question! Why should I like or dislike any one?"

There was perhaps the smallest shade of bitterness in her voice as she asked the question she had so often asked herself. Why should she like Giovanni Saracinesca, for instance?

"I do not know what the world would be like if we had no likes and dislikes," said Giovanni, suddenly. "It would be a poor place; perhaps it is only a poor place at best. I merely wondered whether Del Ferice amused you as he amuses everybody."

"Well, then, frankly he has not amused me to-day," answered Corona, with a smile.

"Then you are glad he is gone?"

"I do not regret it."

"Duchessa," said Giovanni, suddenly changing his position, "I am glad he is gone, because I want to ask you a question. Do I know you well enough to ask you a question?"

"It depends—" Corona felt the blood rise suddenly to her dark forehead. Her hands burned intensely in her gloves. The anticipation of something she had never heard made her heart beat uncontrollably in her breast.

"It is only about myself," continued Giovanni, in low tones. He had seen the blush, so rare a sight that there was not another man in Rome who had seen it. He had not time to think what it meant. "It is only about myself," he went on. "My father wants me to marry; he insists that I should marry Donna Tullia—Madame Mayer."

"Well?" asked Corona. She shivered; a moment before, she had been oppressed with the heat. Her monosyllabic question was low

and indistinct. She wondered whether Giovanni could hear the beatings of her heart, so slow, so loud they almost deafened her.

"Simply this. Do you advise me to marry her?"

"Why do you ask me, of all people?" asked Corona, faintly.

"I would like to have your advice," said Giovanni, twisting his brown hands together and fixing his bright eyes upon her face.

"She is young yet. She is handsome—she is fabulously rich. Why should you not marry her? Would she make you happy?"

"Happy? Happy with her? No indeed. Do you think life would be bearable with such a woman?"

"I do not know. Many men would marry her if they could—"

"Then you think I should?" asked Giovanni. Corona hesitated; she could not understand why she should care, and yet she was conscious that there had been no such struggle in her life since the day she had blindly resolved to sacrifice herself to her father's wishes in accepting Astrardente. Still there could be no doubt what she should say: how could she advise any one to marry without the prospect of the happiness she had never had?

"Will you not give me your counsel?" repeated Saracinesca. He had grown very pale, and spoke with such earnestness that Corona hesitated no longer.

"I would certainly advise you to think no more about it, if you are sure that you cannot be happy with her."

Giovanni drew a long breath, the blood returned to his face, and his hands unlocked themselves.

"I will think no more about it," he said. "Heaven bless you for your advice, Duchessa!"

"Heaven grant I have advised you well!" said Corona, almost inaudibly. "How cold this house is! Will you put down my cup of tea? Let us go near the fire; Strillone is going to sing again."

"I would like him to sing a 'Nunc dimittis, Domine,' for me," murmured Giovanni, whose eyes were filled with a strange light.

Half an hour later Corona d'Astrardente went down the steps of the Embassy wrapped in her furs and preceded by her footman. As she reached the bottom Giovanni Saracinesca came swiftly down and joined her as her carriage drove up out of the dark courtyard. The footman opened the door, but Giovanni put out his hand to help Corona to mount the step. She laid her small gloved fingers upon the sleeve of his overcoat, and as she sprang lightly in she thought his arm trembled.

"Good night, Duchessa; I am very grateful to you," he said.

"Good night; why should you be grateful?" she asked, almost sadly.

Giovanni did not answer, but stood hat in hand as the great carriage rolled out under the arch. Then he buttoned his greatcoat, and went out alone into the dark and muddy streets. The rain had ceased, but everything was wet, and the broad pavements gleamed under the uncertain light of the flickering gas-lamps.

MAURICE FRANCIS EGAN

(1852–1924)

BORN of Irish parents in Philadelphia, 1852, Maurice Francis Egan received a sound education at La Salle College, Georgetown, and the University of Pennsylvania. As editor of the *Freeman's Journal* and professor at Notre Dame, he revealed a sweet reasonableness and witty brilliance which made him an admirable diplomat and an adviser of several Presidents. He received the Laetare Medal from the University of Notre Dame in 1910 and was United States Minister to Denmark, 1907–1918. He died in Brooklyn in 1924.

Egan's works were popular. His many books for children, which form the great bulk of his writings, are testimonials to his amiable outlook on life, at once receptive and well balanced. His book, *The Gentleman,* a treatise on manners, was once read to all Catholic high school students and probably had more effect on generations of immigrants than is readily apparent. As a critic Egan was noted for wit and urbanity, rather than great depth. His study of a saint, *Everybody's St. Francis,* is a tenderly appreciative book, and his autobiography, *Recollections of a Happy Life,* is both superb history and gracious self-revelation.

III

THE WOLF OF GUBBIO AND THE COMING OF SANTA CLARA*

FRANCIS was now free to preach; formerly a bishop or a parish priest might object to an unaccredited layman's assuming the prerogatives of the ordained. As the Catholic Church, the central basis of which is authority, refuses the Bible to the unlearned

unless it is accompanied by an authoritative interpretation, so a preacher unauthorized by superior authority is suspect. Francis had desired the blessing of Innocent III for his way of life; but even more he had desired the permission he now received.

In 1211 the Benedictines, to whom the chapel of the Portiuncula belonged, gave it to Francis; but he refused to own it, and

*From *Everybody's St. Francis* by Maurice F. Egan, copyright, 1912, by The Century Company, 1940, by Roger B. de Monvel, reprinted by permission of D. Appleton-Century Company, Inc., pp. 90–109.

rented it for a basket of fish, to be sent annually to its owners. On the altar was a picture of the "Assumption of Our Lady," and from the symbols in the picture the chapel was known as that of "Our Lady of the Angels." In the wood near the place, which Francis loved, the brethren built a hut of interwoven branches, thatched with mud and leaves. They slept on straw, and the ground served both for tables and for chairs. There were no inclosures about their cabins except hedges. The cabin, the earliest model of a Franciscan establishment, and that which Francis hoped would always be the model, was called *luogo*. The word "convent," afterward substituted, implied a giving way to the relaxation Francis feared from the influence of prudent prelates and the learned; for it must be admitted that, excepting the people who concerned themselves with making cheerful songs and the pious interpretation of the word of God, Francis had a pathetic horror of the learned. As the colony of the Portiuncula grew, new buildings were made of wood, plastered with mud. The friars must dwell in them as pilgrims and strangers.

The influence of Francis was so great at this time that all received his decisions with joy, and the wretched cabins in the wood seemed to be the vestibules of paradise. He was looked on as the living symbol of Christ, for, it must be repeated, that abstractions did not appeal to the medieval folk. Here was a man who did what Christ had counseled — not commanded — those who would follow him perfectly to do. His example in the way of perfection was not for everybody. It was enough for these brethren that they had answered the call. Their lamps must shine before all men, because Christ lived in them, but gently, sweetly, as light falls.

In the beginning there were murmurs against this imprudent, unwise, and unworldly way of life. Common sense was against it; but, then, from the point of view of the Roman patrician, the aristocratic citizen of Jerusalem, and the well-fed money-changers, Christ himself was not a person of common sense. This opinion was not that of Brother Bernard, the kind and patient, or

of Brother Giles, the loving and literal, or of Brother Junipero, who was one of the *jongleurs du bon Dieu,* but perhaps it was of Brother John, who wore a hat and left the community because he could not see how sensible men could live without money. If the farmers did not employ the brothers, they had to live on what they could beg. Roots and edible leaves, without the condiments that Francis loved in his salads, were, with cold water, often their only portion. The gray of the olive-tree, the speckled red-and-white roses, and the changing sky, held great consolation for the little band, and Francis, singing of the wonders of God in nature, kept love aflame within their hearts.

Today we ask with Brother John, who was probably not the Judas some of the shocked brethren believed him to be, but only a practical person who wished to have his own way: How could they be happy on nothing a day?

It must be remembered that at this time Francis was not thinking of improving the general condition of labor. A beggar who asked alms and a great prince, with a magnificent court, were equal in his eyes, though he loved the beggar more because he was poor. Francis did not work for the laborer alone; he worked for everybody, and everybody must pray or beg or work for everybody else, that the kingdom of Christ on earth might be fulfilled. As he grew older, and the counsels of prudence and common sense prevailed among his brethren, and they became learned, and ceased to wear the meanest clothes and to live in mud-thatched huts, his heart wept. One day he left his cell for a few moments, and a friar came to him.

"Whence came you, Brother?" he asked.

"I came from your cell," the friar replied.

"Since you have called it mine," Francis answered, "let another dwell there, and not I."

His brothers who were near him many times heard him say, "Foxes have holes, and the birds of the air have nests; but the Son of man hath not where to lay his head."

What could people of common sense do with such a man? He had forced the hard-headed Innocent III to bless his "impossibilities" cordially, and all of a sudden the whole world was running after him. Unless we have something in our hearts that yearns to love as he loved, we must put this phenomenon down to the mysteries of the medieval heart. New brethren came flocking to Portiuncula. Brother Thomas of Celano in his rhetorical way tells us that the brethren really loved one another. They recited the breviary as though they were priests, ever and anon crying out in spiritual and vocal unison, "Our Father who art in heaven!"

ANECDOTES OF FRANCIS

The heart of the time would be wholly exalted or not at all. Francis said to the man who was willing to give his money to his relatives, but not to the poor: "Go, Brother Fly! Go!" With Francis, "Brother Fly" was a term of reproach. Fired by his preaching, an ardent young peasant, driving two oxen, came in his way.

"What shall I do to be saved?" asked the honest man.

"Give all you have to the poor."

The peasant unharnessed one of the oxen.

"This one," he said, "I will take with me when I go to the Portiuncula; that one I will give to the poor."

Francis, who had rejected all the property of rich disciples, smiled at the simplicity of the man. "I accept," he said; "yet first let us see your father and mother."

But the old folks made difficulties. They regretted the loss of their son, but quite as much they seemed to regret the loss of the ox.

"Let us make a bargain," Francis said. "I will take your son, and give you back his ox." The chronicler leads us to believe that the old couple were willing to agree to this.

The power of Francis with all animate things was marvelous. This is one fact that permeates all the legends, and on which all his biographers agree. And he had the gift of reading the minds of those he loved. There is a story of a young friar who believed that Francis disliked him. One day when this brother was particularly unhappy, thinking that the dislike of Francis meant some serious fault on his part, some ingrained sin, for he knew that Francis loved all created things, the dew of refreshment fell upon him. Francis read his mind and said: "Come to me. Whenever you desire to talk of heavenly things, come to me." and the forlorn young man was made happy.

THE WOLF OF GUBBIO

Whether the story of the conversation of Francis with the wolf of Gubbio is true or not, or, as has been suggested, it is a sublimated version of his interview with the haughty patricians of Assisi and their former slaves, the plebeians, it is certain that the children and the simple-hearted prefer to believe that the wolf was a real wolf; and the children and the simple-hearted are nearer to God than most of us. The story of Francis, who was a saint largely because he was *un uomo de genio,* is so wonderful that to be on the side of the children and of the angels is the only way of understanding it. It cannot be in the least comprehended from the modern analytical point of view. The devil, as Coventry Patmore says, was the first analyst, and we all know what happened to Marguerite after she tore the daisy to pieces.

The story of the wolf of Agobio (Gubbio) is told in the twenty-first chapter of "I Fioretti." It seems that at one time Francis dwelt in the city of Gubbio. Now, the citizens were very unhappy because there was a wolf near the town, and the wolf gave them no peace by day or night. Mothers were afraid to let their children play about. The men were armed, but so furious was this beast that even weapons seemed useless against him, or at least the men were afraid to use them. The fright of the men might not have moved Francis, but the terror of the mothers and children he could not endure; and, then, in his opinion both the citizens and the wolf were to blame. The wolf had never been spoken to of Christ, and he acted only according to his nature; for wolves must eat. The citizens had not remembered that he was God's creature, and that, therefore, they should have made a friend of him. Francis determined to force the beast to hear reason. Despite the advice of the people, he went out to meet the wolf, making the sign of the cross. His brethren accompanied him part of the way, but waited at a safe distance with the people who had come out to view the fearful sight.

The wolf rushed at Francis with open mouth. Francis made over him the sign of the cross, and said gently:

"I command thee, Brother Wolf, on the part of Christ, that you do not do harm to me or anybody."

Upon this the terrible wolf lay down like a lamb at the feet of Francis. He had been addressed properly,—a thing which had never happened before,—and he was willing to hear reason.

"Brother Wolf," continued Francis, "you have done great evil here, hunting and killing God's own without His permission, and not only eating animals, but men created in the image of God; and so you have made yourself a thief and a murderer of the worst kind, and deserve to be hanged like a criminal. And everybody hates you, and voices that hatred. But I would make peace between you and the men of Gubbio, if you will offend no more. They will pardon you, and neither men nor dogs shall molest you."

The wolf, who had not eaten people maliciously or for amusement, but because he was hungry, showed by the expression of his eyes and the movements of his head and tail that he agreed with Francis and was willing to accept his decision. But Francis, according to the manner of the Middle Ages, exacted a symbol of the good faith of the wolf. Brother Wolf must give his paw upon it, on condition that Francis would see that the people of Assisi fed him every day. This peace having been arranged, the wolf, much to the amazement of the citizens, meekly followed Francis to hear him preach. Francis told them that sin was the occasion of the evils that befell them. The flames of God's punishment, he said, with the wolf standing near him and listening attentively, are more terrible than the teeth of an animal that can destroy only the body. "Go, then dear brethren, to God, and do penance for your offenses against Him, and He will save you from the flames of hell."

And then Francis asked Brother Wolf again to put his right paw into his right hand, in the presence of witnesses, as a pledge that he would keep his part of the agreement; for Francis no doubt felt that it would be hard, unless his brother was impressed with the nature of the oath, to keep him from returning to his pagan ways; and perhaps, after all, the wolf might be tempted to find amusement by chasing the terrified men of Assisi into their houses.

Everybody in Gubbio, happy at the prospect of peace, blessed Francis as with one voice. After this, Brother Wolf became a great favorite in Gubbio; he went from house to house, a cherished friend, and the children played with him as though he were a big dog, and the dogs themselves, out of respect for Francis, did not bark at him. Two years later, when Brother Wolf died of old age, Gubbio grieved heartily because "While he went about the place gently," he recalled "vividly the virtue and holiness of St. Francis."

FRANCIS AND THE TURTLE-DOVES

Francis believed that God gave special grace to those who loved his little sisters and brothers, the birds and the beasts. Even Brother Fly, though Francis evidently did not look upon him as the elect, like the lambs and the doves, was not to be called accursed. One day Francis met a youth of amiable appearance on his way to market with a number of turtle-doves in a cage. Now, Francis loved doves, they were so gentle and so affectionate, and had not the Madonna herself offered them in the temple?

"O buono giovane," he said, "give unto me these birds, which are in holy writ compared to chaste and humble souls, so that they may not fall into cruel hands and be killed."

And the young man, by the grace of God, gave the cage of doves to Francis. And then Francis looked into the youth's eyes and said sweetly:

"Little son, thou wilt later be a brother in

this order, and serve Jesus Christ most graciously."

And so in time the good youth became one of the blessed order of Francis, and died in the grace of God, which Francis had sought for him because he enabled him to set the doves free. And to the doves he said:

"O my little pure doves, my little sisters, simple, innocent, chaste, why did you let yourselves be taken? See, I snatch you from death, and give nests to you, wherein you may increase and multiply, according to the commandment of the Creator."

Francis made nests for them at the Portiuncula, and without fear they lived with their families among the brethren, by whom they were fed. And after they had been fed, they would not go away until Francis had given them his blessing.

The mighty love in the heart of Francis drew all pure-hearted things to him, and gave him power to work what men called miracles. There are many records of his way with sinners; for no sinner was hopeless in his eyes, and there was no sinner who might not be called his brother.

III. WHAT MAKES A GENTLEMAN*

CARDINAL NEWMAN made a famous definition and description, both in the same paragraph, of a gentleman. "It is almost," he said, in his "Idea of a University," "a definition of a gentleman to say he is one who never inflicts pain." And this truth will be found to be the basis of all really good manners. Good manners come from the heart, while etiquette is only an invention of wise heads to prevent social friction, or to keep fools at a distance. Nobody but an idiot will slap a man on the back unless the man invites the slap by his own familiarity. It seems to me that the primary rule which, according to Cardinal Newman, makes a gentleman is more disregarded in large schools than anywhere else. There is no sign which indicates ignorance or lack of culture so plainly as the tendency to censure, to jibe, to sneer, — to be always on the alert to find faults and defects. On the other hand, a true gentleman does not censure, if he can help it: he prefers to discover virtues rather than faults; and, if he sees a defect, he is silent about it until he can gently suggest a remedy.

The school-boy is not remarkable for such reticence. And this may be one of the reasons why he has the reputation of being selfish, ungrateful, and sometimes cruel. He is not any of these things; he is, as a rule, only

thoughtless. It has been said that a *blunder* is often worse than a *crime;* and thoughtlessness sometimes produces effects that are more enduringly disastrous than crimes. Forgetfulness among boys or young men is thoughtlessness. If an engineer forget for a *moment,* his train may go to RUIN. If a telegrapher forget to send a message, death may be the result; but neither of them can acquire such control over himself that he will always *remember,* if he does not practise the art of thinking every day of his life. It is thoughtfulness, consideration, that makes life not only endurable, but pleasant. As Christians, we are bound to do to others as we would have them do to us. But as members of a great society, in which each person must be a factor even more important than he imagines, we shall find that, even if our Christianity did not move us to bear and forbear from the highest motives, ordinary prudence and regard for our own comfort and reputation should lead us to do these things. The Christian gentleman is the highest type: he may be a hero as well as a gentleman. Culture produces another type, and Cardinal Newman thus describes him. The Cardinal begins by saying that "it is almost a definition of a gentleman to say he is one who never inflicts pain. This description," he continues, "is both refined and, as far as it goes, accurate. The gentleman is mainly occupied in merely removing the

*Egan, Maurice F., *The Gentleman* (New York: Benziger Brothers, 1893), pp. 47–63.

obstacles which hinder the free and unembarrassed action of those about him; and he concurs with their movements rather than takes the initiative himself. The benefits may be considered as parallel to what are called comforts or conveniences in arrangements of a personal nature; like an easy-chair or a good fire, which do their part in dispelling cold or fatigue, though nature provides both means of rest and animal heat without them. The true gentleman in like manner carefully avoids whatever may cause a jar or a jolt in the minds of those with whom he is cast, — all clashing of opinion or collision of feeling, all restraint or suspicion or gloom or resentment, — his great concern being to make every one at their ease or at home. He has his eyes on all the company: he is tender towards the bashful, gentle towards the distant, and merciful towards the absurd; he can recollect to whom he is speaking; he guards against unreasonable allusions or topics which may irritate; he is seldom prominent in conversation, and never wearisome. He makes light of favors which he does them, and seems to be receiving when he is conferring. He never speaks of himself except when compelled, never defends himself by a mere retort; he has no ears for slander or gossip, is scrupulous in imputing motives to those who interfere with him, and interprets everything for the best. He is never mean or little in his disputes, never takes unfair advantage, never mistakes personalities or sharp sayings for arguments, or insinuates evil which he dare not say out. From a long-sighted prudence he observes the maxim of the ancient sage, that we should ever conduct ourselves towards our enemy as if he were one day to be our friend."

The Cardinal's definition of a gentleman does not end with these words: you can find it for yourself in his "Idea of a University," page 204. It will be found, on examination, to contain the principles which give a man power to make his own life and that of his fellow-beings cheerful and pleasant. And life is short enough and hard enough to need all the kindness, all the cheerfulness, all the gentleness, that we can put into it.

If a friend passes from among us, one of the most enduring of our consolations is that we never gave him needless pain while he lived. And who can say which of our friends may go next? He who sits by you to-night, he who greets you first in the morning, may suffer from a hasty word or a thoughtless act that you can never recall.

It is in the ordinary ways of life that the true gentleman shows himself. He does not wait until he gets out of school to pay attention to the little things. He begins here, and he begins the moment he feels that he ought to begin. Somebody once wrote that the man who has never made a mistake is a fool. And another man added to this, that a wise man makes mistakes, but *never* the *same* mistake *twice*. A gentleman at heart may blush when he thinks of his mistakes, but he never repeats them. It is a mistake made by thoughtless young people to stand near others who are talking. It is a grave sin against politeness for them to listen, as they sometimes do, with eyes and ears open for fear they should miss any of the words not intended for them. The young man thus engaged is an object of pity and contempt. Politeness may prevent others from rebuking him publicly, but it does not change their opinion of him, nor does it enter their minds to excuse him on the plea that he "didn't think."

It does not seem to strike some of you that the convenience of those who work for you ought to be considered, and that unnecessary splashings of liquids and dropping of crumbs and morsels of food is the most reprehensible indication of thoughtlessness.

We often forget that criticism does not mean fault-finding. It means rather the art of finding virtues; and after any private entertainment, at which each performer has done his best for his audience, it is very bad taste to point out all the defects in his work: you may do this at rehearsal, but not after the work is done; you may discourage him by touching on something that he cannot help. A friend of mine once played a part in *Box and Cox,* but on the day after the performance he was much cast down by the comments in one of the daily papers. "Mr. Smith," the critic said, "was admirable, but he should not have made himself ridiculous by wearing such an abnormally *long false nose.*" As the nose happened to be Mr. Smith's own, he was discouraged. Criticism of music especially, unless it be intelligent, is likely to make the critic seem ignorant. For instance, there was on one occasion on a musical programme a *ballade* by Chopin in A flat major. The young woman who played it on the piano was afterwards horrified to find herself described as having sung a *lively* ballad called "A Fat Major"! The musical critic had better know what he is talking about or be silent. No, no, gentlemen, let us not be censorious about the efforts of those who do their best for us; and good-fellowship — what the French call *esprit de corps* — ought to show itself in our manners. Anybody can blame injudiciously, but few can praise judiciously. At college boys especially must remember that the college is part of ourselves, and that any reproach on our *alma mater* is a reproach on *ourselves*. Its reputation is our reputation, and the critically censorious student will find that, in the end, it is the wiser course to dwell on the best side of his college life. The world hates a faultfinder; he will soon see himself left entirely alone with those acute perceptions that help him to find out all that is bad in his fellow-creatures and nothing that is good. To be a gentleman, one must be tolerant, and above all, grateful.

In the world outside there are many kinds of entertainment. We disposed of the dinner-party in a preceding page. One's conduct anywhere must be guided by good sense and the usages of the occasion. At a concert, for instance, the main object of each person present is to hear the music. Anything that interferes with this is a breach of good manners. To chatter during a song or while a piece of music is played shows selfish disregard for the comfort of others and a contemptible indifference to the feelings of the performer. Music may be a great aid to conversation, but conversation is no assistance to music; and people who go to a concert do not pay for their tickets to hear somebody in the next seat tell his private affairs in a loud voice. There are some human creatures who seem to imagine that they may reveal everything possible to their next neighbor in a crowded theatre without being heard by anybody else. There is an old anecdote, but a true one, of a very fashionable lady in Boston who attended an organ recital in the Music Hall there. She was supposed to be an amateur critic of classical music, but her reputation was shattered by an unlucky pause in the tones of the organ. The music ceased unexpectedly, and the only sound heard was that of her voice, soaring above the silence and saying to her friend, "We fry ours in Lard." Her reputation was ruined in musical circles. One goes to a concert or an opera to listen, not to talk. It is only the vulgar, the ostentatious, the ignorant, that distinguish themselves in public places by a disregard of the rights of others. To enter a concert-room late and to interrupt a singer, to enter any public hall while a speaker is making an address, is to excite the disapproval of all well-bred people. Sir Charles Thornton, for a long time British minister at Washington, was noted for his care in this particular; he would stand for half an hour outside the door of a concert-room rather than enter while a piece of music was in progress.

Weddings, I presume, may be put down under the head of entertainments. The etiquette of the assistants is very simple. A wedding invitation requires no answer; a card sent by mail and addressed to the senders of the invitation, who are generally the father and mother of the bride, is quite sufficient. It is unnecessary to say that it is not proper during a marriage ceremony to stand on the seats of the pews in order to get a good look at the happy pair. A tradition exists to the effect that a man during a wedding ceremony once climbed on a confessional. It is added, too, — and I am glad of it, — that he fell and broke his neck. But there is no knowing what some barbarians will do: watch them on Sundays, chewing toothpicks, standing in ranks outside of the churches, and believing that the ladies are admiring their best clothes.

My list of entertainments would be incomplete without the dancing party. St. Francis de Sales says of dancing, that a little of it ought to go a great way. Society ordains that every man shall learn to dance; but if he can talk intelligently, society will forgive him for not dancing. Dancing, after all, is only a substitute for conversation; and, properly directed, it is a very good substitute for scandal, mean gossip, or the frivolous chatter which makes assemblies of young people unendurable to anybody who has not begun to be afflicted with softening of the brain.

Public dances — dances into which anybody can find entrance by paying a fee — are avoided by decent people. A young man who has any regard for his reputation will avoid them; and as nearly every young man has his way to make in the world, he can not too soon realize how the report that he frequents such places will hurt him; for, as I said, there are no secrets in this world, — everything comes out sooner or later.

It is no longer the fashion for a young man to invite a young woman to accompany him to a dance, even at a private house. He must first ask her mother. This European fashion has — thank heaven! — reached many remote districts of late, where young people hitherto ignored the existence of their parents when social pleasures were concerned. The young girl who doesn't want "the old man to know" had better be avoided. And in the best circles young women are not permitted to go to the theatre or to dances without a *chaperon*, — that is, the mother or some elderly lady is expected to accompany the young people. This, of course, makes trips to the theatre expensive; but the young man who cannot afford to take an extra aunt or mother had better avoid such amusements until he can.

As to whether you are to take part in the round dances or not, that will be settled by your confessor: I have no right to dictate on that subject. But if you are invited to a dance, pay your respects to your hostess *first,* and say something pleasant. You must remember that she intends that you shall be useful, — that you shall dance with the ladies to whom she introduces you, and that you shall not think of your own pleasure entirely, but help to give others pleasure by dancing with the ladies who have no partners. In a word, you must be as unselfish in this frivolous atmosphere as

on more serious occasions. When the refreshments are served, you must think of yourself last. If you want to gorge yourself, you can take a yard or two of Bologna sausage to your room after the entertainment is over. A young man over twenty-one should wear an evening suit and no jewelry at a dance. Infants under that age are supposed to be safely tucked in bed at the time the ordinary dance begins.

At a dance or at any other entertainment no introduction should be made thoughtlessly. If a gentleman is presented to a lady, it should be done only after her permission has been asked and received. And the form should be, "Mrs. Jones, allow me to present Mr. Smith." A younger man should always be introduced to an older man, one of inferior position to one of superior position. If you are introducing a friend to the mayor of your city, you ought not to say, "Let me introduce the Mayor to you." On the contrary, the form should be "Mr. Mayor, allow me to present my friend Mr. Smith."

On being introduced to a lady, it is not the fashion for a man to extend his hand, — for hand-shaking on first introduction is a thing of the past. If the lady extends her hand, it is proper to take it but the pump-handle style is no longer practised, except perhaps in some unknown wilds of Alaska. After a man is introduced to a lady and he meets her again, he must not bow until she has bowed to him. In France the man bows first; in America and England we give that privilege to the woman. An American takes his hat entirely from his head when he meets a lady; a foreigner raises it but slightly, but he bows lower than we do. In introducing people, we ought always to be careful to give them their titles, and to add, if possible, the place from which they come. If Mr. Jones, of Chicago, is introduced to Mr. Robinson, of New York, the subject for conversation is already arranged. We know what they will talk about. If the wife of the President introduced you to him, she would call him the President; but if you addressed him, you would call him "Mr. President," as you would address the mayor of a city as "Mr. Mayor." Mrs. Grant was the only President's wife who did not give her husband his title in introductions; she called him simply and modestly, "Mr. Grant."

An English bard sings:

"I know a duke; well — let him pass —
I may not call his grace an ass,
Though if I did, I'd do no wrong —
Save to the asses and my song.

"The duke is neither wise nor good:
He gambles, drinks, scorns womanhood;
And at the age of twenty-four
Is worn and battered as threescore.

"I know a waiter in Pall Mall,
Who works and waits and reasons well
Is gentle, courteous, and refined,
And has a magnet in his mind.

"What is it makes his graceless grace
So like a jockey out of place?
What makes the waiter — tell who can —
The very flower of gentleman?

"Perhaps their mothers! — God is great!
It can't be accident or fate.
The waiter's heart is true, — and then,
Good manners make our gentlemen."

AGNES REPPLIER

(1858–   )

PHILADELPHIA was the birthplace of Agnes Repplier. She was born there April 1, 1858. Judging from her witty book, *Our Convent Days,* Agnes Repplier's education at the Convent of the Sacred Heart did much to form her style and opinions which have added so much to the gaiety of nations in an age all too somber and inhuman.

Her life as an essayist has been distinguished in the extreme. Her sparkling essays have made her now a national figure. In addition to the Laetare Medal and the medal of the National Institute of Arts, which have come to her, she has received honorary degrees from the Universities of Pennsylvania, Yale, Columbia, and Princeton.

Agnes Repplier's style is her own. Though formed in the best tradition of the English essayists, her expression takes its interest and incandescence from the balanced mind of an author who looks upon humanity and its peoples with no detachment but with a merry eye. This truly humanistic approach to men and things gives Agnes Repplier a currency which neither time nor events can obscure.

In addition to her many sparkling essays, Miss Repplier has written some excellent biographies: notably the life of *Mère Marie of the Ursulines* and the biography of *Père Marquette.*

REVEREND MOTHER'S FEAST*

MOTHER'S feast" — in other words the saint's day of the Superioress — was dawning upon our horizon, and its lights and shadows flecked our checkered paths. Theoretically, it was an occasion of pure joy, assuring us, as it did, a *congé,* and not a *congé* only, but the additional delights of a candy fair in the morning, and an operetta, "The Miracle of the Roses," at night. Such a round of pleasures filled us with the happiest anticipations; but — on the same principle that the Church always prefaces her feast days with vigils and with fasts — the

---

*Repplier, Agnes, Litt.D., *In Our Convent Days* (Boston and New York: Houghton, Mifflin and Co., 1905), pp. 183–213.

convent prefaced our *congé* with a competition in geography, and with the collection of a "spiritual bouquet," which was to be our offering to Reverend Mother on her fete.

A competition in anything was an unqualified calamity. It meant hours of additional study, a frantic memorizing of facts, fit only to be forgotten, and the bewildering ordeal of being interrogated before the whole school. It meant for *me* two little legs that shook like reeds, a heart that thumped like a hammer in my side, a sensation of sickening terror when the examiner — Madame Bouron — bore down upon me, and a mind reduced to sudden blankness, washed clean of any knowledge upon any subject, when the simplest question was asked. Tried by this process, I was only one degree removed from idiocy. Even Elizabeth, whose legs were as adamant, whose heart-beats had the regularity of a pendulum, and who, if she knew a thing, could say it, hated to bound states and locate capitals for all the school to hear.

"There are to be prizes, too," she said mournfully. "Madame Duncan said so. I don't like going up for a prize. It's worse than a medal at Primes."

"Oh well, maybe you won't get one," observed Tony consolingly. "You didn't, you know, last time."

"I did the time before last," said Elizabeth calmly. "It was 'La Corbeille de Fleurs.' "

There was an echo of resentment in her voice, and we all — even Tony — admitted that she had just cause for complaint. To reward successful scholarship with a French book was one of those black-hearted deeds for which we invariably held Madame Bouron responsible. She may have been blameless as the babe unborn; but it was our habit to attribute all our wrongs to her malign influence. At least, we knew its shiny black cover, and its frontispiece, representing a sylphlike young lady in a floating veil bearing a hamper of provisions to a smiling and destitute old gentleman. There was nothing in this picture, nor in the accompanying lines, "Que vois-je? Mon Dieu! Un ange de Ciel, qui vient à mon secours," which tempted us to a perusal of the story, even

had we been in the habit of voluntarily reading French.

As for the "spiritual bouquet," we felt that our failure to contribute to it on a generous scale was blackening our reputations forever. Every evening the roll was called, and girl after girl gave in her list of benefactions. Rosaries, so many. Litanies, so many. Aspirations, so many. Deeds of kindness, so many. Trials offered up, so many. Acts, so many. A stranger listening to the replies, might have imagined that the whole school was ripe for Heaven. These blossoms of virtue and piety were added every night to the bouquet; and the sum total, neatly written out in Madame Duncan's flowing hand, was to be presented, with an appropriate address, to Reverend Mother on her feast, as a proof of our respectful devotion.

It was a heavy tax. From what resources some girls drew their supplies remained ever a mystery to us. How could Ellie Plunkett have found the opportunity to perform four deeds of kindness, and resist seven temptations, in a day? We never had any temptations to resist. Perhaps when one came along, we yielded to it so quickly that it had ceased to tempt before its true character had been ascertained. And to whom was Ellie Plunkett so overweeningly kind? "Who wants Ellie Plunkett to be kind to her?" was Tony's scornful query. There was Adelaide Harrison, too, actually turning in twenty acts as one day's crop, and smiling modestly when Madame Duncan praised her self-denial. Yet, to our unwarped judgment, she seemed much the same as ever. We, at least, refused to accept her estimate of her own well-spent life.

"Making an act" was the convent phraseology for doing without something one wanted, for stopping short on the verge of an innocent gratification. If I gave up my place in the swing to Viola Milton, that was an act. If I walked to the woods with Annie Churchill, when I wanted to walk with Elizabeth, that was an act. If I ate my bread unbuttered, or drank my tea unsweetened, that was an act. It will be easily understood that the constant practice of acts deprived life of everything that made it worth living. We are so trained in this system of renunciation that it was impossible to enjoy even the very simple pleasures that our convent table afforded. If there were anything we particularly liked, our nagging little consciences piped up with their intolerable "Make an act, make an act;" and it was only when the last mouthful was resolutely swallowed that we could feel sure we had triumphed over asceticism. There was something maddening in the example set us by our neighbors, by those virtuous and pious girls who hemmed us in at study time and at our meals. When Mary Rawdon gently waved aside the chocolate custard — which was the very best chocolate custard it has ever been my good fortune to eat — and whispered to me as she did so, "An act for the bouquet;" I whispered back, "Take it, and give it to me." and held out my plate with defiant greed. Annie Churchill told us she hadn't eaten any butter for a week; whereat Tony called her an idiot, and Annie — usually the mildest of girls — said that "Envy at another's spiritual good" was a very great sin, and that Tony had committed it. There is nothing so souring to the temper as abstinence.

What made it singularly hard to sacrifice our young lives for the swelling of the spiritual bouquet was that Reverend Mother, who was to profit by our piety, had so little significance in our eyes. She was as remote from the daily routine of the school as the Grand Lama is remote from the humble Thibetans whom he rules; and if we regarded her with a lively awe, it was only because of her aloofness, of the reserves that hedged her majestically round. She was an Englishwoman of good family, and of vast bulk. There was a tradition that she had been married and widowed before becoming a nun; but this was a subject upon which we were not encouraged to talk. It was considered both disrespectful and indecorous. Reverend Mother's voice was slow and deep, a ponderous voice to suit her ponderous size; and she spoke with what seemed to us a strange and barbarous accent, pronouncing certain words in a manner which I have since learned was common in the days of Queen Elizabeth, and which a few ripe scholars are now endeavoring to reintroduce. She was near-sighted to the verge of blindness, and always at Mass used a large magnifying glass, like the one held by Leo the Tenth in Raphael's portrait. She was not without literary tastes of an insipid and obsolete order, the tastes of an English gentlewoman, reared in the days when young ladies read the "Female Spectator," and warbled "Oh, no, we never mention her." Had she not "entered religion," she might have taken Moore and Byron to her heart, — as did one little girl whose "Childe Harold" lay deeply hidden in a schoolroom desk, — but the rejection of these profane poets had left her stranded upon such feeble substitutes as Letitia Elizabeth Landon, whose mysterious death she was occasionally heard to deplore.

Twice on Sundays Reverend Mother crossed our orbit; in the morning when she instructed the whole school in Christian doctrine, and at night, when she presided over Primes. During the week we saw her only at Mass. We should never even have known about Letitia Elizabeth Landon, had she not granted an occasional audience to the graduates, and discoursed to them sleepily upon the books she had read in her youth. Whatever may have been her qualifications for her post (she had surpassing dignity of carriage, and was probably a woman of intelligence and force), to us she was a mere embodiment of authority, as destitute of personal malice as of personal charm. I detested Madame Bouron, and loved Madame Rayburn. Elizabeth detested Madame Bouron, and loved Madame Dane. Emily detested Madame Bouron, and loved Madame Duncan. These were emotions, amply nourished, and easily understood. We were capable of going to great lengths to prove either our aversion or our love. But to give up chocolate custard for Reverend Mother was like suffering martyrdom for a creed we did not hold.

"It's because Reverend Mother is so fond of geography that we're going to have the competition," said Lilly. "Madame Duncan told me so."

"Why can't Reverend Mother, if she likes it so much, learn it for herself?" asked Tony sharply. "I'll lend her my atlas."

"Oh, she knows it all," said Lilly, rather scandalized. "Madame Duncan told me it was her favourite study, and that she knew the geography of the whole world."

"Then I don't see why she wants to hear us say it," observed Elizabeth, apparently under the impressions that competitions, like gladiatorial shows, were gotten up solely for the amusement of an audience. It never occurred to her, nor indeed to any of us, to attach any educational value to the performance. We conceived that we were butchered to make a convent holiday.

"And it's because Reverend Mother is so fond of music that we are going to have an operetta instead of a play," went on Lilly, pleased to have information to impart.

I sighed heavily. How could anybody prefer anything to a play? I recognized an operetta as a form of diversion, and was grateful for it, as I should have been grateful for any entertainment, short of an organ recital. We were none of us surfeited with pleasures. But to me song was at best only an imperfect mode of speech; and the meaningless repetition of a phrase, which needed to be said but once, vexed my impatient spirit. We were already tolerably familiar with "The Miracle of the Roses." For two weeks past the strains had floated from every music room. We could hear, through the closed doors, Frances Fenton, who was to be St. Elizabeth of Hungary, quavering sweetly, —

> "Unpretending and lowly,
> Like spirits pure and holy,
> I love the wild rose best,
> I love the wild rose best,
> I love the wi-i-ild rose best."

We could hear Ella Holrook announcing in her deep contralto, —

> " 'Tis the privilege of a Landgrave
> To go where glory waits him,
>   Glory waits him;"

and the chorus trilling jubilantly, —

> "Heaven has changed the bread to roses,
> Heaven has changed the bread to roses."

Why, I wondered, did they have to say everything two and three times over? Even when the Landgrave detects St. Elizabeth in the act of carrying the loaves of bread to the poor, his anger finds a vent in iteration.

> "Once again you've dared to brave my anger,
> Yes, once again you've dared to brave my anger;
>   My power you scorn,
>   My power you scorn."

To which the saint replies gently, but tediously, —

> "My lord they are,
> My lord they are
> But simple roses,
> But simple ro-o-oses,
> That I gathered in the garden even now."

"Suppose that bread hadn't been changed to roses," said Elizabeth speculatively, "I wonder what St. Elizabeth would have done."

"Oh, she knew it had been, because she prayed it would be," said Marie, who was something of a theologian.

"But suppose it hadn't."

"But it had, and she knew it had, because of her piety and faith," insisted Marie.

"I shouldn't have like to risk it," murmured Elizabeth.

"I think her husband was a pig," said Tony. "Going off to the Crusade, and making all that fuss about a few loaves of bread. If I'd been St. Elizabeth — "

She paused, determining her course of action, and Marie ruthlessly interposed. "If you're not a saint, you can't tell what you would do if you were a saint. You would be different."

There was no doubt that Tony as a saint would have to be so very different from the Tony whom we knew, that Marie's dogmatism prevailed. Even Elizabeth was silenced; and, in the pause that followed, Lilly had a chance to impart her third piece of information. "It's because Reverend Mother's name is Elizabeth," she said, "that we're going to have an operetta about St. Elizabeth; and Bessie Treves is to make the address."

"Thank Heaven, there is another Elizabeth in the school, or I might have to do it," cried our Elizabeth, who coveted no barren honours; and — even as she spoke — the blow fell. Madame Rayburn appeared at the schoolroom door, a folded paper in her hand. "Elizabeth," she said, and, with a hurried glance of apprehension, the saint's unhappy namesake withdrew. We looked at one another meaningly. "It's like giving thanks before you're sure of dinner," chuckled Tony.

I had no chance to hear any particulars until night, when Elizabeth watched her opportunity, and sallied forth to brush her teeth while I was dawdling over mine. The strictest silence prevailed in the dormitories, and no child left her alcove except for the ceremony of tooth-brushing, which was performed at one of two large tubs, stationed in the middle of the floor. These tubs — blessed be their memory! — served as centres of gossip. Friend met friend, and smothered confidences were exchanged. Our gayest witticisms, — hastily choked by a toothbrush, — our oldest and dearest jests were whispered brokenly to the accompaniment of little splashes of water. It was the last social event of our long social day, and we welcomed it as freshly as if we had not been in close companionship since seven o'clock in the morning. Elizabeth, scrubbing her teeth with ostentatious vigour, found a chance to tell me, between scrubs, that Bessie Treves had been summoned home for a week, and that she, as the only other bearer of Reverend Mother's honoured name, had been chosen to make the address. "It's the feast of St. Elizabeth," she whispered, "and the operetta is about St. Elizabeth, and they want an Elizabeth to speak. I wish I had been christened Melpomene."

"You couldn't have been christened Melpomene," I whispered back, keeping a watchful eye upon Madame Chapelle, who was walking up and down the dormitory, saying her beads. "It isn't a Christian name. There never was a St. Melpomene."

"It's nearly three pages long," said Elizabeth, alluding to the address, and not to the tragic Muse. "All about the duties of women, and how they ought to stay at home and be kind to the poor, like St. Elizabeth, and let their husbands go to the Crusades."

"But there are no Crusades any more for their husbands to go to," I objected.

Elizabeth looked at me restively. She did not like this fractious humour. "I mean let their husbands go to war," she said.

"But if there are no wars," I began, when Madame Chapelle, who had not been so inattentive as I supposed, intervened. "Elizabeth and Agnes, go back to your alcoves," she said, "You have been quite long enough brushing your teeth."

I flirted my last drops of water over Elizabeth, and she returned the favour with interest, having more left in her tumbler than I had. It was our customary good-night. Sometimes, when we were wittily disposed, we said *"Asperges me."* That was one of the traditional jests of the convent. Generations of girls had probably said it before us. Our language was enriched with scraps of Latin and apt quotations, borrowed from Church services, the Penitential Psalms, and the catechism.

For two days Elizabeth studied the address, and for two days more she rehearsed it continuously under Madame Rayburn's tutelage. At intervals she recited portions of it to us, and we favoured her with our candid criticisms. Tony objected vehemently to the first line: —

"A woman's path is ours to humbly tread."

She said she didn't intend to tread it humbly at all; that Elizabeth might be as humble as she pleased (Elizabeth promptly disclaimed any personal sympathy with the sentiment), and that Marie and Agnes were welcome to all the humility they could practise (Marie and Agnes rejected their share of the virtue), but that she — Tony — was tired of behaving like an affable worm. To this, Emily, with more courage than courtesy, replied that a worm Tony might be, but an affable worm, never; and Elizabeth headed off any further retort by hurrying on with the address.

"A woman's path is ours to humbly tread,
And yet to lofty heights our hopes are led.
We may not share the Senate's stern debate,

Nor guide with faltering hand the helm of state;
Ours is the holier right to soften party hate,
And teach the lesson, lofty and divine,
Ambition's fairest flowers are laid at Virtue's
    shrine."

"Have you any idea what all that means?" asked Marie discontentedly.

"Oh, I don't have to say what it means," returned Elizabeth, far too sensible to try anything she would not be called upon to explain. "Reverend Mother makes that out for herself.

"Not ours to guide the battle's storm,
Where strength and valour deathless deeds
    perform.
Not ours to bind the blood-stained laurel wreath
In mocking triumph round the brow of death.
No! 'tis our lot to save the failing breath
'Tis ours to heal each wound, and hush each
    moan,
To take from other hearts the pain into
    our own."

"It seems to me," said Tony, "that we are expected to do all the work, and have none of the fun."

"It seems to me," said Marie, "that by the time we have filled ourselves up with other people's pains, we won't care much about fun. Did Reverend Mother, I wonder, heal wounds and hush up moans?"

"St. Elizabeth did," explained Elizabeth. "Her husband went to the Holy Land, and was killed, and then she became a nun. There are some lines at the end, that I don't know yet, about Reverend Mother, —

"Seeking the shelter of the cloister gate,
Like the dear Saint whose name we venerate.

"Madame Rayburn wants me to make an act, and learn the rest of it at recreation this afternoon. That horrid old geography takes up all my study time."

"I've made three acts to-day," observed Lilly complacently, "and said a whole pair of beads this morning at Mass for the spiritual bouquet."

"I haven't made one act," I cried aghast. "I haven't done anything at all, and I don't know what to do."

"You might make one now," said Elizabeth thoughtfully, "and go talk to Adelaide Harrison."

I glanced at Adelaide, who was sitting on the edge of her desk, absorbed in a book. "Oh, I don't want to," I wailed.

"If you wanted to, it wouldn't be an act," said Elizabeth.

"But she doesn't want me to," I urged. "She is reading 'Fabiola.'"

"Then you'll give her the chance to make an act, too," said the relentless Elizabeth.

Argued into a corner, I turned at bay. "I won't," I said resolutely; to which Elizabeth replied: "Well, I wouldn't either, in your place," and the painful subject was dropped.

Four days before the feast the excitement had reached fever point, though the routine of school life went on with the same smooth precision. Every penny had been hoarded up for the candy fair. It was with the utmost reluctance that we bought even the stamps for our home letters, those weekly letters we were compelled to write, and which were such pale reflections of our eager and vehement selves. Perhaps this was because we knew that every line was read by Madame Bouron before it left the convent; perhaps the discipline of those days discouraged familiarity with our parents; perhaps the barrier which nature builds between the adult and the normal child was alone responsible for our lack of spontaneity. Certain it is that the stiffly written pages despatched to father or to mother every Sunday night gave no hint of our abundant and restless vitality, our zest for the little feast of life, our exultations, our resentments, our thrice-blessed absurdities. Entrenched in the citadel of childhood, with laws of our own making, and passwords of our own devising, our souls bade defiance to the world.

If all our hopes centered in the congé, the candy fair, and the operetta, — which was to be produced on a scale of unwonted magnificence, — our time was sternly devoted to the unpitying exactions of geography. Every night we took our atlases to bed with us, under the impression that sleeping on a book would help us to remember its contents. As the atlases were big, and our pillows very small, this device was pregnant with discomfort. On the fourth night before the feast, something wonderful happened. It was the evening study hour, and I was wrestling sleepily with the mountains of Asia, — hideous excrescences with unpronounceable and unrememberable names, — when Madame Rayburn entered the room. As we rose to our feet, we saw that she looked very grave, and our minds took a backward leap over the day. Had we done anything unusually bad, anything that could call down upon us a public indictment, and was Madame Rayburn for once filling Madame Bouron's office? We could think of nothing; but life was full of pitfalls, and there was no sense of security in our souls. We waited anxiously.

"Children," said Madame Rayburn, "I have sorrowful news for you. Reverend Mother has been summoned to France. She sails on her feast day, and leaves for New York to-morrow."

We stared open-mouthed and aghast. The ground seemed sinking from under our feet, the walls crumbling about us. Reverend Mother sailing for France! And on her feast day, too, — the feast for which so many ardent preparations had been made. The *congé*, the competition, the address, the operetta, the spiritual bouquet, the candy fair, — were they, too, sailing away into the land of lost things? To have asked one of the questions that trembled on our lips would have been an unheard-of liberty. We listened in respectful silence, our eyes riveted on Madame Rayburn's face.

"You will all go to the chapel now," she said. "To-night we begin a novena to *Mater Admirabilis* for Reverend Mother's safe voyage. She dreads it very much, and she is sad at leaving you. Pray for her devoutly. Madame Dane will bring you down to the chapel."

She turned to go. Our hearts beat violently. She knew, she could not fail to know, the thought that was uppermost in every mind. She was too experienced and too sympathetic to miss the significance of our strained and wistful gaze. A shadowy smile crossed her face. "Madame Bouron would have told you to-morrow," she said, "what I

think I shall tell you to-night. It is Reverend Mother's express desire that you should have your *congé* on her feast, though she will not be here to enjoy it with you."

A sigh of relief, a sigh which we could not help permitting to be audible, shivered softly around the room. The day was saved; yet, as we marched to the chapel, there was a turmoil of agitation in our hearts. We knew that from far-away France — from a mysterious and all-powerful person who dwelt there, and who was called Mother General — came the mandates which governed our community. This was not the first sudden departure we had witnessed; but Reverend Mother seemed so august, so permanent, so immobile. Her very size protested mutely against upheaval. Should we never again see that familiar figure sitting in her stall, peering through her glass into a massive prayer-book, a leviathan of prayer-books, as imposing in its way as she was, or blinking sleepily at us as we filed by? Why, if somebody were needed in France, had it not pleased Mother General to send for Madame Bouron? Many a dry eye would have seen her go. But then, as Lilly whispered to me, suppose it had been Madame Rayburn. There was a tightening of my heart-strings at the thought, a sudden suffocating pang, dimly foreboding the grief of another year.

The consensus of opinion, as gathered that evening in the dormitory, was not unlike the old Jacobite epitaph on Frederick, Prince of Wales. Every one of us was sincerely sorry that Madame Bouron had not been summoned, —

"Had it been his father,
We had much rather;"

but glad that Madame Dane, or Madame Rayburn, or Madame Duncan, or some other favourite nun had escaped.

"Since it's only Fred
Who was alive, and is dead,
There is no more to be said."

The loss of our Superioress was bewildering, but not, for us, a thing of deep concern. We should sleep as sweetly as usual that night.

THE LUXURY OF CONVERSATION*

IN AN age when everybody is writing Reminiscences, and when nothing is left untold, we hear a great deal about the wit and brilliancy of former days and former conversations. Elderly gentlemen, conscious of an ever increasing dullness in life, would fain have us believe that its more vivacious characteristics vanished with their youth, and can never be tempted to return. Mournful prophecies anent the gradual decay of social gifts assail us on every side. Mr. Justin McCarthy, recalling with a sigh the group of semi-distinguished men who were wont to grace George Eliot's Sunday afternoons, can "only hope that the art of talking is not destined to die out with the art of letter-writing." Mr. George W. E. Russell entertains similar misgivings. He found his ideal talker in Mr. Matthew Arnold, "a man of the world without being frivolous, and a man of letters without being pedantic;" and he considers this admirable combination as necessary as it is rare. American chroniclers point back to a little gleaming band of Northern lights, and assure us sadly that if we never heard these men in their prime, we must live and die uncheered by wit or wisdom. We are born in a barren day.

But conversation, the luxury of conversation, as De Quincey happily phrases it, does not depend upon one or two able talkers. It is not, and never has been, a question of stars, but of a good stock company. Neither can it decay like the art — or the habit — of letter-writing. The conditions are totally different. Letters form a by-path of literature, a charming, but occasional, retreat for people of cultivated leisure. Conversation in its happiest development is a link, equally exquisite and adequate, between mind and mind, a system by which men approach one another with sympathy and enjoyment, a field for the finest amenities of civilization, for the keenest and most intelligent display of social activity. It is also our solace, our inspiration,

and our most rational pleasure. It is a duty we owe to one another; it is our common debt to humanity. "God has given us tongues," writes Heine, "wherewith we may say pleasant things to our neighbours." To refuse a service so light, so sweet, so fruitful, is to be unworthy of the inheritance of the ages.

It is claimed again, by critics disposed to be pessimistic, that our modern development of "specialism" is prejudicial to good conversation. A man devoted to one subject can seldom talk well upon another. Unless his companions share his tastes and his knowledge, he must — a sad alternative — either lecture or be still. There are people endowed with such a laudable thirst for information that they relish lectures, — professional and gratuitous. They enjoy themselves most when they are being instructed. They are eager to form an audience. Such were the men and women who experienced constant disappointment because Mr. Browning, a specialist of high standing, declined to discuss his specialty. No side-lights upon "Sordello" could be extracted from him. We realize how far the spirit of the lecture had intruded upon the spirit of conversation forty years ago, when Mr. Bagehot admitted that, with good modern talkers, "the effect seems to be produced by that which is stated, and not by the manner in which it is stated," — a reversal of ancient rules. We are aware of its still further encroachment when we see a little book by M. Charles Rozan, characteristically christened "Petites Ignorances de la Conversation," and find it full of odds and ends of information, of phrases, allusions, quotations, facts, — all the minute details which are presumably embodied in the talk of educated men. The world today devoutly believes that everything can be taught and learned. When we have shown how a thing is done, we can of course do it. There are even little manuals composed with serious simplicity, the object of which is to enable us to meet specialists on their own grounds; to discuss art with artists, literature with authors, politics with

*Repplier, Agnes, Litt.D., *Compromises* (Boston and New York: Houghton, Mifflin and Co., 1904), pp. 1–19.

politicians, science with scientists, — the last, surely, a dangerous experiment. "Conversation," I read in one of these enchanting primers, "cannot be entirely learned from books," — a generous admission in a day given over to the worship of print.

But in good truth, the contagious ardour, the urbane freedom of the spoken word lift it immeasurably from the regions of pen and ink. Those "shy revelations of affinity," which now and then open to the reader sweet vistas of familiarity and friendship, are frequent, alluring, persuasive, in well-ordered speech. It is not what we learn in conversation that enriches us. It is the elation that comes of swift contact with tingling currents of thought. It is the opening of our mental pores, and the stimulus of marshaling our ideas in words, of setting them forth as gallantly and as graciously as we can. "A language long employed by a delicate and critical society," says Mr. Bagehot, "is a treasure of dexterous felicities;" and the recognition of these felicities, the grading of terms, the enlarging of a narrow and stupid vocabulary make the charm of civilized social contact. Discussion without asperity, sympathy without fusion, gayety unracked by too abundant jests, mental ease in approaching one another, — these are the things which give a pleasant smoothness to the rough edge of life.

So much has been said about good talkers, — brilliant soloists for the most part, — and so little about good talk! So much has been said about good listeners, and so little about the interchange of thought! "Silent people never spoil company," remarked Lord Chesterfield; but even this negative praise was probably due to the type of silence with which he was best acquainted, — a habit of sparing speech, not the muffled stillness of genuine and hopeless incapacity. A man who listens because he has nothing to say can hardly be a source of inspiration. The only listening that counts is that of the talker who alternately absorbs and expresses ideas. Sainte-Beuve says of Fontenelle that, while he had neither tears nor laughter, he smiled at wit, never interrupted, was never excited, nor

ever in a hurry to speak. These are endearing traits. They embody much of the art of conversation. But they are as remote from unadorned silence as from unconsidered loquacity.

The same distinction may be drawn between the amenity which forbids bickering, and the flabbiness which has neither principles to uphold, nor arguments with which to uphold them. Hazlitt's counsel, "You should prefer the opinion of the company to your own," is good in the main, but it can easily be pushed too far. Proffered by a man who bristled with opinions which he never wearied of defending, it is perhaps more interesting than persuasive. If everybody floated with the tide of talk, placidity would soon end in stagnation. It is the strong backward stroke which stirs the ripples, and gives animation and variety. "Unison is a small quality altogether obnoxious in conversation," said Montaigne, who was at least as tolerant as Hazlitt was combative, but who dearly loved stout words from honest men. Dr. Johnson, we know, was of a similar way of thinking. He scorned polite tepidity; he hated chatter; he loved that unfeeling logic which drives mercilessly to its goal. No man knew better than he the unconvincing nature of argument. He had too often thrust his friends from the fortress of sound reason which they were not strong enough to hold. But his talk, for all its aggressiveness, and for all its tendency to negation, was real talk; not — as with Coleridge — a monologue, nor — as with Macaulay — a lecture. He did not infringe upon other people's conversational freeholds, and he was not, be it always remembered, anecdotal. The man who lived upon "potted stories" inspired him with righteous antipathy.

Perhaps the saddest proof of intellectual inertia, of our failure to meet one another with ease and understanding, is the tendency to replace conversation by story-telling. It is no uncommon thing to hear a man praised as a good talker, when he is really a raconteur. People will speak complacently of a "brilliant dinner," at which some strings of anecdotes, disconnected and illegitimate, have usurped the field, to the total exclusion of

ideas. After an entertainment of this order —
like a feast of buns and barley sugar — we
retire with mental indigestion for a fortnight.
That it should be relished betrays the crudeness of social conditions. "Of all the bores,"
writes De Quincey with unwonted ill-temper,
"whom man in his folly hesitates to hang,
and Heaven in its mysterious wisdom suffers
to propagate his species, the most insufferable
is the teller of good stories." This is a hard
saying. The story, like its second cousin the
lie, has a sphere of usefulness. It is a help in
moments of emergency, and it serves admirably to illustrate a text. But it is not, and
never can be, a substitute for conversation.
People equipped with reason, sentiment, and
a vocabulary should have something to talk
about, some common ground on which they
can meet, and penetrate into one another's
minds. The exquisite pleasure of interchang-
ing ideas, of awakening to suggestions, of
finding sympathy and companionship, is as
remote from the languid amusement yielded
by story-telling as a good play is remote from
the bald diversion of the music hall.

Something to talk about appears to be the
first consideration. The choice of a topic, or
rather the possession of a topic which will
bear analysis and support enthusiasm, is essential to the enjoyment of conversation. We
cannot go far along a stony track. Diderot
observed that whenever he was in the company of men and women who were reading
Richardson's books, either privately or aloud,
the talk was sure to be animated and interesting. Some secret springs of emotion were
let loose by this great master of sentiment.
Our ancestors allowed themselves a wider
field of discussion than we are now in the
habit of conceding; but after all, as Stevenson reminds us, "it is not over the virtues of
a curate-and-tea-party novel that people are
abashed into high resolutions." We may not
covet Socratic discourses at the dinner table,
but neither can we long sustain what has
been sadly and significantly called "the burden of conversation" on the lines adopted
by William the Fourth, who, when he felt
the absolute necessity of saying something,
asked the Duke of Devonshire where he
meant to be buried.

The most perfect and pitiful pictures of intercourse stripped bare of interest have been
given to us in Miss Austen's novels. Reading
them, we grow sick at heart to think what
depths of experience they reflect, what hours
of ennui lie back of every page. The conversation of the ladies after Mrs. John Dash-
wood's dinner must stand forever as a perfect
example of sustained stupidity, of that almost
miraculous dullness which can be achieved
only by "want of sense, want of elegance,
want of spirits, and want of temper." Equal
to it in its way is the brief description
of Lady Middleton's first call upon the
Dashwoods.

"Conversation was not lacking, for Sir John
was very chatty, and Lady Middleton had
taken the wise precaution of bringing with
her their eldest child, a fine little boy about
six years old. By this means there was one
subject always to be recurred to by the ladies
in case of extremity, for they had to enquire
his name and age, admire his beauty, and
ask him questions which his mother answered for him, while he hung about her
and held down his head, to the great surprise
of her ladyship, who wondered at his being
so shy before company, as he could make
noise enough at home. On every formal visit
a child ought to be of the party, by way of
provision for discourse. In the present case,
it took up ten minutes to determine whether
the boy were most like his father or mother,
and in what particular he resembled either,
for of course everybody differed, and everybody was astonished at the opinion of the
others."

How real it is! How many of us have lived
through similar half-hours, veiling with recent melancholy the impetuous protest of our
souls!

Charles Greville is responsible for the
rather unusual statement that a dinner at
which all the guests are fools is apt to be as
agreeable as a dinner at which all the guests
are clever men. The fools, he says, are tolerably sure to be gay, and the clever men are
perfectly sure to be heavy. How far the gayety
of fools is an engaging trait it might be difficult to decide (there is a text which throws
some doubt upon the subject), but Greville

appears to have suffered a good deal from the ponderous society of the learned. We are struck in the first place by the very serious topics which made the table-talk of his day. Do people now discuss primogeniture in ancient Rome over their fish and game? It sounds almost as onerous as the Socratic discourses. Then again it was his special hardship to listen to the dissertations of Macaulay, and he resented this infliction with all the ardour of a vain and accomplished man. "Macaulay's astonishing knowledge is every moment exhibited," he writes in his Memoirs, "but he is not agreeable. He has none of the graces of conversation, none of the exquisite tact and refinement which are the result of a felicitous intuition, or of a long acquaintance with good society. . . . *His information is more than society requires.*"

The last line is a master-stroke of criticism. It embodies all that goes before and all that follows, — for Greville airs his grievance at length, — and it is admirably illustrated in his account of that famous evening at Holland House, when Lady Holland, in captious mood, rebelled against a course of instruction. Somebody having chanced to mention Sir Thomas Munro, the hostess rashly admitted that she had never heard of him, whereupon Macaulay "explained all he had said, done, written, or thought, and vindicated his claim to the title of a great man, till Lady Holland, getting bored, said she had had enough of Sir Thomas, and would hear no more. This might have dashed and silenced an ordinary talker; but to Macaulay it was no more than replacing a book upon a shelf, and he was just as ready as ever to open on any other topic." The Fathers of the Church were next discussed (it was not a frivolous company), and Macaulay at once called to mind a sermon of Saint Chrysostom's, in praise of the Bishop of Antioch. "He proceeded to give us the substance of this sermon till Lady Holland got tired of the Fathers, and put her extinguisher on Chrysostom as she had done on Munro. Then with a sort of derision, and as if to have the pleasure of puzzling Macaulay, she turned to him and said: "Pray what was the origin of a doll? When were dolls first mentioned

in history?" Macaulay, however, was just as much up in dolls as in Fathers, and instantly replied that the Roman children had their dolls, which they offered to Venus when they grew older. He quoted Persius, —

'Veneri donatae a virgine puppae,'

and I have not the least doubt that if he had been allowed to proceed, he would have told us who was the Chenevix of ancient Rome, and the name of the first baby that ever handled a doll."

This was indeed more information than society required. It is not surprising that Sydney Smith, perhaps the most charming talker of his day, was quickly silenced by such an avalanche of words, and sat mute and limp in the historian's company. Upon one occasion Greville went to visit the Marquis of Lansdowne at Bowood, and found Macaulay among the guests. "It was wonderful how quiet the house seemed after he had gone," comments the diarist grimly, "and it was not less agreeable."

That a rude invasion of the field is fatal to the enjoyment of intercourse we know from the sentiment of revolt expressed on every side. How little the people who heard Mme. de Staël's brilliant conversation appear to have relished the privilege! Mackintosh admitted that she was agreeable in a tête-à-tête, but too much for a general assembly. Heine hated her, as a hurricane in petticoats. "She hears but little, and never the truth, because she is always talking." Byron, who felt a genuine admiration for her cleverness, and was grateful for her steadfast friendship, confessed ruefully that she overwhelmed him with words, buried him beneath glittering snow and nonsense. The art of being amusing in a lovable way was not hers; yet this is essentially the art which lifted French conversation to its highest level, which made it famous three hundred years ago, and which has preserved it ever since as a rational and engaging occupation. A page of history lies revealed and elucidated in Saint-Simon's little sentence anent Mme. de Maintenon's fashion of speech. "Her language was gentle, exact, well chosen, and naturally eloquent and brief."

No wonder she reigned long. Eloquent and brief! What a magnificent "blend"! How persuasive the "well-chosen" words, immaculately free from harsh emphasis and the feminine fault of iteration! Who would not be influenced by a woman who talked always well, and never too much; who, knowing the value of flattery, administered it with tact and moderation; and who shrank instinctively from the exaggerated terms which destroy balance and invite defeat? From the reign of Louis the Fourteenth to the Revolution, conversation was cultivated in France with intelligent assiduity. Its place in the fabric of civilization was clearly understood. No time was begrudged to its development, no labour was spared to its perfecting. Mr. Henry James is of the opinion that it flowered brilliantly in the middle of the eighteenth century. "This was surely," he says, "in France at least, the age of good society, the period when the right people made haste to be born in time. The sixty years that preceded the Revolution were the golden age of fireside talk, and of those amenities that are due to the presence of women in whom the social art is both instinctive and acquired. The women of that period were, above all, good company. The fact is attested in a thousand documents. Chenonceaux offered a perfect setting to free conversation; and infinite joyous discourse must have mingled with the liquid murmur of the Cher."

"Joyous discourse" is a beguiling phrase. It carries with it the echo of laughter long since silenced, — light laughter following the light words, so swiftly spoken, yet so surely placed. The time was coming fast when this smooth graciousness of speech would inspire singular mistrust, and when Rousseau — ardently embracing nature — would write of the "fine and delicate irony called politeness, which gives so much ease and pliability to the intercourse of civilized man, enabling him to assume the appearance of every virtue without the reality of one." Later on, illusions being dispelled, the painful discovery was made that the absence of politeness does not necessarily imply the presence of virtue, and that taciturnity may be wholly disassociated with the truth. We owe to one another all the wit and good humour we can command; and nothing so clears our mental vistas as sympathetic and intelligent conversation. It can never languish in an age like ours, teeming with new interests widely shared, and with new wonders widely known. We must talk, because we have so much to talk about; and we ought to talk well, because our inspirations are of a noble order. Each new discovery made by science, each fresh emotion awakened by contemporaneous history, each successive pleasure yielded by literature or by art is a spur to rational speech. These things are our common heritage, and we share them in common, through the medium of the aptly spoken word.

HENRY HARLAND

(1861–1905)

HENRY HARLAND was born at St. Petersburg, March 1, 1861. His father was a competent New York lawyer, but both his father and mother were New England to the core. Henry was educated at the College of the City of New York and also studied at Harvard and in Italy. While in Italy he became convinced of the truth of Catholicism but deferred his reception into the Church until 1897 when he and his wife were baptized.

Harland prepared himself as a novelist by years of short story writing. The exquisite perfection of his work attracted the attention of London critics and in a short time Harland became one of the central figures in London literary circles. The quarterly magazine which he projected, *The Yellow Book,* became the outstanding literary periodical of its time. His novels *The Cardinal's Snuff Box, The Lady Paramount,* and *My Friend Prospero* exhale Harland's love of form and the faint lavender of his exquisite humor.

Though *The Lady Paramount* is said to be his best novel, it is in some ways, merely a comedy of manners and must give place to *The Cardinal's Snuff Box* as a study of character. His final novel, *The Royal End,* was incomplete when Harland died. It was finished by his wife.

THE CARDINAL'S SNUFF BOX*

XV

BEATRICE was talking with a priest — nay, I am not sure it wouldn't be more accurate to say conspiring with a priest: but you shall judge.

They were in a room of the Palazzo Udeschini, at Rome — a reception room, on the *piano nobile.* Therefore you see it: for are not all reception-rooms in Roman palaces alike?

Vast, lofty, sombre; the walls hung with dark-green tapestry — a pattern of vertical stripes, dark green and darker green; here and there a great dark painting, a Crucifixion, a Holy Family, in a massive dim-gold frame; dark-hued rugs on the tiled floor; dark pieces of furniture, tables, cabinets, dark and heavy; and tall windows, bare of curtains at this season, opening upon a court — a wide stone-paved court, planted with fantastic-leaved eucalyptus trees, in the midst of which a brown old fountain, indefatigable, played its sibilant monotone.

In the streets there were the smells, the noises, the heat, the glare of August — of August in Rome, "the most Roman of the months," they say; certainly the hottest, noisiest, noisomest, and most glaring. But here all was shadow, coolness, stillness, fragrance — the fragrance of the clean air coming in from among the eucalyptus-trees.

Beatrice, critical-eyed, stood before a pier-glass, between two of the tall windows, turning her head from side to side, craning her neck a little — examining (if I must confess it) the effect of a new hat. It was a very stunning hat — if a man's opinion hath any pertinence; it was beyond doubt very complicated. There was an upward-springing black brim; there was downward-sweeping black feather; there was a defiant white aigrette — not unlike the Shah of Persia's; there were glints of red.

The priest sat in an arm-chair — one of those stiff, upright Roman armchairs, which no one would ever dream of calling easy-chairs, high-backed, covered with hard leather, studded with steel nails — and watched her, smiling amusement, indulgence.

He was an oldish priest — sixty, sixty-five. He was small, lightly built, lean-faced, with delicate-strong features: a prominent, delicate nose; a well-marked, delicate jaw-bone, ending in a prominent, delicate chin; a large, humorous mouth, the full lips delicately chiselled; a high, delicate, perhaps rather narrow brow, rising above humorous grey eyes, rather deepset. Then he had silky-soft smooth white-hair, and, topping the occiput, a tonsure that might have passed for a natural bald spot.

He was decidedly clever-looking; he was aristocratic-looking, distinguished-looking; but he was, above all, pleasant-looking, kindly-looking, sweet-looking.

He wore a plain black cassock, by no means in its first youth — brown along the seams, and, at the salient angles, at the shoulders, at the elbows, shining with the lustre of hard service. Even without his cassock, I imagine, you would have divined him for a clergyman — he bore the clerical impress, that odd indefinable air of clericism which everyone recognises, though it might not be altogether easy to tell just where or from what it takes its origin. In the garb of an Anglican — there being nothing, at first blush, necessarily Italian, necessarily un-English, in his face — he would have struck you, I think, as a pleasant, shrewd old parson of the scholarly-earn-

*Harland, Henry, *The Cardinal's Snuff Box* (London and New York: John Lane Co., 1900), pp. 115–126.

est type, mildly donnish, with a fondness for gentle mirth. What, however, you would scarcely have divined — unless you had chanced to notice, inconspicuous in this sober light, the red sash round his waist, or the amethyst on the third finger of his right hand — was his rank in the Roman hierarchy. I have the honor of presenting his Eminence Egidio Maria Cardinal Udeschini, formerly Bishop of Cittareggio, Prefect of the Congregation of Archives and Inscriptions.

That was his title ecclesiastical. He had two other titles. He was a Prince of the Udeschini by accident of birth. But his third title was perhaps his most curious. It had been conferred upon him informally by the populace of the Roman slum in which his titular church, St. Mary of the Lilies, was situated: the little Uncle of the Poor.

As Italians measure wealth, Cardinal Udeschini was a wealthy man. What with his private fortune and official stipends, he commanded an income of something like a hundred thousand lire. He allowed himself five thousand lire a year for food, clothing, and general expenses. Lodging and service he had for nothing in a palace of his family. The remaining ninety-odd thousand lire of his budget? Well, we all know that titles can be purchased in Italy; and that was no doubt the price he paid for the title I have mentioned.

However, it was not in money only that Cardinal Udeschini paid. He paid also in labour. I have said that his titular church was in a slum. Rome surely contained no slum more fetid, none more perilous — a region of cut-throat alleys, south of the Ghetto, along the Tiber bank. Night after night, accompanied by his stout young vicar, Don Giorgio Appolloni, the Cardinal worked there as hard as any hard-working curate: visiting the sick, comforting the afflicted, admonishing the knavish, persuading the drunken from their taverns, making peace between the combative. Not infrequently, when he came home, he would add a pair of stilettos to his already large collection of such relics. And his home-comings were apt to be late — oftener than not, after midnight; and sometimes, indeed, in the vague twilight of

morning, at the hour when, as he once expressed it to Don Giorgio, "the tired burglar is just lying down to rest." And every Saturday evening the Cardinal Prefect of Archives and Inscriptions sat for three hours boxed up in his confessional, like any parish priest — in his confessional at St. Mary of the Lilies, where the penitents who breathed their secrets into his ears, and received his fatherly counsels. . . . I beg your pardon. One must not, of course, remember his rags or his sores, when Lazarus approaches that tribunal.

But I don't pretend that the Cardinal was a saint; I am sure he was not a prig. For all his works of supererogation, his life was a life of pomp and luxury, compared to the proper saint's life. He wore no hair shirt; I doubt if he knew the taste of the Discipline. He had his weaknesses, his foibles — even, if you will, his vices. I have intimated that he was fond of a jest. "The Sacred College," I heard him remark one day, "has fifty centres of gravity. I sometimes fear that I am its centre of levity." He was also fond of music. He was also fond of snuff.

"'Tis an abominable habit," he admitted. "I can't tolerate it at all — in others. When I was Bishop of Cittareggio, I discountenanced it utterly among my clergy. But for myself — I need not say there are special circumstances. Oddly enough, by the bye, at Cittareggio each separate member of my clergy was able to plead special circumstances for himself. I have tried to give it up, and the effort had spoiled my temper — turned me into a perfect old shrew. For my friends' sake, therefore, I appease myself with an occasional pinch. You see, tobacco is antiseptic. It's an excellent preservative of the milk of human kindness."

The friends in question kept him supplied with sound rappee. Jests and music he was abundantly competent to supply himself. He played the piano and the organ, and he sang — in a clear, sweet, slightly faded tenor. Of secular composers his favourites were "the lucid Scarlatti, the luminous Bach." But the music that roused him to enthusiasm was Gregorian. He would have none other at St. Mary of the Lilies. He had trained his priests and his people there to sing it admirably — you should have heard them sing Vespers; and he sang it admirably himself — you should have heard him sing a Mass — you should have heard that sweet old tenor voice of his in the Preface and the Pater Noster.

So, then, Beatrice stood before a pier-glass, and studied her new hat; whilst the Cardinal, amused, indulgent, sat in his high-backed arm-chair, and watched her.

"Well — ? What do you think?" she asked, turning towards him.

"You appeal to me as an expert?" he questioned.

His speaking-voice, as well as his singing-voice, was sweet, but with a kind of trenchant edge upon it, a genial asperity, that gave it character, tang.

"As one who should certainly be able to advise," she said.

"Well, then —" said he. He took his chin into his hands, as if it were a beard, and looked up at her, considering; and the lines of amusement — the "parentheses" — deepened at either side of his mouth. "Well, then, I think if the feather were to be lifted a little higher in front, and brought down a little lower behind —"

"Good gracious, I don't mean my hat," cried Beatrice. "What in the world can an old dear like you know about hats?"

There was a further deepening of the parentheses.

"Surely," he contended, "a cardinal should know much. Is it not 'the badge of all our tribe,' as your poet Byron says?"

Beatrice laughed. Then, "Byron —?" she doubted, with a look.

The Cardinal waved his hand — a gesture of amiable concession.

"Oh, if you prefer, Shakespeare. Everything in English is one or the other. We will not fall out, like the Morellists, over an attribution. The point is that I should be a good judge of hats."

He took snuff.

"It's a shame you haven't a decent snuff-box," Beatrice observed, with an eye on the enamelled one, cheap and shabby, from which he helped himself.

"The box is but the guinea-stamp; the snuff's the thing. — Was it Shakespeare or Byron who said that?" enquired the Cardinal.

Beatrice laughed again.

"I think it must have been Pulcinella. I'll give you a lovely silver one, if you'll accept it."

"Will you? Really?" asked the Cardinal, alert.

"Of course I will. It's a shame you haven't one already."

"What would a lovely silver one cost?" he asked.

"I don't know. It doesn't matter," answered she.

"But approximately? More or less?" he pursued.

"Oh a couple of hundred lire, more or less, I daresay."

"A couple of hundred lire?" He glanced up, alerter. "Do you happen to have that amount of money on your person?"

Beatrice (the unwary woman) hunted for her pocket — took out her purse — computed its contents.

"Yes," she innocently answered.

The Cardinal chuckled — the satisfied chuckle of one whose unsuspected tactics have succeeded.

"Then give me the couple of hundred lire."

He put forth his hand.

But Beatrice held back.

"What for?" she asked, suspicion waking.

"Oh, I shall have uses for it."

His outstretched hand — a slim old tapering, bony hand, in colour like dusky ivory — closed peremptorily, in a dumb-show of receiving; and now, by the bye, you could not have failed to notice the big lucent amethyst, in its setting of elaborately-wrought pale gold, on the third finger.

"Come! Give!" he insisted, imperative.

"You have caught me finally," she sighed, and gave.

"You shouldn't have jingled your purse — you shouldn't have flaunted your wealth in my face," laughed the Cardinal, putting away the notes. He took snuff again. "I think I honestly earned that pinch," he murmured.

LOUISE IMOGEN GUINEY

(1861–1920)

THE daughter of a major general, Louise Imogen Guiney was born in Boston, in 1861. Her education was acquired at Elmhurst Academy, Providence, Rhode Island, and from private tutors. The story of her life is interior and comparatively uneventful, except for her appointment as postmistress of Auburndale, which was achieved over the protests of bigots and not inconsiderable publicity.

After some years Miss Guiney resigned as postmistress of Auburndale and took a position on the staff of the Boston Public Library.

In order to further her research on the *Recusant Poets,* Miss Guiney went to England. She remained there until her death in 1920.

The poems of Imogen Guiney are well worth reading. They show her virile soul and gallant outlook on life. *Happy Ending,* which contains the best of her collected lyric poems, was published by Houghton, in 1927.

Of Miss Guiney's prose works the *Recusant Poets* is considered best. In her sympathetic understanding of these poets, Miss Guiney has demonstrated an admirable mastery of style and a penetrating analysis which is at times almost intuitional.

THE WILD RIDE*

I hear in my heart, I hear in its ominous
    pulses,
All day, on the road, the hoofs of invisible
    horses;
All night, from their stalls, the importunate
    tramping and neighing.

Let cowards and laggards fall back! but alert
    to the saddle,
Straight, grim, and abreast, go the weather-
    worn, galloping legion,
With a stirrup cup each to the lily of women
    that loves him.

The trail is through dolor and dread, over
    crags and morasses;

There are shapes by the way, there are
    things that appall or entice us:
What odds? We are knights, and our souls
    are but bent on the riding.

I hear in my heart, I hear in its ominous
    pulses,
All day, on the road, the hoofs of invisible
    horses;
All night, from their stalls, the importunate
    tramping and neighing.

We spur to a land of no name, out-racing
    the storm-wind;
We leap to the infinite dark, like the sparks
    from the anvil.
Thou leadest, O God! All's well with Thy
    troopers that follow.

*The above and following poems have been selected from *Happy Ending,* The Collected Lyrics of Louise Imogen Guiney (Boston and New York: Houghton and Mifflin, 1927).

IRISH PEASANT SONG

I Try to knead and spin, but my life is low
    the while.
Oh! I long to be alone, and walk abroad a
    mile;
Yet if I walk alone, and think of naught
    at all,
Why from me that's young should the wild
    tears fall?

The shower-stricken earth, the earth-colored
    streams,
They breathe on me awake, and moan to
    me in dreams;

And yonder ivy fondling the broke castle-
    wall,
It pulls upon my heart till the wild tears
    fall.

The cabin-door looks down a furze-lighted
    hill,
And far as Leighlin Cross the fields are
    green and still;
But once I hear the blackbird in Leighlin
    hedges call,
The foolishness is on me, and the wild tears
    fall!

WHEN ON THE MARGE OF EVENING

When on the marge of evening the last blue
    light is broken,
And winds of dreamy odor are loosened
    from afar,
Or when my lattice opens, before the lark
    has spoken,
On dim laburnum-blossoms, and morning's
    dying star,

I think of thee, (O mine the more if other
    eyes be sleeping!)
Whose great and noonday splendor the many
    share and see,
While sacred and forever, some perfect law
    is keeping
The late and early twilight alone and sweet
    for me.

TO A DOG'S MEMORY

The gusty morns are here,
When all the reeds ride low with level spear;
And on such nights as lured us far of yore,
Down rocky alleys yet, and through the
    pine,
The Hound-star and the pagan Hunter
    shine;
But I and thou, ah, field-fellow of mine,
Together roam no more.

Soft showers go laden now
With odors of the sappy orchard-bough,
And brooks begin to brawl along the march;
The late frost streams from hollow sedges
    high;
The finch is come, the flame-blue dragon-fly,
The cowslip's common gold that children
    spy,

The plume upon the larch.

There is a music fills
The oaks of Belmont and the Wayland hills
Southward to Dewing's little bubbly stream,
The heavenly weather's call! O, who alive
Hastes not to start, delays not to arrive,
Having free feet that never felt a gyve
Weigh, even in a dream?

But thou, instead, hast found
The sunless April uplands underground,
And still, wherever thou art, I must be.
My beautiful! arise in might and mirth,
For we were tameless travellers from our
    birth;
And keep the watch for me.

TWO EPITAPHS

I

Two white heads the grasses cover;
Dorcas, and her lifelong lover.
While they graced their country closes
Simply as the brooks and roses,
Where was lot so poor, so trodden,
But they cheered it of a sudden?
Fifty years at home together,

Hand in hand, they went elsewhither.
Then first leaving hearts behind
Comfortless. Be thou as kind.

2

Praise thou the Mighty Mother for what is
        wrought, not me,
A nameless nothing-caring head asleep against
        her knee.

THE KING

A man said unto his angel:
"My spirits are fallen through,
And I cannot carry this battle;
O brother, what shall I do?

"The terrible Kings are on me,
With spears that are deadly bright.
Against me so from the cradle
Do fate and my fathers fight."

Then said to the man his angel:
"Thou wavering, foolish soul,
Back to the ranks! What matter
To win or to lose the whole,

"As judged by the little judges
Who hearken not well, nor see?
Not thus by the other issue,
The Wise shall interpret thee.

"Thy will is the very, the only,
The solemn event of things;

The weakest of hearts defying
Is stronger than all these Kings.

"Thou out of the past they gather,
Mind's Doubt and bodily Pain,
And pallid Thirst of the Spirit
That is kin to the other twain,

"And Grief, in a cloud of banners,
And ringletted Vain Desires,
And Vice, with the spoils upon him
Of thee and thy beaten sires,

"While Kings of eternal evil
Yet darken the hills about,
Thy part is with broken sabre
To rise on the last redoubt;

"To fear not sensible failure,
Nor covet the game at all,
But fighting, fighting, fighting,
Die, driven against the wall!"

CLEMENT FRANCIS KELLEY

(1870–   )

CLEMENT FRANCIS KELLEY was born October 23, 1870, at Vernon River, Prince Edward Island. His education was wide and though he is essentially a man of thought, the charm of his mind and imagina-tion have been no bar to a positive genius for practical things.

Soon after his ordination in 1893 Father Kelley became an army chaplain in the Spanish American War. With the end of the war he returned to his parish in Lapeer, Michigan, where he remained until 1907. Love of the missions led him to the organization of the Extension Society and the *Extension Magazine,* of which he was the first editor. In 1915 he was created a Domestic Prelate and in 1924 became Bishop of Oklahoma.

Because of his administrative talents and

the creative quality of his imagination, Bishop Kelley remains one of the most significant prelates of our day. His charm as a writer is undeniable. Whether in *Charred Wood, Letters to Jack,* or *The Bishop Jots It Down* (his autobiography), Bishop Kelley demonstrates a literary talent of a high order. As a *raconteur* he has few equals among American Catholics.

CHAPTER II

THE DREAM*

IN CATHOLIC clerical life the hour of passing from youth to age depends more on geographical location than on advancing years. While a priest remains a curate, or assistant, he is young. When, with a smile of satisfaction, he reads the bishop's letter appointing him to a pastorate, he has in his hands an official diploma of admission into the academy of venerables. In, say, Boston, Chicago, or New York, a sacerdotal youth may have white hairs. In Oklahoma he may officially become a venerable without the slightest change in their color. In the Detroit of my day a young priest was fortunate, even blessed, if he did not step from recruit to veteran standing in a month.

This situation was, however, recognized even then as unusual, and allowance was made for it, but the allowance produced a new difficulty. When was a pastor obviously too young to be considered out of his teeth-cutting period? It was a real difficulty and hard to solve, but there was a sort of common understanding that, when admittedly old pastors began to listen to a junior with some slight show of respect for his opinions, the end of the first period was in sight for him. The Academy might then be assumed to be only a short way ahead. But no one ever decided how long the short way should be. For me it came to a sudden end when I was already thirteen years a pastor.

Now a young priest is always very, very young to his presumed elders and is supposed to know it, which means that he is expected to do his work as well as his inexperience will permit and not occupy his mind overmuch with what is obviously none of his business. He may, of course, dream of other things, but telling his dream in the presence of his seniors is considered by them something akin to the indiscretion of Joseph telling his to his brethren. What I mean is that the adage "children should be seen and not heard" is in high favor with the venerables. It used to be in particularly high favor with bishops. It was in super-particularly high favor with mine. But out of the lecturing episode of my clerical youth came a dream that somehow I could not help telling. My peaceful war experience had not made me a hero, but I claim a hero's crown for telling that dream; yes, and another for having had the audacity to write and publish it.

The dream? It had been growing on me from the day when I read a letter of appeal for the Society for the Propagation of the Faith sent out by Abbé Magnien. I was then too poor to help but hopeful enough to promise that some day I should. I felt as I read the Abbé's circular that the whole Church in America ought to help. It was not gratitude for what the great Society had done for the Church of America that moved me, but the thought that we had a duty to vindicate our Catholicity in missionary action within and even beyond our borders. There was for me an effective lecture on that par-

*From *The Bishop Jots It Down,* pp. 113–123, by Francis Clement. Kelly, Harper & Brothers, Publishers; New York: 1939.

ticular mark of the Church in the appeal of the Grand Old Man of Baltimore.

Then came travel and lecturing. I saw America, not the America of the great cities but the real America which feeds and sustains the other — the America of the small towns, villages, and countryside. In the West and South I ran into many small groups of Catholics threatened with being swallowed up by indifference, pastorless people as well as churchless people. And the conviction came to me that our leaders had missed something great because they had been overwhelmed by numbers pouring out of ships into the cities. We had, I thought, been forced to neglect the minority that had gone to the little places. But these were the hope of the cities of the future, the fathers and mothers of the next and succeeding generations of city dwellers. Could we afford to lose them? I was sure we could not.

There is something substantial behind every dream no matter how fantasy may distort it. Dreams are the plays of the subconscious memory. The substantial behind mine was the Catholicity of the Church. So deep-rooted became my desire to help the rural places that I felt no discouragement would prevent me from planting a seed in soil I hoped would be fertile enough to give it strength and growth.

There came to Trinity Rectory one evening when I was there a stern, dignified, and aloof-appearing man. He was John Hennessy, Bishop of Wichita. His bearing did not invite confidences — even conversation for that matter. But young men with dreams are not afraid. I talked of mine in his presence. He showed interest. To the Dean's astonishment he even invited me to pay him a visit if my lecturing brought me near Wichita. I thanked him for the invitation without determining to accept it. I was afraid to accept it. But when I did actually find myself near Wichita I recalled it and paid him a visit. He questioned me closely about the thing that was interesting me. I was launched into the subject of home missions before I knew it, because I was soon aware of the fact that I had a sympathetic listener. To my surprise the Bishop took up the discussion when and where I left off and suggested that I should make an effort to found a Society dedicated to the work.

"What we need first of all," he said, "is financial help to put up chapels for small groups scattered here and there all over the West. Someone like you must make a study of the situation and begin the work."

When I suggested that I was too unimportant a person to do more than make the study, he answered, "For some good purpose of Divine Providence you have been forced out to see conditions from one end of the country to the other. Learn all you can about home mission societies elsewhere and write on the subject. That is the way to begin."

I did make the study but remained doubtful that I was indicated as the founder of such a work. Then something else happened, and again in Kansas. I visited Ellsworth to lecture for the high school of the town and there met the pastor, Father Arthur Luckey. What happened to me in Ellsworth was read by thousands when the appeal I felt forced to write was published in the Ecclesiastical Review of Philadelphia and reprinted many times in pamphlet form. For years after the Church Extension was founded that appeal was known as the "Little Shanty Story" because it began:

"I know a little 'shanty' in the West, patched and desolate, through whose creaks and cracks the blizzard moans and chills, cellarless, stairless, and dreary. Built on low prairie land, the excuse for a garden about it floods with water when the rains come, so that the tumbling old fence, with its network of weeds, falling, fails to hide the heartbreaking desolation. The 'shanty' has three rooms; the first a combination of office, library, and bedroom. In one corner is a folding bed; in another a desk; in another, curtained off with cheap print, is an improvised wardrobe. Against a wall stands a poor bookcase, while a few chairs are scattered about. The next room is also a combination, for eating and sleeping. A table is near the wall, a bed in the corner, and close by are a washstand and a few chairs. Back of all is the third room, kitchen, coal bin, utility, and — what not.

"Whose shanty is it? Who lives here?

"A pioneer on the vast plains, advance guard of civilization, trying in a sod hut to compromise between the longings within him and the wilderness that overwhelms by its lonely savagery without?

"No!

"The hut of a negro huddled away on the outskirts of a great city?

"No!

"A squatter on the railroad right-of-way?

"No!

"It is the rectory of a Catholic parish in a town of two thousand inhabitants, in a well-settled state of the Union. And today it is the home of an educated, cultured gentleman, a priest, who has left his worldly chances behind him — for this!

"Across the street stands a shaky, once white building surmounted by a cross, the only sign of its high and holy mission. Outside it is as ugly as the gargoyles of Notre Dame, without the artistic beauty that surrounds them, to make it all magnificent by contrast. The steps shake as you mount them. The floor trembles at your tread. The rough, unsightly pews are the acme of discomfort, and a house painter's desecrating brush has touched the altar and the Holy of Holies. No vestry. The confessional is literally a box. The vestments are few and tattered. Not a footstep sounds from fortnight to fortnight across the threshold of the Hidden God but His priest's, as alone he comes daily to offer up the mighty redeeming Sacrifice, or steals before the altar, to watch and pray, and perchance — who could blame him? — to sob down his discouragement before this tawdry throne of his Master.

"Why alone?

"Because his people do not care. The decades of neglect, when neglect was the only thing possible, have left the scattered few unmindful. Do not think, gentle reader, that I am drawing with rough charcoal and tinting with pigments from my imagination. I am drawing with a well-tempered pen, and using the colors of fact.

"One priest died in this place a short year before this priest came, died of a fever bred by malarial surroundings, died while his sister was speeding from cultured Boston to share his exile, only to find that she had passed her brothers' body on his last journey home. Other priests followed; none of them stayed long enough to die except this one. He will stay. The timid, shrinking eye fights to master the determined expression of a Western mouth and jaw, and they win. He is working, and working hard, against the odds of indifference and irreligion, working to save for the children the inestimable gift of Faith which the parents have forgotten how to appreciate. Yes, he will win as surely as God reigns and His grace lives."

That Little Shanty Story founded The Catholic Church Extension Society both in the United States and Canada because it played a sympathy if not a symphony on the heartstrings of many people. In the spring of 1905 nothing was wanting for the founding of the society but a distinguished sponsor, definitely the archbishop of one of the large metropolitan sees of the United States. I wanted to go out searching for one but had no money to pay my way around. To my rescue came a group of the Knights of Columbus in Michigan and Ohio. They gave me a one hour job and paid well for it. I was invited to preach on my hobby at their summer outing at Cedar Point, Ohio, with the collection as recompense. That collection netted me about two hundred dollars. I could travel as far as that sum would carry me.

Naturally New York was my first objective. I wanted Archbishop Farley to be the honorary head of the society. His refusal was kindly expressed but clearly definite. I tried Archbishop Ryan of Philadelphia. His refusal, too, was kind and to it he added the saving bit of humor that was expected of the Episcopal wit of the day. But it too was definite. Archbishop Bourgade of Santa Fe was willing to help but did not think himself important enough to lead. Archbishop Williams of Boston was growing old. I knew that he would not consider adding burdens to the great one he already was carrying. I felt the same about Cardinal Gibbons. While I was hesitating about approaching Archbishop Ireland of St. Paul I learned that the "Little Shanty Story" had met with the approbation of Archbishop Quigley of Chicago. Why not Chicago? It was the very gateway to the whole home mission field. At the suggestion of Archbishop Bourgade I put all my hopes on Chicago.

It was at the University of Notre Dame that I met Archbishop Quigley for the first time. He was seated on a rear veranda of the presbytery chatting with President Morrissey and Dr. Zahm, the scientist, when I was presented by the future president, Dr. Cavanaugh. The sun was setting, but for yet a little while I had a chance to study the face of the Archbishop. It was a good face to look at because it seemed to be set in quiet repose. One had the feeling that its owner was a tranquil man who might let his heart's influence count. He had keen measuring eyes, both dark and deep; one did not know how deep they might be. His movements were slow and purposeful. His hand went out toward an ash tray now and then, for when I arrived he was enjoying an after-dinner cigar, but they did not move at all when he spoke. He was a good listener, like a judge hearing a case and anxious to follow and check the points of law involved in it, or an Oxford examiner intent on finding out from the way the student handles himself, rather than from a display of technical learning, if he really merits the honors he seeks. I got the impression that my arguments would count with the Archbishop much less than my personality. That worried me, for my confidence was all in the arguments. Truth was that the Archbishop knew them as well as I did, since for years he had had the same thought on the subject which in me was only developing. But what I had seen in my travels around the West and South interested him, and it was plain that he loved a story with a lesson to end it. The strong impression I got from watching and hearing him was that he was a man of wide vision. His title and dignity meant little, but his object, and the means to attain it, meant everything. He was not one from whom to expect such trifles as personal favors, and certainly not one who would ever expect to receive any; a man who could not be flattered or moved by such things. I must admit that he frightened me. But I knew that here was a personality and a protector well worth winning. He proved easy to win, not because I had winning ways but because he himself had been over the ground. When the light faded and a bell called him to the chapel for the opening of the retreat he was there to attend, his mind was made up and he said so. I had found my protector and knew that if I lost him later it would not be because he failed to stick but because I failed to make good.

All my dealings with Archbishop Quigley, up to his last illness, confirmed my first impressions. I had his confidence in one matter only, the special business he had taken up to do with me. In that I had it to the full. In all the other things which pertained to his office I was an outsider. I spent at least one evening a week alone with him. Business always came first in these visits. He would not even offer me a cigar until I had said "that's all" to the business part of the discussion. Then he would rise from his chair, walk over to a humidor on a side table, hand me a cigar and say, "Very well. We'll have a smoke now."

My evenings with Archbishop Quigley are now very happy memories. I think of him as a friend who gave nothing to me personally but whose friendship was all the better because it included me in something greater. James Edward Quigley was the finest, the strongest, and the noblest influence in my life save that of the stern father who resembled him in so many ways and the saintly mother who contributed to my life what none but mothers can give.

The Catholic Church Extension Society was founded in Archbishop Quigley's house in Chicago on the 18th of October, 1905. I was given mountains to climb. I knew well what was on the other side of them but I never expected to see it. Yet I think that, through a narrow pass high up on the most desolate part of one of them, perhaps I caught a glimpse of it. Cryptic? No! I am only thinking of the advance guard of a new generation of priests, imitating the poor man of Assisi in a modern world; or, if you will, imitating the Apostle to the Gentiles in his own good way — priests of the highways and hedges.

It was, however, one thing to have a plan in mind or on paper and quite another to put it into active operation. At a preliminary meeting in Chicago I had secured a few men to advise with, and, if success came later, to become directors of the work. But I knew that in the beginning both burden and responsibility would be mine and mine alone. I was ready to face the fact that if failure did result, it would find me stripped of all defense except the melancholy excuse of good intentions. The thing to do was to imitate Cortez and destroy my ships. I made ready to do it. But before I did, I took a rapid glance over my defenses against possible, perhaps even probable, failure.

My first and greatest defense was the cause itself. I might be condemned for unskillful planning or over-confident generalship, but no one to whom I intended to appeal could logically condemn the objective. That much was certain.

My second defense was the interest of Archbishop Quigley, as well as his fine reputation for saneness of outlook and sterling good sense. No one ever thought of him as a dreamer. But, on the other hand, I had in him picked a future superior, and I could look back uneasily over incidents which showed a certain lack of skill in dealing with superiors. There was, I felt, something in my character or personality that made such relations all the more difficult because there was nothing outwardly wanting in them of absolute correctness. I felt that to superiors I was a sort of problem, too obviously real to be cast aside but just as obviously too complicated to solve. Knowledge of the handicap first dawned upon me in the Army. My colonel told me one day that General Coppinger did not like me. "It's about that new chaplains' uniform," he said. "The general thinks you were the one responsible for its adoption."

"But I was not," I answered, a bit warmly. "I was not even one of the committee that called on General Miles to ask for it."

"Yes, I know that," he said. "But you were the first chaplain the general saw wearing it, and when he said that he didn't like it you defended it. Yesterday he came over here for Mass and saw you wearing it before you put on your cassock."

"Of course I was wearing it," I answered. "It's regulation. Of course I defended it. It's right. But I was not responsible for its adoption. Why is it that I always seem to get in bad with some people?"

"You don't get in bad with me," the colonel consoled, "but I'm not a general. Better keep away from generals."

I was a bit blue over the matter. "I wonder what's really wrong with me?" I said, "I like and admire General Coppinger."

"Ever see a king snake?" the colonel asked.

"No. Why?"

"Nothing. I was just thinking about them. They look like ugly customers to folks who don't know them. But there are always a few who do know and who let them go ahead quietly attending to their business of exterminating rats and rattlers. Changing old customs and getting down to work hard at it is always a business of exterminating something — maybe only a prejudice. By the way, the general's coming over to dine at our mess tomorrow. What are you going to wear?"

"This uniform," I answered promptly.

"I thought so." He shook his head. "Well, I guess that's about what you ought to do. Better right than President, eh? But it ain't always comfortable, this business of being right. So long!"

Suppose Archbishop Quigley turned out to be another general? I could take the chance safely enough at the beginning, but what might happen later? I decided that I had to take all the chances, and was not sorry later that I did. The Archbishop turned out to be the happy exception to prove an unhappy rule because he was an almost perfect imitation of the Church herself, careful neither to give too much nor to inquire too little, but when inquiry was over and done with, and the gift made, to follow them both with the unquestioning confidence that awakens loyalty and stimulates courage. Just the same I knew that I had in myself a complicated personal problem. I was afraid of myself, afraid that I might fail to win confidence, afraid of my impetuous nature, afraid of the test that had come of my ability to make good. I knew that I had to be a founder, an executive, an editor, an advertiser, a diplomat, all in one. My friends warned me. They were a discouraging lot. I almost blew out the torch I had lighted to destroy my ships. But the dream returned, stood between my friends and me, and blotted them out with all their fears and all their misgivings. This thing was God's, not mine. If He wanted a fool or a child to do it, that was His business. He had His way of picking poor material and working it over to suit His purpose. I was quite sure that I was poor material, but why worry? The skeleton of a failure often marks the beginning of the right trail.

"I can't understand you priests," said a business friend as he shook hands in farewell when I was leaving Lapeer for Chicago. "Here you are abandoning your new church and your fine new home almost the day after you got into them, to start all over again in a Chicago flat with nothing but a dream and not much of a dream at that."

A dream? The man did not know the compelling force and persistent glory of a dream. While I am now, as a bishop, committed to a dislike for dreamers, only yesterday a mother, my own sister, pouring out of her artist soul a prayer of resignation over her afflicted son, brought tears acknowledging the truth and power of a dream from my eyes. She called her poem, "Pilgrim of Shadows."

"As petals fold the fragrance of a rose
Till burgeoning, so did he hold the Dream
Within his heart; and never garden close
Held bud of sweeter promise. It would seem
That all his days were fashioned to attain
One gracious goal: for this his cloistered years,
His exile, and his deep bewildered pain
In lonely, seeking hours; perhaps his tears,
Glimpsing the glory he had failed to win.
And dare we say he failed, whose chalice waits

The touch of priestly fingers? Nay, within
His soul, unstained, the vision compensates;
Always for him pale altar candles gleam;
Always he keeps inviolate — the Dream."

Had I been leaving for a promotion few would have thought or expressed any wonderment. But the business that has to wait for eternity to pay its dividend is another matter. Those who follow the red-gold lure of the Cross are mysterious, even to some who ought to understand.

I had a friend in Detroit, Edward H. Doyle, who would have his joke. He was one of those who thought I was risking too much by the burning of my ships.

"Did you ever hear the definition for a promoter made by my unusual friend, Marcus Pollasky?" he asked when I called at his office in the Majestic Building to say good-by.

"Never. What is it?"

"He was on the witness stand in a court case. The examining lawyer asked his name and his business. Marcus gave his name and said that his business was that of a promoter."

"What is your definition of a promoter, Mr. Pollasky?"

"A promoter? Why, a promoter is a man who has nothing to sell and who sells it to a man who doesn't want to buy it."

I saw the point and tried to explain what my kind of promoter was and what he had to sell. My friend listened politely for awhile. Really I was only trying to give him information, not to "sell him" anything. "That will do. That will do," he interrupted. "Before you go you ought to meet my friend Marcus. He was right. But I'll buy it."

Buy it expensively he did. In him I landed my first big fish. It weighed ten thousand dollars.

The society stayed only one year in Lapeer. Then it was moved to Chicago and I had to go with it. The Bishop of Detroit granted me the usual *Exeat* transferring me to the archdiocese of Chicago. I must admit that he seemed to take his loss in a spirit of resignation.

JAMES J. DALY

(1872–   )

THE masculine qualities of the Middle West suspire from the works of Father James Daly, S.J. He was born in Chicago and educated first in the public schools and later at St. Ignatius College, Chicago. Father Daly was a delicate lad and this circumstance turned his mind toward reading and literary pursuits. At eighteen he joined the Society of Jesus and has done significant work for his community as teacher, literary editor of *America,* and as an associate editor of *Queen's Work* and *Thought.*

When almost sixty years of age Father Daly published his first book, *A Cheerful Ascetic.* In the ten years following he wrote, *Boscobel and Other Rimes, The Road to Peace,* and *The Jesuit in Focus.*

Father Daly's prose style is clear and forceful. It has a silver quality which has made some critics refer to him as "the American Newman." His poetry lacks the ultimate lyric touch, but gives abundant evidence of Father Daly's religious outlook, balanced mind, and abundant good humor.

ALL SAINTS*

IN OCTOBER the soul feels celestial stirrings. Is it the *memento mori* of the falling leaf? The year has spent its exuberance of strength in a careless riot of energy, and now pauses in a sudden access of surprise on the chill edge of snowy silences. *De me fabula* murmurs the soul and shudders. But October also reminds us of other things than death. Its cold breezes may hint to the body of the icy mountain passes of winter which must be traversed soon; but to the soul it carries faint importings of ultramontane felicities. Its transfiguring golden mists bathe the immaterial landscape and strike the distant hilltop into a dream-city of towers and pinnacles.

> *Celestis urbs Jerusalem,*
> *Beata pacis visio,*

the lips murmur half-consciously, showing whither the mind has flown. And is there no *Sursum Corda* in the glory of autumnal color? Field and wood and wayside, hill and valley, are decked out as if a pageant were passing this way, and the very airs seem on tiptoe of hushed expectancy or wonder. Per-haps the angels — for it is their month — are swinging down the broad aerial avenues, shining battalion on shining battalion, the Angels, the Archangels, the Virtues, the Powers, the Principalities, the Dominations, the Thrones, the Cherubim and the Seraphim, glittering regiments of mighty spirits from the fortresses of heaven. And when their silvery cavalcades have passed, and their dedicated month is over, and the vivid scarlets and rich purples of their triumph are fading, and the winter is closing in upon us, comes the Feast of All Saints.

Then wavering intimations become solid assurances. The vibrating and level accents of a divine Voice, coming to us in words and forms which the Spirit of Truth fits closely to their burden, announce that, somewhere in the domains of God, men and women, of the same clay as ours, having lived and died, live, again, sharing in Christ's triumph over death and sin. And, as the north wind of November braces the shrinking nerves to meet the rigors of advancing winter, the message of All Saints stiffens the fiber of the soul to resistance against beleaguering fears of death.

We look forward with humility and trepidation, yet with confident hope, to reaching

---

*Daly, James J., S.J., *The Road to Peace* (Milwaukee: The Bruce Publishing Co., 1936), pp. 187–191.

the very heart of happiness which consists in seeing God, not in fragmentary and dim reflections, but as He is. God's love for us is a mystery and a joy, balanced by the mystery and the sorrow of our coldness toward Him. The mere thought, that some day the icy shackles will drop away from our soul and allow it to leap into its Father's arms, ought to make the grayest life golden. Alas, of that dizzy vision we get only fleeting and illusive glimpses above the rolling fogs of our mortality. We cannot construct its beauty, delicately intense, out of our crude experiences. Christ could not describe it to us: the incapacity was ours, not His. Blind infants that we are, how could He show us the color of that glory? Our discontent is boundless: but we can trust Omnipotence to remove it.

My window opens on the autumn night,
  In vain I watch for sleep to visit me;
How should sleep dull mine ears, and dim
    my sight,
  Who saw the stars, and listened to the sea?

Ah, how the City of our God is fair!
  If, without sea, and starless though it be,
For joy of the majestic beauty there,
  Men shall not miss the stars, nor mourn
    the sea.

But there are flaming, fiery edges of that central joy, which the mind can reach to in a fashion, because it has earthly experiences whereon to climb. The saints will be there, and we shall know them, and they will know us. To meet the white chivalry of God, with our Lord and Our Blessed Lady at their head, to meet them without shyness or fearful reserve, to be the object of their ravishing courtesies, to love them and be beloved of them, the true nobles of our race: this is a joy within the grasp of human yearning. How touching the ancient prayer in the Canon of the Mass, *Nobis quoque peccatoribus!* How it translates our yearning into words!

On ourselves, too, who are sinners but yet Thy servants, and who put our trust in Thy tender mercies, vouchsafe to bestow some lot and fellowship with Thy holy Apostles and Martyrs: with John, Stephen, Matthias, Barnabus, Ignatius, Alexander, Marcellinus, Peter, Felicitas, Perpetua, Agatha, Lucy, Agnes, Cecilia, Anastasia, and all Thy saints. Into their company do Thou, we beseech Thee, admit us, not weighing our merits but freely pardoning us our sins. Through Christ our Lord.

We remember again the colloquy at Ostia in the twilight by the sea when Monica and Augustine conversed, mother and son, about the high intimacies of God: speech failed, the words flagged, and the converse tapered off into silence and ecstasy. So must have been the evenings in Nazareth when the day's work was done; a few sentences, a few words, and then the soaring heights beyond the stars! *Cor ad cor loquitur,* "Heart speaketh to heart," where saints foregather.

This hope is also laid up in our bosom, that we shall meet again those who are dear to us and are here no longer. Kind, beautiful eyes, that in a distant past kindled into a rare light at our approach and filled with tears at our going forth, closed now these many years and withdrawn behind the veil of death, will light again with the joy of meeting, nevermore to know the need of tears. How they loved and believed in us! To think that God will make us so worthy of their love that for eternity it will never find cause to weary, to falter, to doubt!

"What a *surprise* it will be to meet!" exclaims Coventry Patmore. "At least that is always my feeling after a long separation. Doubtless one of the purposes of death is to supply this exquisite feeling in the highest perfection, when those who have loved each other come together again. And, as every feeling will be always new and fresh in heaven, those who attain to it may hope to live forever with this acute delight of recognition in their hearts."

It is this hope which makes every friendship possible on endurable terms. Who would venture to set up his rest on a flower that will perish with the coming of night? St. Edmund in his last will wrote of St. Richard as one *quem jam diu nobis invisceravimus,* a phrase whose strength we fail utterly to reproduce when we translate it "whom our heart-strings have long since entwined about." Only those who are to be saints can afford to love so intensely and love wisely. What fools we are if the casual death can tear and blast the vital tendrils of the soul! Therefore the world knows pagan coldness, and pagan cynicism, and pagan despair.

In one of his charming letters the poet Cowper views as intolerable and not Christian the thought that we may not know our friends in heaven:

"To think that, when we leave them, we lose them forever, that we must remain eternally ignorant whether they, that were flesh of our flesh, and bone of our bone, partake with us of celestial glory, or are disinherited of their heavenly portion, must shed a dismal gloom over all our present connections. For my own part, this life is such a momentary thing, and all its interests have so shrunk in my estimation, that, like a worm in the bud of all my friendships and affections, this very thought would eat out the heart of them all, had I a thousand; and, were their date

to terminate with this life, I think I should have no inclination to cultivate and improve such a fugitive business."

The Church, which poor, soul-harassed Cowper needed so much, leaves no room for uneasy speculations. As Christ knows and is known by His Mother, so we shall know and be known by ours. "There a vast concourse of dear ones are awaiting us," says a lesson in the Divine Office for the Octave of All Saints; "there a large and numerous gathering of parents and brothers and sons, at ease about their own immortal life, solicitous still about ours, are looking forward to their meeting with us." And in the Mass for the Dead the Church provides special prayers for the parents of the priest, in which he begs God, through Christ our Lord, to grant that he "may see them in the brightness of eternal joy."

Sursum corda! Habemus ad Dominum.

THE SECRET OF DELIGHT*

Whenever I see a lovely thing —
A flower, the flash of a tanager's wing,
A tendril of mist curling up to the dawn,
The young moon's scimitar newly drawn,
The mood of water and dying skies,
The tide of pity in saintly eyes,

The authentic luster of heavenly grace
Upon a praying child's grave face —
When beauty takes me unawares
From ambuscades of darkling cares,
I know the secret of my delight:
It never is old or stale or trite.
For I know, or ever the hills were laid,
Or time began, God's goodness made —
In the raptures of eternity —
These trysts for loveliness and me.

*The above and following poems have been selected from *Boscobel and Other Rimes* by James J. Daly, S.J. (Milwaukee: The Bruce Publishing Co., 1934).

RECEPTION COMMITTEES

When Presidents and Kings come home
    Who meets them at the gate?
A squad of soldiers and a groom
    And counsellors sedate.

When bankers finish work downtown
    And motor home at four,
They are received with solemn frown
    By lackeys at the door.

But poor men coming home at night
    Are met by flying feet,
Dear little feet winged with delight,
    Bringing love down the street
To be the first to meet them
And kiss them and greet them
    In everybody's sight.

THE RICH FRIEND

I often of an afternoon
  Stroll down a pleasant street,
Where birds make festival in June
  And wren and robin meet.

Some of the houses are Queen Anne,
  And some are French chateaux;
Some are Colonial with their fan,
  Some have Greek porticoes.

Each dwelling sports its garden blooms,
  With trees that seem to lean
Like prim retainers waving plumes
  Above an Indian queen.

Judges and presidents of banks
  Thus please the public eye;
And I am sure they earn the thanks
  Of poor men passing by.

And yet, I dare say, few presume
  To thank them for the show:
They are important persons whom
  Not everyone may know.

But one house with its open door
  Kindly invites my feet;
Its massive walls and turrets soar
  Above the stately street.

He is the richest of mankind
  Who lives there all alone,
A willing Prisoner self-confined
  In those high walls of stone.

He made the hills and ocean tides,
  The blue walls of the sky,
But in that house of stone abides
  For every passer-by.

DEO GRATIAS!

I would not be a child again
  To start my cruise on seas untried;
For I have traveled leagues since then,
  Befriended by the wind and tide.

I have not gained the Blessed Isles,
  But I can see the lights afar,

And, grim, behind me stretch the miles
  Where nights came down without a star.

I shot my arrows in the air;
  I sowed in water; but I know
Some shots have hit, and unaware
  I garnered where I did not sow.

JAMES M. GILLIS
(1876–   )

FATHER GILLIS was born in Boston on November 12, 1876. His schooling was extensive. He received the S.T.L. from the Catholic University as well as honorary degrees from several universities.

In 1898 Father Gillis entered the Missionary Society of St. Paul the Apostle and was ordained priest in 1901. Father Gillis has held many positions of trust in his Community. He has been novice master and professor of Dogma at St. Paul's College, and after years on the Paulist mission band was made editor of the *Catholic World,* a position he still fills with genuine distinction. His syndicated column, *Sursum Corda,* has a wide following. As preacher and lecturer Father Gillis has few equals in America.

Of his published works *False Prophets* is an outstanding example of Father Gillis at his best. It is genuinely witty and devastatingly analytical. Father Gillis' editorials in the *Catholic World* are models for controversial writing. They reveal his toughmindedness and dialectical acuity which for over twenty years has made the *Catholic World* one of the prominent literary magazines of the United States.

H. G. WELLS*

I

ONE fact of primary importance, to be kept constantly in mind if we are to understand Mr. H. G. Wells, is that his genius is expansive and grandiose. This actual world, physical and intellectual, is too small for him. It cramps him. Like Alexander, he sighs for more worlds. Unlike Alexander, he is not content with sighing; he creates more worlds. And he continues the process of creation indefinitely. His readers never know what new words are to "swim into their ken," until they have read the latest of his semiannual volumes.

The worlds that Wells creates are, of course, incomparably better than the one created by God. The populations of Wells's worlds are as superior to the scrubby human beings who infest this earth, as we, in turn, are superior to the Cromagnon man or the Neanderthaler. His wars also are greater than ours. Our biggest was the World War. His is the War of the Worlds — not nations against nations, but planets against planets. Wells always "thinks big." He knows no boundaries. He is at home in the "great open spaces" — between the stars. How inept, therefore, and woefully inadequate is such a compliment as that of Anatole France, who says, "Wells is the greatest intellectual force in the English-speaking world." The "English-speaking world!" What a sphere of influence for a man whose vision comprises universes! A bungling compliment, indeed, to one whose *bête noire* is nationalism; whose immediate goal is internationalism; whose ultimate or, at least, penultimate ambition is interplanetarianism.

A more appropriate encomium for Wells is that of one who has had a better opportunity to understand him — his publisher. That discerning gentleman knows that Mr. Wells can find outlet for his exuberant genius, not merely by flitting to other worlds, but by leaping into future time. Mr. Flower explains: "Many things that Wells says are

impossible. Presently they become remotely possible, and then ultimately they are achieved; the reason being that Wells is a genius a little before his time. The world catches up with him in jerks." *There* is a fancy almost worthy of Wells himself — the world hurtling through space with inconceivable speed, yet forced to take an occasional leap, a "jerk" now and then, to keep up with the more than cosmic velocity of the mental action of this prodigious man. The fancy (if it be but a fancy) is strikingly Wellsian. It smacks of science. It suggests interplanetary action. It implies earthquakes, tidal waves, and cataclysms — Wellsian revolutions. Truly a dazzling conception — the world hitch-kicking through space to catch up with Herbert George Wells.

However, even his publishers do not thoroughly comprehend the peculiar character of the genius of Wells. They advertise his books in groups, under different headings, thus:

"Mr. Wells has written

The following novels:

The following fantastic and imaginative romances:

The following books upon social, religious, and political questions:"

This grouping and separating are doubtless necessary, but to the unsophisticated they may be misleading. Not that I would maintain that Mr. Wells's political and historical and sociological works should be listed under the heading "Fantastic and Imaginative Romances." But I do declare that to make a strict line of demarcation between his serious books and his fantastical books is to run the risk of misunderstanding all his books. Parts of *The Outline of History* are as fanciful and as romantic as *The Food of the Gods* or *The War of the Worlds*. In his description of the first human beings, or semi-human beings, on this planet, he employed his imagination as liberally as in his description of the Men in the Moon, or on Mars. His *God the Invisible King* is as fantastic a god as his Martians are fantastic men. His

*Gillis, James M., *False Prophets* (New York: The Macmillan Co., 1925), pp. 20–44.

prophecies of the remote future, and his descriptions of the remote past, are equally daring. His account of how the "Old Man of the Tribe" developed into God is as much a fairy tale as his story of the Brobdingnagian growth of those who ate *The Food of the Gods.*

One should, therefore, read his most matter-of-fact volumes, constantly remembering that at any moment the history, or the sociology, or the philosophy, or the theology may become wholly or partially imaginative. The element of fantasy is never long absent from any of his books. Indeed, it would be a psychological impossibility for a man with his riotous imagination to achieve a chapter, perhaps even a paragraph, without evincing the fact that the fanciful is his *metier.* Consequently, all minute and meticulously scientific criticism of Mr. Wells's historical and sociological works would be out of the question, if not absurd.

II

But besides Mr. Wells's irrepressible *attrait* for the fanciful, there are other reasons why it would be unfair to expect scientific or historical accuracy in his work. He writes too much. He has really no time for rigorously accurate scholarship. He has been writing for thirty years, and has produced sixty volumes—to say nothing of articles for magazines, letters to newspapers, speeches, and a mountainous mass of other ephemeral stuff. No man can write so much and always know what he is writing about. True, there have been some whose literary output was even more enormous than that of Wells. Sir Walter Scott wrote more rapidly and more voluminously than Wells, but he wrote as a story-teller speaks, reckless of historical accuracy. Anthony Trollope wrote 250 words every 15 minutes by the clock. But Trollope's novels are like Ford cars—it is a mere question of human endurance and mechanical contrivance whether you get 100 or 1,000 in a given time. Arnold Bennett boasts that for some length of time he produced 500,000 words a year. Before he dies, instead of flaunting that fact, he may lament it. Here in America, we, too, have some

literary Marathon champions. E. Phillips Oppenheim is said to have written 250 volumes. If he could, like Napoleon, dictate to four secretaries at once, he might have written 1,000 volumes—250 or 1,000 of Phillips Oppenheim is about the same.

But when we come to works of scholarship, there is a different story to tell. Edward Gibbon, having decided to write the history of *The Decline and Fall of the Roman Empire,* spent twelve years before publishing the first volume, and twenty-five years before finishing the work. Theodore Mommsen lived to be eighty-six years of age, and wrote only on *The History of Rome,* and immediately allied Roman topics. Janssen spent forty years preparing to write the *History of the German People,* and then he covered only two centuries. But Wells writes a *History of Life and Mankind* beginning perhaps six hundred million years ago, and coming down to the Treaty of Versailles. Any one who demands that such a work should stand the test of scientific history is cruel. Any one who thinks it accurate is gullible.

Yet the Wellsian enthusiasts seem to take the *Outline,* and indeed all of Wells's books, with solemn seriousness. Wells himself sets the example. Perhaps the most appalling unhumorous thing he ever wrote is his statement of what he means to do even with his novels: "We are going to write, subject only to our limitations, about the whole of human life. We are going to deal with political questions and religious questions and social questions. We are going to write about business and finance and politics and precedence, and pretentiousness, and decorum and indecorum, until a thousand pretences and ten thousand impostures shrivel in the cold clear air of our elucidations." It is well that amongst all these multitudinous subjects he is not going to forget "pretentiousness."

Still, that catalogue of subjects to be treated in novels, comprehensive as it seems, is jejune in comparison with the absolute universality of knowledge he displays in *The Outline of History.* He is equally at home in Archaeology, Paleontology, Biology, Painting, Poetry, Music, Anthropology, Psychology, Ethics, Comparative Religion, Theology, Numismatics, and Zoology. He speaks with equal confidence of Heliolithic Culture and of Tel-el-Amarna, of the Tatar language and the Rosetta Stone, of Transubstantiation and of Quadrupedal Reptiles, of the Seljukian Turks and of Sakya Muni, of the Irish Republic and the Incas of Peru. He is equally familiar with Romulus and Remus and Roosevelt. He knows the weight of the earth and the temperature of the sun; he knows the history of the Swastika sign and the habits of the saber-toothed tiger. Even the questions advertising The Children's Book of Knowledge would be ridiculously easy for him. He knows all about Ecumenical Councils and the Oneida Community, Maimonides and the Doctrine of Karma, the Battle of Lexington, Psychical Research, Human Sacrifice in Prehistoric Mexico, Anglo-Norman Feudalism, the Hairy Ainus, Beowulf, Halicarnassus; — all are discussed with the same unhesitating omniscience. It is said that some of the statesmen at the Versailles conference stumbled over a thousand geographical and sociological questions. Yet they had the assistance of hundreds of "experts." President Wilson himself took over a shipload of learned men. If it is a fair question, I should like to know why Lloyd George did not invite Wells to answer all questions, and so dispense with the battalions of authorities.

True, Mr. Wells himself had coadjutors. Sometimes their corrections are given in footnotes on the pages of the *Outline*. But almost always Wells disagrees with his experts. Sometimes he debates with them in the footnotes. More often he simply lets his statements stand in the text, in spite of the footnotes. He trusts that the Wellsian admirer will know whom to believe when "H.G.W." and "E.B." are at odds.

III

But the most astounding of all evidences of Wells's godlike omniscience is the fact that he knows not only historic and prehistoric facts, but thoughts that were in the minds of men so remotely prehistoric that they had not even learned to speak. Of course,

he does say, "the historian can only speculate on what thoughts were in the mind of a king who lived three hundred years ago." Mr. Wells must be not only an historian, but a clairvoyant. He can tell what was in the mind of primordial man. He declares, "Something must be said about the things that were going on inside these brains of which we have traced the growth and development through a period of 500,000 years from the apeman stage." And, bravely enough, he explains that "primordial man, before he could talk, probably saw very vividly, and mimicked very cleverly. . . . He feared the dark, no doubt, and thunderstorms. . . . No doubt he did things to propitiate what he feared, or to change his luck, and please the imaginary powers in rock and beast and river. . . . If a stick hurt him, he kicked it. If the river foamed and flooded, he thought it was hostile. . . . No doubt he had a certain amount of fetishism in his life; he did things which we should now think unreasonable, to produce desired ends. No doubt he was excited by his dreams. Since he buried his dead, and since even the later Neanderthal men seem to have buried their dead, and apparently with food and weapons, it has been argued that they had a belief in a future life. But it is just as reasonable to suppose that early men buried their dead with food and weapons because they doubted if they were dead."

So Mr. Wells runs on and on, building up paragraphs and pages of imaginary biography of men who lived a million years ago. It may be pertinent to ask how can he know all these things. For example, how can he know that primordial man was afraid in the dark? How can he know that primordial man kicked a stick that tripped him, or if he did kick it, why should that bit of impatience be any more significant than if a modern man slams a door, or bangs his fist upon the table, or smashes a vase with his cane when he is irritated? And the peculiar notion that primitive men may have thought that the dead were not dead — what does it signify?

Mr. Wells places an abnormal importance upon these insignificant actions, because he is adroitly building up a theory of the origin of religion. Kicking a stick implies that the stick has a soul — it means animism. Imputing anger to a raging river implies propitiation — it means sacrifice. Doing unreasonable things implies magic and fetishism. Thinking the dead not to be dead implies ancestor worship. Out of these things — animism, fetishism, propitiation, ancestor worship — Mr. Wells is going to show the origin of religion. He is, in effect, performing logical legerdemain. If his hand is quicker than your eye, he fools you.

But if you are critical and skeptical, his sleight-of-hand performance becomes a fiasco. As a matter of fact, impatience with inanimate objects, a stick, or a stone, is evidence of hysteria or neurasthenia, which are diseases of an excessive civilization, rather than of savagery. Children of civilization, whose homes are illuminated at night, are more afraid in the dark than the children of savages, who have little or no artificial light. Savages do not fear thunderstorms any more than we, perhaps less. Primitive man buried his dead because the unburied dead became intolerable. How could any man, even a savage, think the dead were not dead, when his eyes and his nose both gave testimony to the gruesome fact not only of death but of decomposition? Savages probably placed a dead man's spear on his grave for the same reason that we put cannons on a soldier's monument; they may have put food on a grave for the same reason that we put flowers on a grave. Mr. Wells's carefully worked-out theory on the origin of religion is "buncombe."

But the *pièce de résistance* of his theology is the famous "Old Man Theory." I call it "his" theology, but of course it is his only at second hand, like all the rest of his theories about primitive man. He borrowed the theory of animism and fetishism from Frazer and Tylor. He borrows the "Old Man Theory" from Herbert Spencer and Grant Allen. As usual, however, Mr. Wells's description is the most graphic and picturesque. Hear him: "Certain very fundamental things must have been in men's minds, long before the coming of speech. Chief among these must have been

the fear of the Old Man of the Tribe. The young of the primitive squatting-place grew up under that fear. Objects associated with him were probably forbidden. Everyone was forbidden to touch his spear or to sit in his place just as today little boys must not touch father's pipe or sit in his chair. Only by respecting this primal law could the young male hope to escape the Old Man's wrath." (Notice, in passing, that "Old Man" is constantly capitalized.) "And the Old Man must have been an actor in many a primordial nightmare. A disposition to propitiate him even after he was dead is quite understandable. One was not sure that he was dead. He might only be alseep or shamming. Long after an Old Man was dead, when there was nothing to represent him but a mound, and a megalith, the women would convey to their children" ("convey," somehow without speech) "how awful and wonderful he was. And being still a terror to his own little tribe, it was easy to go on hoping that he would be a terror to other and hostile people. In his life he had fought for his tribe, even if he had bullied it. Why not when he was dead? One sees that the Old Man idea was an idea very natural to the primitive mind, and capable of great development."

Great development indeed! Mr. Wells does not cease developing the idea until he has apotheosized the Old Man. The Old Man turns out to be God. Any fairly attentive reader of the *Outline*, could see that such would be the case, after Mr. Wells's first few lines, just as the inveterate habitue of the movies can tell how the story is coming out, after a hundred feet of the first reel have been run.

But even the most elementary criticism will upset the theory. It is notorious that savage people have little patience with the aged. A very considerable part of Sir J. G. Frazer's book, *The Golden Bough*, is devoted to a description of the "practice of putting kings to death either at the end of a fixed period, or whenever their health and strength began to fail." Only Christianity, and indeed a very highly perfected Christianity, leads men to be tolerant of old people, especially when the old people blither and blather and are cantankerous. Amongst savages, as soon as a man is too old to fight any powerful young fellow, the old man is knocked on the head. Mr. Wells knows that. He says so. "Some younger male will stand up to the Old Man and kill him and reign in his stead. There is short shrift for the old at the squatting-place. So soon as they grow weak and bad-tempered, trouble and death come upon them." How Mr. Wells can say this on page 82 and yet on page 125 show the process of making a god of the Old Man, is inexplicable, except that like all legerdemain artists, he expects to divert the attention of the audience so that they shall forget what they have seen a moment ago and notice only what is before their eyes at this instant — and see that wrong.

To me it is marvelous that the most simple of all explanations of the origin of religion seems not to occur to such writers as Wells and Tylor and Grant Allen and Herbert Spencer. Robinson Crusoe could teach them. When Crusoe saw the footprint on the beach, he said, "Some one made it." When a savage sees a hut, or a spear, or an arrowhead, he says, "Some one made it." When he sees a mountain or an ocean, or a tree, or a waterfall he says, "Some one made it." That is the origin of belief in God, and religion. But the explanation is too simple for the learned. They must have something more recondite. If they are both learned and romantic, they must have something bizarre. If they are learned and romantic and "scientific" — like Wells — they must build an argument from a stick, or a spear, or an "angry" river, or an Old-Man-that-Bullies-the-Tribe. Meanwhile the fact remains — as big as a mountain or an ocean, — that men from the beginning have believed in God because they instinctively understand the fundamental scientific law of cause and effect. The mountain had a Maker, the ocean had a Maker — God. A simple, but sufficient theology.

Now, for fear that some may imagine that Wells despises the savage for making a god, let me hasten to explain that he believes that every man should make his own god. As for himself, Wells sometimes has a God, again he has no God, and then he has a God once more — it depends largely upon external circumstances, and the effect produced upon his mind by world events. Before the war he had no God. During the war, he had a God. Now, since the Treaty of Versailles, and the dismal state of Europe resulting therefrom, Wells once more has no God. At least, one cannot find any God in his latest works. But he may have a God again at any moment. In this matter, as in others, one can never tell until one reads his latest book. Like some other excessively rapid thinkers, he drops his convictions as swiftly as he acquires them. It is part of the evolutionary theory that growth and development demand the elimination and extinction of forms of life proved to be inadaptable. So of ideas and convictions. They were useful yesterday, they are a draw-back today. Drop them. They may be helpful to-morrow. Pick them up again. Truth comes and goes. "Fly away, Jack; fly away, Jill. Come back, Jack; come back, Jill."

Still Mr. Wells did declare at one time, with an appearance of permanent conviction: "Religion is the first thing and the last thing, and until a man has found God and been found by God he begins at no beginning and he works to no end." That sounds like the first page of the Catechism. A Christian reader might well cry "Bravo!" But wait and see what Mr. Wells means by "finding God." He means that literally and truly you must discover God for yourself. I have my God, and you must have your God. My God is no good for you — your God is no good for me. I must not take your God, or St. Augustine's God, or St. Paul's God. I must not even take Jesus Christ's God. I must discover God for myself. Wells thus works a metaphor to death. Naturally we refuse to follow him. Indeed, in a sense, every man must "discover" his own God, but if I attempt literally to make my own God, I fear I shall make a botch of the attempt. Even Plato and Aristotle and Socrates, who all believed in God, had some very curious elements in their concept of God. For Christians, the God of Jesus Christ will suffice. His God is good enough for us, and better than any we could make for ourselves.

Wells bungled his God even more than Plato or Aristotle. In fact, he has made two gods. There is a god in your heart and a god beyond the stars. The two are in conflict. The god in your heart is a rebel against the other god. The high God, Who is Almighty and Omniscient, does not interest Wells. His god by preference is the god of the heart, who is not omnipotent and not omniscient, not the Creator of the universe. Strangely enough, though not omnipotent nor omniscient, he is omnipresent. But his power is limited. He has not yet come to his strength. Wells sometimes calls him "The Old Experimenter." He is a god who is doing the best he can. We have all heard the "agnostic's prayer," "O God, if there be a God, save my soul, if I have a soul." Wells's prayer, I imagine is somewhat like that, and yet different. "O God, help me! Or, at least, help me if you can!"

Students of the history of religion will easily recognize Wells's two-god theory. It is Gnostic, and Manichaean. It suggests Ormuzd and Ahriman, or Creator and Demiurge. Wells confesses that he got it from Shelley. Shelley may have got it from the Persians. But the idea of an omnipresent but not omnipotent God is a little something of Wells's own. That is possibly what he means by discovering his own God.

IV

For Christianity, Mr. Wells has only vituperative contempt. As usual, the contempt is based on ignorance, for he shows "an ingenious unfamiliarity with the creed of Christianity." With characteristic inconsistency he sometimes praises Christ and sometimes questions His very existence. He says in *First and Last Things*, that it is a matter of no importance whether Christ ever lived or not. Granting that He did live, Wells thinks that the Christ of the Gospels had no very definite teaching. But after Christ, St. Paul, a man of subtle intellect and considerable education, elaborated the Gospel into a theological system. This system was then further developed in the first four centuries and was codified and crystallized by the time of the Council of Nicaea, A.D. 325.

It is not my intention to discuss at length the extent to which these views are either false or fallacious. I desire but to indicate that this cut-and-dried explanation of the origin and growth and corruption of the Christian religion was, as usual, borrowed, not invented, by Wells. There is nothing in his concept of Christianity that was not written by the Tübingen school seventy years ago. But, old or new, original or borrowed, the explanation is unscientific, in that it does not account for the continuous existence of the Christian religion. A convinced evolutionist, like Mr. Wells, should understand that a system which becomes crystallized in the fourth century cannot be a living organism in the twentieth century. Systems are like species; when they are no longer vital they yield in the struggle for existence. When they yield they die and become extinct. Crystallized systems are like fossil remains. Mr. Wells should know that the Church is not extinct and not fossilized. Only a few years ago he wrote that the twentieth century was destined to see an enormous revival of Catholicism. Perhaps he has already forgotten that prophecy. A man who cannot remember on page 125 what he said on page 82, can hardly be expected to remember in 1924 what he said in 1920. But it is surprising that at the moment he penned that prophecy, the thought did not flash through his brain, "Let me see — crystallized at Nicaea in the fourth century? Yet due for an enormous revival in the twentieth century? is this good evolutionistic doctrine?" But pshaw! Why am I constantly forgetting my own warning that his serious writings are not serious?

Before dropping the question of Mr. Wells's attitude toward Christianity, let me show by a few quotations not only how hopelessly prejudiced is his view, but how thoroughly lacking he is in humor when he deals with what arouses his "vituperative contempt." At least half a dozen times during his consideration of Christ and Christianity in *The Outline of History*, Wells proclaims that he is disinterested, that he is no theologian, that a history is not a theological treatise, and that he will avoid theological controversy. Then, close upon the heels of these ingenuous protestations, he writes sentences like these:

"It is a matter of fact that in the gospels all that body of theological assertion which constitutes Christianity finds little support."

"Christ did not say a word about the worship of His mother Mary, in the guise of Isis, the Queen of heaven."

"All that is most characteristically Christian in worship and usage, He ignored. Skeptical writers" (Heaven forfend that Wells should be thought skeptical) "have had the temerity to deny that Jesus can be called a Christian at all."

"There was nothing in His teaching that a follower of Gautama Sakya might not receive very readily, nothing to prevent a primitive Buddhist from also being a Nazarene, and nothing to prevent a personal disciple of Jesus from accepting all the recorded teaching of Buddha."

The Crucifixion was attended by "foolish stories of physical disturbances. We are told that a great darkness fell upon the face of the earth, and that the veil of the temple was rent in twain. . . . It is difficult to believe nowadays that the order of nature indulged in such meaningless comments."

"The gospels contain the teachings of Jesus on the one hand, and the glosses and interpretations of the disciples on the other."

"Was Jesus God? It is not the function of the historian to answer such questions. The reader is referred to the Athanasian creed for the exact expression of the mystery. To Gibbon he must go for a derisive statement of these controversies. The present writer can deal with them neither with awe nor derision. They seem to him, he must confess, a disastrous ebullition of the human mind entirely inconsistent with the plain account of Jesus preserved for us in the gospels."

"These attempts to say exactly how God was related to Himself were presumptuous and intellectually monstrous; nevertheless we are bound to recognize that beneath these preposterous refinements of impossible dogmas, there lay often a real passion for truth."

He is not a theologian. The *Outline* is not a theological discussion. He is an historian and it is not the function of the historian to answer such questions. But he *will* say that miracles of nature are "foolish stories" and "meaningless"; that Jesus ignored all that is most characteristic of Christianity; that the gospels are partly His teaching and partly the interpolations of ignorant men; that Christ was no Christian, that St. Paul was no Christian, that a primitive Christian and a primitive Buddhist are identical, that creeds are "persumptuous and intellectually monstrous," and that the divinity of Christ is but one of a number of "preposterous refinements of impossible dogmas," which are "disastrous ebullitions of the human mind." It is a great satisfaction to know that Mr. Wells recognizes limitations of the historian, and that he so modestly confesses his ignorance of theology.

I accuse Mr. Wells of lack of humor. I may as well speak my full mind and accuse him of lack of honesty. In view of his violent attack upon Christianity, his protestations of neutrality, so oft repeated, can be nothing less than hypocritical. When he says "We shall treat Jesus of Nazareth as being what He appeared to be, a man. . . . If the light of Divinity shine through our recital we will neither help nor hinder it," does even his most devoted admirer imagine that Wells's mind is still unconvinced as to whether his narrative shall show the divinity in Christ? When he further proclaims that he will discuss Christ impartially, as "we have already done in the case of Buddha, and as we shall do later with Mohammed," we Christians are frank enough to say that to treat Christ with as much aloofness and scientific coldbloodedness as we treat Buddha or Mohammed is for us an impossibility. Our emotions and our feelings for Christ are such that we cannot consider him dispassionately. But neither can Wells treat Christ, or Christianity, dispassionately. Even so loyal a Wellsian as Heywood Broun, in his "American Foreword" to Sidney Dark's *Outline of Wells,* is sensible enough to see, and to say, "Wells is no neutral. Even in his novels, he is a passionate partisan!" If he knows that, his protestations of neutrality are hyprocritical. If he doesn't know it, some one ought to tell him that all the rest of the world knows it.

For Catholicism, as one might surmise, Mr. Wells has the same "vituperative contempt" as for Christianity. And the same "passionate partisanship" against it. The limits of this discussion do not permit me to accumulate evidences of his constant anti-Catholic prejudice. I shall give but one example of it, an example that will sufficiently demonstrate his spirit. He says in Chapter XXXV (or XXXIV in the one volume edition) of the *Outline*: "It is certain that the Catholic Church through its schools and universities opened up the prospect of the modern educational state in Europe." So far so good. But wait! "It is equally certain that the Catholic Church never intended to do anything of the sort. Its purpose in spreading education was the subjugation of minds!"

Readers of G. K. Chesterton's *Orthodoxy* may remember his description of the bewilderment that came upon him, while he was still an agnostic, from reading the self-contradictory ideas of the enemies of Christianity. He was given to understand that "not only had Christianity the most flaming vices, but it had apparently a mystical talent for combining vices which seemed inconsistent with each other." Mr. Chesterton says that this was the lesson he learned by reading all the agnostics "from Huxley to Bradlaugh." But Wells has discovered a still more "mystical talent" in Catholicity, the talent of identifying virtues and vices.

v

It is a curiously invariable fact that those who treat Christianity and Catholicity with "vituperative contempt," have also indifference or disdain for the virtue of purity, and a fondness for "advanced" ideas on sex morality. I do not mean that we should impute personal immorality to Mr. Wells. Like G. B. Shaw, he may, with his inevitable inconsistency, practice virtue while condoning vice, and be a living model of bourgeois respectability while advocating a more than Bohemian recklessness of morals.

I say that he condones vice. In *The Research Magnificent* William Porphyry Benham travels much, leaving his wife solitary at home. In her husband's absence she "receives the embraces" of another man. Now we might grant Wells the right to record the wife's infidelity without moralizing. It is the current opinion that although a novelist is like God, in that he creates men and women, he is unlike God in that he is unconcerned about what his creatures do. But Wells is not content to stand aloof. He defends the action of Mrs. Benham. "A woman" (he explains) "cannot wait about like an umbrella in a stand."

And in a more recent novel, *Men Like Gods,* he explains, through the mouth of Mr. Barnstaple, that the women in his new Utopia associate sexually sometimes with one man, and again with another — or others. "Why!" exclaims Father Amerton (who, as every one knows, is a caricature of the late Father Vaughan), "That is free love." Barnstaple, with hot indignation, retorts, "That's the trouble with you priests. You are nasty-minded." And he continues to vituperate Father Amerton. "You are a dirty priest. What you call Christianity is a black and ugly superstition, a mere excuse for malignity and persecution." When Mrs. Benham practices adultery, Wells defends her. When Father Amerton protests against free love, Barnstaple calls him "dirty." Is Wells an artist, standing aloof from his creatures, letting them act in accordance with their characters, or is he a "passionate partisan"?

Connected (at least in the minds of Christians) with the question of sex morality is the question of motherhood. We consider motherhood a sacred vocation. Wells considers it a gainful occupation. He is an ardent and indefatigable advocate of state endowment of motherhood. He makes of motherhood a profession — like law or medicine — or a business — like stenography or bookkeeping. Years ago, he declared with vigor that there is no more reason why every family should rear its own children than there is why every family should conduct its own gas house or water works or electric power house. He favored the segregation of children in large asylums. They were to be brought up by the State. Now, apparently, he concedes that, in some cases, at least, children may be brought up in private, but under the supervision of the State. He has the details of the system fairly well worked out. "The amount to be paid" (to the mothers) "should vary with the financial standing of the home. People of that excellent class which spends over a hundred a year, ought to get about that much from the State. People of the class which spends five shillings a week per head on them, should get about that, and so on. To endow only poor and bad-class mothers, would be supremely idiotic. . . . If the supply of babies rises too fast, diminish the payment." This from a man who calls a priest "dirty" because he believes that love and marriage between one man and one woman is a sacrament!

VI

But sex morality is comparatively a small matter. Mr. Wells has lost the fundamental basis of *all* morality, the distinction between good and bad. He makes Mr. Polly say (and Mr. Polly is generally understood to be an authentic though rather ludicrous exponent of Wellsian philosophy), "One starts with ideas that things are good and things are bad. . . . I've always been the skeptaceous sort and it always seemed rot to me to pretend men know good from evil." It is Wells's idea that the right and wrong of any action can only be judged by its immediate results, a principle that will ruin morality and civilization.

Since that is his philosophy, what wonder that Wells, like so many other false prophets and false moralists, is growing more and more deeply pessimistic? That an evolutionist can despair of the world is a mystery. It would seem that the theory of evolution might be summed up in three words, "Onward and Upward." But the man who wrote *The Outline of History* as a thesis to demonstrate that the progress of the world and of man is as inevitable as the attraction of gravitation, is in despair about the world and man and life. He speaks of man's life contemptuously as "this little stir amid the slime, a fuss in the mud." He thinks the world a "very sinister and dreadful world." He is convinced that all civilization is crumbling. If these things be so, the much vaunted evolution of the earth and of the race was hardly worth all the pain and all the time it has taken. If it ends now, the ultimate result is a fiasco, or a tragedy. But we who do not consider evolution a key to all mysteries, and a solution of the Riddle of the Universe, are not despondent. We believe in God — not an impotent God who is only doing the best He can, but a God Who has ten thousand times set the world right again when everything seemed wrong, a God Who can and will bring the race out of the morass into which it has so willfully strayed.

It would scarcely be fair to say that Wells, though a pessimist, has entirely abandoned hope. There is, he admits, one last chance for civilization — Education. In a famous phrase he declares that the fate of civilization depends on the outcome of the "race between education and catastrophe." Specifically, he urges that "every one should know three or four languages well, German, French, Italian, English, and should also have more than a smattering of Russian, or Hindustanee or Chinese." The prophet of a new world, the creator of one Utopia after another, having before his eyes Germany, the most highly "educated" nation that ever existed, and believing that Germany deliberately brought about the most enormous catastrophe in history, still thinks that the world can be saved by "education"!

The truth in the matter is obvious, so obvious that Wells and other false prophets must exercise considerable ingenuity to avoid seeing it. The truth is this: Education will not avert catastrophe. Nor will eugenics and the endowment of motherhood. Nor will the League of Nations. Nor will any other artificial device save mankind. The only force that can rehabilitate the world is the institution that Wells treats with "vituperative contempt." The only Saviour of mankind is the One Whom Wells pretends to consider coldly and impartially, the One Whose actual existence or non-existence Wells says is a matter of no moment — Jesus Christ.

MICHAEL WILLIAMS
(*1878–*   )

HALIFAX, Nova Scotia, was the birth-place of Michael Williams, February 5, 1878. During his years as a student at St. Joseph's College he demonstrated a marked talent for writing and he left school without taking a degree.

Williams became a reporter on the *Boston Post, New York World* and *Evening Telegram* and he was city editor of the *San Francisco Examiner* during the earthquake of 1906.

In his youth Williams was a radical idealist, a follower of Upton Sinclair, and an ardent bohemian. With his return to the Church in 1915, Williams soon became one of the outstanding leaders among American Catholics. In 1924 he was made the first editor of the *Commonweal*. With Father James M. Gillis and Father Talbot he is responsible for creating interest in many of the societies and causes which have been of utmost service to the Church in the United States.

As a writer Williams is trenchant yet wittily urbane. *The High Romance,* 1918, remains his best work, though *The Little Flower of Carmel,* 1926, and *Little Brother Francis of Assisi,* 1928, are justly more popular.

THE SPRINGS OF GOODNESS*

I PARTICULARLY remember the singular sensation I experienced of realizing how still, and how silent, the city was. It seemed as though I were in the very centre of a circle of stillness and silence.

Now and then, this profound silence would be broken by a sound beginning very far away, like the rumour of a sound. It would then come near and nearer, rise to its highest, and then pass, and grow lower, softer, and fade away — like the ghost of a sound. . . . Automobiles coming home with merrymakers from the beach resorts. At that time, the fashion in motor horns ran to something that reminded me, especially at night, of some strange animal — a sort of melodious, gobbling sound, rising and falling, and with something ominous under the rather musical effect.

And as I heard the motor cars, one by one, with a sort of clockwork regularity, passing by, I could imagine, with a vividness like a moving picture play, the scenes in the roadhouses by the beach beyond the great park where the smooth broad roads glimmered pale beneath the high, black trees. At sloppy tables I saw the drinkers, while on the polished floors men and women danced — or, rather, they "ragged," as they call the up-to-date perversion of the dance; while the piano player, a young, pallid fellow with a fuming cigarette stuck to his lower lip, banged out the ragtime music.

But the last of the motor cars passed by. The intensified silence drew its circle closer about me.

Night was passing. Dawn was at hand. The southern and eastern parts of the sky were paling, and there the stars were dim. Elsewhere, however, the stars were still big and clear, and the sky darkly and profoundly blue. A couplet from Wordsworth came into my mind: "Dear God! the very houses seem asleep; and all that mighty heart is lying still!"

No doubt, within many indeed of these quiet, darkened houses — in Chinatown, or the Tenderloin quarter, for example — evil was awake and busy — as horrible dreams may go on behind a sleeper's placid forehead — but outwardly all was calm, and broodingly silent. There came upon me a keen realization of the wonder of the city's suspended conscious-

*Williams, Michael, *The Book of the High Romance,* (New York: The Macmillan Co., 1924), pp. 102–108. By permission of the publisher.

ness. There was a singular magic in the suggestion of rest that emanated from those shadowy congeries of vacant, criss-crossing streets, and houses darkly slumbering. In this curious space between night and day it seemed to me that sleep had finally conquered all resistance, had worn down the stubbornness of the most determined noctambulists, just as a quiet, strong-willed nurse or mother might subdue her obstreperous children.

A sense of awe came next. I felt as if I must be the only person left awake in all San Francisco, and as if I had no right to be awake. I felt like an intruder. It was as if I had blundered into some lodge-room or chapel where a secret rite was about to be celebrated. There was something in all this quietude which troubled me deeply. The city no longer seemed merely resting, placidly slumbering, relaxed and at peace. It became to me like a city held in a trance. It brought back to me the uneasy, curious feelings I had once experienced when I saw a hypnotist put a number of men and women into deep entrancement and without using any audible words plant his suggestions in their minds. Only now I felt my awe more profoundly. I seemed aware of strange things happening behind the veil of the dusky dawn and the unbroken quiet of the city's sleep. I seemed to be on the point of actually knowing just *how* all the hundreds of thousands of men and women and children slumbering all about me were being surcharged, like so many living batteries, with new energy generated by the tremendous, invisible dynamos of sleep and silence. Streams of fresh life were pulsing into them all for the use of the coming day. Power for thought and for action. Power more potent, and infinitely more subtle, than all the electrical currents that could be generated by a hundred Niagaras! And soon these living batteries, each with a place in the vast, complex, living machine of the city, would awaken and take its part in the diurnal working of the great organisms and so expend the energy now pouring into them.

This energy, I wondered — as who of us hasn't wondered! — from where did it come? And what, really, was it? And where was it driving the human machines?

This everlasting, triadic question to which there is no answer — the whence, and why and where!

How futile to ask it.

It was just as futile as it would be to go upon one of the city's many hills, and ask the why and wherefore of the tides of the sea, or the system of the stars, or the secret of the rising sun.

And yet, as I dreamed my way homeward through the silent city under the mystical stars, I was seized with a deep, thrilling impression that I was about to *understand* the cosmic mystery — that the secrets of the sky and of the earth and water, and the secret of man, were about to be revealed. There was the thought that between the sleepers in the city, and the stars and the sea and the earth, there was in this moment the closest kind of communion — as though the tide of life flowing into the sleepers was gathering its force from sea and air, and earth and stars — and that now: this instant, all were in rapport — and had come to a crisis; like a clock that had reached its time to strike the hour.

And this mystical moment left the glow of a thought in my mind, as a meteor leaves a trail of light, though its central brightness disappears. It seemed to me that I understood at least one chief factor that entered into the wonder of the city's sleep. This factor was my realization of how united at this moment all the hundreds of thousands of individualities were in the condition of sleep. So far as ordinary consciousness was concerned, and the ordinary affairs of life, egoism — that potent source of human discordance — was in abeyance. All the warring and irreconcilable elements that spring from egoism were withdrawn from manifestation.

What would be the result should the sleepers awaken *bereft of egoism* — united in waking life as now they were united in slumber — and if they should employ *in unity and for unity* the energy they were now deriving together from the secret springs of sleep and silence?

Once more my mind gave up a memory — that paragraph of Goethe's which one reads with yearning wistfulness, and the wish:

"Oh, if it could only happen!" I suppose you know the paragraph; it runs something like this: "There is in man a force — a spring of goodness — which counterbalances egoism; and if by a miracle it could for a moment suddenly be active in all men, the earth would be at once free from evil."

I was dreaming, as who does not. Dreaming vainly, perhaps, yet I don't disown or repudiate my dream — I only acknowledge that I have not realized my share of it. Yes, that's a good way to express the matter — for my dream was but a share of a bigger dream — which is the dream of this age. It is with us all, in greater or lesser degree. It is the dream of human Betterment — the dream of Brotherhood! I don't use the word "dream" as a symbol of something unreal. No — dreams such as this are what Shelley said poetry was — the mirrors of the great shadows which the future casts upon the troubled surface of the present. All the many dreams by which we think to effect the common end are parts and fragments of the one, great dream. Like the co-operating thoughts of one, gigantic mind, they work together to realize the world's desire, even when they appear to contradict and neutralize each other.

For I believed — and here let me say that I still believe — no matter what anybody may say — no matter how many facts may seem to argue against the truth of my belief — I believed them, and I believe now, that the inscrutable forces of Good are powerful today with the power of the rising tide. They are changing doubt to hope, and fear to faith, and anger and hatred into love, more mightily, perhaps, than at any other time since when the Prince of Peace and Lord of Love Himself expressed the world's desire, when He said: "Thy kingdom come: Thy will be done in earth as in heaven." The Kingdom of Peace and of brotherly love. Good Will, to the sway of which the whole creation moves!

My credo . . . and we'll get back to the story. . . .

CHARLES PHILLIPS

(*1880–1934*)

ONE of the great Catholic teachers of the twentieth century, Charles Phillips, was born at New Richmond, Wisconsin, November 20, 1880. His primary education was obtained in the public schools of New Richmond, his college years were spent at De La Salle College, Toronto, Ontario. Phillips was a born journalist and for many years was on the staff of several papers of note. During World War I he served as secretary of the Knights of Columbus and the Red Cross, and at the conclusion of the war proceeded to Poland and Russia where his outstanding services were recognized both by the common people and their governments.

Perhaps his greatest work was done as a professor in the English Department of Notre Dame. Whole generations of men knew him and loved him and he repaid their admiration and love by giving them an abiding admiration for great Catholic literature.

Charlie's room in one of the towers of Sorin Hall, overflowing with books and interesting souvenirs of his travels, was the meeting place of all the university men with literary ambitions. The news of his death came with a sense of personal loss to large groups of students scattered over the world.

The poetry of Charles Phillips was heavily charged with his admiration and emotions. It also indicated his virile faith and not inconsiderable culture.

The New Poland, an analysis of the aspirations of reconstituted Poland after World War I, is Mr. Phillips' best prose work. It is a vigorous example of special pleading which, as events have proved, was in vain.

PHILOSOPHER AT THE KEYBOARD*

HOME life for Paderewski is both play and work, although he is more inclined to forget to stop working than to stop playing. A few turns on the lawn at croquet with his valet, who is an accomplished linguist and who has refused flattering offers rather than leave Paderewski's service, may easily satisfy him, but when he gets to the piano . . . he forgets. Madame has to intervene sometimes, especially during Christmas holidays, when work is forbidden. One time when she was away from home he practiced until three in the morning. He got a round scolding for that.

A good part of his days at home will see him, as Modjeska saw him, "composing and practicing . . . the piano sending up its brilliant notes." He rises usually about ten, has his "first breakfast," and, if the farm does not engage him, remains in his studio. At luncheon, "second breakfast," he appears — looking to an American familiarly like pictures of Mark Twain, dressed all in white — gay, light-hearted, as refreshed as if he had just got up. If he goes back then to his music, after perhaps a turn at billiards or outdoors, he does not reappear till dinnertime. Sometimes he takes a drive or a long walk in the afternoon.

What goes on mornings and afternoons in that music room up in the second floor we shall see. If we listen now we shall hear. Either he is practicing as virtuoso, keeping fresh in the large repertoire of his recitals, experimenting with new pieces for it, or he is composing, trying out his own inventions, digging, delving, cutting deeper and deeper into the tonal secrets of some teasing phrase that, like the elusive word of the poet, strives for utterance. Perhaps it is some separate phrases from Liszt's sonata that we hear, some prismatic bars cut into filigree from the crystal ingots of Chopin, some bits of Debussy — for, as we learned, whatever he has to say of Debussy's opera

he likes Debussy's piano music; or it may be some difficult passages from his own Variations. Hour after hour he works. He refuses to spare himself. There are guests downstairs, there is excursion and entertainment for them, there is the billiard room to tempt him, there are the gardens and there is the farm beckoning to him. There is everything and anything but practice. But he sticks to the piano. He conquers it daily. "I have put up some good fights."

"People," he says, speaking of music students, "are far too inclined to look upon music as a pastime rather than as a serious study. This does not mean that the student should eliminate joy or pleasure from his work at the keyboard, but he should rather find his true happiness in labor of a more serious kind. Students spend too much time in playing and too little in work." They think, he says, that the hours upon hours they must spend at the keyboard are hours thrown away, that nothing is accomplished. But, he says, "the very essence of success is practice," and "system is the most essential thing in practice." "Students who are gifted are very likely to be so enchanted with a composition that they dream away the priceless practice minutes without any more definite purpose than that of amusing themselves."

"Music study is work," he told James Francis Cooke in one of his interviews with him. "Those who work are the only ones who ever win the greatest awards. It is very delightful to sit at the keyboard and revel in some great masterpiece, but when it comes to the systematic study of some exacting detail of fingering, pedaling, phrasing, touch, dynamics: that is work and nothing but work." "Art without technique," in Paderewski's opinion, "is invertebrate, shapeless, characterless." And technique comes only one way, by systematic work.

The thing that Paderewski's intimates most remark upon, however, is not so much his phenomenal capacity for work as his ability to come from his work, reappear

---

*Phillips, Charles, *Paderewski*, The Story of a Modern Immortal (New York: The Macmillan Co., 1934), Chapter XXV, pp. 247–255.

among his guests, not fatigued but refreshed. Ready for play, he plays with a relish. He seems to have mastered the secret of shutting his mind to a given preoccupation, definitely and positively when the time comes, and of opening it freely to some other interest. Now, in his own home, he returns to his guests and takes them with pride through the house to show them his art treasures.

The interior of the Villa Riond-Bosson is roomy and comfortable and in spite of the fact that it is literally crammed with treasures it is furnished with a simplicity that is harmonious and uncrowded. A characteristic of the decoration is the amaranth tinting of the walls: amaranth is one of the Polish national colors. A lofty open staircase with light streaming from above, many fine mirrors, wide areas, room opening into room, altogether give the house a spacious welcoming air. The walls hold some fine old tapestries, the collection of paintings and portraits is priceless. Here we recognize the Alma-Tadema portrait, and here the Burne-Jones profile. Emil Fuchs, the sculptor, whose bust of Paderewski is here at Riond-Bosson, agrees with James Huneker that the Burne-Jones portrait is the best of all the portraits of the artist, "the one nearest to the idealization that one would wish to see handed down to posterity." Few of the portraitists or the sculptors who have tried to portray Paderewski have succeeded. They have not caught "the essential man" who, as Fuchs has said, "so far transcends the frame and features which first meet the eye, that to exact a copy of his small chin and broad cheek bones, and such folds and wrinkles as he may have acquired with time" is to belie the real Paderewski.

The bust by Emil Fuchs seen here at Riond-Bosson has more of "the essential man" than most attempts, and this is perhaps because there is in it more of mystery and less of mere photographic representation of features than in others. In a portrait of Paderewski, Fuchs says, "there must be mystery, because mystery envelopes the entire personality of the man and his music." Every feature in the face of a Paderewski portrait, in marble or on canvas, "ought to convey that high sensitiveness which is the chief charm of his art. That is what distinguishes him from all other musicians. . . . An artist in reproducing the features of Paderewski must, first of all, stress the great forehead with the two marked eminences over the eyebrows, said to be the storehouse of music. Then there are the eyes, so captivating with their dreamy look, and peculiar for their combination of dark color and light lashes, with the lids so prominent that they give an effect of the impenetrable when they are really meant to look kind. An emphasis laid upon the sensitive mouth and the small mustache turned in at the corners would complete the picture of the man who is so remarkable a combination of knowledge, determination, patriotism and sublime poetry."

Among the portraits and sculptures of Paderewski at Riond-Bosson is a bust by his many-gifted friend Alfred Nossig; it is youthful and full of feeling. Nossig, author of the libretto of *Manru,* is not only a writer but a painter and sculptor as well. Another of the more successful portraits is that by Styka, still another by Sigismond Ivanowski. Ivanowski once remarked on what a difficult subject Paderewski is: "a man of astounding gifts and kaleidoscopic moods, it is difficult to give any unified impression of. him . . . he has a personality too large to be captured easily. My portrait of him is the outcome of five years' close and earnest study and literally hundreds of sketches."

There are scores of signed portraits at Riond-Bosson, a gallery of world celebrities all magnetized by the charm of the "genial" pole, as Gounod called him in autographing his picture for him. Here are two Popes, Benedict XV and Pius XI, half a dozen kings and queens, among them Victoria and Edward VII of England, Margharita of Italy, Albert and Elizabeth of Belgium, two Presidents of the United States, Woodrow Wilson and Herbert Hoover (Paderewski's young friend of the San Jose concert), Mussolini, Venizelos, Marshal Foch . . . many others. Here is an exquisite photograph of Modjeska with her soft "Creole eyes"; another of Madame Paderewski as a girl, beautiful dreamy eyes, dusky hair, delicate features; and still another of Madame, a sketch by Siemiradzki, the Polish Alma-Tadema, who in this portrayal has caught the loveliness of her eyes as Modjeska saw them one day on a Tatra mountain road when they spoke together of a certain "extraordinary young man." The collection of Paderewski's signed portraits makes an interesting commentary on the man.

There are some very fine paintings by famous artists, the most striking of all of them Malczewski's "The Vigil of the Siberian Exile," which occupies an entire panel in the richly dark dining salon, a painting which, without a word being said, speaks volumes out of the past from which Paderewski came, the past of Poland's sad days, of his grandfather's banishment, of his mother's birth in exile. A carefully assembled collection of old Swiss prints is another of Paderewski's treasures, and a group of Fragonards, which have the place of honor in the salon and the drawing room. Upstairs, where the study is, and the library with its rare books and manuscripts, an exhibit of Chinese bronzes and vases give us another angle on the artist's hobbies. This Chinese collection is one of his prides, and whenever he shows one particular piece in it he tells of an amusing coincidence which happened when he acquired it. It is a rare *cloisonné* image of a Chinese god. It was owned by his dentist, M. Foucou; but, curiously enough, the name of the god was the same, Fou-Kou, and the special mission of that god, according to antiquarians' belief, is to attract other works of ancient art. "As you may see," Paderewski remarks, "Fou-Kou does not fail in his mission." In the music room is another Oriental treasure, a collection of Chinese music-records. He is intensely interested in Chinese music, and whenever he visits San Francisco he spends time in the Chinese theatres listening to their puzzling cacophony, in which, according to the belief of some, lies the secret of the lost musical notation of the ancient Greeks. There is, of course, a complete collection also of Paderewski's own records, but some of these records of his own

he does not enjoy listening to; the recollection of their making is too disagreeable, they had to be made over too many times before they satisfied him. He does not like making records, the acoustical difficulties are so great. They must be perfect or he will not release them. "I would rather play at twenty concerts than play once for a phonograph." Nevertheless his library of records now numbers fifty-six, a collection which by itself will remain a monument to him for posterity to enjoy.

But if the host of Riond-Bosson makes a grimace at some of his own piano records, he laughs heartily when he shows his guests his collection of caricatures. They are mostly of himself, and they picture him in every imaginable aspect and posture of the exaggerated. His famous hair especially has been the joy of the cartoonists.

Here is another room. It is a small drawing room now, and it is filled with mementoes of the artist's career, tributes and souvenirs showered upon him, the souvenirs and tributes that he laid at the feet of his son, among them the wreath given him by the Boston Symphony Orchestra. This was Alfred's room, the invalid boy whom Madame Helena mothered from childhood. For a long time after the boy's death this room was kept locked. Now it is filled with fresh flowers every day; and here is Alfred's wheel chair, his table, all the things he loved, kept exactly as he left them. . . .

Paderewski's library gives us an entirely new side of him. He loves good books and is an omnivorous reader. As he himself has said, "But I play everything," so it may be said that he reads everything. Everything interests him, from poetry and novels, to history and philosophy, and all of this in no less than eight languages; for, speaking seven, he has added to them a reading knowledge of Hebrew in order to indulge his taste for Biblical studies. During his earliest visits to England and America he made a thorough study of the English classics; that goes back to 1896. Since then the scope of his reading has embraced a huge and varied list. He likes Heine, he loves the Polish poets, especially Mickiewicz and Asnyk. Among his compositions are his settings for several of Asnyk's love lyrics. Asnyk, hearing him play some of them for the first time, exclaimed, "Ah, that man knows women!" But his reading of poetry goes far beyond the lyrical. He is a Dante enthusiast. He will discuss ardently the lastest philosophers as well as the oldest. He once corrected a slip of memory of the great Bergson; Poincaré the mathematician, who, after the manner of Pythagoras, finds harmony and beauty in mathematical speculation, is a favorite topic; he smiles at the new French philosopher who argues that the world, to save itself, must return to Judaism; he raises a dozen questions over the latest philosophical speculations out of Spain.

Paderewski did not take up the study of Spanish until he was in his sixties, yet he speaks it fluently and reads Spanish works that even Spaniards find difficult. One of his favorite Spaniards is the Argentine novelist Enrique Rodriguez Larreta, one time Argentina's ambassador at Paris, whose "La Gloria de Don Ramiro," he especially likes. He has been enthusiastically recommending it to his friends ever since it appeared in 1908. The coloring of the book is one thing that fascinates him; he will quote for you the great scene describing the passage of the Grand Inquisitor Gasper de Quiroga to the *auto-da-fé* at Toledo: "Coming after the gloomy procession, his crimson robes had the rousing effect of a blare of trumpets." That satisfies his sense of music as well as of color. He will roll off his tongue the mellifluous accents of Larreta's picture of a sunset at Avila: *Al sol acababa de ocultarse, y blanda, lentemente, las parroquias tocaban las oraciones.* He will make you hear the rich vowel-music of *Era un coro, un llanto continuo de campanas cantantes.* . . .

It is a liberal education to spend an evening with Paderewski when he discusses literature, history, philosophy. A spirit definitely romantic glows back of the clear flashing of his brilliant mind. In politics he may be called a realist, because there he deals mercilessly with facts, yet at heart he is as much a romanticist in politics as he is in music. His career in statecraft as in art is a notable illustration of the power of intuition when

reason controls it. He would argue that the true romanticist is the only true realist. His agreement would be with Newman, that there are "two modes of apprehending propositions, rational and real . . . real is the stronger . . . the more vivid and forcible . . . intellectual ideas cannot compete in effectiveness with the experience of concrete facts." Paderewski would stress the word "experience." He may quote Goethe writing to Eckerman: "Understanding may serve to fix our affections when we already love, but the understanding is not that which is capable of firing our hearts and awakening a passion." Or Schlegel, saying that romanticism is love: *"Nicht ein Sinnliches, sondern das Geistige. . . . Nein, es ist der heilige Hauch, der uns in den Tönen der Musik berührt"* — "not something sensual but the holy breath born in upon us in the tones of music." The Saint of Geneva, Francis de Sales will speak for him: "The highest peak of the soul's activities [*extrémité et cime de notre âme*] is a certain pinnacle of reason and the spiritual faculty [*certaine éminence at suprême pointe de la raison et faculté spirituelle*] guided not at all either by discourse or by the light of reason" [*qui n'est point conduite par la lumière du Discours, ni de la raison*].

Paderewski goes deep into these thoughts. All life to him, but especially the life which finds its expression in culture, in art, in music, moves on the lines of St. Augustine's text: "Thou madest us for Thyself and our heart is restless until it repose in Thee." That to him explains the whole impulse back of music, back of all art; it is what, as he would show you, the German critic Walzel has called "the intense longing of man as a reasonable thinking being for the Endless and the Eternal." The artist is the one most tortured with this longing, but the one also given the gift of imagination, of seeing at least a glimpse of the way to repose. When Arthur Symons says that "imagination is sight, not wonder, a thing seen, not an opening of the eyes to see it," we understand how Paderewski sees and reveals life in music, and how he opens our eyes to a glimpse of the way. "Art," in Paderewski's own words, "is *the expression of the immortal part of man.* Art is the most important means of human culture. Culture begins the moment you start to work above your needs, and because of a something compelling you to work in that direction. *It is culture that makes man feel that he is made after God's own image.* Through art so many dark corners of the universe which human beings can only look into and conceive through emotion, are made more clear. And music seems the living art that creates the most powerful emotions." Here the philosopher at the keyboard might well quote Browning to us — music

> *. . . is earnest of a heaven,*
> *Seeing we know emotions strange by it,*
> *Not else to be revealed;*

but I prefer Paderewski's own simple words: "Art is the expression of the immortal part of man."

ROSE IN THE RAIN*

Fall, rose petal, fall;
  Your hour is done —
You have had your all
  Of sky and sun.

Now you must take the winds that burn
  And the buffeting rain,
Endure the storm, and learn
  What tears are, and pain.

Rose, rose in the rain that drums
  Cold death on you, teach me
How to take death when it comes,
  Bravely, unflinchingly —

Not grievingly, but strong and tall
  As you are, flinging off
Petal and leaf . . . how all
  The vanities you doff

Of color and pride, and face
  Head high, the flail
Of the whipping wind, the wild lace
  And lash of the gale!

Rose, rose in the rain,
  Teach me when I'm undone
To stand, and to drink of the cup
    of tears and pain
  As I've quaffed the cup of the sun.

*The above and following poems have been selected from *High in Her Tower*, by Charles Phillips (New York: F. T. Kolars and Co., 1927).

MUSIC

There is a hunger in my heart,
  A longing in my soul, to hear
The voice of Heaven o'er the noise
  Of earth that so assails mine ear:

For we are children of the skies,
  Exiles and wanderers from home —
See how the stars like candles burn
  In windows far from where we roam:

Like candles lit to show the way,
  Dear kindly beacons, sure and bright!
But O the heavy journeying,
  And O the silence of the night! —

The vasty silences that lie
  Between the going and the goal!
Will not God reach a friendly hand
  To lift and lead my tired soul?

Will not God speak a friendly word
  Above the tumult and the din
Of earthly things — one little word
  Above the voice of care and sin?

— He speaks. He answers quick my prayer.
  He opens Heaven's lattice wide;
He bids me bathe my brow in airs
  Of Heaven, like a flowing tide!

He speaks; He gives unto my soul,
　　Unto my listening ear, its meed:
He breathes upon me with the breath
　　Of Music — and my soul is freed

And I am lifted up and held
　　A little while, a child, to see
The beauty of my Father's House
　　Which shall no more be shut from me!

SOLITAIRE

Color of wave or sky,
　　Flush of wind on the grass,
Beauty of earth that takes my heart —
　　But O, the hearts that pass,
The souls that go me by!

— Or one now halts apart
　　A little while, and I,
Revealing and concealing, stand,
　　And with a smile, a sigh,
Clasp to my breast the dart,

Hold with a trembling hand,
　　Cherished and dear to me,
The hope, the look, the sudden trance
　　Of eyes that do not see
Nor mark, nor understand.

Beauty of life — the lance
　　Of beauty in my breast;
Love and its sweet applause;
　　Endearing dear behest
Of love, lost in a glance —

Or one more closely draws
　　And draws me closer still,
But by the inexorable laws long set
　　Of life and living and will
Goes on, and may not pause.

Remember? Or forget? —
　　But passes, as the light
Dies down, and will not stay:
　　Stars in the fading night,
Suns that forever set.

Each his appointed way,
　　Each in self-secret sealed,
Nor even he who halts, who turns
　　Revealing and concealed,
May tell me or may say . . .

Light that illumes and burns,
　　Dawn that blooms in the rose,
Stars of the wave and sky,
　　But O, the eyes that close,
The hearts that pass me by!

WILLOW RIVER

Rome I have loved and by the Tiber's stream
Dreamed once again the poet's classic dream
Where living spires above dead splendors
　　gleam.

Firenze under the white Appenine snows
Holds still my heart as long as Arno flows
Deep swelling with the tide of Dante's woes.

Seine of the bridges, that from towered Rouen
Links the dear glory of the martyred Jeanne
With boulevarded Paris in its span —

Vienna of St. Stephen's . . . music, light,
And the blue Danube, swift in silver flight,
Whispering dark secrets to the singing night.

Vistula, that I've followed from the falls
Of ice-fed Tatra, past old Krakow's walls,
Through Poland's sunlit fields where
　　Baltic calls —

And Holy Kiev of the golden domes
Where still down Lavra's darkened
　　catacombs
Grave Nestor's spirit by the Dnieper roams:

But O great Tiber, Arno dear, O Seine,
O, dreaming Danube, and wide-watered
    plain
Of Polish prairie and the flowered Ukraine,

Not all your storied streams nor all your
    flood
Of fabled wave — though stars of glory stud
Your heroed bosoms — stir my homing blood

As one fond vagrant glimpse of this least tide,
Unmapped, uncharted, hidden from the pride
Of traveled scene, whose quiet waters glide

Deep in the timbered prairie, where a day
Of long lost summertime, a boy at play,
I dreamed great worlds and rivers far away.

HOLIDAY

I would that I could find
    In the bright Christmas frost
That gift more dear than gold refined —
    The friends that I have lost!

Now all the bells ring out,
    Now voices rise in song;
Care scampers at the merry rout,
    Forgot are grief and wrong.

The hollyberry gleams,
    The candles dance and glow,
And lighthearts run with happy dreams
    Across the sparkling snow.

Life blows a rosy cheek!
    Life laughs through starry frost! . . .
But where I kneel, still, still I seek
    The friends that I have lost.

EUCHARIST

I will have this Sacrament —
    Eucharist of raying light,
Particle on particle,
One to all and all to one,
Hidden flower or skyey pine,
All to one and one to all;

Even so, the blade, the weed,
Feeding on the Entire Sun,
One to all and all to one.

I will have this Sacrament . . .
One to all and all to one.

SIX SONGS AT BETHLEHEM

I. Road Song

The shepherds had an angel's song
    An angel's radiant light
To guide them the dark hills along
    Through Bethlehem's holy night.

The Magi had a mighty star
    Spanning the skies with fire
To lead them from the East afar
    To find their heart's desire.

So I in light and song rejoice,
    So I my guide am given —
Light of your loving eye, your voice
    Sweet with the sound of Heaven!

II. Good Tidings

We have our flocks to tend,
    Night watch to keep:
Darkly the heavens bend,
    Weary the shepherds sleep,
Lost seems the way, the end
    Unfathomed deep.

"Good tidings of great joy we bring!"
　The angels cry —
And rosy is the world with light,
　And golden is the sky!

O angel voices, still you sing
　From heaven on high,
And you are near us in the night
　When evil passes by!

III. The Crib

How warm, how bright, O babe divine,
　Thy crib before the altar lies —
Yet cold and bleak a bed was thine
　'Neath Bethlehem's wintry skies.

So was my heart, bleak, cold and drear,
　A sorry place of woe and sin
Until — the angels singing near —
　You entered soft within!

IV. Love-Laden

Love-laden, as the shepherds come,
　Each with his gift, a little lamb,
Lord let me come, my offering
　All that I have, all that I am.

Love-laden as the shepherds go
　Into the shadowed night awhile,

Lord, let me go, my soul new born
　By the sweet grace of Bethlehem's smile.

V. My Gift

I would I were the little lamb
　The wondering shepherds bore
To Bethlehem's lowly crib, a gift
　From out their meagre store.

I would I were the ox so calm
　Breathing his sweet warm breath
Upon the Little Baby there
　Who softly slumbereth.

I would I were the beasties good,
　The stable or the stall —
But I can only be myself
And give my heart, my all.

VI. The Woods Are Still With Mystery

The woods are still with mystery,
The fields are white with purity,
And over all a quiet lies,
Peace and the hush of brooding skies.

These are the gifts the dumb earth brings,
Tribute of elemental things,
Peace in the woods, the holy glow
Of peace on widening fields of snow.

JOHN LA FARGE
(*1880–*　　)

FATHER LA FARGE, S.J., talented member of a talented family, was born February 13, 1880, in Newport, Rhode Island. He took his B.A. degree at Harvard, 1897, and pursued graduate studies at Innsbruck University. After his ordination in the Society of Jesus, Father La Farge spent some time in further study and in teaching. His greatest work was the resocializing of the missions in southern Maryland. He organized the Cardinal Gibbons Institute and the Colored Layman's Retreat Union. Upon completion of this splendid work for racial justice and Catholic solidarity, Father La Farge became an associate editor of *America,* in which position he continued his apostolate by means of numerous articles and lectures. In 1945 he was appointed editor of *America.*

Father La Farge has written extensively on social problems and racial justice, and his books have been largely instrumental in altering Catholic prejudice and snobbery. His style is more logical than colorful, but his pointed manner of treating facts has removed much of their controversial character and has paved the way for a dispassionate examination of the record.

G. K. CHESTERTON*

THE convert is a man who has found a solution. The convert is a discover of the meaning of life. He is a man — or a woman, as the case may be — who has discovered the plan behind the world's apparent disorder. He has discovered the Way where others are still finding only the wilderness. He has stumbled upon the Light, where others still grope in puzzled darkness.

For all of us want to find the meanings of things. A student told me the other day how scholars have been laboring for years to decipher the meaning of the curious pictured inscriptions found in the ancient temples of Mexico. Men ask the meaning of history. During the last week millions of people throughout our country have been asking the meaning of the recent change in the stock market: what are the causes of such a phenomenon; what influences are behind the scenes, what further events might it lead to?

And, in the same way, as long as the world rolls on, people will seek the meaning of birth and death, old age and youth, of love and passion and temptation, of human suffering and of sin. Where man comes from; whither he is going; why there is life, or hope, or good, or evil in the world — there is no end of questioning.

Gilbert Keith Chesterton, a man known to pretty nearly everyone who reads the English language, the author of essays, poems, stories and magazine articles in delightful profusion, the humorist, the philosopher, the genial companion of genuine and human men — Chesterton is a man who looked passionately for the meaning of life, for the meaning of all these things that I have mentioned, and of many more besides.

Speaking of the three great ancient masterpieces of literature, he exclaimed: "The *Iliad* is only great because all life is a battle, the *Odyssey* because all life is a journey, the *Book of Job* because all life is a riddle." But for the solution of that riddle

*La Farge, S.J., *Four Great Converts*, pamphlet (New York: American Press).

the ready-made answers of Materialism and Skepticism could not content Chesterton's daring and independent mind. No intelligence, according to him, was needed to be an unbeliever. "A man can be a Christian," he remarks, "to the end of the world, for the simple reason that a man could have been an atheist from the beginning of it. The materialism of things is on the face of things: it does not require any science to find it out."

On the other hand, in his opinion, "the thing from which England — and we could say the same of any other country — suffers most now more than any other evil is not the assertion of falsehoods, but the endless and irrepressible repetition of half-truths." It was these thousands of half-truths that Chesterton set out to examine and evaluate. And, as he did so, he came upon a very curious thing. It is that the ultimate truth, as known to us in the imperfect knowledge of this life, usually contains an element of paradox. This idea Chesterton expresses in his writings in a great variety of ways.

The attempts of rationalists to map out the universe, to plot and measure the infinite by the puny footrule of man's intelligence, he saw as futile. This attempt at a self-contained pseudo-scientific explanation of the unexplainable he symbolized by the self-contained circle, taken as the sign of overdrawn, exaggerated reason and madness. On the other hand, the cross he took as the symbol of mystery and health. "For the circle is perfect and infinite in its nature; but it is fixed forever in its size; it can never be larger or smaller. But the cross, though it has at its heart a collision and a contradiction, can extend its four arms forever without altering its shape. Because it has a paradox in its center, it can grow without changing. The circle returns upon itself and is bound. The cross opens its arms to the four winds; it is a sign post for free travelers."

The central paradox, therefore, at the heart of the cross — a paradox only for our own limited intelligence, not for the all-embracing mind of God — was that union of the human and the Divine, of the temporal and the eternal, of the finite and the infinite, which we call Christianity. Boldly stemming the current of those innumerable half-truths that have swept down into confusion and skepticism so many a brilliant intellect, so many a high heart of our age, Chesterton set his face to Christianity, to seek there the solution of the meaning of life.

"The Christian ideal has not been tried and found wanting," he remarked. "It has been found difficult; and left untried." But for Chesterton, with his vigorous nature, his rich, hearty temperament, his virile mind, the difficulty of a thing was the joy of it. The fact that the world in so many ways rejected Christianity, was his call to go out at dawn and travel the high roads till he found it. He tells of this early stadium of his spiritual quest in the sixth chapter of his "Orthodoxy."

"All I had hitherto heard of Christian theology had alienated me from it. . . . I was a pagan at the age of twelve, and a complete agnostic by the age of sixteen. . . . I read the scientific and skeptical literature of my time — all of it, at least, that I could find written in English and lying about; and I read nothing else; I mean I read nothing else on any other note of philosophy. . . . I never read a line of Christian apologetics. . . . It was Huxley and Herbert Spencer and Bradlaw who brought me back to orthodox theology. . . . The rationalist made me question whether reason was of any use whatever and when I had finished Herbert Spencer I had got as far as doubting (for the first time) whether evolution had occurred at all. As I laid down the last of Colonel Ingersoll's atheistic lectures the dreadful thought broke across my mind, 'Almost thou persuadest me to be a Christian.'"

Christianity, he found, was "attacked on all sides and for all contradictory reasons." No sooner had one rationalist demonstrated that it was too far to the east than another demonstrated with equal clearness that it was much too far to the west. "It was too gloomy; yet too cheerful; too pacific, yet too warlike. The very people who proclaimed the universal morality of mankind were those who insisted that morals were changing from age to age."

Thus he came to find a hidden equilibrium behind the apparent contradictions of Christianity: the romance, he called it, of Orthodoxy, which, in his words, "was sanity; and to be sane is more dramatic than to be mad." The orthodox Church never took the tame course or accepted the earthly power of the Arians. . . . It is easy to be a madman: it is easy to be a heretic. It is always easy to let the age have its head; the difficult thing is to keep one's own. . . . It is always simple to fall; there are an infinity of angles at which one falls, only one at which one stands."

The contrast between the essential joy of Christianity and the essential sadness of paganism impressed him deeply as an illustration of the essential rightness of that religious past towards which his new gaze was turning. "Everything human," he writes, "must have in it both joy and sorrow; the only matter of interest is the manner in which the two things are balanced or divided. And the really interesting thing is this, that the pagan was (in the main) happier and happier as he approached the earth, but sadder and sadder as he approached the heavens. 'The gaiety of paganism' is all a gaiety about the facts of life, not about its origin. . . . When the pagan looks at the core of the cosmos he is struck cold. Behind the gods, who are despotic, sit the fates, who are deadly. Nay the fates are worse than deadly; they are dead. . . . Joy, which was the small publicity of the pagan, is the gigantic secret of the Christian."

I have dwelt at length on the first stage of Chesterton's conversion, viz., from agnosticism to the Christian point of view, because it is the passage of thought that he himself has most fully described; and, moreover, was really for him the turning point. His further progress into the acceptance of the full message of Christianity, by his entering the Catholic Church, was but a logical progress along the same line.

It was not a rapid progress. Between his turning away from skepticism and the final unquestioning adherence of that keen intellect to the fulness of Catholic teaching there elapsed a period of many years. Apparently the very obviousness of the path delayed him. As he remarked: "There is . . . about all complete conviction a kind of huge helplessness. The belief is so big that it takes a long time to get into action. And this hesitation chiefly arises, oddly enough, from an indifference where one should begin. All roads lead to Rome; which is one reason why many people never get there."

Again, his patient mind wanted to think everything through. As he wrote some time after his conversion: "Saving the grace of God, a mystery not within our measure, I believe the practical problem of whether people will become Catholics is simply the problem of whether they will think hard enough to become Catholics."

He thought through the whole tangled field of comparative religion. The result of his quest are summed in his greatest work so far: "The Everlasting Man." And at the end of that book he sums up what he found after passing through the wilderness of primitive beliefs and the labyrinth of pagan philosophy:

"Right in the middle of all these things stands up an enormous exception. It is quite unlike anything else. It is a thing final like the trump of doom, though it is also a piece of good news; or news that seems too good to be true. It is nothing less than the loud assertion that this mysterious maker of the world has visited his world in person. It declares that really and even recently, or right in the middle of historic times, there did walk into the world this original invisible being; about whom the thinkers make theories and the mythologists hand down myths; the Man Who Made the World. The most any religious prophet has said was that he was the true servant of such a being. The most that any visionary had ever said was that men might catch glimpses of the glory of that spiritual being; or much more often

of lesser spiritual beings. The most that any primitive myth had ever suggested was that the Creator was present at the Creation. But that the Creator was present at scenes a little subsequent to the supper parties of Horace, and talked with tax-collectors and government officials in the detailed daily life of the Roman Empire, and that this fact continued to be firmly asserted by the whole of that great civilization for more than a thousand years — that is something utterly unlike anything else in nature. It is the one great startling statement that man has made since he spoke his first articulate word, instead of barking like a dog. . . .

"It came on the world with a wind and rush of running messengers proclaiming that apocalyptic portent; and it is not unduly fanciful to say that they are running still. What puzzles the world, and its wise philosophers and fanciful pagan poets, about the priests and people of the Catholic Church is that they still behave as if they were messengers. A messenger does not dream about what his message might be, or argue about what it probably would be; he delivers it as it is. It is not a theory or a fancy but a fact. . . . All that is condemned in Catholic tradition, authority, and dogmatism and the refusal to retract or modify, are but the natural human attributes of a man with a message relating to a fact."

But more was needed to be done than simply to think things through. When the mind, deductive and analytic, has done all that it can to clear away misconceptions and to unveil the splendor of the truth, the power of Divine grace is still needed before the truth of the teachings of Jesus Christ, as revealed through the Church, can be fully embraced. Before the soul finally can make that act of unquestioning faith, there may be but a moment; as in the case of St. Paul. But more often a long period must elapse; a period of self-discipline, of overcoming of worldliness and the delicate, but strong threads of human respect, of spiritual chastening, and, above all, of persistent and hopeful prayer for light. Such, for instance, was the experience of that other great convert,

Cardinal Newman. Such the experience of Chesterton, and of countless others who have walked the same path.

When the final light does come, it comes usually quite simply and unexpectedly. Gilbert K. Chesterton was instructed and received into the Catholic Church in the year 1922 by an unobtrusive, humble parish priest, Father O'Connor: quietly, with no publicity or display. Once a Catholic, Chesterton was **as** entirely at home in the Church as though he had dwelt in it from childhood.

If one could sum up in one word Chesterton's master impression of the Church, as he now sees it from within, I think I could safely say that it is spiritual liberty. "We say," he remarks at the close of his "Everlasting Man," "we say not lightly but very literally, that the truth has made us free. . . . Religion is revelation. In other words, it is a vision, and a vision received by faith; but it is a vision of reality. The faith consists in a conviction of its reality. That, for example is the difference between a vision and a day-dream. And that is the difference between religion and mythology."

Certainly, as the constant outpourings of his pen suggest, Chesterton's mind was never so free, so buoyant as it is today. That others who have groped like him, who have spiritually suffered like him, may enjoy with him that freedom and that vision of the truth, is the aim of his activity and the passion of his life.

With a striking image, Chesterton sums up his idea of the relation of definite, dogmatic, teaching to human liberty.

"Christ founded the Church with two great figures of speech; in the final words to the Apostles who received authority to found it. The first was the phrase about founding it on Peter as on a rock, the second as the symbol of the keys. . . . The keys have been conspicious enough in the art and heraldry of Christendom; but not everyone has noted the peculiar aptness of the allegory. . . . The Early Christian was very precisely a person carrying about a key, or what he said was a key. The whole Christian movement consisted in claiming to possess that key. It was not merely a vague forward movement, which might be better represented by a battering ram. It was not something that swept along with it similar or dissimilar things, as does a modern social movement. As we shall see in a moment, it rather definitely refused to do so. It definitely asserted that there was a key and that it possesses that key and that no other key was like it; in that sense it was as narrow as you please. Only it happened to be the key that could unlock the prison of the whole world; and let in the white daylight of liberty."

CARLETON J. H. HAYES
(1882–   )

CARLETON J. H. HAYES was born May 16, 1882, at Afton, New York. His university years were spent at Columbia University and culminated in the Ph.D. degree. He fought in World War I with the rank of captain, and has long been a professor in the school of History at Columbia. Dr. Hayes is active in many organizations, particularly the American Historical Association and its Catholic counterpart. At the beginning of World War II he was sent to Spain as ambassador where he played a shrewd role in the power politics of the period.

Carleton Hayes' historical writings are crisp and interesting. His Catholicism is to be seen in his attitudes and judgments and does not display itself by name but by implication. His *Brief History of the Great War, Political and Social History of Modern Europe, Ancient and Medieval History,* and his popular account of his mission in Spain are some of the works of Dr. Hayes.

WARTIME MISSION IN SPAIN*

CHAPTER I

IV

ARRANGEMENTS were made, soon after the Senate's confirmation of my appointment, for my departure for Spain. At first there was some talk of sending the Hayes family by a Portuguese or Spanish boat, chiefly in order that we might take with us all our personal luggage and likewise those housekeeping articles, such as silver, linen, blankets, etc., which the Government did not furnish for the Embassy. There was, however, a widespread belief throughout the State Department, which I then shared, that the Germans might invade Spain at any moment and that consequently my mission to that country would be brief and even might be over before I got there. With this prudently in mind, I had obtained from Columbia a leave of absence only for the summer and autumn of 1942. If we couldn't reach Spain, or if we should shortly have to leave it in a hurry, the less luggage we carried with us the better. Besides, as the President had said, "time was of the essence," and a boat trip to Spain took much time.

Hence it was ultimately decided that we should go by Pan-American clipper from New York to Lisbon, and thence by rail or air to Madrid. We were allowed fifty-five pounds of luggage per person. By the time all my ceremonial clothes were packed, little space remained for anything else. As a result, the other members of the family, on our entry into Madrid, had but scant advantage, in the way of clothes, over the uprooted war refugees who had entered before us.

We had been warned of the serious shortage of foodstuffs in Spain and of conditions there bordering on famine and starvation. So we placed a large order with an American wholesale grocery firm for flour, sugar, cereals, oils, canned milk, butter, vegetables, and other supplies to be shipped, together with our extra clothing, a few house-furnish-

ings, and our automobile, by Portuguese boat from Philadelphia. On urgent recommendations from Washington and from the Rockefeller Foundation in New York, we carried with us an assortment of vitamin tablets (which we never used) and a supply of vaccines against smallpox, typhoid fever, and typhus. Despite remarkable subsequent improvement of living and sanitary conditions in Spain, and despite repeated reporting of the facts by the Embassy, none of the several hundred American officials who landed in Madrid during the next three years failed to bring a mental picture of "starving Spain" and a bottle of vitamin pills. By now there must be a big surplus of vitamins in Spain.

In view of current opinion about Spain and its dangers, I was a bit surprised by the number of persons who appealed to me to help them get jobs in the Embassy at Madrid and to take them over with me. Evidently Spain fascinated them, but I don't know whether the fascination was associated with novel wartime perils in Spain or with those proverbial old castles in Spain. At any rate, I couldn't have taken the applicants if I had wished to do so.

My own family were to go with me: my wife; my son, Carroll, then sixteen years of age and a student in the Canterbury School in Connecticut; and my daughter, Mary Elizabeth, eighteen years of age, and just completing her freshman year in Barnard College. In addition, I had decided to take with me a personal secretary, and for this post I had selected Michael George, a son of the Foreign Service Officer in charge of the Spanish desk in the State Department. Michael was a young man who had lived and worked in Spain, who spoke fluently both Spanish and French, and who at the moment was attending the Georgetown School of Foreign Service.

On the afternoon of Tuesday, May 12, 1942, we received instruction in New York to be ready to depart on the Clipper at four o'clock the next morning. We passed on the word to Michael at Washington, and he

---

*From *Wartime Mission in Spain*, pp. 11-19, by Carlton J. H. Hayes. By permission of The Macmillan Company, Publishers, New York: 1945.

arrived late that night. There was, of course, no sleep for us. At the strange and almost ominous hour of four the five of us bade farewell to home and passed through the deserted streets and avenues of New York. It was seven o'clock when the clipper, with drawn curtains, actually took off with us from La Guardia Field.

We found the clipper flight pleasant and comfortable, though somewhat monotonous and more tiring than we at first realized. We stopped for three hours in the afternoon at Bermuda, where we were officially welcomed and shown about the harbor in a launch. The next morning we were having breakfast at Horta in the Azores, and late the same afternoon we arrived in Lisbon. Here we were met by the American Minister to Portugal, the Honorable Bert Fish, with members of his staff, and were driven to the Palace Hotel in Estoril, a delightful seaside suburb.

The next day, in company with Mr. Fish and his Counselor, Mr. Hugh Millard, I called on Dr. Salazar, the Portuguese prime minister and "dictator." He didn't look like a regular dictator. Rather, he appeared a modest, quiet, and highly intelligent gentleman and scholar. I knew that he had been literally dragged from a professorial chair of political economy in the venerable University of Coimbra a dozen years previously in order to straighten out Portugal's finances, and that his almost miraculous success in this respect had led to the thrusting upon him of other major functions, including those of Foreign Minister and constitution-maker. We conversed more as professors than as diplomats; and the first half hour of our conversation was devoted to professional "shop talk" — universities, books, science, Jacques Maritain's philosophy. He quizzed me about the position of the Catholic Church in the United States, and I had the pleasure of informing him that its hundred-odd bishops and the mass of American Catholics, like the rest of the American people, were solidly behind our Government in the prosecution of the war and in the will to overcome the menace of a world dominated by pagan Nazism.

During the second half hour the conversation with Dr. Salazar veered to political and international affairs. He asked my opinion of the current status of war-preparedness in the United States and of when our full armed strength would be employed and how long the war would last. I stressed the fact, in reply, that we were ahead of schedule in our preparedness, that President Roosevelt's seemingly incredible forecasts were being really surpassed in the production of airplanes, tanks, ships, and munitions of all kinds, and in the training of millions of soldiers. I said I had no idea how long the war would last, but however short or long it proved to be, the United States, with *all* its might and resources, was in it to the finish and to *victory*. He expressed misgivings about what Russian and other Communists might do with a victory in which they shared, adding, however, that the long-range chances favored the English-speaking peoples.

But what, Dr. Salazar queried, would we do with the peace? Would the United States stay with it, as with the war, or would America relapse into isolation as in 1919 and again lose peace for the entire world? I said I was going to make bold and ask him a question. What kind of a peace did he want? He indicated it should embody guarantees of the independence of states, small as well as large, through a strong Association of Nations and one not dominated by only two Great Powers. The League of 1920 broke down, he remarked, primarily because it was but a "Franco-British syndicate." The United States *must* be in the new Association, along with the defeated countries, if the Association was not to suffer the same sorry fate as the League. He took some comfort, he admitted, from information that Wendell Willkie and other Republican leaders, as well as our Democratic President, were now anti-isolationist. He emphasized the need of more specific statements of our war aims and peace plans. They would be helpful and should be reassuring to lesser Powers like Portugal.

Dr. Salazar also emphasized the need of

better relations between the United States and Spain, particularly in the economic domain. We should not merely buy from Spain what we wanted, but supply Spain with what she most required — oil and cereals and fertilizer. The Iberian peninsula was in many respects a unit, and what helped Spain would also help Portugal. Commercial ties could draw Spain as well as Portugal toward America.

While I was in Lisbon, I paid my respects to Admiral Leahy, our Ambassador to Vichy, who was awaiting ship for a sad return home. He was much broken by the recent death of his wife, but extremely interesting and illuminating on the French situation. He voiced the opinion that Vichy's collaboration with the Axis was not likely to extend to the French fleet, though it might affect certain French African bases.

Finding that rail service to Madrid was extremely slow and unsatisfactory, I booked passage for us on a plane of the Spanish "Iberia Company" for the next day, Saturday, May 16, 1942, which happened to be my sixtieth birthday. We left the airport at Lisbon at 9:30 that morning. In two hours and a half we would be due in Madrid.

v

Since that first conversation with Mr. Sumner Welles on March 18, and throughout the crowded intervening two months, certain convictions had gradually crystallized in my mind about policies and methods which I would try to follow in Spain if I ever got there. I fully recognized, of course, that our basic policy toward Spain was not, and should not be, determined by me. It could be determined, properly and with due reference to the exigencies of the war and the over-all world situation, only by the President, the Department of State, and the Chiefs of Staff. In basic policy, therefore, I would simply obey orders. If it was decided in Washington to abandon Spain to the Axis or to make war on Spain, and I was accordingly ordered to break off relations with the Spanish Government and leave the country, I would promptly break and (if possible) leave.

It had been made abundantly clear to me, however, that the basic policy of the President and the Joint Chiefs of Staff, and consequently of the State Department, was to keep Spain out of the war, as a neutral barrier to further German advance in the Mediterranean and Africa, and not to break, but rather to maintain, friendly relations with its Government. On just how this was to be done, I had received no instructions. As Ambassador, I would have to devise and employ the tactics best calculated to implement the basic policy — the strategy — which my superiors determined. If these didn't like my tactics they could countermand them or recall me.

I would, then, do everything I could (1) to keep Spain from joining the Axis, (2) to encourage Spain to offer all possible resistance to any Axis invasion or threat of invasion, and (3) to obtain from Spain every possible facility for our economic and military warfare against the Axis, and in particular against Germany. The success of this program would depend, I recognized, on our ability not only to influence Spanish "public opinion" in our favor but also to obtain the co-operation of the existing Spanish Government. We might not like the dictatorship of General Franco. It certainly, from what I had read and heard about it, did not conform with American ideals. Yet it was the actual Government of Spain and the Government to which President Roosevelt had accredited me. It was this Government which would decide for Spain whether or not to join the Axis, whether or not to resist German invasion, whether or not to accord special facilities to us. I would have to deal with the Spanish Government which was, and not with what many of my countrymen back home hoped would be a different regime.

In tactics, therefore, I would proceed on the assumption that our enemy was not the Spanish Government but the Axis. I would wage war in Spain against the Axis, not against Spaniards. To this end, I would sedulously refrain from interfering, or giving the appearance of interfering, in the internal affairs of Spain. I would show no partiality for or against any domestic party or faction — Nationalist, Monarchist, Republican, Socialist, Communist. I would consign the Spanish Civil War to history and leave the future of Spain to Spaniards.

In this way only could I hope to get the co-operation we needed from the existing Spanish Government. While I most surely would not dissemble, with General Franco or Serrano Suner or anyone else, my own loyalty to democracy and repugnance to Fascism and totalitarianism, I would assume that these isms were foreign products and that to no Spaniard were they really congenial. With officials of the Spanish Government, as with private citizens, I would seek to develop the most courteous and cordial personal relations. I would especially stress the historic and cultural ties between Spain and America, and the advantages to be derived by Spain and the Spanish people from close commercial relations with the English-speaking countries. In soliciting any sort of co-operation from the Spanish Government, I would always endeavor to present the matter as being in the interest of Spain quite as much as in that of the United States or the United Nations. I well knew that no Government will ever do anything which it does not regard at the moment as in its own interest.

For the execution of this strategy and these tactics I counted on the loyal and efficient support of the experienced foreign-service staff of our Embassy at Madrid and our consulates throughout Spain, and in this, as events proved, I was not to be disappointed. And I rightfully counted, too, on helpful collaboration of the British and other Allied Missions in Spain, especially on those from Hispanic America.

Almost two years afterwards, my good friend Charles A. Beard wrote me: "I belong to the old school of dodos who do not regard an Ambassador of the United States as a filibuster with a roving commission to reform the country to which he is accredited and otherwise make as much trouble as he can. I labor under the impression that he is to work within the frame of his Government's policy toward the accomplishment of certain major ends. Naturally in so far as that policy is under fire at home, he is likely to come under fire, but in all such cases personal criticisms seem to me to arise from a misapprehension of the Ambassador's duties."

What Beard thus wrote on March 24, 1944, exactly expressed my abiding conviction about ambassadorial functions. And whatever may be current or future criticism of the policy of our Government and of myself toward Spain and its Government, that policy was no novelty. Long ago it had been clearly stated by James Monroe. In the same message containing the famous "Monroe Doctrine," which he sent to the Congress on December 2, 1823, President Monroe made these remarks: "The late events in Spain . . . show that Europe is still unsettled. . . . Our policy in regard to Europe, which was adopted at an early stage of the wars which have so long agitated that quarter of the globe, nevertheless remains the same, which is, not to interfere in the internal concerns of any of its powers; to consider the Goverment *de facto* as the legitimate Government for us; to cultivate friendly relations with it, and to preserve those relations by a frank, firm, and manly policy, meeting, in all instances, the just claims of every power; submitting to injuries from none."

That had been said in 1823, but it provided the text and indicated the methods for me, as I, with my family, took off from Lisbon on May 16, 1942, on the last leg of the journey to a mission of dubious and perhaps crucial nature in Spain.

The pilot of the Spanish plane which bore us was a big fellow who looked exactly like the ideal Aryan German of the Nazis. Presently, however, as we passed beyond the smiling Portuguese landscape, dotted with whitewashed cottages, and reached the grimmer Castilian countryside with its steep high hills and barren wastes and huddled towns, I learned from the pilot that he was a native of Andalusia, that he had never been in Germany, that he spoke English fluently, and that he was pro-Ally. He was, in fact, a fine and agreeable Spaniard. Perhaps, I thought to myself, this mission to Spain may yet succeed.

CHARLES L. O'DONNELL
(1884–1934)

FATHER O'DONNELL was a prophet in his own country. All his triumphs and joys were bound together by the pleasant Indiana countryside. It was in Greenfield, Indiana, that he was born in 1884. His childhood memories and education were anchored there and his college years were spent at Notre Dame, where he took his A.B. When his thoughts turned toward the priesthood it was natural for him to join the Congregation of the Holy Cross, which he did in 1910.

In the Congregation his career was distinguished: he became provincial in 1920 and president of Notre Dame in 1928. His eminence as a poet made him the only possible selection as first president of the Catholic Poetry Society. Father O'Donnell was equally successful as educator and preacher. His sermon at the burial of Knute Rockne remains a memorable experience for all who heard it.

The poetry of Father O'Donnell, though not a massive body of work, has a validity entirely suitable to his own nature and priestly eminence. It is Incarnational poetry, charged with strong emotional feeling. *The Rime of the Rood* contains his best poems. On the occasion of the centennial celebration of the University of Notre Dame, the Reverend Charles M. Carey, C.S.C., compiled and edited the collected poems of Father O'Donnell. This volume was published by the University Press, Notre Dame, Indiana, 1942.

CLOISTER*

"Show me your cloister," asks the Lady
Poverty of the friars. And they, leading her
to the summit of a hill, showed her the wide
world, saying: "This is our cloister: O Lady
Poverty!"

Well, that were a cloister: for its bars
Long strips of sunset, and its roof the stars.

*The above and following poems have been selected from *Cloister and Other Poems,* by Charles L. O'Donnell, C.S.C. (New York: The Macmillan Co., 1922).

Four walls of sky, with corridors of air
Leading to chapel, and God everywhere.

Earth beauteous and bare to lie upon,
Lit by the little candle of the sun.

The wind gone daily sweeping like a
        broom —
For these vast hearts it was a narrow room.

A ROAD OF FRANCE

All day the carts go by along the road
That bear a regal though a sorry load.
Young pine trees, stripped of all except their
        crown
Which in the trodden dust is trailing down.

Young kings, that knew the mountains and
        the stars,
Dragged captive at the chariot wheels of
        Mars.
Alas, I think, while gazing upon these —
If this were but a sacrifice of trees!

RESTORATION

From these dead leaves the winds deride
  And on the brown earth fling,
Yea, from their dust, new hosts shall rise
  At the trumpet call of Spring.

Thus may the winds our ashes take,
  But in that far dusk dim,
When God's eye hath burnt up the worlds,
  This flesh shall stand with Him.

A ROSARY MOULDED OF ROSE LEAVES

Could anything more lovely be
Than is a rose-leaf rosary —

Wherein a garden bows its head,
And folds its hands and prays, though dead?

A cloister close, where roses wear —
The world forsook — the veil of prayer.

Out of the grave of summer rise
These postulants of Paradise.

Roses that morning robed in white
Go softly here in stoles of light.

Roses the heart of June has bled,
With deeper Passion here are red.

In raptures glorious enfolden,
The golden rose is yet more golden.

The shrouding mysteries they wear
But show their loveliness more fair.

Could anything so proper be
As is a rose-leaf rosary? —

Roses that worshiped God an hour,
Turned into prayers that are a flower.

PROEM*

In the Bread and in the Cup
  Wherein He is hid,
Daily I lift Him up
  As once the Cross did.

There is nothing in me
  Apart from Him —
I am only a tree,
  Root, trunk, and limb.

Oh, pause and see, now,
  You who pass by the road —
You may pluck from my bough
  The bloom that is God!

*The above and following poems have been selected from *The Collected Poems of Charles L. O'Donnell* (Notre Dame, Indiana: The University Press, 1942).

IMMORTALITY

I shall go down as the sun goes
  Over the rim of the world —
Will there be quiet around me,
  As of sunset banners furled?

I shall take flight as a bird wings
  Into the infinite blue —

What if my song come ringing
  Down through the stars and the dew?
I shall mount, strong as the promise
  Forged in love's white, first fire —
A soul through the rustling darkness
  On pinions of desire.

VER

Sandalled with violets, adown the breaking
    way
She cometh, misty-eyed with hopes of May;
The changing splendor of the morning skies
Holds less of promise than her waiting eyes.

Across the black, ploughed fields her scarf
    of rain
In floating folds enwraps the leaping grain,

While 'neath the velvet press of her thin
    feet,
Quickens to growth the yet unbladed wheat.

And as she dreameth, down the blue, far rills
Rise windy banks of unborn daffodils,—
Soft! is it growing grass or young birds' call
Lisping to her, the Mother of them all?

IN THE NIGHT

The joyful heart is slow to sleep,
  Repose it does not crave;
But weary are the eyes that weep
  By sick-bed or by grave.

I lay awake the livelong night,
  By joy too much made glad;
But with the coming of the light
  I found my heart more sad.

The wings of joy are light and fleet,
  They pass and leave no trace;

Deep prints are marked by sorrow's feet
  Upon the spirit's face.

But God can fill the hollows up
  With undeparting peace,
And they who drain their sorrow's cup
  Know pain at last will cease.

The joyful heart, so slow to sleep,
  May find its morning night,—
The heavy eyes of those who weep
  May never lose the light.

GOD IN MAN

A shuttered house He occupies
Whose home is wider than the skies.
(On Thabor, all its windows lit,
Three men were blinded, seeing it).

He hid His Godhead in some sort,
Successfully, by all report.
(Some jars of water once, they say,
Rebelled and gave the truth away).

QUESTIONNAIRE

What did you think of, Mary,
  As He looked up from your breast?
I saw His eyes like stars
  In the early evening west.

And when you bathed His limbs
  In waters warm and sweet?
I loved Him, adorable, perfect
  From head to perfect feet.

What waking vision stirred you
  As He slept, small and weak?
For hours and hours I watched
  The little curve of His cheek.

And when the first words came
  At length from His learning lips?
I could feel my blood listening
  Down to my finger-tips.

On that amazing day
  Along the temple hall
He taught the Scribes, you thought? —
  My Boy grows straight and tall.

At Cana when your words
  Hurried His coming hour,
You saw? — I saw His hands,
  Beautiful, with power.

Oh, and when at the last
  He was slain by the crowd?
Never of my dear Son
  Was I so fond, so proud.

Then, when His cheek to yours
  Lay lifeless and cold?

I thought how never now
  Would my Son grow old.

But, ah, on Easter morn
  You had your heart's desire!
He came to me at dawn
  And helped me with the fire.

Did you know that He was God?
  From Gabriel's word, of course,
Alpha, Omega, of all
  The End and the Source.

But, women of all the world
  That ever children bore,
Remember, He is my Son,
  And human, forevermore.

MARGINALS

1

Veronica, the twilight comes apace
  To meet her Lord, the sun, who goes to
    die:
Behold, the wounded splendor of his face
  Staining her veil of sky.

2

Low in the tangled forest of the sky
  The branching clouds an ancient doom
    prepare,

And soon, like Absalom, the sun will die,
  Hung by his golden hair.

3

Now darkness, like King David, walks the
    skies,
  His crownless head is bowed with grief
    and years,
Only the night winds hear his broken sighs,
  Only the stars are witness to his tears.

HARVEST

I shall have nothing but my sorrow
  When judgment comes, whenever that
    may be,
No fruit, no flowers, no sheaves — myrrh
    only,
  And bitter as the sea.

Shall He regard me with stern anger
  Finding what He shall find,
Or look with eyes that understanding
  Pity makes blind?

I only know, there is nothing in my garden
  That will grow, to the grave;
I shall bring Him at last only my sorrow,
  All that my life could save.

RESOLUTION

Love, You have struck me straight, my Lord!
  Past innocence, past guilt,
I carry in my soul the sword
  You buried to the hilt.

And though to eyes in terrible pain
  Heaven and earth may reel,
For fear You may not strike again
  I will not draw the steel.

JOYCE KILMER
(1886–1918)

NEW BRUNSWICK, New Jersey, was the birthplace of Joyce Kilmer. Rutgers was responsible for his early education and Columbia University for his college years, which culminated in the bachelor of arts degree.

In 1913 Kilmer and his wife Aline became Catholics. His career was short but not uneventful. He was a teacher of Latin, book reviewer, book salesman, lexicographer, and finally poetry editor for the *Literary Digest*. He enlisted as a scout in the American Army in 1917 and was killed in action near the River Ourcq July 28, 1918.

With Kilmer's death something gallant and loveable went from American letters. The promise Kilmer has displayed in his early poems would undoubtedly have matured into something truly splendid.

His poetry displays a wisdom and understanding beyond his years and brief experience of life. Though *Trees* has been universally acclaimed, *Rouge Bouquet* and *Prayer of a Soldier in France* easily stand at the top of his poems. His complete works, edited by Robert Cortes Holliday, were published by the George H. Doran Company, New York, 1918.

ROUGE BOUQUET*

In a wood they call the Rouge Bouquet
There is a new-made grave today,
Built by never a spade nor pick
Yet covered with earth ten metres thick.
There lie many fighting men
Dead in their youthful prime,
Never to laugh nor love again
Nor taste the Summertime.
For Death came flying through the air
And stopped his flight at the dugout stair,
Touched his prey and left them there,
Clay to clay.

He hid their bodies stealthily
In the soil of the land they fought to free
And fled away.
Now over the grave abrupt and clear
Three volleys ring;
And perhaps their brave young spirits hear
The bugle sing:
"Go to sleep!
Go to sleep!
Slumber well where the shell screamed and
    fell.
Let your rifles rest on the muddy floor,
You will not need them any more.
Danger's past;
Now at last,
Go to sleep!"

*The above and following poems have been selected from *Complete Works of Joyce Kilmer,* edited by Robert Cortes Holliday (New York: George H. Doran Co., 1918).

There is on earth no worthier grave
To hold the bodies of the brave
Than this place of pain and pride
Where they nobly fought and nobly died.
Never fear but in the skies
Saints and angels stand
Smiling with their holy eyes
On this new-come band.
St. Michael's sword darts through the air
And touches the aureole on his hair
As he sees them stand saluting there,
His stalwart sons;
And Patrick, Brigid, Columkill
Rejoice that in veins of warriors still

The Gael's blood runs.
And up to Heaven's doorway floats,
From the wood called Rouge Bouquet,
A delicate cloud of buglenotes
That softly say:
"Farewell!
Farewell!
Comrades true, born anew, peace to you!
Your souls shall be where the heroes are
And your memory shine like the morning
　　star.
Brave and dear
Shield us here.
Farewell!"

PRAYER OF A SOLDIER IN FRANCE

My shoulders ache beneath my pack
(Lie easier, Cross, upon His back).

I march with feet that burn and smart
(Tread, Holy Feet, upon my heart).

Men shout at me who may not speak
(They scourged Thy back and smote Thy
　　cheek).

I may not lift a hand to clear
My eyes of salty drops that sear.

(Then shall my fickle soul forget
Thy Agony of Bloody Sweat?)

My rifle hand is stiff and numb
(From Thy pierced palm red rivers come).

Lord, thou didst suffer more for me
Than all the hosts of land and sea.

So let me render back again
This millionth of Thy gift. Amen.

A BLUE VALENTINE

(For Aline)

Monsignore,
Right Reverend Bishop Valentinus,
Sometime of Interamna, which is called
　　Ferni,
Now of the delightful Court of Heaven,
I respectfully salute you,
I genuflect
And I kiss your episcopal ring.

It is not, Monsignore,
The fragrant memory of your holy life,
Nor that of your shining and joyous
　　martyrdom,

Which causes me now to address you.
But since this is your august festival,
　　Monsignore,
It seems appropriate to me to state
According to a venerable and agreeable
　　custom,
That I love a beautiful lady.
Her eyes, Monsignore,
Are so blue that they put lovely little blue
　　reflections
On everything that she looks at,
Such as a wall
Or the moon
Or my heart.

It is like the light coming through blue
    stained glass,
Yet not quite like it,
For the blueness is not transparent,
Only translucent.
Her soul's light shines through,
But her soul cannot be seen.
It is something elusive, whimsical, tender,
    wanton, infantile, wise
And noble.
She wears, Monsignore, a blue garment,
Made in the manner of the Japanese.
It is very blue —
I think that her eyes have made it more blue,
Sweetly staining it
As the pressure of her body has graciously
    given it form.
Loving her, Monsignore,
I love all her attributes;
But I believe
That even if I did not love her
I would love the blueness of her eyes,
And her blue garment, made in the manner
    of the Japanese.

Monsignore,
I have never before troubled you with a
    request.
The saints whose ears I chiefly worry with
    my pleas are the most exquisite and
    maternal Brigid,
Gallant Saint Stephen, who puts fire in my
    blood,
And your brother bishop, my patron
The generous and jovial Saint Nicholas of
    Bari.
But, of your courtesy, Monsignore,
Do me this favour:
When you this morning make your way
To the Ivory Throne that bursts into bloom
    with roses because of her who sits
    upon it,
When you come to pay your devoir to Our
    Lady,
I beg you, say to her:
"Madame, a poor poet, one of your singing
    servants yet on earth,
Has asked me to say that at this moment he
    is especially grateful to you
For wearing a blue gown."

THE SINGING GIRL

(For the Rev. Edward F. Garesché, S.J.)

There is a little maiden
    In blue and silver drest,
She sang to God in Heaven
    And God within her breast.

It flooded me with pleasure,
    It pierced me like a sword,
When this young maiden sang: "My soul
    Doth magnify the Lord."

The stars all sing together
    And hear the angels sing,
But they said they had never heard
    So beautiful a thing.

Saint Mary and Saint Joseph
    And Saint Elizabeth,
Pray for us poets now
    And at the hour of death.

SISTER MADELEVA
(1887–   )

DAUGHTER of pioneer Americans, Sister Madeleva was born in Wisconsin, 1887. The green hills of her native state fostered her love of beauty and of verse.

Her education was wide. It began at St. Mary's College, Notre Dame, Indiana, from which she received her A.B. in 1909. Since that time Sister Madeleva has taught and traveled on three continents.

In 1925 she took her Ph.D. at the University of California, and in addition to this has studied at Oxford and London. Her wisdom and capacities have grown with the years. As president of St. Mary's College, since 1934, she has been a stimulating force in the educational world.

Sister Madeleva's verse has a wide appeal. She is without doubt the most popular of Catholic American poets. Her verse reads easily, is deeply religious, and carries a note of mystical aspiration which sheds a luster on all the works of creation.

Though primarily a seer and a poet, *Chaucer's Nuns and Other Essays* is a good example of Sister Madeleva's ability to write fine, sinewy prose.

THE SHOPPER*

I knew the hills of Nazareth
Had miracles to tell.
I hoped the shops of Nazareth
Had memories to sell.
I climbed the streets of Nazareth
And bought a camel's bell.

At Cana's well in Galilee
One draws no wine today
And wedding guests in Galilee
Have no great word to say.
A beggar child in Galilee
Sold me a pot of clay.

In cobble-stoned Jerusalem
For hours and hours I stood.
I brought back from Jerusalem
The simplest thing I could,
A donkey from Jerusalem
Cut out of olive wood.

A house of bread is Bethlehem
And though I came from far
I did not shop in Bethlehem
Except to buy a bar
Of sunset over Bethlehem
And the first evening star.

*The above and following poems have been selected from *Gates and Other Poems,* by Sr. M. Madeleva. By permission of The Macmillan Company, Publishers, New York: 1938.

CHERWELL RIVER, OXFORD

I am a silken highway none walks upon
Only, in beauty going, you, white swan,
Through the clear dawn.

I am a sleeping mirror, unconscious till
You lean above my face to gaze your grave
　　　　eyes' fill
In me, silver-still.

I am a dreaming fountain, limpid, cold,
Sealed, save to you. Come, beauteous, bold
To me to hold.

PENELOPE*

Penelope never has raveled as I have raveled;
She never has fashioned the fabrics that I
have spun;
And neither her heart nor her lover has trav-
eled as mine has traveled
Under the sun.

Her web of delay, deliberate, passionate,
splendid,
Was tense with allurement, I doubt not; was
wet with tears;
But love found it raveled, unfinished — a
burial robe — and ended
Those piteous years.

My fingers run wildly through warps of bewildering wonder,
Or dream over woof of caught silence or
sudden song;
They tighten on patterns of laughter or fear
that is stricken thunder! —
O Love, how long?

Is it naught that I pause in my web as yon
suitor woos me;
That I ravel at night with regret the design
of day;
That loneliness sickens, grief dazes, and
doubt pursues me
With You away?

With a lifetime of years do I lash myself to
You and bind You,
Do I dare all the seas of the world without
compass or star;
Past the lands of Calypso and Circe and
Scylla I seek You and find You
Be it never so far!

So I fare on the deific pathway my Love has
traveled
As I fashion the web that Penelope could
not have spun
And ravel the heavenly robe of delay that she
could not have raveled
Under the sun.

*The above and following poems have been selected
from *Penelope and Other Poems*, by Sr. M. Madeleva
(New York and London: D. Appleton and Co., 1927).

QUESTIONS OF A NUN'S HABIT

You do not think it is because I do not share
A woman's subtle weakness for the piquancy
of dress,
Its swift, sure coquetry, its studied careless-
ness,
That I wear what I wear?
You do not think it is because I do not dare
Its recklessness?
What do you say
Of wearing one's bridal gown
To town,
To church on Good Friday?
Of wearing one's shroud
Every day, all day,
In the heat and the crowd,
On Easter and Christmas day?
You do not tell me that I have bad taste,

Or none at all, or that I am less than fastidi-
ous and proud.
Is it because you do not wish to waste
Words upon one whose world in secret you
deplore?
You are not sorry for me.
You do not think me dressed quite un-
becomingly?
(You would give much to be attired so
adequately?)
Of all the dozen gowns I ever wore
And have abandoned, orchid and shadow-
gray and powder blue,
This is the only one that you need envy me.
— You have not ever cared to find me beau-
tiful before,
Have you?

MAYTIME

If Maytime in this golden land
Is sweet as death
How heavenly fair it must have been
In Nazareth!

If flowers here a glory are,
What had they been
Abloom about the feet of her
Who is their Queen!

The little winds that here blow wild,
Grown gentle there,

Adoringly had touched her cheek
And kissed her hair.

And O, if heavens here are blue,
What lovelier skies
Had they beheld, deep mirrored in
Their Lady's eyes!

When Maytime here is loveliest
I catch my breath
To think how fair it must have been
In Nazareth.

MY WINDOWS

These are my two windows; one
Lets in the morning and the sun
Lets in tranquillity and noon,
Lets in all magic and the moon.

One, looking on my garden, shows
Me miracles: a sudden rose,

A poppy's flame, a tulip's cup,
A lily's chalice lifted up.

Wonder-windows! who could guess
The secret of their loveliness?
Beyond transfigured sky and clod
My two windows show me God.

THE BISHOP CALLS

Frederic is at the door to meet him,
With James and John in the hall to greet him;
Mary Lucia, darling thing,
Is on her knees to kiss his ring.

Frederic climbs in the chair beside him;
James and Lucia almost hide him,
Perched at each arm; upon his lap
Sits John enthroned, sweet little chap.

There the four settle themselves sedately
Around the bishop, serene and stately.
The grown-ups gasp in amused dismay;
His Lordship insists that they are to stay.

Perhaps you consider this quite appalling
In children when the bishop is calling,
Because you do not know, I suppose,
The things that a child or a bishop knows.

KNIGHTS ERRANT*

Death is no foeman, we were born together;
He dwells between the places of my breath,
Night vigil at my heart he keeps and whether
I sleep or no, he never slumbereth.
Though I do not fear thee, Knight of the
    Sable Feather,
Thou wilt not slay me, Death!

But one rides forth, accoutered all in wonder:
I know thee, Life, God's errant that thou art,
Who comest to make of me celestial plunder;
To wound me with thy Love's immortal
    smart!
Life, thou wilt rend this flesh and soul
    asunder;
Love, thou wilt break my heart!

*The above and following poems have been selected
from *Knights Errant and Other Poems*, by Sr. M. Madeleva (New York and London: D. Appleton and Co.,
1923).

THE LIGHT

You do not know; you cannot, cannot guess
Across what burning sands I came to you;
Over what difficult hills, upon what new
Hard ways of loneliness.

You did not think of gifts—my piteous three;
Worthy I thought them,—kings had such
     of old,—

Do you keep but the frankincense and gold,
And leave the myrrh to me.

Bid me, I will return into the night;
Remember only, you who merciful are,
I found you by the shining of a star,
So I must walk forever in its light.

MARCH

Of what tumultuous grief these tears are
     token!
I wipe them with the wind which is my hair;
And now my alabaster box is broken,
Spilling the breath of lilies everywhere.

Winter, my Lord, let all the seasons tell,
I do these things against thy burial.

IN THE HILL COUNTRY

Men heeded not this thing,—
A young Maid into Juda hurrying,—
But when birds waked to sing,
And buds to blossoming,

When every leaf and petal, wind and wing,
Thrilled with articulate joy, "Our King, our
     King!"
Men said that it was spring.

SWADDLING CLOTHES

My days are all white with wonder, the
     wonder of stitching and sewing,
Making a spotless garment for Mary's spot-
     less Son;
My hours are bright with joy as I watch the
     small robe growing,
The little robe of love that will compass the
     infinite One.
Love is the cloth it is made from; my heart
     possesseth no other;
Love is the pattern, too, that I trace with
     unfaltering care;

Love is my double thread, the love of the
     Son and the mother;
Woven throughout of love, think you it will
     be fair?
Aye, and the mother Mary will let her little
     One wear it,—
He Who hath never in aught save dignity
     been arrayed,—
All upon Christmas morning; O heart of me,
     canst thou bear it,
The joy of thy God appareled in raiment thy
     love hath made!

N O V E M B E R   A F T E R N O O N S

Now they have come, these afternoons in
　　November,
When all the air is still and branches are bare,
And the long, lovely light that I remember
Invades with luminous peace the untroubled
　　air.

Off to the west a dozen trees together
Stand in gray loveliness, bemused with light;
Slender and silver they stand in the autumn
　　weather,

Waiting the inevitable winter, the inevitable
　　night.

Blossoming light they bear as a single flower,
And silence more singing-sweet than a lone
　　bird's call.
Off to the west I stand, sharing their hour,
At peace with beauty and needing no song
　　at all.

R I D D L E S   O N E ,   T W O ,   A N D   T H R E E

My lover is a fool more wise
Than Solomon;
My lover is a bird that flies
Into the sun.

He is a lighted lamp, my love,
A midnight cry,
A mortal worm that died to prove
He could not die.

My lover is a cedar tree
With branches spread;

A sweet and bitter fruit is he,
Alive and dead.

My lover is a quiet rain
Falling on fleece;
My lover is or endless pain
Or endless peace,

Or sometimes an instinctive mole
breaking the clod;
My lover is a thief who stole
The name of God.

E A S T E R   C H R O N I C L E

Today is Easter; I am at Solesmes.
The air is still and delicate and sweet.
Violets cloud the path before my feet
And edge the village with their purple hem.
Alone, bemused with song, I gather them,
Thinking how, on this morning, I should
　　meet
Blossoming sound, antiphonal, complete,
Blossoming color, leaf and flower and stem.

It has unfolded for me like a flower,
This great Gregorian chant: the solemn Mass,
The morning Office, hour by heavenly hour.
There shall remain when lesser praise shall
　　pass
This music that is peace and prayer and
　　power,
These April violets in the quickened grass.

ALINE KILMER

(*1888–*)

ALINE MURRAY was born at Norfolk, Virginia, 1888. In her early years she attended Rutgers Prep School and she later finished her Education at the Vaile–Deane School. In 1908 she married Joyce Kilmer and entered the Church with him in 1913.

After the death of Joyce Kilmer in 1918, Mrs. Kilmer was much in demand as a lecturer on poetry and the arts.

Mrs. Kilmer is a first-class poet in her own right. *Candles That Burn,* an extremely personalized record of her family life, is tender, humorous, and emotionally beautiful. Though her fame has been overshadowed by that of her much admired husband, it may be said that Mrs. Kilmer deserves the higher rank as poet.

As an essayist Mrs. Kilmer also has great charm. *Hunting a Hair Shirt and Other Essays* is in the best vein of the personal essay.

CANDLES THAT BURN*

Candles that burn for a November birthday,
　Wreathed round with asters and with
　　goldenrod,
As you go upward in your radiant dying
　Carry my prayer to God.

Tell Him she is so small and so rebellious,
　Tell Him her words are music on her lips,
Tell Him I love her in her wayward beauty
　Down to her fingertips.

Ask Him to keep her brave and true and
　lovely,

*The above and following poems have been selected from *Candles That Burn,* by Aline Kilmer (New York: George H. Doran Co., 1919).

Vivid and happy, gay as she is now,
Ask Him to let no shadow touch her beauty,
　Nor sorrow mar her brow.

All the sweet saints that came for her baptizing,
　Tell them I pray them to be always near.
Ask them to keep her little feet from stumbling,
　Her gallant heart from fear.

Candles that burn for a November birthday,
　Wreathed round with asters and with
　　goldenrod,
As you go upward in your radiant dying,
　Carry my prayer to God.

FOR TWO BIRTHDAYS

Whenever I light the candles for your birthday
　My memory lights two more,
Two ghostly candles burning with your
　candles
Where hers burned once before.

Whenever I see you at your birthday table,
　Across from you I see
A gentle ghost that sits among us laughing
　Laughing adorably.

She would have been the gayest at the party,
　She always was the gladdest thing on earth:
Now she is gayer still, for she is taken
　Into celestial mirth.

With God and all the saints and all the angels
　She shares her birthday cake.
So let us keep your birthday candles burning
　Joyously, for her sake.

TO TWO LITTLE SISTERS OF THE POOR

Sweet and humble and gladly poor,
The Grace of God came in at my door.

Sorrow and death were mine that day,
But the Grace of God came in to stay;

The Grace of God that spread its wings
Over all sad and pitiful things.

Sorrow turned to the touch of God,
Death became but His welcoming nod.

Grey-eyed, comforting, strong and brave,
You came to ask but instead you gave.

Quickly you came and went, you two,
But the grace of God stayed after you.

MY MIRROR

There is a mirror in my room
Less like a mirror than a tomb,
There are so many ghosts that pass
Across the surface of the glass.

When in the morning I arise
With circles round my tired eyes,
Seeking the glass to brush my hair
My mother's mother meets me there.

If in the middle of the day
I happen to go by that way,
I see a smile I used to know —
My mother, twenty years ago.

But when I rise by candlelight
To feed my baby in the night,
Then whitely in the glass I see
My dead child's face look out at me.

WITH DEEPER MENACE*

When I was in Rome I tried so hard
  To do as the Romans do;
A bit of dance and a bit of song
  With laughter sifting through,

A careless kiss serenely given
  And a heart held fancy-free —
It was all very well for the Roman-born,
  But it was not good for me.

For I couldn't dance and I never could sing
  And my laughter wouldn't ring true,
And whenever I gave my lips away
  My foolish heart went, too.

So now I'll sit by the Roman Road
  And watch the world go by.
When I see a lass that looks like me:
  "Don't go to Rome!" I'll cry.

*The above and following poems have been selected
from The Poor King's Daughter, by Aline Kilmer (New
York: George H. Doran Co., 1925).

FAVETE LINGUIS

Speak not the word that turns the flower to
    ashes,
  Praise not the beauty passing as you gaze.
Let your eyes drink of loveliness in silence:
  It will but wither even as you praise.

See there the plum tree heavy with its blos-
    som
  Swings like the full moon, glimmering and
    round:
You lift your lute to celebrate its beauty
  And all its petals flutter to the ground.

PRELUDE

So many sing of splendid loves,
  Of Guinevere and Lancelot,
Of Aucassin and Nicolette
  They love to sing. But I do not.

I sing of little loves that glow
  Like tapers shining through the rain,
Of little loves that break themselves
  Like moths against the window-pane.

TO APHRODITE: WITH A MIRROR

Here, Cyprian, is my jewelled looking-glass,
  My final gift to bind my final vow:
I cannot see myself as I once was;
  I would not see myself as I am now.

FOR THE BIRTHDAY OF A MIDDLE-AGED CHILD

I'm sorry you are wiser,
  I'm sorry you are taller;
I liked you better foolish,
  And I liked you better smaller.
I'm sorry you have learning
  And I hope you won't display it;
But since this is your birthday
  I suppose I mustn't say it.

I liked you with your hair cut
  Like a mediaeval page's,
And I hate to see your eyes change
  From a seraph's to a sage's.
You are not half so beautiful
  Since middle-age befell you;
But since this is your birthday
  I suppose I mustn't tell you.

NINE: THE HELPLESSNESS OF ADULTS*

WHO was the happy idiot who first conceived it — that wide-spread fallacy that teaches us that children are helpless? Probably someone whose offspring had driven him into imbecility (blest man!) and who found, in this blissful state, that the slings and arrows of outrageous children could touch him not and trouble not again.

The truth of the matter is, of course, that children are not helpless at all. We are. We are so completely helpless that in many cases we can only wonder at the magnanimity of children in allowing us to live at all. When their advantage is so great, what but magnanimity prevents their pressing it to the extent of their enormous power? Indeed, children are not given credit for their generous impulses. Still, this does not strike me as one of those wrongs that cry aloud to be adjusted. The balance is already so heavily in their favour that they can afford to wait for redress until greater evils have been remedied.

This is the nefarious method employed by children. In some underhand way, yet to be accounted for, they get a firm grip on our affections. We never notice what is happening until it is too late. Then they go recklessly ahead. Their tyranny is awful. Sometimes, besotted creatures that we are, we like it. When your young son stands swaying on the very edge of the top step and says, in his

*Kilmer, Aline, *Hunting a Hair Shirt and Other Spiritual Adventures* (New York: George H. Doran and Co., 1923), pp. 83–90.

imperious way, "Now you may carry me downstairs," you are pleased to the core. But when he wakes at midnight and screams for the grey flannel elephant that he left in the sandpile, are you pleased? You get it. Undoubtedly you get it. If you say that you do not there is no one so credulous as to believe you. You go in trailing bath-robe and flapping Japanese slippers and doggishly fetch that elephant — in your teeth, as it were. Is it for love of your young son that you do this? It is not. It is because, if you should not get it, he would continue to make night hideous and there would be no sleep for you. And, what is worse, the neighbours would be disturbed. But what would he care for that? What are the broken slumbers of the whole world to him?

I speak who know. I am not an outsider or casual observer of children. I happen to have children of my own — according to the standard of the times, many children — and to have been thrown, perforce, into more or less close contact with them. And I have discovered that their only weakness, and consequently the sole hope of the world, lies in the fact that, like the downtrodden middle-class (with which, in the words of Clarence Day, "I proudly and reverently take my stand") they know nothing of the value of concerted action. They are totally unorganised. This is the great work that the future holds for us — to prevent the organization of children. I am not, I think, strikingly weak-minded, nor are my children abnormally powerful. But I know well that if they should all mutiny at once I should be obliged to walk the plank. With this contingency in mind I shall, in accordance with the best tradition of mystery stories, place a copy of this paper in the hands of my lawyer, or the friend in whom I have most confidence. In case of my sudden disappearance it is to be opened and the world can know approximately what has become of me. But it will be too late then to help me.

To take up the argument. A child is helpless in inverse ratio to his age. He is at the zenith of his powers while he is an infant in arms. What on earth is more powerful than a very young baby? "Babies," said a small boy of my acquaintance, gazing reflectively at a new and screaming infant of my own, "babies," he said, "are the worst race in the world." Now he has a little brother and he does not say such things aloud. It is sometimes dangerous to put an unpleasant truth into words. It gives it substance. And it was a truth that he stated, for babies are the worst race (shall we say?) in the world. They are the worst in that they are the most irresponsible. And irresponsibility is always a menace. As they become older they grow less and less powerful. They assume responsibilities until finally they are completely enmeshed and absolutely helpless. In fact, they are adults. It is true that in rare cases this does not happen. There are people of whom you remark sadly, or perhaps a trifle wistfully, "as irresponsible as a baby!" And you have always an underlying fear of such people. A perfectly just and reasonable fear. But, of course, it is only a figure of speech. No adult is really quite so irresponsible as a baby.

The extent to which children control our destinies is dreadful to think upon. They can decide our entire manner of life. You may recollect how, when you tried apartment-house life with your young family, including a baby who burned the midnight oil, you were driven from pillar to post by public opinion. Anonymous letters even were brought to bear. Also there was the ever-present danger of windows. Of course, windows can be barred, but a clever child can always manage to get his head, or other valuable parts of his anatomy, wedged between the bars. Finally, in despair, you moved to the country. But life was not much simpler there. You could, without too much misgiving, allow your baby to live in spite of his habits, but other complications arose. Your young daughter, radiant with the joy of life, sought expression of this joy in a casual moment by lifting herself buoyantly over the stair-rail in the upper hall and falling with a dull thud into the hall below. You poured out a liqueur glassful of brandy to revive her, but she was unable to drink it. While you sat on the floor and keened, with her unconscious form clasped to your bosom, your even younger son drank the brandy and in the ensuing fit of drunkenness wrenched a button from his garments and thrust it up his microscopic nose. When the excitement had died down you waited, limp and dejected, for the verdict of the X-ray. You were completely exhausted by the emotional strain. For by this time such slaves are we that the final evil for us is that anything should befall them.

If children knew, oh, if they only knew their power! It is something absolutely glorious in its immensity. But they do not even see it dimly until it is gone forever. Sometimes, it is true, to the child who is growing a little older, a little less irresponsible, a little more articulate, comes a fleeting glimpse of the splendour that is slipping away from him. (When I say "a little more articulate" I do not wish to be interpreted as pitying the child who is too young to express himself in words. Far from it. He does not need speech in order to get everything he wants, and what man can do more?) But, indeed, as shades of the prison-house begin to darken, swift gleams of the departing glory flash across. When my four-year-old daughter explained to me that she tore up and ate one of my best-loved books because she was playing that she was the baby and "the baby doesn't care what

he tears up and eats," I was, in spite of my baffled fury, smitten with a sentimental sorrow for her. I felt like exclaiming "Ichabod!" In fact, I did say "Ichabod!" rather sheepishly. But she only laughed. It had not quite departed.

When I had reached this point in writing down the burning thoughts that sear my brain whenever I hear people make such idiotic remarks as: "How can anyone be harsh to them? Poor little helpless things!" I thought with pride that I would show it to Evadne. She, of all my friends, would realise the great truth of it. She is a little older than I and has even more children.

Evadne read it. But when she had read it she did not look pleased. She lifted a white, stricken face to mine. "Great Heavens!" she gasped, or words to that effect, for Evadne has been a mother so long that she has learned to use strong language. "Great Heavens! You have destroyed the work of centuries. Do you suppose it was for nothing that that belief was started? Do you, in your conceit, imagine that you are the only one who knows it is a fallacy? Why, the children themselves are the only ones it has ever deceived. And now, you fool, you utter fool, you've told them!"

HEYWOOD BROUN

(1888–1939)

ONE of the most beloved columnists of the incredible twenties, Heywood Broun, was born in Brooklyn, 1888. After graduation from Harvard, 1910, he became a reporter. His exceptional talent for warm feeling and forthright expression soon made him a writer with a following. He was one of the first of the popular columnists and was also in great demand as a lecturer. Broun

was converted to Catholicism, May, 1939.

Broun's writing is simple and ordinarily does not get far beneath the surface of things, except in a sentimental way. His writings on the great feast days of Christianity, such as Christmas and Good Friday, show quite clearly, however, that there was a deeper side to the man than anything shown in his frequent popular crusades.

22. FRANKINCENSE AND MYRRH*

ONCE there were three kings in the East and they were wise men. They read the heavens and they saw a certain strange star by which they knew that in a distant land the King of the world was to be born. The star beckoned to them and they made preparations for a long journey.

From their palaces they gathered rich gifts, gold and frankincense and myrrh. Great sacks of precious stuffs were loaded upon the backs of the camels which were to bear them on their journey. Everything was in readiness, but one of the wise men seemed perplexed and would not come at once to join his two companions, who were eager and impatient to be on their way in the direction indicated by the star.

They were old, these two kings, and the other wise man was young. When they asked him he could not tell why he waited. He knew that his treasuries had been ransacked for rich gifts for the King of Kings. It seemed that there was nothing more which he could give, and yet he was not content.

He made no answer to the old men who shouted to him that the time had come. The camels were impatient and swayed and snarled. The shadows across the desert grew longer. And still the young king sat and thought deeply.

At length he smiled, and he ordered his servants to open the great treasure sack upon the back of the first of his camels. Then he went into a high chamber to which he had not been since he was a child. He rummaged about and presently came out and approached the caravan. In his hand he carried something which glinted in the sun.

The kings thought that he bore some new gift more rare and precious than any which they had been able to find in all their treasure rooms. They bent down to see, and even the camel drivers peered from the backs of the great beasts to find out what it was which gleamed in the sun. They were curious about this last gift for which all the caravan had waited.

And the young king took a toy from his hand and placed it upon the sand. It was a dog of tin, painted white and speckled with black spots. Great patches of paint had worn away and left the metal clear, and that was why the toy shone in the sun as if it had been silver.

The youngest of the wise men turned a key in the side of the little black and white dog and then he stepped aside so that the kings and camel drivers could see. The dog leaped high in the air and turned a somersault. He turned another and another and then fell over upon his side and lay there with a set and painted grin upon his face.

A child, the son of a camel driver, laughed and clapped his hands, but the kings were stern. They rebuked the youngest of the wise men and he paid no attention but called to his chief servant to make the first of all the camels kneel. Then he picked up the toy of tin and, opening the treasure sack, placed his last gift with his own hands in the mouth of the sack so that it rested safely upon the soft bags of incense.

"What folly has seized you?" cried the eldest of the wise men. "Is this a gift to bear to the King of Kings in the far country?"

And the young man answered and said: "For the King of Kings there are gifts of great richness, gold and frankincense and myrrh.

"But this," he said, "is for the child in Bethlehem!"

*From *Collected Edition of Heywood Broun,* Copyright, 1941, by Heywood Hale Broun. By permission of Harcourt, Brace and Company, Inc., pp. 106–107.

71. AL'S HOUR*

CHICAGO, July 1 (1932) — I'd rather be right than Roosevelt. And if I just had to be a Democrat, why, then I'd be Al Smith.

If and when Al fails to get the nomination I know a young producer who would love to feature him in an intimate revue, for in spite of competition Alfred E. Smith has proved himself the greatest performer of all the troupe now playing in Chicago.

This might seem merely the reiteration of a well-known circumstance, but for the fact that there was doubt this time before Al came through. He didn't rehearse very well. The Huey Longs, Alfalfa Bills and other acts from the small time seemed to have caught the public eye before the big show went on.

Even some of Al's best friends went around before the first night shaking their heads and saying that the hop on the fast one wasn't there any more. He was a good fellow when he had it, was about the best that they could muster.

And then Senator Walsh said: "The chair recognizes the Hon. Alfred E. Smith, a delegate from the State of New York." And there was for a split second that curious humid hush which comes just before the wind sweeps over the valley and the lightning begins to shoot its fangs at chimneys and tall maples.

It was so in the Chicago Stadium, for the storm broke in the topmost gallery and swept down across the forest of delegates and up to the platform wall and over. Al stood there with the wind of popular acclaim beating around his head and shoulders. And he liked it.

I don't know how he felt about it, but any man would be a fool to swap those minutes for a term, for two terms, for an eternity in the White House. When did 20,000 people ever reach out in that way and pat a President between the shoulder blades and cry out to him, "Ataboy!"? No, we vote for Presidents; we pull the lever and put 'em away and forget about them.

The galleries cried "Al! Al!" as if their hearts would break. And the man from Fulton Market smiled for a while and then began to weep. Suddenly he broke through the din with that curious voice, half Caruso and half Tenth Avenue. When Al speaks the nose has it. It cuts like a sharp blade, a fish knife, through the uproar. Al carries his own gavel in his larynx.

He began to operate on Cordell Hull, who was already cut and bleeding. "The fact," rasped Smith, "that the Senator only found out in the last three days that there is sentiment for repeal is just too bad." With a right and a left, a left and right, Smith tore into the arguments of the Tennessee dry and the crowd stood up as if this were truly a main bout for a title and not merely a political convention.

Cordell Hull had quoted from a statement of Al's made during the 1928 campaign which was obviously far less dripping in its temper than the majority prohibition plank for which Smith was now speaking.

"That was four years ago," said Smith savagely. "Did the Senator agree with me then? He did not. And because I happened to be four years ahead of my time, look what happened to me."

I think it is true that Al does move, and I am for the men who know the difference between last year's little old camel and a present porcupine. And even so, I believe that the most progressive and radical of us should still adhere to some fixed point and tie the craft of our hopes to some ancient pier upon occasion, so that those who have been far away upon returning will know where to find us.

Al referred to the Republican Convention and said: "I promised myself to listen to it on the raddio." And the walls came tumbling down.

I suppose that, among the many reasons which induced millions to vote against Al Smith four years ago, not an inconsiderable number of thousands were alienated by the fact that he chose to call the instrument which brings crooners to our homes "the raddio." I

---

*Ibid., pp. 270–273.

did not sit in upon party councils, but it is inevitable that this fact was brought to his attention by friends and advisers. But Al is no man to swap a pronunciation while crossing a stream. He will change neither a "d" nor a devotion no matter how the vote may go. "Raddio" it was and "raddio" it shall remain though it splits the Solid South and tears untrammeled Democracy asunder.

Accordingly, when his name was placed in nomination I did a thing which is against the rules of the Convention Correspondents' Union and of other organizations to which I am committed. I joined the parade upon the floor and shouted: "Smith! Smith! Smith!"

My cold-blooded, or at least my fairly tepid, newspaper judgment assures me that he isn't going anywhere. And yet the 20,000 and one other never had a misgiving. We'd like to go along.

---

158. PASSION IN THE ANDES*

SOME few years ago I went on a spring cruise. The steamer touched the northern tip of South America and paused for a day at the port so that passengers might travel up the mountain to Caracas. When we reached Venezuela word came that Gomez, the old dictator, lay dying in the capital. And as we went up the winding road, which drops a sheer two or three thousand feet on convenient corners, I noticed that all those who walked along the highway were clad in black or purple. Young and old all seemed to be hurrying to some central point. And, naturally, it was my notion that they were hurrying to the palace to learn the fate of Gomez.

Of course, we went faster that the pedestrians, much faster than was my will and pleasure. I remember mountains above me and hills leaping like waterfalls to meet the sea. Sky and sea and chasm pin-wheeled across my vision. And all because an old dictator drew close to his appointed hour.

In the great square of the city these signs of mourning and of tribulation became banked into moving masses of people. And I thought to myself, "Perhaps the potentate is already dead, and it is for that reason that the garb of grief is everywhere."

But at the door of the cathedral the driver stopped and said something to my companion. My friend translated and explained, "The driver says this is the service to mark the three hours of agony on the cross."

And it came to me that they mourned not for Gomez but for the Son of God. Out of bright sunlight I came into cool darkness flecked, but not wholly broken, by the light of many hundred candles. And all about the walls and statues and across the shoulders of the worshipers I saw the badge of purple. Holy Week had come to the foothills of the Andes.

I had seen church services in far and near places, and many were impressive, but here for the first time I saw a people who seemed to feel that the Passion of the Lord was actually occurring once again.

Pilate was not a famous dead procurator of Judea who washed his hands in an ancient city long ago. It was but yesterday that Jesus stood before the Romans on trial for His life and was condemned. And at the very moment the living Christ hung on the cross.

An Indian woman, older than any being I had ever seen before, lifted her head from the floor as she prayed that death should not achieve its victory. Children in their purple smocks looked at the dancing lights and wondered. But they were silent.

It was as if someone of their own lay dying in a room at home. And all of them lived in a world in which each year Jesus again walked the earth and Judas brought betrayal in a pleasant garden. Many stood outside upon the steps under the hot sun and peered through the doors and down the dark aisles. They waited for some word from the mourn-

*Ibid., pp. 482–484.

ers. Almost they seemed to say, "What is the news? How fares our Lord on Calvary?"

The faith of the faithful burns high along that mountain shelf. Some part of the agony is theirs, but the joy of resurrection bursts in their heart like an apple tree suddenly come to bloom. To them the miracle is without question. They have lived through it, and rebirth becomes a part of their own experience.

Only one sleepy sentry stood outside the palace of Gomez. My friend spoke to him. "Gomez is very old," said the soldier, "and like you and me and the beggar in the street, he must die some day. But he is of strong will. He will breathe until he has seen another Easter morning." I suppose that before death the old man wanted once again to dip his hands in life.

---

186. THE HAND OF HEROD*

A NEWS dispatch from Paris says that the authorities have decided that midnight Masses may not be celebrated in any of the churches of the city during the Christmas season. It is explained that it would be impossible to keep the light from filtering out through the great stained glass windows of a cathedral. A candle by a shrine sheds a beam which is too broad for the warring world in which we live. If the figure of the Christ child were illuminated it might serve as a beacon for the way of wise flying men from out of the East. And their gifts would not be gold and frankincense and myrrh.

Once again the hand of Herod is raised for the slaughter of the innocents. But those things which were are with us now. I have seen men and women moved by devotion into such a mood that they felt themselves not only followers but contemporaries in the life of Jesus. To them His death was a present tragedy and Easter morning marked a literal triumph. And to those who are like-minded there lies reassurance in the revelation of the past. Herod was a ruler who for a little time had might and power vested in himself. His word was absolute and his will was cruel. As captain over thousands he commanded his messengers to find and kill the newborn king. An army was set in motion against an infant in a manger.

But though the hand of Herod fell heavily upon Bethlehem and all the coasts thereof, Joseph, the young child and his mother es-

caped into Egypt. "In Rama was there a voice heard, lamentation and weeping and great mourning, Rachel weeping for her children, and would not be consoled, because they are not." The blood of the young was spilled upon the ground even as it is being shed today. And it may well have seemed, some two thousand years ago, that there was no force which could stay the ravages of the monarch and his minions.

Around the child there stood on guard only Joseph and Mary, three wise men and shepherds from the field who had followed the course set for them by a bright star. Death came to Herod, and the bright star was a portent of the perfect light which was to save the world from darkness. The light of the world was not extinguished then, and it lives today and will again transfix the eyes of men with its brilliance.

In the dark streets of Paris on Christmas Eve, even as in the little town of Bethlehem, a star will animate the gloom. The call comes once more to kings and shepherds to journey to the manger and worship at the shrine of the Prince of Peace. Quite truly the civic authorities of Paris have said that it is impossible to blackout the light which shines from the altar.

And if I were in France I would go at midnight to the little island on the Seine and stand before Notre Dame de Paris. At first the towers of that great Gothic structure might seem to be lost in the blackness of the night. And it has been ruled that no congre-

*Ibid., pp. 545–547.

gation shall raise its voice to welcome the tidings of great joy. But then I think all the windows will take on magnificence, and that the air will resound with the message which has been given to the sons of men and will be offered again to the fellowship of all mankind. "Glory to God in the highest and on earth peace, good will toward men." And that choral cry will rise above the hum of Herod's grim messengers. It will be much louder than the crash of guns and the roar of cannon. No hymn of hate can prevail if we will only heed the eternal cadence of the Christmas carol.

KATHERINE BRÉGY

(*1888–*   )

BORN of distinguished parents in Philadelphia, May 29, 1888, Katherine Brégy was carefully educated at home and in private schools. She traveled abroad at an early age and demonstrated her genius for people by becoming an intimate of the Meynell circle. Through the good offices of Wilfred Meynell her first book of essays, *Poets' Chantry,* was published in England. Miss Brégy, who had been brought up in the Episcopalian Church, became a Catholic in 1906.

When a desire to further Catholic letters in America brought together a choice circle of writers, Katherine Brégy became one of the genuinely active members. In 1925 a second book of essays, *Poets and Pilgrims,* was published, and in 1933 a volume of medieval studies, *From Dante to Jean d'Arc.* Her delicate but valid poetry has been collected in *Ladders and Bridges.*

Miss Brégy's essays are beautifully constructed. They take their excellence from a genuine love of people and literature which makes Miss Brégy's comments at once discerning and delightful.

ROBERT SOUTHWELL*

AS THE highest Gospel was a biography, so," asserts Carlyle, "is the life of every good man still an indubitable gospel." It is, indeed, the simplest and first of all evangels, the evangel of fact: and when by happy consummation it becomes also the evangel of beauty the crown is assured. The world is hungry for inspiration, and sooner or later will capitulate. The meek shall possess the land, the martyr shall reign, even the poet shall be listened to at last.

There is Robert Southwell, for instance — onetime priest of the Society of Jesus, onetime prisoner in the Tower of London town, onetime laureate of the Elizabethan Catholics — whose story no one can read today without more than an intellectual interest. To say that he is best worth knowing for the sublimity of his personal character is to indicate the chasm separating him from the great body of Elizabethan songsters. His memory is not, as so frequently happens, sanctified by his art; rather is his art sanctified by the life which produced it. And yet one would not willingly forget that the young priest's immortality is mainly due to the unique charm of his literary work. "It marks not only the large Roman Catholic element in the country but also the strange contrasts of the times," comments Dr. Stopford Brooke, "that eleven editions (of his works) were published between 1595 and 1609, at a time

*Brégy, Katherine, *The Poets' Chantry* (St. Louis: B. Herder Co., 1913), pp. 1–17.

when the *Venus and Adonis* of Shakespeare led the way for a multitude of poems that sung of love and delight in England's glory." Such *was* once his popularity; and, although that may have lapsed for ever now, the critics are not alone in insisting upon Father Southwell's permanent place in our literature. His poetry, so strangely free from the glad, passionate earthliness of most Elizabethan lyrics, is full of quaint, fanciful grace — of the grace, too, that follows deep religious fervour. The hopes, the fears, the pathetic weariness of Catholics in those evil days, all entered into his work; these and the tender mysticism which bound them like a spell to the Old Religion. Yet, when all is said, the man's life is in itself our choicest heritage — his life as poet, as priest, and at last, as martyr.

Robert Southwell's birth is usually placed somewhere in 1561; a year which saw two events memorable in English history — the arrival on Scottish shores of the young Mary Stuart, and Elizabeth's final break with the Papacy in her refusal to send envoys to the Council of Trent. He was the third son of Richard Southwell, head of a prominent Catholic family of Horsham St. Faith's, Norfolk; it is interesting also to note that his maternal grandmother was a Shelley, and of the same family which later gave birth to the "Skylark" poet. Robert's adventures seem to have begun in the very cradle, whence he was stolen by some wandering gypsies; but, as the theft was promptly discovered, it bore no serious consequence. Far more significant is the fact that at a very early age the boy was sent to school at Douay, where a seminary had been established to supply the needs of English Catholics. Here, in the person of Leonard Lessius, he first came into intimate contact with the Society of Jesus, destined to be so potent a factor in his life. Later, at Paris, his studies were continued under the guidance of Thomas Darbyshire, a zealous soul and one of the first Englishmen to enter that Order. The Catholic mind will scarcely need any comment on the ardour and self-consecration of these early Jesuits, but it is edifying to read the following tribute from such a critic as Dr. Alexander B. Grosart, in his "Memorial Introduction" to *Southwell's*

Poems: "The name of Ignatius Loyola was still a recent 'memory' and power, and his magnificent and truly apostolic example of burning love, compassion, faith, zeal, self-denial, charged the very atmosphere with sympathy as with electricity. . . . The Society was then in its first fresh 'love' and force, unentangled with political action (real or alleged); and I pity the Protestant who does not recognise in Loyola and his disciples noble men . . . with the single object to win allegiance to Jesus Christ." There is nothing to surprise in the fact that the colossal Jesuit hope of winning back Europe to Catholic Christianity should have appealed to the earnest young English student, or that their lives should have excited his passionate admiration; but it is worth noting that while still in his early teens Robert Southwell should have formed a life-purpose, from which he never wavered. To "leave all," to take up the Cross, and bear it back to the old forsaken shrines, became the one dream of this elect young soul. He applied for admission into the Society of Jesus; and, being refused because of his youth, wrote an impassioned lament expressing his disappointment. Delay tried, but did not in the least shake, his determination, so finally the coveted consent was obtained, and on the 17th October, 1578, his name was formally entered "amongst the children" of St. Ignatius. Two years later he took minor orders in Rome, and made his first vows as a scholastic of the Society. Then followed four peaceful years of study, during which Southwell was occupied with philosophy and divinity, and, incidentally it seems, with verse-making. In this case the "poetic temperament" was evidently quite compatible with hard work, for the brilliancy of his labours soon won him the prefecture of the English College at Rome. It was in 1584 — probably his own twenty-fourth year — that Robert Southwell received the final rites of ordination, and stood prepared to begin his apostolic ministry.

Almost simultaneously, a law was passed in England (27 Elizabeth, c. 2) declaring any native-born subject who had entered the Catholic priesthood since the first year of the Queen's accession, and who thereafter resided *more than forty days* on English soil, to be a traitor, and liable to the penalty of death. Severe as it was, it nowise dampened the ardour of the Jesuits in general, nor of Robert Southwell in particular. The English Mission — if most interesting — was obviously one of the most perilous in Europe; religious fanaticism had been aggravated and embittered by political hostility; the air was dark with conspiracies for and against the imprisoned Queen of Scots; and the whole country was, to quote Mr. Turnbull's *Memoir,* "in a ferment of political intrigues." Alarmed by Catholic successes abroad, Elizabeth redoubled the rigour of her Uniformity Acts; the celebration of Mass was forbidden even in private houses, the fines of recusants were increased, and over every Catholic lowered the shadow of high treason. But what was a stone about the neck of the layman became a knife at the throat of the priest; upon him fell the real weight of the persecution, for him the main work of martyrdom was reserved. Against Jesuits, as supposed tools of the Papacy to sow treason in England, popular hatred was even more intense; they were "tracked by pursuivants and spies, dragged from their hiding-places, and sent in batches to the Tower." Then from dungeon to scaffold was but a little way. And all this was done, of course, in the name of justice, on purely political grounds! "To modern eyes," as Green very aptly remarks, "there is something even more revolting than open persecution in a policy which branded every Catholic priest as a traitor, and all Catholic worship as disloyalty."

But had not Ignatius Loyola besought for his followers this legacy of persecution? And never a prayer so promptly answered! Seventy priests had already gone into banishment, not to mention those who had suffered death, when, on 8 May, 1586, two more intrepid missionaries set out for the island. One of them was Father Garnett, subsequently head of the English Jesuits; the other, Robert Southwell. In spite of spies, who somehow ascertained their coming, the priests succeeded in landing in July, and in reaching the house of Lord Vaux of Harrowden, whither they were later joined by others

of the Society. There was plenty of work for them to do; there was also plenty of danger. Father Southwell, who passed in secular society by the name of Cotton and who is described as a man of middle height and auburn hair, seems to have been watched rather narrowly from the beginning. It was worse than a dog's life for them all, and the necessary precautions were irksome. Father Gerard, one of his companions, tells how the young priest tried to familiarise himself with terms of sport for the purpose of conversing with Protestant nobles, and adds that he "used often to complain of his bad memory for such things." On the other hand, one can well imagine how comforting the presence of this earnest, sympathetic soul was to his co-religionists, to whom he ministered largely in London, with occasional journeys to the north of England. "He much excelled," says Father Gerard, "in the art of helping and gaining souls, being at once prudent, pious, meek, and exceedingly winning."

Almost the first of Father Southwell's cares was to win back the wavering faith of his father and his brother. The former, who had married a Protestant lady of the Court, was restored to his birthright by a most eloquent and inimitable epistle from his son. "Howsoever," it concludes, after playing upon almost every key of emotion, "the soft gales of your morning pleasures lulled you into slumbers, however, the violent heat of noon might awake affections, yet now in the cool and calm of the evening retire to a Christian rest, and close up the day of your life with a clear sunset."

In 1589 Father Southwell became chaplain and confessor to the Countess of Arundel, whose husband, Philip Howard, was then confined in the Tower. There followed several years of comparative safety at Arundel House in the Strand, during which began his real literary activity. *Triumphs Over Death,* perhaps his first known work, was occasioned by the death of a certain "noble lady" of the Howards, and was designed as a comfort and check to inordinate grief. *Notes on Theology,* and other prose works mostly of a theological nature, date also from these years. But it is improbable that any of his English poems were yet composed. From Father Gerard we learn that Southwell set up a private printing press; from which it would appear that the "apostolate of the press" is not altogether a recent idea. However, *Mary Magdalen's Funeral Tears,* one of his most popular compositions, and model of Thomas Nash's *Christ's Tears Over Jerusalem,* was printed by Cawood with a licence. None of these works was signed, but the Government seems somehow to have suspected the authorship.

The letters written by Father Southwell during these years reveal the Catholic life of the day with terrible simplicity. Mary Stuart had bowed her weary head upon the block; the Spanish Armada had come and gone, uniting Catholic and Protestant in a common zeal to protect England; it would seem that Elizabeth had no longer much need to fear the Old Religion. Yet the persecutions went on with pitiless insistence. "The condition of Catholic recusants here," wrote Father Southwell in 1590, "is the same as usual, deplorable and full of fears and dangers, more especially since our adversaries have looked for wars. As many as are in chains rejoice, and are comforted in their prisons; and they that are at liberty set not their hearts upon it, nor expect it to be of long continuance. All, by the great goodness and mercy of God, arm themselves to suffer anything that can come, how hard soever it may be, as it shall please our Lord. . . . A little while ago they apprehended two priests, who have suffered such cruel treatment in the prison of Bridewell as can scarce be believed. . . . Some are there hung up for whole days by the hands, in such manner that they can but just touch the ground with the tips of their toes. . . . This purgatory we are looking for every hour, in which Topcliffe and Young, the two executioners of the Catholics, exercise all kinds of torments. But come what pleaseth God, we hope we shall be able to bear all *'In Him that strengthens us.'* " Even through this darkness, eyes of faith caught gleams of a coming sunrise. "It seems to me," he wrote later that year, in words which were to prove so deeply prophetic, "that I see the beginning of a religious life set on foot in England, of which we now sow the seeds with tears, that others hereafter may with joy carry in the sheaves to the heavenly granaries. . . . With such dews as these the Church is watered. . . . We also look for the time (if we are not unworthy of so great a glory) when our day (like that of the hired servant) shall come."

His day was, in fact, not long to be deferred. In 1592 Father Southwell made a dangerous acquaintance in the person of Richard Bellamy of Uxenden Hall, one of whose kinsmen had been executed in connection with the "Babington Conspiracy," and every member of whose family was under suspicion as to his belief. The young Jesuit said Mass at their home and ministered to the whole household, until the storm-cloud suddenly broke above their heads. Anne Bellamy, a young daughter, was chosen as the Government's first victim. She was confined in the Gatehouse at Westminster under the care of one Nicholas Jones, and the story of her double fall is as brief as it is ugly. Having lost both faith and virtue, the girl was soon persuaded to the final baseness of betraying her family and her friends. From her the savage Topcliffe learned that Richard Bellamy was in the habit of receiving Father Southwell and other priests at his home; he learned the manner of their coming and other details; then, like Judas of old, he acted quickly.

On 20 June, Southwell rode over to Uxenden with Thomas Bellamy—some say in hopes of ministering to Anne, who herself had written for him—and fell directly into Topcliffe's snare. "I never did take so weighty a man, if he be rightly used," wrote that officer to the Queen; and the sinister meaning of his words was soon apparent. The young priest was brutally tortured in his captor's own house; then sent to Westminster, under the care of the scoundrel who had now become Anne Bellamy's husband. In September a new entry appeared in the records of the grim Tower of London, that of "Robert Southwell, alias Cotton, a Jesuit and infamous traitor"; and the old gruesome story was repeated. His fortitude during these ordeals coerced the admiration of Cecil himself.

"There is," the latter wrote, "at present confined one Southwell, a Jesuit, who, thirteen times most cruelly tortured, cannot be induced to confess anything, not even the colour of a horse whereon on a certain day he rode, lest from such indication his adversaries might conjecture in what house, or in what company of Catholics, he that day was."

Persecution makes of some men misanthropes; of others, saints; of Father Southwell it made a poet. Broken by torture, imprisoned in the darkness and filthiness of the dungeon, he still worked for his beloved people — and, unable to speak, he sang. His spirit was like that pure frankincense of which Lyly tells us that it "smelleth most sweet when it is in the fire." Dr. Grosart opines that the entire body of his poetical work was produced in prison, and this, being true, adds enormously to its interest and its pathos. The Government, no doubt in hopes of forcing some revelation, kept him awaiting trial over three years. During most of this time he was confined in a dungeon so unspeakably noisome that Richard Southwell finally petitioned the Queen that his son be put to death if he deserved it, or else, as he was a gentleman, that he be treated as such. This protest availed somewhat, for the prisoner was allowed to receive clothing and a few other necessaries and even some books; of which, however, he asked only for the Bible and *St. Bernard*.

At last, in 1595 — and without any previous warning, says the St. Omer M.S. — he was hurried off to Westminster and placed on trial for High Treason. The courtesy, dignity and Christian meekness of Father Southwell throughout this travesty of justice were most impressive. When questioned, he pleaded "not guilty of any treason"; but he freely acknowledged the only crime with which he was charged — that of fulfilling the duties of a Catholic priest to his suffering co-religionists. The result was fore-ordained; England had a law, "and by that law he ought to die." Once more torture did its revolting work upon his much-tried body; then at dawn next morning, his gaoler bore him the final summons. "You could not

bring me more joyful tidings," the priest answered simply.

So at daybreak, on 22 or 23 February, 1595, he was placed in a sledge and drawn to Tyburn for execution. Bishop Challoner tells us that a notorious highwayman was executed on the same day to divert popular attention from Father Southwell's doom; nevertheless, the usual mob awaited him. The priest was to pour out his life-blood for these English people, the poet who had sung to them from his dungeon, gazed down upon the upturned faces — upon the hostile, the friendly, the merely curious. Then, signing himself with the Cross, he began to speak. "Whether we live, we live unto the Lord; or whether we die, we die unto the Lord. Therefore whether we live or whether we die we are the Lord's." The words were scarcely uttered before the sheriff attempted some interruption; but silence being regained, the young priest continued, craving of the "most clement God and Father of Mercies," forgiveness "for all things wherein I may have offended since my infancy. Then, as regards the Queen (to whom I have never done nor wished any evil), I have daily prayed for her, and now with all my heart do pray, that from His great mercy . . . He may grant that she may use the ample gifts and endowments wherewith He hath endowed her to the immortal glory of His name, the prosperity of the whole nation, and the eternal welfare of her soul and body. For my most miserable and with all tears to be pitied country, I pray the light of truth whereby, the darkness of ignorance being dispelled, it may learn in and above all things to praise God, and seek its eternal good in the right way."

There is a quite superlative pathos in these prayers of the condemned man for the Queen and country which thus repudiated him. Far ahead into the future of England his thoughts were wandering, when suddenly he returned to the awful present. "For what may be done to my body," he cried, "I have no care. But since death, in the admitted cause for which I die, cannot be otherwise than most happy and desirable, I pray the God of all comfort that it may be to me the complete cleansing of my sins, and a real solace and increase of faith to others. For I die because I am a Catholic priest, elected unto the Society of Jesus in my youth; nor has any other thing, during the last three years in which I have been imprisoned, been charged against me. This death, therefore, although it may now seem base and ignominious, can to no rightly thinking person appear doubtful but that it is beyond measure an eternal weight of glory to be wrought in us, who look not to the things which are visible, but to those which are unseen."

The simple spiritual grandeur of this valediction sank into the hearts of the listening multitude, and won them, in spite of Protestant detractors, to the martyr's side. The executioner did his work clumsily, which added extra torment to Father Southwell's death; but to the last he calmly commended his soul to its Maker. One is comforted in this dark history to read that the mob itself prevented his body being taken down before dead, as the sentence had directed. "May my soul be with this man's!" exclaimed Lord Mountjoy, a bystander; and when the poor, severed head was held aloft to the public gaze, not one voice was heard to cry "Traitor."

The world, after its wont, was kinder to the man's work than to the man himself. Three volumes of his production — already even popular, as it seems — were published immediately after Father Southwell's death; and they were followed by a host of others. In a very eminent degree was this young Jesuit the "poet of Roman Catholic England"; but he was not merely the poet of any single class. He spoke to the sorrowful and serious of soul, to the meek and the devout; and the Old Faith and the New ceased their warfare to listen. The longest and most ambitious of his poems, but by no means his best, is *St. Peter's Complaint*. The ever sympathetic Dr. Grosart anticipates a very natural objection in pointing out that "regarded as so many distinct studies of the tragic incident, it is ignorance and not knowledge that will pronounce it tedious or idly paraphrastic," for the constant play of fancy is too redundant for modern readers. Such striking passages as the following, however, do much to relieve the monotony: —

At Sorrow's door I knocked, they craved my
　　name:
I answered, one unworthy to be known.
What one? say they. One worthiest of blame.
But who? A wretch, not God's nor yet his own.
A man? Oh no! a beast; much worse. What
　　creature?
A rock. How called? The rock of scandal, Peter!

Throughout his shorter poems Father Southwell shows to truer advantage. It was inevitable that the minor notes of life should have struck deepest echo in our poet's heart. Their very titles, *Scorn Not the Least, Life Is But Loss, What Joy to Live?* etc, carry a message which those that run may read. But their sadness is utterly without bitterness or pessimism, their weariness of life always presses on to a hope beyond. A few lines from *Times Go by Turns* will serve to illustrate the beauty, even the cheerfulness, of his thought: —

Not always fall of leaf, nor ever spring,
No endless night, yet not eternal day;
The saddest birds a season find to sing,
The roughest storm a calm may soon allay;
Thus with succeeding turns God Tempereth all,
That man may hope to rise, yet fear to fall.

But the most masterful of Father Southwell's lyrics — *the* lyric, indeed, to claim which Drummond of Hawthorden tells us Ben Jonson would willingly have destroyed more than one of his own poems, — is the famous

BURNING-BABE

As I in hoary winter's night stood shivering in
　　the snow,
Surprised I was with sudden heat, which made
　　my heart to glow;
And lifting up a fearful eye to view what fire
　　was near,
A pretty Babe all burning bright did in the
　　air appear,
Who, scorched with excessive heat, such floods
　　of tears did shed,
As though His floods should quench His flames,
　　which with His tears were fed.
"Alas!" quoth He, "But newly born, in fiery
　　heats I fry,
Yet none approach to warm their hearts or feel
　　My fire but I!

My faultless breast the furnace is, the fuel
    wounding thorns,
Love is the fire, and sighs the smoke, the ashes
    shame and scorns;
The fuel Justice layeth on, and Mercy blows
    the coals;
The metal in the furnace wrought are men's
    defiled souls,
For which, as now on fire I am, to work them
    to their good,
So will I melt into a bath to wash them in
    My blood":
With these He vanished out of sight, and
    swiftly shrunk away,
And straight I called unto mind that it was
    Christmas Day.

This deeply religious fervour permeates the poet's entire work, not merely the *Maeoniae,* a series on the life of our Saviour and His Mother, but even the shortest lyric, without, I think, one single exception. He bitterly regretted the worldliness of most Elizabethan verse, complaining in one of his Introductions that "The finest wits are now given to write passionate discourses." Today, perhaps, we see the deep human value of many of these same "passionate discourses" more clearly than did the pious young priest; nor can we resist smiling a little at his ingenious recasting of Master Dyer's "Fancy," wherein the subject is made to mourn a lack of *grace* instead of *love!* But the constancy and depth of this devotion, and the delicacy of imagination which accompanied it, both charm and coerce our imagination. They are the characteristics of his prose as well as his verse — they are the dominant, unmistakable notes of his personality. And if, in his own words, his work be "coarse in respect of others' exquisite labours," we shall not easily forget the circumstances which called it into being the "evident fact," to quote Mr. Saintsbury, "that the author thought of nothing else than of merely cultivating the Muses."

Two obvious defects to be found in Southwell's works are extravagance of metaphor and an almost monotonous habit of playing upon words; for both of which, however, the age must be held responsible. When one recalls the years during which he wrote — the vogue of the sonnet-sequences, of *Euphues,*

Arcadia, and the *Faerie Queene* — it is understood that "conceits" were in the very air. Sir Philip Sidney himself, we remember, has somewhere compared a white horse speckled with red to "a few strawberries scattered in a dish of cream!" And the fundamental merit of Father Southwell's poetry has ever been recognised by the best critics, his literary influence being today more and more appreciated. This influence is very manifest in the poems of Richard Crashaw; and the lines from *Scorn Not the Least —*

He that the growth on cedars did bestow,
Gave also lowly mushrooms leave to grow —

find an echo in Blake's *Tiger.* "As a whole," summarises Dr. Grosart, "his poetry is healthy and strong, and I think has been more potential in our literature than appears on the surface. I do not think it would be hard to show that others of whom more is heard drew light from him, as well early as more recent, from Burns to Thomas Hood."

Biography is, after all, the best history; and the life of Robert Southwell reveals one phase of Elizabethan England better than a dozen commentaries. It is not, indeed, the phase oftenest remembered. In the stirring political drama of the day, in the clash of arms and clash of wits through which England was led to unprecedented material splendour, he played but little part. Still further was he from the wild Bohemianism of Greene and Marlowe, or the mature artistic glory of those who congregated at the old Mermaid Tavern. But there was a darker, sadder undercurrent to this rushing tide of Elizabethan life. There was the ardent Catholic minority, nowise deaf to the call of the young intellectual life, nor blind to the signs of England's growing strength — sensitive, indeed, to every vital influence — yet compelled into hostile inactivity. Adherents of the Old Faith were shut out from both the great Universities; they had no part in the administration of justice; they were ineligible for any public office in the kingdom. Thus a great body of men with the culture of the new Learning and the passion of the Renaissance were found marching not *with* but *against* the trend of their age. Some of them sought adventure overseas, or plunged into purely secular activity; others, already forced into disloyalty, spent their time plotting a change in government, and were the easy prey of each new conspiracy. Still others, purified by persecution, rose above the heat and bitterness of personal feud to apostolic zeal and endurance, and fought the losing fight so nobly that in their very defeat lay the assurance of an abiding victory. Of these last was Robert Southwell.

FRANCIS X. TALBOT

(*1889–*   )

ONE of the men who shaped the course of the Catholic literary revival in the United States, Father Talbot, S.J., retired as editor in chief of *America* in 1945. His retirement will be regretted by many writers and many movements which found it profitable to draw on him for inspiration and energy.

Father Talbot was born in Philadelphia, 1889, and educated there. Upon entering the Society of Jesus (1906) his talent for writing matured swiftly in the years he spent as a teacher and associate editor of *America,* 1922, and as literary editor, 1923–1935.

While he was literary editor, Father Talbot was indefatigable in encouraging American writers and in bringing the best English and Continental authors to the notice of the Catholic public. It was chiefly through his efforts that the Catholic Poetry Society became a lively organization with a magazine of its own to encourage the creation of poetry.

These good works were continued in the ten years Father Talbot spent as editor in chief.

Father Talbot has written plays, and has edited several collections of essays and poems. His eminence as a writer is particularly evident in *St. Isaac Jogues* which was published by Harper Brothers, 1935. In this study of Jogues, based on the *Jesuit Relations,* Father Talbot demonstrates an amazing verve and descriptive abilities of the highest order. The story moves with compelling speed and leaves the reader with an impression of great events and almost unbelievable endurance and sanctity.

CHAPTER IX

BOWED BENEATH THE TOMAHAWKS*

RECOVERED to a great extent from the wreckage of their tortures, Father Jogues and René Goupil were left in comparative freedom to wander about Ossernenon. It was all strange to René, whose only experience among the savages was in the Frenchified Christian village of Sillery. Jogues, on the contrary, found the place but little different from the Huron villages of Ihonatiria and Ossossané. The cabins of the Iroquois were of the same pattern as those of the Hurons, long houses of bark, from fifty to one hundred paces in length and some twenty feet in width and in height. Down the central aisle smoldered the line of fires, and along the sides were the heapings of twigs, covered with hides and furs, that served as beds. The poles of the framework of the shed and the rafters were littered with innumerable accessories and possessions. The earthen floor was filthy with rubbish and refuse, crawling with vermin, thick with brown dust. The

---

*From *Saint Among Savages,* pp. 229–240, Harper and Brothers, Publishers, 1935.

air was stale and stinking with the nauseating odors of bodies and decaying goods and excrement and dogs and furs and clothes. And now, with September far advanced, and with the heavy rains, the flimsy houses were damp and cold.

Ossernenon was a village of forty or more cabins, of varying sizes, located more or less regularly in plots with paths intersecting. Most of the cabins were situated within the walls of the palisades, which stretched nearly three hundred paces from east to west and half that distance across. The stockade was strongly built of rough tree trunks, closely knitted together, inclining slightly outward. On the inner side of the wall was a hanging platform on which the warriors might perch in defense. Along the outside base of the lines of poles was a deep trench, and beyond this another wall for an outer defense. To the east and west, narrow gates, three or four feet broad, opened toward the cleared fields that extended along the ridge of the hill above the valley, and another rear gate led out toward the south, to a spring and a tiny rivulet which trickled along the base of a ridge which, a musket-shot distant, sloped up gently away from the village

Jogues and René were at liberty to stroll up this pleasant hillside to the pines and oaks and beeches that crowded its summit, or to walk along the trampled spaces of the fields which commanded the valley. They were sent, at times, down the hollowed road between the trees to the flatlands along the river bank where were the rows of cornstalks and the maturing vegetables. Here they cultivated the soil and gathered the harvest of corn under the command of the squaws. Oftentimes they looked up at the hills which reared up across to the north of the valley, beyond which lay the trail to the St. Lawrence. They remembered the six weeks back, when they had descended the slanting paths into this vale of slavery, the torture by the ford of the rippling river, the climb up the road to the village, the running of the gauntlet to the gates of the palisades. That tribulation was passed. There remained for them the long, dreary winter of captivity.

Because of his six years of residence among the Hurons, Father Jogues was not only inured to the hardships of the savage mode of life, but was skillful in dealing with the savage mind. Goupil, however, was sickened by the food and the filth. He was unable to comprehend the effect of his conscious and unconscious actions on the Mohawks. In the hospitals at Sillery and Quebec, he had won the affections of the Algonquins by his gentleness and his piety and his kindness; but these virtues enraged the Mohawks. Being a sensitive-souled man who had always been treated courteously, he cowered under the rage of the savages and their open hate and maliciousness. Accordingly, he was despised by them as spiritless and no better than a cringing squaw. He was awkward in his gait, and, though strong, clumsy in the odd duties they ordered him to perform. So mutilated was he in his features because of the batterings he received in running the gauntlet, and so scarred was he in his body by the cuts and burnings, that he created a feeling of disgust in the Iroquois.

René was incapable of realizing the extent or the depth of the suspicions of the savages, and the violent extremes to which their suspicions would fling them. He had not learned the caution which was habitual to Jogues and Coûture in avoiding small irritations. He did not comprehend the charge of being a sorceror, and how easy it was to act like one, in the estimation of the savages. When he prayed, René would move his lips and occasionally break out into sighs and heavy breaths and exclamations. He would raise his eyes to heaven, or lower his head in deep veneration. He would strike his breast in repentance, or nod his head in reverence at the sacred Name, or make the sign of the cross. He knelt, a posture painful to the savages, for long spells of time, and clasped his hands on his breast. Father Isaac warned him time and again to avoid these and similar manifestations of his devotion, and explained to him the misinterpretations which the Mohawks would deduce, that he was weaving spells against them and invoking hostile demons to come and ruin them.

The virulence of the Mohawks' hatred concentrated on Goupil. Even the chiefs who championed peace with the French were quite willing to allow him to be killed. If he died, but Ondessonk and Ihandich were preserved, that could be explained to the French as the unfortunate act of a senseless young brave. Due apologies and presents could be made. Ondessonk was a Blackrobe, the Mohawks reasoned, and thus a man of importance and repute at Three Rivers and Quebec. It would be difficult to quiet the indignation of the French if he were murdered.

As a precaution, then, the council ordered that Ondessonk and René be separated. They had been under the charge of a chief of the Bear clan, a bitter enemy of the French. He was impelled to greater rage and resentment latterly, because one of his family, a promising young warrior, was slain by the French at the attack on Fort Richelieu. This chief had power of death over his French prisoners. The other chiefs feared he might exercise it and slay both Ondessonk and René. After the great council, therefore, they ordered that Ondessonk be removed to another cabin and given in charge of a less rabid master. This change foreboded no good, Jogues concluded. While they were together, Father Jogues could shield Goupil and could instruct him how to behave, for he relates: "René did not quite realize the danger in which we were. I saw it better than he; and this often led me to tell him that we should hold ourselves in readiness."

Jogues' fears were further intensified by an incident which happened in René's cabin. The young man, in his gentleness and simplicity, had made friends with the very little children. He was playing with a toddling boy of three or four years, the son, probably, of the warrior slain at Fort Richelieu. He lifted the little fellow in his arms and made him chuckle and chortle by putting the old cap he was wearing on the child's head. Then, as he used to do at Sillery with the children of the Algonquins, he guided the tiny hand of the child to the forehead and breast and shoulders in the sign of a cross.

A scream of anger slashed through the cabin. The grandfather of the baby had been sitting in the dark, watching Goupil and the child. He took a leap at the Frenchman and tore the baby out of his arms, yelling curses and threats. His features were twisted with rage, he trembled with his anger. The Frenchman had made the evil sign on the boy, with the intention of killing him. The Dutch had warned against this sign; it was an invocation to the devils, a diabolical superstition; it always brought ruin and death. The old man put the child aside, and beat and kicked Goupil out of his sight.

When Jogues learned of this, he sought Goupil and led him off, away from the cabin, and outside the palisades. They went out of the south gate, across the rivulet, and ascended the ridge of higher ground to a grove of fir. They had discovered this spot some days before. It was quiet there rather screened from the spying eyes of the savages. They were able to talk and pray in comparative privacy.

Father Isaac spoke plainly: they were in great danger of death because of the insane attitude of the old man; it was not impossible that the old master might cause René to be killed. René protested that he feared nothing the Mohawks could do to him, as long as he was in God's good grace. He then went to confession, which he did every other day, and Father Jogues gave him absolution. They had talked about death and its immanence before, but that afternoon in the fir-grove they renewed their intention that, "mindful of the indulgence at the moment of death, the sacred Name of Jesus would be the last word of our lives." They knelt together on the soft brown needles and prayed. "We offered ourselves to Our Lord with great devotion," Jogues related, "beseeching Him to receive our lives and our blood, and to unite them with His life and His blood for the salvation of these poor peoples."

The afternoon was growing late when they lifted themselves from their knees and walked out from the grove. As was their custom, they began to say their beads on their way to the cabin. Two savages were coming up the path toward them. One of them was from René's cabin. He was one of the tallest, and claimed to be the strongest, man of the Mohawk nation. He was the brother of the

tall chief who had been killed at Fort Richelieu and the son of the old chief whom René
had especially angered. Both the savages wore
rough, woolen blankets wrapped about their
shoulders and covering their folded arms.
They awaited Ondessonk and René. The
big brave scowled down ferociously on
them. "Go back to the village," he curtly
commanded.

Jogues read a portent of danger in the face
and the tone of the man. He whispered to
René: "My dear brother, we don't know
what these men intend to do. There is very
much disturbance going on about us. These
men have some evil design. Let us commend
ourselves to God and to the Most Blessed
Virgin, our good Mother, now, more earnestly than ever. They walked briskly down
the hill path, murmuring the Hail Mary.
They were now nearing the open space at
the foot of the hill, and were in full sight of
the palisades, about which loitered the men
and squaws and children in the sun of the
September afternoon. "Hail Mary, full of
grace, the Lord is with thee, blessed art thou
among women, and blessed is the fruit of
thy womb, Jesus," Father Jogues repeated.
Goupil took it up: "Holy Mary, mother of
God, pray for us sinners now and at the
hour of our death. Amen." They finished the
fourth decade.

"You walk ahead," the giant Mohawk commanded Ondessonk. "You wait behind," he
said to Goupil. Jogues searched the man's
face and eyes for an explanation, but the
savage merely glared at him with a masked
expression, motionless, and with the blanket
held tightly over his arms and hands. Jogues
turned and took five or six steps toward the
brook. He heard a rustle behind him and
wheeled around. He saw the tall Mohawk
throw back his blanket, swing the tomahawk
he held concealed, raise it, and crash it down
on René's head. As the blow fell, he heard
René call out: "Jesus, Jesus, Jesus." René
staggered a step or two under the impact of
the blow, then fell.

In that instant Father Jogues said the words
of absolution over Goupil. Then he dropped
to his knees, facing the two Mohawks. He
looked up at them, and said, hoarsely, "Give

me just a moment or two." He removed his
cap, bent his head, said an act of contrition,
and commended himself to God before he
died. He waited; he lifted his head. The
Mohawks towering above René watched him.
Father Jogues spoke to them: "Do whatever
you please. I do not fear death." The savage
who struck René answered: "Get up. You
are not going to be killed this time. I have no
power over you. You belong to another
family."

Father Jogues bounded to his feet, to René,
who lay face downward in the dust, his hair
soaked with blood. He lifted René, and saw
that he still breathed. With his right hand,
he made the sign of the cross over the split
head and again spoke the words of final
absolution. The Mohawks also saw that their
victim still lived. They tore Ondessonk from
the body, and crashed two more sharp, thud-
ding blows on the skull.

The savages squatting about the gate and
the palisades came racing across to the spot
of the murder, shouting raucously, some in
protest, some in alarm, some cheering. They
mobbed about the body and the two braves,
and trampled over Ondessonk. He tried to
force his way to René, but a man of his cabin
restrained him and bade him rise. "Go back
to the cabin immediately," the man ordered,
tense with apprehension. "Remain there. Do
not leave it." The mob milled and pushed
about him, talking and shouting around his
ears. All the hundreds of people of the village
swarmed densely before his dazed eyes. They
closed in about René's body. The man of his
cabin shoved him roughly toward the gate.
Blinded with his tears, though clear in mind,
he marched back to the cabin.

At the door, the old chief, his master, welcomed him. The man scrutinized him; he
was surprised that Ondessonk was so calm.
He placed a hand on his heart. It beat
steadily, it did not pound with fear or emotion of any sort. Amazed, he called others in
the cabin to witness. They felt about his ribs
and marveled greatly that Ondessonk's heart
was not agitated. The old man was kindly
and warned him: "Do not go out from the
cabin or out of the village, unless you are
accompanied by some one of our family.

They intend to strike you to death. Watch out for yourself."

They left him alone, in the gloom of the cabin, sitting before the flickering fire. René was dead. He was free from all his sufferings, from the dreads and anxieties, free at last and happy with God. René's soul went straight to God. He was pure as an angel, innocent, sinless, brave; he loved God so much. His last words were "Jesus, Jesus." He was rescued by Jesus and the Blessed Mother. This day was Monday, September 29; it was the feast of St. Michael the Archangel, most fittingly a day for this angel of innocence to shed his blood. René, poor René; it was better for him to die. Now he was happy. He was so steadfast, so loyal, so pious, so simple, so beautiful a soul. René seemed to be close, united to him, as he sat there looking into the flames. René was dead. The grief of it overwhelmed his soul and wracked him.

They came to him, after a little while, and told him that he must leave this family and cabin and go to another cabin. That meant his death, he thought to himself. The people with whom he lived were friendly and sympathetic. He knew the man who now ordered him; he knew him as being hostile. The man spoke roughly and menacingly. Father Jogues cared not; he commended himself to God and to René; he was ready for the death stroke.

He followed the man out of the cabin, into the gloaming September evening. Outside the stockade was great excitement. He could hear a crowd running up and down and shouting. He came to a cabin and entered with his guide. It was the house of one of the great sachems, a man of influence as an elder and as a soothsayer. He was the old chief who had spoken so bitterly against the French, the one who had ordered the Algonquin woman to cut off his thumb. Jogues knew with certainty that he was doomed.

The long cabin was filled with turbulent men and women and children of all ages. Their voices shrilled and grunted, their faces looked fierce in the fretful flames of the fires. They mobbed about him, taunting and threatening him. Stoic as a savage, he remained silent and unafraid. He sat motionless before a fireplace. The crowd raged about him. He is a dead man, they told him. He will follow his comrade. A former Huron, who had been kind enough to give him a pair of old moccasins, asked them back, explaining: "Very soon you will have no more use for them. Some one else would be taking them away from you if I didn't." Jogues stripped off the shoes and handed them back.

The tumult of the evening died down, the cabin settled to quiet. Jogues stretched himself on a skin and tried to sleep. He did not know what the night would bring. He might be called out to death; some madman might strike him where he lay. He thought of René, and the spirit of his brother hovered over him and consoled him. He would be happy to be with René. Truly, he thought, "René proved that he was no unworthy son of the Society of Jesus. I love him and I venerate him, not only as a brother, but as a martyr; not only as a martyr of obedience, but a martyr of faith and of the cross."

What had happened to the body of René? He must go out to find it, Jogues decided, and give it a decent burial. This must be his first duty. He watched for the dawn through a slit in the bark side of the cabin. While it was still tenuous and gray, he went out into the morning. Some dim figures moved about. They recognized him; some were amazed that he still lived, some were surprised at his foolhardiness in showing himself openly. He padded in his bare feet toward the south gate beyond which René was murdered.

He saw standing there the old chief from whose charge he had been taken. The man was troubled at this apparition of Ondessonk, for he wished him well. To Jogues' inquiries, he related that the young men and a troop of children had stripped the body and tied a rope around the neck, and dragged it hither and thither about the stockade and through the streets. They had pulled it out toward the west field, later in the evening, and across to the rim of the ravine where they threw the refuse. The old chief believed that they had tumbled the body down the side of the ravine toward the little stream which flowed to the river.

Jogues thanked him and turned to go out of the gate. The old man called him back in alarm. "You have no sense," he burst out at Ondessonk. "Where are you hurrying to? You are no more than alive yourself. You are liable to be killed at any moment. Don't you see that they are seeking you, to murder you? And yet you want to go out to find the body of a dead man who is already half corrupted and which has been dragged away, far from the village. You have no sense at all. Look, don't you see those young braves going out of the gate and how fierce they look? They will kill you as soon as you step out of the stockade."

Father Jogues stood for a moment undecided. He must go. "An overwhelming care and anxiety possessed me," he revealed, "to discover what had been done with the body of my beloved friend and companion. I made up my mind to seek out the body, no matter what the danger to myself, and, if I could possibly do so, to bury it in the earth. Our Lord gave me courage enough to wish to die in this act of charity. I had no fear of anything that might happen to me. For truly it was a pain to live in such bitter anguish, and it was a profit to die in doing such a work of charity." Under the compulsion of these thoughts, despite the warning of his friend, he strode off toward the west gate. The kindly old man no longer had authority over Ondessonk, but he had a care for his safety, and so ordered an Algonquin whom he had adopted, to follow and protect him.

Jogues, with the Algonquin plodding after him, passed beyond the stockade. In the soft dust of the field he noted the swaths crossing and crisscrossing where René had been dragged. Sullen, surly men and squaws watched him; they waited to see if any of the braves would follow and strike him down. He walked fearless, as if unconscious of the enemies all about. He came to the edge of the field fringed with trees, and the dark, sharp declivity that fell down almost straight to the bottom of the ravine. Buzzards circled in the heavens above, and the dogs prowled about amid the shrubs. Jogues and the Algonquin slid down the preciptious clay, from tree to tree. Some fifty or sixty feet below they came on the naked, rigid, dirt-smeared body of René. It lay stark on the damp grass by the stream. Dogs and rodents had been at it and had torn a part of the loins. The rope was still tight about the throat.

Stricken with grief, appalled, Father Jogues folded the sacred remains in his arms. He wept bitter tears over the gashed head. He must hurry. He looked about, fearful that he was being spied upon. No one was visible save the silent Algonquin. He had no tool with him to dig a grave. He must hide the body somewhere, and come back with a spade to bury it. The bed of the stream would be a good place for concealment. Only a shallow trickle of water flowed down, and the hollow was strewn with gray cobblestones. With the help of the Algonquin, he lifted the body over the crumbling bank and lowered it five or six feet to the bottom of the rivulet. He bent the stiff arms and legs straight and laid René on the rocky bed of the stream. Then he lined the body about with rounded stones, and piled other stones in a mound over it, so that it was completely concealed from the eye and safe from the clawing of animals.

Quiet in soul, he ascended from the gloom of the ravine and strode across the field to his cabin. As he entered, two youngish warriors confronted him. He recognized them; they were two brothers who had been with the band which captured him and who had been especially cruel to him. They announced that they had orders to lead him with them to the next village of Andagaron. He perceived at once that they were lying, that they had evil intentions against him. He betrayed no trepidation, no surprise. Casually he told them: "I am not my own master. Ask those who have charge over me. If they send me, or tell me to go, I will accompany you willingly." They were abashed at his attitude and his answer. They had hoped to trick him out of sight of the village, without letting the chief who was his master know of their designs.

His former master heard of the attempt and tried to dissuade the two braves from committing the murder. He also warned the present master, and insisted that he protect

Ondessonk. The old chief agreed, protesting, nevertheless, that he had no love for the French and not much affection for Ondessonk. But his sister, an old sqaw of power among her people, pitied the Frenchman. She called him "Nephew," and he addressed her as "Aunt." She took it on herself to watch over his safety, and for the rest of that day harbored him safely in the cabin.

He was restless, feverish to escape from her surveillance and to go bury René. He could find no chance all the day. Night came on. He planned to rise before the village awoke, steal out alone, and inter the body secretly, where none of the savages could find and dishonor it. She divined his anxiety and kept him in her sight. The next day she thought it might be safer to get him out of the cabin where a continual rabble was about him, threatening and cursing him. She put him under guard of two of her sons, who were bound by honor to preserve his life, and sent him down to work in the plot of ground she cultivated in the flat by the river.

While he worked, he happened to look up. The two braves who had tried to lure him off the day before were dashing across the field toward him. One of them flourished his hatchet. Father Joques prepared for death. The old chief, his master, also saw the two men. He sprang to interpose himself. He howled out at the man, shouting a torrent of abuse and waving his arms. The fellow halted, then brazenly turned away. Again Jogues felt himself saved by the power of God. "Through such occurrences did the Almighty teach me," he stated, "that I should cast all my anxiety on Him, knowing that He has care over me and that I should not fear the face of man, knowing that, since the Almighty is the protector of my life, not a hair could fall from my head without His willing it."

That afternoon a violent storm burst over the village. Blasts of rain beat down torrentially on the bark of the cabin, thunder cracked and rumbled over the valley and the hills. Jogues sat alone in the damp gloom of the lodge, and planned. Night came on and the storm continued intermittently. He dozed a bit, but waited for the first lifting of the morning. In the haze of the dawn he crawled out of the door of the cabin, taking with him a spade which he had borrowed from another hut, the better to conceal his purpose. He slunk out of the western gates of the palisades. Seeing himself free, he dashed across the wet stubble of the open field toward the ravine. He was a fleet runner and agile; recklessly he cast himself over the edge of the ravine and slid down the steep muddy banks. At the bottom of the gorge he found the rivulet swollen into a torrent by the rains. The water swirled by turbulently, up to the level of the banks.

He shivered in the raw October morning. He waded in the stream to the place where he had concealed Goupil under the stones. He toppled in the rush of the waters. He sounded the bed with his naked feet, searching for the mound of stones. Strange, he could not locate it. He calculated anew, and stepped about in the stream, and poked around the bottom with a rod, and peered down into the water, which beat waist-high about him. At last, he traced out the line of rocks with his feet. They were scattered. He bent over and felt with his hands; the cold water splashed about his face and shoulders. The mound was torn apart. The body was gone. René was not there.

"They have carried off René, my brother," he cried aloud in his first anguish. Then he thought: "No, the swollen waters might have tumbled the stones loose and carried the body downstream toward the river." He followed down the current for some yards, feeling with his feet and the stick. Climbing to the bank, he walked along it, scanning the stream and the bush. He descended to the flats over which the stream flowed into the Mohawk River, then crossed to the far bank, and up to the spot where he had left the body. He waded into the freezing water, and fought against its force, and stumbled over the ragged stones and slipped on the cobbles. "What groans did I not utter then? What tears did I not shed, mingling them with the waters of the stream? All the while, I chanted to Thee, O my God, the psalms that are recited by Holy Church in the service of the dead."

Again returned his first thought. The Mohawks had stolen away the body to spite him and to dishonor René the more. He clambered to the soggy grass along the banks, searching among the weeds and undergrowth. He scoured all the bottom of the ravine, seeking some trace of where the body had been dragged, among the trees, in the tall grass, under the vines. He was chilled to the bone. Nevertheless, he trudged up the course of the stream, along the two forks, of which one led to the village and the other into a deep gorge, on both banks, darting hither and thither, everywhere looking, always praying and weeping in his agony. Nowhere could he discover René in all the ravine.

Desolated in soul and numbed in body, he slowly dragged himself up the steep ascent toward the village. It made no difference now that the light of the morning was about him.

He cared not who saw him, whether he was killed or let live. He must find out what they did with René's body. About the palisades, some braves were lounging. He asked them about René. They jeered at him and mimicked his words. He pleaded with all he met, but no one would answer his questions until he found an Algonquin squaw who was friendly. She told him that it was useless for him to search any more. The young men discovered where he had laid the corpse, she related, and had carried it off and thrown it in a river a mile or two below the village. This was a river, she explained, which he had never seen and which he could reach only with difficulty. It was useless for him to try to go there, for the corpse was already washed away. He suspected that she lied. But he could learn no more and could do no more for René.

CARDINAL SPELLMAN

(*1889–*   )

HIS EMINENCE, Francis Cardinal Spellman, Archbishop of New York, was born at Whitman, Massachusetts, May 4, 1889. In the public school of his home town he received his primary education. His university course was taken at Fordham University. In preparation for the priesthood he studied at the Propaganda in Rome where he was ordained May 14, 1916. Since his ordination Cardinal Spellman's rise has been rapid. He was consecrated bishop at Rome September 8, 1932, after a brilliant career as an attaché to the Vatican Secretariat of State. He became Archbishop of New York April, 1939, and was elevated to the Sacred College, 1946.

The outward events of Cardinal Spellman's life, in spite of their extraordinary character, are an inadequate index of his enormous capacity for affairs and a manner of dealing with people and events which amounts to genius. His Eminence has been friend and adviser to two popes, but this or any other fact of his busy life has failed to dilute his American qualities. He still remains "as American as baseball."

As a man of letters the Cardinal has made great progress since his early works of translation. His war books, *Action This Day, The Road to Victory*, and *The Risen Soldier* have made him one of the most popular of American Catholic writers. To a fine talent for description has been added a depth of feeling and communicated wisdom which cannot fail to inspire Catholics with a love of the faith.

Chapter IX

THIS PLACE MUST LAST*

WITHOUT leaving the First Army, whose front extended through France, Belgium, Holland, Luxembourg and Germany, I continued on my way to Belgium, and I thought of one soldier who claimed the world's courting record because, stationed in Germany, he was engaged to a nurse on duty in Holland, and every time he called on her he had to travel through three countries. The Belgians greeted us gratefully and even gaily, though one could sense that their new joy was but slowly seeping through the century-old fear of the Germans, who so often and so ruthlessly had invaded their soil. Homemade American flags flew from many of their houses, and though some were short in the number of stripes, and all were short in the number of stars, these flags were pleasant to see, for they reflected the good-will of the people and their hope in us for happiness. Along the roadways were signs: "For you, Americans, Beer and Lemonade," and "We give our hearts to the American people as souvenirs of our liberation." In the town of Eupen, one of the towns taken from Germany and given to Belgium by the Treaty of Versailles, a clothesline stretched across a street with the sign "Siegfried Line," and hanging from it was an effigy of Hitler. We drove through cities and villages and through apple and plum country, where one could actually pick the fruit without being killed by booby traps, for the Germans had no time to hang them, as they did in Italy, 'midst dusty grapes and ripening figs.

In a chateau in which I stayed, the people wanted to know whether the Americans would remain in Belgium to protect them after the war. That night I was in favor of it, if only out of gratitude for a good night's sleep in a bed which must have been like the one in which Little Red Riding Hood's grandmother had slept. One had to jump, or else climb on a little stool, to get into it. As good as the bed looked to me, it looked even better to Father Stephen Kenny, who was with me, for it was the first one he had seen in four months. Before we went to sleep he told me about one of the Chaplains, who had made the mistake of being the first American to enter a certain Belgian town. He had not realized that he was ahead of the patrols, and found himself just behind the retreating Germans. The people came cautiously out of their houses, some with upraised hands, many waving towels and handkerchiefs, trying to surrender to him! There were tears in the eyes of the old and cheers in the voices of the young when they realized they were liberated. Bells rang out, and jubilantly the Belgians flocked to church, where they offered a Mass of thanksgiving for their freedom and sang hymns and their national anthem.

In Belgium, I heard the same kind of disturbing, distressing stories that I had heard both in liberated and unliberated countries; stories of hatred and distrust among conationals and even between neighbors and members of the same family. In some instances these have become deep and bitter as the hatred against foreign aggressors and oppressors, and while we need not be alarmists we must be alarmed, for war's virus has poisoned human blood-streams, infecting minds and hearts, dividing peoples whose common interests and destinies should unite them! But my heart was consoled by one story of great faith, loyalty and devotion. In a small Belgian town, for more than four years an old priest harbored a dozen Jewish children. He provided for them out of his own resources, helping to care for their physical and spiritual needs as best he could. On his calendar he marked their Sabbath and holy days, and many refugees and American servicemen observed their holy days in his house. On the Day of Atonement, so that they might not leave his roof hungry after their fast, he spent all that day collecting food for them. Not only the very young, but also the very old, were of his brood and came

---

*Spellman, Francis J., *No Greater Love* (New York: Charles Scribner's Sons, 1945), pp. 130–147.

under his compassionate protection, and hundreds of refugees with his aid escaped the Gestapo. Finally, the Nazis became suspicious and the priest had to go into hiding, but first he secured the children's safety in the rectory of another church. When the town was liberated he returned and again took into his care stranded, homeless Jewish children and arranged for their adoption by Jewish families.

In Charleroi, I visited an armory which had been converted into a prison for alleged collaborationists accused of traffic with the enemy. Women, wives, mothers and sisters, with anguished faces, hovered around the jail, their tear-brimmed eyes clinging plaintively to the barred windows, while they waved frantically towards the grim brick walls in the hope that their loved ones might see them through the narrow slits in the masonry. I had no knowledge of the guilt or innocence of the imprisoned, but some of the relatives were strong in asserting that the only crime of their dear ones was that they had not been killed by the Nazis. One Belgian merchant wryly observed, "It's impossible to differ even slightly with any one without running the danger of being shot, and that's the only way to have the last word in an argument."

From the fevered, faltering lips of many eye-witnesses I heard of the cruelty and torture inflicted by the invaders. One Chaplain in the White Army, as the Belgian partisan forces are called, was tortured and had both hands pierced before he was shot by the Nazis. Another priest, a Jesuit, was saturated with gasoline and thrown into a fire. Fortunate were they who died from a head-shattering or chest-piercing bullet, in comparison with those whose lives were leached by torture practiced by some of the world's worst sadists. So revolting and diabolical are the atrocities that were deliberately inflicted on innocent civilians throughout Europe, that unless there was evidence substantiating the facts these tales would be unbelievable!

Here, and in many other countries, political and religious differences and internal rancors have impeded national unity and deflated the value of human life. In America, deep as our differences may be and bitter as they can be, they still are settled in courts of law in accordance with the principles of law. In America, minorities have the protection of the law and all Americans have the obligation to protect every citizen in all his civic rights. And woe betide America if disunion, dishonesty, greed, violence and corruption knock down and undermine the foundation of her stability and greatness!

My first stop in Holland was in Mastrich, a city I had known in peacetime. It still appeared neat and clean, and the red-white-and-blue horizontal-striped flag of the Netherlands flew from every home, even though every home and heart has been broken by the horror of the Nazi invasion. One old Hollander, weeping, said of our boys, "Their smiling faces, their kindness, their generosity and especially their simplicity have won our hearts, and deep is our gratitude to them." Almost every family in this small country was undernourished, and the women and children live in cruel fear for their men abducted by the Nazis and forced into slave labor within the danger zones.

In Holland I was the guest of General Charles Corlett, known to all the Army by his nickname, "Pete." The last place we had met was in Alaska, and in the meantime he had become one of the heroes of Guadalcanal. When I mentioned the mud through which we had jeeped our way to find him, he reminded me that it was nothing as compared to Alaskan mud. But it did not cheer the soldiers slogging their way day after day through Holland to know that somewhere else the mud was thicker and deeper!

"Pete" told me about Captain Rooney of New York, Field Artillery Chaplain, whose specialty in the war seemed to be caring for the tiniest folk. He was driving through one town when the enemy began to pound the road with shells. Running to take shelter, Captain Rooney saw a frightened little girl crouched in the very middle of the road. The shells were hitting so close to the youngster that he thought she would be hit before he could cover the half-block to reach her. He took the child in his arms, covered her completely with his stooped body and got safely to shelter. From sheer relief, the youngster began to cry and the Chaplain started to console her. Suddenly, he began to laugh. The child immediately forgot her fears and laughed too. The story that prompted the Chaplain's laugh, and turned the psychological trick, was his recollection of an American youngster whom he had once tried to sooth by saying: "I wouldn't cry that way if I were you," and the little girl had answered: "This is the way I cry; you can cry the way you want to!" During another bombardment, Chaplain Rooney heard a mother cry out wildly that her baby was alone on the top floor of the house. He ran through the shelling, got the baby and carried her to safety. Awarded the Silver Star "for unselfish devotion to humanity," the Chaplain said: " 'Tis nothing — just the luck of the Irish."

But I know it is not luck but great-spirited courage that makes many Chaplains and each boy a hero. One boy, both of his legs blown off, both hands mangled, with mortar shells crashing around him, cried hoarsley to his comrades, "Get into your holes; don't worry about me!" A Chaplain raised the boy in the cradle of his arms, prayed and gently talked to him. "I want terribly to live," the youngster whispered, "but if God wants me, I am ready." Then, with utter simplicity and faith, he asked God to save from pain and death as many as He could, to bless every one, everywhere, "and the enemy too," he breathed softly, "for they know not what they do." He died. The doctor, with tear filled eyes — eyes accustomed daily to seeing boys gutted, ravaged and torn — turned to the Chaplain and said: "After that, it is not hard to believe in God. I am humbled, for I have seen the glory of God, reflected in this boy!"

Another story, tinged with a twist of humor, was told by a Chaplain who spent Christmas afternoon with the boys at the front, visiting them in their foxholes, ministering to their physical and spiritual comfort. A nineteen-year-old doughboy asked him if it was too late to make his First Communion. "It's never too late and there never will be

a better day," the Chaplain answered, and jumped into the foxhole. The communicant, being a good soldier, kept one eye on the Chaplain, one eye on a German machine gun across No Man's Land, and one finger on the trigger of his gun!

Driving through grief-worn, war-weary Belgium, I saw many of her famous, graceful cities bearing gaping, disfiguring war wounds and I met many of the afflicted of those cities, also worn and war-wounded. I talked with some of Belgium's brave Underground fighters, who had fought fiercely from the Ardennes to the Lys, and I visited their devotional center hidden deep within the beautiful Ardennes. Steps of beaten earth led to its rustic altar, and the statues were carved from the trees of the forests. During the years of occupation and oppression, village priests in jute paratroop uniforms crept silently through the woods to celebrate Mass for the Resistance troops. From one of them, I heard a story that portrayed the supreme devotion of the Belgian people to their God, to their country and to the men who fought and died to preserve it. These men are a bold challenge to the Godless who, in their conquests, captured and crushed men's bodies but never their great souls. A village priest, watching from his garden, saw a powerful formation of American bombers roaring through the heavens, returning to their bases from a raid on Germany. One of the Liberators appeared to be in difficulty, and black smoke trailed the limping plane. Suddenly, four parachutes appeared in the sky. But one of them did not open! As it plummeted earthwards, the priest, in dread anticipation of death, gave absolution as he ran into the meadow towards the fallen parachuter. The boy was still breathing, and reverent hands lifted him and carried him into a nearby house. A thin trickle of blood was oozing from a wound which appeared to be only a scratch on the boy's head, and the priest hoped prayerfully for life. But before the doctor reached the boy's side, the lad was dead. His skull had been fractured in the crash.

The Mayor and the villagers wanted to bury this boy with military honors, but when the German officers arrived they even refused to permit the priest to bless his grave. But the Belgians, in their Christian revenge against this cruel, stupid irreverence, thronged to the parish church, where Masses were offered throughout the day for the fallen American aviator. This was a tribute of affection and gratitude that the Germans could not prevent, nor did they know that one little old lady had dared quietly and simply to slip a simple signet ring from the boy's finger and give it to the priest, some day to send to his mother. And I know that now this ring has begun its journey home!

In Belgium, Holland and Germany, I saw German prisoners of various types and under various conditions, some isolated in wards in our large military hospitals, others, in field tents, lying side by side with our own wounded, receiving identical treatment from our doctors, nurses and medical personnel. Nearly all of these prisoners were physically exhausted, nerve-shattered, listless and hopeless. Drained of arrogance and relieved to be captured, to me they seemed surprised and bewildered at the humane treatment they received. Five members of one prisoner's family had been killed in the bombing of Hamburg, and one of them was his two-year-old daughter. When he was told that when the war was over he would be returned to Germany, he answered, "I never want to see Germany again. There, I suffered sorrow, hunger and disease; I knew fear; I saw mutilation and slaughter; I lived in mud and blood. I am dying to die!"

In a little village near Aachen, I passed a column of about five hundred German prisoners, some very young and some very old, among them a small group of fanatical SS. troops and a dozen ramrod-straight stern Prussian officers, still defiant and confident that Germany would win, even while the crunching vise of war was crushing her to death. There were others, crumpled, collapsed, entirely bereft of their combat spirit, stragglers who had surrendered to our medics. Expressionless children and hausfraus stood by the gates of their homes and quietly wept or tried to smile, as these prisoners marched to a collecting point to be trucked to prisoner-of-war camps. They tossed apples, pears or schwarzbrot to the men, and the hunger-bitten prisoners ate fiercely.

The Nazis tried to weaken the morale of our American prisoners of war by circulating propaganda that because our soldiers had been captured they were cowards. But I know that none of them were cowards and that many of them were heroes forced to surrender and to accept a captivity of gnawing loneliness, of living death and sometimes of sudden death. One courageous, beloved soldier, Major General Maurice B. Rose, gave bitter public proof of this when he was ruthlessly shot by the Germans while being taken prisoner.

I had promised to say Mass in Luxembourg for our soldiers of the fifth Corps commanded by Major General Leonard Gerow. Bad weather prevented us from flying and we had to drive three hours over mud-clogged, rain-beaten roads. It was cold and windy, with rain turning to sleet and hail, and then turning back again to pelting rain. Passing from Germany into Luxembourg, I drove through the town of Spa, where Hitler had had his headquarters. It was also in Spa, during the first World War, that the Kaiser learned from General von Hindenburg that there was no longer any hope of saving Germany from defeat. It was not strange that my thoughts refused to stay with today, but flashed back to disasters past, and forward to the problems and dangers of tomorrow. I thought of our boys, conditioned for war by months of rigid discipline, tedious, timeless testing and training. Their bodies had been tempered to withstand the rigors of extreme weather and of foxhole living, habituated to sleepless days and nights and alerted to combat. Their hands were readied to the tools of war; their feet hardened to mount guard on a lonely sentry post, to make forced marches or keep a rigid battle-stance when the slightest movement would mean death. Thus they were conditioned for war.

But what, I wondered, of the conditioning of these millions of fighting men for peace? When the guns cease firing, are we prepared to train these men for the tasks of conserving the peace with the same realism and vigor with which they were trained for war? Are we prepared to develop men's minds towards peace with the same intensity with which we disciplined men's bodies for war? Will we guide and equip them for the pace of peace with the same determination with which we geared them to the pace of war? Will we forge the links in the chain for peace with the same ardor with which we forged the links in the chain for war? Will leaders of nations continue to try to establish and enforce peace by decree from above, instead of building the foundation for an enduring peace upon the mutual understanding, good-will and well-being of the families and communities who gave their sons to war?

In war, Americans of every race, creed and color were worthy to be sent to fight and die and be buried side by side. In peace shall we forget too soon the inglorious indignities wrought by man upon man, the lavish loss and wanton waste of cherished lives, the destruction of cities, the desolation of lands and nations, the degradation of moral and spiritual values?

We have already begun the process of forgetting if we think that peace will come by formulas, covenants or decrees, that peace means only the re-construction of devastated areas and the revival of trade; or that peace is propaganda, for mere words and phrases are no more tools of peace than they are the implements of war. Down through the centuries, bloody battles have been fought all over the world, but it is sad and ominous that the countries which boast that they have made the greatest contributions to civilization are those which have excelled in the vengeance and violence of war. To win the battles of peace we need the same determination and tactical genius that are needed to win the battles of war. Men must be conditioned for the pusuits of peace with the same steadfastness and perseverance with which they were disciplined for combat in war, and training for a permanent peace can be achieved at a fraction of the cost of preparing for periodic wars!

Driving through so many towns whose names stud our history books was like taking an Alice-in-Wonderland trip, except that today it is a trip through blood-and-sweat-and-tears land. I have heard it said in sad cynicism that the greatest punishment for Mussolini and Hitler would have been to have made them listen to their own and each other's speeches. But one punishment, I believe would have exceeded all others: to have forced them to retread the paths they have drenched in blood, to stand among the ravages and ruins of proud cities they have gored and see the hollowed shells of once-hallowed homes of worship and of love, to heed the sick, the maimed, the broken and bereaved, *to watch the children!* and, in the wake of all, to look upon the dead — the luxuriant youth laid waste by them!

When we finally reached the woods of Luxembourg, I found awaiting me two thousand boys unmindful of the hail and driving rain. A sheet of canvas strung from four trees covered the improvised altar within the forest but afforded little protection, and my vestments and the boy's uniforms were drenched by the water which literally streamed down our bared heads and faces. A band played the soft, soul-stirring strains of "Ave Maria," and I was inspired, as always I have been throughout the world, by the faith of our men of the front lines, so humble and sincere. After Mass, talking with the boys, sharing hot coffee and doughnuts distributed from Red Cross Clubmobiles, we heard the thunder and rumble of artillery, and only then did we realize that, strangely, there had been no shelling during the entire service!

Again I was on my way. On the main Aachen-Liège highway, I stopped at a new American cemetery, stretching across a wide wind-swept field marked off by sparse hedges and crude fences of fieldstones. On one side, the terrain sloped gently to the beautiful valley of the Meuse, and on the opposite side there opened a vista of green fields and low rolling hills dotted with old farm buildings and even older churches. At a turn in the road, I lingered at a wayside Calvary erected by the pious farmer-folk of the region, and said a Rosary for all our dead and their bereaved belovèd.

Here was a military cemetery in the making, a new sanctuary, where not only the bodies of our soldiers were being buried but, with them, the hearts and hopes of those who loved them. Some day, it too would be trim and well-kept, with tall trees restlessly moaning and rustling in the wind. Some day, its serried white crosses and Stars of David would be set off by freshly raked gravel paths and cool green lawns, as in Brookwood outside London, as in the American Cemetery by the lake near Oran, or as in the one at sun-baked Ponte Olivo looking down across the plain of Gela toward the lapping blue waters of the Mediterranean. But on this day it was a lonely expanse of sticky black mud, with yawning holes of familiar shape and depth dug in low rows lined by white tape.

In one corner, the day's harvest of the dead lay piled. Some were just as they had come, fresh-fallen from the field of battle, bloodstained and gory. Some, from the field and evacuation hospitals, still wore their splints and bandages or dressings, now sadly soiled, disarranged and shaken loose, mute, melancholy evidence of the fervent but vain attempts of medical corpsmen to save them. Others lay wrapped in their mud-spattered, soggy white ducking sacks, which serve as mattresses for the living and as burial shrouds for the dead. Some lay twisted and horribly contorted; some were bloated; some were burned and charred.

Here lay the youth of a "decadent democracy," modern youth accustomed from earliest years to the ease, the comfort, the so-called luxuries of typical American living, yet capable of going out, with an infectious grin, a witty wisecrack and a hasty prayer, and dying for an ideal; dying for the America they knew and loved, dying for lands and peoples unknown to them. Across the swirling, swollen Meuse behind them were the lands they had liberated, where the streets had been thronged with people who greeted them with wild shouts of acclaim, music and laughter, with tears, kisses, handclasps and a torrent of grateful words. They had tasted the brief, exhilarating glory of the liberator and, then, they too had been freed from the bondage of war — forever freed!

On the other side of the farthermost hill lay the land those still living would conquer and, in conquering, liberate from the thralldom of Nazi paganism. I thought of Rupert Brooke and his little corner of the earth that would be forever England. I thought of Allan Seeger and his youthful springtime rendezvous at some disputed barricade. I thought of the gentle, kindly Joyce Kilmer and his trumpet-note of young death floating clear in the wood of Rouge Bouquet. I thought of all the others of that great and youthful host who, so little time ago, had also died to make the world safe for democracy — and for us.

The silence was broken only by the mournful sound of picks and shovels hacking at the soft yielding earth — gateway to the only peace thousands of our boys, who fought for peace, would ever know. Sad and still, I stood with them in the dank mud while the chill, grey, dripping fog and narrow-searching cold hugged me, and I prayed that love and tolerance may quench the fires of bigotry and of hate and that in their ashes we may plant the seeds of peace.

I looked again upon the stricken, scarred, shocking remains of fun-loving, peace-loving Americans lately turned soldier who, stout-hearted, strong-limbed, vibrant and daring, had fallen facing the foe upon the soil to which they had carried the flag of freedom. Our martyred dead have made our nation consecrate and it falls upon us, the living, to preserve it! Standing with our hallowed, silent dead, the memory of them forever graven within me, I pondered this trust they have laid upon us. Sorrow welled high in my heart and I understood but this:

No greater love a man can have than this,
That he should lay his life down for his
　　　friend —
Now, as I live again the varied scenes
And world-wide pattern of our fighting men,
It seems no other thought so amply fills
The measure of their sacrifice, or plumbs

So well the depth of love that has inspired
Heroic giving of themselves for us.

No greater love than this: it is a truth
Perhaps more deeply lived by some, yet lived
By all the firm and serried ranks of those
Who form a sword of light, a sword of souls,
Forged in the battle-heat of shell and bomb,
Beat out upon the anvil of our need,
Tempered by justice, and in justice drawn
Against a dreadful foe; and though it break,
Yet in its breaking is its mission won —
Even in death. These souls, this sword, shall
    find
The sheath of final peace, in sacrifice.

Behold the making of this mystic blade:
He was a tiny babe. His sister asked,
"Mother, he is so small, will he grow big?"
The mother smiled and kissed her baby son
Before reply: "Yes, sweetheart, he will grow,
And some day in the shadow of his strength
Many shall rest, even as you and I
Now rest within his father's kindly care."
He was a boy, just one among the throng,
The treasure-trove that is a nation's wealth —
A boy with all a boy's strange wandering
    ways,
Finding adventure in the fields and woods,
Turning from games to books reluctantly,
Eager to live before he sensed the price
That life would ask of him. How could he
    know,
As he stood daily at his desk in school,
The spark that he was nursing in his soul —
"I pledge allegiance to my country's flag
And to the principles for which it stands,
One nation, indivisible," he pledged,
"With liberty and justice here for all."
This was the spark of freedom that would
    grow,
As the boy also grew, in God's good sight.
He found a world without, to which his
    thoughts
Within, at home, at play with other boys,
Gave glad assent. Too soon his mother found
Her son was child no more. In school, he
    grew
In knowledge; in the field, at sports he strove
With other boys, he worked to "make the
    team,"

To win the game, and learn the game of life,
Winning or losing, to play it clean and
    square —
And learn to win by loss as well as gain.
The boy was growing, to become a man,
Not in the mold of Nazi-Fascist thought,
But in the way America provides
For bodies' growth in strength and minds'
    in truth.
Then came another dawning time of hope:
As hills become apparent through a mist,
So, vaguely yet, loomed in his heart the
    dream —
Ideas, ideals, ambitions beckoned him,
Gave impulse to his thoughts; and in those
    thoughts
Was born resolve to take his rightful place,
A man with men. Another picture stood
Upon his bureau now, another heart
Took place, besides his mother's in his own,
And life and love were sweet, and home
    secure.

December Seventh, Nineteen-Forty-One!
A nation, that had knelt to pray, rose up
Reborn, to meet the challenge of brute force,
And from a million homes, as from the hills
The brooks break forth in spring, the young
    men came,
Stern-faced. Now in the fire that others lit
The precious ore of lives was forged and
    shaped
Into the giant blade that, swung athwart
The sky and hurtling o'er the sea, has dealt
A mightier blow, in this dark hour of war,
Than ever yet was struck by men for man.

What fire tempers hearts, what greater flame
Than hate prepared this blade? The flame
    of Love!
No greater gift the human heart can make
Than life-itself. And so in faith we pray
That He who was Himself broken upon
The Cross will gather up and mend forever
These broken blades that now we venerate.
And that is why above the holy sod
Where these blades sheathèd rest, we place
    with prayer
The symbol of the Greatest Love that men
Have ever known — fired by the Flame
    Divine,

These found within themselves, by Heaven's
　　grace
A strength beyond the strength to live, a
　　strength
Which is the strength, for what we love, to
　　die.

Come then, let us not think of these our
　　dead
Save only in the light of Easter morn,
For God with love embraces those
Whose lives with Him are lived and in Him
　　die.
Truly, in death these dear ones have found
　　Life;
Truly, in Life our martyrs have found peace.

Some say our dead were born expendable;
In this sense only speak they true: There is
No wiser spending of this earthly span
Than, like the Master, greater love to prove
By dying for the cause one holds most dear.
The night breeze moves above our dead
　　tonight,
Tomorrow's light with warmth will touch
　　their graves,
Yet none of them so silently shall sleep
But that the angel's lips shall o'er them
　　breathe
The Master's benediction: Greater love
Than this no man can have, that he lay down
His life that other men may live in peace.

AN AMERICAN CREED*

FROM close contacts with men of our armed forces, I am convinced that our soldiers are doing more for us than defending our land, our lives and our ideals. They are inspiring us to a renewal of faith in our country. Like Crusaders of old, they have gone into battle for the country they love, and for the cause in which they believe.

Living with our soldiers has inspired me to write an American creed with which I close this letter to you:

I believe in America.
In her high destiny under God to stand before the people of the earth as a shining example of unselfish devotion to the ideals that have, under God, made us a great nation; the Christian ideal of liberty in harmonious unity, builded of respect for God's image in man and every man's right to life, liberty and happiness.
I believe in America.
For the blood in the veins of America, our heart's blood comes from the wounds of many peoples, chaliced in humanity's name upon the altar of liberty.
I believe in America.

Not because of the tremendous resources of her fields and mountains, rivers and lakes, valleys and plains, but rather because America has been and must ever continue to be, under God, the Beacon of Liberty, the Hope of the Oppressed, the Refuge of the Weak, the Pledge and the Proof that humanity can live in mutual respect based on the law of God, voiced through the conscience of man, and in mutual esteem, based on the responsibility of democratic life.
Lastly, I believe in America:
Because I believe in God and God's Providence that has been over us from the earliest days of our beginning. Believing in God, I am confident both of His merciful forgiveness of our national sins and His awareness of our national virtues. Believing in God's Providence, I am confident of our high resolve that this fair land, the visible setting of the vast, immaterial soul of the American nation, shall never lose its initial consecration to the common Fatherhood of God, so that we and our children's children shall live in peace and harmony among ourselves and with our neighbors. In this America, I believe; for this America, I live; for this America, I and millions of others stand ready to die.

*Spellman, Francis J., Action This Day (New York: Charles Scribner's Sons, 1943), pp. 240–241.

DANIEL SARGENT

(1890-   )

DANIEL SARGENT, convert from Unitarianism, was born August 22, 1890. He was educated at Groton and Harvard. He came to his alma mater as an instructor, 1914–1916, and after distinguished service in World War I returned to the faculty of History and Literature at Harvard University. He is a member of the Catholic Poetry Society and the Catholic Historical Association.

Sargent's poetry is richly musical and covers a wide range of subjects.

As a prose writer he deserves a higher rank than his poetry would warrant. His life of Thomas More is a fine piece of biographical writing, and his book, *Our Land and Our Lady,* does much to indicate the source of our pride in our country and its early history.

CHAPTER VI

MARYLAND*

THEY have their exits and their entrances — was said of men, but it is just as true of nations. First Spain held the stage in our country, then France, now it was England. England had been blundering in the wings, and she came on the stage almost without meaning to, but the stage was certainly hers. She had all Spain's lands east of the Mississippi — that is she had the Florida of Menéndez — and she had the French lands east of the Mississippi. And she had a strength, like that of a suddenly grown boy who has a strength and does not know it. While she was not looking, her strange squatter colonies had grown powerful and populous. They could act for her, and who could act against her? And what then was to be her project? What would she do on the stage?

England does not really concoct projects, except purely down-to-the-ground commercial ones. She does things, and then lets the historians decide what they were, and her pragmatic moralists decide how they were justified. If a cautious prophet had been asked, however, what he thought England would do in the new territory, he would

have made with every sense of security one cautious — laughably cautious — prophecy: England will put an end to any relation that Our Lady has or has had with these lands. But let not even the cautious be prophets. Thirty years later Our Lady had appeared and reappeared resplendent in this domain that had fallen to England's lot. She was not the acknowledged sovereign, the "conquistadora," as she had been among the Spaniards and French. But she had made her entry with the English as she had made her entry with the Spanish and French. It seemed as if she met each nation on the threshold of our country, and in her manner, infinite in variety, worked with them.

When the first English came to our shores, sailing under the Italian Cabots, England was in her own conception Our Lady's special realm, Our Lady's Dower. Whether other parts of Christendom would have been willing to concede her that preeminence I very much doubt, for as every people now in the world considers that it is honest and sincere in comparison with its perfidious neighbors, so every part of old Christendom assumed as a matter of course that it was most especially Our Lady's. Yet England had still at that time some title to be called Our Lady's Dower. When an Englishman in

---

*Sargent, Daniel, *Our Land and Our Lady* (New York–Toronto: Longmans, Green and Co., 1939), pp. 119–142.

1500 made his written testament he began it true to English custom: "First, I bequeathe my soul to God Almighty and to our holy lady Saint Mary, and to all the fair company of hevene." When a group of Englishmen happened to form a corporation or guild at that late date, it would begin its charter after this manner: "In the worshippe of our lord and of our levedy Sainte Marie." England, at the time of Columbus, had still her shrine of Our Lady at Walsingham, which was so important that Erasmus — who hated vulgar pilgrimages — had to make a pilgrimage to it, and did there write a Greek poem in Our Lady's honor. And England's niggard King, Henry VII, who sent the first English ships to the New World, was himself bountiful to that shrine. And so confidently did Englishmen think of the road to that shrine as a permanent road, that the Milky Way, the starry road in the sky, also never changing, they called Walsingham Way. England of old had been an innovator in rites that celebrated Our Lady's Immaculate Conception. Then England had her Duns Scotus in order to define that Immaculate Conception. And though Duns Scotus had passed, Our Lady stayed.

But before the English had come to our shores really to settle those shores, all this had changed. Walsingham had been destroyed. "Weep, weep, O Walsingham," sang the popular song.

> "Weep, weep, O Walsingham
> Whose days are nights:
> Blessings turned to blasphemies,
> Holy deeds to despite;
> Sin is where Our Lady sate
> Heaven turned is to Hell;
> Satan sits where Our Lady did sway —
> Walsingham, O, farewell."

No longer did England touch the sky where Our Lady ruled. Her sky was her earthly sovereign's sky, King Henry VIII's, Queen Elizabeth's.

Yet, curiously enough, this change seemed destined to make the English colonies on the other side of the Atlantic Our Lady's Dower, by transporting there those who wished still to belong to Our Lady. When England took to herself a nationalistic religion, and a national church, she left out of its tidy happiness two groups of people, two discontented classes, two species of non-conformists, one of which wished that the old religion, untrimmed, were back, the other that every trace of it were abolished. The first were much the more numerous. They were the Catholics; the second were fewer and much more aggressive — they were the Calvinists. These more numerous non-conformists, who were — it goes without saying — those who wished that England were still Our Lady's Dower, had particularly no place in England. Yet they were pertinaciously English. It occurred, therefore, to some of England's statesmen that one way to let them stay English, yet have them out of the country, was to send them across the water as colonists. Let them be transatlantic Englishmen. They were the obvious colonists. Let them build far away, where it would do no harm, Our Lady's Dower.

Sir Humphrey Gilbert, Protestant, planned to use them this way, and the Queen — Queen Elizabeth — fell in with his plan. In 1582 he filled a ship called, indirectly, after Our Lady, the Delight, with a hundred of these outlaw Catholics. It sailed toward the State of Maine, but sank off the coast of Nova Scotia, and Sir Humphrey Gilbert sank too.

Then some Catholic nobles began to make this scheme which had originally been a Protestant scheme their Catholic scheme. The Earl of Arundel, Henry Wardour, a Catholic, planned a settlement of Catholics also in Maine. A cross was set up, a bay was called Pentecost Bay, but the ship sailed back to England — we know not why. And this was in 1604, still three years before the real settling of Jamestown.

Yet it was not the Catholics who became the great English colonizers of America; it was the other non-conformists, the Calvinists. The Catholics liked England too well to leave it. They had put their roots of affection into the soil as Catholics always do; and they stayed at home, hoping for better days. Also they had no patrons with money enough to send them across the water. On the other hand, Calvinists tend to be unsocial to their environment and to their neighbors; thus they were readier to immigrate. And there were rich English capitalists who were shrewd enough to see what admirable and useful transatlantic Englishmen they would make. To begin with they were thrifty, good for trade. Then by their religion they hated Spain, and, though not corsairs, would not interfere with the corsair activity of the English merchants if it were against the Spaniards. And these moneyed merchants, though not religious, did not like Catholics, for the name Catholic reminded them of the source of their wealth — loot from the Church — which was something that they tried to forget. They preferred to be with Calvinists, even though they had an antipathy for fanaticism.

It is well to take a look at one of these English speculators close to in order to appreciate how it came about that such 'men chose the Calvinists as partners, and could continue with them. And which of them is better to look at than one, the most conspicuous of them all, the Earl of Warwick?

I have an idea that the Earl of Warwick was, to walk with and dine with, and fight on the same side with, a charming man. He had none of the self-righteousness of the worst of the Calvinists, none of the lack of urbanity of the best of them. He was a sociable being. He was travelled, well read, witty, courageous in battle, as adventurous as a naughty schoolboy, carefree, ready to be friendly and hospitable in his pleasures, not intellectually proud, nor spiritually, and not argumentative. And though he was an unscrupulous money-getter, money-getting was a game with him; he was not avaricious. And though he played the hypocrite, he did it lightly, merely allowing others to be fooled by him, if they were fool enough. There was adventure in him.

At the same time, the history of the man stands, and it is not lovable. To begin with — though we blame it on him — his grandfather was the notorious Richard Rich who perjured himself at the trial of Saint Thomas More in order to win royal favor, and who gained excessive reward by securing the ex-chancellor's conviction. Richard Rich became Sir Richard Rich and had a son who kept his father's ill-gotten wealth, and added to it, without adding to his ignominy. Then came the Rich which I refer to as the Earl of Warwick. He was in reality the second of that title. He was Robert Rich, the second Robert Rich.

The second earl dared take risks that his forbears avoided. He was an enterprising developer of England's foreign trade, and when that foreign trade took the forms of piracy, so much the better; there was more of a lark in it. He was one of those who sent the English colony to Jamestown. He lost money on Jamestown, but I suspect he expected to. Jamestown was worth losing money on. It was a place from which the Caribbean could be raided, and through the possession of which any such losses could be made up; for Jamestown, as the early governor said, needed for its prosperity but two things — a good tobacco crop and "a fair war" with Spain. Even when there was no fair war, an unfair war could be arranged. The Earl of Warwick turned pirate, but not openly. He sailed under the flag of the Duke of Savoy, who was then at war with Spain, and did his piracy with proper respectability.

In founding Jamestown, the Earl of Warwick and his companions had not utilized the Puritans. They were not exactly his kind, and he had not discovered his affinity with them. But the colonists which he had to use, being vaguely irreligious, were not of a usefulness that recommended them to him. They were generally good-for-nothings, lazy, vicious, giving no strength to the settlement. After that experiment he preferred to use Puritans. They were earnest, obstinate, law-abiding. He became therefore the great promoter of the Calvinistic colonies, of Plymouth, of Boston, of Rhode Island (though the last was not exactly Calvinistic) — and of Connecticut. It was his particular grant of land which was, so it is now thought, the grant that was given to the Massachusetts Bay Colony. He became, though continuing to be a black-leg and epicurean, an ally of the Puritans. He became what Clarendon called the "Temporal Head of the Puritans," and very temporal at that. He played Puritanism for profit, and was, so also said Clarendon, the only Englishman who made money out of the War of the Revolution against King Charles.

Associated with the Earl of Warwick were other financial promoters, some of them more unscrupulous, some less, but all of them less daring than he. These men wedded the Calvinists with the gold ring of money, and the marriage lasted. Together they formed a Protestant, or anti-Catholic, front, which gave a strength to the English colonies, for the merchants supplied the shrewdness and the Puritans the fanaticism. Although not the only element on the English Atlantic seaboard, the two working together gave the spiritual tone to all the colonies. Together they drew over the Anglican colonists into non-conformism, and created that anti-prelatic spirit on this side of the ocean which frightened the Church of England from ever daring to send a bishop into the colonies, even though in various of those colonies the Church of England was by law the established Church.

Thus instead of becoming Our Lady's Dower, trans-atlantic England became quite the opposite. It would be an insult to it to say that it was a fortress against her, for even the Calvinists in their beliefs had a place to honor her, but she was not its sovereign. And she was not the joy of the land. The Calvinists did not wish to derive any joy from her or from any other human being. They resented joy. What Henry Adams said of them is somewhat true! "The Puritans abandoned the New Testament and the Virgin in order to go back to the beginning and renew the quarrel with Eve." The Puritans certainly rejected the traditional joyfulness of Christendom, and the cause of it also. And their spirit dominated in all the colonies.

Yet strangely enough into this anti-Marial stronghold was inserted a Marial colony. It was not one of the old English Catholic nobles who had established it, but one of these new men of energy, the class that was making imperial England, the moneyed men. He

was George Calvert, one of the most enterprising of the class to which he belonged, a wise promoter of foreign trade, an active shareholder in many a commercial venture. But he was more than that: he was a man of probity, and a man wise in the affairs of state, the principal secretary of state to Charles I. He was able to found such a colony because he was an able man of affairs, but also because he had the King's respect. And the reason he wanted to found it was that, unlike many of the merchants, he gave ultimate things some thought, and having decided that truth and salvation lay in the Catholic Church, he determined to enter it, cost what it might. And then he determined to help his fellow-Catholics.

It did cost him something to become a Catholic; he had to cease to hold public office, but Charles I was truer to him than to some of his friends, and simply for friendship gave him the title Lord Baltimore, protected him from penal laws, left him in his very great wealth, and allowed him, in an act of confidence hard to explain, to establish a colony north of Virginia in the New World over which he could be feudal lord with the rarest privileges of autonomy such as belonged in England only to the County Palatine of Durham. His obligations to the King were to be a payment of a share of the precious metals, if such were there to be found, but otherwise only a nominal payment of arrow-heads — symbolic as an act of fealty. This colony was not to be a specifically Catholic refuge, but it was a refuge to which Catholics could escape from persecution as well as others of any other persecuted sect, for the religion of the colony was written down merely as the "true Christian Religion" without any definition as to what that religion was. In other words it was to be a place where people could live together, provided they wanted to live a Christian life, even though they differed in their conception of it, and even though they differed in their conception of it zealously.

It has been suggested that the conception of such a colony, tolerating all but fanaticism, was derived from the Utopia of Saint

Thomas More. That the head of the English Jesuits at this time was Father Henry More, descendant of Saint Thomas, and that it was the Jesuits who accompanied the colonizing expedition when it took place, lends color to this suggestion. And if it is so, then the colony of Lord Baltimore derives from Saint Thomas More, whereas the other English colonies derive from Sir Richard Rich, who betrayed him — which is hard — all too hard on the other colonies. But mayhap the idea of toleration came from Lord Baltimore's practical sense, from his knowledge of affairs, and from his experience with human beings. At any rate, the idea became his. And he being a man who accomplished things, the colony came into being. In 1634 the Ark and the Dove arrived in the bay which the Spaniards a hundred years before had christened the Bay of the Mother of God — Chesapeake Bay. They were the ships of Lord Baltimore, though he was dead. With them was one of his sons, Leonard. His other son, Cecil, who had married the daughter of the Earl of Arundel and thus connected the project with the earlier Catholic colonizing projects, remained in England with the office of governor. On the Feast of the Annunciation, March 25, the colonists landed on St. Clement's Island in the Potomac River, and there the two Jesuit priests celebrated the colony's first Mass. It was an act which belonged specifically not to the whole colony, but to the Catholics of it, who were the influential minority. Yet it was astounding on the anti-Catholic seaboard of the English New World to have such an act take place without interference or heckling or grimaces of discontent. Such did not occur. Then the colony was given a name. It was Maryland. The name in the minds of the Catholics recalled Our Lady, but officially it was but a compliment to Henrietta Maria, Queen of England. Thus Our Lady did enter into the English colonies, but not ostentatiously — "as still as dew that falleth on the grass."

This colony with its feudal origin, was, curiously enough, the most democratic of all the English colonies in America, for the Proprietor allowed it to make its own laws like New England town meetings, and unlike the early New England town meetings, there was no restricted franchise. Every man had his vote, irrespective of wealth, or church membership. As a check on any wildness of omnipotent legislation, there was first the governor's veto, and second the unwritten precept of the first Lord Baltimore that theological bickering was to be prohibited. This later precept became a part of the common law of Maryland. Within the first decade of Maryland's founding, the courts of Maryland had established it. There was in Maryland a Catholic named Lewis who happened to overhear a Protestant hour of worship echoing through an open window. It was not a Protestant minister's voice, for there was no Protestant minister in the colony, but the Protestant laymen were reading aloud some minister's quite impassioned sermon. Lewis, listening to the reading, heard the Pope and the Jesuits being reviled again, and losing his temper he shouted out that the author of such stuff was an instrument of the Devil. For this offense he was tried and by Catholic judges was convicted and forced to pay a fine of 500 pounds of tobacco. It was not a question of the truth or falsity of his words: he had "disturbed the peace by unreasonable disputation." The Catholics of Maryland acted with extraordinary discretion. They were not half-hearted in their faith. They called manfully and openly Maryland's first little capital city St. Mary's, but they made no attempt to give Catholics special privileges. The priests of the colony received no public funds, no public recognition. They supported themselves as private owners of farms. Their chapels even were private, and were on private property though the Catholics used them as parish churches.

So discreet and neighborly were the Catholics of Maryland that it would have seemed that they were due to receive the neighborliness of all. And such was the case with the Protestants who had to associate with them in Maryland. But with outsiders it was different. During the Civil Wars in England, between King and Parliament, Governor Berkeley of Virginia who sided with the King drove some Puritans who were of the

Parliament Party out of Virginia. Maryland in trustfulness offered them an asylum in her territory. There they were, in any ordinary sense, not ill treated, but they considered that a positive outrage was done them in making them take an oath "not to insult any other man's religion, not even the Roman Catholic one." They rose in rebellion, and soon the Marylanders, Protestant and Catholic, were ranged in battle against these difficult guests. According to the Puritan account the war cry of the Marylanders was: "Hey for St. Marie." Their answer was: "In the name of God fall on: God is our strength." The Puritans won the battle. The Marylanders, St. Mary's party, surrendered on promise of quarter, and found immediately that ten of their number were condemned to death, of whom four were executed. It seemed as if Our Lady's colony was to cease to be Our Lady's.

But a curious thing happened. Oliver Cromwell — of all people — bade the Puritans to put an end to their quarrelsomeness. He restored the colony to Lord Baltimore. Something of the original spirit of the colony continued.

The next menace came from another source. In 1689, King William III came to the throne of England, whereupon a Marylander called Coode complained to him that Maryland, infested with Catholics, had stood out against him in favor of James II whom he had dethroned. Coode had been once a Catholic, then had pretended to be a Protestant, but according to the Protestants his pretense was not good; he was an atheist. One thing sure, he was a troublemaker, and a clever one. Whether William III was deceived by him, or pretended to be deceived by him we do not know, but at any rate he saw to it that the charter of Maryland was abrogated. The province was taken from the Calverts, and it reverted to the Crown. In so doing it lost its privileges which the first Calvert had secured for it. Automatically the English National Church became established there, and all the inhabitants had to support it, except the Puritans and the Protestant nonconformists, who were exempted therefrom by special decree of the King. Legally now

the Catholics were, as they were in England, outlaws. They could have no civil rights, they could not practice the liberal professions, they could not attend Mass. Priests were forbidden them. If a Catholic taught school he was liable to a year's imprisonment. The Catholic who employed a Catholic teacher, even as a private tutor, had to pay thirty shillings for every day he had so employed him. If a Catholic sent his son to Europe the fine was 100 pounds.

All this was true legally. In reality there were enough Protestant Marylanders who liked the old ways of Maryland too well to let the laws be applied. They knew there were Jesuits still in Maryland — everyone knew it — but they chose not to notice them, or not to notice that they were Jesuits: they were neighbors that had long been there. Of course, the Catholics who were poor and unknown, who were indentured servants, who were newcomers, suffered great spiritual privations. They could not go, as the rich did, to Europe for the Sacrament of Confirmation. They could not possibly give their children anything but a Protestant education. They could enjoy no social life. Such did not exist. But for the old Maryland Catholic families, and for the rich and well-thought of, life was tolerable. The Carrolls, the richest of the Catholic families, did not hesitate to send their children to a Jesuit primary school and they were not fined. And they sent their sons regularly to St. Omer's in France to complete their education without giving a second thought to the penalty of 100 pounds.

Yet how long would this condition of affairs continue? In 1754 a double tax was levied on Catholics, even on the Carrolls, and the Carroll's grew restive. In 1760 while the war with France was going on, in the excitement of the moment, it was proposed in the Maryland Assembly to confiscate the lands of all Catholics. France was Catholic, therefore the Maryland Catholics were their allies. Such reasoning was nonsense, and the best Marylanders knew it, but the Catholics could not help seeing that they were dependent on the good-will of a political body over which they had no influence, into which they could not enter, and which like any other body could in times of weakness try to feel strong with fanaticism.

Contrary to what might have been expected and hoped by Catholics, the victory of England over France in the Seven Years' War, and the Peace of 1763, did not bring a lull in the rising tide of anti-Catholic feeling in Maryland, nor in the pressure exerted by other provinces on Maryland, that she join their utterly intolerant rank, that she conform to the anti-Catholic conformity. Three hundred Catholic Marylanders, seeing the lowering sky, moved off into Kentucky where on a frontier their Catholicism would not be watched. He who was then chief of the Carrolls, the father of Charles Carroll of Carrollton, negotiated with the King of Spain for the purchase of lands in Spanish Louisiana. He was ready in a sad readiness to move there, and was dissuaded from the move only by the tardiness of Spain's King and by the expostulations of his son.

In 1774 there came a climax to this anti-Catholic madness. It was England's Parliament that brought the climax by passing in that year the Quebec Act, which countenanced the toleration of Catholics and of Catholic priests both in Canada and in the region west of the Alleghanies. This move was dictated both by justice and by expediency. By the treaty of peace, eleven years before, England had bound herself to respect the religion of the French citizens in the New World whom she had taken over, and those regions were inhabited by French citizens who were Catholics. And how could she ever make them happy and contented under the English flag without some act of friendliness? And she needed to have them friendly, and with them the Indians. Nevertheless, the act was interpreted in the English colonies as a surrender to the Babylon of Catholic Rome, and the roar which arose along the Atlantic seaboard was like the breaking of a tidal wave which had for generations been rolling from a distant horizon. Ezra Stiles, President of Yale College, cried out that it established "Romish Religion and Idolatry" over two-thirds of English America. Samuel Adams demanded — merely I believe for the sake of oratory — that an investigation of Mas-

sachusetts towns be made to discover whether or not they were infested with "Popery" — and this at a time when fifty or sixty Catholics, cringing and helpless, were all that were in the province. A Philadelphian was equally alarmed! "We may live to see our churches converted into mass-houses and our lands plundered of tythes for the support of a Popish clergy. The Inquisition may erect her standard in Pennsylvania, and the city of Philadelphia may yet experience the carnage of St. Bartholomew's Day." All this sounds like hysteria, but in soberer terms the same consternation was expressed by the Continental Congress meeting then in Philadelphia. It addressed the people of Great Britain: "We think the Legislature of Great Britain is not authorized by the Constitution to establish a religion, fraught with sanguinary and impious tenets — ."

Sanguinary tenets! The Catholic Marylanders were holders of these sanguinary tenets. Their doom was sealed. The ship was sinking under the Marylanders. And yet the next instant the ship was safe. The colonies suddenly took up arms against their mother country, and it was as if the wind had changed, as if the change of wind had blown the sea smooth. And the Marylanders found the sky smiling on them. Their neighbors were saying to themselves, "We need Catholic help."

Washington needed the military help of the Catholic nations, France and Spain. Let the Continental troops at Boston give up their practice of burning the effigy of the Pope on Guy Fawkes' Day. Let the Abenakis of Maine be allowed a Catholic chaplain which they ask for in order that they may march to Cambridge.

And the Continental Congress realized the need they had for Maryland's aid. Maryland was in population far more Protestant than Catholic, yet Maryland's richest man and chief citizen was a Catholic — Charles Carroll of Carrollton. He was more than that: he was the richest man in all the colonies, and though not so forceful a personality as John Adams, or the great men of Virginia, he was probably the most urbane man in North America, for he had received an education in France, and also in England, having in that latter country studied law even though he knew that, as a Catholic, he could not practice it. Charles Carroll was in control of valuable iron works. He was also in control of Maryland's public opinion. He was already disposed, even eager, to join the colonists against England. In no way must he be offended. And he was not. He was in every way honored.

And then there was the question of Canada. Should Canada join whole-heartedly against them, then their northern frontier was in dire danger. Canada was composed of French Catholics who were not such fools as not to remember the Protestant fanaticism of the English colonists. So the most persuasive embassy possible was sent northward. It was composed of Samuel Chase of Maryland, an urbane man, not fanatic, and of Benjamin Franklin, even more urbane, and of Charles Carroll of Carrollton who was a Catholic. And finally to give the embassy a clerical look, there was added to it a secretary, a priest whom John Adams commended for his learning and personally chose: John Carroll, a cousin of Charles. The embassy failed, but it had its significance as a gesture.

This change of front might well have been laughed at by some. Benedict Arnold after he had turned traitor raged at it. It happened that shortly before his treason the members of the Continental Congress a fairly large number of them — had attended a Requiem Mass for the repose of the soul of Miralles, the envoy of the King of Spain to Washington's army, at St. Joseph's Church in Philadelphia. The attendance of course was an act of diplomatic courtesy, but even then it had little precedent. Arnold in order to justify his own betrayal of the colonies pointed to this betrayal by the members of the Congress of their Protestant allegiance. "Do you know that the eye that guides this pen," he wrote in 1780, "lately saw your mean and profligate Congress at Mass for the soul of a Roman Catholic in purgatory?"

Yet this change of face was more significant than merely to be laughed at. It was not mere opportunism. There was a spiritual awakening behind it. The sudden war with

its new circumstances and problems waked the colonial leaders out of an outgrown provincialism, and also presented the colonists with new leaders. These men were not playing the hypocrite. They could not help seeing that "Down with the Pope" could not serve as their battle cry against Protestant England, and they began to suspect that it was not their battle cry at all. Liberty had become their battle cry. They did not recognize their cry as a Catholic one. They were quite unaware that liberty with a large L was but a cutting from a plant in Catholic . theology. They considered it as something from ancient Greece or Rome. Yet in the name of Liberty how could they treat Catholics as helots?

The coming of the war saved the Marylanders from a persecution that might have annihilated them. The winning of the war had a further consequence; it made the Marylanders conspicuous, because of their tradition — never quite obliterated — of toleration. The builders of the new nation were quite aware that one of the great difficulties in regard to establishing concord and peace among the thirteen colonies was the fact that there were deep and genuine religious differences among those who inhabited those States. This was a day before religious indifferentism had set in. Two-thirds of the books in English North America were, the historians tell us, religious books, which can legitimately be classed as religious even though at least half of them were only negatively so, being attacks on the Catholic Church. Theology was taken very seriously. Maryland was the only colony where there was a long tradition of men keeping the peace even though they disagreed vehemently on matters of faith. She could not help being looked at.

At first those who looked at Maryland and looked at themselves decided that the matter must not be made a national matter at all. Every State except Pennsylvania had its established Church. Let each State continue to have the established Church it wanted. As the Federal constitution was first adopted it did not mention religion at all. But there always was a possibility that in some future time the National Government might become affiliated with some one of the sects. Some such sect might become the Federal Church. Although each sect would have been satisfied with such a solution provided that it was the sect that was so honored, mutual jealousy led them to prevent forever any such victory for any one of them. So the Maryland solution of the problem — Lord Baltimore's solution — was incorporated verbally into the constitution. It was not the Catholics who insisted on this. Of what importance were they alone? It was the Protestants. Yet it is significant that Maryland citizens were especially called upon to phrase Maryland's custom into our first amendment. Charles Carroll of Carrollton, now a Senator, was chairman of the committee appointed to draught the amendment. His cousin Daniel Carroll made in his favor the most important speech in the House of Representatives. The amendment was phrased: "Congress shall make no laws respecting an establishment of religion, or prohibiting free exercise thereof." It was passed. It entered our Constitution on the same wind that brought over the Ark and the Dove.

Maryland's way had become the way of the Federal Government. Such was the extraordinary turn-over that took place when our new nation saw itself not merely as a string of colonies dependent on England and threatened by France and Spain, but as a nation among nations; when it came to act as if it were of age, on a scene that was the world. And all this change had come about in fifteen years.

This marvel was matched by another marvel. In the very year in which George Washington became the first President, John Carroll, the priest whom John Adams had found to be a "Gentleman of learning and abilities" and whom he had sent as secretary on the diplomatic mission to Montreal, and whom Franklin on that mission had found to be a most kindly and considerate nurse — for Franklin at the age of seventy was camping out on his way to Canada like a school-boy and needed a nurse — was appointed Bishop of Baltimore, with the United States as his diocese.

The land which had so detested the name of bishop that even the English King had dared not send an Anglican bishop to its shores, had been by the curious train of events drawn to approve of such an appointment and invite it. Our young nation in its new pride was obsessed with the word independence. If she were to have Catholics in her midst they must have the privileges of other Catholics. They should have their own bishop, or even more important, they should not have to look to an English bishop, who living in England would have a shadow of English control over our land. Mr. John Carroll, as he was called, was not only a resident bishop, a new dignity to our country, but he was an American of Americans; his family name stood for American Independence. His cousin Charles had signed it to the Declaration. His Cousin Daniel had presented a large part of the land for the future city of Washington where the seat of that Independence should be established. It is true that the news of his appointment as bishop did not make a great noise everywhere in the colonies. Catholics were but one in every hundred of the population, and their general importance was much less than that proportion would indicate. They were not even thought about. There were no thoughts in which they could be thought about. They were like books that cannot be catalogued. But those who knew of it, men like John Adams, President Washington, Benjamin Franklin (who was on his death bed when the news came), were gratified. It was like the ratification of the permanent independence of their land.

Bishop-elect was the title which Mr. Carroll had gained in 1789. The next year he was consecrated. In order to find bishops to consecrate him he had to leave the United States, no bishop of any kind having ever set foot on what was then the United States, — Florida and New Mexico being still Spain's. — He went to Europe and was consecrated in England in the chapel of Lulworth Castle by an aged Benedictine, Bishop Walmesley. The chapel was dedicated to Our Lady and the day was the feast of her Assumption. "Mr. Carroll," as soon as he became Bishop

Carroll, adopted a seal for his diocese on which was pictured Our Lady surrounded by stars. Under her were St. Peter's keys.

One of the first people to congratulate him after his consecration was an Earl of Arundel, descendant of the Earl of Arundel who had planned to make the New England in the New World into the Catholic England which Old England for a time had ceased to be. Nothing like what he had planned had ever come to pass. The English across the water had not become a Catholic New England — most certainly not. Yet the Earl had some-thing on which to thank and congratulate the new bishop, for the bishop stood for the fruition of at least some of the prayers and the efforts of the Earl's ancestors. It was the remnant of Catholic England that had created Maryland. Our Lady had been able, through the English as through the French and the Spanish, to go her sovereign way. She had, through the handful of English who named their colony somewhat hiddenly after her, presented her particular charge and treasure, the Catholic priesthood, to a new nation which did not know what it was.

THEODORE MAYNARD

(1890–   )

THEODORE MAYNARD is a man of three continents. He was born in Madras November 3, 1890. His years in England anchored his love of beauty in the lovely English countryside and as an American he has done great things for Catholic letters on this continent. He was converted to Catholicism in 1913.

In England Maynard was a close friend of Chesterton and his circle. In America he has done much in helping to popularize the English authors of his time.

Maynard's university education was all acquired in the United States. He took his A.B. degree at Fordham, his M.A. at Marquette, and his Ph.D. at the Catholic University.

In his early years as a lecturer in the United States, Maynard produced several books of excellent poetry. Whether in the tight form of the sonnet or the less precise meters of the long lyric, Maynard reveals a competence rare among American Catholic poets. He paints in large or small strokes with equal facility and felicity. His best poems are well represented in *Poems,* which has a commendatory introduction by Chesterton.

Maynard is equally at home in the field of prose. In his essays, such as *Carven From The Laurel Tree,* Maynard demonstrates a humor and mastery of prose which have flowered in biographies of such well-known men as St. Vincent de Paul and De Soto.

His Autobiography, *The World I Saw,* is a charming introduction to the works of Maynard.

THE LAST KNIGHT*

I ride, I ride, with my memories of Avalon,
    The last of the hundred knights that were
        my peers,
With the jesting and the jousting and the
    glory of the tournaments,

The laughter of the ladies ringing in
    my ears.

But I have made an end of all my challenges;
    The gallant days have gone beyond
        recall —
Although I ride through the furthest bounds
    of Heathenesse,

*The above and following poems are from *Poems* by Theodore Maynard, Copyright, 1919, by J. B. Lippincott Co.

Silence and the sleep of death enwrap
  them all.

Why should they stir, when all the lords of
  Christendom,
  Save I, are sealed beneath the heavy stone?
Why should they shout from the turrets of
  their citadels
  At one old fool who rides the world alone?

Better, by God, were their ancient hate and
  arrogance —
  Our churches wrecked, and our fruitful
  fields laid bare;
The ambush and the sortie and the charges
  of our chivalry,
  The clangour of the battlefields that filled
  the air!

But now they have conquered. In a cold and
  and cruel quietness
  They hold their peace with a scorn too
  deep for scorn!
I ride, I ride — but this dotard of a paladin
  Can bring no answer to his angry horn.

Could I find a man with belief enough for
  blasphemy,
  I would love him well for his hatred of
  my creed.

But the minds of men are rotted with their
  tolerance,
  And doubt eats their wills like a hungry
  weed!

I ride, I ride — for until a paynim fight with
  me,
  My weary bones shall never find their
  grave.
Though rest be sweet I can never have a
  resting-place
  Until my sword is red with a stroke it gave.

Perhaps I shall find it — as a man finds
  fairyland —
  And see it glimmering as the fall of eve,
Perhaps a paynim knight will answer to my
  challenging,
  And men will die for the lie that they
  believe.

That would be something! For if I could but
  see again
  A faith, though false, — then the true
  would surely thrive,
And doubt give way to dogma, and truth
  come to be again
  Passionate and lovely in a soul alive!

ENCHANTMENT

Because my childhood only knew
  The burning sands and white,
Where cactus and palmyra grew
  In bright and bitter light —

That day the English cliffs were seen,
  With meadows cool and kind
All covered with the grass so green,
  Comes often to my mind.

A little Anglo-Indian boy
  The Dorset field I trod,
Beholding buttercups with joy
  And daisies meek like God.

I found, a little older grown,
  In Surrey woods of pine
A stranger thing to keep and own
  Than that young zest of mine.

A wind that smote me as I sat,
  With buffets strong and sharp,
When the wind of love awoke thereat
  To play my heart as a harp.

But yet those vales are not so dear,
  As where the gales are loud
And skies are iron and austere
  From Cirencester to Stroud.

Where little houses built of stone
In crowded hamlets stand,
Because they fear to stand alone
In that enchanted land.

My mind with pain and happiness,
In thinking on it, fills
Where the grave silence comes to bless
The everlasting hills.

REMEMBRANCE

Let not the world remember you,
By any greater thing or less,
Than that upon a reed I blew
A song to praise your loveliness!

Let not the world remember me
(If immortality should crown
A line of verse, when empery
In the vast waves of time goes down)

By any greater thing or less
Than one good song I made and sung
To praise your love and loveliness,
One evening when the world was young!

APOCALYPSE

*"And I saw a new heaven and a new earth;
for the first heaven and the first earth were
passed away." — Apoc. xxi, I.*

Shall summer woods where we have laughed
our fill;
Shall all your grass so good to walk upon;
Each field which we have loved, each little
hill
Be burnt like paper — as hath said Saint
John?

Then not alone they die! or God hath told
How all His plains of mingled fire and
glass,
His walls of hyacinth, His streets of gold,
His aureoles of jewelled light shall pass,

That He may make us nobler things than
these,
And in her royal robes of blazing red

Adorn His bride. Yea, with what mysteries
And might and mirth shall she be
diamonded!

And what new secrets shall our God disclose;
Or set what suns of burnished brass to
flare;
Or what empurpled blooms to oust the rose;
Or what strange grass to glow like angels'
hair!

What pinnacles of silver tracery,
What dizzy rampired towers shall God
devise
Of topaz, beryl and chalcedony
To make Heaven pleasant to His chil-
dren's eyes!

And in what cataclysms of flame and foam
Shall the first Heaven sink — as red as
sin —
When God hath cast aside His ancient home
As far too mean to house His children in!

THE WORLD'S MISER

I

A miser with an eager face
Sees that each roseleaf is in place.

He keeps beneath strong bolts and bars
The piercing beauty of the stars.

The colours of the dying day
He hoards as treasure — well He may! —

And saves with care (lest they be lost)
The dainty diagrams of frost.

He counts the hairs of every head,
And grieves to see a sparrow dead.

II

Among the yellow primroses
He holds His summer palaces,

And sets the grass about them all
To guard them as His spearmen small.

He fixes on each wayside stone
A mark to shew it as His own,

And knows when raindrops fall through air
Whether each single one be there,

That gathered into ponds and brooks
They may become His picture-books,

To shew in every spot and place
The living glory of His face.

TO A BAD ATHEIST

*Who wrote what he called a trinity of meek
retorts to the preceding poem, which were not
meek, but full of pride and abominable heresy.*

You do not love the shadows on the wall,
Or mists that flee before a blowing wind,
Or Gothic forests, or light aspen leaves,
Or skies that melt into a dreamy sea.
In the hot, glaring noontide of your mind
(I have your word for it) there is no room
For anything save sawdust, sun and sand.

No monkish flourishes will do for you;
Your life must be set down in black and
    white.
The quiet half-light of the abbey close,
The cunning carvings of a chantry tomb,
The leaden windows pricked with golden
    saints —

All these are nothing to your ragtime soul!
Yet, since you are a solemn little chap,
In spite of all your blasphemy and booze,
That dreadful sword of satire which you
    shake
Hurts no hide but your own, — you cannot
    use
A weapon which is bigger than yourself.

Yet some there were who rode all clad in
    mail, —
With crosses blazoned on their mighty
    shields,
Roland who blew his horn against the Moor,
Richard who charged for Christ at Ascalon,
Louis a pilgrim with his chivalry,
And Blessed Jeanne who saved the crown
    of France —
Pah! you may keep your whining Superman!

THE RETURN

Beyond these hills where sinks the sun in
    amber,
  Imperial in purple, gold and blood,
I keep the garden walks where roses clamber,
  Set in still rows with shrub and flower
    and bud.

After the clash of all the swords that sunder,
  After the headstrong pride of youth that
    fails,
After the shattered heavens and the thunder
  Remain the summer woods and
    nightingales!

So when the fever has died down that urges
  My lips to utterance of whirling words,
Which, blown among the winds and stormy
    surges,
  Skim the wild sea-waves like the wild
    sea-birds.

So when has ceased the tumult and the riot,
  A man may rest his soul a little space,
And seek your solitary eyes in quiet,
  And all the gracious calmness of your face.

Chapter XVI

THE FATHER OF WATERS*

THE next day, upon which De Soto was
    hoping to see the chief, a large company
of Indians came, fully armed and in war-
paint, with the purpose of attacking the
Christians. But when they saw that the
Governor had drawn up his army in line
of battle, they remained at cross-bowshot
away for half an hour, discussing the situation. They did not like the look of the men
in iron and on horseback.

Then six chiefs came forward saying that
they only wished to find out who this strange
breed of men were, for they had a tradition
from their ancestors that they were to be
subdued by a white race. This may have
been nothing but an attempt to veil their
craft by flamboyant flattery. If they really
had such a tradition it offered another curious parallel with Peru.

The Governor, suspecting that they would
attack if he gave them the chance, felt it
necessary to act with caution. The chief,
whom he had particularly wished to meet,
had not come to see him; nor did he send

any message. The Spaniards saw as they
moved forward that this land was thickly
settled; therefore, capable of making a formidable resistance unless good feeling could
be established. De Soto wished above everything else to avoid fight. He had had enough
of it. The Indians were redoubtable warriors,
and always inflicted severe losses upon them.
Already more than a third of his men had
been killed, and a few had deserted. Every
casualty was now serious. For while they
had so far always defended themselves with
success — in the sense of beating off their
assailants — the time would inevitably come,
if conflict continued, when the army would
be so depleted as to be an easy prey for the
first hostile tribe encountered. He wished to
make friends with the Indians. As it seemed
difficult to do that, he advanced slowly, by
short stages, turning a little to the north to
avoid the natives, and to find a good approach to the Great River. They reached it
on May 21st, a Saturday.

There has been a good deal of discussion
as to the exact spot at which De Soto looked
first with astonished eyes upon that volume
of water. It has been often maintained — so
often that it has come to be generally ac-

*Maynard, Theodore, De Soto and The Conquistadores
(London: Longmans, Green and Co., 1930), pp. 228–
238.

cepted — that the place was the Fourth Chickasaw Bluff, at the present city of Memphis. But this has been questioned. Indeed a somewhat acrimonious controversy has raged between those who wish to retain the honor for Tennessee and those who claim it for the State of Mississippi. Without going into the matter here, in what would be tedious detail, it must be said that those who locate the discovery at a more southern spot seem to have distinctly the best of the argument.

What is infinitely more important than establishing — if it can be established — the exact location of the discovery is a vivid realization of the valor and hardihood of the pioneers who had persisted in advancing through the wilderness, in the face of furious opposition, and after having endured, within four months, the successive disasters of Mabilla and Chicaça. To the loyalty, fortitude and courage of the Spanish army admiration is due; but there are no words adequate to express what should be said of its commander, the brain, the heart, and the unfaltering will of the expedition.

In the halls of the Capitol there hangs a famous painting, familiar to all visitors to Washington, and often reproduced for the benefit of American school-children. It will be seen from what has been recorded in these pages that it is grossly unhistorical. And by putting De Soto and his men back into the finery with which they landed in Florida, a great injustice has been done them. Sentimentalism has once again killed romance.

The weather was indeed brilliant, but the Spanish Army presented a most bedraggled appearance. Their armor, rusty and dinted though it was, remained for the most part intact. But the gaily-sashed doublets of taffeta had long ago yielded to shreds of Indian fibre-blankets or the skins of wild animals, bald with wear. Many had not even so much as this, but wore habiliments somewhat similar to those assumed by Adam and Eve after the Fall, cloaks and aprons of pampas grass, Spanish moss, or ivy. Few of them had any horses; those that still remained were scrawny, poorly shod, and distempered.

The bloodhounds and the Irish greyhounds, savage from scarcity of food, were held in leashes baying hoarsely. The pigs, like the other animals and their masters, were thin; and they were young, for only the smallest porkers had been able to squeeze through the interstices of their sties in the last fire. These rooted where they could, or greedily snatched at offal. The white habits of the Dominicans and the black cassocks of the priests were lost or torn to tatters. They were as wild and matted of hair and beard as the others, barelegged, wearing buckskin drawers and, as the only sign of their holy office, the rude skin vestments painted with a cross in which they said their "Dry Mass." These they were perforce often obliged to use as their daily garments. Even to the Indians of the river the Spaniards must have seemed like savages.

These were the men who had discovered the Mississippi. Through the humid air they looked at the enormous mass of water, turbid, tawney, warm. It was a dirty giant, sprawling out here into the bayou and morass, revealing there little level islands of mud, choked elsewhere with cane-brakes. The swiftness of its current was shown by the uprooted trees carried along like broken twigs. Over its surface and from the swampy banks rose a thin white mist.

People who speak of De Soto to-day immediately, and rightly, at once connect his name with the finding of the Great River. To him it was a stupendous sight, which might be worth gazing at for ten minutes, but which was after all primarily only an obstacle to be crossed. The chroniclers all dismiss it in a line or two. Ranjel and Elvas both refer to it casually as being about a league away from a village in which they found some corn. They did not appreciate their own achievement.

De Soto was now confronted with the task of building boats. Had the Indians been friendly, the army could have crossed in canoes; but it was evidently difficult to conciliate these savages. The Spaniards therefore picked out a spot suitable for their purpose. It was a low-lying patch of land by the side of the water, under a bluff upon which cross-bowmen could be posted to protect the carpenters while they were at work. The locality was well wooded, and timber was cut for the construction of the barges and to make houses for the men.

The local chief, a very exalted personage long awaited by the Governor, at last arrived. He came with about two hundred large war canoes, that held in all about seven thousand men. The canoes were made from trees hollowed out with fire, in much the same way as those already seen at Cutifachiqui.

The Indians were all observed to be tall, well-built warriors, painted with ochre, and with their heads adorned with colored plumes. In their hands they bore shields made of interwoven canes and decorated with feathers. They were so tough that a cross-bow quarrel could hardly pierce them. At the stern of the largest of the canoes, in which the high chief sat, was an awning. This brilliant flotilla, "like a famous armada of galleys," was in strong contrast to the wasted and miserable appearance of the Christians.

But though the chief indulged in the customary Indian eloquence, protesting that it was his intention to serve the Governor, who he had heard was one of the most powerful men upon earth, he declined to land — very possibly because he had heard other things about him. He sent, however, three canoes to the shore full of presents of fish and loaves made of pressed prunes.

Some gesture was made, unfortunately, that revealed, or seemed to reveal, to the Spaniards, that all this was by way of a ruse. For the cross-bowmen, who had been posted in readiness, and were watching every movement of the savages, began to fire. Elvas records the perfect discipline with which the Indians retired, not a man leaving the paddle, though the one next to him was struck down by one of the Spanish bolts. Every day afterwards, promptly at the same hour, three o'clock in the afternoon, they would come up in their "famous armada of galleys," and pay their respects to the Christians by shooting at them from long range. But they never dared to come close enough to do much damage.

After a month of laborious and harassed work, under blazing skies and enervating humidity, four large barges were completed; and on Tuesday, June 18th, the crossing of the Mississippi was effected. Three hours before daybreak — the hour was chosen in order to get the operation finished before the Indians came to contest the passage — they tied the barges one behind the other, putting four picked cavaliers and some cross-bowmen in the hinder three, and the rowers all in the leading vessel of the train.

The strong currents of the river made it impossible for them to cross directly to the opposite shore; and they landed so far down that the Spaniards standing on the bluff could hardly make out at that distance whether they were human beings or not. In this way all the men were carried over, and everything had been accomplished by noon. Having landed without mishap on firm ground they "gave thanks to God that nothing more difficult could confront them."

They were vastly mistaken. It was well for them that De Soto had the foresight to have the barges knocked to pieces on the western shore in order to keep the nails and the bolts for another emergency. They were needed.

Two weeks later, after having passed through the abandoned villages of the Aquixo territory, and crossing again the swamps that reminded them of Florida — for all that day they had to wade waist-deep in water — they reached land, high, dry and level. It was near the St. Francis river. Walnut and mulberry trees abounded there, and the fields were well cultivated. The villages were so thickly set that from a slight eminence a man might see two or three of them at once.

After a two days' march through this country De Soto reached the settlement that was the headquarters of Casqui, the chief of the district. He received the Governor well and made him a fine — though somewhat quaint — speech. "Very high, powerful, and renowned Master, I greet your coming. As soon as I had notice of you, your power and perfections, although you entered my territory capturing and killing the dwellers upon it, who are my vassals, I determined to conform my wishes to your will, and hold right all that you do, believing that it should be so for a good reason, providing against some future event, to you perceptible but from me concealed; since an evil may well be permitted to avoid another greater, that good can arise, which I trust will be so; for from so excellent a prince, no bad motive is to be suspected."

From which it may be seen that Casqui was something of a philosopher as well as a discreet politician. He added to his eloquent words presents of skins, shawls and fish. The villages along the way had done the same thing, for the Indians had recognized in the Spaniards "men from heaven, whom their arrows could not harm."

De Soto, however, knew too much about the wiles of the Indians to relax his vigilance. He refused to take up his quarters in the village, thinking it safer — after Chicaça — to encamp in a grove of trees, a quarter of a league away.

There the inhabitants would come to entertain him with their songs, and to show their reverence by prostrating themselves on the ground before him. And one day the chief arrived with some blind men whom he asked the Governor to cure. Was he not the Child of the Sun? A trifle of this sort would be nothing to him. Would he not leave them a sign, since he had to go away, from which they might derive support in their wars, and upon which the people might call when they needed rain? The chief had been observing the Spanish crucifixes.

The Governor had no objection to Casqui's notion of his divine origin; but he was scandalized at the suggestion that he possessed the power of working miracles. However, he would give them the sign that they needed; and so had a tall cross constructed from the tallest pine procurable. This, he told them, was what they had to adore.

Standing beside it, De Soto remembered his missionary obligations. He had never actually forgotten them, but the business of conquest had given him few opportunities for attempting the conversion of the heathen. The army had moved rapidly from place to place; and had generally had too much fighting to do. But now he preached a sermon to the natives, saying that there was One who could make their blind whole. "This was He who had created the sky and the earth and man in His own image. Upon the tree of the cross He had suffered to save the human race, and had risen from the grave on the third day — what of man there was in Him dying; what of deity being immortal — and, having ascended into heaven, was there with open arms to receive all that would be converted to Him." Really, none of the friars could have put it better! And it carried more weight with the Indians coming from the redoubtable Governor's own lips.

De Soto and his men knelt before the rough cross, telling the natives that Christians venerated it in memory of that other cross upon which Christ had died. And Casqui and his people imitated the example of the Spaniards. "Their faith" says Ranjel, "would have surpassed that of the conquerors if they had been taught"; and, adds Oviedo tartly, "would have brought forth more fruit than those conquerors did."

They left Casqui's village on Sunday, the 26th of June. On the same day, far off in Peru, there was given by Francisco Pizarro, a signal example of Christian faith and devotion, *Conquistador* style. Young Almagro, the friend of the old Marshall executed by Hernando Pizarro, and his friends forced their way into the house of the man they most hated, shouting "Where is the Marquis? Death to the tyrant!" There was a scuffle in the passage in which several men on both sides were slain, and Pizarro, having no time to don his armor, fought with a cloak round his arm until a sword point caught him in the throat. Stretched upon the floor, he had just sufficient strength left to make the sign of the cross in his own blood. He dragged himself forward and kissed it; then with the name of Jesus upon his lips the Lion of Peru died.

In this he was like his cousin, Cortes — strong in faith, though not always showing the conduct of a good Christian. The same thing may be said of the apostolic De Soto. After having preached to the heathen, he accepted from Casqui — who expressed a desire to unite his own blood to that of so illustrious a man — a daughter to be his wife. He did not think it necessary to carry his exposition of Christian doctrine far enough to explain that, already having one wife, a second was forbidden by his religion.

He did even worse. From Pacaha, the next chief whom he visited, he accepted two sisters, and in the sight of all men set up a harem. Elvas gives their names; Maconoche was one, Mochila the other. "They were symmetrical, tall and full: Maconoche bore a pleasant expression; in her manners and features appeared the lady; the other was robust."

Meanwhile Dona Isabella went up every day to a tower in the harbor in Havana to scan the horizon for her husband's sails.

WILLIAM THOMAS WALSH
(*1891–*   )

ON SEPTEMBER 11, 1891, William Thomas Walsh was born at Waterbury, Connecticut. He took his B.A. degree at Yale, 1913, and was employed in newspaper work until he became professor of English at Manhattanville College. Though most of his hours were given to study and research, he still spent much time with his beloved cello and his delightful family.

His first book, *Isabella of Spain* (1930), a splendid example of research and descriptive writing, marked him as an important author. This was admirably borne out with the publication of *Philip II* (1935), and *Teresa of Ávila* (1946).

Doctor Walsh's style is richly colorful but strong. His creative imagination is always at the service of his scholarship. His historical works are well documented.

Although his poetry is not of such high order as his prose works, it is sincere and beautiful.

PHILIP'S THIRD MARRIAGE (1560)*

THE year after his return to Spain was one of the happiest in Philip's life. The violent and wilful character of his father, revere him as he might, no longer overshadowed and suppressed him. He was no longer shackled, even at a distance, to an old and ailing wife whom he could only respect. England and Cecil seemed very far away. He was once more breathing the keen air of the Castilian hills where his very being had its roots. Here there was no stench of heresy. Here there were people he understood. Spain was still Catholic and free. He had laid its enemies low. At thirty-three he was one of the most powerful kings in the world. And he was soon to have a young wife whose portrait by Marco Sidonio hung in his bedroom, and seemed to promise a great deal.

The buoyancy and confidence he felt were reflected in his attitude toward the Cortes, which met at Toledo toward the end of 1559. Philip, with his usual fondness for play, went to the ancient capital on the Tagus on November fourth, incognito, with only five or six attendants, apparently to pick out his residence. Having decided on the Alcázar, he went off to hunt until the twentieth, when he made his formal entry.

When the Cortes met, he made a long and vigorous address, of which the Cabrera gives the substance. He reminded the delegates

*Walsh, William Thomas, *Philip II* (London and New York: Sheed and Ward, 1937), pp. 258–264.

that, although he was ruler also over Flanders and the estates of Italy and many others, "my love and estimation prefers you to all, and I have come to remedy the evils which have commenced here, so much in offense to God and to me. . . . Europe is now free from cares and from wars, and enjoys the general peace which I gave it by my arms, my treasures, and the glory of my victories, reducing the enemies of the Crown to the knowledge of their own perversity and my justice, power and fortune.

"Consider the religious disorders in Germany and other places, through the malice of the heretics, disobedient men and persecutors of the Roman Church, in whose obedience I live, as my predecessors did, and will until death. I have asked the Sovereign Pontiff for the reassembling of the Council of Trent, the reformation of the clergy and monasteries of Spain, that they may serve God with greater integrity, purity and perfection.

"As for what touches me alone, I have summoned you to see to it that you live as good Christians and good vassals of mine, for the better you are, the greater will be my excellence and glory. To this end it is necessary that, accommodating yourselves to the ways of Castile and of the time, you make laws that will reform what is evil and will strive after what is good, with penalties to command fear — oppress, no, for laws too rigorous destroy the republic as much as the crimes for whose remedies they are established. A few are enough, if they are enforced; otherwise they defeat their own purpose. . . . Do not rush to the correction of that which, if not corrected, will cost you no loss of reputation; and do not change old laws unless they are harmful; for thus, by your example, your descendants will give up your new ones when they become old. Let what you do be in accord with the law of God, suitable for good example and useful for good living, in accord with the natural law.

"Laws must be made for subjects, just as medicines are prescribed for the particular disease and complexion of the sick. They must not be obscure, for that opens the way to wrong interpretation.

"My royal patrimony has been impaired by sales and forced loans, continued from the King Don Fernando, my grandfather, through all the reign of the Emperor, my lord, whose charges, obligations and enemies I have inherited. Animated and guided by his example, I wish to fulfill the hopes His Caesarial Majesty gave the world that I would be a good prince, when he renounced his most noble estates to me. My victories will be much better, if they are not against Christians, and if my arms can be turned against the Turks and Moors who trouble these kingdoms, which they have put to so much expense by so many and such necessary wars." He concluded by asking them for money to build a fleet for the defense of his Mediterranean shores.

The King's words, "so grave and free," as Cabrera says, delighted the Castilians. "He seemed to them to speak like a sovereign lord revealing his greatness of soul. They thanked him and promised to serve him faithfully"; but it was not until June seventeenth, 1560, that they agreed to give him, during the next three years, the ordinary and extraordinary service of 1,200,000 ducats.

There was more than sentiment in this, for the Turkish threat to the freedom of the West had never been more acute than at that moment. One of the consequences of the war with Pope Paul IV was the scourging of the coasts of Italy in 1558 by a hundred Turkish galleys from Constantinople under the renegade Piali Pasha, the ruthless Barbary corsair Dragut Reis, and Sinan, the chivalrous Jew. They did this, Cabrera notes, "to please the French and at their request," and after unspeakable atrocities in Philip's kingdoms of Sicily and Naples, overran Minorca, attacked Nice and Villafranca, and finally, worst blow of all, took Tripoli from the Knights of Saint John. Malta was now the only remaining outpost in Spain's Mediterranean line of defense.

Immediately after the treaty of Cateau-Cambresis, Philip had promised the Grand Master of Saint John his aid in the recovery of Tripoli. He was determined, though the effort required was great and plunged him still further into debt, to keep his word. With the money voted by the Cortes he managed to have an armada of 100 sails ready for sea by the middle of November. In all there were fifty-four galleys and thirty ships under the command of his viceroy of Sicily, the Duke of Medina-Celi, seconded by young Juan Andrea Doria of Genoa, nephew of Philip's host of 1549. On board were 14,000 good fighting men, the majority of them Spaniards.

Besides giving money for this fleet, the Cortes of October passed a few laws concerning the Moriscos. These ostensible but not always sincere Christians were so numerous in the south and east that in any conflict against Islam they were found to be objects of suspicion, and sometimes a real danger, to the Spanish State. The Cortes forbade them to keep Negro slaves, and renewed the law of 1553, prohibiting them from carrying arms, save with a license from the Captain-General. Philip explained that this law was directed only against persons under suspicion, not to all, for he knew "that there were many noble persons who comported themselves as good Christians."

With the Cortes over and his fleet on the seas, Philip could now settle down to the peaceful routine that he loved: the life of a constitutional monarch. For the moment, Europe was comparatively at peace. It was a good time to strengthen his ties with France and England and the Empire, meanwhile co-operating with the new Pope for the peace and security of Italy and the speedy assembly of the General Council at Trent. He wished to put an end to certain abuses that had grown up in his absence and to continue the reforms, judicial and economic, that he had begun in 1551. Finally, he was about to undertake his third venture in matrimony.

The French marriage was extremely popular in Spain. The Castilians had had no Queen living among them since the death of Philip's first wife fourteen years before; they loved youth and beauty, both of which Elizabeth of Valois possessed. The fact that the match had been arranged to end the long feud between the two countries appealed enormously both to sentiment and to common sense. People were already calling her the Queen of Peace — *Isabel de la Paz* — and preparing to give her a royal welcome. There was a great flurry in Toledo when it became known that she had left Paris, where her mother was visiting the heretical Queen of Navarre. She crossed the Pyrenees with the Duke of Bourbon and other lords, spent Christmas at Pampeluna, and finally reached Roncevalles. There, on January fourth (1560) in the valley where an imaginative person could still hear the horn of the dying Roland echoing and re-echoing among the hallowed rocks, she was welcomed to Spain by the Cardinal of Burgos and the Duke of Infantado, who conducted her through Navarre with great splendor, followed by a long train of mules bearing her trousseau in boxes.

Philip meanwhile left Toledo. With the Princess Juana, Don Carlos, and many lords and cavaliers, amid the usual abundance of music and gorgeous color so dear to the Castilian heart, he rode west to meet her at Guadalajara. Arriving before she did, he waited for her at the sumptuous palace of the Duke of Infantado, one of the most splendid in Spain. The townspeople were almost beside themselves with joy and pride. They had even made an artificial hill at the entrance, and transplanted living oaks to fashion a little park for the bride. When at last she appeared, riding a white palfrey, weary no doubt after more than a month on rough wintry roads in all sorts of weather, they went forth to welcome her and to conduct her to the palace. Faithful to the prescriptions of Castilian court etiquette, the Princess Juana met her in the court and led her up to the great hall, where Don Felipe and Don Carlos were waiting.

Philip saw coming toward him a very slender but fairly tall girl with black hair, dark and lovely eyes, and skin so brown that it might almost be called swarthy — decidedly a southern, Italian type, a true daughter of the Medici. She moved as lightly and as gracefully as a bird. Everything about her suggested youth, joy and goodness. There was almost always a suggestion of a tender smile on her lips. She was not over eighteen.

When she came near Philip, she stopped and looked at him intently and searchingly. All the speeches that her mother and some of the Spanish grandees had taught her were forgotten. She could only stare at the blond majesty before her until, if we may believe the gossipy Brantôme, the King said, "What are you looking at? To see if I have any gray hairs?"

A different meeting, this, from that one at Winchester, when he had kissed Mary Tudor on the mouth by way of taking England by storm. This girl with her extremely slender waist was more to his liking. It seems probable that she had completely won his heart when they were married by the Cardinal of Burgos on February second.

After many feasts, and much lavish entertainment by the Duke of Infantado, one of the richest of the great family of Mendozas, the fair King and the dark Queen left the palace, followed by innumerable boxes full of apparel and gifts. They were attended by a cortege brilliant enough to startle the very sun as they now cantered, now walked their horses, over the sandy plains and snowy hills, and along the banks of the Henares, stopping only at Alcalá to send the Duke back to get some rest, for his efforts to please his sovereign seem to have exhausted him.

At last they came within sight of their capital, that antique city whose shaggy crest of a hundred towers and spires, zigzagging the crown of a rugged promontory, seemed almost pendant in air above the wide barren countryside. El Greco has well expressed the sense of mystery that brooded over Toledo. Never was any city more fought for, more dearly bought with human blood. Long before the Incarnation, the Romans stormed it and called it Toletum. The Visigoths sacked it, and ruled it for centuries. The Berbers wrested it from the Goths and rebuilt it after their own taste, imposing Moorish architecture upon the Roman and early Christian. The Crusaders of the eleventh century won it from the caliphs, to raise Gothic spires above the mosaics and Moorish arches and to change the mosques and synagogues into churches.

High on the peak of the hill the Alcázar stood like a dark and menacing sentinel above the houses that spread below in a great fan-shaped semi-circle, tier on tier, down the steep crooked streets to the ancient walls and the crooked Tagus, and the strong arches of the Roman bridge of Alcántara, where Ferdinand and Isabel had entered in triumph three-quarters of a century ago.

Just as the Catholic sovereigns had seen the northern gate open and dancing boys come forth to the sound of oriental music, so now Philip and Isabel saw filing from the gate and over the bridge into the vega eight companies of infantry, in bright colors, which shifted into squadron formation and began to skirmish. Then some cavalry appeared, half of the riders in Moorish array, half in Hungarian; to give pleasure to the Queen they executed various maneuvers and exchanged volleys of musketry. As the warriors filed back to the city and the Alcázar, beautiful damsels came forth to do the sword dance of the ancient Spaniards. Others did gypsy dances. Still others the Dance of the Twenty-Four *a la morisca,* with a tremendous accompaniment of bag-pipes, flutes and kettle-drums.

Now came the Justica, twenty-four gentlemen in green velvet, with passementeries of gold, and black velvet cloaks studded with jewels. These were followed by twenty-four ministers of the *Hermandad* with their green *pendon.* Next appeared one hundred and thirty-eight men from the Royal Mint, carrying their crimson banner embroidered with gold, together with the royal arms and the semblances of various coins. Forty others followed, dressed in scarlet, half of them wearing blue berets, surmounted by a *fleur de lis,* and bearing the azure standard of the hospital of *la Piedad.* "And they sang, with great *concierto,* well composed songs in praise of the Queen and of her most felicitous coming, and in their manner of singing imitated marvelously the birds, with much fidelity."

When the Queen arrived outside the *Puerta de Visagra* (Via Sagrada or Via Sacra, the Holy Way, at the north of the city), officials came forth in yellow suits with long gowns of azure trimmed with gold, to kiss her hand and to administer the oath that she would respect all their customs and privileges. This done, she advanced on her white hackney through the Holy Gate and its elaborate triumphal arch, under a canopy of brocade richly worked with her initial and her husband's: F. and I., Felipe and Isabel.

Viva la Reina! The crowd of townspeople, soldiers, beggars, merchants, workmen on holiday, Jews and Moors, and gypsies from Triana, shouted themselves hoarse, so fresh and exquisite she seemed. The accounts of her instant popularity are unanimous; but the chief chroniclers were so interested in setting down what all the various officials and entertainers wore that they neglected the far more important duty of telling posterity anything about the new Queen's costume.

But where is the King? He has slipped away, apparently, to disguise himself, and is going festively about the streets of the city with two or three of his friends, including Ruy Gómez no doubt, to enjoy better as a mere spectator the reception his people are giving his bride. Perhaps he is that student by the gate with his bonnet over his eyes. Perhaps he is peeping from the hood of what seems to be a Franciscan monk, a little farther along. At all events, he is somewhere in the noisy crowd, "seeing the beautiful and joyful entry, the decorations of the balconies and the streets, and the many costly and various liveries, all mingling in a flowery background like a tapestry of Flanders."

The Queen, attended by the Cardinal of Burgos, the Admiral of Castile, four dukes, (including Alba), a Neapolitan prince and sundry marqueses and counts, went slowly up the rough streets, under arch after arch made by the guilds of workmen. Two of the most notable ones were those of the Sword Cutlers and the Smiths, both "costly and curious, with eulogistic inscriptions in Latin, Greek and Castilian, and poetical and historical figures of good and proper significations." At the Gate of Forgiveness Isabel

dismounted; leaning on the arm of His Eminence of Burgos, she entered the Holy Church "to give thanks to God for her happiness."

The vast Cathedral, one of the most beautiful in Spain and well worth the two-and-a-half centuries of labor expended upon it, was illuminated with thousands of tapers.

After the ceremony, the royal cortege left the Church, and proceeded up the hill to the Alcázar, with its four towers thrust into the sky like the lances of the crusaders. In the plaza were statues of Hercules and other heroes, concealing fireworks, many and curious, that were set off as the Queen approached, to the huge delight of the people. And there, once more, were patient Lady Juana and squinting Don Carlos, with a throng of noble dames and grandees, to bid her welcome to Toledo. The crowd shouted outside, and the very hill seemed to become vocal with music, as the bride crossed the patio and passed among the corinthian columns of the arcade to be welcomed by her husband.

Feasts and balls, games, bull-fights and tournaments followed day after day for weeks. Philip himself entered the lists on foot, and jousted on horseback for the honor of his lady. Day and night the austere city resounded with music and laughter. One feast alone cost 100,000 ducats, or some millions of dollars in our money. Both King and people were so delighted with the Queen that the festivities might have gone on for months if royal persons had been gifted with immunity to disease. But Isabel presently became feverish, and then a rash appeared. She was immediately put to bed, where Philip, in spite of the warnings of the physicians that it might be smallpox, insisted upon attending her himself.

A swift courier having carried the news across the Pyrenees, Catherine de' Medici, still lingering near the border, was gravely alarmed, fearing at first that her daughter had been smitten with the foul and incurable "Italian disease" with which her grandfather Francis I had paid for his sins of venery and might have handed on to his children even unto the third and fourth generations. This apprehension of the Queen-Mother proved unfounded. Isabel's sickness was diagnosed as a light case of smallpox; and as she was careful to follow her mother's advice about using the whites of eggs, her soft dark skin remained unscarred. Catherine was greatly relieved, for she counted on her daughter's beauty to bring and keep Philip II within the sphere of her own political influence.

ISABELLA THE CRUSADER*

CHAPTER VII

ISABEL looked down from the Alcázar of Segovia on the frosty morning of December thirteenth upon a town full of people. Into the four gates of the stern city, built upon a cliff, were coming noblemen and commoners from all the countryside, with much flourishing of pennons, and much music of trumpets, flageolets, and kettle-drums, for no ceremony in Spain was complete without music.

There was a mighty shout as the gate of the castle opened, and Dona Isabel came forth on a white palfrey, with the Governor Cabrera on one side of her, and Archbishop Carrillo on the other. She was then twenty-three years old, a beautiful and stately figure, clad from head to foot in white brocade and ermine. Gems sparkled at her throat, at her bridle, at the arch of her foot; and her mount was caparisoned with cloth of gold. Slowly she advanced along the narrow stony street near the head of a gorgeous procession. Just in front of her on a great horse rode a herald, holding point upward the Castilian sword of justice, naked, menacingly bright in the sunlight, symbol that the young woman on the white jennet had the power of life and death over all who beheld her. After him went two pages, bearing on a pillow the gold crown of her ancestor, King Fernando the Saint. After the Princess came prelates and priests in chasubles worked in gold threads over purple silks, nobles in rich velours, glistening with gold chains and precious stones, councilmen of Segovia in ancient heraldic costumes, spearmen, cross-bowmen, men at arms, flag-bearers, musicians, a great rabble following.

"Viva la Reina! Castile for the Queen Lady Isabel!" cried the people.

Arriving at the plaza, she dismounted and ascended a high platform, draped with stuffs of rich colors, and seated herself on a throne, where, amid shouts and trumpet blasts, the great crown of her ancestors was placed on her light auburn hair. The bells of all the churches and convents of the city began to ring joyously, muskets and arquebusses were fired from the keep of the Alcázar, heavy lombards thundered from the city walls.

Isabel was a queen at last.

After all the nobles present had kissed her hand and sworn allegiance to her, she walked to the Cathedral, where she humbly prostrated herself before the high altar, giving thanks to God for bringing her safely through so many perils, and asking the grace to rule according to His will.

A few days later she learned that her husband was riding from the north as fast as horses could carry him. The news of Enrique's death and of his wife's coronation had reached him in Perpignan, where he had gone early in autumn to save his father from capture by his enemies. Having rescued the aged King, Fernando had commenced to restore order in Aragon in the way that he and Isabel agreed was necessary in those abnormal times. He had found the city of Saragossa in a state of anarchy, cowed and exploited by Ximenes Gordo, a rich Converso, who had taken command of the city troops and imposed his turbulent will on the people. The young Prince, on his arrival, invited the tyrant to visit him, and when Gordo came, had him seized and delivered to the

*Walsh, William Thomas, *Isabella the Crusader* (New York: Sheed and Ward, 1935), pp. 58–67.

ministrations of a priest and a hangman. The body was exposed in the market-place that noon.

When Fernando learned from a letter of Carrillo of his wife's coronation, he was indignant because the sword of justice had been carried before her. It was not customary in Aragon or in Castile to carry the sword before queens. In Aragon, too, there was a Salic law, excluding women from the throne. Fernando evidently thought, notwithstanding the terms of his marriage agreement with Isabel, that he would be the real King of Castile, after Enrique's death, and it was a great shock to him to find that the gentle lady he had married intended to take the burden of government into her own hands. Gossip, controversies, and intrigues among the nobles made the matter worse, and when Fernando arrived at Segovia, the court was divided into two factions, bitterly disputing the merits of husband and wife.

A reconciliation was effected, however, by the efforts of Don Pedro Gonzalez de Mendoza, Cardinal of Spain, representing the Queen, and Archbishop Carrillo, speaking for King Fernando. But it was Isabel herself who, with her tact and dignity, maneuvered her husband into a position where he could only acquiesce as gracefully as possible. According to her secretary, Pulgar, she spoke to him in these words:

"This subject, Senor, need never have been discussed, because where there is such union as by the grace of God exists between us, there can be no difference. Already, as my husband, you are King of Castile, and your commands have to be obeyed here; and these realms, please God, will remain after our days for your sons and mine. But since it has pleased these cavaliers to open up this discussion, perhaps it is just as well that any doubt they have be clarified, as the law of these our kingdoms provides. This, Senor, I say, because, as you perceive, it has not pleased God thus far to give us any heir but the Princess Dona Isabel, our daughter. And it could happen that after our days some one might come who, being descended from the royal house of Castile, might allege that

these realms belonged to him even by the collateral line, and not to your daughter the Princess, on account of her being a woman. . . . Hence you see well, Senor, what great embarrassments would ensue for our descendants. And . . . we ought to consider that, God willing, the Princess our daughter has to marry a foreign prince, to whom will belong the government of these realms, and who may desire to place in command of our fortresses and royal patrimony other people of his nation, who will not be Castilians; whence it may follow that the kingdom may pass into the hands of a foreign race. And that would be a great burden on our consciences, and a disservice to God, and a great loss to our successors and subjects. And it is well that this declaration be made now, to avoid any misunderstandings in the future."

Fernando evidently could think of no reply. "The King, knowing this to be true, was much pleased," says the chronicler, "and gave orders that nothing further be said on the subject."

Fernando had disappointed Isabel more than once since their marriage. She had suffered keenly on learning the truth about the forged dispensation his father had sent from Aragon. She was even more deeply wounded when she learned that he had an illegitimate child, born about the time of his marriage. Henceforth she was to know the torment of a jealousy for which Fernando only too often provided the occasion, for he had four children born out of wedlock. Nevertheless she continued to love him to the day of her death. Never again, with one notable exception, would they have any serious difference of opinion. Henceforth, in most public affairs, they were to act as one person, both signatures on all documents, both faces on all coins. "Even if necessity parted them, love held their wills in unison. . . . Many persons tried to divide them, but they were resolved not to disagree."

They could not afford to have differences if they wished to accomplish the gigantic task that awaited them. To bring order out of anarchy, to restore the prestige of the crown, to recover from robber barons the crown lands illegally granted by Enrique, to deflate the currency and restore prosperity to the farms and industries, to settle the Jewish problem, the Moorish problem, the Converso problem — this was a task that seemed impossible for a young woman and a young man with neither troops nor money. France and Portugal were their enemies. Castile was in a state of chaos.

The young Queen commenced her reign resolutely, however, by sweeping out of sight the worst of the parasites who had made her brother's court so infamous. She appointed able and trustworthy men to the chief offices: Mendoza, the Cardinal of Spain, as Chancellor; Count Haro as Constable of Castile; Fernando's uncle Fadrique as Admiral of Castile; Gutierre de Cárdenas as Treasurer and Bursar. She and Fernando began to have thieves and murderers executed right and left, until "the men and citizens and laborers and all the people in general who longed for peace were joyful, and gave thanks to God, because they had lived to see a time in which it pleased Him to have mercy on these kingdoms. . . . And the King and Queen, with this justice which they administered, gained the hearts of all in such a manner that the good had love for them, and the evil had fear."

The great barons who had looted the country under the weak Enrique were not willing, however, to lose their power without a struggle. The young Marqués of Villena threatened to proclaim Juana, La Beltraneja, Queen of Castile if Isabel did not grant him the Grand Mastership of the order of Santiago and several cities. Archbishop Carrillo, angered because Fernando had offered him certain lands different from those he had promised, left the court in a huff, and remained at his home at Alcalá de Henares, performing alchemistic experiments with a friend of his, Doctor Alarcon. And both the Archbishop and young Villena were said to be in correspondence with Alfonso V of Portugal.

Cardinal Mendoza, whose elevation to the Primacy and growing influence with Isabel and Fernando had aroused the jealousy of the old Archbishop, now rode to Alcalá, and attempted to conciliate the old warrior by offering to efface himself and to let Carrillo play the first part in a reform Cortes to be assembled at Segovia in the spring.

The Archbishop gave an evasive answer, which was somewhat too ceremonious to be reassuring. Mendoza, disappointed, returned to the young sovereigns to report that he feared something was brewing between Carrillo and Villena and Alfonso V of Portugal. To make matters worse, several miniature wars had broken out among the nobles. Three of them were quarreling over the Grand Mastership of Santiago. Two of them were conducting a war for the possession of Seville. Two others were fighting at Córdoba.

At this juncture Isabel and Fernando, then at Valladolid, received a letter from King Alfonso of Portugal, announcing that he was about to marry La Beltraneja, and, therefore, was entitled to call himself King of Castile and Leon. He added that many of the great Castilian nobles, including the Archbishop of Toledo, were ready to join him.

Isabel could not believe that her old friend Carrillo had gone over to her enemies. She had her secretary write a passionate letter of appeal to him. The Archbishop made no reply. People were saying all over Castile, "Whoever gets the Archbishop will win."

The Queen decided, in spite of the advice of her councillors, to ride to Alcalá and make a personal appeal to him. She sent Count Haro ahead to make arrangements for her visit.

Carrillo received the Count with gloomy courtesy, and was obviously moved by the nobleman's appeal to his generosity and his loyalty. However, his attitude changed after he had consulted certain friends, who may have been emissaries of Villena and of Portugal. He now declared that if Queen Isabel came in at one gate of Alcalá, he would go out the other. "I took her from the distaff and gave her a sceptre, and I will send her back to the distaff!" he said.

Haro rode back to Colmenar, where the Queen was in a church praying and waiting for his return.

She did not receive her envoy until Mass was over. When she heard his report, she turned pale, and put her hands to her hair, says Pulgar, as if to hold her wits together. Closing her eyes, she remained silent till she had regained control of herself. Then, looking up, she said, "My Lord Jesus Christ, in Your hands I place all my affairs, and I implore Your protection and aid!" and, mounting her horse, rode on toward Toledo.

There she learned that Alfonso V, with 20,000 men had crossed the border from Portugal into Estremadura on May 25, and marching to Plasencia, where his Castilian allies joined him, had publicly married La Beltraneja, and had had himself and his fifteen-year-old bride proclaimed King and Queen of Castile and Leon.

Fernando rode frantically through the north, seeking to raise an army. He had become unpopular in Castile, however, since his attempt to usurp the crown, and it was evident that any successful appeal to the country must come from Isabel herself. It appeared only too likely, however, that Alfonso would soon have both her and the kingdom in his power.

Queen Isabel, wearing a breastplate of steel over her plain brocade dress, pressed her lips silently together as she mounted her horse and took the road to the north.

TRIUMPH OF THE REFORM*

THE first sign of any turning in the tide of misery barely perceptible just after Christmas. On the morning of Saint John's day a postman stopped at the convent with a letter from Madrid containing the only good news Teresa had received in many a long week. Gracián and Mariano were to be freed. Thus she began the year 1579 with a ray of hope that was soon to be confirmed, on the vigil of the Feast of Saint Joseph, with a vision in which she saw her Patron and our Lady praying to Christ for the Discalced, and heard Him say that she would be freed from her "prison" in twenty days: that she should have recourse to Philip II, who would be a father to the Reform; and that her Order would continue, despite the joy of hell and many people of the world at its persecution, for at the very moment when the Nuncio ordered its destruction, God confirmed it.

All these prophecies came to pass. The Duke of Alba had already won over the Royal Council to the cause of the Reform. One of Teresa's most valorous champions at Court was the Count of Tendilla, who had threatened to let Gracián taste his poniard if he deserted her; in fact, it was another of this choleric nobleman's outbursts, this time to Sega, that led to the King's intercession. The Nuncio was so offended that he went to the Escorial and demanded an apology. Perhaps in doing so he cast some reflection upon Madre Teresa and her Discalced. King Philip who had been convinced of their sanctity since the Apostolic Visitor Fernández had told him of their way of life — Philip II, "who was always the father of truth and justice, and champion of reform and virtue," treated his visitor to one of his rare exhibitions of anger. There was such a terrible quality in the wrath of this patient self-disciplined man that when he gave the lie to Cardinal Espinosa, for example, that ecclesiastical politician went home heartbroken and died the next day. Now, in the same deadly tone he said to the Nuncio, "The Count owes you satisfaction, and I will see that he gives it, for no one in my kingdom is allowed to show disrespect to the representative of the Holy Father with impunity. But I am aware of the hostility of the Mitigated friars against the Reform, and this looks bad, for the Discalced lead austere lives of perfection. *See that you favor virtue, for people tell me you are no friend of the Discalced.*"

*Walsh, William Thomas, *Saint Teresa of Ávila* (Milwaukee: The Bruce Publishing Co., 1943), pp. 550–567.

The Count, at the King's command, wrote an apology to Monsignor Sega, who then, at the end of his patience, declared that he would be only too happy if His Majesty would appoint some persons in whom he had confidence to investigate the whole matter with him. Philip seized upon the suggestion and named four assessors: Don Luis Manrique, his almoner; Canon Villavicencio, an Augustinian court preacher, and two Dominican fathers, Fray Pedro Hernández and Fray Hernando del Castillo. These four, after some stormy sessions with the Nuncio, finally pointed out to him that he had formed his prejudiced opinion of the Discalced without reading all the evidence, and asked him to examine certain testimonials. Sega consented, and had the surprise of his life. A good and honest man at heart, though not of a judicial temperament, he saw at once that he had been misinformed, acknowledged the error, and set about making amends. On April 26 the assessors formally declared in favor of setting up a separate province for the Reform. On July 3 the Nuncio joined with them in petitioning the King to request this of the Pope. It was almost a foregone conclusion that an appeal from both the King and the Nuncio would find a favorable reception at Rome, and on June 22, 1580, Pope Gregory XIII issued the bulls making the reform permanent, and establishing it as a separate province in Spain.

This victory for La Madre, after so many years of conflict and suffering, was crowned by the assembling of the first legal Chapter General of the Reform at Alcalá on February 1, 1581. Gracián was elected Provincial, and the new province was established on March 3 by the Apostolic Commissary Juan de las Cuevas. Teresa went to great pains to see that the new Constitutions would be such as to protect and perpetuate the Reform. She read the Pope's brief for the first time Wednesday in Holy Week, 1581, at Palencia. Now at last, as she wrote Mother María de San José, she could say with Holy Simeon her *nunc dimittis:* let them not pray that her life be prolonged, for her work was done.

As one of many legacies to her sons, she wrote a memorandum of four things our Lord told her in prayer at the hermitage called Nazareth in the garden of San José de Ávila — four counsels whose observance would make the Reform flourish, and whose neglect would cause its failure:

1. There must be suitable superiors.
2. Have many houses, but few friars in each.
3. Have little to do with seculars, and this only for the good of their souls.
4. Teach rather with good works than with words.

With these celebrated *Avisos,* which were placed at the head of the *Constitutions,* Teresa committed the future of her Order to God. There was no longer any doubt that the Reform would survive. The Nuncio Sega, now that his eyes were open, did not stop at half measures, but appointed Father Angel de Salazar Vicar-General and Visitor of the Discalced, with instructions to show the nuns and friars every consideration. Fray Angel, being in ill health, made Gracián his deputy in Andalucía, while he himself "visited" in Castilla. One of his first acts was to give Madre Teresa permission to leave San José, in fact he ordered her to inspect several of her convents, commencing with the one at Malagón, where the illness and departure of Mother Brianda had left matters in a sorry state.

Teresa was not much pleased. She sent Fray Angel's letter of instructions to Gracián, asking him to tear it up afterwards, and remarking, "By this letter Your Paternity will see what has been arranged for the poor old hag. According to the indications (though it may be only a suspicion) it is more a matter of the desire of these my Calced brothers to see me far away from them than the necessity of Malagón. This has hurt me a little, I mean the rest of it, not the thing itself, the going to Malagón; though I should be sorry to go as prioress, for I am not up to it, and I am afraid of failing in the service of our Lord."

The "poor old hag" may have been wrong about the motives of Father Salazar. As if aware of this herself, she said in another letter, "Truly he is of such a very good disposition that he doesn't know how to say no." It was true that the convent at Malagón needed attention. Furthermore, the fame of La Madre was now such that many important people were asking her superiors for her companionship and spiritual help; among others the Bishop Don Álvaro de Mendoza, his sister Doña María, and the Duchess of Alba, grieving because her husband and son had been imprisoned by Philip II. It was Alba that Teresa had chiefly in mind when she left Ávila on June 25, 1579, for Malagón; and not the Duchess so much as a postulant, the daughter of a benefactor, the Lawyer Godoy, who seemed to be out of her mind, and used to scream at the top of her voice, pretending to be sick.

La Madre was not to see Alba, however, for more than three years. After a few days at Malagón, she proceeded to Valladolid, where she spent most of the month of July. Her correspondence of that time is full and various. We learn that Casilda's family are withholding her dowry, and begin to expect the inevitable. Father Gracián's sister, now a nun in the convent, is a "little saint." La Madre has met Fray Nicholas of Joseph-Mary Doria, and likes him very much, though he has not Gracián's charm and sweetness; however, he is talented, humble, and sincere, and will be a great help to her Paul, who has chosen him for his *socius* — Doria, who is to be his nemesis. She sends two of her books to the Bishop of Évora. The two friars have arrived in Italy. Brother Lorenzo should not worry about the pranks of his son Francisco; boys will be boys. She plans to stop at Alba on the way to Salamanca. There is not a word about the most sensational event of that year in Spain; the arrest, on July 28, on King Philip's orders and under his personal direction, of the Princess of Éboli and her paramour, Antonio Pérez.

Teresa arrived in Salamanca about the middle of August, 1579. She was there until the end of October, repairing the harm done by an inefficient prioress and seeking to liberate the nuns from the house of Pedro de la Banda. When she found another, the prospective sellers changed their minds. "There is no trusting these Sons of Adam." she lamented to Gracián, in a letter in which she also complained that he did not return her affection. No other place was to be found. If these sisters only had as good a house as the one in Sevilla! And yet Mother María de San José was dissatisfied, and had committed the blunder of telling the nuns at Sevilla that their home was unhealthy: that was enough to make them ill. Teresa then made some surprising criticisms of her former protégé. "She has lost much credit with me. I fear the devil has begun with that house, and that he wants to destroy it altogether. . . . I see the childishness of that house, and I can't endure it, and this Prioress is more clever than her estate calls for. And so I have been afraid . . . as I told her there, that she has never been frank with me. . . . I tell you I have put up with a great deal from her in that place. As she has written me several times with great repentance, I thought she had amended, since she acknowledged it. . . . I have written her terrible letters, and I might as well have been hitting an anvil." It was three o'clock in the morning when Teresa finished this letter, on the Feast of Saint Francis, 1579. A few days later she departed for Salamanca, for the last time.

November found her once more at San José de Ávila, but not for long. She had a stroke of *Perlesía,* and a heart attack; but before she had fairly recovered she was on the roads again, in a downpour of rain that continued for three days. After a brief stop at Toledo, she pressed on to Malagón, arriving there November 25. This time, though still so ill and aching that she was hardly able to get out of bed, she made certain reforms that she had postponed on her last visit. She found it hard to replace Mother Brianda, and the difficulty was increased by the interference of certain unidentified priests. Fray Antonio had caused much mischief by his visit the previous year.

The house at Malagón, looking out upon the noisiest street in the town, had always been unsatisfactory, and Doña Luisa de la Cerda had agreed to build another, which was to have been finished in the latter part of 1579. When Teresa arrived unexpectedly on Saint Catherine's day, November 25, she was planning to have the nuns move in at once, only to learn from the workmen that the building would not be ready for occupancy for six months.

She replied that she would give them thirteen days, for she intended to open the new convent on the Feast of the Immaculate Conception, December 8. Then, taking a broom and a basket, she went to work herself cleaning up debris; it was eleven o'clock at night before she stopped to read her office. At sixty-four she seemed as active as in the old days at San José or Medina. She gave orders like a sea captain, performed prodigies of labor, fell on her knees and asked pardon if her sharp tongue offended anyone. Perfect health seemed hers those busy days; it was not until all was done that her fever and pains returned. When the eve of our Lady's feast came, only eleven of the nuns' cells were ready, but it was enough to accommodate the community for the present, with some doubling up; and on the eighth, as she had planned, Teresa and the sisters went in procession to the new house, behind the splendor of the Blessed Sacrament.

She wrote an enthusiastic report of all this to Father Gracián. "The change was made with great rejoicing. . . . It made them very happy, and they seemed like nothing but little lizards coming out into the sun in the summertime. . . . Oh *mi Padre*, how necessary my coming here has been!" Sister Jerónima del Espíritu Santo (Acevedo), who was later to establish the mother house in Italy, was made prioress, and charged with rectifying the errors of poor Brianda. All seemed well. "God grant it may always be so," said Teresa.

Of all her convents this was her favorite. Here alone she was free to create, not merely to adapt. The two-story building of stone and cement was built around a central patio surrounded by a cloister, upon one of whose wings the confessionals still open, with their tiny screened windows designed by Teresa herself. The garden is large and beautiful, shaded by trees. The refectory is well lighted

and ventilated, and still contains the tables chosen by her; and adjoining this are the kitchen and laundry. The cell she occupied on the upper story is said to be just as she left it. This, as Padre Silverio says, is the ideal Teresian convent. It was a daily joy for her to see it assume its final shape, to find the life of prayer she planned for all her daughters made easier by the position of every window, every stairway, and every stone and stick. "How well I remember," she wrote Gracián, December 18, "what a letter from your Paternity made me suffer on Christmas Eve a year ago! God be praised that times are so much better." Yet there was no complete satisfaction in this life. She was learning more and more from the nuns of the laxity and disorder which prevailed under her cousin Sister Beatriz of Jesus, who had administered the convent for Mother Brianda. "She has never said a word to me, even now, though she sees that they all tell me about it and that I know it. I have decided that she has very little virtue or discretion."

When Mother María de San José took the part of the nuns at Malagón, Teresa reproved her vigorously. She hoped that God would make her a saint, "for wicked as you are, I wish I had several like you, for I wouldn't know what to do if a foundation were to be made now, for I don't find anyone fit to be prioress, though there ought to be; and since they are not experienced and I see what has happened here, I have felt great fear that the devil may trick us with good intentions into doing his work. And so it is needful to walk always in fear, and close to God, and trust little in our understandings; for, however good they may be, if this is not so, God will forsake us to go astray in the very thing we think we are most sure of. . . . Some of the things Your Reverence wrote me about astonished me. Where was your understanding? . . . O, God help me, the silly things that letter contained, all to get your own way! The Lord give us light, for without it there is no having strength or skill, except for evil. I am glad Your Reverence is so disillusioned, for it will help you in many things; for to improve, it is useful to have made mistakes, and so experience is gained. God keep you — I didn't think I could write so long a letter."

On the day after opening of the new house, her maladies all returned and she had another attack of *Perlesia*. At Christmas, however, her joy was such that all the nuns felt and shared it; and when, after making a slip in reading the lesson for the day, she prostrated herself on the floor of the choir, they were all dissolved in tears, and none could speak a word.

She left Malagón on February 13, 1580, to found a house at Villanueva de la Jara, in La Mancha of Toledo, where a priest had told her he had assembled in a hermitage nine holy women who wanted to adopt her rule and obedience. She was not much interested until our Lord told her to go; then she departed in such good health that it seemed as if she had never been ill in her life. As her cart rumbled through the frozen countryside, crowds gathered everywhere to see her, for her reputation was now secure, and the news of her coming had spread everywhere. In a house at Villarrobledo, where she stopped to eat, people broke through the windows and the walls to get a glimpse of her, until the police arrested a few. In another town she had to depart three hours before dawn to escape the crowd. She was asked to bless people, and in one place a herd of cattle. At the Discalced Monastery of *Nuestra Señora del Socorro,* all her friars came forth in procession to receive her, and after kneeling to ask her benediction, escorted her to the church, singing the *Te Deum.* This was the monastery that Catalina de Cardona had caused to be built in the midst of a desert, and though she had died in 1577, the fathers were still called "the Friars of the Good Woman," by the people round about, and many pilgrims visited the cave where she had lived, at the entrance of the Church. When Teresa received Communion there, she saw the hermit woman in her glorified body attended by angels, rejoicing, and heard her say that she must continue her foundations.

Teresa was clutching an image of the Child Jesus to her breast when she arrived at Villanueva, a short distance away, just before High Mass on the first Sunday of Lent, February 21, 1580. The whole population, headed by their clergy, assembled in procession to receive her and to follow the Blessed Sacrament with her to the new convent, where she gave the habit to nine women weeping with joy.

While she was superintending the digging of a well some days later, a workman dropped a windlass, which struck her with tremendous force and knocked her flat on the ground. She got up uninjured; everyone said that Saint Joseph — it was on the eve of his feast — had protected her, though afterwards a painful abcess resulted. But Teresa was well pleased with the new community at Villanueva, and well she might be, for under her rule the nine holy women led a heavenly existence, of which many miraculous details were reported and believed. Although food was very scarce following the sterile year 1579, and money was even scarcer, the nuns trusted in God so completely that they got along with six *fanegas* of wheat instead of the sixty they ordinarily required, and seemed none the worse for it; for like the widow of Elias, they found their wheat bin always full. Their one little pear tree bore enough fruit for two months to supply their needs, with plenty left over to sell and give to the poor. Money was mysteriously found lying about, especially when the nuns had recourse to the Niño that La Madre had carried in the procession. A broken pot would stay together whenever cooking was to be done, and then fall apart again. All the accepted laws of economics and even of nature seemed to yield before the love and trust of these simple souls.

Teresa was ill again when she left the hallowed place March 20, accompanied by Sister Beatriz of Jesus, Fray Antonio of Jesus, and a nurse. They arrived in Toledo on Saturday in Passion Week, March 25. On Maundy Thursday she had another stroke of *Perlesia,* which left her prostrate for a month. She still had a fever and was very weak when she went with Father Gracián to see Archbishop Quiroga, the Inquisitor General. The Holy Office was examining her autobiography again, but the Archbishop assured her there was nothing to worry about. Several copies of the famous book had been read and approved by various personages of deeper spiritual discernment than the Princess of Éboli. The Duke of Alba, for example, was reading it in his prison at Ubeda. Teresa had a profound influence on this great soldier and opportunist statesman. He took with him on his last campaign (the conquest of Portugal, for which the King released him) a picture of Christ that she had given him; and he used to say later that by looking at it he was able to practice mental prayer even in the confusion of war.

When Teresa left Toledo June 7, she was attended by a nurse who was to be her companion for the remainder of her days and to leave some of the most interesting data concerning her. This was the kind and gracious Ana de San Bartolomé whom we now call Blessed. Born Ana García, the child of poor village laborers, she had entered San José de Ávila as the first lay sister in 1572. Now twenty-eight years old, with little or no formal education, she had so good a mind and such sound judgment that she became Teresa's confidential secretary as well as nurse, learning to write miraculously by merely copying La Madre's letters. It was she who dressed the old lady in the darkness before dawn, and helped her off with her tunic in the small hours of the next morning; she who wrote out most of the last energetic letters; she who went foraging for an egg or two or a piece of bread as they passed through villages impoverished by famine and drought.

From Villanueva they went to Medina, where Sister Ana de la Trinidad was cured of a violent erisipelas by the caressing touch of Teresa's hand on her swollen face; then to Valladolid, and thence to Segovia, stopping on the way in inns which were hot and stifling even at night.

At Segovia, where she stayed from about June 13 to July 8, La Madre had the great sorrow of learning of her brother's death. Lorenzo's health had been failing gradually since his return from America in 1575.

Generous to a fault, he found himself hard pressed at times for money, and constantly bedeviled by his younger brother Pedro de Ahumada, who had followed him back from the Indies, a penniless wreck of a man, a hopeless neurotic who, on being denied a pension by Philip II, became so embittered that he went about grumbling at everything and everybody. Teresa thought he was insane in his attachment to Lorenzo. She sent the latter long letters begging him have patience with their unfortunate brother, who could not help his infirmity, and to give him money in installments, instead of the lump sum that Pedro had let slip through his hands in 1580. This was the state of affairs when Lorenzo became acutely ill on June 26, 1580. His heart had been weakened by the high altitudes in the Andes, and it probably did him no good to live so near Ávila, which is half a mile above sea level. In six hours he was dead, of what would probably now be called coronary thrombosis. Teresa, many miles away, turned pale at that moment, and told the nuns at Segovia that she had seen him die, and pass through purgatory into heaven. A few days later she saw him with Saint Joseph, both very radiant, beside the priest at Mass.

Many of her friends died in 1580, the terrible year of the *catarro universal,* a virulent form of influenza. The Holy Cavalier, Father Francis de Salcedo, was one of them. Philip II might have died in Portugal if his young fourth wife had not knelt by his bedside and offered her life in place of his, so necessary to Spain and to the Church; and God took her at her word.

The death of Father Baltasar Alvarez occurred at Belmonte a month after Lorenzo's, on July 25, 1580. Since 1574 he had been rector at Salamanca and visitor for the Jesuit houses in Aragon. His last years were saddened by suspicions of certain other Jesuits that his high state of contemplation, in which he had followed the lead of Teresa, was a delusion of the devil. There was talk of sending him to Peru in 1579, but nothing came of it. Although his death grieved Teresa, she saw him in glory and splendor, and wrote, "I rejoice that he has left this life of misery and is now in safety. Life passes so quickly that we ought to think more of how to die than how to live. . . . I am four years older than my brother, yet I never manage to die."

Lorenzo having named her his executrix, Fray Angel de Salazar gave her permission to go to Ávila to look after the interests of her nephew Francisco. (The younger son, Lorenzo, had returned to Peru in 1578.) After a brief stay there, she took the young heir to Valladolid by way of Medina, for the signing of some papers concerning his father's estate. Gracián went with her to help with the business matters, which were very distasteful to her.

Soon after their arrival in August, Teresa was stricken by the epidemic *catarro*. She was so ill that the nuns at Valladolid felt sure she was going to die. Heretofore, although she had passed her sixty-fifth year, she had always retained an appearance of the bloom of youth; illnesses, fasts, vigils, scourgings, and incredible labors had left her cheek unwrinkled and her black eyes youthful. Now, as she slowly mended, María Bautista and the nuns noticed for the first time that she looked like an old woman.

During the long slow convalescence that kept her in Valladolid until after Christmas, 1580, she had many anxieties. Some relatives were beginning to grumble about a bequest Lorenzo had made for a chapel at San José de Ávila, to be paid for out of the money still owing to him from the convent at Sevilla. "Oh my daughters, what weariness and contention these temporal possessions bring with them!" she wrote to the nuns at Ávila, October 7. Lorenzo's son Francisco was one of her chief worries. At first he seemed to have a vocation, and Gracián took him to Pastrana. But the young man left in a month, finding the life far too strenuous. Teresa wrote Gracián that he seemed to have been transformed into a different creature. He would have nothing to do with any Discalced friars or nuns, least of all with her. He intended to marry, and take care of the property his father had left him. His digestion was ruined, he had headaches, and something was wrong with his heart. Happily

these afflictions were but temporary, for only three months after he left the monastery, he married a lovely girl of fourteen, Doña Orofrisia de Mendoza y de Castilla. La Madre was delighted with this match. Her letter to her nephew in Peru, informing him of his brother's good fortune, is very Spanish, very bourgeois, and very feminine:

"Her mother is first cousin of the Duke of Albuquerque, niece of the Duke of Infantazgo, and other very important titled people. In short, as for father and mother, they say there are none better in Spain. In Ávila she is related to the Marqués de la Navas, and to him of Velada, and very much to the wife of Don Luis, the one descended from Mosén Rubí. They gave her four thousand ducats. He writes me that he is very happy, which is the main thing. I am told that Doña Beatriz, her mother, is of such worth and discretion that she will be able to manage them both, and that it will be arranged, from what they say, that it won't cost much. Doña Orofrisia has only one brother, heir of an entailed estate, and a sister is a nun. If the heir has no son, he will inherit it. A thing that may possibly be."

Before the end of 1580 Teresa had made up her mind to found two more convents. She desired three, in fact, but the one at Madrid had to wait upon the return of Philip II from Portugal, and he was there until 1583. Burgos and Palencia, however, were within the bounds of possibility. "More than six years ago," she wrote, "some very religious persons of the Company of Jesus, old men and learned and spiritual, told me that our Lady would be much served if a house of this sacred Order were established in Burgos, giving me certain reasons for it that moved me to desire it." The suggestion for Palencia had come from her old friend Don Álvaro de Mendoza, who was now bishop of that place. When she hesitated during her convalescence, expecting to die, Father Ripalda, S.J., told her that old age was making her cowardly. "I saw plainly that that was not true," she said, "for now I am older and I am not cowardly." When our Lord said, "What are you afraid of? When have I ever failed you?" she resolved to essay both foundations, commencing with Palencia.

She was pleased when this foundation was made on the Feast of King David, to whom she had great devotion (because,. she explained, he, too, was a sinner!). It was fitting, too, that the advance preparations should have been made by a holy priest of Jewish descent, the Canon Francisco Reinoso, nephew of Father Jerónimo Reinoso, friend of Saint Pius V and afterward bishop of Córdoba. He had already rented and prepared a house, and unlike Fray Mariano in Sevilla, had even the beds made up and all necessities on hand on the cold foggy twenty-ninth of December when six tired nuns and the lay sister Ana arrived. Everyone was happy, for there was no opposition anywhere, the Bishop was greatly loved, and "the population," added Teresa, "is the best and noblest I have seen."

Since the house was only rented, it was necessary later to find another. She was offered two adjoining the famous hermitage called the Church of Our Lady of the Street, in the most populous part of the town. This she disliked so much that Canon Reinoso found her one that seemed far more attractive, although the owner asked a stiff price, and she agreed to take it. Next day at Mass she began to feel uneasy. As a thought of the humble house near *Nuestra Señora de la Calle* came to her mind, she heard the voice of our Lord saying in reference to it, "This is the one for thee." She went to confession to Father Reinoso, "a most prudent and saintly man, and endowed with the gift of good counsel in everything," who naturally was somewhat perplexed. While he and his friend Canon Salinas were hesitating, Christ said to her, "They don't understand how much I am offended there, and this will be a reparation." At this juncture, the owner of the house she had agreed to take raised his price by 300 ducats, thus giving her the right to withdraw. She then took the house next to the hermitage. Afterwards she wondered why she had not preferred it from the start. She learned, too, that its dark and lonely rooms had been used by men and women as an all-night rendezvous. The Carmelites put an end to that scandal when they took possession on the Feast of Corpus Christi, in the presence of most of the townspeople. Gracián traveled all night to be present.

It was at Palencia that Teresa first heard that Pope Gregory XIII had decreed the permanence of her Reform by setting up a separate province for the Discalced. The future of the Order being now assured, the friars resumed their foundations. John of the Cross had already made one at Baeza; Valladolid, Valencia, and Salamanca soon followed. *"Nunc dimittis!"* she could well say with a full and grateful heart, *"nunc dimittis."* A sister who entered her cell unnoticed saw her write in complete absorption, and sigh profoundly as she laid down her pen; and was frightened when there came from her mouth rays of something like the splendor of sunlight.

Having had an unexpected offer of a house and its upkeep from a widow in Soria, Teresa left Palencia for that place at the beginning of June, 1581, but not without regrets. She had found the people of Sevilla cold and unfeeling. Toledo was ugly and barren of taste. But Palencia — "I don't want to omit saying many praises of the charity I found in Palencia, in particular and in general. Truly it seemed to me like something of the primitive church, at least not very often found nowadays in the world, to see that we were not getting an income, and that they would have to give us our food, and not only not forbidding it, but saying that God was doing them the very greatest favor. And if it be examined with light, they spoke truth; for even if it was no more than to have another church where the Most Blessed Sacrament was multiplied, it was much." No other city ever drew such a tribute from her.

She went to Soria with Father Doria (Gracián was busy founding a college at Valladolid) and seven nuns. The house being well equipped, they made the fifteenth foundation without difficulty, calling it the Monastery of the Most Blessed Trinity. The first Mass was said on the Feast of the Prophet Eliseus, June 14, 1581, and the first sermon preached on the Feast of the Transfiguration by Father Francisco de la Garrera, S.J.

At Soria that summer La Madre had her last conversation with Father Francisco de Ribera, S.J., who was to be her first and one of her best biographers. And on the day after she left the place, she had a strange encounter, at dusk, in a little town of Burgo de Osma, with the Jeronymite Father Yepes, her second biographer, whom she delicately warned of a great penance he would have to endure. The following day she pressed on toward Ávila. The roads were uncommonly bad, and the muleteer incompetent, so that the nuns had often to get out and walk past a dangerous cliff or a defile, and barely escaped being dumped into the mud and over a precipice. When they reached Segovia on Saint Bartholomew's Eve, August 23, 1581, Teresa was in such a state that the sisters prevailed on her to stay and rest for eight days before resuming the journey.

It was a sad situation that confronted her when she finally arrived at San José, September 5; the first fruit of her sacrifice and prayer now relaxed and undisciplined, the nuns discontented and half starved, the debts piling up, the buildings unrepaired. At the bottom of the physical misery there was, as always, a spiritual negligence. She was not long in tracing this to Father Julian of Ávila, who, in his dotage, had become what she feared most, an overindulgent and over-friendly confessor. He had dispensed the nuns from this rule and that rule until the Constitutions seemed hardly in force, and God, being no longer well served, had stopped providing.

The nuns were so glad to see their Madre that they elected her prioress, saying there was never any lack of food where she presided. This confidence was not in vain. As soon as Teresa had restored the harmony of discipline and prayer, during the autumn of 1581, the rest seemed to take care of itself; God fed them as He fed the birds of the air.

"I am astonished at what the devil can do," she reported to Gracián, "and almost all the blame belongs to the confessor, though he is such a good man; but he has allowed them all to eat meat, and this was one of the petitions they made. What a life!"

The affable old chaplain did not enjoy the reforming process.

"How, peevish Julian goes about these days. One can't growl at la Mariana every time she wants to see him. . . . It is all holy, but God deliver me from confessors of many years. We shall be lucky if we succeed in rooting this up. What would happen if they were not such good souls! After I had written this, certain things happened here with one nun that displeased me very much, and so I have mentioned it, and I didn't mean to speak of it. . . . The remedy . . . will be to send the two away from here; for although it is holy, it cannot be tolerated. . . ."

Teresa's health was better that fall, but she was never without some suffering. In September she had the grief of hearing that Casilda had left the convent at Valladolid. In October she was profoundly disturbed by a scandal of which her twenty-one-year-old niece Beatriz (daughter of Juan de Ovalle and Juana) appears to have been the innocent victim. A certain Don Gonzalo, a frequent visitor to their house, had a jealous wife who proclaimed everywhere that her husband was "carrying on a wicked friendship" with the young woman. "And she affirms and says this so publicly," continued La Madre, "that for the most part they must believe it. And so, as for the girl's reputation, it must already be so lost that there is no use talking about it, but of the many offenses that are committed against God. I am so sorry that a thing of mine should be the occasion of this, and so I have tried to get her parents to send her away, for certain learned men have told me they are obliged to do so; and even if they weren't, it seems to me common sense to flee, as from a wild beast, from the tongue of an impassioned woman. Others tell them that this would make what is a lie seem true, and they should not make any change. They tell me husband and wife are living apart." Juana de Ahumada insisted that her daughter was wholly innocent, and Teresa believed this, for she offered to take the girl into one of her convents. Finally the parents sent her to stay with an uncle. Don Gonzalo's wife soon died, whereupon he made a proposal of marriage to Beatriz, which she refused. In 1585 she entered the convent at Alba, and became an exemplary nun.

Alba was always in La Madre's thoughts, but somehow she never managed to get there. Life was so full of crosses. Her relatives had begun a lawsuit over the estate of Lorenzo. She suspected Father Nicholas Doria and Mother Maria de San José of having agreed to keep her in the dark about a certain money transaction.

It must have been a relief from such sordid interludes when John of the Cross made his appearance in Ávila on the seventh of November. It was the first time she had seen him since his arrest in 1577, and it was the last time they were to meet in this world. As prior of *Los Mártires* at Granada, he had come to beg her to found a convent there, to combat the vicious immorality of the Moorish city. This was out of the question, for she had promised to go to Burgos. However, when he left on November 28, she sent two nuns with him to make the foundation. It was January 21 when they reached Granada. How the stubborn Archbishop opposed them, and how a thunderstorm set fire to his library and jolted him out of bed, leading him to change his mind, are told at length in the pages of Ribera and Yepes.

One of the last thoughts of John of the Cross before leaving Ávila had been to try to save money from his scanty travel allowance to send to Gracián, who was in need —

Gracián, who had never lifted a finger to get him out of prison and who did not put in an appearance on this occasion until "Seneca" had departed. Was Teresa contrasting the two in her mind when she wrote Gracián, just before he came, "O Jesus! How few people in this world are perfect!"?

As if to exemplify the fact, she drew back, in a final moment of hesitation, from the thought of the bitter cold of Burgos in winter, and her own infirmities.

"Never mind the cold," said Christ. "I am the true warmth. Satan is exerting all his strength to hinder the foundation: do thou exert thyself on My behalf that it may be made, and go thyself without fail, for the fruits of it will be great."

Gracián gave a grudging consent to go with her. He reminded her that she had only the verbal permission of the Archbishop, and secondhand at that, through the Bishop of Palencia.

"No look, Padre," said Teresa, "the affairs of God have no need of such prudence. . . . The foundation is going to be a great service to Him, and if we delay it any longer it won't be done. Let us make the attempt, and do you keep silent, for the more we suffer the better it will be; and you must know, *Padre*, that the devil is making a great effort to keep it from being talked about; but in spite of this, let Your Reverence command what you will, for that will be the best thing."

As usual he commanded what she had made up her mind to do.

BIRDS OVER NEW YORK*

Who would have thought that birds would
    haunt this place,
This wilderness of asphalt, brick and plaster,
This forest of inedible skyscrapers
Bearing no fruit for angels, men or birds

(Only for coupon-clippers, entrepreneurs
And usurers of fifty-seven varieties);
This garden redolent with gasolene,
And whiskey, garlic, chow-mein, zabaglione,
Gefulte-fish, tobacco, applestrudel?
Can it be possible birds would come to this
From meadows where the sun shines all day
    long

*The above and following poems have been selected from *Lyric Poems*, by William Thomas Walsh (New York: P. J. Kenedy and Sons, 1939).

In a clear sky,   .
And there are pools to splash in, edged with
    violets,
And fields of rye and wheat and stacked corn,
And crimson cherries to peck from Maine to
    Georgia?
And for the gulls, salt marshes
Well garnished with fat worms and bay-
    berries?
And old maids' gardens where the humming
    bird
Glides like a ghost upon red hollyhocks,
Like the ghost of a little song on rows of
    hollyhocks
When the dew dries?

Ah, there is a bird of sense.
You will never find him fluttering
At the window of a lawyer's office,
Or pecking pathetically
At the balls of a pawnshop.
Oh, no, he knows better.
He is a rare bird, and has sense.
But what are you others doing here?
Answer me that.

I do not mean canaries in a bird store,
Or those two green and purple parrots
I saw in Harlem, picking lucky numbers
Out of a box, at a nickel apiece,
For a fortune-telling negro in Turkish
    costume —
These are involuntary visitors
Of our metropolis.

Nor do I mean the great and stately gulls
That course the hungry waters fingering
The edges of this island, day and night —
This is their habitat, the tide washes
Their prey to Hell's Gate or the Palisades,
And outside waits the unforgotten sea.
But I refer to thousands of free-born birds
Created for green hillsides, woods and lakes.
Yet denizens of ugliness.
Is there a subtle sympathy in birds
For man's perverse and migratory heart
That they should follow him to this?
There is a broker's clerk who feeds the
    sparrows
Upon a Wall Street roof, all winter long;
And in the Bronx I used to see a woman,

Old and withered and wretchedly clad,
Lean from a window five, six stories up,
To throw upon the clean fresh-fallen snow
Handfuls of bread that must be precious to
    her,
And sparrows fought for it,
And she would prattle to them, tenderly,
As to a child.

All afternoon the pigeons over Harlem
Fly back and forth, and back and forth, in
    the sun,
All in a flock, as if one mind impelled them.
Two blocks they flutter, turn, and catch the
    light
That changes them from drab to flaming
    silver,
And then they wheel and flutter back again,
Dull gray; and this goes on for hours,
Gray and silver, silver and gray.
Pigeons in parks are tamer. In Riverside
I saw them perch upon the arms and
    shoulders
Of an old man who fed them.
He had the beard and face of a Hebrew
    prophet,
And there was something in him of which
    birds
Were not afraid; and one was blue, one
    brown,
And one like mother-of-pearl with a green
    collar.

Once in a dingy street of tenements
I saw a white dove light majestically
Upon a cornice, and there for hours he sat,
Brooding upon a crowd of children, playing.
Ah, so the Holy Ghost
Comes quietly to this city.
Even here, even more silently, more white
He steals into its sanctuaries,
Into His chosen hearts.

Not far from quite the worst street in the
    world
(Its windows placarded with blasphemies,
And loitering in its doorways, half-clad girls,
White, black and yellow, painted, soliciting,
And in its alleys, blood of murdered men)
There is a convent garden where peace reigns
Among old trees, and flowers for the altar

Make strips of color on the shadowed grass;
And I have seen there woodpeckers, and robins
And orioles, and once a small green finch;
And every spring wild thrushes find that place
(How, Heaven knows) and build their nests, and sing
As gloriously as in a virgin forest.
Saint Francis would like it here.

Yes, there are swallows too, great handfuls of them
Pelted out of the darkening sky at dusk
From all the corners of the wind, twenty,
Thirty, fifty of them at once,
From every quarter of New York.
They swirl about Grant's Tomb, then dart aloft
Tracing a giant parabola on the sunset,
And then swoop down, to roost among the frescoes
And twitter in the eaves till darkness falls
And silence.
Yesterday,
I saw four hawks come soaring up the Hudson,
And one of them swerved east and made his course

Among the homing swallows.
But they were not afraid, and he flapped on
Into the cloudy north.
If these were Roman times, some augurer
Might read for us such writings on the sky.
Some Jeremias could disclose to us
That while this city piles up sin on sin
And laughs at God,
Death waits in silence for it, patiently,
Death waits in the outraged sea, and in the sky,
And under the solid rock,
And the masked stonier hearts of men.

Some day, God willing, I will flee this city,
And the ocean of people will close over my place
As if I had never been there,
While I find peace and rest among the hills
Where I was born;
But not until I see the birds depart,
Not till you go, my birds!
You read the face of the sky.
The signs of the season
Better than men.
Bad as we are, we are not wholly lost,
Perhaps, while birds are with us.
But when I see the birds begin their flight,
I too shall go. It will not be too soon.

RENUNCIATION

Your face is like a poem
   Too beautiful to die.
It will not yield its secret
   To such as I.

Your face is like a chalice
   That I may never touch.
I thirst; but this, this vintage
   Is not for such.

Then let us pass in silence,
   In silence let us part;
It is the kiss ungiven
   That lives in the heart.

PERCEPTIONS

I have seen Christ in children's eyes,
In the tears of a woman,
In the face of my mother,
In the smile of a girlish nun.

And once I heard Him in music,
And once in the sound the sunlight made
Caressing a white rose.
But once, when the Host was raised at Mass,

I thought I was at the bottom of Mount
   Tabor
And saw far above in the sun
His white robes and almost His glorified face
Through the mist of my tears.

Once in a prison cell I saw the Christ
Wearing the garb of a murderer
Condemned to the gallows.
I saw Him tortured and whipped in a
   hypocrite's glance,
And once on a harlot's face, when a good
   woman passed.
Oh, often on crowded streets I have seen
   Him,

Yes, Him, the Ineffable,
Thousands, thousands of Christs,
Bearing the crosses of thieves, lechers and
   fools
Through long and sweaty centuries —
Your cross, and my cross, and all crosses;
And I thought it was night, and I knelt at
   the base
Of the Mount of Olives under the grief-
   smitten stars,
And then at last I almost understood
   Gethsemani
Through the mist of my tears,
Through the veil of my sins.

SONG

When I was an urchin,
  Oh, how I could sing
For the first leaf of April,
  The first bird of spring!

When I was a stripling
  The spring made me sad.
I wanted the whole world;
  'Twas not to be had.

But now, being older,
  I never repine,
For now I want nothing,
  And all the world's mine.

FULTON SHEEN
(1895–   )

THE outstanding radio orator of our time, Fulton John Sheen was born at Elpaso, Illinois, May 8, 1895. His vocation for the priesthood claimed him early, and in his preparatory years Father Sheen demonstrated such brilliance that he was selected for special studies, after his ordination in 1919. His graduate work was pursued at the Catholic University, the University of Louvain, and the Angelico in Rome.

Since the conclusion of his studies, Father Sheen has been in constant demand as a lecturer, radio speaker, and teacher. In partial recognition of his outstanding work and talents he was created a Domestic Prelate, with the rank of monsignor. For a decade he has been a professor of philosophy at the Catholic University of America.

Father Sheen's many books indicate but do not give the full force of the man. He is at his best as a speaker and has perhaps the widest radio audience of any man in America. His published sermons are a testimony to the unfailing brilliance of his mind.

THE HYMN OF LIFE*

THE universe reveals the profound truth that all things, from the grain of sand on even to the angels, are singing a beautiful hymn of life to the Creator. This hymn has many verses, each one more beautiful than the preceding, and all leading up to a climax in man in the natural order and to Christ in the supernatural. All life reveals itself as a process of unification. To make unity out of multiplicity, homogeneity out of heterogeneity, the same out of the different, the permanent out of the passing — that is the fundamental movement of life. This world would be like a gigantic puzzle-picture if there were no unifying force to put the pieces together. A mosaic is unintelligible if it is seen only in its details, but it takes on a new beauty when seen in its unity. The Mosque of Omar in Jerusalem has the magnificent beauty of its tinted windows ruined by the folly of petty lines running in crazy-fashion about the walls. They lead nowhere; they are like blind leaders of the blind — there is nothing to unify them. Life is beautiful only when it is reduced to unity.

The plant unifies the chemicals; the animal unifies the plants and chemicals; man unifies all three. The chemical finds its existence perfected in the animal, and the animal finds its existence perfected in man. Those things which are separated in the lower kingdom are united in the higher. The kingdom which is above subsists through that which is below, and that which is below exists to serve that which is above. As the servant serves the master, so in the hierarchy of creation the mineral serves the plant, the plant serves the animal, and all three serve man. Each exists for the other and all exist for man. Man, the "paragon of animals," combines the perfections of them all. He has the existence of the stone, the life of the plant, the consciousness of the animal, and his own peculiar perfection, intellect and will. Imagine this unification working itself out this way. Picture

four vases — one of clay, another of brass, another of silver, and another of gold. Suppose the contents of the first poured into the second, the second into the third, and the third into the fourth, the golden vase, and you have some idea of the manner in which chemical, plants and animals gradually unify themselves in man. The universe is like a pyramid gradually reaching to a point at the base of which is the mineral or chemical kingdom and the peak of which is man.

All things point to man and seem to tend towards him, but not by chance or accident. Everything tends towards him because everything was made for him. But why should the whole universe wait on man, and why should it be his footstool? By what right does he lord over all that he surveys? Man rules the universe in virtue of a Divine Gift. The Magna Charta over Creation was given him in the Garden of Paradise when God said to him: "Increase and multiply and fill the earth and subject it and rule over the fishes of the sea and the birds of the air and all living things which move upon the earth. I give to you every herb bearing fruit upon the earth and all trees which have in themselves a seed of their kind — all are yours to eat, and all the birds of heaven and all things which move upon the earth and in which there is a living soul." It was the consciousness of this lordship over the universe which prompted David the prophet to cry out: "What is man that thou shouldst be mindful of him? or the son of man that thou shouldst visit him? Thou hast made him a little less than the angels; Thou hast crowned him with glory and with honor and hast set him over the work of Thy hands. Thou hast subjected all things under his feet, all sheep, all oxen, moreover the beasts also of the fields, the birds of the air, and the fishes of the sea that pass through the paths of the sea." It is not because man is mightier than the mineral or the animal, that he may dominate and rule these things; as a matter of fact, he is not mightier. The lightning can kill him — but man knows that he is being killed. In other

*From *The Life of All Living,* pp. 205–223, by Fulton Sheen, Copyright, 1929, by The Century Company, reprinted by permission of the publishers.

words, it is thanks to the Divine Mandate to his immortal soul that man exercises dominion over all creation. It is by right and not by might. He has a higher kind of life and hence may subdue all things unto himself. The world is his:

Nothing hath got so far
But Man hath caught and kept it as his prey;
His eyes dismount the highest star;
He is in little all the sphere;
Herbs gladly cure our flesh, because that they
Find their acquaintance there.

The stars have us to bed,
Night draws the curtain, which the sun
    withdraws;
Music and light attend our head,
All things unto our flesh are kind
In their descent and being; to our mind
In their ascent and cause.

Each thing is full of duty;
Waters united are our navigation;
Distinguished, our habitation;
Below, our drink; above, our meat;
Both are our cleanliness. Hath one such beauty?
Then how are all things neat!

More servants wait on Man
Than he'll take notice of: in ev'ry path
He treads down that which doth befriend him
When sickness makes him pale and wan.
Oh mighty love! Man is one world, and hath
Another to attend him.

Since then, my God, Thou hast
So brave a palace built, O dwell in it,
That it may dwell with Thee at last!
Till then afford us so much wit,
That, as the world serves us, we may serve Thee,
And both Thy servants be.

The dominion over nature has been a slow process for man. It has become particularly rapid in the last two centuries. As a matter of fact, there has been more mechanical progress in the last two hundred years than there has been heretofore in the whole history of the world, and there has been probably among the masses less spiritual progress in that period than at any other time, for prosperity does not necessarily imply progress in the paths of God. Mechanical progress is a sign of worldliness, as spiritual progress is a sign of other-worldliness. But whatever one's opinion be on this point, the fact is that man is more and more subduing the universe and bringing all things under his domination. New continents are explored; seas traversed in every sense; their currents studied; the mysteries of heaven unveiled; the course of the stars measured; their constitution analyzed; light imprisoned and made the designers of scenes; electricity harnessed to carry our thoughts from one continent to another; and the air conquered with wings of steel. The forces of nature which at so many times seemed beyond the control of man, are not unified and harnessed and directed to his own purposes. And the pity of it all is that an ungrateful world, forgetful that God whispered these hidden secrets to man, cries out: "a conflict between religion and science!" How could there be conflict since God is the source of both? How could science be an enemy of religion when God commanded man to be a scientist the day He told him to rule the earth and subject it? The truth is that men praised God for nature far more before the age of scientific discoveries; now they glorify man's ingenuity rather than the bounty of God.

The fact is man is king of the visible universe and all things were created for him. "All are yours." But what was God's plan in creating all things for man? Certainly not mere egotistical domination, for this would have been a deformity in the Divine Plan. God gave man the whole of visible creation on condition that he exercise in the name of all creation a three-fold sacred office — that of priest, pontiff, and king. Its priest: to give to God all the sacred things a creature can give to a Creator; its pontiff: to be a bridge between the finite and the infinite; its king: because the lord and master of all visible creation. All things were made by God but not all things can speak. The mineral hidden in the bowels of the earth has no tongue; the plant has no other voice than its flower; the animal has no other language than a cry. Being dumb they need a spokesman. Their voices would have fallen at the door of the eternal mansion, if man did not transform their mute gaspings into his own language, and give them the imprint of his intelligence and his love. What joy does a conqueror receive from the smiling valleys which he has won unless he hears from a thousand throats a "Viva" in his honor? What joy would God receive, humanly speaking, from the minerals, the plants and the animals unless there was an intelligent act of gratitude? Hence it is that God has given man the power to unite all things within himself, by his intellect, in order that he might be spokesman of the world; that he might know the world, admire for the world, speak for the world, adore for the world, render thanks for the world, pray for the world, and like the three youths in the fiery furnace, sing a living Benedicite to the Creator of the world! If the mineral could speak it would thank God for its existence; if the plant could speak it would thank God for its life; if the animal could speak it would thank God for its sentiency; but man can speak, and it is in the name of all these things beneath him he must speak thanks to God. Such is the noble office of man, the spokesman of all creation! Such is his high destiny!

The universe is a great sacrament. A Sacrament in the strict sense of the term is a material sign used as a means of conferring grace, and instituted by Christ. In the broad sense of the term everything in the world is a sacrament inasmuch as it is a material thing used as a means of spiritual sanctification. Everything is and should be a stepping stone to God: sunsets should be the means of reminding us of God's beauty as a snowflake should remind us of God's purity. Flowers, birds, beasts, men, women, children, beauty, love, truth, all these earthly possessions are not an end in themselves, they are only means to an end. The temporal world is a nursery to the eternal world, and the mansions of this earth a figure of the Father's heavenly mansions. The world is just a scaffolding up which souls climb to the kingdom of Heaven, and when the last soul shall have climbed through that scaffolding, then it shall be torn down and burnt with fervent fire, not because it is base, but simply because it has done its work.

Man therefore partly works out his salvation by *sacramentalizing the universe;* man sins by refusing to sacramentalize it, or, in other words, by using creatures as selfish ends rather than God-ward means. Manichaeism is wrong because it considers matter as an evil instead of a "sacrament." Epicureanism is wrong because it considers pleasures as a God, instead of a means to God. Sacramentalizing the universe ennobles the universe, for it bestows upon it a kind of transparency which permits the vision of the spiritual behind the material. Poets are masters in sacramentalizing creation for they never take anything in its mere material expression; for them things are symbols of the divine. Saints surpass poets in that gift, for saints see God in everything, or better, see God through everything. The poor, the lame, the blind to them are transparent like a window-pane; they are revelations of Christ as Christ Himself told us they really were: "I was sick and you visited Me."

Why should man be bound to the office of holding commerce with God? Why should not man be independent of God? Man could not be independent of God any more than a ray of sunlight could be independent of the sun. The absolute independence of the ray would mean its destruction, for it is only by being dependent on the sun that it survives. So it is with man in his relation with God. Let us make this clear by an example. If I should invent some great machine which would not only shorten human labor but add great material benefit to mankind, the government would give me patent rights on that invention. The rights would entitle me to all returns on my invention and would protect me against illegal encroachments of others. Now, we are "God's invention." Being His invention He has "rights" on us, which means that He is entitled to the service of our intellect and our will, and it is this service which constitutes the true perfection and liberty of man and the foundation of all religion. In other words, God is entitled to our worship for the same reason every author is entitled to a royalty on his book — it is his creation.

If man is that by which all visible creation is unified, should there not be someone who will unify all men into a brotherhood under a common Father? If man is the king of all visible creation shall not man have a King? If man is lord and master of all that he surveys, and if everything that has not perfect life in itself, finds its perfection in a higher life, is it not fitting that man have a Lord, a Master, and King in Whom he will find his perfection?

All creation belongs to man by a Divine concession, and all men belong to Jesus Christ for a twofold reason: first, because He is King by Divine Right, born of an Eternal Father: "The Father loveth the Son and He hath given all things unto His Hand." He "is set above all principality and power and virtue and every name that is named, not only in this world but in that which is to come; and He hath subjected all things under His feet." It is in His Son, Jesus, that God has resolved to "re-establish all things," or rather, according to the Greek text, "to gather all things under Christ, as under only one Head."

But Christ is Our King, for a second reason, and that is, because He has conquered us from sin. There were four elements which contributed to our fall: a disobedient man, Adam; a proud woman, Eve; a tree, and the fruit of a tree. Now, only God in His sweet revenge can use the instruments of ruin as the instruments of reparation, and in His Supreme Wisdom He chose the same four: an obedient man, Christ; a humble virgin, Mary; a tree, the cross; the fruit of the tree, Christ and the Eucharist.

We are Christ's because this mighty King — King not only by Divine and Eternal Birth, but King also by request — won us to Himself at the battle of Calvary, the site whereon took place the only real struggle for existence. It was a struggle; it was more — a battle; a battle fought not with spitting steel but with dripping blood; a battle waged not with five stones as David waged war against Goliath, but with five wounds — hideous scars on hands and feet and side; a battle in which the armor was not steel glistening under a noon-day sun, but flesh hanging like purple rags under a darkened sky; a battle whose cry was not "Crush and kill," but "Father, forgive them, for they know not what they do"; a battle that was won not by saving a Life, but by giving It — a strange battle in which "He who slew the foe, lost the day." The cross is the Throne of the King of Kings; His blood is His royal purple; His crucifixion is His installation — and He, the King of Kings, reigns from the sign of contradiction!

As all creation revolves about man, so too, man revolves about Jesus Christ. Man is the pivot about which the whole order of nature swings; Jesus Christ is the pivot about which all supernature swings. This is the point to which we must ever recur, for without Christ this world of ours loses its intelligibility and meaning.

The modern world is vainly digging up the earth in searching for the Missing Link, when it should be digging up the soil of Calvary. We should seek the Link: not the link which is to bind us to the beast, but the link which is to bind us to God. Our family tree does not look the more beautiful because there is a beast hanging in it. The real family tree — the Tree of the whole human family — is the Cross, and Jesus Christ is the Link — because He alone binds us to God. Man is finite; God is infinite. Nothing finite can be the bridge between the two. In the event that God demands a satisfaction proportionate to the sin — for the finite has nothing in common with the Infinite — nothing infinite can be the balanced bridge, because it has nothing in common with the finite. The link must be something finite and infinite, and this is Jesus Christ, Our Lord — finite in His Human nature, infinite in His Divine, and one in the Unity of His Person.

HELEN C. WHITE
(*1896*–   )

IT IS seldom that the scholar, the critic, and the novelist are united forcefully but amiably in the personality of a woman as they are in the character of Helen C. White.

New England, Radcliffe, and Smith are in her background and education. In 1924 Miss White took her Ph.D. at the University of Wisconsin. Since 1937 she has been a Professor in the English Department.

Widely traveled and subtle minded, Helen White has become one of the notable figures in the Return to Tradition. Her books, published by Macmillan, include *The Metaphysical Poets* (1936); *Not Built With Hands* (1935); *A Watch in the Night* (1933); and *To the End of the World* (1939).

In the *Metaphysical Poets,* Helen White has splendidly combined her deep knowledge of spiritual life and a critical maturity seldom found in the field of literary criticism, a revelation to the gentiles and the Dr. Johnsons.

Of her historical novels, *Not Built With Hands* is probably the best. It gives a romantic picture of the great Hildebrand and paints a portrait of Matilda which though dashingly done is femininely winning.

MYSTICISM AND POETRY*

POETRY and mysticism have, to begin with, this in common, that both alike belong to the field of contemplation rather than of action. Both are concerned primarily with the recognition of pattern, of significance, ultimately of value, in the world about them and within them. As distinguished from the man of action, say, the contemplative is concerned not with the conquest of the external world but with the understanding of it. Not possession but appreciation is his goal. The poet does not wish to carry the sunset home in his hat but with the eyes of his body and his mind to seize upon it so that the memory of it will abide with him. The mystic does not think of his God as a faithful genie to answer the rubbing of some Aladdin's lamp of prayer. He does not pray that his God will do his will, but only that He will give him Himself that he may behold Him face to face. The hunger for God is the basic human hunger, so every mystic of every tradition agrees. "Thou madest us for Thyself, and our heart is restless, until it repose in Thee," is the way Saint Augustine puts it. "Beauty is its own excuse for being," said the poet Emerson as he looked upon the woodland flower. But in each case the satisfaction of the hunger, the final justification of the experience, is to be found in the experience itself.

Once aboard ship I heard a spiritual globe-trotter, famous for the catholicity and zest of his religious appreciation, tell a curious audience of American tourists about the almost miraculous energy and accomplishments of an Oriental mystic. It was at the height of our late prosperity when anything seemed possible to the aggressive disciple of the strenuous life, and it was frightening to see the intentness with which that audience listened to the speaker's suggestion of undreamed-of energies to be discovered in the mystic's contact with God. One of that audience at least was reminded of the enthusiasm with which Milton's fallen angels set about prospecting the burning field of hell for gold and silver and precious stones. So the dupes of a power-maddened age listened with bated breath to this news of a super-source of power waiting to be tapped and exploited. Damming Niagara Falls to turn a wheel seemed

*From *The Metaphysical Poets,* pp. 1–11, by Helen C. White. By permission of The Macmillan Company, Publishers; New York: 1936.

a puny thing to the possibilities of this super-dynamo of God, and focussing the rays of the universal sun to roast an egg a triumph of the fitness of things. But eight centuries ago the Moslem woman Rabi'a had prayed, "O God! if I worship Thee for fear of Hell, send me to Hell; and if I worship Thee in hopes of Paradise, withhold Paradise from me; but if I worship Thee for Thine own sake, then withhold not from me the Eternal Beauty." And the story is told of the mystic, Thomas Aquinas, that as he knelt in the Church of Saint Dominic in Naples, weary from the labor of his great defence of the Real presence in the Sacrament, he heard the voice of his Master speak from the crucifix before him. And the Voice asked him what reward he would have for the work he had done so well. The answer which the great theologian is said to have returned on that occasion is the one answer of which the mystic could approve, "I will have Thyself."

In other words, for poet and mystic alike, it is the contemplation of the object, and not its conquest or its use toward some other end, that is the purpose of their being. The triumph of utilitarianism in the last century set up a final criterion for all human activity, "What use is it?" The humanitarianism of the Victorians gave that standard some elements of breadth and generosity. But the scepticism of altruism that is so widespread today has made of it something narrower and harder. The man in the street in a certain light-hearted revue of a summer or two ago in London expressed a common attitude when he confronted a lively travesty of the glories of the national history with the persistent challenge, "What good did it do me?" It is significant of their basic relation that poetry and mysticism alike suffer in an age that glorifies action at the expense of contemplation, utility at the expense of understanding or delight, and material achievement at the cost of worship. For in their essence both poetry and mysticism are contemplative activities, finding in the attainment of their object their own excuse for being.

The mystic and the poet are alike, also, in that neither is willing to remain passive. So often unresisting submission to the flood of experience seems the sole alternative to aggressive conquest of one's environment, to the imposition of one's own mood upon the offerings of the day, to the bending of one's surroundings, animate and inanimate, to one's private purpose, that it is worthwhile remembering that there is another way in which the opportunities of experience may be even more richly fulfilled. The contemplative does not remain helpless before the impact of experience. True, he does not repel it, but neither does he fall bewildered before it. He receives it, with a thousand tentacles of awareness taking possession of what cannot be possessed in any other way. In a certain sense, perhaps, he surrenders to the fullness of the moment, but it is a selective surrender. What he gives up is no jot of his own identity or of his own integrity but only those preoccupations, those reserves, those impediments of appetite and passion, that insulate the private spirit. To the contemplation of a beautiful sunset, for instance, I bring myself, together with those misgivings, those anxieties, those irritations, perhaps those greeds or resentments, that clog and imprison and heat the potential self. These I surrender, or rather am relieved of, in a sudden inrush of sense and feeling that takes possession of the released spirit. The word that bruised, the thought that fettered, are forgotten in the light of color, the spacious freedom of the effortless clouds, the coolness of the vast and unbroken air. But I am there still, in a thousand suggestions and recollections of other sunsets seen, far perhaps from this inland prairie, at sea, or from foreign hill-tops, or behind dimly glimpsed and still alien mountains. There are memories of paintings which have hinted of things to look for in color and the stratification of the clouds. There are the words of poets — it was Coleridge who first in "The Lime Tree Bower" opened to me the cool delight of that greenish yellow that comes only when the first glory of the sunset is spent. There are the fantasies of childhood when the eyes of unspoiled wonder beheld the souls of the day's dead go riding joyously through the light-foaming gates of heaven, or in the remoter swirls of orchid and topaz saw the Valkyries of the singers and the Aurora of the sculptors urging unimagined steeds and chariots through the melting distance. Then there are those deeper thoughts of light fading here to shine on other worlds — and with these delight and release pass into awe and that simple lifting of the heart that is perhaps the most universal and the most basic of the forms of worship of the race.

All of this is, of course, highly selective. Past experience, taste, ignorance even, play their part in the choice of impressions to be received and still more to be registered. In that sense even the fullest surrender to the moment is imperfect. For in the very act of selection experience is shaped by the patterning habits of the mind that receives it. And still more when the individual consciousness takes possession of the impressions of the moment, registering them and, as it were, naturalizing them in its own contexts of association, then obviously the role of the contemplative consciousness assumes a character far from passive. Finally, when the contemplative, so to speak, assimilates the experience, or at least that portion of it which he is capable of assimilating, the active element in the process of contemplation becomes quite obvious. For, the very delight of the artist in the materials of beauty, like the awe of the worshipper, involves a process of identification, of reference, of determination of context. In other words, the poet and the mystic find in the experience its pattern, its value, its significance. "What a beautiful sunset!" "The heavens declare the glory of God." Each in its degree is a conclusion of meaning, of value. In reaching such a conclusion, the mind and the heart of the contemplative act upon the materials of the experience, and to that extent elements of aggression do enter into the act of contemplation. But it is upon the materials of the experience as they exist that the poet or the mystic works. And in that sense the operations of the contemplative differ fundamentally from those of the man of action.

In other words, contemplation belongs to the realm of the mind and the spirit. But what one may call the process of contemplation is still essentially different from the usual working of the mind in two very important respects. The first is that character of total-working that is perhaps the most striking element in contemplation whether it be the contemplation of the mystic or the contemplation of the poet. No one who has ever tried to analyze a poem as one must, say, when one is trying to help an inexperienced reader to get hold of it, can fail to appreciate the indissoluble integrity of the poet's experience. He did, it is true, see certain things, and feel certain things, and think certain things, but he did these things all at once. Nothing makes a teacher of poetry feel so helpless when, for instance, he is trying to share with a novice even his partial understanding of the poet's experience as this overwhelming sense of the integrity of the experience. And still more is this true when the expression of experience with which he is dealing is the report of a mystical experience. Even something so matter-of-fact, so humbly point-by-point, as the account which Bernard of Clairvaux in one of his sermons on the Canticle of Canticles gave to his brethren of what seems to have happened when he was at the height of contemplation, leaves the reader who has caught a glimpse of what Bernard is talking about overpowered with the sense of something beyond the ordinary faculties of the mind. For the mind of man like his body can operate upon the facts of experience only piecemeal. All human action is by very necessity of the basic limitations of human capacity partial and exclusive. We take up one thing at a time, so look away from the rest. As Henri Bergson so shrewdly pointed out to the bafflement of all of us who wrestle with the demon of absent-mindedness, we forget in order to think.

Now the common man, who is neither poet nor mystic but who by virtue of the fact that he is the common man often shows surprising evidence of having the roots of many of these more ambitious trees in his own low ground, has some vague sense of this state of affairs. For instance, nothing is more frequent in the experience of the teacher of literature than the student who objects, "But it spoils the poetry to analyze it." To a certain extent he is right. The process of analysis does do violence to the essential nature of the experience involved. And it is always a good deal of a question whether the student who has been forced to inquire into the grounds of his elementary and hazy reaction to the totality of a poem will be able to reconstitute that integrity of experience on the higher level of awareness to which the teacher is endeavoring to lead him. Similarly, every lover of the mystics who has tried to share his degree of understanding of their value with his non-mystical brother is familiar with the repeated gibe of the sceptic that mysticism is essentially a surrender of thought to emotion. Indeed, this latter misapprehension is so widespread, the misuse of the term "mystical" as a stick with which to belabor whichever of the "isms" of the present day the speaker most emotionally dislikes, so common, that sometimes it seems as if it might be wiser to give up the term "mysticism" altogether and fall back upon the less inclusive and less misunderstood term, "contemplation." But, however annoying, both misunderstandings, like so many of the philosophic misapprehensions of the common man, rest on a very just, if hazy, perception of a fact, namely, that both the experience of the poet and that of the mystic have an integrity of character that eludes the process of analysis. So it is not surprising that the sentimental uninstructed lover of poetry assumes that the integrity will be damaged by that process of analysis, or that the sceptic of rationalistic prejudices takes it for granted that what will not survive it never existed anyway.

In this both the student and the sceptic pay homage, even if unconsciously, to the totality of an experience which neither understands, and both recognize the presence of something that is not entirely accounted for or taken possession of by our ordinary analytic methods of point-by-point dissection and diagrammatic summation. Nevertheless both of them mistake the essential nature of the experience of the poet and the mystic in that they assume that totality of character is identical with and restricted to the unanalyzed continuity of that succession of sensations and perceptions which constitutes the raw-material of experience. In other words, neither recognizes that out of the process of taking possession of that material with all the capacities of the human personality operating at once, there results a new totality, a reintegration of the elements of experience on a higher level, the level of the poet and the mystic.

Now, it is true that in trying to follow that process of reintegration the student of either poetry or mysticism is forced, at least at the beginning, to take up its elements one at a time. And it is probably true that whenever he is trying to explain or to give an account of a piece of poetic or mystical expression, he will be forced to take up one aspect of the activity of the human personality at a time and carry through his exposition more or less in terms of a point-by-point analysis. For instance, in discussing a poem he will be forced to consider imagery before he takes up implied meanings, or vice versa. He cannot discuss both at once without risk of confusion. That is one reason why the critic and the expositor in either field must so often feel himself an obstruction rather than a bridge in this process of communication between the two levels of experience, that of the poet and mystic and that of the common man. For the human personality in either the mature poetic or the mature mystical experience acts as a living unit, and the result is a single and, in the degree of its realization, a whole experience. In spite of the misgivings of the sceptic, the keen and logically alert mind with which Saint Augustine listened to the arguments of the Manichaeans was not put to sleep that wonderful day in the house at Ostia when talking with his mother Monica "of what sort the eternal life of the saints was to be," he seemed to himself to have risen to the very gates of heaven. Nor did Plato lay aside that gift of his for catching the movement of truth in the flash of something seen in a moment's image when he discoursed of the ideal beauty at that immortal banquet which has ever since haunted alike the dreams of poet and mystic. For both of these are whole men, possessed of an uncommon capacity for integrating the energies of the human personality.

No less baffling to the common man than this totality and integrity of contemplative experience is a certain character of "otherness," of something from without and beyond at least the everyday range of either poet or mystic. It is very difficult to find neutral terms to describe an element which depends to so large an extent for its definition upon the psychology, to say nothing of the metaphysics, of the critic. But of the presence of the element, however one may choose to identify it, there can be no question. Everyone who writes discovers now and then that he has written something so much better than the habitual product of his mind or imagination that not even literary vanity can forbear asking whether this be really he who has written so well. And the same holds true of the mystic. Bernard of Clairvaux, seeking to find words for what happens within his own soul in moments of mystical experience, is finally driven to offer as his final bit of evidence the greater purity and peace that he discovers within himself at such times. "Yet it has not come from within me, for it is good, and I know that in me dwelleth no good thing," he says, drawing upon St. Paul in his extremity. Many terms have been used to describe this feeling of inspiration or possession from the daemon of Socrates to the unconscious of Dr. Freud, but the experience itself is almost universally acknowledged whenever the deeper levels of mind or imagination or feeling are involved in the creation of a work of art.

For the writer or the mystic the predominating mood in the presence of this phenomenon would seem to be one mainly of wonder, the essential character of the experience, surprise. It is not just that the candid spirit knows that nothing so good or great can come out of his normal and habitual self. It is rather that when he was seeking something different, perhaps even something inferior, this happened. There has been a good deal of quite reasonable laughter over the tales of Tennyson, for instance, reading his own verse with obvious delight and even admiration. But we may be sure that there is something more involved in such situations than the obvious vanity. Indeed, probably vanity, however omnipresent, is quite the least of it. We may be sure that just as important for the poet is the surprise at what has suddenly come into his work, beyond his shrewdest calculation, beyond, probably, even his wildest hope. Something of astonishment is, we may be certain, the essential character of all inspiration, and I am not sure but that in the poet's delight in his own work there may not be quite as much of the humility of surprise as of any other emotional or spiritual ingredient.

One of the particular grounds of this astonishment is to be found in the element of sudden fulfillment of hope deferred, of which so many of the mystics speak and which is so familiar in the experience of the creative imagination in any field. One of the best descriptions of the phenomenon, indeed, is to be found in the account which the great French mathematician, Poincaré, gives of his struggles with difficult problems in mathematical creation. The main lines of the experience are widely familiar. The scholar wrestles with a problem in mathematics, the writer tries to bring a situation alive in a story, to round out the beginning of an image, to follow through the curve of a feeling in a poem, or the mystic strives to rise from one level of prayer to another, say from that which finds its expression in words to that in which the inspiration soars fully and warmly without the intervention of words into a closer communion with the Object of all prayer. It does not matter what the field of endeavor is, the process seems to be much the same. The weary and defeated and overlabored spirit confesses its bafflement and for the time being gives over the struggle. Empty, in despair or in acquiescence, it just waits. Perhaps even it turns to other matters, trivial and irrelevant to the essential purpose. And then the wonderful thing happens. Suddenly, the answer to the problem flashes across the seemingly empty mind, and it is as if the sand of the desert had bloomed in a moment with a thousand undreamed-of flowers. Or the scene that had stopped still and turned to stone before one's frantic eyes but a few hours back is suddenly struck to life, and the story out of the imageless air unfolds its seemingly predestinate course. Or the poet with heart bursting from the pressure of feelings but half uttered and then frozen into silence hears the rest of his music, as sudden, as surprising as that first music when the morning stars sang together. Or the contemplative, knocking in vain on the doors of divine indifference suddenly finds that lo, He whom he sought to soar to is here beside him in his own spirit, answering the prayer which mortal frailty had given up all hope of ever being able to frame. It is no wonder that the poet swears that he has caught the music of the spheres, and the mystic is sure that his God has come down from his heaven and entered beneath his low roof, and that even the positivist marvels a little at the mysteries of the mind of man. In such moments the meanest of us is a little more than himself, and the proudest is awed by the sudden inrush of a power beyond the most arrogant of his dreams.

NOT BUILT WITH HANDS*

CHAPTER IX

IT WAS only in June that Matilda finally dared to go to Rome. Hopeless as her affairs still seemed, the very setting-out was yet something in the nature of a release. For the agony of those helpless months in which she had waited at Canossa for news of the King's movements was now over. Again, the heat had driven Henry to withdraw his troops to Lombardy, and the immediate and direct threat to the peace of her realm was past. But still more important, Henry had once again invested the city of Rome with all the forces he could muster, and once again he had been forced to withdraw without accomplishing anything.

As she waited now in the Lateran Palace for the Pope to receive her, Matilda reflected that she could fairly claim some of the credit of that result. True, rumor said that Robert Guiscard the Norman had marshaled the forces with which he had returned from the East and the vassals who had come to meet him before the walls of Rome and before Tivoli, and that those displays of festive strength had made an impression on the imagination of Henry and played no small part in the forming of his decision to retreat, however much he might attribute it to the weather. But Matilda knew that neither the Normans nor the weather had played so large a part in the determination of Henry's course as the fact that the Romans had withstood all his blandishments, verbal and monetary alike, and had refused to open their gates to him. And knowing the Romans as she had known them all her life, turbulent and venal and unstable, she reflected grimly that the gold which she had scraped together so painfully had played its part in their determination. The sword she could not wield herself she had put into the Pope's hand.

It was a beautiful day without, and she walked through the open door into the loggia opening on one of the inner courts of the Lateran. It was a shabby little garden as if there had not been much of time or energy to spend on it of late, but in its ground ivies and its laurels, its roses and its iris, and its carved marble wellhead, there was something of the peace and the gentle grace of all gardens. And though the arches of the loggia in their bare stone lines, with blank slabs of unadorned stucco work between, suggested the monastery rather than the imperial palace, they lacked neither the dignity nor the restfulness of austerity.

This bare and somewhat haggard peace seemed the fitting symbol of the state of mind in which she had arrived in Rome, where the mere fact of her presence was such

*Pp. 438–445. By permission of The Macmillan Company, Publishers; London: 1935.

a triumph, and there was nothing else but helplessness and penury for her to glory in.

"His Holiness bade me welcome you," said a thin but bright voice behind her.

Matilda turned to look at an extraordinary face, regarding her with lively curiosity. Two features immediately leaped out to her surprised eye. The first was a slightly curly down of bright red beard over a delicately pink chin. The second was a pair of gleaming eyes, almost fierce in their intensity of regard.

As Matilda stared at this startling apparition in a monk's gray robe and cowl, the fierce eyes twinkled, and the stranger answered the question in her eyes, "My Lady Countess, I am Bruno of Segni."

"Ah, I remember, the Pope wrote that like his namesake the Blessed Gregory you are writing a commentary on Isaias. It must be very hard to keep your mind on a piece of writing at such a time as this," she said, watching the color deepen in the thin cheeks. What bright brown hair the little man had, who looked so much like the Judas in a tapestry that hung in her mother's house at Pisa!

There was a gleam in the tense eyes, and then the monk smiled. "But this is such a time as Isaias himself wrote in. It is the same sort of day of judgment as his when men's sins have come upon their heads, and the just and the unjust alike are in danger of perishing but for the goodness of God."

"That is certainly what it does seem like, a day of judgment," she agreed. "I suppose that is why it is hard for me to imagine thinking of any other day. And yet," she added hastily, as the gleaming eyes dilated, "I suppose the present makes it easier to understand the past."

But the little man shook his head, "I am not sure that it is not rather that the days of Isaias make it easier to understand ours. For we walk blindly through today into an unknown tomorrow. But these past times are finished, and we see how the sins of men brought their inescapable punishment. But for today, we do not know what the end will be."

"Sometimes," said Matilda grimly, "I am afraid we do."

She was at once ashamed of that discour-aged rejoinder, but Bruno seemed completely unaware of what she had said. "It is a very exciting time to be alive today," he said abruptly, his eyes shining. "For the hand of the Lord may be seen bringing mighty things to pass. If you had seen the hosts of Baal turn from the walls of Rome — "

But he did not finish his sentence, for a light step came behind them, and the voice of the Pope made Matilda turn. "God is indeed good, my daughter, to bring you here."

She knelt to kiss his ring, and then she looked up into his face. It was not only that he was tired, but there was a certain look of high patience in that face that spoke more movingly than any words, of pain the sting of which could not be plucked out. The tears came into her eyes, and his face for all the sharpness of its look blurred. As she struggled to her feet, he took her hand and held it until she was leaning against the stone pillar of the arch.

"God has been very good to me, Matilda, in giving me faith such as yours," he said, sitting down on a chair against the wall and motioning to Matilda to sit down again on the low stone seat that ran below the arches. "I need not tell you that Alberic brought your treasure at a time when I did not know where I could turn for silver to buy bread for my people."

"They have stood faithfully against Henry from all I hear," she said tentatively, searching his face for some hint of what was in his heart when he fronted the future which so frightened her.

He shook his head. "They will not do so indefinitely. Not, God knows, that I blame them for finding the strain of the siege and the fear of it hard to bear. But they on whom it presses hardest, the poor and the helpless women, they are the most patient, you know. It is the merchants who see their trade stopped and the nobles who must compose their jealousies and spend their treasures against the siege who wax most impatient."

"But traditionally, you remember, the ancient families of Rome have always been jealous of Emperor or King." This was but cold comfort for a generous heart straining for a deeper sympathy, and Matilda knew it.

But sometimes, she thought sadly, there is more to be depended upon in the persistence of the selfish interests of men than in their more unstable loyalties.

"They are jealous of any power that imposes restraint upon their greed and turbulence," he answered. "I don't suppose you have heard of what the Council of Clergy did in May?"

Matilda shook her head. "They voted a motion declaring that the goods of the Church ought not to be alienated for military purposes. In other words, the resources of the Church are not to be spent for the defence of the Church."

"And they were not thinking just of the levies Henry has been making upon the German bishoprics?" Matilda asked astonished.

"These were the Roman clergy. Some of them," said the Pope judicially, "were idealists who hate to see priests in arms and the charity of the faithful spent in blood. But those who pressed their fellows to such a decision at this time were men who had listened to the agents of Henry. They have been all through Rome, telling the simple that it is only the obstinacy of the Pope who exposes them to this hazard, that if they open to the King, here will be peace."

"It is as if," said Bruno of Segni, "a robber should say to an honest man, 'Give me your treasure, and there will be no violence.'"

Matilda laughed, but the Pope shook his head gravely, and a note of bitterness, rare for him, came into his voice, "God knows I wish it were that. If I could give the nothing of personal wealth I possess, if I could give my life to Henry, I would be glad to do so. But it is as if a bandit should come to the door of some lonely grange and say to the master, 'Now, I am a lover of peace, and I do not wish any bloodshed. So give me your wife and your children and your servants to me for slaves, and I will take them and go quietly away.' That is what Henry really says, and it is that which no householder worthy of the trust God has given him could yield so long as he had even his bare hand to hold between his family and the robber."

There was an uncomfortable silence as the Pope finished; so Matilda said hastily, "But Henry has gone back to Germany for this year."

"For this year," repeated the Pope quietly, smoothing his red robe over his knee.

"The Norman Guiscard will help you next year," suggested the monk.

"Guiscard!" In her astonishment Matilda almost gasped the name of the dreaded invader against whose forces she had fought her first battle. It brought back, too, the memory of that first girlish triumph and the unshadowed pride of inexperience. She winced at the overpowering bitterness of the memory of that first careless certainty, when she had ridden into Rome with the sword of a Norman knight rubbing at her knee and the populace cheering in the summer streets.

But the Pope seemed unaware of her exclamation, for he turned to Bruno. "Guiscard has indeed professed willingness to help us, but I have a letter from Desiderius of Monte Cassino today. And he tells me that all of the Norman lands are in a turmoil. While Robert has been trying to conquer the Eastern Emperor, his vassals at home have been making good their independence and snatching all of his possessions that they can lay hands on."

Matilda smiled grimly, and a look of compassion came into the face of the speaker as he added, "You have probably heard how even his own nephew, Jordan of Capua, has gone over to Henry without waiting for his return to consult him."

Matilda looked at him quickly. "But Jordan had sworn fealty to Your Holiness."

The Pope shrugged his shoulders. "I have given up counting the number of those who have sworn fealty to St. Peter and forgotten their word."

"The faithless in the hour of judgment —" began Bruno, but the Pope raised his hand.

"No," he said firmly. "Who knows if, but for our sins, they might not have escaped this temptation of forswearing? I should not fear to fail if I did not know that ultimately it is my own sins and my own shortcomings that are to blame."

It was then that Matilda made up her mind

to speak of the fear that had been troubling her ever since the Pope first spoke of Robert Guiscard.

"My Lord," she began, "have you ever thought of what might happen if Robert Guiscard and his Normans should enter Rome?"

The Pope looked at her in unaffected bewilderment. She had known it would be hard to voice her suspicion, but now she was completely at a loss. She began over again. "I mean, have you thought of what he might do?"

"Might do?" repeated the Pope. "But Robert Guiscard would come to Rome only as the sworn defender of the Church. Remember that, though he never makes a promise unless he sees some profit, Robert Guiscard has never been accused by his worst enemies of breaking his word." There was a trace of indignation in the Pope's defence of his ally.

It gave Matilda courage to defy misunderstanding. "My lord," she said, rising and standing before him with her right hand outstretched and her left tight-clutched within her mantle, "I beg you to forgive me for persisting, but everybody in the south knows that the Normans are savages, brave it is true, but cruel and without pity. Think of what would happen—"

But a dark flush burned in the shadowed cheek of the Pope, and he raised his hand to stop her. "Do you think it would fare better with Rome if Henry were suffered to sack it? You have not heard yet what Guibert who calls himself Clement is doing. If it is not the green fields burned with fire, it is cattle slain. If it is not the cattle, it is the peasants themselves, hanged for trying to protect their miserable hovels or burned with the hay in their byres."

Her heart softened at the agony with which he said this last; yet she persisted. "But they are doing the work of Antichrist who do these things, and the deed is worthy of the cause. Oh, my lord, let me see once more if I cannot rally my misguided lands to your defence."

The indignation had gone out of his voice when he answered, "My beloved daughter

and my valiant soldier, you know that not a day passes without my prayer that you will save your lands. And no misfortune of my own so grieves me as the thought of the poverty and misery you bear as the price of your fidelity to me."

He paused, and the tears came into Matilda's eyes so that she could not look at him.

"You may be sure that I will spare neither myself nor anything of mine to save the least of these my people from suffering. But I cannot surrender those things which are not mine but God's to Henry or anybody else, if there is any way in which I can save them — order and peace and justice."

Then as Matilda gazed at him without saying anything, Gregory added in a lighter tone, "Not, you understand, that I think Guiscard or his Norman savages you fear. I grant he has long been a thorn in my side with his raids into the lands of the Church, but he has sworn to forbear any more attacks on Church property and to defend the Church against her enemies. We Italians are too prone to think any people but ourselves savages, you know."

They talked for a few minutes more. The Pope was sure that the next time Henry would be determined to break into the city, and he was afraid the Romans would not hold out.

"My lord," said Matilda at last, seeing the slow afternoon shadows lengthening on the broad paved walk in the open garden, "I do not see any way in which I can possibly get help, and I am going home to get it."

The Pope smiled, and for a moment something of the playfulness of happier hours looked out of his gaunt and shadowed face. "Spoken like a Christian, my child. When we meet in that City, we shall not grieve for the times we were beaten, but we shall rejoice that we were not overcome. God bless you."

When she turned back to the door to look at him again, he was still standing with his right hand outstretched in blessing and that look of stillness making a light in his dark and troubled face. She turned back quickly that he might not see her tears.

LEONARD FEENEY

(*1897–*)

IT WAS a happy day for America and the Church when Leonard Feeney was born at Lynn, Massachusetts, in 1897. He was a whimsical but religious boy and it must have surprised some people when he entered the Society of Jesus in 1914. He was ordained in 1928.

Since that date Father Feeney has been literary editor of *America,* teacher, writer, lecturer, and adviser to many aspiring young Catholic writers.

Of all the American Catholic writers of our time, Father Feeney is the most American and the most Catholic. He demonstrates as no drama could the importance of being Feeney. His humor is whimsically himself. While his essays and poems prove the lucid depth of his mind, all his experience and knowledge flow into print through a consciousness as delightful as it is American.

Father Feeney's poems are spare but not anemic. His many faceted humor finds precise expression in his delicious poems for children. *Song for a Listener* and *Boundaries* contain the best of his poems.

His prose is equally delightful. Such essays as *The Brown Derby* and *Fish on Friday* are excellent examples of Father Feeney's wit and Americanism. His life of Mother Seton, *Elizabeth Seton, an American Woman,* translates a pioneer of the soul into understandable American perspective. The strokes of her portrait are leisurely, but the result is as magnificently sharp as Grant Wood's American Gothic.

RABBIT*

Rabbit's eyes are pink
And they are, I think
Less to watch with than to wink
With: they are ornamental:
Sight in them is incidental.
All sensation goes
In through rabbit's ears and nose.
Rabbit runs around

With jump and rebound,
Sniffing every sound,
Listening to the light
Falling on the clover.
Rabbit wants to be afraid;
He delights in fright,
And is soft all over.
He is lovable and white
And by God was made,
Out of man some tenderness to take:
Just for pity's sake.

*The above and following poems have been selected from: *The Leonard Feeney Omnibus* (New York: Sheed and Ward, 1943).

SNAILS

Snails obey the Holy
Will of God slowly.

THE MOTH

The little muslin moth,
Whose food is flame and cloth,
Flitting in rapid flight
From linen-chest to light,
In its intense desire
To be dissolved in fire,
Many manoeuvres made
Around my red lamp-shade,

That so enchanted me —
To it I faithfully
Promise appropriate praise
In my verse, one of these days,
As soon as I can get,
And put on paper down,
Some nimble epithet
And little noiseless noun.

BOUNDARIES

Over us and under
Is a world of wonder:
In between we blunder,
Blunder in between
The unseen and unseen,
And on someone's word
Hear of the unheard.
From our faiths and hopes
In prophets and in popes,
And in microscopes,
Mites and sprites we know
Are above, below,
And vice versa so.

Amoebas and archangels
Send us their evangels:
In between the ropes
Where we stand and stare
At the empty air;
Seeing only sights
That are lit by lights,
Hearing only sounds
That are kept in bounds
By celestial sheriffs
On their ghostly rounds
In between the seraphs
And the fleas on hounds.

I BURNED MY BRIDGES

I burned my bridges when I had crossed
I never brooded on what I lost,
Nor ruined with rapine my holocaust.

Youth is a rapture we must forget;
Wither and wrinkle without regret,
Hobble to Heaven and do not fret.

Yet in my soul there is something still
Deeper than memory, mind and will,
Something alive that I cannot kill.

Part of me, put not in my keeping,
Awakes unwakened when I am sleeping,
Under my laughter it goes on weeping.

For by-gone beaches and limbs of brown
When hoops were rolling around the town,
And London Bridges were falling down.

VIRGIN MOST PRUDENT

May after May I see by candlelight
  Above an icon that I kneel below,
Her head in shadow nodding left and right,
  Most sweetly and discreetly nodding No.

Year after year I must agree to let her
  Decide what to provide me for my good;
Pray as I may, I cannot ever get her
  To grant what would be wonderful if she
    would.

Spring comes, and little birds make warble.
Snow thaws, but not Our Lady of the
  Snows.
Tapers I melt before relentless marble.
Poems I write from what to live is prose.

AFTER THE LITTLE ELEVATION

O wheat-like, white, little, still-as-death,
Circumferenced Jesus of Nazareth;
My duty, Your beauty to recondite,
To fashion You, frangible, frail and light.

You come translucent to hold and handle
To peer clear through, Dear, and see a candle,
With a tractable trait to elate my heart
Who make You and take You and break
    You apart:—

Yet sever You never, St. Thomas said,
For wetness to water is not more wed
Than these twin fragments I now expand,
In my left, in my right, in my either hand.

The Saints have gazed at in other guise
This Body, ecstasies with other eyes;
But sinners with semblances rest content:
Its measure and mould as a Sacrament.

So daily at dawn, by the grace of Mary,
With well-worn words in a voice I vary,
I Give God God, and at God's behest,
For whatever may ease her or please her best.

SONG FOR A LISTENER*

1

This is a song of something said
For ears left hanging on the head
Weary of words that will not wed;

A song in which I trust is found
The pretty echo and rebound
Of sound of sense and sense of sound.

Our tuneless asses cannot climb
Parnassus, so perhaps it's time
For reason to return to rhyme.

2

The squirrel's scamper no one sees,
The measured arc, the branch, the breeze:
The perfect leap among the trees.

The stars, long snubbed, themselves resign,
Beginning about eight or nine,
To simply stick it out and shine.

The unmolested little mouse
Goes bric-a-brac throughout the house
Where artificial cats carouse.

3

One gathers wisdom coarse as this;
Two lips resisting cause a kiss,
And bondage is bereft of bliss.

And soldered selves each other slay
In incommunicable clay.
I thought it was the other way:

*Stanzas 1–11.

That out of selves new selves could come,
The hive, the hubbub and the hum,
The little dolly and the drum.

4

The heart is bruised below, above;
The ill-conditioned state thereof
Unfits it for the beat of love.

Much rubbish mixed with faint desire,
It seems more fuel now than fire,
And tries at all its tasks to tire.

In lacquered bosoms when it swings,
If cooled by hands aflame with rings,
Psychiatrists will tell it things.

5

There's no more music in the voice.
Music is now a nightmare noise,
And rowdy instruments employs.

The breath of life from being blown
Incessant through the saxophone
Has worn the body down to bone.

Starvation is a fad in food:
There is disgrace in amplitude;
Only the skeleton is wooed.

6

Our lanky lads and skinny lasses
Come crowding into college classes
To find what flunks them and what passes.

They are compelled in curious courses
To trace through manuscripts and sources
The origins of river horses, —

Which, after long didactic fusses
Conjoined with therefores and with thuses,
Are labeled: hippopotamuses.

7

A tattered scarecrow tends the farm,
And nothing's kept from hurt or harm;
The cows can roam, the bees can swarm.

The gay harmonica is stuffed,
The artful lips no longer puffed,
The sweet sonata never snuffed.

And barefoot boys, who whistle well,
Have ceased to whistle, so they tell,
Since what befell us all befell.

8

Because the title was alluring,
Because one's friend was reassuring
And said that it was worth enduring, —

Miss Tupper's lecture one attended,
And Smotherhood one heard defended,
And one was grateful when it ended;

And with Miss Tupper on the brain
One walked home in the streaming rain
Till two and two made four again.

9

Because his lyre was newly strung,
Because the poet still was young
One reads some lines that Spoundel sung;

And found that what he thought untoward
He wallowed in, and thanked the Lord
He was not bored with being bored, —

And made elliptical allusions
To obfuscate his own confusions
And ostracize his own exclusions.

10

Because the curtain rose at four
And S.R.O. was on the door
One went to witness "Nevermore";

And saw O'Reilly on the stage
Attempting to become of age
And read the simplest primer page.

He hoped that we would not be pained
To hear the alphabet explained;
And hoped we would be entertained.

11

Allow me when the dawn comes down
Over the mountain to the town
To light my candle, get my gown.

And as I climb the crimson stairs,
Unleash the bloodhounds of my prayers
On these defeats and these despairs.

For well I know how worn and thin
The simple certitude within
Though braggartly stuck out the chin.

FISH ON FRIDAY*

TO THOUSANDS of our fellow Americans we Catholics are known merely as the people who eat fish on Friday. It amuses us (up to a point) to be thought of in this way, as some queer sort of "Sixth Day Adventists" waiting with out-stretched frying-pans for the weekly arrival of the fishmonger, or rushing periodically to market and calling for halibut or clamoring for clams in order to fulfill a strange religious superstition.

It is a pity so little is known about us. We now number twenty million in this country, and sooner or later we are bound to be reckoned with as a Christian body in terms of something more substantial than our Friday fare. For it never fails to happen that people who know only a little about us get that little wrong. As a matter of fact we do not eat fish on Friday. That is to say, not unless we like fish and want to eat it of our own accord. I am one of those many moderately good Catholics in whom the persuasive power of Canon Law has not developed a taste for fish either on Friday or any other day, and stands no chance of doing so. It is true I do not eat meat on Friday, but the distinction between abstaining from meat and partaking of fish is not too difficult to comprehend and ought to offer food for thought.

Oddly enough the learned explanations of why we eat fish on Friday are more stupid than the stupid ones. The ordinary friendly Protestant who sits beside us in restaurants and notices our hebdomadal horror of meat puts us down as "just a little bit on the queer on that point," somewhat in the manner of the orthodox Jews who are "a little bit queer" on the subject of ham all the year round.

We like this simple explanation of our Friday observance best of all those which do not explain it. A misunderstanding is never unpleasant provided it is straightforward and uninvolved. What drives us to desperation is a treatise on the subject of "Catholics and Friday Fish" by a savant, a theological psychologist, or a student of "comparative religion."

We are amazed to learn from Professor Puffles that the practice of eating fish was introduced into the Christian ritual because the Apostles were fishermen: or to be informed by more erudite authorities that whereas pictures of little fishes were enscrolled on the walls of the Catacombs, the early Christians became gradually devoted to fish worship, which aroused in them intermittently a religious symptom known as "an icthophagus esophagus."

What annoys us in the theories of these polysyllablists is not what they say but what they imply. They imply, of course, that the Christian tradition is merely a superior form of myth, and if archeologists and other diggers had time to go into the matter, it could probably be shown that the Roman Pontiff is a development of the god Neptune and that the Holy Virgins of the Litanies were were originally a school of mermaids.

The true explanation of the ICTHUS inscribed as a devotional rebus in the Catacombs has no more to do with our practice of eating fish than the presence of an embroidered pelican on the back of a Benediction vestment has to do with our failure to eat pelicans, whether embroidered or otherwise. If our religious development followed the psychological rules which professors of religion imagine, we would most certainly be consuming lambs and devouring doves on Friday instead of avoiding them in favor of fish, because of all the animal symbols employed by Christians in their sacred liturgy unquestionably the commonest and most pronounced have been the lamb and the dove.

In my younger days when our adversaries were the good old (and thoroughly honorable) Protestant Evangelicals, who had sense enough to see that what we were doing on Friday was not eating fish but abstaining from meat, there was often quoted against us the text from Saint Matthew: "Not that which goeth into the mouth defileth a man": and I remember the great flurry which occurred in the "Question Box Departments" of Catholic magazines in trying to answer this difficulty.

*Feeney, Leonard, *Fish on Friday* (New York: Sheed and Ward, 1934), pp. 3–16.

What a pity the Catholic Apologete of those days had not tact enough to be less apologetic! Instead of trying to belabor the exegesis of a Scriptural text — to nobody's satisfaction, not even our own — he could have pointed out the enormous compliment we were paying to meat by considering its absence from our table to be a hardship. One does not offer God by way of penance what one thinks is bad but what one thinks is good. And nobody really understands how good meat is until he tries going without it one day a week. And why has it not been noticed that whenever a big feast of the Church — let us say Christmas — falls on Friday we become joyously carnivorous out of schedule, openly abandon our loyalty to fish and transfer it to roast turkey? Indeed the truth of the matter is if we dared to tell non-Catholics the number of reasons which will legitimately permit us to eat meat on Friday they would be scandalized. And I have always considered this a most amusing situation, namely, the constant danger we are in of giving scandal to those outside our Faith should we neglect to do what they think it absurd for us to do even if we did it.

There is, in view of these considerations, a resolution we ought to make. And it is this: not to waste our time and the time of unbelievers in discussing our religion with them any longer in terms of its non-essentials. There is no use trying to explain Friday fish, devotional prayers, incense, holy water, candles, relics, medals and such incidentals to anyone who has not studied the Catholic Faith "from the ground up." We can only beget confusion of mind in those who question us and arouse inordinately our own risibilities.

I remember once being asked by a very ponderous Protestant Divine: "When you read Matins in your Breviary do you believe everything that is written in the lessons of the Second Nocturne concerning the lives of the Saints?"

"Well," I replied, "that all depends on what you mean by the word 'believe.' I do not BELIEVE them as part of the Christian Revelation. Nevertheless I credit them with some authority, let us say as the best record of a saint's life available when an account of it was being prepared for recitation in the Divine Office."

"You know," he added, paying not the slightest attention to the explanation I had given, "the French pay compliment to a skillful liar by saying, 'He can lie like a Second Nocturne.' "

I laughed out loud. But my reverend adversary, strange to say, did not laugh at all. He looked very serious.

Now why did I laugh, and why did he not laugh at a joke which was entirely on me? For the simple reason that I have in common with those of my Faith a sense of humor radically different from that of an outsider. There are — let there be no mistake about it — Catholic quips and drolleries which no one but a Catholic can tell and no one but a Catholic can see the point of. I hate to analyze a joke, but let me do so for once in order to illustrate what I mean.

Every Catholic knows that our Church sometimes speaks directly in the name of God. To each phrase of God's revelation we attach a sacredness that would not warrant our making a joke about it. If anyone (even a Frenchman) should say about a liar, "He can lie like the Apostles' Creed," I should not only resent that remark, I should not only think it not in the least funny, but I should promptly wither my opponent with one of the retorts I keep at hand for just such a situation.

But the lessons of the Second Nocturne do not always come to us directly from God. Many of them were written not by inspired writers, but by some holy old monks whose purposes were not historical but panegyrical, who were trying to compose not chronicles but eulogies. Now there is between a good panegyrist and a good prevaricator an apparent similarity in that both over-tell their story, the former to delight, the latter to deceive. That is why a comparison of the two is so funny. But the universal law of all humor achieved by comparison demands that underneath an apparent similarity there be a real difference. And if one doesn't see the real difference one doesn't see the joke.

Furthermore every authentic Catholic joke

is at once humorous and pathetic. One smiles not in ridicule but in tenderness at the poor old scribe who wrote lessons for the Second Nocturne in order to commemorate a saint whom he loved, and who tried so hard to tell the truth that he told it too well. For charity is the most childlike of all virtues, and it thinks sometimes, in its innocence, it can do service, for every other virtue besides itself, even for the virtue of veracity.

This idea as it exists in the minds of simple Christian folk was brought home to me strikingly on a certain lovely morning in Galway when I went for a walk and asked an Irish peasant to tell me how far it was to — let us call the place, for I forget it, Corofin.

"Good morning! How far is it to Corofin?" He was sitting on a wall. He raised his hat and gave me a bow.

"About a half mile down the road, Father. And God speed you!"

"Thank you."

I walked a half mile. I walked another half mile, examining sign posts as I went. And another half mile. And another. And not until I had duplicated this distance twelve times did I arrive at Corofin, for it was six full miles away.

When I returned in the late afternoon I met the same Irishman sitting on the wall. I went up to him indignantly.

"What did you mean by telling me Corofin was only a half mile away?" I shouted. "It was six miles away! You knew that when I spoke to you! Why didn't you tell me the truth?"

"Well, you poor man," he answered quietly and with great seriousness, "I didn't want to knock the heart out of you, and you looking so tired in the early morning. I gave you a half mile to Corofin. That got you started. Somebody else gave you another half mile. That drove you on a bit further. In Ireland we do be always wanting to soften the journey of a stranger by giving him little dribbles of encouragement. Sure there'd be nobody going any place here on a hot day if people knew how far they had to go to get there."

"Now listen," I said, refusing to smile,

"I don't think that's really funny. It may be Irish, but it isn't honest. I just came from England. In England one doesn't get fooled that way. An Englishman takes great care in giving any information that is asked of him and he takes great pride in giving it truthfully."

"Do you know the trouble with the English, Father?" he replied vehemently, as he pounded the wall with his fist. "Do you know the trouble with the English? They wouldn't think enough of you to tell you a lie!"

I am not defending the naïveté of this Galway playboy nor holding it up as either a convincing or authentic example of Christian perfection. To be an ideal Catholic it is not enough to be a Celt. One needs also to be a saint. But surely there can be detected in him a thorough sense of self-forgetfulness not found in any save the children of the Faith, whose failing it is to love a person more than a thing and a man more than a measurement. Undisciplined Christian generosity of this sort has its drawbacks, I admit, but I prefer it greatly to the cold exactitudes of post-Reformation skeptics whose social courtesies are governed solely by an undistracted interest in their own good breeding. True, they are pleasant people to meet on a short walk, especially when one is in need of more information than of affection, but in the long run give me "a half mile down the road to Corofin" any day, and I'll walk the rest of the way myself.

It can be seen from this homely example that one source of Catholic humor is human nature itself in the act of being transformed (with all its absurdities, stupidities, scruples and superstitions) into something serene and noble. For a religion as universal as ours embraces all classes and patiently tolerates among its members even the most ridiculous types provided they be men of good-will.

But this is to take Catholic humor in its passive sense. This is not what makes a Catholic laugh. It is what makes him laughable. I am anxious to discover, in some fashion or other, what is the inner secret of our joy and what it is that makes us laugh by ourselves and within ourselves, even when we are alone.

I am sure the reason lies in our knowing through the light of Faith paradoxes too magnificent to be contradictions. And this is the secret not only of our mirth but of our sorrow as well. There is an empty amusement and an empty sadness that come from a mere knowledge of life's contradictions. But these are the portion of the skeptic and the stoic who seldom laugh and seldom weep. But the Christian may look into a world of mystery in which all contradictions are reconciled even though paradoxes remain. And the fruit of his wisdom is his gayety and his tears, for laughter and tears are the safety valves of sanity and by these beautiful outlets the strain within our nature is relieved.

I may illustrate this animadversion by another little story.

There is a convent not far from where I live to which I have gone on occasions to give a retreat. At this convent one meets a very nice old lay sister who has charge of the priest's dining-room, and whom I may call Sister Mary.

Sister Mary spends half the day indoors and half the day outdoors, for her duties are twofold: to feed the chaplain and to feed the chickens. Now this in itself is a paradoxical situation and I am sure accounts for the merry twinkle in Sister Mary's eyes, who, knowing nothing of either Evolution or Relativity, has faith enough to see, apart from apparent similarities, the enormous difference between a chaplain and a chicken. Indeed I have often thought it would be delightful if Sister Mary should some day get her functions confused and should walk out to the hen-coop with a cup of coffee and come clucking into the chaplain's refectory throwing handfuls of corn.

"Sister Mary," I said to her one day as I sat beaming over a splendid dinner which she had just brought in on a tray, "if you were going to order a nice meal for yourself what dishes would you choose? What would you like best to eat?"

She rubbed her hands on her apron and stood for a while speculating, and then said finally and decisively: "I think I'd love a

nice thick beefsteak!" Whereupon she began to laugh, and laughed and laughed until tears streamed from her eyes.

I must confess I was not prepared for such a mirthful explosion and it puzzled me. I knew, of course, the traditional Christian custom (which nuns observe most scrupulously) of laughing whenever anything pleasant is either spoken of or thought of. But this was sheer hysterics and seemed unwarranted by anything either Sister Mary or I had said which was so dreadfully funny.

It was only after I returned to my room and had time to meditate on the matter that I arrived at a solution of my perplexity. I am sure the reason for Sister Mary's hilarity, even to the point of turning herself into a fountain, was her use of the word "love" in the sentence, "I think I'd love a nice thick beefsteak."

One begins to see how funny this concept is when one remembers the love employments of Sister Mary's heart during the rest of the day. My question, I daresay, had distracted her from some holy thought. She is not often asked about the amours of her appetite. But being asked she must admit that the same heart which loves God and His angels and archangels in her moments of contemplation has lowlier and less ethereal preferences when she studies a bill of fare. Now it is a shatteringly laughable experience to transfer one's attachment suddenly from something sublime and eternal to something desperately temporal and comestible, to be loving at one moment a living angel and at another a dead cow. But because a Seraph is just as real to Sister Mary as a sirloin, she saw the absurdity of their conflict on her heart's affections and went into a paroxysm.

It is interesting to notice that in non-Catholic circles and in Catholic circles which have been influenced by non-Catholic culture (and many of us have adopted, more than we are willing to admit, the moods of the pagans and the manners of the heretics in whose midst we live) there is no genuine humor of this kind. An honest Christian joke in which the very roots of one's being are shaken with laughter has been supplanted, in this country at least, by what is known as a wise-crack. A wise-crack is a bogus form of humor in which a ridiculous sense of the sublime is combined with a sublime sense of the ridiculous. Its physical reaction is not a laugh but a snicker. Being rarely capable of more than two variations, the one uncharitable, the other unchaste, it is noticeably the most tiresome form of humor ever invented. It will eventually destroy one's power to laugh altogether as well as raise havoc with one's nervous system. There is no reckoning how much fundamental harm is being done to the amusement audiences of America by reading and listening to professional wise-crackers to whom their own fun-making is a drudgery and who after a short spasm of popularity succumb to melancholia, alcoholia and other poisons.

But where am I who, a few pages back, started to write on fish? I am where every Catholic finds himself who undertakes to write anything. I am writing on everything.

For if one is a Catholic one cannot think without being cosmical, or without being comical either, because Faith links all realities together and fills the world with surprises.

Nevertheless in deference to one of the favorite penitential practices of my co-religionists I feel bound to say something directly favorable about my subject before I conclude. So I shall say this: On that day of the week when meat is forbidden me I like to go to a Catholic kitchen and listen to little fish being fried in their skins. Because I think one of the very nicest noises of all noises is the sound of hot silver sizzling in a pan. But the palatability of these little creatures when they arrive on my dinner plate depends upon whatever success I have in obliterating their natural flavor with strong doses of fish-sauce. Which reminds me that I have never yet seen a bottle of fish-sauce which did not claim to have won a medal at the World's Fair.

GENTLEMEN WITH A GRUDGE*

UPON attaining the use of reason in a positive and permanent form, I found that among seasons, summer was most to my liking. During my favorite months — the hot ones — I used to don a pair of overalls and a farm-boy's hat, and plucking a blade of grass on which to chew, would go wandering in our neighborhood so as to explore its houses and inhabitants by way of discovering what sort of world it was I had to live in.

A favorite rendezvous of mine was a nearby shop which aspired to be a general store in a very small way. This shop had only one window and a little side entrance, and exteriorly it gave the impression of being a fruit store, for there were always oranges and bananas exposed for sale at the door. But inside, it proved to be a bit of everything. It was a grocery shop if you had forgotten to order a can of peas; it had a plaything department selling tops and marbles for boy's

games; and it would do for a drug store if you needed liniment or iodine in an emergency. It always seemed to me to be a brave little shop, trying to be all these things at once. It was open days and nights, and even Sunday mornings.

The full fledged fruit shops of our town were exclusively in the hands of the Italians, but this amateur fruit shop was owned by a Yankee. He was a tall man, with loose-fitting clothes, a walrus moustache, and spectacles, and his name was one of those odd Yankee names that would so amuse the Irish, a name in which the syllables are words and give you a strange association of ideas, like Frothingham, Saltonstall, Winterbottom. The proprietor's name was Wigglesworth.

Though I had read no Dickens at the time I first met Mr. Wigglesworth, once I had gone through David Copperfield and Nicholas Nickleby, I knew that he was definitely a Dickens character. For he had that odd quality which a Dickens character can display, of being sufficiently crazy to amuse you,

*Feeney, Leonard, Survival Till Seventeen (New York: Sheed and Ward, 1941).

without being sufficiently dangerous to do you any harm. Mr. Wigglesworth's mild dementia was revealed in his fondness for making speeches to an audience of one. If the audience happened to be only one small boy, but lately possessed of the use of reason, it made no difference to Mr. Wigglesworth. He went right on orating in adult language as though addressing the Senate or the House of Representatives. He would discourse on war, on politics, on marriage, on literature, on anything that supplied him with enthusiasm. He liked especially to air his grudges, his grudges against life in general and particular, to tell what was wrong with men and their affairs, and how it could be corrected. One of his chief grudges was the bad fruit Americans are given to eat.

"The United States," Mr. Wigglesworth once said to me as I sat on one of his onion crates, chewing a straw, "the United States, my boy, is a nation of unripe bananas!"

While saying this, he made a most contemptuous gesture toward the front door of his establishment, by way of indicating that his own bananas, hanging on a stalk there, were included in the censure.

"Yes, sir!" Mr. Wigglesworth repeated, because he always repeated anything that seemed to him like a weighty pronouncement, "this is a nation of unripe bananas!"

"Is it?" I said.

"Is it!" Mr. Wigglesworth replied, because he always repeated you as well as himself, "Good God, did you ever see the things the way they ship them to us from South America?"

"No, sir."

"No, sir? Well, you ought to! They're absolutely green, my boy, so green and hard you couldn't crack one with a rock. Imagine a banana taken off the tree in that condition!"

I at once closed my eyes, and endeavored to visualize the fruit interiorly, and to appreciate its horrible state.

"Bananas, my boy," Mr. Wigglesworth then went on, having sensed that he had begun to impress me, "should be left on the tree until they are *ripe!*" — and he would rip off the word as though snapping a whip — "not torn off the tree while they are *green!*

put in a cellar till they become *yellow!* and hung up for sale until they become *rotten.* Do you see what I mean?" and he made an odd gesture of futility, like a scarecrow gyrating in a storm.

I assured him that I was *trying* to see what he meant, and then sat quietly and awaited further developments of a theme upon which I knew he would be glad to expatiate.

Having refreshed his mouth, inside with a bite of tobacco, and outside with a rub from a red handkerchief, and having adjusted his collar so as to give more comfort to the throat, Mr. Wigglesworth continued.

"There isn't a single person in the forty-eight states of this Union, my boy — excepting someone who has travelled to South America, like myself — who has ever tasted the flavor of a real ripe banana, a golden banana that has been left on the tree for the sun to work on, to mellow it, bring it to maturity, with a full rich flavor, and a firm brown skin. No, sir, there's not a person in this country that knows what a banana like that tastes like. They either eat green bananas, and that gives them appendicitis; or else they eat rotten bananas, and that gives them dysentery. Now which will you take?"

I said I thought I should take the second, if forced to a choice.

"What!" Mr. Wigglesworth shrieked out, "You would?" And then a sudden reserve which all adults arrive at eventually when they are dealing with children, restrained him. He looked at me with a hesitant regard, and knew immediately two things: first, that I did not know what the disease he had mentioned was; and second, that it was well for me not to know. Children catch these flashes of caution in the conversation of their elders with unerring accuracy. That is why it is foolish for a grown-up to answer all the questions of a child.

One could not fail, however, to admire Mr. Wigglesworth's consistency and sincerity when dealing with his customers. If, in the course of one of his banana harangues, a lady customer should enter the shop to buy bananas, Mr. Wigglesworth's strong aversions concerning the unsuitability of that fruit for human consumption would not in the least diminish.

"Which do you want?" he would say to the woman, "that yellow bunch, which is unripe, or that spotted bunch, which is rotten?"

This disarming frankness on the part of her tradesman would seem to give the woman only more confidence in Mr. Wigglesworth and his wares. She would order the unripe ones, or the rotten ones, as the case might be, then pay him the price and depart cheerfully. Mr. Wigglesworth would then clink a cash drawer with a bell attached to it, deposit the dishonest money therein, slam the drawer until it closed again, and continue to be thoroughly disgusted with his profession.

"What can I do, my boy?" Mr. Wigglesworth would muse, as he surveyed the woman he had cheated, while she went waddling down the street, "I give them advice, but they won't take it! But I repeat, the United States is a nation of unripe bananas!"

"Or else rotten ones, Mr. Wigglesworth!" I would add.

"You're right, son!" Mr. Wigglesworth would say, as he patted me on the head, for he loved one who would agree with him, "Or else rotten ones!" And there the subject might end for the moment.

I have said that Mr. Wigglesworth liked you when you agreed with him. But with all the good will in the world, it was difficult to do this consistently. For he had the habit of planting false leads in his conversation which made the trend of his thought difficult to follow, and threw his listener completely off the track. I shall give an example of what I mean.

"I see," Mr. Wigglesworth said one day, while misting and drying his spectacles, "that young Slocum's gone and got himself engaged to be married. The darn fool! That kid ain't set for marriage yet, not by a long shot. Furthermore, he ain't got any money. Furthermore, I understand the girl he's going to marry has a perfectly impossible disposition. Cranky as a rattlesnake, so I hear. That ain't no kind of a girl to marry. I fell in love

with a cranky girl myself when I was young. I even went so far as to become engaged to her, before I discovered how disagreeable she was. And then do you know what I did?"

"You threw her over, Mr. Wigglesworth?"

"Nope! I married her, went right ahead and married her. Shows what a darn fool I was. Not only was she cranky, my boy, but do you know what she was? She was a hypocrite. She told me she had a thousand dollars in the bank, all her own. That's what she told me."

"And was that a lie, Mr. Wigglesworth?"

"Bless your heart, no! She had one thousand, one hundred and three dollars in the bank, all in her own name, certified to by a bank book. That's what she had. But do you know what she promised me? She promised that when we were married she would turn the whole sum of money over to me; said she would sign it all over to me just as soon as we were married. That's what she promised."

"But she didn't do it, Mr. Wigglesworth?"

"Didn't do it? I'll tell you she did. Every darn cent of it. She signed on the dotted line the day after the minister hitched up. But that ain't what I'm comin' to. What I'm comin' to, son, is this. Do you know what that woman, that woman with the cranky disposition, whom I married through sheer pity, do you know what she went around sayin' about me after we were married? She went around sayin' that I married her for her money! That's what she said. Good God, what can you do with a woman like that?"

I was not able to answer this last question. But it echoed a thought that was already simmering in my own mind. I had already heard of a lady who drank "kerosene oil" for asthma. Now I had met a man who hated bananas and was being falsely accused by his wife. It set me believing at an early age that human existence was bound to be full of such alarms and disappointments.

Mr. Wigglesworth passed out of my life as casually as he had entered it. I can go back to my native city and locate the shop where I first met him, but it is no longer the shop of Mr. Wigglesworth's day and mine. It is now a large establishment, with two windows instead of one, and with a door for entrance at the center and is owned by a chain-store grocery company.

One feature of Mr. Wigglesworth's companionship I shall always be grateful for. He never spoke to me as though it were necessary for me to be stupid by way of being young. He spoke to me always as though I had intelligence, intelligence which needed to be guided in many points, and supplied with a vocabulary in others, but intelligence none the less. This is the greatest compliment a child can receive. As a child I always hated to be talked down to. I hated all nursery nonsense directed towards my ears. I hated

in every way to be babied. I particularly hated to have things over-explained to me. Mr. Wigglesworth never treated me as though I were a dunce. He treated me as though I were a man, and that's what I liked, and was the reason why I visited him wearing a laborer's overalls, and chewing a conversational straw.

Whether or not Mr. Wigglesworth died with his antipathy for bananas still unabated, I do not know. I thought of him particularly after the first World War when the popular song was being sung: "Yes, we have no bananas!" I thought how much Mr. Wigglesworth, if he lived, would have rejoiced in that song.

SISTER MARIS STELLA

(*1899–   *)

SOME of the best writing in America today is being done by nuns. Not least among these writers is Sister Maris Stella, of St. Catherine's College, St. Paul, Minnesota.

Sister Maris Stella was born in Iowa, December 21, 1899, and was educated in the public schools of that state until her third year in high school when she entered Derham Hall, on the grounds of St. Catherine's College, St. Paul, Minnesota.

Two years after graduation from high school, Sister Maris Stella entered the Novitiate of St. Joseph. After receiving the habit in 1921, she pursued her college studies at St. Catherine's, taking her B.A. in 1924.

A brief apprenticeship as teacher at the college was followed by years of study at Oxford, from which Sister Maris Stella received two degrees (B.A., 1929; M.A., 1933).

With the completion of her formal education she became a member of the English faculty at St. Catherine's and has been head

of her department at that college since 1929.

A Phi Beta Kappa, Sister Maris Stella plays a lively part in many learned and cultural societies. She has been a fairly regular contributor to such magazines as *Poetry, Sign, The Commonweal, The Catholic World,* and *America.*

Sister Maris Stella has published but one book of verse, *Here Only a Dove,* 1939.

Though she has published only one book of poems, it is of such distinguished workmanship as to place her among the best Catholic poets of our time, with Father Feeney, Jessica Powers, and Thomas Merton.

In her poems the language and figures are freshly memorable and her sonnet rhythms, if somewhat after the pattern of Francis Jammes, are miraculously original in English poetry. Many poets have slavishly followed the metrical innovations of Hopkins, but Sister Maris Stella has improved upon them.

HERE ONLY A DOVE*

Everything one sees or feels or hears
in this world is an illusion. Everything
that fills up space or time or eyes or ears —
all of it is illusion, vanishing
out of our sight, dissolving into air,
or dying away in silence. There have been

trees coiled around by fog wraiths until where
the trees were there was nothing to be seen.
There was a church the gannets wheeled
    above,
crying out continually their dissonant cry,
circling the windy spire. Here only a dove
rings its monotonous bell. Soon it will fly
away as all things fly except the mind's
question and the immortal answer it finds.

*The above and following poems have been selected from *Here Only a Dove,* by Sister Maris Stella (Paterson, N. J.: St. Anthony Guild Press, 1939).

RIDDLES

Out of this tangle of threads to find the
    thread
that will untangle the threads. Out of the
    maze
to find the amazing path and so be led
back to the beginning by incredible ways.
Out of the confusion of keys to find the key
that fits each keyhole, unlocks every lock.
Among a multitude of suns to see

only the sun. To find the moveless rock
under the shifting stones, under the sand,
the rock no shifting sands can ever shake,
nor great wind crying out over a shaken land,
nor lightning blast, nor breaking water break.
To find in multiplicity but one
end, beginning, thread, path, key, rock,
    sun. . . .

EPITAPH FOR A CAT WITH BLUE EYES

This cat had eyes of color to be seen
in water above rocks, a lucid blue
shot through with jewel-specks of gold and
    green
you marveled at each time she looked at you.
And if you found her on a window sill
staring up at the sun, you would forget
the words that reasonable people will
employ to heap affection on a pet.

For when she turned her head and opened
    wide
her strange eyes, looking through you and
    beyond
and into space, remote and deified,
you would not ever venture to be fond;
or have audacity to patronize
this purring idol with sea-colored eyes.

PIGEON

Straight into the sun the pigeon darted.
I could not see, I could not follow his flight
high above the place from which he started
vanishing upward into a dazzle of light.
A moment ago he strutted here on the
    lawn —
a pigeon with a hard and beady eye —
picking for bits no snow had settled on,
a mundane bird not meant to tread the sky.
But suddenly he opened wide his wings,

flapping at first and scattering snow with his
    feet;
sweeping in gradual curves and arcs and
    rings,
he climbed up steadily with a strong wing-
    beat.
No fleck of cloud showed in the burnished
    blue
as straight into the sun the pigeon flew.

O NEVER, NEVER AGAIN

O never, never again in the bright air
    streaming
this year's blue lilies delicately will blow.
O never, never again in the waters gleaming
the image of their loveliness will go.
Nor ever again these little leaves will flutter
in ribbons of light on the thin lombardies,
nor ever again on rainy nights will utter

this sibilant music the wet cedar trees.
O never, never again in the undreamed days
will come reiteration of the flower
that here has blown among us. But always
I shall remember. I shall remember this hour.
And there will linger in successive springs
the fragrance of these heart-remembered
    things.

LANDSCAPE WITH CHILDREN

Always waiting at the back of the mind
where old shapes are the familiar scenery,
hills lie beyond the water, and I find
cows there and crocuses, and three
children with tin lunch pails picking their
    way
along new grass cropped short by munching
    cows.
Three children gather silken crocuses. (They

call them wind flowers.) The warm wind
    blows
out of the past, ruffling the water still,
ruffling the children's hair, tossing the bob-
    white-whistle, blackbird-meadowlark-
    mirth until
I am aware at least of how the light
fades out of that horizon. And I know
those hills are far away and filled with snow.

FAIRY RING

The children searching for the fairy rings
had in their minds not fairy rings but fairies
flying about the timber on little wings.
They looked warily among the green goose-
    berries,

up in the wild plum trees, in the sunflowers,
in acorn cups, and in a hollow tree
where yellowhammers lived. They looked
    for hours

and hours until a man they met said he
knew where a fairy ring was. He knew
    where.
The children followed him without a sound
into a little sunny clearing. There
with bright eyes wide, they peered but only
    found

a ring of ugly toadstools in the light
and not a fairy, not one fairy in sight.

THE BUTTERFLY TREE

The children always had their favorite trees:
there was an oak with a long rope swing;
there were the slippery elms and hickories
and weeping willows by the willow spring.

And there was the tree they called the butter-
    fly tree
where late one summer crowds of butterflies
    came,
and the children flocked like butterflies to see
this miracle that gave the tree its name.

Thousands and thousands of brown butter-
    flies dropped
like bloom from branches, waving their
    wings and flying
high up in the air above. They never stopped
until nightfall when birds left off their
    crying,

all except owls. And afterwards it seemed
these butterflies were a dream the children
    had dreamed.

JOHN GILLAND BRUNINI

(*1899–*)

THE present editor of *Spirit*, John Gilland Brunini, was born in Vicksburg, Mississippi, October 1, 1899. His education was fostered at St. Aloysius College, Vicksburg, and completed at Georgetown University, 1919, when he received the A.B. With the publication of the *Mysteries of the Rosary*, 1932, Brunini became a well-known figure in the world of Catholic poets. He is executive secretary of the Catholic Poetry Society and editor of *Spirit*, the creative magazine sponsored by the society.

Brunini's poetry displays a fine meditative quality: it is deeply religious and linked with all the most valid beauties of our culture.

Whereon to Stand, Brunini's first prose work of note, is an admirable presentation of the Catholic faith. The tone of the book is imperturbably good-humored, and because of its unimpassioned writing it is bound to appeal to all men of good will who have long felt the need of a book in which simple exposition took the place of special pleading. It is significant that just such a book should have been written by a Catholic layman.

THE MYSTICAL BODY*

PENTECOST, with Christmas, Easter and the Ascension, is a major feast of the Church. It is at once a commemoration of the Descent of the Holy Ghost on the apostles and the birthday of the Church. Often called Whitsunday, because in former times the newly baptized put on white garments which they wore for eight days, Pentecost corresponded to the closing Hebrew festival of the Paschal season. This the book of Exodus calls "the feast of weeks" and the book of Numbers "the day of firstfruits." The Jewish observance, set for the fiftieth day after the Sunday following the Passover Sabbath, embraced not one but two days during which the saying of certain prayers was recommended.

The Acts of the Apostles does not directly mention the fact that the Mother of God, the apostles, and the disciples were gathered together on the first Pentecost to observe the ancient feast. The account, however, does imply that they were at prayer when they assembled in the room called "the cenacle" and "the days of the Pentecost were accomplished." "And suddenly there came a sound from heaven, as of a mighty wind coming: and it filled the whole house where they were sitting. And there appeared to them parted tongues, as it were of fire: and it sat upon every one of them. And they were all filled with the Holy Ghost."

From this moment of the Descent of the Holy Ghost, the Catholic Church dates the beginning of her life. For He had been earlier promised to the apostles as the Spirit of Truth Who would infuse the light of faith and confirm and strengthen in them that supernatural virtue. He would sanctify them in truth. He would abide with and in them for all time, and would endow them with the gift of tongues. This, an extraordinary miracle which man could recognize with his natural faculties, was overshadowed by others, not perceptible to the senses, brought to the apostles by the Holy Ghost. But the greatest gift, the greatest mystery of Pentecost, is the unique and vigorous supernatural life — intimately binding together its members — which on that day was established, and ever since has animated the Catholic Church.

The mystery of that supernatural life is embodied in the doctrine of the Mystical Body of Christ, a term selected to note the

*From *Whereon to Stand*, pp. 117–127, by John Gilland Brunini, Harper & Brothers Publishers, New York: 1946.

difference between it and His real physical body in any state, whether mortal here on earth, glorious now in heaven, or in the Eucharist. The Eucharist — being the real body and blood of Christ, under the appearance of bread and wine perpetually present in the tabernacles of Catholic Churches — fulfills Christ's promise that He would be with His Church forever. Of a different order is the Mystical Body of Christ.

When Jesus used the imagery of the vine and the branches in His Last Supper discourse, He explained that His Father was the husbandman, He Himself the true vine, and the apostles the branches. Those branches which did not bear fruit, the husbandman would remove. But fruitful boughs would live, and live because they were one with and received their life from the vine. The same life animating the branches and the vine, the apostles and their successors would abide in Christ, the vine. So, too, would the faithful, the fruit of the branches. "You have not chosen me: but I have chosen you; and have appointed you," He told them, "that you should go and should bring forth fruit; and your fruit should remain." The apostles' fruit remains only when it shares the life that runs through the vine and the branches. The principle of this life is the Holy Ghost, the Love of God.

When into Paul himself had been infused the life of the Holy Ghost, he gave the Romans a more specific application of the analogy of the vine, branches and fruit. "Now if any man have not the Spirit of Christ, he is none of his," he told them. "And if Christ be in you, the body indeed is dead, because of sin: but the spirit liveth, because of justification." The body, in other words, is dead because it is subject to death; the soul lives because it is freed of sin through the Redemption and is given sanctifying grace — the principle of supernatural life — by the Holy Ghost.

In his first epistle to the Corinthians, Paul used another analogy. The vine symbol pointed to the community of supernatural life existing alike in all parts of the vine, branches and fruit. But this community, he emphasized in a different way of teaching, one which considers the diversities of the individual men — apostles, teachers, laymen, and all the classes in a universal Church — who are followers of Christ. This comparison was a body of which Christ Himself is the Head and all others its members.

There are diversities of grace, Paul wrote, for certain men receive different ones from God, but there is "the same Spirit" in all members. There are also diversities in men's operations, in their vocations, in their works, "but the same God, who worketh all in all. And the manifestation of the Spirit is given to every man unto profit. To one indeed, by the Spirit, is given the word of wisdom . . . and to another, the working of miracles; to another, prophecy. . . . But all these things, one and the same Spirit worketh, dividing to every one according as he will." Thus Paul illustrates the fact that the Mystical Body of Christ is animated by the operation of the spirit, just as the soul or mind of man determines the action of the various members of his body. Paul, then, in a mysterious and true manner, designates the Holy Ghost as the Soul of the Mystical Body.

The Body, Paul continues, "is one and hath many members; and all the members of the body, whereas they are many, yet are one body: so also is Christ." This, Paul states, is Christ wedded to the Church, all of whose flock are at one and the same time members of the Mystical Body of Christ, just as a hand, or an eye or an arm, is part of a physical body. Although there are many members, he reiterates that there is but one body, and an interdependence in the body among all the members. Since it is controlled by the head, Christ Himself is at once the Head, and, together with the Church, the Mystical Body.

This doctrine carries in its train many other truths which shed light on the entire Christian revelation and explained the supernatural life of both the Church and those who adhere to her. It in particular illuminates Christ's kingship. The rebellion of man, initiated by Adam, was in essence a repudiation of the dominion of Christ, the Word of God in whom all things were created. He came into the world to purchase back that which had been lost and to invite all men, by their acceptance of His kingship, to become incorporate in His Mystical Body and to share in its supernatural life.

The Church's teaching of the Mystical Body, too, brings out her true composition. For her members are all members of the Mystical Body and one in life so that, as Paul says, God, having tempered and welded the body together, "there might be no schism in the body." The natural fellowship that exists in any earthly association is thus supernaturally lifted up and ennobled. It flowers in the solicitude which one member must have for the other. "And if one member suffer any thing, all the members suffer with it: or if one member glory, all the members rejoice with it."

This supernatural fellowship among the faithful, this participation in a common life and good, is summed up in the Church's doctrine called "the Communion of Saints." One member of a body performs its own, but not all the same, function. All do not have the same dignity nor operate in manners equally useful and worthy of honor. In a storm, the eyes of a body direct the legs to carry the body to shelter, and the eyes can see because the heart, among others, fulfills its task. None works alone for its own particular advantage but legs, eyes, heart and all members work in unison for the good of the entire body.

Every good deed of every member of the Church, whether it be the relief of the poor, resistance to temptation, abstaining from legitimate pleasure, the prayers of the cloistered who devote their lives exclusively to the spiritual aid of their fellows, therefore profits the body with all its members. There follows thus a constant contribution to the body and a distribution throughout it which spreads from one member to all members the benefits of grace and life. While there is one Mystical Body of Christ, one Church, the Church — according to the conditions of her members — has three phases: The Church Triumphant, the Church Militant, and the Church Suffering.

"If one member glory," Paul said, alluding to the Church Triumphant, which embraces all those holy men and women who have attained through the justness of their lives the glory of heaven and the happiness of the Beatific Vision. These the Church calls saints. But because they are glorified and perfected for eternity in grace, and at the same time they remain members of the Mystical Body in considerable measure contribute to its health. They never cease praying and obtaining benefits for their fellow members who need assistance, whether these be on earth, the Church Militant, or in Purgatory, the Church Suffering.

The members of the Body who are on earth — the men and women who are now working out their salvation — are indeed the solicitude of those who have been saved. The Church Militant consists of all those on earth who must fight the evils of the world, the flesh, and the devil. These are the embattled, who show their militancy in remaining loyal to the good and resisting evil, and who fight as the soldiers of Christ seeking fulfillment in His eternal love. They, sometimes the besieged by temptation, sometimes the prudently fearful, sometimes the courageous and unselfish, pray for assistance to their fellow members of the Mystical Body who are in heaven. But the members of the Church Militant do not pray for those the Church designates as saints because these have reached their final perfection of being.

Those souls who are in Purgatory, one-time members of the Church Militant now destined for heaven but not yet worthy of entering into the presence of God owing to their impurities, constitute the Church Suffering. Purgatory means a place where things are purified, and the penalties of transgressions are suffered, for although God forgives guilt, He nevertheless punishes sin. God forgave Moses and Aaron their doubts, which were sins against faith, but He punished them, not permitting either to enter into "the promised land." David, who confessed to Him and to Nathan his sin with Bethsabee, was also forgiven, but Nathan correctly foretold that the king would be punished by the death of the child of that sin.

The removal of the soul's guilt from sin

is not to be confused with the punishment God exacts for it. Man may win freedom from guilt through penance, good works and especially the sacraments. Since murder, blasphemy, adultery far outweigh the daily faults of human frailty — impatience, discourtesy, unkindness — all sins are manifestly not equal before God. Into little sins man falls so frequently that he is inclined to overlook and forget them. But while the guilt he incurs by them is not sufficient to cause his damnation, at the same time punishment for them is due in justice.

Because all that comes into the presence of God must be entirely pure, the soul, which on earth has not made satisfaction for what the Church calls the "temporal punishment" due for sin, must be purged. Origen, one of the earliest doctors of the Church, compared a soul at its body's death to a man who has built a house partly of gold, silver, and precious stones, partly of wood, hay and stubble. Because he has built of valuable material, he does not deserve exclusion from heaven, which he would deserve had he used only the worthless or faulty materials. Yet these latter, which cannot be accepted, must be burned out of the building.

The Church has always taught that Purgatory is a place of torments, and asserts that chief among these is the soul's separation from God. Theological opinion, it is true, is practically unanimous in declaring that there is real fire in Purgatory. But mainly, the soul, acutely and overwhelmingly aware of its longing for God, suffers through its separation from Him.

Purgatory and hell differ radically because the latter's punishment is for eternity and the former's is temporal, for sentence there is governed by time just as is earthly imprisonment. Because Purgatory is a middle state and will sooner or later, not being eternal, pass, hope — which is impossible in hell — strengthens and sustains its sufferers. While these are unable to shorten their sentence by their own acts, they remain incorporated in the Mystical Body, and can rely for aid on other members of that Body. For in the torment of their fellows in Purgatory all members of the Body also suffer.

Belief in such a process of soul cleansing, which the Church declares is the essence of Purgatory, is deeply ingrained in the consciousness of humanity. It was not only accepted by the Israelites, but it is implicit in certain passages of Vergil's *Aeneid,* in the *Antigone* of Euripides, and in writings of Sophocles — all before the coming of Christianity. Judas Macchabeus, the commander of the Israelite forces, after a battle ordered prayers for his fallen men saying, "It is therefore a holy and wholesome thought to pray for the dead, that they may be loosed from sin." The Church Militant, both officially and through its individual members constantly prays and offers works of atonement for those who, in the Church Suffering, await heaven. For the latter the Church Triumphant also prays and intercedes.

The triumphant members of the Mystical Body also, in this interdependence between souls in heaven, purgatory and on earth, intercede for all in the Church Militant. From their solicitude, the sinners among the members of the Church on earth are not excluded. For a branch remains a part of the vine, even though it may be shriveled and sapless, and not sharing the life that produces fruit. This comparison, applied to a member who through sin cuts himself off from the life of the vine, is apt but not quite accurate. A shriveled branch may never again have sap flowing through it, whereas a sinning member of the Mystical Body regains sanctifying grace — his "sap" — immediately on repentance. A shriveled branch of a real vine is, for practical purposes, no longer a part of the vine; but a man who has lost sanctifying grace through sin remains, so long as he is alive, a member of the Mystical Body; he is kept as a member "in expectation," so to speak; in expectation of the time when he will regain living membership in the Mystical Body. And even while shriveled he is not deprived of the advantages of being a branch of the Vine.

Among these advantages are included the means which may be used to restore the life and health of the soul, especially the means of the sacraments whose administration Christ gave to His Church. Through the sacrament of Baptism, members are incorporated into the vine or the Mystical Body — "For in one Spirit," Paul explains, "were we all baptized into one body." But from then on all the other sacraments, together with countless other aids, are used by the Church for the sanctification of its members. The sacrament of Penance is always available. Through it a member who has sinned and shut off the sap of supernatural life can reopen the veins, causing the flow to resume.

As blood courses through the physical body of a man, so does sanctifying grace flow throughout the Mystical Body of Christ, going to all parts and all members who have kept the channels free. Since only through the Mystical Body can man become a member of the Church Triumphant, to win salvation, he must first be a member of the Church Militant.

Yet the Church does not interpret this truth to mean that only professed Catholics will reach heaven. She has always taught that nothing else is needed for salvation than an act of perfect love of God, which is charity. If this is true love it implicitly desires the sacrament of Baptism. Whoever performs this act of love, immediately receives, through "baptism of desire," the gift of sanctifying grace. Thereby he becomes one of the children of God and should he die in this disposition he will assuredly attain heaven. At the same time, since one cannot truly love God unless he follows God's will and is contrite for his sins, charity carries its own obligation. Should he, aware that God has commanded all to join the Church, remain outside her fold, his charity would become "sounding brass"; it would cease to exist.

There is a positive divine precept to belong to the true Church. By the institution of Christ, no one can be saved unless he is a member of that concrete, visible society which is the Catholic Church. This means actual, visible communion with her whenever this is possible. Meanwhile, it remains true that this communion is impossible for many who are kept from the Church by ignorance of which they are blameless; for many who are sincerely convinced that they are doing all God wills them to do; and for many, too,

who are prevented by other circumstances for which they are not responsible.

Nevertheless, even when for such reasons membership in the true Church is impossible, there still exists the obligation under pain of damnation to belong to this Church by interior, spiritual communion. Men come to this communion by an act of perfect love of God — love of Him above all simply for His own sake or because of His supreme lovableness — and thus are in the state of grace. This communion with the Church into which they are drawn is of a spiritual nature, and one of which they, by the very nature of the case, are not aware. It is a spiritual communion with that visible society of the Mystical Body, animated by the Holy Spirit and united with Christ as its Head. It gives those who do not profess to be Catholics participation in its supernatural life, without which there is no salvation.

In the case of those whom God saves apart from her visible communion, the Church therefore teaches that He does so through the grace by which they are brought into spiritual communion with her. But she declares that their position is one through which they suffer by serious deprivations. Thus they cannot avail themselves of the ordinary channels of grace nor of countless means of sanctification which the Church offers them. When she asserts that she is the one, true Church and that salvation must be through her, she may be — and is — called harsh and intolerant. This is the harshness and intolerance of Christ Who said, "If you believe not that I am he, you shall die in your sin." She cannot be any less stern nor more compromising than He. Were she to declare that any road to heaven is good, rather than that there is only one, she would fail in the trust Christ reposed in her. Even where her claims are unwelcome and arouse antagonisms, she must make them, as she has in the past, come rack, come rope, come avalanche of stones.

This dogma has been proclaimed at every period of the Church's history; it is not one which has been added somewhere during the centuries as a coat of paint is laid over another. It was stated just as emphatically by the apostles and their successors, by the teachers of the earliest centuries, by those of the Middle Ages, and by those of recent times. "If any man followeth one that maketh schism," St. Ignatius of Antioch wrote, "he doth not inherit the kingdom of God. If anyone walketh in strange doctrine, he hath no fellowship with the Passion." "Outside this house, that is the Church," Origen declares, "none is saved." And St. Cyprian advises that no man could have "God for his father, who had not the Church for his mother." In like manner Paul warned the Ephesians against those "children tossed to and fro and carried about with every wind of doctrine." He bade the faithful to do all in love of God so that "we may in all things grow up in him who is the head, even Christ, from whom the whole body, being compacted and fitly joined together, by what every joint supplieth, according to the operation in the measure of every part, maketh increase of the body."

Paul thus indicated the growth of the Mystical Body and implied that the Church cannot be considered simply as a society of men and women with only an external form. He also pointed to her inward life — the indwelling of the Holy Ghost, the gifts of faith, hope and charity, the grace of the sacraments, and all the many spiritual advantages through which the children of God differ from the children of the world. The Mystical Body is threefold in its growth. It grows in number of members and also through their progress in personal holiness. But it also grows as the whole Body tends steadily toward the ultimate spiritual perfection, toward the "perfect man" of Paul, toward the perfect imitation of Christ, the head of the Mystical Body.

Because the mystery of the Mystical Body is better understandable through analogy, this explanation of Christ's continuous mission on earth in terms of a living body is more generally used than others. He Who came to found His Church and through her to claim His Own is its head. The work which He has entrusted to her visible head, the Pope, and to the bishops and pastors of the faithful and through them to all the faithful, is His work. It is the work of salvation. Of His kingdom all are members, and between them and those forces in the world opposed to Christ is that warfare which He predicted when He said that He came to bring "not peace, but the sword."

Man's time on earth has been variously described as "an exile," "a vale of tears," and "a period of testing." It is an exile because man was shut off from his inheritance through Adam and must regain it as an individual. It is a valley of tears because sorrow and pain are in the world and man's lower appetites, when they seek unreasonable satisfaction, precipitate the hardships of his struggle toward perfection and away from sin. It is a period of testing because during it man is given the opportunity and the means to work out his salvation once and for all time, in accord with the will and help of God. He must logically never cease fighting all things that threaten that salvation, whether these be the obvious evils of the world or subtle evils that take on the guise of the good.

That there would be the sword, not peace, was underscored in Eden when God spoke of the enmity which would exist between Satan and the woman, and again when He declared that Satan could not prevail against the Church, which with Christ is the Mystical Body. Men too, as members of Christ, become the enemies of Satan and in this conflict they are intimately allied with Satan's archenemy, Mary, the Mother of God. For in her motherhood of God she crushed the serpent — the Prince of Evil, who always attempts to depopulate the kingdom of Christ and win His children to his own kingdom of darkness.

Mary, who participated in the Redemption as Co-Redeemer on Calvary, participates too in the life of the Mystical Body. St. John Chrysostom explains this in his comparison of Mary to Eve: "He (Christ) has turned against Satan the arms with which he once overcame. You ask me how: I will tell you. A woman, a tree and death represented our defeat. These three have all become for us principles of victory. In the place of Eve, we have Mary; in place of the tree of knowledge of good and evil, the wood of the Cross; in place of the death of Adam, the death of the Savior." The Church has always taught to this effect. While St. Jerome wrote in Palestine, "Death by Eve, life by Mary," St. Augustine in Africa was writing: "It is a great mystery that as it was through a woman that death befell us, so through a woman it was that life was born to us — perdition by Eve, salvation by Mary." Before the end of the second century, so did Justin teach in the East, Tertullian in the West, and St. Irenaeus in both the East and the West.

This place which is Mary's in the order of Redemption Mary has also in the application of that Redemption through the Mystical Body of Christ. Bodily, not spiritually, she is the mother of the Head of the Mystical Body of Christ. But she is spiritually the mother of the members of that Head, that is, of men — "because by her charity," as Augustine explains, "she co-operated in bringing about the birth in the Church of the faithful who are the members of that Head, whilst bodily she is the Mother of the Head himself." Therefore in the supernatural order man owes the life of his soul to Mary. While sanctifying grace depends primarily upon Christ, Who is God and from Whom all life comes, Mary is the mother of all whom Christ incorporates in His Mystical Body, and has been so ever since He assigned this role to her on Calvary when He said to John: "Behold thy mother." As He is the Head, the Holy Ghost is the soul and the Father is indeed the Father of the Mystical Body, she — whom the Church delights to call the Mirror of Justice, Gate of Heaven and Comforter of the Afflicted — is its Mother.

This relationship between the Trinity and Mary, concerning the Mystical Body, is essentially a mystery, partially explained by means of substantially true comparisons which cannot be followed through in all details. Other figures of speech also the apostles realized could aid the understanding of the same truths and thus, as did Christ, they frequently spoke of Him as the Spouse of the Church, and of the Church as the bride of Christ. On this simile is based the whole of the Canticle of Canticles, known in the King James Bible as the Song of Songs.

Again both Christ and the apostles described the Church as God's temple in which the faithful are "living stones." Peter, who called Christ the stone which the builders rejected, as Jesus Himself had spoken of Himself, bids the faithful: "Be you also as living stones built up, a spiritual house, a holy priesthood. . . . To you therefore that believe, he is honour, but to them that believe not, the stone which the builders rejected, the same is made head of the corner: and a stone of stumbling, and a rock of scandal, to them who stumble at the word, neither do believe, whereunto also they are set."

Similarly Paul writes to the Corinthians that "you are the temple of God" and he reminds the Ephesians that they are "built upon the foundation of the apostles and prophets, Jesus Christ Himself being the chief corner stone: in whom all the building, being framed together, groweth up into an holy temple in the Lord."

EMMET LAVERY

(1902–   )

A DRAMATIST who can spell Poughkeepsie, Emmet Godfrey Lavery, was born in Poughkeepsie, New York. His first inclination was toward the law, and in pursuit of this he received his LL.B. from Fordham. His talent for writing and the drama, which had shown themselves during his university course, became the consuming impulses of his life.

His initial play, *The First Legion,* was

produced on Broadway where it had a great success. This drama is a creditable presentation of life in a Jesuit rectory. Quite naturally small differences of character suffer some distortion, but the play is "good theater" and does much to reveal the human aspects of life in a great community whose existence is a willful enigma to the multitude.

In 1938 Lavery also published *Second Spring*, a play based on the life of Cardinal Newman. This is not as valid as *The First Legion*, due mainly to the injustice with which Lavery delineates the character of Manning. To make of him an ambitious wire puller with implications of oily hypocrisy is bound to reduce the intensity of the conflict between the two men which arose from differing conceptions of the priest's role: Manning's being basically social, Newman's aristocratic and intellectual.

SECOND SPRING*

ACT TWO

Scene 2

TIME: *July 1852.*

SETTING: *Oscott: a simple chamber, distinguished largely by the Cardinal's chair and desk.*

At Rise: Cardinal Wiseman is seated at the head of the table, wearing the zucchetto (little red cap) of a Cardinal and a matching cassock.

At his side is Dr. Ullathorne, Bishop of Birmingham, dressed in street clothes which include, of course, the Roman collar and a bit of red at the throat.

Wiseman, poised, scholarly, aristocratic, is the personification of the cardinalate at its best. A gentleman to the fingertips, he has the breadth and the depths of a great statesman.

Ullathorne (aged 46) is cut from a different block of wood, but is no less imposing. He has the look of old oak about him. There is a Scottish virility about him and a fine rough naturalness that are as striking as Wiseman's delicacy of touch. He is, moreover, a direct descendant of Sir Thomas More.

WISEMAN (impressively): And when the Bishops meet here at Oscott tomorrow for the first synod since the fall of the Ancient Church, England will know that the Catholic hierarchy has returned to stay.

ULLATHORNE (drily): Aye. You've seen to that, My Lord Cardinal. But what is it we are aspiring to this time — a martyr's crown again?

WISEMAN (softly): No. A different crown this time. The conversion of all England!

ULLATHORNE: Ah, the martyr's crown by another name, perhaps? (Drily) The Bishops will like that.

WISEMAN: There is no cause for alarm. Times have changed. There is a different spirit in the air. I feel it. I am certain of it.

ULLATHORNE: I pray you are right, Your Eminence. But I can smell no Popery in the air just the same!

WISEMAN: I am not denying that, My Lord. But the right word — the right touch — and we shall have England at our feet again.

ULLATHORNE (gloomily): Or at our throats!

WISEMAN (smiling): We shall see. I shall put my trust in Dr. Newman.

(Ullathorne gets up and strolls about nervously, gesturing vigorously with his walking stick.)

ULLATHORNE: Ah, Newman! Well, that's a different proposition. But Newman is off to Ireland again in a few days.

WISEMAN: I have asked him to wait over and speak to the meeting of the Bishops.

ULLATHORNE: Hmmm. You are a man of long views, Your Eminence. If any single individual can realize this for you, it would be Newman.

WISEMAN: I was counting on your approval.

ULLATHORNE (brusquely): I could love that man as my own brother. I am proud to be his Bishop. But tell me this, Your Eminence — he was so happy with his Oratorians in

---

*Lavery, Emmet, *Second Spring* (New York, London, Toronto: Longmans, Green and Co., 1938), pp. 89–99.

their house at Birmingham, why did you throw him to the lions in Dublin?

WISEMAN (reproachfully): My Lord!

ULLATHORNE: Well, I'll not mince words about the matter.

WISEMAN: Surely you remember the circumstances. We didn't force Newman on them. Dr. Cullen himself asked that Newman might be loaned to set the Catholic University on its feet in Dublin. Wouldn't you like to have Newman spared for this honor.

ULLATHORNE: Yes, spared is the word. I know Archbishop Cullen!

WISEMAN: But, My Lord, Newman himself is most enthusiastic and already they have named him Rector of the University.

ULLATHORNE: Humph. How liberal they are — with titles! (Then challengingly) But do you think the Irish really want a University?

WISEMAN: Why not? (Then briskly.) Surely you are not doubting my sincerity in the matter?

ULLATHORNE: Oh, no. Not yours, Your Eminence. But I can't help wondering about theirs. Mind you, I don't deny it would be a grand thing for Ireland and a great thing for Newman. But I can't help wondering: do the Irish really want a University all their own, with an Englishman for Rector and an Oxford man at that? I'll believe it when I see it.

(A servant appears in the doorway and addresses Cardinal Wiseman.)

SERVANT: Dr. Newman is here, Your Eminence.

WISEMAN (getting up eagerly): Excellent. Show him in at once.

(The servant exits and Wiseman speaks earnestly to Ullathorne.)

WISEMAN: You won't say anything to discourage him?

ULLATHORNE: No. You can rely on me, Your Eminence. But I hate to see a good man wasted . . . on Dr. Cullen!

WISEMAN: But he won't be wasted, Dr. Ullathorne. Now we have to remember Dr. Newman isn't an easy man to place. Well, here is a job he could do and do well. (Then, significantly.) But I'll remember what you

have said and I'll see to it that he is able to meet those Irish Bishops on their own level!

(Ullathorne looks at Wiseman in pleased surprise but has no opportunity to follow up his unspoken question. Newman, a man of 51, is now shown in. He is wearing the plain cassock of an Oratorian with the white collar which overlaps the neck of the cassock.)

SERVANT: Dr. Newman.

NEWMAN (kneeling and kissing Cardinal's ring): My Lord Cardinal.

WISEMAN (lifting him up): It is good to have you back at Oscott for a few days.

NEWMAN: Thank you, Your Eminence. It seems only a few days ago that I came here from Littlemore to be confirmed and to study before I went to Rome. Yet it's quite six years or more. (Then turns to Ullathorne and kneels to kiss his ring): Ah, my Lord. I am most happy to see you again.

ULLATHORNE (lifts Newman up quickly): Well, the truth is, we have been talking about you behind your back, but strangely enough, it was nothing but good. But just wait till the next time! (He goes out briskly, trying not to let on how very much he likes Newman. Wiseman laughs and waves Newman to a chair.)

WISEMAN: Isn't Bishop Ullathorne magnificent? I seldom agree with him yet I constantly defer to him.

NEWMAN: We all love him at Birmingham. Perhaps it is because every time we look at him, we seem to see the face of Thomas More smiling out at us.

WISEMAN (softly): Yes. The blood of martyrs flows in the veins of Bishop Ullathorne. If only we could make a faith like his and Thomas More's bloom again throughout the length of England — (Then crisply) Well, tomorrow is our great chance, Dr. Newman. The eyes of England will be upon us. How do you plan to plant the seed?

(Newman takes some manuscript out of a folder and passes it over to Wiseman.)

NEWMAN (simply): I have written it all down in a few words here.

WISEMAN (eagerly): Excellent. Tell me — (starts to thumb pages rapidly) do you call upon England to submit in no uncertain terms?

NEWMAN: Oh, no, Your Eminence. The thought never occurred to me.

WISEMAN (amazed): Dr. Newman! But you must. This is not the time for half measures. The Church of England stands crumbling on the precipice. One strong word from you and we may demolish it for all time!

NEWMAN (softly): Only to see it replaced by what? People who believe in nothing at all.

WISEMAN (excitedly): You forget. There will be conversions by the thousands. All of England may come over!

NEWMAN: No, Your Eminence. Not in your lifetime nor in mine, either. And if they are not yet prepared to change their faith for ours, who am I to try to take away from them the faith they already have?

WISEMAN: But you can make them see the true light, if you only will.

NEWMAN (eagerly): Ah, but how, Your Eminence? By ridiculing them? Sometimes I think we should all ask ourselves every time we enter the pulpit: what is the purpose in this sermon? Is it to antagonize those outside the fold or is it to convince them?

WISEMAN (much taken aback): I must confess, Dr. Newman, this is something of a surprise, a not too pleasant surprise. I thought you intended speaking to England with the voice of Peter and in tones of authority. But this I cannot understand. You call it Second Spring — but what does it mean, Second Spring?

NEWMAN (very simply): I thought it quite simple, Your Eminence. I thought we might speak of love instead of hate and of peace instead of war. Just now you were wishing that the faith of Thomas More might bloom again throughout all of England. And you were asking me how I planned to plant the seed. Well, the truth is: Your Eminence, the seed was planted by the martyrs long ago and now it is just beginning to flower. (Then, with simple eloquence.) So when I look at the Bishops assembling here tomorrow, I see no Papal aggression, I hear no trumpets calling for an imperious conquest of all England. I see something instead which is like one of the wonders of nature. I see a flower in its second blooming. The past has returned. The

dead lives. The English Church was and was not and is once again! It is the coming in of a Second Spring!

(Wiseman, cold at first to Newman's explanation, is on his feet now with eager questions on his lips. But Newman does not have a chance to catch Wiseman's changing attitude now. There is an interruption. The door opens and Manning rushes in — Manning in a Roman collar and cassock.)

MANNING: Cardinal Wiseman! (He comes over quickly to Wiseman and kneels.)

WISEMAN (pleased to see him, lifts him to his feet cordially): Father Manning!

MANNING (turning to Newman): Newman! How good to see you — (crosses quickly to shake Newman by the hand, then turns to Wiseman.) Forgive me, Your Eminence. I thought you were alone. They said to come right in and I was so eager to see you, I —

WISEMAN (beaming as he looks from Newman to Manning): I am eager to see you, too, Father Manning. I want all the latest gossip from Rome — and don't hold anything back. Now, will you two keep each other company while I go over Dr. Newman's sermon? I shall be with you shortly. (He goes out. Manning looks at Newman humorously.)

MANNING: Dear, dear, I forgot about the sermon! (Pats papers in his pocket.) Wait till he sees mine. I'm afraid it doesn't say a thing.

NEWMAN: Don't worry! Mine didn't either — at least, it didn't say anything he seemed to like.

MANNING: Oh, you never can tell about Wiseman. He's deep. Let's see, you preach on the 13th, don't you?

NEWMAN: Yes; when are you down for?

MANNING: The 11th. Seems like old times, doesn't it? Both of us doing the same work again . . . in the same place . . .

(The two converts have been sizing each other up a bit. And they apparently like what they see. They should, too, for each man is now at the prime of his life.)

NEWMAN: Yes, it is like old times, isn't it? Tell me, Manning, do you like it in Rome? I found it rather lonely at times.

MANNING: Oh, I like it so much. Of course, you were at Propaganda, and I am at the Academia. It's a little different there.

NEWMAN (smiling): Yes. I understand it's a regular nursery for Cardinals!

MANNING (lightly): Well, there's no denying you do meet the right people there and it's very exciting. Of course, I have only been there half a year.

NEWMAN: What are you going to do when you come back?

MANNING: I'm not sure yet. I might do some kind of mission work among the poor in London. Lots of room for it.

NEWMAN (diffidently): I — I don't suppose you'd reconsider becoming Vice-Rector of a University, would you — an Irish one at that?

MANNING (rather touched): Newman! Oh, that reminds me — congratulations, my dear fellow. I hear you've made a stir in Dublin.

NEWMAN: Well, I've done no more than give a few lectures at present, but there's a great dream in the making there. And do you know what it is? It's to be another Oxford — in Ireland!

MANNING (smiling): Oxford! Can't you ever forget Oxford?

NEWMAN (simply): I've never tried to.

MANNING (taken aback): Oh. Well, it's a magnificent idea, certainly, but do you think anyone but the Irish can teach the Irish?

NEWMAN (tensely): We can try. We are going to have the best staff of professors this side of Louvain and we are going to teach the whole man. There's to be room for science as well as theology, for history as well as psychology — and for the laity as well as for the clergy. Well, what do you say? Together we might accomplish things we could never achieve separately.

MANNING (good naturedly): Hold on. You go too fast for me. And if I'm not careful, you'll sweep me off my feet just as you used to at Oxford.

NEWMAN: Which means I am still without a Vice-Rector?

MANNING: Oh, it isn't that I shouldn't like to, Newman. It would be fun rattling those Irish! Remember, you have to be firm with them. But I shouldn't make a very good teacher. I rely too much on authority.

NEWMAN (quickly): Manning, you're much smarter about things like this than I am. You can always tell the winning side, even from a long way off. Don't you think we have a chance in Ireland?

MANNING: Oh. Of course, of course. (He's not too convincing here.) But you're much better off without me in Dublin. I'd have you in hot water all the time!

(Newman is more than a little apprehensive that Manning has sized up the Irish University as a losing cause but has no chance to pursue the topic. Wiseman enters quickly, waving manuscript excitedly.)

WISEMAN: Newman — Newman — how can you ever forgive me for doubting your judgment? This is beautiful — exquisite —

MANNING: Oh! Well, my congratulations.

WISEMAN: Yes, you may well congratulate Dr. Newman, Father Manning — for I may whisper to you now what I shall soon ask His Holiness to do without delay! (Then to Newman.) You won't have to worry any more, Dr. Newman, about meeting the Irish Bishops on an equal level. I shall urge the Holy Father to make the Rector of the Catholic University a Bishop as soon as the time is ripe.

NEWMAN (amazed): Your Eminence —

WISEMAN: You shall see, Dr. Newman — our second spring shall be your second spring as well!

(Manning, amazed at the sudden turn of developments, is trying to find new words with which to congratulate Newman.)

NEWMAN: Oh, Your Eminence, I thank you from my heart, but I don't want to be a Bishop.

MANNING: My dear Newman, of course you do. Anybody would!

(But Manning is expressing his own reactions, not Newman's. He feels there is a point past which modesty need not go. He shakes Newman's hand vigorously.)

WALTER FARRELL
(1902–   )

CHICAGO, Illinois, was the birthplace of Father Walter Farrell, O.P. Having entered the Dominican Order, he was ordained to the priesthood in 1927 and was sent abroad for graduate studies. He took his S.T.D. in Fribourg, 1930, and his S.T.M. in Rome, 1940. He has been professor of the Dominican House of Studies, Washington, D. C., and Regent of Studies for the Dominican Province of St. Joseph in the United States.

Father Farrell has written extensively in the *Thomist* and other scholarly journals, but his chief contribution to the Catholic Revival of letters has been his *Companion to the Summa* in four volumes.

This work makes the theology of St. Thomas available to Catholic readers in a form which is agreeable to the educated who have had preliminary training in formal philosophy. In easy style, illuminated by an abundance of apt examples, Father Farrell extends the teachings of St. Thomas to many Catholic levels of awareness which without Father Farrell's intervention would never have known the enlightenment of the Perennial Doctor.

CHAPTER II

HE WHO IS*

(Q. 2)

IT IS more than the perennial vigor of human hope that makes human life a long process of constant beginnings. A beginning never becomes a prosaic thing, though we see its counterparts on all sides every day; it is in itself glamorous, enticing, irresistible, for it is in itself mysterious. The feeble spark of young life in a mother's womb, the first tentative plan of the architect, the first step of the infant, the first scribbled words of a book fascinate us. They swing open doors and we cannot resist straining our eyes to peer down the long corridors of the future they reveal to us. It is not an explanation of this attraction to say that this moment of beginning is tightly packed with love's rewards, love's labors and love's hopes. It is all of this; but it is much more. It is that inexplicable thing that we call mystery, the thing that calls our minds out on the long road along whose winding way the explanation of the mystery may be found.

The woman who gives birth to a child is not only a cause of a wondrous effect, she herself has become what she was not before, a mother. It is not only the marble under the sculptor's chisel that has become something new; the sculptor has undergone a process of becoming in producing his masterpiece, he has fulfilled a formerly unfulfilled capacity within himself. For in these human beginnings the process of becoming wraps its arms around both cause and effect to pile wonder on wonder and yet leave the mystery intact, the mystery of the beginning of that which becomes both in the cause and the effect, the mystery of the beginning not of becoming but of being itself.

Beginnings are not only mysterious, they are also difficult. Perhaps it is because they are mysterious that beginnings are so hard; at least, it is a fact that it is always difficult to begin at the beginning. That is a divine way of doing things, the divine way that made the Son of God start human life as an infant. For divinity itself is the Beginning and is naturally careful of beginnings, even of human beginnings which are but frag-

---

*Farrell, Walter, O.P., *A Companion to the Summa* (New York: Sheed and Ward, 1941), pp. 25–46.

ments gathered up from the feasts of the past. Surely the Catholic Doctor must be careful, even exhaustively careful, of beginnings: so careful that his works must be aimed, not merely at the learned or saintly, but at those humble beginners who are his particular care as an exponent of the things that pertain to God.

Beginnings are hard for us even when we ourselves are capable, the material on which we work it apt, and the work we have to do is no more than to coax to full bloom hidden beauties in the material and in ourselves. To our minds, the uncreated beginning faced the extreme difficulty, not of drawing out hidden powers, but of establishing that which is. Beginners in the way of God, which is to say beginners in the way of human living, face a man-made difficulty that springs from the reluctance of their teachers to begin at the beginning, a difficulty that is only hinted at when we call it a lack of order in the presentation of truth. That reluctance is not difficult to understand: there is an attractive, though completely false, air of excitement in dodging difficulty, shutting one's eyes to mystery and plunging into the middle of things.

That excitement has so gripped the modern mind that the beginning of things has become irritating to the point of consuming much of modern energy just in the elimination of it. These reasons for a beginning, which are sometimes called the proofs for the existence of God, have been excluded on the grounds that the human intellect cannot be trusted outside the boundaries of direct sense experience. Of course, many other objections have been made to them: scientific objections, such as their pitiful dependence on an Aristotelian science long since defunct; they are not the product of scientific investigation; they are in evident conflict with the history of religion and the theory of evolution, both of which show that the Christian God is a very modern luxury.

If the philosopher's patience is worn thin enough, he may protest that the results of such proofs are meaningless, devoid of qualitative content; which means this philosopher has been much too lazy to think. In despera-

tion, the philosopher may simply toss the proofs out the window regardless of their truth of falsehood; the God they speak of is of no value or service to humanity. And this will be a philosopher who takes all the important things for granted.

These proofs may be a nuisance to one who tries, philosophically, to keep up with the times at whatever cost; but they cannot be denied modernity if by modern we mean to occupy a place in the minds and words of men of our day. They are strong enough, independent enough, to live through this age and all ages. They ask no favors. They ask only what cannot be denied — and then make the most of it.

Specifically these proofs for the existence of God start with a simplicity worthy of the divinity they demonstrate, demanding just two things: a fact evident to the senses and the first principles of the intellect. Understand, now, this sensible fact is not carefully selected, difficult to see or subject to controversy; but an obvious, tangible reality of experience, such a fact as the wink of an eye, the birth of a child, the withering of a leaf, the beauty of a face or the smooth flight of a bird. The first principles of knowledge demanded are only those fundamentals without which intellectual operation of any kind is impossible, the principles which are the rock bottom of being as well as of thought and without which science itself is invalid, nay unthinkable. In thoroughly modern fashion, these reasons proceed carefully, cautiously, adhering strictly to the evidence in hand. They are not dependent on a system of science, a weight of tradition or subjective dispositions to make their way in the world. They are genuine.

The proofs for the existence of God do not belong on the dubious fringe of philosophy but in a place of honor; they have fought a bitter battle in defense of the intellect of man. A complete treatment of the existence of a beginning of things must always be a three-sided fight which must be won on all fronts or the intellect is lost. On one side are the champions of the ineptitude of man who insist that man's one distinctive power of intellect has no intrinsic value; of course it cannot prove the existence of God. At the opposite extreme is the camp of optimists and emotionalists, one group insisting the existence of God needs no proof since it is self-evident, the other tacitly admitting the intellectual incapacity of man but holding for an emotional assurance of the Supreme Being. In the middle, carrying the brunt of the offensive today, are those who champion man by destroying God, claiming there is no God, at least no such God as the Christians worship.

The fight is bitter. Because not all men and women have the appetite for fighting, or the time and ability to carry on the fight to the end, and because so very much hangs on the outcome of the battle, infallible authority has come forth to protect those who by force of circumstance are non-combatants. By that authority, the man who cannot follow the intricacies of proof, either by reason of inability or lack of leisure time, knows beyond question that the reason of man, by its own power, can certainly know the existence of God and that God, the supreme Being, certainly exists.

The gesture of authority is necessary, not because the truth it defends is beyond the range of the guns of reason, but because it is essential that *every* man *know* of God's existence for his individual life, just as it is essential for the world about man that God *exist*. The thinker who has seen and grasped the proof has no need of authority; he holds that truth by a clear insight into a natural truth. This man can prove the existence of God; by that proof he has also shown that the existence of God is not self-evident, it does not rest on an emotional assurance, it does not escape the powers of the mind of man. It is a proved fact.

Of course this man did not arrive at the proof of the existence of God effortlessly, as he might come to the point of raising a beard. The proof demands hard work, the hard work of thinking; certainly this man would have to have some preliminary notions accurately in mind before he could take a step towards the proof itself.

There is, for instance, the simple, but decidedly abstract notion of potentiality and actuality, a notion that is perhaps grasped more easily by seeing it in the complex notion of change. Let us look at these notions in a rather clumsy example. Let us take a large, perfectly plain block of marble; then put a sculptor to work on it and have him make a statue of that block of marble. We say, rightly, that in the original marble block there is the potentiality of becoming a statue, the principle or aptitude for receiving this further perfection, the quality of being changed. It may be worth noting that by "perfection" here we mean any respect in which a thing can be completed or become more determinate in its being. When the process is complete, that potentiality has been realized, the marble block has become a statue.

We call this process of realizing potentialities "becoming," and whole philosophies have been built upon it. More simply, we call it "change"; in its positive form we give it the name of "development." Whatever we call it, it is nothing more or less than the motion from potentiality to actuality, from the mere capability of receiving perfection to the perfection received. This is *motion* in its widest sense; it takes place in every change, of canvas and tubes of paint into a masterpiece, of a farmhand into a doctor of medicine, of an acorn into an oak, as well as in a journey from Chicago to New York. Obviously, this process of change involves three things: (1) a potential or starting point which is prior to the change and contains the potentiality, a thing which is already something but with the capacity for becoming something else, for receiving an added perfection; (2) the reality of the process or movement of change which proceeds from the potential to the actual; (3) the product of the change, the actual needed perfection. It is essential that we hold fast to the obvious fact of a distinct difference between the potentiality and its goal of realization. If this difference be denied, we are forced into a denial of both ends of a change, potentialities and actualities, or into an identification of these two. In either case we are in the impossible position of holding to a motion as eerie as a faceless smile, a motion that has come from nowhere and goes nowhere, or of holding to the absurdity that contradictories are identical, that there is no distinction between the undeveloped and the developed, between farmhands and doctors, marble blocks and statues.

The particular value of clarity in this notion of change lies in the fact that it brings out the complete necessity of explaining every realized potentiality, every perfection, by an explanation external to the realized potentiality itself. It makes more obvious the truth that a developed perfection is not its own explanation, it has not developed itself, nor is it explained by the potentiality which it perfected.

Another value, for our purpose of proving the existence of God, is had from the difference this process of becoming, or change, brings out between action of God and of creatures. It is on the basis of this process of becoming that we argue from effects to causes in created causes and their effects. Where the cause is divine, the fundamental question remains the same, that is, the explanation of a perfection that is not self-explanatory, that has not produced itself. In this latter case, however, it is not a question of a cause drawing a potentiality to perfection, but of a cause producing that which possesses the potentialities. In a word, the question in this case is not of the cause of becoming (or change) but of the cause of being itself; the transition is not from potentiality to actualization of potentiality, but from non-being to being.

One other preliminary notion that must be clarified before proceeding to the actual proofs for the existence of God is the limitation of all proofs for existence. As a matter of fact, there are only two possibilities for proof of the existence of anything: the direct proof offered by sense experience, such as a man has of the existence of a door by ramming his nose against it; and the inferential or a posteriori proof, such as a detective might have of the existence of a murderer when he finds an armless paralytic dangling on a four-foot rope from a rafter fifteen feet above the floor. The detective, by his type of proof, may never come to more than an extremely great

probability because it may be impossible to rule out all possibilities, this proof by inference, the a posteriori proof, gives complete certitude.

No other proof of existence is possible, no a priori proof is valid, because existence in no way enters into the very nature of created things; we cannot argue from the nature of things to their existence, as we can argue from the nature of man to the spirituality of his soul. As we shall see, when the proof for God's existence is completed, existence does enter into the very nature of God; but we cannot presuppose that when starting off on the task of proving God does exist. In other words, a conclusion about existence cannot be drawn from premises which do not assert the existence of anything; to assert the existence of something in the conclusion of a line of reasoning, you must assert the existence of something somewhere among the premises.

The contrary is the sophism inherent in all a priori or ontological proofs for God's existence, the sophism which Kant attributed to all proofs for God's existence. He argued that some concept of God is essential at the start of any proof for the existence of God and such a concept includes the notion of God's existence. Kant is right, of course, in maintaining that some concept of God is necessary from the very beginning of these proofs; after all, the proofs are trying to prove *something*. But it is quite enough, for the purpose of the proofs that that concept be no more than a statement of the absence of contradiction between God and existence; in other words, that concept, required to begin the proofs, need be no more than a construct which demands only the possibility of the union of the subject and predicate in the proposition "God exists."

Experience assures us emphatically that we *do* not have a direct sense knowledge of God's existence. When, in the course of this volume, we learn more about the divine nature, we shall see why we *cannot* have a sense knowledge of God. For the present, it is sufficient to accept the dictum of experience and concentrate our efforts along the only line of proof left open to us, the inferential or a posteriori proof, the proof of the cause from the effects.

The first proof proceeds from the fact of motion or, to put the same thing in another way, from the fact of the passivity of things. Its extremely simple formulation can be made in these terms: because nothing that is moved moves or changes itself, the unquestionable fact of movement or change in the world about us, forces us to conclude to the existence of a first mover who is not himself moved. That is all of the proof. Its very brevity is reason enough for a somewhat lengthy explanation of it.

The phrase, "nothing moves or changes itself," means only that a thing cannot be, relative to the same goal, merely movable and already moved, merely changeable and already changed; for the starting point and the goal of the process of becoming are necessarily different. The mere aptitude for receiving motion is not its own completion. The common sense fundamental back of this phrase, then, is simply that what is not possessed cannot be bestowed; and the very notion of potentiality is the absence of perfection that can be possessed but so far is not, for, unless we maintain that contraries are identical, a potentiality is not its actualization.

Actually this argument goes back a step farther, beyond the cause of change to the cause of that which is changed, back of the cause of becoming to the cause of being. For the immediate cause of change alone is itself in the process of becoming by its very causality; the mover of a potentially movable thing is himself moved by the very movement by which he moves this thing, he becomes something other than he was. The peddler does something to himself as well as to his pushcart when he bends his strength to its movement. Unless we come to a cause that does not itself become something other than it was, the process of becoming or change cannot start. Briefly, what is in question here is not the process of motion, but the existence of that perfection which is motion.

It is obvious, then, that the term "mover" is used of the first and of secondary movers

not in an identical, but only in a proportional, sense; for the first mover is the cause of being and is himself unchanged, while secondary movers are causes of change and are themselves changed in their action. It is to this unique first mover that the argument concludes.

A not uncommon fallacy today is to suppose that since this particular movement is caused by another, this latter by another, and so on, there is no need for further explanation since it is taken for granted that the world is eternal. From this point of view, since you can never come to the end of the chain of movers, there is no mystery about the present movement. The fallacy lies in the fact that without a beginning the whole thing could not start; no one of these previous movers is sufficient explanation of itself and its effect on others, yet a sufficient explanation must be found if the fact of movement is to be intelligible, if we are not to have something coming from nothing. The haze of distance or the weight of time do not do away with the necessity of explanation any more than they offer a positive explanation. To be satisfied with this is to be satisfied with the removal of the question to more obscure quarters, comforted by its consequent vagueness. The plain fact is that unless we come to a mover that is in no way dependent we have not explained the existence of the movers who are undoubtedly dependent either for their actual movement or for the power to move; where the effects are patently present the cause ultimately explaining them is not to be denied.

Two things are to be particularly noted about this first proof for the existence of God: the narrowness of the conclusion and the independence of the argument from the element of time. The argument adheres rigidly to the limits of its premises; it concludes to a first mover unmoved — and to nothing more. There is nothing more which can be concluded from the sensible fact of motion with which the argument started. Because there is movement, there is a cause of cosmic movement which is itself unmoved. The argument is not a sputtering flame to be extinguished by the simple expedient of blanketing it with centuries. There is no question here of movement beginning in time. It is not a question of a present reality demanding a cause in the past. It is simply a question of the universe as given, movement or change as experienced, and the conclusion that such a movement or change is unintelligible without a first mover communicating movement to all things. Time makes no difference. If the eternity of the world were to be proved tomorrow beyond all doubt, this proof would be in no way affected; the fact of change is there, the effect is with us, its cause cannot be denied.

The background for the other four proofs is exactly the same as for this first one. Keeping the preliminary notions, explained above, well in mind and holding to the detailed explanation of this first proof, the others can be seen readily. The point at issue is always the same; the existence of perfection that did not previously exist.

The second proof proceeds from causality or the activity of things. Here it is a question of the existence of an efficient cause, the external agent by whose operation a thing exists, the question of the existence of the hen that laid an egg, of the thunderbolt which struck a man dead, the storm that has battered a ship into helplessness. The starting point is again the sensible world.

We see in that sensible world an order of efficient causes dependent one on the other for their causality — the powder which propels the shell, which in turn crashes into a storage tank of gasoline, and this throwing out a sheet of flame in the heart of a city, and so on. We find nothing that is the cause of itself. Precisely because of this impossibility of a cause causing itself, the efficient causes of the sensible world force the conclusion upon us that a first efficient cause exists which is itself uncaused.

Here it is said that it is impossible for a cause to cause itself for the same fundamental reason as was exposed in the first argument, namely, because the starting point and the goal of change, the potentiality and its realization, cannot be identical. Otherwise we are identifying opposites, saying that the potentiality is the actuality. Here again,

as in the first proof, the argument is really stronger than it looks; for the only alternative is not merely identifying opposites, it is identifying non-reality with reality, nonbeing with being, for the transition is not from potentiality to actuality but from the purely privative condition of nothingness to existence. Here again it must be noted that the term "cause" is used, not identically, but proportionally, of the first and secondary causes.

A difficulty may be offered to this argument, the difficulty of living causes where the dependence is not so immediately obvious. And the answer is that no one living cause explains the efficacy of the species to which it belongs and from which it derives its power to cause. Yet that efficacy must have its explanation. Infinite regress gets us nowhere: without the first uncaused cause there will be no effects produced by any cause no matter how many eons are placed between the beginning of things and the world of today. It is not a question of time, nor is the question made more difficult by adding on a few million years to the age of the world. Again attention must be called to the strict adherence of the conclusion to the evidence in hand: the argument concludes to the existence of a cause that is itself uncaused, nothing more. Either of these two arguments is sufficient to demonstrate the existence of God; their effectiveness is not a matter of accumulative evidence. They are merely different angles, shafts of light focusing on the same spectacle of divinity but taking their rise from different starting points in the sensible world.

The third proof proceeds from our experience of the contingency or defectibility of things. It can be stated briefly like this: if any beings exist whose essence is not one with their existence (that is, which are contingent), then a being exists whose essence is its existence (that is, an absolutely necessary being). The fact is that in the world about us we see things that can have or lose existence, that begin to exist and cease to exist, that are born and that die. If everything were of this nature, that is if existence is not essentially natural to anything, then nothing would ever exist; which is patently false in view of the existing world. The argument proceeds as do the preceding ones: if things are capable of beginning to exist or of ceasing to exist, then, since they do in fact exist and cease to exist, that capability is fulfilled, that potentiality is realized, and a potentiality cannot realize itself. Much less can nothingness produce that which is the subject of realized potentialities.

The object of physically necessary substances is answered as was the fundamental objection to the preceding arguments. No such physically necessary being explains its own necessity but *receives* it (an actualized potentiality). So the necessity of the species is not explained by the species itself; "a multitude of contingent things do not make a necessary thing any more than a multitude of idiots make one intelligent man." This necessity must be explained by a necessary being that does not *receive* necessity, but that *is* its necessity. Again the element of time makes no difference. An infinite chain of beings that *receive* their necessity, or of beings which are not necessary, neither complicates nor explains the difficulty; it merely attempts to dodge the problem by hiding under the accumulation of immediate causes or the accumulation of the years.

These first three proofs have argued to the existence of God from the passivity, the activity and the contingency of things. The fourth proof argues from the perfection of things. But the argument still proceeds from the world of reality, not necessarily the world of sense experience, sense impressions, but nonetheless from the world of reality. For the real world also includes the things we understand as well as the things we feel, such things as love, justice, friendship, things that we can never grow in the garden or meet on the street but which are, for all that, decidedly realities.

The perfections in question here are only the absolute perfections that carry the note of perfection in themselves, not the relative which are perfections only because of their order to something else. Examples of such absolute perfections are animality, rationality, life, existence. And these can be roughly classified by stressing the point that they are in themselves either strictly limited or completely limitless.

As examples of the strictly limited, we may mention animality or humanity. A man is no less an animal than a lion; nor has a sickly boy less humanity than a strapping giant. These things imply definitely fixed limits. They either are or are not fully possessed; there is never any question of having a little or a great deal of them. To exceed or to fall away from the fixed limit means the complete loss of that perfection. As examples of the limitless perfections, there are life, goodness, existence, and so on. If there are limits to these perfections in this or that individual or species, the limitation does not come from the perfection itself. We note the source of the limitation in our very manner of speech when we speak of human life and animal life, though it never occurs to us to speak of human rationality or animal animality.

Since it is precisely from these unlimited perfections that the proof of the existence of God proceeds, it may be worthwhile pointing out some of their characteristics. Perhaps the most noticeable is that these perfections are possessed by different kinds of being in an analogous, not an identical, way; thus, for instance, we speak of a good stone, a good fruit, a good horse or a good professor according as each has its due perfection. Obviously the goodness of the professor is not identically the same as the goodness of fruit. There is proportionality there, but not identity. The second particularly noteworthy characteristic is that these perfections are realizable in different degrees; thus, in the course of one lifetime a man may be bad, of mediocre virtue, of more than average virtue, and ultimately a saint.

The fourth proof for the existence of God can be stated succinctly. In the world about us we see these perfections existing in things in greater and lesser degrees: that is, we see things that are more and less good, more and less true, and so on; we see life within human limits, animal limits, plant limits. Now these limited degrees of limitless perfections can be explained only by the existence of something to which these perfections pertain in their fullness, something which does not possess this or that degree of goodness, truth, life, but which is, by its very nature, limitless goodness, limitless truth, limitless life.

Certainly these limited degrees of limitless perfections are not explained by the natures which possess them. For what flows from the essential principles of a nature is had in its fullness; humanity is not something a man achieves after a long struggle. Moreover, perfections which flow from nature do not vary: the spoiled lapdog is not less animal as the days pass, the puppy does not grow into his animality. Yet, as a matter of fact, in the world about us these limitless perfections of goodness, life and the rest are not had in their fullness and they vary with an infinite variety.

The explanation, then, must be sought outside of the natures which possess a limited edition of a limitless virtue, that is, in some extrinsic source which has the perfection perfectly. Otherwise we meet the fundamental obstacle erected by an identification of contraries, of a potentiality bringing about its own realization, indeed, of the absence of perfection bringing about the presence of perfection. In a word, these limited editions of limitless virtues are received virtues; in the ultimate analysis, they are explicable only by some being who has not received them but to whom they belong, in their limitlessness, by the very nature of that being. Nor is this a question of a jump from the ideal to the real order. These effects — human life, the goodness of a man — are decidedly in the real order. It is not a matter of having an ideal rule by which we may measure these perfections; but of having a real, existing cause by whose action these realities have been brought into being.

This fourth proof proceeded from multiplicity to unity, from the multiplicity of shared or received perfections to the unity of essentially possessed perfection. The fifth proof proceeds from an ordered multiplicity to an ordering unity. The order of the world, which is at the starting point of this proof, furnished one of the most constant evidences of the existence of God to men through the ages. It appealed to Greek poets and philosophers; in unphilosophic form it was preserved in the Sacred Writings of the Jews; primitive peoples appealed to it in their origin myths. It has been not only one of the most ancient of the proofs but one of the most popular. It has been accepted as genuine by the uneducated who were unable to follow its philosophical implications; and, at the same time, was the only proof given a measure of respect by the great Kant.

It was perhaps to be expected that modern philosophy, with its contempt for the past should most strenuously assail this particular proof. Some will say that it was destroyed by the theory of evolution which, telling a tale of the process of development, made unnecessary all explanation of the beginning of that process. Again, the facts of reality are said to be adequately explained by blind chance or by necessity. We shall look at these last two modern (and ancient) objections more closely after we have seen the proof itself.

The fifth proof for the existence of God proceeds just as did the other four, demanding no more, resting on just as solid a foundation. It has the same starting point of facts in the world in which we live; it makes use of the same fundamental principle of reason and of things, namely, that opposites are not identical. Here the point in question is the existence of an order; the search for its explanation leads us to a supreme intelligence.

The argument might be phrased briefly like this. In the world about us we see things devoid of intelligence acting for an end, a fact which is evident from their always, or generally, acting in the same orderly way to attain that which is best for them. Evidently these actions are placed, not by accident, but on purpose. As things devoid of intelligence do not act for an end unless they be directed by some intelligence, we must conclude that a supreme intelligence exists which directs all natural things to their end.

An immediately obvious difficulty against this argument seems to be that it presumes the order of the world; this order is by no means a fact of experience. If there is such an order in the world, we have not discovered it yet. As a matter of fact, this objection has its roots in the lush soil of confusion, the confusion of external and internal finality. To solve the mystery of external finality we would have to know all the answers to such questions as the external reason for the bite of a mosquito, the existence of a snake, the destruction wrought by a hurricane. We simply do not know these things; certainly we do not know all of them and probably we never shall. It is asking a good deal to demand an exhaustive measurement of divine plans by such an instrument as the mind of a man. As a matter of fact, we do not have to plumb the mystery of external finality for the purposes of this argument.

It is quite sufficient that we establish the fact of internal finality. That we can and do know without doubt. We do know that the eye is constructed for purposes of seeing, the ear for hearing; that a mosquito bites for purposes of nourishment, that the snake's fangs are weapons of defense, and so on. Knowledge such as this is sufficient for the starting point of this fifth proof for the existence of God. Indeed, only one such instance of internal finality would give grounds enough for the proof. This fact of internal finality is quite sufficient to absolve this argument from the charge of anthropomorphism which some philosophers have levelled against it. The argument does not demand that we search the soul of a snake or a mosquito to unearth motives, intentions or plans; it asks merely that we recognize the fact of a constant order of cause to effect.

This internal order is not to be explained by chance. Such an explanation is an insult to common sense: my ear might just as well have turned out to be an organ of smell; on such grounds, is it not surprising that so many animals have ears? The ratio of the chances for a simultaneous chance development of the thirteen conditions immediately necessary for sight has been figured out as 9,999,985 to 15; yet the thing happens every day!

Putting aside the appeal of common sense, which is strangely suspect by the modern philosopher, the explanation of the order of the world by chance is philosophically unsound. Certainly chance exists. It is just chance that a bald-headed man is caught in a thunder-shower without his hat; but obviously if there were no reason for his being out, no reason for the shower, the heavy drops would not now be smacking off the smooth surface of his head. In other words, the very existence of chance presupposes the existence of the essential; chance is no more than the clash of two causes attempting to pursue their own purposive ways; it is an accident which happens to the essential, not which explains or does away with the essential. If everything happens by chance, then all nature is reduced to the level of the accidental; things are not essentially what they are, but only accidentally so, the mirage may melt away before the groping fingers of our mind.

Such an explanation is no explanation at all; it is a contradiction. It is the by now familiar absurdity of explaining the perfect by the imperfect, the greater by the less, order by the lack of order. Or, to put it bluntly, it identifies opposites — potentiality with its realization or potentiality with the lack of all being. And we are faced with the old dilemma of denying the potentialities of the medical student and the perfections of the doctor or of denying the difference between the two; that is, we are back to the impossible attempt to deny facts.

The modern, intent on dodging the infinite, is not at all dashed by the breakdown of an explanation which he will confidently use again as soon as the thunder of reason's guns has died down. For the moment he solves the problem by denying it: the order of the world is explained by the necessity of nature; God is unnecessary because the world is self-sufficient. In plain language, this means that order is discernible in the world, science can continue with its investigation of this order, because things are what they are; this is their nature, they are determined by necessary physical laws to this way of being and of acting, nature itself supplies the necessary determination.

No real question is solved by pretending it does not exist; and this is a real question. The solution offered on the grounds of necessity merely pushes the question back. Whence comes this determination, this necessary inclination to determined action? What is the source of the necessity of nature and of physical laws? Obviously it does not explain itself; chance will not do as an explanation; the only possible solution is a cause above nature, an intelligence that is supreme. Not any intelligence will do. For if that intelligence is not supreme, then it is not intelligence but a nature which has intelligence, that is, a nature determined, inclined, ordered to know; and we have the same problem all over again — whence comes this determination, this inclination, this order? This ultimately explanatory intelligence must be, not have, intelligence; it must not be ordered to knowing but must be its own knowledge.

Such are the proofs for the existence of God. They have their foundations deep in the solid earth while their superstructure sweeps up to the heights of divinity. These proofs are not airy abstractions, they are not vague constructs made to substitute, in the dim light of argumentation, for solid reality. They are inferential proofs, a posteriori proofs, inductions based on the facts of the sensible world and the first principles of reason. The facts upon which they are based are in no sense disputed facts; given the movement of an eyelash, the perfection of a stone or the contingency of a sigh, these proofs hold. Surely, in all common sense, the foundation asked from the senses for these proofs cannot be denied.

On the other hand, the principle of reason involved in these proofs is no less indisputable. It cannot be denied without the denial of all intellectual activities, without the denial of the world of reality; indeed, it cannot be denied without being affirmed.

For this principle is simply that a thing is what it is, a thing cannot be and not be at the same time, it cannot be itself and something else; in other words, the principle insists that differences are not identities, that potentialities are not their actualizations, that non-being is not identical with being.

The philosopher who, for reasons best known to himself, decides to challenge these proofs has entered a war of cosmic proportions; fortunately for himself, he cannot win. Such a victory would be his own annihilation. These proofs are not aimed at a cumulative effect; they are totally different from the mass of arguments gathered in support of the hypothesis of evolution, they are not the frail threads woven into the strong cloth of a prosecuting attorney's circumstantial argument. From all of them, or from any of them, the existence of God is established; from any one of them as a starting point, it can be shown that God is existence itself, the perfect being, *ens a se.*

No fault can be found with their procedure, for they adhere rigidly to the evidence in hand and conclude within the proper limits of this evidence. The knowledge they give is not that of probability, not even of very high probability; rather it is knowledge of metaphysical certitude, excluding every other possibility, leaving only the first mover, the first cause, the necessary being and so on as the ultimate answer to the facts of the world of reality.

That these proofs have been shrugged off as meaningless to men, devoid of qualitative content, is something the thinking man will always be unable to understand; and for the very good reason that such an attitude is unintelligible. The following chapters will bring out at length the implications of these notions; but without further elaboration these arguments bow down under the weight of the ripe fruit of profound significance. Thus, for instance, the fact of the existence of a first unmoved mover means that there is no movement, from the crushing force of a tidal wave to the rise and fall of a breast in sleep, which does not depend every instant on God; there is no change, from the imperceptible coloring of a leaf in autumn to the upheaval of a social revolution in which God does not play a major part. The existence of a first uncaused cause means that in the swaying struggle of men's lives, the triumphs of their greatest thoughts and works, their masterpieces, their literature, their architecture, the soarings of the poet or the crisp command of the soldier, there is no instant from which God can be excluded. No walls are thick enough, no wastes lonely enough, no army powerful enough, no governmental edict sweeping enough, no hatred bitter enough to exclude the action of the first cause.

The existence of an absolutely necessary being means there is a divine sustaining hand whose withdrawal means annihilation; it means that we cannot contact anything of reality without confronting divinity; that God is closer to us than we are to ourselves, that every moment of life, every particle of dust, every stitch of a garment is permeated with divinity or it could not continue to be. That there is an all perfect being means that all the beauty, the love, the goodness that lift the heart of a man out of himself are but shadows of the infinite on the pool of life, vague hints of the ineffable that lies at the beginning and end of life. That a supreme intelligence exists makes it plain that the hairs of our head are indeed numbered; that there is no step, no breath, no success or failure that is without its meaning, without its place in the divine plan, a supreme order, that necessarily goes beyond the human mind's power of assimilation.

These proofs may be attacked as wild abstractions of reason without solid foundation or as cold reasonings that have no meaning, no interest to men. Both accusations are completely false: these are scientific proofs based on the world of reality; they are of an inexhaustible significance and interest to men. If the truth were honestly faced, it would be evident that the real grounds for the modern unease in their presence is the fact that they lead the mind of man to the ultimate mystery. Every beginning is mysterious because every beginning has a drop of the exotic perfume of divinity on its garments. Every beginning is a bridge spanning the chasm between what can be and what is, by its very existence proclaiming the perfection and the mystery of its builder, the ultimate Beginning who laid the foundations upon which every such bridge must be built. The most prosaic beginning intrigues our mind, for the humblest beginning poses a question that only divinity answers and only divinity can fully understand that answer. By a beginning something has come into being that did not exist before; it is a sleight of hand trick, a bit of magic that cannot be true, a mouse giving birth to a mountain unless we come to the Beginning that never began and always is, to the limitlessness that explains the limited, to the utterly independent which is the sole support of the dependent. When we have arrived at that ultimate answer, we are face to face with the incomprehensible precisely because we are in the presence of the limitless.

To the man who confusedly identifies human excellence with absolute supremacy, this sort of thing is intolerable; what overflows the measure of the human mind simply cannot exist, for this would be a refutation of the excellence of man. Some other solution must be had, something not mysterious, something that can be weighed, measured and put in its place by the human god of the universe. It may be this man will try to satisfy his mind, and his heart, by the absurdities of order explained by chance, by the blindness of necessity that has no source, or the deceit of substituting a process for an explanation. But such things can satisfy the mind of a man only by destroying it; they do not solve the problem of a beginning, they dodge it, deny it, destroy it, whereas the mind of man can be satisfied only with an answer. If we are to have that answer, we must face the fact of mystery, for mystery can be eliminated only at the cost of eliminating the beginning and so eliminating all that follows from that beginning. Perhaps, some day, the modern man will learn that mystery is not the prison of the mind of man, it is his home.

JESSICA POWERS

CONTEMPLATIVE nuns have no past, only a Presence. As a consequence of her entry into the Carmelite Order, the age and past of Jessica Powers dissolve into the enlightenment and girlish laughter which arise behind the seeming gloom of the monastic grill. But her poems still remain after her to demonstrate her sharp intuitions and unspoiled love of beauty. Disciple of Hopkins, Miss Powers displays her discipleship with living fire. Flight and birds are her preoccupation in so many figures she uses, but their magic does not grow stale with use nor the sharpness of Jessica Powers' crystallizations of experience less intense in personalized expression.

NIGHT OF STORM*

The times are winter. Thus a poet signed
  Our frosty fate. Life is a night of snow.
Man sees no path before him, nor behind;
  His faithless footprints from his own heels
    blow.
Where can an exile out of heaven go,
  With murk and terror in a trackless place
  And stinging bees swept down upon his
    face?

Or what is else? There is your world within.
  And now the soul is supplicant: O most
Wretched and blind, come home! Where love
    has been
  Burns the great lantern of the Holy Ghost.
Here in His light, review your world of frost:
  A drifting miracle! What had been night
  Reels with unending eucharists of light.

*The above and following poems have been selected from The Lantern Burns, by Jessica Powers (New York: The Monastine Press, 1939).

SONG OF THE IMMORTAL SOUL

O birds of the blue air that call to me!
O orioles of brilliant song and dress!
O whippoorwills that sob against a tree
And larks of incoherent happiness!
O mourning doves that make a lonely call!
O wild geese geometric on the sky!
O robins sweet in April twilight! All

You little birds of God that sing and fly,
From you I hide this bright bird of my
    breast;
For if you saw his far-winged journeying,
Your flight might fail; your song die
    unexpressed
If, listening at the stars, you heard him sing.

THE BOOKS OF SAINT JOHN OF THE CROSS

Out of what door that came ajar in heaven
  Drifted this starry manna down to me,
To the dilated mouth both hunger given
  And all satiety?

Who bore at midnight to my very dwelling
  The gift of this imperishable food?
My famished spirit with its fragrance filling;
  Its savor certitude.

The mind and heart ask, and the soul replies
  What store is heaped on these bare shelves
    of mine?
The crumbs of the immortal delicacies
  Fall with precise design.

Mercy grows tall with the least heart
    enlightened,
  And I, so long a fosterling of night,
Here feast upon immeasurably sweetened
  Wafers of light.

THE FIRST PENTECOST

All the Apostles looked at one another;
　Words curled in fire through the returning
　　gloom.
　Something had changed and colored all the
　　room.
The beauty of the Galilean mother
Took the breath from them for a little space.
　Even a cup, a chair or a brown dress
　Could draw their tears with the great
　　loveliness
That wrote tremendous secrets every place.

That was the day when Fire came down from
　　heaven,
　Inaugurating the first spring of love.
Blood melted in the frozen veins, and even
　The least bird sang in the mind's inmost
　　grove.
The seed sprang into flower, and over all
Still do the multitudinous blossoms fall.

THE KINGDOM OF GOD

Not toward the stars, O beautiful naked
　　runner,
　Not on the hills of the moon after a wild
　　white deer,
Seek not to discover afar the unspeakable
　wisdom, —
　The quarry is here.

Beauty holds court within, —
　A slim young virgin in a dim shadowy
　　place.
Music is only the echo of her voice,
　And earth is only a mirror for her face.

Not in the quiet arms, O sorrowful lover;
　O fugitive, not in the dark on a pillow of
　　breast;
Hunt not under the lighted leaves for God, —
　Here is the sacred Guest.

There is a Tenant here.
　Come home, roamer of earth, to this room
　　and find
A timeless Heart under your own heart
　beating,
　A Bird of beauty singing under your mind.

AT EVENING WITH A CHILD

. . . For Maureen

We walk along a road
At the day's end, a little child and I;
And she points out a bird, a tree, a toad,
A stretch of colored sky.

She knows no single word
But "Ah" (with which all poems must
　commence,
At least in the heart's heart), and I am
　stirred
By her glad eloquence.

Her feet are yet unsure
Of their new task, her language limited,
But her eyes see the earth in joy secure.
And it is time I said:

Let the proud walls come down!
Let the cold monarchy be taken over!
I give my keys to rust, and I disown
Castles of stone for ambushed roads in clover.

　All the vast kingdoms that I could attain
　Are less to me than that the dusk is mild
　And that I walk along a country lane
　At evening with a child.

BIRD AT EVENING

Here is a very Magdalen of bird
  Weeping her music at the feet of day,
Who in a moment more will be interred
  And in his shroud of silver laid away.

This is the bird that lately had anointed
  The radiant flesh with the cool oil of song.
These feet are still; the night is three days
  long.

Henceforth the story of this bird shall live
Enclosed forever in day's narrative.
  This shall be told of her
Wherever any poet is appointed
  As day's biographer.

THOMAS MERTON

(1915–   )

IN THE *Culture of Cities* Lewis Mumford laments our lack of quiet and the absence of places of tranquillity and retreat in a world given over to the crash and chatter of machines. Real poets are the first to sense this need: So many lovely things to see and no time, no quiet in which to sum them up, or interpret them in the memorable cartouche. Perhaps that is one of the secondary reasons which impelled Thomas Merton to retire to the Trappist Monastery at Gethsemani, Kentucky. Cambridge University has known Thomas and the pages of the *New Yorker* saw some of his poems, but what are these things compared with a growth in Reality which is so utterly real as to forestall the forgetfulness of the grave even while the life of the body still cries for the posthumous immortality of a tombstone.

His is a poetic talent far beyond average. Scholars who review his works in smart claptrap articles for the magazines will air their knowledge of the metaphysical poets, Eliot, Auden, and Spender, and even Father Hopkins. The work of a first-rate poet is like the embassage of angels, original as all surprise, though some memory of speech warmed over clothes the message. "Comparisons are odorous, *me falta palabras*."

Both in his formally religious poems and his verse, which sums up deeply personalized estimates of experience, Thomas Merton is prodigal of surprise — thought, figures, anguished movement of both thought and phrase are the seal of a first-class poet who not only loves things and sees into them but refers them to a living center of interpretation which fires them with authentic revelation. This quality gives religious value to *The Oracle* not one whit less elevated than the lightning which flails out of *The Sponge Full of Vinegar,* unless we believe with the signboards that modern girls have no more value than their forms or empty eyes. It is the center of reference which inspires the glosses for all things, all situations.

For the genuinely religious poet asks no especially religious subject in order to cry out in the wilderness.

POEM: 1939*

The white, the silent stars
Drive their wheeling ring,
Crane down out of the tall black air
To hear the swanworld sing.

*The above and following poems have been selected
from: *A Man in the Divided Sea*, by Thomas Merton
(Norfolk, Conn.: New Directions, 1946).

But the long, deep knife is in,
(O bitter, speechless earth)
Throat grows tight, voice thin,
Blood gets no regrowth,

As night devours our days,
Death puts out our eyes,
Towns dry up and flare like tongues
But no voice prophesies.

THE ORACLE

The girls with eyes of wicks of lights,
Thin as the rushes, and as many,
Make in their minds uncertain shapes of
    music,
And slyly string their phony harps with
    twine.

The girls with eyes of drops of water,
Thin as the fires, and as frightened,
Bring pennies and their empty zodiacs.
Horses, loose on a plain, drum
The secret dance their thought does now!

Come up and light your harmless questions.
Burn them to the Brazen Face,
And wait, in terror, for the Brazen Voice.

"You girls with eyes of wicks of lights,
Shake me: I ring like a bank.
I shout like the assembly: 'Go, be presidents
You shall all marry rectangles!'

"But you with eyes of drops of water,
Punch my brass eyes with your little fists;
I am a box, my voice is only electric.
So keep your pennies for the poor;
Sew, in your houses, and cry."

But already, down the far, fast ladders of
    light
The stern, astounding angel
Starts with a truer message,
Carrying a lily.

THE BETRAYAL

The sense that sits in the thin skins of lips
Was waiting with a traitor's kiss that made
    You sweat with death,
When envy, in the Lenten night,
Shone sharp as lightnings: and we came with
    blades.

What hate, what worlds of wormwood did
    our tongues distill!
We cried with voices dry as shot,
In Pilate's yard where pride of life
And love of glory laced Your brows in Blood.

What were our curses, dark as vinegar,
We swore, with tongues as sharp as thongs,
On Golgotha, where pride of life,
With easy slanders nailed You to the wood!

And all we uttered, all, was nails and gall,
With our desires cruel as steel.
We digged Your hands, and filled them full
    of Blood.
With little smiles as dry as dice
We whipped and killed You for Your lovely
    world.

You died, and paid Your traitors with a prayer
And cured our swearing darkness with Your wounds' five lights.
Eyes see Your holy hands, and, in them, flowers.

You let the doubter's fingers feel the sun in Your side.
Ears have Your words, and tongues believe You wheat:
You feed with life the lips that kissed You dead!

THE SPONGE FULL OF VINEGAR

When Romans gambled in the clash of lancelight,
Dicing amid the lightnings for the unsewn mantle,
Thirst burned crimson, like a crosswise firebird
Even in the eyes of dying Christ.
But the world's gall, and all its rotten vinegar
Reeked in the sponge, flamed on His swollen mouth,
And all was paid in poison, in the taste of our feasts!
O Lord! When I lie breathless in Thy churches

Knowing it is Thy glory goes again
Torn from the wise world in the daily thundercrack of Massbells,
I drink new fear from the four clean prayers I ever gave Thee!
For even the Word of Thy Name, caught Thy grace,
And offered up out of my deepest terror,
Goes back gallsavored of flesh.
Even the one good sacrifice,
The thirst of heaven, comes to Thee: vinegar!
Reeks of the death-thirst manlife found in the forbidden apple.

THE EVENING OF THE VISITATION

Go, roads, to the four quarters of our quiet distance,
While you, full moon, wise queen,
Begin your evening journey to the hills of heaven,
And travel no less stately in the summer sky
Than Mary, going to the house of Zachary.

The woods are silent with the sleep of doves,
The valleys with the sleep of streams,
And all our barns are happy with peace of cattle gone to rest.
Still wakeful, in the fields, the shocks of wheat
Preach and say prayers:
You sheaves, make all your evensongs as sweet as ours,
Whose summer world, all ready for the granary and barn,
Seems to have seen, this day,
Into the secret of the Lord's Nativity.

Now at the fall of night, you shocks
Still bend your heads like kind and humble kings
The way you did this golden morning when you saw God's Mother passing,
While all our windows fill and sweeten
With the mild vespers of the hay and barley.

You moon and rising stars, pour on our barns and houses
Your gentle benedictions.
Remind us how our Mother, with far subtler and more holy influence,
Blesses our rooves and eaves,
Our shutters, lattices and sills,
Our doors, and floors, and stairs, and rooms, and bedrooms,
Smiling by night upon her sleeping children:
O gentle Mary! Our lovely Mother in heaven!

SISTER MARY MAURA

(*1916–*)

BROOKLYN, New York, is not usually associated with poetry but it is the birthplace of Sister Maura who was born there May 5, 1916. After her profession as a school Sister of Notre Dame, Sister Maura continued her studies at Notre Dame of Maryland and in addition to the degree of bachelor of arts received there, she has a master of arts degree from the Catholic University of America and is now completing her work as a doctor of philosophy at Johns Hopkins University. Sister Maura is a member of the Catholic Poetry Society and the Modern Language Association. As a teacher she spent some years at the Notre Dame Preparatory School and is at the present time instructor in English at the College of Notre Dame of Maryland.

Sister Maura's poetry as seen in her one published book, *Initiate the Heart,* is completely mature. As a craftsman she shows subtlety and complete mastery of many forms. Her best quality is her social intuitiveness which finds in dramatic situations food for thought and religious implications.

SOMEWHERE THE COCK CROW*

Panel of a Fifteenth Century Diptych: A Donor with St. John the Baptist

This much is left: the man and grave St. John,
his patron. To what young Virgin's face
he looks, no man will know. He broods upon
the culminating years — through harsh, thick brace
of furrows on the brow; the long, bruised stare;
by flesh as stretched as silence on a moan;
by hint of lips, and more by hands of prayer,
so pressed that carvings mark the knuckle bone.

Somewhere, somewhere a cock must crow: the eyes
listen, the mouth listens, and the flat ears
listen. This is a man without disguise
at what dark dawn before a route of tears.
So Adam waited, so does Adam's son,
aching between sin ended, grief begun.

*The above and following poems have been selected from *Initiate the Heart,* by Sister Mary Maura, S.S.N.D. By Permission of The Macmillan Company, Publishers; New York: 1946.

BEFORE SNOW

Here a portent broods
not dread, nor fear,
only the grey
turn of the year.
Through the gaunt trees
patrolling the west
uncertain clouds bar
a vast unrest.
The air broods soft

as a great cat's paw,
but the fur bodes cold
and stings like a claw

Once the snow falls
there will be peace. . . .
So the taut heart strains
before release.

EPITAPH FOR A NUN

Ignore the coiffure intricate;
the wimple's white design
is but the chastened mark of love,
the signet and the sign.
To mocker and to reverent,
to scorner and sincere,
she wore the blazoned lettering —
God suffices here.

This was the reason for her poise,
her questing for perfection,
this is the vision that she veiled,
the bourne of her election.
Ignore the coiffure intricate
that was her meek adorning,
pray by the fathomless darks she knew —
night was her morning.

COME CHRISTMAS

They waited for the street car,
the rabbi and the nun,
he was so old he must have known
his son's son's youngest son.
She and her companion were
description proof as far as dress,
one thought of Canterbury Tales
and Chaucer's prioress.

The car was crowded and the rabbi stood,
jostled and awkward on tired feet;
she took his hand and paid his fare,
she helped him find a seat.
He murmured some old blessing,
and she bent low her head
as one who knows the value of
the swift prayer surely said.

There was a stir within the car
and man to man was not a stranger
seeing Isaiah prophesy,
and a virgin stand at her own heart's manger.

OUR LADY OF THE REFUGEES

Mother who knew
what hardship shakes
a woman bundling clothes,
and putting by her wheaten cakes;
Mother who urged the donkey,
(making happy riot
on the straggling stones)
urged the beast to be more quiet;
Mother who heard the Child
whimper beneath the thin blue shawl,
our aching prayers cry out to thee,
  Mother, pray for them all.

A thousand Bethlehems
mask dark tonight,
the eyes of friendly little homes
have lost their light;
pathetic heaps of poor, dear things
are laid aside; a small bird sang
where a latched door swings.
Mother, whose sad Egyptian flight
preceded all of these
guide them in faith beneath familiar stars,
Our Lady of the Refugees.

INITIATE THE HEART

Consider the season's wheel:
the turn of summer creeping over
leaves one incurved tendril on the vine,
one pointed peak of sweet, late clover.

Initiate the heart to change
for it is wiser so,
accepting the splendor of the hour
white with clematis or snow.

Fortify the will with peace;
no season taking root,
tranquil in mist, in warmth, in frost,
each bears fruit.

JOHN W. LYNCH
(*1904–*   )

FATHER LYNCH was born in Oswego, New York, 1904. He was educated at Niagara University, and the seminary of Our Lady of the Angels. Ordained priest for the Diocese of Syracuse, he has been a curate at St. Patrick's Church, Binghamton, New York.

In 1941 Father Lynch produced his book-length poem on the life of the Blessed Virgin, *A Woman Wrapped in Silence*. The poem is written in blank verse and though it shows more than ordinary talent in handling the broad strokes of the portrait of Our Lady, its ruminative measures are more akin to prose than poetry.

A WOMAN WRAPPED IN SILENCE*

This was a little child who knew not man,
Nor life, nor all the needed frauds of life,
Nor any compromise, and when she turned
To raise the earthen jar, and faced the airs
Of Spring, she smiled for young security,
And she was glad. These were her own,
  these lanes
Of Nazareth. She'd known the slope and feel
Of them for all her years, and they had
  known
Of her, and she was walking now and was
Familiar, and the well she sought not far
Beyond the clustered houses was so old
It had become a part of permanence.
The sky around it was so clear, serene

With blue, and famed with hills that had
  been hers
For always, and which lifted up a silence
She had loved. These thresholds were her
  friends,
These white walls leaning, and the narrow
  doors,
And she could watch the shadows and the
  slant
Of sun, and turn a corner so, and hear
The farther crowing of a cock, and guess
That in the marketplace were dusty sheep
She could not hear; and passing on, she
  marked
With deeper care that from an opened
  window
Rose the sound of psalms. She was at home.

*From *A Woman Wrapped in Silence*, pp. 1–9, by John W. Lynch. By permission of The Macmillan Company, Publishers; New York: 1942.

These few streets and the ruts in them were
  home,
And she was sure, and young, and now the
  others
At the well had called to her, and said
Among them it was Mary who had come.
They mentioned Joseph to her with a smile
And nod, and one remarked that she had
  seen
Him at a friend's house yesterday, and that
His work was moving on, and he had plans
He'd spoken of, and that he'd asked for her.

They turned with understanding in their eyes
And looked to her. She was a woman here
Who'd made a bond with Joseph. She could
  sense
Their knowing that, they saw her now as
  his,
Belonging, with a place and name declared
And set and sealed beyond the need to think
It could be ever altered or would change.
She held that in her thoughts. She'd made a
  bond
With Joseph. He had given her his word
And she'd consented. She had made a bond.
And after she had moved away and placed
The filled jar to her shoulder, and had gone
A distance up the little sloped return,
It came to her that this content, this ease,
This quiet in her was not of the hills,
Or roofs, or streets that were her childhood's
  paths,
But was of Joseph. Joseph was her peace.
He was her home, and holding in her now,
His name was warm and strong and innocent
Of fears. She could be confident of him,
She could be glad for Joseph, she could
  trust. . . .

And then she was remembering the day
He came to pledge to her. Joachim,
Her father, had stood forward solemnly.
Behind him, Mary Cleophas and all
The rest of kinsfolk, cousins, and the friends
Who were as dear. And he had come, and
  was
Not bold, and offered Joachim the gift
Of *mohar,* and had said it was a sign.
And afterward, the lesser gifts of *mattan*
He had brought for all to share in him.

They were not rich, his gifts, and he had
  spoken
Softly, and she could remember how
His voice had trembled, and he'd said that
  prayers
Were on his heart.

        O, Joseph, Joseph! She
Had known there would be prayers. And
  when the time
Of waiting ended, and procession formed
To lead her to his house, she'd have no fears.

And smiling in the peace that mantled her,
She reached her father's door again and
  stepped
Within to old repeated tasks and cares
That for these brief months still would be
  her own.
No change had come because the plighted
  word
Of Joseph had been said, and villagers
Could recognize she was betrothed to him.
The spinning must be done, the weaving
  threads
Be caught and mended, and the knots untied,
The pans and ovens filled with bread, the
  crusts
Must still be hoarded, and the counted needs
Of poetry be met. She walked upon
The stairs and watched for Joachim, and
  called
Across the street to neighbors and received
Their news, and when the day was bright,
  she closed
The shutters to the sun. She woke, and slept,
And moved, and bound her hair up in a
  braid.
She saved the moments out that gave her
  heart
To God, as she had always done, and all
Around her, Nazareth was small and old
And settled on its hills, and kept the old
Ways it had learned. She was a young girl
  here. . . .

But when across the years we see her so,
Our generation finds it hard to think
Of her as one with us. Our stains have made
Us hesitant, and sad remembrance curls
And turns within to slow the prideful
  binding

To ourselves, as if the very claim
Could soil in her the grace whose essence is
It is not soiled. This name is benediction
On our blood, defence and refuge, hope
And harbor, and our one fair memory
Of innocence, and we have known too long
Its silence on the world's wild clamoring
Not now to know this name is uttered prayer
And not a name.

        And yet, the gifts that were
To weigh her heart will find already there
Bewilderment, and seated fears, and sight
That moved no farther than her vision ran,
And God gave her to see. Not true to think
Her tears were not as salt as tears may be,
And not as real. It is not true to say
Her sweetness made a cushion for the blows
That fell on her, and left her warmed and
        snug
Against the starkness of the staring night.
This voice could laugh, and sob, and sing,
        and cry:
This was a woolen garment that she wore
About her tired shoulders, and the hands
That brushed the weight of hair from off her
        brow
Were roughened with the water jars, and
        knew
The feel of sunlight and the form of bread.

Not strange is this, and we have always
        known
It true, that she was one with us, and yet,
We've built so many towers in our skies,
So often flung the great stones up for her
To ease the heart's full need, and be a praise
To stand above the years' long pondering;
So often have we turned the litanies,
Strung out so many garlands, while her bells
Have called to us, and kneeling we have
        sighed
In such dear confidence. . . .

        We scarce remember
Now that once this name was spoken softly
In a time before the Aves rang.
Perhaps across some threshold it was said,
So casually, by one who called to her,
"Mary." Then, she must have turned and
        come,

Obedient from where the children played
Together in the dusk: and no one knew
That more was said than just a young girl's
        name.

No, not true to think that then her feet
Were visibly upon the serpent's head,
And stars ringed visibly about her brow.
Except for gentleness and modesty,
The grace she held in fullness, was as grace
We hold, a silent gift, unknown, if knowing
Be the shattering of earthly molds,
And loosing of the need for watchfulness.
No deep, relentless tide of ecstasy
Swept over her, to carry her beyond
The world she knew, and make her stranger
        here.
The dawn was cold, and in the dark, the
        wind
Still spoke of other dawns, and all her days
Were labor and were vigilance. And peace
That made its quietness in her was peace
God gave, since she had made a place for it
By tired hands and a heart that did not tire.

His way with men has been to take men's
        way,
And that's the glory and the scandal both. . . .
O, not the thunders and the lifted gates
He chose, and not exotic retinue
To bring Him flaming through the breathless
        towns
With swift compulsion and command, not
        this,
But briefest pausing in the pulse of life,
With all our old simplicities unmarred,
With no rejections of the flesh we bear,
The hearts we love with, and the pain we
        know.
He slept our sleep, and with us dreamed our
        dreams.

And when the hour had come that was to
        move
The long days onward up to Bethlehem,
Until a faint new cry should break across
Our air that had not heard such cry before,
Weighted with ungarnered potencies,
High portent unreleased, and tremulous
With mercies still unsaid, a moment paused
Above a quiet place, and found, just this,

A woman wrapped in silence, and the seed
Of silence was her heart that tried to give
All that it held to give, and ever more.
Spilled all about her, pooled in radiance,
The guardian brightness of God's favor lay,
Like light, too luminous to bear the trace
Of shadow, too intense, too strong for sight.
No vision here is ours. Nor Gabriel's,
Who, shaded in his sanctity, was sent
To stand here, lonely and apart, to speak
In whisper that which only God could see.

Hail, full of grace, the Lord is with thee:
Blessed art thou among women.

O, Luke had words to tell, but Luke's good
    words
Are faltering, and halt before they lead
Beyond the outer margins of the light:
And only this we know, and knowing now
Keep higher hopes and on our race may hold
A stronger blessedness: O, only this . . .
Within the light, the mercies of the Three
Were offered unto her: Who made all power,
Paused, and suppliant, was powerless . . .
The Holy Ghost shall come upon thee, and
the power of the most High shall over-
shadow thee. And therefore also the Holy
which shall be born of thee shall be called
the Son of God. And behold thy cousin
Elizabeth, she also hath conceived a son in
her old age; and this is the sixth month with
her that is called barren; because no word
shall be impossible with God.
Not, "Aye," returned; not "Aye, for all the
    tribes
And all the worlds await." But secretly,
Uneager, prideless, unafraid, the brightness
Flamed to greater radiance, and then . . .

Behold the handmaid of the Lord, be it
done to me according to thy word.

This is conclusion, and the fires that scorched
The Prophet's lips, the old consuming fires
That burned in Israel's blood might now be
    cooled;

For prophecies are ending, and the dreams
That throbbed above the great unfinished
    music
Of the psalms are quieted, and psalms
At last resolve, like chords that come to rest.
This is fulfillment, and upreaching hands
May now be folded, and the long desires
That beat, half heard in need, through all
    the veins,
May now be eased. New testament is made,
New visitation, and a full new world
That holds much more of mystery, and more
Of consequence than that which answered
    first
From nothingness.

And yet the quiet here
Retains no trace of great archangel wings,
And now that all the words are said that
    waited
To be said, the voices leave no trail
Of echo after them to tell that once
They spoke. Dust is floating undisturbed,
And from a distance comes the muffled noise
Of moving wheels and sound of daily things.
A moment came, and that is all, a moment
Came and passed, and in the passing left
A young girl here who was not now alone.
This was not she who lifted up her head,
And yet it was, and crowded days that stretch
Beyond will still be bound for her in sun
And in the dark. Her steps will fall upon
The dust and leave an imprint there, and
    tasks
Will weary her. Dedicate, and now
So utterly bequeathed, her strengths are yet
Her strengths.

This is God's chosen way with men,
To take men's way; and so the streets she
    walks
And all the roads, the shepherds and the
    shepherds'
Sheep, the winds, the firelight, Israel's hills,
Will find just this, no more, a woman plain
Upon the earth, and in her arms, a Child.

HAROLD C. GARDINER
(*1904–*   )

THE present literary editor of *America* was born in Washington, D. C., February 6, 1904. He made his first vows in the Society of Jesus in 1924, his final vows in 1939. He was ordained in 1935. The foundation for his education was laid at Woodstock College. After receiving the S.T.L. and M.A. from Woodstock, Father Gardiner pursued graduate studies for the Ph.D. at Cambridge University in England. He has taught at Canisius College and Fordham University.

As literary editor of *America,* Father Gardiner has played a prominent role in developing a mature appreciation of Catholic literature. Through his influence Catholic literary criticism, in particular, has been lifted to a plane which is worthy of our intellectual background and tradition. This widening of horizons has been the largest single force in preparing the way for the future endeavors of Catholic novelists.

PRINCIPLE V:
FICTION'S FUNCTION NOT TO TEACH*

I WOULD like now to discuss a point that often, indeed, touches on morality, but which is, essentially, a question of the author's artistic approach to the whole question of truth and beauty. Upon a proper adjudication of his approach, of his soundness in striking a balance between the two, will also, to a great extent, depend the justice of the reader's demands on the author.

What can the reader demand? He can and must demand, as the preceding discussion has tried to show, that the author treat human life as human life, and that, therefore, he treat sin for what it is; he must demand that the author, in treating sin this way, not so glamorize it as to run the risk of making the reader's life less human. But — and this is the point of this further discussion — the reader cannot, in literature, demand that the author teach him how to live. In other words — and here is another principle for both reviewers and readers — we do not and cannot go to fiction for instruction.

This statement would, indeed, seem to need no laboring, but I feel that much of the difficulty felt by some who have ob-

jected to the recent novels that have occasioned this treatment has arisen from the fact that the aggrieved readers have forgotten that all literature, and fiction, perhaps, above all, is written to please and not to teach. Indeed, one correspondent gives voice to that very confusion, when she writes that when and if she ever wants to find out how to wean a baby daughter, she will go to a standard manual for mothers or to her doctor, and not to Betty Smith.

Precisely, and so would I, were such a happy fate possible for me. But the point is that such an attitude is casting upon the author (Betty Smith or any other) a burden that is unfair and overwhelming. Miss Smith never set out to tell us, in the pages of her novel, how children ought to be weaned, or how public schools ought to be run or how life ought to be lived; she simply wanted to say and did say that this was actually how the child was weaned, and this was how a particular life was lived.

Well, then, do we learn nothing from fiction? Is it, then, merely an escape, time wasted that adds nothing to the fullness of human life? By no means; not if it is read. I do learn from fiction, but I learn in the

*Gardiner, Harold C., S.J., *Tenets for Readers and Reviewers* (New York: The America Press), pp. 18–23.

fashion that is art's unique own; I learn through being pleased; I find truth through the door of beauty. And if I strike upon something beautiful, let me have no fears that I can miss truth, for they are both but different facets of the same Thing.

Ah, but there is the rub! We grant you, you say, that we ought not to go to novels to find the truth of instruction; we will be content to find the mere truth of fact — but where, oh where, in so much modern fiction is there any vestige of beauty?

Let me try to unravel that by a concrete example. A recent novel that I praised in review (America, August 28, 1943) was Marquand's So Little Time. Writing of it in the Herald Tribune Books for December 26, 1943, Isabel Patterson rather echoes America's judgment when she says:

Nobody in the story had any [truths, ideas to orient themselves by]. There is not a trace of intellectual activity in the characters; they do not think, therefore they do not feel anything but a rather dull discomfort and boredom. . . . So Little Time is a group portrait of people in a huddle, wondering what for. . . .

Precisely, you say, and where is there the dimmest glimmering of beauty there? It isn't *there,* but it emerges from the book; it is in the overtones, it is in the wistful gropings of the rootless characters, it is in the whole poignant contrast that the author never points explicitly but which lurks beneath every page — the contrast between what these huddled people actually are and what, as human beings, they could have been. There is beauty; the beauty of the potentiality of the human soul, unrealized, frustrated, dissipated on the husks, but still fundamentally and eternally there.

And it is through this obscured door of a dimly suggested beauty that the author actually does, though it may not have been his intention, teach a deep lesson. But if I approach the book with the exclusive expectation and demand that the author instruct me in life, I would be asking him to assume a responsibility that simply is not his, that of being a moral guide. He cannot be an immoral guide; but the truth he hints

at and suggests cannot be indicated by pointer-and-blackboard method — it must emerge from the beauty (tenuous and fitful, perhaps, as what beauty is not, save One?) of the characters, of the situation, of the overtones.

There must be this kind of beauty in any true art, and in literary art above all, for without it the truth contained will never be more than the truth of fact, never the truth of ideal. But when the truth of fact is informed by this idea of beauty, then the truth of ideal springs from the wedding of the two. Geoffrey Wilson's love affair (never trespassing the principles laid down earlier in this series) with the actress in So Little Time was a truth of fact — it did happen in the author's mind. But it was more than that; informed and suffused with the author's own oblique commentary on the emptiness of Geoffrey's life, the episode merges into a statement of an ideal truth — that the holiness and sharing of marriage would have been the character's salvation, had he only known how to turn to it. Francie Nolan's experience with the pervert in the famous "Tree" was a truth of fact; transformed by the author's appreciation of the girl's instinctive modesty and of her mother's protective love, even that realistic scene shades off into a truth of ideal.

The misapprehension of going to fiction to be instructed was the main reason, I feel, for the furore that was raised some years ago over The Keys of the Kingdom. Those who read it first and foremost as a treatise on moral or pastoral theology forgot that Cronin was not saying that this is the way priests and nuns ought to talk and act. This was the way his creations did act and think, and that artistic fact, seen through the aura of devotion and zeal that permeated the book, showed us, *by contrast or by confirmation,* what the ideal of priestly and religious life is.

Now this critical stand that the purpose of fiction is not primarily to instruct, but to please, is not at all the "art for art's sake" heresy. It is not, for example, Poe's, who pushed to the extreme the theory that the end of art is pleasure, not truth. The fact of the matter is that truth is an element in intellectual pleasure; I cannot take a legitimate intellectual pleasure in something that I know to be intellectually or morally untrue. Literature, dealing with human life, must deal with facts and their interpretation, meaning and bearing; it must teach, it cannot help it. But it must never seem to teach, and the reader must not approach it with the demand that it instruct him as its primary duty.

Here lies a cardinal and practical difficulty for reviewers, especially Catholic ones. If the reviewer knew that all his readers were those who already know how to live life, and were going to fiction, not for a blueprint, but for the enlargement of their own lives either by way of confirmation or contrast, he could judge the book with much more accuracy as to its actual effect. Since some, however, apparently do read fiction to learn how to live, he must often rather temper his purely critical judgment with an eye to practical prudence. But it is totally unfair to expect that that practical prudence will be plenary enough to forestall all and any demurrers.

Truth, then, must be in a novel, but it does not *make* a novel; it is essential, but artistically secondary, subordinate to and presupposed by the fact that the aim of art is to please. But it is so important that if falsehood, untruth, is portrayed in the story, it fails as art, no matter what the specious pleasure derived, for though the end of art be to please, it must please legitimately and rationally.

That is why an historical novel is an exacting task; the author has to keep two truths clearly before him: first of all, the truth of historical fact, which he may, indeed, embellish and expand, but which he can never contravene; second, the truth of ideal, which he shares in common with the purely imaginative writer. *The Robe* and *The Apostle* both fail as works of art, quite apart from their doctrinal shortcomings, because they deny the truth of certain definite historical happenings. The pleasure they give, therefore, is in so far an illegitimate one.

The purely imaginative writer is spared this risk. The truth of the facts depends on his creation; the bickerings of Father Chisholm and the Mother Superior in the earlier controversial novel actually happened, in the author's mind and heart, and the critic cannot dismiss them by saying "these things don't happen." One correspondent objected to praise of *Kansas Irish,* as I have mentioned above, on the ground that the book was false. How could it have been false to the facts, when the author was telling what he actually witnessed in his own family? The question is: did those facts so impress him and does he so transmit them as to give us from them the further truth, the truth of ideal? If so, and if his book is so written as to give pleasure, then his work has accomplished the end which is art's only legitimate one, to give pleasure *humano modo,* not to instruct.

Here again we verge onto the inescapable matter of individual taste. Though the end of art be to please legitimately, not all art is going to please everybody. You may simply not like a certain type of book, but that will be no guarantee that the book is not art. The somber or tragic tale may repel you, but as long as it can be pointed out that the tale does contain the elements of truth and beauty that I have been insisting on, the novel will be, objectively, a work of art, whether you derive pleasure from it or not.

Taste is a personal matter, though it is true that there is an objective hierarchy of taste. The whole point of this discussion is, not by any means to bludgeon people into liking or saying that they like what they actually don't, but rather to discuss what I honestly feel to be some general principles on which taste can be properly built and judgments in reviewing (and reading) may be more sanely and critically passed.

That there is need of such temperance is but too sadly proved by the utterly uncharitable tone of some of the correspondence (predominantly in agreement) which has occasioned my going into this thorny question — and, of course, not a few of these letters have been unsigned. Such one-sided criticism (if it may be so called), when applied publicly to a discussion of current fiction, inevitably leads to the suspicion that there are Catholic bigots, too. It is not that way that we are going to influence modern literary thought, whether through creation or through criticism. Nor is it a question of yielding the outposts to the children of this world; it is a matter of knowing principles clearly and holding them tenaciously, but of being judicious in their application. Catholic critics and readers must, to pull their weight, begin and continue, with God's help, to judge books on that basis.

ROBERT LOWELL

(*1917–*   )

BORN into the most exclusive Brahmin circle of Boston in 1917, Robert Lowell was schooled in its exclusive pieties. St. Mark's School laid the foundation of his mental disciplines and was largely instrumental in developing his poetic talent, which is of first class intensity. Lowell entered the Catholic Church in 1941.

It will be fashionable to compare Lowell's poetry with the work of T. S. Eliot, but such comparison is inadequate and illusory. Lowell's poetry, in both form and content, is distinctly original; it does not derive. In exalted moments it is "icily magnificent" and profoundly intellectual, but it exudes, as well, some of the tart quality of the wild New England crab apple, which if it is wry to the mouth in its fruit has also a season of reluctant flower. Like the prose works of Arthur Koestler, Lowell's poetry gives us an excellent example of the modern mind at work: impressions of tortured uncertainty and mental complexity sifting the loess of tradition in search of the bones of the absolute.

For *Lord Weary's Castle,* Lowell was awarded the Pulitzer Prize in poetry, 1947.

THE HOLY INNOCENTS*

Listen, the hay-bells tinkle as the cart
Wavers on rubber tires along the tar
And cindered ice below the burlap mill
And ale-wife run. The oxen drool and start
In wonder at the fenders of a car,
And blunder hugely up St. Peter's hill.
These are the undefiled by woman — their
Sorrow is not the sorrow of this world:
King Herod shrieking vengeance at the curled
Up knees of Jesus choking in the air,

A king of speechless clods and infants. Still
The world out-Herods Herod; and the year,
The nineteen-hundred forty-fifth of grace,
Lumbers with losses up the clinkered hill
Of our purgation; and the oxen near
The worn foundations of their resting-place,
The holy manger where their bed is corn
And holly torn for Christmas. If they die,
As Jesus, in the harness, who will mourn?
Lamb of the shepherds, Child, how still you
   lie.

*The above and following poems have been selected from *Lord Weary's Castle,* by Robert Lowell (New York: Harcourt, Brace and Co., 1944).

CHRISTMAS IN BLACK ROCK

Christ God's red shadow hangs upon the wall
The dead leaf's echo on these hours
Whose burden spindles to no breath at all;
Hard at our heels the huntress moonlight
    towers
And the green needles bristle at the glass
Tiers of defense-plants where the treadmill
    night
Churns up Long Island Sound with piston-
    fist.
Tonight, my child, the lifeless leaves will
    mass,
Heaving and heaping, as the swivelled light
Burns on the bell-spar in the fruitless mist.

Christ Child, your lips are lean and evergreen
Tonight in Black Rock, and the moon
Sidles outside into the needle-screen
And strikes the hand that feeds you with a
    spoon

Tonight, as drunken Polish night-shifts walk
Over the causeway and their juke-box booms
Hosannah in excelsis Domino.
Tonight, my child, the foot-loose hallows
    stalk
Us down the blind alleys of our rooms;
By the mined root the leaves will overflow.

December, old leech, has leafed through Au-
    tumn's store
Where Poland has unleashed its dogs
To bay the moon upon the Black Rock shore:
Under our windows, on the rotten logs
The moonbeam, bobbing like an apple, snags
The undertow. O Christ, the spiralling years
Slither with child and manger to a ball
Of ice; and what is man? We tear our rags
To hand the Furies by their itching ears,
And the green needles nail us to the wall.

VI

OUR LADY OF WALSINGHAM

There once the penitents took off their shoes
And then walked barefoot the remaining
    mile;
And the small trees, a stream and hedgerows
    file
Slowly along the munching English lane,
Like cows to the old shrine, until you lose
Track of your dragging pain.
The stream flows down under the druid tree,
Shiloah's whirlpools gurgle and make glad
The castle of God. Sailor, you were glad
And whistled Sion by that stream. But see:

Our Lady, too small for her canopy,
Sits near the altar. There's no comeliness
At all or charm in that expressionless
Face with its heavy eyelids. As before,
This face, for centuries a memory,
Non est species, neque decor,
Expressionless, expresses God: it goes
Past castled Sion. She knows what God
    knows,
Not Calvary's Cross nor crib at Bethlehem
Now, and the world shall come to Walsing-
    ham.

THE FIRST SUNDAY IN LENT

I

In the Attic

The crooked family chestnut sighs, for March,
Time's fool, is storming up and down the
town;
The gray snow squelches and the well-born
stamp
From sermons in a scolded, sober mob
That wears away the Sabbath with a frown,
A world below my window. What will clamp
The weak-kneed roots together when the
damp
Aches like a conscience, and they grope to rob
The hero under his triumphal arch?

This is the fifth floor attic where I hid
My stolen agates and the canister
Preserved from Bunker Hill — feathers and
guns,
Matchlock and flintlock and percussion-cap;
Gettysburg etched upon the cylinder
Of Father's Colt. A Lüger of a Hun,
Once blue as Satan, breaks Napoleon
In a stained print of Waterloo to trap
A chipmunk on a saber where it slid.

On Troy's last day, alas, the populous
Shrines held carnival, and girls and boys
Flung garlands to the wooden horse; so we
Burrow into the lion's mouth to die.
Lord, from the lust and dust thy will
destroys
Raise an unblemished Adam who will see
The limbs of the tormented chestnut tree
Tingle, and hear the March-winds lift and
cry:
"The Lord of Hosts will overshadow us."

IV

A PRAYER FOR MY GRANDFATHER TO OUR LADY

Mother, for these three hundred years or more
Neither our clippers nor our slavers reached
The haven of your peace in this Bay State:
Neither my father nor his father. Beached
On these dry flats of fishy real estate,
O Mother, I implore
Your scorched, blue thunderbreasts of love to
pour
Buckets of blessings on my burning head
Until I rise like Lazarus from the dead:
Lavabis nos et super nivem dealbabor.

"On Copley Square, I saw you hold the door
To Trinity, the costly Church, and saw
The painted Paradise of harps and lutes
Sink like Atlantis in the Devil's jaw
And knock the Devil's teeth out by the roots;
But when I strike for shore
I find no painted idols to adore:
Hell is burned out, heaven's harp-strings are
slack.
Mother, run to the chalice, and bring back
Blood on your finger-tips for Lazarus who
was poor."

CHILDREN OF LIGHT

Our fathers wrung their bread from stocks
and stones
And fenced their gardens with the Redman's
bones;
Embarking from the Nether Land of Hol-
land,
Pilgrims unhouseled by Geneva's night,
They planted here the Serpent's seeds of
light;
And here the pivoting searchlights probe to
shock
The riotous glass houses built on rock,
And candles gutter by an empty altar,
And light is where the landless blood of Cain
Is burning, burning the unburied grain.

THE SOLDIER

In time of war you could not save your skin.
Where is that Ghibelline whom Dante met
On Purgatory's doorstep, without kin
To set up chantries for his God-held debt?
So far from Campaldino, no one knows
Where he is buried by the Archiano
Whose source is Camaldoli, through the snows,
Fuggendo a piedi e sanguinando il piano,
The soldier drowned face downward in his blood.
Until the thaw he waited, then the flood
Roared like a wounded dragon over shoal
And reef and snatched away his crucifix
And rolled his body like a log to Styx;
Two angels fought with bill-hooks for his soul.

AS A PLANE TREE BY THE WATER

Darkness has called to darkness, and disgrace
Elbows about our windows in this planned
Babel of Boston where our money talks
And multiplies the darkness of a land
Of preparation where the Virgin walks
And roses spiral her enamelled face
Or fall to splinters on unwatered streets.
Our Lady of Babylon, go by, go by,
I was once the apple of your eye;
Flies, flies are on the plane tree, on the streets.

The flies, the flies, the flies of Babylon
Buzz in my ear-drums while the devil's long
Dirge of the people detonates the hour
For floating cities where his golden tongue
Enchants the masons of the Babel Tower

To raise tomorrow's city to the sun
That never sets upon these hell-fire streets
Of Boston, where the sunlight is a sword
Striking at the withholder of the Lord:
Flies, flies are on the plane tree, on the streets.

Flies strike the miraculous waters of the iced
Atlantic and the eyes of Bernadette
Who saw Our Lady standing in the cave
At Massabielle, saw her so squarely that
Her vision put out reason's eyes. The grave
Is open-mouthed and swallowed up in Christ.
O walls of Jericho! And all the streets
To our Atlantic wall are singing: "Sing,
Sing for the resurrection of the King."
Flies, flies are on the plane tree, on the streets.

THE DEAD IN EUROPE

After the planes unloaded, we fell down
Buried together, unmarried men and women;
Not crown of thorns, not iron, not Lombard crown,
Not grilled and spindle spires pointing to heaven
Could save us. Raise us, Mother, we fell down
Here hugger-mugger in the jellied fire:
Our sacred earth in our day was our curse.

Our Mother, shall we rise on Mary's day
In Maryland, wherever corpses married
Under the rubble, bundled together? Pray
For us whom the blockbusters marred and buried;
When Satan scatters us on Rising-day,
O Mother, snatch our bodies from the fire:
Our sacred earth in our day was our curse.

Mother, my bones are trembling and I hear
The earth's reverberations and the trumpet
Bleating into my shambles. Shall I bear,
(O Mary!) unmarried man and powder-puppet,
Witness to the Devil? Mary, hear,
O Mary, marry earth, sea, air and fire;
Our sacred earth in our day is our curse.

JOSEPH DEVER
(*1919-*)

SOMERVILLE, MASS., was the birthplace of Joseph Gerard Dever. He was educated in the parochial schools of Somerville, and completed his mature education at Boston College. His talent for verse and exuberant prose demonstrated itself while Dever was still in college.

During the years of World War II, as a protégé of Harold C. Gardiner, S.J., Dever developed his flair for short-story writing and in a world-wide story contest sponsored by *Yank,* the army magazine, won first place with his much-discussed *Fifty Missions.*

In his first novel, *No Lasting Home,* Dever shows competence and verve. His character delineations have both depth and freshness. He is modern without pose or preciosity; gently humorous as becomes one who holds to standards without sacrificing that pinch of tenderness for humanity which marks the true Christian.

Through the scenes of the human comedy Joseph Dever detects the concomitant action of the divine comedy: this quality gives him both his present excellence and future promise.

CHAPTER XXVIII*

IN THE sweetly coolish light of the following morning Barbara moaned with the gouging, dry nausea of a hangover. Ed remained with her as long as he could — holding to her lips steaming black coffee, holding to her forehead an ice-lumpy towel, holding her head as she moaned in anguish both of the body and the soul, talking to her soothingly — "taking her, Barbara, in sickness, till death do us part."

"Must you go away again, Ed?" she asked. "Can't you take me with you, Ed? I'll be an utterly good wife then, Ed, really I will, if I'm with you. But I must be with you, Ed, I must. I can't live on without you, Ed. Really!"

He held her close and smoothed her warm, dampish brow. "Don't worry, Barb," he said. "Try and rest now. I can't take you with me this time but I'm going to see that you'll be safe and well taken care of till I come home. Come on now, honey, rest. . . .

"Rest, rest," he continued in a gradually lowering, singsong voice. He stroked her brow softly, coolly, as he whispered. Soon she slept, deep and abandoned unto peace as a baby, with a faint, sweet smile touching gently the corners of her mouth.

Ed glanced at his watch. It was 9:15. He'd just have time to get out to the Exercises if

*Dever, Joseph, *No Lasting Home* (Milwaukee: Bruce, 1947).

he grabbed a cab at the Square. What about Barbara. He couldn't leave her entirely alone. She was sleeping deeply now. Maybe Mrs. Gannon next door would look in on her once in a while. He'd hurry back from the Exercises . . . Gerry was graduating, and he had to go!

He writhed into a clean, stiffly starched set of sun tans, tied his tie, combed his hair, cocked his overseas cap on the side of his head, took one last tiptoeing look at the slumbering Barbara, and hurried out the back door. He dashed across the empty lot between the houses and was soon scraping on Mrs. Gannon's back screen door.

The inner door opened. Mrs. Gannon squealed with joy, swept open the screen, and threw her arms around Ed.

"Eddie, Eddie, my boy, oh, it's so good to see you. Come in. Come in, have a cup of tea and tell me where you've been and what you've done!"

Ed explained that he would have to run if he wanted to make Gerry's graduation. He said that Barbara had been under the weather but was now resting comfortably. He wondered if Mrs. Gannon would be able to look in on her every so often while he was over at Ignatian. He promised he'd hurry back. He'd drop in to see her then and tell her all about the places he'd been and the things he'd seen.

"Why surely, Eddie," Mrs. Gannon said.

"You hurry right on out there. I'll go over to Barbara in a while and bring her some hot soup."

"Oh, thank you, Mrs. Gannon, thank you so much!" Ed said, as he backed out the screen door twisting his cap impatiently.

"And give my congratulations to Gerald, won't you now? Oh, you'll be so proud of him . . . my, if his mother was only alive!"

"Yeh, Mrs. Gannon — well, I better go now. See you this afternoon. Thanks again."

He waved at her with his cap, cocked it on, and broke into a run toward the Square and a taxi. He had not forgotten to ask her about Martha — it was just that he could not bring himself to ask — he had noticed a momentary look of pity in Mrs. Gannon's eyes when he had mentioned Barbara. She probably knew all about her. But she would really keep an eye on Barbara while he was gone — he must hurry back — perhaps Gerry would come with him.

He hailed a cab at the Square, snapped out the words "Ignatian College," and settled back on the brown-leather cushions restlessly.

"Can you make it by ten?" he asked as the cab shot toward the Charles River Parkway. "I've got to make the kid brother's graduation."

The cab driver nodded with a faint, customer smile and stepped on the accelerator.

Perhaps Gerry will help me figure out what to do with Barbara while I'm overseas, Ed thought. There must be some nice family that will take her in and kind of keep an eye on her while I'm gone. Maybe Harlan Rock's family would be interested. Maybe Father Boley will have an idea. She'll have to be in a good home while I'm gone . . . oh, well, this is Gerry's graduation morning. Thank God, it's come at last.

After Eddie had left, Mrs. Gannon stood at the back door for a while shaking her gray head slowly and dabbing the corners of her eyes with the end of her apron. She had almost told Ed that Martha was home on leave from the UTO and that she had left for Ignatian College also to attend Gerry's graduation less than an hour ago. Ed was certain to meet her over there, but she just hadn't been able to tell him.

She sighed heavily and went back into the house. That fine Eddie Creedin, she thought. To think he might have been my own son-in-law! Well, it was for this graduation day that he did it all — if only Mary Creedin were alive. God rest her soul.

She dabbed her eyes again and lit the gas under a large kettle of chicken soup. "Well, we'll get some hot nourishment into the wild one, anyway," she sighed. "Sure and she's Eddie's wife no matter what else she is. God help us!"

For a short while after Ed had left her, Barbara slumbered fitfully on. Her mind was clearing — the hangover was wearing off and her nausea, while still bothersome, had none the less abated.

She stirred in her bed restlessly. Her sensitivities were now emerging sharply from their foggy cocoon of alcohol. She dwelt mentally on the happenings of the previous night, on Ed's selflessness and devotion. And she was overwhelmed with excruciating remorse.

But beneath her remorse she knew one truth purely, inexorably — she knew that she now loved Ed with all the life she had within her. She knew, too, that as soon as Ed went away she would slip into her errant ways again — she hated herself for it and was physically powerless before it; but she knew the weakness of herself without him and she resolved out of her love for him never to hurt or embarrass or burden him again.

What could she do? She could pray . . . Ed would like that . . . she could pray. "Hail Mary . . ." she said. The words plummeted from her lips like stones. She broke into a fit of weeping.

Self-abhorrence filled her, how could she do it, how could she destroy herself as quickly and as painlessly as possible? Gas — yes, that was it. The kitchen range. She pushed herself out of bed and stumbled into the kitchen. To steady herself she caught hold of the chromium pipe, which ran around the top of the gas-range burners. She bit her lower lip and turned all four handles.

The gas hissed ominously from the burners. She'd write Ed a note — quickly while she had time. She shuddered with chills as she reeled over to the kitchen mantelpiece for a stub of pencil and a scrap of paper. The faint, yet growing escapings of gas were in her nostrils as she slumped into a chair and began painfully to scrawl on the paper. The gas hissed diabolically behind her. She began to cough as she wrote:

"Dearest Ed: I'm doing this because I have come to love you more than anything else on this earth. I'm positive I would only disgrace you again after you had gone. . . ." What would she say next? The gas was collecting in the high-ceilinged kitchen — she coughed more frequently now. "God help me," she whispered involuntarily. God. That was it, God! She remembered Father Boley's remarks to her one night about the vastness of God's mercy; in a confused yet none the less poignant way she now applied them to herself. "God's mercy is greater than yours, Ed," she continued writing. "Yours was great — perhaps I shall be forgiven. — Barbara."

"Forgiven," she whispered, and coughed violently. She buried her face in her hands. "Forgiven, forgiven," the words rung wildly in her mind. "But will I be? Will I be forgiven?" she asked herself feverishly. A deep and terrifying sense of her wrong in trying to destroy herself overcame her. She lifted her head out of her hands, coughing rackingly. "What am I doing, oh, what am I doing!" She pushed herself up and fell toward the gas stove.

"I can't do this! God forgive me," she whispered chokingly and reached for one of the gas cocks. She turned it off and was clawing for the second one when she collapsed inertly at the foot of the stove.

About an hour later Mrs. Gannon started out the back door bearing a bowl of steaming soup covered by a small dish of salty crackers. In her other hand she carried a hot cup of tea covered by another small dish.

She walked across the empty, weed-riotous lot, which was spotty with rusting tin cans, piles of refuse, and the occasional grease-crusted chassis of an abandoned automobile.

At the back door of the Creedin apartment she smelt gas. There must be a leak in the cellar, she decided. She would tell Barbara about that. She knocked on the kitchen door softly. If Barbara was still asleep she would push on in and awaken her gently.

The smell of gas was much stronger now — she began to cough.

"Jesus, Mary, and Joseph!" she screamed, pushing in the door, dropping the dishes with a crash and backing frantically out of the hall as a wall of fumes hit her in the face and seeped chokingly into her throat.

She stumbled down the back stairs coughing violently and repeating what was at once a call for both heavenly and earthly help: "Jesus, Mary, and Joseph!"

There was an empty garbage tin standing just beside the stairs. She picked it up and heaved it through the Creedins' kitchen window. Then she ran for her telephone, screaming for the neighbors all the way.

The Somerset Fire Department rescue squad arrived four minutes later. Three gasmasked rescuers rushed into the Creedin kitchen where a pretty, pale, redheaded girl lay stretched out on the floor. One of the rescuers turned off the hissing gas jets on the kitchen stove. The other two carried Barbara Creedin out into the backyard where an oxygen pump awaited them. All their efforts and those of a doctor to revive her failed.

Soon a policeman arrived and was asking questions. One of the neighbors referred him to Mrs. Gannon.

He asked her about Barbara's people.

She told him her soldier husband, Ed, was now home on furlough.

"Where can he be reached?" the policeman asked.

Mrs. Gannon hesitated. She would not spoil Ed's fine morning, the morning for which he had worked and sacrificed for years; she would not spoil it with the bitter, black storm of his wife's awful death. She would call the college a little later. By that time the Exercises would be over. . . .

"Sure and I don't know," Mrs. Gannon answered.

When Pfc. Ed Creedin stepped out of the taxi on College Road the solemn boom-bells in the clock building were tolling the hour of ten.

He was just in time. The tulips along the way were tossing their gorgeous heads, the grass seemed greenly cool in a way that might almost slake a thirst — the sunshine, the pure-blue sky —

He hurried along past St. Ignatius' Hall to the stadium amid throngs of well-dressed mothers, fathers, sisters, sweethearts, aunts, uncles, and cousins who had come to see their loved ones take their bachelor degrees before going to war.

He slipped into a line that had formed before the stadium gate, his invitation in hand. A lovely blond girl in a billowing yellow summer dress stood in front of him. It was really spring! He moved forward step by step to the gate.

"Here they come!" someone said.

"All right, will you step back a minute, please!" an officious looking gentleman in a cap and gown said. "Let the graduates pass!"

The apple-cheeked young men in the caps and gowns descended upon them — walking briskly along in a column of twos.

As Ed scanned the faces eagerly for a sight of Gerry, he saw in his mind's eye this same column of twos dressed in khaki, moving briskly along a parade ground, over an obstacle course, running up a beach into a thousand hell-spitting mouths of steel. He winced and continued looking for Gerry.

The tall ones were first. There was Harlan Rock — tall and serious, looking straight ahead. It would be good to see him afterward.

He waited excitedly for the bobbing heads to descend. There, there he was! No eyes straight ahead for Gerry — he was looking all around as he walked.

The eyes met longingly, eagerly — they smiled at each other. The caps and gowns swept by, through the gate and down the hill to the seats around the platform.

Ed filed through the gate and eventually climbed to a seat high in the grandstand. They were friends again — he had known Gerry would come around — he knew he would understand. He had come to understand — this was his big day — their big day.

Then the blessings, the speeches, the awards.

Harlan Rock was valedictorian. He exhorted his classmates in a strong, resonant voice to live up to the principles of eternal life learned here at the college — he exhorted them to do all the things that valedictorians always exhort fellow classmates to do. He did what he was supposed to do up there, and Ed loved the speech because he knew it was the time and the place for such beautiful, and in the face of global war, seemingly impractical ideals.

Then there was the guest speaker, an eminent clerical editor who also exhorted them to do many wonderful things which Ed knew would be difficult when the first sergeant shook them out of bed at 4:15 in the morning for another twelve hours of kitchen police.

Yet Ed knew that this was the time and the place for such exhortations — these kids would be forced to temper burning idealism with cold realities soon enough. Perhaps, too, he admitted, such idealisms of goodness, truth, and beauty would eventually save them from cynicism when the going got roughest. If it did that, and it probably would, he admitted, then it was all very wonderful. But when's the Cardinal going to speak? Bring on the Cardinal.

He had heard that ancient Patrick Cardinal O'Garrity, Ignatian's most distinguished alumnus and venerable patriarch of the archdiocese, always gave an impromptu speech at the Ignatian graduations, and invariably stole the show.

Now the president of the college introduced him and, assisted by a pair of attendant clerics, the giant, gray-haired old man moved to the edge of the platform, leaned on his cane, and looked steadily into the universe of faces before him.

"Boys," he began, with a salute of rhetorical thunder that had not lost its vigor despite his years. "Boys, I'm an old man! I've seen a lot of wars — I've seen them come and I've seen them go.

"I sat with my Ignatian classmates many years ago — even as you are sitting there now. There was a war waiting for them then; there is one waiting for you now.

"But if I know one thing in looking back

over all my years, boys, it is that all wars pass away and you and I do not. There will not always be wars, boys, but there will always be you and I, in an eternal life for which we are destined by our God-made nature.

"So fear not, you young men of whom your people are asking so much, in the very springtime of your years. Remember that it has all been done before by others before you, that it will undoubtedly be done again in the next generation, and the next.

"But, boys, listen to an old man — you will live longer than wars and rumors of wars, remember that — remember that you are the salt of the earth, the flower of the flock. Remember that wars will pass away and you will not. For you are Christ's and Christ is God's. God bless you with the blessing of a tired old man who is ready to go home to his Father's house."

The old Cardinal blessed the students and the entire gathering with a stiffened, outstretched right arm. With tears in his dimming blue eyes he was led back to his chair of honor.

Ed's eyes were wet. "Lord, it is good for us to be here," was the phrase that he wanted to call forth to his lips. He wished so much that his mother, his father, Aunt Annie, and, yes, Barbara could be here with him. But he was seeing and hearing it for them all.

They were handing out diplomas now. He saw Harlan get his and then began watching for Gerry.

There he went. Ed's heart leaped up within him. For this he had lain upon his own particular rugged cross. For this — the sight of a boy getting his college diploma. A great joy pulsed through all of his being.

He looked at the unassuming men in their plain black soutanes sitting down there beside the graduates. Father Boley was among them undoubtedly — they also had sacrificed for the bright young men springing up to the platform. This, too, was their simple yet eternal joy. He felt a deep sympathy with those selfless men in black soutanes that only a selfless man can know.

Now the graduates were standing and singing their Alma Mater song. Ed stood with the spectators in passive tribute to the college and the graduates.

Their young voices were carried on the tender May winds up and over the grandstand. Their voices swelled in the last crescendo of their *ave atque vale*. They held the last sweet word of their college careers on the vehicle of the last sweet note of their song. And holding that note, they held for an instant the soft, white hand of boyhood. When they dropped their voices and their song they dropped the last intimation of boyhood they were to know. They were men now, bachelors of arts and sciences. They were soldiers, sailors, marines, and the war would be long, the loneliness vast, the bloodshed torrential, the ultimate peace precarious. But they were Christ's and Christ was God's.

They looked at each other sheepishly and shook each other's hands wondering what the war and the world would bring them.

Ed swayed along with the crowd which was snaking out of the grandstand onto the field. Where is he? he thought happily, where's that college graduate brother of mine?

He stumbled gleefully among the happy graduates, their families, and their friends.

"Hey, Ed, over here!" he heard Gerry say.

He turned and saw him. They rushed toward each other, shook each other's hands violently, laughed, cried — the estrangement was over; they were brothers and friends again, forever.

"Well," Ed said, "you take over from here. You're on your own and I'll be expecting big things of you. Put her there!"

They shook hands again.

"Gee, Ed, thanks so much for all you've done," Gerry said, "and I'm real sorry for the way I've treated you — I just can't tell you how sorry I am for being such a stubborn, selfish ass."

"Forget it, kid," Ed said. "Your mother should be happy today, your father, your Aunt Annie . . . I know I am."

"Yes, and so are we!" the voice of Father Boley said from behind him. "Congratulations to both of you!" He put his arms around Ed's and Gerry's shoulders. "Here's someone else that wants to congratulate you both!"

"Hello, Ed. Hello, Gerry," Martha Gannon said. "My congratulations to you both."

She smiled at Ed and then at Gerry, discreetly, as if she had already seen him previously.

Ed looked into her face and saw the calm loveliness of a fast-maturing woman whom he had once loved as a young girl. "Well, my gosh, Martha, how are you? It's been a hundred years since I've seen you!"

"Yes, it does seem to have been that long, doesn't it? I'm fine, Ed, and I needn't ask you how the army is — I've seen so much of it in going around with the troupe that I'll spare you the agony."

Ed laughed and then he thought of Barbara at home lying in bed sick and waiting for him, and his mood changed. He must get back there quickly — he mustn't impose too much on Mrs. Gannon.

"Well, folks," he said, "I really think I should be going. Barbara isn't feeling too well today and I promised I'd hurry back. Nice to have seen you again, Martha. Lots of luck in your career."

"Thank you, Eddie. Lots of luck to you as a flying medic."

"Coming with me, Gerry?" Ed asked.

"You go ahead, Ed. I want to look up Harlan Rock and some of the boys. I'll give you a ring this afternoon — we'll get together tonight. Barbara, too. Okay?"

"Sounds swell," Ed said. "How about you, Father, will you join us?"

"Perhaps. I've still got those perennial freshmen on my hands. But we'll get together soon before you go — wait. I'll walk up the hill with you. Behave yourselves, you two." He looked with mock sternness at Gerry and Martha.

This was the first palpable indication Ed had received of the strengthening relationship between Gerry and Martha. Since he had last seen his brother there had been an intensified exchange of letters between Martha and Gerry, culminating in Gerry's inviting her to his graduation prom, which had taken place the previous night. She had arranged her long overdue leave so as to be in Boston at that time.

As Ed climbed the hill with Father Boley he stole a glance back over his shoulder.

Gerry had Martha by the hand and both were sauntering through the knots of relatives and graduates in search of Harlan Rock.

"Don't look down there," Father Boley said with an affectionate and compassionate grin. "Your life is up here, not down there."

Ed smiled shyly, caught in a momentary act of vain regret. He looked up ahead and could see the Gothic towers, a lace fringe of eternal granite against the deliriously blue sky.

"I wish my life *was* up here," he said, "up here with you and all the others. I really wish it, Father, I do."

The priest nodded. He did not know what to say. He was convinced now after his extensive army correspondence with Ed that the boy, even though married, still had leanings toward a vocation to the religious life. It seemed to Father Boley that Ed himself was aware of this other quite unattainable calling — that of a lay brother perhaps, since he was without the extensive formal education so necessary to the studies of the priesthood.

Ed had given up so much for the love of his brother — it was just a step from that to giving up everything for the love of God.

"Walk a little while with me before you go," he said. "It's so good to see you again."

"That's just how I feel myself, Father."

Ed told the priest about Barbara as they wandered off College Road and down into the fragrant, rainbowish gardens surrounding Ignatian Hall. He told the priest of Barbara's dire need of a sanctuary after he had gone, a sanctuary which was her only alternative to self-destruction.

"I didn't quite know it was that serious," Father Boley said. "But I should have known — I've been so darned busy. Yes . . . we'll find some good family to take her in. I'm sure we can find one — I can think of a few possibilities already. I'll look into it, Ed, right away.

"You know," the priest continued, "it looks as if I'm not going to be able to join you boys. I've done everything in my power to secure a release from the provincial so as to join the chaplain corps — but he thinks I just can't be spared. All the younger men have gone or are going, and some of us simply have to hold the fort. It looks as if I'll be right here while all of you are roaming the world and snuffing out the barbarians."

"You won't be missing much, Father. The army's a pretty dreary life no matter what you're wearing on your shoulders."

"Perhaps you're right," Father Boley agreed. "But you young men are under compulsion to serve, so I suppose the only way to bear it would be to try and look on it all as a great adventure."

Just then an old lay brother who had just come into the garden with a spade and a bucket sprinkler recognized Father Boley and called to him.

"Father, I've just now come from the Porter's Lodge and they're trying to locate some soldier that's supposed to be with you. Perhaps this is the young man."

"Thank you, Brother. Come along, Ed, we'll see what it is."

Ed paled and followed after the priest. Barbara . . .

They hurried into the Porter's Lodge. Father Boley asked if they were looking for Pfc. Ed Creedin. Yes, they were. There was an urgent telephone call from Somerset for him. The switchboard operator, another ancient lay brother, put through the call to Somerset immediately. Ed recognized the number as that of the Gannon house.

"Right in there," the porter said, motioning to a booth at one end of the small closet-like room which housed the switchboard.

Ed went into the booth and closed the door. Father Boley stood outside silently. After several moments Father Boley heard the dead-weight clatter of the receiver against the hook.

For a moment Ed leaned his head against the side window of the booth. Father Boley rushed to the booth and pushed open the folding door.

"What is it, Eddie?"

Ed came out of the booth dull-eyed and speechless.

"Oh-uh-Father," Ed said, "Barbara turned on the gas in the kitchen — she's dead, Father!"

"Christ have mercy on us!" the priest exclaimed. "Come upstairs to my room, Eddie — I'll get a collar on. We'll call a cab and go home right away. Come on, Eddie, here in the elevator. That's a good boy. The poor soul!" he whispered as the elevator shot up to the fourth floor. "The poor little soul. God have mercy upon her!"

Ed Creedin struggled with an arid tongue and could say nothing.

PART

V

THE LITURGICAL REVIVAL

THE study of the liturgy is profoundly indebted to the Continental scholars of the nineteenth century. Their work in History, Scripture, and the History of Dogma set the scene for special research in liturgy itself and the Liturgical Movement which flowed out of such particularized study in the twentieth century. Scattered passages in the works of Cardinal Newman and other great thinkers of his time foreshadowed the drift and complexion of this movement long before it came into existence, but as a movement it remains a twentieth century phenomenon.

The pontificate of Pius X was the prelude to the revival. In his zeal for liturgical reform, this holy Pope demonstrated less concern for the letter than the spirit and intent of liturgy. His labors of reform revealed the impelling simplicity and magnificence of the liturgical year freed from all the efflorescence of accumulated piety. It was more than a revival of simplicity, however, more than a recreation of the primitive spirit. It was at once an analysis and appraisal of the place and purpose of liturgy and restoration of all things in Christ after the exaggerated laicism of the nineteenth century with its emphasis on private piety and public *laissez faire*.

Its first fruits were seen in the studies in Church music carried to a superb conclusion by the monks of Solesmes and the formation, particularly among the Benedictines, of groups of scholars devoted to the complete understanding of the cultures and events which had formed the liturgy and given it its particular implications and overtones.

Under Benedictine leadership the Abbey of Maria Laach in Germany became a world center of liturgical study. The diocesan clergy, however, showed no reluctance for the movement and it was largely through their efforts,

in the works of Adam, Guardini, and Pius Parsch, that an understanding of the liturgy, and love of it as well, came down to the common people.

Outside of Germany and Austria, the Liturgical Movement had its greatest following in the United States. Through the interest and encouragement of Abbot Alcuin Deutch, of St. John's Abbey, Collegeville, Minnesota, Father Virgil Michel, O.S.B., became the father of the Liturgical Movement in America. He was soon joined by Rev. William Busch and Monsignor Hellriegel and through their combined efforts liturgical study groups sprang up as if by magic in seminaries and parishes, and an excellent monthly review, *Orate Fratres,* published at St. John's Abbey, devoted itself to liturgical research and analysis.

The progress of the movement in Germany and Austria was brought to a halt by the persecution of the Nazis, but in England and the United States the revival of liturgy has grown even during the recent years. Through the influence of this movement the public life of the Church, one of the modes in which Christ lives in time, is so well understood today that few Catholics can be excused for their failure to understand the meaning and purpose of the Mass and the Divine Office. Such understanding is an obvious gain, particularly where it has led to a more intelligent participation in the abounding life of the Church.

The movement, it must be emphasized, is not in any sense merely analytical and scholarly. It leads inevitably to the strengthening of the individual will in revealing to the Christian what he is and through what divine atmosphere he continually moves. Christ's life and existence are not envisaged as something which took place only in history and a period of time, but as an eternal drama, a mystical reality perpetually revealing itself in the seasons of the liturgical year. Christ *is* born again each year, He suffers and dies again, and in the cool of the Easter dawn He rises from the dead. After His ascension the Holy Ghost descends upon the Apostles, brings the Church into being, perpetually animating her and dwelling in the souls of her children. In this fashion the eternal *now* of Christ is borne home to the consciousness of those who struggle to create the pattern of Christ in themselves.

KARL ADAM

(*1876–*   )

ONE of the great molders of liturgical thought, Karl Adam, was born at Oberfalz in Bavaria in 1876. He pursued his classical studies in Amberg, and with their completion studied for the priesthood at Ratisbon Theological college. He was ordained in 1900, and after two years of parish work was selected to do research in Patrology and the History of Dogma. At the conclusion of these labors Father Adam was made professor of Dogma at Munich, and in 1919 became professor of Moral Theology at Tübingen.

His writings were largely instrumental in giving the Liturgical Movement a popular following in Germany and the United States.

CHAPTER II

CHRIST IN THE CHURCH*

"Behold, I am with you all days even unto the consummation of the world" (Mt. xxviii, 20).

IF WE ask the Catholic Church herself to tell us, according to her own notion of herself, what constitutes her essential nature and what is the substance of her self-consciousness, she answers us through the mouth of the greatest of her teachers, that the Church is the realisation on earth of the kingdom of God. "The Church of to-day, of the present, is the Kingdom of Christ and the Kingdom of Heaven": such is the emphatic assertion of St. Augustine (*De civ. Dei* xx, 9, I). The "Kingdom of Heaven" and "Kingdom of God," taken up from the prophecy of Daniel (vii, 9–28) and proclaimed by Christ, that Kingdom which grows great like the mustard seed, and like leaven permeates the world, and which like a field of corn shelters both wheat and cockle until the harvest, this "Kingdom of Heaven" is, so the Church believes, implanted in her own being and there manifested. The Church believes that she is the manifestation of that newness, that supernature and that divinity which come in with the Kingdom of God, the manifestation of holiness. She is the new supernatural reality brought by Christ into the world and arrayed in the garment of the transitory; she is the divine attesting itself under earthly veils.

And inasmuch as the fulness of this divine power was creatively revealed in the Person of Christ, Paul, the Apostle of the Gentiles, expresses its deepest mystery when he borrows Hellenistic forms and calls the Church the Body of Christ (I Cor. xii, 27; Col. i, 18, 24; Eph. i, 22; iv, 12): "For in one Spirit were we all baptized into one body, whether Jews or Gentiles, whether bond or free; and in one Spirit we have all been made to drink" (I Cor. xii, 13).

Christ the Lord is the real self of the Church. The Church is the body permeated through and through by the redemptive might of Jesus. So intimate is this union of Christ with the Church, so inseparable, natural and essential, that St. Paul in his Epistles to the Colossians and Ephesians explicitly calls Christ the Head of the body. As the Head of the body Christ makes the organism of the Church whole and complete. And Christ and the Church can no more be regarded separately than can a head and its body (Col. i, 18; ii, 19; Eph. iv, 15 ff.).

This conviction that the Church is permeated by Christ, and of necessity organically united with Him, is a fundamental point of

*From *The Spirit of Catholicism*, pp. 14–30, by Dr. Karl Adam, translated by Dom Justin McCann, O.S.B. By Permission of The Macmillan Company, New York, 1929.

Christian teaching. From Origen to Augustine and Pseudo-Dionysius and thence to Thomas Aquinas, and thence on to our own unforgettable Mohler, this conviction stands in the centre of the Church's doctrine. Her teachers delight to express in ever new forms that sentence of Augustine wherein he celebrated the mystical oneness of Christ and the Church: the two are one, one body, one flesh, one and the same person, one Christ, the whole Christ. Nor could this intimate connexion of Christ and the Church, this their intimate oneness, receive profounder or plainer expression than in the figure of a marriage of Christ and the Church which St. Paul, inspired by the language of several of the prophets (Osee i–iii; Jer. ii, 2; Is. liv, 5) is the first to employ (II Cor. xi, 2). According to St. Paul the Church is the Bride of Christ, for whom He gave Himself. And with a like train of thought the Seer of the Apocalypse celebrates the "marriage of the Lamb," and sings of His "bride" that hath prepared herself (xix, 7–8). Later mystical theology wove out of these scriptural thoughts its wondrously sweet bridal mysticism, in which Christ is the Lord, the Church His bride, and the two in closest union generate the children of life.

This supernatural being of the Church expresses itself chiefly in her most primary creations, in dogma, morals and worship.

Her dogma aims at being nought else than the exact formulisation and description of all that precious reality, and all that abounding life which have entered this our actual world along with the Uncreated Word. The dogmas of Christology, in the narrower sense, delineate the Person of the God-man and describe the radiation of the glory of God in the face of Christ Jesus. The dogmas of Soteriology set forth His redemptive activity in His life, passion and death, and at the right hand of the Father. The dogmas that concern the Trinity lead us to the fundamental source of this divine life, to the bosom of the Father, and join the actual manifestation of Jesus to the eternal processions of the inner life of the Trinity. The dogmas of Mariology describe the bodily and natural relations of the Humanity of Jesus and His redemptive work

to His own blessed Mother. The dogmas of grace secure the character of the redemption as unmerited and due wholly to God, and fix the new basic mood of the redeemed, namely, love, peace, and joy in the Holy Ghost. The dogmas that deal with the Church, the sacraments and the sacramentals, show how the new life that welled up in Christ is communicated to the men of all times and places. The dogmas of the Last Things set forth Jesus as the Judge and Fulfiller, and show how, when His redemptive work is complete, He gives back His lordship to the Father, that "God may be all in all."

Thus all the dogmas of the Catholic Church are stamped with the name of Christ; they would express each and every aspect of His teaching, they would bring the living, redeeming, ruling, judging Christ before our eyes according to all the dimensions of His historical manifestation.

And not otherwise is it with the Church's morality and with her worship. The fundamental object of all her educative work, of all her instruction, preaching and discipline, is to make the Christian a second Christ, an *alter Christus,* to make him, as the Fathers express it, "Christ-like." This one highest aim of its endeavour gives Christian morality its inner unity. There is no two-fold morality in the Church, since there is but one Christ to be formed. But the ways and manners in which men strive towards this goal are infinitely various, as various as the human personalities which have to mature and grow up to the stature of Christ. Very many of the faithful will be able to form the image of Christ in themselves only in very vague and general outline. Yet, just as nature at times sees fit to give of her best and to manifest her superabundant power in some perfect types, even so the fulness of Christ which works in the Church breaks out ever and again in this or that saintly figure into brilliant radiance, in marvels of self-surrender, love, purity, humility and devotion. Professor Merkle's book may provide even outsiders with some insight into the deep earnestness and heroic strength with which the Church in every century of her existence has striven after the realisation of the image of Christ, after the translation of His spirit into terms of flesh and blood, after the incarnation of Jesus in the individual man.

And the worship of the Church breathes the same spirit, and is as much interwoven with Christ and full of Christ as is her morality. Just as every particular prayer of the liturgy ends with the ancient Christian formula: *Per Christum Dominum nostrum,* so is every single act of worship, from the Mass down to the least prayer, a memorial of Christ, an ἀνάμνησις Χριστοῦ. Nay, more, the worship of the Church is not merely a filial remembrance of Christ, but a continual participation by visible mysterious signs in Jesus and His redemptive might, a refreshing touching of the hem of His garment, a liberating handling of His sacred Wounds. That is the deepest purpose of the liturgy; namely, to make the redeeming grace of Christ present, visible and fruitful as a sacred and potent reality that fills the whole life of the Christian. In the sacrament of Baptism — so the believer holds — the sacrificial blood of Christ flows into the soul, purifies it from all the infirmity of original sin and permeates it with its own sacred strength, in order that a new man may be born thereof, the re-born man, the man who is an adopted son of God. In the sacrament of Confirmation, Jesus sends His "Comforter," the Spirit of constancy and divine faith, to the awakening religious consciousness, in order to form the child of God into a soldier of God. In the sacrament of Penance Jesus as the merciful Saviour consoles the afflicted soul with the word of peace: Go thy way, thy sins are forgiven thee. In the sacrament of the Last Anointing the compassionate Samaritan approaches the sick-bed and pours new courage and resignation into the sore heart. In the sacrament of Marriage He engrafts the love of man and wife on His own profound love for His people, for the community, for the Church, on His own faithfulness unto death. And in the priestly consecration by the imposition of hands, He transmits His messianic might, the power of His Mission, to the disciples whom He calls, in order that He may by their means pursue without interruption His work of raising the new men, the children of God, out of the kingdom of death.

The sacraments are nought else than a visible guarantee, authenticated by the word of Jesus and the usage of the apostles, that Jesus is working in the midst of us. At all the important stages of our little life, in its heights and in its depths, at the marriage-altar and the cradle, at the sick-bed, in all the crises and shocks that may befall us, Jesus stands by us under the veils of the grace-giving sacrament as our Friend and Consoler, as the Physician of soul and body, as our Saviour. St. Thomas Aquinas has described this intimate permeation of the Christian's whole life by faith in the sacraments and in his Saviour with luminous power. And Goethe, too, in the seventh book of the second part of his *Dichtung und Wahrheit* speaks warmly of it, and closes his remarks with the significant words: "How is this truly spiritual whole broken into pieces in Protestantism, a part of these symbols being declared apocryphal and only a few admitted as canonical. How shall we be prepared to value some highly when we are taught to be indifferent to the rest?"

But the sacraments which we have enumerated are not the deepest and holiest fact of all. For so completely does Jesus disclose Himself to His disciples, so profound is the action of His grace, that He gives himself to them and enters into them as a personal source of grace. Jesus shares with His disciples His most intimate possession, the most precious thing that He has, His own self, His personality as the God-man. We eat His Flesh and drink His Blood. So greatly does Jesus love His community, that He permeates it, not merely with His blessing and His might, but with His real Self, God and Man; He enters into a real union of flesh and blood with it, and binds it to His being even as the branch is bound to the vine. We are not left orphans in this world. Under the forms of bread and wine the Master lives amid His disciples, the Bridegroom with His bride, the Lord in the midst of His community, until that day when He shall return in visible majesty on the clouds of heaven.

The Sacrament of the Altar is the strongest, profoundest, most intimate memorial of the Lord, until He come again. And therefore we can never forget Jesus, though centuries and millennia pass, and though nations and civilisations are ever perishing and rising anew. And therefore there is no heart in the world, not even the heart of father or mother, that is so loved by millions and millions, so truly and loyally, so practically and devotedly, as is the Heart of Jesus.

Thus we see that in the sacraments, and especially in the Sacrament of the Altar, the fundamental idea of the Church is most plainly represented, the idea, that is, of the incarnation of Christ in the faithful. And therefore the Catholic can only regard that criticism of the sacraments as superficial, which derives them, not merely in this or that external detail, but in their proper content and dominant meaning, from non-Christian conceptions and cults, as for instance from the pagan mysteries. On the contrary the sacraments breathe the very spirit of primitive Christianity. They are the truest expression and result of that original and central Christian belief that the Christian should be inseparably united with Christ and should live in Christ. In Catholic sacramental devotion Christ is immediately conceived and experienced as the Lord of the community, as its invisible strength and principle of activity. In the sacraments is expressed the fundamental nature of the Church, the fact that Christ lives on in her and that the divine is incarnated in human form.

Therefore dogma, morality and worship are primary witnesses to the consciousness of the Church that she is of supernatural stock, that she is the Body of Christ. But more than this, the same consciousness determines the spirit of her ordinances and laws, the special manner and method in which she would have her supernatural life realised, and especially her conception of authority and of sacrament. We have spoken of the supernatural life in the Church; let us now throw light on the special forms in which this life is presented.

Since the Church would be nought else but the Body of Christ, the realisation in history of His divine and human Being, therefore the glorified Christ is the proper source of her power and authority, so much so that this authority is exercised only in His name and in the true and deepest sense belongs only to Him. The whole constitution of the Church is completely aristocratic and not democratic, her authority coming from above, from Christ, and not from below, from the community. The new powers come from Christ, the Incarnate God, and from Him flow through the apostles to the Church. The government of the Church is, so to say, in the vertical and not in the horizontal line. That ancient African writer, Tertullian, defined this vertical system as early as the second century in the pregnant sentence: "The Church is from the apostles, the apostles from Christ, Christ from God." The apostles did not act in their own right, but as "sent" and as representatives of Christ: "He that heareth you, heareth me, and he that despiseth you, despiseth me; and he that despiseth me, despiseth Him that sent me" (Luke x, 16; cf. Mt. x, 40). And the apostles on their part, as the New Testament in general and the pastoral epistles in particular show us, appointed by imposition of hands, wherever they founded new communities, the "firstlings," i.e., the first converts, to be leaders (προεστῶτες) who should, as St. Peter so strikingly and beautifully says (I Peter v, 2): "shepherd the flocks of God" in their stead. So the apostolic authority did not reside in the communities, but in the elders, leaders, overseers, who were chosen by the apostles in the name of Christ to take their place. And after the death of the apostles it was these elders who transmitted the authority which had been committed to them, by the imposition of hands, and organised the new communities round men empowered with this authority. Certainly the communities played their part in the matter, and helped by their advice to determine who should be entrusted with the commission. But in itself the power was exclusively an apostolic power, a thing reserved to the bishops who derived from the apostles. We may assert that the whole literature of early Christianity attests this conception. It is developed with classic lucidity in one of the earliest of Christian writings, the First Epistle of St. Clement (Ad Cor. xliv, 3).

Therefore ecclesiastical authority rests upon the apostolic succession (*successio apostolica*), upon the uninterrupted communication by imposition of hands of that commission which the apostles received from Christ. This apostolic commission, as passed on from bishop to bishop right down to our own day, is, if we regard its inmost nature, nothing else than the messianic authority of Jesus. By means of the apostolic succession, this authority is perpetuated and imparts the truth and grace of Jesus to humanity. And, therefore, behind ecclesiastical authority stands Jesus Himself. As the scholastics put it, Jesus is the "principal cause" (*causa principalis*) of all functions exercised by the Church, their ultimate source and the basis of their efficacy. Man is only an instrument, the *causa instrumentalis,* through whom Christ Himself acting in the Church teaches and sanctifies and governs. And so in the functioning of the Church, the human self, the human personality, the individual as such, falls wholly into the background. Not any human personality, but the redemptive might of Jesus controls the Church. The expression and resultant of this force is Church authority. The official authority of the Church is essentially a service of Christ (*ministerium Christi*), that is to say, a service which is fulfilled only in the name and by the commission of Christ, and derives its importance exclusively from the authority of Christ. It is true that the personality of the official may considerably affect the manner and method in which he carries out the will of Christ. Nevertheless the substance of his function, the core of his activity, is wholly independent of personal traits and weaknesses. For it is not the particular man and his personality that preaches, baptizes, and governs in the Church, but Christ alone. Therefore, Church authority, as thus conceived, derives immediately from the fundamental conviction that the Church is inwardly permeated by her "Lord." This is no unevangelical borrowing from pagan sources, or from Jewish or Roman law, but an expression of that primitive Christian thought: "It is Christ who evangelizes, Christ who baptizes." (*Christus est, qui evangelizat, Christus est, qui baptizat.*) So the aim of the Church in her official system is simply to secure that great and primary Christian idea that there is properly only one authority, only one teacher, only one sanctifier, only one pastor: Christ, the Lord.

Consequently, such a conception of authority does not paralyse and petrify the believer, but enfranchises him, directing his gaze to Christ and Christ alone. No human authority, no extraneous personality, may stand between Christ and the believing subject. Divine truth, grace and life must flow into the soul directly from Christ Himself. Therefore — however paradoxical it may seem — the authority of the Church secures the liberty of the individual Christian, by its impersonal and extra-personal character. It protects that liberty from the spiritual domination and claims to mediatorship of alleged leading personalities, and sets Christ and the believer in direct contact with each other. Therefore the effect of such authority is not to separate, but to unite; or rather, it protects and secures that mysterious magnetic field and those wondrous magnetic forms which originate in the polarity of Christ and the soul. It protects and secures that direct contact and interplay of life between the Head and its members.

That is as true of the Church's teaching office as of her priestly and pastoral authority. The basis of her teaching authority is that sentence of the Lord: "One only shall be your teacher, Christ" (Mt. xxiii, 10). When the Catholic priest proclaims the word of God, he that preaches is not a mere man, but Christ Himself. For the Catholic consciousness, therefore, a sermon by the pope in the Sistine Chapel has no more weight than the words of a simple parish priest in a remote village church. For it is not Peter, or Paul, or Pius that preaches, but Christ: *Christus est, qui evangelizat.* All the doctrinal controversies of Christianity are dominated by this Christo-centric conception of the Church's teaching authority. It is because Christ is the sole canon of her preaching, that the Church adheres so obstinately and so rigidly to His traditional message. It is for this reason that she can endure no modernism, no fraternising with the spirit of the age. Her teaching is, and aims at being, nothing else but a handing on of that message of Christ which was proclaimed by the apostles. St. Paul enjoined his disciple, Timothy, to guard that which had been committed to him (*Timothee, custodi depositum!* II Tim. i, 14; cf. I Tim. iv, 16; vi, 14). That is exactly the doctrinal programme of the Church. Her conservatism and her traditionalism derive directly from her fundamentally Christocentric attitude.

Rooted in this fundamental attitude the Church has always resisted the domination of leading personalities, of schools or movements. When any school of thought seemed to be obscuring or menacing the traditional faith, she has not hesitated to override even her greatest sons, an Origen, an Augustine, yes, in some points even a Thomas Aquinas. And whenever men have sought to interpret Christ's message, not by tradition, by firm adherence to history to the original faith and to the uninterrupted fellowship, but by means of private speculation, from out of the limited experience of their little individual selves, then the Church has proclaimed her emphatic anathema. And she would utter this same anathema, even if an angel came down from heaven teaching aught else than what she has received from the apostles. The doctrinal history of the Church is simply an obstinate adherence to Christ, a constant carrying out of the command of Jesus: "One only shall be your teacher, Christ."

Just as Christ stands behind the teaching office of the Church, so also He stands, as "Lord" of the community, behind her sacramental activity. Only one who overlooks this decisive fact can allege that "the scholastic conception of the efficacy of the sacraments reveals the primitive idea of the automatic effect, of the 'manna' of the sacred action." According to Catholic theology the sacraments work *ex opere operato,* and not *ex opere operantis;* that is to say that the sacramental grace is not produced and effected through the personal, moral and religious efforts of the recipient, but rather through the

objective accomplishment of the sacramental sign itself. In every sacrament there is something objectively given (*opus operatum*), namely, the special conjunction according to the institution of Christ of a material element (the "matter") and certain words (the "form"). When this conjunction is effected in the recipient according to the intentions of the Church, then the sacrament is a "work of Christ" (*opus Christi*), which independently of the subjective share of the recipient (*opus operantis*) by force of its valid accomplishment causes the sacramental grace. Thus, in the case of baptism, when the water is poured upon the forehead of a child in the name of the Trinity, the child by the very performance of this act is admitted into the family of God. The heavens at once open and the Father's voice proclaims: "Thou art my beloved child."

Therefore the sacramental action does in fact transmit the Saviour's grace "without any subjective factor," at least so far as regards the sanctification of an infant child. When it is a question of the sanctification of an adult, who has attained religious and moral consciousness, the recipient must prepare himself subjectively for the grace which is objectively imparted in the sacramental act, by acts of faith, contrition and repentance. Therefore, according to the teaching of the Church, this ethico-religious effort of the adult is not the effective cause of his sanctification, its *causa efficiens,* but only its preparatory cause, *causa dispositiva.* The effective cause of grace is exclusively Christ Himself, who proclaims and effects His gracious will through signs determined by Himself. Primarily, therefore, and *in actu primo,* grace is a free gift and favour, a thing already guaranteed by the sacramental act apart from all personal effort. But whether I shall effectively grasp this grace which is thus provided and profit by it, that depends upon my subjective dispositions. Therefore practically (*in actu secundo*) my subjective sanctification is not the work of grace alone, but the resultant of two factors, the grace of Christ and my good will. Can it then be alleged that this sacramentalism is akin to primitive magic, to the belief in a "manna" or something of the sort which makes certain special objects the conveyors of supernatural forces?

In fact, the criticism which thinks it right to speak of the sacraments as having a "magical character" divorces them from their proper and sole source, namely from Christ, the true and only giver of grace, and gives them an independent status. So that they become, not signs of grace, but independent sources of it, instruments endued with their own power, sacred charms. In reality, however, no sacrament stands thus in its own right, or can so stand for a single moment. It has its whole meaning and its whole power in and through Christ alone. As St. Thomas teaches, it is no more than the instrument (*causa instrumentalis*) of Christ the Giver of grace, the visible sign whose physical being He employs in order to effect in the soul of the believer the supernatural results which are indicated in the symbolical form of the sign. Nay, more, according to that Scotist view which is now advocated by many theologians, the sacrament itself possesses no strictly "physical" causality in any way immanent in its sign. On the contrary, the sacramental grace flows directly from Jesus into the soul of the believer. The sacrament is no more than an appointed sign of Christ, an objectivisation of the gracious will of Jesus, a visible and perceptible "I will, be thou made clean!"

Certainly it is true that even according to this view there remains something objective and impersonal in the notion of a sacrament. It remains true that the grace of Christ is not causally connected with the ethico-religious activity of the believer or the priest, but with the objective accomplishment of the sign. But why is that so? The very impersonal and objective character of the sacrament, like the impersonality of the Church's teaching activity, expresses that profoundest claim of the Church, her most intimate union with Christ, her working purely out of the fulness of Christ, her sanctifying through the might of Christ alone. Precisely because it is not the human element in her which sanctifies men, but the power of Christ alone, therefore the blessing of Christ is not tied to

human activity, not to the faith and repentance of the sinner, not even to the prayers and sacrifices of saintly, magnanimous souls and specially gifted personalities, whether saintly prophets, bishops, or priests, but to a wholly impersonal thing, a dead sign, which has no other merit save that of being a sign of Christ, a valid expression of His gracious will. The purpose, therefore, of the formula *ex opere operato,* is to secure the deepest essence of Christianity, that thing for which St. Paul suffered and fought, the absolute unmeritedness of grace, and the thought that Christ is "all in all." And since this idea of the impersonality of the sacraments springs directly from the heart of Christianity, it is consequently as old as Christianity itself, and as old as the Body of Christ, the Church. Students of biblical theology emphasise the fact that the sacramental doctrine of St. John and St. Paul has already got this impersonal conception, that it recognises an efficacy *ex opere operato,* at least in effect, and is therefore completely Catholic in its character. And how could it be otherwise? When Christ is placed in the centre, when we are told emphatically that of His fulness we have all received, then all human intermediaries must stand aside. There can be no human mediators, as Augustine remarked against the Donatists. Christ is the sole worker. When individual Christians in the Corinthian Church attached themselves to various gifted personalities and formed a Peter party and a Paul party and an Apollo party, as though they would found their salvation upon these personalities, then St. Paul with the burning zeal of his witness for Christ cried out against this humanisation of the Gospel, "What is Apollo and what is Paul? . . . His servants, through whom ye were made believers . . . other foundation can no man lay but that which has been laid, which is Christ Jesus" (I Cor. iii, 4–5, 11). The sacramental idea is nothing but the realisation and maintenance of this basis of Christianity. In her age-long conflicts with Montanists, Novatians, Donatists, and again later on with Waldenses, Albigenses and Hussites, the Church reiterated the sentence of St. Augustine: "The sacraments sanctify through themselves, and not through men" (*sacramenta per se sancta, non per homines*). For man does not baptize, and man does not absolve, but Christ alone. When the Christian sacrament by this its impersonal character eliminates all human intermediaries, it secures an immediate and free exchange of life between the Head and the members. And so the freedom of the personal religious life is nowhere so perfectly safeguarded as in Catholic piety. And the forms of piety, in which the Catholics' sacramental experience of Christ achieves self-expression, are as manifold as the innumerable leaves of the trees.

There is yet something to be said about the relation of the pastoral office of the Church to the Head of the Church. St. John tells us (xxi, 15 ff.) that the risen Christ enjoined the apostle Peter: "Feed my lambs, feed my sheep." Peter is not to feed his own sheep, but Christ's sheep. So that the pastoral authority is plainly a delegated authority and the pastor a deputy of Christ. That is the sort of authority which St. Paul exercises against the incestuous Corinthian; he gives him over "to Satan for the destruction of the flesh, that the spirit may be saved in the day of our Lord Jesus Christ," and he does this "in the name of our Lord Jesus Christ," and "with the power of our Lord Jesus." Every disciplinary measure of the Church is inspired by her conviction that she is acting in the name and in the power of Jesus. It is true that the pastoral authority of the Church does not, like her teaching or priestly authority, point directly to certain supernatural realities which have been determined once for all by Christ's revelation, to the realities, that is, of doctrine and sacrament. Its object is rather to introduce these supernatural realities into practical life, to apply Christian rules and principles to the progressive and constantly changing life of nations and individuals. And in consequence there is no absolute certainty that all the particular measures of the pastoral authority are according to the mind and spirit of Christ.

So it is possible, as St. Augustine often insists, that the human element may obtrude itself and colour the administration of Church discipline, and that there may be errors and mistakes. Yet, even though there be mistakes of detail, the luminous goal, the directive principles and the decisive means of Church discipline are — so the Catholic is convinced — determined by Christ, and pertain to His truth, love and power. The Catholic knows that the rule of the Church incarnates absolute truth, justice and love, and so he has solved the problem of Dostoievski: Is not all human exercise of authority tantamount to a usurpation? Yes, if it be merely human, it is. For every merely human governance necessarily rests on might, whether it be the tyranny of an individual or the despotism of a community. Only in theocracy is a man free from men, for he serves not men but God. Therein lies the secret of that childlike obedience, so incomprehensible to the outsider, which the Catholic gives to his Church, an obedience whereby he freely and cheerfully submits his own little notions and wishes to the will of Christ expressed in the action of authority; an obedience whereby his own small and limited self is enlarged to the measure of the great self of the Church. That is no corpse-like obedience or slave mentality, but a profoundly religious act, an absolute devotion to the Will of Christ which rules the Church, a service of God. And so this obedience is not cowardly and weak, but strong and ready for sacrifice, manly and brave even in the presence of kings. It is faithful even to the surrender of earthly possessions, yes, even to the sacrifice of life itself, offering itself to the Christ who lives in the Church. This fidelity is instinct with the noble spirit of the faith. If a storm were to burst to-morrow over the Christian churches and their members were called upon to testify even unto death, I know not if all these communities would stand firm, strong and faithful, ranged round the one Christ; I know not if the bonds that in times of peace hold their members together would not be broken and utterly shattered, and those Christians blown like chaff before the wind. But one thing I know, that the bond which binds the Church and her members together will be broken by no devil and no demon. For it is not of this world. It is woven by the Church's "Lord," by the God-man, Christ Jesus.

ILDEFONS HERWEGEN

(1878–1946)

ILDEFONS HERWEGEN, Abbot of Maria Laach and scholarly leader of the liturgical renaissance in Germany, was born November 27, 1878, at Köln-Junkersdorf, where he spent his youth and received his early education. It was during the first period of his life that the monuments of early Christian culture fired his imagination with a love of the liturgy. A natural concomitant of this interest was a vocation for the priesthood. His first ecclesiastical studies were made at Seckau. There growth in the humanities kept pace with a complete Benedictine formation. On December 8, 1896, he pronounced his monastic vows at Maria Laach. The bases of his learning were widened appreciably with courses in Philosophy and Theology which were pursued in his own monastery and also in Beuron. His love of early Christian culture led him to Rome for exploration and study.

After his ordination in 1901, he spent twelve years in scholarly research at Maria Laach and Bonn University. In 1913 he was elected Abbot of Maria Laach, an office which he filled with distinction through all the tragic years which intervened until his death in 1946.

Abbot Herwegen was mighty in word and work. Under his rule the Abbey of Maria Laach assumed something of its medieval splendor, and the Liturgical Academy became a power house of ideals and ideas.

Though his scholarly works were strong buttresses of the movement, a small monograph, *The Art Principle of the Liturgy,* written by Abbot Herwegen at the time of the last war, came to be considered, even by himself, as a key to the total interior meaning of the liturgy. It was translated into English by the Rev. William Busch and published by the Liturgical Press, Collegeville, Minnesota.

THE ART-PRINCIPLE OF THE LITURGY*

THE golden portal, hallowed by our Lord Himself, by which we enter into the history of the Christian liturgy, is the Cenacle of Mount Sion. Here on the very threshold of the Church's history, in the primitive community of Jerusalem, the very first scene that we behold is one of assembly in public prayer. The Acts of the Apostles says briefly: "And they were persevering in the doctrine of the apostles, and in the communication of the breaking of bread, and in prayers" (ii, 42). The sacred narrative adds that the faithful gathered for common prayer in the temple, but celebrated "the breaking of bread" in their private homes, and thus distinguishes between the didactic synagogue service and the eucharistic sacrifice, a distinction corre-

sponding to the main division of our Mass service to the present day.

The first part of our Mass service, made up of chant, reading and prayer, was originally a service to which Jews and pagans might be admitted. But "the breaking of bread," the sacrificial part of the Mass beginning with the offertory, was an exclusively Christian service, celebrated in private homes, the upper room of the oriental dwelling or the atrium of the Roman one. About the beginning of the second century, owing to the legislation of Trajan against the Christians, the two services were joined into one which was now celebrated behind closed doors and to which Christians alone were admitted.

Thus the main outlines of our present Mass service may be discerned in the Acts of the Apostles. However, whether we regard the service of prayer and instruction as conducted in the hall of Solomon in the temple, or the

*Herwegen, Dom Ildefons, *The Art-Principle of the Liturgy,* translated from the fourth and fifth German editions by William Busch (Collegeville, Minn.: The Liturgical Press, 1931), pp. 7–19.

service conducted by St. Paul at night in Troas, or the eucharistic banquet as celebrated by the Christian community of Corinth, the very limited information of this kind given us in the New Testament writings is not apt in any case to convey the impression of anything aesthetic. The question naturally arises: what justification is there for speaking of the liturgy as art, and indeed as an art-synthesis in the Wagnerian sense?

In order to answer this question we must first know what the liturgy is and we must understand its mode of expression.

The liturgy is the entire system of the Church's official acts of worship. Catholic worship includes the eucharistic sacrifice, the sacraments whose graces flow therefrom, and various forms of prayer. And since the Church is Christ living on in His mystical body, the sacrifice and prayer of the Church are the sacrifice and prayer of Christ. The liturgy is founded in the spousal union of Christ and His Church and is therefore by its very nature our inmost bond of union with Him. All the sacraments, by which the graces of His redemption come to us, are included in the liturgy.

The liturgy is therefore the life-breath of the Church, the very spirit and life of Christ who is the prototype of the entire cosmos of creation. Hence it must somehow reflect the splendor of the eternal Word, it must contain the element of beauty.

We do indeed find this innate beauty glittering in the first utterances of the primitive liturgy, in prayers perhaps not yet official formulas of public worship.

The editors of the *Monumenta Liturgica* are probably not mistaken in regarding as part of a sacred hymn the fourteenth verse of Chapter 5 of the Epistle to the Ephesians:

Arise, thou that sleepest,
And arise from the dead,
And Christ shall enlighten thee.

The same is true of the sixteenth verse of Chapter 3 of the First Epistle to Timothy:

And evidently great is the mystery of godliness,
Which was manifested in the flesh,
Was justified in the spirit,

Appeared unto angels,
Hath been preached unto the gentiles,
Is believed in the world,
Is taken up in glory.

In like manner we may regard as hymns the doxologies which occur in the apostolic letters, for they have a distinctly liturgical character. Let us cite, for example, the first verse of Chapter 3 of the Second Epistle to the Corinthians: "Blessed be the God and Father of our Lord Jesus Christ, the Father of all mercies and the God of all comfort, who comforteth us in all our tribulations." Consider also the greeting formulas, like that of the Epistle to the Romans: "Grace to you and peace from God our Father and from the Lord Jesus Christ."

A more distinct instance is that from the Didache (about the end of the first century) in a directly liturgical formula: "As for the Eucharist, we give thanks in this wise. First for the Chalice: 'We thank Thee, our Father, for the holy vine of David Thy servant, which Thou hast made known to us by Jesus, Thy servant. Glory to Thee for evermore.' For the bread: 'We thank Thee, our Father, for the life and knowledge which Thou has made known to us by Jesus, Thy servant. Glory to Thee for evermore. As the elements of this bread, scattered on the mountains, were brought together into a single whole, may Thy Church in like manner be gathered together from the ends of the earth into Thy kingdom; for Thine is the glory and the power, through Jesus Christ, for evermore.' "

We may also cite two examples of petition formulas from the prayer contained in the epistle of St. Clement of Rome: "We beseech Thee, O Master, be our help and succour. Be the salvation of those who are in tribulation, take pity on the lowly, raise up them that fall, reveal Thyself to those who are in need, heal the ungodly, and restore those who have gone out of the way. Appease the hunger of the needy, deliver those among us who suffer in prison, heal the sick, comfort the faint-hearted; so that all people may know that Thou art the only God, and that Jesus Christ is Thy servant, and that we are Thy people and the sheep of Thy pasture." "Remember not the sins of Thy servants and handmaids, but cleanse us by Thy truth and direct our steps so that we may walk in holiness of heart and do that which is good and acceptable in Thy sight and in the eyes of our princes."

These few texts are enough to show that it is precisely the prayer character of the liturgy that explains the unfolding of its intrinsic beauty. In prayer the soul ascends from earth to God and learns to know Him and to love Him in His infinite beauty. And in the measure that words can express the inward things of mind and heart, the language of prayer should reflect the light of the All-beautiful. The sublimity of Christian thought naturally finds its most exalted expression in Christian prayer, and especially in the early Christian days when those endowed with charismatic gifts gave utterance to their ecstasies in the assemblies of the faithful. We still have some echo of these in the Prefaces of the Mass.

But these charismatic gifts were personal and extraordinary. A more regular and permanent school of prayer for the early Christians was that furnished by the inspired psalms of the Old Testament. The Psalms of David, chanted of old in the Jewish temple, continued to sound in the catacombs and in the basilicas on the lips of the Christians. Throughout the centuries the Church has always found the richly colored poetry of the Psalms full of inspiration and prayer-value. And poetry indeed is a notable feature of liturgical prayer. Yet the poetry that speaks for the Church cannot be merely individual and subjective. It must be an objective poetry, expressing the thought and desire which all Christians have in common, speaking in a lofty and universal language so that each and every soul may find his own experiences set forth therein. The poet of the liturgy must be an interpreter of the heart of mankind, like the royal bard of Israel.

The Christian hymns which we know to have been composed in Milan in the fifth century were not admitted into the Roman liturgy until the eleventh century because they were thought to be somewhat too individual in character, although in fact there is nothing of subjective triviality in them.

From primitive Christian days then, the glorious Psalms supplied the major part of the common prayer of the faithful. They were distributed throughout the days of the week and combined with a series of hymns in such a way that a sort of definite spiritual physiognomy was given not only to each day of the week but furthermore to the various canonical hours of each day. Moreover, the natural phenomena of light, the dawn and sunset, and the darkness and silence of night were made the symbols of mystical concepts with an exquisite sense of the interrelations of the natural and the supernatural.

The very nature of poetry precludes a strict systematic unity in the structure of liturgical compositions, especially in the case of longer ones where the component parts are apt to receive a certain amount of independent treatment. The unity which is to be sought is of a higher, lyrical kind. It is a unity of mood which takes its coloring from the time, the place and many other circumstances, sometimes almost imperceptible, and blends them into one composition. It is precisely this poetic liberty, this weaving of many motives into harmonious unity that gives to liturgical prayer its wonderful richness, its suggestiveness and its adaptability to all times. Admirable examples in this regard are to be found among the ferial Masses of the Lenten season. Let us cite the Mass of Wednesday of the second week in Lent. The stational church in this case is that of St. Cecilia, a Roman lady, a virgin-martyr, the thought of whom pervades the Mass formulary in a subdued way like a delicate odour of incense.

The faithful are assembled in this basilica by the Tiber, the very building, it is said, which had been the dwelling of the noble Cecilia and the scene of her glorious martyrdom. The Introit and Offertory chants have the penitential motif which belongs to the Lenten season. "Forsake me not, O Lord my God; do not Thou depart from me; attend unto my help, O Lord, the power of my salvation." "To Thee, O Lord, have I lifted up my soul; in Thee, O my God, I put my trust; let me not be ashamed; neither let my enemies laugh at me; for none of them that wait on Thee shall be confounded."

These are Lenten prayers; but how fittingly they apply to the case of Cecilia in the hour of her trial. The Collect refers directly to the season of Lent. The Epistle is the prayer of Mardochaeus from the Book of Esther. Does not the figure of the queenly Esther, the protectress of her people, suggest the patron saint of the day, the Roman Cecilia? The final sentence of the Epistle: "Close not, O Lord, the lips of them that sing to Thee," recalls the song which Cecilia sang in her heart to God while the musical instruments sounded for her wedding-feast. The Gradual and Tract continue the Lenten motif and bring us to the Gospel, a passage in which our Lord predicts His passion. Again the figure of Cecilia is suggested. For the mother of James and John asks of the Master that her sons may be at His right and left when He comes into His kingdom. One thinks of Cecilia with Tiburtius and Valerian at her right and left, the two whom she brought to her divine Bridegroom and who drank with her of the chalice of suffering. The final "Prayer over the people," addressing God as "the restorer and lover of innocence," again calls up the thought of Cecilia.

In this Mass formulary the thoughts of sin and guilt, the sentiments of contrition and penance, the remembrance of the redeeming passion of Christ, are woven into a unity which is sustained by the local atmosphere of the stational church and the memory of the virginity and martyrdom of Cecilia.

Thus far we have been speaking only of liturgical texts, and the examples adduced are enough to show that liturgical prayer contains beauty-values which naturally tend to find expression in art-forms. But in the liturgy word and action are organically united. Indeed one of the ancient names for the Mass was *actio*. The liturgy is dramatic prayer. The eucharistic sacrifice especially is drama in the highest sense. All the sacraments and sacramentals have their visible and dramatic signs. In the liturgical drama there is a distribution of roles, first that of the central figure, the priest, then that of several clerics each with his proper part, and finally that of the whole assembly. The action proceeds through outward forms which are symbolic, thus speaking in a high poetic language, awakening a mystic sense and producing a spiritual elevation. It employs certain traditional gestures which are venerable with age, the bended knees, the folded hands, the outstretched arms and since the fourth century the forms of court ceremonial of Byzantium, Milan and Ravenna, notably the use of incense, gestures of reverence and liturgical vestments. Gallican influences also contributed greatly to heighten the dramatic effectiveness of the Roman liturgy.

We cannot here examine these matters in detail. But our brief observations will enable anyone to recognize without difficulty that the liturgy contains the innate germs of beauty, art-potencies which require only time for their development.

To return now to the original question as to the liturgy and aesthetics, it is obvious that nothing short of some catastrophe in the early Church could have prevented the gradual and natural development of these art-potencies. The fact is that as the Church grew the liturgy did develop and did become a supreme work of art, and we need not hesitate to say (without any mention as yet of the musical side of the liturgy) a complete art-synthesis.

I should insist that the liturgy became all this, and that it was not primarily intended by the Church to be a work of art. Its inherent beauty eventually and inevitably made it a work of art. But the creative principle, working from within, which brought this about was that something which is the very essence of the Christian religion. What was that inner force? What is the creative art-principle of the liturgy?

The purpose of the Christian religion is to assimilate man to God through Christ; to form mankind, therefore, in the likeness of Christ. *Christianus alter Christus* — the Christian is another Christ. The purpose of the Christian religion is to sanctify, to spiritualize, to deify mankind, to bring us as transfigured Christians to the transfigured Christ. This is accomplished through sacrifice and sacrament and prayer, that is, through the liturgy. The purpose of the liturgy is the transfiguration of human souls. It is this transcendent purpose that has brought out the inherent beauty of the liturgy and made it a consummate work of art. In a word: the idea of Christian transfiguration is the art-principle of the liturgy.

In order to understand this statement it will be necessary to advert again to the mind of the early Christians.

The first Christians, in their great desire for union with Christ, expected His *parousia,* a second coming of the Lord, at a not far distant date. Their great love of Him on the one hand, and the sharp trial of persecution on the other, caused them to long for that day when He would come again to establish His beatific kingdom.

But as years went by the faithful became aware that the second coming was not to be as their enthusiasm had bidden them to hope. Yet the vision of the glorified Redeemer in the light of which they had walked, continued to rest like the glow of sunset upon the declining years of Christian antiquity.

The art of the catacombs speaks eloquently in this regard. It is entirely an art of the world beyond. The catacomb paintings represent in rich variety the favorite theme of resurrection and union with Christ. The figure of the *Orans,* the praying one, standing with outstretched arms amid the flowers and the birds, and with the simple inscription: *in pace,* is an image of the Christian soul whose mortal remains are here laid to rest. The brilliant peacock is an accepted symbol of the transfiguration idea (for example in the cubiculum of the five saints in the catacomb of Calixtus). The beloved figure of the Good Shepherd depicted in a floral setting, expresses the thought of Him who brings His sheep into the heavenly fold (as in several arcosolia in the catacomb of Domitilla). The martyrs are never pictured in the realistic scene of their passion; they appear with hands extended to receive the palm and crown of victory which Christ holds out to them.

The art of the basilicas, corresponding to the altered circumstances of the Church in her victory under Constantine, speaks in a more majestic language. In the apse of the basilicas appears the *crux gemmata,* the cross bedight with pearls and precious stones, a symbol of Christ the king and conqueror. And later there appears the figure of the Lord Himself, shown as the *pantokrator,* the supreme ruler, with the inscription: *Dominus legem dat.* The idea of transfiguration appears not in pictorial art only, but everywhere throughout the liturgy. Observe how the feast of Easter stands as the center of the liturgical year. Or consider the entire composition of the rite of Baptism. One imagines the stately basilica with its glistening mosaics, one sees the bishop at the altar surrounded by his priests and deacons and lesser clerics in ordered rank and splendid vesture, one hears the chant of the choir and of the whole assembly, and one understands why in the writings of the post-Constantinian period the thought so frequently recurs that the basilica, the church-edifice here on earth, prefigures the eternal court of heaven. In the fifth and sixth centuries the liturgy had reached the term of its development as a complete art-synthesis.

For a deeper understanding of the transfiguration motive as it appears in the liturgy it will be necessary to dwell upon another thought which was stressed in the ancient Church especially for the sake of its ethical value.

The Church, the *familia Dei,* the community of the children of God, stood opposed to the saeculum, the world, as that term is employed, notably in St. John's Gospel, to mean the realm of evil. The Christian had renounced the world, in the sense of the evil world. This thought is expressed dramatically in the rite of Baptism. The candidate turns his back upon the West, the region of darkness, and solemnly renounces Satan and all his pomps. And then he turns toward the East, the region of light, and dedicates himself to Christ. Light and darkness, life and death, Christ and Satan, henceforward irreconcilable opposites, the two standards which determine the orientation of Christian life and all its energies and endurances, whether in the life of the individual Christian or in the larger life of the Church as a whole. Whatever is not Christ's is Satan's; whatever separates one from Christ is the work of Satan. This is the awful result of the primal catastrophe of original sin. Sin has subjected all creation in some measure to the dominion of Satan. Christ by His atoning death has emancipated mankind and all creation from the servitude of sin. The power of the great sacrifice of Calvary is to be communicated to all creatures through the Church which is the mystical Christ, to mankind in the sacraments and to inanimate creatures in a great variety of blessings. This continual infusion of the graces of Christ's redemption produces a gradual elevation, a transfiguration, of mankind first of all, and also of the entire material universe. And since grace is normally imparted in liturgical acts, the liturgy is the agency, the primary means of this inward transfiguration. Now, in order to satisfy the elementary requirements of art, the outward form of the liturgical act, the union of word and deed, must express the general idea of transfiguration in a manner appropriate to the particular transfiguration process that is effected by a given liturgical act.

PIUS PARSCH

(1884–　)

CREATOR of the popular Liturgical Movement on the Continent, Pius Parsch was born in Neustift in the Sudetenland, May 18, 1884. He was ordained to the priesthood in 1909. Cloisterneuburg near Vienna, the scene of his apostolic labors, grew into a center of liturgical action which influenced the movement throughout the world. Father Parsch saw very early in his priestly career the necessity of emphasizing the Christo-centric character of true piety, and he achieved that end in making the Christian community conscious of its solidarity by means of community singing and community prayers. A popular explanation of the significance of the liturgical year was his first achievement. This step was followed by a translation of the missal into German and the creation of an inexpensive leaflet missal, making the text of the Mass available to the Christian community. Translation of the Breviary, for Sundays and feast days, the singing of Mass itself, and the practice of the Dialogue Mass were further steps in making the parish at Cloisterneuburg a model of liturgical propriety and Christian dynamism.

Father Parsch writes with genuine unction, revealing itself even in his most didactic pages. While admirably illustrating the inspirational character of the liturgical life, he retained his complete amiability and superb common sense. His complete understanding of the intimate relationship between the Scriptures and the liturgy enabled him to demonstrate with enlightening clarity the interaction of dogma and life. Belief and action became the cornerstones of his system, and it was significantly discerning in that Father Parsch envisaged the praying community as the most significant factor in action.

THE EARLY HISTORY OF THE MASS*

WHEN our Lord instituted the Mass as a living memorial of Himself, as the making present again of His sacrifice of the Cross, and as the banquet which imparts a heavenly life, He gave to His Church a treasure to be guarded to the end of time. He gave to the Church a jewel of priceless value for which the Church has fashioned a worthy setting. That is to say, our Lord gave to the Church the Mass in its core and essence, the essential elements which we find in the Last Supper; but not all the prayers and ceremonies which we have at present. These latter are the setting which the Church has provided in the course of time, and they are not precisely the same throughout all the periods of history nor in all places. Thus, for example, in the lands and in the churches where the Mass is celebrated in the Greek language, the prayers and ceremonies are not exactly the same as those that we have in the Latin Mass. Hence in order to understand well the Mass service we should know something of its historical development.

1. The Last Supper

The Mass of the Last Supper was celebrated by our Lord Himself. We notice first of all its two principal component parts, the Consecration and the Communion. "Whilst they were at supper, Jesus took bread, and blessed, and broke, and gave to His disciples, and said: 'Take ye and eat; this is My body.' And taking the chalice, He gave thanks, and gave to them, saying: 'Drink ye all of this; for this is My blood of the new testament . . .'" (Matt. 26, 26). Here at once are the two chief component parts of the Mass, Consecration and Communion.

But besides these we also observe other non-essential elements which may be regarded as corresponding somewhat to the ceremonies that were added later. Thus at the Last Supper our Lord washed the feet of the apostles and explained the meaning of this action. "He that is washed needeth not but to wash his feet, but is clean wholly" (John 13, 10). He means thereby that one should purify one's soul before taking part in this august sacrifice; and we do this in the prayers at the foot of the altar. We read also that the Lord "broke" the bread, and this, too, is done in the Mass. He also addressed a sermon to the apostles, the beautiful discourse of farewell which St. John records, and there is still preaching and instruction in the Mass service. Finally, the evangelists tell us that at the end of the Supper a hymn or psalm was sung, and our Mass service today includes the chant of psalm pieces, Thus the Mass of the Last Supper included besides the essential parts other minor features from which our later ceremonies developed.

2. The Mass in Apostolic Days.

In what manner did the apostles celebrate the Mass? We are not informed as to when precisely they first carried out the Lord's bidding: "Do this in commemoration of Me" (Luke 22, 10). No doubt it was soon after Pentecost. We may imagine the ceremony as a very simple one. Very likely St. Peter or some other of the apostles arose one night in the Christian assembly in Jerusalem and spoke some such words as these: "Brethren, in the night in which the Lord Jesus was betrayed, He took bread, and broke, and said: 'This is My body which is given for you.' And He added: 'Do this in commemoration of Me' (1 Cor. 12, 24). Let us now celebrate the memorial of His passion and resurrection and ascension." Thus the apostle may well have spoken; and bread and wine were brought, and consecrated, and distributed to those who were present. We cannot determine what prayers or ceremonies may have accompanied this sacrificial action. But of two things we may be quite certain; it was celebrated with great reverence, and it corresponded to the action of the Last Supper

---

*Parsch, Pius, *Study the Mass* (Collegeville, Minn.: The Liturgical Press, 1941), pp. 12–17.

and to the usages of Jewish worship. The first Christians knew that their Christian sacrifice had been instituted during the observance of the Jewish paschal supper, and they knew that they were acting in the spirit of the Lord in combining their memorial sacrifice with a community repast. Thus they instituted their charity-banquet or *agape*. They gathered in the house of one or another of the faithful and brought with them food which they shared in common in evidence of their mutual charity and fellowship in Christ, and in connection with this meal they celebrated the Mass which they called the Lord's Supper (1 Cor. 12, 20).

In the writings of the New Testament we find various allusions to this eucharistic service joined with the *agape*. In the Acts of the Apostles we read that the Christians in Jerusalem continued "daily with one accord in the temple, and breaking bread from house to house, they took their meat with gladness and simplicity of heart" (Acts 2, 46). Again, we read the account of St. Paul's visit in Troas in Asia Minor, on his third missionary journey: "And on the first day of the week, when we were assembled to break bread, Paul discoursed with them, being to depart on the morrow. And he continued his speech until midnight." And after recounting the accident that befell one of the young men, the narrative continues to tell of St. Paul: "And breaking bread and tasting, and having talked a long time until daylight, so he departed." Further information regarding the *agape* service is given us by St. Paul in his first epistle to the Corinthians (1 Cor. 11, 17). And already there are some shadows in the pictures. It had come about that some of the Christians, especially the more wealthy ones, neglected to share with others. "For every one taketh before his own supper; and one indeed is hungry, and another is drunk." These abuses for which St. Paul blames the Christians of Corinth, quite likely were found also in other places. And therefore gradually within the first century the Mass was separated from the *agape*. For it was recognized that in the circumstances people might not always be in proper disposition for the holy sacrifice. The *agape*

service continued for some time to be held in the evening. But the eucharistic sacrifice was now celebrated in the morning with the precept of previous abstention from food and drink.

3. The Origin of the Fore-Mass.

Besides the "Lord's Supper" which the early Christians celebrated in connection with their charity-repast or *agape,* they had another service in their divine worship which was made up of prayer and instruction. Their sacrificial banquet was celebrated in the homes of the faithful and all outsiders were rigidly excluded. But their service of prayer and instruction was at first conducted, for some short time at least, in the temple or the synagogues, and its structure resembled that of the Jewish service which the first Christians, being of Jewish origin, took over from their past. The Jewish synagogue service consisted of: 1) prayer, 2) readings from the Law and the Prophets, and 3) sermons or instructions based on these readings. The Christians took over this kind of service and refashioned it in a Christian way. And then, when the eucharistic sacrifice was separated from the *agape* and provided with fixed prayers and ceremonies, the prayer and instruction service was placed before it as an introductory service which we may call the Fore-Mass. This Fore-Mass, the first part of our present service, from the beginning to the Credo, resembled the Jewish synagogue service and retains the same general structure to our present day, namely: 1) prayer (from the prayers at the foot of the altar to the Collect inclusive), 2) readings (Epistle and Gospel), and 3) sermon (which is a part of the Mass). The purpose of the Fore-Mass is evidently, first, the elevation of the soul by prayer and, second, the strengthening of faith by the readings and sermons, and both together are a preparation from the actual sacrifice which begins with the Offertory.

The prayer portion of the Fore-Mass is a progressive movement of the soul Godward. In the prayers at the foot of the altar we express our sorrow for sin, in the Kyrie our longing for God, in the Gloria our praise of His glory, and in the Collect our petition for His aid. After this Godward effort on our part the divine reply comes to us in the instruction part of the Fore-Mass, in the inspired words of the Epistle and Gospel which, with the sermon, are intended to strengthen our faith, to form Christ in our hearts by faith in preparation for His coming in sacramental communion. The prayers and readings of the Fore-Mass are not always the same. Some of them vary according to the seasons and feasts of the year.

4. The Mass in the Second Century

We have seen how the sacrifice of the Mass was at first celebrated in connection with a charity-repast, and then separated from the latter and preceded by an introductory service or Fore-Mass. And so by the year 150, just about a century after the apostles, we find the general outline of the entire service already fixed as it is today. One of the fathers of the second century, St. Justin, has left us a description of the Mass which he wrote about the year 150.

Let us read a part of St. Justin's description. "On the day called of the Sun (Sunday), an assembly in one place is made of all who live in the towns and in the country; and the commentaries of the apostles (Gospels) or the writings of the prophets are read as long as time allows. Then, when the reader has stopped, the president (bishop) makes an admonition and exhortation regarding the remembrance of these admirable things in a speech. Then we all stand up together and send up prayers . . . for ourselves . . . and for all others everywhere, that we, having learned true things, may be worthy to be found good workers in deeds and keepers of the commands, and so may be saved with eternal salvation. When we have finished the prayers, we greet each other with a kiss (of peace). Then bread and a cup of wine are brought to the president of the brethren, and he, taking these, sends up praise and glory to the Father of all through the name of the Son and of the Holy Ghost, and makes thanksgiving (makes the Eucharist) at length, because we are granted these favors by Him. When he has ended the prayers and thanksgiving (Eucharist), all the people cry out saying: 'Amen'. . . . After the president has given thanks (made the Eucharist) and all the people have cried out, those who are called by us deacons give to each one present to share the eucharistic bread and wine and carry them to those not present. And this food is called by us Eucharist, of which no one else may have a share, except he who believes that our teaching is true and has been cleansed by the washing for the forgiveness of sins and regeneration and so lives as Christ taught. For we do not receive these things as common bread or common drink; but as Jesus Christ, our Savior, having been made flesh by a word of God, had flesh and blood for our salvation, so we have learned that the food made a Eucharist by a word of prayer that comes from Him, from which our blood and flesh are nourished, by change are the flesh and blood of the incarnate Jesus."

In this passage from St. Justin we find that the Mass in the second century was like the Mass today. We notice the distinction between the introductory service and the actual sacrifice. In the former we find readings from the Old and New Testaments and a sermon by the bishop. Then there followed a prayer for all classes of people which is omitted in our Mass today, although we still find it in our Mass service on Good Friday. In the sacrificial part of the service we notice in St. Justin's description the Offertory, the Consecration and the Communion.

ROMANO GUARDINI

(1885–   )

THE Liturgical Movement owes much to the subtle and scholarly mind of Romano Guardini. Father Guardini was born at Verona in Italy. When he was still a child the family moved to Germany. He completed his studies for the priesthood in his adopted fatherland, and as a young priest became the leader in the Catholic Youth Movement which achieved such profound success before the advent of Hitler. His theological and liturgical writings made him a commanding figure in Catholic Germany, and many young priests were influenced by his lectures in Dogmatic Theology during the years he gave this course at Berlin. With the rise of Adolf Hitler, Father Guardini's best work came to an end in Germany, though his influence still lives in the Liturgical Movement.

THE PRIMACY OF THE LOGOS OVER THE ETHOS*

THE liturgy exhibits one peculiarity which strikes as very odd those natures in particular which are generously endowed with moral energy and earnestness — and that is its singular attitude towards the moral order.

People of the type instanced above chiefly regret one thing in the liturgy, that its moral system has few direct relations with everyday life. It does not offer any easily transposable motives, or ideas realisable at first hand, for the benefit of our daily conflicts and struggles. A certain isolation, a certain remoteness from actual life characterise it; it is celebrated in the somewhat sequestered sphere of spiritual things. A contrast exists between the study, the factory, and the laboratory of to-day, between the arena of public and social life and the Holy Places of solemn, divine worship, between the intensely practical tendency of our time, which is opposed to life by its wholly material force and acrid harshness, and the lofty, measured domain of liturgical conceptions and determination, with its clearness and elevation of form.

From this it follows that we cannot directly translate into action that which the liturgy offers us. There will always be a constant

need, then, for methods of devotion which have their origin in a close connection with modern life, and for the popular devotions by which the Church meets the special demands and requirements of actual existence, and which, since they directly affect the soul, are immediately productive of practical results. The liturgy, on the contrary, is primarily occupied in forming the fundamental Christian temper. By it man is to be induced to determine correctly his essential relation to God, and to put himself right in regard to reverence for God, love and faith, atonement and the desire for sacrifice. As a result of this spiritual disposition, it follows that when action is required of him he will do what is right.

The question, however, goes yet deeper. What is the position of the liturgy generally to the moral order? What is the quality of the relation in it of the will to knowledge, as of the value of truth to the value of goodness? Or, to put it in two words, what is the relation in it of the Logos to the Ethos? It will be necessary to go back somewhat in order to find the answer.

It is safe to affirm that the Middle Ages, in philosophy at least, answered the question as to the relation between these two fundamental principles by decisively ranking knowledge before will and the activity attendant

*From *The Spirit of the Liturgy*, by Romano Guardini, translated by Ada Lane (London: Sheed and Ward, 1930).

upon the functioning of the latter. They gave the Logos precedence over the Ethos. That is proved by the way in which certain frequently discussed questions are answered, and by the absolute priority which was assigned to the contemplative life over the active; this stands out as the fundamental attitude of the Middle Ages, which took the Hereafter as the constant and exclusive goal of all earthly striving.

Modern times brought about a great change. The great objective institutions of the Middle Ages — class solidarity, the municipalities, the Empire — broke up. The power of the Church was no longer, as formerly, absolute and temporal. In every direction individualism became more strongly pronounced and independent. This development was chiefly responsible for the growth of scientific criticism, and in a special manner the criticism of knowledge itself. The inquiry into the essence of knowledge, which formally followed a constructive method, now assumes, as a result of the profound spiritual changes which have taken place, its characteristic critical form. Knowledge itself becomes questionable, and as a result the centre of gravity and the fulcrum of the spiritual life gradually shifts from knowledge to the will. The actions of the independent individual become increasingly important. In this way active life forces its way before the contemplative, the will before knowledge.

Even in science, which after all is essentially dependent upon knowledge, a peculiar significance is assigned to the will. In place of the former penetration of guaranteed truth, of tranquil assimilation and discussion, there now develops a restless investigation of obscure, questionable truth. Instead of explanation and assimilation, education tends increasingly towards independent investigation. The entire scientific sphere exhibits an enterprising and aggressive tendency. It develops into a powerful, restlessly productive, labouring community.

This importance of the will has been scientifically formulated in the most conclusive manner by Kant. He recognised, side by side with the order of perception, of the world of things, in which the understanding alone

is competent, the order of practicality, of freedom, in which the will functions. Arising out of the postulations of the will he admits the growth of a third order, the order of faith, as opposed to knowledge, the world of God and the soul. While the understanding is of itself incapable of asserting anything on these latter matters, because it is unable to verify them by the senses, it receives belief in their reality, and thus the final shaping of its conception of the world, from the postulations of the will which cannot exist and function without these highest data from which to proceed. This established the 'primacy of the will.' The will, together with the scale of moral values peculiar to it, has taken precedence of knowledge with its corresponding scale of values; the Ethos has obtained the primacy over the Logos.

The ice having been broken, there now follows the entire course of philosophic development which sets, in the place of the pure will logically conceived by Kant, the psychological will, constituting the latter the unique rule of life — a development due to Fichte, Schopenhauer, and von Hartmann — until it finds its clearest expression in Nietzsche. He proclaims the 'will to power.' For him, truth is that which makes life sound and noble, leading humanity further towards the goal of the 'Superman.'

Such is the origin of pragmatism, by which truth is no longer viewed as an independent value in the case of a conception of the universe or in spiritual matters, but as the expression of the fact that a principle or a system benefits life and actual affairs, and elevates the character and stability of the will. Truth is fundamentally if not entirely — though here we overstep the field marked out for our consideration — a moral, though hardly a vital fact.

This predominance of the will and of the idea of its value gives the present day its peculiar character. It is the reason for its restless pressing forward, the stringent limiting of its hours of labour, the precipitancy of its enjoyment; hence, too, the worship of success, of strength, of action; hence the striving after power, and generally the exaggerated opinion of the value of time, and the compulsion to exhaust oneself by activity till the end. This is the reason, too, why spiritual organisations such as the old contemplative orders, which formerly were automatically accepted by spiritual life everywhere and which were the darlings of the orthodox world, are not infrequently misunderstood even by Catholics, and have to be defended by their friends against the reproach of idle trifling. And if it is true that this attitude of mind has already become firmly established in Europe, whose culture is rooted in the distant past, it is doubly true where the New World is concerned. There it comes to light unconcealed and unalloyed. The practical will is everywhere the decisive factor, and the Ethos has complete precedence over the Logos, the active side of life over the contemplative.

What is the position of Catholicism in relation to this development? It must be premised that the best elements of every period and of every type of mind can and will find their fulfilment in this Religion, which is truly capable of being all things to all men. So it has been possible to adapt the tremendous development of power during the last five centuries in Catholic life, and to summon ever fresh aspects from its inexhaustible store. A long investigation would be needed if we were to point out how many highly valuable personalities, tendencies, activities and views have been called forth from Catholic life as a result of this responsiveness to the needs of all ages. But it must be pointed out that an extensive, biased, and lasting predominance of the will over knowledge is profoundly at variance with the Catholic spirit.

Protestantism presents, in its various forms, ranging from the strong tendency to the extreme of free speculation, the more or less Christian version of this spirit, and Kant has rightly been called its philosopher. It is a spirit which has step by step abandoned objective religious truth, and has increasingly tended to make conviction a matter of personal judgment, feeling, and experience. In this way truth has fallen from the objective plane to the level of a relative and fluctuating value. As a result, the will has been obliged to

assume the leadership. When the believer no longer possesses any fundamental principles, but only an experience of faith as it affects him personally, the one solid and recognisable fact is no longer a body of dogma which can be handed on in tradition, but the right action as a proof of the right spirit. In this connection there can be no talk of spiritual metaphysics in the real sense of the word. And when knowledge has nothing ultimately to seek in the Above, the roots of the will and of feeling are in their turn loosened from their adherence to knowledge. The relation with the supertemporal and eternal order is thereby broken. The believer no longer stands in eternity, but in time, and eternity is merely connected with time through the medium of conviction, but not in a direct manner. Religion becomes increasingly turned towards the world, and cheerfully secular. It develops more and more into a consecration of temporal human existence in its various aspects, into a sanctification of earthly activity, of vocational labour, of communal and family life, and so on.

Everyone, however, who has debated these matters at any considerable length clearly perceives the unwholesomeness of such a conception of spiritual life, and the flagrance of its contradiction of all fundamental spiritual principles. It is untrue, and therefore contrary to Nature in the deepest sense of the word. Here is the real source of the terrible misery of our day. It has perverted the sacred order of Nature. It was Goethe who really shook the latter when he made the doubting Faust write, not 'In the beginning was the Word,' but 'In the beginning was the Deed.'

While life's centre of gravity was shifting from the Logos to the Ethos, life itself was growing increasingly unrestrained. Man's will was required to be responsible for him. Only one Will can do this, and that is creative in the absolute sense of the word, *i.e.,* it is the Divine Will. Man, then, was endowed with a quality which presumes that he is God. And since he is not, he develops a spiritual cramp, a kind of weak fit of violence, which takes effect often in a tragic, and sometimes (in the case of lesser minds) even a ludicrous manner. This presumption is guilty of having put modern man into the position of a blind person groping his way in the dark, because the fundamental force upon which it has based life — the will — is blind. The will can function and produce, but cannot see. From this is derived the restlessness which nowhere finds tranquillity. Nothing is left, nothing stands firm, everything alters, life is in continual flux; it is a constant struggle, search, and wandering.

Catholicism opposes this attitude with all its strength. The Church forgives everything more readily than an attack on truth. She knows that if a man falls, but leaves truth unimpaired, he will find his way back again. But if he attacks the vital principle, then the sacred order of life is demolished. Moreover, the Church has constantly viewed with the deepest distrust every ethical conception of truth and of dogma. Any attempt to base the truth of a dogma merely on its practical value is essentially un-Catholic. The Church represents truth — dogma — as an absolute fact, based upon itself, independent of all confirmation from the moral or even from the practical sphere. Truth is truth because it is truth. The attitude of the will to it, and its action towards it, is of itself a matter of indifference to truth. The will is not required to prove truth, nor is the latter obliged to give an account of itself to the will, but the will has to acknowledge itself as perfectly incompetent before truth. It does not create the latter, but it finds it. The will has to admit that it is blind and needs the light, the leadership, and the organising, formative power of truth. It must admit as a fundamental principle the primacy of knowledge over the will, of the Logos over the Ethos. This 'primacy' has been misunderstood. It is not a question of a priority of value or of merit. Nor is there any suggestion that knowledge is more important than action in human life. Still less does a desire exist to direct people as to the advisability of setting about their affairs with prayer or with action. The one is just as valuable and meritorious as the other. It is partly a question of disposition; the tone of a man's life will accentuate either knowledge or action; and the one type of disposition is worth as much as the other. The

'Primacy' is far rather a matter of culture — philosophy, and indeed it consists of the question as to which value in the whole of culture and of human life the leadership will be assigned, and which therefore will determine the decisive tendency; it is a precedence of order, therefore, of leadership, not of merit, significance, or even of frequency.

But if we concern ourselves further with the question, the idea occurs that the conception of the Primacy of the Logos over the Ethos could not be the final one. Perhaps it should be put thus: in life as a whole, precedence does not belong to action, but to existence. What ultimately matters is not activity, but development. The roots of and the perfection of everything lie, not in time, but in eternity. Finally, not the moral, but the metaphysical conception of the world is binding, not the worth-judgment, but the import-judgment, not struggle, but worship.

These trains of thought, however, trespass beyond the limits of this little book. The further question — if a final precedence must not be allotted to love — seems to be linked with a different chain of thought. Its solution perhaps lies within the possibilities we have already discussed. When one knows, for instance, that for a time truth is the decisive standard, it is still not quite established whether truth insists upon love or upon frigid majesty; the Ethos can be an obligation of the law, as with Kant, or the obligation of creative love. And even face to face with existence it is still an open question whether this obligation is a final rigid inevitability, or if it is love transcending all measure, in which the impossible itself becomes possible, to which hope can appeal against all hope. That is what is meant by the question whether love is not the greatest of these. Indeed, it is. Nothing less than this was announced by the 'good tidings.'

In this sense, too, as far as the primacy of truth — but 'truth in love' — is concerned, the present question is to be resolved.

As soon as this is done the foundation of spiritual health is established. For the soul needs absolutely firm ground on which to stand. It needs a support by which it can raise itself, a sure external point beyond itself, and that can only be supplied by truth. The knowledge of pure truth is the fundamental factor of spiritual emancipation. 'The truth shall make you free.' The soul needs that spiritual relaxation in which the convulsions of the will are stilled, the restlessness of struggle quieted, and the shrieking of desire silenced; and that is fundamentally and primarily the act of intention by which thought perceives truth, and the spirit is silent before its splendid majesty.

In dogma, the fact of absolute truth, inflexible and eternal, entirely independent of a basis of practicality, we possess something which is inexpressibly great. When the soul becomes aware of it, it is overcome by a sensation as of having touched the mystic guarantee of universal sanity; it perceives dogma as the guardian of all existence, actually and really the rock upon which the universe rests. 'In the beginning was the Word' — the Logos. . . .

For this reason the basis of all genuine and healthy life is a contemplative one. No matter how great the energy of the volition and action and striving may be, it must rest on the tranquil contemplation of eternal, unchangeable truth. This attitude is rooted in eternity. It is peaceful, it has that interior restraint which is a victory over life. It is not in a hurry, but has time. It can afford to wait and to develop.

This spiritual attitude is really Catholic. And if it is also a fact, as some maintain, that Catholicism is in many aspects, as compared with the other denominations, 'backward,' by all means let it be. Catholicism could not join in the furious pursuit of the unchained will, torn from its fixed and eternal order. But it has in exchange preserved something that is irreplaceably precious, for which, if it were to recognise it, the non-Catholic spiritual world would willingly exchange all that it has; and this is the primacy of the Logos over the Ethos, and by this, harmony with the established and immutable laws of all existence.

Although as yet the liturgy has not been specifically mentioned, everything which has been said applies to it. In the liturgy the Logos has been assigned its fitting precedence over the will. Hence the wonderful power of relaxation proper to the liturgy, and its deep reposefulness. Hence its apparent consummation entirely in the contemplation, adoration and glorification of Divine Truth. This is also the explanation of the fact that the liturgy is apparently so little disturbed by the petty troubles and needs of everyday life. It also accounts for the comparative rareness of its attempts at direct teaching and direct inculcation of virtue.

The liturgy has something in itself reminiscent of the stars, their eternally fixed and even course, of their inflexible order, of their profound silence, and of the infinite space in which they are poised. It is only in appearance, however, that the liturgy is so detached and untroubled by the actions and strivings and moral position of men. For in reality it knows that those who live by it will be true and spiritually sound, and at peace to the depths of their being; and that when they leave its sacred confines to enter life they will be men of courage.

WILLIAM BUSCH
(1882–   )

PIONEER of the Liturgical Movement in the United States, Rev. William Busch was born at Red Wing, Minnesota, October 6, 1882. He was educated at St. Joseph's School, Red Wing, St. Thomas College, the St. Paul Seminary, and Louvain University, where he majored in History. After ordination in 1907, he was stationed as curate at St. Luke's Church, St. Paul, and since 1913 has been professor of Church History at the St. Paul Seminary. In his classes at the seminary, as associate editor of *Orate Fratres,* as translator and lecturer, Father Busch has labored incessantly to further the Liturgical Movement. He has inspired several generations of students with a modicum of his own fervor and his book *The Mass-Drama* has become something of a source book to all who love the liturgy.

CONFLICT AND VICTORY—THE MYSTERY OF DEATH AND LIFE*

ONE notices of late a certain change in the style of our crucifixes, a departure from what has long been customary in Christian art. The recent style is less realistic; indeed it does not aim simply to portray the actual moments of Calvary, the agony and death of the Lord. It is rather an attempt to combine the two events of His death on the cross and His resurrection. Therefore His sacred figure is shown not in the tension of agony nor in the rigor of death, but upright and powerful even though fixed by the nails. The outstretched arms do not bear the weight of the body and rather suggest the wide embrace in which the Lord draws all things to Himself. The head is erect, the eyes wide open, the crown is not one of thorns but a jeweled diadem, the cross itself is of wrought metal or decorated wood and perhaps set with gems. The Christ of this crucifix is not a dead but a living Christ, the Lord who died indeed on the cross but who rose again, the conqueror of death, the redeemer and life-giver, Christ the Victor and King.

One may be inclined to associate this change in the style of the crucifix with the establishment a few years ago of the feast of the Kingship of Christ, and indeed there is a relationship. However, it would be more correct to say that here are two evidences, among many more, of the liturgical revival that is now spreading throughout the Church. The feast of Christ the King is a new emphasis of a truth that is written plainly all throughout the text of our liturgy, to which we are now giving a deeper interest. And the new style in the crucifix is not new but old; it is a return to the style that prevailed in ancient years when the liturgy first attained to its full development. If we may judge from the Roman catacombs, the crucifixion of the Lord was not represented in early Christian art, certainly not in a realistic way. And when the era of persecution had ended and the Church had triumphed in the days of Constantine, the cross was displayed as an emblem of victory and the crucifix was fashioned in a style like that to which we are now returning.

We are gradually coming to see once more that in our understanding of the holy sacrifice of the Mass we must give due attention to both the death and the resurrection of our Lord. We say commonly that the Mass is Calvary again; yes, but it is both Good Friday and Easter Sunday. Father D'Arcy speaks of those to whom the Mass is "on the whole a Sorrowful Mystery, a sacrifice un-

*Busch, William, *The Mass-Drama,* second edition (Collegeville, Minn.: The Liturgical Press, 1933).

bloody indeed, but otherwise dark with the darkness of Calvary." But it is not so to those whose piety is illuminated and guided by close and constant study of the official Mass-Liturgy.

In the days when our attention was held by the needs of controversy with unbelief we regarded the Resurrection chiefly as a proof of the divinity of Christ. "If Christ be not risen again," says St. Paul, "then is our preaching vain, and your faith is vain; yea, and we are found false witnesses of God, because we have given testimony against God, that He hath raised up Christ." This is the thought upon which we have chiefly rested our attention. But St. Paul continues with a further thought: "And if Christ be not risen again, your faith is vain, for you are yet in your sins." Here he uses the word *vain* in a somewhat different way. In the first case he means: your faith is without foundation. In the second sense he means: your faith is also vain in the sense that it is useless, it is without effect, you are still in your sins, you are unredeemed — if Christ has died and not risen again. It was necessary both that He die and rise again. Did not the Lord Himself say to the two disciples on the road to Emmaus: "Ought not Christ to have suffered these things, *and so to enter into His glory?*" We are reminded here of what we may call the negative and the positive aspects of our redemption, which also are pointed out to us in the Easter Preface: "Who by dying hath overcome our death, and by rising again hath restored our life." St. Paul means to say: Since Christ has truly risen your faith is not a vain and empty thing; it does possess that power which is revealed in His resurrection. Because He is risen you are redeemed. As He lives you also shall live, not merely in a future life beyond the grave, but here and now. You are dead to a life that is past, an unredeemed life, and you are risen with Christ to the supernatural life of His sanctifying grace.

Our Savior by His death on the cross paid the debt of mankind's sin. Too often we are content to stop there when we think of the meaning of our redemption. We say truly that His resurrection is the greatest of His

miracles, the splendid proof of His divine mission, the sure foundation of our faith, the pledge of our own resurrection into the life beyond the grave. Less frequently, as the Abbé Anger observes, do we consider the rôle of the Resurrection in the work of our sanctification. Risen from the dead, victorious and immortal, Christ is now in full truth, both in His divinity and humanity, our source of life. He is, as St. Paul says, "the new Adam"; He has become "a quickening spirit" who communicates to all the members of His mystical body that Spirit which He possesses in plenitude. Not only does He take away sin; He makes us sharers in His own divine life. "Who was delivered up for our sins," says St. Paul, "and rose again for our justification." And St. Thomas explains: "The passion of Christ works our salvation, strictly speaking, as regards the taking away of what is evil; but His resurrection as regards the beginning and example of what is good."

If we have not reflected sufficiently on the meaning of the Resurrection in this aspect, it is largely because we have not given enough attention to the mind of the Church as revealed in our liturgy. The rite of Baptism is constructed entirely on the double basis of the death and resurrection of our Lord. It may all be summarized in the words of St. Paul: "Know ye not that all we who are baptized in Christ Jesus are baptized in His death? For we are buried together with Him by baptism into death; that as Christ is risen from the dead by the glory of the Father, so we may walk in newness of life." The Mass-text also is built upon this principle and gives direct expression to it in many ways.

The Preface of the Mass during Easter time, as we have observed above, echoes distinctly the thought contained in these words of St. Paul. Nor is this peculiar to the Mass during Easter time. In every Mass, at the heart of the Canon-prayer, immediately after the Consecration, we say that the Mass is offered always in memory of the blessed passion of Christ and of His resurrection from the dead and of His ascension into heaven. The Christ of the Mass is the Christ who died and rose again and who lives forevermore.

In order to see how intimately the Resurrection enters into the whole fabric of the Mass-Liturgy, let us examine the main lines of its structure. The Mass of the Faithful is divided into two main parts, the sacrifice-oblation (our gift to God) and the sacrifice-banquet (God's gift to us). The meaning of these two elements is stated briefly by Father D'Arcy in approximately the following words: The act of sacrificial homage furthers union with God through the offering of a gift which symbolizes interior self-offering (sacrifice-oblation). The gift is sanctified and made holy with God's holiness, since it passes into His possession if it is accepted by Him. His acceptance, so to speak, passes through the gift to the offerer; and the union is ratified when the worshipper eats of what is holy with God's holiness (sacrifice-banquet). Compare here the words of the Canon-prayer after the Consecration which beg for the divine acceptance of our Sacrifice, and those which pray "that as many of us as, by participation at this altar, shall have received the most sacred body and blood of Thy Son may be filled with every heavenly blessing and grace."

We say that the essence of the Mass is in the words of Consecration by which our Lord is present as the eternal Priest and Victim. Holy Communion is not an essential part, but it is an integral part of the Mass. Father De la Taille asks the question: Was the sacrifice of Christ complete by His death on the cross? And he answers that as oblation or immolation it was complete so that nothing could be added. But he goes on to say that from the side of God there still remains the divine acceptance. "In order that the sacrifice may be completed and perfected, that it may reach its goal, we must not forget the part which God has in it." In the Old Testament we read of the fire that descended from heaven, and consumed the victim. So, to the oblation of Christ, our High-priest, there was of necessity to be an answer of divine acceptance. "No created fire, it is true, came down to devour the body of Christ in the sepulcher. But there came the fire of divine glory, consuming the mortality and corruptibility of the Savior, making Him pass, whole and entire,

body and soul, into the proper condition of only Son, Lord, Christ. The Gift has reached its goal."

In the sacrifice of the Mass this divine acceptance is included essentially in the words of Consecration by which Christ is present as the Victim both offered and accepted. But for the sake of human understanding it is necessary that what is contained essentially in these words be distributed throughout the literary and ceremonial expression of the liturgy. Hence the prayer for divine acceptance after the Consecration and the prayer for blessing upon those who partake of the accepted Victim. And thus we see the meaning of the Resurrection as revealed throughout the sacrifice-banquet. We eat of the accepted Victim and are made holy with the holiness of God. Our Lord was delivered up for our sins and rose again for our justification. Here are the negative and positive aspects of the redemption, and they are related as are the sacrifice-oblation and the sacrifice-banquet. We share first in Christ's passion and death, and then in the glory of His resurrection. In the sacrifice-banquet He becomes unto us "a quickening spirit." In our Lord's own words: "He that eateth Me, the same also shall live by me."

The genius of St. Thomas was able to say all this in two wonderful lines of his hymn, the *Adoro Te*.

O Thou memorial of our Saviour's dying!
O Bread that living art and vivifying!

The first line tells of the sacrifice-oblation and the second of the sacrifice-banquet; the first tells of the Death and the second of the Resurrection. Holy Communion therefore always has the quality of Easter. "Christ our Pasch is sacrificed," and like the disciples at Emmaus we "recognize Him in the breaking of bread." In the ancient liturgy a favorite hymn at Communion time was Psalm 33 which contains the verse: "O taste and see that the Lord is sweet." In the Greek text there is here a beautiful example of play upon words. The phrase: that the Lord is sweet — *hoti chrestos ho kyrios* — gains a new meaning by the change of one letter — *hoti Christos ho Kyrios* — which means: that Christ is the Lord, i.e., that Christ is God — "O taste and see that Christ is God!" The sacrifice-banquet of the Mass is the actual experience of divine life.

While we consider these things we have already passed over into the thought that the sacrifice of the Mass, which is the renewal of the death and resurrection of our Lord, is also for each and all of us the daily drama of our Christian life, and indeed the very secret of that extraordinary life which as Christians we have in Christ. It was necessary that Christ suffer and so enter into His glory, and the same principle applies to all whom He has called to follow Him and to lose their life and find it. What he did for us was not done merely in our stead and for our benefit; it is done over and over in order that mankind, incorporated in Him, may be drawn actively into the mystery of His death and resurrection and from generation to generation may find redemption and glory in Him.

As we dwell on this thought we see why Pope Pius X declared that active participation in the liturgy of the Church is the primary and indispensable source of the true Christian spirit. We recognize that the holy sacrifice of the Mass is the secret and fountain-head of Christian asceticism, and at the same time our understanding of asceticism gains a certain rectification. As we were inclined to think of the Mass only as Calvary, without sufficient regard to the Resurrection, we have also considered asceticism chiefly as mortification, without due thought of its positive goal.

Asceticism is often regarded as something altogether negative, as the practice of rigorous self-denial, the renunciation of comfort and pleasure, the deliberate choice of privation and pain. People who lack the supernatural point of view consider this to be entirely unreasonable, the result of misguided zeal or of religious fanaticism. And even Christians who know how to admire heroic virtue sometimes fail to understand the true nature of Christian asceticism because they regard only its negative aspect.

Christian asceticism is both negative and positive. Its process is always a double one. Both aspects are essential; but the ultimate goal is positive. Self-denial, in the sense of the renunciation of things naturally good and licit, is not practiced for its own sake, but as the way to a higher and richer life. The process is one of dying in order to live. No doubt our devotional literature here and there has not always managed to measure out the exact balance of emphasis. But those who are familiar with the teachings of ascetical theology, and those especially whose piety is formed and guided by the liturgy, are not likely to make any such misjudgment. Christian asceticism is in last analysis conformity of life to the asceticism of Christ, the secret of which is to be found in His death and resurrection and is expressed in the Easter Sequence:

Together death and life in a strange conflict strove;
The Prince of Life who died, now lives and reigns.

The Greek word *askesis* is positive in its meaning. It expresses the idea of exercise or training of any sort, the method by which one acquires proficiency in any art, whether of the body or the mind. Hence an *ascete* might be an artisan, a soldier, a rhetorician, a professional man. Especially he might be an athlete, one trained to proficiency in physical contest, one who contends for a prize. As applied to the exercise or training of the body, *askesis* meant what we call physical culture, and the term was used equally to mean the culture of the mind. Aristotle refers to both when he says that the Spartans made the mistake of limiting themselves to physical *askesis* and the art of war; so that they failed ultimately because they had neglected the higher mental and moral *askesis*. His words remind us that the two do not always go together, and also that, however desirable both are in themselves, it may be necessary sometimes to renounce the lower for the sake of the higher. This higher asceticism which the Greek philosopher has in mind is exemplified in many a serious worker who practices abnegation and spends himself for some intellectual or moral good. Thus asceticism both in the natural and the supernatural order has a positive goal, but its process includes certain negative features. The effort required for the attainment of proficiency involves a certain self-discipline. Physical culture affords many examples, especially in the case of the training of the athlete, as St. Paul points out, for example, in the Lesson for Septuagesima Sunday. "Every one that striveth for the mastery refraineth himself from all things; and they indeed that they may receive a corruptible crown; but we an incorruptible one."

The Epistle of Septuagesima is not the only instance of this kind in the liturgy and in ancient Christian literature. Other examples from St. Paul are his words to Timothy: "He that striveth for the mastery is not crowned except he strive lawfully," and the reference to his own life: "I have fought the good fight, I have finished my course, I have kept the faith; for the rest, there is laid up for me a crown of justice." Or again, he says that the wrestling of the Christian is "not against flesh and blood, but against . . . the spirits of wickedness," and therefore he urges the putting on of "the armor of God." In ancient Christian literature the word athlete is used regularly of those who were highly trained and proficient in the art of Christian life. This is true especially during the years of persecution when Christian life meant not only that contest with self and with inward foes which St. Paul has chiefly in mind, but the conflict with a bitterly hostile world. The Christian athlete was especially he who strove literally in the arena and won the crown of martyrdom.

St. Ignatius of Antioch says in his letter to St. Polycarp: "Bear the infirmities of us all as a perfect athlete. . . . Be temperate as an athlete of God. . . . It is the part of a noble athlete to be wounded and yet conquer." In the account of the martyrs of Lyons and Vienna we read that the neophyte Maturus proved himself "a glorious combatant," and little Blandina, the slave girl who so inspired her companions, is called "a noble athlete."

Tertullian, in his letter to the martyrs in prison, dwells at greater length on this thought of St. Paul. "You are about to pass through a noble contest in which the living God acts the part of the judge, in which the Holy Ghost is your trainer, in which the prize is an eternal crown. . . . Therefore, your Master, Jesus Christ, who has anointed you with His Spirit and led you forth to the arena, has seen it good before the day of the conflict to take you from a condition more pleasant in itself, and has imposed on you a harder treatment that your strength may be greater. For the athletes, too, are set apart to a more stringent discipline that they may have their physical powers built up. They are kept from luxury, from daintier meats, from more pleasant drinks; they are pressed, racked, worn out; the harder their labors in the preparatory training, the stronger is the hope of victory. 'And they,' says the Apostle, 'that they may receive a corruptible crown.' We, with the crown eternal in view, look upon the prison as our training ground, that at the goal of final judgment we may be brought forth well disciplined by many a trial, since virtue is built up by hardships, as by voluptuous indulgence it is overthrown."

St. Cyprian writes in the same way to the Christians of Thibaris: "Men are trained and prepared for secular contest and they account it a great mark of honor if it so happen that they are crowned in the sight of the people and in the presence of the emperor. Behold a sublime and mighty contest, glorious with the prize of a heavenly crown, in which God beholds us contending. . . . How great the dignity of glory, how great the happiness, to strive in the presence of God and to be crowned by Christ our judge."

In the days when the persecutions were active and bitter, schools were established precisely for the training of Christians for martyrdom. The training was of course chiefly that of the will by the study of the teaching and example of Christ the Lord and by participation in the mysteries of the liturgy. But it included also a training in physical endurance that would enable them to stand firm in the hour of trial. And apart from these special measures the regular catechumenate provided a system of Christian *askesis;* that is, it was a system not merely of doctrinal instruction but of a spiritual exercise and practical training in the art of Christian life. As such it was closely bound up with the public worship or the liturgy of the Church, as one may even now discover by a study of the Mass, and particularly of its proper parts during the season of Lent.

The reason for this union of liturgy and asceticism is plain to anyone who knows the ancient meaning of the two words. The liturgy is the normal way of Christian asceticism, the divinely established *askesis* in which Christians are incorporated into the passion and victory of Christ. The secret of all Christian life lies in our incorporation into Christ, the new Adam, the Head of a redeemed race. His redeeming work has its culmination in those hours of His agony and triumph in which He was "put to death indeed in the flesh, but enlivened in the spirit." The fundamental principle of Christian asceticism, union with Christ in the conflict and victory of His death and resurrection, is also the underlying principle of all the liturgy. Baptism incorporates us into Christ precisely by union with Him in the mystery of His death and resurrection. We are "baptized in His death . . . buried together with Him by baptism into death; that as Christ is risen from the dead by the glory of the Father, so we may walk in newness of life." The same is true in varying ways of all the sacraments. But the Eucharist especially is the sacrifice-sacrament which is at once the memorial of our Savior's passion and death and of His resurrection the cause of our liberation from sin and the source of supernatural life and the pledge of ever-lasting glory. We have seen how this principle underlies the entire structure of the Mass-Drama and determines the division into the sacrifice-oblation and the sacrifice-banquet. It governs also the entire structure of the liturgical year which has its crisis in the paschal mystery. The goal of Lent is not Good Friday, but Good Friday joined with Easter Sunday. Lent and Easter should not be regarded as two separate seasons, for they are related as are the sacrifice-oblation and the sacrifice-banquet, and both are governed by the same double idea, that by the passion and cross of our Lord we are brought to the glory of His resurrection. Therefore the liturgy has us begin even on Septuagesima Sunday with St. Paul's lesson of the Christian athlete. And for the same reason the liturgy has given to the Easter season an atmosphere of joy, a sense of victory, which is the pledge of eternal glory in Christ.

In the record of the martyrs of Lyons and Vinne we read of St. Blandina that, though she was only a little slave girl of whom great heroism would hardly be expected, yet, "strengthened by the power of Christ, our invincible Athlete, she strove gloriously and won the crown of immortality." Here again is the thought of Christ as the Strong One into whose conflict and victory we are incorporated. Cardinal Newman has expressed this thought in his *Dream of Gerontius:*

> O wisest love! that flesh and blood
>> Which did in Adam fail
> Should strive afresh against the foe,
>> Should strive and should prevail.

And it is the same thought that we have seen in the words of the Easter Sequence quoted above. It is the deep truth which finds expression also in the recent style of the crucifix, the secret of Christian life, the mystery of the death and resurrection of our Lord. The word *mystery* as used in the liturgy means more than a truth addressed to the mind and which we cannot fully understand; it means also a divine deed, especially the drama of redemption, the work of the God-man which had its crisis in His death and resurrection and which is continued in the drama of worship, the eucharistic Sacrifice, wherein the Church, the mystical Christ, continues to act under His headship. And the word *secret* means more than something hidden. It means, certainly in this case, something that deserves to be sought for, and which when found is light and life.

VIRGIL MICHEL
(*1890–1938*)

A TIRELESS worker in the liturgical field and one of the most influential of American liturgists, Rev. Virgil George Michel, O.S.B., was born at St. Paul, Minnesota, June 26, 1890. His early love of the Benedictine Order drew him into the novitiate at St. John's Abbey in 1909, he was professed in 1910 and ordained June 15, 1916. Father Michel's studies were extensive. In addition to the degrees taken at St. John's Abbey School (A.B. and M.A.) he received his Ph.D. from the Catholic University and spent some time in graduate studies and research in Belgium and Italy. As a teacher of Philosophy at St. John's and later as prefect of studies, Father Virgil became one of the most noted of American liturgists. He was the founder of *Orate Fratres* and his unceasing writing and lecturing may be said to have scattered interests into a massive movement which has swept the continent. In the midst of his labors Father Virgil died in 1938.

CHAPTER V

THE LITURGICAL YEAR*

I. CENTERED IN CHRIST

THE daily round of sacrificial worship that the Church offers to God in her liturgy, specifically in the Mass and the divine office, varies in its general atmosphere from day to day in accordance with the succession of feasts that make up the liturgical year. In both missal and breviary there are prayers that recur regularly and are called the *ordinary* prayers of the Mass and the office. Many other prayers in each vary with the succession of feasts and seasons. They are called the proper of the season. It is these proper parts of Mass and office that constitute the characteristic elements of the liturgical year. The divine office is a radiation of the sacrifice of the Mass, so that the two belong together. Still more true is it that the liturgical year is inseparable from Mass and office. The liturgical year is realized precisely in the Church's daily offering of the sacrifice of the altar and of the divine praises to the Father. Without the Mass in particular the liturgical year would have no real liturgical signifi-

cance. In treating here of the liturgical year we shall confine our attention chiefly to the proper parts that give expression to the varying aspects of the liturgical cycle, but it must always be kept in mind that the essential element in the liturgical year is the daily sacrifice. The variable parts of Mass and office that constitute the proper of the liturgy are as such only the background or stage setting within which the official worship of the Church unfolds itself, as within integral elements of her liturgy.

The liturgical year, beginning with the first Sunday of Advent and ending with the last Sunday after Pentecost, does not everywhere give equal emphasis to all the truths and mysteries of Christ's redemption. The different truths and mysteries of our faith are presented singly and in succession in both missal and breviary. One by one they are marshalled forth, commemorated, lived in the way that is peculiar to the divine liturgy of the Church. But in the ordered succession of these Christ is at all times central.

There is a rhythmic ebb and flow running through the liturgical year as through all else in .this world. The universe of the

*From *The Liturgy of the Church,* pp. 84–98, by Dom Virgil Michel, O.S.B. By permission of The Macmillan Company, New York, 1937.

heavens has its changing cycles and periods; the solar system gives us our four seasons and the earth gives us the regular recurrence of night and day, the rhythms of which are copied by the various forms of life here on earth. In life itself there have been the vast cycles of species coming into existence in geological time and again disappearing; the stages of youth, maturity, old age in the individual; the seasonal changes in many forms of life; the daily periods of wakefulness and sleep; and the smaller alternations of the rhythmic pulsebeat of breath and blood. Likewise in the liturgical or church year we have the larger seasonal divisions of Advent, Christmas, Epiphany, Septuagesima, Lent, Passiontide, Eastertide, and Pentecost with its longer aftermath; and again the regularly recurring Day of the Lord, and within each day the recurring rhythm of the different hours of the divine office. In all these cycles there is also a progressive change of sentiments and moods, based on special dogmas and mysteries, a changing series of eternal truths accompanied by a corresponding atmosphere of joy and adoration, admiration and wonder, sympathy and compunction, mortification and repentance. The whole spiritual life in all its wondrous variations thereby comes to view and realizes itself in the members of the mystical body ever in intimate union with their divine head Christ.

The symbolism of the sun as representative of Christ, the eternal Sun of Justice, has been mentioned in the preceding chapter. This symbolism finds realization in the prime fact that the liturgical year centers about Christ, just as do the seasons of the natural year around the celestial sun. "The liturgical year is the revolution of the year round Christ, the reproduction of the principal events of his life," as Dom Cabrol says. It was mentioned before that the liturgy puts us in touch with the wonderful richness of the life of Christ. This is done particularly in the whole liturgical cycle. We there have a panorama of the life of Christ in its historical development from his birth to his resurrection. All the mysteries of the redemption are there placed before

us, and in them we see the wonderful dispensation of God's love towards man.

"The first half of the cycle," says Dom Festugière in dividing the year from the standpoint of temporal duration, "that in which the series of mysteries is truly condensed, serves to give us in short, but according to their temporal succession, all the phases of the life of Jesus. In the second half, which commences supposedly after the career of Jesus is ended, and which consequently symbolizes the life of the Church herself, the liturgy by means of the gospels freely composes a vista of sacred events that invite the Christians to contemplate the visage of their divine Model under the most varied aspects, and to imbue themselves with his teachings and examples."

The liturgical year thus gives us a sublime manifestation of Christ's devotion to his Father. Christ permeates the liturgical year, even as he is always present in the liturgy. "Always, therefore, is Christ in the liturgy: Jesus Christ in the beatitude of heaven, Jesus Christ in his temporal abasement, Jesus Christ in the work of the redemption, Jesus Christ living in the Church in the course of the centuries. He is the immortal King of the ages, to whom the liturgy incessantly sings its hymn of honor and glory." This is only to be expected, since the liturgy is the life of the Church, and since it is the mission of the Church by means of her liturgy to bring about an ever increasing fullness of Christ in her children, the members of this same Christ.

II. LIVING IN CHRIST

The recurring celebration of the various mysteries of the life of Christ in the course of the liturgical cycle can therefore be no mere historical commemoration of the events of his career. Between a memorial celebration of the birth of our Savior on Christmas day and, say, of the birth of Washington as the father of our country, there must be all the difference that exists between the liturgy as something divine-human and the purely earthly events of man. A celebration of the latter kind may also have its wholesome moral and psychological effect in the revitalization of the ideals surrounding the event commemorated, but it can have nothing more than that, nothing of the spiritual supernatural actuality that is of the nature of the Church's liturgy such as was described in the preceding chapter.

The symbolical representation of the historical Christ must have also the deeper purpose that exists in all the liturgical worship of his Church. It must have also the higher purpose of producing in the Church, in the members of the living body of Christ, the living actuality of Christ's mystical presence, and that, in all the richness of the life of the Redeemer and in all its aspects. As Abbot Caronti says so well: "The liturgical year, this drama of marvellous beauty, is undoubtedly the official glorification of God which it is the duty of the Church to enact. It has a great historical and dogmatic value; but in the intention of our mother the Church its purpose is also to produce in souls the moral effects which assimilate them to Christ. That which happens in the course of the liturgical periods must reproduce itself in the soul; and no event is celebrated, no truth is commemorated, no great occurrence is narrated, that is not destined to produce its sanctifying effect in the intimacy of the soul, that is not destined also to effect a living practice of some virtue."

By truly participating in the liturgy, then, and drawing from it not only our prime spiritual inspirations but especially also a real share in the very life of Christ, in the divine life of God, the mysteries of the life of Christ, or of our salvation and redemption, become a living present actuality in our souls. That is the true meaning and true nature of the liturgical mysteries celebrated on the altar with the very powers of Christ himself — the enactment in the mystical body of the *opus redemptionis,* the divine redemptive action of the God-Man. "The epenetic liturgy, joined to the sacrificial liturgy, causes the person of Jesus to reign really and mystically over every one of our days; by means of the cycle of feasts, it reproduces mystically, every year here on earth, the phases of the life of Jesus. In fine,

it continues really and mystically the prayer and the teaching of Jesus."

These mysteries we enact in ourselves by means of the liturgy, that is, Christ enacts them in the members who are actively united to him in the celebration of the liturgical mysteries; our lives begin to reflect, to contain more and more in themselves, the very life of Christ; we live Christ. "I live, now not I; but Christ liveth in me." This is at once the best possible response of ours to the saying of our Lord: "I have given you an example, that as I have done to you, so do you also," of which we find an echo in the first letter of St. Peter, quoted in the vespers chapter of the second Sunday after Easter: "Dearly beloved, Christ also suffered for us, leaving us an example that you should follow his steps."

The various phases of the liturgy of the year are therefore so many different attempts to enact the life of Christ in us, of developing more and more the presence of Christ in his mystical body, of entering upon the reality of the divine mystery of which we treated in the preceding chapter — the realization of the Divine in man. "The ecclesiastical year," writes Dom Sticker, "represents the chief events of the work of the redemption in order that we may gratefully commemorate the various redemptive acts which God performed for us through Christ, and which have an eternal significance for us. In the ecclesiastical year we go through a continuous memorial celebration. But as we 'commemorate' these great acts of the Redemption in a holy fellowship, something wonderful transpires: the event that we celebrate becomes again a salutary presence in us. With that I have touched upon the profoundest essence of the ecclesiastical year. It is a continuous celebration of divine mystery."

III. GROWTH IN CHRIST

We have seen before that the realization of the divine mystery in us, of the sacred union of members with Christ through participation in the liturgical mysteries, is something gradual that is destined for continuous growth and greater fulfilment. The gradual development of the mysterious life of Christ as unfolded in the liturgical cycle is thus admirably adapted to our nature insofar as our finite being cannot possess its fulness of the Divine at once. It cannot grasp the Divine in one act, it can never grasp or possess it fully, but it can always attain to a greater possession and realization of it. This realization in us, this union with God that is an increasing possession of God by us and of us by him, takes on a fuller form in the course of the year, as one after the other of the aspects of the Divine are allowed to shed their efficacious rays of grace on our souls.

However, our nature ever remains finite, no matter how intimate and abundant is its participation in the divine life. It can never grasp this life adequately or in its totality in the course of any year, not even in the course of a lifetime, even while, just because it is finite, it is capable of ever realizing more than it does at any one time. Hence, again, it is admirably in harmony with our human nature that the liturgical cycle is repeated year after year, just as the divine sacrifice is repeated in the Church day after day. As we are unable to exhaust our capacity for the Divine in a day or a year, the Church of Christ, with the infinite patience and the tender love of her divine Founder, continues to present to us the divine means of living Christ, thereby truly fulfilling her mission of achieving the ever increasing plentitude of the Redeemer.

It is for this reason that the recurring daily and annual cycles of the liturgy never grow old for those who enter into their participation with the understanding and love of their divine Head. Ancient as the hills, the liturgy is still ever new, it has ever a new store of the divine life to hold out to our grasp, and with the recurring years the realization of its meaning grows ever richer. Therein lies the difference between the divine and the human, the inexhaustible and the purely finite. Taking our comparisons from our own life of today, we see just the opposite characteristic, *e.g.*, in the popular cinema of our times. How many films should any thinking man care to see

a second time, or a third or fourth? Even in different photoplays there is a certain recurrent sameness, which to the intelligent mind becomes tiresome and deadening, so that the constantly regular enthusiast or "movie fan" is by many considered a bit abnormal or subnormal.

Now the eternal mysteries of God cannot really change fundamentally. To have recourse to them regularly should therefore be equally tiresome, were it not for the fact of their inner spiritual vitality, of the divine efficacy in them. If they realize their purpose one year, their possibilities have not at all been exhausted; they have in fact been enhanced, for their inner divine efficacy is infinite, and its realization grows in proportion to the participation already entered into wholeheartedly. As they recur the next year, they will find in us an increased capacity for realizing them, and will thus year after year produce a continuous growth in the intimate possession of the Christ-life. They build up stone upon stone in the human temple of God, wherever one enters truly into the living spirit of the annual liturgical celebration of the redemptive mysteries. The growth which can thus be developed by the help of the ecclesiastical cycle of the liturgy is endless; it admits of continuous increase; it is truly a divine light that with increasing years opens ever new vistas to the spiritual eye of the soul.

Thus not only the Church at large, but also the individual, comes under the full influence of the divine energy acting in the liturgy. "This succession of mystic seasons," said Dom Guèranger, "imparts to the Christian the elements of that supernatural life, without which every other life is but a sort of death, more or less disguised." The individual soul, as well as the Church as an organic unity, realizes this mystic growth by submitting to the guidance of the liturgical cycle. Both take their cue from it for their mode of developing the successive phases of Christ in the yearly routine. However, here again the submission is not merely passive, but is the same peculiar mixture of reception and active disposition and co-operation that was mentioned before. The liturgical year has been well styled the spiritual itinerary of the member of the mystical Christ. As the member goes on the journey as mapped out by the Church, Christ is indeed his sole support, but, not unlike the child that learns to walk while upheld by its mother's supporting arms, the individual must put forth effort step by step in co-operation with the workings of the Spirit of Christ in him.

In reference to the liturgical year the comparison has been made of the gardener who in the various types of work he must do is guided by the days and seasons of the solar year. "A gardener, who works with nature and her rhythm must indeed dig, sow, trim; but all the rest, and just that which is ultimately the energizing factor, is the work of the sun and of nature living by the sun. Under the influence of the latter the plant develops as of itself, it grows and blossoms and bears fruits, and is of a beauty and perfection that are striven after in vain by human effort and art. It is the gardener's part, that in his labors he be guided not by his own whims but by nature, that he expose his young shoots properly to the sun, which alone and freely gives them their increase. The Church is a gardener in her holy year, and everyone is in regard to his soul like a gardener if he associates himself simply and unaffectedly with the Church. He cannot force his sanctification by his own powers; he becomes holy. His holiness is an organically growing life of which the Lord says: Which of you by taking thought, can add to his stature one cubit? (Matt. 6:27)."

IV. Parts of the Church Year

To many it may come as a surprise to hear that the church year as we now have it and understand it was perhaps more than any other aspect of the liturgy a matter of very gradual development. In the earliest Christian times even the feast of Christmas was entirely unknown. Yet elements of the church year go back directly to the Old Testament out of which the New was evolved. "The general ground-plan of the Christian church year," writes Dom Haer-ing, "was already laid down in the Old Testament law pertaining to feast days, sab-baths, and the division of the weeks. The celebration of the highest Jewish feasts, Easter and Pentecost, was carried over from the Old Testament. But the idea of a church year was not clearly grasped until towards the end of the sixteenth century. And only after the civil year was made to begin with the first of January, in accordance with the Gregorian calendar, was the idea of a church year more clearly understood and adapted to pastoral needs."

The greatest feast in the liturgical year is that of Easter: "This is the day that the Lord hath made, let us rejoice and be glad therein. Alleluia" (gradual, etc.). It is also the first great festival in point of origin. After the first Pentecost the apostles went about preaching the gospel and "breaking bread." The Sabbath of the Old Law gave way to the Sunday because of the occurrence of the mysteries of the resurrection and the pentecostal descent on a Sunday. Each Sunday became a special commemoration of the redemptive mysteries of Christ, all of which were concentrated *in toto* in the eucharistic celebration. Naturally the annual recurrence of the anniversary of the first Easter was celebrated with special solemnity. It was called the Paschal mystery, which at the time included the events of the three days leading up to the resurrection itself. The institution of the Eucharist, the passion and death, and the resurrection — all of these received their anniversary commemor-ation in a solemn manner on the feast of Easter, even as they did with less solemnity every Sunday of the year.

The extension of the Easter solemnity over the forty days ending with Pentecost was natural in the light of the Gospel nar-ratives. "The date of Easter necessarily de-termined that of Pentecost, which was kept on the fiftieth day after the resurrection. It was the festival of the descent of the Holy Ghost upon the apostles, who were then assembled in the Cenacle. These fifty days formed, as it were, an uninterrupted festival, a jubilee, a time of rejoicing, during which there was no fasting, all penitential exercises ceased, and even the very attitude of prayer was less humble." In the spirit of Christ and in imitation of his suffering, a period of preparation for the Easter celebration was soon observed as a time of special penance and mortification. The length of this Lenten period varied greatly for a long time.

In the first Christian centuries apparently no celebration of the birth of Christ was held. In the East the feast of Epiphany came into vogue but it emphasized the appearance of the Savior the manifestations of his divinity as, e.g., at his baptism in the Jordan. Only in the fourth century was the feast of Christmas instituted in the West and celebrated on December 25. Gradually a preceding period was set aside as one of preparation for the advent of the Redeemer on the anniversary of his birth, and the general structure of the Christmas period was modeled on that of the Easter period.

Thus the liturgical cycle of the church year, which leads the member of Christ through the successive phases of Christ's life, divides naturally into two periods, that of Christmas and that of Easter. The one centers in the mystery of the incarnation, Christ's coming onto the earth and his revelation of himself as the light of the world; and the other centers in the mystery of the completed redemption, his passion and death, which attain their glory in his resurrection and ascension, with the completing touch put on the Church by the descent of the Holy Ghost on Pentecost, after which comes the mystical reign of Christ in his Church to the end of time. Each of these two periods may be divided into a preparatory season, Advent and Septuagesima to Holy Week, respectively; a main period of the characteristic feasts, Christmas and Epiphany on the one hand, Easter, Ascension and Pentecost on the other; and the aftermath, the echo of the feasts, the Sundays after Epiphany and after Pentecost respectively.

In the preparatory periods the mood is one of compunction and mental preparation for the great grace and deliverance wrought by the mysteries of the main feasts. Hence they are periods of sorrow and penance and

the color of the time is violet. The main feasts are feasts of joy and deliverance, true manifestations of the divine love, and the sentiments are those of joy and jubilation. Here the color of the day is white, with the red of flaming love for Pentecost. During the aftermaths we have a sort of continuing echo of the feasts themselves. There is no emphatic further mystery to celebrate in them, but rather the calm onward march of events in the life of Christ and the Church. Here the color of the time is green, symbolizing at once the absence of outstanding mysteries and the progressive development of the fruits of the previous feasts growing into a rich harvest of the life divine.

The mysteries and feasts thus celebrated in accord with the succession of liturgical seasons are said to make up the temporal cycle of the liturgical year, by all odds its most important part. There is also a so-called sanctoral cycle, in which various feasts of our Lord, less related to the mysteries celebrated in the temporal cycle, and of the blessed Virgin and of innumerable saints are celebrated. These feasts are usually dated in accordance with the secular calendar. In their celebration God is honored in his saints and they make intercession to him in our behalf. As with all the liturgy, their purpose is the glorification of God and the sanctification of man, but with the aid now of those members of Christ who have attained their final crown and resting place in the plenitude of their divine Head.

Even among these feasts there are some whose dates seem aptly chosen in relation to the temporal cycle. Thus the feast of the Immaculate Conception occurs shortly before Christmas and that of the Presentation in the Temple after Epiphany. The feasts of John, the beloved disciple, of the Holy Innocents, and of Stephen the first martyr, seem to fit in well with the celebration of Christ's appearance on earth; and the feasts of Corpus Christi and of the apostles Peter and Paul are well placed shortly after Pentecost, in the time commemorative of the spread and growth of the kingdom of God on earth. In a similar way the feasts of Christ the King, of All Saints and of All Souls come naturally towards the end of the Sundays after Pentecost, the end of the entire liturgical year. While the general placement of feasts in the temporal cycle follows the temporal succession of the events of Christ's life in a very foreshortened manner, there is one peculiar exception in the fixing of the feast of the Annunciation on March 25, nine months before the feast of Christ's birth. To this may be added the feast of the Visitation (July 2) and that of John the Baptist (June 24).

GERALD ELLARD
(1894–   )

ONE who became, as he says, a writer by chance or indirection, Father Gerald Ellard, S.J., was born October 8, 1894, at Commonwealth, Wisconsin. In 1912 Father Ellard joined the Society of Jesus, was professed July 13, 1914, and ordained June 16, 1926. Teaching and study engrossed his first years as a priest. After obtaining his B.A. at Gonzaga in 1919, Father Ellard proceeded to St. Louis University for his M.A. Further graduate studies at the University of Munich culminated with Father Ellard's reception of the Ph.D.

His interest in the liturgy arose from the conviction that Catholics should participate instead of being mere spectators at the Mass. Father Ellard's understanding of the liturgy is scholarly and complete, but his great contribution to the movement in the United States has been practical, in that it has enlarged the layman's conception of his priesthood and the necessity of his fullest participation in the life of the Church. *Christian Life and Worship, Men at Work at Worship,* and *The Dialog Mass* are some of Father Ellard's important works.

In some parishes a practice has become established whereby the people together with the server make the responses in private Masses. . . .
In some places . . . the people recite aloud and in unison, together with the priest, the Gloria, Credo, Sanctus, Benedictus and Agnus Dei.
Reply . . . Your Eminence has the full right to control this form of liturgical piety.
— Rites Congregation, for Pius XI, 1935.

CHAPTER VIII

THE WORKER GETS A VOICE*

LETTERS from Spain told of the rapid spread there during the recent Civil War, in both military and civil life, of active lay participation in the Church's public worship. Thereby some interesting Mass-history was repeating itself, for the Dialog Mass, or *Missa Recitata* as more formally styled, can, in fairly accurate fashion, be called a by-product of the World War. In the Church's program of chant restoration, not yet realized with anything like completeness, the Holy See decreed, "in order that the *faithful* [that is, the entire congregation] *may more actively* participate in divine worship, let them be made once more to sing" all the short responses, and the unchanging choral parts,

*Ellard, Gerald, S.J., Ph.D., *Men at Work at Worship* (New York: Longmans, Green and Co., 1940), pp. 131–142.

such as the *Gloria, Credo, Sanctus, Benedictus* and *Agnus Dei* (Pius X, XI). What is called the Dialog Mass provides for the laity at *Low Mass* the same scope of group participation as envisaged by the chant reforms for High Mass. Just how the Dialog Mass is conducted in its two usual forms is indicated in these directions of the Archbishop of Rouen (February 1934): "We authorize our priests to organize it only when they are sure it will be done correctly — *i.e.,* with uniform and regular pronunciation of *all* the Latin words, and with careful attention to the words of the priest, so as not to delay him. All this will suppose careful preparation, and cooperation with the priest at the altar. There are two kinds of 'dialogs,' the maximum and the minimum. The latter includes the ordinary responses made by the Mass server; the former includes over and above these, the *Gloria, Credo, Sanctus, Agnus Dei* as well as the *Confiteor* and the *Domine non sum dignus,* which precedes the people's Communion. We authorize these two methods." The story of this radical mode of Mass-attendance is here sketched in a few paragraphs.

"My inspiration came from the Gregorian *Motu Proprio* of Pius X," declared a Belgian priest reporting at a local Eucharistic Congress at Malines, 1909, on *his* novel method of having children take part in Mass. "I applied to the daily Low Mass what His Holiness had said of the Sunday High Mass." Similar experiments similarly inspired were elsewhere in progress: a priest from the south of France had his success in this matter signalized at the International Eucharistic Congresses at Montreal (1910) and Madrid (1911). Then began, especially in Belgium and Holland, the specialists' study of the matter in its historical setting, doctrinal implications, rubrical propriety. As was to be expected, learned men were to be found arguing against it, others, in this case with better arguments, defending it.

By the outbreak of the World War this little battle of books was about over, and 1915 saw the publication within hearing of the guns in northern France of the first Dialog Mass booklets. Before those guns were stilled, Belgium, Holland, France, Germany, Austria and Italy had all felt the sweep of the 'new' Mass, the 'people's' Mass, the 'Mass with the layman's voice.' The World War brought few blessings, but it did give us this one. One of the greatest heroes of the war, Cardinal Mercier, was among the first who sought the mind of the Holy See as to the full propriety of the Dialog Mass. Subsequently, a National Council held under his presidency at Malines, 1920, enacted the following decree on the Dialog Mass, which was subsequently approved by the Vatican:

"To instil insensibly, as it were, into the minds of the faithful that collective and truly Christian spirit, and to prepare the way for that active participation which the Holy See (*Pontificalia documenta*) desires, we must praise the practice, at least in educational institutions and religious houses, whereby those present at Mass answer the responses in unison with the servers."

The learned Benedictine liturgist, whom we are following in many details of this exposition, dwells on the next big impetus given this cause by a letter which Father Angelo Santi, S.J., as president of the Italian St. Cecilia Society, addressed to the Italian hierarchy in the interests of a National Congress of Church Music to be held at Turin, September 1920. Said Father Santi in part:

"Finally the Association requests the Most Reverend Bishops to be pleased to use their authority in recommending to the religious communities of men and women, to educational institutions, to societies and Catholic circles, to work uniformly to promote the active participation of all in Low Mass by making the responses and reciting with the priest the *Gloria, Credo, Sanctus* and *Agnus Dei.*"

The semi-official papal newspaper, *L'Osservatore Romano,* in printing this letter, added editorially that the Dialog Mass had already been introduced by many bishops into their dioceses.

The year 1922, the first of the pontificate of Pius XI, had witnessed the International Eucharistic Congress at Rome. In connection with this it was reported that the Holy Father celebrated Mass in St. Peter's, with the people answering him in unison. A similar episode is recounted as happening during the Holy Year of 1925: a large group of French pilgrims, after similarly participating in the Pontiff's Mass, heard themselves commended by His Holiness for the way in which they had sustained *their* part in his and their joint Sacrifice.

But the new and rapidly-spreading enthusiasm for joint-recitation with the priest at Mass was in parts of Italy in danger of getting out of hand, and in places went to the extreme of having whole congregations recite the entire Canon aloud, not excluding the words of Consecration. The Holy See, consulted repeatedly by bishops about the Dialog Mass, took from the outset the position it still occupies, the cardinal point of which is quoted at the head of this chapter. This position covers these points:

A. The Canon may not be recited aloud by priest or people.
B. The introduction of Dialog Mass must not engender disturbance or confusion.
C. With the safeguard of local episcopal direction, "the custom . . . in itself praiseworthy" (Decree of 1935), may be introduced without other restriction.

In connection with the prohibition of reciting the Canon of the Mass aloud, it is interesting to note that the Lenten Pastoral of His Excellency, the Most Reverend Dionysius Vismara, Bishop of Hyderabad, India, as reported in *The Bombay Examiner,* recommends a very brief explanation of the Canon prayers: "A priest or catechist during the Mass explains (very briefly) what is going on, especially the prayers of the Canon, which are not allowed to be said in an audible voice, and leads the actions and the prayers of the people. As to the other parts of the Mass, the faithful assisting may well answer the priest's prayers with the server, and also recite the *Gloria, Credo, Sanctus* and *Agnus Dei*."

To conclude this survey in brief: The fifteen-year period, 1922-1937, witnessed the initial appearance of the Dialog Mass in some form in practically every corner of the Catholic world. In the year last indicated centers were set up at Lourdes and Rome, with papal approbation, to foster by non-authoritarian means a uniform mode of Dialog Mass throughout the world.

What of the Dialog Mass in the United States? Its introduction here was inspired by contact with European centers, where it was being fostered. Specifically, the great Benedictine Abbey of Maria Laach in the Rhineland was in this matter exerting a strong influence on isolated places in America. By 1925 our liturgical review, *Orate Fratres,* was being planned by American sons of St. Benedict, and from the appearance of the first issue late in 1926 the Dialog Mass and the chanted High Mass have been consistently held up before American Catholics as the ideal methods of active lay participation in the holy Sacrifice. As early as 1926 the official *Manual* of the Sodality of the Blessed Virgin recommended Dialog Mass, the local bishop so permitting, as the most proper form for special sodality Masses. What was perhaps the first really conspicuous Dialog Mass in the United States was celebrated by the Reverend M. B. Hellriegel in connection with the First Sodality Convention, St. Louis, July, 1928. Just ten years later what was unquestionably the *largest* Dialog Mass yet held on our continent was the Children's Mass at Canada's National Eucharistic Congress, 1938. Under the aegis of their beloved Cardinal-Primate acting as Papal Legate, *seventy-five thousand children* made the responses and recited "their" Mass with the august celebrant. But what of the intervening years?

In 1930, at our Sixth National Eucharistic Congress in Omaha, Bishop White (Spokane) could say sweepingly:

"There is lacking among the vast majority of Catholics in our country that active participation in the Mass that the Church so eagerly desires. . . . From what proportion of the ordinary Sunday congregation is there any intelligent response (I do not mean vocal, but devotional) to the celebrant's successive liturgical invitations and salutations — *Oremus, Dominus vobiscum, Orate, fratres, Sursum corda?*"

What has been done since then, what is being done, to give the layman his voice in the Mass? Until such time as Rome may take the matter more closely in hand, the hierarchy, shepherds of our souls, are in the vast majority of cases allowing the Dialog Mass here to go through the preparatory stage it went through in Belgium, that is, of permitting it to become a feature of school Masses and children's Masses for some time, before making it a matter of positive recommendation for parochial observance. For the space of a few years after its first beginnings in the United States, say 1928–1933 or so, there was a very rapid spread, in more or less haphazard fashion, in schools and religious houses, and to a less, but still considerable, extent in parish churches of Dialog Mass in all manner of arrangements. But when Dom Lefebvre reported at the 1933 Liturgical Week in Louvain, "In the United States of America the Dialog Mass has spread rapidly in colleges and in sodalities of the Blessed Virgin, and not a few retreat masters have put it into their retreats. The ordinaries have never refused the necessary permission," those closer to the scene knew that by that date the Dialog Mass here had already suffered a sharp decline.

The decline was due principally to this factor. Wherever introduced the Dialog Mass rested chiefly, if not exclusively, for its conduct on groups of children in the upper grades and in high school. It was generally overlooked that, while it is easiest to begin recited participation with groups of "regimented" children, it is nowhere harder to gauge the *psychological* effects of Dialog Mass than with such groups. This for the simple reason that *they* do not suffer from the ills which the Dialog Mass is intended to cure — those of super-individualism. The Dialog Mass, as Pius XI said of collective prayer in general, is "to form the *social* conscience," and the pupils of a common school, associating in study and play with each other the greater part of every day, have a highly developed sense of being a group together. When the novelty of the first introduction of Dialog Mass had worn off, and before it was retained long enough to become a habit, it was found exacting, and self-sacrificing — and was often discontinued.

But how different in the matter of group

association is the pastor's adult congregation at the Sunday Mass. *The Sunday Mass is the one and only thing that brings that group, as a whole, together.* If they learn to collaborate jointly *with one another, with the priest,* and *consciously to collaborate with Jesus Christ, Priest,* in celebrating the common sacrifice, they will have the bond of a living Action, and "the holiest of actions," linking their lives together at one point. They will be on the way toward the formation of a social conscience, in addition to a personal one, and the continuous repetition of the joint-Action will afford them the abiding sense of union needed for the many other actions in Christianizing our times. But to resume our narrative.

Following upon the decline of Dialog Mass just mentioned, there ensued a time of questioning, of study and preparation. We are now witnessing in colleges, schools and religious houses a wide resurgence of the Mass in dialog, now better prepared for, better regulated, better understood in its wider bearings. Taking the country as a whole, however, this resurgence has had little effect on parochial observance. One priest summed up the situation in a sizable city of the East as follows: "In this city and suburbs there are thirty-four churches. Four use the Dialog Mass now; of the remaining thirty, three used it for a time and dropped it as impractical; of the remaining twenty-seven, three seem to be interested in it. Of the four churches now using the Dialog Mass, one uses it every day (Sundays and weekdays); one uses it every Sunday at the Children's Mass, and occasionally on weekdays; one uses it on Sundays only at the Children's Mass; one uses it occasionally on weekdays." That summation is perhaps typical of the country as a whole at the present time. A partial survey of Chicago's parish churches lists twenty-eight in which the Dialog Mass is now used, but in nearly all cases it is limited to responses in English at the Children's Mass. Not long after Archbishop Spellman was invested with the see of New York, permission for the Dialog Mass began to be multiplied in that metropolis.

Beyond the vast difference in group-effectiveness touched upon above, what are the hindrances or difficulties attaching to the introduction and continued use of the Dialog Mass? One hindrance, in the eyes of clergy and laity alike, is its novelty, with the seeming condemnation of ways long tried. One notes with profit in this connection the calmness of tone and the objections forestalled in a letter to his *clergy* by the Cardinal-Archbishop of Genoa in 1933:

"It is the duty of priests to associate the faithful with the active celebration of the divine Mysteries, and not merely content themselves with silent assistance. The recitation of the rosary, morning prayers, acts of faith, etc., are *good things*. But it *is a better thing* for the people to join their voice with that of the server and priest at the altar. Let us not be exclusivists. But let us be convinced that the more active and conscious the participation of our faithful is in the divine services, the greater progress will they make in their spiritual formation. A good assistant, a good pastor of a church cannot ordinarily be satisfied with the silence of the people during the sacred functions."

But, since Dialog Mass is not obligatory, why make people change lifelong habits of prayer? With all the "new" praying out loud, some feel they cannot pray at all — because they can no longer say their customary silent prayers in peace! Pius XI was very much alive to this difficulty, and urged priests to elevate deficient and imperfect prayer little by little.

"The Church [said he] is very inclusive. In fact, her inclusiveness is occasionally very astonishing. She accepts all manners of prayer, even very deficient and imperfect prayer, for she has pity on the weakness of poor man. 'Very well,' she says, 'since you cannot pray otherwise, pray as you do, as long as you really pray.' But when one wishes to know what *she* understands by prayer, that is an entirely different matter: and *it is in the liturgy that one discovers her way.*

"It is necessary to imitate Holy Church, and not to prohibit what she consents to accept in the matter of prayer. *But one should seek to elevate this prayer little by little, and to teach the faithful to pray as she prays.*"

How the fatherly heart of the Pontiff would have rejoiced to note the careful provision for all made by the pastor of a large Chicago parish:

"Our Sunday is observed in the following manner: 6:00, silent Mass; 7:30, Dialog Mass in Latin, when the men receive Communion, and the women will do the same beginning next month; 9:00, Solemn Mass for the parish, with full participation of the children and many adults; 10:30 and 12:00, Dialog Mass in English . . ."

The size of the church edifice sometimes offers a problem in the conduct of Dialog Mass, but this is easily obviated in some places by the public address system. Hindrances of undue delay or disorder in the service are traceable to hasty and insufficient preparation, and disappear of themselves, as more attention is given to these matters. In fine, care and an understanding of the ultimate objective prove that the difficulties attending the change-over from silent to active group-participation in Low Mass are neither serious nor permanent.

At the opening of this chapter the more or less fortuitous connection of Dialog Mass with the stress of war times was touched upon. But the real warfare of modern times is the battle for or against God and His Christ. "This modern revolution," said the voice of the Pontiff who led us for so long, "has already broken out or threatens almost everywhere, and it exceeds in amplitude and violence anything yet experienced in the preceding persecutions launched against the Church. Entire peoples find themselves in danger of falling back into a barbarism worse than that which oppressed the greater part of the world at the coming of the Redeemer" (Pius XI, *On Atheistic Communism*). Even now, from the outposts of the Christianizers, where the fight is already joined, we constantly receive in this country such messages as this of a *Pax Romana* congress in Paris, 1937: "Not far from where the German swastika and the Russian hammer and sickle are flaunted proudly in the sky, hundreds of voices, men and women, were raised in a *Missa Recitata*." Or messages like this, of the training of the Christianizers:

"It is necessary to recall here the large part played in the Young Christian Workers' movement by the conception of the Church as the Mystical Body of Christ. . . . How the balance is being readjusted is being shown by the liturgical movement. It is also a fact that this movement is closely associated with the demand for social justice. And the reverse can also be observed. The demand for social justice has thrown fresh light on corporate worship. . . . The members of Catholic Action are passing beyond the stage at which worship is merely a formal obligation demanding no more than a respectful demeanor, and are experiencing the reality of that Presence whose Mystical Body the Church is. Especially is this the case among the . . . Workers *in whose responses, given during the recitation of the liturgy,*[1] one finds a new note of joyful spirituality and a realistic appreciation of the holy Sacrifice's practical implications."

"Instead of the Mass being something extra, outside his ordinary life, it is an integral part of that life. His daily toil with its strain exhaustion, suffering is an extension of the Sacrifice of the altar."

That is why, as another observer reports: "At Brussels, in the black winter dawns, one may see the young work-men and the young working-girls coming each morning, in their overalls, to Mass; before they go to their factories and their shops and their mills, they receive Christ in the Eucharist, to carry Him with them into that bitterly drab, dehumanised life of theirs which He and they are fighting to transform. *One can hear them answer the priest in the dialogue of the Mass.* The liturgy, the social prayer of the Church, is the soul of their social movement, as it must be the soul of all Catholic action."

The lay Christianizers of other lands are already in the thick of the battle for which we leisurely prepare. They have tested and proved and cherish the soul-to-soul liaison value of the Dialog Mass.

And when our turn comes?

PAUL BUSSARD
(*1904*–   )

KNOWN for editorial discernment on more than one continent, Rev. Paul Bussard was born November 22, 1904, at Essex, Iowa. After moving to Marshall, Minnesota, with his family, Father Bussard continued his education in Minnesota schools. He entered St. Thomas College, 1922, proceeded to the St. Paul Seminary and was ordained in June, 1928. During his four years as an assistant priest in the cathedral parish, Father Bussard founded the *Leaflet Missal*. His gifts of mind marked him for graduate studies which were pursued at the Catholic University, Bonn University, and the Liturgical Academy at Maria Laach. Returning to St. Paul, Minnesota, Father Bussard combined forces with Father Louis Gales, founder of the *Catholic Digest*. As chief editor of the *Digest* Father Bussard has amply demonstrated his competence as a writer.

Of his liturgical writings, *The Sacrifice* is his finest achievement. Written in clear and delightful style it expounds many of the theories of the Liturgical Academy at Maria Laach.

CHAPTER I: INTRODUCTORY*

BEFORE the actual Sacrifice of the Mass begins, there is an introductory service originally introduced to instruct the Catechumens. This service begins with the prayers at the foot of the altar and ends with the Creed. The introductory service is very important, but of course not as important as the Mass of the Faithful, which comes immediately after. We are, all of us, familiar with at least some parts of the Catechumens' service. But there is a great deal to be known about it, and a great deal to be done. To begin with, suppose we try to visualize this service in the Early Church.

Suppose you were a pagan living some 1,600 years ago. Imagine that you had heard how bravely these Christians had died in the persecutions, that some of your friends had become Christians or Catholics. The words meant the same thing. Suppose you had thought and worried about the riddle of life without making much headway. Imagine, and it isn't hard to imagine, that you were afraid of death and quite in the dark about what might happen after death. Suppose you had wished that God would send a messenger who could not be mistaken, who would tell you about all things with authority and certainty. Then imagine that you had been told about the Catholics, that they were absolutely certain that they knew these darksome things, that they knew that God had sent a Messenger and that His authority was beyond question because He had so vividly proved it. That this Messenger had died a violent death and then had come to life again! That He was God, and that He continued to be present among the Catholics in a way which was invisible but was tremendously actual to them.

You wished to learn more. You went to a priest. You became a Catechumen, that is, you were permitted to go to a service where selections of Scripture were read to you and explained, you were taught to sing

some of the Psalms and some of the hymns that had just been written. Then when that was finished one of the officials said to you and to all those about you, *"Ite, missa est,"* and you had to go away, because you were not yet baptized. But those who were baptized were allowed to stay for another service about which you had not yet been instructed. Perhaps you had learned that it was the *Mysterium Fidei,* the Mystery of Faith, and that you must have Faith and be baptized before you could take part in it. And you might have known, too, in a vague way, that it was in this *Mysterium* that the faithful were given a share in the acts of the Saviour and in His divine life.

You would certainly have been a very good Catechumen. You would have been very glad indeed to go to the Catechumens' service every day during Lent. You would have learned more and more about the marvelous truth which God's Messenger was making known to you through the Church. And you would have been learning, too, to cast off the bad moral practices of paganism and to walk worthy of the vocation to which you were being called.

Then when Easter Saturday came you would have been baptized and on Easter Sunday you would have taken part in the *Mysterium* of Faith for the first time. The Mass of the Catechumens would have been a way to, a preparation for, an introduction to, the Mass of the Faithful. It was that in the fourth century. It is quite the same thing in the twentieth. For although it has, of necessity, changed and developed many of its details, its general purpose and character are just as they have always been.

One might spend a great deal of time talking about the historical origins of the Mass of the Catechumens. It is certain, for example, that a good part of it was taken from the old Jewish synagogue service. You see, under the Old Law there was only one place in Palestine where sacrifice was offered up. Of course it was the sacrifice of the Old Testament, but even so it was offered

---

*Bussard-Kirsch, *The Meaning of the Mass* (The Catholic University of America Press; distributed by P. J. Kenedy & Sons, New York, N. Y., 1942), pp. 3–14.

only in one place, the Temple at Jerusalem. Naturally, it was very difficult for most Jewish people, and impossible for some, to go there. In the meanwhile they might forget the Law and the Prophets. That would never do. So in every community where there were enough people to have a synagogue, they had a service quite distinct from that which went on in the Temple in Jerusalem. When persons went to the synagogue, they sang a few Psalms, listened to some readings from the Old Testament, and heard one of the elder members of the community explain the passages which had been read.

It was quite natural for the Jews who had become Christians to continue with that service. It was indeed a very good thing for them to do. But of course it had to be adapted to the New Law. It had to include readings from the New Testament as well as from the Old. They kept on singing the Psalms. In fact we are still singing them at the present time, though not with as much understanding as our ancestors had. They kept reading passages from the Old and the New Testament. And of course they kept the explanation. That is the Sermon today.

Although scholars debate and investigate the exact sources of all that we have in the Mass of the Catechumens, this need not concern us very much at the present moment. It is good to know, though, that the fulfillment of the Old Law is to be seen in the Mass of the Catechumens as well as in many other things.

When the Greeks and Romans were learning to become Catholics, they went to this service taken over from the more ancient synagogue service. Now we may ask, why was it taken over, and why did the Greeks and Romans go? Remember, they knew very little about the Catholic Church. They had to learn to be Catholics. And they went to the Mass of the Catechumens in order to learn.

They had two things to learn: first, how to pray; second, what the truths of Christ are, what were the dignity and the duties

of one who is baptized. They were taught to pray by praying in word and in song with the community. They were taught the truths of Revelation, the dignity and duties of a Catholic, by hearing Sacred Scripture read and explained.

We shall learn more about this later on. At the moment it is clear that the Mass of the Catechumens has a very definite purpose. The Church has always kept the Mass of the Catechumens. Throughout all these centuries this part of the Mass has remained much the same. It has, therefore, the same purpose now as it always had. And everyone knows that the process of learning about the Incarnation and the Redemption, the dignity and duties of a Catholic, does not cease when one is baptized, or when one is confirmed. It goes on and on throughout all of one's life. A good understanding of the Catechumens' Mass, and close attention to it when we are there, will make this process of learning a fact rather that a mere theory in our lives.

The double purpose of the Mass of the Catechumens is made clear by the text itself. The Mass begins, as you know, with the prayers at the foot of the altar. Then follow the Introit, Kyrie, Gloria, and Collect. If you read these over in your Missal, you will readily see that they are all prayers, and that they are very good prayers too. You will notice secondly that they are prayers not so much for a single individual but rather for a community or congregation of individuals. I mean that if an individual were going to pray to God all alone by himself, he would not be very likely to choose these prayers for himself. He would find others more appropriate for just one person. But if a congregation were going to pray together, they would find it very difficult to discover anything more fitting.

This congregational character of the prayers is shown, also, by the circumstance that most of these prayers are supposed to be sung rather than just said. The Introit, for example, should be sung. The Kyrie loses much of its force if it is not sung and the Gloria likewise. Even the Collect should be chanted by the celebrant. Now it is very seldom that a single person, praying to God all alone, sings his prayer. But when a great many persons pray, they usually find it natural to sing. You see, a solemn Mass is the normal manner of offering the Sacrifice. Although low Mass is more usual and common today, the Church still looks upon it, and rightly so, as an exception.

These first five parts of the Mass of the Catechumens are prayers then. But if you read the next three parts you will see that they are not prayers at all. First the Epistle. It is not a prayer. It is a lesson. It begins, for instance, with the words, "The lesson is from St. Paul's Epistle to the Romans . . ." Then the Gospel. That is not a prayer either. It is another lesson. And the Sermon, which comes just after the Gospel, and which is really part of the Mass of the Catechumens, is not a prayer but a Sermon.

But, you will say, between the Epistle and Gospel there is a Gradual and that is a prayer. Well, perhaps; but you must remember that the Gradual is supposed to be sung, and that it was originally *the only solo* in all the Mass (except, of course, the parts the celebrant chants alone). It is there to relieve the strain of attention. It is difficult to listen to two lessons, and then a Sermon *attentively*. The Gradual, a solo, makes it easier.

The Mass of the Catechumens, then, is made up of five prayers and three lessons. It is designed to make us pray together and then to teach us the truth God gave the Church, and so to prepare us for participation in the Mystery of Faith.

The service designed to introduce Catechumens to the Sacrifice of the Mass corresponds in its up and down movements, with the up and down movements that almost every prayer has by nature.

You see, since a prayer places us in relation to, or in union with God, it must go back and forth between God and us. That is, of course, a figure of speech, because all of us know that God is everywhere, and there is no need of a prayer "going up." But as long as we are on earth it will be necessary to speak in figures of speech. So it is all right to say that a prayer must go up and come down. At any rate it must go from us to God and then from God to us.

It would be just as accurate to say that every prayer has a giving and a receiving part. In the first we give something to God; in the second God gives something to us. This is describing another aspect of prayer.

Probably the clearest example of this is the song the angels sang at the birth of Christ: "Glory to God in the highest, and on earth peace to men of good will." Now this has two very distinct parts. The first is "Glory to God in the highest." That is what we give to God. It is the reason for our existence on earth as well as for our presence at Mass. It is the reason for the existence of the earth, too, for that matter. And it is the very profound reason for the Incarnation. Of course, we can not add anything to the intrinsic glory of God. God is infinitely perfect. We can not add anything to that infinite perfection. But we can add something to His external glory. Thus we say a saint gives more glory to God than a sinner.

There is our purpose in life. We give glory to God who is in the highest. And perhaps the joy of the angels' song at the Incarnation was because, from now on, more perfect glory would be given to God in the highest through Christ, His Son, our Lord.

The second part is "peace on earth to men of good will." In the word "peace" all blessings of God are included: peace, and union with God through grace, information and knowledge and wisdom, forgiveness, blessing, and the pledge of unending peace in eternity.

Not all these things are given in the Mass of the Catechumens. The thing that is given is *instruction*. You remember there are three lessons, three things which teach us, three things from which we are to *learn*. By paying attention to the Mass of the Catechumens we advance in wisdom, just as by taking part in the sacrifice of the Mass we advance in grace. This is the true and indispensable source from which all Christians must draw who wish to advance "in wisdom . . . and grace with God and Men." (St. Luke 2, 52.)

Now almost every prayer in the Missal has that same double direction in miniature. Almost every prayer has a request at the end. It asks God for something. You might examine the Our Father, the Hail Mary, the Confiteor, any Collect in the Missal, the ceremony of Benediction, and almost every other prayer, and satisfy yourself that this is generally true.

That is why it is necessary to take active part in both the Sacrifice and in the Mass of the Catechumens. We are not just bystanders, mere spectators. We must know what we say, and desire that which we receive. And the more we give, the more we increase our capacity to receive and to advance in wisdom.

In view of the fact that the Mass of the Catechumens means to teach us, it is very necessary that we understand. At once we are faced with a difficulty. Everyone knows that the prayers of the Mass are in Latin. Everyone knows, too, that very few persons know Latin well enough to understand when they hear it spoken. How did it ever come about that Latin is the language we must use?

The question will be cleared up somewhat if we say at the outset that the Church uses many languages; that she allows the Sacrifice of the Mass to be offered in many languages. That does not concern us very much though, because in the western part of the world Latin is almost the only language used in the Mass.

If you look back over history it will help. The Church is so old, you know. Had you been a Catholic three hundred years after Our Lord ascended into Heaven, you would not have been speaking English for the very good reason that there wasn't any English to speak, or French or German either. Some spoke Latin, some spoke Greek. For the first few centuries Greek was the most common language; so the Church used Greek in her service. Then Latin became

more popular and the Church used Latin, although one thing at least, the Kyrie Eleison, was never translated into Latin. It is Greek to this day. Latin was made the language of the West and for over a thousand years everyone spoke Latin.

Then our modern languages began to grow and assume importance. People began to speak them instead of Latin. They developed and became very great languages indeed. But the Church has always kept on speaking Latin.

If printing had not been invented Latin might prove a great difficulty for us. But now that books are so common it is really not any difficulty at all. Everyone can afford to own a book now. A thousand years ago very few people had books because they were very, very expensive.

It seems quite providential that books became cheap when languages began to multiply. For with the help of a Missal in English anyone can follow what is said.

So, although Latin is the language of the Mass, everyone who uses a Missal overcomes that apparent difficulty. The Missal is a very important book too. I might go on writing about its history, its sublime passages, its jewelled prayers, its profound lessons, and you might go on reading what I write; but it would be much better and very much more effective if you would just begin to use a Missal when you go to Mass. Then you would see those things for yourself.

Using a Missal, then, is the most practical way you can become a good Catechumen under the present circumstances. No one ever regrets that he becomes a good Catechumen. Many have said that if a person went to Mass every Sunday and every weekday as far as possible, using a Missal carefully, at the end of the year he would know an astonishingly great deal about the Church. Not only that, he would be just as eager to begin the next year in the same fashion.

Explanations of the Mass generally spend much time on externals like the vestments worn and the vessels used in the celebration of Mass. Knowledge of these things may be useful, but it is much less important than the text of the Mass itself.

How did it come about that the vestments which we see worn today became a universal custom? Well, in the beginning you may be sure that the Apostles said Mass in the clothes they wore all the time. They had no such things as special vestments for Mass. But it was quite natural that they, and their successors, should wear the best clothes they had. That is just what they did. It was a long time ago; and we all know how rapidly fashions in dress change. They change much more rapidly now than they did centuries ago, but even they changed. The Church, however, did not change. The vestments her ministers wear now are simply the sort of clothes men wore in the early centuries of the Christian era. If a contemporary of Julius Caesar should see a priest vested for the Mass, he would feel quite at home because those are the sort of clothes he was accustomed to see in his lifetime.

This leads us to discuss two kinds of vestments. They are called Roman and Gothic. Both names are quite wrong. Roman vestments are not Roman, and Gothic vestments are not Gothic. What is usually meant by Roman vestments are the stiff cardboard-like style, so cut as to deserve the name "fiddleback," simply because the back has the outline of a bass viol. Until a few years ago this kind was almost universal in America. Just why they came to be called Roman is hard to say, for you may be sure that no contemporary of Julius Caesar would ever have been seen in garments cut in such a style. As a matter of fact they are only two or three centuries old.

The other kind — Gothic — are long, flowing, full-cut vestments. They are not decorated with heavy braid; they depend for their effect upon the grace of the folds and the beauty of line. These are called Gothic, but they are no more Gothic than you or I. They are actually Old Roman; I mean they are the kind of garments worn by the contemporary of Julius Caesar. This contempo-

rary would recognize a priest vested in "Gothic" vestments, but he would never recognize a priest vested in "Roman" vestments.

Many are hoping that the so-called Gothic vestments will become more widespread. The question is not so very important; no one need get greatly excited about either kind; it is simply a question of good taste and the approval of the Sacred Congregation of Rites.

The large outer vestment is called the chasuble. The word means "little house." Originally the chasuble was a garment which reached from the neck down almost to the ground. Under it is worn the stole, a long narrow vestment hung about the neck. The stole is worn at other times as well as at Mass — whenever any Sacrament is administered. About the left arm the maniple is worn — a vestment which originally was for practical use like a handkerchief. The long white vestment is called the alb (the word *albus* means "white"), and beneath it a square piece of linen (called the amice) is placed over the shoulders and about the neck. The cincture serves the purpose of gathering up and holding the alb in place.

There are five colors in use at the present time. During the preparation for Christmas and Easter (Advent and Lent) the violet of penance is worn. (It is wrong to call this color purple.) During the celebration of Christmas and Easter white is worn, and during the prolongation of those two great festivals (time after Epiphany and the time after Pentecost) green is worn. At Pentecost red is worn, and black is used at funerals. White is worn on the feasts of Our Lord and of the Blessed Virgin. On saints' days white is worn unless the saint is a martyr in that case, red. Other colors have been used at different times, and that of course could be allowed by the Church. Some have advocated the use of blue vestments on feasts of the Blessed Virgin. Perhaps that will someday become the custom.

INDEX OF AUTHORS AND TITLES

The names of authors are printed in **black** type, the titles of books are printed in *italics*, and the titles of individual selections are printed in ordinary roman type.